EASIER ENGLISH
Dictionary of
Business

fourth edition

EASIER ENGLISH
Dictionary of
Business

fourth edition

A. Ivanovic M.B.A.
P. H. Collin

BLOOMSBURY

A BLOOMSBURY REFERENCE BOOK

Originally published by Peter Collin Publishing
as *English Business Dictionary*

First published 1985
Second edition 1994, 1995, 1997, 1999
Third edition 2001
Fourth edition 2004
This edition published in the United States of America 2005

Bloomsbury Publishing Plc
38 Soho Square, London W1D 3HB

Bloomsbury Reference titles are distributed
in the United States of America by
Independent Publishers Group
814 N. Franklin St., Chicago, IL 60610
1-800-888-4741
www.ipgbook.com

ISBN 1 904970 08 7

All papers used by Bloomsbury Publishing are natural, recyclable products
made from wood grown in well-managed forests. The manufacturing
processes conform to the environmental regulations of the country of origin.

Text processing and computer typesetting by Bloomsbury
Printed in the United States of America by Quebecor World Fairfield

Preface

This dictionary provides the user with the basic vocabulary used in business in both American and British English. The dictionary contains words and phrases which cover all aspects of business life from the office to the Stock Exchange and international trade fairs.

It is designed for anyone who needs to check the meaning or pronunciation of a business term, but especially for those for whom English is an additional language. Each entry is explained in clear, straightforward English.

Pronunciations, irregular plurals and verb forms, constructions used with particular words, differences between American and British usage, and other useful points are included. At the back of the book, the user will find supplements giving useful information about how to speak and write numbers, telephoning, and writing business letters, together with a list of world currencies, weights and measures, and local times around the world.

Thanks are due to Steven Gregory for his helpful comments and advice on the fourth edition of the dictionary. Thanks also to Julie Plier and John Surdyk, whose advice has been invaluable for this American edition.

Pronunciation

The following symbols have been used to show the pronunciation of the main words in the dictionary.

Stress is indicated by a main stress mark (') and a secondary stress mark (‚). Note that these are only guides, as the stress of the word changes according to its position in the sentence.

Vowels		*Consonants*	
æ	back	b	buck
ɑ	harm	d	dead
aɪ	type	ð	other
aʊ	how	dʒ	jump
ɔ	course	f	fare
ɔɪ	annoy	g	gold
e	head	h	head
eɪ	make	j	yellow
ɜr	word	k	cab
i	keep	l	leave
ə	about	m	mix
ɪ	fit	n	nil
oʊ	go	ŋ	sing
u	pool	p	print
ʊ	book	r	rest
ʌ	shut	s	save
		ʃ	shop
		t	take
		tʃ	change
		θ	theft
		v	value
		w	work
		x	loch
		ʒ	measure
		z	zone

A

A /eɪ/, **AA**, **AAA** *noun* letters that show how reliable a particular bond is considered to be ○ *These bonds have a AAA rating.*

> "…the rating concern lowered its rating to single-A from double-A, and its senior debt rating to triple-B from single-A" [*Wall Street Journal*]
>
> COMMENT: The AAA rating is given by Standard & Poor's or by Moody's, and indicates a very high level of reliability for a corporate or municipal bond in the U.S.

A1 /,eɪ 'wʌn/ *adjective* **1.** in very good condition ○ *We sell only goods in A1 condition.* **2.** □ **ship which is A1 at Lloyd's** a ship which is in the best possible condition according to Lloyd's Register

AAA /,trɪp(ə)l 'eɪ/ *abbreviation* American Accounting Association

ABA *abbreviation* American Bankers Association

abandon /ə'bændən/ *verb* **1.** to give up or not continue doing something ○ *We abandoned the idea of setting up a New York office.* ○ *The development program had to be abandoned when the company ran out of cash.* □ **to abandon an action** to give up a court case **2.** to leave something ○ *The crew abandoned the sinking ship.*

abandonment /ə'bændənmənt/ *noun* an act of giving up voluntarily something that you own, such as an option or the right to a property □ **abandonment of a ship** giving up a ship and cargo to the underwriters against payment for total loss

abatement /ə'beɪtmənt/ *noun* an act of reducing

ABA transit number /,eɪ bi eɪ 'trænzɪt ,nʌmbər/ *noun* a number allocated to an American financial institution, such as a bank (NOTE: The number appears on U.S. checks in the top right-hand corner, above the "check routing symbol".)

above par /ə,bʌv 'pɑr/ *adjective* referring to a stock with a market price higher than its par value

above-the-line advertising /ə,bʌv ðə ,laɪn 'ædvərtaɪzɪŋ/ *adjective, adverb* **1.** used to describe entries in a company's profit and loss accounts that appear above the line separating entries showing the origin of the funds that have contributed to the profit or loss from those that relate to its distribution. Exceptional and extraordinary items appear above the line. ○ *Exceptional items are noted above the line in company accounts.* ◊ **below the line 2.** relating to revenue items in a government budget **3.** advertising for which payment is made (such as an ad in a magazine or a stand at a trade fair) and for which a commission is paid to an advertising agency. Compare **below the line**

abroad /ə'brɔːd/ *adverb* to or in another country ○ *The consignment of cars was shipped abroad last week.* ○ *The chairman is abroad on business.* ○ *He worked abroad for ten years.* ○ *Half of our profit comes from sales abroad.*

absence /'æbs(ə)ns/ *noun* the fact of not being at work or at a meeting □ **in the absence of** when someone is not there ○ *In the absence of the chairman, his deputy took the chair.*

absent /'æbsənt/ *adjective* not at work or not at a meeting ○ *He was absent owing to illness.* ○ *Ten of the workers are absent with flu.* ○ *The chairman is absent in Holland on business.*

absentee /,æbsən'tiː/ *noun* a person who is absent or an employee who stays away from work for no good reason

absenteeism /,æbs(ə)n'tiːz(ə)m/ *noun* the practice of staying away from work for no good reason ○ *Low productiv-*

ity is largely due to the high level of absenteeism. ○ *Absenteeism is high in the week before Christmas.*

absenteeism rate /ˌæbs(ə)nˈtiːz(ə)m ˌreɪt/ *noun* the percentage of the work force which is away from work with no good excuse ○ *The rate of absenteeism or the absenteeism rate always increases in fine weather.*

absolute /ˈæbsəlut/ *adjective* complete or total

absolute monopoly /ˌæbsəlut məˈnɑpəli/ *noun* a situation where only one producer produces or only one supplier supplies something ○ *The company has an absolute monopoly of imports of French wine.* ○ *The supplier's absolute monopoly of the product meant that customers had to accept her terms.*

absorb /əbˈsɔrb/ *verb* to take in a small item so that it forms part of a larger one □ **to absorb overhead** to include a proportion of overhead costs into a production cost (this is done at a certain rate, called the "absorption rate") □ **overhead has absorbed all our profits** all our profits have gone in paying overhead expenses □ **to absorb a loss by a subsidiary** to include a subsidiary company's loss in the group accounts □ **a business which has been absorbed by a competitor** a small business which has been made part of a larger one

absorption /əbˈsɔrpʃən/ *noun* the process of making a smaller business part of a larger one, so that the smaller company in effect no longer exists

absorption costing /əbˈsɔrpʃən ˌkɑstɪŋ/ *noun* a form of costing for a product that includes both the direct costs of production and the indirect overhead costs as well

absorption rate /əbˈzɔrpʃən ˌreɪt/ *noun* a rate at which overhead costs are absorbed into each unit of production

abstract /ˈæbstrækt/ *noun* a short form of a report or document ○ *to make an abstract of the company accounts*

abstract of title /ˌæbˌstrækt əv ˈtaɪt(ə)l/ *noun* a summary of the details of the ownership of a property which has not been registered

a/c, acc *abbreviation* account

ACAS /ˈeɪkæs/ *abbreviation* Advisory, Conciliation and Arbitration Service

accelerate /əkˈseləreɪt/ *verb* to make something go faster

acceleration clause /əkˌseləˈreɪʃən ˌklɔz/ *noun* a clause in a contract that provides for immediate payment of the total balance if there is a breach of contract

accept /əkˈsept/ *verb* **1.** to take something which is being offered □ **to accept delivery of a shipment** to take goods into the warehouse officially when they are delivered **2.** to say "yes" or to agree to something ○ *She accepted the offer of a job in Australia.* ○ *He accepted $2,000 instead of one week's notice.*

acceptable /əkˈseptəb(ə)l/ *adjective* easily accepted ○ *Both parties found the offer acceptable.* ○ *The terms of the contract of employment are not acceptable to the candidate.*

acceptance /əkˈseptəns/ *noun* **1.** the act of signing a bill of exchange to show that you agree to pay it □ **to present a bill for acceptance** to present a bill for payment by the person who has accepted it **2.** □ **acceptance of an offer** the act of agreeing to an offer □ **to give an offer a conditional acceptance** to accept an offer provided that specific things happen or that specific terms apply □ **we have their letter of acceptance** we have received a letter from them accepting the offer

acceptance against documents /əkˌseptəns əˌgenst ˈdɑkjəmənts/ *noun* a transaction where the seller takes charge of the shipping documents for a consignment of goods when a buyer accepts a bill of exchange ○ *Acceptance against documents protects the seller when sending goods which are not yet paid for.*

acceptance bank /əkˈseptəns bæŋk/, **acceptance house** *noun* a firm, usually a merchant bank, which accepts bills of exchange at a discount, in return for immediate payment to the issuer

acceptance sampling /əkˈseptəns ˌsæmplɪŋ/ *noun* the process of testing a small sample of a batch to see if the whole batch is good enough to be accepted

access /ˈækses/ *noun* □ **to have access to something** a way of obtaining or reaching something ○ *She has access to large amounts of venture capital.* ■ *verb* to call up data which is stored in a computer ○ *She accessed the address file on the computer.*

accession /ək'seʃ(ə)n/ *noun* the act of joining an organization

access time /'ækses ˌtaɪm/ *noun* the time taken by a computer to find data stored in it

accident /'æksɪd(ə)nt/ *noun* something unpleasant which can be caused by carelessness or which happens by chance such as a plane crash

accident insurance /ˌæksɪd(ə)nt ɪn'ʃʊrəns/ *noun* insurance which will pay the insured person when an accident takes place

accident policy /ˌæksɪd(ə)nt 'pɒlɪsi/ *noun* an insurance contract which provides a person with accident insurance

accommodation /əˌkɒmə'deɪʃ(ə)n/ *noun* **1.** money lent for a short time **2.** □ **to reach an accommodation with creditors** to agree terms for settlement with creditors **3.** *U.K.* same as **accommodations**

"…any non-resident private landlord can let furnished or unfurnished accommodation to a tenant" [*Times*]

accommodation address /əˌkɒmə 'deɪʃ(ə)n əˌdres/ *noun* an address used for receiving messages, but which is not the real address of the company

accommodation bill /əˌkɒmə 'deɪʃ(ə)n ˌbɪl/ *noun* a bill of exchange where the person signing (the "drawee") is helping another company (the "drawer") to get a loan

accommodations /əˌkɒmə 'deɪʃ(ə)nz/ *plural noun* a place to stay temporarily or live in ○ *Visitors have difficulty in finding hotel accommodations during the summer.*

accompany /ə'kʌmp(ə)ni/ *verb* to go with ○ *The chairman came to the meeting accompanied by the finance director.* ○ *They sent a formal letter of complaint, accompanied by an invoice for damage.* (NOTE: accompanied **by** something)

accordance /ə'kɔːd(ə)ns/ *noun* □ **in accordance with** in agreement or conformity with, as a result of what someone has said should be done ○ *In accordance with your instructions we have deposited the money in your checking account.* ○ *I am submitting the claim for damages in accordance with the advice of our legal advisers.*

accordingly /ə'kɔːdɪŋli/ *adverb* in agreement with what has been decided ○ *We have received your letter and have altered the contract accordingly.*

according to /ə'kɔːdɪŋ tu/ *preposition* **1.** in accordance with ○ *The computer was installed according to the manufacturer's instructions.* **2.** as stated or shown by someone

"…the budget targets for employment and growth are within reach according to the latest figures" [*Australian Financial Review*]

account /ə'kaʊnt/ *noun* **1.** a record of financial transactions over a period of time, such as money paid, received, borrowed or owed ○ *Please send me your account* or *a detailed* or *an itemized account.* **2.** (*in a store*) an arrangement in which a customer acquires goods and pays for them at a later date, usually the end of the month ○ *to have an account* or *a charge account with Nordstroms* ○ *Put it on my account* or *charge it to my account.* ○ *They are one of our largest accounts.* □ **to open an account** (*of a customer*) to ask a store to supply goods which you will pay for at a later date □ **to open an account, to close an account** (*of a store*) to start or to stop supplying a customer on credit □ **to settle an account** to pay all the money owed on an account □ **to stop an account** to stop supplying a customer until payment has been made for goods supplied **3.** □ **on account** as part of a total bill □ **to pay money on account** to pay to settle part of a bill □ **advance on account** money paid as a part payment **4.** a customer who does a large amount of business with a firm and has an account with it ○ *Smith Brothers is one of our largest accounts.* ○ *Our sales people call on their best accounts twice a month.* **5.** □ **to keep the accounts** to write each sum of money in the account book ○ *The bookkeeper's job is to keep the accounts.* □ **profit and loss account (P&L account)** statement of company expenditure and income over a period of time, almost always one calendar year, showing whether the company has made a profit or loss (the balance sheet shows the state of a company's finances at a certain date; the profit and loss account shows the movements which have taken place since the last balance sheet) **6.** □ **overdrawn account** an account where you have taken out more money than you have put in, i.e. the bank is effectively lending you money

□ **to open an account** to start an account by putting money in ○ *She opened an account with the Northeast Credit Union.* □ **to close an account** to take all money out of a bank account and stop the account ○ *We closed our account with U.S. Trust.* **7.** a period during which shares are traded for credit, and at the end of which the shares bought must be paid for **8.** a notice □ **to take account of inflation, to take inflation into account** to assume that there will be a specific percentage of inflation when making calculations ■ *verb* □ **to account for** to explain and record a money transaction ○ *to account for a loss* or *a discrepancy* ○ *The reps have to account for all their expenses to the sales manager.*

accountability /ə,kaʊntə'bɪlɪti/ *noun* the fact of being responsible to someone for something, e.g., the accountability of directors to the stockholders

accountable /ə'kaʊntəb(ə)l/ *adjective* referring to a person who has to explain what has taken place or who is responsible for something (NOTE: You are accountable **to** someone **for** something.)

accountancy /ə'kaʊntənsi/ *noun* same as **accounting**

accountant /ə'kaʊntənt/ *noun* **1.** a person who keeps a company's accounts or deals with an individual person's tax affairs ○ *The chief accountant of a manufacturing group.* ○ *The accountant has shown that there is a sharp variance in our labor costs.* **2.** a person who advises a company on its finances ○ *I send all my income tax questions to my accountant.* **3.** a person who examines accounts

account book /ə'kaʊnt bʊk/ *noun* a book with printed columns which is used to record sales and purchases

account end /ə,kaʊnt 'end/ *noun* the end of an accounting period

account executive /ə'kaʊnt ɪg,zekjətɪv/ *noun* an employee who looks after customers or who is the link between customers and the company

accounting /ə'kaʊntɪŋ/ *noun* **1.** the work of recording money paid, received, borrowed, or owed ○ *accounting methods* ○ *accounting procedures* ○ *an accounting machine* **2.** the work of an accountant ○ *They are studying accounting* or *They are accounting students.* Also called **accountancy**

accounting department /ə'kaʊntɪŋ dɪ,pɑrtmənt/ *noun* a department in a company which deals with money paid, received, borrowed, or owed

accounting manager /ə'kaʊntɪŋ ,mænɪdʒər/ *noun* the manager of an accounting department. Also called **accounts manager**

accounting period /ə'kaʊntɪŋ ,pɪriəd/ *noun* a period of time at the end of which a company's accounts are closed, usually monthly, quarterly, and annually

accounting staff /ə'kaʊntɪŋ stæf/ *noun* people who work in the accounting department

accounts /ə'kaʊnts/ *noun* detailed records of a company's financial affairs

accounts department /ə'kaʊnts dɪ,pɑrtmənt/ *noun* same as **accounting department**

accounts manager /ə'kaʊnts ,mænɪdʒər/ *noun* same as **accounting manager**

accounts payable /ə,kaʊnts 'peɪəb(ə)l/ *noun* money owed by a company

accounts receivable /ə,kaʊnts rɪ'sivəb(ə)l/ *noun* money owed to a company. Abbreviation **AR**

accreditation /ə,kredɪ'teɪʃ(ə)n/ *noun* the process of certifying the competence of a person in a certain area

accredited /ə'kredɪtɪd/ *adjective* used to describe an agent who is appointed by a company to act on its behalf

accrual basis /ə'kruəl ,beɪsɪs/ *noun* **1.** an accounting method in which receipts and payments are accounted for when they are entered in the books, whether or not the money has actually been received or paid out **2.** a gradual increase by addition □ **accrual of interest** the automatic addition of interest to capital

accrue /ə'kru/ *verb* **1.** to record a financial transaction when it takes place, and not when payment is made or received **2.** to increase and be due for payment at a later date ○ *Interest accrues from the beginning of the month.*

accrued dividend /ə,krud 'dɪvɪdend/ *noun* a dividend earned since the last dividend was paid

accrued interest /ə,krud 'ɪntrəst/ *noun* interest which has been earned by an interest-bearing investment ○ *Accrued interest is added quarterly.*

acct. *abbreviation* account

accumulate /ə'kjumjəleɪt/ *verb* to grow in quantity by being added to, or to get more of something over a period of time ○ *We allow dividends to accumulate in the fund.*

accumulated profit /ə,kjumjəleɪtɪd 'prɑfɪt/ *noun* a profit which is not paid as dividend but is taken over into the accounts of the following year

accumulated reserves /ə,kjumjəleɪtɪd rɪ'zɜrvz/ *plural noun* reserves which a company has put aside over a period of years

accumulation unit /ə,kjumjə 'leɪʃ(ə)n ,junɪt/ *noun* a share of participation in a variable annuity

accurate /'ækjərət/ *adjective* correct ○ *The sales department made an accurate forecast of sales.* ○ *The designers produced an accurate copy of the plan.*

accuse /ə'kjuz/ *verb* to say that someone has committed a crime ○ *She was accused of stealing from the petty cash box.* ○ *He was accused of industrial espionage.* (NOTE: You accuse someone **of** a crime or **of** doing something.)

achieve /ə'tʃiv/ *verb* to succeed in doing something, to do something successfully ○ *He has achieved his long-term training objectives.* ○ *The company has achieved great success in the Far East.* ○ *We achieved all our objectives in 2004.*

"…the company expects to move to profits of FFr 2m next year and achieve equally rapid growth in following years" [*Financial Times*]

achievement /ə'tʃivmənt/ *noun* success or something that has been achieved

achiever /ə'tʃivər/ *noun* a person who is successful or who tends to achieve his or her objectives ○ *It was her reputation as a high achiever that made us think of headhunting her.* ◊ **VALS**

acid test ratio /,æsɪd 'test ,reɪʃiou/ *noun* same as **liquidity ratio**

acknowledge /ək'nɑlɪdʒ/ *verb* to tell a sender that a letter, package, or shipment has arrived ○ *He has still not acknowledged my letter of the 24th.* ○ *We acknowledge receipt of your letter of June 14th.*

acknowledgment /ək'nɑlɪdʒmənt/ *noun* the act of acknowledging ○ *She sent*

an *acknowledgement of receipt.* ○ *The company sent a letter of acknowledgement after I sent in my job application.*

acquire /ə'kwaɪr/ *verb* to buy ○ *to acquire a company* ○ *We have acquired a new office building in the center of town.*

acquirer /ə'kwaɪrər/ *noun* a person or company which buys something

acquisition /,ækwɪ'zɪʃ(ə)n/ *noun* **1.** something bought ○ *The chocolate factory is our latest acquisition.* **2.** the takeover of a company. The results and cash flows of the acquired company are brought into the group accounts only from the date of acquisition: the figures for the previous period for the reporting entity should not be adjusted. The difference between the fair value of the net identifiable assets acquired and the fair value of the purchase consideration is goodwill. **3.** the act of getting or buying something

acquisition rate /,ækwɪ'zɪʃ(ə)n reɪt/ *noun* a figure that indicates how much new business is being won by a company's marketing activities

acre /'eɪkə/ *noun* a measure of the area of land (NOTE: The plural is used with figures, except before a noun: *he has bought a farm of 250 acres, he has bought a 250 acre farm.*)

across-the-board /ə,krɔs ðə 'bɔrd/ *adjective* applying to everything or everyone ○ *an across-the-board price increase* or *wage increase*

act /ækt/ *noun* a law passed by parliament which must be obeyed by the people ■ *verb* to do something ○ *The board will have to act quickly if the company's losses are going to be reduced.* ▢ **to act on something** to do what you have been asked to do by someone ○ *to act on a letter* ○ *The lawyers are acting on our instructions.*

acting /'æktɪŋ/ *adjective* working in place of someone for a short time ○ *acting manager* ○ *the Acting Chairman*

action /'ækʃən/ *noun* **1.** a thing which has been done ▢ **to take action** to do something ○ *You must take action if you want to stop people cheating you.* ○ *You must take action if you want to improve productivity.* **2.** a case in a law court where a person or company sues another person or company ▢ **to take legal action** to sue someone ○ *an action for libel* or *a libel action* ○ *an action for damages* ○ *She* *brought an action for wrongful dismissal against her former employer.*

actionable /'ækʃənəb(ə)l/ *adjective* used to describe writing, speech, or an act which could provide the grounds for bringing an action against someone ○ *Was the employer's treatment of the employee actionable?*

action-centered leadership /,ækʃən ,sentərd 'lidərʃɪp/ *noun* a theory of leadership which focuses on what leaders actually have to do in order to be effective, rather than on the personal qualities that they need to be good leaders, and which believes that leadership can be taught (NOTE: Action-centered leadership is usually illustrated by three overlapping circles, which represent the three key activities undertaken by leaders: achieving the task, building and maintaining the team and developing the individual.)

action learning /'ækʃən ,lɜrnɪŋ/ *noun* the process of learning by doing or participating in an activity

action rationality /,æɪʃ(ə)n ,ræʃ(ə)n 'ælɪti/ *noun* a decision-making model that is designed to increase the motivation for action by presenting only a limited range of alternatives and stressing only the positive outcomes

active /'æktɪv/ *adjective* involving many transactions or activities ○ *an active demand for oil stocks* ○ *an active day on the Stock Exchange* ○ *Computer stocks are very active.*

active partner /,æktɪv 'pɑrtnər/ *noun* a partner who works in a company that is a partnership

activity /æk'tɪvɪti/ *noun* something which is done ○ *out-of-work activities*

"...preliminary indications of the level of business investment and activity during the March quarter will provide a good picture of economic activity in the year" [*Australian Financial Review*]

activity chart /æk'tɪvɪti tʃɑrt/ *noun* a plan showing work which has been done, made so that it can be compared to a previous plan showing how much work should be done

act of God /,ækt əv 'gɑd/ *noun* something you do not expect to happen and which cannot be avoided, e.g., a storm or a flood (NOTE: Acts of God are not usually covered by insurance policies.)

actual /'æktʃuəl/ *adjective* real or correct ○ *What is the actual cost of one unit?* ○ *The actual figures for directors' expenses are not shown to the stockholders.*

actuals /'æktʃuəlz/ *plural noun* real figures ○ *These figures are the actuals for last year.*

actuarial /,æktʃu'eriəl/ *adjective* calculated by an actuary ○ *The premiums are worked out according to actuarial calculations.*

actuarial tables /,æktʃueriəl 'teɪb(ə)lz/ *noun* lists showing how long people are likely to live, used to calculate life insurance premiums and annuities

actuary /'æktʃuəri/ *noun* a person employed by an insurance company or other organization to calculate the risk involved in an insurance, and therefore the premiums payable by people taking out insurance

ACU *abbreviation* Asian Currency Unit

ad /æd/ *noun* same as **advertisement** (*informal*) ○ *We put an ad in the paper.* ○ *She answered an ad in the paper.* ○ *He found his job through an ad in the paper.*

ADA *abbreviation* Americans with Disabilities Act

adaptable /ə'dæptəb(ə)l/ *adjective* able to change or be changed

adaptation /,ædæp'teɪʃ(ə)n/ *noun* the process of changing something, or of being changed, to fit new conditions ○ *adaptation to new surroundings*

ad banner /'æd ,bænər/ *noun* same as **banner**

ad click /'æd klɪk/ *noun* same as **click-through**

ad click rate /'æd klɪk ,reɪt/ *noun* same as **click-through rate**

add /æd/ *verb* to put figures together to make a total ○ *If you add the interest to the capital you will get quite a large sum.* ○ *Interest is added monthly.*

add up *phrasal verb* **1.** to put several figures together to make a total ○ *He made a mistake in adding up the column of figures.* □ **the figures do not add up** the total given is not correct **2.** to make sense ○ *The complaints in the letter just do not add up.*

add up to *phrasal verb* to make a total of ○ *The total expenditure adds up to more than $1,000.*

added value /ˌædɪd 'vælju/ *noun* an amount added to the value of a product or service, equal to the difference between its cost and the amount received when it is sold. Wages, taxes, etc. are deducted from the added value to give the profit.

adding /'ædɪŋ/ *adjective* which adds, which makes additions ○ *an adding machine*

addition /ə'dɪʃ(ə)n/ *noun* **1.** a thing or person added ○ *The management has stopped all additions to the staff.* ○ *We are exhibiting several additions to our product line.* ○ *The marketing director is the latest addition to the board.* **2.** □ **in addition to** added to, as well as ○ *There are twelve registered letters to be sent in addition to this packet.* **3.** an arithmetic operation consisting of adding together two or more numbers to make a sum ○ *You don't need a calculator to do simple addition.*

additional /ə'dɪʃ(ə)nəl/ *adjective* extra which is added ○ *additional costs* ○ *They sent us a list of additional charges.* ○ *Some additional clauses were added to the contract.* ○ *Additional duty will have to be paid.*

additional premium /ə,dɪʃ(ə)nəl 'primiəm/ *noun* a payment made to cover extra items in existing insurance

address /ə'dres/ *noun* the details of number, street and town where an office is located or a person lives ○ *My business address and phone number are printed on the card.* ■ *verb* to write the details of an address on an envelope or package ○ *a letter addressed to the managing director* ○ *an incorrectly addressed package* ○ *Please address your inquiries to the manager.*

address book /ə'dres bʊk/ *noun* a special notebook, with columns printed in such a way that names, addresses and phone numbers can be entered

addressee /ˌædre'si/ *noun* a person to whom a letter or package is addressed

address list /ə'dres lɪst/ *noun* a list of names and addresses of people and companies

adequate /'ædɪkwət/ *adjective* more or less satisfactory ○ *The results of the tests on the product were adequate.*

ad hoc decision /ˌæd hɑk dɪ'sɪʒ(ə)n/ *noun* a decision taken to solve a particular problem

adhocracy /æd'hɑkrəsi/ *noun* a form of organization characterized by a flexible, organic structure, often comprising experts attached to project groups without functional divisions

adjourn /ə'dʒɜrn/ *verb* to stop a meeting for a period ○ *The chairman adjourned the meeting until three o'clock.* ○ *The meeting adjourned at midday.* □ **adjourn a case sine die** to postpone the hearing of a case without fixing a new date for it

adjournment /ə'dʒɜrnmənt/ *noun* an act of adjourning ○ *He proposed the adjournment of the meeting.*

adjudicate /ə'dʒudɪkeɪt/ *verb* to give a judgment between two parties in law or to decide a legal problem ○ *to adjudicate a claim* ○ *to adjudicate in a dispute* □ **he was adjudicated bankrupt** he was declared legally bankrupt

adjudication /ə,dʒudɪ'keɪʃ(ə)n/ *noun* the act of giving a judgment or of deciding a legal problem

adjudication of bankruptcy /ə,dʒudɪkeɪʃ(ə)n əv 'bæŋkrʌptsi/ *noun* a legal order making someone bankrupt

adjudication order /ə,dʒudɪ'keɪʃ(ə)n ,ɔrdər/ *noun* an order by a court making someone bankrupt

adjudication tribunal /ə,dʒudɪ'keɪʃ(ə)n traɪ,bjun(ə)l/ *noun* a group which adjudicates in industrial disputes

adjudicator /ə'dʒudɪkeɪtər/ *noun* a person who gives a decision on a problem ○ *an adjudicator in an industrial dispute*

adjust /ə'dʒʌst/ *verb* to change something to fit new conditions ○ *Prices are adjusted for inflation.*

adjuster /ə'dʒʌstər/ *noun* a person who calculates losses for an insurance company

adjustment /ə'dʒʌstmənt/ *noun* the act of adjusting ○ *to make an adjustment to salaries* ○ *an adjustment of prices to take account of rising costs*

adjustor /ə'dʒʌstər/ *noun* same as **adjuster**

adman /'ædmæn/ *noun* a man who works in advertising (*informal*) ○ *The admen are using balloons as promotional material.*

admin /'ædmɪn/ *noun* **1.** the work of administration, especially paperwork (*informal*) ○ *All this admin work takes a* *lot of my time.* ○ *There is too much admin in this job.* ○ *Admin costs seem to be rising each quarter.* ○ *The admin people have sent the report back.* **2.** administration staff or the administration department ○ *Admin say they need the report immediately.* ○ *She did not answer my note but sent it on to admin.* (NOTE: no plural; as a group of people it can have a plural verb)

administer /əd'mɪnɪstər/ *verb* to organize, manage or direct the whole of an organization or part of one ○ *She administers a large pension fund.* ○ *It will be the HR manager's job to administer the induction program.*

administered price /əd'mɪnɪstərd praɪs/ *noun* a price fixed by a manufacturer which cannot be varied by a retailer (NOTE: The U.K. term is **resale price maintenance.**)

administration /əd,mɪnɪ'streɪʃ(ə)n/ *noun* **1.** the action of organizing, controlling or managing a company **2.** a person or group of people who manage or direct an organization ○ *It is up to the administration to solve the problem, not the government.* **3.** the running of a company in receivership by an administrator appointed by the courts **4.** an appointment by a court of a person to manage the affairs of a company

administration costs /əd,mɪnɪ 'streɪʃ(ə)n ,kɔsts/, **administration expenses** /əd,mɪnɪ'streɪʃ(ə)n ɪk,spensɪz/ *plural noun* the costs of management, not including production, marketing, or distribution costs

administrative /əd'mɪnɪstrətɪv/ *adjective* referring to administration ○ *administrative details* ○ *administrative expenses*

administrator /əd'mɪnɪstreɪtər/ *noun* **1.** a person who directs the work of other employees in a business ○ *After several years as a college teacher, she hopes to become an administrator.* **2.** a person appointed by a court to manage the affairs of someone who dies without leaving a will **3.** *U.K.* a person appointed by a court to administer a company which is insolvent (NOTE: The U.S. term is **receiver.**)

admission /əd'mɪʃ(ə)n/ *noun* **1.** ○ *free admission on Sundays* ○ *There is a £1 admission charge.* ○ *Admission is free on presentation of this card.* □ **admission,**

admission charge, admission fee the price to be paid before going into an area or building, e.g., to see an exhibition **2.** an act of saying that something really happened ○ *He had to resign after his admission that he had passed information to the competition.*

admit /əd'mɪt/ *verb* to say that something is correct, to say that something really happened ○ *The chairman admitted he had taken the cash from the company's safe.* (NOTE: **admitting – admitted**)

admittance /əd'mɪt(ə)ns/ *noun* the act of allowing someone to go in ○ *no admittance except on business*

adopt /ə'dɑpt/ *verb* to agree to something or to accept something

adoption curve /ə'dɑpʃən kɜrv/ *noun* a line on a graph showing how many consumers adopt or buy a new product at various time periods after the launch date ○ *The adoption curve shows that most people who buy the product do so at a fairly late stage.*

ADP *abbreviation* automatic data processing

ADR *abbreviation* American Depositary Receipt

ad valorem duty /,æd və'lɔrəm ,duti/ *noun* the duty calculated on the sales value of the goods

ad valorem tax /,æd və'lɔrem tæks/ *noun* a tax calculated according to the value of the goods taxed

advance /əd'væns/ *noun* **1.** money paid as a loan or as a part of a payment to be made later ○ *She asked if she could have a cash advance.* ○ *We paid her an advance on account.* ○ *Can I have an advance of $100 against next month's salary?* **2.** an increase **3.** □ **in advance** early, before something happens ○ *freight payable in advance* ○ *prices fixed in advance* ■ *adjective* early, or taking place before something else happens ○ *advance payment* ○ *Advance vacation bookings are up on last year.* ○ *You must give seven days' advance notice of withdrawals from the account.* ■ *verb* **1.** to pay an amount of money to someone as a loan or as a part of a payment to be made later ○ *The bank advanced him $100,000 against the security of his house.* **2.** to increase ○ *Prices generally advanced on the stock market.* **3.** to make something happen earlier ○ *The date of the shipping* *has been advanced to May 10th.* ○ *The meeting with the German distributors has been advanced from 11:00 to 9:30.*

advanced manufacturing technology /əd,vænst ,mænjəfæktʃərɪŋ tek'nɑlədʒi/ *noun* modern computer-based technology that can be introduced at every stage of the manufacturing process, from design through to assembly, to make production faster and more efficient. Abbreviation **AMT** (NOTE: Advanced manufacturing technology includes such things as computer-aided design, computer-aided engineering, computer-integrated manufacturing, automated materials handling systems, electronic data interchange and robotics.)

advantage /əd'væntɪdʒ/ *noun* something useful which may help you to be successful ○ *Knowledge of two foreign languages is an advantage.* ○ *There is no advantage in arriving at the exhibition before it opens.* ○ *Fast typing is an advantage in a secretary.* □ **to take advantage of something** to use something which helps you

adventure training /əd'ventʃər ,treɪnɪŋ/, **adventure learning** /əd'ventʃər ,lɜrnɪŋ/ *noun* a type of training in which employees engage in group games and physically demanding outdoor activities such as climbing and rappelling away from their usual work environment (NOTE: The goal of adventure training is to develop skills in leadership, problem-solving, decision-making, and interpersonal communication and to build team spirit.)

adverse /'ædvɜrs/ *adjective* unfavorable □ **adverse balance of trade** a situation in which a country imports more than it exports □ **adverse trading conditions** bad conditions for trade

advert /'ædvɜrt/ *noun U.K.* same as **advertisement** (*informal*)

advertise /'ædvərtaɪz/ *verb* to arrange and pay for publicity designed to help sell products or services or to find new employees ○ *to advertise a vacancy* ○ *to advertise for a secretary* ○ *to advertise a new product*

advertisement /əd'vɜrtɪsmənt/ *noun* **1.** a notice which shows that something is for sale, that a service is offered, that someone wants something, or that a job is vacant **2.** a short movie on television or a

short announcement on the radio which tries to persuade people to use a product or service

advertisement billboard /əd,vɜrtɪsmənt 'bɪlbɔrd/ *noun* a large board for posters

advertisement manager /əd'vɜrtɪsmənt ,mænɪdʒər/ *noun* the manager in charge of the advertisement section of a newspaper

advertisement panel /əd'vɜrtɪsmənt ,pæn(ə)l/ *noun* a specially designed large advertising space in a newspaper

advertiser /'ædvərtaɪzər/ *noun* a person or company that advertises ○ *The catalog gives a list of advertisers.*

advertising /'ædvərtaɪzɪŋ/ *noun* the business of announcing that something is for sale or of trying to persuade customers to buy a product or service ○ *She works in advertising* or *She has a job in advertising.* ○ *Their new advertising campaign is being launched next week.* ○ *The company has asked an advertising agent to prepare a presentation.* □ **to take advertising space in a paper** to book space for an advertisement in a newspaper

advertising agency /'ædvərtaɪzɪŋ ,eɪdʒənsi/ *noun* an office which plans, designs, and manages advertising for other companies

advertising budget /'ædvərtaɪzɪŋ ,bʌdʒət/ *noun* money planned for spending on advertising ○ *Our advertising budget has been increased.*

advertising campaign /'ædvərtaɪzɪŋ kæm,peɪn/ *noun* a coordinated publicity or advertising drive to sell a product

advertising jingle /'ædvərtaɪzɪŋ ,dʒɪŋg(ə)l/ *noun* a short and easily remembered tune or song to advertise a product on television, etc.

advertising manager /'ædvərtaɪzɪŋ ,mænɪdʒər/ *noun* the manager in charge of advertising a company's products

advertising medium /'ædvərtaɪzɪŋ ,midiəm/ *noun* a type of advertisement, e.g., a TV commercial ○ *The product was advertised through the medium of the trade press.* (NOTE: The plural for this meaning is **media**.)

advertising rates /'ædvərtaɪzɪŋ reɪts/ *noun* the amount of money charged for advertising space in a newspaper or advertising time on TV

advertising space /'ædvərtaɪzɪŋ speɪs/ *noun* a space in a newspaper set aside for advertisements

advertorial /ˌædvər'tɔːriəl/ *noun* text in a magazine which is not written by the editorial staff but by an advertiser

advice /əd'vaɪs/ *noun* **1.** a notification telling someone what has happened **2.** an opinion as to what action to take ○ *The accountant's advice was to send the documents to the police.* □ **to take legal advice** to ask a lawyer to say what should be done ◇ **as per advice** according to what is written on the advice note

advice note /əd'vaɪs nəʊt/ *noun* the written notice to a customer giving details of goods ordered and shipped but not yet delivered. Also called **letter of advice**

advise /əd'vaɪz/ *verb* **1.** to tell someone what has happened ○ *We have been advised that the shipment will arrive next week.* **2.** to suggest to someone what should be done ○ *The lawyer advised us to send the documents to the police.*

  advise against *phrasal verb* to suggest that something should not be done ○ *The HR manager advised against dismissing the staff without notice.*

adviser /əd'vaɪzər/, **advisor** *noun* a person who suggests what should be done ○ *He is consulting the company's legal adviser.*

advisory /əd'vaɪz(ə)ri/ *adjective* as an adviser ○ *She is acting in an advisory capacity.*

advisory board /əd'vaɪz(ə)ri ˌbɔːd/ *noun* a group of advisers

affair /ə'feə/ *noun* business or dealings ○ *Are you involved in the copyright affair?* ○ *His affairs were so difficult to understand that the lawyers had to ask accountants for advice.*

affect /ə'fekt/ *verb* to cause some change in something, especially to have a bad effect on something ○ *The new government regulations do not affect us.*

affidavit /ˌæfɪ'deɪvɪt/ *noun* a written statement which is signed and sworn before a judge or other person authorized to administer oaths, and which can then be used as evidence in court

affiliate /ə'fɪlieɪt/ *noun* a company which partly owns another company, or is partly owned by the same holding company as another

affiliated /ə'fɪlieɪtɪd/ *adjective* connected with or owned by another company ○ *Smiths Inc. is one of our affiliated companies.*

affiliate partner /ə'fɪliət ˌpɑːtnər/ *noun* a company which puts advertising onto its website for other companies, who pay for this service

affiliate program /ə'fɪliət ˌprəʊgræm/ *noun* a form of advertising on the web, in which a business persuades other businesses to put banners and buttons advertising its products or services on their websites and pays them a commission on any purchases made by their customers. Also called **associate program**

affinity card /ə'fɪnɪti kɑːd/ *noun* a credit card where a percentage of each purchase made is given by the credit card company to a stated charity

affirmative /ə'fɜːmətɪv/ *adjective* meaning "yes" □ **the answer was in the affirmative** the answer was yes

affirmative action /əˌfɜːmətɪv 'ækʃən/ *noun* the practice of providing opportunities for disadvantaged groups such as ethnic minorities, women or people with disabilities

affluence /'æfluəns/ *noun* wealth and a high standard of living

  "For many older Koreans, who 20 years ago worked more than 60 hours a week to barely scrape by, such affluence is unimaginable." [*BusinessWeek*]

affluent society /ˌæfluənt sə'saɪɪti/ *noun* a type of society where most people are rich

afford /ə'fɔːd/ *verb* to be able to pay for or buy something ○ *We could not afford the cost of two telephones.* ○ *The company cannot afford the time to train new staff.* (NOTE: Only used after **can, cannot, could, could not, able to**)

AFL-CIO *noun* an organization former by the merger U.S. labor unions. Full form **American Federation of Labor – Congress of Industrial Organisations**

after-hours buying /'æftə aʊəz/, **after-hours selling, after-hours dealing** *noun* the activity of buying, selling or dealing in stocks after the Stock Exchange has officially closed for the day, such deals being subject to normal Stock Exchange rules. In this way, dealers can take advantage of the fact that because of time differences, the various stock exchanges around the world are open almost all twenty-four hours of the day.

after-hours trading /ˌæftə aʊrz ˈtreɪdɪŋ/ *noun* trading after the Stock Exchange had closed

after-sales service /ˌæftər seɪlz ˈsɜːrvɪs/ *noun* a service of a machine carried out by the seller for some time after the machine has been bought

after-tax profit /ˌæftə ˈtæks ˌprɑfɪt/ *noun* a profit after tax has been deducted

against /əˈgenst/ *preposition* **1.** in view of the fact that something else is owed or has been pledged ○ *Can I have an advance against next month's salary?* ○ *The bank advanced him $10,000 against the security of his house.* **2.** compared with

"…investment can be written off against the marginal rate of tax" [*Investors Chronicle*]

age bracket /ˈeɪdʒ ˌbrækɪt/, **age group** /ˈeɪdʒ gruːp/ *noun* a group of people of about the same age ○ *the 25–30 age group*

age discrimination /ˈeɪdʒ dɪskrɪmɪˌneɪʃ(ə)n/ *noun* unfair treatment resulting from prejudice against a person on the grounds of his or her age (NOTE: Countries such as Australia and the United States have passed laws to make age discrimination illegal)

"The U.S. Equal Employment Opportunity Commission reports that during fiscal 2002, complaints of age discrimination were up 14.5% from the prior year" [*BusinessWeek*]

ageism /ˈeɪdʒɪz(ə)m/ *noun* unfair discrimination against older people

age limit /ˈeɪdʒ ˌlɪmɪt/ *noun* the top age at which you are allowed to do a job ○ *There is an age limit of thirty-five for the position of buyer.*

agency /ˈeɪdʒənsi/ *noun* **1.** an office or job of representing another company in an area ○ *They signed an agency agreement* or *an agency contract.* **2.** an office or business which arranges things for other companies

agency labor /ˈeɪdʒənsi ˌleɪbər/ *noun* staff supplied by an employment agency

agenda /əˈdʒendə/ *noun* a list of things to be discussed at a meeting ○ *The conference agenda* or *the agenda of* ○ *After two hours we were still discussing the first item*

on the agenda. ○ *We usually put finance at the top of the agenda.* ○ *The chair wants two items removed from* or *taken off the agenda.*

agent /ˈeɪdʒənt/ *noun* **1.** a person who represents a company or another person in an area ○ *to be the agent for BMW cars* ○ *to be the agent for IBM* **2.** a person in charge of an agency ○ *an advertising agent* ○ *The real estate agent sent me a list of properties for sale.* ○ *Our trip was organized through our local travel agent.* **3.** □ **(business) agent** the chief local official of a labor union ○ *Management would only discuss the new payment program with agents officially representing the workers.*

agent's commission /ˌeɪdʒənts kəˈmɪʃ(ə)n/ *noun* money, often a percentage of sales, paid to an agent

aggregate /ˈægrɪgət/ *adjective* total, with everything added together ○ *aggregate output*

aggregate demand /ˌægrɪgət dɪˈmænd/ *noun* the total demand for goods and services from all sectors of the economy including individuals, companies, and the government ○ *Economists are studying the recent fall in aggregate demand.* ○ *As incomes have risen, so has aggregate demand.*

aggregate supply /ˌægrɪgət səˈplaɪ/ *noun* all goods and services on the market ○ *Is aggregate supply meeting aggregate demand?*

aggregator /ˈægrɪgeɪtər/ *noun* an organization that acts as a link between producers and customers in business dealings over the Internet. The aggregator selects products for sale over the Internet, sets prices, and ensures that orders are fulfilled.

aging schedule /ˈeɪdʒɪŋ ˌskedʒəl/ *noun* a list which analyzes a company's debtors, showing the number of days their payments are outstanding

AGM *abbreviation U.K.* Annual General Meeting

agora /ˈægərə/ *noun* a marketplace on the Internet

agree /əˈgriː/ *verb* **1.** to decide and approve something together with another person or other people ○ *The figures were agreed between the two parties.* ○ *We have agreed the budgets for next year.* ○ *The*

terms of the contract are still to be agreed.
2. □ **to agree on something** to come to a decision that is acceptable to everyone about something ○ *We all agreed on the need for action.* **3.** □ **to agree to something** to say that you accept something that is suggested ○ *After some discussion he agreed to our plan.* □ **to agree to do something** to say that you will do something ○ *She agreed to be chairman.* ○ *Will the finance director agree to resign?* **4.** to be the same as ○ *The two sets of calculations do not agree.*

   agree with *phrasal verb* **1.** to say that your opinions are the same as someone else's ○ *I agree with the chairman that the figures are lower than normal.* **2.** to be the same as ○ *The auditors' figures do not agree with those of the accounts department.*

agreed /ə'griːd/ *adjective* having been accepted by everyone ○ *We pay an agreed amount each month.* ○ *The agreed terms of employment are laid down in the contract.*

agreed price /ə,griːd 'praɪs/ *noun* a price which has been accepted by both the buyer and seller

agreed takeover bid /ə,griːd 'teɪkoʊvər ,bɪd/ *noun* a takeover bid which is accepted by the target company and recommended by its directors to its stockholders

agreement /ə'griːmənt/ *noun* a spoken or written contract between people or groups which explains how they will act ○ *a written agreement* ○ *an unwritten* or *verbal agreement* ○ *to draw up* or *to draft an agreement* ○ *to break an agreement* ○ *to sign an agreement* ○ *to reach an agreement* or *to come to an agreement on something* ○ *a collective wage agreement*

agricultural co-operative /,ægrɪkʌltʃ(ə)rəl koʊ 'apərətɪv/ *noun* a farm run by groups of workers who are the owners and share the profits

agricultural economist /,ægrɪkʌltʃ(ə)rəl ɪ'kanəmɪst/ *noun* a person who specializes in the study of finance and investment in agriculture

agriculture /'ægrɪkʌltʃər/ *noun* use of land for growing crops or raising animals, etc. ○ *Agriculture is still an important part of the nation's economy.*

ahead /ə'hed/ *adverb* in front of, better than ○ *We are already ahead of our sales forecast.* ○ *The company has a lot of work ahead of it if it wants to increase its market share.*

AICPA *abbreviation* American Institute of Certified Public Accountants

aim /eɪm/ *noun* something which you try to do ○ *One of our aims is to increase the quality of our products.* □ **the company has achieved all its aims** the company has done all the things it had hoped to do ■ *verb* to try to do something ○ *Each member of the sales team must aim to double their previous year's sales.* ○ *We aim to be No. 1 in the market within two years.*

air /er/ *noun* a method of traveling or sending freight using aircraft ○ *to send a letter* or *a shipment by air* ■ *verb* □ **to air a grievance** to talk about or discuss a grievance ○ *The management committee is useful because it allows the workers' representatives to air their grievances.*

air cargo /'er ,kargoʊ/ *noun* freight sent by air

air carrier /'er ,kæriər/ *noun* a company which sends cargo or passengers by air

air forwarding /'er ,fɔrwərdɪŋ/ *noun* the process of arranging for freight to be shipped by air

air freight /'er freɪt/ *noun* the transportation of goods in aircraft, or goods sent by air ○ *to send a shipment by air freight* ○ *Air freight tariffs are rising.*

airfreight /'erfreɪt/ *verb* to send freight by air ○ *to airfreight a consignment to Mexico* ○ *We airfreighted the shipment because our agent ran out of stock.*

airline /'erlaɪn/ *noun* a company which carries passengers or cargo by air

airmail /'ermeɪl/ *noun* a postal service which sends letters or packages by air ○ *to send a package by airmail* ○ *Airmail charges have risen by 15%.* ■ *verb* to send letters or packages by air ○ *We airmailed the document to New York.*

airmail envelope /'ermeɪl ,envəloʊp/ *noun* a very light envelope for sending airmail letters

airmail letter /'ermeɪl ,letər/ *noun* a letter sent by air

airmail transfer /'ermeɪl ,trænsfər/ *noun* an act of sending money from one bank to another by airmail

airport bus /ˈerpɔrt bʌs/ *noun* a bus which takes passengers to and from an airport

airport security /ˌerpɔrt sɪˈkjʊrɪti/ *noun* actions taken to protect aircraft and passengers against attack

airport tax /ˈerpɔrt tæks/ *noun* a tax added to the price of an air ticket to cover the cost of running an airport

airport terminal /ˌerpɔrt ˈtɜrmɪn(ə)l/ *noun* the main building at an airport where passengers arrive and depart

air terminal /ˈer ˌtɜrmɪn(ə)l/ *noun* a building in a town where passengers meet to be taken by bus to an airport outside the town

all /ɔl/ *adjective, pronoun* everything or everyone ○ *All (of) the managers attended the meeting.* ○ *A salesman should know the prices of all the products he is selling.*

all-in /ˌɔl ˈɪn/ *adjective U.K.* same as **all-inclusive**

all-inclusive /ɔl ɪnˈkluːsɪv/ *adjective* including everything ○ *Sign up now for an all-inclusive vacation package.*

all-in rate /ˌɔl ɪn ˈreɪt/ *noun* a price which covers all the costs connected with a purchase, such as delivery, tax and insurance, as well as the cost of the goods themselves

allocate /ˈæləkeɪt/ *verb* **1.** to provide a particular amount from a total sum of money for a particular purpose ○ *We allocate 10% of revenue to publicity.* ○ *$2,500 was allocated to office furniture.* **2.** to divide something in various ways and share it ○ *How are we going to allocate the available office space?*

allocation /ˌæləˈkeɪʃ(ə)n/ *noun* the process of providing sums of money for particular purposes, or a sum provided for a purpose ○ *the allocation of funds to a project*

allot /əˈlɒt/ *verb* to to divide up and share

allotment /əˈlɒtmənt/ *noun* the process of dividing something up and sharing it, especially money between various departments, projects, or people ○ *The allotment of funds to each project is the responsibility of the finance director.*

all-out strike /ˌɔl aʊt ˈstraɪk/ *noun* a complete strike by all employees

allow /əˈlaʊ/ *verb* **1.** to say that someone can do something ○ *Junior members of*
staff are not allowed to use the chairman's elevator.* ○ *The company allows all members of staff to take six days' vacation at Christmas.* **2.** to give ○ *to allow 5% discount to members of staff* **3.** to agree to or accept legally ○ *to allow a claim* or *an appeal*

allow for *phrasal verb* **1.** to give a discount for something, or to add an extra sum to cover something ○ *to allow for money paid in advance* ○ *Add on an extra 10% to allow for postage and packing.* ○ **delivery is not allowed for** delivery charges are not included **2.** to include something in your calculations □ **allow 28 days for delivery** calculate that delivery will take up to 28 days

allowable /əˈlaʊəb(ə)l/ *adjective* legally accepted. Opposite **disallowable**

allowable expenses /əˌlaʊəb(ə)l ɪkˈspensɪz/ *plural noun* business expenses which can be claimed against tax

allowance /əˈlaʊəns/ *noun* **1.** money which is given for a special reason ○ *a travel allowance* or *a traveling allowance* **2.** *U.K.* a part of an income which is not taxed ○ *allowances against tax* or *tax allowances* ○ *personal allowances* (NOTE: The U.S. term is **exemption**) **3.** money removed in the form of a discount ○ *an allowance for depreciation* ○ *an allowance for exchange loss*

all-risks policy /ˌɔl ˈrɪsks ˌpɑlɪsi/ *noun* an insurance policy which covers risks of any kind, with no exclusions

all-time /ˌɔl ˈtaɪm/ *adjective* □ **all-time high**, **all-time low** highest or lowest point ever reached ○ *Sales have fallen from their all-time high of last year.*

"…shares closed at an all-time high yesterday as expectations grew of lower interest rates" [*Times*]

alphabetical order /ˌælfəbetɪk(ə)l ˈɔrdər/ *noun* the arrangement of records such as files and index cards in the order of the letters of the alphabet

alter /ˈɔltər/ *verb* to change ○ *to alter the terms of a contract*

alteration /ˌɔltəˈreɪʃ(ə)n/ *noun* a change which has been made ○ *He made some alterations to the terms of a contract.* ○ *The agreement was signed without any alterations.*

alternate /'ɔltərnət, ɔl'tɜrnət/ *adjective* other, which can take the place of something

alternate director /ɔl,tɜrnɪt daɪ'rektər/ *noun* a person nominated by a director to attend meetings in his or her place

alternative /ɔl'tɜrnətɪv/ *noun* a thing which can be done instead of another ○ *What is the alternative to firing half the staff?* □ **we have no alternative** there is nothing else we can do ■ *adjective U.K.* same as **alternate** □ **to find someone alternative employment** to find someone another job

alternative minimum tax /ɔl,tɜrnətɪv ,mɪnɪməm 'tæks/ *noun* a way of calculating U.S. income tax that is intended to ensure that wealthy individuals, corporations, trusts, and estates pay at least some tax regardless of deductions, but that is increasingly targeting the middle class. Abbreviation **AMT**

Altman Z-score /,ɔltmən 'zi ,skɔr/ *noun* a calculated score using data from a financial statement that is intended to evaluate a company's financial health or predict its likelihood of entering bankruptcy. Also called **Z-score**

altogether /,ɔltə'geðər/ *adverb* putting everything together ○ *The staff of the three companies in the group come to 2,500 altogether.* ○ *The company lost $2m last year and $4m this year, making the loss $6m altogether for the two years.*

a.m. /,eɪ 'em/ *adverb* in the morning, before 12 midday ○ *The flight leaves at 9.20 a.m.* ○ *Telephone calls before 6 a.m. are charged at the cheap rate.* (NOTE: The U.S. spelling is **A.M.**)

amalgamate /ə'mælgəmeɪt/ *verb* to join together with another group ○ *The amalgamated group includes six companies.*

ambition /æm'bɪʃ(ə)n/ *noun* what someone wants to do or achieve in their life ○ *We insist that our sales representatives have plenty of ambition.* ○ *Her ambition is to become the senior partner in the firm.*

ambitious /æm'bɪʃəs/ *adjective* full of ambition, wanting to do or achieve something ○ *He is ambitious, but not very competent.*

amend /ə'mend/ *verb* to change and make more correct or acceptable ○ *Please amend your copy of the contract accordingly.*

amendment /ə'mendmənt/ *noun* a change to a document ○ *to propose an amendment to the constitution* ○ *to make amendments to a contract*

American Bankers Association /ə,merɪkən 'bæŋkəz ə,sousieɪʃ(ə)n/ *noun* an association that represents U.S. banks and promotes good practice. Abbreviation **ABA**

American Depositary Receipt /ə,merɪkən dɪ'pazɪtri rɪ,sit/ *noun* a document issued by an American bank to U.S. citizens, making them unregistered stockholders of companies in foreign countries. The document allows them to receive dividends from their investments, and ADRs can themselves be bought or sold. Abbreviation **ADR**

COMMENT: Buying and selling ADRs is easier for American investors than buying or selling the actual shares themselves, as it avoids stamp duty and can be carried out in dollars without incurring exchange costs.

American Economics Association /ə,merɪkən ,ikə'namɪks ə,sousieɪʃ(ə)n/ *noun* an association that represents U.S. economists, mainly academicians. Abbreviation **AEA**

American Federation of Labor and Congress of Industrial Organizations *noun* full form of **AFL-CIO**

American Institute of Certified Public Accountants /ə,merɪkən ,ɪnstɪtjut əv ,sɜrtɪfaɪd ,pʌblɪk ə'kauntənts/ *noun* the national association for certified public accountants. Abbreviation **AICPA**

American Stock Exchange /ə,merɪkən 'stak ɪks,tʃeɪndʒ/ *noun* the smaller of the two Stock Exchanges based in New York (the other is the New York Stock Exchange or NYSE). Abbreviation **Amex** (NOTE: Also called **Curb Exchange** or **Little Board,** as opposed to the **Big Board,** or **NYSE.**)

Americans with Disabilities Act /ə,merɪkənz wɪθ ,dɪsə'bɪlɪtiz ,ækt/ *noun* a civil rights law passed in the United States in 1990 that is designed to prevent discrimination and enable somebody with a physical or mental disability to participate fully in all aspects of society. This includes an equal opportunity to work at a job for which he or she is qualified. Abbreviation **ADA**

Amex /'æmeks/ *abbreviation* American Stock Exchange (*informal*)

AmEx /'æmeks/ *abbreviation* American Express

amortizable /ˌæmɔrˈtaɪzəb(ə)l/ *adjective* being possible to amortize ○ *The capital cost is amortizable over a period of ten years.*

amortization /əˌmɔrtaɪˈzeɪʃ(ə)n/ *noun* an act of amortizing ○ *amortization of a debt*

amortize /əˈmɔrtaɪz/ *verb* **1.** to repay a loan by regular payments, most of which pay off the interest on the loan at first, and then reduce the principal as the repayment period progresses ○ *The capital cost is amortized over five years.* **2.** to depreciate or to write down the capital value of an asset over a period of time in a company's accounts

amount /əˈmaʊnt/ *noun* a quantity of money ○ *A small amount has been deducted to cover our costs.* ○ *A large amount is still owing.* ○ *What is the amount to be written off?*

  amount to *phrasal verb* to make a total of ○ *Their debts amount to over $1m.*

AMT *abbreviation* **1.** advanced manufacturing technology **2.** alternative minimum tax

analysis /əˈnæləsɪs/ *noun* a detailed examination and report ○ *a job analysis* ○ *market analysis* ○ *Her job is to produce a regular sales analysis.* (NOTE: The plural is **analyses**.)

analyst /'ænəlɪst/ *noun* a person who analyzes ○ *a market analyst* ○ *a systems analyst*

analytical /ˌænəˈlɪtɪk(ə)l/ *adjective* using analysis

analytics /ˌænəˈlɪtɪks/ *noun* the evaluation of the effectiveness of a website, considering, e.g., the number of visitors, their route to the site, and how long they stayed

analyze *verb* to examine someone or something in detail ○ *to analyze a statement of account* ○ *to analyze the market potential*

ancillary-to-trade /ænˌsɪləri tə ˈtreɪd/ *noun* a service which supports trade, e.g.,

banking and advertising ○ *The recession has affected ancillaries-to-trade and the industries they support and supply.* ○ *Advertising was the fastest expanding ancillary-to-trade at that time.*

angel /'eɪndʒəl/ *noun* an investor in a company in its early stages, often looking for returns over a longer period of time than a venture capitalist

announce /əˈnaʊns/ *verb* to tell something to the public ○ *to announce the first year's trading results* ○ *The director has announced a program of investment.*

announcement /əˈnaʊnsmənt/ *noun* an act of telling something in public ○ *the announcement of a cutback in expenditure* ○ *the announcement of the appointment of a new managing director* ○ *The managing director made an announcement to the staff.*

annual /'ænjuəl/ *adjective* for one year ○ *an annual statement of income* ○ *They have six weeks' annual leave.* ○ *The company has an annual growth of 5%.* ○ *We get an annual bonus.* □ **on an annual basis** each year ○ *The figures are revised on an annual basis.*

annual accounts /ˌænjuəl əˈkaʊnts/ *plural noun* the accounts prepared at the end of a financial year ○ *The annual accounts have been sent to the stockholders.*

annual depreciation /ˌænjuəl dɪˌpriːʃiˈeɪʃ(ə)n/ *noun* a reduction in the book value of an asset at a particular rate per year. ◊ **straight line depreciation**

Annual General Meeting /ˌænjuəl ˌdʒen(ə)rəl ˈmiːtɪŋ/ *noun U.K.* same as **annual meeting**

annual income /ˌænjuəl ˈɪnkʌm/ *noun* money received during a calendar year

annualized /'ænjuəlaɪzd/ *adjective* shown on an annual basis

> "…he believes this may have caused the economy to grow at an annualized rate of almost 5 per cent in the final quarter of last year" [*Investors Chronicle*]

annualized percentage rate /ˌænjuəlaɪzd pəˈsentɪdʒ ˌreɪt/ *noun* a yearly percentage rate, calculated by multiplying the monthly rate by twelve. Abbreviation **APR** (NOTE: The annualized percentage rate is not as accurate as the Annual Percentage Rate (APR), which includes fees and other charges.)

annually /'ænjuəli/ *adverb* each year ○ *The figures are updated annually.*

annual meeting /ˌænjuəl ˌdʒen(ə)rəl 'mitɪŋ/ *noun* an annual meeting of all stockholders of a company, when the company's financial situation is presented by and discussed with the directors, when the accounts for the past year are approved and when dividends may be declared and audited. Also called **annual stockholders' meeting** (NOTE: The U.K. term is **Annual General Meeting**.)

Annual Percentage Rate /ˌænjuəl pər'sentɪdʒ reɪt/ *noun* a rate of interest (such as on the installment plan) shown on an annual compound basis, and including fees and charges. Abbreviation **APR**

annual report /ˌænjuəl rɪ'pɔrt/ *noun* a report of a company's financial situation at the end of a year, sent to all the stockholders

annual stockholders' meeting /ˌænjuəl ˌdʒen(ə)rəl 'mitɪŋ/ *noun* same as **annual meeting**

annuitant /ə'njuɪtənt/ *noun* a person who receives an annuity

annuity /ə'njuɪti/ *noun* **1.** money paid each year to a retired person, usually in return for a lump-sum payment. The value of the annuity depends on how long the person lives, as it usually cannot be passed on to another person. Annuities are fixed payments, and lose their value with inflation, whereas a pension can be index-linked. ○ *to buy* or *to take out an annuity* ○ *She has a government annuity* or *an annuity from the government.* **2.** a type of insurance contract in which the insurance company agrees to make regular payments to someone, usually after retirement. ◊ **fixed annuity, variable annuity**

annuity for life /əˌnjuɪti fə 'laɪf/ *noun* annual payments made to someone as long as they are alive

annul /ə'nʌl/ *verb* to cancel or to stop something being legal ○ *The contract was annulled by the court.* (NOTE: **annulling – annulled**)

annulment /ə'nʌlmənt/ *noun* the act of canceling ○ *the annulment of a contract*

answer /'ænsər/ *noun* a reply, a letter or conversation coming after someone has written or spoken ○ *my letter got no answer* or *there was no answer to my letter* ○ *I am writing in answer to your letter of Oc-*tober 6th. ○ *I tried to phone his office but there was no answer.* ■ *verb* to speak or write after someone has spoken or written to you □ **to answer a letter** to write a letter in reply to a letter which you have received □ **to answer the telephone** to lift the telephone when it rings and listen to what the caller is saying

answering service /'æns(ə)rɪŋ ˌsɜrvɪs/ *noun* an office which answers the telephone and takes messages for someone or for a company

antedate /ˌænti'deɪt/ *verb* to put an earlier date on a document ○ *The invoice was antedated to January 1st.*

anti- /ænti/ *prefix* against

anti-dumping /ˌænti 'dʌmpɪŋ/ *adjective* **1.** protecting a country against dumping ○ *anti-dumping legislation* **2.** intended to stop surplus goods being sold in foreign markets at a price that is lower than their marginal cost

"…just days before the Department of Commerce decides on anti-dumping duties for Chinese wooden bedroom furniture." [*Forbes*]

anti-dumping duty /ˌænti 'dʌmpɪŋ/ *noun* same as **countervailing duty**

anti-inflationary /ˌænti ɪn'fleɪʃ(ə)n(ə)ri/ *adjective* restricting or trying to restrict inflation ○ *anti-inflationary measures*

anti-inflationary measure /ˌænti ɪn'fleɪʃ(ə)n(ə)ri ˌmeʒər/ *noun* a measure taken to reduce inflation

anti-site /'ænti saɪt/ *noun* same as **hate site**

anti-trust /ˌænti 'trʌst/ *adjective* attacking monopolies and encouraging competition ○ *anti-trust measures*

anti-trust laws /ˌænti 'trʌst lɔz/, **anti-trust legislation** /ˌledʒɪ'sleɪʃ(ə)n/ *plural noun* laws in the United States which prevent the formation of monopolies

any other business /ˌeni ˌʌðə 'bɪznɪs/ *noun* an item at the end of an agenda, where any matter can be raised. Abbreviation **AOB**

AOB *abbreviation* any other business

apologize /ə'pɑlədʒaɪz/ *verb* to say you are sorry ○ *to apologize for the delay in answering* ○ *she apologized for being late*

appeal /ə'pil/ *noun* **1.** the fact of being attractive **2.** the act of asking a law court or a government department to change its decision ○ *He lost his appeal for damages against the company.* □ **she won her case on appeal** her case was lost in the first court, but the appeal court said that she was right ■ *verb* **1.** to attract ○ *The idea of working in Australia for six months appealed to her.* **2.** to ask a law court or a government department or to alter its decision ○ *The union appealed against the decision of the tribunal.* (NOTE: You appeal **to** a court or a person **against** a decision.)

appear /ə'pɪr/ *verb* to seem ○ *The company appeared to be doing well.* ○ *The managing director appears to be in control.*

appendix /ə'pendɪks/ *noun* **1.** additional sheets at the back of a contract **2.** additional pages at the back of a book

applicant /'æplɪkənt/ *noun* a person who applies for something ○ *an applicant for a job* or *a job applicant*

application /ˌæplɪ'keɪʃ(ə)n/ *noun* **1.** the act of asking for something, usually in writing, or a document in which someone asks for something, e.g., a job ○ *She sent off six applications for job* or *six job applications.* **2.** effort or diligence ○ *She has shown great application in her work on the project.*

application form /ˌæplɪ'keɪʃ(ə)n ˌfɔrm/ *noun* a form to be filled in when applying for a job

application service provider /ˌæplɪkeɪʃ(ə)n 'sɜrvɪs prəˌvaɪdər/ *noun* a company that provides access over the Internet to software solutions, which other companies license for use but do not own or maintain. Abbreviation **ASP**

apply /ə'plaɪ/ *verb* **1.** to ask for something, usually in writing ○ *to apply in writing* ○ *to apply in person* ○ *The more ambitious of the employees will apply for the management trainee program.* ○ *About fifty people have applied for the job, but there is only one vacancy.* **2.** to affect or to relate to ○ *This clause applies only to deals outside the EU.* (NOTE: [all senses] **applies – applying – applied**)

appoint /ə'pɔɪnt/ *verb* to choose someone for a job ○ *We have appointed a new distribution manager.* ○ *They've appointed Janet Smith (to the post of) manager.* (NOTE: You appoint a person **to** a job.)

appointee /əˌpɔɪn'tiː/ *noun* a person who is appointed to a job

appointment /ə'pɔɪntmənt/ *noun* **1.** an arrangement to meet ○ *to make* or *to fix an appointment with someone for two o'clock* ○ *He was late for his appointment.* ○ *She had to cancel her appointment.* **2.** the act of being appointed to a job, or of appointing someone to a job □ **on his appointment as manager** when he was made manager **3.** a job

appointments book /ə'pɔɪntmənts bʊk/ *noun* a desk calendar in which appointments are noted

apportion /ə'pɔrʃ(ə)n/ *verb* to share something, e.g., costs, funds, or blame ○ *Costs are apportioned according to projected revenue.*

apportionment /ə'pɔrʃ(ə)nmənt/ *noun* the sharing of costs

appraisal /ə'preɪz(ə)l/ *noun* a calculation of the value of someone or something

appraise /ə'preɪz/ *verb* to assess or to calculate the value of something or someone

appraisee /əˌpreɪ'ziː/ *noun* an employee who is being appraised by his or her manager in an appraisal interview

appreciate /ə'priːʃieɪt/ *verb* **1.** to notice how good something is **2.** (*of currency, shares, etc.*) to increase in value

appreciation /əˌpriːʃi'eɪʃ(ə)n/ *noun* **1.** an increase in value. Also called **capital appreciation 2.** the act of valuing something highly ○ *She was given a pay raise in appreciation of her excellent work.*

apprentice /ə'prentɪs/ *noun* a young person who works under contract for a period in order to be trained in a skill ■ *verb* □ **to be apprenticed to someone** to work with a skilled worker to learn from them

apprenticeship /ə'prentɪsʃɪp/ *noun* the time spent learning a skilled trade ○ *He served a six-year apprenticeship in the steel works.*

appro /'æproʊ/ *noun* same as **approval** (*informal*)

approach /ə'proʊtʃ/ *noun* an act of getting in touch with someone with a proposal ○ *The company made an approach to the supermarket chain.* ○ *The board turned down all approaches on the subject of mergers.* ○ *We have had an approach from a Japanese company to buy our car* division. ○ *She has had an approach from a firm of headhunters.* ■ *verb* to get in touch with someone with a proposal ○ *He approached the bank with a request for a loan.* ○ *The company was approached by an American publisher with the suggestion of a merger.* ○ *We have been approached several times but have turned down all offers.* ○ *She was approached by a headhunter with the offer of a job.*

appropriate *adjective* /ə'proupriət/ suitable ○ *I leave it to you to take appropriate action.* ■ *verb* /ə'prouprieit/ to put a sum of money aside for a special purpose ○ *to appropriate a sum of money for a capital project*

appropriation /ə,proupri'eɪʃ(ə)n/ *noun* the act of putting money aside for a special purpose ○ *appropriation of funds to the reserve*

appropriation account /ə,proupri 'eɪʃ(ə)n ə,kaunt/ *noun* the part of a profit and loss account which shows how the profit has been dealt with, e.g., how much has been given to the stockholders as dividends and how much is being put into the reserves

approval /ə'pruv(ə)l/ *noun* **1.** the act of saying or thinking that something is good ○ *to submit a budget for approval* **2.** □ **on approval** in order to be able to use something for a period of time and check that it is satisfactory before paying for it ○ *to buy a photocopier on approval*

approve /ə'pruv/ *verb* **1.** □ **to approve of something** to think something is good ○ *The chairman approves of the new company letterhead.* ○ *The sales staff do not approve of interference from the accounts division.* **2.** to agree to something officially ○ *to approve the terms of a contract* ○ *The proposal was approved by the board.*

approximate /ə'prɑksɪmət/ *adjective* not exact, but almost correct ○ *The sales division has made an approximate forecast of expenditure.*

approximately /ə'prɑksɪmətli/ *adverb* not quite exactly, but close to the figure shown ○ *Expenditure on marketing is approximately 10% down on the previous quarter.*

approximation /ə,prɑksɪ'meɪʃ(ə)n/ *noun* a rough calculation ○ *Each department has been asked to provide an approx-*imation of expenditure for next year.* ○ *The final figure is only an approximation.*

APR *abbreviation* Annual Percentage Rate

aptitude /'æptɪtud/ *noun* the ability to do something

aptitude test /'æptɪtud test/ *noun* a test to see if a candidate is suitable for a certain type of work. Compare **attainment test**

AR *abbreviation* accounts receivable

arbitrage /'ɑrbɪ,trɑrʒ/ *noun* the business of making a profit from the difference in value of various assets, e.g., by selling foreign currencies or commodities on one market and buying on another at almost the same time to profit from different exchange rates, or by buying currencies forward and selling them forward at a later date, to benefit from a difference in prices

arbitrage syndicate /'ɑrbɪtrɑrʒ ,sɪndɪkət/ *noun* a group of people who together raise the capital to invest in arbitrage deals

arbitrageur /'ɑrbɪtreɪdʒər/, **arbitrager** /,ɑrbɪtrɑr'ʒɜr/ *noun* a person whose business is arbitrage

COMMENT: Arbitrageurs buy stock in companies which are potential takeover targets, either to force up the price of the stock before the takeover bid, or simply as a position while waiting for the takeover bid to take place. They also sell stock in the company which is expected to make the takeover bid, since one of the consequences of a takeover bid is usually that the price of the target company rises while that of the bidding company falls. Arbitrageurs may then sell the stock in the target company at a profit, either to one of the parties making the takeover bid, or back to the company itself.

arbitrate /'ɑrbɪtreɪt/ *verb* (*of an outside party*) to try to settle an industrial dispute by talking to representatives of both sides, who agree in advance to abide by the arbitrator's decision

arbitration /,ɑrbɪ'treɪʃ(ə)n/ *noun* the settling of a dispute by an outside party agreed on by both sides ○ *to take a dispute to arbitration* or *to go to arbitration* ○ *arbitration in an industrial dispute* ○ *The two sides decided to submit the dispute to arbitration* or *to refer the question to arbitration*

arbitration board /ˌɑrbɪˈtreɪʃ(ə)n bɔrd/ *noun* a group which arbitrates

arbitrator /ˈɑrbɪtreɪtər/ *noun* a person not concerned with a dispute who is chosen by both sides to try to settle it ○ *an industrial arbitrator* ○ *They refused to accept* or *they rejected the arbitrator's ruling.*

architect /ˈɑrkɪtekt/ *noun* somebody who develops a plan or strategy for a business activity, then sees that it is carried through to completion ○ *The New York-based firm is looking for a marketing strategy architect.*

archive /ˈɑrkaɪv/ *noun* 1. a collection of documents and records preserved for their historic interest 2. a set of copies of computer files, often stored in compressed form 3. a directory of files that Internet users can access

"...hackers could delete ballots on a particular machine without any worries that the library archives would foil them." [*Forbes*]

archives /ˈɑrkaɪvz/ *noun* old documents which are kept safely ○ *The company's archives go back to its foundation in 1892.*

area /ˈeriə/ *noun* 1. a measurement of the space taken up by something (calculated by multiplying the length by the width) ○ *a no-smoking area* ○ *The area of this office is 3,400 square feet.* ○ *We are looking for a store with a sales area of about 100 square meters.* 2. a subject ○ *a problem area* or *an area for concern* 3. a district or part of a town ○ *The office is in the commercial area of the town.* ○ *Their factory is in a very good area for getting to the motorways and airports.* 4. a part of a country, a division for commercial purposes ○ *Her sales area is the Northwest.* ○ *He finds it difficult to cover all his area in a week.* 5. a part of a room, factory, restaurant, etc. ○ *a no-smoking area*

area code[1] /ˈeriə koʊd/ *noun* a special telephone number which is given to a particular area ○ *The area code for Boston is 617.*

area code[2] /ˈeəriə koʊd/ *noun* special series of numbers which you use to make a call to another town or country

area manager /ˌeriə ˈmænɪdʒər/ *noun* a manager who is responsible for a company's work in a specific part of the country

argue /ˈɑrgju/ *verb* to discuss something about which you do not agree ○ *they argued over* or *about the price* ○ *We spent hours arguing with the managing director about the site for the new factory.* ○ *The union officials argued among themselves over the best way to deal with the ultimatum from the management.*

argument /ˈɑrgjəmənt/ *noun* 1. an act of discussing something without agreeing ○ *She was sacked after an argument with the managing director.* 2. a reason for supporting or rejecting something ○ *The document gives the management's arguments in favor of flexible working hours.*

arising /əˈraɪzɪŋ/ *adjective* which comes from ○ *differences arising from the contract*

around /əˈraʊnd/ *preposition* approximately ○ *The office costs around $2,000 a year to heat.* ○ *Her salary is around $85,000.*

arrange /əˈreɪndʒ/ *verb* to organize ○ *We arranged to have the meeting in their offices.* (NOTE: You arrange **for** someone to do something; you arrange **for** something to be done; or you arrange **to do** something.)

arrangement /əˈreɪndʒmənt/ *noun* 1. the way in which something is organized ○ *The company secretary is making all the arrangements for the meeting.* 2. the settling of a financial dispute ○ *He came to an arrangement with his creditors.*

arrangement fee /əˈreɪndʒmənt fi/ *noun* a charge made by a bank to a client for arranging credit facilities

arrears /əˈrɪrz/ *plural noun* 1. money which is owed, but which has not been paid at the right time ○ *a salary with arrears effective from January 1st* ○ *We are pressing the company to pay arrears of interest.* ○ *You must not allow the mortgage payments to fall into arrears.* 2. □ **in arrears** owing money which should have been paid earlier ○ *The payments are six months in arrears.* ○ *He is six weeks in arrears with his rent.*

arrival /əˈraɪv(ə)l/ *noun* reaching a place ○ *We are waiting for the arrival of a consignment of spare parts.*

arrive /əˈraɪv/ *verb* to reach a place ○ *The consignment has still not arrived.* ○ *The shipment arrived without any documentation.* ○ *The plane arrives in Sydney* *at 4:00.* ○ *The train leaves Paris at 9:20 and arrives at Bordeaux two hours later.* (NOTE: You arrive **at** *or* **in** a place or town, but only **in** a country.)

arrive at *phrasal verb* to work out and agree on something ○ *They very quickly arrived at an acceptable price.* ○ *After some discussion we arrived at a compromise.*

article /ˈɑrtɪk(ə)l/ *noun* **1.** a product or thing for sale ○ *to launch a new article on the market* ○ *a black market in luxury articles* **2.** a section of a legal agreement such as a contract or treaty ○ *See article 8 of the contract.*

article numbering system /ˌɑrtɪk(ə)l ˈnʌmbərɪŋ ˌsɪstəm/ *noun* a universal system of identifying articles for sale, used especially in Europe and Japan, using a series of digits which can be expressed as bar codes

articles of association /ˌɑrtɪk(ə)lz əv əˌsoʊsiˈeɪʃ(ə)n/ *plural noun U.K.* same as **bylaw**

articles of incorporation /ˌɑrtɪk(ə)lz əv ɪnˌkɔrpəˈreɪʃ(ə)n/ *plural noun* a document which sets up a company and lays down the relationship between the stockholders and the company (NOTE: The U.K. term is **Memorandum of Association**.)

articulated lorry /ɑrˌtɪkjʊleɪtɪd ˈlɑri/, **articulated vehicle** /ɑrˈtɪkjʊleɪtɪd ˈviːk(ə)l/ *noun U.K.* same as **tractor-trailer**

artisan /ˌɑrtɪˈzæn/ *noun* a worker who has special training in a manual skill

asap /ˌeɪ es eɪ ˈpiː, ˈeɪsæp/, **ASAP** *abbreviation* as soon as possible

Asian Currency Unit /ˌeɪʒ(ə)n ˈkʌrənsi ˌjuːnɪt/ *noun* a unit of account for dollar deposits held in Singapore and other Asian markets. Abbreviation **ACU**

Asian dollar /ˌeɪʒ(ə)n ˈdɑlər/ *noun* an American dollar deposited in Singapore and other Asian markets, and traded in Singapore

aside /əˈsaɪd/ *adverb* to one side, out of the way □ **to put aside**, **to set aside** to save (money) ○ *He is putting $50 aside each week to pay for his car.*

ask /æsk/ *verb* **1.** to put a question to someone ○ *He asked the information office for details of companies exhibiting at the motor show.* ○ *Ask the salesclerk if the*

bill includes sales tax. **2.** to tell someone to do something ○ *He asked the switchboard operator to get him a number in Germany.* ○ *She asked her secretary to fetch a file from the managing director's office.* ○ *Customs officials asked him to open his case.*

ask for *phrasal verb* **1.** to say that you want or need something ○ *They asked for more time to repay the loan.* **2.** to put a price on something for sale ○ *They are asking $24,000 for the car.*

asking price /ˈæskɪŋ ˌpraɪs/ *noun* a price which the seller is hoping will be paid for the item being sold ○ *the asking price is $24,000*

ASP *abbreviation* application service provider

as per /ˌæz ˈpɜr/ ▶ **per**

aspirations /ˌæspɪˈreɪʃ(ə)nz/ *plural noun* ambitions or hopes of advancement in your job

assay mark /ˈæseɪ mɑrk/ *noun* a mark put on gold or silver items to show that the metal is of the correct quality

assemble /əˈsemb(ə)l/ *verb* to put a product together from various parts ○ *The engines are made in Japan and the bodies in Scotland, and the cars are assembled in France.*

assembly /əˈsembli/ *noun* **1.** the process of putting an item together from various parts ○ *There are no assembly instructions to show you how to put the computer together.* ○ *We can't put the machine together because the instructions for assembly are in Japanese.* **2.** an official meeting

assembly line /əˈsembli laɪn/ *noun* a production system where a product such as a car moves slowly through the factory with new sections added to it as it goes along ○ *She works on an assembly line* or *She is an assembly line worker.*

assertiveness /əˈsɜrtɪvnəs/ *noun* the ability to state opinions or show that you can make decisions

assertiveness training /əˈsɜrtɪvnəs ˌtreɪnɪŋ/ *noun* the process of training employees to have more confidence in themselves

assess /əˈses/ *verb* to calculate the value of something or someone ○ *to assess damages at $1,000* ○ *to assess a property for the purposes of insurance*

assessing /ə'sesɪŋ/ *noun* the process of valuing a property for local taxes

assessment /ə'sesmənt/ *noun* a calculation of value ○ *a property assessment* ○ *a tax assessment* ○ *They made a complete assessment of each employee's contribution to the organization.*

assessor /ə'sesər/ *noun* a person who makes assessments, e.g., for tax or insurance purposes

asset /'æset/ *noun* something which belongs to a company or person, and which has a value ○ *He has an excess of assets over liabilities.* ○ *Her assets are only $640 as against liabilities of $24,000.*

asset stripper /'æset ˌstrɪpər/ *noun* a person who buys a company to sell its assets

asset stripping /'æset ˌstrɪpɪŋ/ *noun* the practice of buying a company at a lower price than its asset value, and then selling its assets

asset value /ˌæset 'vælju/ *noun* the value of a company calculated by adding together all its assets

assign /ə'saɪn/ *verb* **1.** to give something to someone by means of an official legal transfer ○ *to assign a right to someone* ○ *to assign shares to someone* **2.** to give someone a job of work to do and make him or her responsible for doing it ○ *She was assigned the task of checking the sales figures.*

assignation /ˌæsɪg'neɪʃ(ə)n/ *noun* a legal transfer ○ *the assignation of stock to someone* ○ *the assignation of a patent*

assignee /ˌæsaɪ'niː/ *noun* a person who receives something which has been assigned to him or her

assignment /ə'saɪnmənt/ *noun* **1.** the legal transfer of a property or right ○ *the assignment of a patent or of a copyright* ○ *to sign a deed of assignment* **2.** a particular task given to someone ○ *Her first assignment was to improve the company's image.* ○ *The oil team is on an assignment in the North Sea.*

assignor /ˌæsaɪ'nɔr/ *noun* a person who assigns something to someone

assist /ə'sɪst/ *verb* to help ○ *Can you assist the stock controller in counting the stock?* ○ *She assists me with my income tax returns.* (NOTE: You assist someone **in** doing something or **with** something.)

assistance /ə'sɪst(ə)ns/ *noun* help ○ *Some candidates need assistance in filling in the form.*

assistant /ə'sɪst(ə)nt/ *noun* a person who helps or a clerical employee

assistant manager /əˌsɪst(ə)nt 'mænɪdʒər/ *noun* a person who helps a manager

associate /ə'soʊsiət/ *adjective* linked ■ *noun* **1.** a person who works in the same business as someone ○ *She is a business associate of mine.* **2.** a title given to a junior member of a professional organization. Senior members are usually called "fellows".

associate company /əˌsoʊsiət 'kʌmp(ə)ni/ *noun* a company which is partly owned by another company

associated /ə'soʊsieɪtɪd/ *adjective* linked

associated company /əˌsoʊsieɪtɪd 'kʌmp(ə)ni/ *noun* a company which is partly owned by another company (though less than 50%), which exerts some management control over it or has a close trading relationship with it ○ *Smith Inc. and its associated company, Jones Brothers*

associate director /əˌsoʊsiət daɪ'rektər/ *noun* a director who attends board meetings, but has not been elected by the stockholders

association /əˌsoʊsi'eɪʃ(ə)n/ *noun* a group of people or companies with the same interest ○ *an employers' association* ○ *Our company has applied to join the trade association.*

Association of University Technology Managers /əˌsoʊsieɪʃ(ə)n əv ˌjuːnɪvɜrsɪti tek'nɑlədʒi ˌmænɪdʒərz/ *noun* an association for technology transfer professionals at colleges and universities in the United States. Abbreviation **AUTM**

assortment /ə'sɔrtmənt/ *noun* a combination of goods sold together ○ *The box contains an assortment of chocolates with different centers.*

asst *abbreviation* assistant

assume /ə'sjum/ *verb* **1.** to suppose, to believe something to be true ○ *I assume you have enough money to pay these expenses?* ○ *We assume the shipment has arrived on time.* **2.** to take for yourself ○ *He has assumed responsibility for marketing.* ○ *The company will assume all risks.*

assumption /ə'sʌmpʃ(ə)n/ *noun* **1.** a general belief ○ *We are working on the assumption that the exchange rate will stay the same.* **2.** the act of taking for yourself ○ *assumption of risks* **3.** the transfer of the rest of a mortgage to someone

assurance /ə'ʃʊrəns/ *noun* a type of insurance which pays compensation for an event that is certain to happen at some time, especially for the death of the insured person. Also called **life assurance, life insurance**

assure /ə'ʃʊər/ *verb U.K.* to insure someone, or someone's life, so that the insurance company will pay compensation when that person dies ○ *He has paid the premiums to have his wife's life assured.* (NOTE: **Assure, assurer** and **assurance** are used in Britain for insurance policies relating to something which will certainly happen (such as death); for other types of policy (i.e. those against something which may or may not happen, such as an accident) use the terms **insure, insurer** and **insurance**. In the U.S. **insure, insurer** and **insurance** are used for both.)

assurer /ə'ʃʊrər/, **assuror** *noun U.K.* an insurer or a company which insures

at best /ˌæt 'best/ *adverb* □ **buy at best** an instruction to a stockbroker to buy securities at the best price available, even if it is high □ **sell at best** an instruction to a stockbroker to sell securities at the best price possible

ATM *abbreviation* automated teller machine

ATM card /'kæʃ kɑrd/ *noun* a plastic card used to obtain money from an ATM

atomistic competition /ˌætəmɪstɪk ˌkɑmpə'tɪʃ(ə)n/ *noun* same as **perfect competition**

atomize /'ætəmaɪz/ *verb* to divide up a large organization into several smaller operating units

at par /ˌæt 'pɑr/ *phrase* equal to the face value

at sight /ˌæt 'saɪt/ *adverb* immediately, when it is presented ○ *a bill of exchange payable at sight*

attach /ə'tætʃ/ *verb* to fasten or to link ○ *I am attaching a copy of my previous letter.* ○ *Please find attached a copy of my letter of June 24th.* ○ *The company attaches great importance to good time-keeping.*

attaché case /ə'tæʃeɪ keɪs/ *noun* a small case for carrying papers and documents

attachment /ə'tætʃmənt/ *noun* the act of holding a debtor's property to prevent it being sold until debts are paid

attachment of earnings /əˌtætʃmənt əv 'ɜrnɪŋz/ *noun* legal power to take money from a person's salary to pay money, which is owed, to the court

attainment /ə'teɪnmənt/ *noun* the act of reaching a certain standard or goal

attainment test /ə'teɪnmənt test/ *noun* a test designed to measure the skills which someone is currently using. Compare **aptitude test**

attempt /ə'tempt/ *noun* an act of trying to do something ○ *The company made an attempt to break into the American market.* ○ *The takeover attempt was turned down by the board.* ○ *All his attempts to get a job have failed.* ■ *verb* to try ○ *The company is attempting to get into the tourist market.* ○ *We are attempting the takeover of a manufacturing company.* ○ *He attempted to have the sales director sacked.*

attend /ə'tend/ *verb* to be present at ○ *The chairman has asked all managers to attend the meeting.* ○ *None of the stockholders attended the annual meeting.*

attend to *phrasal verb* to give careful thought to something and deal with it ○ *The managing director will attend to your complaint personally.* ○ *We have brought in experts to attend to the problem of installing the new computer.*

attendance /ə'tendəns/ *noun* the fact of being present at a meeting or at work ○ *Some of the employees were reprimanded for poor attendance.* ○ *The supervisor kept a strict record of the workers' attendance.* ○ *Promotion to the post of supervisor depends to a certain extent on a person's attendance record.* ○ *Attendance at the staff meeting is not compulsory.*

attention /ə'tenʃən/ *noun* careful thought or consideration □ **for the attention of (attn., fao)** words written on a letter to show that a certain person must see it and deal with it ○ *Mark your letter "for the attention of the Managing Director".*

attention management /əˌtenʃən 'mænɪdʒmənt/ *noun* the use of techniques designed to make sure that employees' minds remain focused on their work and on the aims of the organization they work for, since inattentiveness results in wasted time (NOTE: Getting people to be emotionally involved in their work and organizational goals is an important element in attention management.)

attitude research /'ætɪtud rɪ,sɜrtʃ/, **attitude survey** /'ætɪtud ,sɜrveɪ/ *noun* research that is intended to reveal what people think and feel about an organization, its products or services, and its activities (NOTE: Attitude research can be used to discover the opinions either of consumers and the general public or of an organization's own employees.)

attn. *abbreviation* for the attention of

attorney /ə'tɜrni/ *noun* a person who is legally allowed to act on behalf of someone else

attorney-at-law /ə,tɜrni ət 'lɔr/ *noun* a lawyer who has a state license to practice in a court

attract /ə'trækt/ *verb* **1.** to make someone want to join or come to something ○ *The company is offering free holidays in Mexico to attract buyers.* ○ *We have difficulty in attracting skilled staff to this part of the country.* **2.** to bring something or someone to something ○ *The deposits attract interest at 15%.*

attractive /ə'træktɪv/ *adjective* attracting something or someone □ **attractive prices** prices which are cheap enough to make buyers want to buy □ **attractive salary** a good salary to make high-quality applicants apply for the job

attributable profit /ə,trɪbjʊtəb(ə)l 'prɑfɪt/ *noun* a profit which can be shown to come from a particular area of the company's operations

attribution theory of leadership /,ætrɪbjuʃ(ə)n ,θɪri əv 'lidəʃɪp/ *noun* the theory that leaders observe the behavior of the people they lead, decide what it is that is causing them to behave in that particular way, e.g., what is causing them to perform well or perform badly, and base their own actions on what they believe those causes to be

attrition /ə'trɪʃ(ə)n/ *noun* **1.** a decrease in the loyalty of consumers to a product, due to factors such as boredom or desire for a change ○ *We must adapt our products if we are to avoid attrition.* ○ *Attrition showed the company that brand loyalty*

could not be taken for granted. **2.** the process of losing employees because they resign or retire, not because they are dismissed (NOTE: The U.K. term is **natural wastage**)

auction /'ɔkʃən/ *noun* a method of selling goods where people who want to buy compete with each other by saying how much they will offer for something, and the item is sold to the person who makes the highest offer ○ *Their furniture will be sold in the auction rooms next week.* ○ *They announced a sale by auction of the fire-damaged stock.* ○ *The equipment was sold by auction* or *at auction.* □ **to put an item up for auction** to offer an item for sale at an auction ■ *verb* to sell something at an auction ○ *The factory was closed and the machinery was auctioned off.*

auctioneer /,ɔkʃə'nɪr/ *noun* the person who conducts an auction

audio-typing /'ɔrdioʊ ,taɪpɪŋ/ *noun* the act of typing to dictation from a recording on a dictating machine

audio-typist /'ɔrdioʊ ,taɪpɪst/ *noun* a typist who types to dictation from a recording on a dictating machine

audit /'ɔdɪt/ *noun* **1.** the examination of the books and accounts of a company ○ *to carry out the annual audit* **2.** a detailed examination of something in order to assess it ○ *A thorough job audit was needed for job evaluation.* ○ *A manpower audit showed up a desperate lack of talent.* ■ *verb* to examine the books and accounts of a company ○ *Messrs. Smith have been asked to audit the accounts.* ○ *The books have not yet been audited.*

auditing /'ɔrdɪtɪŋ/ *noun* the work of examining the books and accounts of a company

auditor /'ɔrdɪtər/ *noun* a person who audits

COMMENT: In the U.S., audited accounts are only required by corporations which are registered with the SEC, but in the U.K. all limited companies with a turnover over a certain limit must provide audited annual accounts.

auditors' qualification /,ɔrdɪtərz ,kwɑlɪfɪ'keɪʃ(ə)n/ *noun* a form of words in a report from the auditors of a company's accounts, stating that in their opinion the accounts are not a true reflection of the company's financial position. Also called **qualification of accounts**

auditors' report /ˌɔrdɪtərz rɪˈpɔrt/ *noun* a report written by a company's auditors after they have examined the accounts of the company (NOTE: If the auditors are satisfied, the report certifies that, in their opinion, the accounts give a "true and fair" view of the company's financial position.)

audit trail /ˈɔdɪt treɪl/ *noun* the records that show all the stages of a transaction, e.g., a purchase, a sale or a customer complaint, in the order in which they happened (NOTE: An audit trail can be a useful tool for problem-solving and, in financial markets, may be used to ensure that the dealers have been fair and accurate in their proceedings.)

"…provides real-time fax monitoring and audit trail to safeguard information privacy and accuracy" [*Forbes*]

AUT *abbreviation* authorised unit trust

authenticate /ɔˈθentɪkeɪt/ *verb* to say that something is true or genuine

authorised unit trust /ˌɔθəraɪzd ˈjunɪt ˌtrʌst/ *noun U.K.* the official name for a unit trust which has to be managed according to EU directives. Abbreviation **AUT**

authority /ɔˈθɑrɪti/ *noun* the power to do something ○ *a manager with authority to sign checks* ○ *He has no authority to act on our behalf.* ○ *Without the necessary authority, the manager could not command respect.* ○ *Only senior managers have the authority to initiate these changes.*

authorization /ˌɔθəraɪˈzeɪʃ(ə)n/ *noun* permission or power to do something ○ *Do you have authorization for this expenditure?* ○ *He has not been given authorization to act on our behalf.*

authorize /ˈɔrθəraɪz/ *verb* **1.** to give permission for something to be done ○ *to authorize payment of $10,000* **2.** to give someone the authority to do something ○ *to authorize someone to act on the company's behalf*

authorized /ˈɔrθəraɪzd/ *adjective* permitted

authorized capital /ˌɔrθəraɪzd ˈkæpɪt(ə)l/ *noun* the total value of the shares of stock that a corporation is allowed to issue, as stated in its articles of incorporation

authorized dealer /ˌɔθəraɪzd ˈdilər/ *noun* a person or company (such as a bank) that is allowed by the country's central bank to buy and sell foreign currency

authorized stock /ˌɔθəraɪzd ˈstɑk/ *noun* the number of shares of stock that a corporation is allowed to issue, as stated in its articles of incorporation

AUTM *abbreviation* Association of University Technology Managers

autocratic management style /ˌɔtəkrætɪk ˈmænɪdʒmənt ˌstaɪl/ *noun* a style of management where the managers tell the employees what to do, without involving them in the decision-making processes. Opposite **democratic management style**

automated /ˈɔtəmeɪtɪd/ *adjective* worked automatically by machines ○ *a fully automated car assembly plant*

automated teller machine /ˌɔtəmeɪtɪd ˈtelər məˌʃin/ *noun* a machine which gives out money when a special card is inserted and special instructions given. Abbreviation **ATM**

automatic /ˌɔtəˈmætɪk/ *adjective* working or taking place without any person making it happen ○ *There is an automatic increase in salaries on January 1st.*

automatically /ˌɔrtəˈmætɪkli/ *adverb* without a person giving instructions ○ *The invoices are sent out automatically.* ○ *Addresses are typed in automatically.* ○ *A demand note is sent automatically when the invoice is overdue.*

automatic data processing /ˌɔtəmætɪk ˈdeɪtə ˌprɑsesɪŋ/ *noun* data processing done by a computer. Abbreviation **ADP**

automatic vending machine /ˌɔtəmætɪk ˈvendɪŋ məˌʃin/ *noun* a machine which provides drinks, cigarettes etc., when a coin is put in

automation /ˌɔrtəˈmeɪʃ(ə)n/ *noun* the use of machines to do work with very little supervision by people

autonomous /ɔˈtɑnəməs/ *adjective* which rules itself ○ *The work force in the factory is made up of several autonomous work groups.*

autonomous work group /ɔr ˌtɑnəməs ˈtimwɜrkɪŋ/ *noun* a group of employees who can work independently, taking decisions together as a group. Also called **self-managing team**

autonomy /ɔ'tɑnəmi/ *noun* working by yourself, without being managed

availability /ə,veɪlə'bɪlɪti/ *noun* the fact of being easy to obtain □ **offer subject to availability** the offer is valid only if the goods are available

available /ə'veɪləb(ə)l/ *adjective* able to be obtained or bought ○ *an item which is no longer available* ○ *funds which are made available for investment in small businesses* ○ *This product is available in all branches.* ○ *These articles are available to order only.*

available capital /ə,veɪləb(ə)l 'kæpɪt(ə)l/ *noun* capital which is ready to be used

average /'æv(ə)rɪdʒ/ *noun* **1.** a number calculated by adding several figures together and dividing by the number of figures added ○ *the average for the last three months* or *the last three months' average* ○ *sales average* or *average of sales* **2.** □ **on average, on an average** in general ○ *On average, $15 worth of goods are stolen every day.* **3.** the sharing of the cost of damage or loss of a ship between the insurers and the owners ■ *adjective* equal to the average of a set of figures ○ *the average increase in salaries* ○ *The average cost per unit is too high.* ○ *The average sales per representative are rising.* ■ *verb* **1.** to amount to something when the average of a set of figures is worked out ○ *Price increases have averaged 10% per annum.* ○ *Days lost through sickness have averaged twenty-two over the last four years.* **2.** to work out an average figure for something

   average out *phrasal verb* to come to a figure as an average ○ *It averages out at 10% per annum.* ○ *Sales increases have averaged out at 15%.*

average adjustment /,æv(ə)rɪdʒ ə'dʒʌstmənt/ *noun* a calculation of the share of the cost of damage or loss of a ship that an insurer has to pay

average cost pricing /,æv(ə)rɪdʒ 'kɔst ,praɪsɪŋ/ *noun* pricing based on the average cost of producing one unit of a product

average due date /,æv(ə)rɪdʒ 'du ,deɪt/ *noun* the average date when several different payments fall due

averager /'ævərɪdʒər/ *noun* a person who buys the same stock at various times and at various prices to get an average value

average-sized /,ævərɪdʒ 'saɪzd/ *adjective* of a similar size to most others, not very large or very small ○ *They are an average-sized company.* ○ *She has an average-sized office.*

averaging /'ævərɪdʒɪŋ/ *noun* the buying or selling of stocks at different times and at different prices to establish an average price

avoid /ə'vɔɪd/ *verb* to try not to do something ○ *My goal is to avoid paying too much tax.* ○ *We want to avoid direct competition with Smith Inc.* ○ *The company is struggling to avoid bankruptcy.* (NOTE: You avoid something or avoid **doing** something.)

avoidance /ə'vɔɪd(ə)ns/ *noun* the act of trying not to do something or not to pay something ○ *tax avoidance*

avoirdupois /,ævərdə'pɔɪz/ *noun* a non-metric system of weights used in the U.K., the U.S., and other countries, whose basic units are the ounce, the pound, the hundredweight and the ton (NOTE: The system is now no longer officially used in the U.K.)

award /ə'wɔrd/ *noun* something given by a court, tribunal or other official body, especially when settling a dispute or claim ○ *an award by an industrial tribunal* ○ *The arbitrator's award was 'set aside on appeal.* ○ *The latest pay award has been announced.* ■ *verb* to decide the amount of money to be given to someone ○ *to award someone a salary increase* ○ *He was awarded $10,000 damages in the libel case.* ○ *The judge awarded costs to the defendant.* □ **to award a contract to someone** to decide that someone will be given the contract

away /ə'weɪ/ *adverb* not here, somewhere else ○ *The managing director is away on business.* ○ *My secretary is away sick.* ○ *The company is moving away from its down-market image.*

ax /æks/ *noun* □ **the project got the ax** the project was stopped ■ *verb* to cut or to stop ○ *to ax expenditure* ○ *Several thousand jobs are to be axed.* (NOTE: [all senses] The U.K. spelling is **axe**.)

B

B2B /ˌbi tə 'bi/ *adjective* referring to products or services that are aimed at other businesses rather than at consumers (NOTE: The word is most commonly used of business-to-business dealings conducted over the Internet.)

"...rather than opening markets to greater competition, B2B exchanges could become powerful monopolistic tools" [*Economist*]

B2B commerce /ˌbi tə bi 'kɑmɜrs/ *noun* business done by companies with other companies, rather than with individual consumers

B2B exchange /ˌbi tə bi ɪks'tʃeɪndʒ/ *noun* same as **exchange**

B2B web exchange /ˌbi tə bi 'web ɪks,tʃeɪndʒ/ *noun* same as **exchange**

B2B website /ˌbi tə bi 'websaɪt/ *noun* a website that is designed to help businesses trade with each other on the Internet

B2C /ˌbi tə 'si/ *adjective* referring to products or services that are aimed at consumers rather than at other businesses (NOTE: The word is most commonly used of business-to-consumer dealings conducted over the Internet.)

"While B2C companies were the target of choice last May, this spring they ranked fourth: The leaders were B2B outfits, e-marketplaces, and online service companies" [*BusinessWeek*]

B2C website /ˌbi tə si 'websaɪt/ *noun* an online store that sells products to consumers via its website

baby boomer /'beɪbi ˌbumər/ *noun* a person born during the period from 1945 to 1965, when the populations of the U.S. and U.K. increased rapidly

back /bæk/ *noun* the opposite side to the front ○ *Write your address on the back of the envelope.* ○ *Please endorse the check on the back.* ■ *adjective* referring to the past ○ *a back payment* ■ *adverb* so as to make things as they were before ○ *He will*

pay back the money in monthly installments. ○ *The store sent back the check because the date was wrong.* ○ *The company went back on its agreement to supply at $1.50 a unit.* ■ *verb* **1.** to help someone, especially financially ○ *The bank is backing us to the tune of $10,000.* ○ *She is looking for someone to back her project.* **2.** □ **to back a bill** to sign a bill promising to pay it if the person it is addressed to is not able to do so

back out *phrasal verb* to stop being part of a deal or an agreement ○ *The bank backed out of the contract.* ○ *We had to cancel the project when our German partners backed out.*

backbone /'bækboʊn/ *noun* a high-speed communications link for Internet communications across an organization or country or between countries

back burner /ˌbæk 'bɜrnər/ *noun* □ **to put something on the back burner** to file a plan or document as the best way of forgetting about it ○ *The whole project has been put on the back burner.*

backdate /bæk'deɪt/ *verb* **1.** to put an earlier date on a document such as a check or an invoice ○ *Backdate your invoice to April 1st.* **2.** to make something effective from an earlier date than the current date ○ *The pay increase is backdated to January 1st.*

backdoor selling /ˌbækdɔr 'selɪŋ/ *noun* the practice of bypassing an organization's bureaucracy and selling direct to the chief decision-maker in it ○ *If we did not resort to backdoor selling the right department might never hear of us.* ○ *The chairman was asked out for a meal by the sales director of the other company to try a little backdoor selling.*

back-end loaded /ˌbæk end 'loʊdɪd/ *adjective* referring to an insurance or investment plan where commission is charged when the investor withdraws his or her money from the plan. Compare **front-end loaded**

backer /ˈbækər/ *noun* **1.** a person or company that backs someone ○ *One of the company's backers has withdrawn.* **2.** □ **the backer of a bill** the person who backs a bill

background /ˈbækɡraʊnd/ *noun* **1.** past work or experience ○ *My background is in the steel industry.* ○ *The company is looking for someone with a background of success in the electronics industry.* ○ *She has a publishing background.* ○ *What is his background?* ○ *Do you know anything about his background?* **2.** past details ○ *He explained the background of the claim.* ○ *I know the contractual situation as it stands now, but can you fill in the background details?*

backhander /ˈbæk,hændər/ *noun* a bribe or money given to persuade someone to do something for you (*informal*) ○ *He was accused of taking backhanders from the company's suppliers.*

backing /ˈbækɪŋ/ *noun* support, especially financial support ○ *She has the backing of an Australian bank.* ○ *The company will succeed only if it has sufficient backing.* ○ *She gave her backing to the proposal.*

back interest /,bæk ˈɪntrəst/ *noun* interest which has not yet been paid

backlog /ˈbæklɒɡ/ *noun* an amount of work, or of items such as orders or letters, which should have been dealt with earlier but is still waiting to be done ○ *The warehouse is trying to cope with a backlog of orders.* ○ *We're finding it hard to cope with the backlog of paperwork.*

back office /,bæk ˈɒfɪs/ *noun* **1.** the part of a brokerage firm where the paperwork involved in buying and selling stocks is processed **2.** the part of a bank where checks are processed, statements of account drawn up and other administrative tasks are done **3.** the general administration department of a company

back orders /ˈbæk ,ɔrdərz/ *plural noun* orders received and not yet fulfilled, usually because the item is out of stock ○ *It took the factory six weeks to clear all the accumulated back orders.*

back pay /ˈbæk peɪ/ *noun* a salary which has not been paid ○ *I am owed $500 in back pay.*

back payment /ˈbæk ,peɪmənt/ *noun* **1.** a payment which is due but has not yet been paid **2.** the act of paying money which is owed

backpedal /ˈbæk,pedəl/ *verb* to go back on something which was stated earlier ○ *When questioned by reporters about the discrepancies, the CFO backpedaled fast.* (NOTE: **backpedaling – backpedaled**)

back rent /ˈbæk rent/ *noun* a rent due but not paid ○ *The company owes $100,000 in back rent.*

back tax /ˈbæk tæks/ *noun* tax which is owed

back-to-back loan /,bæk tə ,bæk ˈloʊn/ *noun* a loan from one company to another in one currency arranged against a loan from the second company to the first in another currency. Also called **parallel loan** (NOTE: Back-to-back loans are used by international companies to get round exchange controls.)

backtrack /ˈbæktræk/ *verb* to go back on what has been said before

back up /,bæk ˈʌp/ *verb* **1.** to support or help ○ *She brought along a file of documents to back up his claim.* ○ *The employee said his union had refused to back him up in his argument with management.* **2.** to copy a file or disk onto another file or disk ○ *He forgot to back up his files.*

backup /ˈbækʌp/ *adjective* supporting or helping ○ *We offer a free backup service to customers.* ○ *After a series of sales tours by representatives, the sales director sends backup letters to all the contacts.*

backup copy /ˈbækʌp ,kɑpi/ *noun* a copy of a computer disc to be kept in case the original disc is damaged

back wages /,bæk ˈweɪdʒɪz/ *plural noun* same as **back pay**

backwardation /,bækwəˈdeɪʃ(ə)n/ *noun* **1.** a penalty paid by the seller when postponing delivery of stock to the buyer **2.** a situation in which the cash price is higher than the forward price. Opposite **forwardation**

backward integration /,bækwərd ,ɪntɪˈɡreɪʃ(ə)n/ *noun* a process of expansion in which a business which deals with the later stages in the production and sale of a product acquires a business that deals with an earlier stage in the same process, usually a supplier ○ *Buying up rubber plantations is part of the tire company's backward integration policy.* ○ *Backward integration will ensure cheap supplies but forward integration would bring us nearer to the market.* Also called **vertical integration**. Opposite **forward integration**

bad bargain /ˌbæd ˈbɑːgɪn/ *noun* an item which is not worth the price asked

bad buy /ˌbæd ˈbaɪ/ *noun* a thing bought which was not worth the money paid for it

bad check /ˌbæd ˈtʃek/ *noun* a check which is returned to the drawer for any reason

bad debt /ˌbæd ˈdet/ *noun* a debt which will not be paid, usually because the debtor has gone out of business, and which has to be written off in the accounts ○ *The company has written off $30,000 in bad debts.*

baggage check /ˈbægɪdʒ tʃek/ *noun* a room where suitcases can be left while passengers are waiting for a plane or train (NOTE: The U.S. term is **baggage room**.)

bail /beɪl/ *verb*
bail out *phrasal verb* **1.** to rescue a company which is in financial difficulties **2.** □ **to bail someone out** to pay money to a court as a guarantee that someone will return to face charges ○ *She paid $3,000 to bail him out.*
"...the government has decided to bail out the bank which has suffered losses to the extent that its capital has been wiped out" [*South China Morning Post*]

bail-out /ˈbeɪ laʊt/ *noun* a rescue of a company in financial difficulties

balance /ˈbæləns/ *noun* **1.** the amount which has to be put in one of the columns of an account to make the total debits and credits equal □ **balance in hand** cash held to pay small debts □ **balance brought down** *or* **forward** the closing balance of the previous period used as the opening balance of the current period □ **balance carried down** *or* **forward** the closing balance of the current period **2.** the rest of an amount owed ○ *You can pay $100 deposit and the balance within 60 days.* □ **balance due to us** the amount owed to us which is due to be paid ■ *verb* **1.** to be equal, i.e. the assets owned must always equal the total liabilities plus capital □ **the February ac-**counts do not balance the two sides are not equal **2.** to calculate the amount needed to make the two sides of an account equal ○ *I have finished balancing the accounts for March.* **3.** to plan a budget so that expenditure and income are equal ○ *The president is planning for a balanced budget.*

balanced scorecard /ˌbælənst ˈskɔːkɑːd/ *noun* a system of measurement and assessment that uses a variety of indicators, particularly customer relations, internal efficiency, financial performance and innovation, to find out how well an organization is doing in its attempts to achieve its main objectives

balance of payments /ˌbæləns əv ˈpeɪmənts/ *noun* a comparison between total receipts and payments arising from a country's international trade in goods, services, and financial transactions. Abbreviation **BOP**

balance of payments deficit /ˌbæləns əv ˈpeɪməntz ˌdefɪsɪt/ *noun* a situation in which a country imports more than it exports

balance of payments surplus /ˌbæləns əv ˈpeɪmənts ˌsɜːpləs/ *noun* a situation in which a country sells more to other countries than it buys from them

balance of trade /ˌbæləns əv ˈtreɪd/ *noun* a record of the international trading position of a country in merchandise, excluding invisible trade. Also called **trade balance**

balance sheet /ˈbæləns ʃiːt/ *noun* a statement of the financial position of a company at a particular time, such as the end of the financial year or the end of a quarter, showing the company's assets and liabilities ○ *Our accountant has prepared the balance sheet for the first half-year.* ○ *The company balance sheet for the last financial year shows a worse position than for the previous year.* ○ *The company balance sheet for 1984 shows a substantial loss.*

COMMENT: The balance sheet shows the state of a company's finances at a certain date. The profit and loss account shows the movements which have taken place since the end of the previous accounting period. A balance sheet must balance, with the basic equation that assets (i.e. what the company owns, including money owed to the company) must equal liabilities (i.e. what the company owes to its creditors) plus capital (i.e. what it owes to its shareholders). A balance sheet can be drawn up either in the horizontal form, with liabilities and capital on the right-hand side of the page (in the U.K., they are on the left-hand side) or in the vertical form, with assets at the top of the page, followed by liabilities, and capital at the bottom. Most are usually drawn up in the vertical format, as opposed to the more old-fashioned horizontal style.

balloon /bə'lun/ *noun* **1.** a loan where the last repayment is larger than the others **2.** a large final payment on a loan, after a number of periodic smaller loans

balloon mortgage /bə,lun 'mɔrgɪdʒ/ *noun* a mortgage in which the final payment (called a "balloon payment") is larger than the others

ballot /'bælət/ *noun* **1.** an election where people vote for someone by marking a cross on a paper with a list of names ○ *Six names were put forward for three vacancies on the committee so a ballot was held.* **2.** a vote where voters decide on an issue by marking a piece of paper ■ *verb* to take a vote by ballot ○ *The union is balloting for the post of president.*

ballot box /'bælət bɑks/ *noun* a sealed box into which ballot papers are put

ballot paper /'bælət ,peɪpər/ *noun* a paper on which the voter marks a cross to show who they want to vote for

ballot-rigging /'bælət ,rɪgɪŋ/ *noun* the illegal arranging of the votes in a ballot, so that a particular candidate or party wins

ballpark figure /'bɔlpɑrk ,fɪgər/ *noun* a general figure which can be used as the basis for discussion

BAM *abbreviation* business activity monitoring

ban /bæn/ *noun* an order which forbids someone from doing something ○ *a government ban on the import of weapons* ○ *a ban on the export of farm animals* □ **to impose a ban on smoking** to make an order which forbids smoking □ **to lift the ban on smoking** to allow people to smoke □ **to beat the ban on something** to do something which is banned – usually by doing it rapidly before a ban is imposed, or by finding a legal way to avoid a ban ■ *verb* to forbid something ○ *The council has*

banned the sale of alcohol at the sports ground. ○ *The company has banned drinking on company premises.* (NOTE: **banning – banned**)

band /bænd/ *noun* a range of figures with an upper and a lower limit, to which something, e.g., the amount of someone's salary or the exchange value of a currency, is restricted but within which it can move ○ *a salary band*

bandwidth /'bændwɪdθ/ *noun* a measurement of the capacity of a fiber-optic cable to carry information to and from the Internet (NOTE: The higher the bandwidth, the faster information passes through the cable.)

bank /bæŋk/ *noun* **1.** a business which holds money for its clients, lends money at interest, and trades generally in money ○ *the First National Bank* ○ *City Bank* ○ *She put all her earnings into the bank.* ○ *I have had a letter from my bank telling me my account is overdrawn.* **2.** □ **the World Bank** central bank, controlled by the United Nations, whose funds come from the member states of the UN and which lends money to member states ■ *verb* to deposit money into a bank or to have an account with a bank ○ *He banked the check as soon as he received it.* ○ *I bank at or with Union State Bank.* □ **where do you bank?** where do you have a bank account?

bank on *phrasal verb* to feel sure that something will happen ○ *He is banking on getting a loan from his father to set up in business.* ○ *Do not bank on the sale of your house.*

bankable /'bæŋkəb(ə)l/ *adjective* acceptable by a bank as security for a loan

bankable paper /,bæŋkəb(ə)l 'peɪpər/ *noun* a document which a bank will accept as security for a loan

bank account /'bæŋk ə,kaʊnt/ *noun* an account which a customer has with a bank, where the customer can deposit and withdraw money ○ *to open a bank account* ○ *to close a bank account* ○ *How much money do you have in your bank account?* ○ *If you let the balance in your bank account fall below $1,000, you have to pay a fee.*

bank advance /'bæŋk əd,væns/ *noun* same as **bank loan** ○ *She asked for a bank advance to start her business.*

bank balance /'bæŋk ˌbæləns/ *noun* the state of a bank account at any particular time ○ *Our bank balance went into the red last month.*

bank base rate /ˌbæŋk 'beɪs ˌreɪt/ *noun* a basic rate of interest, on which the actual rate a bank charges on loans to its customers is calculated. Also called **base rate**

bank book /'bæŋk bʊk/ *noun* a book given by a bank or savings and loan which shows money which you deposit or withdraw from your savings account or savings and loan account. Also called **passbook**

bank borrowing /ˌbæŋk 'bɒrəʊɪŋ/ *noun* money borrowed from a bank ○ *The new factory was financed by bank borrowing.*

bank borrowings /'bæŋk ˌbɒrəʊɪŋz/ *plural noun* money borrowed from banks

bank card /'bæŋk kɑrd/ *noun* a credit card or debit card issued to a customer by a bank for use instead of cash when buying goods or services (NOTE: There are internationally recognized rules that govern the authorization of the use of bank cards and the clearing and settlement of transactions in which they are used.)

bank charge /'bæŋk tʃɑrdʒ/ *noun* same as **service charge**

bank charter /ˌbæŋk 'tʃɑrtər/ *noun* an official government document allowing the establishment of a bank

bank check /'bæŋk tʃek/ *noun* a bank's own check, drawn on itself and signed by a bank official

bank clerk /'bæŋk klɜrk/ *noun* a person who works in a bank, but is not a manager

bank credit /'bæŋk ˌkredɪt/ *noun* loans or overdrafts from a bank to a customer

bank deposits /bæŋk dɪ'pɑzɪts/ *plural noun* all money placed in banks by private or corporate customers

bank draft /'bæŋk dræft/ *noun* an order by one bank telling another bank, usually in another country, to pay money to someone

banker /'bæŋkər/ *noun* **1.** a person who is in an important position in a bank **2.** a bank ○ *the company's banker is First State Bank*

banker's bill /'bæŋkərz bɪl/ *noun* an order by one bank telling another bank,

usually in another country, to pay money to someone. Also called **bank bill**

banker's order /'bæŋkərz ˌɔrdər/ *noun* an order written by a customer asking a bank to make a regular payment ○ *He pays his subscription by banker's order.*

banker's reference /ˌbæŋkərz 'ref(ə)rəns/ *noun* details of a company's bank, account number, etc., supplied so that a client can check if the company is a risk

bank giro /'bæŋk ˌdʒaɪrəʊ/ *noun* a method used by clearing banks to transfer money rapidly from one account to another

bank holiday /ˌbæŋk 'hɒlɪdeɪ/ *noun U.K.* a weekday which is a public holiday when the banks are closed ○ *New Year's Day is a bank holiday.* ○ *Are we paid for bank holidays in this job?*

bank identification number /ˌbæŋk ˌaɪdentɪfɪ'keɪʃ(ə)n ˌnʌmbər/ *noun* an internationally organized six-digit number which identifies a bank for charge card purposes. Abbreviation **BIN**

banking /'bæŋkɪŋ/ *noun* the business of banks ○ *He is studying banking.* ○ *She has gone into banking.* □ **a banking crisis** a crisis affecting the banks

banking account /'bæŋkɪŋ əˌkaʊnt/ *noun* an account which a customer has with a bank

banking hours /'bæŋkɪŋ ˌaʊrz/ *plural noun* the hours when a bank is open for its customers ○ *You cannot get money out of the bank after banking hours.*

bank loan /'bæŋk loʊn/ *noun* a loan made by a bank to a customer, usually against the security of a property or asset ○ *She asked for a bank loan to start her business.* Also called **bank advance**

bank manager /'bæŋk ˌmænɪdʒər/ *noun* the person in charge of a branch of a bank ○ *They asked their bank manager for a loan.*

bank mandate /'bæŋk ˌmændeɪt/ *noun* a written order to a bank, asking it to open an account and allow someone to sign checks on behalf of the account holder, and giving specimen signatures and relevant information

banknote /'bæŋknoʊt/ *noun* **1.** a piece of printed paper money ○ *a counterfeit £20 banknote* (NOTE: The U.S. term is **bill**.) **2.** a non-interest bearing note, issued by a Federal Reserve Bank, which can be used as cash

Bank of England /ˌbæŋk əv ˈɪŋlənd/ *noun* the U.K. central bank, owned by the state, which, together with the Treasury, regulates the nation's finances

COMMENT: The Bank of England issues banknotes which carry the signatures of its officials. It is the lender of last resort to commercial banks and supervises banking institutions in the U.K. Its Monetary Policy Committee is independent of the government and sets interest rates. The Governor of the Bank of England is appointed by the government.

bank rate /ˈbæŋk ˈreɪt/ *noun* the discount rate of a central bank

bank reconciliation /ˌbæŋk ˌrekənsɪliˈeɪʃ(ə)n/ *noun* the act of making sure that the bank statements agree with the company's ledgers

bank reserves /ˌbæŋk rɪˈzɜːvz/ *noun* cash and securities held by a bank to cover deposits

bankroll /ˈbæŋkrəʊl/ *verb* to provide the money that enables something or someone to survive (*informal*) ○ *How long can he go on bankrolling his daughter's art gallery?*

bankrupt /ˈbæŋkrʌpt/ *noun, adjective* (a person) who has been declared by a court not to be capable of paying his or her debts and whose affairs are put into the hands of a receiver ○ *a bankrupt property developer* ○ *She was adjudicated* or *declared bankrupt.* ○ *He went bankrupt after two years in business.* ■ *verb* to make someone become bankrupt ○ *The recession bankrupted my father.*

bankruptcy /ˈbæŋkrʌptsi/ *noun* the state of being bankrupt ○ *The recession has caused thousands of bankruptcies.* (NOTE: The plural is **bankruptcies**.)

COMMENT: In the U.K., bankruptcy is applied only to individual persons, but in the U.S. the term is also applied to corporations. In the U.K., a bankrupt cannot hold public office (for example, they cannot be elected an MP) and cannot be the director of a company. They also cannot borrow money. In the U.S., there are two types of bankruptcy: involuntary, where the creditors ask for a person or corporation to be made bankrupt; and voluntary, where a person or corporation applies to be made

bankrupt (in the U.K., this is called voluntary liquidation).

bankruptcy order /ˈbæŋkrʌptsi ˌɔːdər/ *noun* same as **declaration of bankruptcy**

bank statement /ˈbæŋk ˌsteɪtmənt/ *noun* a written statement from a bank showing the balance of an account at a specific date

bank transfer /ˈbæŋk ˌtrænsfɜːr/ *noun* an act of moving money from a bank account to another account

banner /ˈbænər/ *noun* an online interactive advertisement that appears on a webpage, usually at the top or bottom, and contains a link to the website of the business whose products or services are being advertised (NOTE: Banner ads often use graphics images and sound as well as text.)

banner advertising /ˈbænər ˌædvərtaɪzɪŋ/ *noun* a website advertising which runs across the top of a webpage, similar to newspaper headlines

banner exchange /ˈbænər ɪksˌtʃeɪndʒ/ *noun* an agreement between two or more businesses, in which each allows the others' advertising banners to be displayed on its website

bar /bɑːr/ *noun* a thing which stops you doing something ○ *Government legislation is a bar to foreign trade.*

bar chart /ˈbɑːr tʃɑːrt/ *noun* a chart where values or quantities are shown as columns of different heights set on a base line, the different lengths expressing the quantity of the item or unit. Also called **bar graph**, **histogram**

bar code /ˈbɑːr kəʊd/ *noun* a system of lines printed on a product which, when read by a computer, give a reference number or price

barely /ˈbeəli/ *adverb* almost not ○ *There is barely enough money left to pay the staff.* ○ *She barely had time to call her lawyer before the police arrived.*

bargain /ˈbɑːgɪn/ *noun* **1.** an agreement on the price of something ○ *to strike a bargain* or *to make a bargain* □ **to drive a hard bargain** to be a difficult person to negotiate with **2.** something which is cheaper than usual ○ *That car is a (real) bargain at $500.* ■ *verb* to try to reach agreement about something, especially a price, usually with each person or group involved putting forward suggestions or offers which are discussed until a compromise is arrived at ○ *You will have to bargain with the dealer if you want a discount.* ○ *They spent two hours bargaining about* or *over the price.* (NOTE: You bargain **with** someone **over** or **about** or **for** something.)

bargain basement /ˌbɑːɡɪn ˈbeɪsmənt/ *noun* a basement floor in a store where goods are sold cheaply □ **I'm selling this at a bargain basement price** I'm selling this very cheaply

bargain counter /ˈbɑːɡɪn ˌkaʊntər/ *noun* a counter in a store where goods are sold cheaply

bargain hunter /ˈbɑːɡɪn ˌhʌntər/ *noun* a person who looks for cheap deals

bargaining /ˈbɑːɡɪnɪŋ/ *noun* the act of trying to reach agreement about something, e.g., a price or a wage increase for workers

bargaining position /ˈbɑːɡɪnɪŋ pə ˌzɪʃ(ə)n/ *noun* the offers or demands made by one group during negotiations

bargaining power /ˈbɑːɡɪnɪŋ ˌpaʊr/ *noun* the strength of one person or group when discussing prices or wage settlements

bargain offer /ˌbɑːɡɪn ˈɒfər/ *noun* the sale of a particular type of goods at a cheap price ○ *This week's bargain offer – 30% off all carpet prices.*

bargain price /ˌbɑːɡɪn ˈpraɪs/ *noun* a cheap price ○ *These carpets are for sale at a bargain price.*

bargain sale /ˌbɑːɡɪn ˈseɪl/ *noun* the sale of all goods in a store at cheap prices

bar graph /ˈbɑː ɡræf/ *noun* same as **bar chart**

barrel /ˈbærəl/ *noun* **1.** a large round container for liquids ○ *to sell wine by the barrel* ○ *He bought twenty-five barrels of wine.* **2.** an amount of liquid contained in a barrel ○ *The price of oil has reached $30 a barrel.*

"…if signed, the deals would give effective discounts of up to $3 a barrel on Saudi oil" [*Economist*]

"U.S. crude oil stocks fell last week by nearly 2.6m barrels" [*Financial Times*]

"…the average spot price of Nigerian light crude oil for the month of July was 27.21 dollars a barrel" [*Business Times (Lagos)*]

barrier /ˈbæriər/ *noun* anything which makes it difficult for someone to do something, especially to send goods from one place to another □ **to impose trade barriers on certain goods** to restrict the import of some goods by charging high duty ○ *They considered imposing trade barriers on some food products.* □ **to lift trade barriers from imports** to remove restrictions on imports ○ *The government has lifted trade barriers on foreign cars.*

barrier to entry /ˌbæriər tu ˈentri/ *noun* a factor that makes it impossible or unprofitable for a company to try to start selling its products in a particular market (NOTE: Barriers to entry may be created, for example, when companies already in a market have patents that prevent their goods from being copied, when the cost of the advertising needed to gain a market share is too high, or when an existing product commands very strong brand loyalty.)

barrier to exit /ˌbæriər tu ˈeɡzɪt/ *noun* a factor that makes it impossible or unprofitable for a company to leave a market where it is currently doing business (NOTE: Barriers to exit may be created, for example, when a company has invested in specialist equipment that is only suited to manufacturing one product, when the costs of retraining its work force would be very high, or when withdrawing one product would have a bad effect on the sales of other products in the range.)

barter /ˈbɑːtər/ *noun* a system in which goods are exchanged for other goods and not sold for money ■ *verb* to exchange goods for other goods and not for money ○ *They agreed upon a deal to barter tractors for barrels of wine.*

barter agreement /ˌbɑːtər əˈɡriːmənt/ *noun* an agreement to exchange goods by barter ○ *The company has agreed a barter deal with Bulgaria.*

bartering /ˈbɑːtərɪŋ/ *noun* the act of exchanging goods for other goods and not for money

base /beɪs/ *noun* **1.** the lowest or first position ○ *Turnover increased by 200%, but started from a low base.* **2.** a place where a company has its main office or factory, or a place where a businessperson's office is located ○ *The company has its base in London and branches in all the European* *countries.* ○ *She has an office in Madrid which he uses as a base while traveling in Southern Europe.* ■ *verb* **1.** □ **to base something on something** to calculate something using something as your starting point or basic material for the calculation ○ *We based our calculations on the forecast turnover.* □ **based on** calculating from ○ *based on last year's figures* ○ *based on population forecasts* **2.** to set up a company or a person in a place ○ *The European manager is based in our New York office.* ○ *Our overseas branch is based in the Bahamas.* ■ *adjective* lowest or first, and used for calculating others

base pay /'beɪs peɪ/ *noun* pay for a job which does not include extras such as overtime pay or bonuses

base rate /'beɪs reɪt/ *noun* same as **bank base rate**

base year /'beɪs jɪr/ *noun* the first year of an index, against which changes occurring in later years are measured

basic /'beɪsɪk/ *adjective* **1.** normal **2.** most important **3.** simple, or from which everything starts ○ *She has a basic knowledge of the market.* ○ *To work at the cash desk, you need a basic qualification in math.*

basically /'beɪsɪkli/ *adverb* seen from the point from which everything starts

basic commodities /ˌbeɪsɪk kə'mɑdətiz/ *plural noun* ordinary farm produce, produced in large quantities, e.g., corn, rice or sugar

basic discount /ˌbeɪsɪk 'dɪskaʊnt/ *noun* a normal discount without extra percentages ○ *Our basic discount is 20%, but we offer 5% extra for rapid settlement.*

basic industry /ˌbeɪsɪk 'ɪndəstri/ *noun* the most important industry of a country, e.g., coal, steel or agriculture

basic pay /ˌbeɪsɪk 'peɪ/ *noun* a regular salary without extra payments or benefits

basic price /ˌbeɪsɪk 'praɪs/, **basic rate** /ˌbeɪsɪk 'reɪt/ *noun* the price of a product or service that does not include any extras ○ *This is a rather high basic price.* ○ *Please make clear whether $1,000 is the basic rate or whether it is inclusive of spare parts.*

basic product /ˌbeɪsɪk 'prɑdʌkt/ *noun* the main product made from a raw material

basics /'beɪsɪks/ *plural noun* simple and important facts or principles ○ *She has studied the basics of foreign exchange dealing.* □ **to get back to basics** to consider the main facts or principles again

basic salary /ˌbeɪsɪk 'sæləri/ *noun* same as **basic pay**

basic wage /ˌbeɪsɪk 'weɪdʒ/ *noun* same as **basic pay** ○ *The basic wage is £110 a week, but you can expect to earn more than that with overtime.*

basis /'beɪsɪs/ *noun* **1.** a point or number from which calculations are made ○ *We forecast the turnover on the basis of a 6% price increase.* (NOTE: The plural is **bases**.) **2.** the general terms of agreement or general principles on which something is decided or done ○ *This document should form the basis for an agreement.* ○ *We have three people working on a freelance basis.* (NOTE: The plural is **bases**.) □ **on a short-term** *or* **long-term basis** for a short or long period ○ *He has been appointed on a short-term basis.*

basket /'bæskɪt/ *noun* a group of prices or currencies taken as a standard ○ *the price of the average shopping basket* ○ *The pound has fallen against a basket of European currencies.* ○ *The market basket has risen by 6%.*

"…the weekly adjusted average total basket price of œ37.89 was just 3p more than the week before Christmas" [*The Grocer*]

basket case /'bæskɪt keɪs/ *noun* company which is in financial difficulties and is not likely to recover (*informal*)

basket of currencies /ˌbæskət əv 'kʌrənsiz/ *noun* same as **currency basket**

batch /bætʃ/ *noun* **1.** a group of items which are made at one time ○ *This batch of shoes has the serial number 25–02.* **2.** a group of documents which are processed at the same time ○ *Today's batch of invoices is ready to be mailed.* ○ *The factory is working on yesterday's batch of orders.* ○ *The accountant signed a batch of checks.* ○ *We deal with the orders in batches of fifty at a time.* ■ *verb* to put items together in groups ○ *to batch invoices or checks*

batch number /'bætʃ ˌnʌmbər/ *noun* a number attached to a batch ○ *When making a complaint always quote the batch number on the packet.*

batch processing /'bætʃ ˌprɑsesɪŋ/ *noun* a system of data processing where information is collected into batches before being loaded into the computer

batch production /'bætʃ prəˌdʌkʃən/ *noun* production in batches

bath /bæθ/ ◇ **take a bath** (*informal*) **1.** to suffer a severe financial loss **2.** to choose to take a group of charges against one period of earnings so that the earnings appear down for that period

battery /'bæt(ə)ri/ *noun* a series of similar things ○ *Candidates have to pass a battery of tests.*

BBB *abbreviation* Better Business Bureau

BC *abbreviation* blind copy

b/d *abbreviation* barrels per day

bear /ber/ *noun* a person who sells stock, commodities or currency because he or she thinks their price will fall and it will be possible to buy them again more cheaply later. Opposite **bull** ■ *verb* **1.** to give interest ○ *government bonds which bear 5% interest* **2.** to have something, especially to have something written on it ○ *an envelope which bears a Houston postmark* ○ *a letter bearing yesterday's date* ○ *The check bears the signature of the company secretary.* ○ *The share certificate bears his name.* **3.** to pay costs ○ *The costs of the exhibition will be borne by the company.* ○ *The company bore the legal costs of both parties.* (NOTE: **bearing – bore – has borne**)

bearer /'berər/ *noun* a person who holds a check or certificate □ **the check is payable to bearer** the check will be paid to the person who holds it, not to any particular name written on it

bearing /'berɪŋ/ *adjective* producing ○ *certificates bearing interest at 5%* ○ *interest-bearing deposits*

bear market /'ber ˌmɑrkɪt/ *noun* a period when stock prices fall because stockholders are selling since they believe the market will fall further. Opposite **bull market**

bear raid /'ber reɪd/ *noun* the act of selling large numbers of shares of stock to try to bring down prices

beat /bit/ *verb* □ **to beat a ban** to do something which is forbidden by doing it rapidly before the ban is enforced

become /bɪ'kʌm/ *verb* to change into something different ○ *The export market has become very difficult since the rise in the dollar.* ○ *The company became very profitable in a short time.* (NOTE: **becoming – became – has become**)

begin /bɪ'gɪn/ *verb* to start ○ *The company began to lose its market share.* ○ *He began to write the report which the stockholders had asked for.* ○ *The auditors' report began with a description of the general principles adopted.* (NOTE: You begin something *or* begin **to do** something *or* begin **with** something. Note also: **beginning – began – has begun**.)

beginner /bɪ'gɪnər/ *noun* a person who is starting in a job

beginning /bɪ'gɪnɪŋ/ *noun* the first part ○ *The beginning of the report gives a list of the directors and their shareholdings.*

beginning inventory /bɪ'gɪnɪŋ ˌɪnvənt(ə)ri/ *noun* on a balance sheet, the closing stock at the end of one accounting period that is transferred forward and becomes the opening stock in the one that follows (NOTE: The U.K. term is **opening stock**.)

behalf /bɪ'hæf/ *noun* □ **on behalf of** acting for someone or a company ○ *lawyers acting on behalf of the Texan company* ○ *I am writing on behalf of the minority stockholders.* ○ *She is acting on my behalf.*

behind /bɪ'haɪnd/ *preposition* at the back or after ○ *The company is No. 2 in the market, about $4m the competition.* ■ *adverb* □ **the company has fallen behind with its deliveries** it is late with its deliveries

believe /bɪ'liv/ *verb* to think that something is true ○ *We believe he has offered to buy 25% of the stock.* ○ *The chairman is believed to be in South America on business.*

belong /bɪ'lɑŋ/ *verb* **1.** □ **to belong to** to be the property of ○ *The company belongs to an old American banking family.* ○ *The patent belongs to the inventor's son.* **2.** □ **to belong with** to be in the correct place with ○ *Those documents belong with the sales reports.*

below /bɪ'loʊ/ *preposition* lower down than or less than ○ *We sold the property at below the market price.* ○ *You can get a ticket for New York at less than $150 on the*

Internet. ○ *The company has a policy of paying staff below the market rates.*

below the line /bɪˌloʊ ðə ˈlaɪn/ *adjective, adverb* used to describe entries in a company's profit and loss account that show how the profit is distributed, or where the funds to finance the loss originate. ◊ **above-the-line advertising** 1

below-the-line advertising /bɪˌloʊ ðə laɪn ˈædvərtaɪzɪŋ/ *noun* advertising which is not paid for and for which no commission is paid to the advertising agency, e.g., work by staff who are manning an exhibition. Compare **above-the-line advertising**

below-the-line expenditure /bɪˌloʊ ðə laɪn ɪkˈspendɪtʃər/ *noun* **1.** payments which do not arise from a company's usual activities, e.g., severance payments **2.** extraordinary items which are shown in the profit and loss account below net profit after taxation, as opposed to exceptional items which are included in the figure for profit before taxation

benchmark /ˈbentʃmɑrk/ *noun* a point or level which is important, and can be used as a reference when making evaluations or assessments

benchmarking /ˈbentʃmɑrkɪŋ/ *noun* the practice of measuring the performance of a company against the performance of other companies in the same sector. Benchmarking is also used widely in the information technology sector to measure the performance of computer-based information systems.

beneficiary /ˌbeniˈfɪʃəri/ *noun* a person who gains money from something ○ *the beneficiaries of a will*

benefit /ˈbenəfɪt/ *noun* **1.** payments which are made to someone under a national or private insurance plan ○ *She receives $75 a week as an unemployment benefit.* **2.** something of value given to an employee in addition to their salary ■ *verb* **1.** to make better or to improve ○ *A fall in inflation benefits the exchange rate.* **2.** □ **to benefit from** *or* **by something** to be improved by something, to gain more money because of something ○ *Exports have benefited from the fall in the exchange rate.* ○ *The employees have benefited from the profit-sharing program.*

"…the retail sector will also benefit from the expected influx of tourists" [*Australian Financial Review*]

benefit-cost analysis /ˈbenəfɪt kɔst/ *noun* same as **cost-benefit analysis**

benefits plan /ˈbenəfɪts plæn/ *noun* a Canadian government programme intended to promote the employment of Canadian citizens and to provide Canadian manufacturers, consultants, contractors and service companies with opportunities to compete for projects

bequeath /bɪˈkwið/ *verb* to leave property, money, etc. (but not freehold land) to someone in a will

bespoke /bɪˈspoʊk/ *adjective* made to order or made to fit the requirements of the customer

best /best/ *adjective* very good, better than all others ○ *His best price is still higher than all the other suppliers.* ○ *Last year was the company's best year ever.* ■ *noun* a very good effort ○ *The salesmen are doing their best, but the stock simply will not sell at that price.*

best-before date /ˌbest bɪˈfɔr ˌdeɪt/ *noun* the date stamped on the label of a food product, which is the last date on which the product is guaranteed to be of good quality. ◊ **sell-by date, use-by date**

best-in-class /ˌbest ɪn ˈklæs/ *adjective* more effective and efficient, especially in acquiring and processing materials and in delivering products or services to customers, than any other organization in the same market or industrial sector

best practice /ˌbest ˈpræktɪs/ *noun* the most effective and efficient way to do something or to achieve a particular goal (NOTE: In business, best practice is often determined by benchmarking, that is by comparing the method one organization uses to carry out a task with the methods used by other similar organizations and determining which method is most efficient and effective.)

"For the past 25 years, managers have been taught that the best practice for valuing assets…is to use a discounted-cash-flow (DCF) methodology." [*Harvard Business Review*]

best-seller /ˌbest ˈselər/ *noun* an item (especially a book) which sells very well

best-selling /ˌbest 'seliŋ/ *adjective* selling better than any other ○ *These computer disks are our best-selling line.*

best value /ˌbest 'vælju/ *noun* a system adopted by the U.K. government to ensure that local authorities provide services to the public in the most efficient and cost-effective way possible

bet /bet/ *noun* an amount deposited when you risk money on the result of a race or of a game ■ *verb* to risk money on the result of something ○ *He bet $100 on the result of the election.* ○ *I bet you £25 the dollar will rise against the pound.*

better /'betər/ *adjective* very good compared with something else ○ *This year's results are better than last year's.* ○ *We will shop around to see if we can get a better price.*

Better Business Bureau /ˌbetər 'bɪznɪs ˌbjʊroʊ/ an organization of local businesses whose purpose is to establish a good relationship between businesses and consumers by promoting ethical business practices

betting tax /'betɪŋ tæks/ *noun* a tax levied on betting on horses, dogs, etc. (NOTE: **betting – bet – has bet**)

beware /bɪ'wer/ *verb* to be careful

b/f *abbreviation* brought forward

bi- /baɪ/ *prefix* twice □ **bi-monthly** twice a month □ **bi-annually** twice a year

bias /'baɪəs/ *noun* the practice of favoring one group or person rather than another ○ *A postal survey will do away with bias.* ○ *The trainee interviewers were taught how to control bias and its effects.* ○ *Management has shown bias in favor of graduates in its recent appointments.*

bid /bɪd/ *noun* **1.** an offer to buy something at a specific price. ◊ **takeover bid** □ **to make a bid for something** to offer to buy something ○ *We made a bid for the house.* ○ *The company made a bid for its competition.* □ **to make a cash bid** to offer to pay cash for something □ **to put in** *or* **enter a bid for something** to offer to buy something, usually in writing **2.** an offer to sell something or do a piece of work at a specific price ○ *She made the lowest bid for the job.* □ **to put a project out for bids, to ask for** *or* **invite bids on a project** to ask contractors to give written estimates of cost for a job □ **to put in** *or* **submit a bid** to make an estimate of cost for a job ■

verb **1.** to offer to buy □ **to bid for something** (*at an auction*) to offer to buy something □ **he bid $1,000 for the jewels** he offered to pay $1,000 for the jewels **2.** □ **to bid on a contract** to submit an estimate of cost for work to be carried out under contract

bidder /'bɪdər/ *noun* **1.** a person who makes a bid, usually at an auction ○ *Several bidders made offers for the house.* □ **the property was sold to the highest bidder** to the person who had made the highest bid or who offered the most money **2.** a person or company that submits an estimate of cost (NOTE: The U.K. term is **tenderer**)

bidding /'bɪdɪŋ/ *noun* **1.** the act of making offers to buy, usually at an auction □ **the bidding started at $1,000** the first and lowest bid was $1,000 □ **the bidding stopped at $250,000** the last bid, i.e. the successful bid, was for $250,000 □ **the auctioneer started the bidding at $100** the auctioneer suggested that the first bid should be $100 **2.** the act of submitting an estimate of cost (NOTE: The U.K. term is **tendering**.)

bid price /'bɪd praɪs/ *noun* a price at which investors sell shares of stock in a mutual fund (NOTE: The opposite, i.e. the buying price, is called the **offer price**; the difference between the two is the **spread**.)

Big Bang /bɪg 'bæŋ/ *noun* **1.** the change in practices on the London Stock Exchange, with the introduction of electronic trading on October 27th 1986 **2.** a similar change in financial practices in another country

COMMENT: The changes on the London Stock Exchange included the abolition of stock jobbers and the removal of the system of fixed commissions. The Stock Exchange trading floor closed and deals are now done by phone or computer or on the Internet.

Big Board /'bɪg 'bɔrd/ *noun* same as **New York Stock Exchange** (*informal*)

"…at the close, the Dow Jones Industrial Average was up 24.25 at 2,559.65, while New York S.E. volume totalled 180m shares. Away from the Big Board, the American S.E. Composite climbed 2.31 to 297.87" [*Financial Times*]

big box store /ˌbɪg bɑks 'stɔr/ *noun* a large retail superstore that sells a very wide range of merchandise from groceries to refrigerators or televisions

big business /ˌbɪg ˈbɪznɪs/ *noun* very large commercial firms

big picture /ˌbɪg ˈpɪktʃər/ *noun* a broad view of a subject that takes into account all the factors that are relevant to it and considers the future consequences of action taken now (*informal*)

bilateral /baɪˈlæt(ə)rəl/ *adjective* between two parties or countries ○ *The minister signed a bilateral trade agreement.*

bill /bɪl/ *noun* **1.** a written list of charges to be paid ○ *The sales assistant wrote out the bill.* ○ *Does the bill include sales tax?* ○ *The bill is made out to Smith Inc.* ○ *The builder sent in his bill.* ○ *She left the country without paying her bills.* **2.** *U.K.* same as **check** ○ *Does the bill include service?* **3.** a written paper promising to pay money □ **bills payable (B** *or* **P)** bills, especially bills of exchange, which a company will have to pay to its creditors □ **bills receivable (B** *or* **R)** bills, especially bills of exchange, which are due to be paid by a company's debtors □ **due bills** bills which are owed but not yet paid. ◊ **bill of exchange 4.** a piece of printed paper money ○ *a $5 bill* (NOTE: The U.K. term is **note** or **banknote**.) **5.** a draft of a new law which will be discussed in Congress ■ *verb* to present a bill to someone so that it can be paid ○ *The plumbers billed us for the repairs.*

billboard /ˈbɪlbɔrd/ *noun* a large outdoor poster site (measuring 12 x 25 feet) ○ *The railroad track was lined with billboards specially set up for election propaganda.* ○ *A shortage of billboards has led to an increase in press advertising.* (NOTE: The U.K. term is **hoarding**.)

bill broker /ˈbɪl ˌbroʊkər/ *noun* a discount house, a firm which buys and sells bills of exchange for a fee

billing /ˈbɪlɪŋ/ *noun* the work of writing invoices or bills

billion /ˈbɪljən/ *noun* one thousand million (NOTE: In the U.S., it has always meant one thousand million, but in U.K. English it formerly meant one million million, and it is still sometimes used with this meaning. With figures it is usually written **bn**: **$5bn** say "five billion dollars".)

"…gross wool receipts for the selling season to end June 30 appear likely to top $2 billion" [*Australian Financial Review*]

"…at its last traded price the bank was capitalized at around $1.05 billion" [*South China Morning Post*]

bill of exchange /ˌbɪl əv ɪksˈtʃeɪndʒ/ *noun* a document, signed by the person authorizing it, which tells another person or a financial institution to pay money unconditionally to a named person on a specific date (NOTE: Bills of exchange are usually used for payments in foreign currency.) □ **to accept a bill** to sign a bill of exchange to show that you promise to pay it □ **to discount a bill** to buy or sell a bill of exchange at a lower price than that written on it in order to cash it later

COMMENT: A bill of exchange is a document drawn up by a seller and signed by a purchaser, stating that the purchaser accepts that he owes the seller money, and promises to pay it at a later date. The person drawing up the bill is the "drawer"; the person who accepts it is the "drawee". The seller can then sell the bill at a discount to raise cash. This is called a "trade bill". A bill can also be accepted (i.e. guaranteed) by a bank, and in this case it is called a "bank bill".

bill of lading /ˌbɪl əv ˈleɪdɪŋ/ *noun* a list of goods being shipped, which the transporter gives to the person sending the goods to show that the goods have been loaded

bill of sale /ˌbɪl əv ˈseɪl/ *noun* a document which the seller gives to the buyer to show that the sale has taken place

bin /bɪn/ *noun* **1.** a large container **2.** a separate section of shelves in a warehouse

BIN *abbreviation* bank identification number

bin card /ˈbɪn kɑrd/ *noun* a stock record card in a warehouse

bind /baɪnd/ *verb* **1.** to tie or to attach **2.** to make it a legal duty for someone or something to act in a particular way ○ *The company is bound by its bylaws.* ○ *He does not consider himself bound by the agreement which was signed by his predecessor.* (NOTE: [all senses] **binding – bound**)

binder /ˈbaɪndər/ *noun* **1.** a temporary agreement for insurance sent before the insurance policy is issued (NOTE: The U.K. term is **cover note**.) **2.** money paid as part of the initial agreement to purchase property (NOTE: The U.K. term is **deposit**.)

binding /'baɪndɪŋ/ *adjective* being a legal requirement that someone does something ○ *a binding contract* ○ *This document is not legally binding.* □ **the agreement is binding on all parties** all parties signing it must do what is agreed

bioethics /'baɪoʊˌeθɪks/ *noun* the study of the moral and ethical choices faced in medical research and in the treatment of patients, especially when the application of advanced technology in involved

biometrics /ˌbaɪə'metrɪks/ *noun* the use of measurable biological characteristics such as fingerprints or iris patterns to identify a person to an electronic system

biomimicry /'baɪoʊˌmɪmɪkri/ *noun* the imitation of natural processes in the organization of business activities, with the goal of reducing waste and limiting their impact on the environment

BIS *abbreviation* Bank for International Settlements

bit /bɪt/ *noun* a piece of information or knowledge

black economy /ˌblæk ɪ'kɑnəmi/ *noun* goods and services which are paid for in cash, and therefore not declared for tax. Also called **hidden economy, parallel economy, shadow economy**

Black Friday /ˌblæk 'fraɪdeɪ/ *noun* a sudden collapse on a stock market (NOTE: Called after the first major collapse of the U.S. stock market on 24th September, 1869.)

black list /'blæk lɪst/ *noun* a list of goods, people, or companies which have been banned

blacklist /'blæklɪst/ *verb* to put goods, people, or a company on a black list ○ *Their firm was blacklisted by the government.*

black market /ˌblæk 'mɑrkət/ *noun* the buying and selling of goods or currency in a way which is not allowed by law ○ *There is a flourishing black market in spare parts for cars.* □ **to pay black market prices** to pay high prices to get items which are not easily available

Black Monday /ˌblæk 'mʌndeɪ/ *noun* Monday, 19th October, 1987, when world stock markets crashed

Black-Scholes Option Pricing Model /ˌblæk skoʊlz 'praɪsɪŋ ˌmɑd(ə)l/ *noun* a formula for fairly valuing stock options using interest rates and other variables

Black Tuesday /ˌblæk 'tjuzdeɪ/ *noun* Tuesday, 29th October, 1929, when the U.S. stock market crashed

blame /bleɪm/ *noun* the act of saying that someone has done something wrong or that someone is responsible ○ *The sales staff got the blame for the poor sales figures.* ■ *verb* to say that someone has done something wrong or is responsible for a mistake ○ *The managing director blamed the chief accountant for not warning her of the loss.* ○ *The union is blaming the management for poor industrial relations.*

blamestorming /'bleɪmstɔrmɪŋ/ *noun* a group discussion of the reasons why a project has failed or is late and who is to blame for it (*slang*) (NOTE: The term is modeled on the word "brainstorming.")

"…more often than not what actually went on was blamestorming – people sitting in meetings, allegedly to share ideas but really saying "Who dropped the ball? Who made the mistake?"" [*BusinessWeek*]

blank /blæŋk/ *adjective* with nothing written on it ■ *noun* a space on a form which has to be completed ○ *Fill in the blanks and return the form to your local office.*

blank check /ˌblæŋk 'tʃek/ *noun* a check with the amount of money and the payee left blank, but signed by the drawer

blanket agreement /ˌblæŋkɪt ə'grimənt/ *noun* an agreement which covers many different items

blanket insurance (coverage) /ˌblæŋkɪt ɪn'ʃʊrəns ˌkʌvər/ *noun* insurance which covers various items such as a house and its contents

blanket refusal /ˌblæŋkɪt rɪ'fjuz(ə)l/ *noun* a refusal to accept many different items

blind copy /ˌblaɪnd 'kɑpi/ *noun* a copy of an e-mail that its main addressee does not know has been sent

blindside /'blaɪndsaɪd/ *verb* to attack a competitor unexpectedly and in a way which it is difficult to respond to

blind testing /ˌblaɪnd 'testɪŋ/ *noun* the practice of testing a product on consumers without telling them what brand it is

blip /blɪp/ *noun* **1.** a short period when movement forward or upward is stopped ○ *This month's bad trade figures are only a blip.* **2.** bad economic figures (a higher inflation rate, lower exports, etc.), which only have a short-term effect

"...whether these pressures are just a cyclical blip in a low inflation era, or whether the U.K. is drifting back to the bad old days will be one of the crucial questions for the stock market this year" [*Financial Times*]

blister pack /'blɪstər pæk/ *noun* a type of packing where the item for sale is covered with a stiff plastic cover sealed to a card backing. Also called **bubble pack**

block /blɒk/ *noun* **1.** a series of items grouped together **2.** a very large number of shares of stock, typically 10,000 or more ○ *I bought a block of 15,000 shares.* ■ *verb* to stop something taking place ○ *He used his casting vote to block the motion.* ○ *The planning committee blocked the redevelopment plan.*

block capitals /ˌblɒk 'kæpɪt(ə)lz/, **block letters** /ˌblɒk 'letərz/ *plural noun* capital letters such as A, B, C ○ *Write your name and address in block letters.*

blocked currency /ˌblɒkt 'kʌrənsi/ *noun* a currency which cannot be taken out of a country because of government exchange controls ○ *The company has a large account in blocked rubles.*

block vote /ˌblɒk 'voʊt/ *noun* the casting of a large number of votes (such as of a labor union delegation) all together in the same way

blog /blɒg/ *noun* same as **web log** (*informal*)

Blue Book /ˌblu 'bʊk/ *noun* a document reviewing monetary policy, prepared for the Federal Reserve

blue chip /'blu tʃɪp/ *noun* a very safe investment, low-risk stock in a good company

blue-chip investments /ˌblu tʃɪp ɪn 'vestmənts/, **blue-chips** /'blu tʃɪps/ *plural noun* low-risk investments in good companies

blue-collar union /ˌblu 'kɒlə ˌjunjən/ *noun* a labor union formed mainly of blue-collar workers

blue-collar worker /ˌblu 'kɒlə ˌwɜrkər/ *noun* a manual worker in a factory

Blue Laws /'blu lɔz/ *plural noun* regulations governing business activities on Sundays

blueprint /'bluprɪnt/ *noun* a plan or model of something ○ *The agreement will be the blueprint for other agreements in the industry.*

blue-sky thinking /ˌblu ˌskaɪ 'θɪŋkɪŋ/ *noun* extremely idealistic and often unconventional ideas

"Researchers are also doing blue-sky thinking about technologies that might step to the fore once magnetic recording has reached its limit." [*BusinessWeek*]

Bluetooth /'blutuθ/ *trademark* a type of technology allowing for communication between cell phones, computers, and the Internet

blur /blɜr/ *noun* a period in which a great many important changes take place in an organization very quickly

blurb /blɜrb/ *noun* a brief description of a book, printed in a publisher's catalog or on the cover of the book itself

bn /'bɪljən/ *abbreviation* billion

board /bɔrd/ *noun* **1.** ♦ **board of directors** ○ *He sits on the board as a representative of the bank.* ○ *Two directors were removed from the board at the annual meeting.* **2.** a group of people who run an organization, trust, or association **3.** □ **on board** on a ship, plane or train **4.** an official group of people **5.** a large flat piece of wood or card ■ *verb* to go on to a ship, plane or train ○ *Customs officials boarded the ship in the harbor.*

boarding card /'bɔrdɪŋ 'kard/, **boarding pass** /'bɔrdɪŋ pɑrs/ *noun* a card given to passengers who have checked in for a flight or for a sailing to allow them to board the plane or ship

board meeting /'bɔrd ˌmitɪŋ/ *noun* a meeting of the directors of a company

board of directors /ˌbɔrd əv daɪ 'rektərz/ *noun* **1.** *U.K.* a group of directors elected by the stockholders to run a company ○ *The bank has two representatives on the board of directors.* **2.** a group of people elected by the stockholders to draw up company policy and to appoint the president and other executive officers who are responsible for managing the company

"...a proxy is the written authorization an investor sends to a stockholder meeting conveying his vote on a corporate resolution or the election of a company's board of directors" [*Barrons*]

boardroom /'bɔrdrum/ *noun* a room where the directors of a company meet

boardroom battle /,bɔrdrum 'bæt(ə)l/ *noun* an argument between directors

boilerplate /'bɔɪlərpleɪt/ *noun* a basic standard version of a contract that can be used again and again

bona fide /,bʊonə 'faɪdi/ *adjective* trustworthy, which can be trusted □ **a bona fide offer** an offer which is made honestly

bond /band/ *noun* **1.** a contract document promising to repay money borrowed by a company or by the government on a specific date, and paying interest at regular intervals **2.** □ **goods (held) in bond** goods held by customs until duty has been paid □ **entry of goods under bond** bringing goods into a country in bond □ **to take goods out of bond** to pay duty on goods so that they can be released by customs

COMMENT: Bonds are in effect another form of long-term borrowing by a company or government. They can carry a fixed interest or a floating interest, but the yield varies according to the price at which they are bought; bond prices go up and down in the same way as stock prices.

bonded /'bandɪd/ *adjective* held in bond

bonded warehouse /,bandɪd 'werhaʊs/ *noun* a warehouse where goods are stored until excise duty has been paid

bondholder /'bandhoʊldər/ *noun* a person who holds government bonds

bonus /'boʊnəs/ *noun* an extra payment in addition to a normal payment

bonus issue /,boʊnəs 'ɪʃu/ *noun U.K.* a scrip issue or capitalization issue, in which a company transfers money from reserves to share capital and issues free extra shares to the stockholders. The value of the company remains the same, and the total market value of stockholders' shares remains the same, the market price being adjusted to account for the new shares.

bonus share /'boʊnəs ʃer/ *noun U.K.* an extra share given to an existing stockholder

book /bʊk/ *noun* **1.** a set of sheets of paper attached together □ **a company's books** the financial records of a company

2. a statement of a dealer's exposure to the market, i.e. the amount which he or she is due to pay or has borrowed ■ *verb* to order or to reserve something ○ *to book a room in a hotel* or *a table at a restaurant* or *a ticket on a plane* ○ *I booked a table for 7.45.* ○ *He booked a ticket through to Cairo.* □ **to book someone into a hotel, on** or **onto a flight** to order a room or a plane ticket for someone else ○ *He was booked on the 09.00 flight to Zurich.* □ **the hotel, the flight is fully booked, is booked up** all the rooms or seats are reserved ○ *The restaurant is booked up over the Christmas period.*

booking /'bʊkɪŋ/ *noun* an arrangement by which something such as a room or seat is kept for someone's use at a specific time ○ *Hotel bookings have fallen since the end of the tourist season.* □ **to confirm a booking** to say that a booking is certain

booking clerk /'bʊkɪŋ klɜrk/ *noun U.K.* a person who sells tickets in a booking office

bookkeeper /'bʊkkipər/ *noun* a person who keeps the financial records of a company or an organization

bookkeeping /'bʊkkipɪŋ/ *noun* the work of keeping the financial records of a company or an organization

booklet /'bʊklət/ *noun* a small book with a paper cover

book sales /'bʊk seɪlz/ *plural noun* sales as recorded in the sales book

book value /'bʊk ,vælju/ *noun* the value of an asset as recorded in the company's balance sheet

bookwork /'bʊkwɜrk/ *noun* the keeping of financial records

boom /bum/ *noun* a time when sales, production or business activity are increasing ○ *a period of economic boom* ○ *the boom of the 1990s* □ **the boom years** years when there is an economic boom ■ *verb* to expand or to become prosperous ○ *business is booming* ○ *sales are booming*

boomerang worker /'buməræŋ ,wɜrkər/ *noun* an employee who returns to work for a previous employer (*slang*)

boom industry /'bum ,ɪndəstri/ *noun* an industry which is expanding rapidly

booming /'bumɪŋ/ *adjective* expanding or becoming prosperous ○ *a booming industry* or *company* ○ *Technology is a booming sector of the economy.*

boost /buːst/ *noun* help given to increase something ○ *This publicity will give sales a boost.* ○ *The government hopes to give a boost to industrial development.* ■ *verb* to make something increase ○ *We expect our publicity campaign to boost sales by 25%.* ○ *The company hopes to boost its market share.* ○ *Incentive schemes are boosting production.*

"…the company expects to boost turnover this year to FFr 16bn from FFr 13.6bn last year" [*Financial Times*]

boot /buːt/ *noun* the process of starting or restarting a computer and loading the operating system ■ *verb* to start or restart a computer and load the operating system, or be started up in this way

boot camp /buːt kæmp/ *noun* a demanding program for new employees, designed to teach them technical skills and introduce them to the corporate culture of the organization they are joining (NOTE: boot camps are modeled on the basic training of the U.S. Marine Corps)

booth /buːð/ *noun* **1.** a small place for one person to stand or sit **2.** a section of a commercial fair where a company exhibits its products or services (NOTE: The U.K. term is **stand**.)

BOP *abbreviation* balance of payments

border crosser /ˈbɔːdər ˌkrɔsər/ *noun* an employee who has a variety of skills and is able to move from job to job within a company (*slang*)

borderless world /ˌbɔːdələs ˈwɜːld/ *noun* the global economy in the age of the Internet, which is thought to have removed all the previous barriers to international trade

borderline case /ˌbɔːdəlaɪn ˈkeɪs/ *noun* **1.** a situation which is not easy to resolve, being either one way or the other **2.** a worker who may or may not be recommended for a particular type of treatment, such as for promotion or dismissal

borrow /ˈbɑːroʊ/ *verb* to take money from someone for a time, possibly paying interest for it, and repaying it at the end of the period ○ *She borrowed $1,000 from the bank.* ○ *The company had to borrow heavily to repay its debts.* ○ *They borrowed $25,000 against the security of the factory.*

borrow short *phrasal verb* to borrow for a short period

borrower /ˈbɑːroʊər/ *noun* a person who borrows ○ *Borrowers from the bank pay 12% interest.*

borrowing /ˈbɑːroʊɪŋ/ *noun* the act of borrowing money ○ *The new factory was financed by bank borrowing.*

"…we tend to think of building societies as having the best borrowing rates and indeed many do offer excellent terms" [*Financial Times*]

borrowing costs /ˈbɑːroʊɪŋ kɔsts/ *plural noun* the interest and other charges paid on money borrowed

borrowing power /ˈbɑːroʊɪŋ ˌpaʊr/ *noun* the amount of money which a company can borrow

borrowings /ˈbɑːroʊɪŋz/ *plural noun* money borrowed ○ *The company's borrowings have doubled.*

COMMENT: Borrowings are sometimes shown as a percentage of shareholders' funds (i.e. capital and money in reserves); this gives a percentage which is the leverage of the company.

boss /bɑs/ *noun* an employer or person in charge of a company or an office (*informal*) ○ *If you want a pay raise, go and talk to your boss.*

Boston Box /ˌbɑstən ˈbɑks/ *noun* a system used to indicate a company's potential by analyzing the relationship between its market share and its growth rate (NOTE: The Boston Box was devised by the Boston Consulting Group in the 1970s to help companies decide which businesses they should invest in and which they should withdraw from. In this system businesses with a high market share and high growth rate are called stars, businesses with a low market share and low growth rate are called dogs, businesses with a high market share and a low growth rate are called cash cows and businesses with a low market share and a high growth rate are called question marks.)

Boston matrix /ˌbɑstən ˈmeɪtrɪks/ *noun* a type of product portfolio analysis, in which products are identified as stars, question marks, cash cows, or dogs. Full form **Boston Consulting Group Share/Growth Matrix**

bottleneck /ˈbɑt(ə)lnek/ *noun* a situation which occurs when one section of an operation cannot cope with the amount of work it has to do, which slows down the later stages of the operation and business activity in general ○ *a bottleneck in the supply system* ○ *There are serious bottlenecks in the production line.*

bottom /ˈbatəm/ *noun* the lowest part or point □ **the bottom has fallen out of the market** sales have fallen below what previously seemed to be the lowest point □ **rock-bottom price** the lowest price of all □ **to go bottom up** to crash or to go into liquidation ■ *verb* to reach the lowest point

bottom line /ˌbatəm ˈlaɪn/ *noun* **1.** the last line on a balance sheet indicating profit or loss **2.** the final decision on a matter ○ *The bottom line was that the work had to completed within budget.*

bottom price /ˈbatəm praɪs/ *noun* the lowest price

bottom-up approach /ˌbatəm ˈʌp ə ˌproutʃ/ *noun* a style of leadership that encourages employees at all levels to take part in decision-making and problem-solving. Opposite **top-down approach**

"The managers use a fundamental, bottom-up approach, and do not target country, sector, or industry weightings." [*Forbes*]

bought /bɔrt/ ▸ **buy**

bought ledger /ˈbɔrt ˌledʒər/ *noun* a book in which purchases are recorded. Same as **purchase ledger**

bounce /baʊns/ *verb* to be returned by the bank to the person who has tried to cash it, because there is not enough money in the payer's account to pay it ○ *She paid for the car with a check that bounced.*

boutique /buˈtik/ *noun* a small financial institution offering specialist advice or services

box file /ˈbaks faɪl/ *noun* a cardboard box for holding documents

box number /ˈbaks ˌnʌmbər/ *noun* a reference number used when asking for mail to be sent to a post office or when asking for replies to an advertisement to be sent to the newspaper's offices ○ *Please reply to Box No. 209.*

box office /ˈbaks ˌɔfɪs/ *noun* an office at a theater where tickets can be bought

boycott /ˈbɔɪkat/ *noun* a refusal to buy or to deal in certain products ○ *The union organized a boycott against* or *of imported cars.* ■ *verb* to refuse to buy or deal in a product ○ *We are boycotting all imports from that country.* □ **the management has boycotted the meeting** the management has refused to attend the meeting

B/P *abbreviation* bills payable

BPO *abbreviation* business process outsourcing

B/R *abbreviation* bills receivable

bracket /ˈbrækət/ *noun* a group of items or people taken together □ **people in the middle-income bracket** people with average incomes, not high or low □ **she is in the top tax bracket** she pays the highest level of tax

bracket together *phrasal verb* to treat several items together in the same way ○ *In the sales reports, all the European countries are bracketed together.*

brain drain /ˈbreɪn dreɪn/ *noun* the movement of clever people away from a country to find better jobs in other countries

brainstorming /ˈbreɪnˌstɔrmɪŋ/ *noun* an intensive discussion by a small group of people as a method of producing new ideas or solving problems

branch /bræntʃ/ *noun* **1.** the local office of a bank or large business, or a local store which is part of a large chain **2.** the local office of a union, based in a factory

branch out *phrasal verb* to start a new but usually related type of business ○ *From car retailing, the company branched out into car leasing.*

branch manager /ˌbræntʃ ˈmænɪdʒər/ *noun* a person in charge of a branch of a company

branch office /ˌbræntʃ ˈɔfɪs/ *noun* a less important office, usually in a different town or country from the main office

brand /brænd/ *noun* a make of product, which can be recognized by a name or by a design ○ *the top-selling brands of toothpaste* ○ *The company is launching a new brand of soap.*

brand awareness /ˈbrænd əˌwernəs/ *noun* consciousness by the public of a brand's existence and qualities ○ *How can you talk about brand awareness when most people don't even know what the product is supposed to do?* ○ *Our sales staff must work harder to increase brand awareness in this area.*

branded goods /ˌbrændɪd ˈgʊdz/ *plural noun* goods sold under brand names

brand image /ˌbrænd ˈɪmɪdʒ/ *noun* an opinion of a product which people associate in their minds with the brand name. Brand image is developed and protected carefully by companies to make sure that their product or service is adopted by its target customers.

brand leader /ˌbrænd ˈliːdər/ *noun* the brand with the largest market share

brand loyalty /ˌbrænd ˈlɔɪəlti/ *noun* the feeling of trust and satisfaction that makes a customer always buy the same brand of product

brand name /ˈbrænd neɪm/ *noun* a name of a particular make of product

brand new /ˌbrænd ˈnuː/ *adjective* quite new, very new

brand recognition /ˌbrænd ˌrekəgˈnɪʃ(ə)n/ *noun* the ability of the consumer to recognize a brand on sight

brand X /ˌbrænd ˈeks/ *noun* the anonymous brand used in TV commercials to compare with the named brand being advertised

breach /briːtʃ/ *noun* a failure to carry out the terms of an agreement

breach of contract /ˌbriːtʃ əv ˈkɒntrækt/ *noun* the failure to do something which has been agreed upon in a contract

breach of trust /ˌbriːtʃ əv ˈtrʌst/ *noun* a situation where a person does not act correctly or honestly when people expect him or her to

breach of warranty /ˌbriːtʃ əv ˈwɒrənti/ *noun* the act of supplying goods which do not meet the standards of the warranty applied to them

breadwinner /ˈbredwɪnər/ *noun* a person who earns the main income in a family

break /breɪk/ *noun* **1.** a pause between periods of work ○ *She keyboarded for two hours without a break.* **2.** a lucky deal or good opportunity ■ *verb* **1.** □ **to break even** to balance costs and receipts, but not make a profit ○ *Last year the company only just broke even.* ○ *We broke even in our first two months of trading.* (NOTE: **breaking – broke – has broken**) **2.** to fail to carry out the duties of a contract ○ *The company has broken the contract* or *the agreement by selling at a lower price.* (NOTE: **breaking – broke – has broken**) □ **to break an engagement to do something** not to do what has been agreed **3.** to

cancel a contract ○ *The company is hoping to be able to break the contract.* (NOTE: **breaking – broke – has broken**)

break down *phrasal verb* **1.** to stop working because of mechanical failure ○ *The fax machine has broken down.* **2.** to stop ○ *Negotiations broke down after six hours.* **3.** to show all the items in a total list of costs or expenditure ○ *We broke the expenditure down into fixed and variable costs.*

break off *phrasal verb* to stop ○ *We broke off the discussion at midnight.* ○ *Management broke off negotiations with the union.*

break up *phrasal verb* **1.** to split something large into small sections ○ *The company was broken up and separate divisions sold off.* **2.** to come to an end ○ *The meeting broke up at 12.30.*

breakdown /ˈbreɪkdaʊn/ *noun* **1.** an act of stopping working because of mechanical failure ○ *We cannot communicate with our Nigerian office because of the breakdown of the telephone lines.* **2.** an act of stopping talking ○ *a breakdown in wage negotiations* **3.** an act of showing details item by item ○ *Give me a breakdown of investment costs.*

breakeven analysis /breɪkˈiːv(ə)n ə ˌnæləsɪs/ *noun* **1.** the analysis of fixed and variable costs and sales that determines at what level of production the break-even point will be reached ○ *The break-even analysis showed that the company will only break even if it sells at least 1,000 bicycles a month.* **2.** a method of showing the point at which a company's income from sales will be equal to its production costs so that it neither makes a profit nor makes a loss (NOTE: Break-even analysis is usually shown in the form of a chart and can be used to help companies make decisions, set prices for their products, and work out the effects of changes in production or sales volume on their costs and profits.)

breakeven point /breɪkˈiːv(ə)n pɔɪnt/ *noun* the point or level of financial activity at which expenditure equals income, or the value of an investment equals its cost so that the result is neither a profit nor a loss. Abbreviation **BEP**

breaking bulk /ˌbreɪkɪŋ ˈbʌlk/ *noun* the practice of buying in bulk and then selling in small quantities to many customers

break-up value /'breɪk ʌp ˌvælju/ *noun* **1.** the value of the material of a fixed asset ○ *What would the break-up value of our old machinery be?* ○ *Scrap merchants were asked to estimate the tractors' break-up value.* **2.** the value of various parts of a company taken separately

bribe /braɪb/ *noun* money given secretly and usually illegally to someone in authority to get them to help ○ *The minister was dismissed for taking a bribe.* ■ *verb* to pay someone money secretly and usually illegally to get them to do something for you

bribery /'braɪb(ə)ri/ *noun* the illegal or dishonest act of offering somebody cash or a gift in order to persuade them to give you an unfair advantage

bricks-and-mortar /ˌbrɪks ən 'mɔːtər/ *adjective* conducting business in the traditional way in buildings such as stores and warehouses and not being involved in e-commerce. Compare **clicks-and-mortar**

bridge financing /'brɪdʒ ˌfaɪnænsɪŋ/ *noun* loans to cover short-term needs

brief /briːf/ *noun* instructions given to someone ○ *He went into the negotiations with the brief to get a deal at any price.* ■ *verb* to explain something to someone in detail ○ *The salespeople were briefed on the new product.* ○ *The managing director briefed the board on the progress of the negotiations.*

briefing /'briːfɪŋ/ *noun* an act of telling someone details ○ *All sales staff have to attend a sales briefing on the new product.*

brightsizing /'braɪtˌsaɪzɪŋ/ *noun* the practice of reducing the size of the work force by making the most capable or intelligent employees redundant (NOTE: This usually happens accidentally when a company has a policy of laying off its most recently recruited employees first, since these are often the best trained and best educated members of its staff.)

bring /brɪŋ/ *verb* to come to a place with someone or something ○ *He brought his documents with him.* ○ *The finance director brought her assistant to take notes of the meeting.* (NOTE: **bringing – brought**)

bring down *phrasal verb* **1.** to reduce ○ *Gas companies have brought down the price of oil.* **2.** to add a figure to an account at the end of a period to balance expenditure and income ○ *balance brought down: $365.15* **3.** same as **bring forward 2**

bring forward *phrasal verb* **1.** to make something take [place earlier ○ *to bring forward the date of repayment* ○ *The date of the next meeting has been brought forward to March.* **2.** to take an account balance from the end of the previous period as the starting point for the current period ○ *Balance brought forward: $365.15*

bring in *phrasal verb* to earn an amount of interest ○ *The stock brings in a small amount.*

bring out *phrasal verb* to produce something new ○ *They are bringing out a new model of the car for the Motor Show.*

bring up *phrasal verb* to refer to something for the first time ○ *The chairman brought up the question of redundancy payments.*

brisk /brɪsk/ *adjective* characterized by a lot of activity ○ *sales are brisk* ○ *a brisk market in technology shares* ○ *The market in oil stocks is particularly brisk.*

broadband /'brɔːdbænd/ *noun* a data transmission system that allows large amounts of data to be transferred very quickly

broadside /'brɔːdsaɪd/ *noun* a large format publicity leaflet

brochure /brəʊ'ʃʊr/ *noun* a publicity booklet ○ *We sent off for a brochure about vacations in Greece or about postal services.*

brochure site /brəʊ'ʃʊr ˌsaɪt/ *noun* a website that gives details of a company's products and contact information

brochureware /brəʊ'ʃʊrwer/ *noun* a website that provides information about products and services in the same way as a printed brochure (NOTE: The word is often used negatively to refer to electronic advertising for planned but nonexistent products.)

broke /brəʊk/ *adjective* having no money (*informal*) ○ *The company is broke.* ○ *She cannot pay for the new car because she is broke.*

go broke *phrasal verb* to become bankrupt

broken lot /ˌbrouʊkən 'lɑt/ *noun* same as **odd lot** ○ *We'll give you a discount since it is a broken lot, with two items missing.*

broker /'broukər/ *noun* **1.** a dealer who acts as a middleman between a buyer and a seller **2.** □ **(stock)broker** a person or firm that buys and sells stocks or bonds on behalf of clients

brokerage /'broukərɪdʒ/, **broker's commission** /ˌbroukərz kə'mɪʃ(ə)n/ *noun* **1.** payment to a broker for a deal carried out **2.** same as **broking**

brokerage firm /'broukərɪdʒ fɜrm/, **brokerage house** /'broukərɪdʒ haus/ *noun* a firm which buys and sells stocks for clients

broking /'broukɪŋ/ *noun* the business of dealing in stocks

brought down /'brɔrt daun/, **brought forward** /'brɔrt ˌfɔrwərd/ *noun* the balance in an account from the previous period taken as the starting point for the current period ○ *balance brought down* or *forward:$365.15* Abbreviation **b/d, b/f**

brownfield site /'braunfild saɪt/ *noun* a site for a new housing development which was originally the site of a factory. Compare **greenfield site**

brown goods /'braun gudz/ *plural noun* electrical equipment for home entertainment, e.g., television sets, hi-fi equipment. Compare **white goods**

brown paper /ˌbraun 'peɪpər/ *noun* thick paper for wrapping packages

browser /'brauzər/ *noun* a piece of software that enables computer users to have access to the Internet and World Wide Web

Brundtland Report /'brʌntlənd rɪˌpɔrt/ *noun* a report by a UN commission that was published in1987, in which "sustainability" was defined and which became the basis for many UN summits on the environment

bubble /'bʌb(ə)l/ *noun* a continued rise in the value of an asset, such as a stock price, which is caused by people thinking that the price will continue to rise. Also called **speculative bubble**

bubble envelope /ˌbʌb(ə)l 'envəloup/ *noun* an envelope lined with a sheet of plastic with bubbles in it, which protects the contents of the envelope

bubble pack /'bʌb(ə)l pæk/ *noun* same as **blister pack**

bubble wrap /'bʌb(ə)l ræp/ *noun* a sheet of clear plastic with bubbles of air in it, used as a protective wrapping material

buck /bʌk/ *noun* a dollar (*informal*) □ **to make a quick buck** to make a profit very quickly ■ *verb* □ **to buck the trend** to go against the trend

buddy system /'bʌdi ˌsɪstəm/ *noun* an on-the-job training system, where a trainee works with an experienced employee ○ *The buddy system teaches the trainee the practical realities of the job.* ○ *The company operates both a buddy system and some off-the-job classroom instruction for its trainees.*

budget /'bʌdʒət/ *noun* **1.** a plan of expected spending and income for a period of time ○ *to draw up a budget for salaries for the coming year* ○ *We have agreed on the budgets for next year.* **2.** □ **the Budget** the annual plan of taxes and government spending. In the U.S. the Office of Management and Budget prepares the budget based on requests for funds by the various agencies. The President then submits the budget to Congress, which passes legislation to appropriate and authorize the funds. In the U.K. the budget is proposed by a finance minister and drawn up by the Chancellor of the Exchequer. ○ *The minister put forward a budget aimed at boosting the economy.* □ **to balance the budget** to plan income and expenditure so that they balance ○ *The president is planning for a balanced budget.* ■ *verb* to plan probable income and expenditure ○ *We are budgeting for $10,000 of sales next year.*

budget account /'bʌdʒət əˌkaunt/ *noun* a bank account where you plan income and expenditure to allow for periods when expenditure is high, by paying a set amount each month

budgetary /'bʌdʒɪt(ə)ri/ *adjective* referring to a budget

budgetary control /ˌbʌdʒɪt(ə)ri kən'troul/ *noun* controlled spending according to a planned budget

budgetary policy /ˌbʌdʒɪt(ə)ri 'pɑlisi/ *noun* the policy of planning income and expenditure

budgetary requirements /ˌbʌdʒɪt(ə)ri rɪ'kwaɪrmənts/ *plural noun* the rate of spending or income required to meet the budget forecasts

budget deficit /ˈbʌdʒɪt ˌdefɪsɪt/ *noun* a deficit in a country's planned budget, where income from taxation will not be sufficient to pay for the government's expenditure

budget department /ˈbʌdʒət dɪ ˌpɑrtmənt/ *noun* a department in a large store which sells cheaper goods

budgeting /ˈbʌdʒətɪŋ/ *noun* the preparation of budgets to help plan expenditure and income

budget surplus /ˌbʌdʒət ˈsɜrpləs/ *noun* a situation where there is more revenue than was planned for in the budget

budget variance /ˌbʌdʒət ˈveriəns/ *noun* the difference between the cost as estimated for a budget and the actual cost

build /bɪld/ *verb*

build into *phrasal verb* to include something in something which is being set up ○ *You must build all the forecasts into the budget.* □ **we have built 10% for contingencies into our cost forecast** we have added 10% to our basic forecast to allow for items which may appear suddenly

build up *phrasal verb* **1.** to create something by adding pieces together ○ *She bought several shoe stores and gradually built up a chain.* **2.** to expand something gradually ○ *to build up a profitable business* ○ *to build up a team of sales representatives*

building and loan association /ˌbɪldɪŋ ən ˈloʊn əˌsoʊsieɪʃ(ə)n/ *noun* same as **savings and loan**

building materials /ˈbɪldɪŋ məˌtɪriəlz/ *plural noun* materials used in building, e.g., bricks and cement

building permit /ˈbɪldɪŋ ˌpɜrmɪt/ *noun* an official document which allows someone to build on a piece of land

building site /ˈbɪldɪŋ saɪt/ *noun* a place where a building is being constructed ○ *All visitors to the site must wear safety helmets.*

building society /ˈbɪldɪŋ səˌsaɪəti/ *noun U.K.* same as **savings and loan**

buildup /ˈbɪldʌp/ *noun* a gradual increase ○ *a buildup in sales or a sales buildup* ○ *There will be a big publicity buildup before the launch of the new mod-*

el. ○ *There has been a buildup of complaints about customer service.*

built-in /ˌbɪlt ˈɪn/ *adjective* forming part of the system or of a machine ○ *The PC has a built-in modem.* ○ *The accounting system has a series of built-in checks.* ○ *The microwave has a built-in clock.*

built-in obsolescence /ˈbɪlt ɪn ɑbsə ˌles(ə)ns/ *noun* a method of ensuring continuing sales of a product by making it in such a way that it will soon become obsolete

bulk /bʌlk/ *noun* a large quantity of goods □ **in bulk** in large quantities ○ *to buy rice in bulk*

bulk buying /ˌbʌlk ˈbaɪɪŋ/ *noun* the act of buying large quantities of goods at low prices

bulk carrier /ˌbʌlk ˈkæriər/ *noun* a ship which carries large quantities of loose goods such as corn or coal

bulk discount /ˌbʌlk ˈdɪskaʊnt/ *noun* a discount given to a purchaser who buys in bulk

bulk purchase /ˌbʌlk ˈpɜrtʃɪs/ *noun* an act of buying a large quantity of goods at low prices

bulk shipment /ˌbʌlk ˈʃɪpmənt/ *noun* a shipment of large quantities of goods

bull /bʊl/ *noun* a person who believes the market will rise, and therefore buys stocks, commodities, or currency to sell at a higher price later. Opposite **bear**

"…lower interest rates are always a bull factor for the stock market" [*Financial Times*]

bullion /ˈbʊliən/ *noun* a gold or silver bars ○ *A shipment of gold bullion was stolen from the security van.* ○ *The price of bullion is fixed daily.*

bullish /ˈbʊlɪʃ/ *adjective* optimistic, feeling that prices of stocks will rise

"…another factor behind the currency market's bullish mood may be the growing realisation that Japan stands to benefit from the current combination of high domestic interest rates and a steadily rising exchange rate" [*Far Eastern Economic Review*]

"…currency traders chose to ignore better unemployment statistics from France, preferring to focus on the bullish outlook for the dollar" [*Times*]

bull market /ˈbʊl ˌmɑrkɪt/ *noun* a period when stock prices rise because people are optimistic and buy shares. Opposite **bear market**

bumper /'bʌmpər/ *noun* a very large crop ○ *a bumper crop of corn* □ **1999 was a bumper year for computer sales** 1999 was an excellent year for sales

bumping /'bʌmpɪŋ/ *noun* **1.** a lay-off procedure that allows an employee with greater seniority to displace a more junior employee ○ *The economic recession led to extensive bumping in companies where only the most qualified were retained for some jobs.* ○ *The labor unions strongly objected to bumping practices since they considered that many employees were being laid off unfairly.* **2.** the situation where a senior employee takes the place of a junior (in a restaurant)

buppies /'bʌpiz/ *plural noun* young professional African-American people with relatively high incomes (NOTE: Short for **Black Upwardly-Mobile Professionals**)

bureau /'bjʊroʊ/ *noun* an office which specializes in a specific service

bureaucracy /bjʊ'rɑkrəsi/ *noun* a system of administration where an individual person's responsibilities and powers are strictly defined and processes are strictly followed

bureaucratic /ˌbjʊrə'krætɪk/ *adjective* following strict administrative principles

bureau de change /ˌbjʊroʊ də 'ʃɑnʒ/ *noun* an office where you can change foreign currency

burn /bɜrn/ *verb*

burn down *phrasal verb* to destroy (a building) completely in a fire ○ *The warehouse burned down and all the stock was destroyed.* ○ *The company records were all lost when the offices were burned down.*

burn out *phrasal verb* to become tired and incapable for further work because of stress (NOTE: **burning – burnt or burned**)

bushel /'bʊʃ(ə)l/ *noun* a measure of dry goods, such as corn (= 35 litres)

business /'bɪznɪs/ *noun* **1.** work in buying, selling, or doing other things to make a profit ○ *We do a lot of business with Japan.* ○ *Business is expanding.* ○ *Business is slow.* ○ *Repairing cars is 90% of our business.* ○ *We did more business in the week before Christmas than we usually do in a month.* ○ *Strikes are very bad for business.* ○ *What's your line of business?* □ **to be in business** to run a commercial firm □ **on business** doing commercial work ○ *She had to go abroad on business.* ○ *The chairman is in Holland on business.* **2.** a commercial company ○ *He owns a small car repair business.* ○ *She runs a business from her home.* ○ *I set up in business as an insurance broker.* **3.** the affairs discussed ○ *The main business of the meeting was finished by 3 p.m.*

business activity monitoring /'bɪznɪs æk,tɪvɪti ,mɑnɪt(ə)rɪŋ/ *noun* the process of monitoring the activities of a business using specialized software in order to get real-time information about the effectiveness of its operations. Abbreviation **BAM**

business address /'bɪznɪs ə,dres/ *noun* the details of number, street, and city or town where a company is located

business agent /'bɪznɪs ,eɪdʒənt/ *noun* the chief local official of a labor union

business call /'bɪznɪs kɔl/ *noun* a visit to talk to someone about business

business card /'bɪznɪs kɑrd/ *noun* a card showing a businessperson's name and the name and address of the company he or she works for

business case /'bɪznɪs keɪs/ *noun* a statement that explains why a particular course of action would be advantageous or profitable to an organization (NOTE: A business case depends on the preparation and presentation of a viable business plan and is intended to weed out ideas that may seem promising but have no real long-term value to an organization.)

business center /'bɪznɪs ,sentər/ *noun* the part of a town where the main banks, stores, and offices are located

business class /'bɪznɪs klæs/ *noun* a type of airline travel which is less expensive than first class and more comfortable than economy class

business college /'bɪznɪs ,kɑlɪdʒ/ *noun* same as **business school**

business community /'bɪznɪs kə,mjunɪti/ *noun* the business people living and working in the area

business computer /'bɪznɪs kəm,pjutər/ *noun* a powerful small computer that runs software written to manage a business

business correspondence /'bɪznɪs kɔrɪ‚spɑndəns/ *noun* letters concerned with a business

business correspondent /'bɪznɪs kɔrɪ‚spɑndənt/ *noun* a journalist who writes articles on business news for newspapers

business cycle /'bɪznɪs ‚saɪk(ə)l/ *noun* the period during which trade expands, slows down, and then expands again. Also called **trade cycle**

business efficiency exhibition /‚bɪznɪs ɪ'fɪʃ(ə)nsi eksɪ‚bɪʃ(ə)n/ *noun* an exhibition which shows products such as computers and word-processors which help businesses to be efficient

business environment /‚bɪznɪs ɪn 'vaɪrənmənt/ *noun* the elements or factors outside a business organization which directly affect it, such as the supply of raw materials and product demand ○ *The unreliability of supplies is one of the worst features of our business environment.*

business equipment /'bɪznɪs ɪ ‚kwɪpmənt/ *noun* the machines used in an office

business expenses /'bɪznɪs ɪk ‚spensɪz/ *plural noun* money spent on running a business, not on stock or assets

business game /'bɪznɪs geɪm/ *noun* a learning game in which trainees are presented with a typical business situation and compete with one another to find the best way of dealing with it

business hours /'bɪznɪs ‚aʊrz/ *plural noun* the time when a business is open, usually 9:00 a.m. to 5:00 p.m.

Business Information Center /‚bɪznɪs ‚ɪnfər'meɪʃ(æə)n ‚sentər/ *noun* a regional location in the U.S. designed to provide information, education, and training to entrepreneurs who want to start and operate successful businesses. The centers operate under the direction of the Small Business Administration (SBA), which receives help from community organizations and volunteers.

business intelligence /'bɪznɪs ɪn ‚telɪdʒ(ə)ns/ *noun* information that may be useful to a business when it is planning its strategy

"…a system that enables its employees to use cell phones to access the consulting firm's business information database."

[*InformationWeek*]

business letter /'bɪznɪs ‚letər/ *noun* a letter which deals with business matters

business lunch /'bɪznɪs lʌntʃ/ *noun* a meeting between business people where they have lunch together to discuss business deals

businessman /'bɪznɪsmæn/ *noun* a man engaged in business

business park /'ɔfɪs pɑrk/ *noun* same as **office park**

business plan /'bɪznɪs plæn/ *noun* a document drawn up to show how a business is planned to work, with cash flow forecasts, sales forecasts, etc., often used when trying to get a loan, or when setting up a new business

business portfolio analysis /‚bɪznɪs pɔrt'foʊlioʊ ə‚næləsɪs/ *noun* a method of categorizing a firm's products according to their relative competitive position and business growth rate in order to lay the foundations for sound strategic planning

business practices /'bɪznɪs ‚præktɪsɪz/ *noun* ways of managing or working in business, industry or trade

business premises /'bɪznɪs ‚premɪsɪz/ *plural noun* building used for commercial use

business process outsourcing /‚bɪznɪs ‚prɑses 'aʊtsɔrsɪŋ/ *noun* the practice of contracting tasks such as payroll or billing to a company that specializes in those tasks, either as a cost-saving measure or in order to focus on the business's main activity

business rate /'bɪznɪs reɪt/ *noun* a tax levied on business property (NOTE: The U.S. term is **local property tax**.)

business school /'bɪznɪs skul/ *noun* an educational institution at college or university level that offers courses in subjects related to business such as management, technology, finance, and interpersonal skills (NOTE: Business schools provide courses of varying length and level, up to Master of Business Administration, and besides catering to full-time students, also offer part-time courses and distance learning to people already in employment.)

"Business school gives one the chance to be exposed to various opportunities from a unique vantage point. It is like being offered a smorgasbord of career paths from which to choose." [*BusinessWeek*]

business science /ˌbɪznɪs ˈsaɪəns/ *noun* the study of business or management techniques ○ *He has a master's degree in business science.*

business social responsibility /ˌbɪznɪs ˌsoʊʃəl rɪˌspɑnsɪˈbɪlɪti/ *noun* abbreviation **BSR**. same as **corporate social responsibility**

business-to-business /ˌbɪznɪs tə ˈbɪznɪs/ *adjective* full form of **B2B**

business-to-consumer /ˌbɪznɪs tə kənˈsumər/ *adjective* full form of **B2C**

business transaction /ˈbɪznɪs trænˌzækʃən/ *noun* an act of buying or selling

business traveler /ˈbɪznəs ˌtræv(ə)lər/ *noun* a person who is traveling on business

business trip /ˈbɪznɪs trɪp/ *noun* a trip made to discuss business matters with clients

business unit /ˈbɪznɪs ˌjunɪt/ *noun* a unit within an organization that operates as a separate department, division, or stand-alone business and is usually treated as a separate profit center

businesswoman /ˈbɪznɪsˌwʊmən/ *noun* a woman engaged in business

bust /bʌst/ *verb*

　go bust *phrasal verb* to become bankrupt (*informal*) ○ *The company went bust last month.*

busy /ˈbɪzi/ *adjective* occupied in doing something or in working ○ *He is busy preparing the annual accounts.* ○ *The manager is busy at the moment, but she will be free in about fifteen minutes.* ○ *The busiest time of year for stores is the week before Christmas.* ○ *Summer is the busy season for hotels.* □ **the line is busy** the telephone line is being used

busy season /ˈbɪzi ˌsiz(ə)n/ *noun* the period when a company is busy

buy /baɪ/ *verb* to get something by paying money ○ *to buy wholesale and sell retail* ○ *to buy for cash* ○ *She bought 10,000 shares.* ○ *The company has been bought by its leading supplier.* (NOTE: **buying – bought**) ■ *noun* something which should be bought ○ *That stock is a definite buy.*

　buy back *phrasal verb* **1.** to buy some-

thing which you sold earlier ○ *She sold the store last year and is now trying to buy it back.* **2.** to buy its own stock

buy forward *phrasal verb* to buy foreign currency before you need it, in order to be sure of the exchange rate

buy in *phrasal verb* (*of a seller at an auction*) to buy the thing which you are trying to sell because no one will pay the price you want

buyback /ˈbaɪbæk/ *noun* **1.** a type of loan agreement to repurchase bonds or securities at a later date for the same price as they are being sold **2.** an international trading agreement where a company builds a factory in a foreign country and agrees to buy all its production

"...the corporate sector also continued to return cash to shareholders in the form of buy-backs, while raising little money in the form of new or rights issues" [*Financial Times*]

buyer /ˈbaɪər/ *noun* **1.** a person who buys □ **there were no buyers** no one wanted to buy **2.** a person who buys stock on behalf of a trading organization for resale or for use in production **3.** in B2B selling, a person who has made a commitment to buy, but has not finalized the deal

buyer's market /ˈbaɪərz ˌmɑrkət/ *noun* a market where products are sold cheaply because there are few people who want to buy them. Opposite **seller's market**

buyer's risk /ˌbaɪərz ˈrɪsk/ *noun* the risk taken by a buyer when accepting goods or services without a guarantee

buying /ˈbaɪɪŋ/ *noun* the act of getting something for money

buying department /ˈbaɪɪŋ dɪˌpɑrtmənt/ *noun* U.K. same as **purchasing department**

buying power /ˈbaɪɪŋ ˌpaʊr/ *noun* the ability to buy ○ *The buying power of the dollar has fallen over the last five years.*

buyout /ˈbaɪaʊt/ *noun* the purchase of a controlling interest in a company

buy-side /ˈbaɪ saɪd/ *noun* an investing entity such as a mutual fund or insurance company that buys securities for investment on its own account. ◊ **sell-side**

bylaw /ˈbaɪlɔ/ *noun* **1.** a rule made by a local authority or organization, and not by central government **2.** a rule governing the internal running of a corporation, such as the number of meetings, the appointment of officers (NOTE: In the U.K., these are called **Articles of Association**.)

byproduct /ˈbaɪˌprɑdʌkt/ *noun* a product made as a result of manufacturing a main product

C

C2C commerce /ˌsi tə si ˈkɑmərs/ same as **consumer-to-consumer commerce**

CA *abbreviation* chartered accountant

CAAC *abbreviation* Civilian Agency Acquisition

cabinet /ˈkæbɪnət/ *noun* a group of senior officials appointed by a president, prime minister, or other government leader to head a department and advise on policy ○ *The President will meet with the cabinet on Monday*

CAD/CAM *noun* the combined use of data and technologies from computer-aided design and computer-aided manufacturing in a fully automated system that covers every part of the manufacturing process from design to production. Full form **computer-aided design/computer-aided manufacturing**

cafeteria plan /ˌkæfəˈtɪriə plæn/ *noun* same as **flexible benefit plan**

calculate /ˈkælkjʊleɪt/ *verb* **1.** to find the answer to a problem using numbers ○ *The bank clerk calculated the rate of exchange for the dollar.* **2.** to estimate ○ *I calculate that we have six months' stock left.*

calculation /ˌkælkjʊˈleɪʃ(ə)n/ *noun* the answer to a problem in mathematics ○ *According to my calculations, we have six months' stock left.* □ **we are $20,000 off in our calculations** we have made a mistake in our calculations and arrived at a figure which is $20,000 too much or too little

calendar year /ˌkælɪndə ˈjɪr/ *noun* a year from the 1st January to 31st December

call /kɔl/ *noun* **1.** a conversation on the telephone □ **to make a call** to dial and speak to someone on the telephone □ **to take a call** to answer the telephone □ **to log calls** to note all details of telephone calls made **2.** a demand for repayment of a loan by a lender **3.** an official request for something **4.** a demand to pay for new shares which then become paid up **5.** same as **call option** ■ *verb* **1.** to telephone someone ○ *I'll call you at your office tomorrow.* □ **to call collect** to make a phone call, asking the person receiving it to pay for it **2.** □ **to call on someone** to visit someone ○ *Our salespeople call on their best accounts twice a month.* **3.** to ask for or order something to be done ○ *to call a meeting* □ **the union called a strike** the union told its members to go on strike

call back *phrasal verb* to telephone in reply to a phone call ○ *The CEO rang – can you call him back?*

call in *phrasal verb* **1.** to visit ○ *Their sales representative called in twice last week.* **2.** to telephone to make contact ○ *We ask the reps to call in every Friday to report the week's sales.* **3.** to ask for a debt to be paid

call off *phrasal verb* to ask for something not to take place ○ *The union has called off the strike.* ○ *The deal was called off at the last moment.*

call-back pay /ˈkɔl bæk ˌpeɪ/ *noun* pay given to an employee who has been called back to work after his or her usual working hours

call center /ˈkɔl ˌsentər/ *noun* a department or business that operates a large number of telephones and specializes in making calls to sell products or in receiving calls from customers to provide information or after-sales services (NOTE: A call center often acts as the central point of contact between an organization and its customers.)

call divert /ˌkɔl daɪˈvərt/ *noun* a telephone facility in which calls are automatically switched from one number to another

caller /'kɔlər/ *noun* **1.** a person who telephones **2.** a person who visits

calling line identification /'kɔlɪŋ laɪn aɪdentɪfɪˌkeɪʃ(ə)n/ *noun* ♦ computer telephony integration

call money /'kɔl ˌmʌni/ *noun* money loaned for which repayment can be demanded without notice. Also called **money at call, money on call**

call option /'kɔl ˌɑpʃən/ *noun* an option to buy stocks at a future date and at a specific price. Also called **call**. Opposite **put option**

call rate /'kɔl reɪt/ *noun* the number of calls per day or per week which a salesperson makes on customers

campaign /kæm'peɪn/ *noun* a series of coordinated activities to reach an objective ■ *verb* to work in an organized way to get something ○ *They are campaigning for better pay for low-paid workers.*

cancel /'kæns(ə)l/ *verb* **1.** to stop something which has been agreed or planned ○ *to cancel an appointment* or *a meeting* ○ *The government has canceled the order for a fleet of buses.* ○ *The manager is still ill, so the interviews planned for this week have been canceled.* (NOTE: **canceling – canceled**. The U.K. spelling is **cancelling – cancelled**.) **2.** □ **to cancel a check** to stop payment of a check which has been signed

cancel out *phrasal verb* (*of two things*) to balance each other or act against each other so that there is no change in the existing situation ○ *The two clauses cancel each other out.* ○ *Higher costs have canceled out the increased sales revenue.*

cancellation /ˌkænsə'leɪʃ(ə)n/ *noun* the act of stopping something which has been agreed or planned ○ *the cancellation of an appointment* ○ *the cancellation of an agreement*

cancellation clause /ˌkænsə'leɪʃ(ə)n ˌklɔz/ *noun* a clause in a contract which states the terms on which the contract may be canceled

candidate /'kændɪdeɪt/ *noun* a person who applies for or is considered suitable for a job or for a training course ○ *Ten out of fifty candidates were shortlisted.* ○ *The candidates for department manager were each given a personality test and an intelligence test.* ○ *I don't consider him as suitable candidate for management training.*

can-do /'kæn du/ *adjective* go-ahead, liking to cope with new challenges ○ *She's a can-do individual.*

cannibalization /ˌkænɪbəlɪz(ə)m/, **cannibalism** *noun* a situation where a company launches a new product which sells well at the expense of another established product ○ *Though the new product sold well, the resultant cannibalization damaged the company's overall profits for the year.* ○ *Cannibalism became a real problem because the new product made the existing line seem obsolete.*

canvass /'kænvəs/ *verb* to visit people to ask them to buy goods, to vote, or to say what they think ○ *He's canvassing for customers for his hairdresser's store.* ○ *We've canvassed the staff about raising the prices in the staff restaurant.*

canvasser /'kænvəsər/ *noun* a person who canvasses

canvassing /'kænvəsɪŋ/ *noun* the practice of asking people to buy, to vote, or to say what they think ○ *door-to-door canvassing* ○ *canvassing techniques*

cap /kæp/ *noun* an upper limit placed on something, such as an interest rate. The opposite, i.e. a lower limit, is a "floor"). ■ *verb* to place an upper limit on something ○ *to cap a local authority's budget* ○ *to cap a department's budget* (NOTE: **capping – capped**)

capable /'keɪpəb(ə)l/ *adjective* **1.** □ **capable of** able or clever enough to do something ○ *She is capable of very fast keyboarding speeds.* ○ *The sales force should be capable of selling all the stock in the warehouse.* ○ *She is capable of very fast typing speeds.* **2.** efficient ○ *She is a very capable departmental manager.* (NOTE: You are capable **of** something or **of doing** something.)

capacity /kə'pæsəti/ *noun* **1.** the amount which can be produced, or the amount of work which can be done ○ *industrial* or *manufacturing* or *production capacity* □ **to work at full capacity** to do as much work as possible **2.** the amount of space □ **to use up spare** *or* **excess capacity** to make use of time or space which is not fully used **3.** ability ○ *She has a particular capacity for detailed business deals with overseas companies.* **4.** □ **in one's capacity** as acting as ○ *I signed the document in my capacity as chairman.*

"…analysts are increasingly convinced that the industry simply has too much capacity" [*Fortune*]

capacity planning /kəˈpæsɪti ˌplænɪŋ/ *noun* forward planning to relate production needs to anticipated demand

capacity requirements planning /kəˌpæsɪti rɪˌkwaɪrmənts ˈplænɪŋ/ *noun* planning that determines how much machinery and equipment is needed in order to meet production targets

capacity utilization /kəˌpæsəti ˌjutɪlaɪˈzeɪʃ(ə)n/ *noun* a measurement that shows how much of the plant and equipment of a company or industry is actually being used to produce goods or services. It is usually expressed as a ratio between actual output over a particular period and the maximum output the plant or equipment designed to produce during the same period.

capita /ˈkæpɪtə/ ◊ **per capita**

capital /ˈkæpɪt(ə)l/ *noun* **1.** the money, property, and assets used in a business ○ *a company with $10,000 capital* or *with a capital of $10,000* □ **capital structure of a company** the way in which a company's capital is made up from various sources **2.** money owned by individuals or companies, which they use for investment □ **movements of capital** changes of investments from one country to another □ **flight of capital** the rapid movement of capital out of one country because of lack of confidence in that country's economic future

capital account /ˈkæpɪt(ə)l əˌkaʊnt/ *noun* **1.** an account of dealings such as money invested in or taken out of the company by the owners of a company **2.** items in a country's balance of payments which do not refer to the buying and selling merchandise, but refer to investments **3.** the total equity in a business

capital allowances /ˌkæpɪt(ə)l əˈlaʊənsɪz/ *plural noun* the allowances based on the value of fixed assets which may be deducted from a company's profits and so reduce its tax liability

capital appreciation /ˌkæpɪt(ə)l əˌpriʃiˈeɪʃ(ə)n/ *noun* same as **appreciation**

capital asset pricing model /ˌkæpɪt(ə)l ˌæset ˈpraɪsɪŋ ˌmɑd(ə)l/ *noun* an equation that shows the relationship between expected risk and expected

return on an investment and serves as a model for valuing risky securities. Abbreviation **CAPM**

capital assets /ˌkæpɪt(ə)l ˈæsets/ *plural noun* the property, machines, and other assets which a company owns and uses but which it does not buy and sell as part of its regular trade. Also called **fixed assets**

capital base /ˌkæpɪt(ə)l ˈbeɪs/ *noun* the capital structure of a company (stockholders' capital plus loans and retained profits) used as a way of assessing the company's worth

capital bonus /ˌkæpɪt(ə)l ˈboʊnəs/ *noun* an extra payment by an insurance company which is produced by a capital gain

capital city /ˌkæpɪt(ə)l ˈsɪti/ *noun* the main city in a country, where the government is located

capital commitments /ˌkæpɪt(ə)l kəˈmɪtmənts/ *plural noun* expenditure on assets which has been authorized by directors, but not yet spent at the end of a financial period

capital employed /ˌkæpɪt(ə)l ɪmˈplɔɪd/ *noun* an amount of capital consisting of stockholders' funds plus the long-term debts of a business. ◊ **return on capital employed**

capital equipment /ˌkæpɪt(ə)l ɪˈkwɪpmənt/ *noun* equipment which a factory or office uses to work

capital expenditure /ˌkæpɪt(ə)l ɪkˈspendɪtʃər/ *noun* money spent on fixed assets such as property, machines and furniture. Also called **capital investment**, **capital outlay**. Abbreviation **CAPEX**

capital gain /ˌkæpɪt(ə)l ˈgeɪn/ *noun* an amount of money made by selling a fixed asset. Opposite **capital loss**

capital gains tax /ˌkæpɪt(ə)l ˈgeɪnz ˌtæks/ *noun* a tax on the difference between the gross acquisition cost and the net proceeds when an asset is sold. Abbreviation **CGT**

capital goods /ˈkæpɪt(ə)l gʊdz/ *plural noun* machinery, buildings, and raw materials which are used to make other goods

capital-intensive industry /ˌkæpɪt(ə)l ɪnˈtensɪv ˌɪndəstri/ *noun* an industry which needs a large amount of capital investment in plant to make it work

capital investment /ˌkæpɪt(ə)l ɪn 'vestmənt/ *noun* same as **capital expenditure**

capitalism /'kæpɪt(ə)lɪz(ə)m/ *noun* the economic system in which each person has the right to invest money, to work in business, and to buy and sell, with no restrictions from the state

capitalist /'kæpɪt(ə)lɪst/ *adjective* working according to the principles of capitalism ○ *the capitalist system* ○ *the capitalist countries* or *world* ■ *noun* a person who invests capital in business enterprises

capitalist economy /ˌkæpɪt(ə)lɪst ɪ 'kɒnəmi/ *noun* an economy in which each person has the right to invest money, to work in business, and to buy and sell, with no restrictions from the state

capitalization /ˌkæpɪt(ə)laɪ'zeɪʃ(ə)n/ *noun* the value of a company calculated by multiplying the price of its stock on the stock exchange by the number of shares issued. Also called **market capitalisation**

   "...she aimed to double the company's market capitalization" [*Fortune*]

capitalization issue /ˌkæpɪtəlaɪ 'zeɪʃ(ə)n ˌɪʃu/ *noun* same as **bonus issue**

capitalization of reserves /ˌkæpɪt(ə)laɪzeɪʃ(ə)n əv rɪ'zɜːrvz/ *noun* the issuing of free bonus shares to stockholders

capitalize *verb* to invest money in a working company □ **the company is capitalized at $10,000** the company has a working capital of $10,000

  capitalize on *phrasal verb* to make a profit from ○ *We are seeking to capitalize on our market position.*

capital letters /ˌkæpɪt(ə)l 'letərz/ *noun* letters written as A, B, C, D, etc., and not a, b, c, d ○ *Write your name in block capitals at the top of the form.*

capital levy /ˌkæpɪt(ə)l 'levi/ *noun* a tax on the value of a person's property and possessions

capital loss /ˌkæpɪt(ə)l 'lɒs/ *noun* a loss made by selling assets. Opposite **capital gain**

capital market /ˌkæpɪt(ə)l 'mɑːrkɪt/ *noun* an international market where money can be raised for investment in a business

capital outlay /ˌkæpɪt(ə)l 'aʊtleɪ/ *noun* same as **capital expenditure**

capital project /ˌkæpɪt(ə)l 'prɑːdʒekt/ *noun* a large-scale and complex project, often involving construction or engineering work, in which an organization spends part of its financial resources on creating capacity for production

capital project management /ˌkæpɪt(ə)l ˌprɑːdʒekt 'mænɪdʒmənt/ *noun* the control and organization of capital projects

capital requirements /ˌkæpɪt(ə)l rɪ 'kwaɪrmənts/ *plural noun* the amount of capital which a firm needs to operate normally

capital reserves /ˌkæpɪt(ə)l rɪ'zɜːrvz/ *plural noun* money from profits, which forms part of the capital of a company and can be used for distribution to stockholders only when a company is wound up. Also called **undistributable reserves**

capital structure /ˌkæpɪt(ə)l 'strʌktʃər/ *noun* the relative proportions of equity capital and debt capital within a company's balance sheet

CAPM *abbreviation* capital asset pricing model

captain of industry /ˌkæptɪn əv 'ɪndəstri/ *noun* a head of a major industrial company

captive market /ˌkæptɪv 'mɑːrkət/ *noun* a market where one supplier has a monopoly and the buyer has no choice over the product which he or she must purchase

capture /'kæptʃər/ *verb* to take or get control of something □ **to capture 10% of the market** to sell hard, and so take a 10% market share □ **to capture 20% of a company's shares** to buy stock in a company rapidly and so own 20% of it

car assembly plant /ˌkɑːr ə'sembli ˌplænt/ *noun* a factory where cars are put together from parts made in other factories

card /kɑːrd/ *noun* **1.** stiff paper ○ *We have printed the instructions on thick white card.* **2.** a small piece of cardboard or plastic, usually with information printed on it ○ *He showed his staff card to get a discount in the store.* **3.** a postcard **4.** □ **to get your cards** to be dismissed

card catalog /'kɑːrd ˌkætəlɒg/ *noun* a series of cards with information written on them, kept in special order so that the information can be found easily ○ *We use an alphabetical card-index system for staff records.*

cardholder /'kɑrd,hoʊldər/ *noun* **1.** a person who holds a credit card or bank ATM card **2.** a frame which protects a card or a message

card-index /'kɑrd ,ɪndeks/ *verb* to put information onto a card catalog

card-index file /'kɑrd ,ɪndeks faɪl/ *noun* information kept on filing cards

card-indexing /'kɑrd ,ɪndeksɪŋ/ *noun* the process of putting information onto a card catalog ○ *No one can understand her card-indexing system.*

card-not-present merchant account /,kɑrd nɑt ,prez(ə)nt 'mɜrtʃənt ə,kaʊnt/ *noun* an account that enables businesses operating on the web to receive payments by credit card without the buyer or card being physically present when the transaction is made

card phone /'kɑrd foʊn/ *noun* a public telephone which works when you insert a phonecard

career /kə'rɪr/ *noun* a job which you are trained for and which you expect to do all your life ○ *He made his career in electronics.* ○ *She has had a varied career, having worked in education and industry.* ○ *The company offered its employees no advice on their future careers.*

career break /kə'rɪr breɪk/ *noun* a period when an employee leaves a career job for several years to undertake another activity such as studying for a degree or having a baby and then returns at the same level

career change /kə'rɪr tʃeɪndʒ/ *noun* a change in a person's profession or in the type of job they do, that often involves going to work for a different employer (NOTE: career changes may be planned as part of someone's career development, or may be forced on somebody as a result of dismissal, ill-health, or a change in their personal circumstances.)

career development /kə'rɪr dɪ,veləpmənt/ *noun* the planning of an employee's future career in an organization ○ *a career development programme* ○ *If the company does not spend more time on career development, many employees will leave.* ○ *Career development involves a very comprehensive training programme.*

career path /kə'rɪr pæθ/ *noun* a planned logical sequence of jobs within one or more professions through which a person can progress in the course of their working life (NOTE: it is much easier to plan a career path when the market is stable and there is little change in business conditions; in uncertain times people need to be more adaptable and the idea of a planned career path has much less value, according to some experts)

caretaker /'kerteɪkər/ *noun U.K.* same as **janitor**

cargo /'kɑrgoʊ/ *noun* a load of goods which are sent in a ship or plane, etc. □ **the ship was taking on cargo** the ship was being loaded with goods □ **to load cargo** to put cargo on a ship

cargo plane /'kɑrgoʊ pleɪn/ *noun* a plane which carries only cargo and not passengers (NOTE: The plural is **cargoes**.)

cargo ship /'kɑrgoʊ ʃɪp/ *noun* a ship which carries cargo, not passengers

car-hire /'kɑr haɪr/ *noun U.K.* same as **car rental**

car hire firm /'kɑr haɪr ,fɜrm/ *noun U.K.* same as **car rental agency**

car insurance /'kɑr ɪn,ʃʊrəns/ *noun* the insuring of a car, the driver and passengers in case of accident

carnet /'kɑrneɪ/ *noun* an international document which allows dutiable goods to cross several European countries by road without paying duty until the goods reach their final destination

car rental /'kɑr ,rent(ə)l/ *noun* the business of renting cars to people

car rental agency /,kɑr 'rent(ə)l ,eɪdʒənsi/ *noun* a company which specializes in offering cars for rent

carriage /'kærɪdʒ/ *noun* **1.** the transporting of goods from one place to another ○ *to pay for carriage* **2.** the cost of transportation of goods ○ *to allow 10% for carriage* ○ *Carriage is 15% of the total cost.* □ **carriage prepaid** a note showing that the transportation costs have been paid in advance

carriage forward /,kærɪdʒ 'fɔrwərd/ *noun* a deal where the customer pays for transporting the goods

carriage free /,kærɪdʒ 'fri/ *adverb* the customer does not pay for the shipping

carriage paid /ˌkærɪdʒ ˈpeɪd/ *noun* a deal where the seller has paid for the shipping

carrier /ˈkæriər/ *noun* **1.** a company that transports goods ○ *We only use reputable carriers.* **2.** a vehicle or ship that transports goods

carrier's risk /ˌkæriərz ˈrɪsk/ *noun* the responsibility of a carrier to pay for damage or loss of goods being shipped

carry /ˈkæri/ *verb* **1.** to take from one place to another ○ *a tanker carrying oil from the Gulf* ○ *The truck was carrying goods to the supermarket.* (NOTE: **carries – carrying – carried**) **2.** to vote to approve (NOTE: **carries – carrying – carried**) □ **the motion was carried** the motion was accepted after a vote **3.** to produce ○ *The bonds carry interest at 10%.* (NOTE: **carries – carrying – carried**) **4.** to keep in stock ○ *to carry a line of goods* ○ *We do not carry pens.* (NOTE: **carries – carrying – carried**) ■ *noun* the cost of borrowing to finance a deal (NOTE: **carries – carrying – carried**)

carry down, carry forward *phrasal verb* to take an account balance at the end of the current period as the starting point for the next period □ **balance carried forward, balance c *or* f** the amount entered in an account at the end of a period or page of an account book to balance the debit and credit entries; it is then taken forward to start the next period or page

carry on *phrasal verb* to continue or to go on doing something ○ *The staff carried on working in spite of the fire.* □ **to carry on a business** to be active in running a business

carry over *phrasal verb* **1.** □ **to carry over a balance** to take a balance from the end of one page or period to the beginning of the next **2.** □ **to carry over stock** to hold stock from the end of one stocktaking period to the beginning of the next

carrying /ˈkæriɪŋ/ *noun* transporting from one place to another ○ *carrying charges* ○ *carrying cost*

cartage /ˈkɑrtɪdʒ/ *noun* the activity of carrying goods by road

cartel /kɑrˈtel/ *noun* a group of companies which try to fix the price or to regulate the supply of a product so that they can make more profit

carter /ˈkɑrtər/ *noun* a person who transports goods by road

carton /ˈkɑrt(ə)n/ *noun* **1.** thick cardboard ○ *a folder made of carton* **2.** a box made of cardboard ○ *a carton of milk*

case /keɪs/ *noun* **1.** a typical example of something ○ *The company has had several cases of petty theft in the mail room.* **2.** reasons for doing something ○ *The negotiators put forward the union's case for a pay raise.* **3.** □ **the case is being heard next week** the case is coming to court next week ■ *verb* to pack (items) in a case

case study /ˈkeɪs ˌstʌdi/ *noun* a true or invented business situation used in business training to practice decision-making ○ *The marketing case study consisted of a long history of the company, the present situation, and a choice of strategic plans.* ○ *The case study was about territory-planning in a city in which there were a number of accounts of varying importance.*

cash /kæʃ/ *noun* **1.** money in the form of coins or bills **2.** the using of money in coins or bills □ **to pay cash down** to pay in cash immediately ■ *verb* □ **to cash a check** to exchange a check for cash

cash in *phrasal verb* to sell stock or other property for cash

cash in on *phrasal verb* to profit from ○ *The company is cashing in on the interest in computer games.*

cash out *phrasal verb* to add up the cash in a store at the end of the day

cash up *phrasal verb U.K.* same as **cash out**

cashable /ˈkæʃəb(ə)l/ *adjective* able to be cashed ○ *A crossed check is not cashable at any bank.*

cash account /ˈkæʃ əˌkaʊnt/ *noun* an account which records the money which is received and spent

cash advance /ˌkæʃ ədˈvæns/ *noun* a loan in cash against a future payment

cash-and-carry /ˌkæʃ ən ˈkæri/ *noun* a large store selling goods at low prices, where the customer pays cash and takes the goods away immediately ○ *We get our supplies every morning from the cash-and-carry.*

cashback /ˈkæʃbæk/ *noun* a discount system where a purchaser receives a cash discount on the completion of the purchase

"... he mentioned BellSouth's DSL offer of $75 a month, plus a one-month cash-back rebate." [BusinessWeek]

cash balance /'kæʃ ˌbæləns/ *noun* a balance in cash, as opposed to amounts owed

cash basis /'kæʃ ˌbeɪsɪs/ *noun* an accounting method in which receipts and payments are accounted for when the money is actually received or paid out, not necessarily when they are entered in the books

cash book /'kæʃ bʊk/ *noun* a book in which all cash payments and receipts are recorded. In a double-entry bookkeeping system, the balance at the end of a given period is included in the trial balance and then transferred to the balance sheet itself.

cash box /'kæʃ bɑks/ *noun* metal box for keeping cash

cash budget /'kæʃ ˌbʌdʒət/ *noun* a plan of cash income and expenditure

cash card /'kæʃ kɑrd/ *noun U.K.* same as **ATM card**

cash cow /'kæʃ kaʊ/ *noun* a product or subsidiary company that consistently generates good profits but does not provide growth

cash deal /ˌkæʃ 'dil/ *noun* a sale done for cash

cash desk /'kæʃ desk/ *noun U.K.* same as **checkout**

cash discount /ˌkæʃ 'dɪskaʊnt/ *noun* a discount given for payment in cash. Also called **discount for cash**

cash dispenser /'kæʃ dɪˌspensər/ *noun U.K.* same as **automated teller machine**

cash economy /ˌkæʃ ɪ'kɑnəmi/ *noun* a black economy, where goods and services are paid for in cash, and therefore not declared for tax

cash float /'kæʃ floʊt/ *noun* cash put into the cash box at the beginning of the day or week to allow change to be given to customers

cash flow /'kæʃ floʊ/ *noun* cash which comes into a company from sales (cash inflow) or the money which goes out in purchases or overhead expenditure (cash outflow) □ **the company is suffering from cash flow problems** cash income is not coming in fast enough to pay the expenditure going out

cash flow forecast /'kæʃ floʊ ˌfɔrkæst/ *noun* a forecast of when cash will be received or paid out

cash flow statement /'kæʃ floʊ ˌsteɪtmənt/ *noun* a record of a company's cash inflows and cash outflows over a specific period of time, typically a year

cashier /kæ'ʃɪr/ *noun* **1.** a person who takes money from customers in a store or who deals with the money that has been paid **2.** a person who deals with customers in a bank and takes or gives cash at the counter

cashier's check /kæˌʃɪrz 'tʃek/ *noun* a bank's own check, drawn on itself and signed by a cashier or other bank official

cash in hand /ˌkæʃ ɪn 'hænd/ *noun* money and bills, kept to pay small amounts but not deposited in the bank

cash items /'kæʃ ˌaɪtəmz/ *plural noun* goods sold for cash

cashless society /ˌkæʃləs sə'saɪəti/ *noun* a society where no one uses cash, all purchases being made by credit cards, charge cards, checks or direct transfer from one account to another

cash limit /kæʃ 'lɪmɪt/ *noun* a fixed amount of money which can be spent during some period

cash offer /'kæʃ ˌɔfər/ *noun* an offer to pay in cash, especially an offer to pay cash when buying stock in a takeover bid

cash on delivery /ˌkæʃ ɑn dɪ'lɪv(ə)ri/ *noun* payment in cash when goods are delivered. Abbreviation **COD**

cash payment /'kæʃ ˌpeɪmənt/ *noun* payment in cash

cashpoint /'kæʃˌpɔɪnt/ *noun U.K.* a place where there are cash dispensers where a card holder can get cash by using his ATM card

cash position /'kæʃ pəˌzɪʃ(ə)n/ *noun* a state of the cash which a company currently has available

cash price /'kæʃ praɪs/ *noun* a lower price or better terms which apply if the customer pays cash

cash purchase /'kæʃ ˌpɜrtʃɪs/ *noun* a purchase made for cash

cash register /'kæʃ ˌredʒɪstər/ *noun* a machine which shows and adds the prices of items bought, with a drawer for keeping the cash received

cash reserves /'kæʃ rɪ,zɜrvz/ *plural noun* a company's reserves in cash deposits or bills kept in case of urgent need ○ *The company was forced to fall back on its cash reserves.*

cash sale /'kæʃ seɪl/ *noun* a transaction paid for in cash

cash-strapped /'kæʃ stræpt/ *adjective* short of money

cash terms /'kæʃ tɜrmz/ *plural noun* lower terms which apply if the customer pays cash

cash till /'kæʃ tɪl/ *noun* same as **cash register**

cash transaction /'kæʃ træn,zækʃən/ *noun* a transaction paid for in cash

cash voucher /'kæʃ ,vaʊtʃər/ *noun* a piece of paper which can be exchanged for cash ○ *With every $20 of purchases, the customer gets a cash voucher for $2.*

cash with order /,kæʃ wɪð 'ɔrdər/ *noun* terms of sale showing the payment has to be made in cash when the order is placed. Abbreviation **CWO**

casting vote /,kæstɪŋ 'voʊt/ *noun* a vote used by the chairman in the case where the votes for and against a proposal are equal ○ *The chairman has the casting vote.* ○ *She used her casting vote to block the motion.*

casual /'kæʒuəl/ *adjective* **1.** informal or not serious **2.** not permanent, or not regular

casual labor /,kæʒuəl 'leɪbər/ *noun* workers who are hired for a short period

casual laborer /,kæʒuəl 'leɪbərər/ *noun* a worker who can be hired for a short period

casual work /'kæʒuəl wɜrk/ *noun* work where the employees are hired only for a short period

casual worker /,kæʒuəl 'wɜrkər/ *noun* an employee who can be hired for a short period

catalog /'kætəlɔg/ *noun* a publication which lists items for sale, usually showing their prices ○ *an office equipment catalog* ○ *They sent us a catalog of their new range of products.* ■ *verb* to put an item into a catalog

catalog price /'kætəlɔg praɪs/ *noun* a price as marked in a catalog or list

catchment area /'kætʃmənt ,eriə/ *noun* the area around a store or shopping center, where the customers live

category /'kætɪg(ə)ri/ *noun* a type or sort of item ○ *We deal only in the most expensive categories of watches.* ○ *The company has vacancies for most categories of office staff.*

cater /'keɪtər/ *verb*
  cater for *phrasal verb* to deal with or provide for ○ *The store caters mainly for overseas customers.*

caterer /'keɪtərər/ *noun* a person or company that supplies food and drink, especially for parties

catering /'keɪtərɪŋ/ *noun* the activity of supplying food and drink for a party etc ■ *adjective* □ **catering to** providing for ○ *a store catering to overseas visitors*

catering trade /'keɪtərɪŋ treɪd/ *noun* the food trade, especially businesses supplying food that is ready to eat

cause /kɔz/ *noun* a thing which makes something happen ○ *What was the cause of the bank's collapse?* ○ *The police tried to find the cause of the fire.* ■ *verb* to make something happen ○ *The recession caused hundreds of bankruptcies.*

caveat /'kæviæt/ *noun* warning □ **to enter a caveat** to warn someone legally that you have an interest in a case, and that no steps can be taken without your permission

caveat emptor /,kæviæt 'emptɔr/ *phrase* a Latin phrase meaning "let the buyer beware," which indicates that the buyer is responsible for checking that what he or she buys is in good order

caveat venditor /,kæviæt ven'dɪtɔr/ *phrase* a Latin phrase meaning "let the seller beware", which indicates that the seller is legally bound to make sure that the goods he sells are in good order

CB *abbreviation* cash book

CBD *abbreviation* central business district

cc a way of including other parties in an e-mail conversation even if the message is not addressed to them directly. Cc is a convention carried through from traditional business practices when carbon copies were kept of typewritten letters sent to customers or suppliers. (NOTE: **cc** is put at the bottom of a letter, under the signature, to show who has been sent a copy of it)

CCA *abbreviation* current cost accounting

CD *abbreviation* certificate of deposit

c/d *abbreviation* carried down

cede /sid/ *verb* to give up property to someone else

ceiling /'silɪŋ/ *noun* the highest point that something can reach, e.g., the highest rate of a pay increase ○ *to fix a ceiling for a budget* ○ *There is a ceiling of $100,000 on deposits.* ○ *Output reached its ceiling in June and has since fallen back.* ○ *What ceiling has the government put on wage increases this year?*

ceiling price /'silɪŋ praɪs/ *noun* the highest price that can be reached

cell manufacturing, cellular manufacturing *noun* an approach to manufacturing in which workers and machines are organized into compact work centers that have everything they need to produce an item or range of similar items

cell phone /'seljʊlə 'telɪfoʊn/, **cellular telephone** /'sel 'telɪfoʊn/ *noun* a small portable phone which can be used away from home or the office ○ *If I'm not in the office for some reason you can always reach me on my cell phone.* (NOTE: The U.K. term is **mobile phone**.)

cent /sent/ *noun* a small coin, one hundredth of a dollar ○ *The stores are only a 25-cent bus ride away.* ○ *They sell oranges at 99 cents each.* (NOTE: **Cent** is usually written ¢ in prices: **25¢**, but not when a dollar price is mentioned: **$1.25**.) ■ ♦ **percent**

center /'sentər/ *noun* **1.** an important town ○ *Pittsburgh became a major industrial center in the 19th century.* ○ *Nottingham is the center for the shoe industry.* **2.** a department, area, or function to which costs and/or revenues are charged (NOTE: [all senses] The U.S. spelling is **center**.)

center of excellence /,sentər əv 'eksələns/ *noun* an organization which is recognized as being successful and having a world-wide reputation in its field, and so receives special funding

centimeter /'sentɪmitə/ *noun* a measurement of length (one hundredth of a meter) ○ *The paper is fifteen centimeters wide.* (NOTE: **centimeter** is usually written **cm** after numbers: *260 cm*. The usual U.K. spelling is **centimetre**.)

central /'sentrəl/ *adjective* organized from one main point

central bank /,sentrəl 'bæŋk/ *noun* the main government-controlled bank in a country, which controls that country's financial affairs by fixing main interest rates, issuing currency, supervising the commercial banks and trying to control the foreign exchange rate

central business district /,sentrəl 'bɪznɪs ,dɪstrɪkt/ *noun* the area in the center of a city or town where the majority of businesses and stores have traditionally been located. Many businesses relocated to the suburbs during the last century but are returning to restored and revitalized downtown areas. Abbreviation **CBD**

central government /,sentrəl 'gʌv(ə)nmənt/ *noun* the main government of a country as opposed to municipal, local, provincial or state governments

centralization /,sentrəlaɪ'zeɪʃ(ə)n/ *noun* the organization of everything from a central point

centralize /'sentrəlaɪz/ *verb* to organize from a central point ○ *All purchasing has been centralized in our main office.* ○ *The company has become very centralized, and far more staff work at headquarters.*

centralized distribution /,sentrəlaɪzd ,dɪstrɪ'bjuʃ(ə)n/ *noun* a system of distribution of goods to retail stores in a chain, from a central or local warehouse, so avoiding direct distribution from the manufacturer, and making stock control easier

central limit theorem /,sentrəl 'lɪmɪt ,θɪrəm/ *noun* a theorem that demonstrates the tendency of random samples of a population to eventually produce a normal curve approximating the population's true mean as the sample size increases. Abbreviation **CLT**

central office /,sentrəl 'ɔfɪs/ *noun* the main office which controls all smaller offices

central purchasing /,sentrəl 'pɜrtʃɪsɪŋ/ *noun* purchasing organized by a central office for all branches of a company

CEO *abbreviation* chief executive officer

CERES *noun* an association of environmental organizations, investment funds, and advocacy groups whose goal is to improve the environment by encouraging companies to be environmentally responsible. Full form **Coalition for Environmentally Responsible Economies**

certain /'sɜːt(ə)n/ *adjective* **1.** sure ○ *The chairman is certain we will pass last year's total sales.* **2.** □ **a certain** one particular □ **a certain number**, **a certain quantity** some ○ *A certain number of lines are being discontinued.*

certificate /sər'tıfıkeıt/ *noun* **1.** an official document carrying an official declaration by someone, and signed by that person **2.** an official document which shows that something is owned by someone or that something is true

certificate of airworthiness /sər‚tıfıkət əv 'erwɜːrðinəs/ *noun* a document to show that an aircraft is safe to fly

certificate of approval /sə‚tıfıkət əv ə'pruːv(ə)l/ *noun* a document showing that an item has been approved officially

certificate of competency /sər‚tıfıkət əv 'kɑmpıt(ə)nsi/ *noun* a certificate issued by the Small Business Administration to a small business that has met certain requirements, giving the business a fair opportunity to compete for and receive government contracts. Abbreviation **COC**

certificate of deposit /sər'tıfıkət əv dı'pɑzıt/ *noun* a document from a bank showing that money has been deposited at a guaranteed interest rate for a certain period of time. Abbreviation **CD**

"...interest rates on certificates of deposit may have little room to decline in August as demand for funds from major city banks is likely to remain strong. After delaying for months, banks are now expected to issue a large volume of CDs. If banks issue more CDs on the assumption that the official discount rate reduction will be delayed, it is very likely that CD rates will be pegged for a longer period than expected" [*Nikkei Weekly*]

COMMENT: A CD is a bearer instrument, which can be sold by the bearer. It can be sold at a discounted value, so that the yield on CDs varies.

certificate of origin /sər‚tıfıkət əv 'orıdʒın/ *noun* a document showing where imported goods come from or were made

certificate of registration /sər‚tıfıkət əv ‚redʒı'streıʃ(ə)n/ *noun* a document showing that an item has been registered

certification /sə‚tıfı'keıʃ(ə)n/ *noun* the act of giving an official certificate of approval

certified /'sɜːtıfaıd/ *noun* having passed special examinations in a subject

certified accountant /‚sɜːtıfaıd ə'kaʊntənt/ *noun U.K.* an accountant who has passed the professional examinations and is a member of the Chartered Association of Certified Accountants. ◊ **certified public accountant**

certified check /‚sɜːtıfaıd 'tʃek/ *noun* a check which a bank says is good and will be paid out of money put aside from the payer's bank account

certified copy /‚sɜːtıfaıd 'kɑpi/ *noun* a document which is certified as being the same as another

certified mail /‚sɜːtıfaıd 'meıl/ *noun* a mail service where the letters are signed for by the person receiving them ○ *We sent the documents (by) certified mail.*

certified public accountant /‚sɜːtıfaıd ‚pʌblık ə'kaʊntənt/ *noun* an accountant who has passed the examinations of the AICPA and been given a certificate by a state, allowing him or her to practice in that state. Abbreviation **CPA**

certify /'sɜːtıfaı/ *verb* to make an official declaration in writing ○ *I certify that this is a true copy.* ○ *The document is certified as a true copy.* (NOTE: **certifies – certifying – certified**)

cession /'seʃ(ə)n/ *noun* the act of giving up property to someone, especially a creditor

c/f *abbreviation* carried forward

CFO *abbreviation* chief financial officer

CGT *abbreviation* capital gains tax

chain /tʃeın/ *noun* a series of stores or other businesses belonging to the same company ○ *a chain of hotels* or *a hotel chain* ○ *the chairman of a large do-it-yourself chain* ○ *He runs a chain of shoe stores.* ○ *She bought several garden centers and gradually built up a chain.*

chain of command /‚tʃeın əv kə'mænd/ *noun* a series of links between directors, management and employees, by which instructions and information are passed up or down

chain store /'tʃeɪn stɔr/ *noun* one store in a chain. Also called **multiple store**

chair /tʃer/ *noun* the position of the chairman, presiding over a meeting ○ *to be in the chair* ○ *Mr. Smith was in the chair.* ○ *Mrs. Brown was voted into the chair.* □ **Mr. Jones took the chair** Mr. Jones presided over the meeting. □ **to address the chair** to speak to the chairman and not to the rest of the people at the meeting ○ *Please address your remarks to the chair.* ■ *verb* to preside over a meeting ○ *The meeting was chaired by Mrs. Smith.*

chairman /'tʃermən/ *noun* **1.** a person who is in charge of a meeting ○ *Mr Howard was chairman* or *acted as chairman* **2.** a person who presides over the board meetings of a company ○ *the chairman of the board* or *the company chairman* □ **the chairman's report, the chairman's statement** an annual report from the chairman of a company to the stockholders

"...the corporation's entrepreneurial chairman seeks a dedicated but part-time president. The new president will work a three-day week" [*Globe and Mail (Toronto)*]

chairman and managing director /ˌtʃermən ən ˌmænɪdʒɪŋ daɪ'rektər/ *noun U.K.* a managing director who is also chairman of the board of directors

chairmanship /'tʃermənʃɪp/ *noun* the fact of being a chairman ○ *The committee met under the chairmanship of Mr Jones.*

chairperson /'tʃerpɜrs(ə)n/ *noun* a person who is in charge of a meeting (NOTE: The plural is **chairpersons**.)

chairwoman /'tʃerwʊmən/ *noun* a woman who is in charge of a meeting (NOTE: The plural is **chairwomen**.)

challenger /'tʃælɪndʒər/ *noun* a company which challenges other companies which are already established in the marketplace

Chamber of Commerce /ˌtʃeɪmbər əv 'kɑmɜrs/ *noun* an organization of local business people who work together to promote and protect common interest in trade

chambers /'tʃeɪmbərz/ *plural noun* office of a lawyer or judge □ **the judge heard the case in chambers** he heard the case in his private office, and not in court

chance /tʃæns/ *noun* **1.** the fact of being possible ○ *The company has a good chance of winning the contract.* ○ *His pro-*

motion chances are small. **2.** the opportunity to do something ○ *She is waiting for a chance to see the managing director.* ○ *He had his chance of promotion when the finance director's assistant resigned.* (NOTE: You have a chance **of doing** something or **to do** something.)

chandler /'tʃændlər/ *noun* a person who deals in goods, especially supplies to ships ○ *There is a ship chandler's near the yacht club.*

chandlery /'tʃændləri/ *noun* a chandler's store

change /tʃeɪndʒ/ *noun* **1.** money in coins or small bills. ◊ **exchange** □ **to give someone change for $20** to give someone coins or bills in exchange for a twenty dollar bill **2.** money given back by the seller, when the buyer can pay only with a larger bill or coin than the amount asked ○ *She gave me the wrong change.* ○ *You paid the $5.75 check with a $10 bill, so you should have $4.25 change.* □ **keep the change** keep it as a tip (said to e.g. waiters, taxi-drivers) **3.** an alteration of the way something is done or of the way work is carried out ■ *verb* **1.** □ **to change a $50 bill** to give someone smaller bills or coins in place of a $50 bill **2.** to give one type of currency for another ○ *to change £1,000 into dollars* ○ *We want to change some traveler's checks.* **3.** □ **to change hands** (*of a business, property, etc.*) to be sold to a new owner ○ *The store changed hands for $100,000.*

change machine /'tʃeɪndʒ məˌʃin/ *noun* a machine which gives small change for a bill or larger coin

change management /ˌtʃeɪndʒ 'mænɪdʒmənt/ *noun* the control and organization of the changes that take place within a business during a period when it is adapting itself to deal with new situations

change of ownership /ˌtʃeɪndʒ əv 'oʊnəʃɪp/ *noun* (*of a business*) the process of being sold to a new owner ○ *The change of ownership has had an effect on staff morale.*

changer /'tʃeɪndʒər/ *noun* a person who changes money

channel /'tʃæn(ə)l/ *noun* a means by which information or goods pass from one place to another □ **to go through the official channels** to deal with government officials, especially when making a request ■ *verb* to send in some direction ○ *They are channeling their research funds into developing European communication systems.* (NOTE: **channeling – channeled**. The U.S. spelling is **channeling – channeled**.)

channel captain /'tʃæn(ə)l ˌkæptɪn/ *noun* a business which controls or has the most influence in a distribution channel ○ *The production company became a channel captain by acquiring a number of important retail outlets.* ○ *Only businesses with enough financial resources to acquire other companies can become channel captains.*

channel of distribution /ˌtʃæn(ə)l əv ˌdɪstrɪ'bjuʃ(ə)n/ *noun* same as **distribution channel**

channel stuffing /'tʃæn(ə)l ˌstʌfɪŋ/ *noun* the practice of offering distributors or retailers incentives to purchase more goods than they need at the end of a fiscal year in order to artificially inflate sales and earnings

chapter /'tʃæptər/ *noun* a section of an Act of Congress

"…the company filed under Chapter 11 of the federal bankruptcy code, the largest failure ever in the steel industry" [*Fortune*]

"…the firm, whose trademark dates back to 1871, has been desperately trying to cut costs to compete with manufacturers in cheaper countries, but has also been hit by management problems. It said the filing for Chapter 11 protection should have little impact on customers and employees and would allow it to restructure" [*Times*]

Chapter 7 /ˌtʃæptə 'sevən/ *noun* a section of the U.S. Bankruptcy Reform Act 1978, which sets out the rules for the liquidation, a choice available to individuals, partnerships, and corporations

Chapter 11 /ˌtʃæptə 'ten/ *noun* a section of the U.S. Bankruptcy Reform Act 1978, which allows a corporation to be protected from demands made by its creditors for a period of time, while it is reorganized with a view to paying its debts

Chapter 13 /ˌtʃæptər θɜr'tin/ *noun* a section of the U.S. Bankruptcy Reform Act 1978, which allows individuals with debts falling below specified levels to keep their property by repaying creditors out of future income

charge /tʃɑrdʒ/ *noun* **1.** money which must be paid, or the price of a service ○ *to make no charge for delivery* ○ *to make a small charge for rental* ○ *There is no charge for this service* or *No charge is made for this service.* **2.** a debit on an account ○ *It appears as a charge on the accounts.* **3.** management or control □ **to be in charge of something** to be the manager or to deal with something ○ *She is in charge of all our HR documentation.* □ **to take charge of something** to start to deal with something or to become responsible for something ○ *When the manager was ill, his deputy took charge of the department.* **4.** a formal accusation in a court ○ *He appeared in court on a charge of embezzling* or *on an embezzlement charge.* **5.** a sum deducted from revenue in the profit and loss account ■ *verb* **1.** to ask someone to pay for services later □ **to charge the packing to the customer, to charge the customer with the packing** the customer has to pay for packing **2.** to ask for money to be paid ○ *to charge $5 for delivery* ○ *How much does he charge?* □ **he charges $16 an hour** he asks to be paid $16 for an hour's work **3.** to pay for something by putting it on a charge account ○ *Can you charge the meal to my room?* ○ *I want to charge these purchases to the company account.* **4.** to accuse someone formally of having committed a crime ○ *He was charged with embezzling his clients' money.* **5.** to record an expense or other deduction from revenue in the profit and loss account

chargeable /'tʃɑrdʒəb(ə)l/ *adjective* able to be charged ○ *repairs chargeable to the occupier*

charge account /'tʃɑrdʒ əˌkaʊnt/ *noun* an arrangement which a customer has with a store to buy goods and to pay for them at a later date, usually when the invoice is sent at the end of the month

charge card /'tʃɑrdʒ kɑrd/ *noun* same as **credit card**

chargee /tʃɑr'dʒi/ *noun* a person who has the right to force a debtor to pay

charges forward /ˌtʃɑrdʒɪz 'fɔrwərd/ *noun* charges which will be paid by the customer

chart /tʃɑrt/ *noun* a diagram displaying information as a series of lines, blocks, etc.

charter /'tʃɑrtər/ noun **1.** a document giving special legal rights to a group **2.** in the U.S., a formal document incorporating an organization, company, or educational institution **3.** the action or business of hiring transportation for a special purpose ■ verb to hire for a special purpose ○ to charter a plane or a boat or a bus

chartered /'tʃɑrtərd/ adjective **1.** in the U.K., used to describe a company which has been set up by charter, and not registered under the Companies Act ○ a chartered bank **2.** in the U.S., used to describe an incorporated organization, company, or educational institution that has been set up by charter **3.** □ **a chartered ship** or **bus** or **plane** a ship, bus or plane which has been hired for a special purpose

chartered accountant /ˌtʃɑrtərd ə'kaʊntənt/ noun U.K. same as **certified public accountant**

charterer /'tʃɑrtərər/ noun a person who hires a ship etc. for a special purpose

chartering /'tʃɑrtərɪŋ/ noun the act of hiring for a special purpose

charter party /'tʃɑrtər ˌpɑrti/ noun a contract between the owner and the charterer of a ship

chartist /'tʃɑrtɪst/ noun a person who studies stock market trends and forecasts future rises or falls

chase /tʃeɪs/ verb to try to speed up work by asking how it is progressing ○ We are trying to chase down the accounts department for the check. ○ We will chase your order with the production department.

chaser /'tʃeɪsər/ noun a letter to remind someone of something (especially to remind a customer that an invoice has not been paid) ○ The computer automatically sends chasers after sixty days to customers who have not paid.

chattels /'tʃæt(ə)lz/ plural noun goods, movable property but not real estate

cheap /tʃip/ adjective, adverb not costing a lot of money or not expensive □ **to buy something cheap** at a low price ○ He bought two companies cheap and sold them again at a profit. □ **they work out cheaper by the box** these items are cheaper per unit if you buy a book of them

cheap labor /ˌtʃip 'leɪbər/ noun workers who do not earn much money

cheaply /'tʃipli/ adverb without paying much money ○ The salesman was living cheaply at home and claiming an enormous hotel bill on expenses.

cheap money /ˌtʃip 'mʌni/ noun money which can be borrowed at a low rate of interest

cheapness /'tʃipnəs/ noun the fact of being cheap ○ The cheapness of the pound means that many more tourists will come to London.

cheap rate /'tʃip reɪt/ noun a rate which is not expensive ○ Cheap rate phone calls start at 8 p.m.

cheat /tʃit/ verb to trick someone so that he or she loses money ○ He cheated the Inland Revenue out of thousands of pounds. ○ She was accused of cheating clients who came to ask her for advice.

check /tʃek/ noun **1.** a sudden stop □ **to put a check on imports** to stop some imports coming into a country **2.** investigation or examination ○ a routine check of the fire equipment ○ The auditors carried out checks on the petty cash book. **3.** a list of charges in a restaurant **4.** a note to a bank asking them to pay money from your account to the account of the person whose name is written on the note ○ a check for $10 or a $10 check □ **check to the bearer** a check with no name written on it, so that the person who holds it can cash it □ **to endorse a check** to sign a check on the back to show that you accept it □ **to pay a check into your account** to deposit a check □ **the bank referred the check to the drawer** the bank returned the check to the person who wrote it because there was not enough money in the account to pay it □ **to sign a check** to sign on the front of a check to show that you authorize the bank to pay the money from your account □ **to stop a check** to ask a bank not to pay a check which has been signed and sent **5.** a mark on paper to show that something is correct ○ Make a check in the box marked "R". (NOTE: The U.K. term is **tick**.) ■ verb **1.** to stop or delay something ○ to check the entry of contraband into the country ○ to check the flow of money out of a country **2.** to examine or to investigate something ○ to check that an invoice is correct ○ to check and sign for goods □ **she checked the computer printout against the invoices** she examined the printout and the invoices to see if the figures were the same **3.** to mark something with a sign to show that it is correct ○ *check the box marked "R"* (NOTE: The U.K. term is **tick.**)

check in *phrasal verb* **1.** (*at a hotel*) to arrive at a hotel and sign for a room ○ *He checked in at 12:15.* **2.** (*at an airport*) to give in your ticket to show you are ready to take the flight **3.** □ **to check baggage in** to pass your baggage to the airline to put it on the plane for you

check out *phrasal verb* **1.** (*at a hotel*) to leave and pay for a room ○ *We will check out before breakfast.* **2.** to go through a checkout and pay for the goods bought

check account /'tʃek əˌkaʊnt/ *noun* same as **checking account**

check book /'tʃek bʊk/ *noun U.K.* same as **checkbook**

checkbook /'tʃekbʊk/ *noun* a booklet with new blank checks

check card¹ /'tʃek kɑrd/ *noun* a plastic card issued by a bank that allows someone to directly access his or her checking account to get cash or make purchases

check card² /'tʃek kɑrd/, **check guarantee card** /ˌtʃek ˌgærən'ti kɑrd/ *noun U.K.* same as **check card**

check-in /'tʃek ɪn/ *noun* a place where passengers give in their tickets for a flight ○ *The check-in is on the first floor.*

check-in counter /'tʃek ɪn ˌkaʊntər/ *noun* a place where plane passengers have to check in

checking /'tʃekɪŋ/ *noun* an examination or investigation ○ *The inspectors found some defects during their checking of the building.*

checking account /'tʃekɪŋ əˌkaʊnt/ *noun* an account in a bank from which the customer can withdraw money when he or she wants. Checking accounts do not always pay interest. ○ *to pay money into a checking account*

check-in time /'tʃek ɪn ˌtaɪm/ *noun* a time at which passengers should check in

checklist /'tʃeklɪst/ *noun* a list of points which have to be checked before something can be regarded as finished, or as part of a procedure for evaluating something

checkoff /'tʃekɔf/ *noun* a system where union dues are automatically deducted by the employer from an employee's pay-

check ○ *Checkoffs are seen by most employees as worthwhile as long as their interests are well represented by the union.* ○ *After checkoffs and tax deductions the employees' pay had been reduced by one third.*

checkout /'tʃekaʊt/ *noun* the place where goods are paid for in a store or supermarket ○ *We have opened two more checkouts to cope with the Saturday rush.*

check requisition /'tʃek ˌrekwɪzɪʃ(ə)n/ *noun* an official note from a department to the company accounts staff asking for a check to be written

check routing symbol /ˌtʃek 'raʊtɪŋ ˌsɪmbəl/ *noun* a number shown on a U.S. check which identifies the Federal Reserve district through which the check will be cleared, similar to the U.K. "bank sort code"

check sample /'tʃek ˌsæmp(ə)l/ *noun* a sample to be used to see if a consignment is acceptable

check stub /'tʃek stʌb/ *noun* a piece of paper left in a checkbook after a check has been written and taken out

cheque /tʃek/ *noun U.K.* same as **check**

cherry-picking /'tʃeri ˌpɪkɪŋ/ *noun* the practice of choosing only the best or most valuable items from among a group

"Though it doesn't cherry-pick the best applicants--students are selected randomly by zip codes--its student body tends to be better off than those at the toughest schools." [*Forbes*]

chief /tʃif/ *adjective* most important ○ *He is the chief accountant of an industrial group.* ○ *She is the chief buyer for a department store.*

chief executive /ˌtʃif ɪg'zekjʊtɪv/, **chief executive officer** /ˌtʃif ɪg'zekjʊtɪv ˌɒfɪsə/ *noun* the most important director in charge of a company. Abbreviation **CEO**

chief financial officer /ˌtʃif faɪ'nænʃəl ˌɒfɪsər/ *noun* an executive in charge of a company's financial operations, reporting to the CEO. Abbreviation **CFO**

chief information officer /ˌtʃif ˌɪnfə'meɪʃ(ə)n ˌɒfɪsər/ *noun* the most senior person with responsibility for an organization's information systems and sometimes also for its e-business technology. Abbreviation **C.I.O.**

chief marketing officer /ˌtʃif ˈmarkɪtɪŋ ˌɔfɪsər/ *noun* the most senior person with responsibility for promoting and advertising an organization's products or services. Abbreviation **CMO**

chief operating officer /ˌtʃif ˈɑpəreɪtɪŋ ˌɔfɪsər/ *noun* a director in charge of all a company's operations (same as a "managing director"). Abbreviation **COO**

chief technology officer /tʃif tek ˌnɑlədʒi ˈɔfɪsər/, **chief technical officer** /tʃif ˌteknɪk(ə)l ˈɔfɪsər/ *noun* the most senior person with responsibility for an organization's research and development activities and sometimes for its new product plans. Abbreviation **C.T.O.**

Chinese walls /ˌtʃaɪniz ˈwɔlz/ *plural noun* imaginary barriers between departments in the same organization, set up to avoid insider dealing or conflict of interest. For example, if a merchant bank is advising on a planned takeover bid, its investment department should not know that the bid is taking place, or they would advise their clients to invest in the company being taken over.

CHIPS *noun* the computerized clearing bank system used in the U.S. Full form **Clearing House Interbank Payments System**

chit /tʃɪt/ *noun* a check (for food or drink in a club)

choice /tʃɔɪs/ *noun* **1.** a thing which is chosen ○ *You must give the customer time to make their choice.* **2.** a range of items to choose from ○ *We have only a limited choice of suppliers.* ■ *adjective* (*of food*) specially selected ○ *choice meat* ○ *choice wines* ○ *choice foodstuffs*

choose /tʃuz/ *verb* to decide to do a particular thing or to buy a particular item (as opposed to something else) ○ *There were several good candidates to choose from.* ○ *They chose the only woman applicant as sales director.* ○ *You must give the customers plenty of time to choose.* (NOTE: **choosing – chose – has chosen**)

chop /tʃɑp/ *noun* a mark made on a document to show that it has been agreed, acknowledged, paid, or that payment has been received

Christmas bonus /ˌkrɪsməs ˈboʊnəs/ *noun* an extra payment made to staff at Christmas

chronological order /ˌkrɑnəlɑdʒɪk(ə)l ˈɔrdər/ *noun* the arrangement of records such as files and invoices in order of their dates

churn /tʃɜrn/ *verb* **1.** to be in a situation where many employees stay for only a short time and then leave and have to be replaced **2.** to buy many different products or services one after the other without showing loyalty to any of them (NOTE: Churning often happens when companies have competitive marketing strategies and continually undercut their competitors' prices. This encourages customers to switch brands constantly in order to take advantage of cheaper or more attractive offers.)

churning /ˈtʃɜrnɪŋ/ *noun* a practice employed by stockbrokers, where they buy and sell on a client's discretionary account in order to earn their commission. The deals are frequently of no advantage to the client.

"…more small investors lose money through churning than almost any other abuse, yet most people have never heard of it. Churning involves brokers generating income simply by buying and selling investments on behalf of their clients. Constant and needless churning earns them hefty commissions which bites into the investment portfolio" [*Guardian*]

churn rate /ˈtʃɜrn reɪt/ *noun* **1.** a measurement of how often new customers try a product or service and then stop using it **2.** a measurement of how many stocks and bonds are traded in a brokerage account and how often they are traded

"The customer churn rate…also increased, from 2.2 percent in the year ago quarter to 3.4 percent this quarter." [InformationWeek]

CIF /ˌsi aɪ ˈef/, **c.i.f.** *abbreviation* cost, insurance, and freight

CIO *abbreviation* chief information officer

circular /ˈsɜrkjələr/ *adjective* sent to many people ■ *noun* a leaflet or letter sent to many people ○ *They sent out a circular offering a 10% discount.* ○ *Senior management sent out a circular to all the employees explaining the changes in the payment plan.*

circularize /ˈsɜrkjələraɪz/ *verb* to send a circular to ○ *The committee has agreed to circularize the members of the society.* ○

They circularized all their customers with a new list of prices.

circular letter /ˌsɜrkjələr 'letər/ *noun* a letter sent to many people

circular letter of credit /ˌsɜrkjələr ˌletər əv 'kredɪt/ *noun* a letter of credit sent to all branches of the bank which issues it

circulate /'sɜrkjəleɪt/ *verb* **1.** □ to circulate freely (*of money*) to move about without restriction by the government **2.** to send or to give out without restrictions □ **to circulate money** to issue money, to make money available to the public and industry **3.** to send information to ○ *They circulated a new list of prices to all their customers.* ○ *They circulated information about job vacancies to all colleges in the area.*

circulating capital /ˌsɜrkjʊleɪtɪŋ 'kæpɪt(ə)l/ *noun* capital in the form of cash or debtors, raw materials, finished products and work in progress which a company requires to carry on its business

circulation /ˌsɜrkjə'leɪʃ(ə)n/ *noun* **1.** the act of sending information ○ *The company is trying to improve the circulation of information between departments.* **2.** movement □ **to put money into circulation** to issue new bills to business and the public ○ *The amount of money in circulation increased more than was expected.* **3.** the number of readers of a newspaper or magazine. It is audited and is not the same as "readership."

circulation battle /ˌsɜrkjə'leɪʃ(ə)n ˌbæt(ə)l/ *noun* a competition between two papers to try to sell more copies in the same market

circulation of capital /ˌsɜrkjʊleɪʃ(ə)n əv 'kæpɪt(ə)l/ *noun* a movement of capital from one investment to another

City /'sɪti/, **City of London** *noun* a large town ○ *The largest cities in Europe are linked by hourly flights.*

civil /'sɪv(ə)l/ *adjective* relating to ordinary people

civil action /ˌsɪv(ə)l 'ækʃən/ *noun* a court case brought by a person or a company against someone who has done them wrong

civil engineer /ˌsɪv(ə)l ˌendʒɪ'nɪr/ *noun* a person who specializes in the construction of roads, bridges, railways, etc.

civil engineering /ˌsɪv(ə)l ˌendʒɪ'nɪrɪŋ/ *noun* the construction of roads, bridges, railways, etc.

Civilian Agency Acquisition Council /sə,vɪliən ˌeɪdʒənsi ˌækwɪ'zɪʃ(ə)n ˌkaʊns(ə)l/ *noun* a group of representatives from U.S. government agencies and departments that works with the Defense Acquisition Regulations Council (DARC) to develop and maintain the Federal Acquisition Regulations (FAR) system. Abbreviation **CAAC**

civil law /ˌsɪv(ə)l 'lɔr/ *noun* laws relating to people's rights and to agreements between individuals

civil servant /ˌsɪv(ə)l 'sɜrvənt/ *noun* a person who works in the civil service

civil service /ˌsɪv(ə)l 'sɜrvɪs/ *noun* the organization and personnel which administer a country ○ *You have to pass an examination to get a job in the civil service* or *to get a civil service job.*

claim /kleɪm/ *noun* **1.** an act of asking for something that you feel you have a right to □ **the union put in a 6% wage claim** the union asked for a 6% increase in wages for its members **2.** an act of stating that something is a fact ○ *Her claim that she had been authorized to take the money was demonstrably false.* **3.** an act of asking for money from an insurance company when something you insured against has taken place □ **to put in a claim** to ask the insurance company officially to pay damages ○ *to put in a claim for repairs to the car* ○ *She put in a claim for $250,000 damages against the driver of the other car.* □ **to settle a claim** to agree to pay what is asked for ○ *The insurance company refused to settle his claim for storm damage.* ■ *verb* **1.** to ask for money, especially from an insurance company ○ *He claimed $100,000 damages against the cleaning firm.* ○ *She claimed for repairs to the car against her insurance policy.* **2.** to say that you have a right to something or that something is your property ○ *She is claiming possession of the house.* ○ *No one claimed the umbrella found in my office.* **3.** to state that something is a fact ○ *He claims he never received the goods.* ○ *She claims that the stock is her property.*

claim back *phrasal verb* to ask for money to be paid back

claimant /'kleɪmənt/ *noun* a person who makes a claim against someone in the civil courts (NOTE: This term has now replaced **plaintiff**. The other side in a case is the **defendant**.)

claimer /'kleɪmər/ *noun* same as **claimant**

claim form /'kleɪm fɔrm/ *noun* a form which has to be filled in when making an insurance claim

claiming /'kleɪmɪŋ/ *noun* the act of making a claim

claims department /'kleɪmz dɪ‚pɑrtmənt/ *noun* a department of an insurance company which deals with claims

claims manager /'kleɪmz ‚mænɪdʒər/ *noun* the manager of a claims department

class /klæs/ *noun* a category or group into which things are classified

class action /‚klɑrs 'ækʃən/, **class suit** /klɑrs 'sut/ *noun* a legal action brought on behalf of a group of people

classification /‚klæsɪfɪ'keɪʃ(ə)n/ *noun* arrangement into classes or categories according to specific characteristics ○ *the classification of employees by ages or skills* ○ *Jobs in this organization fall into several classifications.*

classified advertisements /‚klæsɪfaɪd əd'vɜrtɪsmənts/, **classified ads** /‚klæsɪfaɪd 'ædz/ *plural noun* advertisements listed in a newspaper under special headings such as "property for sale" or "jobs wanted" ○ *Look in the small ads to see if anyone has a filing cabinet for sale.*

classified directory /‚klæsɪfaɪd daɪ'rekt(ə)ri/ *noun* a list of businesses grouped under various headings such as computer stores or newsagents

classify /'klæsɪfaɪ/ *verb* to put into classes or categories according to specific characteristics (NOTE: **classifies – classifying – classified**)

clause /klɔz/ *noun* a section of a contract ○ *There are ten clauses in the contract of employment.* ○ *There is a clause in this contract concerning the employer's right to dismiss an employee.* ■ *verb* to list details of the relevant parties to a bill of exchange

claused bill of lading /‚klɔzd bɪl əv 'leɪdɪŋ/ *noun* a bill of lading stating that goods did not arrive on board in good condition

claw /klɔ/ *verb*

claw back *phrasal verb* to take back money which has been allocated ○ *Income tax claws back 25% of pensions paid out by the government.* ○ *Of the $1m allocated to the project, the government clawed back $100,000 in taxes.*

clawback /'klɔbæk/ *noun* **1.** money taken back, especially money taken back by the government from grants or tax concessions which had previously been made **2.** the allocation of new shares to existing stockholders, so as to maintain the value of their holdings

clean /klin/ *adjective* with no problems or no record of offenses

clean bill of lading /‚klin bɪl əv 'leɪdɪŋ/ *noun* a bill of lading with no note to say the shipment is faulty or damaged

clear /klɪr/ *adjective* **1.** easily understood ○ *When the check bounced, it was a clear sign that the company was in trouble.* ○ *He made it clear that he wanted the manager to resign.* ○ *You will have to make it clear to the staff that productivity is falling.* **2.** (*of a period of time*) free, total ■ *verb* **1.** to sell something cheaply in order to get rid of stock ○ *"Demonstration models to clear".* **2.** □ **to clear goods through customs** to have all documentation passed by customs so that goods can enter or leave the country **3.** □ **to clear 10%, $5,000 on the deal** to make 10% or $5,000 clear profit □ **we cleared only our expenses** the sales revenue only paid for the costs and expenses without making any profit **4.** □ **to clear a check** to pass a check through the banking system, so that the money is transferred from the payer's account to another ○ *the check took ten days to clear* or *the bank took ten days to clear the check*

clearance /'klɪrəns/ *noun* **1.** □ **to effect customs clearance** to clear goods through customs **2.** □ **clearance of a check** the passing of a check through the banking system, transferring money from one account to another ○ *You should allow six days for check clearance.*

clearance certificate /'klɪrəns sə‚tɪfɪkət/ *noun* a document showing that goods have been passed by customs

clearance sale /'klɪrəns seɪl/ *noun* a sale of items at low prices to get rid of stock

clearing /'klɪrɪŋ/ *noun* 1. □ **clearing of goods through customs** passing of goods through customs 2. □ **clearing of a debt** paying all of a debt 3. an act of passing of a check through the banking system, transferring money from one account to another

clearing bank /'klɪrɪŋ bæŋk/ *noun* a bank which clears checks, especially one of the major U.K. High Street banks, specializing in usual banking business for ordinary customers such as loans, checks, overdrafts and interest-bearing deposits

clearinghouse /'klɪrɪŋhaʊs/ *noun* a central office where clearing banks exchange checks, or where stock exchange or commodity exchange transactions are settled

Clearing House Interbank Payments System /,klɪrɪŋ haʊs ,ɪntərbæŋk 'peɪmənts ,sɪstəm/ *noun* abbreviation **CHIPS**

clear profit /,klɪr 'prɑfɪt/ *noun* a profit after all expenses have been paid ○ *We made $6,000 clear profit on the deal.*

clerical /'klerɪk(ə)l/ *adjective* (*of work*) done in an office or done by a clerk

clerical assistance /,klerɪk(ə)l ə 'sɪst(ə)ns/ *noun* help with office work

clerical error /,klerɪk(ə)l 'erər/ *noun* a mistake made by someone doing office work

clerical staff /'klerɪk(ə)l stæf/ *noun* people who work in offices

clerical work /'klerɪk(ə)l wɜrk/ *noun* work done in an office

clerical worker /'klerɪk(ə)l ,wɜrkər/ *noun* a person who works in an office

clerk *U.S.* /klɑrk/ *noun* a person who works in an office ■ *verb* to work as a clerk

C-Level /'si ,lev(ə)l/ *noun* executives or senior officers of a corporation considered as a group ■ *adjective* relating to or suitable for executives or senior officers of a corporation ○ *C-Level decision making*

CLI *abbreviation* calling line identification

clickable corporation /,klɪkəb(ə)l ,kɔrpə'reɪʃ(ə)n/ *noun* a company that operates on the Internet

click rate /'klɪk reɪt/ *noun* same as **click-through rate**

clicks and bricks /,klɪks ən 'brɪks/ *noun* a way of doing business that combines e-commerce and traditional stores

clicks and mortar /,klɪks ən 'mɔrtər/ *noun* a combination of computers and store premises, as in a group which sells over the Internet but also maintains a chain of normal stores

"…there may be a silver lining for "clicks-and-mortar" stores that have both an online and a high street presence. Many of these are accepting returns of goods purchased online at their traditional stores. This is a service that may make them more popular as consumers become more experienced online shoppers" [*Financial Times*]

clicks-and-mortar /,klɪks ən 'mɔrtər/ *adjective* conducting business both through e-commerce and also in the traditional way in buildings such as stores and warehouses. Compare **bricks-and-mortar**

clicks-and-mortar business /,klɪks ən 'mɔrtər ,bɪznɪs/ *noun* a business that uses both e-commerce and buildings such as stores to market its products

click-through /'klɪk θru/ *noun* an act of clicking on a banner or other onscreen advertising that takes the user through to the advertiser's website (NOTE: The number of times users click on an advertisement can be counted, and the total number of click-throughs is a way of measuring how successful the advertisement has been.)

click-through rate /'klɪk θru ,reɪt/ *noun* a method of charging an advertiser for the display of a banner advertisement on a website. Each time a visitor clicks on a displayed advertisement which links to the advertiser's main site, the advertiser is charged a fee. A click-through rate of just a few percent is common and most advertisers have to pay per thousand impressions of their banner ad, sometimes written CTM (click-through per thousand). (NOTE: The click-through rate is expressed as a percentage of ad views and is used to measure how successful an advertisement has been.)

client /'klaɪənt/ *noun* a person with whom business is done or who pays for a service ○ *One of our major clients has defaulted on her payments.*

client base /'klaɪənt beɪs/ *noun* same as **client list**

clientele /ˌklaɪənˈtel/ *noun* all the clients of a business or all the customers of a store

client list /ˈklaɪənt lɪst/ *noun* a list of clients of an advertising agency

climb /klaɪm/ *verb* to go up ○ *The company has climbed to No. 1 position in the market.* ○ *Profits climbed rapidly as the new management cut costs.*

clinch /klɪntʃ/ *verb* to settle (a business deal), to come to an agreement ○ *He offered an extra 5% to clinch the deal.* ○ *They need approval from the board before they can clinch the deal.*

clipping /ˈklɪpɪŋ/ *noun* a piece cut out from a publication which refers to an item of particular interest

clipping service /ˈklɪpɪŋ ˌsɜːvɪs/ *noun* the service of cutting out references to a client in newspapers or magazines and sending them to him

clock /klɒk/ *verb*
  clock in, clock on *phrasal verb U.K.* same as **punch in**
  clock out, clock off *phrasal verb U.K.* same as **punch out**

clock card /ˈklɒk kɑːd/ *noun U.K.* same as **time-card**

close *noun* /kləʊz/ the end of a day's trading on the Stock Exchange ○ *At the close stocks had fallen 20%.* ■ *adjective* /kləʊs/ □ **close to** very near, almost ○ *The company was close to bankruptcy.* ○ *We are close to meeting our sales targets.* ■ *verb* /kləʊz/ **1.** □ **to close the accounts** to come to the end of an accounting period and make up the profit and loss account **2.** to bring something to an end □ **she closed her bank account** she took all the money out and stopped using the account **3.** (*business, store*) to stop doing business for the day ○ *The office closes at 5.30.* ○ *We close early on Saturdays.* **4.** □ **the stock closed at $15** at the end of the day's trading the price of the stock was $15
  close down *phrasal verb* **1.** to shut a store, factory, or service for a long period or for ever ○ *The company is closing down its Denver office.* ○ *The accident closed down the station for a period.* **2.** (*of a store, factory, or service*) to stop doing business or operating

close company /ˌkləʊs ˈkʌmp(ə)ni/ *noun* a privately owned company controlled by a few stockholders (in the U.K.,

fewer than five) where the public may own a small number of the shares (NOTE: The U.S. term is **close corporation** or **closed corporation**.)

closed /kləʊzd/ *adjective* **1.** not open for business, or not doing business ○ *The office is closed on Mondays.* ○ *These warehouses are usually closed to the public.* ○ *All the banks are closed on Christmas Day.* **2.** restricted

closed-end credit /ˌkləʊzd end ˈkredɪt/ *noun* a loan, plus any interest and finance charges, that is to be repaid in full by a specified future date. Loans that have real estate or motor vehicles as collateral are usually closed-end. ◊ **revolving credit** (NOTE: Most loans for the purchase of property or motor vehicles are closed-end credits.)

closed market /ˌkləʊzd ˈmɑːkət/ *noun* a market where a supplier deals only with one agent or distributor and does not supply any others direct ○ *They signed a closed-market agreement with an Egyptian company.*

closed shop /kləʊzd ˈʃɒp/ *noun* a system where a company agrees to employ only union members for specific jobs ○ *The union is asking the management to agree to a closed shop.*

COMMENT: Closed shops are illegal in many countries.

closing /ˈkləʊzɪŋ/ *adjective* **1.** final or coming at the end **2.** at the end of an accounting period ○ *At the end of the quarter the bookkeeper has to calculate the closing balance.* ■ *noun* **1.** the shutting of a store or being shut **2.** □ **the closing of an account** the act of stopping supply to a customer on credit

closing bid /ˈkləʊzɪŋ bɪd/ *noun* the last bid at an auction, the bid which is successful

closing date /ˈkləʊzɪŋ deɪt/ *noun* the last date ○ *The closing date for bids to be received is May 1st.*

closing-down sale /ˌkləʊzɪŋ ˈdaʊn ˌseɪl/ *noun* the sale of goods when a store is closing for ever

closing price /ˈkləʊzɪŋ praɪs/ *noun* the price of a stock at the end of a day's trading

closing stock /ˌkləʊzɪŋ ˈstɒk/ *noun* a business's remaining stock at the end of an accounting period. It includes finished products, raw materials, or work in progress and is deducted from the period's costs in the balance sheets. ○ *At the end of the month the closing stock was 10% higher than at the end of the previous month.*

closing time /'klouzɪŋ taɪm/ *noun* the time when a store or office stops work

closure /'klouʒər/ *noun* the act of closing

CLT *abbreviation* Central Limit Theorem

cm *abbreviation* centimeter

CMO *abbreviation* chief marketing officer

C/N *abbreviation* credit note

Co. *abbreviation* company ○ *J. Smith & Co.*

co- /kou/ *prefix* working or acting together

c/o *abbreviation* care of

Coalition for Environmentally Responsible Economies /ˌkouəlɪʃ(ə)n fər ɪnˌvaɪrənmentəli rɪˌspɑnsɪb(ə)l ɪ 'kɑnəmiz/ full form of **CERES**

COBRA /'koubrə/ *noun* a U.S. law which allows employees who leave their jobs to continue employer-sponsored group health care coverage under their former employer for as long as 18 months. Full form **Consolidated Omnibus Reconciliation Act**

co-browsing /ˌkou 'brauzɪŋ/ *noun* the synchronization of two or more browsers so that their users can see the same web pages at the same time. Also called **page pushing**

COC *abbreviation* certificate of competency

co-creditor /ˌkou 'kredɪtər/ *noun* a person who is a creditor of the same company as you are

COD, c.o.d. *abbreviation* cash on delivery

code /koud/ *noun* **1.** a system of signs, numbers, or letters which mean something **2.** a set of rules

codec /'koudek/ *noun* a device that compresses and decompresses the audio and video signals used in videoconferencing and that can be located either in the users' software or their hardware

code of conduct /ˌkoud əv 'kɑndʌkt/ *noun* the guidelines showing how someone (such as salesclerks or railroad station staff) should behave toward customers

code of practice /ˌkoud əv 'præktɪs/ *noun* rules drawn up by an association which the members must follow when doing business

coding /'koudɪŋ/ *noun* the act of putting a code on something ○ *the coding of invoices*

co-director /'kou daɪˌrektər/ *noun* a person who is a director of the same company as you

coefficient of correlation /kouɪ ˌfɪʃ(ə)nt əv ˌkɔrə'leɪʃ(ə)n/ *noun* a measurement of correlation or relationship between two sets of data on a continuum from −1 to +1

coffee break /'kɔfi breɪk/ *noun* a rest time during work when the employees can drink coffee or tea

cognitive processing /ˌkɑgnətɪv 'prɑsesɪŋ/ *noun* the way in which a person changes external information into patterns of thought and how these are used to form judgments or choices

cohesion fund /kou'hiʒ(ə)n fʌnd/ *noun* a fund that is designed to even out economic and social inequalities among member countries of the European Union by providing financial help for major environmental and transportation projects

cohort /'kouhɔrt/ *noun* a group of people who do the same thing at the same time (such as a group of managers who joined a company as trainees together)

cohort study /'kouhɔrt ˌstʌdi/ *noun* a study in which a group of individuals who have something in common with each other, e.g., children with the same birth date, are observed over several years

coin /kɔɪn/ *noun* a piece of metal money ○ *He gave me two 10-cent coins in my change.*

coinage /'kɔɪnɪdʒ/ *noun* a system of metal money used in a country

co-insurance /ˌkou ɪn'ʃurəns/ *noun* an insurance policy where the risk is shared among several insurers

COLA /'koulə/ *abbreviation* cost-of-living allowance

cold /kould/ *adjective* without being prepared

cold call /ˌkould 'kɔl/ *noun* a telephone call or sales visit where the salesperson has no appointment and the client is not an established customer ■ *verb* to make a cold call

cold start /ˌkoʊld 'stɑrt/ *noun* the act of beginning a new business or opening a new store with no previous turnover to base it on

cold storage /ˌkoʊld 'stɔrɪdʒ/ *noun* the keeping of food in a cold store to prevent it or other goods from going bad

cold store /'koʊld stɔr/ *noun* a warehouse or room where food can be kept cold

collaborate /kə'læbəreɪt/ *verb* to work together ○ *We collaborated with a French firm on a building project.* ○ *They collaborated on the new aircraft.* (NOTE: You collaborate **with** someone **on** something.)

collaboration /kə,læbə'reɪʃ(ə)n/ *noun* the act of working together ○ *Their collaboration on the project was very profitable.*

collaborative working /kə,læb(ə)rətɪv 'wɜrkɪŋ/ *noun* a method of working in which people at different locations or from different organizations work together, usually using videoconferencing, email, networks and other electronic communications tools

collapse /kə'læps/ *noun* **1.** a sudden fall in price ○ *the collapse of the market in silver* ○ *the collapse of the dollar on the foreign exchange markets* **2.** a sudden failure ○ *the collapse of the pay negotiations* ○ *Investors lost thousands of pounds in the collapse of the company.* ■ *verb* **1.** to fall suddenly ○ *The market in silver collapsed.* ○ *The yen collapsed on the foreign exchange markets.* **2.** to fail suddenly ○ *The company collapsed with $250,000 in debts.* ○ *Talks between management and unions collapsed last night.*

collateral /kə'læt(ə)rəl/ *adjective* used to provide a guarantee for a loan ■ *noun* a security, such as negotiable instruments, stock, or goods, used to provide a guarantee for a loan

colleague /'kɑlig/ *noun* **1.** a person who does the same type of work as another ○ *His colleagues gave him a present when he got married.* ○ *I know Jane Gray – she was a colleague of mine at my last job.* ○ *She was unpopular with her colleagues in the machine room.* **2.** a person who works in the same organization as another

collect /kə'lekt/ *verb* **1.** to get money which is owed to you by making the person who owes it pay □ **to collect a debt** to go and make someone pay a debt **2.** to take things away from a place ○ *We have to collect the stock from the warehouse.* □ **letters are collected twice a day** postal workers take letters from the mail box to the post office for dispatch ■ *adverb, adjective* used to describe a phone call which the person receiving the call agrees to pay for

collect call /kə'lekt kɔl/ *noun* a telephone call which the person receiving the call agrees to pay for

collecting agency /kə'lektɪŋ ,eɪdʒənsi/ *noun U.K.* same as **collection agency**

collection /kə'lekʃən/ *noun* **1.** the act of getting money together, or of making someone pay money which is owed ○ *tax collection* or *collection of tax* □ **bills for collection** bills where payment is due **2.** the fetching of goods ○ *The stock is in the warehouse awaiting collection.* □ **to hand something in for collection** to leave something for someone to come and collect **3.** the act of taking letters from a letter box or mail room to the post office for dispatch ○ *There are four collections a day from the letter box at the corner of the street.* ○ *There are six collections a day from the letter box.*

collection agency /kə'lekʃən ,eɪdʒənsi/ *noun* an agency which collects money owed to other companies for a commission

collection charge /kə'lekʃən ,tʃɑrdʒɪz/, **collection rate** /kə'lekʃən reɪt/ *noun* a charge for collecting something

collections /kə'lekʃənz/ *plural noun* money which has been collected

collective /kə'lektɪv/ *adjective* referring to a group of people together

collective ownership /kə,lektɪv 'oʊnəʃɪp/ *noun* ownership of a business by the employees who work in it

collective wage agreement /kə,lektɪv 'weɪdʒ ə,grimənt/ *noun* an agreement signed between management and the labor union about wages

collector /kə'lektə/ *noun* a person who makes people pay money which is owed ○ *He works as a debt collector.*

collocation hosting /ˌkɑləkeɪʃ(ə)n 'hoʊstɪŋ/ *noun* a (**hosting option**) in which a business places its own servers with a hosting company and controls everything that happens on its website. The hosting company simply provides an agreed speed of access to the Internet and an agreed amount of (**data transfer**), and ensures that the business's server is up and running.

color /'kʌlə/ *noun* a shade which an object has in light (red, blue, yellow, etc.) (NOTE: The usual U.K. spelling is **colour**)

color printer /ˌkʌlər 'prɪntər/ *noun* a printer which prints material in color ○ *All our publicity leaflets are printed on the color printer here in the office.*

color swatch /'kʌlər swɑtʃ/ *noun* a small sample of color which the finished product must look like

column /'kɑləm/ *noun* **1.** a series of numbers arranged one underneath the other ○ *to add up a column of figures* ○ *Put the total at the bottom of the column.* **2.** a section of printed words in a newspaper or magazine

combination /ˌkɑmbɪ'neɪʃ(ə)n/ *noun* **1.** several things which are joined together ○ *A combination of cash flow problems and difficult trading conditions caused the company's collapse.* **2.** a series of numbers which open a special lock ○ *I have forgotten the combination of the lock on my briefcase.* ○ *The office safe has a combination lock.*

combine *noun* /'kɑmbaɪn/ a large financial or commercial group ○ *a German industrial combine* ■ *verb* /kəm'baɪn/ to join together ○ *The work force and management combined to fight the takeover bid.*

comeback /'kʌmbæk/ *noun* a means of getting compensation for a complaint or claim ○ *If you throw away the till receipt you will have no comeback if the goods turn out to be faulty.*

command economy /kəˌmænd ɪ'kɑnəmi/ *noun* same as **planned economy**

commerce /'kɑmɜrs/ *noun* the buying and selling of goods and services

commerce service provider /ˌkɑmɜrs 'sɜrvɪs prəˌvaɪdər/ *noun* an organization that provides a service that helps companies with some aspect of e-commerce, e.g., by acting as an Internet payment gateway

commercial /kə'mɜrʃ(ə)l/ *adjective* **1.** referring to business **2.** profitable □ **not a commercial proposition** not likely to make a profit ■ *noun* an advertisement on television

commercial aircraft /kəˌmɜrʃ(ə)l 'erkræft/ *noun* an aircraft used to carry cargo or passengers for payment

commercial artist /kəˌmɜrʃ(ə)l 'ɑrtɪst/ *noun* an artist who designs advertisements, posters, etc. for payment

commercial attaché /kə'mɜrʃ(ə)l əˌtæʃeɪ/ *noun* a diplomat whose job is to promote the commercial interests of his or her country

commercial bank /kə'mɜrʃ(ə)l bæŋk/ *noun* a bank which offers banking services to the public, as opposed to a merchant bank

commercial break /kəˌmɜrʃ(ə)l 'breɪk/ *noun* the time set aside for commercials on television ○ *The advertiser wished to specify exactly when in the commercial break the advertisements were to appear.* ○ *The advertising manager placed one advertisement in each commercial break of the day on the radio channel.*

commercial college /kə'mɜrʃ(ə)l ˌkɑlɪdʒ/ *noun* a college which teaches business studies

commercial course /kə'mɜrʃ(ə)l kɔrs/ *noun* a course where business skills are studied ○ *He took a commercial course by correspondence.*

commercial directory /kə'mɜrʃ(ə)l daɪˌrekt(ə)ri/ *noun* a book which lists all the businesses and business people in a town

commercial district /kə'mɜrʃ(ə)l ˌdɪstrɪkt/ *noun* the part of a town where offices and stores are located

commercial failure /kə'mɜrʃ(ə)l 'feɪljər/ *noun* a financial collapse or bankruptcy

commercialization /kəˌmɜrʃ(ə)laɪ'zeɪʃ(ə)n/ *noun* the act of making something into a business run for profit ○ *the commercialization of museums*

commercialize /kə'mɜrʃəlaɪz/ *verb* to make something into a business ○ *The vacation town has become unpleasantly commercialized.*

commercial law /kəˌmɜrʃ(ə)l 'lɔ/ *noun* the laws regarding business

commercial lawyer /kə,mɜrʃ(ə)l 'lɔjər/ *noun* a person who specializes in company law or who advises companies on legal problems

commercial load /kə,mɜrʃ(ə)l 'loʊd/ *noun* the amount of goods or number of passengers which a bus, train, or plane has to carry to make a profit

commercially /kə'mɜrʃ(ə)li/ *adverb* in a business way □ **not commercially viable** not likely to make a profit

commercial port /kə,mɜrʃ(ə)l 'pɔrt/ *noun* a port which has only goods traffic and no passengers

commercial property /kə,mɜrʃ(ə)l 'prɑpəti/ *noun* a building, or buildings, used as offices or stores

commercial traveler /kə,mɜrʃ(ə)l 'træv(ə)lər/ *noun* a salesperson who travels round an area visiting customers on behalf of his or her company (NOTE: The modern term for a commercial traveler is **sales representative.**)

commercial value /kə,mɜrʃ(ə)l 'vælju/ *noun* the value that a thing would have if it were offered for sale □ **"sample only – of no commercial value"** these goods are intended only as a sample and would not be worth anything if sold

commercial vehicle /kə,mɜrʃ(ə)l 'viːk(ə)l/ *noun* a van or truck used for business purposes

commercial version /kə,mɜrʃ(ə)l 'vɜrʃ(ə)n/ *noun* the version of a computer program that is sold to customers, as opposed to a test or beta version, which is used for development and testing

commission /kə'mɪʃ(ə)n/ *noun* **1.** money paid to a salesperson or agent, usually a percentage of the sales made ○ *She gets 10% commission on everything she sells.* ○ *He is paid on a commission basis.* □ **he charges 10% commission** he asks for 10% of sales as his payment **2.** a group of people officially appointed to examine some problem ○ *He is the chairman of the government commission on export subsidies.*

commission agent /kə'mɪʃ(ə)n ,eɪdʒənt/ *noun* an agent who is paid a percentage of sales

commissioner /kə'mɪʃ(ə)nər/ *noun* an important official appointed by a government or other authority, or a member of a commission

Commission of the European Community /kə,mɪʃ(ə)n əv ði ,jʊərəpiən kə'mjuːnɪti/ *noun* same as **European Commission**

commission rep /kə'mɪʃ(ə)n rep/ *noun* a representative who is not paid a salary but receives a commission on sales

commission sale /kə'mɪʃ(ə)n seɪl/ *noun* a sale where the salesperson is paid a commission

commit /kə'mɪt/ *verb* **1.** to carry out a crime ○ *She was accused of committing several thefts from the storeroom.* **2.** to agree to do something (NOTE: **committing- committed**) □ **to commit funds to a project** to agree to spend money on a project

commitment /kə'mɪtmənt/ *noun* **1.** something which you have agreed to do ○ *to make a commitment* or *to enter into a commitment to do something* ○ *The company has a commitment to provide a cheap service.* **2.** money which you have agreed to spend

commitments /kə'mɪtmənts/ *plural noun* things which you have agreed to do, especially money which you have agreed to spend □ **to meet your commitments** to pay money which you had agreed to pay

committee /kə'mɪti/ *noun* an official group of people who organize or plan for a larger group ○ *to be a member of a committee* or *to sit on a committee* ○ *He was elected to the committee of the staff club.* ○ *The new plans have to be approved by the committee members.* ○ *She is the secretary of the finance committee.* □ **to chair a committee** to be the chairman of a committee

Committee on Accounting Procedure /kə,mɪti ɒn ə'kaʊntɪŋ prə,sɪdʒər/ *noun* in the United States, a committee of the American Institute of Certified Public Accountants that was responsible between 1939 and 1959 for issuing accounting principles, some of which are still part of the Generally Accepted Accounting Principles

commodity /kə'mɑdəti/ *noun* something sold in very large quantities, especially a raw material such as a metal or a food such as wheat

COMMENT: Commodities are either traded for immediate delivery (as "actuals" or "physicals"), or for delivery in the future (as "futures"). Commodity markets deal either in metals (aluminum, copper, lead, nickel, silver and zinc) or in "soft" items, such as cocoa, coffee, sugar and oil.

commodity exchange /kəˈmɒdəti ɪksˌtʃeɪndʒ/ *noun* a place where commodities are bought and sold

commodity futures /kəˌmɒdəti ˈfjuːtʃəz/ *plural noun* commodities traded for delivery at a later date ○ *Silver rose 5% on the commodity futures market yesterday.*

commodity market /kəˈmɒdəti ˌmɑːkət/ *noun* a place where people buy and sell commodities

commodity trader /kəˈmɒdəti ˌtreɪdər/ *noun* a person whose business is buying and selling commodities

common /ˈkɒmən/ *adjective* 1. happening frequently ○ *Unrealistic salary expectations in younger staff was a common problem they had to deal with.* ○ *Being caught by the customs is very common these days.* 2. belonging to several different people or to everyone

common carrier /ˌkɒmən ˈkæriər/ *noun* a firm which carries goods or passengers, and which anyone can use

common law /ˌkɒmən ˈlɔː/ *noun* 1. a law as laid down in decisions of courts, rather than by statute 2. a general system of laws which formerly were the only laws existing in England, and which in some cases have been superseded by statute (NOTE: You say **at common law** when referring to something happening according to the principles of common law.)

common ownership /ˌkɒmən ˈoʊnəʃɪp/ *noun* a situation where a business is owned by the employees who work in it

common pricing /ˌkɒmən ˈpraɪsɪŋ/ *noun* the illegal fixing of prices by several businesses so that they all charge the same price

common seal /ˌkɒmən ˈsiːl/, **company's seal** /ˌkʌmp(ə)niz ˈsiːl/ *noun* a metal stamp for stamping documents with the name of the company to show that they have been approved officially ○ *to attach the company's seal to a document*

common stock /ˌkɒmən ˈstɒk/ *noun* stock in a company that gives stockholders a right to vote at meetings and to receive dividends (NOTE: The U.K. term is **ordinary shares**.)

communautaire /kəˌmjuːnoʊˈteər/ *adjective* sympathetic to the European Union; (person) who works happily with EU officials

communicate /kəˈmjuːnɪkeɪt/ *verb* to exchange views or information with someone ○ *We need to find better ways of communicating with staff* ○ *In her presentation she communicated her knowledge of details and her enthusiasm for the project well.*

communication /kəˌmjuːnɪˈkeɪʃ(ə)n/ *noun* 1. the passing on of views or information ○ *A house journal was started to improve communication between management and staff.* ○ *Customers complained about the lack of communication about the unexpected delay.* □ **to enter into communication with someone** to start discussing something with someone, usually in writing ○ *We have entered into communication with the relevant government department.* 2. an official message ○ *We have had a communication from the local tax inspector.*

communications /kəˌmjuːnɪˈkeɪʃ(ə)nz/ *plural noun* 1. the fact of being able to contact people or to pass messages ○ *After the flood all communications with the outside world were broken.* 2. systems or technologies used for sending and receiving messages, e.g., postal and telephone networks 3. messages sent from one individual or organization to another

communication skills /kəˌmjuːnɪˈkeɪʃ(ə)n skɪlz/ *plural noun* the ability to pass information to others easily and intelligibly

community /kəˈmjuːnəti/ *noun* a group of people living or working in the same place

community-based /kəˈmjuːnəti ˌbeɪst/ *adjective* used to describe an organization or activity that involves the people of a community and whose goal is to improve some aspect of the community

community initiative /kəˈmjuːnəti ɪˈnɪʃətɪv/ *noun* a particular scheme set up by a business organization with the goal of making a positive contribution to the life of the community by helping local people take practical action to solve their problems

community involvement /kə‚mjunəti ɪn'vɑlvmənt/ *noun* the contribution that business organizations make to the life of their local community in the form of community initiatives (NOTE: Community involvement developed as a result of the growing emphasis on the social responsibility of business in the 1960s and 1970s and often involves companies not only giving money to finance local projects but also sending trained staff to help set them up.)

commute /kə'mjut/ *verb* **1.** to travel to work from home each day ○ *He commutes from the country to his office in the center of town.* ○ *She spends two hours a day commuting to and from work.* ○ *We have bought a house within commuting distance of Washington.* **2.** to exchange one form of payment for another ○ *I decided to commute part of my pension rights into a lump sum payment.*

"Commuting is never business use. A trip to work is personal and not deductible. And making a business phone call or holding a business meeting in your car while you drive will not change that fact" [*Nation's Business*]

commuter /kə'mjutər/ *noun* a person who commutes to work

commuter belt /kə'mjutər belt/ *noun U.K.* an area of country where the commuters live round a town

commuter train /kə'mjutər treɪn/ *noun* a train which commuters take in the morning and evening

Companies Act /'kʌmp(ə)niz ækt/ *noun* an Act of the U.K. Parliament which regulates the workings of companies, stating the legal limits within which companies may do their business

companies' register /‚kʌmp(ə)niz 'redʒɪstər/ *noun U.K.* a list of companies, showing their directors and registered addresses

Companies Registration Office /‚kʌmp(ə)niz ‚redʒɪ'streɪʃ(ə)n ‚ɒfɪs/ *noun U.K.* an office of the Registrar of Companies, the official organization where the records of companies must be deposited, so that they can be inspected by the public. Abbreviation **CRO**. Also called **Companies House**

company /'kʌmp(ə)ni/ *noun* **1.** a business organization, a group of people organized to buy, sell, or provide a service, usually for profit □ **to set up a company** to start a company legally **2.** □ **a tractor, aircraft, chocolate company** company which makes tractors, aircraft or chocolate

company apartment /‚kʌmp(ə)ni ə'pɑrtmənt/ *noun* an apartment owned by a company and used by members of staff from time to time (NOTE: The U.K. term is **company flat**.)

company car /‚kʌmp(ə)ni 'kɑr/ *noun* a car which belongs to a company and is lent to an employee to use for business or other purposes

company director /‚kʌmp(ə)ni daɪ'rektə/ *noun* a person appointed by the stockholders to help run a company

company doctor /‚kʌmp(ə)ni 'dɑktər/ *noun* **1.** a doctor who works for a company and looks after sick workers ○ *The staff are all sent to see the company doctor once a year.* **2.** a specialist businessperson who rescues businesses which are in difficulties

company handbook /‚kʌmp(ə)ni 'hændbʊk/ *noun* a booklet containing information about the company's structure, employees' rights, grievance procedure, etc.

company law /‚kʌmp(ə)ni 'lɔr/ *noun* laws which refer to the way companies work

company officers /‚kʌmp(ə)ni 'ɒfɪsərz/ *noun* the main executives or directors of a company

company promoter /‚kʌmp(ə)ni prə'moʊtər/ *noun* a person who organizes the setting up of a new company

company report /‚kʌmp(ə)ni rɪ'pɔrt/ *noun* a document that sets out in detail what a company has done and how well it has performed (NOTE: Companies are legally required to write annual reports and financial reports and to submit them to the authorities in the country where they are registered, but they may also produce other reports on specific subjects, for example, on the environmental or social impact of a project they are undertaking.)

company secretary /‚kʌmp(ə)ni 'sekrɪt(ə)ri/ *noun* a person who is responsible for a company's legal and financial affairs

company's infrastructure /ˌkʌmpəniz ˈɪnfrəˌstrʌktʃər/ *noun* the way in which the company is organized

company town /ˈkʌmp(ə)ni taʊn/ *noun* a town in which most of the property and stores are owned by a large company which employs most of the population

comparability /ˌkɒmp(ə)rəˈbɪlɪti/ *noun* the fact of being able to be compared

comparable /ˈkɒmp(ə)rəb(ə)l/ *adjective* possible to compare ○ *The two sets of figures are not comparable.* □ **which is the nearest company comparable to this one in size?** which company is most similar in size to this one?

comparative advantage /kəmˌpærətɪv ədˈvæntɪdʒ/ *noun* the fact of being able to produce a good or service at a lower cost than other producers. Also called **comparative cost**

comparative cost /kəmˌpærətɪv ˈkɒst/ *noun* same as **comparative advantage**

compare /kəmˈpeər/ *verb* to look at several things to see how they differ ○ *The finance director compared the figures for the first and second quarters.*

compare with *phrasal verb* to examine two things to see where they are the same and where they differ ○ *How do the sales this year compare with last year's?* ○ *Compared with the previous month, last month was terrific.*

comparison /kəmˈpærɪs(ə)n/ *noun* the act of comparing one thing with another ○ *Sales are down in comparison with last year.* □ **there is no comparison between overseas and home sales** overseas and home sales are so different they cannot be compared

comparison-shop /kəmˈpærɪs(ə)n ʃɒp/ *verb* to compare prices and features of items for sale in different stores to find the best deal

compassionate leave /kəmˌpæʃ(ə)nət ˈliv/ *noun* time off work granted to an employee to deal with personal or family problems

compensate /ˈkɒmpənseɪt/ *verb* to give someone money to make up for a loss or injury ○ *In this case we will compensate a manager for loss of commission.* ○ *The company will compensate the employee for the burns suffered in the accident.*

(NOTE: You compensate someone **for** something.)

compensation /ˌkɒmpənˈseɪʃ(ə)n/ *noun* **1.** □ **compensation for damage** payment for damage done □ **compensation for loss of office** payment to a director who is asked to leave a company before their contract ends □ **compensation for loss of earnings** payment to someone who has stopped earning money or who is not able to earn money **2.** a salary

"…compensation can also be via the magistrates courts for relatively minor injuries" [*Personnel Management*]

compensation deal /ˌkɒmpən ˈseɪʃ(ə)n dil/ *noun* a deal where an exporter is paid (at least in part) in goods from the country to which he or she is exporting

compensation package /ˌkɒmpən ˈseɪʃ(ə)n ˌpækɪdʒ/ *noun* the salary, pension, and other benefits offered with a job

"…golden parachutes are liberal compensation packages given to executives leaving a company" [*Publishers Weekly*]

compete /kəmˈpit/ *verb* □ **to compete with someone** *or* **with a company** to try to do better than another person or another company ○ *We have to compete with cheap imports from the Far East.* ○ *They were competing unsuccessfully with local companies on their home territory.* □ **the two companies are competing for a market share** *or* **for a contract** each company is trying to win a larger part of the market, trying to win the contract

competence /ˈkɒmpɪt(ə)ns/ *noun* **1.** the ability to do the tasks required in a job ○ *The training sessions are intended to increase staff competence.* **2.** □ **the case falls within the competence of the court** the court is legally able to deal with the case

competence framework /ˈkɒmpɪt(ə)ns ˌfreɪmwɜrk/ *noun* the set of duties or tasks performed as part of a job with the standards which should be achieved in these duties

competency /ˈkɒmpɪt(ə)nsi/ *noun* same as **competence**

competent /ˈkɒmpɪt(ə)nt/ *adjective* **1.** able to do something, efficient ○ *she is a competent manager* **2.** able to do the tasks required in a job □ **the court is not competent to deal with this case** the court is not legally able to deal with the case

competition /ˌkɑmpə'tɪʃ(ə)n/ *noun* **1.** a situation where companies or individuals are trying to do better than others, e.g., trying to win a larger share of the market, or to produce a better or cheaper product or to control the use of resources **2.** □ **the competition** companies which are trying to compete with your product ○ *We have lowered our prices to beat the competition.* ○ *The competition have brought out a new range of products.*

competition-oriented pricing /kɑmpə,tɪʃ(ə)n ,ɔrientɪd 'praɪsɪŋ/ *noun* the act of putting low prices on goods so as to compete with other competing products

competitive /kəm'petətɪv/ *adjective* **1.** involving competition **2.** intended to compete with others, usually by being cheaper or better □ **competitive price** a low price aimed to compete with a rival product □ **competitive product** a product made or priced to compete with existing products

competitive analysis /kəm,petətɪv ə 'næləsɪs/ *noun* analysis for marketing purposes that can include industry, customer, and competitor analysis and aims to discover how competitive an organization, project, or product is, especially by evaluating the capabilities of key competitors

competitive bid /kəm,petɪtɪv 'bɪd/ *noun* a form of bid in which different organizations are asked to bid for a contract

competitive edge /kəm,petətɪv 'edʒ/ *noun* a factor that gives a special advantage to a nation, company, group, or individual when it is competing with others ○ *Any competitive edge we have in this market is due to our good after-sales service.* ○ *Why does this product have the competitive edge over similar products?*

competitive forces /kəm,petətɪv 'fɔrsɪz/ *plural noun* economic and business factors that force an organization to become more competitive if wants to survive and succeed

competitive intelligence /kəm ,petətɪv ɪn'telɪdʒəns/ *noun* information, especially information concerning the plans, activities, and products of its competitors, that an organization gathers and analyzes in order to make itself more competitive (NOTE: Competitive intelligence may sometimes be gained through industrial espionage.)

competitively /kəm'petətɪvli/ *adverb* □ **competitively priced** sold at a low price which competes with the price of similar products from other companies

competitiveness /kəm'petətɪvnəs/ *noun* the fact of being competitive

competitiveness index /kəm 'petətɪvnəs ,ɪndeks/ *noun* a list that uses economic and other data to rank countries in order according to the competitiveness of their industries and products

competitive pricing /kəm,petətɪv 'praɪsɪŋ/ *noun* the practice of putting low prices on goods so as to compete with other products

competitive tender /kəm,petɪtɪv 'tendər/ *noun* same as **competitive bid**

competitor /kəm'petɪtər/ *noun* a person or company that is competing with another ○ *Two German firms are our main competitors.*

competitor analysis /kəm,petɪtər ə 'næləsɪs/ *noun* the process of analyzing information about competitors and their products in order to build up a picture of where their strengths and weaknesses lie

competitor profiling /kəm,petɪtər 'proʊfaɪlɪŋ/ *noun* same as **competitor analysis**

complain /kəm'pleɪn/ *verb* to say that something is no good or does not work properly ○ *The office is so cold the staff have started complaining.* ○ *She complained about the service.* ○ *They are complaining that our prices are too high.* ○ *If you want to complain, write to the manager.*

complaint /kəm'pleɪnt/ *noun* a statement that you feel something is wrong ○ *complaints from the work force about conditions in the factory* ○ *She sent her letter of complaint to the managing director.* □ **to make** *or* **to lodge a complaint against someone** to write and send an official complaint to someone's superior

complaints department /kəm 'pleɪnts dɪ,pɑrtmənt/ *noun* a department in a company or store to which customers can send or bring complaints about its products or service

complaints management /kəm 'pleɪnts ,mænɪdʒmənt/ *noun* the management of complaints from customers

complaints procedure /kəm'pleɪnts prə,sidʒər/ *noun* a way of presenting complaints formally from a labor union to a management ○ *The labor union has followed the correct complaints procedure.*

complementor /'kamplɪmentər/ *noun* a company that makes something that your product needs in order to function successfully. For example, software companies are complementors to computer companies. (NOTE: Software companies, for example, are complementors to computer companies.)

complete /kəm'plit/ *adjective* whole, with nothing missing ○ *The order is complete and ready for sending.* ○ *The shipment will be delivered only if it is complete.* ■ *verb* **1.** to finish ○ *The factory completed the order in two weeks.* ○ *How long will it take you to complete the job?* ○ *He has completed his probationary period.* **2.** to sign a contract for the sale of a property and to exchange it with the other party, so making it legal

completely /kəm'plitli/ *adverb* all or totally ○ *The cargo was completely ruined by water.* ○ *The warehouse was completely destroyed by fire.*

completion /kəm'pliʃ(ə)n/ *noun* the act of finishing something □ **completion of a contract** the act of signing a contract for the sale of a property whereby the buyer pays and the seller transfers ownership to the buyer

completion date /kəm'pliʃ(ə)n deɪt/ *noun* a date when something will be finished

complex /'kampleks/ *noun* a series of large buildings ○ *a large industrial complex* (NOTE: The plural is **complexes**.) ■ *adjective* with many different parts ○ *a complex system of import controls* ○ *The specifications for the machine are very complex.*

compliance /kəm'plaɪəns/ *noun* agreement to do what is ordered

compliance department /kəm'plaɪəns dɪ,pɑrtmənt/ *noun* a department in a stockbroking firm which makes sure that the Stock Exchange rules are followed and that confidentiality is maintained in cases where the same firm represents competitors

complimentary /,kamplɪ'ment(ə)ri/ *adjective* free

complimentary ticket /,kamplɪment(ə)ri 'tɪkət/ *noun* a free ticket, given as a present

compliments slip /'kamplɪmənts slɪp/ *noun* a piece of paper with the name of the company printed on it, sent with documents or gifts etc. instead of a letter

comply /kəm'plaɪ/ *verb* to agree to do what is ordered (NOTE: **complies – complying – complied**) □ **to comply with a court order** to obey an order given by a court

component /kəm'poʊnənt/ *noun* a piece of machinery or a part which will be put into a final product ○ *The assembly line stopped because the supply of a vital component was delayed.*

components factory /kəm'poʊnənts ,fækt(ə)ri/ *noun* a factory which makes parts which are used in other factories to make finished products

composition /,kampə'zɪʃ(ə)n/ *noun* an agreement between a debtor and creditors, where the debtor settles a debt by repaying only part of it

compound /kəm'paʊnd/ *verb* to agree with creditors to settle a debt by paying part of what is owed

compound interest /,kampaʊnd 'ɪntrəst/ *noun* interest which is added to the capital and then earns interest itself

comprehensive /,kamprɪ'hensɪv/ *adjective* which includes everything

comprehensive insurance /,kamprɪhensɪv ɪn'ʃʊrəns/, **comprehensive policy** /,kamprɪhensɪv 'palɪsi/ *noun* an insurance policy which covers you against all risks which are likely to happen

compromise /'kamprəmaɪz/ *noun* an agreement between two sides, where each side gives way a little ○ *Management offered $5 an hour, the union asked for $9, and a compromise of $7.50 was reached.* ■ *verb* to reach an agreement by giving way a little ○ *She asked $15 for it, I offered $7 and we compromised on $10.*

comptometer /kamp'tamɪtər/ *noun* a machine which counts automatically

comptroller /kən'troʊlər/ *noun* a financial controller

compulsory /kəm'pʌlsəri/ *adjective* which is forced or ordered

compulsory liquidation /kəm
ˌpʌlsəri ˌlɪkwɪˈdeɪʃ(ə)n/ *noun* liquidation which is ordered by a court

compulsory purchase order /kəm
ˌpʌlsəri ˈpɜːtʃɪs ˌɔːdər/ *noun* an order from a local authority by which property is purchased whether the owner wants to sell or not (as when buying properties to widen a road)

compulsory winding up /kəm
ˌpʌlsəri ˌwaɪndɪŋ ˈʌp/ *noun* liquidation which is ordered by a court

compulsory winding up order
/kəmˌpʌlsəri ˌwaɪndɪŋ ˈʌp ˌɔːdər/ *noun* an order from a court saying that a company must be wound up

computable /kəmˈpjutəb(ə)l/ *adjective* possible to calculate

computation /ˌkʌmpjuˈteɪʃ(ə)n/ *noun* a calculation

computational error
/ˌkʌmpjuteɪʃ(ə)nəl ˈerər/ *noun* a mistake made in calculating

compute /kəmˈpjut/ *verb* to calculate, to do calculations

computer /kəmˈpjutər/ *noun* an electronic machine which calculates or stores information and processes it automatically

computer-based training /kəm
ˌpjutər beɪst ˈtreɪnɪŋ/ *noun* training that is carried out on computer, using programs that are usually interactive so that the trainees can select from multiple-choice options or key in their own answers

computer bureau /kəmˈpjutər
ˌbjuroʊ/ *noun* an office which offers to do work on its computers for companies which do not own their own computers

computer department /kəmˈpjutər
dɪˌpɑːtmənt/ *noun* a department in a company which manages the company's computers

computer error /kəmˌpjutər ˈerər/ *noun* a mistake made by a computer

computer file /kəmˈpjutər faɪl/ *noun* a section of information on a computer, e.g., the payroll, list of addresses, or list of customer accounts

computer hardware /kəmˌpjutər
ˈhɑːdwer/ *noun* machines used in data processing, including the computers and printers, but not the programs

computerize /kəmˈpjutəraɪz/ *verb* to change something from a manual system

to one using computers ○ *We have computerized all our records.* ○ *Stock control is now completely computerized.*

computerized /kəmˈpjutəraɪzd/ *adjective* carried out by computers ○ *a computerized invoicing* or *filing system*

computer language /kəmˈpjutər
ˌlæŋgwɪdʒ/ *noun* a system of signs, letters, and words used to instruct a computer

computer listing /kəmˌpjutər ˈlɪstɪŋ/ *noun* a printout of a list of items taken from data stored in a computer

computer-literate /kəmˌpjutər
ˈlɪt(ə)rət/ *adjective* referring to a person who knows how to use more or less any type of computer

computer magazine /kəmˈpjutər
ˌmægəzin/ *noun* a magazine with articles on computers and programs

computer manager /kəmˈpjutər
ˌmænɪdʒər/ *noun* a person in charge of a computer department

computer network /kəmˌpjutər
ˈnetwɜːk/ *noun* a computer system where several PCs are linked so that they all draw on the same database

computer printer /kəmˌpjutər
ˈprɪntər/ *noun* a machine which prints information from a computer

computer printout /kəmˌpjutər
ˈprɪntaʊt/ *noun* a printed copy of information from a computer ○ *The sales director asked for a printout of the agents' commissions.*

computer program /kəmˈpjutər
ˌproʊgræm/ *noun* instructions to a computer telling it to do a particular piece of work ○ *to buy a graphics program* ○ *The accounts department is running a new payroll program.*

computer programmer /kəmˌpjutər
ˈproʊgræmər/ *noun* a person who writes computer programs

computer programming /kəm
ˌpjutər ˈproʊgræmɪŋ/ *noun* the work of writing programs for computers

computer-readable /kəmˌpjutər
ˈridəb(ə)l/ *adjective* able to be read and understood by a computer ○ *computer-readable codes*

computer run /kəmˈpjutər rʌn/ *noun* a period of work done by a computer

computer services /kəm,pjutər 'sɜrvɪsɪz/ *plural noun* work using a computer, done by a computer bureau

computer system /kəm'pjutər ,sɪstəm/ *noun* a set of programs, commands, etc., which run a computer

computer tape /kəm'pjutər teɪp/ *noun* magnetic tape used in computers

computer telephony integration /kəm,pjutər tə,lefəni ,ɪntɪ'greɪʃ(ə)n/ *noun* a technology that links computers and telephones and enables computers to dial telephone numbers and send and receive messages (NOTE: One product of computer telephony integration is calling line identification, which identifies the telephone number a customer is calling from, searches the customer database to identify the caller, and displays his or her account on a computer screen.)

computer terminal /kəm'pjutər ,tɜrmɪn(ə)l/ *noun* a keyboard and screen, by which information can be put into a computer or can be called up from a database ○ *computer system consisting of a microprocessor and six terminals*

computer time /kəm'pjutər taɪm/ *noun* the time when a computer is being used, paid for at an hourly rate

computer worm /kəm'pjutər wɜrm/ *noun* a type of computer virus that does damage by making as many copies of itself as it can as quickly in order to clog up communication channels on the Internet

"New features in a free Windows upgrade will give your PC a lot of much-needed protection from viruses, worms, and other nuisances." [*Fortune*]

computing /kəm'pjutɪŋ/ *noun* the operating of computers

computing speed /kəm'pjutɪŋ spid/ *noun* the speed at which a computer calculates

concealment /kən'silmənt/ *noun* the act of hiding for criminal purposes

concealment of assets /kən,silmənt əv 'æsets/ *noun* the act of hiding assets so that creditors do not know they exist

concentration /,kɑnsən'treɪʃ(ə)n/ *noun* **1.** the degree to which a small number of businesses control a large section of the market ○ *Too much concentration created resentment among small businesses trying to enter the market.* ○ *Concentration has meant too little competition*

and therefore higher prices to the consumer. **2.** the action of grouping a large number of things together. Also called **market concentration**

concept /'kɑnsept/ *noun* an idea

concept testing /'kɑnsept ,testɪŋ/ *noun* the evaluation of a new product idea, usually by consulting representatives from all the main departments in a company, and/or by interviewing a sample of consumers ○ *The new product idea did not survive concept testing because it didn't answer an existing demand.* ○ *After thorough concept testing the idea of a disposable pen was rejected as the company's production capacity was too limited.*

concern /kən'sɜrn/ *noun* **1.** a business or company **2.** the fact of being worried about a problem ○ *The management showed no concern at all for the workers' safety.* ■ *verb* to deal with or be connected with ○ *The sales staff are not concerned with the cleaning of the store.* ○ *She filled in a questionnaire concerning computer utilization.*

concert /'kɑnsət/ *noun* □ **to act in concert** (*of several people*) to work together to achieve a goal

concert party /'kɑnsət ,pɑrti/ *noun* an arrangement where several people or companies work together in secret, usually to acquire another company through a takeover bid

concession /kən'seʃ(ə)n/ *noun* **1.** the right to use someone else's property for business purposes **2.** the right to be the only seller of a product in a place ○ *She runs a jewelry concession in a department store.* **3.** an allowance, e.g., a reduction in tax or price

concessionaire /kən,seʃə'ner/ *noun* a person or business that has the right to be the only seller of a product in a place

concessionary /kən'seʃ(ə)nəri/ *adjective* which is allowed as a concession

concessionary fare /kən,seʃ(ə)nəri 'fer/ *noun* a reduced fare for some types of passenger such as pensioners, students or employees of a transportation company

concessionary ticket /kən,seʃ(ə)nəri 'tɪkɪt/ *noun* a cheaper entrance ticket to an exhibition for pensioners, students, etc.

conciliation /kən,sɪli'eɪʃ(ə)n/ *noun* the practice of bringing together the parties in a dispute with an independent third party, so that the dispute can be settled through a series of negotiations

conclude /kən'klud/ *verb* **1.** to complete successfully ○ *to conclude an agreement with someone* **2.** to believe from evidence ○ *The police concluded that the thief had got into the building through the main entrance.*

condition /kən'dıʃ(ə)n/ *noun* **1.** something which has to be carried out as part of a contract or which has to be agreed before a contract becomes valid □ **on condition that** provided that ○ *They were granted the lease on condition that they paid the legal costs.* **2.** a general state or the general way of life in a place ○ *item sold in good condition* ○ *The union has complained of the bad working conditions in the factory.* ○ *What was the condition of the car when it was sold?* ○ *Adverse trading conditions affected our profits.*

conditional /kən'dıʃ(ə)n(ə)l/ *adjective* provided that specific conditions are taken into account □ **to give a conditional acceptance** to accept, provided that specific things happen or that specific terms apply □ **conditional on** subject to (certain conditions) □ **the offer is conditional on the board's acceptance** the offer is only valid provided the board accepts

conditional offer /kən,dıʃ(ə)nəl 'ɔfər/ *noun* an offer to buy provided that specific terms apply

conditional sale /kən,dıʃ(ə)nəl 'seıl/ *noun* a sale which is subject to conditions, such as a installment plan agreement

conditions of contract /kən,dıʃ(ə)nz əv 'kɑntrækt/ *noun* the conditions which are listed in a contract and which are legally binding

conditions of employment /kən,dıʃ(ə)nz əv ım'plɔımənt/ *plural noun* the terms of a contract of employment

conditions of sale /kən,dıʃ(ə)nz əv 'seıl/ *plural noun* agreed ways in which a sale takes place, e.g., discounts or credit terms

condominium /,kɑndə'mıniəm/ *noun* a system of ownership, in which a person owns an apartment in a building, together with a share of the land, stairs, roof, etc.

conduct /kən'dʌkt/ *verb* to carry on ○ *to conduct negotiations* ○ *The chairman conducted the negotiations very negligent-*

ly. ○ *She conducted the training session very efficiently.* ■ *noun* a way of behaving ○ *He was fired for bad conduct at the staff Christmas party.*

conducted tour /kən,dʌktıd 'tʊr/ *noun* a tour with a guide who shows places to the tourists

confer /kən'fɜr/ *verb* to discuss a problem with another person or within a group ○ *The interview board conferred in the next room before announcing the names of the successful candidates.* (NOTE: **conferring – conferred**)

conference /'kɑnf(ə)rəns/ *noun* **1.** a meeting of people to discuss problems ○ *Many useful tips can be picked up at a sales conference.* ○ *The conference of HR managers included talks on payment and recruitment policies.* □ **to be in conference** to be in a meeting **2.** a meeting of an organization such as an association, society or union

conference call /'kɑnf(ə)rəns kɔl/ *noun* a telephone call that connects three or more lines so that people in different places can talk to one another (NOTE: Conference calls reduce the cost of meetings by making it unnecessary for the participants to spend time and money on getting together in one place.)

conference phone /'kɑnf(ə)rəns foʊn/ *noun* a telephone arranged in such a way that several people can speak into it from around a table

conference proceedings /'kɑnf(ə)rəns prə,sidıŋz/ *plural noun* a written report of what has taken place at a conference

conference room /'kɑnf(ə)rəns rum/ *noun* a room where a small meeting can take place

conference timetable /,kɑnf(ə)rəns 'taım,teıb(ə)l/ *noun* a list of events and speakers at a conference

confidence /'kɑnfıd(ə)ns/ *noun* **1.** the state of feeling sure or being certain ○ *The sales teams do not have much confidence in their manager.* ○ *The board has total confidence in the managing director.* **2.** □ **in confidence** in secret ○ *I will show you the report in confidence.*

confidence interval /,kɑnfıd(ə)ns 'ıntəv(ə)l/ *noun* a range of statistical values within which a result is expected to fall with a specific probability

confident /'kɑnfɪd(ə)nt/ *adjective* certain or sure ○ *I am confident the turnover will increase rapidly.* ○ *Are you confident the sales team can handle this product?*

confidential /ˌkɑnfɪ'denʃəl/ *adjective* not to be told or shown to other people ○ *The references sent by the applicant's last employer were in an envelope marked "Private and Confidential".* ○ *Whatever an employee says in an appraisal interview should be treated as confidential.* ○ *The consultants sent a confidential report to the chairman.*

confidentiality /ˌkɑnfɪdenʃi'ælɪti/ *noun* the fact of being secret □ **she broke the confidentiality of the discussions** she told someone about the secret discussions

confidential report /ˌkɑnfɪdenʃəl rɪ'pɔrt/ *noun* a secret document which must not be shown to other people

confirm /kən'fɜrm/ *verb* to say again that something agreed before is correct ○ *to confirm a hotel reservation* or *a ticket* or *an agreement* or *a booking* □ **to confirm someone in a job** to say that someone is now permanently in the job

confirmation /ˌkɑnfə'meɪʃən/ *noun* **1.** the act of making certain □ **confirmation of a booking** the act of checking that a booking is certain **2.** a document which confirms something ○ *She received confirmation from the bank that the deeds had been deposited.*

conflict /'kɑnflɪkt/ *noun* antagonism between people, e.g., between management and workers ○ *There was conflict between the two groups of workers.*

conflict management /'kɑnflɪkt ˌmænɪdʒmənt/ *noun* a system of work that involves identifying possible sources of conflict within an organization and dealing with and settling conflicts when they occur

conflict of interest /ˌkɑnflɪkt əv 'ɪntrəst/ *noun* a situation where a person or firm may profit personally from decisions taken in an official capacity

conflict of interest(s) /ˌkɑnflɪkt əv 'ɪntrəsts/ *noun* a situation in which a person or institution has difficulty in making a fair and impartial decision on some issue through having divided loyalties or being likely to benefit if the issue is decided in one way rather than another, as, e.g., when someone is connected with two or more companies who are competing with each other (NOTE: the correct thing to do in such cases is for the person concerned to declare any interests, to make known the way in which those interests conflict and to abstain from participating in the decision-making process)

conformance /kən'fɔrməns/ *noun* the process of acting in accordance with a rule ○ *The machine used is not in conformance with safety regulations.*

conformity /kən'fɔrmɪti/ *noun* compliance with a standard, regulation, or requirement ○ *The court found that the rate increases were not in conformity with the law*

confuse /kən'fjuz/ *verb* to make it difficult for someone to understand something, to make something difficult to understand ○ *to introduce the problem of tax will only confuse the issue* ○ *The chairman was confused by all the journalists' questions.*

conglomerate /kən'glɑmərət/ *noun* a group of subsidiary companies linked together and forming a group, each making very different types of products

conglomerate diversification /kən ˌglɑmərət daɪˌvɜrsɪfɪ'keɪʃ(ə)n/ *noun* a form of (**diversification**) in which a company sets up subsidiary companies with activities in many different areas of business

conjoint analysis /kənˌdʒɔɪnt ə'næləsɪs/ *noun* a research method aimed at discovering the best combination of features for a product or service, e.g., price and size

connect /kə'nekt/ *verb* **1.** to link or to join ○ *She is connected to the business as a consultant.* **2.** □ **the flight from New York connects with a flight to Athens** the plane from New York arrives in time for passengers to catch the plane to Athens

connecting flight /kəˌnektɪŋ 'flaɪt/ *noun* a plane which a passenger will be on time to catch and which will take him to his final destination ○ *Check at the helicopter desk for connecting flights to downtown.*

connection /kə'nekʃən/ *noun* a link, something which joins ○ *Is there a connection between his argument with the director and his sudden move to become warehouse manager?* □ **in connection**

with referring to ○ *I want to speak to the managing director in connection with the sales forecasts.*

connections /kə'nekʃ(ə)nz/ *noun* people you know, customers or contacts ○ *He has useful connections in industry.*

connectivity /ˌkanek'tɪvəti/ *noun* **1.** the ability of an electronic product to connect with other similar products, or the extent to which individuals, companies and countries can connect with one another electronically **2.** the ability of individuals, organizations and countries to connect with each other and communicate electronically

connexity /kə'neksɪti/ *noun* the fact of being closely linked by worldwide communications networks

conscientious /ˌkanʃi'enʃəs/ *adjective* referring to a person who works carefully and well ○ *She's a very conscientious worker.*

consensus /kən'sensəs/ *noun* an opinion which most people agree on ○ *management by consensus*

consent /kən'sent/ *noun* agreement that something should be done ○ *Change of use requires the consent of the local planning authorities.* ■ *verb* to agree that something should be done ○ *The management consented to the union's proposals.*

consequential loss /ˌkansɪkwenʃəl 'lɔs/ *noun* loss which occurs as the result of some other loss. Also called **indirect loss**

conservative /kən'sɜrvətɪv/ *adjective* careful, not overestimating ○ *His forecast of expenditure was very conservative* or *She made a conservative forecast of expenditure.* □ **a conservative estimate** a calculation which probably underestimates the final figure ○ *Their turnover has risen by at least 20% in the last year, and that is probably a conservative estimate.*

"…we are calculating our next budget income at an oil price of $15 per barrel. We know it is a conservative projection, but we do not want to come in for a shock should prices dive at any time during the year" [*Lloyd's List*]

conservatively /kən'sɜrvətɪvli/ *adverb* not overestimating ○ *The total sales are conservatively estimated at $2.3m.*

consider /kən'sɪdə/ *verb* to think seriously about something □ **to consider the terms of a contract** to examine a contract and discuss whether the terms are acceptable

considerable /kən'sɪd(ə)rəb(ə)l/ *adjective* quite large ○ *We sell considerable quantities of our products to Africa.* ○ *They lost a considerable amount of money on the commodity market.*

considerably /kən'sɪd(ə)rəbli/ *adverb* quite a lot ○ *Sales are considerably higher than they were last year.*

consideration /kənˌsɪdə'reɪʃ(ə)n/ *noun* **1.** serious thought ○ *We are giving consideration to moving the head office to Scotland.* **2.** something valuable exchanged as part of a contract

consign /kən'saɪn/ *verb* □ **to consign goods to someone** to send goods to someone for them to use or to sell for you

consignation /ˌkansaɪ'neɪʃ(ə)n/ *noun* the act of consigning

consignee /ˌkansaɪ'ni/ *noun* a person who receives goods from someone for their own use or to sell for the sender

consignment /kən'saɪnmənt/ *noun* **1.** the sending of goods to someone who will sell them for you □ **goods on consignment** goods kept for another company to be sold on their behalf for a commission **2.** a group of goods sent for sale ○ *A consignment of goods has arrived.* ○ *We are expecting a consignment of cars from Japan.*

consignment note /kən'saɪnmənt noʊt/ *noun* a note saying that goods have been sent

consignor /kən'saɪnər/ *noun* a person who consigns goods to someone

COMMENT: The goods remain the property of the consignor until the consignee sells or pays for them.

consolidate /kən'salɪdeɪt/ *verb* **1.** to include the accounts of several subsidiary companies as well as the holding company in a single set of accounts **2.** to group goods together for shipping

consolidated accounts /kənˌsalɪdeɪtɪd ə'kaʊnts/ *plural noun* accounts where the financial position of several different companies, i.e. a holding company and its subsidiaries, are recorded together

Consolidated Omnibus Reconciliation Act /kənˌsalɪdeɪtɪd ˌɑmnɪbʌs ˌrekənsɪli'eɪʃ(ə)n ˌækt/ full form of **COBRA**

consolidated profit and loss account /kən,sɑlɪdeɪtɪd ,prɑfɪt ən 'lɔs ə ,kaʊnt/ *noun U.K.* profit and loss accounts of the holding company and its subsidiary companies, grouped together into a single profit and loss account (NOTE: The U.S. term is **profit and loss statement** or **income statement**.)

consolidated shipment /kən ,sɑlɪdeɪtɪd 'ʃɪpmənt/ *noun* a single shipment of goods from different companies grouped together

consolidation /kən,sɑlɪ'deɪʃ(ə)n/ *noun* the grouping together of goods for shipping

consolidator /kən'sɑlɪdeɪtər/ *noun* **1.** a firm which groups together orders from different companies into one shipment **2.** a firm which groups together bookings made by various travel agents so as to get cheaper group fares on normal scheduled flights

consortium /kən'sɔrtiəm/ *noun* a group of companies which work together ○ *A consortium of Canadian companies* or *A Canadian consortium has bid for the job.* (NOTE: The plural is **consortia**.)

constant /'kɑnstənt/ *adjective* unchanging ○ *The calculations are in constant dollars.*

constitution /,kɑnstɪ'tjuʃ(ə)n/ *noun* written rules or regulations of a society, association, club, or state ○ *Under the society's constitution, the chairman is elected for a two-year period.* ○ *Payments to officers of the association are not allowed by the constitution.*

constitutional /,kɑnstɪ'tjuʃ(ə)nəl/ *adjective* according to a constitution ○ *The reelection of the chairman is not constitutional.*

construct /kən'strʌkt/ *verb* to build ○ *The company has tendered for the contract to construct the new bridge.*

construction /kən'strʌkʃən/ *noun* the activity of building □ **under construction** being built ○ *the airport is under construction*

construction company /kən 'strʌkʃ(ə)n ,kʌmp(ə)ni/ *noun* company which specializes in building

construction industry /kən 'strʌkʃ(ə)n ,ɪndəstri/ *noun* all companies specializing in building

constructive /kən'strʌktɪv/ *adjective* which helps in the making of something ○ *She made some constructive suggestions for improving management-worker relations.* ○ *We had a constructive proposal from a distribution company in Italy.*

constructive dismissal /kən ,strʌktɪv dɪs'mɪs(ə)l/ *noun* a situation where an employee does not leave his or her job voluntarily, but because of pressure from the management

constructor /kən'strʌktər/ *noun* a person or company which constructs

consult /kən'sʌlt/ *verb* to ask an expert for advice ○ *We consulted our accountant about our tax.*

consultant /kən'sʌltənt/ *noun* a specialist who gives advice ○ *an engineering consultant* ○ *a management consultant* ○ *a tax consultant*

consulting /kən'sʌltɪŋ/ *adjective* giving specialist advice ○ *a consulting engineer*

consulting engineer /kən,sʌltɪŋ ,endʒɪ'nɪr/ *noun* an engineer who gives specialist advice

consumable goods /kən,suməb(ə)l 'gʊdz/ *plural noun* same as **consumer goods**

consumables /kən'suməb(ə)lz/ *plural noun* items that have to be bought on a regular basis because they are used up, e.g., paper

consumer /kən'sumər/ *noun* a person or company that buys and uses goods and services ○ *Gas consumers are protesting at the increase in prices.* ○ *The factory is a heavy consumer of water.*

consumer council /kən,sumər 'kaʊns(ə)l/ *noun* a group representing the interests of consumers

consumer credit /kən,sumər 'kredɪt/ *noun* the credit given by stores, banks, and other financial institutions to consumers so that they can buy goods

consumer durables /kən,sumər 'djʊrəb(ə)lz/ *plural noun* items which are bought and used by the public, e.g., washing machines, refrigerators, or ovens

consumer goods /kən,sjumər 'gʊdz/ *plural noun* goods which are bought by members of the public and not by companies. Also called **consumable goods**

consumer panel /kən'sumər
ˌpæn(ə)l/ *noun* a group of consumers who
report on products they have used so that
the manufacturers can improve them or
use what the panel says about them in advertising

Consumer Price Index /kən,sumər
'praɪs ˌɪndeks/ *noun* a U.S. index showing how prices of consumer goods have
risen over a period of time, used as a way
of measuring inflation and the cost of living. Abbreviation **CPI** (NOTE: The U.K.
term is **retail prices index**.)

consumer protection /kən,sjumər
prə'tekʃən/ *noun* the activity of protecting consumers against unfair or illegal
traders

consumer research /kən,sumər rɪ
'sɜrtʃ/ *noun* research into why consumers
buy goods and what goods they may want
to buy

consumer resistance /kən,sumər rɪ
'zɪstəns/ *noun* a lack of interest by consumers in buying a new product ○ *The new
product met no consumer resistance even
though the price was high.*

consumer society /kən,sumər sə
'saɪəti/ *noun* a type of society where consumers are encouraged to buy goods

consumer spending /kən,sumər
'spendɪŋ/ *noun* spending by private
households on goods and services

**consumer-to-consumer com-
merce** /kən,sumər tə kən'sumər
ˌkɑmɜrs/ *noun* business, especially e-
business, done by one individual with another and not involving any business organization

consumption /kən'sʌmpʃ(ə)n/ *noun*
the act of buying or using goods or services ○ *a car with low gasoline consumption*
○ *The factory has a heavy consumption of
coal.*

contact /'kɑntækt/ *noun* **1.** a person
you know or a person you can ask for help
or advice ○ *He has many contacts in the
city.* ○ *Who is your contact in the ministry?* **2.** the act of getting in touch with
someone □ **I have lost contact with them**
I do not communicate with them any longer □ **he put me in contact with a good
lawyer** he told me how to get in touch with
a good lawyer ■ *verb* /'kɑntækt, kən
'tækt/ to get in touch with someone, to
communicate with someone ○ *He tried to*

contact his office by phone. ○ *Can you
contact the managing director at his club?*

contain /kən'teɪn/ *verb* to hold something inside ○ *a barrel of oil contains 42
gallons* ○ *Each crate contains two computers and their peripherals.* ○ *We have
lost a file containing important documents.*

container /kən'teɪnər/ *noun* **1.** a box,
bottle, can, etc., which can hold goods ○
*The gas is shipped in strong metal contain-
ers.* ○ *The container burst during shipping.* **2.** a very large metal case of a standard size for loading and transporting goods
on trucks, trains, and ships ○ *container
berth* ○ *containerport* ○ *container terminal* ○ *to ship goods in containers* □ **a con-
tainer-load of spare parts** a shipment of
spare parts sent in a container

containerization /kən,teɪnəraɪ
'zeɪʃ(ə)n/ *noun* the act of shipping goods
in containers

containerize /kən'teɪnəraɪz/ *verb* to
put or ship goods in containers

container ship /kən'teɪnə ʃɪp/ *noun* a
ship made specially to carry containers

container terminal /kən'teɪnər
'tɜrmɪn(ə)l/ *noun* an area of a harbor
where container ships are loaded or unloaded

contempt of court /kən,tempt əv
'kɔrt/ *noun* an act of being rude to a court,
e.g., bad behavior in court or a refusal to
carry out a court order

content /'kɑntent/ *noun* the ideas inside
a letter, etc. □ **the content of the letter** the
real meaning of the letter

content management /'kɑntent
ˌmænɪdʒmənt/ *noun* the management of
the textual and graphical material contained on a website (NOTE: Owners of
large sites with thousands of pages often
invest in a content management application system to help with the creation and
organization of the content of these
sites.)

content management system
/ˌkɑntent 'mænɪdʒmənt ˌsɪstəm/ *noun*
software that allows a user to manage the
textual and graphical material contained
on a website

contents /'kɑntents/ *plural noun* things
contained by something, what is inside
something ○ *The contents of the bottle
poured out onto the floor.* ○ *Customs offi-*

cials inspected the contents of the crate. □ **the contents of the letter** the words written in the letter

contested takeover /kən,testɪd 'teɪkoʊvər/ *noun* a takeover bid where the board of the target company does not recommend it to the stockholders and tries to fight it. Also called **hostile bid**

context /'kɑntekst/ *noun* additional information about a product that is considered to be helpful to customers and is shown on a website. For example, reviews by other customers displayed on the site for a particular book.

contingency /kən'tɪndʒənsi/ *noun* a possible state of emergency when decisions will have to be taken quickly □ **to add on 10% to provide for contingencies** to provide for further expenditure which may be incurred

contingency fund /kən'tɪndʒənsi fʌnd/ *noun* money set aside in case it is needed urgently

contingency plan /kən'tɪndʒənsi plæn/ *noun* a plan which will be put into action if something unexpected happens

contingency reserve /kən'tɪndʒənsi rɪ,zɜrv/ *noun* money set aside in case it is needed urgently

contingent expenses /kən,tɪndʒənt ɪk'spensɪz/ *plural noun* expenses which will be incurred only if something happens

contingent liability /kən,tɪndʒənt ,laɪə'bɪləti/ *noun* a liability which may or may not occur, but for which provision is made in a company's accounts, as opposed to "provisions," where money is set aside for an anticipated expenditure

contingent policy /kən,tɪndʒənt 'pɑlɪsi/ *noun* an insurance policy which pays out only if something happens, such as if a person named in the policy dies before the person due to benefit

contingent workforce /kən,tɪndʒənt 'wɜrkfɔrs/ *noun* temporary workers, independent contractors, on-call workers, and contract company workers

continual /kən'tɪnjuəl/ *adjective* which happens again and again ○ *Production was slow because of continual breakdowns.*

continually /kən'tɪnjuəli/ *adverb* again and again ○ *The photocopier is continually breaking down.*

continuation /kən,tɪnju'eɪʃ(ə)n/ *noun* the act of continuing

continuation sheet /kən,tɪnjʊ 'eɪʃ(ə)n ʃit/ *noun* the second (or third) page of a document

continue /kən'tɪnju/ *verb* to go on doing something or to do again something which you were doing earlier ○ *The meeting started at 10 a.m. and continued until 6 p.m.* ○ *Negotiations will continue next Monday.*

continuous /kən'tɪnjuəs/ *adjective* with no end or with no breaks ○ *a continuous production line*

continuous feed /kən,tɪnjuəs 'fid/ *noun* a device which feeds continuous stationery into a printer

continuous improvement /kən ,tɪnjuəs ɪm'pruvmənt/ *noun* a procedure and management philosophy that focuses on looking all the time for ways in which small improvements can be made to processes and products, with the goal of increasing quality and reducing waste and cost (NOTE: Continuous improvement is one of the tools that underpin the philosophies of total quality management and lean production; in Japan it is known as kaizen.)

continuous service /kən,tɪnjuəs 'sɜrvɪs/ *noun* a period of employment with one employer, which begins on the day on which the employee starts work and ends on the day which they resign or are dismissed

continuous stationery /kən,tɪnjuəs 'steɪʃ(ə)n(ə)ri/ *noun* paper made as one long sheet used in computer printers

contra /'kɑntrə/ *verb* □ **to contra an entry** to enter a similar amount in the opposite side of an account

contra account /'kɑntrə ə,kaʊnt/ *noun* an account which offsets another account, e.g., where a company's supplier is not only a creditor in that company's books but also a debtor because it has purchased goods on credit

contraband /'kɑntrəbænd/ *noun* goods brought into a country illegally, without paying customs duty

contract *noun* /'kɑntrækt/ **1.** a legal agreement between two parties ○ *to draw up a contract* ○ *to draft a contract* ○ *to sign a contract* □ **the contract is binding on both parties** both parties signing the contract must do what is agreed □ **under contract** bound by the terms of a contract ○ *The firm is under contract to deliver the goods by November.* □ **to void a contract** to make a contract invalid **2.** □ **by private contract** by private legal agreement **3.** an agreement for the supply of a service or goods ○ *to enter into a contract to supply spare parts* ○ *to sign a contract for $10,000 worth of spare parts* □ **to put work out to contract** to decide that work should be done by another company on a contract, rather than by employing members of staff to do it □ **to award a contract to a company, to place a contract with a company** to decide that a company shall have the contract to do work for you □ **to bid on a contract** to put forward an estimate of cost for work under contract ■ *verb* /kən'trækt/ to agree to do some work on the basis of a legally binding contract ○ *to contract to supply spare parts* or *to contract for the supply of spare parts* □ **the supply of spare parts was contracted out to Smith Inc.** Smith Inc. was given the contract for supplying spare parts. □ **to contract out of an agreement** to withdraw from an agreement with the written permission of the other party

COMMENT: A contract is an agreement between two or more parties which creates legal obligations between them. Some contracts are made "under seal", i.e. they are signed and sealed by the parties; most contracts are made orally or in writing. The essential elements of a contract are: (a) that an offer made by one party should be accepted by the other; (b) consideration (i.e. payment of money); (c) the intention to create legal relations. The terms of a contract may be express or implied. A breach of contract by one party entitles the other party to sue for damages or to ask for something to be done.

contract out *phrasal verb* to hire another organization or person to carry out part or all of a certain piece of work ○ *The catering firm has contracted out the distribution of its products to a delivery firm.* ○ *We shall contract out any work we are not specialized in.* ○ *The supply of spare parts was contracted out to Smith Inc.*

contract distribution /kən,trækt ,dɪstrɪ'bjuʃ(ə)n/ *noun* the practice of outsourcing a company's distribution activi-

ties to another company contract (NOTE: Contract distribution can help to reduce costs and stockholdings and improve flexibility of delivery.)

contract hire /'kɑntrækt haɪr/ *noun U.K.* same as **equipment leasing**

contracting party /kən,træktɪŋ 'pɑrti/ *noun* a person or company that signs a contract

contract law /'kɑntrækt lɔ/ *noun* laws relating to private agreements

contract note /'kɑntrækt noʊt/ *noun* a note showing that stock has been bought or sold but not yet paid for, also including the commission

contract of employment /,kɑntrækt əv ɪm'plɔɪmənt/ *noun* a contract between an employer and an employee stating all the conditions of work. Also called **employment contract**

contract of service /,kɑntrækt əv 'sɜrvɪs/ *noun* a legal agreement between an employer and an employee whereby the employee will work for the employer and be directed by them, in return for payment

contractor /kən'træktər/ *noun* a person or company that does work according to a written agreement

contractual /kən'træktʃuəl/ *adjective* according to a contract ○ *contractual conditions* □ **to fulfill your contractual obligations** to do what you have agreed to do in a contract

contractual liability /kən,træktʃuəl ,laɪə'bɪləti/ *noun* a legal responsibility for something as stated in a contract

contractually /kən'træktʃuəli/ *adverb* according to a contract ○ *The company is contractually bound to pay our expenses.*

contractual obligation /kən ,træktʃuəl ,ɑblɪ'geɪʃ(ə)n/ *noun* something that a person is legally forced to do through having signed a contract to do □ **to fulfill your contractual obligations** to do what you have agreed to do in a contract □ **he is under no contractual obligation to buy** he has signed no agreement to buy

contract work /'kɑntrækt wɜrk/ *noun* work done according to a written agreement

contra entry /'kɑntrə ,entri/ *noun* an entry made in the opposite side of an account to make an earlier entry worthless, i.e. a debit against a credit

contrarian /kən'treriən/ *adjective* going against a trend

contrary /'kɑntrəri/ *noun* the opposite □ **failing instructions to the contrary** unless different instructions are given □ **on the contrary** quite the opposite ○ *The chairman was not annoyed with his assistant – on the contrary, he promoted him.*

contribute /kən'trɪbjut/ *verb* to give money or add to money ○ *We agreed to contribute 10% of the profits.* ○ *They had contributed to the pension fund for 10 years.*

contributed content website /kən‚trɪbjutɪd ‚kɑntent 'websaɪt/ *noun* a website that allows visitors to add their contributions to its content, e.g., to write reviews of books that are advertised on the site

contribution /‚kɑntrɪ'bjuʃ(ə)n/ *noun* money paid to add to a sum

contribution analysis /‚kɑntrɪ'bjuʃ(ə)n ə‚næləsɪs/ *noun* an analysis of how much each of a company's products contributes to fixed costs, based on its profit margin and sales ○ *Contribution analysis helps to streamline production and marketing.* ○ *Thorough contribution analysis led to six products being dropped from the product range.*

contribution margin /‚kɑntrɪ'bjuʃ(ə)n ‚mɑrdʒɪn/ *noun* a way of showing how much individual products or services contribute to net profit

"The provider of rehabilitation services cited the negative impact of Part B therapy caps on estimated Contract Therapy contribution margins." [*BusinessWeek*]

contribution of capital /‚kɑntrɪbjuʃ(ə)n əv 'kæpɪt(ə)l/ *noun* money paid to a company as additional capital

contribution pricing /‚kɑntrɪ'bjuʃ(ə)n ‚praɪsɪŋ/ *noun* a pricing method based on maximizing the contribution of each product to fixed costs

contributor /kən'trɪbjutə/ *noun* a person who gives money

contributor of capital /kən‚trɪbjutər əv 'kæpɪt(ə)l/ *noun* a person who contributes capital

contributory /kən'trɪbjut(ə)ri/ *adjective* causing or helping to cause ○ *Falling exchange rates have been a contributory factor in the company's loss of profits.*

contributory negligence /kən‚trɪbjut(ə)ri 'neglɪdʒəns/ *noun* negligence partly caused by the plaintiff and partly by the defendant, resulting in harm done to the plaintiff

contributory pension plan /kən‚trɪbjut(ə)ri 'penʃən plæn/ *noun* a pension plan in which the employee pays a proportion of his or her salary into the pension fund

control /kən'troʊl/ *noun* **1.** the power or ability to direct something ○ *The company is under the control of three stockholders.* ○ *Top management exercises tight control over spending.* □ **to lose control of a business** to find that you have less than 50% of the stock in a company, and so are no longer able to direct it ○ *The family lost control of its business.* **2.** the act of restricting or checking something or making sure that something is kept in check □ **under control** kept in check ○ *Expenses are kept under tight control.* ○ *The company is trying to bring its overhead back under control.* □ **out of control** not kept in check ○ *Costs have gotten out of control.* ■ *verb* **1.** □ **to control a business** to direct a business ○ *The business is controlled by a company based in Luxembourg.* ○ *The company is controlled by the majority stockholder.* **2.** to make sure that something is kept in check or is not allowed to develop ○ *The government is fighting to control inflation* or *to control the rise in the cost of living.* (NOTE: **controlling – controlled**)

control group /kən'troʊl grup/ *noun* a small group which is used to check a sample group

controlled /kən'troʊld/ *adjective* ruled or kept in check

controlled economy /kən‚troʊld ɪ'kɑnəmi/ *noun* an economy where most business activity is directed by orders from the government

controller /kən'troʊlər/ *noun* **1.** a person who controls something, especially the finances of a company **2.** the chief accountant in a company

controlling interest /kən‚troʊlɪŋ 'ɪntrəst/ *noun* □ **to have a controlling interest in a company** to own more than 50% of the stock so that you can direct how the company is run

control systems /kən'troʊl ˌsɪstəmz/ *plural noun* the systems used to check that a computer system is working correctly

convene /kən'vin/ *verb* to ask people to come together ○ *to convene a meeting of shareholders* ○ *to convene a meeting of union members*

convenience /kən'viniəns/ *noun* □ **at your earliest convenience** as soon as you find it possible

convenience store /kən'viniəns stɔ/ *noun* a small store selling food or housewares, open until late at night, or even 24 hours per day

convenient /kən'viniənt/ *adjective* suitable or handy ○ *A bank draft is a convenient way of sending money abroad.* ○ *Is 9:30 a convenient time for the meeting?*

convenor /kən'vinər/ *noun* a trade unionist who organizes union meetings

convergence /kən'vɜrdʒəns/ *noun* a situation where the economic factors applying in two countries move closer together, e.g., when basic interest rates, or budget deficits become more and more similar

conversion /kən'vɜrʃ(ə)n/ *noun* a change

conversion of funds /kən,vɜrʃ(ə)n əv 'fʌndz/ *noun* the act of using money which does not belong to you for a purpose for which it is not supposed to be used

conversion price /kən'vɜrʃ(ə)n praɪs/, **conversion rate** /kən'vɜrʃ(ə)n reɪt/ *noun* **1.** a price at which preferred stock is converted into common stock **2.** a rate at which a currency is changed into a foreign currency

convert /kən'vɜrt/ *verb* **1.** to change money of one country for money of another ○ *We converted our pounds into Swiss francs.* **2.** □ **to convert funds to your own use** to use someone else's money for yourself

convertibility /kən,vɜrtə'bɪləti/ *noun* the ability of a currency to be exchanged for another easily

convertible currency /kən ,vɜrtəb(ə)l 'kʌrənsi/ *noun* a currency which can easily be exchanged for another

conveyance /kən'veɪəns/ *noun* a legal document which transfers a property from the seller to the buyer

conveyancer /kən'veɪənsər/ *noun* a person who draws up a conveyance

conveyancing /kən'veɪənsɪŋ/ *noun* the work of legally transferring a property from a seller to a buyer

COO *abbreviation* chief operating officer

cooling-off laws /ˌkulɪŋ 'ɔf lɔz/ *plural noun* state laws allowing cancellation of an order within a specific period after signing an agreement ○ *Cooling-off laws are making buyers less hesitant about placing large orders.*

cooling-off period /ˌkulɪŋ 'ɔf ˌpɪriəd/ *noun* **1.** (*during an industrial dispute*) a period when negotiations have to be carried on and no action can be taken by either side **2.** a period during which someone who is about to enter into an agreement may reflect on all aspects of the arrangement and change his or her mind if necessary ○ *New York has a three day cooling-off period for telephone sales.*

co-op /'koʊ ɑp/ *noun* same as **cooperative**

cooperate /koʊ'ɑpəreɪt/ *verb* to work together ○ *The regional governments are cooperating in the fight against piracy.* ○ *The two firms have cooperated on the computer project.*

cooperation /koʊˌɑpə'reɪʃ(ə)n/ *noun* the act of working together ○ *The project was completed ahead of schedule with the cooperation of the work force.*

cooperative /koʊ'ɑp(ə)rətɪv/ *adjective* **1.** willing to work together ○ *The work force has not been cooperative over the management's productivity plan.* **2.** used to describe a business in which the profits are shared among the workers ■ *noun* a business run by a group of employees who are also the owners and who share the profits ○ *an industrial cooperative* ○ *The product is marketed by an agricultural cooperative.* ○ *They set up a workers' cooperative to run the factory.*

cooperative society /koʊ'ɑp(ə)rətɪv səˌsaɪəti/ *noun* an organization where customers and employees are partners and share the profits

co-opt /ˌkoʊ 'ɑpt/ *verb* □ **to co-opt someone onto a committee** to ask someone to join a committee without being elected

co-owner /ˌkoʊ 'oʊnər/ *noun* a person who owns something with another person

○ *The two sisters are co-owners of the property.*

co-ownership /ˌkoʊ ˈoʊnəʃɪp/ *noun* an arrangement where two people own a property or where partners or employees share in the ownership of a company

copartner /koʊˈpɑrtnər/ *noun* a person who is a partner in a business with another person

copartnership /koʊˈpɑrtnəʃɪp/ *noun* an arrangement where partners or employees share in the ownership of a company

cope /koʊp/ *verb* to manage to do something ○ *The new assistant manager coped very well when the manager was on vacation.* ○ *The warehouse is trying to cope with the backlog of orders.*

copier /ˈkɑpiər/ *noun* a machine which makes copies of documents

copier paper /ˈkɑpiər ˌpeɪpər/ *noun* special paper used in photocopiers

coproperty /koʊˈprɑpəti/ *noun* ownership of property by two or more people together

coproprietor /ˌkoʊprəˈpraɪətər/ *noun* a person who owns a property with another person or several other people

copy /ˈkɑpi/ *noun* **1.** a document which is made to look the same as another □ **carbon copy** copy made with carbon paper **2.** a document **3.** a book, a newspaper ○ *Have you kept yesterday's copy of the "Times"?* ○ *I read it in the office copy of "Fortune".* ○ *Where is my copy of the telephone directory?* ■ *verb* to make a second document which is like the first ○ *He copied the company report and took it home.* (NOTE: **copies – copying- copied**)

copyholder /ˈkɑpihoʊldər/ *noun* a frame on which a document can be put, which stands next to a keyboard, so that the operator can read the text to be copied more easily

copying machine /ˈkɑpiɪŋ məˌʃin/ *noun* a machine which makes copies of documents

copy paper /ˈkɑpi ˌpeɪpər/ *noun* special paper used in photocopiers

copyright /ˈkɑpiraɪt/ *noun* **1.** an author's legal right to publish his or her own work and not to have it copied, lasting seventy years after the author's death □ **work which is out of copyright** work by a writer who has been dead for seventy years □ **work still in copyright** work by a living writer, or by a writer who died less than seventy years ago **2.** a legal right which protects the creative work of writers and artists and prevents others from copying or using it without authorization, and which also applies to such things as company logos and brand names ■ *verb* to confirm the copyright of a written work by inserting a copyright notice and publishing the work ■ *adjective* covered by the laws of copyright ○ *It is illegal to photocopy a copyright work.*

copyrighted /ˈkɑpiˌraɪtɪd/ *adjective* in copyright

copyright holder /ˌkɑpiraɪt ˈhoʊldər/ *noun* a person who owns a copyright and who can expect to receive royalties from it

copyright notice /ˌkɑpiraɪt ˈnoʊtɪs/ *noun* a note in a book showing who owns the copyright and the date of ownership

copywriter /ˈkɑpiˌraɪtər/ *noun* a person who writes advertisements

core /kɔr/ *noun* the central or main part

core business /ˈkɔr ˌbɪznɪs/ *noun* the most important work that an organization does, that it is most expert at, that makes it different from other organizations, that contributes most to its success and, usually, that it was originally set up to do (NOTE: The concept of core business became prominent in the 1980s when attempts at diversification by large companies proved less successful than expected.)

core capability /ˌkɔr ˌkeɪpəˈbɪləti/ *noun* same as **core competency**

core competency /ˌkɔr ˈkɑmpɪt(ə)nsi/ *noun* a skill or an area of expertise possessed by an organization that makes it particularly good at doing some things and makes an important contribution to its success by giving it competitive advantage over other organizations

core product /ˌkɔr ˈprɑdʌkt/ *noun* **1.** the main product which a company makes or sells **2.** a basic product, without added benefits such as credit terms, installation service, etc.

core skills /ˌkɔr ˈskɪlz/ *noun* basic skills, which are needed by everyone

core time /ˈkɔr taɪm/ *noun* a period when people working under a flextime system must be present at work

core values /ˌkɔr ˈvæljuz/ *plural noun* **1.** the main commercial and moral principles that influence the way an organization is run and the way it conducts its business, and that are supposed to be shared by everyone in the organization from senior management to ordinary employees (NOTE: Core values are often reflected in an organization's mission statement.) **2.** a set of concepts and ideals that guide someone's life and help them to make important decisions

core workers /'kɔr ˌwɜrkərz/ *plural noun* workers who are in full-time employment (as opposed to part-timers or casual workers who are called "peripheral workers")

corner /'kɔrnər/ *noun* a situation where one person or a group controls the supply of a certain commodity ○ *The syndicate tried to create a corner in the silver market.* ■ *verb* □ **to corner the market** to own most or all of the supply of a commodity and so control the price ○ *The syndicate tried to corner the market in silver.*

corner store /'kɔrnər stɔr/ *noun* a small privately owned general store

corp *abbreviation* corporation

corporate /'kɔrp(ə)rət/ *adjective* **1.** referring to corporations or companies, or to a particular company as a whole **2.** referring to business in general ○ *corporate America* ○ *corporate Britain*

corporate brand /ˌkɔrp(ə)rət 'brænd/ *noun* the overall image that a company presents to the outside world, or the image of it that exists in the minds of its customers, its employees, and the public, and that encapsulates what it does and what it stands for

"A corporate brand, which is based on the characteristics of the firm as well as its products, can play a critical role in a company's brand portfolio." [*Harvard Business Review*]

corporate citizenship /ˌkɔrp(ə)rət 'sɪtɪzənʃɪp/ *noun* the impact of a company's operations, investments, and philanthropy on a community or society

corporate climate /ˌkɔrp(ə)rət 'klaɪmət/ *noun* the general feeling and atmosphere within an organization that is mainly created by the attitudes of its managers toward their work, their staff and their customers and that can affect such things as productivity, creativity, and customer focus

corporate communication /ˌkɔrp(ə)rət kəˌmjunɪ'keɪʃ(ə)n/ *noun* the activities undertaken by an organization to pass on information both to its own employees and to its existing and prospective customers and the general public

corporate culture /ˌkɔrp(ə)rət 'kʌltʃər/ *noun* **1.** the way of managing a corporation, by increasing the importance of the corporation itself, and therefore the loyalty of the work force to the corporation **2.** the often unspoken beliefs and values that determine the way an organization does things, the atmosphere that exists within it, and the way people who work for it behave (NOTE: The culture of an organization is often summed up as "the way we do things around here.")

"Executives may have no idea how differently minority colleagues can view the corporate culture that treats whites so well." [*Fortune*]

corporate evolution /ˌkɔrp(ə)rət ˌivə'luʃ(ə)n/ *noun* the process of change and development that takes place in organizations as a result of the use of information technology

corporate governance /ˌkɔrp(ə)rət 'gʌv(ə)nəns/ *noun* a theory of the way companies should be run

corporate hospitality /ˌkɔrp(ə)rət ˌhɑspɪ'tæləti/ *noun* entertainment provided by an organization, originally intended to help salespeople build relationships with customers, but now increasingly used as an incentive for staff and in team-building and training exercises for employees

corporate identity /ˌkɔrp(ə)rət aɪ'dentəti/ *noun* the way in which a corporation is distinguished from others

corporate image /ˌkɔrp(ə)rət 'ɪmɪdʒ/ *noun* an idea which a company would like the public to have of it

corporate income tax /ˌkɔrp(ə)rət 'ɪnkʌm ˌtæks/ *noun* a tax paid on the income of a business

corporate name /ˌkɔrp(ə)rət 'neɪm/ *noun* the name of a large corporation

corporate plan /ˌkɔrp(ə)rət 'plæn/ *noun* a plan for the future work of a whole company

corporate planning /ˌkɔrp(ə)rət 'plænɪŋ/ *noun* the process of planning the future work of a whole company

corporate portal /ˌkɔːp(ə)rət ˈpɔːt(ə)l/ *noun* a main website that allows access to all the information and software applications held by an organization and provides links to information from outside it (NOTE: A corporate portal is a development of intranet technology and, ideally, should allow users to access groupware, email, and desktop applications, and to customize the way information is presented and the way it is used.)

corporate profits /ˌkɔːp(ə)rət ˈprɑːfɪts/ *plural noun* the profits of a corporation

corporate raider /ˌkɔːp(ə)rət ˈreɪdər/ *noun* a person or company which buys a stake in another company before making a hostile takeover bid

corporate restructuring /ˌkɔːp(ə)rət riˈstrʌktʃərɪŋ/ *noun* a fundamental change in the way in which an organization is structured that may involve increasing or decreasing the various layers of staff between the top and the bottom of the hierarchy or re-assigning roles and responsibilities within it (NOTE: Corporate restructuring has generally come to mean reorganizing after a period of unsatisfactory performance, and often involves the closure of parts of the business and the laying-off of personnel.)

corporate social responsibility /ˌkɔːp(ə)rət ˌsəʊʃ(ə)l rɪˌspɑːnsɪˈbɪlɪti/ *noun* the extent to which a business organization behaves in a socially, environmentally, and financially responsible way. Abbreviation **CSR**. Also called **business social responsibility**

corporate strategy /ˌkɔːp(ə)rət ˈstrætədʒi/ *noun* the plans for future action by a corporation

corporate vision /ˌkɔːp(ə)rət ˈvɪʒ(ə)n/ *noun* the overall goal or purpose of an organization that all its business activities are designed to help it achieve (NOTE: An organization's corporate vision is usually summed up in its vision statement.)

corporate volunteerism /ˌkɔːp(ə)rət ˌvɑːlənˈtɪrɪz(ə)m/ *noun* the participation by a business in volunteer programs in its community, e.g., by giving employees paid time away from work for volunteering, or by donating management or technical expertise to community service organization

corporation /ˌkɔːpəˈreɪʃ(ə)n/ *noun* **1.** a large company **2.** a company which is incorporated in the United States **3.** a municipal authority

corporation income tax /ˌkɔːpəreɪʃ(ə)n ˈɪnkʌm ˌtæks/ *noun* a tax on profits made by incorporated companies

corporation loan /ˌkɔːpəˈreɪʃ(ə)n ləʊn/ *noun* a loan issued by a local authority

corporation tax /ˌkɔːpəˈreɪʃ(ə)n tæks/ *noun* a tax on profits and capital gains made by companies, calculated before dividends are paid. Abbreviation **CT**

correct /kəˈrekt/ *adjective* accurate or right ○ *The published accounts do not give a correct picture of the company's financial position.* ■ *verb* to remove mistakes from something ○ *The accounts department have corrected the invoice.* ○ *You will have to correct all these typing errors before you send the letter.*

correction /kəˈrekʃ(ə)n/ *noun* **1.** an act of making something correct ○ *She made some corrections to the text of the speech.* **2.** a change in the valuation of something that is thought to be overvalued or undervalued which results in its being more realistically valued

"…there were fears in October that shares were overvalued and bears were ready to enter the market. This only proved to be a small correction" [*Investors Chronicle*]

correlation /ˌkɑːrəˈleɪʃ(ə)n/ *noun* the degree to which there is a relationship between two sets of data ○ *Is there any correlation between people's incomes and the amount they spend on clothing?* ◊ **coefficient of correlation**, **multiple correlation**

correspond /ˌkɔːrɪˈspɑːnd/ *verb* **1.** □ **to correspond with someone** to write letters to someone **2.** □ **to correspond with something** to fit or to match something

correspondence /ˌkɔːrɪˈspɑːndəns/ *noun* letters, emails or other messages exchanged □ **to be in correspondence with someone** to write letters to someone and receive letters back

correspondence clerk /ˌkɔːrɪˈspɑːndəns ˌklɜːrk/ *noun* a clerk whose responsibility it is to answer correspondence

correspondent /ˌkɒrɪˈspɒndənt/ *noun* a journalist who writes articles for a newspaper on specialist subjects ○ *He is the Paris correspondent of the Daily Telegraph.*

corrupt /kəˈrʌpt/ *adjective* **1.** (person, especially an official) who takes bribes; referring to the taking of bribes ○ *They accused the government official of corrupt practices.* **2.** (data on a computer disk) which is faulty and therefore cannot be used ■ *verb* to make data unusable ○ *The faulty disk drive corrupted our files.*

cosmetic /kɑzˈmetɪk/ *adjective* referring to the appearance of people or things ○ *We've made some cosmetic changes to our product line.* ○ *Packaging has both practical as well as cosmetic importance.*

cost /kɒst/ *noun* **1.** the amount of money which has to be paid for something ○ *What is the cost of a first class ticket to New York?* ○ *Computer costs are falling each year.* ○ *We cannot afford the cost of two cars.* □ **to cover costs** to produce enough money in sales to pay for the costs of production ○ *The sales revenue barely covers the costs of advertising* or *the advertising costs.* □ **to sell at cost** to sell at a price which is the same as the cost of manufacture or the wholesale cost **2.** □ **cost of borrowing** Same as **borrowing costs** ■ *verb* **1.** to have as its price ○ *How much does the machine cost?* ○ *This cloth costs $10 a yard.* **2.** □ **to cost a product** to calculate how much money will be needed to make a product, and so work out its selling price

cost, insurance, and freight /ˌkɒst ɪnˌʃʊrəns ən ˈfreɪt/ *noun* the estimate of a price, which includes the cost of the goods, the insurance, and the transportation charges. Abbreviation **CIF, c.i.f.**

cost accountant /ˈkɒst əˌkaʊntənt/ *noun* an accountant who gives managers information about their business costs

cost accounting /ˈkɒst əˌkaʊntɪŋ/ *noun* the process of preparing special accounts of manufacturing and sales costs

cost analysis /ˈkɒst əˌnæləsɪs/ *noun* the process of calculating in advance what a new product will cost

cost-benefit analysis /ˌkɒst ˈbenəfɪt əˌnæləsɪs/ *noun* the process of comparing the costs and benefits of various possible ways of using available resources. Also called **benefit-cost analysis**

cost center /ˈkɒst ˌsentər/ *noun* **1.** a person or group whose costs can be itemized and to which costs can be allocated in accounts **2.** a unit, a process, or an individual that provides a service needed by another part of an organization and whose cost is therefore accepted as an overhead of the business

cost-cutting /ˈkɒst ˌkʌtɪŋ/ *noun* the process of reducing costs ○ *As a result of cost-cutting, we have had to lay off half the staff.*

cost driver /ˈkɒst ˌdraɪvər/ *noun* a factor that determines how much it costs to carry out a particular task or project, e.g., the amount of resources needed for it, or the activities involved in completing it

cost-effective /ˌkɒstɪ ˈfektɪv/ *adjective* giving good value when compared with the original cost ○ *We find advertising in the Sunday newspapers very cost-effective.*

cost-effectiveness /ˌkɒstɪ ˈfektɪvnəs/, **cost efficiency** /ˌkɒstɪ ˈfɪʃənsi/ *noun* the quality of being cost-effective ○ *Can we calculate the cost-effectiveness of air freight against shipping by sea?*

cost factor /ˈkɒst ˌfæktər/ *noun* the problem of cost

cost inflation /ˌkɒst ɪnˈfleɪʃ(ə)n/ *noun* same as **cost-push inflation**

costing /ˈkɒstɪŋ/ *noun* a calculation of the manufacturing costs, and so the selling price, of a product ○ *The costings give us a retail price of $2.95.* ○ *We cannot do the costing until we have details of all the production expenditure.*

costly /ˈkɒstli/ *adjective* costing a lot of money, or costing too much money ○ *Defending the court case was a costly process.* ○ *The mistakes were time-consuming and costly.*

cost of capital /ˌkɒst əv ˈkæpɪt(ə)l/ *noun* interest paid on the capital used in operating a business

cost of entry /ˌkɒst əv ˈentri/ *noun* the cost of going into a market for the first time

cost of goods sold /ˌkɒst əv ɡʊdz ˈsoʊld/ *noun* same as **cost of sales**

cost of living /ˌkɒst əv ˈlɪvɪŋ/ *noun* money which has to be paid for basic items such as food, heating or rent ○ *to allow for the cost of living in the salary adjustments*

cost-of-living allowance /ˌkɔst əv 'lɪvɪŋ əˌlaʊəns/ *noun* an addition to normal salary to cover increases in the cost of living. Abbreviation **COLA**

cost-of-living bonus /ˌkɔst əv 'lɪvɪŋ ˌboʊnəs/ *noun* money paid to meet an increase in the cost of living

cost-of-living increase /ˌkɔst əv 'lɪvɪŋ ˌɪnkris/ *noun* an increase in salary to allow it to keep up with the increased cost of living

cost-of-living index /ˌkɔst əv 'lɪvɪŋ ˌɪndeks/ *noun* a way of measuring the cost of living which is shown as a percentage increase on the figure for the previous year. It is similar to the consumer price index, but includes other items such as the interest on mortgages.

cost of sales /ˌkɔst əv 'seɪlz/ *noun* all the costs of a product sold, including manufacturing costs and the staff costs of the production department, before general overhead is calculated. Also called **cost of goods sold**

cost per click-through /ˌkɔst pər 'klɪk ˌθru/ *noun* a method of pricing online advertising, based on the principle that the seller gets paid whenever a visitor clicks on an advertisement

cost plus /ˌkɔst 'plʌs/ *noun* a system of calculating a price, by taking the cost of production of goods or services and adding a percentage to cover the supplier's overhead and margin ○ *We are charging for the work on a cost plus basis.*

cost price /'kɔst praɪs/ *noun* a selling price which is the same as the price, either the manufacturing price or the wholesale price, which the seller paid for the item

cost-push inflation /ˌkast 'pʊʃ ɪn ˌfleɪʃ(ə)n/ *noun* inflation caused by increased wage demands and increased raw materials costs, which lead to higher prices, which in turn lead to further wage demands. Also called **cost inflation**

costs /kɔsts/ *plural noun* the expenses involved in a court case ○ *The judge awarded costs to the defendant.* ○ *Costs of the case will be borne by the prosecution.* □ **to pay costs** to pay the expenses of a court case

cottage industry /ˌkatɪdʒ 'ɪndəstri/ *noun* the production of goods or some other type of work, carried out by people working in their own homes

cotton mill /'katən mɪl/ *noun* a factory where raw cotton is processed

council /'kaʊnsəl/ *noun* an official group chosen to run something or to advise on a problem

Council of Economic Advisers /ˌkaʊns(ə)l əv ˌikənamɪk əd'vaɪzərz/ *noun* a group of academic and industry economists who advise the President of the United States on economic matters. Abbreviation **CEA**

counsel /'kaʊnsəl/ *noun* a lawyer acting for one of the parties in a legal action ○ *defense counsel* ○ *prosecution counsel* ■ *verb* to advise □ **he counseled caution** he advised us to act carefully

counseling /'kaʊnsəlɪŋ/ *noun* the act of giving professional advice to others on personal matters ○ *An office is being set up for counseling employees who have professional or social problems.* ○ *Counseling helps employees get accustomed to their new environment, by offering advice and guidance.* (NOTE: The U.K. spelling is **counselling**.)

count /kaʊnt/ *verb* **1.** to add figures together to make a total ○ *She counted up the sales for the six months to December.* **2.** to include something ○ *Did you count my trip to New York as part of my sales expenses?*

count on *phrasal verb* to expect something to happen or to be given to you ○ *They are counting on getting a good response from the TV advertising.* ○ *Do not count on a bank loan to start your business.*

counter- /kaʊntər/ *prefix* against

counterbid /'kaʊntərbɪd/ *noun* a higher bid in reply to a previous bid ○ *When I bid $20 she put in a counterbid of $25.* ■ *verb* to make a higher bid in reply to a previous bid ○ *When I bid $20 he counterbid $25.*

counter-claim /'kaʊntər kleɪm/ *noun* a claim for damages made in reply to a previous claim ○ *Jones claimed $25,000 in damages against Smith, and Smith entered a counter-claim of $50,000 for loss of office.* ■ *verb* to put in a counter-claim for something ○ *Jones claimed $25,000 in damages and Smith counter-claimed $50,000 for loss of office.*

counterfeit /'kaʊntərfɪt/ *adjective* referring to false or imitation money ○

Shops in the area have been asked to look out for counterfeit $20 bills. ■ *verb* to make imitation money

counterfoil /'kaʊntərfɔɪl/ *noun* a slip of paper kept after writing a check, an invoice or a receipt, as a record of the deal which has taken place

countermand /ˌkaʊntər'mænd/ *verb* to say that an order must not be carried out ○ *to countermand an order*

counter-offer /'kaʊntər ˌɔfər/ *noun* a higher or lower offer made in reply to another offer ○ *Smith Inc. made an offer of $1m for the property, and Blacks replied with a counter-offer of $1.4m.*

counterpart /'kaʊntərpart/ *noun* a person who has a similar job in another company □ **John is my counterpart in Smith's** John has the same post as I have here

counterparty /'kaʊntəparti/ *noun* the other party in a deal

counter-productive /ˌkaʊntər prə'dʌktɪv/ *adjective* which has the opposite effect to what you expect ○ *Increasing overtime pay was counter-productive, the workers simply worked more slowly.* ○ *The CFO's talk about profitability was quite counter-productive, as it encouraged the employees to ask for higher wages.*

countersign /'kaʊntərsaɪn/ *verb* to sign a document which has already been signed by someone else ○ *All our checks have to be countersigned by the finance director.* ○ *The sales director countersigns all my orders.*

counter staff /'kaʊntər stæf/ *noun* sales staff who serve behind counters

countervailing duty /'kaʊntəveɪlɪŋ ˌdjuti/ *noun* a duty imposed by a country on imported goods, where the price of the goods includes a subsidy from the government in the country of origin. Also called **anti-dumping duty**

countinghouse /'kaʊntɪŋhaʊs/ *noun* a department dealing with cash (*dated*)

country /'kʌntri/ *noun* land which is separate and governs itself ○ *some African countries export oil* ○ *the Organization of Petroleum Exporting Countries* ○ *The contract covers distribution in the countries of the EU.* □ **the managing director is out of the country** she is on a business trip abroad

country of origin /ˌkʌntri əv 'ɔrɪdʒɪn/ *noun* a country where a product is manufactured or where a food product comes from ○ *All produce must be labeled to show the country of origin.*

couple /'kʌp(ə)l/ *noun* two things or people taken together ○ *We only have enough stock for a couple of weeks.* ○ *A couple of the directors were ill, so the board meeting was canceled.* □ **the negotiations lasted a couple of hours** the negotiations went on for about two hours

coupon /'kupɑn/ *noun* **1.** a piece of paper used in place of money **2.** a piece of paper which replaces an order form

coupon ad /'kupɑn æd/ *noun* an advertisement with a form attached, which you cut out and return to the advertiser with your name and address for further information

courier /'kʊriər/ *noun* a person or company which arranges to carry packages or take messages from one place another in a town ■ *verb* to send by courier ○ *We will courier the package to your hotel.*

course /kɔrs/ *noun* **1.** □ **in the course of** during or while something is happening ○ *In the course of the discussion, the managing director explained the company's expansion plans.* ○ *Sales have risen sharply in the course of the last few months.* **2.** a series of lessons or a program of instruction ○ *She has finished her secretarial course.* ○ *The company has paid for her to attend a course for trainee sales managers.* ○ *Management trainees all took a six-month course in business studies.* ○ *The training officer was constantly on the lookout for new courses in management studies.* ○ *The company sent her on a management course.* **3.** □ **of course** naturally ○ *Of course the company is interested in profits.* ○ *Are you willing to go on a sales trip to Australia? – Of course!*

court /kɔrt/ *noun* a place where a judge listens to a case and decides legally which of the parties in the argument is right □ **to take someone to court** to tell someone to appear in court to settle an argument

court case /'kɔrt keɪs/ *noun* a legal action or trial

court order /ˌkɔrt 'ɔrdər/ *noun* a legal order made by a court, telling someone to do or not to do something

covenant /'kʌvənənt/ *noun* a legal contract ■ *verb* to agree to pay annually a specified sum of money to a person or organization by contract. When payments are made under covenant to a charity, the charity can reclaim the tax paid by the donee. ○ *to covenant to pay $10 per annum*

Coventry /'kɑvəntri/ □ **to send someone to Coventry** to refuse to speak to or to have any dealings with someone, especially a fellow-worker ○ *After he told the management about the thefts, the other workers sent him to Coventry.* ○ *Workers who carried on working were sent to Coventry after the strike ended.*

cover /'kʌvər/ *noun* **1.** the proportion of a target audience reached by advertising **2.** the protection guaranteed by insurance □ **to operate without adequate cover** to operate without being protected by enough insurance □ **to ask for additional cover** to ask the insurance company to increase the amount for which you are insured **3.** an amount of money large enough to guarantee that something can be paid for ○ *Do you have sufficient cover for this loan?* **4.** □ **to send something under separate cover** in a separate envelope □ **to send a magazine under plain cover** in an ordinary envelope with no company name printed on it ■ *verb* **1.** to provide protection by insurance against something ○ *The insurance covers fire, theft and loss of work.* □ **the damage was covered by the insurance** the damage was of a kind that the insurance policy protects against or the insurance company paid enough money to enable the damage to be repaired □ **to be fully covered** to have insurance against all risks **2.** to have, earn or provide enough money to pay for something ○ *We do not make enough sales to cover the expense of running the store.* ○ *Break-even point is reached when sales cover all costs.* □ **to cover a position** to have enough money to be able to pay for a forward purchase **3.** to earn enough money to pay for costs, expenses, etc. ○ *We do not make enough sales to cover the expense of running the store.* ○ *Break-even point is reached when sales cover all costs.* □ **the dividend is covered four times** profits are four times the dividend paid out **4.** to ask for security against a loan which you are making

"...three export credit agencies have agreed to provide cover for large projects in Nigeria" [*Business Times (Lagos)*]

coverage /'kʌv(ə)rɪdʒ/ *noun* protection guaranteed by insurance ○ *Do you have coverage against fire damage?*

cover charge /'kʌvər tʃɑrdʒ/ *noun* (*in restaurants*) a charge for a place at the table in addition to the charge for food

cover letter /'kʌvər ˌletər/ *noun* a letter sent with documents to say why they are being sent ○ *She sent a cover letter with her résumé, explaining why she wanted the job.* ○ *The job advertisement asked for a résumé and a cover letter.*

cover note /'kʌvər noʊt/ *noun* **1.** a letter from an insurance company giving details of an insurance policy and confirming that the policy exists **2.** same as **cover letter**

cowboy /'kaʊbɔɪ/ *noun* a workman who does bad work and charges a high price ○ *The people we got in to repaint the office were a couple of cowboys.*

cowboy outfit /'kaʊbɔɪ ˌaʊtfɪt/ *noun* company which does bad work and charges high prices

CPI *abbreviation* Consumer Price Index

Cr, CR *abbreviation* credit

cradle-to-grave /ˌkreɪd(ə)l tə 'greɪv/ *adjective* used to describe a company's obligation to monitor the production, transport, use, and disposal of specific hazardous materials in order to comply with environmental regulations

crane /kreɪn/ *noun* a machine for lifting heavy objects ○ *The container slipped as the crane was lifting it onto the ship.* ○ *They had to hire a crane to get the machine into the factory.*

crash /kræʃ/ *noun* a financial collapse ○ *The financial crash caused several bankruptcies.* ○ *He lost all his money in the crash of 1929.* ■ *verb* to collapse financially ○ *The company crashed with debts of over $1 million.*

crash-test /'kræʃ test/ *verb* to establish the safety and reliability of something by testing it in different ways

crate /kreɪt/ *noun* a large wooden box ○ *a crate of oranges* ■ *verb* to put goods into crates

creaming /'krimɪŋ/ *noun* the act of fixing a high price for a product in order to achieve high short-term profits

create /kri'eɪt/ *verb* to make something new ○ *By acquiring small unprofitable companies he soon created a large manufacturing group.* ○ *The government program aims at creating new jobs for young people.*

creation /kri'eɪʃ(ə)n/ *noun* the process of making something

creative /kri'eɪtɪv/ *noun* someone who works in the conceptual or artistic side of a business

creative accounting /kri,eɪtɪv ə'kaʊntɪŋ/ *noun* an adaptation of a company's figures to present a better picture than is correct, usually intended to make a company more attractive to a potential buyer, or done for some other reason which may not be strictly legal

COMMENT: Creative accounting is the term used to cover a number of accounting practices which, although legal, may be used to mislead banks, investors, and shareholders about the profitability or liquidity of a business.

creative destruction /kri,eɪtɪv dɪ'strʌkʃ(ə)n/ *noun* a term used to describe the process in which in existing goods, services, or organizations are replaced by new ones as a result of innovation (NOTE: The term was very popular during the dot-com boom of the late 1990s and early 2000s.)

creative director /kri,eɪtɪv daɪ'rektər/ *noun* an employee of an advertising agency who is in overall charge of finding the right words and images to promote the product during an advertising campaign

creative selling /kri,eɪtɪv 'selɪŋ/ *noun* a sales technique where the main emphasis is on generating new business

creativity /,kri.eɪ'tɪvəti/, **creative thinking** /kri,eɪtɪv 'θɪŋkɪŋ/ *noun* **1.** the ability to use the imagination to produce new ideas or things **2.** the ability to generate new ideas, especially by taking a fresh and imaginative approach to old problems or existing procedures (NOTE: Creativity is considered important not just in the development of new products and services, but also in organizational decision-making and problem-solving, and many organizations try to encourage it through their corporate culture and by using techniques such as brainstorming and lateral thinking.)

crèche /kreʃ/ *noun U.K.* same as **day care center**

credentials /krɪ'denʃəlz/ *plural noun* letters or documents which describe a person's qualities and skills ○ *The new production manager has very impressive credentials.*

credere /'kreɪdəri/ *noun* ♦ **del credere agent**

credibility /,kredɪ'bɪləti/ *noun* the state of being trusted

credibility gap /,kredɪ'bɪləti ,gæp/ *noun* a discrepancy between claims for a product made by the manufacturer and acceptance of these claims by the target audience ○ *The credibility gap that we face is partly due to our product's bad performance record.* ◊ **source credibility**

credit /'kredɪt/ *noun* **1.** a period of time allowed before a customer has to pay a debt incurred for goods or services ○ *to give someone six months' credit* ○ *to sell on good credit terms* □ **letter of credit (L or C)** a letter from a bank, allowing someone credit and promising to repay at a later date □ **to open a line of credit, a credit line** to make credit available to someone □ **on credit** without paying immediately ○ *to live on credit* ○ *We buy everything on sixty days' credit.* ○ *The company exists on credit from its suppliers.* **2.** an amount entered in accounts to show a decrease in assets or expenses or an increase in liabilities, revenue, or capital. In accounts, credits are entered in the right-hand column. ○ *to enter $100 to someone's credit* ○ *to pay in $100 to the credit of Mr. Smith* Compare **debit** □ **account in credit** an account where the credits are higher than the debits **3.** an amount that can be subtracted directly to reduce an individual's income tax liability ■ *verb* to put money into someone's account, or to note money received in an account ○ *to credit an account with $100* or *to credit $100 to an account*

credit account /'kredɪt ə,kaʊnt/ *noun U.K.* same as **charge account**

credit agency /'kredɪt ,eɪdʒənsi/ *noun* a company which reports on the creditworthiness of customers to show whether they should be allowed credit

credit balance /'kredɪt ,bæləns/ *noun* a balance in an account showing that more money has been received than is owed ○ *The account has a credit balance of $100.*

credit bank /'kredɪt bæŋk/ *noun* a bank which lends money

credit bureau /'kredɪt ˌbjʊroʊ/ *noun* a company used by businesses and banks to assess the creditworthiness of people

credit card /'kredɪt kɑrd/ *noun* a card issued to customers by a store, bank, or other organization, used to charge purchases to an account for later payment. Also called **charge card**

credit card holder /'kredɪt ˌhoʊldər/ *noun* **1.** a person who has a credit card **2.** a plastic wallet for keeping credit cards

credit card sale /'kredɪt kɑrd ˌseɪl/ *noun* the act of selling where the buyer uses a credit card to pay

credit column /'kredɪt ˌkɑləm/ *noun* the right-hand column in accounts showing money received

credit control /'kredɪt kənˌtroʊl/ *noun* a check that customers pay on time and do not owe more than their credit limit

credit controller /'kredɪt kənˌtroʊlər/ *noun* a member of staff whose job is to try to get payment of overdue invoices

credit entry /'kredɪt ˌentri/ *noun* an entry on the credit side of an account

credit facilities /'kredɪt fəˌsɪlətiz/ *plural noun* an arrangement with a bank or supplier to have credit so as to buy goods

credit freeze /'kredɪt friz/ *noun* a period when lending by banks is restricted by the government

credit history /'kredɪt ˌhɪst(ə)ri/ *noun* a record of how a potential borrower has repaid his or her previous debts

"…failed to consider numerous factors, such as an applicant's credit history and ability to repay based on income." [*Economist*]

credit limit /'kredɪt ˌlɪmɪt/ *noun* the largest amount of money which a customer can borrow □ **he has exceeded his credit limit** he has borrowed more money than he is allowed to

credit note /'kredɪt noʊt/ *noun* a note showing that money is owed to a customer ○ *The company sent the wrong order and so had to issue a credit note.* Abbreviation **C/N**

creditor /'kredɪtər/ *noun* a person or company that is owed money, i.e. a company's creditors are its liabilities

creditors /'kredɪtərz/ *noun* a list of all liabilities in a set of accounts, including overdrafts, amounts owing to other companies in the group, trade creditors, payments received on account for goods not yet supplied, etc.

creditors' meeting /'kredɪtərz ˌmitɪŋ/ *noun* a meeting of all the people to whom an insolvent company owes money, to decide how to obtain the money owed

credit rating /'kredɪt ˌreɪtɪŋ/ *noun* an amount which a credit agency feels a customer will be able to repay

credit rating agency /ˌkredɪt 'reɪtɪŋ ˌeɪdʒənsi/ *noun* a company used by businesses and banks to assess the creditworthiness of people

credit-reference agency /'kredɪt ˌrefər(ə)ns ˌeɪdʒənsi/ *noun U.K.* same as **credit bureau**

credit references /'kredɪt ˌrefər(ə)nsɪz/ *plural noun* details of persons, companies or banks who have given credit to a person or company in the past, supplied as references when opening a charge account with a new supplier

credit sale /'kredɪt seɪl/ *noun* a sale where the purchaser will pay for the goods bought at a later date

credit side /'kredɪt saɪd/ *noun* the right-hand column of accounts showing money received

credit squeeze /'kredɪt skwiz/ *noun* a period when lending by the banks is restricted by the government

credit system /'kredɪt ˌsɪstəm/ *noun* the system that governs the way that loans are made to people and organizations, especially the regulations that relate to loans and to organizations that provide loans

credit transfer /'kredɪt ˌtrænsfɜr/ *noun* an act of moving money from one account to another

credit union /'kredɪt ˌjunjən/ *noun* a group of people who pay in regular deposits or subscriptions which earn interest and are used to make loans to other members of the group

creditworthiness /'kredɪtˌwɜrðinəs/ *noun* the ability of a customer to pay for goods bought on credit

creditworthy /'kredɪtwɜrði/ *adjective* having enough money to be able to buy goods on credit ○ *We will do some checks on her to see if she is creditworthy.*

crew /kruː/ *noun* a group of people who work on a plane, ship, etc. ○ *The ship carries a crew of 250.*

crime /kraɪm/ *noun* an act which is against the law ○ *Crimes in supermarkets have risen by 25%.*

criminal /'krɪmɪn(ə)l/ *adjective* illegal ○ *Misappropriation of funds is a criminal act.*

criminal action /ˌkrɪmɪn(ə)l 'ækʃən/ *noun* a court case brought by the state against someone who is charged with a crime

criminal negligence /ˌkrɪmɪn(ə)l 'neglɪdʒəns/ *noun* failure to do a duty with the result that harm is done to the interests of people

criminal record /ˌkrɪmɪn(ə)l 'rekɔːd/ *noun* same as **police record**

crisis /'kraɪsɪs/ *noun* a serious economic situation where decisions have to be taken rapidly ○ *a banking crisis* ○ *The government stepped in to try to resolve the international crisis.* ○ *Withdrawals from the bank have reached crisis level.* □ **to take crisis measures** to take severe measures rapidly to stop a crisis developing

crisis management /'kraɪsɪs ˌmænɪdʒmənt/ *noun* **1.** management of a business or a country's economy during a period of crisis **2.** actions taken by an organization to protect itself when unexpected events or situations occur that could threaten its success or continued operation (NOTE: Crisis situations may result from external factors such as the development of a new product by a competitor or changes in legislation, or from internal factors such as a product failure or faulty decision-making, and often involve the need to make quick decisions on the basis of uncertain or incomplete information.)

critical mass /ˌkrɪtɪk(ə)l 'mæs/ *noun* the point at which an organization or a project is generating enough income or has gained a large enough market share to be able to survive on its own or to be worth investing more money or resources in

critical path analysis¹ /ˌkrɪtɪk(ə)l 'pæθ əˌnæləsɪs/ *noun* **1.** an analysis of the way a project is organized in terms of the minimum time it will take to complete,

calculating which parts can be delayed without holding up the rest of the project **2.** same as **critical-path method**

critical path analysis² /ˌkrɪtɪk(ə)l 'pæθ əˌnæləsɪs/ *noun* the analysis of the way a project is organised in terms of the minimum time it will take to complete, calculating which parts can be delayed without holding up the rest of the project. Abbreviation **CPM**

critical-path method /ˌkrɪtɪk(ə)l 'pæθ ˌmeθəd/ *noun* a technique used in project management to identify the activities within a project that are critical to its success, usually by showing on a diagram or flow chart the order in which activities must be carried out so that the project can be completed in the shortest time and at the least cost

"…need initial project designs to be more complex or need to generate Critical Path Method charts or PERT reports." [*InformationWeek*]

critical restructuring /ˌkrɪtɪk(ə)l riː'strʌktʃərɪŋ/ *noun* major changes in the economy or society that lead to a basic reshaping of previous forms of organization

critical success factors /ˌkrɪtɪk(ə)l sək'ses ˌfæktəz/ *plural noun* the aspects of a business that are considered to be most necessary for it to be able to achieve its aims and continue to operate successfully over time

criticize /'krɪtɪsaɪz/ *verb* to say that something or someone is wrong or is working badly ○ *The sales manager criticized the sales force for not improving the volume of sales.* ○ *The design of the new catalog has been criticized.*

CRM *abbreviation* customer relations management *or* customer relationship management

cross /krɒs/ *verb*
    cross off *phrasal verb* to remove something from a list ○ *He crossed my name off his list.* ○ *You can cross him off our mailing list.*
    cross out *phrasal verb* to put a line through something which has been written ○ *She crossed out $250 and put in $500.*

cross holding /'krɒs ˌhəʊldɪŋz/ *noun* a situation where two companies own stock in each other in order to stop either from being taken over ○ *The two compa-*

nies have protected themselves from take-over by a system of cross holdings.

cross rate /ˈkrɔs reɪt/ *noun* an exchange rate between two currencies expressed in a third currency

cross-selling /ˌkrɔs ˈselɪŋ/ *noun* the selling of a new product which goes with another product a customer has already bought

crude (oil) /ˈkrud ɔɪl/ *noun* raw petroleum, taken from the ground ○ *The price for Arabian crude has slipped.*

crude petroleum /ˌkrud pəˈtrouliəm/ *noun* raw petroleum which has not been processed

cryptography /ˌkrɪpˈtɑgrəfi/ *noun* the use of codes and ciphers, especially as a way of restricting access to part or all of a website, so that only a user with a key can read the information

CTM /ˌsi ti ˈem/ *noun* click through per thousand. ◊ **click-through rate**

CTR /kənˈtroʊl/ *abbreviation* click-through rate

cubic /ˈkjubɪk/ *adjective* measured in volume by multiplying length, depth and width ○ *The crate holds six cubic meters.*

cubic measure /ˌkjubɪk ˈmeʒər/ *noun* volume measured in cubic feet or meters, calculated by multiplying height, width and length

cue /kju/ *noun* a factor that makes a high-value product different from an ordinary commodity

cum /kʌm/ *preposition* with

cum dividend /kʌm ˈdɪvɪdend/, **cum div** *adverb* including the next dividend still to be paid

cumulative /ˈkjumjəˌleɪtɪv/ *adjective* added to regularly over a period of time

cumulative interest /ˌkjumjəleɪtɪv ˈɪntrəst/ *noun* the interest which is added to the capital each year

cumulative preferred stock /ˌkjumjʊlətɪv prɪˌfɜrd ˈstɑk/ *noun* a preferred stock which will have the dividend paid at a later date even if the company is not able to pay a dividend in the current year

curb exchange /ˈkɜrb ɪksˌtʃeɪndʒ/ same as **American Stock Exchange**

currency /ˈkʌrənsi/ *noun* **1.** money in coins and bills which is used in a particular country **2.** a foreign currency, the currency of another country (NOTE: **Currency** has no plural when it refers to the money of one country: *He was arrested trying to take currency out of the country.*)

currency backing /ˈkʌrənsi ˌbækɪŋ/ *noun* gold or government securities which maintain the strength of a currency

currency basket /ˈkʌrənsi ˌbæskət/ *noun* a group of currencies, each of which is weighted, calculated together as a single unit against which another currency can be measured

currency note /ˈkʌrənsi noʊt/ *noun* a bank bill

currency reserves /ˈkʌrənsi rɪˌzɜrvz/ *noun* foreign money held by a government to support its own currency and to pay its debts

current /ˈkʌrənt/ *adjective* referring to the present time ○ *the current round of wage negotiations*

current account /ˈkʌrənt əˌkaʊnt/ *noun* **1.** an account of the balance of payments of a country relating to the sale or purchase of raw materials, goods, and invisibles **2.** *U.K.* same as **checking account**

current assets /ˌkʌrənt ˈæsets/ *plural noun* the assets used by a company in its ordinary work, e.g., materials, finished goods, cash and monies due, and which are held for a short time only

current cost accounting /ˌkʌrənt ˈkɔst əˌkaʊntɪŋ/ *noun* a method of accounting which notes the cost of replacing assets at current prices, rather than valuing assets at their original cost. Abbreviation **CCA**

current liabilities /ˌkʌrənt laɪəˈbɪlətiz/ *plural noun* the debts which a company has to pay within the next accounting period. In a company's annual accounts, these would be debts which must be paid within the year and are usually payments for goods or services received.

currently /ˈkʌrəntli/ *adverb* at the present time ○ *We are currently negotiating with the bank for a loan.*

current price /ˌkʌrənt ˈpraɪs/ *noun* today's price

current rate of exchange /ˌkʌrənt reɪt əv ɪksˈtʃeɪndʒ/ *noun* today's rate of exchange

current yield /ˌkʌrənt 'jild/ *noun* a dividend calculated as a percentage of the current price of a stock on the stock market

curriculum vitae /kəˌrɪkjələm 'viːtaɪ/ *noun U.K.* same as **résumé**

curve /kɜrv/ *noun* a line which is not straight, e.g., a line on a graph ○ *The graph shows an upward curve.*

cushion /'kʊʃ(ə)n/ *noun* money which allows a company to pay interest on its borrowings or to survive a loss ○ *We have sums on deposit which are a useful cushion when cash flow is tight.*

custom /'kʌstəm/ *noun* **1.** a thing which is usually done ○ *It is the custom of the book trade to allow unlimited returns for credit.* □ **the customs of the trade** the general way of working in a trade **2.** *U.K.* same as **patronage**

custom-built /'kʌstəm bɪlt/ *adjective* made specially for one customer ○ *He drives a custom-built Rolls Royce.*

customer /'kʌstəmər/ *noun* a person or company that buys goods ○ *The store was full of customers.* ○ *Can you serve this customer first please?* ○ *She's a regular customer of ours.* (NOTE: The customer may not be the consumer or end user of the product.)

customer appeal /'kʌstəmər əˌpiːl/ *noun* what attracts customers to a product

customer capital /ˌkʌstəmər 'kæpɪt(ə)l/ *noun* an organization's relationships with its customers considered as a business asset

customer care /ˌkʌstəmər 'keər/ *noun* the activity of looking after customers, so that they do not become dissatisfied

customer-centric model /ˌkʌstəmər 'sentrɪk ˌmɑd(ə)l/ *noun* a business model that is based on an assessment of what the customer needs

customer focus /ˌkʌstəmər 'foʊkəs/ *noun* the aiming of all marketing operations toward the customer

customer loyalty /ˌkʌstəmər 'lɔɪəlti/ *noun* the feeling of customers who always shop at the same store

customer profile /ˌkʌstəmər 'proʊfaɪl/ *noun* a description of an average customer for a product or service ○ *The customer profile shows our average buyer to be male, aged 25–30, and employed in the service industries.*

customer profitability /ˌkʌstəmər ˌprɑfɪtə'bɪləti/ *noun* the amount of profit generated by each individual customer. Usually a small percentage of customers generate the most profit.

customer relationship management /ˌkʌstəmər rɪ'leɪʃ(ə)nʃɪp ˌmænɪdʒmənt/ *noun* an approach to management that focuses on building and maintaining long-term relationships with customers through the use of, e.g., loyalty cards, special credit cards and Internet contacts. Abbreviation **CRM**

customer relations management /ˌkʌstəmər rɪ'leɪʃ(ə)nʃɪp ˌmænɪdʒmənt/, **customer relationship management** *noun* the management of relations between a company and its customers, keeping them informed of new products or services and dealing sympathetically with their complaints or inquiries. Abbreviation **CRM**

customer satisfaction /ˌkʌstəmər ˌsætɪs'fækʃən/ *noun* the act of making customers pleased with what they have bought

customer service /ˌkʌstəmər 'sɜrvɪs/ *noun* a service given to customers once they have made their decision to buy, including delivery, after-sales service, installation, training, etc.

customer service department /ˌkʌstəmər 'sɜrvɪs dɪˌpɑrtmənt/ *noun* a department which deals with customers and their complaints and orders

customization *noun* the process of making changes to products or services that enable them to satisfy the particular needs of individual customers

customize *verb* to change something to fit the special needs of a customer ○ *We use customized computer terminals.*

customs /'kʌstəmz/ *plural noun* the government department which organizes the collection of taxes on imports, or an office of this department at a port or airport ○ *He was stopped by customs.* ○ *Her car was searched by customs.* □ **to go through customs** to pass through the area of a port or airport where customs officials examine goods □ **to take something through customs** to carry something illegal through a customs area without declaring it □ **the crates had to go through a customs ex-**

amination the crates had to be examined by customs officials

customs barrier /'kʌstəmz ˌbæriər/ noun customs duty intended to make trade more difficult

customs broker /'kʌstəmz ˌbroʊkər/ noun a person or company that takes goods through customs for a shipping company

customs clearance /'kʌstəmz ˌklɪrəns/ noun 1. the act of passing goods through customs so that they can enter or leave the country 2. a document given by customs to a shipper to show that customs duty has been paid and the goods can be shipped ○ to wait for customs clearance

customs declaration /'kʌstəmz dekləˌreɪʃ(ə)n/ noun a statement showing goods being imported on which duty will have to be paid ○ to fill in a customs declaration form

customs duty /'kʌstəmz ˌdjuti/ noun a tax on goods imported into a country

customs entry point /ˌkʌstəmz 'entri ˌpɔɪnt/ noun a place at a border between two countries where goods are declared to customs

customs examination /'kʌstəmz ɪɡˌzæmɪneɪʃ(ə)n/ noun an inspection of goods or baggage by customs officials

customs formalities /'kʌstəmz fɔr ˌmælɪtiz/ plural noun a declaration of goods by the shipper and examination of them by customs

customs officer /'kʌstəmz ˌɒfɪsər/ noun a person working for the Customs and Excise Department

customs official /'kʌstəmz əˌfɪʃ(ə)l/ noun a person working for the Customs and Excise Department

customs seal /'kʌstəmz sil/ noun a seal attached by a customs officer to a box, to show that the contents have not passed through customs

customs tariff /'kʌstəmz ˌtærɪf/ noun a list of taxes to be paid on imported goods

customs union /'kʌstəmz ˌjunjən/ noun an agreement between several countries that goods can travel between them, without paying duty, while goods from other countries have to pay special duties

cut /kʌt/ noun 1. the sudden lowering of a price, salary or the number of jobs ○ price cuts or cuts in prices □ he took a cut in salary, he took a salary cut he accepted a lower salary 2. a share in a payment ○ She introduces new customers and gets a cut of the sales rep's commission. ■ verb 1. to lower something suddenly ○ We are cutting prices on all our models. ○ We have taken out the second telephone line in order to try to cut costs. □ to cut (back) production to reduce the quantity of products made 2. to reduce the number of something □ to cut jobs to reduce the number of jobs by making people redundant □ he cut his losses he stopped doing something which was creating a loss

"…state-owned banks cut their prime rates a percentage point to 11%" [Wall Street Journal]

"…the U.S. bank announced a cut in its prime from 10½ per cent to 10 per cent" [Financial Times]

"Opec has on average cut production by one third since 1979" [Economist]

cut in phrasal verb □ to cut someone in on a deal to give someone a share in the profits of a deal (informal)

cut down (on) phrasal verb to reduce suddenly the amount of something used ○ The government is cutting down on welfare expenditure. ○ The office is trying to cut down on electricity consumption. ○ We have installed networked computers to cut down on paperwork.

cutback /'kʌtbæk/ noun a reduction ○ cutbacks in government spending

cut-price /ˌkʌt 'praɪs/ adjective sold at a cheaper price than usual ○ He made his money selling cut-price goods in the local market. ○ You can get cut-price gasoline in some gasoline stations near the border.

cut-price store /ˌkʌt praɪs 'stɔr/ noun a store selling cut-price goods

cut-throat competition /ˌkʌt θroʊt ˌkɒmpə'tɪʃ(ə)n/ noun sharp competition which cuts prices and offers high discounts

cutting /'kʌtɪŋ/ noun U.K. same as **clipping**

cutting-edge /ˌkʌtɪŋ 'edʒ/ adjective using or involving the latest and most advanced techniques and technologies

CV abbreviation curriculum vitae ○ Please apply in writing, enclosing a current CV.

CWO abbreviation cash with order

CXO *noun* any executive or senior officer of a corporation

cybercrime /'saɪbəkraɪm/ *noun* a crime committed using the Internet

"…the treaty…names four types of cybercrime: confidentiality offenses, notably breaking into computers; fraud and forgery; content violations, such as child pornography and racism; and copyright offenses."

cyber mall /'saɪbər mɔl/ *noun* a website that provides information and links for a number of online businesses

cybernetics /ˌsaɪbər'netɪks/ *plural noun* the study of information communication systems and how they can be improved (NOTE: takes a singular verb)

cybershopping /'saɪbəˌʃɑpɪŋ/ *noun* the activity of making purchases using the Internet

cycle /'saɪk(ə)l/ *noun* a set of events which happen in a regularly repeated sequence

cyclical /'sɪklɪk(ə)l/ *adjective* happening in cycles

cyclical factors /ˌsɪklɪk(ə)l 'fæktərz/ *plural noun* the way in which a trade cycle affects businesses

cyclicals /'sɪklɪk(ə)lz/ *plural noun* stock that moves up and down in cycles

"…consumer cyclicals such as general retailers should in theory suffer from rising interest rates. And food retailers in particular have cyclical exposure without price power" [*Investors Chronicle*]

D

daily /'deɪli/ *adjective* done every day □ **daily production of cars** number of cars produced each day □ **daily interest, interest calculated daily** *or* **on a daily basis** a rate of interest calculated each day and added to the principal

daily consumption /ˌdeɪli kən'sʌmpʃən/ *noun* an amount used each day

daily sales returns /ˌdeɪli 'seɪlz rɪˌtɜrnz/ *plural noun* reports of sales made each day

damage /'dæmɪdʒ/ *noun* harm done to things □ **fire damage** damage caused by a fire □ **storm damage** damage caused by a storm □ **to suffer damage** to be harmed ○ *We are trying to assess the damage which the shipment suffered in transit.* □ **to cause damage** to harm something ○ *The fire caused damage estimated at $100,000.* ■ *verb* to harm ○ *the storm damaged the cargo* ○ *They are holding a sale of stock which has been damaged by water.*

damaged /'dæmɪdʒd/ *adjective* which has suffered damage or which has been harmed ○ *goods damaged in transit*

damages /'dæmɪdʒɪz/ *plural noun* money claimed as compensation for harm done ○ *to claim $1000 in damages* ○ *to be liable for damages* ○ *to pay $25,000 in damages* □ **to bring an action for damages against someone** to take someone to court and claim damages

damage survey /'dæmɪdʒ ˌsɜrveɪ/ *noun* a report on the amount of damage done

damp /dæmp/ *verb*

  damp down *phrasal verb* to reduce ○ *to damp down demand for domestic consumption of oil*

D & B *abbreviation* Dun & Bradstreet

danger /'deɪndʒər/ *noun* **1.** the possibility of being harmed or killed ○ *The old machinery poses a danger to the work force.* ○ *The red light means danger.* **2.** the likelihood or possibility of something □ **there is no danger of the sales force leaving** it is not likely that the sales force will leave □ **in danger of** which may easily happen ○ *She is in danger of being dismissed* ○ *The company is in danger of being taken over.*

dangerous /'deɪndʒərəs/ *adjective* which can be harmful □ **dangerous job** a job where the workers may be hurt or killed

danger pay /'deɪndʒər ˌpeɪ/ *noun* extra money paid to employees in dangerous jobs ○ *The work force has stopped work and asked for danger pay.* ○ *He decided to go to work on an oil rig because of the danger pay offered as an incentive.*

DARC *abbreviation* Defense Acquisition Regulations Council

data /'deɪtə/ *noun* information available on computer, e.g., letters or figures ○ *All important data on employees was fed into the computer.* ○ *To calculate the weekly wages, you need data on hours worked and rates of pay.* (NOTE: takes a singular or plural verb)

data acquisition /'deɪtə ækwɪˌzɪʃ(ə)n/ *noun* the act of gathering information about a subject

data bank /'deɪtə bæŋk/ *noun* a store of information in a computer

database /'deɪtəbeɪs/ *noun* a set of data stored in an organized way in a computer system ○ *We can extract the lists of potential customers from our database.*

database management system /ˌdeɪtəbeɪs 'mænɪdʒmənt ˌsɪstəm/ *noun* a computer program that is specially designed to organize and process the information contained in a database

database modeling /'deɪtəbeɪs ˌmɑd(ə)lɪŋ/ *noun* using the information from a database to create a website or to forecast trends in a market

data capture /ˈdeɪtə ˌkæptʃər/, **data entry** /ˌdeɪtə ˈentri/ *noun* the act of putting information onto a computer by keyboarding or by scanning

data cartridge /ˈdeɪtə ˌkɑrtrɪdʒ/ *noun* a stiff box with magnetic tape inside, used for recording data from a computer ○ *Copy the information from the computer onto a cartridge.*

data mining /ˈdeɪtə ˌmaɪnɪŋ/ *noun* the use of advanced software to search online databases and identify statistical patterns or relationships in the data that may be commercially useful

"…it used decision-science-based analytical tools and database marketing. This deep data mining has succeeded because Harrah's has simultaneously maintained its focus on satisfying its customers." [*Harvard Business Review*]

data processing /ˌdeɪtə ˈprɑsesɪŋ/ *noun* the act of selecting and examining data in a computer to produce information in a special form

data protection /ˈdeɪtə prəˌtekʃən/ *noun* **1.** making sure that computerized information about people is not misused **2.** the safeguards that protect people whose personal details are held on computers or in paper-based filing systems against improper use or storage of the data that relates to them (NOTE: The growing use of computers to store information about individuals has led many countries to pass laws designed to protect the privacy of individuals and prevent the disclosure of information to unauthorized people.)

data retrieval /ˌdeɪtə rɪˈtriːv(ə)l/ *noun* the act of getting information from the data stored in a computer

data transfer /ˌdeɪtə trænsˈfɜr/ *noun* **1.** the action or process of moving data from one location to another, e.g., of downloading data from a website onto a computer **2.** the amount of data downloaded from a website (NOTE: This information can be useful as a way measuring the number of visitors a website receives.)

data warehouse /ˈdeɪtə ˌwerhaʊs/ *noun* a large collection data that is collected over a period of time from different sources and stored on a computer in a standard format so that is easy to retrieve.

It can be used, e.g., to support managerial decision-making. (NOTE: Organizations often use data warehouses for marketing purposes, for example, in order to store and analyze customer information.)

data warehousing /ˈdeɪtə ˌwerhaʊzɪŋ/ *noun* the process of collecting data into a data warehouse for use in analyzing business strategy

date /deɪt/ *noun* **1.** the number of the day, month, and year ○ *I have received your letter of yesterday's date.* □ **date of receipt** the date when something is received **2.** □ **to date** up to now □ **interest to date** interest up to the present time **3.** □ **up to date** current, recent or modern ○ *an up-to-date computer system* **4.** □ **out of date** old-fashioned, no longer modern ○ *Their computer system is years out of date.* ○ *They are still using out-of-date machinery.* ■ *verb* to put a date on a document ○ *The check was dated March 24th.* ○ *You forgot to date the check.* □ **to date a check forward** *U.K.* to put a later date than the present one on a check

date coding /ˈdeɪt ˌkoʊdɪŋ/ *noun* the act of showing the date by which a product should be consumed

dated /ˈdeɪtɪd/ *adjective* **1.** with a date written on it ○ *Thank you for your letter dated June 15th.* **2.** out-of-date ○ *The unions have criticized management for its dated ideas.*

date of bill /ˌdeɪt əv ˈbɪl/ *noun* a date when a bill will mature

date of maturity /ˌdeɪt əv məˈtʃʊrɪti/ *noun* same as **maturity date**

date stamp /ˈdeɪt stæmp/ *noun* a stamp with rubber figures which can be moved, used for marking the date on documents

day /deɪ/ *noun* **1.** a period of 24 hours ○ *There are thirty days in June.* ○ *The first day of the month is a public vacation.* □ **days of grace** the time given to a debtor to repay a loan, to pay the amount purchased using a credit card, or to pay an insurance premium ○ *Let's send the check at once since we have only five days of grace left.* ○ *Because the store owner has so little cash available, we will have to allow him additional days of grace.* **2.** a period of work from morning to night □ **she works three days on, two days off** she works for three days, then has two days' vacation □

to work an eight-hour day to spend eight hours at work each day 3. one of the days of the week

day book /'deɪ bʊk/ *noun* a book with an account of sales and purchases made each day

day-care /'deɪ ker/ *noun* a provision of care for small children while their parents are at work ○ *One of the fringe benefits of the job was a free day care centre.* ○ *The excellent day care facilities in the area have increased the availability of staff.*

day care center /'deɪ ker ˌsentər/ *noun* a special room or building on a company's premises where babies and small children can be looked after ○ *The company provides a day care center for its staff.* Compare **nursery**

day in the sun /ˌdeɪ ɪn ðə 'sʌn/ *noun* the period of time during which a product is in demand and sells well in the marketplace (*informal*)

day release /ˌdeɪ rɪ'liːs/ *noun* an arrangement where a company allows an employee to go to college to study for one or two days each week ○ *The junior sales manager is attending a day release course.*

day shift /'deɪ ʃɪft/ *noun* a shift worked during the daylight hours

day-to-day /ˌdeɪ tə 'deɪ/ *adjective* ordinary or going on all the time ○ *He organizes the day-to-day running of the company.* ○ *Sales only just cover the day-to-day expenses.*

day trader /'deɪ ˌtreɪdər/ *noun* a person who buys stock and sells it within the same day

day trading /'deɪ ˌtreɪdɪŋ/ *noun* the activity of buying stock and selling it within the same day

day work /'deɪ wɜrk/ *noun* work done during a day

day worker /'deɪ ˌwɜrkər/ *noun* a person who works the day shift

DCF *abbreviation* discounted cash flow

dead /ded/ *adjective* not working □ **the line went dead** the telephone line suddenly stopped working

dead account /ˌded ə'kaʊnt/ *noun* an account which is no longer used

dead capital /ˌded 'kæpɪt(ə)l/ *noun* money which is not invested to make a profit

dead-cat bounce /ˌded kæt 'baʊns/ *noun* a slight rise in a stock price after a sharp fall, showing that some investors are still interested in buying the stock at the lower price, although further sharp falls will follow

dead end /ˌded 'end/ *noun* a point where you cannot go any further forward ○ *Negotiations have reached a dead end.*

dead end job /ˌded end 'dʒɒb/ *noun* a job where there are no chances of promotion

dead freight /ˌded 'freɪt/ *noun* payment by a charterer for unfilled space in a ship or plane ○ *Too much dead freight is making it impossible for the company to continue to charter ships.*

deadline /'dedlaɪn/ *noun* the date by which something has to be done □ **to meet a deadline** to finish something in time □ **to miss a deadline** to finish something later than it was planned ○ *We've missed our October 1st deadline.*

deadlock /'dedlɒk/ *noun* a point where two sides in a dispute cannot agree ○ *The negotiations have reached deadlock or a deadlock.* □ **to break a deadlock** to find a way to start discussions again after being at a point where no agreement was possible ■ *verb* to be unable to agree to continue negotiations □ **talks have been deadlocked for ten days** after ten days the talks have not produced any agreement

dead loss /ˌded 'lɒs/ *noun* a total loss ○ *The car was written off as a dead loss.*

dead season /'ded ˌsiːz(ə)n/ *noun* the time of year when there are few tourists about

deadweight /'dedweɪt/ *noun* heavy goods, e.g., coal, iron, or sand

deadweight capacity /ˌdedweɪt kə'pæsɪti/ *noun* the largest amount of cargo which a ship can carry safely

deadweight cargo /ˌdedweɪt 'kɑrɡoʊ/ *noun* a heavy cargo which is charged by weight, not by volume

deadweight tonnage /ˌdedweɪt 'tʌnɪdʒ/ *noun* the largest amount of cargo which a ship can carry safely

deadwood /ded'wʊd/ *noun* employees who are old or who do not work well ○ *The new management team is weeding out the deadwood from the sales department.*

deal /diːl/ *noun* **1.** a business agreement, affair or contract ○ *The sales director set up a deal with a Russian bank.* ○ *The deal will be signed tomorrow.* ○ *They did a deal with an American airline.* □ **to call off a deal** to stop an agreement ○ *When the chairman heard about the deal he called it off.* **2.** □ **a great deal, a good deal of something** a large quantity of something ○ *He has made a good deal of money on the stock market.* ○ *The company lost a great deal of time asking for expert advice.* ○ *Leave it to the personnel department – they'll deal with it.* ■ *verb* **1.** □ **to deal with** to organize something ○ *Leave it to the filing clerk – he'll deal with it.* □ **to deal with an order** to work to supply an order **2.** to buy and sell □ **to deal with someone** to do business with someone □ **to deal in leather** *or* **options** to buy and sell leather or options □ **he deals on the Stock Exchange** his work involves buying and selling stock on the Stock Exchange for clients

dealer /ˈdiːlər/ *noun* **1.** a person who buys and sells ○ *a used-car dealer* **2.** a person or firm that buys or sells on their own account, not on behalf of clients

dealership /ˈdiːlərʃɪp/ *noun* **1.** the authority to sell some products or services **2.** a business run by an authorized dealer

dealing /ˈdiːlɪŋ/ *noun* **1.** the business of buying and selling on the Stock Exchange, commodity markets, or currency markets **2.** the business of buying and selling goods □ **to have dealings with someone** to do business with someone

dealing floor /ˈdiːlɪŋ flɔːr/ *noun* **1.** an area of a brokerage firm where dealing in securities is carried out by phone, using monitors to display current prices and stock exchange transactions **2.** a part of a stock exchange where dealers trade in securities

dear /dɪr/ *adjective* **1.** expensive, costing a lot of money ○ *Property is very dear in this area.* **2.** way of starting a letter by addressing someone □ **Dear Sir, Dear Madam** addressing a man or woman whom you do not know, or addressing a company □ **Dear Sirs** addressing a company □ **Dear Mr Smith, Dear Mrs. Smith, Dear Miss Smith** addressing a man or woman whom you know □ **Dear James, Dear Julia** addressing a friend or a person you do business with often

COMMENT: First names are commonly used between business people in the U.K. and U.S.; they are less often used in other European countries (France and Germany), for example, where business letters tend to be more formal.

dear money /ˈdɪr ˌmʌni/ *noun* same as **tight money**

death benefit /ˈdeθ ˌbenəfɪt/ *noun* insurance benefit paid to the family of someone who dies in an accident at work

death by committee /ˌdeθ baɪ kə ˈmɪti/ *noun* the prevention of serious consideration of a proposal by assigning a committee to look at it

death in service /ˌdeθ ɪn ˈsɜːrvɪs/ *noun* an insurance benefit or pension paid when someone dies while employed by a company

death tax /ˈdeθ tæks/ *noun* same as **estate tax, inheritance tax**

deaveraging /diˈæv(ə)rɪdʒɪŋ/ *noun* the act of treating customers in different ways according to the amount they buy, by rewarding the best and penalizing the worst

debenture /dɪˈbentʃə/ *noun* agreement to repay a debt with fixed interest using the company's assets as security ○ *The bank holds a debenture on the company.*

COMMENT: In the U.K., debentures are always secured on the company's assets. In the U.S., debenture bonds are not secured.

debenture bond /dɪˈbentʃə bɑnd/ *noun* **1.** a certificate showing that a debenture has been issued **2.** an unsecured loan

debenture capital /dɪˈbentʃə ˌkæpɪt(ə)l/ *noun* a capital borrowed by a company, using its fixed assets as security

debenture holder /dɪˈbentʃə ˌhoʊldər/ *noun* a person who holds a debenture for money lent

debenture issue /dɪˈbentʃə ˌɪʃu/ *noun* the activity of borrowing money against the security of the company's assets

debenture register /dɪˈbentʃə ˌredʒɪstər/ *noun* a list of debenture holders of a company

debenture stock /dɪˈbentʃə stɑk/ *noun* a capital borrowed by a company, using its fixed assets as security

debit /ˈdebɪt/ *noun* an amount entered in accounts which shows an increase in assets or expenses or a decrease in liabilities, revenue or capital. In accounts, debits are entered in the left-hand column. Compare **credit** ■ *verb* □ **to debit an account** to charge an account with a cost ○ *His account was debited with the sum of $25.*

debitable /ˈdebɪtəb(ə)l/ *adjective* able to be debited

debit balance /ˈdebɪt ˌbæləns/ *noun* a balance in an account showing that more money is owed than has been received ○ *Because of large payments to suppliers, the account has a debit balance of $1,000.*

debit card /ˈdebɪt kɑrd/ *noun* a plastic card, similar to a credit card, but which debits the holder's account immediately through an EPOS system

debit column /ˈdebɪt ˌkɑləm/ *noun* the left-hand column in accounts showing the money paid or owed to others

debit entry /ˈdebɪt ˌentri/ *noun* an entry on the debit side of an account

debit note /ˈdebɪt noʊt/ *noun* a note showing that a customer owes money ○ *We undercharged Mr. Smith and had to send him a debit note for the extra amount.*

debits and credits /ˌdebɪts ən ˈkredɪts/ *plural noun* money which a company owes and money it receives, or figures which are entered in the accounts to record increases or decreases in assets, expenses, liabilities, revenue, or capital

debit side /ˈdebɪt saɪd/ *noun* a left-hand column of accounts showing money owed or paid to others

debt /det/ *noun* money owed for goods or services ○ *The company stopped trading with debts of over $1 million.* □ **to be in debt** to owe money □ **he is in debt to the tune of $250,000** he owes $250,000 □ **to get into debt** to start to borrow more money than you can pay back □ **the company is out of debt** the company does not owe money anymore □ **to pay back a debt** to pay all the money owed □ **to pay off a debt** to finish paying money owed □ **to service a debt** to pay interest on a debt ○ *The company is having problems in servicing its debts.* □ **debts due** money owed which is due for repayment

debt collection /ˈdet kəˌlekʃən/ *noun* the act of collecting money which is owed

debt collection agency /ˈdet kə ˌlekʃən ˌeɪdʒənsi/ *noun* a company which collects debts for other companies for a commission

debt collector /ˈdet kəˌlektər/ *noun* a person who collects debts

debt counseling /ˈdet ˌkaʊnsəlɪŋ/ *noun* the work of advising people who are in debt of the best ways to arrange their finances so as to pay off their debts

debtor /ˈdetər/ *noun* a person who owes money

debtor nation /ˈdetə ˌneɪʃ(ə)n/ *noun* a country whose foreign debts are larger than money owed to it by other countries

"…the United States is now a debtor nation for the first time since 1914, owing more to foreigners than it is owed itself" [*Economist*]

debtors /ˈdetərz/ *noun* all money owed to a company as shown in the accounts

debtor side /ˈdetər saɪd/ *noun* the debit side of an account

debt rescheduling /ˈdet riˌskedʒəlɪŋ/ *noun* the process of reorganizing the way in which debts are repaid. Debt rescheduling may be necessary if a company is unable to pay its debts and may involve postponing debt payments, postponing payment of interest, or negotiating a new loan.

debt-service ratio /ˌdet ˈsɜrvɪs ˌreɪʃioʊ/ *noun* the debts of a company shown as a percentage of its equity

debt servicing /ˈdet ˌsɜrvɪsɪŋ/ *noun* the payment of interest on a debt

debug /diˈbʌg/ *verb* to remove errors from a computer program (NOTE: **debugging – debugged**)

deceit /dɪˈsit/, **deception** /dɪˈsepʃən/ *noun* making a wrong statement to someone in order to trick him into paying money ○ *he obtained $10,000 by deception*

decentralization /diˌsentrəlaɪˈzeɪʃ(ə)n/ *noun* an organization from various points, with little power concentrated at the center ○ *the decentralization of the buying departments*

decentralize /diˈsentrəlaɪz/ *verb* to organize from various points, with little power concentrated at the center ○ *Formerly, the bank was decentralized, with many decisions being taken by branch managers.* ○ *Since the company was de-*

centralized, its headquarters have moved to a tiny office. ○ *The group has a policy of decentralized purchasing where each division has its own buying department.*

decide /dɪˈsaɪd/ *verb* to make up your mind to do something ○ *to decide on a course of action* ○ *to decide to appoint a new managing director*

decider /dɪˈsaɪdə/ *noun* a person who makes decisions, especially the person who makes the decision to buy

deciding factor /dɪˌsaɪdɪŋ ˈfæktər/ *noun* the most important factor which influences a decision ○ *A deciding factor in marketing our range of sports goods in the country was the rising standard of living there.*

decile /ˈdesaɪl/ *noun* one of a series of nine figures below which one tenth or several tenths of the total fall

decimal /ˈdesɪm(ə)l/ *noun* □ **correct to three decimal places** correct to three figures after the decimal point (e.g., 3.485)

decimalisation /ˌdesɪm(ə)laɪˈzeɪʃ(ə)n/, **decimalization** *noun* the process of changing to a decimal system

decimalise /ˈdesɪm(ə)laɪz/, **decimalize** *verb* to change something to a decimal system

decimal point /ˌdesɪm(ə)l ˈpɔɪnt/ *noun* a dot which indicates the division between the whole unit and its smaller parts, e.g., 4.75

COMMENT: The decimal point is used in the U.K. and U.S. In most European countries a comma is used to indicate a decimal, so 4,75% in Germany means 4.75% in the U.K. and the U.S.

decimal system /ˈdesɪm(ə)l ˌsɪstəm/ *noun* a system of mathematics based on the number 10

decision /dɪˈsɪʒ(ə)n/ *noun* a choice made after thinking about what to do ○ *It took the committee some time to come to a decision* or *to reach a decision.*

decision-maker /dɪˈsɪʒ(ə)n ˌmeɪkər/ *noun* a person who takes decisions

decision-making /dɪˈsɪʒ(ə)n ˌmeɪkɪŋ/ *noun* the act of coming to a decision

decision-making unit /dɪˈsɪʒ(ə)n ˌmeɪkɪŋ ˌjuːnɪt/ *noun* a group of people who decide on the purchase of a product. For the purchase of a new piece of equipment, they would be the manager, the financial controller, and the operator who

will use the equipment. Abbreviation **DMU**

decision support system /dɪˌsɪʒ(ə)n səˈpɔːt ˌsɪstəm/ *noun* a system containing information in a form that is designed to assist people in making decisions. Abbreviation **DSS**

decision theory /dɪˈsɪʒ(ə)n ˌθɪəri/ *noun* the mathematical methods for weighing the various factors in making decisions ○ *In practice it is difficult to apply decision theory to our planning.* ○ *Students study decision theory to help them suggest strategies in case-studies.*

decision tree /dɪˈsɪʒ(ə)n triː/ *noun* a model for decision-making, showing the possible outcomes of different decisions ○ *This computer program incorporates a decision tree.*

decisive /dɪˈsaɪsɪv/ *adjective* referring to a person who makes up their mind or who comes to a decision. Opposite **indecisive**

decisiveness /dɪˈsaɪsɪvnəs/ *noun* the ability to come to a decision quickly (NOTE: opposites are **indecision, indecisiveness**)

deck cargo /ˈdek ˌkɑːɡoʊ/ *noun* the cargo carried on the open top deck of a ship

declaration /ˌdekləˈreɪʃ(ə)n/ *noun* an official statement

declaration of bankruptcy /ˌdekləreɪʃ(ə)n əv ˈbæŋkrʌptsi/ *noun* an official statement that someone is bankrupt

declare /dɪˈkleə/ *verb* to make an official statement of something, or announce something to the public ○ *to declare someone bankrupt* ○ *The company declared an interim dividend of 10p per share.* □ **to declare goods to customs** to state that you are importing goods which are liable to duty ○ *Customs officials asked him if he had anything to declare.* □ **to declare an interest** to state in public that you own stock in a company being discussed or that you are related to someone who can benefit from your contacts

declared /dɪˈkleəd/ *adjective* having been made public or officially stated

declared value /dɪˌkleəd ˈvælju/ *noun* the value of goods entered on a customs declaration

decline /dɪ'klaɪn/ *noun* **1.** a gradual fall ○ *the decline in the value of the dollar* ○ *a decline in buying power* ○ *The last year has seen a decline in real wages.* **2.** the final stage in the life cycle of a product when the sales and profitability are falling off and the product is no longer worth investing in ■ *verb* to fall slowly or decrease ○ *Stocks declined in a weak market.* ○ *New job applications have declined over the last year.* ○ *The economy declined during the last government.* ○ *The purchasing power of the pound declined over the decade.*

deconstruction /ˌdikən'strʌkʃ(ə)n/ *noun* the process of reorganizing traditional business structures, often by breaking them up into smaller units, when they no longer fit the requirements of the modern economy

decontrol /dikən'troʊl/ *verb* to stop controls □ **to decontrol the price of gasoline** to stop controlling the price of gasoline so that it can be priced freely by the market

decrease *noun* /'dikris/ a fall or reduction ○ *The decrease in the prices of consumer goods is reflected in the fall in the cost of living.* ○ *Exports have registered a decrease.* ○ *Sales show a 10% decrease on last year.* ■ *verb* /dɪ'kris/ to fall or to become less ○ *Imports are decreasing.* ○ *The value of the pound has decreased by 5%.*

decreasing /dɪ'krisɪŋ/ *adjective* which is falling ○ *the decreasing influence of the finance director*

deduct /dɪ'dʌkt/ *verb* to take money away from a total ○ *to deduct $3 from the price* ○ *to deduct a sum for expenses* ○ *After deducting costs the gross margin is only 23%.* ○ *Expenses are still to be deducted.*

deductible /dɪ'dʌktɪb(ə)l/ *adjective* possible to deduct

deductible expenses /dɪˌdʌktɪb(ə)l ɪk'spensɪz/ *plural noun* expenses which can be deducted against tax

deduction /dɪ'dʌkʃən/ *noun* the removing of money from a total, or the amount of money removed from a total ○ *Net salary is salary after deduction of tax and social security.* ○ *The deduction from her wages represented the cost of repairing the damage she had caused to the machinery.* □ **deductions from salary** *or* **salary deductions** *or* **deductions at source** money which a company removes from salaries to give to the government as tax, national insurance contributions, etc.

deduction at source /dɪˌdʌkʃən ət 'sɔrs/ *noun* (*in the U.K.*) a system of collecting taxes in which the organization or individual that pays somebody an income, e.g., an employer paying wages, a bank paying interest or a company paying dividends, is responsible for deducting and paying tax, not the person who receives the income

deed /did/ *noun* a legal document or written agreement

deed of assignment /ˌdid əv ə'saɪnmənt/ *noun* a document which legally transfers a property from a debtor to a creditor

deed of covenant /ˌdid əv 'kʌvənənt/ *noun* a legal document in which a person or organization promises to pay a third party a sum of money on an annual basis. In certain countries this arrangement may have tax advantages. For example, in the United Kingdom, it is often used for making regular payments to a charity.

deed of partnership /ˌdid əv 'pɑrtnəʃɪp/ *noun* agreement which sets up a partnership

deed of transfer /ˌdid əv 'trænsfɜr/ *noun* a document which transfers the ownership of stock

deep discount /ˌdip 'dɪskaʊnt/ *noun* a very large discount

"...when it needed to make its financial results look good, it shipped a lot of inventory. It did this by offering deep discounts to distributors" [*Forbes*]

de facto standard /ˌdeɪ ˌfæktoʊ 'stændərd/ *noun* a standard that is set by a product or service that is very successful in a particular market

defalcation /ˌdifæl'keɪʃ(ə)n/ *noun* an illegal use of money by someone who is not the owner but who has been trusted to look after it

default /dɪ'fɔlt/ *noun* **1.** a failure to carry out the terms of a contract, especially failure to pay back a debt □ **in default of payment** with no payment made □ **the company is in default** the company has failed to carry out the terms of the contract **2.** □ **by default** because no one else will act □ **he was elected by default** he was elected because all the other candidates withdrew ■ *verb* to fail to carry out the terms of a contract, especially to fail to pay back a debt ○ *There was a major financial crisis when the bank defaulted.* □ **to default on payments** not to make payments which are due under the terms of a contract

defaulter /dɪˈfɔltər/ *noun* a person who defaults

defeat /dɪˈfit/ *noun* the loss of a vote ○ *The chairman offered to resign after the defeat of the proposal at the annual meeting.* ■ *verb* to beat someone or something in a vote ○ *The proposal was defeated by 10 votes to 23.* ○ *He was heavily defeated in the ballot for union president.*

defect /ˈdifekt/ *noun* something which is wrong or which stops a machine from working properly ○ *a computer defect* or *a defect in the computer seems to be the cause of the problem*

defective /dɪˈfektɪv/ *adjective* **1.** faulty, not working properly ○ *The machine broke down because of a defective cooling system.* **2.** not legally valid ○ *His title to the property is defective.*

defend /dɪˈfend/ *verb* to fight to protect someone or something that is being attacked ○ *The company is defending itself against the takeover bid.* ○ *They hired the best lawyers to defend them against the tax authorities.* □ **to defend a lawsuit** to appear in court to state your case when accused of something

defendant /dɪˈfendənt/ *noun* a person against whom a legal action is taken or who is accused of doing something to harm someone (NOTE: The other side in a case is the **claimant**.)

defense /dɪˈfens/ *noun* the act of fighting a lawsuit on behalf of a defendant (NOTE: The U.S. spelling is **defense**.)

Defense Acquisition Regulations Council /dɪˌfens ˌækwɪzɪʃ(ə)nz ˌregjʊ ˈleɪʃ(ə)nz ˌkaʊns(ə)l/ *noun* a group of representatives from various U.S. government departments and agencies involved in defense, that works with the Civilian Agency Acquisition Council (CAAC) to develop and maintain the Federal Acquisitions Regulations (FAR) system. Abbreviation **DARC**

defense counsel /dɪˈfens ˌkaʊnsəl/ *noun* a lawyer who represents the defendant in a lawsuit

defer /dɪˈfɜr/ *verb* to put back to a later date, to postpone ○ *We will have to defer payment until January.* ○ *The decision has been deferred until the next meeting.* (NOTE: **deferring – deferred**)

deferment /dɪˈfɜrmənt/ *noun* the act of leaving until a later date ○ *deferment of payment* ○ *deferment of a decision*

deferral /dɪˈfɜrəl/ *noun* a postponement, a putting back to a later date ○ *tax deferral*

deferred /dɪˈfɜrd/ *adjective* put back to a later date

deferred creditor /dɪˌfɜrd ˈkredɪtər/ *noun* a person who is owed money by a bankrupt but who is paid only after all other creditors

deferred payment /dɪˌfɜrd ˈpeɪmənt/ *noun* **1.** money paid later than the agreed date **2.** payment for goods by installments over a long period

deferred rebate /dɪˌfɜrd ˈribeɪt/ *noun* a discount given to a customer who buys up to a specified quantity over a specified period

deferred shares /dɪˌfɜrd ˈʃerz/, **deferred stock** /dɪˌfɜrd ˈstɑk/ *noun* stock that pays a dividend only after all other dividends have been paid

deficiency /dɪˈfɪʃ(ə)nsi/ *noun* a lack of something, or the amount by which something, e.g., a sum of money, is less than it should be ○ *There is a $10 deficiency in the petty cash.* □ **to make up a deficiency** to put money into an account to balance it

deficit /ˈdefɪsɪt/ *noun* the amount by which spending is higher than income □ **the accounts show a deficit** the accounts show a loss □ **to make good a deficit** to put money into an account to balance it

deficit financing /ˈdefɪsɪt ˌfaɪnænsɪŋ/ *noun* a type of financial planning by a government in which it borrows money to cover the difference between its tax income and its expenditure

deflate /dɪˈfleɪt/ *verb* □ **to deflate the economy** to reduce activity in the economy by cutting the supply of money

deflation /dɪˈfleɪʃ(ə)n/ *noun* a general reduction in economic activity as a result of a reduced supply of money and credit, leading to lower prices ○ *The oil crisis resulted in worldwide deflation.* Opposite **inflation**

deflationary /diˈfleɪʃ(ə)n(ə)ri/ *adjective* causing deflation ○ *The government has introduced some deflationary measures in the budget.*

defraud /dɪˈfrɔːd/ *verb* to cheat someone to get money (NOTE: You **defraud** someone **of** something.)

defray /dɪˈfreɪ/ *verb* to provide money to pay costs ○ *The company agreed to defray the costs of the exhibition.*

degearing /diˈɡɪərɪŋ/ *noun U.K.* a reduction in leverage, reducing a company's loan capital in relation to the value of its common stock

degree /dɪˈɡriː/ *noun* **1.** a title awarded to someone who has successfully completed a course of study at a college or university ○ *He has a degree in business studies.* ○ *She has a degree in social work.* **2.** an amount or level ○ *Being promoted to a management position means a greater degree of responsibility.* ○ *The HR director is trying to assess the degree of discontent among the work force.*

degree mill /dɪˈɡriː mɪl/ *noun* an establishment that claims to be an educational institution and offers to award a qualification for little or no work, often on payment of a large sum of money (*informal*) (NOTE: The qualifications offered by degree mills are mostly considered worthless and are not accepted by employers.)

delay /dɪˈleɪ/ *noun* the time when someone or something is later than planned ○ *There was a delay of thirty minutes before the annual meeting started* or *the annual meeting started after a thirty-minute delay.* ○ *We are sorry for the delay in supplying your order* or *in replying to your letter.* ■ *verb* to make someone or something late ○ *The company has delayed payment of all invoices.* ○ *She was delayed because her taxi was involved in an accident.*

delayering /diˈleɪərɪŋ/ *noun* the process of making the structure of an organization simpler and therefore more efficient

del credere agent /del ˈkreɪdərɪ ˌeɪdʒənt/ *noun* an agent who receives a high commission because he or she guarantees payment by customers

delegate *noun* /ˈdelɪɡət/ a person who represents others at a meeting ○ *The management refused to meet the labor union delegates.* ■ *verb* /ˈdeləˌɡeɪt/ to pass authority or responsibility to someone else ○

to delegate authority □ **she cannot delegate** she wants to control everything herself and refuses to give up any of her responsibilities to her subordinates

delegation /deli ˈɡeɪʃ(ə)n/ *noun* **1.** a group of delegates ○ *A Chinese trade delegation is visiting Washington.* ○ *The management met a union delegation.* **2.** an act of passing authority or responsibility to someone else

delete /dɪˈliːt/ *verb* **1.** to cut out words in a document ○ *They want to delete all references to credit terms from the contract.* ○ *The lawyers have deleted clause two.* **2.** to remove a product from a company's product range ○ *We have decided to delete three old products as the new ones are coming on stream.*

deliver /dɪˈlɪvər/ *verb* to transport goods to a customer □ **goods delivered free** *or* **free delivered goods** goods transported to the customer's address at a price which includes transportation costs □ **goods delivered on board** goods transported free to the ship or plane but not to the customer's warehouse

delivered price /dɪˈlɪvərd praɪs/ *noun* a price which includes packing and transportation

delivery /dɪˈlɪv(ə)ri/ *noun* **1.** the transporting of goods to a customer ○ *allow 28 days for delivery* ○ *packages awaiting delivery* ○ *free delivery* or *delivery free* ○ *a delivery date* ○ *Delivery is not included.* ○ *We have a pallet of packages awaiting delivery.* □ **to take delivery of goods** to accept goods when they are delivered ○ *We took delivery of the stock into our warehouse on the 25th.* **2.** a consignment of goods being delivered ○ *We take in three deliveries a day.* ○ *There were four items missing in the last delivery.* **3.** the transportation of a commodity to a purchaser **4.** the transfer of a bill of exchange or other negotiable instrument to the bank which is due to make payment

delivery note /dɪˈlɪv(ə)ri noʊt/ *noun* a list of goods being delivered, given to the customer with the goods

delivery of goods /dɪˌlɪv(ə)ri əv ˈɡʊdz/ *noun* the transportation of goods to a customer's address

delivery order /dɪˈlɪv(ə)ri ˌɔːrdər/ *noun* the instructions given by the customer to the person holding her goods, to tell her where and when to deliver them

delivery service /dɪˈlɪv(ə)ri ˌsɜrvɪs/ *noun* a transportation service organized by a supplier or a store to take goods to customers

delivery time /dɪˈlɪv(ə)ri taɪm/ *noun* the number of days before something will be delivered

delivery van /dɪˈlɪv(ə)ri væn/ *noun* a van for delivering goods to customers

demand /dɪˈmænd/ *noun* **1.** an act of asking for payment □ **payable on demand** which must be paid when payment is asked for **2.** an act of asking for something and insisting on getting it ○ *The management refused to give in to union demands for a meeting.* ■ *verb* **1.** the need that customers have for a product or their eagerness to buy it ○ *There was an active demand for oil stocks on the stock market.* ○ *The factory had to cut production when demand slackened.* ○ *The office cleaning company cannot keep up with the demand for its services.* □ **there is not much demand for this item** not many people want to buy it □ **this book is in great demand** *or* **there is a great demand for this book** many people want to buy it □ **to meet** *or* **fill a demand** to supply what is needed ○ *The factory had to increase production to meet the extra demand.* **2.** to ask for something and expect to get it ○ *She demanded a refund.* ○ *The suppliers are demanding immediate payment of their outstanding invoices.* ○ *The store stewards demanded an urgent meeting with the managing director.*

demand bill /dɪˈmænd bɪl/ *noun* a bill of exchange which must be paid when payment is asked for

demand deposit /dɪˈmænd dɪˌpɑzɪt/ *noun* money in a deposit account which can be taken out when you want it by writing a check

demand-led inflation /dɪˌmænd led ɪnˈfleɪʃ(ə)n/, **demand-pull inflation** /dɪ ˌmænd pʊl ɪnˈfleɪʃ(ə)n/ *noun* inflation caused by rising demand which cannot be met

demand price /dɪˈmænd praɪs/ *noun* the price at which a quantity of goods will be bought

demarcation /ˌdimɑrˈkeɪʃ(ə)n/ *noun* a clear definition of the responsibilities of

each employee or category of employment ○ *The union insisted on clear demarcation when tasks were assigned to different workers.* ○ *Demarcation ensures that no one does work which is not defined in their job description.*

demarcation dispute /ˌdimɑrˈkeɪʃən dɪsˌpjut/ *noun* an argument between different labor unions over who shall do different parts of a job ○ *Production of the new car was held up by demarcation disputes.*

demassifying /ˌdiˈmæsɪfaɪɪŋ/ *noun* the process of changing a mass medium into one that is customized to fit the needs of individual consumers

demerge /diˈmɜrdʒ/ *verb* to separate a company into several separate parts

demerger /diˈmɜrdʒər/ *noun* the separation of a company into several separate parts, especially used of companies which have grown by acquisition

demise /dɪˈmaɪz/ *noun* **1.** a death ○ *On his demise the estate passed to his daughter.* **2.** the act of granting a property on a lease ■ *verb* to grant property on a lease

democratic management style /ˌdeməkrætɪk ˈmænɪdʒmənt ˌstaɪl/ *noun* a management style in which the managers involve the employees in decision-making processes. Opposite **autocratic management style**

demographic /ˌdeməˈgræfɪk/ *adjective* referring to demography or demographics ○ *A full demographic study of the country must be done before we decide how to export there.*

demographics /ˌdeməˈgræfɪks/ *plural noun* the details of the population of a country, in particular its size, density, distribution, and the birth, death, and marriage rates, which affect marketing (NOTE: takes a singular verb)

demography /dɪˈmɑgrəfi/ *noun* the study of populations and population statistics such as size, density, distribution, and birth, death, and marriage rates

demonetization /diˌmʌnɪtaɪ ˈzeɪʃ(ə)n/ *noun* the act of stopping a coin or bill being used as money

demonetize /diˈmʌnɪtaɪz/ *verb* to stop a coin or bill being used as money

demonstrate /ˈdemənstreɪt/ *verb* to show how something works ○ *He was demonstrating a new tractor when he was* killed. ○ *The managers saw the new stock-control system being demonstrated.*

demonstration /ˌdemən'streɪʃ(ə)n/ *noun* an act of showing or explaining how something works ○ *We went to a demonstration of new laser equipment.*

demonstration model /ˌdemən'streɪʃ(ə)n ˌmɑd(ə)l/ *noun* a piece of equipment used in demonstrations and later sold off cheaply

demonstrator /'demənstreɪtər/ *noun* **1.** a person who demonstrates pieces of equipment **2.** same as **demonstration model**

demote /dɪ'moʊt/ *verb* to give someone a less important job or to reduce an employee to a lower rank or grade ○ *He was demoted from manager to salesman.* ○ *Her salary was reduced when she was demoted.*

demotion /dɪ'moʊʃ(ə)n/ *noun* the act of reducing an employee to a lower rank or giving someone a less important job ○ *Demotion would mean a considerable drop in income.* ○ *Demotion ended his dreams of becoming managing director.*

demurrage /dɪ'mʌrɪdʒ/ *noun* money paid to a customer when a shipment is delayed at a port or by customs

denationalization /'dinæʃ(ə)nəlaɪ'zeɪʃ(ə)n/ *noun* the act of denationalizing ○ *The denationalization of the aircraft industry.*

denationalize /di'næʃənəlaɪz/ *verb* to put a nationalized industry back into private ownership ○ *The government has plans to denationalize the steel industry.*

denial of service attack /dɪˌnaɪəl əv ˌsɜrvɪs ə'tæk/ *noun* an attack by a computer hacker or computer virus in which a very large number of messages are sent to a website in a very short time in order to overload it, so that it stops operating and is unavailable to other users

"New security technologies are needed to prevent the kinds of "denial of service" attacks that closed down Yahoo! (No. 94) and other Internet sites in January." [*BusinessWeek*]

denomination /dɪˌnɑmɪ'neɪʃ(ə)n/ *noun* a unit of money on a coin, banknote or stamp ○ *We collect coins of all denominations for charity.* ○ *Small denomination bills are not often counterfeited.*

depart /dɪ'pɑrt/ *verb* **1.** to leave ○ *The plane departs from Paris at 11.15.* **2.** □ **to depart from normal practice** to act in a different way from the normal way of doing things

department /dɪ'pɑrtmənt/ *noun* **1.** a specialized section of a large organization ○ *Trainee managers work for a while in each department to get an idea of the organization as a whole.* **2.** a section of a large store selling one type of product ○ *You will find beds in the furniture department.*

departmental /ˌdipɑrt'ment(ə)l/ *adjective* referring to a department

departmental manager /ˌdipɑrtment(ə)l 'mænɪdʒər/ *noun* the manager of a department

department store /dɪ'pɑrtmənt stɔr/ *noun* a large store with separate sections for different types of goods

departure /dɪ'pɑrtʃər/ *noun* **1.** the act of going away ○ *The plane's departure was delayed by two hours.* **2.** a new venture or new type of business ○ *Selling records will be a departure for the local bookstore.* **3.** □ **departure from normal practice** an act of doing something in a different way from the usual one

departures /dɪ'pɑrtʃərz/ *noun* a part of an airport terminal which deals with passengers who are leaving

depend /dɪ'pend/ *verb* **1.** □ **to depend on** to need someone or something to exist ○ *The company depends on efficient service from its suppliers.* ○ *We depend on government grants to pay the salary bill.* **2.** to happen because of something ○ *The success of the launch will depend on the publicity campaign.* □ **depending on** which varies according to something ○ *Depending on the circumstances, she may be reprimanded or have the money docked from her pay.*

deploy /dɪ'plɔɪ/ *verb* to send staff to a certain place to carry out a certain job

deposit /dɪ'pɑzɪt/ *noun* **1.** money placed in a bank for safe keeping or to earn interest □ **deposit at 7 days' notice** money deposited which you can withdraw by giving seven days' notice **2.** money given in advance so that the thing which you want to buy will not be sold to someone else ○ *to pay a deposit on a watch* ○ *to leave $10 as deposit* ■ *verb* **1.** to put documents somewhere for safe keeping ○ *We have deposited the deeds of the house with the bank.* ○ *He deposited his will with his solicitor.* **2.** to put money into a bank account ○ *to deposit $100 in a checking account*

deposit account /dɪˈpɑzɪt əˌkaʊnt/ *noun* a bank account which pays interest but on which notice has to be given to withdraw money. Abbreviation **D/A**

depositary /dɪˈpɑzɪtəri/ *noun* a person or corporation which can place money or documents for safekeeping with a depository. ◊ **American Depositary Receipt** (NOTE: Do not confuse with **depository**.)

depositor /dɪˈpɑzɪtər/ *noun* a person who deposits money in a bank, savings and loan, etc.

depository /dɪˈpɑzɪt(ə)ri/ *noun* a person or company with whom money or documents can be deposited (NOTE: Do not confuse with **depositary**.)

deposit slip /dɪˈpɑzɪt slɪp/ *noun* a form you fill out when you put money into a checking or savings account (NOTE: The U.K. term is **paying-in slip**.)

depot /ˈdipoʊ/ *noun* **1.** a central warehouse or storage area for goods, or a place for keeping vehicles used for transportation ○ *a goods depot* ○ *an oil storage depot* ○ *a freight depot* ○ *a bus depot* **2.** a center for transportation ○ *bus depot*

depreciate /dɪˈpriʃieɪt/ *verb* **1.** to reduce the value of assets in accounts ○ *We depreciate our company cars over three years.* **2.** to lose value ○ *a stock that has depreciated by 10% over the year* ○ *The pound has depreciated by 5% against the dollar.*

COMMENT: Various methods of depreciating assets are used, such as the "straight line method", where the asset is depreciated at a constant percentage of its cost each year and the "reducing balance method", where the asset is depreciated at a constant percentage which is applied to the cost of the asset after each of the previous years' depreciation has been deducted.

depreciation /dɪˌpriʃiˈeɪʃ(ə)n/ *noun* **1.** a reduction in value of an asset **2.** a loss of value ○ *a stock that has shown a depreciation of 10% over the year* ○ *the depreciation of the pound against the dollar* **3.** a reduction in value, writing down the capital value of an asset over a period of time in a company's accounts

depreciation rate /dɪˌpriʃiˈeɪʃ(ə)n reɪt/ *noun* the rate at which an asset is depreciated each year in the company accounts

depress /dɪˈpres/ *verb* to reduce something ○ *Reducing the money supply has the effect of depressing demand for consumer goods.*

depressed area /dɪˌprest ˈeriə/ *noun* a part of a country suffering from a depression

depressed market /dɪˌprest ˈmɑrkət/ *noun* a market where there are more goods than customers

depression /dɪˈpreʃ(ə)n/ *noun* a period of economic crisis with high unemployment and loss of trade ○ *The country entered a period of economic depression.*

dept *abbreviation* department

depth /depθ/ *noun* the variety in a product line

deputize /ˈdepjʊtaɪz/ *verb* □ **to deputize for someone** to take the place of someone who is absent ○ *He deputized for the chairman who was sick.*

deputy /ˈdepjʊti/ *noun* a person who takes the place of another ○ *to act as deputy for someone* or *to act as someone's deputy* ○ *He is deputy manager of the accounts department.* ○ *Her title is deputy managing director.*

deregulate /diˈregjʊleɪt/ *verb* to remove government controls from an industry ○ *The U.S. government deregulated the banking sector in the 1980s.*

deregulation /diˌregjʊˈleɪʃ(ə)n/ *noun* the reduction of government control over an industry ○ *the deregulation of the airlines*

derived demand /dɪˌraɪvd dɪˈmænd/ *noun* a demand for a product because it is needed to produce another product which is in demand

describe /dɪˈskraɪb/ *verb* to say what someone or something is like ○ *The leaflet describes the services the company can offer.* ○ *The managing director described the difficulties the company was having with cash flow.*

description /dɪˈskrɪpʃən/ *noun* a detailed account of what something is like □ **false description of contents** the act of wrongly stating the contents of a packet to trick customers into buying it

design /dɪ'zaɪn/ *noun* **1.** the planning or drawing of a product before it is built or manufactured **2.** the planning of the visual aspect of an advertisement ■ *verb* to plan or to draw something before it is built or manufactured ○ *He designed a new car factory.* ○ *She designs garden furniture.*

designate *adjective* /'dezɪgnət/ appointed to a job but not yet working ○ *the chairman designate* (NOTE: always follows a noun) ■ *verb* /'dezɪgneɪt/ to appoint someone to a post

design department /dɪ'zaɪn dɪ ˌpɑrtmənt/ *noun* the department in a large company which designs the company's products or its advertising

designer /dɪ'zaɪnər/ *noun* a person who designs ○ *She is the designer of the new computer.* ■ *adjective* expensive and fashionable ○ *designer jeans*

designer clothes /dɪ,zaɪnər 'kloʊðz/ *noun* clothes which have been designed by a famous designer, with his or her name printed on them

design studio /dɪ'zaɪn ˌstudioʊ/ *noun* an independent firm which specializes in creating designs

desk /desk/ *noun* a section of a newspaper

deskilling /di'skɪlɪŋ/ *noun* the process of reducing the number of skilled jobs and replacing them with unskilled jobs

desk pad /'desk pæd/ *noun* a pad of paper kept on a desk for writing notes

desk planner /'desk ˌplænər/ *noun* a book or chart which shows days, weeks and months so that the work of an office can be shown by diagrams

desk research /'desk rɪˌsɜrtʃ/ *noun* the process of looking for information which is in printed sources such as directories

desk-top publishing (DTP) /ˌdesk tɑp 'pʌblɪʃɪŋ/ *noun* the writing, designing and printing of documents in an office, using a computer, a printer and special software

despatch /dɪ'spætʃ/ same as **dispatch**

destination /ˌdestɪ'neɪʃ(ə)n/ *noun* a place to which something is sent, to which something is going ○ *The ship will take ten weeks to reach its destination.* □ **final des-** tination, **ultimate destination** place reached at the end of a trip after stopping at several places en route

detail /'diteɪl/ *noun* **1.** a small part of a description ○ *The catalog gives all the details of our product range.* ○ *We are worried by some of the details in the contract.* □ **in detail** giving many particulars ○ *The catalog lists all the products in detail.* **2.** the temporary assignment of an employee to a different position for a specified time ○ *The union is complaining that employees are being given details that were never mentioned at the time of their recruitment.* ○ *The manager was sent to another branch on a two-week detail.* ■ *verb* **1.** to list in detail ○ *The catalog details the payment arrangements for overseas buyers.* ○ *The terms of the license are detailed in the contract.* **2.** to give someone a temporary assignment ○ *Two men were detailed to deal with the urgent order.*

detailed /'diteɪld/ *adjective* in detail □ **detailed account** an account which lists every item

determine /dɪ'tɜrmɪn/ *verb* to fix, arrange or decide ○ *to determine prices* or *quantities* ○ *conditions still to be determined*

deutsche mark /'dɔɪtʃ mɑrk/ *noun* a unit of currency used before the euro in Germany

devaluation /ˌdivælju'eɪʃ(ə)n/ *noun* a reduction in the value of a currency against other currencies ○ *the devaluation of the rand*

devalue /di'vælju/ *verb* to reduce the value of a currency against other currencies ○ *The dollar was devalued by 7%.*

develop /dɪ'veləp/ *verb* **1.** to plan and produce ○ *to develop a new product* **2.** to plan and build an area ○ *to develop an industrial estate*

developed country /dɪˌveləpt 'kʌntri/ *noun* a country which has an advanced manufacturing system

developing country /dɪˌveləpɪŋ 'kʌntri/, **developing nation** /dɪˌveləpɪŋ 'neɪʃ(ə)n/ *noun* a country which is not fully industrialized

developing world /dɪˌveləpɪŋ 'wɜrld/ *noun* the countries of Africa, Asia and South America which do not all have highly developed industries

development /dɪ'veləpmənt/ *noun* the work of planning the production of a new product and constructing the first prototypes ○ *We spend a great deal on research and development.*

development area /dɪ'veləpmənt ‚eriə/, **development zone** /dɪ'veləpmənt zoʊn/ *noun* an area which has been given special help from a government to encourage businesses and factories to be set up there

device /dɪ'vaɪs/ *noun* a small useful machine ○ *He invented a device for screwing tops on bottles.*

devise /dɪ'vaɪz/ *noun* the act of giving freehold land to someone in a will

COMMENT: Giving of other types of property is a **bequest**.

diagram /'daɪəgræm/ *noun* a drawing which presents information visually ○ *a diagram showing sales locations* ○ *a diagram of the company's organizational structure* ○ *The first diagram shows how our decision-making processes work.*

diagrammatic /‚daɪəgrə'mætɪk/ *adjective* □ **in diagrammatic form** in the form of a diagram ○ *The chart showed the work flow in diagrammatic form.*

diagrammatically /‚daɪəgrə'mætɪkli/ *adverb* using a diagram ○ *The chart shows the sales pattern diagrammatically.*

dial /'daɪəl/ *verb* to call a telephone number on a telephone ○ *to dial a number* ○ *to dial the operator* (NOTE: **dialing – dialed**. The U.S. spelling is **dialing – dialed**.) □ **to dial direct** to contact a phone number without asking the operator to do it for you ○ *You can dial New York direct from London.*

dialing /'daɪəlɪŋ/ *noun* the act of calling a telephone number

dialogue /'daɪəlɒg/ *noun* a discussion between two people or groups, in which views are exchanged ○ *The management refused to enter into a dialogue with the strikers.*

diarize /'daɪəraɪz/ *verb U.K.* to enter a date you have to remember in a calendar

dictaphone /'dɪktəfoʊn/ *noun* a trademark for a brand of dictating machine

dictate /dɪk'teɪt/ *verb* to say something to someone who then writes down your words ○ *to dictate a letter to a secretary* ○

He was dictating orders into his pocket dictating machine.

dictating machine /dɪk'teɪtɪŋ mə‚ʃin/ *noun* a machine which records what someone dictates, which a typist can then play back and type out

dictation /dɪk'teɪʃ(ə)n/ *noun* an act of dictating □ **to take dictation** to write down what someone is saying ○ *The secretary was taking dictation from the managing director.*

dictation speed /dɪk'teɪʃ(ə)n spid/ *noun* the number of words per minute which a secretary can write down in shorthand

differ /'dɪfə/ *verb* not to be the same as something else ○ *The two products differ considerably – one has an electric motor, the other runs on oil.* ○ *The two managerial vacancies differ considerably – one deals with product design and the other with customer services.*

difference /'dɪf(ə)rəns/ *noun* a way in which two things are not the same ○ *differences in price* or *price differences* ○ *What is the difference between these two products?* ○ *What is the difference between a junior manager and a managerial assistant?*

different /'dɪf(ə)rənt/ *adjective* not the same ○ *Our product range is quite different in design from that of our competitors* ○ *We offer ten models each in six different colors.*

differential /‚dɪfə'renʃəl/ *adjective* showing a difference ■ *noun* □ **to erode wage differentials** to reduce differences in salary gradually

differential pricing /‚dɪfərenʃəl 'praɪsɪŋ/ *noun* the act of giving different products in a range of different prices so as to distinguish them from each other

differential tariffs /‚dɪfərenʃəl 'tærɪfs/ *plural noun* different tariffs for different classes of goods as, e.g., when imports from some countries are taxed more heavily than similar imports from other countries

differentiation /‚dɪfərenʃi'eɪʃ(ə)n/ *noun* the act of ensuring that a product has some unique features that distinguish it from competing products ○ *We are adding some extra features to our watches in the interest of product differentiation.* ○ *The* *goal of differentiation should be to catch the customer's eye.*

difficult /'dɪfɪk(ə)lt/ *adjective* not easy ○ *The company found it difficult to sell into the European market.* ○ *The market for secondhand computers is very difficult at present.*

difficulty /'dɪfɪk(ə)lti/ *noun* a problem, or trouble in doing something ○ *They had a lot of difficulty selling into the European market.* ○ *We have had some difficulties with customs over the export of computers.*

diffusion /dɪ'fjuːʒ(ə)n/ *noun* the process by which a product is gradually adopted by consumers

digit /'dɪdʒɪt/ *noun* a single number ○ *a seven-digit phone number* □ **a seven-digit phone number** a phone number with seven figures ○ *The seven-digit numbers are being replaced by eight digits.*

digital /'dɪdʒɪt(ə)l/ *adjective* converted into a form that can be processed by computers and accurately reproduced

digital cash /ˌdɪdʒɪt(ə)l 'kæʃ/ *noun* a form of digital money that can be used like physical cash to make online purchases and is anonymous because there is no way of obtaining information about the buyer when it is used

digital Darwinism /ˌdɪdʒɪt(ə)l 'dɑːwɪnɪz(ə)m/ *noun* the theory that Internet companies develop in the same way as species, according to Darwin's theory of evolution, and that those that are most successful in adapting to their environment will survive

digital economy /ˌdɪdʒɪt(ə)l ɪ'kɒnəmi/ *noun* an economy that is based on electronic commerce, e.g., trade on the Internet

digital goods /ˌdɪdʒɪt(ə)l 'gʊdz/ *plural noun* goods that are sold and delivered electronically, usually over the Internet

digital money /ˌdɪdʒɪt(ə)l 'mʌni/ *noun* a series of numbers that has a value equivalent to a sum of money in a physical currency

digital nervous system /ˌdɪdʒɪt(ə)l 'nɜːvəs ˌsɪstəm/ *noun* a digital information system that gathers, manages, and distributes knowledge in a way that allows an organization to respond quickly and effectively to events in the outside world

digital strategy /ˌdɪdʒɪt(ə)l 'strætədʒi/ *noun* a business strategy that is based on the use of information technology

digital wallet /ˌdɪdʒɪt(ə)l 'wɒlət/ *noun* a piece of personalized software on the hard drive of a user's computer that contains, in coded form, such items as credit card information, digital cash, a digital identity certificate, and standardized shipping information, and can be used when paying for a transaction electronically. Also called **e-purse**, **electronic purse**

digithead /'dɪdʒɪt,hed/ *noun* a person who is very knowledgeable about technology and mathematics but who is not very good at talking or relating to people (*slang*)

digitizable /'dɪdʒɪtaɪzəb(ə)l/ *adjective* able to be converted into digital form for distribution via the Internet or other networks

dilberted /'dɪlbɜːtɪd/ *adjective* badly treated by your employer, like the cartoon character Dilbert (*slang*) (NOTE: see **Dilbert Principle**)

Dilbert principle /'dɪlbɜːt ˌprɪnsɪp(ə)l/ *noun* the principle that the most inefficient employees are moved to the place where they can do the least damage (NOTE: Dilbert is the main character in a comic strip and cartoon series by Scott Adams which satirizes office and corporate life.)

dilution of equity /daɪˌluːʃ(ə)n əv 'ekwɪti/ *noun* a situation in which a company issues additional shares of stock but without an increase in its assets, so that the current investor's equity in the company is less than before the process

dime /daɪm/ *noun* ten cent coin (*informal*)

diminish /dɪ'mɪnɪʃ/ *verb* to become smaller ○ *Our share of the market has diminished over the last few years.*

dip /dɪp/ *noun* a sudden small fall ○ *Last year saw a dip in the company's performance.* ■ *verb* to fall in price ○ *Stocks dipped sharply in yesterday's trading.* (NOTE: **dipping – dipped**)

diploma /dɪ'pləʊmə/ *noun* a document which shows that a person has reached a certain level of skill in a subject ○ *He is studying for a diploma in engineering.* ○ *The new assistant HR manager has a diploma in human resources management.* ○

A diploma is awarded at the end of the two-year course in accountancy.

diplomat /'dɪpləmæt/, **diplomatist** /dɪ'ploʊmətɪst/ *noun* a person (such as an ambassador) who is the official representative of his country in another country

diplomatic /ˌdɪplə'mætɪk/ *adjective* referring to diplomats □ **to grant someone diplomatic status** to give someone the rights of a diplomat

diplomatic immunity /ˌdɪpləmætɪk ɪ'mjunɪti/ *noun* the condition of being outside the control of the laws of the country you are living in because of being a diplomat ○ *He claimed diplomatic immunity to avoid being arrested.*

direct /daɪ'rekt/ *verb* to manage or organize something ○ *He directs our Southeast Asian operations.* ○ *She was directing the development unit until last year.* ■ *adjective* straight or without interference ■ *adverb* with no third party involved ○ *We pay income tax direct to the government.*

direct action /daɪˌrekt 'ækʃən/ *noun* a strike or go-slow by a work force

direct cost /daɪˌrekt 'kɑst/ *noun* a cost which can be directly related to the making of a product, i.e. its production cost

direct debit /daɪˌrekt 'debɪt/ *noun* a system where a customer allows a company to charge costs to his or her bank account automatically and where the amount charged can be increased or decreased with the agreement of the customer ○ *I pay my electricity bill by direct debit.* Abbreviation **DD**

direct expenses /daɪˌrekt ɪk'spensɪz/ *plural noun* expenses excluding materials, labor or purchase of stock for resale which are incurred in making a product

direction /daɪ'rekʃən/ *noun* **1.** the process of organizing or managing ○ *He took over the direction of a multinational group.* **2.** □ **directions for use** instructions showing how to use something

directive /daɪ'rektɪv/ *noun* an order or command to someone to do something ○ *The Commission issued a directive on food prices.*

direct labor /daɪˌrekt 'leɪbər/ *noun* the cost of the workers employed which can be allocated to a product, not including materials or overhead

direct labor costs /daɪˌrekt 'leɪbər ˌkɔsts/ *noun* the cost of the employees employed which can be allocated to a product, not including materials or overhead

directly /daɪ'rektli/ *adverb* **1.** immediately ○ *She left for the airport directly after receiving the telephone message.* **2.** with no third party involved ○ *We deal directly with the manufacturer, without using a wholesaler.*

direct mail /daɪˌrekt 'meɪl/ *noun* the practice of selling a product by sending publicity material to possible buyers through the mail ○ *These calculators are only sold by direct mail.* ○ *The company runs a successful direct-mail operation.*

direct-mail advertising /daɪˌrekt meɪl 'ædvərtaɪzɪŋ/ *noun* advertising by sending leaflets to people through the mail

direct mailing /daɪˌrekt 'meɪlɪŋ/ *noun* the sending of publicity material by mail to possible buyers

director /daɪ'rektər/ *noun* **1.** a senior employee appointed by the stockholders to help run a company, who is usually in charge of one or other of its main functions, e.g., sales or human relations, and usually, but not always, a member of the board of directors □ **directors' salaries** salaries of directors (which have to be listed in the company's profit and loss account) **2.** the person who is in charge of a project, an official institute, or other organization ○ *the director of the government research institute* ○ *She was appointed director of the trade association.*

directorate /daɪ'rekt(ə)rət/ *noun* a group of directors

directorship /daɪ'rektəʃɪp/ *noun* the post of director ○ *She was offered a directorship with Smith Inc.*

directors' report /daɪˌrektərz rɪ'pɔrt/ *noun* the annual report from the board of directors to the stockholders

directory /daɪ'rekt(ə)ri/ *noun* **1.** a reference book containing information on companies and their products **2.** a list of people or businesses with information about their addresses and telephone numbers

direct selling /daɪˌrekt 'selɪŋ/ *noun* the work of selling a product direct to the customer without going through a store

direct tax /daɪˌrekt 'tæks/ *noun* a tax paid directly to the government, e.g., income tax

direct taxation /daɪˌrekt tæk
'seɪʃ(ə)n/ *noun* a tax which is paid direct
to the government, e.g., income tax ○ *The
government raises more money by direct
taxation than by indirect.*

disaggregation /ˌdɪsægrə'geɪʃ(ə)n/
noun the process of separating the companies that make up a group so that their
strengths and contributions can be analyzed as a basis for rebuilding an effective
business web

disallow /ˌdɪsə'laʊ/ *verb* not to accept a
claim for insurance ○ *She claimed $2,000
for fire damage, but the claim was disal-
lowed.*

disallowable /ˌdɪsə'laʊəb(ə)l/ *adjective* not able to be allowed for tax relief ○
*The use of a car for private travel is a dis-
allowable expense.* Opposite **allowable**

disburse /dɪs'bɜrs/ *verb* to pay money

disbursement /dɪs'bɜrsmənt/ *noun*
the payment of money

discharge /dɪs'tʃɑrdʒ/ *noun*
/'dɪstʃɑrdʒ/ **1.** a payment of debt □ **in full
discharge of a debt** as full payment of a
debt **2.** □ **in discharge of her duties as director** while carrying out her duties as director **3.** dismissal from a job ■ *verb* **1.** □
to discharge a bankrupt to release someone from bankruptcy because they have
has paid their debts **2.** □ **to discharge a
debt, to discharge your liabilities** to pay
a debt or your liabilities in full **3.** to dismiss an employee ○ *to discharge an employee for negligence*

discharged bankrupt /ˌdɪstʃɑrdʒd
'bæŋkrʌpt/ *noun* a person who has been
released from being bankrupt because his
or her debts have been paid

discharge of bankruptcy
/ˌdɪstʃɑrdʒ əv 'bæŋkrʌptsi/ *noun* the legal process of being released from bankruptcy after paying your debts

disciplinary /ˌdɪsɪ'plɪnəri/ *adjective*
referring to punishment

"...disciplinary action is often regarded as
synonymous with dismissal, but the new
ACAS handbook takes a more positive
view" [*Employment Gazette*]

disciplinary procedure /ˌdɪsɪ'plɪnəri
prəˌsidʒər/ *noun* a way of warning a
worker officially that he or she is breaking
rules or is working badly

discipline /'dɪsɪplɪn/ *noun* the self-con-
trol needed to do a job ○ *Working his way*
up the company ladder gave him the discipline to take on further management responsibilities.* ○ *Lack of discipline is responsible for poor attendance figures.* ■
verb to punish an employee for miscon-
duct ○ *Three members of staff were disci-
plined by the manager.*

disclaimer /dɪs'kleɪmər/ *noun* a legal
refusal to accept responsibility

disclose /dɪs'kloʊz/ *verb* to tell something that was previously unknown to other people or secret ○ *The bank has no right
to disclose details of my account to the tax
office.*

disclosure /dɪs'kloʊʒər/ *noun* the act
of telling something that was previously
unknown to other people or secret ○ *The
disclosure of the takeover bid raised the
price of the stock.*

discontinue /ˌdɪskən'tɪnju/ *verb* to
stop stocking, selling or making (a product) ○ *These carpets are a discontinued
line.*

discount *noun* /'dɪskaʊnt/ **1.** the percentage by which the seller reduces the full
price for the buyer ○ *to give a discount on
bulk purchases* □ **to sell goods at a discount** *or* **at a discount price** to sell goods
below the normal price □ **10% discount
for cash** *or* **10% cash discount** you pay
10% less if you pay in cash **2.** the amount
by which something is sold for less than its
value □ **shares at a discount** shares which
are lower in price than their asset value or
their par value ■ *verb* /dɪs'kaʊnt/ **1.** to reduce prices to increase sales **2.** □ **to discount bills of exchange** to buy or sell bills
of exchange for less than the value written
on them in order to cash them later □ **to
discount invoices** to obtain a cash advance
from a discounter against the value of invoices **3.** to react to something which may
happen in the future, such as a possible
takeover bid or currency devaluation □
**shares are discounting a rise in the dol-
lar** shares have risen in advance of a rise in
the dollar price **4.** to calculate the value of
future income or expenditure in present
value terms

discountable /'dɪskaʊntəb(ə)l/ *adjective* possible to discount ○ *These bills are
not discountable.*

discounted cash flow /ˌdɪskaʊntɪd
'kæʃ floʊ/ *noun* **1.** a calculation of forecast sales of a product in current terms

with reductions for current interest rates **2.** the calculation of the forecast return on capital investment by discounting future cash flows from the investment, usually at a rate equivalent to the company's minimum required rate of return. Abbreviation **DCF**

COMMENT: Discounting is necessary because it is generally accepted that money held today is worth more than money to be received in the future. The effect of discounting is to reduce future income or expenses to their "present value". Once discounted, future cash flows can be compared directly with the initial cost of a capital investment which is already stated in present value terms. If the present value of income is greater than the present value of costs, the investment can be said to be worthwhile.

discounted value /ˌdɪskaʊntɪd ˈvælju/ *noun* the difference between the face value of a stock and its lower market price

discounter /ˈdɪskaʊntər/ *noun* a person or company that discounts bills or invoices, or sells goods at a discount

discount for cash /ˌdɪskaʊnt fər ˈkæʃ/ *noun* same as **cash discount**

discount house /ˈdɪskaʊnt haʊs/ *noun* **1.** a financial company which specializes in discounting bills **2.** a store which specializes in selling cheap goods bought at a high discount

discount price /ˈdɪskaʊnt praɪs/ *noun* the full price less a discount

discount rate /ˈdɪskaʊnt reɪt/ *noun* the rate charged by a central bank on any loans it makes to other banks

discount store /ˈdɪskaʊnt stɔr/ *noun* a store which specializes in cheap goods bought at a big discount

discover /dɪˈskʌvə/ *verb* to find something new ○ *We discovered that our agent was selling our competitor's products at the same price as ours.* ○ *The auditors discovered some errors in the accounts.*

discrepancy /dɪˈskrepənsi/ *noun* a lack of agreement between figures in invoices or accounts

discretion /dɪˈskreʃ(ə)n/ *noun* the ability to decide what should be done □ **I leave it to your discretion** I leave it for you to decide what to do □ **at the discretion of someone** according to what someone decides ○ *Membership is at the discretion of the committee.*

discretionary /dɪˈskreʃ(ə)n(ə)ri/ *adjective* possible if someone wants □ **the governor's discretionary powers** powers which the governor could use if he or she thought it necessary □ **on a discretionary basis** referring to a way of managing a client's funds, where the fund manager uses his discretion to do as he wants, without the client giving him any specific instructions

discrimination /dɪˌskrɪmɪˈneɪʃ(ə)n/ *noun* the practice of treating people in different ways because of class, religion, race, language, color, or sex

discuss /dɪˈskʌs/ *verb* to talk about a problem ○ *They spent two hours discussing the details of the contract.* ○ *The committee discussed the question of import duties on cars.* ○ *The board will discuss wage rises at its next meeting.* ○ *We discussed delivery schedules with our suppliers.*

discussion /dɪˈskʌʃ(ə)n/ *noun* the act of talking about a problem ○ *After ten minutes' discussion the board agreed the salary increases.* ○ *We spent the whole day in discussions with our suppliers.*

discussion board /dɪˈskʌʃ(ə)n bɔrd/, **discussion group** /dɪˈskʌʃ(ə)n grup/ *noun* **1.** a group of people who discuss something by sending emails to the group and where each member can respond and see the responses of other members **2.** an area on a website where people can write in their own opinions, ideas and announcements

diseconomies of scale /dɪsɪ ˌkɑnəmiz əv ˈskeɪl/ *plural noun* a situation where increased production leads to a higher production cost per unit or average production cost

COMMENT: After having increased production using the existing work force and machinery, giving economies of scale, the company finds that in order to increase production further it has to employ more workers and buy more machinery, leading to an increase in unit cost.

disembark /ˌdɪsɪmˈbɑrk/ *verb* to get off a boat or plane

disembarkation /ˌdɪsɪmbɑrˈkeɪʃ(ə)n/ *noun* an act of getting off a boat or plane

disembarkation card /ˌdɪsembɑr
'keɪʃ(ə)n kɑrd/ *noun* a card which allows
you to get off a plane or boat, and return
after a short time

disenfranchise /ˌdɪsɪn'fræntʃaɪz/
verb to take away someone's right to vote
○ *The company has tried to disenfranchise
the holders of common stock.*

disequilibrium /ˌdɪsikwɪ'lɪbriəm/
noun an imbalance in the economy when
supply does not equal demand

dishonor /dɪs'ɑnər/ *verb* □ **to dishonor
a bill** not to pay a bill (NOTE: The U.K.
spelling is **dishonour**.)

dishonored check /dɪsˌɑnərd 'tʃek/
noun a check which the bank will not pay
because there is not enough money in the
account to pay it

disincentive /ˌdɪsɪn'sentɪv/ *noun*
something which discourages, especially
something which discourages people from
working ○ *The low salary offered was a
disincentive to work.*

disinflation /ˌdɪsɪn'fleɪʃ(ə)n/ *noun* the
process of reducing inflation in the economy by increasing tax and reducing the level of money supply. Compare **deflation**

disintegration /dɪsˌɪntɪ'greɪʃ(ə)n/
noun the decision to stop producing some
goods or supplies and to buy them in instead ○ *Disintegration has meant we now
have to buy all of our plastic parts.* ○ *Part
of the company's disintegration policy involved selling off the factories.*

disintermediation /dɪsˌɪntəmidi
'eɪʃ(ə)n/ *noun* the removal of any intermediaries from a process so that, e.g.,
manufacturers sell direct to consumers instead of selling their products through
wholesalers and retailers

disinvest /ˌdɪsɪn'vest/ *verb* to reduce
investment by not replacing capital assets
when they wear out

disinvestment /ˌdɪsɪn'vestmənt/
noun a reduction in capital assets by not
replacing them when they wear out

disk /dɪsk/ *noun* a round flat object, used
to store information in computers

disk drive /'dɪsk draɪv/ *noun* a part of a
computer which makes a disk spin round
in order to read it or store information on it

diskette /dɪ'sket/ *noun* a small floppy
disk ○ *She sent a diskette of the accounts
to her accountant.*

dismiss /dɪs'mɪs/ *verb* **1.** □ **to dismiss
an employee** to remove an employee from
a job ○ *She was dismissed for being late.*
2. to refuse to accept ○ *The court dismissed the claim.*

dismissal /dɪs'mɪs(ə)l/ *noun* the removal of an employee from a job, either by
sacking or by not renewing a contract

dismissal procedures /dɪs'mɪs(ə)l
prəˌsidʒərz/ *plural noun* the correct way
to dismiss someone, following the rules in
the contract of employment

disparity /dɪ'spærɪti/ *noun* a difference
(NOTE: The plural is **disparities**.)

dispatch /dɪ'spætʃ/ *noun* **1.** the sending
of goods to a customer ○ *Production difficulties held up dispatch for several weeks.*
2. goods which have been sent ○ *The
weekly dispatch went off yesterday.* ■ *verb*
to send goods to customers ○ *The goods
were dispatched last Friday.*

dispatch department /dɪ'spætʃ dɪ
ˌpɑrtmənt/ *noun* the department which
deals with the packing and sending of
goods to customers

dispatcher /dɪ'spætʃər/ *noun* **1.** a person who sends goods to customers **2.** a
person responsible for the route schedules
of taxis, buses, trucks, etc.

dispatch note /dɪ'spætʃ noʊt/ *noun* a
note saying that goods have been sent

dispatch rider /dɪ'spætʃ ˌraɪdər/ *noun*
a motorcyclist who delivers messages or
packages in a town

dispersion /dɪ'spɜrʃ(ə)n/ *noun* the attempt by a distributor to distribute a product to a market

display /dɪ'spleɪ/ *noun* the showing of
goods for sale ○ *an attractive display of
kitchen equipment* ○ *The store has several
car models on display.* ■ *verb* to show ○
*The company was displaying three new
car models at the show.*

display advertisement /dɪ'spleɪ əd
ˌvɜrtɪsmənt/, **display ad** /dɪ'spleɪ æd/
noun an advertisement which is well designed or printed in bold type to attract attention

display cabinet /dɪ'spleɪ ˌkæbɪnət/
noun a piece of furniture with a glass top
or glass doors for showing goods for sale

display material /dɪ'spleɪ məˌtɪriəl/
noun material used to attract attention to

goods which are for sale, e.g., posters and photographs

display pack /dɪ'spleɪ pæk/ *noun* a special box for showing goods for sale ○ *The watches are prepacked in plastic display boxes.*

display panel /dɪ'spleɪ ˌpæn(ə)l/ *noun* a flat area for displaying goods in a store window

display stand /dɪ'spleɪ stænd/ *noun* a special stand for showing goods for sale

disposable /dɪ'spoʊzəb(ə)l/ *adjective* which can be used and then thrown away ○ *The machine serves soup in disposable paper cups.*

disposable income /dɪˌspoʊzəb(ə)l 'ɪnkʌm/, **disposable personal income** /dɪˌspoʊzəb(ə)l ˌpɜrs(ə)nəl 'ɪnkʌm/ *noun* the income left after tax has been deducted

disposable personal income /dɪˌspoʊzəb(ə)l ˌpɜrs(ə)nəl 'ɪnkʌm/ *noun* the income left after tax and national insurance have been deducted. Also called **take-home pay**

disposal /dɪ'spoʊz(ə)l/ *noun* a sale ○ *a disposal of securities* ○ *The company has started a systematic disposal of its property portfolio.* □ **lease** *or* **business for disposal** a lease or business for sale

dispose /dɪ'spoʊz/ *verb* □ **to dispose of** to get rid of or to sell, especially cheaply ○ *to dispose of excess stock* ○ *to dispose of excess equipment* ○ *He is planning to dispose of his business in the new year.*

dispute /dɪ'spjut, 'dɪspjut/ *noun* a disagreement ○ *dispute between two departments in an organization* □ **to adjudicate** *or* **mediate in a dispute** to try to settle a dispute between other parties ■ *verb* to argue that something is wrong ○ *he disputed the check*

disputes procedure /dɪ'spjuts prə ˌsidʒər/ *noun* a formal way of resolving disputes between a labor union and management

disqualification /dɪsˌkwɑlɪfɪ 'keɪʃ(ə)n/ *noun* the act of making someone disqualified to do something

"Even "administrative offences" can result in disqualification. A person may be disqualified for up to five years following persistent breach of company legislation in terms of failing to file returns, accounts and other documents with the Registrar" [*Accountancy*]

disqualify /dɪs'kwɑlɪfaɪ/ *verb* to make a person unqualified to do something, such as to be a director of a company

disruptive technology /dɪsˌrʌptɪv tek'nɑlədʒi/ *noun* an innovative product that displaces an older established product and brings radical change to an industry

dissolution /ˌdɪsə'luʃ(ə)n/ *noun* the ending of a partnership

dissolve /dɪ'zɑlv/ *verb* to bring to an end ○ *to dissolve a partnership*

distrain /dɪ'streɪn/ *verb* to seize goods to pay for debts

distress /dɪ'stres/ *noun* the act of taking someone's goods to pay for debts

distressed /dɪ'strest/ *adjective* experiencing economic or financial difficulties

distress merchandise /dɪ'stres ˌmɜrtʃəndaɪs/ *noun* goods sold cheaply to pay a company's debts

distress sale /dɪ'stres seɪl/ *noun* a sale of goods at low prices to pay a company's debts

distribute /dɪ'strɪbjut/ *verb* **1.** to pay out dividends ○ *Profits were distributed among the stockholders.* **2.** to send out goods from a manufacturer's warehouse to retail stores ○ *Smith Inc. distributes for several smaller companies.* ○ *All orders are distributed from our warehouse near Oxford.*

distribution /ˌdɪstrɪ'bjuʃ(ə)n/ *noun* **1.** the act of sending goods from the manufacturer to the wholesaler and then to retailers ○ *Stock is held in a distribution center which deals with all order processing.* ○ *Distribution costs have risen sharply over the last 18 months.* ○ *She has several years' experience as distribution manager.* **2.** the act of sharing something among several people

distribution channel /ˌdɪstrɪ 'bjuʃ(ə)n ˌtʃæn(ə)l/ *noun* the route by which a product or service reaches a customer after it leaves the producer or supplier (NOTE: A distribution channel usually consists of a chain of intermediaries, for example wholesalers and retailers, that is designed to move goods from the point of production to the point of consumption in the most efficient way.)

distribution network /ˌdɪstrɪ 'bjuʃ(ə)n ˌnetwɜrk/ *noun* a series of points or small warehouses from which goods are sent all over a country

distribution slip /ˌdɪstrɪˈbjuːʃ(ə)n slɪp/ *noun* a paper attached to a document or to a magazine, showing all the people in an office who should read it

distributive /dɪˈstrɪbjʊtɪv/ *adjective* referring to distribution

distributive trades /dɪˈstrɪbjʊtɪv ˌtreɪdz/ *plural noun* all businesses involved in the distribution of goods

distributor /dɪˈstrɪbjətər/ *noun* a company which sells goods for another company which makes them □ **a network of distributors** a number of distributors spread all over a country

distributorship /dɪˈstrɪbjətərʃɪp/ *noun* the position of being a distributor for a company

district /ˈdɪstrɪkt/ *noun* a section of a country or of a town ○ *district manager*

diversification /daɪˌvɜːsɪfɪˈkeɪʃ(ə)n/ *noun* the process of adding another quite different type of business to a firm's existing trade

diversify /daɪˈvɜːsɪfaɪ/ *verb* **1.** to add new types of business to existing ones ○ *The company is planning to diversify into new products.* **2.** to invest in different types of stock or savings so as to spread the risk of loss

divest /daɪˈvest/ *verb* □ **to divest oneself of something** to get rid of something ○ *The company had divested itself of its U.S. interests.*

divestiture /daɪˈvestɪtʃər/ *noun* a sale of an asset

divestment /daɪˈvestmənt/ *noun* the dropping or sale of a whole product line, to allow the company to concentrate on other products

divide /dɪˈvaɪd/ *verb* to cut into separate sections ○ *The country is divided into six sales areas.* ○ *The two companies agreed to divide the market between them.*

dividend /ˈdɪvɪdend/ *noun* a percentage of profits paid to stockholders □ **to raise** *or* **increase the dividend** to pay out a higher dividend than in the previous year □ **to maintain the dividend** to keep the same dividend as in the previous year □ **to omit the dividend** to pay no dividend □ **the stock is quoted ex dividend** the stock

price does not include the right to the dividend

COMMENT: The dividend is calculated as the proportion of profits a company can pay to its stockholders after tax has been paid, always keeping some of the profit back to reinvest in the company's products or activities. Large companies usually pay dividends twice a year, once after the half-year results have been declared (called the "interim dividend") and gain when the final results are published.

dividend check /ˈdɪvɪdend tʃek/ *noun* a check which makes payment of a dividend

dividend cover /ˈdɪvɪdend ˌkʌvər/ *noun* the ratio of profits to dividends paid to stockholders

dividend forecast /ˈdɪvɪdend ˌfɔːkæst/ *noun* a forecast of the amount of an expected dividend

dividend warrant /ˌdɪvɪdend ˈwɒrənt/ *noun U.K.* same as **dividend check**

dividend yield /ˈdɪvɪdend jiːld/ *noun* a dividend expressed as a percentage of the current market price of a stock

divider /dɪˈvaɪdər/ *noun* a sheet of colored cardboard which fits into a ring binder to separate different series of sheets of paper

division /dɪˈvɪʒ(ə)n/ *noun* **1.** the main section of a large company ○ *the marketing division* ○ *the production division* ○ *the retail division* ○ *the hotel division of the leisure group* **2.** a company which is part of a large group ○ *Smith's is now a division of the Brown group of companies.* **3.** the act of separating a whole into parts ○ *the division of responsibility between managers*

divisional /dɪˈvɪʒ(ə)n(ə)l/ *adjective* relating to a division ○ *a divisional director* ○ *the divisional headquarters*

divisional headquarters /dɪˌvɪʒ(ə)nəl hedˈkwɔːtərz/ *plural noun* the main office of a division of a company

division of labor /dɪˌvɪʒ(ə)n əv ˈleɪbə/ *noun* a production system where work is split up into clearly defined tasks and areas of responsibility

DIY *abbreviation* do-it-yourself

DJSI *abbreviation* Dow Jones Sustainability Index

DM, D-mark *abbreviation* deutsche mark

dock /dɑk/ *noun* a harbor, a place where ships can load or unload ○ *loading dock* ○ *a dock worker* ○ *the dock manager* □ **the docks** part of a town where the harbor is ■ *verb* **1.** to go into dock ○ *the ship docked at 17.00* **2.** to remove money from someone's wages ○ *We will have to dock your pay if you are late for work again.* ○ *He had $20 docked from his pay for being late.*

dock dues /'dɑk duz/ *plural noun* a payment which a ship makes to the harbor authorities for the right to use the harbor

docket /'dɑkɪt/ *noun* a list of contents of a package which is being sent

dockyard /'dɑkjɑrd/ *noun* a place where ships are built

doctor's certificate /'dɑktəz sə,tɪfɪkət/ *noun* a document written by a doctor to say that a worker is ill and cannot work ○ *He has been off sick for ten days and still has not sent in a doctor's certificate.*

document /'dɑkjəmənt/ *noun* a paper, especially an official paper, with written information on it ○ *He left a file of documents in the taxi.* ○ *She asked to see the documents relating to the case.*

documentary /,dɑkjə'ment(ə)ri/ *adjective* in the form of documents ○ *documentary evidence*

documentary evidence /,dɑkjʊment(ə)ri 'evɪd(ə)ns/ *noun* evidence in the form of documents

documentary proof /,dɑkjʊment(ə)ri 'pruf/ *noun* a proof in the form of a document

documentation /,dɑkjʊmen'teɪʃ(ə)n/ *noun* all the documents referring to something ○ *Please send me the complete documentation concerning the sale.*

dog /dɔg/ *noun* a product that has a low market share and a low growth rate, and so is likely to be dropped from the company's product line

dog-eat-dog /,dɔg it 'dɔg/ *noun* marketing activity where everyone fights for their own product and attacks competitors mercilessly (*informal*)

dogsbody /'dɔgzbɑdi/ *noun* a person who does all types of work in an office for very low wages (*informal*)

do-it-yourself /,du ɪt jə'self/ *adjective* done by an ordinary person, not by a skilled worker

dole /doʊl/ *noun* money given by the government to unemployed people □ **he is receiving dole payments, he is on the dole** he is receiving unemployment benefits

dole queue /'doʊl kju/ *noun U.K.* a line of people waiting to collect their unemployment money (NOTE: The U.S. term is **dole line.**)

dollar /'dɑlər/ *noun* a unit of currency used in the U.S. and other countries such as Australia, Bahamas, Barbados, Bermuda, Brunei, Canada, Fiji, Hong Kong, Jamaica, New Zealand, Singapore and Zimbabwe ○ *The U.S. dollar rose 2%.* ○ *They sent a check for fifty Canadian dollars.* ○ *It costs six Australian dollars.* □ **a five dollar bill** a banknote for five dollars

dollar area /'dɑlər ,eriə/ *noun* an area of the world where the U.S. dollar is the main trading currency

dollar balances /'dɑlər ,bælənsɪz/ *noun* a country's trade balances expressed in U.S. dollars

dollar crisis /'dɑlər ,kraɪsɪs/ *noun* a fall in the exchange rate for the U.S. dollar

dollar gap /'dɑlər 'gæp/ *noun* a situation where the supply of U.S. dollars is not enough to satisfy the demand for them from overseas buyers

dollar millionaire /,dɑlər ,mɪljə'ner/ *noun* a person who has more than one million dollars

dollar stocks /,dɑlər 'stɑkz/ *plural noun* stocks in U.S. companies

domestic /də'mestɪk/ *adjective* **1.** referring to the home market or the market of the country where the business is situated ○ *Domestic sales have increased over the last six months.* **2.** for use in the home ○ *Glue which is intended for both domestic and industrial use.*

domestic appliances /də,mestɪk ə'plaɪənsɪz/ *plural noun* electrical machines which are used in the home, e.g., washing machines

domestic consumption /də,mestɪk kən'sʌmpʃən/ *noun* use in the home country ○ *Domestic consumption of oil has fallen sharply.*

domestic market /də,mestɪk 'mɑːkət/ *noun* the market in the country where a company is based ○ *They produce goods for the domestic market.*

domestic production /də,mestɪk prə'dʌkʃən/ *noun* the production of goods for use in the home country

domestic sales /də'mestɪk seɪlz/ *noun* sales in the home country

domestic trade /də'mestɪk treɪd/ *noun* trade within the home country

domicile /'dɑmɪsaɪl/ *noun* the country where someone lives or where a company's office is registered ■ *verb* □ **she is domiciled in Denmark** she lives in Denmark officially □ **bills domiciled in France** bills of exchange which have to be paid in France

donor /'dəʊnər/ *noun* a person who gives, especially someone who gives money

door-to-door /,dɔː tə 'dɔː/ *adjective* going from one house to the next, asking the occupiers to buy something or to vote for someone ○ *door-to-door canvassing* ○ *We have 200 door-to-door salesmen.* ○ *Door-to-door selling is banned in this town.*

door-to-door salesman /,dɔː tə dɔː 'seɪlzmən/ *noun* a man who goes from one house to the next, asking people to buy something

dormant /'dɔːmənt/ *adjective* no longer active or no longer operating

dormant account /,dɔːmənt ə'kaʊnt/ *noun* a past customer who is no longer buying ○ *Let's reestablish contact with some of our dormant accounts.* ○ *All the old reports on dormant accounts have been filed away.*

dossier /'dɑsieɪ/ *noun* a file of documents

dot.com /,dɑt'kɑm/, **dot-com** /dɑt kɑm/ *noun* a business that markets its products through the Internet, rather than by using traditional marketing channels

dot-matrix printer /,dɑt 'meɪtrɪks ,prɪntər/ *noun* a cheap printer which makes letters by printing many small dots (the quality is not as good as laser printers or inkjet printers)

dotted line /,dɑtɪd 'laɪn/ *noun* a line made of a series of dots ○ *Please sign on the dotted line.* ○ *Do not write anything below the dotted line.*

double /'dʌb(ə)l/ *adjective* twice as large or two times the size ○ *Their turnover is double ours.* □ **to be on double time** to earn twice the usual wages for working on Sundays or other holidays □ **in double figures** with two figures, from 10 to 99 ○ *Inflation is in double figures.* ○ *We have had double-figure inflation for some years.* ■ *verb* to become twice as big, or make something twice as big ○ *We have doubled our profits this year* or *our profits have doubled this year.* ○ *The company's borrowings have doubled.*

double-book /,dʌb(ə)l 'bʊk/ *verb* to let the same hotel room, plane seat, etc., to more than one person at a time ○ *We had to change our flight as we were double-booked.*

double-digit /,dʌb(ə)l 'dɪdʒɪt/ *adjective* more than 10 and less than 100 ○ *double-digit inflation*

double-entry bookkeeping /,dʌb(ə)l ,entri 'bʊkkiːpɪŋ/ *noun* the most commonly used system of bookkeeping, based on the principle that every financial transaction involves the simultaneous receiving and giving of value, and is therefore recorded twice

double opt-in /,dʌb(ə)l 'ɑpt ,ɪn/ *noun* a method by which users who want to receive information or services from a website can register themselves as subscribers

double taxation /,dʌb(ə)l tæk 'seɪʃ(ə)n/ *noun* the act of taxing the same income twice

double taxation agreement /,dʌb(ə)l tæk'seɪʃ(ə)n ə,grimənt/, **double taxation treaty** /,dʌb(ə)l tæk 'seɪʃ(ə)n ,triti/ *noun* an agreement between two countries that a person living in one country shall not be taxed in both countries on the income earned in the other country

doubtful debt /,daʊtf(ə)l 'det/ *noun* a debt which may never be paid

doubtful loan /,daʊtf(ə)l 'ləʊn/ *noun* a loan which may never be repaid

Dow □ **the Dow** Same as **Dow Jones Index** □ **the Dow 30** Same as **Dow Jones Industrial Average**

Dow 30 /,daʊ 'θɜːti/ *noun* same as **Dow Jones Industrial Average**

Dow Jones Average /ˌdaʊ ˈdʒəʊnz ˌæv(ə)rɪdʒ/ *noun* same as **Dow Jones Industrial Average**

Dow Jones Index /daʊ ˈdʒəʊnz ˌɪndeks/ *noun* any of a number of indexes published by the Dow Jones Co., based on prices on the New York Stock Exchange.

Dow Jones Industrial Average /daʊ ˌdʒəʊnz ɪnˈdʌstrɪəl ˌæv(ə)rɪdʒ/ *noun* an index of stock prices on the New York Stock Exchange, based on a group of thirty major corporations ○ *The Dow Jones Average rose ten points.* ○ *General optimism showed in the rise on the Dow Jones Average.* Abbreviation **DJIA**

Dow Jones Sustainability Index /ˌdaʊ dʒəʊnz səsˌteɪnəˈbɪlɪti ˌɪndeks/ *noun* any of several indexes published by the Dow Jones Co. that use economic, environmental, and social criteria to assess companies' performance. Abbreviation **DJSI**

down /daʊn/ *adverb, preposition* in a lower position or to a lower position ○ *The inflation rate is gradually coming down.* ○ *Stocks are slightly down on the day.* ○ *The price of gasoline has gone down.* □ **to pay money down** to pay a deposit ○ *They paid $50 down and the rest in monthly installments.*

    down tools *phrasal verb U.K.* to stop working ○ *The entire work force downed tools in protest.*

downgrade /ˈdaʊngreɪd/ *verb* to reduce the importance of someone or of a job ○ *The post was downgraded in the company reorganization.*

download /ˌdaʊnˈləʊd/ *verb* to load data or a program onto a computer from another computer

down market /ˈdaʊn ˌmɑːkət/ *noun* a stock market which is falling or is at its lowest level

downmarket /daʊnˈmɑːkət/ *adverb, adjective* cheaper or appealing to a less wealthy section of the population ○ *The company has adopted a downmarket image.*

down payment /ˌdaʊn ˈpeɪmənt/ *noun* a part of a total payment made in advance ○ *We made a down payment of $100.*

downshifting /ˈdaʊnʃɪftɪŋ/ *noun* the process of giving up all or part of your work and income in exchange for an improved quality of life (NOTE: Downshifting has increased in popularity because of rising stress in the workplace and is integral to the idea of portfolio working, in which people opt out of a formal employment to sell their services to companies as freelances.)

downside /ˈdaʊnsaɪd/ *noun* □ **the sales force have been asked to give downside forecasts** they have been asked for pessimistic forecasts

downside factor /ˈdaʊnsaɪd ˌfæktər/, **downside potential** /ˌdaʊnsaɪd pə ˈtenʃ(ə)l/ *noun* the possibility of making a loss in an investment

downside risk /ˈdaʊnsaɪd rɪsk/ *noun* a risk that an investment will fall in value

downsize /ˈdaʊnsaɪz/ *verb* to reduce the number of people employed in order to make a company more profitable

downsizing /ˈdaʊnsaɪzɪŋ/ *noun* the process of reducing the size of something, especially reducing the number of people employed in a company to make it more profitable

downstream /ˈdaʊnstriːm/ *adjective* referring to the operations of a company at the end of a process (such as selling gasoline through garages considered as an operation of a petroleum company). Compare **upstream**

downstream progress /ˌdaʊnstriːm ˈprəʊgres/ *noun* easy progress by a company toward achieving its aims, when it benefits from favorable conditions and trends. Opposite **upstream progress**

down time /ˈdaʊn taɪm/ *noun* **1.** the time when a machine is not working or not available because it is broken or being mended **2.** time when a worker cannot work because machines have broken down or because components are not available

downtown /ˈdaʊntaʊn/ *adjective, adverb, noun* (in) the central business district of a town ○ *His office is in downtown New York.* ○ *She works in a downtown store.* ○ *They established a business downtown.*

downturn /ˈdaʊntɜːn/ *noun* the movement toward lower prices, sales, or profits ○ *a downturn in the market price* ○ *The last quarter saw a downturn in the economy.*

downward communication /ˌdaʊnwərd kəmjuːnɪˈkeɪʃ(ə)n/ *noun* communication from the top management to the lower levels of employee in an organization ○ *More effective downward communication will be helped by starting a house journal and by more informal talks between directors and employees.*

dozen /'dʌz(ə)n/ *noun* a twelve ○ *to sell in sets of one dozen* □ **cheaper by the dozen** the product is cheaper if you buy twelve at a time

Dr, DR *abbreviation* **1.** debtor **2.** drachma

drachma /'drækmə/ *noun* a former unit of currency in Greece

draft /dræft/ *noun* **1.** an order for money to be paid by a bank ○ *We asked for payment by banker's draft.* □ **to make a draft on a bank** to ask a bank to pay money for you **2.** a first rough plan or document which has not been finished ○ *The finance depart* ○ *A draft of the contract* or *The draft contract is waiting for the CEO's comments.* ○ *He drew up the draft agreement on the back of an envelope.* ■ *verb* to make a first rough plan of a document ○ *to draft a letter* ○ *to draft a contract* ○ *The contract is still being drafted* or *is still in the drafting stage.*

drafter /'dræftər/ *noun* a person who makes a draft ○ *the drafter of the agreement*

drafting /'dræftɪŋ/ *noun* an act of preparing the draft of a document ○ *The drafting of the contract took six weeks.*

drain /dreɪn/ *noun* a gradual loss of money flowing away ○ *The costs of the New York office are a continual drain on our resources.* ■ *verb* to remove something gradually ○ *The expansion plan has drained all our profits.* ○ *The company's capital resources have drained away.*

draw /drɔ/ *verb* **1.** to take money away ○ *to draw money out of an account* □ **to draw a salary** to have a salary paid by the company ○ *The chairman does not draw a salary.* **2.** to write a check ○ *She paid the invoice with a check drawn on a Canadian bank.* (NOTE: **drawing – drew – has drawn**)

draw down *phrasal verb* to draw money which is available under a credit agreement

draw up *phrasal verb* to write a legal document ○ *to draw up a contract* or *an agreement* ○ *to draw up a company's by-laws*

drawback /'drɔbæk/ *noun* **1.** something which is not convenient or which is likely to cause problems ○ *One of the main drawbacks of the plan is that it will take six years to complete.* **2.** a rebate on customs duty for imported goods when these are then used in producing exports

drawee /drɔ'i/ *noun* the person or bank asked to make a payment by a drawer

drawer /'drɔər/ *noun* the person who writes a check or a bill asking a drawee to pay money to a payee □ **the bank returned the check to drawer** the bank would not pay the check because the person who wrote it did not have enough money in the account to pay it

drawing account /'drɔɪŋ ə,kaʊnt/ *noun* a checking account, or any account from which the customer may take money when he or she wants

dress code /'dres koʊd/ *noun* a policy on which type of clothes are considered suitable for a specific activity, especially the clothes worn at work ○ *The dress code is suit and tie for men or smart casual clothes on Fridays.* ○ *The company has a strict dress code for members of staff who meet the public.*

dress-down day /'dres daʊn ,deɪ/ *noun* a day on which employees are allowed to wear informal clothes to work

drift /drɪft/ *verb* to move gradually in a particular direction ○ *Stocks drifted lower in a dull market.* ○ *Strikers are drifting back to work.*

drilling down /,drɪlɪŋ 'daʊn/ *noun* the act of sorting data into hierarchies, each of which is more detailed than the previous one

drive /draɪv/ *noun* **1.** an energetic way of doing things □ **She has a lot of drive** she is very energetic in business **2.** a part of a machine which makes other parts work ■ *verb* **1.** to make a motor vehicle go in a specific direction ○ *He was driving to work when he heard the news on the car radio.* ○ *She drives a company car.* **2.** □ **She drives a hard bargain** she is a difficult person to negotiate with

driver /'draɪvər/ *noun* something or someone that provides an impetus for something to happen

driver's license /'draɪvərz ,laɪs(ə)ns/ *noun* the official document which shows someone is legally allowed to drive a car, truck, or other vehicle ○ *Applicants for the job should hold a valid driver's license.* (NOTE: The U.K. term is **driving license**.)

drop /drɒp/ *noun* a fall ○ *a drop in sales* ○ *Sales show a drop of 10%.* ○ *The drop in prices resulted in no significant increase in sales.* ■ *verb* **1.** to fall ○ *Sales have dropped by 10%* or *have dropped 10%.* ○ *The pound dropped three points against the dollar.* **2.** not to keep in a product range ○ *We have dropped these items from the catalog because they've been losing sales steadily for some time.* (NOTE: **dropping – dropped**)

drop ship *phrasal verb* to deliver a large order direct to a customer

drop shipment /'drɒp ˌʃɪpmənt/ *noun* the delivery of a large order from the manufacturer direct to a customer's store or warehouse without going through an agent or wholesaler

drug(s) trafficker /'drʌgz ˌtræfɪkər/ *noun* a person who deals illegally in drugs ○ *He was stopped at customs because they suspected he was a drug trafficker.*

dry goods /ˌdraɪ 'gʊdz/ *plural noun* cloth, clothes and housewares

dry measure /ˌdraɪ 'meʒər/ *noun* a way of calculating the quantity of loose dry goods (such as corn)

DSS *abbreviation* decision support system

DTI *abbreviation* Department of Trade and Industry

DTP *abbreviation* desk-top publishing

dubious /'dubiəs/ *adjective* doubtful, probably not legal ○ *Dubious business practices can cause a collapse of market confidence.*

duck /dʌk/ ◗ **lame duck**

dud /dʌd/ *noun* something that does not do what it is supposed to do (*informal*) ○ *The much-anticipated software upgrade turned out to be a real dud.*

due /du/ *adjective* **1.** owed ○ *a sum due from a debtor* □ **to fall** *or* **become due** to be ready for payment □ **bill due on May 1st** a bill which has to be paid on May 1st □ **balance due to us** the amount owed to us which should be paid **2.** expected to arrive ○ *She is due to come for interview at 10.30.* **3.** correct and appropriate in the situation □ **in due form** written in the correct legal form ○ *a receipt in due form* ○ *a contract drawn up in due form* □ **after due**

consideration of the problem after thinking seriously about the problem □ **due to** caused by ○ *The company pays the wages of staff who are absent due to illness.* **4.** expected to do something, especially to arrive or appear ○ *The committee is due to report next month.*

due diligence /ˌdu 'dɪlɪdʒəns/ *noun* the examination of a company's accounts prior to a potential takeover by another organization. This assessment is often undertaken by an independent third party.

dues /duz/ *plural noun* **1.** regular payments made to an organization to be a member, e.g., by a union member to the union **2.** orders taken but not supplied until new stock arrives □ **to release dues** to send off orders which had been piling up while a product was out of stock ○ *We have recorded thousands of dues for that item and our supplier cannot supply it.*

dull market /ˌdʌl 'mɑrkət/ *noun* a market where little business is done

dullness /'dʌlnəs/ *noun* the fact of being dull ○ *the dullness of the market*

duly /'duli/ *adverb* **1.** properly ○ *duly authorized representative* **2.** as was expected ○ *We duly received his letter of 21st October.* ○ *We duly met the union representatives to discuss the takeover.*

dumbsizing /'dʌmsaɪzɪŋ/ *noun* the process of reducing the size of a company to such an extent that it is no longer profitable or efficient (*slang*)

dummy /'dʌmi/ *noun* an imitation product to test the reaction of potential customers to its design

dummy pack /'dʌmi pæk/ *noun* an empty pack for display in a store

dump /dʌmp/ *verb* □ **to dump goods on a market** to get rid of large quantities of excess goods cheaply in an overseas market

dump bin /'dʌmp bɪn/ *noun* a display container like a large box which is filled with goods for sale

dumping /'dʌmpɪŋ/ *noun* the act of getting rid of excess goods cheaply in an overseas market ○ *The government has passed anti-dumping legislation.* ○ *Dumping of goods on the European market is banned.* □ **panic dumping of sterling** a rush to sell sterling at any price because of possible devaluation

Dun & Bradstreet /ˌdʌn ən 'brædstrit/ *noun* an organization which produces reports on the financial rating of companies, and also acts as a debt collection agency. Abbreviation **D&B**

DUNS™, D-U-N-S™ *trademark* a trademark for a nine-digit code obtained from Dun & Bradstreet and used for identifying and tracking businesses throughout the world

duplicate *noun* /'djuplɪkət/ a copy ○ *He sent me the duplicate of the contract.* □ **duplicate receipt, duplicate of a receipt** copy of a receipt □ **in duplicate** with a copy ○ *to print an invoice in duplicate* □ **receipt in duplicate** two copies of a receipt ■ *verb* /'djuplɪkeɪt/ **1.** □ **to duplicate with another** (*of a bookkeeping entry*) to repeat another entry or to be the same as another entry **2.** □ **to duplicate a letter** to make a copy of a letter

duplicating paper /'duplɪkeɪtɪŋ ˌpeɪpər/ *noun* a special type of paper for use in a duplicating machine

duplication /ˌdjuplɪ'keɪʃ(ə)n/ *noun* the act of doing something that is already being done in the same way by somebody else, copying □ **duplication of work** the fact of doing the same work twice unnecessarily

DuPont Identity /duˌpɑnt aɪ'dentɪti/ *noun* the relationship of return on equity to profit margin, total asset turnover, and financial leverage

durable /'djʊrəb(ə)l/ *adjective* □ **durable effects** effects which will be felt for a long time ○ *These demographic changes will have durable effects on the economy.*

durables /'djʊrəb(ə)lz/ *plural noun* goods which will be used for a long time, e.g., washing machines or refrigerators

dust cover /'dʌst ˌkʌvər/ *noun* a cover which is put over a machine such as a computer to keep dust off

Dutch /dʌtʃ/ *adjective*

   go Dutch *phrasal verb* to pay your own part of the check in a restaurant

Dutch auction /ˌdʌtʃ 'ɔkʃən/ *noun* an auction in which the auctioneer offers an item for sale at a high price and then gradually reduces the price until someone makes a bid

dutiable goods /ˌdutjəb(ə)l 'gʊdz/ *plural noun* goods on which a customs duty has to be paid

duty /'duti/ *noun* **1.** a tax that has to be paid, especially on imported and exported goods □ **goods which are liable to duty** goods on which customs or excise tax has to be paid **2.** work which has to be done □ **on duty** doing official work which is part of your job ○ *She has been on duty all day.* ○ *Two security guards were on duty at the time of the theft.* **3.** a moral or legal obligation ○ *the employee's duty to his employer* ○ *He felt he had a duty to show his successor how the job was done.*

duty-free /ˌduti 'fri/ *adjective, adverb* sold with no duty to be paid ○ *She bought duty-free perfume at the airport.* ○ *He bought the watch duty-free.*

duty-free store /ˌduti 'fri ˌstɔr/ *noun* a store at an airport or on a ship where goods can be bought without paying duty

duty of care /ˌduti əv 'ker/ *noun* a duty which every person has not to act in a negligent way

duty-paid goods /ˌduti 'peɪd ˌgʊdz/ *plural noun* goods where the duty has been paid

duvet day /'duveɪ deɪ/ *noun U.K.* same as **personal day**

Dynamic HTML /daɪˌnæmɪk ˌeɪtʃ ti em 'el/ *noun* a tool for creating limited animated graphics on a website that can be viewed by most browsers. Its major advantage is that it does not require a plug-in to be viewed by users. Abbreviation **DHTML**

dynamic pricing /daɪˌnæmɪk 'praɪsɪŋ/ *noun* pricing that changes when the demand for something increases or decreases

E

e- /i/ *prefix* referring to electronics or the Internet

e-address /'i ə,dres/ *noun* a series of letters and full stops which make up an address for email ○ *My e-address is: peter&pcp.co.uk.*

e-alliance /'i ə,laɪəns/ *noun* a partnership between organizations that do business over the web. Studies show that the most successful e-alliances have been those that link traditional off-line businesses with businesses that specialize in operating online entities.

e. & o.e. *abbreviation* errors and omissions excepted

ear candy /'ɪr kændi/ *noun* pleasant but meaningless noise or talk

early /'ɜrli/ *adjective, adverb* before the usual time ○ *The mail arrived early.* □ **to take early retirement** to retire from work before the usual age □ **at an early date** very soon ■ *adjective* at the beginning of a period of time ○ *He took an early flight to Paris.* □ **we hope for an early resumption of negotiations** we hope negotiations will start again soon

early adopter /,ɜrli ə'dɑptər/ *noun* an individual or organization that is one of the first to make use of a new technology

"...early adopters of electronic-product-code RFID systems will wait for a return on investment longer than perhaps they'd anticipated." [*InformationWeek*]

early closing day /,ɜrli 'kloʊzɪŋ ,deɪ/ *noun* a weekday, usually Wednesday or Thursday, when some stores close in the afternoon

early majority /,ɜrli mə'dʒɔrəti/ *noun* a category of buyers of a product who buy it later than the early adopters

early retirement /,ɜrli rɪ'taɪrmənt/ *noun* a plan where a company encourages employees to retire earlier than usual, and receive financial compensation for this ○ *early retirement at fifty-five* ○ *He took early retirement.* ○ *The management offered some of the senior staff early retirement.*

early withdrawal /,ɜrli wɪð'drɔrəl/ *noun* the act of withdrawing money from a deposit account before the due date ○ *Early withdrawal usually incurs a penalty.*

earmark /'ɪrmɑrk/ *verb* to reserve for a special purpose ○ *to earmark funds for a project* ○ *The grant is earmarked for computer systems development.*

earn /ɜrn/ *verb* **1.** to be paid money for working ○ *to earn $100 a week* ○ *Our agent in Paris certainly does not earn his commission.* ○ *Her new job is more of a transfer than a promotion, since she doesn't earn any more.* ○ *How much do you earn in your new job?* **2.** to produce interest or dividends ○ *a savings and loan account which earns interest at 10%* ○ *What dividend do these stocks earn?*

earned income /ɜrnd 'ɪnkʌm/ *noun* income from wages, salaries, pensions, fees, rental income, etc., as opposed to "unearned" income from investments

earnest /'ɜrnɪst/ *noun* money paid as an initial payment by a buyer to a seller, to show commitment to the contract of sale

earning capacity /'ɜrnɪŋ kə,pæsɪti/ *noun* the amount of money someone should be able to earn

earning potential /'ɜrnɪŋ pə,tenʃəl/ *noun* **1.** the amount of money a person should be able to earn in his or her professional capacity **2.** the amount of dividend which a stock is capable of earning

earning power /'ɜrnɪŋ ,paʊr/ *noun* the amount of money someone should be able to earn ○ *She is such a fine designer that her earning power is very large.*

earnings /'ɜrnɪŋz/ *plural noun* **1.** salary, wages, dividends or interest received ○ *High earnings in top management reflect* *the heavy responsibilities involved.* ○ *The calculation is based on average earnings over three years.* **2.** money which is earned in interest or dividend **3.** the profit made by a company

"...the U.S. now accounts for more than half of our world-wide sales. It has made a huge contribution to our earnings turnaround" [*Duns Business Month*]

"...last fiscal year the chain reported a 116% jump in earnings, to $6.4 million or $1.10 a share" [*Barrons*]

earnings performance /'ɜrnɪŋz pə ˌfɔrməns/ *noun* a way in which stocks earn dividends

earnings per share /ˌɜrnɪŋz pər 'ʃer/ *plural noun* the money earned in dividends per share, shown as a percentage of the market price of one share. Abbreviation **EPS**

earnings-related pension /ˌɜrnɪŋz rɪˌleɪtɪd 'penʃən/ *noun* a pension which is linked to the size of a person's salary

earnings yield /'ɜrnɪŋz jild/ *noun* the money earned in dividends per share as a percentage of the current market price of the share

ease /iz/ *verb* to fall a little ○ *The stock index eased slightly today.* ■ *noun* a slight fall in prices

easement /'izmənt/ *noun* a right which someone has to use land belonging to someone else (such as for a path across someone's land to a garage)

easily /'izɪli/ *adverb* **1.** without any difficulty ○ *we passed through customs easily* **2.** much, a lot (compared to something else) ○ *He is easily our best salesman.* ○ *The firm is easily the biggest in the market.*

easy /'izi/ *adjective* not difficult

easy monetary policy /ˌizi 'mʌnɪt(ə)ri ˌpɑlɪsi/ *noun* same as **easy money policy**

easy money /'izi 'mʌni/ *noun* **1.** money which can be earned with no difficulty **2.** a loan available on easy repayment terms

easy money policy /ˌizi 'mʌni ˌpɑlɪsi/ *noun* a government policy of expanding the economy by making money more easily available, e.g., through lower interest rates and easy access to credit

easy terms /ˌizi 'tɜrmz/ *plural noun* financial terms which are not difficult to ac-

cept ○ *The store is rented on very easy terms.*

e-business /'i ˌbɪznɪs/ *noun* **1.** a general term that refers to any type of business activity on the Internet, including marketing, branding and research ○ *E-business is a rising part of the economy.* **2.** a company that does its business using the Internet

EC *abbreviation* European Community (NOTE: now called the **European Union**)

ECB *abbreviation* European Central Bank

ECGD *abbreviation* Export Credit Guarantee Department

echelon /'eʃəlɑn/ *noun* a group of people of a certain grade in an organization ○ *the upper echelons of industry* ○ *Communications have improved between the higher and lower echelons in the company.*

ecological priority /ˌikələdʒɪk(ə)l praɪ'ɑrɪti/ *noun* the need for organizations and governments to pay as much attention to protecting the environment as to achieving economic success

e-commerce /'i ˌkɑmɜrs/ *noun* a general term that is usually used to refer to the process of buying and selling goods over the Internet

econometrics /ɪˌkɑnə'metrɪks/ *plural noun* the study of the statistics of economics, using computers to analyze these statistics and make forecasts using mathematical models

economic /ˌikə'nɑmɪk/ *adjective* **1.** providing enough money to make a profit ○ *The apartment is rented for an economic sum.* ○ *It is hardly economic for the company to run its own warehouse.* **2.** referring to the financial state of a country ○ *economic planning* ○ *economic trends* ○ *Economic planners are expecting a consumer-led boom.* ○ *The government's economic policy is in ruins after the devaluation.* ○ *The economic situation is getting worse.* ○ *The country's economic system needs more regulation.*

economical /ˌikə'nɑmɪk(ə)l/ *adjective* saving money or materials or being less expensive ○ *This car is very economical.* □ **economical car** a car which does not use much gasoline □ **an economical use of resources** the fact of using resources as carefully as possible

economic crisis /ˌikɑnəmɪk 'kraɪsɪs/, **economic depression** /ˌikəˌnɑmɪk dɪ 'preʃ(ə)n/ *noun* a situation where a country is in financial collapse ○ *The government has introduced import controls to solve the current economic crisis.*

economic cycle /ˌikənəmɪk 'saɪk(ə)l/ *noun* a period during which trade expands, then slows down and then expands again

economic development /ˌikənəmɪk dɪ'veləpmənt/ *noun* the expansion of the commercial and financial situation ○ *The government has offered tax incentives to speed up the economic development of the region.* ○ *Economic development has been relatively slow in the north, compared with the rest of the country.*

economic growth /ˌikənəmɪk 'grouθ/ *noun* the rate at which a country's national income grows

economic indicator /ˌikənəmɪk 'ɪndɪkeɪtəz/ *noun* various statistics, e.g., for the unemployment rate or overseas trade, which show how the economy is going to perform in the short or long term

economic migrant /ˌikənəmɪk 'maɪgrənt/ *noun* a person who moves because he or she wants to find a job, or simply a better-paying job

economic model /ˌikənəmɪk 'mad(ə)l/ *noun* a computerized plan of a country's economic system, used for forecasting economic trends

economic order quantity /ˌikənəmɪk 'ɔrdər ˌkwantəti/ *noun* the quantity of stocks which a company should hold, calculated on the basis of the costs of warehousing, of lower unit costs because of higher quantities purchased, the rate at which stocks are used, and the time it takes for suppliers to deliver new orders. Abbreviation **EOQ**

economic planning /ˌikənəmɪk 'plænɪŋ/ *noun* the process of planning the future financial state of the country for the government

economics /ˌikə'namɪks/ *noun* the study of the production, distribution, selling and use of goods and services ■ *plural noun* the study of financial structures to show how a product or service is costed and what returns it produces ○ *I do not understand the economics of the coal industry.* (NOTE: [all senses] takes a singular verb)

economic sanctions /ˌikənəmɪk 'sæŋkʃ(ə)ns/ *plural noun* restrictions on trade with a country in order to influence its political situation or in order to make its government change its policy ○ *to impose economic sanctions on a country*

economic stagnation /ˌikənəmɪk stæg'neɪʃ(ə)n/ *noun* a lack of expansion in the economy

economic trend /ˌikənəmɪk 'trend/ *noun* the way in which a country's economy is moving

Economic Value Added /ˌikənəmɪk ˌvælju 'ædɪd/ *noun* full form of **EVA**

economies of scale /ɪˌkanəmiz əv 'skeɪl/ *plural noun* the cost advantages of a company producing a product in larger quantities so that each unit costs less to make. Compare **diseconomies of scale**

economies of scope /ɪˌkanəmiz əv 'skoup/ *plural noun* the cost advantages of a company producing a number of products or engaging in a number of profitable activities that use the same technology

economist /ɪ'kanəmɪst/ *noun* a person who specializes in the study of economics ○ *Government economists are forecasting a growth rate of 3% next year.* ○ *An agricultural economist studies the economics of the agriculture industry.*

economize /ɪ'kanəmaɪz/ *verb* □ **to economize on gasoline** to save gasoline

economy /ɪ'kanəmi/ *noun* **1.** an action which is intended to stop money or materials from being wasted, or the quality of being careful not to waste money or materials □ **to introduce economies or economy measures into the system** to start using methods to save money or materials **2.** the financial state of a country, or the way in which a country makes and uses its money ○ *The country's economy is in ruins.*

economy car /ɪ'kanəmi kar/ *noun* a car which does not use much gasoline

economy class /ɪ'kanəmi klæs/ *noun* a lower-quality, less expensive way of traveling ○ *I travel economy class because it is cheaper.* ○ *I always travels first class because economy class is too uncomfortable.*

economy drive /ɪ'kanəmi draɪv/ *noun* a vigorous effort to save money or materials

economy measure /ɪ'kanəmi ˌmeʒər/ *noun* an action to save money or materials

economy size /ɪˈkɒnəmi saɪz/ *noun* a large size or large packet which is cheaper than usual

EDGAR /ˈedɡər/ *noun* a service provided by the U.S. Securities and Exchange Commission that allows companies to file all required financial disclosures online and allows individual investors to access to the information for free. Full form **Electronic Data Gathering Analysis and Retrieval**

edge /edʒ/ *noun* an advantage ○ *Having a local office gives us a competitive edge over Smith Inc.* □ **to have the edge on the competition** to be slightly more profitable or to have a slightly larger share of the market than a competitor

"...the leading index edged down slightly for the week ended May 13, its first drop in six weeks" [*Business Week*]

"...the evidence suggests that U.S. companies have not lost their competitive edge over the last 20 years" [*Harvard Business Review*]

EDI *abbreviation* electronic data interchange

editor /ˈedɪtər/ *noun* a person in charge of a newspaper or a section of a newspaper ○ *the editor of the "Times"*

editorial /ˌedɪˈtɔːriəl/ *adjective* referring to editors or to editing ■ *noun* the main article in a newspaper, written by the editor

editorial board /edɪˌtɔːriəl ˈbɔːd/ *noun* a group of editors on a newspaper or other publication

EDP *abbreviation* electronic data processing

EEA *abbreviation* European Economic Area

EEC *abbreviation* European Economic Community (NOTE: now called the **European Union (EU)**)

e-economy /ˈiː ɪˌkɒnəmi/ *noun* an economy in which the use of the Internet and information technology plays a major role

EEOC *abbreviation* Equal Employment Opportunity Commission

effect /ɪˈfekt/ *noun* **1.** a result ○ *The effect of the pay increase was to raise productivity levels.* **2.** an operation □ **terms of a contract which take effect** *or* **come into effect from January 1st** terms which start to operate on January 1st □ **prices are increased 10% with effect from January 1st** new prices will apply from January 1st

□ **to remain in effect** to continue to be applied **3.** meaning □ **a clause to the effect that** a clause which means that □ **we have made provision to this effect** we have put into the contract terms which will make this work ■ *verb* to carry out □ **to effect a payment** to make a payment □ **to effect customs clearance** to clear something through customs □ **to effect a settlement between two parties** to bring two parties together and make them agree to a settlement

effective /ɪˈfektɪv/ *adjective* **1.** actual, as opposed to theoretical **2.** □ **a clause effective as from January 1st** a clause which starts to be applied on January 1st **3.** producing results ○ *Advertising in the Sunday papers is the most effective way of selling.* ○ *She is an effective marketing manager.* ◊ **cost-effective**

effective control /ɪˌfektɪv kənˈtroʊl/ *noun* a situation where someone owns a large number of shares in a company, but less than 50%, and so in effect controls the company because no other single stockholder can outvote him or her

effective date /ɪˈfektɪv deɪt/ *noun* the date on which a rule or contract starts to be applied, or on which a transaction takes place

effective demand /ɪˌfektɪv dɪˈmænd/ *noun* the actual demand for a product which can be paid for

effectiveness /ɪˈfektɪvnəs/ *noun* the quality of working successfully or producing results ○ *I doubt the effectiveness of television advertising.* ○ *Her effectiveness as a manager was due to her quick grasp of detail.* ◊ **cost-effectiveness**

effective yield /ɪˌfektɪv ˈjiːld/ *noun* an actual yield shown as a percentage of the price paid after adjustments have been made

effectual /ɪˈfektʃuəl/ *adjective* which produces a correct result

efficiency /ɪˈfɪʃ(ə)nsi/ *noun* the ability to work well or to produce the right result or the right work quickly ○ *a business efficiency exhibition* ○ *The bus system is run with a high degree of efficiency.* ○ *We called in an efficiency expert to report on ways of increasing profitability.*

"...increased control means improved efficiency in purchasing, shipping, sales and delivery" [*Duns Business Month*]

efficient /ɪˈfɪʃ(ə)nt/ *adjective* able to work well or to produce the right result quickly ○ *the efficient working of a system* ○ *An efficient assistant is invaluable.* ○ *An efficient new machine would save time.*

efficient frontier /ɪˌfɪʃ(ə)nt frʌnˈtɪr/ *noun* the combination of stocks, bonds, or other securities that produce the maximum return at a given level of risk

efficiently /ɪˈfɪʃ(ə)ntli/ *adverb* in an efficient way ○ *She organized the sales conference very efficiently.*

Efficient Market Hypothesis[1] /ɪˌfɪʃ(ə)nt ˌmɑrkɪt haɪˈpɑθəsɪs/ *noun* the hypothesis that all relevant information is immediately reflected in the price of a security

Efficient Market Hypothesis[2] /ɪˌfɪʃ(ə)nt ˈmɑrkət haɪˌpɑθəsɪs/, **Efficient Markets Hypothesis** *noun* the hypothesis that all relevant information is immediately reflected in the price of a security. Abbreviation **EMH**

efflux /ˈeflʌks/ *noun* the act of flowing out ○ *the efflux of capital to North America*

effort /ˈefət/ *noun* an act of using the mind or body to do something ○ *The sales staff made great efforts to increase sales.* ○ *Thanks to the efforts of the finance department, overhead has been reduced.* ○ *If we make one more effort, we should clear the backlog of orders.*

EFQM *abbreviation* European Foundation for Quality Management

EFT *abbreviation* electronic funds transfer

EFTA *abbreviation* European Free Trade Association

EFTPOS *abbreviation* electronic funds transfer at point of sale

EFTPS *trademark* a trademark of the U.S. Department of the Treasury for an online service that enables businesses and taxpayers to pay their federal taxes electronically. Full form **Electronic Federat Tax Payment System**

e.g. e.g., or such as ○ *The contract is valid in some countries (e.g. France and Belgium) but not in others.*

EGM *abbreviation* extraordinary general meeting

800 number /eɪt ˈhʌndrəd ˌnʌmbər/ *noun* a telephone number beginning with the digits 800, on which calls can be made free of charge, such as to reply to an ad. The supplier pays for them, not the caller. (NOTE: The U.K. term is **0800 number**.)

802.11 *noun* a set of specifications for wireless local area networks

eighty/twenty law /ˌeɪti ˈtwenti rul/, **80/20 law** *noun* the rule that a small percentage of customers may account for a large percentage of sales. ▷ **Pareto's Law**

elastic /ɪˈlæstɪk/ *adjective* able to expand or contract easily because of small changes in price

elastic demand /ɪˌlæstɪk dɪˈmænd/ *noun* demand which experiences a comparatively large percentage change in response to a change in price

elasticity /ˌɪlæˈstɪsəti/ *noun* the ability to change easily in response to a change in circumstances □ **elasticity of supply and demand** changes in supply and demand of an item depending on its market price

elastic supply /ɪˌlæstɪk səˈplaɪ/ *noun* supply which experiences a comparatively large percentage change in response to a change in price

e-learning /ˈi ˌlɜrnɪŋ/ *noun* learning by means of courses or aids to study provided on the Internet or an intranet (NOTE: E-learning is a development from **computer-based training** and, because it is Internet based, it is very flexible: it allows the learner to proceed at their own pace and can be adapted to suit the changing needs of the company. Full form is **electronic learning**)

elect /ɪˈlekt/ *verb* **1.** to choose someone by a vote ○ *to elect the officers of an association* ○ *She was elected president of the staff club.* **2.** to choose to do something ○ *He elected to take early retirement.*

-elect /ɪlekt/ *suffix* referring to a person who has been elected but has not yet started the term of office

election /ɪˈlekʃən/ *noun* the act of electing someone ○ *the election of officers of an association* ○ *the election of directors by the stockholders*

electric /ɪˈlektrɪk/ *adjective* referring to electricity; worked by electricity ○ *an electric typewriter*

electrical /ɪˈlektrɪk(ə)l/ *adjective* referring to electricity ○ *The engineers are trying to repair an electrical fault.*

electricity /ɪˌlek'trɪsəti/ *noun* a current used to make light, heat or power ○ *The electricity was cut off this morning, so the computers could not work.* ○ *Our electricity bill has increased considerably this quarter.* ○ *Electricity costs are an important factor in our overhead.*

electronic /ˌilek'trɑnɪk/ *adjective* referring to computers and electronics

electronic banking /ˌelektrɑnɪk 'bæŋkɪŋ/ *noun* the use of computers to carry out banking transactions such as withdrawals through cash dispensers or transfer of funds at point of sale

electronic cash /ˌelektrɑnɪk 'kæʃ/ *noun* same as **digital cash**

electronic check /ˌelektrɑnɪk 'tʃek/ *noun* a system that transfers money electronically from the buyer's checking account to the seller's bank account

electronic commerce /ˌelektrɑnɪk 'kɑmɜrs/ *noun* same as **e-commerce**

electronic cottage /ˌelektrɑnɪk 'kɑtɪdʒ/ *noun* someone's home from which they work for a company on a computer, usually linked to the office via a modem

Electronic Data Gathering Analysis and Retrieval /ˌilektrɑnɪk ˌdeɪtə ˌgæθərɪŋ əˌnælɪsɪs ən rɪ'triv(ə)l/ full form of **EDGAR**

electronic data interchange /ˌelektrɑnɪk 'deɪtə ˌɪntərtʃeɪndʒ/ *noun* a standard format used when business documents such as invoices and purchase orders are exchanged over electronic networks such as the Internet. Abbreviation **EDI**

electronic data processing /ˌelektrɑnɪk 'deɪtə ˌprɑsesɪŋ/ *noun* the process of selecting and examining data stored in a computer to produce information. Abbreviation **EDP**

electronic engineer /ˌelektrɑnɪk ˌendʒɪ'nɪr/ *noun* an engineer who specializes in electronic machines

Electronic Federal Tax Payment System /ˌilektrɑnɪk ˌfedər(ə)l 'tæks ˌpeɪmənt ˌsɪstəm/ *trademark* full form of **EFTPS**

electronic funds transfer /ˌelektrɑnɪk ˌfʌndz ˌtrænsfɜr ət ˌpɔɪnt əv 'seɪl/ *noun* the system used by banking organizations for the movement of funds between accounts and for the provision of services to the customer. Abbreviation **EFT**

electronic funds transfer at point of sale /ˌelektrɑnɪk ˌfʌndz ˌtrænsfɜr ət ˌpɔɪnt əv 'seɪl/ *noun* the payment for goods or services by a bank customer using a card that is swiped through an electronic reader on the register, thereby transferring the cash from the customer's account to the retailer's or service provider's account. Abbreviation **EFTPOS**

electronic mail /ˌelektrɑnɪk 'meɪl/ *noun* same as **email** *noun* 1

electronic payment system /ˌelektrɑnɪk 'peɪmənt ˌsɪstəm/ *noun* a means of making payments over an electronic network such as the Internet

electronic point of sale /ˌelɪktrɑnɪk pɔɪnt əv 'seɪl/ *noun* a system where sales are charged automatically to a customer's credit card and stock is controlled by the store's computer. Abbreviation **EPOS**

electronic purse /ˌelektrɑnɪk 'pɜrs/ *noun* same as **digital wallet**

electronics /ˌelek'trɑnɪks/ *plural noun* the scientific study of systems worked by a flow of electrons which are used in manufactured products, such as computers, calculators or telephones ○ *the electronics industry* ○ *an electronics specialist* or *expert* ○ *an electronics engineer* (NOTE: takes a singular verb)

element /'elɪmənt/ *noun* a basic part or the smallest unit into which something can be divided ○ *the elements of a settlement* ○ *Work study resulted in a standard time for each job element.*

elevator pitch /'elɪveɪtər pɪtʃ/ *noun* a very concise description of a business model, often delivered to a potential investor (NOTE: The idea here is that the description should take no longer than the time it takes to ride an elevator between floors.)

eligibility /ˌelɪdʒɪ'bɪlɪti/ *noun* the fact of being eligible ○ *The chairman questioned her eligibility to stand for reelection.*

eligible /'elɪdʒɪb(ə)l/ *adjective* possible to choose ○ *She is eligible for reelection.*

eligible bill /'elɪdʒəb(ə)l bɪl/ *noun* a bill which will be accepted by the Bank of England or the U.S. Federal Reserve, and which can be used as security against a loan

eliminate /ɪ'lɪmɪneɪt/ *verb* to remove ○ *to eliminate defects in the system* ○ *Using a computer should eliminate all possibility of error.* ○ *We have decided to eliminate this series of old products from our range.* ○ *Most of the candidates were eliminated after the first batch of tests.*

email /'imeɪl/, **e-mail** /'i meɪl/ *noun* **1.** a system of sending messages from one computer terminal to another, using a modem and telephone lines ○ *You can contact me by phone or email if you want.* **2.** a message sent electronically ○ *I had six emails from him today.* ■ *verb* to send a message from one computer to another, using a modem and telephone lines ○ *She emailed her order to the warehouse.* ○ *I emailed him about the meeting.*

email address /'imeɪl ə‚dres/ *noun* a series of letters and full stops which make up an address for email ○ *I'll give you my email address.* ○ *My email address is: peter&pcp.co.uk.*

emailing /'imeɪlɪŋ/ *noun* the process of sending something by email

email mailing list /‚imeɪl 'meɪlɪŋ ‚lɪst/ *noun* a marketing technique that involves contacting a group of people from anywhere in the world and inviting them to discuss a particular topic and share information and experience by email (NOTE: An email mailing list is run by a moderator who compiles a list of email addresses for possible members, mails them with the theme for discussion, collects their contributions, and publishes them by email so that other members of the group can respond to them.)

e-mail signature /'i meɪl ‚sɪgnətʃər/ *noun* a piece of text at the bottom of an e-mail, which contains information about the sender

e-marketplace /‚i 'mɑːkətpleɪs/ *noun* a network of connections that brings business-to-business buyers and sellers together on the Internet and enables them to trade more efficiently online

embargo /ɪm'bɑːgoʊ/ *noun* **1.** a government order which stops a type of trade □ **to impose** *or* **put an embargo on trade with a country** to say that trade with a country must not take place ○ *The government has put an embargo on the export of computer equipment.* □ **to lift an embargo** to allow trade to start again ○ *The government has lifted the embargo on the export of computers.* □ **to be under an embargo** to be forbidden **2.** a period of time during which specific information in a press release must not be published (NOTE: The plural is **embargoes**.) ■ *verb* **1.** to stop trade, or not to allow something to be traded ○ *The government has embargoed trade with countries that are in breach of international agreements.* **2.** not to allow publication of information for a period of time ○ *The news of the merger has been embargoed until next Wednesday.*

embark /ɪm'bɑːk/ *verb* **1.** to go on a ship ○ *the passengers embarked at Southampton* **2.** □ **to embark on** to start ○ *The company has embarked on an expansion program.*

embarkation /‚embɑː'keɪʃ(ə)n/ *noun* the act of going on to a ship or plane

embarkation card /‚embɑː'keɪʃ(ə)n kɑːd/ *noun* a card given to passengers getting on to a plane or ship

embezzle /ɪm'bez(ə)l/ *verb* to use illegally money which is not yours, or which you are looking after for someone ○ *He was sent to prison for six months for embezzling his clients' money.*

embezzlement /ɪm'bez(ə)lmənt/ *noun* the act of embezzling ○ *He was sent to prison for six months for embezzlement.*

embezzler /ɪm'bez(ə)lər/ *noun* a person who embezzles

emergency /ɪ'mɜːdʒənsi/ *noun* a dangerous situation where decisions have to be taken quickly □ **to take emergency measures** to take action rapidly to stop a crisis developing ○ *The company had to take emergency measures to stop losing money.*

emergency reserves /ɪ‚mɜːdʒənsi rɪ'zɜːvz/ *noun* ready cash held in case it is needed suddenly

EMH *abbreviation* Efficient Market Hypothesis

emission credits /ɪ'mɪʃ(ə)n ‚kredɪts/ *plural noun* theoretical reductions in emissions of CO_2 and other greenhouse gases which can be bought by a country from others who do not need them and set against its targets. They are allowed under the Kyoto treaty.

emisson /ɪ'mɪʃ(ə)n/ *noun* the release of a pollutant into the atmosphere, e.g., from an industrial facility

emoluments /ɪˈmɑljʊmənts/ *plural noun* pay, salary or fees, or the earnings of directors who are not employees (NOTE: U.S. English uses the singular **emolument**.)

e-money /ˈiː ˌmʌni/ *noun* same as **digital money**

emotional capital /ɪˌmoʊʃ(ə)n(ə)l ˈkæpɪt(ə)l/ *noun* the emotional skills and experiences of employees, which give them the ability to communicate and form interpersonal relationships successfully, considered as an intangible asset of a company. Emotional capital is increasingly being considered to be an important factor in company performance.

emotional intelligence /ɪˌmoʊʃ(ə)n(ə)l ɪnˈtelɪdʒəns/ *noun* the ability to understand your own personal feelings and those of other people, to take other people's feelings into account when reaching decisions and to respond to people's feelings in a restrained and thoughtful way (NOTE: Emotional intelligence can greatly improve people's interpersonal communication and people skills.)

employ /ɪmˈplɔɪ/ *verb* to give someone regular paid work □ **to employ twenty staff** to have twenty people working for you □ **to employ twenty new staff** to give work to twenty new people

"70 per cent of Australia's labour force was employed in service activity" [*Australian Financial Review*]

employed /ɪmˈplɔɪd/ *adjective* **1.** in regular paid work □ **he is not gainfully employed** he has no regular paid work **2.** referring to money used profitably ■ *plural noun* people who are working ○ *the employers and the employed*

employee /ɪmˈplɔɪiː/ *noun* a person employed by another ○ *Employees of the firm are eligible to join a profit-sharing program.* ○ *Relations between management and employees are good.* ○ *The company has decided to take on new employees.*

"…companies introducing robotics think it important to involve individual employees in planning their introduction" [*Economist*]

employee development /ɪmˌplɔɪi dɪˈveləpmənt/ *noun* additional training dedicated to increasing the skills, knowledge and experience of employees in order to improve their performance

employee stock ownership plan /ɪmˈplɔɪi ˌʃer ˈoʊnəʃɪp plæn/, **employee stock ownership program** /ɪmˌplɔɪi ˈʃer ˌoʊnəʃɪp ˌproʊɡræm/ *noun* a plan which allows employees to obtain stock in the company for which they work, though tax may be payable if the stock is sold to employees at a price which is lower than the current market price. Abbreviation **ESOP**

employer /ɪmˈplɔɪə/ *noun* a person or company that has regular employees and pays them

employer's association /ɪmˌplɔɪəz əˌsoʊsiˈeɪʃ(ə)n/ *noun* same as **employers' organization**

employer's contribution /ɪmˌplɔɪəz ˌkʌntrɪˈbjuːʃ(ə)n/ *noun* money paid by an employer toward an employee's pension

employers' liability insurance /ɪmˌplɔɪəz ˌlaɪəˈbɪləti ɪnˌʃʊrəns/ *noun* insurance to cover accidents which may happen at work, and for which the company may be responsible

employers' organization /ɪmˈplɔɪərz ˌɔrɡənaɪzeɪʃ(ə)n/, **employers' association** /ɪmˌplɔɪərz əˌsoʊsiˈeɪʃ(ə)n/ *noun* a group of employers with similar interests

employment /ɪmˈplɔɪmənt/ *noun* regular paid work □ **to be without employment** to have no work

"…the blue-collar unions are the people who stand to lose most in terms of employment growth" [*Sydney Morning Herald*]

employment agency /ɪmˈplɔɪmənt ˌeɪdʒənsi/, **employment bureau** *noun* an office or company that finds jobs for people

employment contract /ɪmˌplɔɪmənt ˈkɑntrækt/ *noun* same as **contract of employment**

employment law /ɪmˈplɔɪmənt lɔ/ *noun* the law as referring to workers, employers and their rights

employment office /ɪmˈplɔɪmənt ˌɔfɪs/ *noun* an office which finds jobs for people

employment opportunities /ɪmˈplɔɪmənt ˌɑpəˌtjunɪtiz/ *plural noun* new jobs being available. Also called **job opportunities**

employment protection /ɪmˈplɔɪmənt prəˌtekʃən/ *noun* the action of protecting employees against unfair dismissal

employment tribunal /ɪmˈplɔɪmənt traɪˌbjunəl/ *noun* a government body in the U.K. that is responsible for dealing with disputes between employees and employers

emporium /ɪmˈpɔriəm/ *noun* a large store (NOTE: The plural is **emporia**.)

empower /ɪmˈpaʊr/ *verb* to give someone the power to do something ○ *She was empowered by the company to sign the contract.* ○ *Her new position empowers her to hire and fire at will.*

empowerment /ɪmˈpaʊrmənt/ *noun* the act of giving someone (such as an employee) the power to make decisions

"…a district-level empowerment programme run in one of the government's executive agencies failed because middle managers blocked it. Empowerment was officially defined by the agency as involving delegation of responsibility and the encouragement of innovation" [*People Management*]

empties /ˈemptiz/ *plural noun* empty bottles or cases

emptor /ˈemptər/ *noun* ♦ **caveat emptor**

enc., encl. *abbreviation* enclosure

encash /ɪnˈkæʃ/ *verb U.K.* to cash a check, to exchange a check for cash

encashable /ɪnˈkæʃəb(ə)l/ *adjective U.K.* possible to cash

encashment /ɪnˈkæʃmənt/ *noun U.K.* an act of exchanging for cash

enclose /ɪnˈkloʊz/ *verb* to put something inside an envelope with a letter ○ *to enclose an invoice with a letter* ○ *I am enclosing a copy of the contract.* ○ *Please find the check enclosed herewith.* ○ *Please enclose a recent photograph with your résumé.*

enclosure /ɪnˈkloʊʒə/ *noun* a document enclosed with a letter or package ○ *a letter with enclosures* ○ *The enclosure turned out to be a free sample of perfume.* ○ *Sales material on other products was sent out as an enclosure.*

encourage /ɪnˈkʌrɪdʒ/ *verb* 1. to make it easier for something to happen ○ *The general rise in wages encourages consumer spending.* ○ *Leaving your credit cards on your desk encourages people to steal* or *encourages stealing.* ○ *The company is*

trying to encourage sales by giving large discounts. **2.** to help someone to do something by giving advice ○ *He encouraged me to apply for the job.*

encouragement /ɪnˈkʌrɪdʒmənt/ *noun* the act of giving advice to someone to help them to succeed ○ *The designers produced a very marketable product, thanks to the encouragement of the sales director.* ○ *My family has been a source of great encouragement to me.*

encryption /ɪnˈkrɪpʃən/ *noun* a conversion of plain text to a secure coded form by means of a cipher system

encumbrance /ɪnˈkʌmbrəns/ *noun* a liability which is attached usually to a property or land, e.g., a mortgage or charge

end /end/ *noun* **1.** the final point or last part ○ *at the end of the contract period* □ **at the end of six months** after six months have passed □ **to come to an end** to finish ○ *Our distribution agreement comes to an end next month.* **2.** □ **in the end** at last, after a lot of problems ○ *In the end the company had to pull out of the U.S. market.* ○ *In the end they signed the contract at the airport.* ○ *In the end the company had to call in the police.* **3.** □ **on end** for a long time, with no breaks ○ *The discussions continued for hours on end.* ○ *The work force worked at top speed for weeks on end to finish the order on time.* ■ *verb* to finish ○ *The distribution agreement ends in July.* ○ *The chairman ended the discussion by getting up and walking out of the room.*

end in *phrasal verb* to have as a result ○ *The annual meeting ended in the stockholders fighting on the floor.*

end up *phrasal verb* to finish ○ *We ended up with a bill for $10,000.*

end of season sale /ˌend əv ˈsiz(ə)n ˌseɪl/ *noun* a sale of goods at a lower price when the season in which they would be used is over, such as summer clothes sold cheaply in the fall

endorse /ɪnˈdɔrs/ *verb* to say that a product is good □ **to endorse a bill** *or a* **check** to sign a bill or check on the back to show that you accept it

COMMENT: By endorsing a check (i.e., signing it on the back), a person whose name is on the front of the check is passing ownership of it to another party, such as the bank, which can then accept it and pay him cash for it. If a check is deposited in an account, it does not need to be endorsed. Cheques can also be endorsed to another person: a check made payable to Mr. A. Smith can be endorsed by Mr. Smith on the back, with the words: "Pay to Brown Ltd.", and then his signature. This has the effect of making the check payable to Brown Ltd., and to no one else. Most cheques are now printed as crossed cheques with the words "A/C Payee" printed in the space between the two vertical lines. These cheques can only be paid to the person whose name is written on the check and cannot be endorsed.

endorsee /ˌendɔːˈsiː/ *noun* a person whose name is written on a bill or check as having the right to cash it

endorsement /ɪnˈdɔːsmənt/ *noun* **1.** the act of endorsing **2.** a signature on a document which endorses it **3.** a note on an insurance policy which adds conditions to the policy

endorsement advertising /ɪnˈdɔːsmənt ˌædvətaɪzɪŋ/ *noun* same as **product endorsement**

endorser /ɪnˈdɔːsər/ *noun* a person who endorses a bill or check which is then paid to him or her

endowment /ɪnˈdaʊmənt/ *noun* the act of giving money to provide a regular income

COMMENT: The borrower pays interest on the mortgage in the usual way, but does not repay the capital; the endowment insurance (life insurance) is taken out to cover the total capital sum borrowed, and when the assurance matures the capital is paid off, and a further lump sum is usually available for payment to the borrower; a mortgage where the borrower repays both interest and capital is called a "repayment mortgage".

endowment insurance /ɪnˈdaʊmənt ɪnˌʃʊərəns/ *noun* an insurance policy where a sum of money is paid to the insured person on a specific date or to his heirs if he dies before that date

endowment mortgage /ɪnˈdaʊmənt ˌmɔːgɪdʒ/ *noun* a mortgage backed by an endowment insurance

endowment policy /ɪnˈdaʊmənt ˌpɒlɪsi/ *noun* same as **endowment insurance**

end product /ˌend ˈprɒdʌkt/ *noun* a manufactured product resulting from a production process

end-to-end /ˌend tə ˈend/ *adjective* **1.** including everything, so as to be complete ○ *end-to-end management software for small businesses* **2.** used to describe the transfer of information between the source and destination in a computer network

end user /ˌend ˈjuːzər/ *noun* a person who actually uses a product

energetic /ˌenəˈdʒetɪk/ *adjective* with a lot of energy ○ *The sales staff have made energetic attempts to sell the product.*

energy /ˈenədʒi/ *noun* **1.** a force or strength ○ *She hasn't the energy to be a good salesman.* ○ *They wasted their energies on trying to sell cars in the German market.* (NOTE: The plural is **energies**.) **2.** power produced from electricity, gasoline or a similar source ○ *We try to save energy by switching off the lights when the rooms are empty.* ○ *If you reduce the room temperature to eighteen degrees, you will save energy.*

energy conservation /ˌenədʒi ˌkɒnsəˈveɪʃ(ə)n/ *noun* the process of saving energy and keeping fuel consumption as low as possible by controlling the amounts of electricity, gas, and other fuels used in the workplace. Energy conservation can help to reduce costs and damage to the environment.

energy-saving /ˈenədʒi ˌseɪvɪŋ/ *adjective* which saves energy ○ *The company is introducing energy-saving measures.*

energy-saving device /ˌenədʒi ˌseɪvɪŋ dɪˈvaɪs/ *noun* a machine which saves energy or labor

enforce /ɪnˈfɔːs/ *verb* to make sure something is done or that a rule is obeyed ○ *to enforce the terms of a contract*

enforcement /ɪnˈfɔːsmənt/ *noun* the act of making sure that something is obeyed ○ *enforcement of the terms of a contract*

engage /ɪnˈgeɪdʒ/ *verb* **1.** to arrange to employ employees or advisors ○ *If we increase production we will need to engage more machinists.* ○ *She was engaged as a temporary replacement for the marketing manager who was ill.* ○ *The company has engaged twenty new sales representatives.* □ **to engage someone to do something** to make someone do something legally ○

The contract engages us to a minimum annual purchase. **2.** to employ ○ *We have engaged the best commercial lawyer to represent us.* ○ *The company has engaged twenty new salesmen.* **3.** □ **to be engaged in** to be busy with ○ *He is engaged in work on computers.* ○ *The company is engaged in trade with Africa.*

engaged /ɪnˈɡeɪdʒd/ *adjective* busy (telephone) ○ *You cannot speak to the manager – his line is engaged.*

engaged tone /ɪnˈɡeɪdʒd təʊn/ *noun* a sound made by a telephone when the line dialed is busy ○ *I tried to phone the complaints department but got only the engaged tone.*

engagement /ɪnˈɡeɪdʒmənt/ *noun* an agreement to do something

engagements /ɪnˈɡeɪdʒmənts/ *noun* arrangements to meet people ○ *I have no engagements for the rest of the day.* ○ *She noted the appointment in her engagements calendar.*

engine /ˈendʒɪn/ *noun* a machine which drives something ○ *A car with a small engine is more economical than one with a large one.* ○ *The elevator engine has broken down again – we shall just have to walk up to the 4th floor.*

engineer /ˌendʒɪˈnɪr/ *noun* a person who looks after technical equipment

engineering /ˌendʒɪˈnɪrɪŋ/ *noun* the science of technical equipment □ **an engineering consultant** an engineer who gives specialist advice

engineering department /ˌendʒɪˈnɪrɪŋ dɪˌpɑːrtmənt/ *noun* a section of a company dealing with equipment

enquire, enquiry /ɪnˈkwaɪr, ɪnˈkwaɪri/ same as **inquire, inquiry**

en route /ˌɒn ˈruːt/ *adverb* on the way ○ *The tanker sank when she was en route to the Gulf.*

entail /ɪnˈteɪl/ *noun* a legal condition which passes ownership of a property only to some specific persons ■ *verb* to involve ○ *Itemizing the sales figures will entail about ten days' work.*

enter /ˈentər/ *verb* **1.** to go in ○ *They all stood up when the chairman entered the room.* ○ *The company has spent millions trying to enter the do-it-yourself market.* **2.** to write ○ *to enter a name on a list* ○ *The clerk entered the interest in my bank book.* ○ *She entered a competition for a vacation*

in Mexico. ○ *They entered the sum in the ledger.* □ **to enter a bid for something** to offer (usually in writing) to buy something □ **to enter a caveat** to warn legally that you have an interest in a case, and that no steps can be taken without your permission

enter into *phrasal verb* to begin ○ *to enter into relations with someone* ○ *to enter into negotiations with a foreign government* ○ *to enter into a partnership with a friend* ○ *The company does not want to enter into any long-term agreement.*

entering /ˈentərɪŋ/ *noun* the act of writing items in a record

enterprise /ˈentərpraɪz/ *noun* **1.** initiative or willingness to take risks or to take responsibility ○ *We are looking for enterprise and ambition in our top managers.* **2.** a system of carrying on a business **3.** a business

enterprise culture /ˈentərpraɪz ˌkʌltʃər/ *noun* a general feeling that the commercial system works better with free enterprise, increased share ownership, property ownership, etc.

enterprise-level /ˈentərpraɪz ˌlev(ə)l/ *adjective* suitable for use by a business, especially a large one

enterprise portal /ˌentərpraɪz ˈpɔːrt(ə)l/ *noun* a website that contains a wide variety of information and services useful to the employees of a particular organization for their work (NOTE: The essential difference between an enterprise portal and an intranet is that an enterprise portal also provides external content that may be useful, e.g. specialist news feeds and access to industry research reports.)

enterprise resource planning /ˌentərpraɪz rɪˈzɔːrs ˌplænɪŋ/ *noun* the use of software to integrate all the functions of a business, e.g., planning, accounting, inventory management, manufacturing, marketing, and human resources. Abbreviation **ERP**

enterprise zone /ˈentərpraɪz zoʊn/ *noun* an area of the country where businesses are encouraged to develop by offering special conditions such as easy planning permission for buildings or a reduction in the business rate

entertain /ˌentəˈteɪn/ *verb* **1.** to offer such things as meals, hotel accommodations and theater tickets for the comfort and enjoyment of business visitors **2.** to be ready to consider (a proposal) ○ *The management will not entertain any suggestions from the union representatives.*

entertainment /ˌentəˈteɪnmənt/ *noun* the practice of offering meals or other recreation to business visitors

entertainment allowance /ˌentəˈteɪnmənt əˌlaʊəns/ *noun* money which managers are allowed by their company to spend on meals with visitors

entertainment expenses /ˌentəˈteɪnmənt ɪkˌspensɪz/ *plural noun* money spent on giving meals to business visitors

enticement /ɪnˈtaɪsmənt/ *noun* the act of attracting someone away from their job to another job which is better paid

entitle /ɪnˈtaɪt(ə)l/ *verb* to give the right to someone to have something ○ *After one year's service the employee is entitled to four weeks' vacation.* □ **he is entitled to a discount** he has the right to be given a discount

entitlement /ɪnˈtaɪt(ə)lmənt/ *noun* a person's right to something

entrance /ˈentrəns/ *noun* **1.** a way in ○ *The taxi will drop you at the main entrance.* ○ *Deliveries should be made to the south entrance.* **2.** *U.K.* same as **admission** (NOTE: The U.S. term is **admission**.)

entrepot port /ˈɑntrəpoʊ pɔrt/ *noun* a town with a large international commercial port dealing in re-exports

entrepot trade /ˈɑntrəpoʊ treɪd/ *noun* the exporting of imported goods

entrepreneur /ˌɑntrəprəˈnɜr/ *noun* a person who is willing to take commercial risks by starting or financing commercial enterprises

entrepreneurial /ˌɑntrəprəˈnɜriəl/ *adjective* taking commercial risks ○ *an entrepreneurial decision*

entrepreneurship /ˌɑntrəprəˈnɜrʃɪp/ *noun* willingness to take commercial risks

entrust /ɪnˈtrʌst/ *verb* □ **to entrust someone with something, to entrust something to someone** to give someone the responsibility for looking after some-

thing ○ *He was entrusted with the keys to the office safe.*

entry /ˈentri/ *noun* **1.** an item of written information put in an accounts ledger (NOTE: The plural is **entries**.) □ **to make an entry in a ledger** to write in details of a transaction **2.** an act of going in or the place where you can go in ○ *to pass a customs entry point* ○ *entry of goods under bond*

entry barrier /ˈentri ˌbæriər/ *noun* same as **barrier to entry**

entry charge /ˈentri tʃɑrdʒ/ *noun* money which you have to pay before you go in

entry level job /ˈentri ˌlev(ə)l dʒɑb/ *noun* a job for which no previous experience is needed ○ *It is only an entry level job, but you can expect promotion within six months.*

entry level pay /ˈentri ˌlev(ə)l peɪ/ *noun* pay for an entry level job

entry visa /ˈentri ˌvizə/ *noun* a visa allowing someone to enter a country

environment /ɪnˈvaɪrənmənt/ *noun* **1.** the area in which an organization works **2.** all the various types of computers, browsers or bandwidth access points by means of which a user may access a website. It is important to test a website within as many different environments as possible to make sure that it can be effectively accessed by a variety of users.

environmental analysis /ɪnˌvaɪrənmənt(ə)l əˈnæləsɪs/ *noun* the analysis of factors outside an organization such as demography or politics, in order to make strategic planning more effective ○ *Our environmental analysis must cover all the countries we sell in.* ○ *Environmental analysis made clear that some markets were too unstable to enter.*

environmental audit /ɪnˌvaɪrənmənt(ə)l ˈɔrdɪt/ *noun* an assessment made by a company or organization of the financial benefits and disadvantages to be derived from adopting a more environmentally sound policy

environmental management /ɪnˌvaɪrənmənt(ə)l ˈmænɪdʒmənt/ *noun* a planned approach to minimizing an organization's impact on the environment

environmental management system /ɪnˌvaɪrənmənt(ə)l ˈmænɪdʒmənt ˌsɪstəm/ *noun* the various procedures and controls that an organization sets up in order to minimize its impact on the environment. Abbreviation **EMS** (NOTE: The ISO 14000 quality standards set out formally how environmental management systems should operate.)

Environmental Protection Agency /ɪn,vaɪrənmənt(ə)l prə'tekʃ(ə)n ,eɪdʒənsi/ *noun* an agency of the U.S. government whose job is to protect human health and the environment. Abbreviation **EPA**

environmental scanning /ɪn ,vaɪrənmənt(ə)l 'skænɪŋ/ *noun* the continuous monitoring of events and trends in the business environment

environmental sustainability /ɪn ,vaɪrənmənt(ə)l səs,teɪnə'bɪlɪti/ *noun* the ability of a business to protect natural resources and ecological systems and still remain profitable

EOC *abbreviation* Equal Opportunities Commission

EOQ *abbreviation* economic order quantity

EPA *abbreviation* Environmental Protection Agency

e-payment /'i ,peɪmənt/ *noun* automatic withdrawal of funds from an account using electronic means, especially via the Internet

epos /'ipɒs/, **EPOS, EPoS** *abbreviation* electronic point of sale

EPS *abbreviation* earnings per share

e-purse /'i ,pɜrs/ *noun* same as **digital wallet**

equal /'ikwəl/ *adjective* exactly the same ○ *Male and female employees have equal pay.* ■ *verb* to be the same as ○ *Production this month has equaled our best month ever.* (NOTE: **equaling – equaled**. The U.K. spelling is **equalling – equalled**.)

Equal Employment Opportunity Commission /,ikwəl ɪm,plɔɪmənt ,ɒpə'tunəti/ *noun* a U.S. government organization set up in 1965 to eliminate discrimination in the workplace. It monitors employers' performance and enforces the Equal Employment Opportunity Act. Abbreviation **EEOC**

equality /ɪ'kwɒlɪti/ *noun* the state of being equal

equality of opportunity /ɪ,kwɒlɪti əv ,ɒpə'tunəti/ *noun* a situation where everyone, regardless of sex, race, class, etc., has the same opportunity to get a job

equalization /,ikwəlaɪ'zeɪʃən/ *noun* the process of making equal

equalize /'ikwəlaɪz/ *verb* to make equal ○ *to equalize dividends*

equally /'ikwəli/ *adverb* so that each has or pays the same, or to the same degree ○ *Costs will be shared equally between the two parties.* ○ *They were both equally responsible for the disastrous launch.*

Equal Opportunities Commission /,ikwəl ,ɒpə'tjunətiz kə,mɪʃ(ə)n/ *noun* a government body set up to make sure that no discrimination exists in employment. Abbreviation **EOC**

equal opportunities program /,ikwəl ,ɒpə'tunətiz ,prəʊɡræm/ *noun* a program to avoid discrimination in employment (NOTE: The U.S. term is **affirmative action**.)

equal pay /,ikwəl 'peɪ/ *noun* the act of paying the same rate to men and women who do the same job

equilibrium /,ikwɪ'lɪbriəm/ *noun* the state of balance in the economy where supply equals demand or a country's balance of payments is neither in deficit nor in excess

equip /ɪ'kwɪp/ *verb* to provide with machinery ○ *to equip a factory with new machinery* ○ *The office is fully equipped with word-processors.*

equipment /ɪ'kwɪpmənt/ *noun* machinery and furniture required to make a factory or office work ○ *office equipment* or *business equipment* ○ *an office equipment supplier* ○ *an office equipment catalog*

equipment leasing /ɪ'kwɪpmənt ,lisɪŋ/ *noun* a system that allows organizations to rent equipment that they need to use for a long period, e.g., cars or office machines, from other organizations instead of buying it, on condition that they sign a contract for the rental with owners (NOTE: Equipment leasing agreements often include arrangements for maintenance and replacement.)

equities /'ekwɪtiz/ *plural noun* stock in a corporation

"…in the past three years commercial property has seriously underperformed equities and dropped out of favour as a result" [*Investors Chronicle*]

equity /'ekwɪti/ *noun* **1.** a right to receive dividends as part of the profit of a company in which you own stock **2.** ownership in a company in the form of stock **3.** the value of a company which is the property of its stockholders (the company's assets less its liabilities, not including the ordinary share capital) **4.** the value of an asset, such as a house, less any mortgage on it

COMMENT: "Equity" (also called "capital" or "shareholders" equity' or "shareholders" capital' or "shareholders" funds') is the current net value of the company including the nominal value of the shares in issue. After several years a company would expect to increase its net worth above the value of the starting capital. "Equity capital" on the other hand is only the nominal value of the shares in issue.

equity capital /'ekwəti ˌkæpɪt(ə)l/ *noun* the nominal value of the stock owned by the stockholders of a company

equity fund /'ekwɪti fʌnd/ *noun* a fund which is invested in equities, not in government securities or other funds

equity investment fund /ˌekwɪti ɪn 'vestmənt ˌfʌnd/ *noun* same as **equity fund**

equivalence /ɪ'kwɪvələns/ *noun* the condition of having the same value or of being the same

equivalent /ɪ'kwɪvələnt/ *adjective* □ **to be equivalent to** to have the same value as or to be the same as ○ *The total dividend paid is equivalent to one quarter of the pretax profits.* ○ *Our managing director's salary is equivalent to that of far less experienced employees in other organizations.*

e-retailer /'i ˌriteɪlər/ *noun* a business that uses an electronic network such as the Internet to sell its goods or services

ergonomics /ˌɜːrgə'nɑmɪks/ *noun* the study of the relationship between people at work and their working conditions, especially the machines they use (NOTE: takes a singular verb)

ergonomist /ɜːr'gɑnəmɪst/ *noun* a scientist who studies people at work and tries to improve their working conditions

ERM *abbreviation* exchange rate mechanism

error /'erər/ *noun* a mistake ○ *He made an error in calculating the total.* ○ *Someone must have made a keyboarding error.*

□ **in error** by mistake ○ *The letter was sent to the Boston office in error.*

error rate /'erər reɪt/ *noun* the number of mistakes per thousand entries or per page

errors and omissions excepted /ˌerərz ənd oʊˌmɪʃ(ə)nz ɪk'septɪd/ *phrase* words written on an invoice to show that the company has no responsibility for mistakes in the invoice. Abbreviation **e. & o.e.**

escalate /'eskəleɪt/ *verb* to increase steadily

escalation /ˌeskə'leɪʃ(ə)n/ *noun* a steady increase ○ *an escalation of wage demands* ○ *The union has threatened an escalation in strike action.* □ **escalation of prices** a steady increase in prices

escalation clause /ˌeskə'leɪʃ(ə)n ˌklɔːz/ *noun* same as **escalator clause**

escalator clause /'eskəleɪtər klɔːz/ *noun* a clause in a contract allowing for regular price increases because of increased costs, or regular wage increases because of the increased cost of living

escape clause /ɪ'skeɪp klɔːz/ *noun* a clause in a contract which allows one of the parties to avoid carrying out the terms of the contract under conditions

escrow /'eskroʊ/ *noun* an agreement between two parties that something should be held by a third party until conditions are fulfilled □ **in escrow** held in safekeeping by a third party □ **document held in escrow** a document given to a third party to keep and to pass on to someone when money has been paid

escrow account /'eskroʊ əˌkaʊnt/ *noun* an account where money is held in escrow until a contract is signed or until goods are delivered

escudo /es'kjuːdoʊ/ *noun* a former unit of currency in Portugal

e-shock /'i ʃɑk/ *noun* the revolutionary impact of e-commerce and its apparently irresistible progress

ESOP *abbreviation* employee stock ownership plan

essential /ɪ'senʃəl/ *adjective* very important ○ *It is essential that an agreement be reached before the end of the month.* ○ *The factory is lacking essential spare parts.*

essential foodstuffs /ɪ,senʃəl
'fudstʌfs/ *plural noun* very important
food, such as bread or rice

essentials /ɪ'senʃəlz/ *plural noun*
goods or products which are very important

establish /ɪ'stæblɪʃ/ *verb* to set up or to
open ○ *The company has established a
branch in Australia.* ○ *The business was
established in Scotland in 1823.* ○ *It is still
a young company, having been established
for only four years.* □ **to establish oneself
in business** to become successful in a new
business

establishment /ɪ'stæblɪʃmənt/ *noun*
1. a commercial business ○ *He runs an important printing establishment.* 2. the
number of people working in a company □
to be on the establishment to be a full-
time employee □ **office with an establishment of fifteen** an office with a budgeted
staff of fifteen

establishment charges /ɪ
'stæblɪʃmənt ,tʃɑrdʒɪz/ *plural noun* the
cost of people and property in a company's
accounts

estate /ɪ'steɪt/ *noun* property left by a
dead person

estate agency /ɪ'steɪt ,eɪdʒənsi/ *noun
U.K.* same as **real estate agency**

estate agent /ɪ'steɪt ,eɪdʒənt/ *noun
U.K.* same as **real estate agent**

estate tax /ɪ'steɪt tæks/ *noun* a tax paid
on the right to pass property on to heirs,
based on the value of the property and paid
before it is passed to the heirs. Also called
death tax

estimate *noun* /'estɪmət/ 1. a calculation of the probable cost, size, or time of
something ○ *Can you give me an estimate
of how much time was spent on the job?* □
these figures are only an estimate these
are not the final accurate figures 2. a calculation by a contractor or seller of a service
of how much something is likely to cost,
given to a client in advance of an order ○
*You should ask for an estimate before com-
mitting yourselves.* ○ *Before we can give
the grant we must have an estimate of the
total costs involved.* ○ *Unfortunately the
final bill was quite different from the estimate.* □ **to put in an estimate** to give
someone a written calculation of the probable costs of carrying out a job ○ *Three
firms put in estimates for the job.* ■ *verb*

/'estɪmeɪt/ 1. to calculate the probable
cost, size, or time of something ○ *to estimate that it will cost $1m* or *to estimate
costs at $1m* ○ *We estimate current sales
at only 60% of last year.* 2. □ **to estimate
for a job** to state in writing the future costs
of carrying out a piece of work so that a
client can make an order ○ *Three firms estimated for the refitting of the offices.*

estimated /'estɪmeɪtɪd/ *adjective* calculated approximately ○ *estimated sales* ○
*Costs were slightly more than the estimat-
ed figure.*

estimated time of arrival
/,estɪmətɪd ,taɪm əv ə'raɪv(ə)l/ *noun* a
time when an aircraft, a bus or a group of
tourists is expected to arrive. Abbreviation
ETA

estimation /,estɪ'meɪʃ(ə)n/ *noun* an
approximate calculation

estimator /'estɪmeɪtər/ *noun* a person
whose job is to calculate estimates for carrying out work

ETA *abbreviation* estimated time of arrival

e-tailer /'i ,teɪlər/ *noun* same as **e-retailer**

e-tailing /'i ,teɪlɪŋ/ *noun* 1. the selling of
goods and services using an electronic network such as the Internet 2. same as **e-
commerce**

etc. /ɪt'setrə/ and so on ○ *The import
duty is to be paid on luxury items including
cars, watches, etc.*

ethical investment /,eθɪk(ə)l ɪn
'vestmənt/ *noun* an investment in companies that follow certain moral standards

ethical screening /,eθɪk(ə)l 'skriːnɪŋ/
noun the process of checking companies
against certain moral standards, and removing those which do not conform

ethics /'eθɪks/ *noun* the moral aspects of
decision-making ○ *Whether or not we use
such aggressive sales tactics is a matter of
ethics.* (NOTE: takes a singular verb)

ethos /'iːθɒs/ *noun* a characteristic way
of working and thinking

e-ticket /'i ,tɪkɪt/ *noun* a reservation, especially for air travel, made on the Internet
for which no paper ticket is issued to the
customer

EU *abbreviation* European Union ○ *EU
ministers met today in Brussels.* ○ *The
U.S. is increasing its trade with the EU.*

euro /'jʊrʊʊ/ *noun* a unit of currency adopted as legal tender in several European countries from January 1st, 1999 ○ *Many articles are priced in euros.* ○ *What's the exchange rate for the euro?* (NOTE: The plural is **euro** or **euros**.)

"...cross-border mergers in the European Union have shot up since the introduction of the euro" [*Investors Chronicle*]

COMMENT: The countries which are joined together in the European Monetary Union and adopted the euro as their common currency in 1999 are: Austria, Belgium, Finland, France, Germany, Ireland, Italy, Luxembourg, the Netherlands, Portugal, and Spain. The conversion of these currencies to the euro was fixed on 1st January 1999 at the following rates: Austrian schilling: 13.7603; Belgian & Luxembourg franc: 40.3399; Finnish Markka: 5.94573; French franc: 6.55957; German mark: 1.95583; Irish punt: 0.787564; Italian lira: 1936.27; Dutch guilder: 2.20371; Portuguese escudo: 200.482; Spanish peseta: 166.386. The CFA franc and CFP franc were pegged to the euro at the same time.

Euro- /jʊrʊʊ/ *prefix* referring to Europe or the European Union

euro account /'jʊrʊʊ ə,kaʊnt/ *noun* a bank account in euros (NOTE: Written **Ä** before numbers: *Ä250:* say: "two hundred and fifty euros".)

Eurocurrency /'jʊrʊʊkʌrənsi/ *noun* any currency used for trade within Europe but outside its country of origin, the Eurodollar being the most important ○ *a Eurocurrency loan* ○ *the Eurocurrency market*

Eurodollar /'jʊrʊʊdɑlər/ *noun* a U.S. dollar deposited in a bank outside the U.S., used mainly for trade within Europe ○ *a Eurodollar loan* ○ *the Eurodollar markets*

Euroland /'jʊrʊʊlænd/ *noun* same as **Eurozone**

euronote /'jʊrʊʊ,nʊʊt/ *noun* a short-term Eurocurrency bearer note

Europe /'jʊrəp/ *noun* **1.** the continent of Europe, the part of the world to the west of Asia, from Russia to Ireland ○ *Most of the countries of Western Europe are members of the EU.* ○ *Poland is in eastern Europe, and Greece, Spain and Portugal are in southern Europe.* **2.** the same area, but not including the U.K. **3.** the European Union, including the U.K. ○ *Canadian exports to Europe have risen by 25%.* **4.** other EU countries but not including the U.K. ○ *U.K. sales to Europe have increased this year.*

European /,jʊrə'piən/ *adjective* referring to Europe ○ *They do business with several European countries.*

European Central Bank /,jʊrəpiən ,sentrəl 'bæŋk/ *noun* central bank for most of the countries in the European Union, those which have accepted European Monetary Union and have the euro as their common currency. Abbreviation **ECB**

"...the ECB begins with some $300 billion of foreign exchange reserves, far more than any other central bank" [*Investors Chronicle*]

"...any change in the European bank's statutes must be agreed and ratified by all EU member nations" [*The Times*]

European Commission /,jʊrəpiən kə'mɪʃ(ə)n/ *noun* the main executive body of the EU, made up of members nominated by each member state. Also called **Commission of the European Community**

European Common Market /,jʊrəpiən ,kamən 'markət/ *noun* formerly, the name for the European Community, an organization which links several European countries for the purposes of trade

European Community /,jʊrəpiən kə 'mjunɪti/ *noun* formerly, the name of the European Union. Abbreviation **EC**

European Economic Area /,jʊrəpiən ,ikənamɪk 'eriə/ an area comprising the countries of the EU and the members of EFTA, formed by an agreement on trade between the two organizations. Abbreviation **EEA**

European Economic Community /,jʊrəpiən ,ikənamɪk kə'mjunɪti/ *noun* a grouping of European countries which later became the European Union. Abbreviation **EEC**. Also called **European Community**

European Foundation for Quality Management /,jʊrəpiən faʊn ,deɪʃ(ə)n fə ,kwaləti 'mænɪdʒmənt/ *noun* an institution founded in the late 1980s by leading companies in Western Europe to oversee standards in quality management and grants awards. It established the EFQM European Excellence Model, which focuses on the key elements that sustain business success. Abbreviation **EFQM**

European Free Trade Association /ˌjʊərəpiən fri ˈtreɪd əˌsoʊsieɪʃ(ə)n/ *noun* a group of countries (Iceland, Liechtenstein, Norway and Switzerland) formed to encourage freedom of trade between its members, and linked with the EU in the European Economic Area. Abbreviation **EFTA**

European Monetary Union /ˌjʊərəpiən ˈmʌnɪt(ə)ri ˌjunjən/ *noun* the process by which some of the member states of the EU joined together to adopt the euro as their common currency on 1st January 1999. Abbreviation **EMU**

European options /ˌjʊərəˈpiən ˌɑpʃənz/ *plural noun* an American term for options which can only be exercised on their expiration date

European Union /ˌjʊərəpiən ˈjunjən/ *noun* a group of European countries linked together by the Treaty of Rome. The European Community was set up in 1957 and changed its name to the European Union when it adopted the single market. It has now grown to include twenty-five member states. These are: Austria, Belgium, Cyprus, the Czech Republic, Denmark, Estonia, Finland, France, Germany, Greece, Hungary, Ireland, Italy, Latvia, Lithuania, Luxembourg, Malta, the Netherlands, Poland, Portugal, Slovakia, Slovenia, Spain, Sweden and the United Kingdom. The member states of the EU are linked together by the Treaty of Rome in such a way that trade is more free, that money can be moved from one country to another freely, that people can move from one country to another more freely and that people can work more freely in other countries of the group (the four fundamental freedoms). Abbreviation **EU**

COMMENT: The European Community was set up in 1957 and changed its name to the European Union when it adopted the Single Market. It has now grown to include fifteen member states. These are: Austria, Belgium, Denmark, Finland, France, Germany, Greece, Ireland, Italy, Luxembourg, the Netherlands, Portugal, Spain, Sweden and the United Kingdom; other countries are negotiating to join. The member states of the EU are linked together by the Treaty of Rome in such a way that trade is more free, money can

be moved from one country to another freely, people can move from one country to another more freely and people can work more freely in other countries of the group.

Eurozone /ˈjʊəroʊzoʊn/ *noun* the European countries which use the euro as a common currency, seen as a group. Also called **Euroland**

"…the European Central Bank left the door open yesterday for a cut in Eurozone interest rates" [*Financial Times*]

"…a sustained recovery in the euro will require either a sharp slowdown in U.S. growth or a rise in inflation and interest rates in the Eurozone beyond that already discounted" [*Investors Chronicle*]

EVA *trademark* a trademark for a method of calculating the profit of an enterprise. It is net operating profit minus the cost of capital. Full form of **Economic Value Added**

evade /ɪˈveɪd/ *verb* to try to avoid something □ **to evade tax** to try illegally to avoid paying tax

evaluate /ɪˈvæljueɪt/ *verb* to examine something to see how good it is

evaluation /ɪˌvæljuˈeɪʃ(ə)n/ *noun* the examination of a product to see how good it is

evasion /ɪˈveɪʒ(ə)n/ *noun* the act of avoiding something

even lot /ˌivən ˈlɑt/ *noun* same as **round lot**

evidence /ˈevɪd(ə)ns/ *noun* written or spoken information ○ *What evidence is there that the new employee is causing all the trouble?*

EWCP *abbreviation* Export Working Capital Program

ex /eks/ *prefix* out of or from □ **price ex works**, **ex factory** a price not including transportation from the maker's factory ■ *adverb* without ■ *preposition*, *prefix* formerly ○ *Mr. Smith, the ex-chairman of the company*

exact /ɪgˈzækt/ *adjective* strictly correct, not varying in any way from, e.g., not any more or less than, what is stated ○ *The exact time is 10.27.* ○ *The salesgirl asked me if I had the exact sum, since the store had no change.*

exactly /ɪgˈzæktli/ *adverb* not varying in any way from, e.g., not any more or less than, what is stated ○ *The total cost was exactly $6,500.*

examination /ɪɡˌzæmɪˈneɪʃ(ə)n/ *noun* an act of looking at something very carefully to see if it is acceptable

examine /ɪɡˈzæmɪn/ *verb* to look at someone or something very carefully ○ *Customs officials asked to examine the inside of the car.* ○ *The police are examining the papers from the managing director's safe.*

example /ɪɡˈzæmpəl/ *noun* something chosen to show how things should be done ○ *The motor show has many examples of energy-saving cars on display.* ○ *Her sales success in Europe is an example of what can be achieved by determination.* □ **for example** to show one thing out of many ○ *The government wants to encourage exports – for example, it gives free credit to exporters.*

exceed /ɪkˈsiːd/ *verb* to be more than ○ *a discount not exceeding 15%* ○ *Last year costs exceeded 20% of income for the first time.* □ **he has exceeded his credit limit** he has borrowed more money than he is allowed

excellent /ˈeksələnt/ *adjective* very good ○ *The quality of the firm's products is excellent, but its sales force is not large enough.*

except /ɪkˈsept/ *preposition, conjunction* not including ○ *sales tax is levied on all goods and services except books, newspapers and children's clothes.* ○ *Sales are rising in all markets except the Far East.*

excepted /ɪkˈseptɪd/ *adverb* not including

exceptional /ɪkˈsepʃən(ə)l/ *adjective* different or not usual

exceptional items /ɪkˌsepʃən(ə)l ˈaɪtəmz/ *plural noun* items which arise from normal trading but which are unusual because of their size or nature; such items are shown separately in a note to the company's accounts but not on the face of the P & L account unless they are profits or losses on the sale or termination of an operation, or costs of a fundamental reorganization or restructuring which have a material effect on the nature and focus of the reporting entity's operations, or profits or losses on the disposal of fixed assets

exception reporting /ɪkˌsepʃən rɪˈpɔːtɪŋ/ *noun* a system of information distribution that passes on only information that is new and out of the ordinary, in order

to avoid overloading recipients with information that is out of date or has already been transmitted to them. ◊ **management by exception**

excess /ˈekses/; /ɪkˈses/ *noun, adjective* an amount which is more than what is allowed ○ *an excess of expenditure over revenue* ○ *Excess costs have caused us considerable problems.* □ **in excess of** above, more than ○ *quantities in excess of twenty-five kilos*

excess capacity /ˌekses kəˈpæsəti/ *noun* spare capacity which is not being used

excess demand /ˌekses dɪˈmænd/ *noun* more demand at the present price than sellers can satisfy ○ *Much more machinery and labor must be acquired to meet excess demand.*

excess fare /ˈekses feər/ *noun* an extra fare to be paid (such as for traveling first class with a second class ticket)

excessive /ɪkˈsesɪv/ *adjective* too large ○ *Excessive production costs made the product uneconomic.*

excess profit /ˌekses ˈprɒfɪt/ *noun* a profit which is higher than what is thought to be normal

excess profits tax /ˌekses ˈprɒfɪts ˌtæks/ *noun* a tax on profits which are higher than what is thought to be normal

excess supply /ˌekses səˈplaɪ/ *noun* more supply at the present price than buyers want to buy

exchange /ɪksˈtʃeɪndʒ/ *noun* **1.** the act of giving one thing for another **2.** a market for stock, commodities, futures, etc. ■ *verb* **1.** □ **to exchange something (for something else)** to give one thing in place of something else ○ *He exchanged his motorcycle for a car.* ○ *Hang on to your sales slip in case you need to exchange the items you bought.* **2.** □ **to exchange contracts** to sign a contract when buying a property, carried out by both buyer and seller at the same time **3.** to change money of one country for money of another ○ *to exchange euros for dollars*

exchangeable /ɪksˈtʃeɪndʒəb(ə)l/ *adjective* possible to exchange

exchange controls /ɪksˈtʃeɪndʒ kənˌtrəʊlz/ *plural noun* government restrictions on changing the local currency into foreign currency ○ *The government had to impose exchange controls to stop the rush* *to buy dollars.* ○ *They say the government is going to lift exchange controls.*

exchange dealer /ɪks'tʃeɪndʒ ˌdilər/ *noun* a person who buys and sells foreign currency

exchange dealings /ɪks'tʃeɪndʒ ˌdilɪŋz/ *plural noun* the buying and selling of foreign currency

exchange economy /ɪks'tʃeɪndʒ ɪ ˌkɑnəmi/ *noun* an economy based on the exchange of goods and services

exchange of contracts /ɪks,tʃeɪndʒ əv 'kɑntrækts/ *noun* the point in the sale of property when the buyer and the seller both sign the contract of sale, which then becomes binding

exchange premium /ɪks'tʃeɪndʒ ˌprimiəm/ *noun* an extra cost above the usual rate for buying a foreign currency

exchanger /ɪks'tʃeɪndʒər/ *noun* a person who buys and sells foreign currency

exchange rate /ɪks'tʃeɪndʒ reɪt/ *noun* **1.** a rate at which one currency is exchanged for another. Also called **rate of exchange 2.** a figure that expresses how much a unit of one country's currency is worth in terms of the currency of another country

exchange rate mechanism /ɪks 'tʃeɪndʒ reɪt ˌmekənɪz(ə)m/ *noun* a former method of stabilizing exchange rates within the European Monetary System, where currencies could only move up or down within a narrow band (usually 2.25% either way, but for some currencies this is widened to 6%) without involving a realignment of all the currencies in the system

exchange transaction /ɪks'tʃeɪndʒ træn,zækʃən/ *noun* a purchase or sale of foreign currency

Exchequer /ɪks'tʃekə/ ◇ **the Exchequer** *U.K.* **1.** the fund of all money received by the government of the U.K. from taxes and other revenues **2.** the British government's account with the Bank of England **3.** the British government department dealing with public revenue

excise /ɪk'saɪz/ *verb* to cut out ○ *Please excise all references to the strike in the minutes.*

excise tax /'eksaɪz ˌtæks/ *noun* a tax on goods such as alcohol and gasoline which are produced in the country

exclude /ɪk'sklud/ *verb* to keep out, or not to include ○ *The interest charges have been excluded from the document.* ○ *Damage by fire is excluded from the policy.*

excluding /ɪk'skludɪŋ/ *preposition* not including ○ *All sales staff, excluding those living in New York, can claim expenses for attending the sales conference.*

exclusion /ɪk'skluʒ(ə)n/ *noun* **1.** the act of not including something **2.** an item reported on the tax return but on which no tax is payable **3.** the action of cutting people off from being full members of society, because of lack of education, alcoholism or drug abuse, unemployment, etc.

exclusion clause /ɪk'skluʒ(ə)n klɔz/ *noun* a clause in an insurance policy or warranty which says which items or events are not covered

exclusive /ɪk'sklusɪv/ *adjective* **1.** limited to one person or group □ **to have exclusive right to market a product** to be the only person who has the right to market a product **2.** □ **exclusive of** not including ○ *The invoice is exclusive of tax.*

exclusive agreement /ɪk,sklusɪv ə 'grimənt/ *noun* an agreement where a person is made sole agent for a product in a market

exclusive distributor /ɪk,sklusɪv dɪ 'strɪbjutər/ *noun* a retailer who is the only one in an area who is allowed by the manufacturer to sell a certain product

exclusivity /ˌeksklu'sɪvəti/ *noun* the exclusive right to market a product

ex coupon /eks 'kupɑn/ *adverb* without the interest coupons or after interest has been paid

excuse *noun* /ɪk'skjus/ a reason for doing something wrong ○ *His excuse for not coming to the meeting was that he had been told about it only the day before.* □ **the managing director refused to accept the sales manager's excuses for the poor sales** she refused to believe that there was a good reason for the poor sales ■ *verb* /ɪk 'skjuz/ to forgive a small mistake ○ *She can be excused for not knowing the French for "photocopier".*

ex-directory /ˌeks daɪ'rekt(ə)ri/ *adjective U.K.* (telephone number) which is not printed in the telephone book. Same as **unlisted**

ex dividend /ˌeks 'dɪvɪdend/, **ex div** /ˌeks 'dɪv/ *adjective* used to describe a stock that does not have the right to receive the next dividend ○ *The stock went ex dividend yesterday.* Abbreviation **xd**

exec /ɪgˈzek/ *noun* an executive or executive officer

execute /ˈeksɪkjut/ *verb* to carry out an order ○ *Failure to execute orders may lead to dismissal.* ○ *There were many practical difficulties in executing the managing director's instructions.*

execution /ˌeksɪˈkjuʃ(ə)n/ *noun* the carrying out of a commercial order or contract

executive /ɪgˈzekjətɪv/ *adjective* putting decisions into action ■ *noun* a person in a business who takes decisions, a manager or director ○ *sales executives* ○ *a senior* or *junior executive*

"...one in ten students commented on the long hours which executives worked" [*Employment Gazette*]

"...our executives are motivated by a desire to carry out a project to the best of their ability" [*British Business*]

executive board /ɪgˈzekjutɪv bɔrd/ *noun* a board of directors which deals with the day-to-day running of the company (as opposed to a supervisory board, which deals with policy and planning)

executive committee /ɪgˌzekjutɪv kəˈmɪti/ *noun* a committee which runs a society or a club

executive director /ɪgˌzekjutɪv daɪˈrektər/ *noun* **1.** a director who works full-time in the company, as opposed to a "non-executive director" **2.** a senior employee of an organization who is usually in charge of one or other of its main functions, e.g., sales or human relations, and is usually, but not always, a member of the board of directors

executive power /ɪgˌzekjutɪv ˈpaʊr/ *noun* a right to act as director or to put decisions into action

executive search /ɪgˈzekjutɪv sɜrtʃ/ *noun* the process of looking for new managers for organizations, usually by approaching managers in their existing jobs and asking them if they want to work for different companies (NOTE: a more polite term for **headhunting**)

executor /ɪgˈzekjutər/ *noun* a person or firm that sees that the terms of a will are carried out ○ *She was named executor of her brother's will.*

executrix /ɪgˈzekjutrɪks/ *noun* a female executor

exempt /ɪgˈzempt/ *adjective* not forced to do something, especially not forced to obey a particular law or rule, or not forced to pay something ○ *Anyone over 65 is exempt from charges* ○ *He was exempt from military service in his country.* □ **exempt from tax** not required to pay tax ○ *As a nonprofit organization we are exempt from tax.* ■ *verb* **1.** □ **to exempt someone or something from something** to allow someone or something not to do something that others are forced to do **2.** to free someone from having to do a task ○ *I hope to be exempted from taking these tests.* ○ *She was exempted from fire duty.*

exemption /ɪgˈzempʃ(ə)n/ *noun* **1.** the act of exempting something from a contract or from a tax **2.** a part of an income that is not taxed (NOTE: The U.K. term is **allowance**)

exempt rating /ɪgˈzempt ˌreɪtɪŋ/ *noun* U.K. the legal right of a business not to add VAT to the prices of some products or services

exempt supplies /ɪgˌzempt səˈplaɪz/ *plural noun* U.K. products or services on which the supplier does not have to charge sales tax, e.g., the purchase of, or rent on, real estate and financial services

exercise /ˈeksərsaɪz/ *noun* a use of something □ **exercise of an option** using an option, putting an option into action ■ *verb* to use ○ *The chairwoman exercised her veto to block the motion.* □ **to exercise an option** to put an option into action ○ *He exercised his option to acquire sole marketing rights for the product.*

exercise price /ˈeksəsaɪz praɪs/ *noun* same as **strike price**

ex gratia /ˌeks ˈgreɪʃə/ *adjective* as an act of favor, without obligation

ex gratia payment /eks ˌgreɪʃə ˈpeɪmənt/ *noun* a payment made as a gift, with no other obligations

exhaust /ɪgˈzɔst/ *verb* to use up totally ○ *We will go on negotiating until all possible solutions have been exhausted.*

exhibit /ɪgˈzɪbɪt/ *noun* **1.** a thing which is shown ○ *The buyers admired the exhibits on our stand.* **2.** a single section of an exhibition ○ *the British Trade Exhibit at the International Computer Fair* ■ *verb* □

to exhibit at the Motor Show to display new models of cars at the Motor Show

exhibition /ˌeksɪˈbɪʃ(ə)n/ *noun* an occasion for the display of goods so that buyers can look at them and decide what to buy ○ *The government has sponsored an exhibition of good design.* ○ *We have a stand at the Ideal Home Exhibition.* ○ *The agricultural exhibition grounds were crowded with visitors.*

exhibition booth /ˌeksɪˈbɪʃ(ə)n buð/, **exhibition stand** *noun* a separate section of an exhibition where a company exhibits its products or services

exhibition room /ˌeksɪˈbɪʃ(ə)n rum/ *noun* a place where goods are shown so that buyers can look at them and decide what to buy

exhibitor /ɪɡˈzɪbɪtər/ *noun* a person or company that shows products at an exhibition

exile /ˈeksaɪl/ *noun* **1.** the state of being sent away from your home country ○ *The ex-finance minister went into exile in Switzerland.* (NOTE: no plural in this meaning) **2.** a person who is sent away from his own country ■ *verb* to send someone away from his home country as a punishment ○ *The former finance minister was exiled for life.*

exit /ˈeɡzɪt/ *noun* **1.** the way out of a building ○ *The customers all rushed toward the exits.* **2.** the act of going out or leaving **3.** the act of leaving a job

ex officio /ˌeks əˈfɪʃiou/ *adjective, adverb* because of an office held ○ *The treasurer is ex officio a member* or *an ex officio member of the finance committee.*

expand /ɪkˈspænd/ *verb* to get bigger, or make something bigger ○ *an expanding economy* ○ *The company is expanding fast.* ○ *We have had to expand our sales force.*

expanded polystyrene /ˌɪkˌspændɪd ˌpɑliˈstaɪriːn/ *noun* light solid plastic used for packing ○ *The computer is delivered packed in expanded polystyrene.*

expansion /ɪkˈspænʃən/ *noun* an increase in size ○ *The expansion of the domestic market.* ○ *The company had difficulty in financing its current expansion program.*

expect /ɪkˈspekt/ *verb* to hope that something is going to happen ○ *We are expecting him to arrive at 10:45.* ○ *They are*

expecting a check from their agent next week. ○ *The house was sold for more than the expected price.*

expectation /ˌekspekˈteɪʃ(ə)n/ *noun* **1.** what someone believes will happen, especially concerning their future prosperity **2.** what someone believes about an item or service to be purchased, which is one of the reasons for making the purchase

expenditure /ɪkˈspendɪtʃər/ *noun* the amount of money spent □ **heavy expenditure on equipment** spending large sums of money on equipment

expense /ɪkˈspens/ *noun* money spent ○ *It is not worth the expense.* ○ *The expense is too much for my bank balance.* ○ *The likely profits do not justify the expense of setting up the project.* ○ *It was well worth the expense to get really high-quality equipment.* □ **at great expense** having spent a lot of money □ **he furnished the office regardless of expense** without thinking how much it cost

expense account /ɪkˈspens əˌkaʊnt/ *noun* an allowance of money which a business pays for an employee to spend on traveling and entertaining clients in connection with that business ○ *I'll put this lunch on my expense account.*

expenses /ɪkˈspensɪz/ *plural noun* money paid to cover the costs incurred by someone when doing something ○ *The salary offered is £10,000 plus expenses.* ○ *She has a high salary and all her travel expenses are paid by the company.* □ **all expenses paid** with all costs paid by the company ○ *The company sent him to San Francisco all expenses paid.* □ **to cut down on expenses** to reduce spending

expensive /ɪkˈspensɪv/ *adjective* which costs a lot of money ○ *First-class air travel is becoming more and more expensive.*

experience /ɪkˈspɪriəns/ *noun* knowledge or skill that comes from having had to deal with many different situations ○ *She has a lot of experience of dealing with German companies.* ○ *I gained most of my experience abroad.* ○ *Considerable experience is required for this job.* ○ *The applicant was pleasant, but did not have any relevant experience.* ■ *verb* to live through a situation ○ *The company experienced a period of falling sales.*

expert /'ekspɜrt/ *noun* a person who knows a lot about something ○ *an expert in the field of electronics* or *an electronics expert* ○ *The company asked a financial expert for advice* or *asked for expert financial advice.* □ **expert's report** a report written by an expert

expertise /ˌekspər'tiz/ *noun* specialist knowledge or skill in a particular field ○ *We hired Mr. Smith because of his financial expertise* or *because of his expertise in finance.* ○ *With years of experience in the industry, we have plenty of expertise to draw on.* ○ *Lack of marketing expertise led to low sales figures.*

expert system /'ekspɜrt ˌsɪstəm/ *noun* software that applies the knowledge, advice and rules defined by experts in a particular field to a user's data to help solve a problem

expiration /ˌekspə'reɪʃ(ə)n/ *noun* the act of coming to an end ○ *the expiration of an insurance policy* ○ *to repay before the expiration of the stated period* □ **on expiration of the lease** when the lease comes to an end

expiration date /ˌekspɪ'reɪʃ(ə)n deɪt/ *noun* **1.** a date when something will end **2.** the last date on which a credit card can be used

expire /ɪk'spaɪə/ *verb* to come to an end ○ *The lease expires in 2010.* □ **his passport has expired** his passport is no longer valid

expiry /ɪk'spaɪri/ *noun* the act of coming to an end ○ *the expiry of an insurance policy*

explain /ɪk'spleɪn/ *verb* to give reasons for something ○ *He explained to the customs officials that the two computers were presents from friends.* ○ *Can you explain why the sales in the first quarter are so high?* ○ *The sales director tried to explain the sudden drop in unit sales.*

explanation /ˌeksplə'neɪʃ(ə)n/ *noun* a reason for something ○ *The tax inspector asked for an explanation of the invoices.* ○ *At the annual meeting, the chairman gave an explanation for the high level of interest payments.* ○ *The human resources department did not accept her explanation for being late.*

exploit /ɪk'splɔɪt/ *verb* to use something to make a profit ○ *The company is exploiting its contacts in the Trade Office.* ○ *We hope to exploit the oil resources in the China Sea.* ○ *The directors exploit their employees, who have to work hard for very little pay.*

exploitation /ˌeksplɔɪ'teɪʃ(ə)n/ *noun* the unfair use of cheap labor to get work done ○ *The exploitation of migrant farm workers was only stopped when they became unionized.*

explore /ɪk'splɔr/ *verb* to examine carefully ○ *We are exploring the possibility of opening an office in Seattle.*

exponential smoothing /ˌekspənenʃ(ə)l 'smuðɪŋ/ *noun* a technique for working out averages while allowing for recent changes in values by moving forward the period under consideration at regular intervals

export *noun* /'eksport/ the practice or business of sending goods to foreign countries to be sold ○ *50% of the company's profits come from the export trade* or *the export market.* ◊ **exports** ■ *verb* /ɪk'sport/ to send goods to foreign countries for sale ○ *50% of our production is exported.* ○ *The company imports raw materials and exports the finished products.*

export agent /'eksport ˌeɪdʒənt/ *noun* a person who sells overseas on behalf of a company and earns a commission ○ *An export agent is developing our business in West Africa.* ○ *She is working in New York as an export agent for a French company.*

exportation /ˌekspə'teɪʃ(ə)n/ *noun* the act of sending goods to foreign countries for sale

export bounty /'eksport ˌbaʊnti/ *noun* a government payment to businesses to encourage specific types of export

export department /'eksport dɪˌpartmənt/ *noun* the section of a company which deals in sales to foreign countries

export duty /'eksport ˌduti/ *noun* a tax paid on goods sent out of a country for sale

exporter /ɪk'sportər/ *noun* a person, company, or country that sells goods in foreign countries ○ *a major furniture exporter* ○ *Canada is an important exporter of oil* or *an important oil exporter.*

export house /'eksport haʊs/ *noun* a company which specializes in the export of goods manufactured by other companies

exporting /ek'spɔrtɪŋ/ *adjective* sending goods out of a country □ **oil-exporting countries** countries which produce oil and sell it to other countries

export license /'ekspɔrt ˌlaɪs(ə)ns/ *noun* a government permit allowing something to be exported ○ *The government has refused an export license for computer parts.*

export manager /'ekspɔrt ˌmænɪdʒər/ *noun* the person in charge of an export department in a company ○ *The export manager planned to set up a sales force in Southern Europe.* ○ *Sales managers from all export markets report to our export manager.*

export permit /'ekspɔrt ˌpɜrmɪt/ *noun* an official document which allows goods to be exported or imported

export restitution /ˌekspɔrt ˌrestɪ'tjuʃ(ə)n/ *noun* (*in the EU*) subsidies to European food exporters

exports /'ekspɔrts/ *plural noun* goods sent to a foreign country to be sold ○ *Exports to Africa have increased by 25%.* (NOTE: Usually used in the plural, but the singular form is used before a noun.)

Export Working Capital Program /ˌekspɔrt ˌwɜrkɪŋ 'kæpɪt(ə)l ˌproʊgræm/ *noun* a short-term loan program guaranteed by the Small Business Administration, that is designed to provide working capital to exporters. Abbreviation **EWCP**

exposition /ˌekspə'zɪʃ(ə)n/ *noun* same as **exhibition**

exposure /ɪk'spoʊʒə/ *noun* **1.** publicity given to an organization or product ○ *Our company has achieved more exposure since we decided to advertise nationally.* **2.** the amount of risk which a lender or investor runs ○ *He is trying to limit his exposure in the property market.*

> COMMENT: Exposure can be the amount of money lent to a customer (a bank's exposure to a foreign country) or the amount of money which an investor may lose if his investments collapse (his or her exposure in the stock market).

express /ɪk'spres/ *adjective* **1.** rapid or very fast ○ *an express letter* **2.** clearly shown in words ○ *The contract has an express condition forbidding sale in Africa.*
■ *verb* **1.** to put into words or diagrams ○ *This chart shows home sales expressed as a percentage of total turnover.* **2.** to send something very fast ○ *We expressed the order to the customer's warehouse.*

express delivery /ɪkˌspres dɪ'lɪv(ə)ri/ *noun* a very fast delivery

express letter /ɪkˌspres 'letər/ *noun* a letter sent very fast

expressly /ɪk'spresli/ *adverb* clearly in words ○ *The contract expressly forbids sales to the United States.*

ext. *abbreviation* extension

extend /ɪk'stend/ *verb* **1.** to offer something ○ *to extend credit to a customer* **2.** to make something longer ○ *Her contract of employment was extended for two years.* ○ *We have extended the deadline for making the appointment by two weeks.*

extended credit /ɪkˌstendɪd 'kredɪt/ *noun* credit allowing the borrower a very long time to pay ○ *We sell to Australia on extended credit.*

extended guarantee /ɪkˌstendɪd ˌgærən'ti/ *noun* a guarantee, offered by a dealer on durable goods such as dishwashers, which goes beyond the time specified in the manufacturer's guarantee

Extensible Business Reporting Language /ɪkˌstensɪb(ə)l ˌbɪznɪs rɪ'pɔrtɪŋ ˌlæŋgwɪdʒ/ *noun* full form of **XBRL**

extension /ɪk'stenʃən/ *noun* **1.** a longer time allowed for something than was originally agreed □ **to get an extension of credit** to get more time to pay back □ **extension of a contract** the continuing of a contract for a further period **2.** (*in an office*) an individual telephone linked to the main switchboard ○ *The sales manager is on extension 53.* ○ *Can you get me extension 21?* ○ *Extension 21 is engaged.*

extensive /ɪk'stensɪv/ *adjective* very large or covering a wide area ○ *an extensive network of sales outlets* ○ *an extensive recruitment drive*

external /ɪk'stɜrn(ə)l/ *adjective* **1.** outside a country. Opposite **internal 2.** outside a company

external analysis /ɪkˌstɜrn(ə)l ə'næləsɪs/ *noun* the analysis of an organization's customers, market segments, competitors, and marketing environment

external audit /ɪkˌstɜrn(ə)l 'ɔdɪt/ *noun* an audit carried out by an independent auditor who is not employed by the company

external auditor /ɪkˌstɜːn(ə)l ˈɔːdɪtər/ *noun* an independent person who audits the company's accounts

external growth /ɪkˌstɜːn(ə)l ˈɡrəʊθ/ *noun* growth by buying other companies, rather than by expanding existing sales or products. Opposite **internal growth**

external search /ɪkˌstɜːn(ə)l ˈsɜːtʃ/ *noun* a method of finding information from external sources such as advertising, or from the web using a search engine

external search engine /ɪkˌstɜːn(ə)l ˈsɜːtʃ ˌendʒɪn/ *noun* a search engine that allows the user to search millions of Internet pages rapidly

external trade /ɪkˌstɜːn(ə)l ˈtreɪd/ *noun* trade with foreign countries. Opposite **internal trade**

extra /ˈekstrə/ *adjective* which is added or which is more than usual ○ *to charge 10% extra for postage* ○ *There is no extra charge for heating.* ○ *Service is extra.* ○ *We get £25 extra pay for working on Sunday.*

extract /ˈekstrækt/ *noun* a printed document which is part of a larger document ○ *He sent me an extract of the accounts.*

extranet /ˈekstrənet/ *noun* a closed network of websites and email systems that is accessible to the people who belong to an organization and to some others who do not, and that allows the outsiders access to the organization's internal applications or information—usually subject to some kind of signed agreement (NOTE: Like intranets, extranets provide all the benefits of Internet technology (browsers, web servers, HTML, etc.) with the added benefit of security, since the network cannot be used by the general public.)

extraordinary /ɪkˈstrɔːd(ə)n(ə)ri/ *adjective* different from normal

Extraordinary General Meeting /ɪk ˌstrɔːd(ə)n(ə)ri ˌdʒen(ə)rəl ˈmiːtɪŋ/ *noun* U.K. a special meeting of stockholders to discuss an important matter (such as a change in the company's bylaws) which cannot wait until the next annual meeting ○ *to call an Extraordinary General Meeting* Abbreviation **EGM**

extraordinary items /ɪk ˈstrɔːd(ə)n(ə)ri ˌaɪtəmz/ *plural noun* formerly, large items of income or expenditure which did not arise from usual trading and which did not occur every year. They were shown separately in the P&L account, after taxation.

extras /ˈekstrəz/ *plural noun* items which are not included in a price ○ *Packing and postage are extras.*

extremely /ɪkˈstriːmli/ *adverb* very much ○ *It is extremely difficult to break into the U.S. market.* ○ *Their management team is extremely efficient.*

eyeballing /ˈaɪbɔːlɪŋ/ *noun* simply looking at statistical data to make a quick and informal assessment of the results (*informal*)

eye service /ˈaɪ ˌsɜːvɪs/ *noun* the practice of working only when a supervisor is present and able to see you (*slang*)

e-zine /ˈiː ziːn/ *noun* a publication on a particular topic that is distributed regularly in electronic form, mainly via the web but also by email

F

face-lift /feɪs lɪft/ *noun* an improvement to the design of products and packaging or of an organization's image ○ *These products need a face-lift if they are going to retain their appeal.*

face time /ˈfeɪs taɪm/ *noun* time spent communicating with other people face-to-face as opposed to time spent communicating with them electronically (*informal*)

face-to-face /ˌfeɪs tə ˈfeɪs/ *adjective* used to describe a credit- or debit-card transaction in which the cardholder is present, as opposed, e.g., to an online transaction

face value /ˌfeɪs ˈvælju/ *noun* the value written on a coin, banknote, or stock certificate

facilitation /fəˌsɪlɪˈteɪʃ(ə)n/ *noun* the process of helping people to do something, e.g., to learn or to find a solution to a problem, without dictating how they do it

facilitator /fəˈsɪlɪteɪtər/ *noun* a person who actively encourages discussion, new initiatives, etc.

facilities /fəˈsɪlətiz/ *plural noun* services, equipment, or buildings which make it possible to do something ○ *Our storage facilities are the best in the region.* ○ *Transport facilities in the area are not satisfactory.* ○ *There are no facilities for disabled visitors.* ○ *There are very good sports facilities on the company premises.*

facility /fəˈsɪləti/ *noun* **1.** something that allows something to be done something easily ○ *We offer facilities for payment.* **2.** the total amount of credit which a lender will allow a borrower **3.** a single large building ○ *We have opened our new warehouse facility.*

facsimile /fækˈsɪmɪli/ *noun* an exact copy of a text or illustration

fact /fækt/ *noun* **1.** a piece of information ○ *The chairman asked to see all the facts on the income tax claim.* ○ *The sales director can give you the facts and figures about the African operation.* **2.** □ **the fact of the matter is** what is true is that **3.** □ **in fact** really ○ *The chairman blamed the finance director for the loss when in fact he was responsible for it himself.*

fact-finding /ˈfækt ˌfaɪndɪŋ/ *noun* the process of looking for information

fact-finding mission /ˈfækt ˌfaɪndɪŋ ˌmɪʃ(ə)n/ *noun* a visit by a person or group of people, usually to another country, to obtain information about a specific issue ○ *The trade official went on a fact-finding tour of the region.*

factor /ˈfæktər/ *noun* **1.** something which is important, or which is taken into account when making a decision ○ *The drop in sales is an important factor in the company's lower profits.* ○ *Motivation was an important factor in drawing up the new payment plan.* **2.** a number used in multiplication to produce another number □ **by a factor of ten** ten times **3.** a person or company which is responsible for collecting debts for companies, by buying debts at a discount on their face value ■ *verb* to buy debts from a company at a discount

COMMENT: A factor collects a company's debts when due, and pays the creditor in advance part of the sum to be collected, so "buying" the debt.

factoring /ˈfæktərɪŋ/ *noun* the business of buying debts from a firm at a discount and then getting the debtors to pay

factoring charges /ˈfæktərɪŋ ˌtʃɑrdʒɪz/ *plural noun* the cost of selling debts to a factor for a commission

factors of production /ˌfæktərz əv prəˈdʌkʃən/ *plural noun* land, labor and capital, i.e. the three things needed to produce a product

factory /'fækt(ə)ri/ *noun* a building where products are manufactured ○ *a car factory* ○ *a shoe factory* ○ *The company is proposing to close three of its factories with the loss of 200 jobs.*

factory floor /,fækt(ə)ri 'flɔr/ *noun* the main works of a factory

factory gate price /,fækt(ə)ri 'geɪt praɪs/ *noun* the actual cost of manufacturing goods before any mark-up is added to give profit (NOTE: The factory gate price includes direct costs such as labor, raw materials, and energy, and indirect costs such as interest on loans, plant maintenance, or rent.)

factory hand /'fækt(ə)ri hænd/ *noun* a person who works in a factory

factory inspector /'fækt(ə)ri ɪn,spektər/ *noun* a government official who inspects factories to see if they are well run

factory inspectorate /'fækt(ə)ri ɪn,spekt(ə)rət/ *noun* all inspectors of factories

factory outlet /'fækt(ə)rɪ ,aʊtlet/ *noun* a store where merchandise is sold direct to the public from the factory, usually at wholesale prices

factory price /'fækt(ə)ri praɪs/ *noun* a price not including transportation from the maker's factory

factory unit /'fækt(ə)ri ,juːnɪt/ *noun* U.K. a single building in an industrial park

factory worker /'fækt(ə)ri ,wɜrkər/ *noun* a person who works in a factory

fact sheet /'fækt ʃiːt/ *noun* a sheet of paper giving information about a product or service which can be used for publicity purposes

fail /feɪl/ *verb* **1.** not to do something which you were trying to do ○ *The company failed to notify the tax office of its change of address.* ○ *They failed to agree on an agenda for the meeting.* ○ *Negotiations continued until midnight but the two sides failed to come to an agreement.* **2.** to be unsuccessful ○ *The prototype failed its first test.* □ **the company failed** the company went bankrupt ○ *He lost all his money when the bank failed.*

failing /'feɪlɪŋ/ *noun* weakness ○ *The chairman has one failing – he goes to sleep at board meetings.* ■ *preposition* if something does not happen □ **failing instructions to the contrary** unless someone gives opposite instructions □ **failing**

prompt payment if the payment is not made on time □ **failing that** if that does not work ○ *Try the company secretary, and failing that the chairman.*

failure /'feɪljər/ *noun* **1.** an act of breaking down or stopping ○ *the failure of the negotiations* **2.** the fact of not doing something which you promised to do □ **failure to pay a bill** not paying a bill

failure fee /'feɪljər fiː/ *noun* a fee charged by a distributor to the manufacturer of a product whose sales are less than those agreed upon in advance

fair /fer/ *noun* same as **trade fair** ○ *The computer fair runs from April 1st to 6th.* ■ *adjective* reasonable, with equal treatment

fair copy /,fer 'kɑpi/ *noun* a document which is written or typed with no changes or mistakes

fair deal /,fer 'diːl/ *noun* an arrangement where both parties are treated equally ○ *The employees feel they did not get a fair deal from the management.*

fair dealing /,fer 'diːlɪŋ/ *noun* the legal buying and selling of stock

fair dismissal /,fer dɪs'mɪs(ə)l/ *noun* the dismissal of an employee for reasons such as the employee's bad conduct, e.g., theft or drunkenness, failure of the employee to work capably or redundancy, which are regarded as valid causes

fairly /'ferli/ *adverb* **1.** quite ○ *She is a fairly fast keyboarder.* ○ *The company is fairly close to breaking even.* **2.** reasonably or equally ○ *The union representatives put the employees' side of the case fairly and without argument.*

fair market value /fer ,mɑrkət 'væljuː/ *noun* same as **fair value**

fair price /,fer 'praɪs/ *noun* a good price for both buyer and seller

fair trade /,fer 'treɪd/ *noun* an international business system where countries agree not to charge import duties on some items imported from their trading partners

fair trading /,fer 'treɪdɪŋ/ *noun* a way of doing business which is reasonable and does not harm the consumer

fair value /,fer 'væljuː/ *noun* **1.** a price paid by a buyer who knows the value of what he or she is buying, to a seller who also knows the value of what is being sold, i.e., neither is cheating the other **2.** a method of valuing the assets and liabilities of a business based on the amount for which they could be sold to independent parties at the time of valuation

fair wear and tear /ˌfeə wer ən 'ter/ *noun* acceptable damage caused by normal use ○ *The insurance policy covers most damage but not fair wear and tear to the machine.*

faith /feɪθ/ *noun* □ **to have faith in something** *or* **someone** to believe that something or a person is good or will work well ○ *The sales force have great faith in the product.* ○ *The sales teams do not have much faith in their manager.* ○ *The board has faith in the managing director's judgment.* □ **to buy something in good faith** to buy something thinking that is of good quality, that it has not been stolen or that it is not an imitation

fake /feɪk/ *noun* imitation, copy made for criminal purposes ○ *The painting was proved to be a fake.* ■ *adjective* copied for criminal purposes ○ *The shipment came with fake documentation.* ■ *verb* to make an imitation for criminal purposes ○ *faked documents* ○ *He faked the results of the test.*

fall /fɔl/ *noun* a sudden reduction or loss of value ○ *a fall in the exchange rate* ○ *a fall in the price of gold* ○ *a fall on the Stock Exchange* ○ *Profits showed a 10% fall.* ■ *verb* **1.** to be reduced suddenly to a lower price or value ○ *Stocks fell on the market today.* ○ *Gold stocks fell 10%* or *fell 45 cents on the Stock Exchange.* ○ *The price of gold fell for the second day running.* ○ *The dollar fell against the euro.* **2.** to happen or to take place ○ *The public holiday falls on a Tuesday.* □ **payments which fall due** payments which are now due to be made

fall away *phrasal verb* to become less ○ *Hotel bookings have fallen away since the tourist season ended.*

fall back *phrasal verb* to become lower or cheaper after rising in price ○ *Stocks fell back in light trading.*

fall back on *phrasal verb* to have to use something kept for emergencies ○ *to fall back on cash reserves* ○ *The management fell back on the usual old excuses.*

fall behind *phrasal verb* **1.** to be late in doing something ○ *They fell behind with their mortgage payments.* □ **the company has fallen behind with its deliveries** it is late with its deliveries **2.** to be in a worse position than □ **we have fallen behind our competitors** we have fewer sales or make less profit than our competitors

fall off *phrasal verb* to become lower, cheaper, or less ○ *Sales have fallen off since the tourist season ended.*

fall out *phrasal verb* □ **the bottom has fallen out of the market** sales have fallen below what previously seemed to be their lowest point

fall through *phrasal verb* not to happen or not to take place ○ *The plan fell through at the last moment.*

fall-back price /'fɔl bæk ˌpraɪs/ *noun* the lowest price which a seller will accept ○ *The buyer tries to guess the seller's fall-back price.* ○ *The fall-back price must not be any lower or there won't be any profit in the deal.*

falling /'fɔlɪŋ/ *adjective* becoming smaller or dropping in price

falling market /ˌfɔlɪŋ 'mɑrkət/ *noun* a market where prices are coming down

falling pound /ˌfɔlɪŋ 'paʊnd/ *noun* the pound when it is losing its value against other currencies

fallout /'fɔlaʊt/ *noun* a bad result or collapse

false /fɔls/ *adjective* not true or not correct ○ *to make a false claim for a product* ○ *to make a false entry in the balance sheet*

false accounting /ˌfɔls ə'kaʊntɪŋ/ *noun* a criminal offense of changing, destroying or hiding accounting records for a dishonest purpose, such as to gain money

false pretenses /ˌfɔls 'prɪtensɪz/ *plural noun* doing or saying something to cheat someone ○ *He was sent to prison for obtaining money by false pretenses.*

false weight /ˌfɔls 'weɪt/ *noun* a weight as measured on a store scales which is wrong and so cheats customers

falsification /ˌfɔlsɪfɪ'keɪʃ(ə)n/ *noun* the act of making false entries in accounts

falsify /'fɔlsɪfaɪ/ *verb* to change something to make it wrong ○ *They were accused of falsifying the accounts.*

family company /'fæm(ə)li ˌkʌmp(ə)ni/ *noun* a company in which most of the stock is owned by members of a family

family-friendly policy /ˌfæm(ə)li ˈfrendli ˌpɑlɪsi/ *noun* a policy that is designed to help employees to combine their work with their family responsibilities in a satisfactory way, e.g., by enabling them to work flexible hours or by helping them with childcare

fancy goods /ˈfænsi gʊdz/ *plural noun* small attractive items

fancy prices /ˌfænsi ˈpraɪsɪz/ *noun* high prices ○ *I don't want to pay the fancy prices they ask in designer stores.*

f. & f. *abbreviation* fixtures and fittings

Fannie Mae /ˌfæni ˈmeɪ/ *noun* same as **Federal National Mortgage Association**

fao *abbreviation* for the attention of

FAR *abbreviation* Federal Acquisition Regulations

fare /feɹ/ *noun* a price to be paid for a ticket to travel ○ *Train fares have gone up by 5%.* ○ *The government is asking the airlines to keep air fares down.*

farm /fɑrm/ *noun* property in the country where crops are grown, where animals are raised for sale ■ *verb* to own a farm ○ *he farms 150 acres*

   farm out *phrasal verb* □ **to farm out work** to hand over work for another person or company to do for you ○ *She farms out the office keyboarding to various local bureaus.*

farming /ˈfɑrmɪŋ/ *noun* the job of working on a farm, of raising animals for sale or of growing crops for food ○ *chicken farming* ○ *fish farming* ○ *mixed farming*

FAS *abbreviation* Federal Accounting Standards

FASB *abbreviation* Financial Accounting Standards Board

fascia /ˈfeɪʃə/, **facia** /ˈfeɪʃə/ *noun* **1.** a board over a store on which the name of the store is written **2.** a board above an exhibition stand on which the name of the company represented is written

fast /fæst/ *adjective, adverb* quick or quickly ○ *The train is the fastest way of getting to our supplier's factory.* ○ *Home computers sell fast in the pre-Christmas period.*

fast-selling item /ˌfæst ˌselɪŋ ˈaɪtəm/ *noun* an item which sells quickly

fast track /ˈfæst træk/, **fast tracking** *noun* rapid promotion for able employees

○ *He entered the company at 21, and by 25 he was on the fast track.*

fault /fɔlt/ *noun* **1.** the fact of being to blame for something which is wrong ○ *It is the stock controller's fault if the warehouse runs out of stock.* ○ *The chairman said the lower sales figures were the fault of a badly motivated sales force.* **2.** an act of not working properly ○ *The technicians are trying to correct a programming fault.* ○ *We think there is a basic fault in the product design.*

faulty /ˈfɔlti/ *adjective* which does not work properly ○ *Faulty equipment was to blame for the defective products.* ○ *They installed faulty computer programs.*

favor /ˈfeɪvə/ *noun* **1.** □ **as a favor** to help or to be kind to someone ○ *He asked me for a loan as a favor.* **2.** □ **in favor of** in agreement with or feeling that something is right ○ *Six members of the board are in favor of the proposal, and three are against it.* ■ *verb* to agree that something is right or suitable ○ *The board members all favor Smith Inc. as partners in the project.* (NOTE: [all senses] The usual U.S. spelling is **favor**.)

favorable /ˈfeɪv(ə)rəb(ə)l/ *adjective* giving an advantage (NOTE: The U.K. spelling is **favourable**.) □ **on favorable terms** on especially good terms ○ *The store is rented on very favorable terms.*

favorable balance of trade /ˌfeɪv(ə)rəb(ə)l ˌbæləns əv ˈtreɪd/, **favorable trade balance** /ˌfeɪv(ə)rəb(ə)l ˈtreɪd ˌbæləns/ *noun* a situation where a country's exports are larger than its imports

favorite /ˈfeɪv(ə)rət/ *noun, adjective* (something) which is liked best ○ *This brand of chocolate is a favorite with the children's market.* (NOTE: The usual U.S. spelling is **favorite**.)

fax /fæks/ *noun* **1.** a system for sending the exact copy of a document via telephone lines ○ *Can you confirm the booking by fax?* **2.** a document sent by this method ○ *We received a fax of the order this morning.* ■ *verb* to send a message by fax ○ *The details of the offer were faxed to the brokers this morning.* ○ *I've faxed the documents to our New York office.* ■ *noun* a machine for sending or receiving faxes

COMMENT: Banks will not accept fax messages as binding instructions (as for example, a faxed order for money to be transferred from one account to another).

fax paper /'fæks ˌpeɪpər/ *noun* special paper which is used in fax machines

fax roll /'fæks roʊl/ *noun* a roll of fax paper

feasibility /ˌfizə'bɪləti/ *noun* the ability to be done ○ *to report on the feasibility of a project*

feasibility report /ˌfizə'bɪləti rɪˌpɔrt/ *noun* a document which says if it is worth undertaking something

feasibility study /ˌfizə'bɪləti ˌstʌdi/ *noun* the careful investigation of a project to see whether it is worth undertaking ○ *We will carry out a feasibility study to decide whether it is worth setting up an agency in South America.*

feasibility test /ˌfizə'bɪləti test/ *noun* a test to see if something is possible

feather-bedding /ˌfeðə 'bedɪŋ/ *noun* the heavy subsidizing of unprofitable industry by government

Fed /fed/ *noun* same as **Federal Reserve Board** (*informal*)

"...indications of weakness in the U.S. economy were contained in figures from the Fed on industrial production for April" [*Financial Times*]

"...the half-point discount rate move gives the Fed room to reduce the federal funds rate further if economic weakness persists. The Fed sets the discount rate directly, but controls the federal funds rate by buying and selling Treasury securities" [*Wall Street Journal*]

federal /'fed(ə)rəl/ *adjective* **1.** referring to a system of government where a group of states are linked together in a federation **2.** referring to the central government of the United States ○ *Most federal offices are in Washington.*

"...federal examiners will determine which of the privately-insured savings and loans qualify for federal insurance" [*Wall Street Journal*]

"...since 1978 America has freed many of its industries from federal rules that set prices and controlled the entry of new companies" [*Economist*]

Federal Accounting Standards /ˌfed(ə)rəl ə'kaʊntɪŋ ˌstændərdz/ *noun* the U.S. regulations governing accounting procedures. Abbreviation **FAS**

Federal Acquisition Regulations /ˌfed(ə)rəl ˌækwɪ'zɪʃ(ə)n ˌregjʊleɪʃ(ə)nz/ *noun* a system of collecting and publishing the policies and procedures used by all the executive agencies of the U.S. government for the purchase of goods and services. Abbreviation **FAR**

Federal National Mortgage Association /ˌfed(ə)rəl ˌnæʃ(ə)nəl 'mɔrgɪdʒ əˌsoʊsieɪʃ(ə)n/ *noun* a privately owned U.S. organization which regulates mortgages and helps offer mortgages backed by federal funds. Abbreviation **FNMA**. Also called **Fannie Mae**

Federal Open Market Committee /ˌfed(ə)rəl ˌoʊpən 'mɑrkət kəˌmɪti/ *noun* the 12-member committee of the Federal Reserve System that sets guidelines regarding the purchase and sale of government securities in the open market as a means of influencing the volume of bank credit and money in the economy. Abbreviation **FOMC**

Federal Reserve /ˌfed(ə)rəl rɪ'zɜrv/, **Federal Reserve System** /ˌfed(ə)rəl rɪ 'zɜrv ˌsɪstəm/ *noun* the system of federal government control of the U.S. banks, where the Federal Reserve Board regulates money supply, prints money, fixes the discount rate and issues government bonds

COMMENT: The Federal Reserve system is the central bank of the U.S. The system is run by the Federal Reserve Board, under a chairman and seven committee members (or "governors") who are all appointed by the President. The twelve Federal Reserve Banks act as lenders of last resort to local commercial banks. Although the board is appointed by the president, the whole system is relatively independent of the U.S. government.

Federal Reserve Bank /ˌfed(ə)rəl rɪ 'zɜrv ˌbæŋk/ *noun* any one of the twelve federally-owned regional banks in the U.S., which are directed by the Federal Reserve Board. Abbreviation **FRB**

Federal Reserve Board /ˌfed(ə)rəl rɪ 'zɜrv bɔrd/ *noun* a government organization which runs the central banks in the U.S. Abbreviation **FRB**

"...pressure on the Federal Reserve Board to ease monetary policy mounted yesterday with the release of a set of pessimistic economic statistics" [*Financial Times*]

federation /ˌfedə'reɪʃ(ə)n/ *noun* a group of societies, companies or organizations which have a central organization which represents them and looks after their common interests ○ *a federation of trades unions* ○ *the employers' federation*

fee /fiː/ *noun* money paid for work carried out by a professional person such as an accountant, a doctor or a lawyer ○ *We charge a small fee for our services.* ○ *The consultant's fee was much higher than we expected.* □ **director's fees** money paid to a director as a lump sum, not a salary

feed /fiːd/ *noun* a device which puts paper into a printer or into a photocopier ○ *the paper feed has jammed* ■ *verb* to put information into a computer or paper into a printer (NOTE: **feeding – fed**)

feedback /ˈfiːdbæk/ *noun* information, especially about the result of an activity which allows adjustments to be made to the way it is done in future ○ *We are getting positive feedback about our after-sales service.* ○ *It would be useful to have some feedback from people who had a test drive but didn't buy the car.* ○ *Are we getting any feedback on customer reaction to our new product?* ○ *The management received a lot of feedback on how popular the new pay program was proving.*

feelgood factor /ˈfiːlɡʊd ˌfæktər/ *noun* a general feeling that everything is going well (leading to increased consumer spending)

fee work /ˈfiː wɜːrk/ *noun* any work on a project carried out by independent workers or contractors, rather than by the organization's employees

feint /feɪnt/ *noun* very light lines on writing paper

fetch /fetʃ/ *verb* **1.** to go to bring something ○ *We have to fetch the goods from the docks.* ○ *It is cheaper to buy at a cash-and-carry warehouse, provided you have a car to fetch the goods yourself.* **2.** to be sold for a certain price ○ *to fetch a high price* ○ *It will not fetch more than £200.* ○ *These machines fetch very high prices on the black market.*

few /fjuː/ *adjective, noun* □ **a few** some ○ *A few of our salesmen drive Rolls-Royces.* ○ *We get only a few orders in the period from Christmas to the New Year.*

fiat money /ˈfiːæt ˌmʌni/ *noun* coins or bills which are not worth much as paper or metal, but are said by the government to

have a value and are recognized as legal tender

fictitious assets /fɪkˌtɪʃəs ˈæsets/ *plural noun* assets which do not really exist, but are entered as assets to balance the accounts

fiddle /ˈfɪd(ə)l/ *noun* an act of cheating (*informal*) ○ *It's all a fiddle.* □ **he's on the fiddle** he is trying to cheat ■ *verb* to cheat (*informal*) ○ *He tried to fiddle his tax returns.* ○ *The salesman was caught fiddling his expense account.*

fide ♦ **bona fide**

fiduciary /fəˈduːʃieri/ *noun, adjective* a person in a position of trust ○ *Directors have fiduciary duty to act in the best interests of the company.*

fiduciary deposits /fəˌduːʃieri dɪˈpɑːzɪts/ *plural noun* bank deposits which are managed for the depositor by the bank

field /fiːld/ *noun* **1.** an area of study or interest □ **first in the field** being the first company to bring out a product or to start a service ○ *Smith Inc. has a great advantage in being first in the field with a reliable electric car.* ○ *What's his field?* **2.** □ **in the field** outside the office, among the customers ○ *We have sixteen reps in the field.*

field research /ˈfiːld rɪˌsɜːrtʃ/ *noun* the process of looking for information that is not yet published and must be obtained in surveys ○ *They had to do a lot of fieldwork before they found the right market for the product.* ○ *Field research is carried out to gauge potential demand.*

field sales force /ˌfiːld ˈseɪlz ˌfɔːrs/ *noun* salespeople working outside the company's offices, in the field ○ *After working for a year in the field sales force, she became field sales manager.* ○ *The field sales force operates in three main areas.*

field sales manager /ˌfiːld ˈseɪlz ˌmænɪdʒər/ *noun* the manager in charge of a group of salespeople

field trial /ˈfiːld traɪəl/, **field test** /ˈfiːld tests/ *noun* a test of a new product or of something such as an advertisement on real customers

field work /ˈfiːld wɜːrk/ *noun* same as **field research** ○ *They had to do a lot of field work to find the right market for the product.*

FIFO /ˈfaɪfoʊ/ *abbreviation* first in first out

fifty-fifty /ˌfɪfti ˈfɪfti/ *adjective, adverb* half □ **he has a fifty-fifty chance of making a profit** he has an equal chance of making a profit or a loss

    go fifty-fifty *phrasal verb* to share the costs equally

figure /ˈfɪgər/ *noun* **1.** a number, or a cost written in numbers ○ *The figure in the accounts for heating is very high.* □ **he put a very low figure on the value of the lease** he calculated the value of the lease as very low **2.** □ **to work out the figures** to calculate something □ **his income runs into six figures** *or* **he has a six-figure income** his income is more than $100,000 □ **in round figures** not totally accurate, but correct to the nearest 10 or 100 ○ *They have a work force of 2,500 in round figures.*

figures /ˈfɪgərz/ *plural noun* **1.** written numbers **2.** the results for a company ○ *the figures for last year* or *last year's figures*

file /faɪl/ *noun* **1.** documents kept for reference □ **to place something on file** to keep a record of something □ **to keep someone's name on file** to keep someone's name on a list for reference **2.** a section of data on a computer, e.g., payroll, address list, customer accounts ○ *How can we protect our computer files?* ■ *verb* **1.** ○ *You will find the salary scales filed by department.* ○ *The correspondence is filed under "complaints".* □ **to file documents** to put documents in order so that they can be found easily ○ *The correspondence is filed under "complaints".* **2.** to make an official request □ *or* **to file for bankruptcy** to ask officially to be made bankrupt or to ask officially for someone else to be made bankrupt **3.** to register something officially ○ *to file an application for a patent* ○ *to file a return to the tax office* ◇ **to file a petition in bankruptcy, to file for bankruptcy 1.** to ask officially to be made bankrupt **2.** to ask officially for someone else to be made bankrupt

file copy /ˈfaɪl ˌkɑpi/ *noun* a copy of a document which is kept for reference in an office

file server /ˈfaɪl ˌsɜrvər/ *noun* a computer connected to a network, running a network operating system software to manage accounts, files, etc.

file sharing /ˈfaɪl ˌʃerɪŋ/ *noun* a feature of computer networking that allows more

than one user to access the same file at the same time

filing /ˈfaɪlɪŋ/ *noun* documents which have to be put in order ○ *There is a lot of filing to do at the end of the week.* ○ *The manager looked through the week's filing to see what letters had been sent.*

filing basket /ˈfaɪlɪŋ ˌbæskɪt/ *noun* same as **filing tray**

filing cabinet /ˈfaɪlɪŋ ˌkæbɪnət/ *noun* a piece of furniture, made of metal, with wide deep drawers so that files (called "suspension files") can be hooked inside them ○ *We need two more four-drawer filing cabinets.* ○ *Last year's correspondence is in the bottom drawer of the filing cabinet.*

filing card /ˈfaɪlɪŋ kɑrd/ *noun* a card with information written on it, used to classify information into the correct order

filing clerk /ˈfaɪlɪŋ klɜrk/ *noun* an office worker who files documents

filing system /ˈfaɪlɪŋ ˌsɪstəm/ *noun* a way of putting documents in order for easy reference

filing tray /ˈfaɪlɪŋ treɪ/ *noun* a container kept on a desk for documents which have to be filed

fill /fɪl/ *verb* **1.** to make something full ○ *We have filled our order book with orders for Africa.* ○ *The production department has filled the warehouse with unsellable products.* **2.** □ **to fill a gap** to provide a product or service which is needed, but which no one has provided before ○ *The new range of small cars fills a gap in the market.* **3.** □ **to fill a post** *or* **a vacancy** to find someone to do a job ○ *Your application arrived too late – the post has already been filled.*

    fill in *phrasal verb* to write the required information in the blank spaces on a form ○ *Fill in your name and address in block capitals.*

    fill out *phrasal verb* to write the required information in the blank spaces on a form ○ *To get customs clearance you must fill out three forms.*

    fill up *phrasal verb* **1.** to make something completely full ○ *He filled up the car with gasoline.* ○ *My appointments book is completely filled up.* **2.** to finish writing on a form ○ *He filled up the form and sent it to the bank.*

filter /'fɪltər/ *noun* a process of analysis applied to incoming information in order to identify any material that could be of interest to an organization

final /'faɪn(ə)l/ *adjective* last, coming at the end of a period ○ *to pay the final instalment* ○ *to make the final payment* ○ *to put the final details on a document* □ **final date for payment** last date by which payment should be made

final accounts /ˌfaɪn(ə)l ə'kaʊntz/ *noun* the accounts produced at the end of an accounting period, including the balance sheet and profit and loss account

final demand /ˌfaɪn(ə)l dɪ'mænd/ *noun* the last reminder from a supplier, after which they will sue for payment

final discharge /ˌfaɪn(ə)l dɪs'tʃɑrdʒ/ *noun* the last payment of what is left of a debt

final dividend /ˌfaɪn(ə)l 'dɪvɪdend/ *noun* a dividend paid at the end of a year's trading, which has to be approved by the stockholders at an annual meeting

finalize /'faɪnəlaɪz/ *verb* to agree final details ○ *We hope to finalize the agreement tomorrow.* ○ *After six weeks of negotiations the loan was finalized yesterday.*

finally /'faɪn(ə)li/ *adverb* in the end ○ *The contract was finally signed yesterday.* ○ *After weeks of trials the company finally accepted the computer system.*

final product /ˌfaɪn(ə)l 'prɑdʌkt/ *noun* a manufactured product, made at the end of a production process

final salary /ˌfaɪn(ə)l 'sæləri/ *noun* the salary earned by an employee on the date of leaving or retiring

final settlement /ˌfaɪn(ə)l 'set(ə)lmənt/ *noun* the last payment which settles a debt

finance /'faɪnæns/ *noun* **1.** *U.K.* money used by a company, provided by the stockholders or by loans ○ *Where will they get the necessary finance for the project?* (NOTE: The U.S. term is **financing**) **2.** money (used by a club, local authority, etc.) ○ *She is the secretary of the local authority finance committee.* **3.** the business of managing money ■ *verb* to provide money to pay for something ○ *They plan to finance the operation with short-term loans.*

Finance Bill /'faɪnæns bɪl/ *noun* **1.** a bill that lists the proposals in the federal budget and that is debated in Congress before being voted into law **2.** a short-term bill of exchange which provides credit for a corporation so that it can continue trading

finance company /'faɪnæns ˌkʌmp(ə)ni/, **finance corporation** /'faɪnæns ˌkɔrpəreɪʃ(ə)n/ *noun* a company that gets funds from investors or banks to make loans on the installment plan or to finance corporations

finance department /'faɪnæns dɪˌpɑrtmənt/, **finance committee** /'faɪnæns kəˌməti/ *noun* the department or committee which manages the money used in an organization

finance market /'faɪnæns ˌmɑrkət/ *noun* a place where large sums of money can be lent or borrowed

finances /'faɪnænsɪz/ *plural noun* money or cash which is available ○ *the bad state of the company's finances*

financial /faɪ'nænʃəl/ *adjective* relating to money

Financial Accounting Standards Board /faɪˌnænʃ(ə)l ə'kaʊntɪŋ/ *noun* an independent association of accounting professionals that sets standards for Generally Accepted Accounting Principles (GAAP) for companies in the U.S. to follow. Abbreviation **FASB**

financial adviser /faɪˌnænʃəl əd'vaɪzər/ *noun* a person or company which gives advice on financial problems for a fee

financial assistance /faɪˌnænʃəl ə'sɪstəns/ *noun* help in the form of money

financial correspondent /faɪˌnænʃəl ˌkɔrɪs'pɑndənt/ *noun* a journalist who writes articles on money matters for a newspaper

financial institution /faɪˌnænʃəl ˌɪnstɪ'tjuʃ(ə)n/ *noun* a bank, investment trust, or insurance company whose work involves lending or investing large sums of money

financial instrument /faɪˌnænʃəl 'ɪnstrʊmənt/ *noun* a document showing that money has been lent or borrowed, invested or passed from one account to another, e.g., a bill of exchange, stock certificate, certificate of deposit, or IOU

financial intermediary /faɪˌnænʃəl ˌɪntə'midiəri/ *noun* an institution which takes deposits or loans from individuals and lends money to clients

financially /fɪ'nænʃəli/ *adverb* regarding money □ **a company which is financially sound** a company which is profitable and has strong assets

financial position /faɪˌnænʃəl pə'zɪʃ(ə)n/ *noun* the state of a person's or company's bank balance in terms of assets and debts ○ *She must think of her financial position.*

financial report /faɪˌnænʃəl rɪ'pɔrt/ *noun* a document which gives the financial position of a company or of a club, etc.

financial resources /faɪˌnænʃəl rɪ'zɔrsɪz/ *plural noun* the supply of money for something ○ *a company with strong financial resources*

financial review /faɪˌnænʃəl rɪ'vjuː/ *noun* an examination of an organization's finances

financial risk /faɪˌnænʃəl 'rɪsk/ *noun* the possibility of losing money ○ *The company is taking a considerable financial risk in manufacturing 25 million units without doing any market research.* ○ *There is always some financial risk in selling on credit.*

Financial Standards Accounting Board /faɪˌnænʃ(ə)l ˌstændərdz ə'kauntɪŋ ˌbɔrd/ *noun* an independent association of accounting professionals that sets standards for generally accepted accounting principles for companies in the U.S. to follow. Abbreviation **FSAB**

financial statement /faɪˌnænʃəl 'steɪtmənt/ *noun* a document which shows the financial situation of a company ○ *The accounting department has prepared a financial statement for the stockholders.*

financial year /faɪˌnænʃəl 'jɪr/ *noun* the twelve-month period for which a company produces accounts. A financial year is not necessarily the same as a calendar year.

financier /faɪ'nænsiər/ *noun* a person who lends large amounts of money to companies or who buys stock in companies as an investment

financing /'faɪnænsɪŋ/ *noun* **1.** the act of providing money for a project ○ *The financing of the project was done by two international banks.* **2.** money used by a

company, provided by the stockholders or by loans (NOTE: The U.K. term is **finance**)

find /faɪnd/ *verb* **1.** to get something which was not there before ○ *We are still trying to find backing for the project.* **2.** to make a legal decision in court ○ *The tribunal found that both parties were at fault.* □ **the judge found for the defendant** the judge decided that the defendant was right

findings /'faɪndɪŋz/ *plural noun* □ **the findings of a commission of enquiry** the recommendations of the commission

fine /faɪn/ *noun* money paid because of something wrong which has been done ○ *She was asked to pay a $25,000 fine.* ○ *We had to pay a £50 parking fine.* ■ *verb* to punish someone by making him or her pay money ○ *to fine someone $2,500 for obtaining money by false pretenses*

fine print /ˌfaɪn 'prɪnt/ *noun* very small characters often used in contracts to list exceptions and restrictions ○ *Did you read the fine print on the back of the agreement?*

fine-tune /ˌfaɪn 'tuːn/ *verb* to make small adjustments to a plan or the economy so that it works better

fine-tuning /faɪn 'tjuːnɪŋ/ *noun* the act of making of small adjustments in areas such as interest rates, tax bands or the money supply, to improve a nation's economy

finish /'fɪnɪʃ/ *noun* **1.** the final appearance ○ *The product has an attractive finish.* **2.** an end of a day's trading on the Stock Exchange ○ *Oil stocks rallied at the finish.* ■ *verb* **1.** to do something or to make something completely ○ *The order was finished in time.* ○ *She finished the test before all the other candidates.* **2.** to come to an end ○ *The contract is due to finish next month.*

finished goods /ˌfɪnɪʃt 'gudz/ *plural noun* manufactured goods which are ready to be sold

finite capacity scheduling /ˌfaɪnaɪt kə'pæsiti ˌskedʒəlɪŋ/ *noun* the process of finding the best way to use limited resources to meet production goals on time

fire /faɪr/ *verb* to dismiss someone from a job ○ *He was fired after being late for work.*

fire certificate /'faɪr sərˌtɪfɪkət/ *noun* a document from the local fire brigade stating that a building meets official requirements as regards fire safety

fire-damaged goods /ˌfaɪr ˌdæmɪdʒd ˈgʊdz/ *noun* goods which have been damaged in a fire

fire door /ˈfaɪr dɔr/ *noun* a special door to prevent fire going from one part of a building to another

fire drill /ˈfaɪr drɪl/ *noun* a procedure to be carried out to help people to escape from a burning building

fire escape /ˈfaɪr ɪˌskeɪp/ *noun* a door or stairs which allow people to get out of a building which is on fire

fire exit /ˈfaɪr ˌegzɪt/ *noun* a door which leads to a way out of a building if there is a fire

fire hazard /ˈfaɪə ˌhæzərd/ *noun* a situation or goods which could start a fire ○ *That warehouse full of paper is a fire hazard.* Also called **fire risk**

fire insurance /ˈfaɪr ɪnˌʃʊrəns/ *noun* insurance against damage by fire

fireproof safe /ˈfaɪrˌpruf seɪf/ *noun* a safe which cannot be harmed by fire

fire risk /ˈfaɪr rɪsk/ *noun* same as **fire hazard**

fire safety /ˌfaɪr ˈseɪfti/ *noun* activities designed to make a place of work safe for the workers in case of fire

fire safety officer /faɪr ˈseɪfti ˌɔfɪsər/ *noun* a person responsible for fire safety in a building

fire sale /ˈfaɪr seɪl/ *noun* **1.** a sale of fire-damaged goods **2.** a sale of anything at a very low price

firm /fɜrm/ *noun* a company, business or partnership ○ *a manufacturing firm* ○ *an important publishing firm* ○ *She is a partner in a law firm.* ■ *adjective* **1.** unchangeable ○ *to make a firm offer for something* ○ *to place a firm order for two aircraft* **2.** not dropping in price and possibly going to rise ○ *Stocks remained firm.* ■ *verb* to remain at a price and seem likely to rise ○ *The stock firmed at $8.00 a share.*

firm up *phrasal verb* to agree on the final details of something ○ *We expect to firm up the deal at the next trade fair.*

firmness /ˈfɜrmnəs/ *noun* the fact of being steady at a particular price, or likely to rise ○ *the firmness of the dollar on foreign exchanges*

"Toronto failed to mirror New York's firmness as a drop in gold shares on a falling bullion price left the market closing on a mixed note" [*Financial Times*]

firm price /ˌfɜrm ˈpraɪs/ *noun* a price which will not change ○ *They are quoting a firm price of $1.23 a unit.*

firm sale /ˌfɜrm ˈseɪl/ *noun* a sale which does not allow the purchaser to return the goods

first /fɜrst/ *noun* a person or thing that is there at the beginning or earlier than others ○ *Our company was one of the first to sell into the European market.*

first-class /ˌfɜrst ˈklæs/ *adjective* top-quality or most expensive ○ *She is a first-class accountant.* ■ *noun, adverb* (the type of travel or type of hotel which is most expensive and comfortable ○ *to travel first-class* ○ *First-class travel provides the best service.* ○ *A first-class ticket to New York costs more than I can afford.* ○ *The CEO prefers to stay in first-class hotels.*

first-class mail /ˌfɜrst klæs ˈmeɪl/ *noun* a more expensive mail service, designed to be faster ○ *A first-class letter should get to Scotland in a day.*

first floor /ˌgraʊnd ˈflɔr/ *noun* a floor (in a shop or office) which is level with the ground ○ *The men's department is on the first floor.* ○ *He has a first-floor office.* (NOTE: The British term is **ground floor**.)

first half /ˌfɜrst ˈhæf/ *noun* a period of six months from January to the end of June

first half-year /ˌfɜrst hæf ˈjɪr/ *noun* the first six months or the second six months of a company's accounting year

first in first out /ˌfɜrst ɪn ˌfɜrst ˈaʊt/ *phrase* **1.** an employment policy, in which the people who have been working longest are the first to be be dismissed **2.** an accounting policy in which it is assumed that inventory in hand were purchased last, and that inventory sold during the period were purchased first. Abbreviation **FIFO**. Compare **last in first out**

first-line management /ˌfɜrst laɪn ˈmænɪdʒmənt/ *noun* the managers who have immediate contact with the work force

first mover /ˌfɜrst ˈmuvər/ *noun* a person or company that is the first to launch a product in a market

first mover advantage /fɜrst 'muvər əd,væntɪdʒ/ *noun* the advantage a company gets in being the first to enter a market

first quarter /,fɜrst 'kwɔrtər/ *noun* the period of three months from January to the end of March ○ *The first quarter's rent is payable in advance.*

fiscal /'fɪskəl/ *adjective* referring to tax or to government revenues

fiscal measures /,fɪskəl 'meʒərz/ *plural noun* tax changes made by a government to improve the working of the economy

fiscal year /,fɪskəl 'jɪr/ *noun* an accounting period of twelve months, not necessarily beginning on January 1
"…last fiscal year the chain reported a 116% jump in earnings" [*Barron's*]

fit /fɪt/ *verb* to be the right size for something ○ *The paper doesn't fit the typewriter.* (NOTE: **fitting – fitted**)
fit in *phrasal verb* to make something go into a space ○ *Will the computer fit in that little space?* ○ *The chairman tries to fit in a game of golf every afternoon.* ○ *My appointments calendar is full, but I shall try to fit you in tomorrow afternoon.*
fit out *phrasal verb* to provide equipment or furniture for a business ○ *They fitted out the factory with a new computer system.* ○ *The store was fitted out at a cost of $10,000.* □ **fitting out of a store** putting shelves or counters in for a new store

fittings /'fɪtɪŋz/ *plural noun* items which are sold with a property but are not permanently fixed, e.g., carpets or shelves. ◊ **fixtures**

Five-Year Plan /,faɪv jɪr 'plæn/ *noun* proposals for running a country's economy over a five-year period

fix /fɪks/ *verb* **1.** to arrange or to agree to ○ *to fix a budget* ○ *to fix a meeting for 3 p.m.* ○ *The date has still to be fixed.* ○ *The price of gold was fixed at $300.* ○ *The mortgage rate has been fixed at 5%.* **2.** to mend ○ *The technicians are coming to fix the phone system.* ○ *Can you fix the photocopier?*
fix up with *phrasal verb* to arrange ○ *My secretary fixed me up with a car at the airport.* ○ *Can you fix me up with a room for tomorrow night?*

fixed /fɪkst/ *adjective* unable to be changed or removed

fixed annuity /,fɪkst ə'nuəti/ a type of insurance contract in which the insurance company invests the premiums and agrees to make regular fixed payments to someone over a period of time. ◊ **annuity, variable annuity**

fixed assets /,fɪkst 'æsets/ *plural noun* property or machinery which a company owns and uses, but which the company does not buy or sell as part of its regular trade, including the company's investments in stock of other companies

fixed capital /,fɪkst 'kæpɪt(ə)l/ *noun* capital in the form of buildings and machinery

fixed costs /,fɪkst 'kɒsts/ *plural noun* business costs which do not change with the quantity of the product made

fixed deposit /,fɪkst dɪ'pɒzɪt/ *noun* a deposit which pays a stated interest over a set period

fixed expenses /,fɪkst ɪk'spensɪz/ *plural noun* expenses which do not vary with different levels of production, e.g., rent, secretaries' salaries, and insurance

fixed income /,fɪkst 'ɪnkʌm/ *noun* income which does not change from year to year, as from an annuity

fixed-interest /,fɪkst 'ɪntrəst/ *adjective* having an interest rate which does not vary ■ *noun* interest which is paid at a set rate

fixed-interest investments /,fɪkst ,ɪntrəst ɪn'vestmənts/ *plural noun* investments producing an interest which does not change

fixed-interest securities /fɪkst ,ɪntrəst sɪ'kjʊrɪtiz/ *plural noun* securities such as government bonds which produce an interest which does not change

fixed-price agreement /,fɪkst 'praɪs ə,grɪmənt/ *noun* an agreement where a company provides a service or a product at a price which stays the same for the whole period of the agreement

fixed rate /,fɪkst 'reɪt/ *noun* a rate, e.g., an exchange rate, which does not change

fixed scale of charges /,fɪkst skeɪl əv 'tʃɑrdʒɪz/ *noun* a rate of charging which does not change

fixed-term contract /,fɪkst tɜrm 'kɑntrækt/ *noun* a contract of employment valid for a fixed period of time ○ *I have a fixed-term contract with the company, and no guarantee of an extension when it ends in May.*

fixed yield /ˌfɪkst ˈjild/ *noun* a percentage return which does not change

fixer-upper /ˈfɪksər/ *noun* **1.** a person who has a reputation for arranging business deals, often illegally **2.** a house or car which is being sold cheaply because it needs repairing

fixing /ˈfɪksɪŋ/ *noun* arranging ○ *the fixing of charges* ○ *the fixing of a mortgage rate*

fixtures /ˈfɪkstʃərz/ *plural noun* items in a property which are permanently attached to it, e.g., sinks and lavatories

fixtures and fittings /ˌfɪkstʃərz ən ˈfɪtɪŋz/ *plural noun* objects in a property which are sold with the property, both those which cannot be removed and those which can. Abbreviation **f. & f.**

flag /flæg/ *noun* a mark which is attached to information in a computer so that the information can be found easily ■ *verb* to insert marks on information in a computer so that the information can be found easily (NOTE: **flagging – flagged**)

flagship /ˈflægʃɪp/ *noun* the key product in a range, on which the reputation of the producer most depends

flat /flæt/ *adjective* **1.** used to describe market prices which do not fall or rise, because of low demand ○ *The market was flat today.* **2.** not changing in response to different conditions ■ *adverb* in a blunt way ○ *He turned down the offer flat.*

"…the government revised its earlier reports for July and August. Originally reported as flat in July and declining by 0.2% in August, industrial production is now seen to have risen by 0.2% and 0.1% respectively in those months" [*Sunday Times*]

flat organization /ˈflæt ˌɔrgənaɪzeɪʃ(ə)n/ *noun* an organization with few grades in the hierarchical structure ○ *A flat organization does not appeal to those who like traditional bureaucratic organizations.*

flat out /ˌflæt ˈaʊt/ *adverb* **1.** working hard or at full speed ○ *The factory worked flat out to complete the order on time.* **2.** in a blunt way ○ *He refused the offer flat out.*

flat pack /ˈflæt pæk/ *noun* a pack of goods in which a piece of furniture is sold

in flat sections, which the purchaser then has to put together ○ *The shelves are sold as a flat pack.*

flat rate /ˌflæt ˈreɪt/ *noun* a charge which always stays the same ○ *a flat-rate increase of 10%* ○ *We pay a flat rate for electricity each quarter.* ○ *He is paid a flat rate of £2 per thousand.*

fleet /flit/ *noun* a group of cars belonging to a company and used by its staff ○ *a company's fleet of representatives' cars*

fleet car /ˈflit kɑr/ *noun* a car which is one of a fleet of cars

fleet discount /ˌflit dɪsˈkaʊnt/ *noun* a special low price that a company gets for renting or purchasing all its cars from the same company

fleet rental /ˌflit ˈrent(ə)l/ *noun* an arrangement to rent all a company's cars from the same company at a special price

flexecutive /flekˈsekjutɪv/ *noun* an executive with many different skills who is able to switch jobs or tasks easily (*slang*)

flexibility /ˌfleksɪˈbɪlɪti/ *noun* the ability to be easily changed ○ *There is no flexibility in the company's pricing policy.*

"…they calculate interest on their "flexible" mortgage on an annual basis rather than daily. Charging annual interest makes a nonsense of the whole idea of flexibility which is supposed to help you pay off your mortgage more quickly" [*Financial Times*]

flexible /ˈfleksɪb(ə)l/ *adjective* possible to alter or change ○ *We try to be flexible where the advertising budget is concerned.* ○ *The company has adopted a flexible pricing policy.*

flexible benefit plan /ˌfleksɪb(ə)l ˈbenefɪt ˌplæn/ *noun* an employment benefit plan that offers an employee a choice between taxable and non-taxable benefits such as life insurance, health insurance, retirement plans, vacation time, and stock options. If the employer does not contribute to a chosen benefit or the contribution is too little, the employee can choose to have the cost or excess cost deducted regularly from his or her pay. Also called **cafeteria plan**

flexible manufacturing system /ˌfleksɪb(ə)l ˌmænjʊˈfæktʃərɪŋ ˌsɪstəm/ *noun* a way of manufacturing using computerized systems to allow certain quantities of the product to be made to a specific order. Abbreviation **FMS**

flexible working hours /ˌfleksɪb(ə)l ˈwɜːkɪŋ ˌaʊrz/, **flexible work** plural noun a system in which employees can start or stop work at different hours of the morning or evening provided that they work a certain number of hours per day or week

flextime /ˈflekstaɪm/ noun a system in which employees can start or stop work at different hours of the morning or evening, provided that they work a certain number of hours per day or week ○ *We work flextime.* ○ *Flextime should mean that employees work when they feel most productive.* Also called **flexible working hours** (NOTE: The U.K. term is flexitime)

flier /ˈflaɪər/, **flyer** /ˈflaɪə/ noun a small advertising leaflet designed to encourage customers to ask for more information about the product for sale

flight /flaɪt/ noun **1.** a trip by an aircraft, leaving at a regular time ○ *Flight AC 267 is leaving from Gate 46.* ○ *He missed his flight.* ○ *I always take the afternoon flight to Rome.* ○ *If you hurry you will catch the six o'clock flight to Paris.* **2.** a rapid movement of money out of a country because of a lack of confidence in the country's economic future ○ *The flight of capital from Europe into the U.S.* ○ *The flight from the peso into the dollar.*

flight information /ˈflaɪt ˌɪnfəmeɪʃ(ə)n/ noun information about flight times

flip /flɪp/ noun a start-up company that is established with the goal of building up market share quickly so that it can be listed on the Stock Exchange or sold off in order to produce personal wealth for its founders ■ verb same as **stag**

flipchart /ˈflɪptʃɑːt/ noun a way of showing information to a group of people by writing on large sheets of paper which can then be turned over to show the next sheet

float /floʊt/ noun **1.** cash taken from a central supply and used for running expenses ○ *The sales reps have a float of $100 each.* **2.** U.K. the process of starting a new company by selling shares in it on the Stock Exchange ○ *The float of the new company was a complete failure.* **3.** the process of allowing a currency to settle at its own exchange rate, without any government intervention ■ verb **1.** □ **to float a**

company U.K. to start a new company by selling shares in it on the Stock Exchange □ **to float a loan** to get a loan on the financial market by asking banks and companies to subscribe to it **2.** to let a currency settle at its own exchange rate on the international markets and not be fixed

floating /ˈfloʊtɪŋ/ noun □ **floating of a company** U.K. the act of starting a new company by selling shares in it on the Stock Exchange ■ adjective not fixed ○ *floating exchange rates* ○ *the floating pound*

"…in a world of floating exchange rates the dollar is strong because of capital inflows rather than weak because of the nation's trade deficit" [*Duns Business Month*]

floating charge /ˈfloʊtɪŋ tʃɑːdʒ/ noun a charge linked to any of the company's assets in a category, but not to any specific item

floating population /ˌfloʊtɪŋ ˌpɒpjə ˈleɪʃ(ə)n/ noun people who move from place to place

floating rate /ˈfloʊtɪŋ reɪt/ noun **1.** same as **variable rate 2.** an exchange rate for a currency, which can vary according to market demand, and is not fixed by the government

flood /flʌd/ noun a large quantity ○ *We received a flood of orders.* ○ *Floods of tourists filled the hotels.* ■ verb to fill with a large quantity of something ○ *The market was flooded with cheap imitations.* ○ *The sales department is flooded with orders or with complaints.*

floor /flɔː/ noun a bottom level of something, e.g., the lowest exchange rate which a government will accept for its currency or the lower limit imposed on an interest rate ○ *The government will impose a floor on wages to protect the poor.*

floor manager /ˈflɔː ˌmænɪdʒər/ noun a person in charge of the sales staff in a department store

floor plan /ˈflɔː plæn/ noun a drawing of a floor in a building, showing where different departments are

floor price /ˈflɔː praɪs/ noun a lowest price, a price which cannot go any lower

floor space /ˈflɔː speɪs/ noun an area of floor in an office or warehouse ○ *We have 3,500 square meters of floor space to rent.*

floor stand /'flɔr stænd/ *noun* a display stand which stands on the floor, as opposed to one which stands on a table or counter

floorwalker /'flɔrwɔkər/ *noun* an employee of a department store who advises customers, and supervises the store assistants in a department

flop /flɑp/ *noun* a failure, or something which has not been successful ○ *The new model was a flop.* ■ *verb* to fail or not be a success ○ *The launch of the new shampoo flopped badly.* ○ *The flotation of the new company flopped badly.* (NOTE: **flopping – flopped**)

floppy disk /,flɑpi 'dɪsk/, **floppy** /'flɑpi/ *noun* a flat circular flexible disk onto which data can be stored in a magnetic form. A floppy disk cannot store as much data as a hard disk, but is easily removed, and is protected by a plastic sleeve.

flotation /flou'teɪʃ(ə)n/ *noun* □ **the flotation of a new company** *U.K.* the act of starting a new company by selling stock in it

flotsam and jetsam /,flɑtsəm ən 'dʒetsəm/ *noun* garbage floating in the water after a ship has been wrecked and garbage washed on to the land

flourish /'flʌrɪʃ/ *verb* to be prosperous, to do well in business ○ *the company is flourishing* ○ *trade with Estonia flourished*

flourishing /'flʌrɪʃɪŋ/ *adjective* profitable □ **flourishing trade** trade which is expanding profitably ○ *He runs a flourishing shoe business.*

flow /flou/ *noun* **1.** a movement ○ *the flow of capital into a country* ○ *the flow of investments into Japan* **2.** □ **discounted cash flow (DCF)** calculation of forecast sales of a product in current terms with reductions for current interest rates ■ *verb* to move smoothly ○ *Production is now flowing normally after the strike.*

flow chart /'flout ʃɑrt/, **flow diagram** /'flou ,daɪəgræm/ *noun* a chart which shows the arrangement of work processes in a series

flow diagram /'flou ,daɪəgræm/ *noun* same as **flow chart**

fluctuate /'flʌktʃueɪt/ *verb* to move up and down ○ *Prices fluctuated between $1.10 and $1.25.* ○ *The pound fluctuated all day on the foreign exchange markets.*

fluctuating /'flʌktʃueɪtɪŋ/ *adjective* moving up and down ○ *fluctuating dollar prices*

fluctuation /,flʌktʃu'eɪʃ(ə)n/ *noun* an up and down movement ○ *the fluctuations of the yen* ○ *the fluctuations of the exchange rate*

fluff /flʌf/ *verb* □ **fluff it and fly it** give a product an attractive appearance and then sell it (*informal*)

fly-by-night /'flaɪ baɪ ,naɪt/ *adjective* company which is not reliable or which might disappear to avoid paying debts ○ *I want a reputable builder, not one of these fly-by-night outfits.*

flying picket /,flaɪɪŋ 'pɪkɪt/ *noun* a picket who travels round the country to try to stop workers going to work

FMS *abbreviation* flexible manufacturing system

FNMA *abbreviation* Federal National Mortgage Association

FOB /'efou'bi/, **f.o.b.** *abbreviation* free on board

focus group /'foukəs grup/ *noun* a group of people who are brought together to discuss informally a market-research question

FOIA *abbreviation* Freedom of Information Act

fold /fould/ *verb* to stop doing business (*informal*) ○ *The business folded up last December.* ○ *The company folded with debts of over $1m.*

-fold /fould/ *suffix* times □ **four-fold** four times

"…the company's sales have nearly tripled and its profits have risen seven-fold since 1982" [*Barrons*]

folio /'fouliou/ *noun* a page with a number, especially two facing pages in an account book which have the same number ■ *verb* to put a number on a page

follow /'falou/ *verb* to come behind or to come afterward ○ *The samples will follow by surface mail.* ○ *We will pay $10,000 down, with the balance to follow in six months' time.*

follow up *phrasal verb* to examine something further ○ *I'll follow up your idea of targeting our address list with a special mailing.* □ **to follow up an initiative** to take action once someone else has decided to do something

follow-up letter /'fɑloʊ ʌp ˌletər/, **follow-up call** noun a letter or call to someone who has not acted on the instructions in a previous letter or call, or to discuss in more detail points which were raised earlier

FOMC abbreviation Federal Open Market Committee

food stamp /'fud stæmp/ noun a coupon issued by the U.S. federal government to poor people so that they can buy food at a discounted price

foolscap /'fulskæp/ noun a large size of writing paper (13 1/2 by 8 1/2 inches) ○ The letter was on six sheets of foolscap.

foolscap envelope /ˌfulskæp 'envəloʊp/ noun a large envelope which takes foolscap paper

foot /fʊt/ noun 1. the bottom part ○ He signed his name at the foot of the invoice. 2. a measurement of length (=12 inches) ○ The table is six feet long. ○ My office is ten feet by twelve. (NOTE: The plural is **feet** for (a) and (c); there is no plural for (b). In measurements, **foot** is usually written **ft.** or ' after figures: **10ft.; 10'.** Note that the foot is now no longer officially used in the U.K.) ■ verb □ **to foot the bill** to pay the costs □ **to foot up an account** to add up a column of numbers

footer /'fʊtər/ noun a section at the bottom of a web page, which usually contains any essential links and information on how to contact the organization that owns the page and on its copyright and privacy policy

footfall /'fʊtfɔl/ noun the number of customers who come into and walk round a store

Footsie /'fʊtsi/ noun an index based on the prices of 100 leading companies (this is the main London index) (informal) Full form **Financial Times-Stock Exchange 100 index**

FOR full form **free on rail**

"Forbes" 500 /ˌfɔrbz faɪv 'hʌndrəd/ noun a list of the largest U.S. corporations, published each year in "Forbes" magazine

forbid /fər'bɪd/ verb to tell someone not to do something, or to say that something must not be done ○ Smoking is forbidden in our offices. ○ The contract forbids resale of the goods to the U.S. ○ Staff are forbidden to speak directly to the press.

(NOTE: **forbidding – forbade – forbidden**)

force /fɔrs/ noun 1. strength □ **to be in force** to be operating or working ○ The rules have been in force since 1986. □ **to come into force** to start to operate or work ○ The new regulations will come into force on January 1st. 2. a group of people ■ verb to make someone do something ○ Competition has forced the company to lower its prices. ○ After the takeover several of the managers were forced to take early retirement.

force down phrasal verb to make something such as prices become lower □ **to force prices down** to make prices come down ○ Competition has forced prices down.

force up phrasal verb to make something become higher □ **to force prices up** to make prices go up ○ The war forced up the price of oil.

forced sale /ˌfɔrst 'seɪl/ noun a sale which takes place because a court orders it or because it is the only way to avoid a financial crisis

force majeure /ˌfɔrs mæ'ʒɜr/ noun something which happens which is out of the control of the parties who have signed a contract, e.g., a strike, war, or storm

forecast /'fɔrkæst/ noun a description or calculation of what will probably happen in the future ○ The chairman did not believe the sales director's forecast of higher turnover. ■ verb to calculate or to say what will probably happen in the future ○ She is forecasting sales of $2m. ○ Economists have forecast a fall in the exchange rate. (NOTE: **forecasting – forecast**)

forecast dividend /ˌfɔrkɑrst 'dɪvɪdend/ noun a dividend which a company expects to pay at the end of the current year. Also called **prospective dividend**

forecasting /'fɔrkɑstɪŋ/ noun the process of calculating what will probably happen in the future ○ Manpower planning will depend on forecasting the future levels of production.

foreclose /fɔr'kloʊz/ verb to sell a property because the owner cannot repay money which he or she has borrowed, using the property as security ○ to foreclose on a mortgaged property

foreclosure /fɔːˈkləʊʒə/ *noun* an act of foreclosing

foreign /ˈfɒrɪn/ *adjective* not belonging to your own country ○ *Foreign cars have flooded our market.* ○ *We are increasing our trade with foreign countries.*

Foreign Corrupt Practices Act /ˌfɒrɪn kəˌrʌpt ˈpræktɪsɪz ˌækt/ a law that prohibits U.S. individuals and companies from bribing any foreign government officials in order to get business

foreign currency /ˌfɒrɪn ˈkʌrənsi/ *noun* money of another country

foreign currency account /ˌfɒrɪn ˈkʌrənsi əˌkaʊnt/ *noun* a bank account in the currency of another country, e.g., a dollar account in a U.K. bank

foreign currency reserves /ˌfɒrɪn ˈkʌrənsi rɪˌzɜːvz/ *plural noun* a country's reserves held in currencies of other countries. Also called **foreign exchange reserves, international reserves**

foreigner /ˈfɒrɪnər/ *noun* a person from another country

foreign exchange /ˌfɒrən ɪks ˈtʃeɪndʒ/ *noun* **1.** the business of exchanging the money of one country for that of another **2.** foreign currencies

"…the dollar recovered a little lost ground on the foreign exchanges yesterday" [*Financial Times*]

foreign exchange broker /ˌfɒrɪn ɪks ˈtʃeɪndʒ ˌbrəʊkər/, **foreign exchange dealer** *noun* a person who deals on the foreign exchange market

foreign exchange dealing /ˌfɒrɪn ɪksˈtʃeɪndʒ ˌdiːlɪŋ/ *noun* the business of buying and selling foreign currencies

foreign exchange market /ˌfɒrɪn ɪks ˈtʃeɪndʒ ˌmɑːkət/ *noun* **1.** a market where people buy and sell foreign currencies ○ *She trades on the foreign exchange market.* **2.** dealings in foreign currencies ○ *Foreign exchange markets were very active after the dollar devalued.*

foreign exchange reserves /ˌfɒrɪn ɪksˈtʃeɪndʒ rɪˌzɜːvz/ *plural noun* foreign money held by a government to support its own currency and pay its debts

foreign exchange transfer /ˌfɒrɪn ɪksˈtʃeɪndʒ ˌtrænsfər/ *noun* the sending of money from one country to another

foreign goods /ˌfɒrɪn ˈɡʊdz/ *plural noun* goods manufactured in other countries

foreign investments /ˌfɒrɪn ɪnˈvestmənts/ *plural noun* money invested in other countries

foreign money order /ˌfɒrɪn ˈmʌni ˌɔːdər/ *noun* a money order in a foreign currency which is payable to someone living in a foreign country

foreign rights /ˌfɒrɪn ˈraɪtz/ *plural noun* a legal entitlement to sell something in a foreign country, e.g., the right to translate a book into a foreign language

foreign trade /ˌfɒrɪn ˈtreɪd/ *noun* trade with other countries

foreman /ˈfɔːmən/, **forewoman** /ˈfɔːwʊmən/ *noun* a skilled worker in charge of several other workers (NOTE: The plural is **foremen** or **forewomen**.)

forex /ˈfɔːreks/, **Forex** *noun* same as **foreign exchange**

"…the amount of reserves sold by the authorities were not sufficient to move the $200 billion Forex market permanently" [*Duns Business Month*]

forfeit /ˈfɔːfɪt/ *noun* the fact of having something taken away as a punishment □ **the goods were declared forfeit** the court said that the goods had to be taken away from the person who was holding them ■ *verb* to have something taken away as a punishment □ **to forfeit a patent** to lose a patent because payments have not been made □ **to forfeit a deposit** to lose a deposit which was left for an item because you have decided not to buy that item

forfeit clause /ˈfɔːfɪt ˌklɔːz/ *noun* a clause in a contract which says that goods or a deposit will be taken away if the contract is not obeyed

forfeiture /ˈfɔːfɪtʃər/ *noun* the act of forfeiting a property

forge /fɔːdʒ/ *verb* to copy money or a signature illegally, to make a document which looks like a real one ○ *He tried to enter the country with forged documents.*

forgery /ˈfɔːdʒəri/ *noun* **1.** making an illegal copy ○ *He was sent to prison for forgery.* **2.** an illegal copy ○ *The signature was proved to be a forgery.*

for hire contract /ˌfər ˈhaɪr ˌkɒntrækt/ *noun* a freelance contract

fork-lift truck /ˌfɔːk lɪft ˈtrʌk/ *noun* a type of small tractor with two metal arms in front, used for lifting and moving pallets

form /fɔːm/ *noun* **1.** □ **form of words** words correctly laid out for a legal docu-

171

ment □ **receipt in due form** a correctly written receipt **2.** an official printed paper with blank spaces which have to be filled in with information ○ *a pad of order forms* ○ *You have to fill in form A20.* ○ *Each passenger was given a customs declaration form.* ○ *The reps carry pads of order forms.* ■ *verb* to start, create or organize something ○ *The brothers have formed a new company.*

forma /ˈfɔːmə/ *noun* ♦ **pro forma**

formal /ˈfɔːm(ə)l/ *adjective* clearly and legally written ○ *to make a formal application* ○ *to send a formal order* ○ *Is this a formal job offer?* ○ *The factory is prepared for the formal inspection by the government inspector.*

formality /fɔːˈmælɪti/ *noun* something which has to be done to obey the law

formally /ˈfɔːməli/ *adverb* in a formal way ○ *We have formally applied for planning permission for the new shopping precinct.*

formation /fɔːˈmeɪʃ(ə)n/, **forming** /ˈfɔːmɪŋ/ *noun* the act of organizing ○ *the formation of a new company*

former /ˈfɔːmər/ *adjective* before or at an earlier time ○ *The former chairman has taken a job with a the competition.* ○ *She got a reference from her former employer.*

formerly /ˈfɔːməli/ *adverb* at an earlier time ○ *He is currently managing director of Smith Inc., but formerly he worked for Jones Brothers.*

for-profit /fər ˈprɒfɪt/ *adjective* established or designed to make a profit ○ *a for-profit clinic*

fortnight /ˈfɔːtnaɪt/ *noun U.K.* two weeks ○ *I saw him a fortnight ago.* ○ *We will be on vacation during the last fortnight of July.*

fortune /ˈfɔːtʃən/ *noun* a large amount of money ○ *He made a fortune from investing in oil stocks.* ○ *She left her fortune to her three children.*

Fortune 500 /ˌfɔːtʃʊn ˌfaɪv ˈhʌndrəd/ *plural noun* (*the 500 largest companies in the USA*) the 500 largest companies in the U.S., as listed annually in Fortune magazine

forum /ˈfɔːrəm/ *noun* an online area where Internet users can read, post, and respond to messages

forward /ˈfɔːwəd/ *adjective* in advance or to be paid at a later date ■ *adverb* **1.** □ **to date a check forward** to put a later date than the present one on a check **2.** □ **to sell forward** to sell foreign currency, commodities, etc., for delivery at a later date **3.** □ **balance brought forward, carried forward** balance which is entered in an account at the end of a period and is then taken to be the starting point of the next period ■ *verb* □ **to forward something to someone** to send something to someone ○ *to forward a consignment to Nigeria* □ **"please forward", "to be forwarded"** words written on an envelope, asking the person receiving it to send it on to the person whose name is written on it

forwardation /ˌfɔːwədˈeɪʃ(ə)n/ *noun* a situation in which the cash price is lower than the forward price (NOTE: The opposite is **backwardation.**)

forward buying /ˌfɔːwəd ˈbaɪɪŋ/ *noun* the act of buying stock, currency, or commodities at today's price for delivery at a later date

forward contract /ˈfɔːwəd ˌkɒntrækt/ *noun* a one-time agreement to buy currency, stock, or commodities for delivery at a later date at a specific price

forward dealing /ˈfɔːwəd ˌdiːlɪŋ/ *noun* the activity of buying or selling commodities forward

forwarder /ˈfɔːwədər/ *noun* a person or company that arranges shipping and customs documents for several shipments from different companies, putting them together to form one large shipment

forward exchange rate /ˌfɔːwəd ɪksˈtʃeɪndʒ reɪt/, **forward rate** *noun* a rate for purchase of foreign currency at a fixed price for delivery at a later date ○ *What are the forward rates for the pound?*

forwarding /ˈfɔːwədɪŋ/ *noun* the act of arranging shipping and customs documents

forwarding address /ˈfɔːwədɪŋ əˌdres/ *noun* the address to which a person's mail can be sent on

forwarding agent /ˈfɔːwədɪŋ ˌeɪdʒənt/ *noun* a person or company which arranges shipping and customs documents

forwarding instructions /ˈfɔːwədɪŋ ɪnˌstrʌkʃənz/ *plural noun* instructions showing how the goods are to be shipped and delivered

forward integration /ˌfɔwərd ˌɪntə ˈgreɪʃ(ə)n/ *noun* a process of expansion in which a company becomes its own distributor or takes over a company in the same line of business as itself ○ *Forward integration will give the company greater control over its selling.* ○ *Forward integration has brought the company closer to its consumers and has made it aware of their buying habits.* Compare **backward integration**

forward market /ˌfɔrwərd ˈmɑrkət/ *noun* a market for purchasing foreign currency, oil, or commodities for delivery at a later date

forward price /ˈfɔrwərd praɪs/ *noun* a price of goods which are to be delivered in the future

forward sales /ˈfɔrwərd seɪlz/ *plural noun* the sales of stock, commodities, or foreign exchange for delivery at a later date

foul bill of lading /ˌfaʊl bɪl əv ˈleɪdɪŋ/ *noun* a bill of lading which says that the goods were in bad condition when received by the shipper

founder /ˈfaʊndər/ *noun* a person who starts a company ■ *verb* to collapse, to fail ○ *The project foundered for lack of funds.*

founder's shares /ˈfaʊndəz ʃerz/ *noun* special stock issued to the person who starts a company

four O's /ˌfɔr ˈoʊz/ *plural noun* a simple way of summarizing the essentials of a marketing operation, which are Objects, Objectives, Organization, and Operations

four-pack /ˈfɔr pæk/ *noun* a box containing four items (often bottles)

four-part /ˈfɔr pɑrt/ *adjective* paper (for computers or typewriters) with a top sheet for the original and three other sheets for copies ○ *four-part invoices* ○ *four-part stationery*

four P's /ˌfɔr ˈpiz/ *plural noun* a simple way of summarizing the essentials of the marketing mix, which are Product, Price, Promotion, and Place

fourth quarter /ˌfɔrθ ˈkwɔrtər/ *noun* a period of three months from 1st October to the end of the year

Fr *abbreviation* franc

fraction /ˈfrækʃən/ *noun* a very small amount ○ *Only a fraction of the new issue was subscribed.*

fractional /ˈfrækʃənəl/ *adjective* very small

fractional certificate /ˈfrækʃənəl sər ˌtɪfɪkət/ *noun* a certificate for part of a share

franc /fræŋk/ *noun* **1.** a former unit of currency in France and Belgium ○ *French francs* or *Belgian francs* **2.** a unit of currency in Switzerland and several other currencies ○ *It costs twenty-five Swiss francs.*

franchise /ˈfræntʃaɪz/ *noun* a license to trade using a brand name and paying a royalty for it ○ *He's bought a printing franchise* or *a pizza franchise.* ■ *verb* to sell licenses for people to trade using a brand name and paying a royalty ○ *His sandwich bar was so successful that he decided to franchise it.*

franchise agreement /ˈfræntʃaɪz əˌgrɪmənt/, **franchise contract** /ˈfræntʃaɪz ˌkɑntrækt/ *noun* a legal contract to trade using a brand name and paying a royalty for it

franchisee /ˌfræntʃaɪˈzi/ *noun* a person who runs a franchise

franchiser /ˈfræntʃaɪzər/ *noun* a person who licenses a franchise

franchising /ˈfræntʃaɪzɪŋ/ *noun* the act of selling a license to trade as a franchise ○ *She runs her sandwich chain as a franchising operation.*

franchising operation /ˈfræntʃaɪzɪŋ ɑpəˌreɪʃ(ə)n/ *noun* an operation involving selling licenses to trade as a franchise

franchisor /ˈfræntʃaɪzər/ *noun* another spelling of **franchiser**

franco /ˈfræŋkoʊ/ *adverb* free

frank /fræŋk/ *verb* to stamp the date and postage on a letter

franking machine /ˈfræŋkɪŋ məˌʃin/ *noun* a machine which marks the date and postage on letters so that the sender does not need to use stamps

fraud /frɔrd/ *noun* an act of making money by making people believe something which is not true ○ *He got possession of the property by fraud.* ○ *She was accused of frauds relating to foreign currency.* □ **to obtain money by fraud** to obtain money by saying or doing something to cheat someone

fraud squad /'frɔd skwɑd/ *noun* the special police department which investigates frauds

fraudulent /'frɔdjʊlənt/ *adjective* not honest, or aiming to cheat people ○ *a fraudulent transaction*

fraudulent conversion /,frɔdjʊlənt kən'vɜrʃ(ə)n/ *noun* the act of using money which does not belong to you for a purpose for which it is not supposed to be used

fraudulently /'frɔdjʊləntli/ *adverb* not honestly ○ *goods imported fraudulently*

fraudulent misrepresentation /,frɔdjələnt mɪs,reprɪzen'teɪʃ(ə)n/ *noun* the act of making a false statement with the intention of tricking a customer

free /fri/ *adjective, adverb* **1.** not costing any money ○ *I have been given a free ticket to the exhibition.* ○ *The price includes free delivery.* ○ *All goods in the store are delivered free.* ○ *A catalog will be sent free on request.* □ **free of charge** with no payment to be made **2.** with no restrictions □ **free of tax** with no tax having to be paid ○ *Interest is paid free of tax.* □ **free of duty** with no duty to be paid ○ *to import wine free of duty* **3.** not busy or not occupied ○ *Are there any free tables in the restaurant?* ○ *I will be free in a few minutes.* ○ *The chairman always keeps Friday afternoon free for a game of bridge.* ■ *verb* to make something available or easy ○ *The government's decision has freed millions of dollars for investment.*

free baggage allowance /,fri 'bægɪdʒ ə,laʊəns/ *noun* the amount of baggage which a passenger can take with him or her free on a plane

freebie /'fribi/ *noun* a product or service supplied free of charge, especially a gift to an agent or journalist (*informal*)

free collective bargaining /,fri kə,lektɪv 'bɑrgɪnɪŋ/ *noun* negotiations between management and labor unions about wage increases and working conditions

free competition /,fri ,kɑmpə'tɪʃ(ə)n/ *noun* the fact of being free to compete without government interference

free currency /,fri 'kʌrənsi/ *noun* a currency which is allowed by the government to be bought and sold without restriction

Freedom of Information Act /,fridəm əv ,ɪnfər'meɪʃ(ə)n ,ækt/ *noun* a federal law the allows any person the right to get U.S. government records upon written request, unless the records are protected by any of nine exemptions. Abbreviation **FOIA**

free enterprise /,fri 'entərpraɪz/ *noun* a system of business free from government interference

free gift /,fri 'gɪft/ *noun* a present given by a store to a customer who buys a specific amount of goods ○ *There is a free gift worth $25 to any customer buying a CD player.*

freeholder /'frihoʊldər/ *noun* a person who owns a freehold property

freehold property /'frihoʊld ,prɑpəti/ *noun* property which the owner holds for ever and on which no rent is paid

free issue /,fri 'ɪʃu/ *noun* same as **scrip issue**

freelance /'frilæns/ *adjective, noun* (an independent worker) who works for several different companies but is not employed by any of them ○ *We have about twenty freelances working for us* or *about twenty people working for us on a freelance basis.* ○ *She is a freelance journalist.* ■ *adverb* selling your work to various firms, but not being employed by any of them ○ *He works freelance as a designer.* ■ *verb* **1.** to do work for several firms but not be employed by any of them ○ *She freelances for the local newspapers.* **2.** to send work out to be done by a freelancer ○ *We freelance work out to several specialists.*

freelancer /'frilænsər/ *noun* a freelance worker

free luggage allowance /,fri 'lʌgɪdʒ ə,laʊəns/ *noun* the amount of luggage which a passenger can take with him free of charge

freely /'frili/ *adverb* with no restrictions ○ *Money should circulate freely within the EU.*

free market /,fri 'mɑrkət/ *noun* a market in which there is no government control of supply and demand, and the rights of individuals and organizations to physical and intellectual property are upheld

free market economy /,fri ,mɑrkət ɪ'kɑnəmi/ *noun* a system where the government does not interfere in business activity in any way

free on board /,fri ɑn 'bɔrd/ *adjective* **1.** including in the price all the seller's costs until the goods are on the ship for transportation. Abbreviation **f.o.b. 2.** including in the price all the seller's costs until the goods are delivered to a place

free paper /ˌfri ˈpeɪpər/ noun a newspaper which is given away free, and which relies for its income on its advertising

freephone /ˈfrifoʊn/, **freefone** noun a system where you can telephone to reply to an advertisement, to place an order, or to ask for information and the seller pays for the call

free port /ˈfri pɔrt/ noun a port where there are no customs duties to be paid

freepost /ˈfripoʊst/ noun a system where someone can write to an advertiser to place an order or to ask for information to be sent, without paying for a stamp. The company paying for the postage on receipt of the envelope.

free sample /ˌfri ˈsæmpəl/ noun a sample given free to advertise a product

freesheet /ˈfriʃit/ noun same as **free paper**

free trade /ˌfri ˈtreɪd/ noun a system where goods can go from one country to another without any restrictions

free trade area /fri ˈtreɪd ˌeriə/ noun a group of countries practicing free trade

free trader /ˌfri ˈtreɪdər/ noun a person who is in favor of free trade

free trade zone /ˌfri ˈtreɪd ˌzoʊn/ noun an area where there are no customs duties

free trial /ˌfri ˈtraɪəl/ noun an opportunity to test a machine or product with no payment involved

free worker /ˈfri ˌwɜrkər/ noun a person who moves frequently from one job or project to another, because they have skills and ideas that many organizations value and prefer to work on a short-term contract rather than to build a career within a single organization

freeze /friz/ noun □ **a freeze on wages and prices** period when wages and prices are not allowed to be increased ■ verb to keep something such as money or costs at their present level and not allow them to rise ○ to freeze wages and prices ○ to freeze credits ○ to freeze company dividends ○ We have frozen expenditure at last year's level. (NOTE: **freezing – froze – frozen**)

freeze out phrasal verb □ **to freeze out the competition** to trade successfully and cheaply and so prevent competitors from operating

freeze on wages /ˌfriz ɑn ˈweɪdʒɪz/ noun same as **wage freeze**

freight /freɪt/ noun **1.** the cost of transporting goods by air, sea, or land ○ At an auction, the buyer pays the freight. **2.** goods which are transported □ **to take on freight** to load goods onto a ship, train, or truck ■ verb □ **to freight goods** to send goods ○ We freight goods to all parts of the country.

freightage /ˈfreɪtɪdʒ/ noun the cost of transporting goods

freight car /ˈfreɪt kɑr/ noun a railroad wagon for carrying freight

freight charges /ˈfreɪt ˌtʃɑrdʒɪz/ plural noun money charged for transporting goods ○ Freight charges have gone up sharply this year.

freight collect /ˈfreɪt kəˌlekt/ noun an arrangement whereby the customer pays for transporting the goods

freight costs /ˈfreɪt kɔsts/ plural noun money paid to transport goods

freight depot /ˈfreɪt ˌdepoʊ/ noun a central point where goods are collected before being shipped

freight elevator /ˈfreɪt ˌeləveɪtər/ noun a strong elevator for carrying goods up and down inside a building

freighter /ˈfreɪtər/ noun **1.** an aircraft or ship which carries goods **2.** a person or company that organizes the transportation of goods

freight forward /ˌfreɪt ˈfɔrwərd/ noun a deal where the customer pays for transporting the goods

freight forwarder /ˈfreɪt ˌfɔrwərdər/ noun a person or company that arranges shipping and customs documents for several shipments from different companies, putting them together to form one large shipment

freightliner /ˈfreɪtlaɪnər/ noun a train which carries goods in containers ○ The shipment has to be delivered to the freightliner depot.

freight plane /ˈfreɪt pleɪn/ noun an aircraft which carries goods, not passengers

freight train /ˈfreɪt treɪn/ *noun* a train used for carrying goods (NOTE: The U.K. term is **goods train**)

frequent /ˈfriːkwənt/ *adjective* which comes, goes or takes place often ○ *There is a frequent ferry service between England and France.* ○ *We send frequent faxes to New York.* ○ *How frequent are the planes to Birmingham?* ○ *We send frequent telexes to New York.*

frequently /ˈfriːkwəntli/ *adverb* often ○ *The photocopier is frequently out of use.* ○ *We email our New York office very frequently – at least four times a day.*

friction-free market /ˌfrɪkʃən fri ˈmɑːkət/ *noun* a market in which there are few differences between competing products, so that the customer has an exceptionally free choice

"…economists predict that a new era of nearly friction-free markets will arrive. Companies that don't move quickly to the new technology risk being left behind." [*BusinessWeek*]

friendly society /ˈfrendli səˌsaɪəti/ *noun* a group of people who pay regular subscriptions which are used to help members of the group when they are ill or in financial difficulties

fringe benefit /ˈfrɪndʒ ˌbenəfɪt/ *noun* an extra item given by a company to employees in addition to a salary, e.g., company cars or health club membership ○ *The fringe benefits make up for the poor pay.* ○ *Use of the company recreation facilities is one of the fringe benefits of the job.*

front /frʌnt/ *noun* **1.** □ **in front of** before or on the front side of something ○ *They put up a "for sale" sign in front of the factory.* ○ *The chairman's name is in front of all the others on the staff list.* **2.** a business or person used to hide an illegal trade ○ *His restaurant is a front for a drugs organization.*

front end /ˈfrʌnt end/ *noun* the part of an organization that meets and deals with customers face-to-face

front-end /ˌfrʌnt ˈend/ *adjective* referring to the start of an investment or insurance

front-end loaded /ˈfrʌnt end ˌləʊdɪd/ *adjective* used to describe an insurance or investment plan in which most of the management charges are incurred in the first year of the investment or insurance, and are not spread out over the whole period. Compare **back-end loaded**

front-line management /ˌfrʌnt laɪn ˈmænɪdʒmənt/ *noun* managers who have immediate contact with the employees

front man /ˈfrʌnt mæn/ *noun* a person who seems honest but is hiding an illegal trade

frozen /ˈfrəʊz(ə)n/ *adjective* not allowed to be changed or used ○ *Wages have been frozen at last year's rates.* □ **his assets have been frozen by the court** the court does not allow him to sell his assets. ◊ **freeze**

frozen account /ˈfrəʊz(ə)n əˌkaʊnt/ *noun* a bank account where the money cannot be moved or used because of a court order

frozen assets /ˌfrəʊz(ə)n ˈæsets/ *plural noun* a company's assets which by law cannot be sold because someone has a claim against them

frozen credits /ˌfrəʊz(ə)n ˈkredɪtz/ *plural noun* credits in an account which cannot be moved

frustrate /frʌˈstreɪt/ *verb* to prevent something, especially the terms of a contract, being fulfilled

ft *abbreviation* foot

fuel /ˈfjuːəl/ *noun* material (like oil, coal, gas) used to give power ○ *The annual fuel bill for the plant has doubled over the last years.* ○ *He has bought a car with low fuel consumption.* ■ *verb* to add to ○ *Market worries were fueled by news of an increase in electricity charges.* ○ *The rise in the share price was fueled by rumors of a takeover bid.* (NOTE: **fueled – fueling**. The U.K. spelling is **fuelled – fuelling**.)

fulfill /fʊlˈfɪl/ *verb* to complete something in a satisfactory way ○ *The clause regarding payments has not been fulfilled.* (NOTE: **fulfilling- fulfilled**. The U.K. spelling is **fulfil**.) □ **to fulfill an order** to supply the items which have been ordered ○ *We are so understaffed that we cannot fulfill anymore orders before Christmas.*

fulfillment /fʊlˈfɪlmənt/ *noun* the act of carrying something out in a satisfactory way (NOTE: The U.K. spelling is **fulfilment.**)

fulfillment house /fʊlˈfɪlmənt haʊs/ *noun* a company which supplies orders on behalf of a mail-order company

full /fʊl/ *adjective* **1.** with as much inside it as possible ○ *The train was full of commuters.* ○ *Is the container full yet?* ○ *We sent a truck full of spare parts to our warehouse.* ○ *When the disc is full, don't forget to make a backup copy.* **2.** complete, including everything □ **we are working at full capacity** we are doing as much work as possible **3.** □ **in full** completely ○ *a full refund* or *a refund paid in full* ○ *Give your full name and address* or *your name and address in full.* ○ *He accepted all our conditions in full.*

full cost pricing /ˌfʊl kɔst ˈpraɪsɪŋ/ *noun* a pricing method based on assessing the full production cost of each product unit and adding a profit margin

full costs /ˌfʊl ˈkɔsts/ *plural noun* all the costs of manufacturing a product, including both fixed and variable costs

full cover /ˌfʊl ˈkʌvər/ *noun* insurance cover against all risks

full employment /ˌfʊl ɪmˈplɔɪmənt/ *noun* a situation where all the people who can work have jobs

full factoring service /ˌfʊl ˈfæktərɪŋ ˌsɜrvɪs/ *noun* a service by which a factor operates a client's purchase ledger and even takes on responsibility for his bad debts

full fare /ˌfʊl ˈfer/ *noun* a ticket for a trip by an adult who is paying the full price

full lot /ˌfʊl ˈlɑt/ *noun* same as **round lot**

full payment /ˌfʊl ˈpeɪmənt/ *noun* the paying of all money owed

full price /ˌfʊl ˈpraɪs/ *noun* a price with no discount ○ *She bought a full-price ticket.*

full rate /ˌfʊl ˈreɪt/ *noun* the full charge, with no reductions

full refund /ˌfʊl ˈrifʌnd/ *noun* a refund of all the money paid ○ *He got a full refund when he complained about the service.*

full repairing lease /ˌfʊl rɪˈperɪŋ ˌlis/ *noun* a lease where the tenant has to pay for all repairs to the property

full-scale /ˈfʊl skeɪl/ *adjective* complete or very thorough ○ *The bank ordered a full-scale review of credit terms.* ○ *The HR department will start a full-scale review of the present pay structure.*

full-service banking /fʊl ˌsɜrvɪs ˈbæŋkɪŋ/ *noun* banking that offers a whole range of services including mortgages, loans, pensions, etc.

full-time /ˈfʊl taɪm/ *adjective, adverb* working all the usual working time, i.e. about eight hours a day, five days a week ○ *She has full-time work* or *She works full-time.* ○ *He is one of our full-time staff.*

full-time employment /ˌfʊl taɪm ɪmˈplɔɪmənt/ *noun* work for all of a working day ○ *to be in full-time employment*

full-timer /ˌfʊl ˈtaɪmər/ *noun* a person who works full-time

fully /ˈfʊli/ *adverb* completely

"…issued and fully paid capital is $100 million" [*Hongkong Standard*]

fully connected world /ˌfʊli kə ˌnektɪd ˈwɜrld/ *noun* a world where most people and organizations are linked by the Internet or similar networks

fully-paid shares /ˌfʊli peɪd ˈʃerz/ *plural noun* shares for which the full face value has been paid

fully paid-up capital /ˌfʊli peɪd ʌp ˈkæpɪt(ə)l/ *noun* all money paid for the issued capital shares

function /ˈfʌŋkʃən/ *noun* **1.** a duty or job **2.** a mathematical formula, where a result is dependent upon several other numbers ■ *verb* to work ○ *The advertising campaign is functioning smoothly.* ○ *The new management structure does not seem to be functioning very well.*

function code /ˈfʌŋkʃən koʊd/ *noun* a computer code that controls an action rather than representing a character

fund /fʌnd/ *noun* **1.** money set aside for a special purpose □ **the International Monetary Fund (IMF)** a type of bank forming part of the United Nations which helps member states in financial difficulties, gives financial advice to members and encourages world trade **2.** money invested in an investment trust as part of a mutual fund, or given to a financial adviser to invest on behalf of a client. ◊ **funds** ■ *verb* to provide money for a purpose ○ *The company does not have enough resources to fund its expansion program.* □ **to fund a company** to provide money for a company to operate

"…the S&L funded all borrowers' development costs, including accrued interest" [*Barrons*]

funded /ˈfʌndɪd/ *adjective* backed by long-term loans ○ *long-term funded capital*

funding /ˈfʌndɪŋ/ *noun* **1.** money for spending ○ *The bank is providing the funding for the new product launch.* **2.** the act of changing a short-term debt into a long-term loan ○ *The capital expenditure program requires long-term funding.*

fund management /ˈfʌnd ˌmænɪdʒmənt/ *noun* the business of dealing with the investment of sums of money on behalf of clients

fund manager /ˈfʌnd ˌmænɪdʒər/ *noun* a person who invests money on behalf of clients

funds /fʌndz/ *plural noun* **1.** money which is available for spending ○ *The company has no funds to pay for the research program.* ◊ **non-sufficient funds** □ **the company called for extra funds** the company asked for more money □ **to run out of funds** to come to the end of the money available □ **to convert funds to another purpose** to use money for a wrong purpose **2.** government stocks and securities

"...small innovative companies have been hampered for lack of funds" [*Sunday Times*]

"...the company was set up with funds totalling NorKr 145m" [*Lloyd's List*]

funny money /ˈfʌni ˌmʌni/ *noun* an unusual type of financial instrument created by a company

furnish /ˈfɜrnɪʃ/ *verb* **1.** to supply or to provide ○ *The IRS has asked us to furnish details of all our transactions since August.* **2.** to put furniture into an office or room ○ *He furnished his office with secondhand chairs and desks.* ○ *The company spent $10,000 on furnishing the chairman's office.*

furnished accommodations /ˌfɜrnɪʃt əˌkɑməˈdeɪʃ(ə)nz/ *noun* an apartment, house, etc., which is rented with furniture in it

further /ˈfɜrðər/ *adjective* **1.** at a larger distance away ○ *The office is further down the High Street.* ○ *The flight from Paris terminates in New York – for further destinations you must change to internal*

flights. **2.** additional or extra ○ *the bank has asked for further details* or *particulars* ○ *Further orders will be dealt with by our New York office.* ○ *Nothing can be done while we are awaiting further instructions.* ○ *He had borrowed $100,000 and then tried to borrow a further $25,000.* ○ *The company is asking for further credit.* ○ *He asked for a further six weeks to pay.* **3.** □ **further to** referring to something in addition □ **further to our letter of the 21st** in addition to what we said in our letter □ **further to your letter of the 21st** here is information which you asked for in your letter □ **further to our telephone conversation** here is some information which we discussed ■ *verb* to help to grow, to promote ○ *He was accused of using his membership of the council to further his own interests.*

future /ˈfjutʃər/ *adjective* referring to time to come or to something which has not yet happened ■ *noun* the time which has not yet happened ○ *Try to be more careful in the future.* ○ *In the future all reports must be sent to Australia by air.*

future delivery /ˌfjutʃər dɪˈlɪv(ə)ri/ *noun* delivery at a later date

futures /ˈfjutʃəz/ *plural noun* stock, currency, or commodities that are bought or sold for now for delivery at a later date ○ *Gold rose 5% on the commodity futures market yesterday.*

"...cocoa futures plummeted in November to their lowest levels in seven years" [*Business in Africa*]

futures contract /ˈfjutʃəz ˌkɑntrækt/ *noun* a contract for the purchase of commodities for delivery at a date in the future

COMMENT: A futures contract is a contract to purchase; if investors are bullish, they will buy a contract, but if they feel the market will go down, they will sell one.

futurize /ˈfjutʃəraɪz/ *verb* to adapt an organization to make sure that it is able to take full advantage of the latest technologies

"Mr. Judge added: "After having overseen one of the biggest mergers in advertising history between Lowe and APL, I am proud of the steps we have taken to futurize the agency."" [*Forbes*]

G

g *abbreviation* gram

G5 *abbreviation* Group of Five

G7 *abbreviation* Group of Seven

G8 *abbreviation* Group of Eight

G10 *abbreviation* Group of Ten

GAAP *abbreviation* Generally Accepted Accounting Principles

gain /geɪn/ *noun* **1.** an increase, or the act of becoming larger □ **gain in experience** the act of getting more experience □ **gain in profitability** the act of becoming more profitable **2.** an increase in profit, price, or value ○ *Oil stocks showed gains on the Stock Exchange.* ○ *Property shares put on gains of 10%-15%.* **3.** money made by a company which is not from the company's usual trading ■ *verb* **1.** to get or to obtain ○ *She gained some useful experience working in a bank.* □ **to gain control of a business** to buy more than 50% of the stock so that you can direct the business **2.** to rise in value ○ *The dollar gained six points on the foreign exchange markets.*

gainful employment /ˌgeɪnf(ə)l ɪm ˈplɔɪmənt/ *noun* employment which pays money

gainfully /ˈgeɪnf(ə)li/ *adverb* □ **gainfully employed** working and earning money

gallon /ˈgælən/ *noun* a measure of liquids (= 4.5 liters) (NOTE: usually written **gal** after figures: **25gal.**) □ **the car does twenty-five miles per gallon, the car does twenty-five miles to the gallon** the car uses one gallon of gasoline in traveling twenty-five miles

galloping inflation /ˌgæləpɪŋ ɪn ˈfleɪʃ(ə)n/ *noun* very rapid inflation which is almost impossible to reduce

game theory /ˈgeɪm ˌθɪəri/ *noun* a mathematical method of analysis used in operational research to predict the outcomes of games of strategy and conflicts of interest. It is used to assess the likely strategies that people will adopt in situations governed by a particular set of rules and to identify the best approach to a particular problem or conflict.

Gantt chart /ˈgænt tʃɑrt/ *noun* a type of chart used in project management to plan and schedule work, setting out tasks and the time periods within which they should be completed (NOTE: A Gantt chart looks like a bar chart in which the bars extend sideways.)

gardening leave /ˈgɑrd(ə)nɪŋ liv/ *noun* a period of leave stipulated in a contract of employment, during which an employee is not allowed into the company offices and cannot take up another job (*informal*)

garnishee /ˌgɑrnɪˈʃi/ *noun* a person who owes money to a creditor and is ordered by a court to pay that money to a creditor of the creditor, and not to the creditor himself

garnishee order /ˌgɑrnɪˈʃi ˌɔrdər/ *noun* a court order, making a garnishee pay money not to the debtor, but to a third party

gasoline /ˈgæsəlin/ *noun* a liquid, made from petroleum, used to drive a car engine (NOTE: The U.K. term is **petrol**.)

gatekeeper /ˈgeɪtˌkipər/ *noun* **1.** a person who acts as a screen between a group and people outside the group (such as an interviewer in the human resources department who screens job applicants) **2.** a person who controls the flow of information within an organization and so has a great influence on its policy

gather /ˈgæðər/ *verb* **1.** to collect together, to put together ○ *He gathered his papers together before the meeting started.* ○ *She has been gathering information on import controls from various sources.* **2.** to understand, to find out ○ *I gather he has* *left the office.* ○ *Did you gather who will be at the meeting?*

GATT *abbreviation* General Agreement on Tariffs and Trade

gazelle /gə'zel/ *noun* a rapidly growing small or medium-sized company, typically with 20% gains per year in sales

GDP *abbreviation* gross domestic product

gear /gɪr/ *verb* **1.** to link something to something else □ **salary geared to the cost of living** salary which rises as the cost of living increases **2.** □ **a company which is highly geared, a highly-geared company** company which has a high proportion of its funds from fixed-interest borrowings

gear up *phrasal verb* to get ready ○ *The company is gearing itself up for expansion into the African market.* □ **to gear up for a sales drive** to make all the plans and get ready for a sales drive

gearing /'gɪrɪŋ/ *noun* **1.** *U.K.* same as **leverage 2.** the act of borrowing money at fixed interest which is then used to produce more money than the interest paid

general /'dʒen(ə)rəl/ *adjective* **1.** ordinary or not special **2.** dealing with everything or with everybody

General Agreement on Tariffs and Trade /,dʒen(ə)rəl ə,grimənt ɑn ,tærɪfs ən 'treɪd/ *noun* an international agreement to try to reduce restrictions in trade between countries (replaced in 1998 by the World Trade Organization). Abbreviation **GATT**. ◊ **World Trade Organization**

general audit /,dʒen(ə)rəl 'ɔrdɪt/ *noun* a process of examining all the books and accounts of a company

general average /,dʒen(ə)rəl 'æv(ə)rɪdʒ/ *noun* a process by which the cost of lost goods is shared by all parties to an insurance policy, such as in cases where some goods have been lost in an attempt to save the rest of the cargo

general delivery /,dʒen(ə)rəl dɪ'lɪv(ə)ri/ *noun* a system in which letters can be addressed to someone at a post office, where they can be collected ○ *They received the mail-order items via general delivery.* (NOTE: The U.K. term is **poste restante**.)

general election /,dʒen(ə)rəl ɪ'lekʃən/ *noun* election of a government by all the voters in a country

general expenses /,dʒen(ə)rəl ɪk'spensɪz/ *plural noun* all kinds of minor expenses, the money spent on the day-to-day costs of running a business

general insurance /,dʒen(ə)rəl ɪn'ʃʊrəns/ *noun* insurance covering all kinds of risk, e.g., theft, loss or damage, but excluding life insurance

general lien /,dʒen(ə)rəl 'liən/ *noun* a right to hold goods or property until a debt has been paid

generally /'dʒen(ə)rəli/ *adverb* normally or usually ○ *The office is generally closed between Christmas and the New Year.* ○ *We generally give a 25% discount for bulk purchases.*

Generally Accepted Accounting Principles /,dʒen(ə)rəli ək,septɪd ə'kauntɪŋ ,prɪnsɪp(ə)lz/ *plural noun* a summary of best practice in respect of the form and content of financial statements and auditor's reports, and of accounting policies and disclosures adopted for the preparation of financial information. GAAP does not have any statutory or regulatory authority in the United Kingdom, unlike in a number of other countries where the term is in use, such as the United States, Canada. Abbreviation **GAAP**

general manager /,dʒen(ə)rəl 'mænɪdʒər/ *noun* a manager in charge of the administration of a company

general meeting /,dʒen(ə)rəl 'mitɪŋ/ *noun* a meeting of all the stockholders of a company or of all the members of an organization

general office /'dʒen(ə)rəl ,ɔfɪs/ *noun* the main administrative office of a company

general store /,dʒen(ə)rəl 'stɔr/ *noun* a small country store which sells a wide range of goods

general strike /,dʒen(ə)rəl 'straɪk/ *noun* a strike of all the workers in a country

general trading /,dʒen(ə)rəl 'treɪdɪŋ/ *noun* dealing in all types of goods

Generation X /,dʒenəreɪʃ(ə)n 'eks/ *noun* the generation of people who were born between 1963 and 1976 and began their working lives from the 1980s onward (NOTE: The people who belong to Generation X are said to have challenged traditional corporate expectations by not being solely motivated by money. Instead they want to establish a balance between their professional and personal lives, being in favor of flexible working practices and valuing opportunities for learning and self-advancement.)

Generation Y /ˌdʒenəreɪʃ(ə)n 'waɪ/ *noun* the generation of people who were born between 1979 and 1994 and began their working lives from 2000 onward (NOTE: The people who belong to Generation Y are skeptical of traditionally-run businesses and traditional advertising. They want employers to tell them the truth, explain to them why they are doing what they are doing, and reward them when they do well. They want their work environment to be flexible and fun.)

generic /dʒəˈnerɪk/ *adjective* which is shared by a group, and does not refer to one individual ■ *noun* **1.** a product sold without a brand name ○ *Generics are cheap since they have no name to advertise.* **2.** a brand name which is now given to a product rather than to a particular brand, e.g., kleenex or thermos

generic product /dʒəˌnerɪk 'prɒdʌkt/ *noun* same as **generic** *noun* 1 ○ *Next to the brightly packaged branded goods the generic products on display were easily overlooked.*

generic term /dʒəˌnerɪk 'tɜrm/, **generic name** /dʒəˌnerɪk 'neɪm/ *noun* same as **generic** *noun* 2

generous /ˈdʒen(ə)rəs/ *adjective* referring to an amount that is larger than usual or expected ○ *She received a generous redundancy payment.* ○ *The staff contributed a generous sum for the manager's retirement present.*

genetically modified organism /dʒɪˌnetɪk(ə)li ˌmɒdɪfaɪd 'ɔrgənɪz(ə)m/ *noun* an organism such as a cotton or soybean plant that has received genetic material from another organism so as to give it desirable commercial characteristics, e.g., resistance to a particular organism or chemical. Abbreviation **GMO**

gentleman /ˈdʒent(ə)lmən/ *noun* □ **"gentlemen"** way of starting to talk to a group of men ○ *"Good morning, gentlemen – if everyone is here, the meeting can start."* ○ *"Well, gentlemen, we have all*

read the report from our Australian office." □ **"ladies and gentlemen"** way of starting to talk to a group of women and men

gentleman's agreement /ˈdʒent(ə)lmənz əˌgriːmənt/ *noun* a verbal agreement between two parties who trust each other

genuine /ˈdʒenjuɪn/ *adjective* true or real ○ *a genuine Picasso* ○ *a genuine leather purse*

genuine article /ˌdʒenjuɪn 'ɑrtɪk(ə)l/ *noun* a real article, not an imitation

genuineness /ˈdʒenjuɪnnəs/ *noun* the state of being real, not being an imitation

genuine purchaser /ˌdʒenjuɪn 'pɜrtʃɪsər/ *noun* someone who is really interested in buying

geographic information system /ˌdʒiəgræfɪk ˌɪnfərˈmeɪʃ(ə)n ˌsɪstəm/ *noun* a type of database which is sorted on geographic data, such as a census, or one which provides maps onscreen. Abbreviation **GIS**

geographic weighting /ˌdʒiəgræfɪk 'weɪtɪŋ/ *noun* a statistical process which gives more importance to some geographic areas than others in the process of reaching a final figure or result

get /get/ *verb* **1.** to receive ○ *We got a letter from the solicitor this morning.* ○ *When do you expect to get more stock?* ○ *He gets $250 a week for doing nothing.* ○ *She got $5,000 for her car.* **2.** to arrive at a place ○ *The shipment got to Canada six weeks late.* ○ *She finally got to the office at 10.30.* (NOTE: **getting – got**)

get across *phrasal verb* to make someone understand something ○ *The manager tried to get across to the work force why some people were being made redundant.*

get along *phrasal verb* **1.** to manage ○ *We are getting along quite well with only half the staff we had before.* **2.** to be friendly or to work well with someone ○ *She does not get along very well with her new boss.*

get back *phrasal verb* to receive something which you had before ○ *I got my money back after I had complained to the manager.* ○ *He got his initial investment back in two months.*

get on *phrasal verb* **1.** to work or manage ○ *How is your new assistant getting* *on?* **2.** to succeed ○ *My son is getting on well – he has just been promoted.*

get on with *phrasal verb* **1.** to be friendly or work well with someone ○ *She does not get on with her new boss.* **2.** to go on doing work ○ *The staff got on with the work and finished the order on time.*

get out *phrasal verb* **1.** to produce something ○ *The accounts department got out the draft accounts in time for the meeting.* **2.** to sell an investment (*informal*) ○ *He didn't like what he read in the company's annual report, so he got out before the company collapsed.*

get out of *phrasal verb* to stop trading in a product or an area ○ *The company is getting out of computers.* ○ *We got out of the South American market.*

get round *phrasal verb* to avoid ○ *We tried to get round the embargo by shipping from Canada.*

get through *phrasal verb* **1.** to speak to someone on the phone ○ *I tried to get through to the complaints department.* **2.** to be successful ○ *She got through her exams, so she is now a qualified engineer.* **3.** to try to make someone understand ○ *I could not get through to her that I had to be at the airport by 2.15.*

gift /gɪft/ *noun* a thing which is given to someone

gift coupon /'gɪft ˌkupɑn/, **gift certificate** /'gɪft sɜr,tɪfɪkət/ *noun* a card that can be used to buy specified goods up to the value printed on it, often issued by chain stores. The person receiving the voucher is able to redeem it in any store in the chain. ○ *We gave her a gift certificate for her birthday.*

gift inter vivos /ˌgɪft ˌɪntər 'vivoʊs/ *noun* a gift given to another living person. Abbreviation **GIV**

gift store /'gɪft stɔr/ *noun* a store selling small items which are given as presents

gift-wrap /'gɪft ræp/ *verb* to wrap a present in attractive paper ○ *Do you want this book gift-wrapped?* (NOTE: **gift-wrapping – gift-wrapped**)

gift-wrapping /'gɪft ˌræpɪŋ/ *noun* **1.** a service in a store for wrapping presents for customers **2.** attractive paper for wrapping presents

gig /gɪg/ *noun* a particular project or assignment undertaken by an independent professional or freelance (*informal*)

gilt-edged /'gɪlt edʒd/ *adjective* used to describe an investment which is very safe

gilt-edged stock /ˌgɪlt edʒd 'stɑk/ *noun* stock in blue-chip companies. Same as **government bonds**

gilts /gɪlts/ *plural noun* bonds issued by the U.K. government. Same as **government bonds**

gimmick /'gɪmɪk/ *noun* a clever idea or trick ○ *a publicity gimmick*

Ginnie Mae /ˌdʒɪni 'meɪ/ *noun* same as **GNMA** (*informal*)

giro /'dʒaɪroʊ/ *noun* **1.** same as **bank giro 2.** a giro check

Girobank /'dʒaɪroʊbæŋk/ *noun* a bank in a giro system ○ *a National Girobank account* ○ *She has her salary paid into her National Girobank account.*

giro system /'dʒaɪroʊ ˌsɪstəm/ *noun* a banking system in which money can be transferred from one account to another without writing a check

give /gɪv/ *verb* **1.** to pass something to someone as a present ○ *The office gave him a clock when he retired.* **2.** to pass something to someone ○ *She gave the documents to the accountant.* ○ *Do not give anybody personal details about staff members.* ○ *Can you give me some information about the new computer system?* **3.** to organize ○ *The company gave a party on a boat to say goodbye to the retiring sales director.* (NOTE: **giving – gave – given**)

give away *phrasal verb* to give something as a free present ○ *We are giving away a pocket calculator with each $10 of purchases.*

giveaway /'gɪvəweɪ/ *adjective* □ **to sell at giveaway prices** to sell at very cheap prices ■ *noun* something which is given as a free gift when another item is bought

giveaway paper /'gɪvəweɪ ˌpeɪpər/ *noun* a newspaper which is given away free, and which relies for its income on its advertising

glad-hand /'glæd hænd/ *verb* to shake hands with and greet people at a business party or meeting

global /'gloʊb(ə)l/ *adjective* **1.** referring to the whole world ○ *We offer a 24-hour global delivery service.* □ **global economy**

the economy of the whole world **2.** referring to all of something ○ *The management proposed a global review of salaries.*

globalization /ˌɡloʊbəlaɪˈzeɪʃ(ə)n/ *noun* the process of making something international or worldwide, especially the process of expanding business interests, operations, and strategies to countries all over the world (NOTE: Globalization is due to technological developments that make global communications possible, political developments such as the fall of communism, and developments in transportation that make traveling faster and more frequent. It can benefit companies by opening up new markets, giving access to new raw materials and investment opportunities, and enabling them to take advantage of lower operating costs in other countries.)

global product /ˌɡloʊb(ə)l ˈprɒdʌkt/ *noun* a product with a famous brand name which is recognized and sold all over the world

global reporting initiative /ˌɡloʊb(ə)l rɪˈpɔrtɪŋ ɪˌnɪʃətɪv/ *noun* an international effort designed to develop guidelines for measuring and reporting on the social, environmental, and economic performance of multi-national companies. Abbreviation **GRI**

glocalization /ˌɡloʊkəlaɪˈzeɪʃ(ə)n/ *noun* the process of adapting globalized products or services to fit the needs of different local markets and communities around the world (NOTE: The word is a combination of globalization and localization.)

glue /ɡlu/ *noun* something such as information that unifies organizations, supply chains, and other commercial groups

glut /ɡlʌt/ *noun* □ **a glut of produce** too much produce, which is then difficult to sell ○ *a coffee glut* or *a glut of coffee* □ **a glut of money** a situation where there is too much money available to borrowers ■ *verb* to fill the market with something which is then difficult to sell ○ *The market is glutted with cheap cameras.* (NOTE: **glutting – glutted**)

gm *abbreviation* gram

GMO *abbreviation* genetically modified organism

GNMA *noun* a U.S. federal organization which provides backing for mortgages.

Full form **Government National Mortgage Association**

GNP *abbreviation* gross national product

go /ɡoʊ/ *verb* **1.** to move from one place to another ○ *The check went to your bank yesterday.* ○ *The plane goes to Frankfurt, then to Rome.* ○ *He is going to our Lagos office.* ○ *She went on a management course.* **2.** to be placed ○ *The date goes at the top of the letter.* (NOTE: **going – went – gone**)

go back on *phrasal verb* not to carry out something after you have promised to do it ○ *Two months later they went back on the agreement.*

go into *phrasal verb* to examine something carefully ○ *The bank wants to go into the details of the inter-company loans.*

go into business *phrasal verb* to start in business ○ *He went into business as a car dealer.* ○ *She went into business in partnership with her son.*

go liquid *phrasal verb* to convert as many assets as possible into cash

go on *phrasal verb* **1.** to continue ○ *The staff went on working in spite of the fire.* ○ *The chairman went on speaking for two hours.* **2.** to work with ○ *The figures for 1998 are all he has to go on.* ○ *We have to go on the assumption that sales will not double next year.* (NOTE: You go on **doing** something.)

go out of business *phrasal verb* to stop doing business ○ *The firm went out of business last week.*

go public *phrasal verb* to become a public company by placing some of its stock for sale on the stock market so that anyone can buy them

go-ahead /ˈɡoʊ əˌhed/ *noun* □ **to give something the go-ahead** to approve something or to say that something can be done ○ *My project got a government go-ahead.* ○ *The board refused to give the go-ahead to the expansion plan.* ■ *adjective* energetic or keen to do well ○ *He is a very go-ahead type.* ○ *She works for a go-ahead clothing company.*

goal /ɡoʊl/ *noun* something which you try to achieve ○ *Our goal is to break even within twelve months.* ○ *The company achieved all its goals.*

godown /ˈɡoʊdaʊn/ *noun* a warehouse (in the Far East)

going /'gəʊɪŋ/ *adjective* current

going concern /,gəʊɪŋ kən'sɜːn/ *noun* a company that is actively trading and making a profit □ **sold as a going concern** sold as an actively trading company □ **to sell a business as a going concern** to sell a business as an actively trading company

going price /,gəʊɪŋ 'praɪs/ *noun* the usual or current price, the price which is being charged now ○ *What is the going price for 1975 Volkswagen Beetles?*

going rate /,gəʊɪŋ 'reɪt/ *noun* the usual or current rate of payment ○ *We pay the going rate for typists.* ○ *The going rate for offices is £10 per square meter.*

going to /'gəʊɪŋ tʊ/ *phrase* □ **to be going to do something** to be just about to start doing something ○ *The firm is going to open an office in New York next year.* ○ *When are you going to answer my letter?*

gold bullion /,gəʊld 'bʊliən/ *noun* bars of gold

gold card /'gəʊld kɑːd/ *noun* a credit card issued to important customers, i.e., those with a high income, which gives certain privileges such as a higher spending limit than ordinary credit cards

golden handcuffs /,gəʊld(ə)n 'hændkʌfs/ *plural noun* a contractual arrangement to make sure that a valued member of staff stays in their job, by which they are offered special financial advantages if they stay and heavy penalties if they leave

golden handshake /,gəʊld(ə)n 'hændʃeɪk/ *noun* a large, usually tax-free, sum of money given to a director who retires from a company before the end of his or her service contract ○ *The retiring director received a golden handshake of $250,000.*

golden hello /,gəʊld(ə)n hə'ləʊ/ *noun* a cash inducement paid to someone to encourage them to change jobs and move to another company

golden parachute /,gəʊld(ə)n 'pærəʃuːt/, **golden umbrella** /,gəʊld(ə)n ʌm'brelə/ *noun* a large, usually tax-free, sum of money given to an executive who retires from a company before the end of their service contract

golden share /,gəʊld(ə)n 'ʃeə/ *noun* a share in a privatized company which is retained by the government and carries spe-

cial privileges such as the right to veto foreign takeover bids

goldmine /'gəʊldmaɪn/ *noun* a mine which produces gold □ **that store is a little goldmine** that store is a very profitable business

gold point /'gəʊld pɔɪnt/ *noun* an amount by which a currency which is linked to gold can vary in price

gold reserves /'gəʊld rɪ,zɜːvz/ *plural noun* the country's store of gold kept to pay international debts

gold standard /,gəʊld 'stændəd/ *noun* an arrangement that links the value of a currency to the value of a quantity of gold

gold stock /,gəʊld 'ʃerz/ *noun* stock in gold mines

gondola /'gɒndələ/ *noun* a free-standing display in a supermarket which shoppers can walk round

good /gʊd/ *adjective* □ **a good deal (of)** a large amount (of) ○ *We wasted a good deal of time discussing the arrangements for the meeting.* ○ *The company had to pay a good deal for the building site.* □ **a good many** very many ○ *A good many staff members have joined the union.*

good buy /,gʊd 'baɪ/ *noun* a thing bought which is worth the money paid for it ○ *That watch was a good buy.*

good industrial relations /gʊd ɪn,dʌstriəl rɪ'leɪʃ(ə)nz/ *plural noun* a situation where management and employees understand each others' problems and work together for the good of the company

goods /gʊdz/ *plural noun* items which can be moved and are for sale □ **goods in bond** imported goods held by customs until duty is paid

goods and chattels /,gʊdz ən 'tʃæt(ə)lz/ *plural noun* movable personal possessions

Goods and Services Tax /,gʊdz ən 'sɜːvɪsɪz ,tæks/ *noun* a Canadian tax on the sale of goods or the provision of services. Abbreviation **GST**

goods depot /'gʊdz ,depəʊ/ *noun* a central warehouse where goods can be stored until they are moved

goods train /'gəʊds treɪn/ *noun U.K.* same as **freight train** (NOTE: The U.S. term is **freight train**)

goodwill /gʊd'wɪl/ *noun* **1.** good feeling toward someone ○ *To show goodwill, the management increased the terms of the offer.* **2.** the good reputation of a business, which can be calculated as part of a company's asset value, though separate from its tangible asset value (the goodwill can include the trading reputation, the patents, the trade names used, the value of a "good site", etc., and is very difficult to establish accurately) ○ *He paid $10,000 for the goodwill of the store and $4,000 for the stock.*

COMMENT: Goodwill can include such things as the trading reputation, the patents, the trade names used and the value of a "good site" and is very difficult to establish accurately. It is an intangible asset, and so is not shown as an asset in a company's accounts, unless it figures as part of the purchase price paid when acquiring another company.

gopher /'goʊfər/ *noun* an employee who carries out simple menial duties such as fetching and carrying things for a manager or another employee (NOTE: The usual U.S. spelling is **gofer**.)

go-slow /ˌgoʊ 'sloʊ/ *noun* the slowing down of production by workers as a protest against the management ○ *A series of go-slows reduced production.* ■ *verb* to protest against management by working slowly

govern /'gʌv(ə)n/ *verb* to rule a country ○ *The country is governed by a group of military leaders.*

governance /'gʌv(ə)nəns/ *noun* the philosophy of ruling, whether a country or a company

"…the chairman has committed the cardinal sin in corporate governance – he acted against the wishes and interests of the shareholders" [*Investors Chronicle*]

"…in two significant decisions, the Securities and Exchange Board of India today allowed trading of shares through the Internet and set a deadline for companies to conform to norms for good corporate governance" [*The Hindu*]

government /'gʌv(ə)nmənt/ *noun* an organization which administers a country ■ *adjective* coming from the government, referring to the government ○ *a government ban on the import of arms* ○ *Government intervention or Intervention by the government helped to solve the dispute.* ○ *Government employees can belong to one of two unions.*

governmental /ˌgʌv(ə)n'ment(ə)l/ *adjective* referring to a government

government annuity /ˌgʌv(ə)nmənt ə'nuəti/ *noun* money paid each year by the government

government-backed /ˌgʌv(ə)nmənt 'bækt/ *adjective* backed by the government

government bonds /ˌgʌv(ə)nmənt 'bɑndz/ *plural noun* bonds or other securities issued by the government on a regular basis as a method of borrowing money for government expenditure

government contractor /ˌgʌv(ə)nmənt kən'træktər/ *noun* a company which supplies the government with goods by contract

government-controlled /ˌgʌv(ə)nmənt kən'troʊld/ *adjective* under the direct control of the government ○ *Advertisements cannot be placed in the government-controlled newspapers.*

government economic indicators /ˌgʌv(ə)nmənt ˌikənɑmɪk 'ɪndɪkeɪtərz/ *plural noun* statistics which show how the country's economy is going to perform in the short or long term

government loan /ˌgʌv(ə)nmənt 'loʊn/ *noun* money lent by the government

Government National Mortgage Association /ˌgʌv(ə)nmənt ˌnæʃ(ə)nəl 'mɔrgɪdʒ əˌsoʊsieɪʃ(ə)n/ *noun* full form of **GNMA**

government pension /ˌgʌv(ə)nmənt 'penʃən/ *noun* a pension paid by the state

government-regulated /'gʌv(ə)nmənt ˌregjʊleɪtɪd/ *adjective* regulated by the government

government sector /ˌgʌv(ə)nmənt 'sektər/ *noun* same as **public sector**

government securities /ˌgʌv(ə)n mənt sɪ'kjʊrɪtiz/ *plural noun* same as **government bonds**

government-sponsored /'gʌv(ə)n mənt ˌspɑnsərd/ *adjective* encouraged by the government and backed by government money ○ *She is working in a government-sponsored program to help small businesses.*

government stock /ˌgʌv(ə)nmənt 'stɑk/ *noun* same as **government bonds**

government support /ˌɡʌv(ə)nmənt səˈpɔːt/ *noun* a financial help given by the government ○ *The aircraft industry relies on government support.*

governor /ˈɡʌv(ə)nə/ *noun* **1.** a person in charge of an important institution **2.** one of the members of the Federal Reserve Board

grace /ɡreɪs/ *noun* a favor shown by granting a delay ○ *to give a creditor a period of grace* or *two weeks' grace*

grade /ɡreɪd/ *noun* a level or rank ○ *to reach the top grade in the civil service* ■ *verb* **1.** to sort something into different levels of quality ○ *to grade coal* ○ *He got good grades in college.* **2.** to make something rise in steps according to quantity □ **graded advertising rates** rates which become cheaper as you take more advertising space

graded hotel /ˌɡreɪdɪd həʊˈtel/ *noun* a good-quality hotel

graded tax /ˌɡreɪdɪd ˈtæks/ *noun* **1.** a tax in which the rate rises as income increases **2.** a tax on property in which vacant land is taxed at a higher rate than structures, in order to encourage development

gradual /ˈɡrædʒuəl/ *adjective* slow and steady ○ *The company saw a gradual return to profits.* ○ *Her CV describes her gradual rise to the position of company chairman.*

gradually /ˈɡrædʒuəli/ *adverb* slowly and steadily ○ *The company has gradually become more profitable.* ○ *She gradually learned the details of the import-export business.*

graduate *noun* /ˈɡrædʒuət/ a person who has obtained a degree ■ *verb* /ˈɡrædʒuˌeɪt/ to get a degree ○ *She graduated from Edinburgh university last year.*

graduated /ˈɡrædʒueɪtɪd/ *adjective* changing in small regular stages

graduated income tax /ˌɡrædʒueɪtɪd ˈɪnkʌm ˌtæks/ *noun* a tax which rises in steps, with those having the highest income paying the highest percentage of tax

graduated taxation /ˌɡrædʒueɪtɪd tækˈseɪʃ(ə)n/ *noun* a tax system in which the tax rates rise in steps, with those having the highest income paying the highest percentage of tax

graduate entry /ˈɡrædʒuət ˌentri/ *noun* the entry of graduates into employment with a company ○ *the graduate entry into the civil service*

graduate trainee /ˌɡrædʒuət treɪˈniː/ *noun* a person in a graduate training program

graduate training program /ˌɡrædʒuət ˈtreɪnɪŋ ˌprəʊɡræm/ *noun* a training program set up by a company to encourage graduates to work for them

gram /ɡræm/ *noun* a measure of weight (one thousandth of a kilo) (NOTE: Usually written **g** or **gm** with figures: *25g.*)

grand /ɡrænd/ *adjective* important □ **grand plan** *or* **grand strategy** a major plan ○ *They explained their grand plan for redeveloping the factory site.* ■ *noun* one thousand dollars (*informal*) ○ *They offered him fifty grand for the information.* ○ *She's earning fifty grand plus car and expenses.*

grand total /ˌɡrænd ˈtəʊt(ə)l/ *noun* the final total made by adding several subtotals

grant /ɡrænt/ *noun* money given by the government to help pay for something ○ *The laboratory has a government grant to cover the cost of the development program.* ○ *The government has allocated grants toward the costs of the program.* ■ *verb* to agree to give someone something ○ *to grant someone a loan* or *a subsidy* ○ *to grant someone three weeks' leave of absence* ○ *The local authority granted the company an interest-free loan to start up the new factory.*

"…the budget grants a tax exemption for $500,000 in capital gains" [*Toronto Star*]

grapevine /ˈɡreɪpvaɪn/ *noun* **1.** an unofficial communications network in an organization ○ *I heard on the grapevine that the managing director has been sacked.* **2.** an informal and unofficial communications network within an organization that passes on information by word of mouth (NOTE: A grapevine may distort information or spread gossip and rumor, but it can also back up the official communications network, provide feedback, and strengthen social relationships within the organization.)

graph /ɡrɑːf/ *noun* a diagram which shows the relationship between two sets of quantities or values, each of which is represented on an axis ○ *A graph was used to show salary increases in relation to increases in output.* ○ *According to the graph, as average salaries have risen so has absenteeism.* ○ *We need to set out the results of the questionnaire in a graph.*

gratia ▸ **ex gratia**

gratis /'grætɪs/ *adverb* free or not costing anything ○ *We got into the exhibition gratis.*

gratuity /grə'tuːɪti/ *noun* a tip, money given to someone who has helped you ○ *The staff are instructed not to accept gratuities.*

gray market /'greɪ ˌmɑrkət/ *noun* an unofficial market run by dealers, where new issues of shares are bought and sold before they officially become available for trading on the Stock Exchange even before the share allocations are known

great /greɪt/ *adjective* large □ **a great deal of** very much ○ *He made a great deal of money on the Stock Exchange.* ○ *There is a great deal of work to be done before the company can be made really profitable.*

Great Depression /greɪt dɪ'preʃ(ə)n/ *noun* the world economic crisis of 1929–33

greenback /'grinbæk/ *noun* a dollar bill (*informal*)

"…gold's drop this year is of the same magnitude as the greenback's 8.5% rise" [*Business Week*]

green card /ˌgrin 'kɑrd/ *noun* an identity card and work permit for a person going to live in the U.S.

greenfield site /'grinfild ˌsaɪt/ *noun* a site for a factory which is in the country, and not surrounded by other buildings. Compare **brownfield site**

greenmail /'grinmeɪl/ *noun* the practice of making a profit by buying a large number of shares in a company, threatening to take the company over, and then selling the shares back to the company at a higher price

"…he proposes that there should be a limit on greenmail, perhaps permitting payment of a 20% premium on a maximum of 8% of the stock" [*Duns Business Month*]

GRI *abbreviation* global reporting initiative

grid /grɪd/ *noun* a system of numbered squares

grid structure /'grɪd ˌstrʌktʃər/ *noun* a structure based on a grid

grievance /'griːv(ə)ns/ *noun* a complaint made by an employee or labor union to the management

"ACAS has a legal obligation to try and resolve industrial grievances before they reach industrial tribunals" [*Personnel Today*]

grievance procedure /'griːv(ə)ns prə ˌsɪdʒər/ *noun* a way of presenting and settling complaints from a labor union to the management

gross /groʊs/ *noun* twelve dozen (144) ○ *He ordered four gross of pens.* (NOTE: no plural) ■ *adjective* total, with no deductions ■ *adverb* with no deductions ○ *My salary is paid gross.* ■ *verb* to make as a gross profit or earn as gross income ○ *The group grossed $25m in 1999.*

"…gross wool receipts for the selling season to end June appear likely to top $2 billion" [*Australian Financial Review*]

gross domestic product /ˌgroʊs də ˌmestɪk 'prɑdʌkt/ *noun* the annual value of goods sold and services paid for inside a country. Abbreviation **GDP**

gross earnings /ˌgroʊs 'ɜrnɪŋz/ *plural noun* total earnings before tax and other deductions

gross income /groʊs 'ɪnkʌm/ *noun* a salary before tax is deducted

gross margin /ˌgroʊs 'mɑrdʒɪn/ *noun* the percentage difference between the received price and the unit manufacturing cost or purchase price of goods for resale. Abbreviation **GM**

gross national product /ˌgroʊs ˌnæʃ(ə)nəl 'prɑdʌkt/ *noun* the annual value of goods and services in a country including income from other countries. Abbreviation **GNP**

gross negligence /ˌgroʊs 'neglɪdʒəns/ *noun* the act of showing very serious neglect of duty toward other people

gross profit /ˌgroʊs 'prɑfɪt/ *noun* a profit calculated as sales income less the cost of the goods sold, i.e. without deducting any other expenses

gross receipts /ˌgroʊs rɪ'sits/ *plural noun* the total amount of money received before expenses are deducted

gross salary /ˌgroʊs 'sæləri/ *noun* a salary before tax is deducted

gross sales /ˌgrəʊs 'seɪlz/ *plural noun* money received from sales before deductions for goods returned, special discounts, etc. ○ *Gross sales are impressive since many buyers seem to be ordering more than they will eventually need.*

gross tonnage /ˌgrəʊs 'tʌnɪdʒ/ *noun* the total amount of space in a ship

gross turnover /ˌgrəʊs 'tɜːnəʊvər/ *noun* the total turnover including sales tax and discounts

gross weight /ˌgrəʊs 'weɪt/ *noun* the weight of both the container and its contents

gross yield /ˌgrəʊs 'jiːld/ *noun* a profit from investments before tax is deducted

ground floor /ˌgraʊnd 'flɔːr/ *noun U.K.* same as **first floor**

ground landlord /'graʊnd ˌlændlɔːd/ *noun* a person or company that owns the freehold of a property which is then rented and sublet ○ *Our ground landlord is an insurance company.*

ground lease /'graʊnd liːs/ *noun* the first lease on a freehold building

ground rent /'graʊnd rent/ *noun* a rent paid by the main tenant to the ground landlord

grounds /graʊndz/ *plural noun* basic reasons ○ *Does she have good grounds for complaint?* ○ *There are no grounds on which we can be sued.* ○ *What are the grounds for the demand for a pay rise?*

ground transportation /'graʊnd trænspɔːˌteɪʃ(ə)n/ *noun* the means of transportation available to take passengers from an airport to the town, e.g., buses, taxis, or trains

group /gruːp/ *noun* **1.** several things or people together ○ *A group of managers has sent a memo to the chairman complaining about noise in the office.* ○ *The respondents were interviewed in groups of three or four, and then singly.* **2.** several companies linked together in the same organization ○ *the group chairman* or *the chairman of the group* ○ *group turnover* or *turnover for the group* ○ *the Granada Group* ■ *verb* □ **to group together** to put several items together ○ *Sales from six different agencies are grouped together under the heading "European sales."*

group accounts /ˌgruːp ə'kaʊntz/ *noun* accounts for a holding company and its subsidiaries

group insurance /ˌgruːp ɪn'ʃʊərəns/ *noun* an insurance plan where a group of employees is covered by one policy

Group of Eight /ˌgruːp əv 'eɪt/ *noun* the G7 expanded to include Russia. Abbreviation **G8**

Group of Five /ˌgruːp əv 'faɪv/ *noun* a central group of major industrial nations (France, Germany, Japan, the U.K. and the U.S.), now expanded to form the G7. Abbreviation **G5**

Group of Seven /ˌgruːp əv 'sev(ə)n/ *noun* a central group of major industrial nations (Canada, France, Germany, Italy, Japan, the U.K. and the U.S.) who meet regularly to discuss problems of international trade and finance. Abbreviation **G7**

Group of Ten /ˌgruːp əv 'ten/ *noun* the major world economic powers working within the framework of the IMF: Belgium, Canada, France, Germany, Italy, Japan, Netherlands, Sweden, the United Kingdom and the United States. There are in fact now eleven members, since Switzerland has joined the original ten. It is also called the "Paris Club", since its first meeting was in Paris. Abbreviation **G10**

group results /ˌgruːp rɪ'zʌlts/ *plural noun* the results of a group of companies taken together

groupthink /'gruːpθɪŋk/ *noun* a type of faulty thinking that can affect people who are working together to make decisions or solve problems. It occurs when people's eagerness to reach agreement with each other is stronger than their need to deal fully with the complexities of the problem, so the result is often an unsatisfactory compromise.

"As a long-term observer of the technology industry, I can point to many cases in which companies have engaged in a form of groupthink that has led their businesses, if not their people, on a downward spiral."

group tool /ˌgruːp 'tuːl/ *noun* an electronic tool, e.g., videoconferencing or e-mail, that makes it possible for people based in different locations to work together on a project

groupware /'gruːpweər/ *noun* software that enables a group of people who are based in different locations to work together and share information (NOTE: Groupware usually provides communal diaries, address books, work planners, bulletin boards, and newsletters in electronic format on a closed network.)

grow /groʊ/ *verb* **1.** to become larger ○ *The company has grown from a small repair store to a multinational electronics business.* ○ *Turnover is growing at a rate of 15% per annum.* ○ *The computer industry grew very rapidly in the 1980s.* (NOTE: **growing – grew – has grown**) **2.** to cause something such as a business to develop or expand

growth /groʊθ/ *noun* **1.** the fact of becoming larger or increasing □ **the company is aiming for growth** the company is aiming to expand rapidly **2.** the second stage in a product life cycle, following the launch, when demand for the product increases rapidly

growth area /ˈgroʊθ ˌeriə/ *noun* an area where sales are increasing rapidly

growth index /ˈgroʊθ ˌɪndeks/ *noun* an index showing how something has grown

growth industry /ˈgroʊθ ˌɪndəstri/ *noun* an industry that is expanding or has the potential to expand faster than other industries

growth rate /ˈgroʊθ reɪt/ *noun* the speed at which something grows

growth stock /ˈgroʊθ stɑk/ *noun* a stock which people think is likely to rise in value

GST *abbreviation* Goods and Services Tax

"…because the GST is applied only to fees for brokerage and appraisal services, the new tax does not appreciably increase the price of a resale home" [*Toronto Globe & Mail*]

guarantee /ˌgærənˈti/ *noun* **1.** a legal document in which the producer agrees to compensate the buyer if the product is faulty or becomes faulty before a specific date after purchase ○ *a certificate of guarantee* or *a guarantee certificate* ○ *The guarantee lasts for two years.* ○ *It is sold with a twelve-month guarantee.* □ **the car is still under guarantee** the car is still covered by the maker's guarantee **2.** a promise that someone will pay another person's debts **3.** something given as a security ○ *to leave stock certificates as a guarantee* ■ *verb* **1.** to give a promise that something will happen □ **to guarantee a debt** to promise to pay another person's

debts if he or she should fail to □ **to guarantee a bill of exchange** to promise that the bill will be paid **2.** □ **the product is guaranteed for twelve months** the manufacturer says that the product will work well for twelve months, and will mend it free of charge if it breaks down

guaranteed minimum wage /ˌgærəntid ˌmɪnɪməm ˈweɪdʒ/ *noun* the lowest wage which is legally guaranteed to workers (no employer can pay a worker less than this wage)

guarantor /ˌgærənˈtɔr/ *noun* a person who promises to pay another person's debts if he or she should fail to ○ *She stood guarantor for her brother.*

guess /ges/ *noun* a calculation made without any real information ○ *The forecast of sales is only a guess.* □ **an informed guess** a guess which is based on some information □ **it is anyone's guess** no one really knows what is the right answer ■ *verb* □ **to guess (at) something** to try to calculate something without any information ○ *They could only guess at the total loss.* ○ *The sales director tried to guess the turnover of the Far East division.*

guesstimate /ˈgestɪmət/ *noun* a rough calculation (*informal*)

guideline /ˈgaɪdlaɪn/ *noun* an unofficial suggestion from the government as to how something should be done ○ *The government has issued guidelines on increases in salaries and prices.* ○ *The increase in retail price goes against the government guidelines.*

guild /gɪld/ *noun* an association of merchants or storekeepers ○ *a trade guild* ○ *the guild of master bakers*

guilder /ˈgɪldər/ *noun* a unit of currency used before the euro in the Netherlands. Also called **florin** (NOTE: Usually written **fl** before or after figures: *fl25, 25fl.*)

"…the shares, which eased 1.10 guilders to fl49.80 earlier in the session, were suspended during the final hour of trading" [*Wall Street Journal*]

guilty /ˈgɪlti/ *adjective* referring to a person who has done something wrong ○ *He was found guilty of libel.* ○ *The company was guilty of not reporting the sales to the auditors.*

H

ha *abbreviation* hectare

haggle /'hæg(ə)l/ *verb* to discuss prices and terms and try to reduce them ○ *to haggle about* or *over the details of a contract* ○ *After two days' haggling the contract was signed.*

half /hæf/ *noun* one of two equal parts into which something is divided ○ *The first half of the agreement is acceptable.* □ **we share the profits half and half** we share the profits equally ■ *adjective* divided into two parts □ **to sell goods off at half price** at 50% of the price for which they were sold before

"...economists believe the economy is picking up this quarter and will do better in the second half of the year" [*Sunday Times*]

half a dozen /ˌhæf ə 'dʌz(ə)n/ *noun* six

half a percent /ˌhæf ə pər'sent/ *noun* 0.5%

half-dollar /ˌhæf 'dɑlər/ *noun* fifty cents

half fare /ˌhæf 'fer/ *noun* a half-price ticket for a child

half-price /ˌhæf 'praɪs/ *noun* a sale of all goods at half the price

half-price sale /ˌhæf praɪs 'seɪl/ *noun* a sale of items at half the usual price

half-year /ˌhæf 'jiər/ *noun* six months of an accounting period □ **to announce the results for the half-year to June 30th, the first half-year's results** results for the period January 1st to June 30th ○ *We look forward to improvements in the second half-year.*

half-yearly /ˌhæf 'jɪrli/ *adjective* happening every six months, or referring to a period of six months ○ *half-yearly accounts* ○ *half-yearly payment* ○ *half-yearly statement* ○ *a half-yearly meeting* ■ *adverb* every six months ○ *We pay the account half-yearly.*

hallmark /'hɔlmɑrk/ *noun* a mark put on gold or silver items to show that the metal is of the correct quality ■ *verb* to put a hallmark on a piece of gold or silver ○ *a hallmarked spoon*

Hambrecht & Quist Technology Index /ˌhæmbrekt ən ˌkwɪst tek 'nɑlədʒi ˌɪndeks/ *noun* a U.S. index based on the prices of 275 technology stocks

hammer /'hæmər/ *noun* □ **to go under the hammer** to be sold by auction □ **all the stock went under the hammer** all the stock was sold by auction ■ *verb* to hit hard □ **to hammer the competition** to attack and defeat the competition □ **to hammer prices** to reduce prices sharply

hammer out *phrasal verb* □ **to hammer out an agreement** to agree something after long and difficult negotiations ○ *The contract was finally hammered out.*

hammered /'hæmərd/ *adjective* □ **they were hammered** (*on the London Stock Exchange*) the firm was removed from the Stock Exchange because it had failed

"...one of Britain's largest independent stockbrokers was hammered by the Stock Exchange yesterday, putting it out of business for good. The hammering leaves all clients of the firm in the dark about the value of their investments and the future of uncompleted financing deals" [*Guardian*]

hammering /'hæmərɪŋ/ *noun* a beating or severe losses □ **the company took a hammering in Europe** the company had large losses in Europe or lost parts of its European markets □ **we gave them a hammering** we beat them commercially

hand /hænd/ *noun* **1.** □ **by hand** using the hands, not a machine ○ *These shoes are made by hand.* □ **to send a letter by hand** to ask someone to carry and deliver a letter personally, not sending it through the mail **2.** □ **in hand** kept in reserve ○ *we have $10,000 in hand* □ **work in hand** work which is in progress but not finished **3.** □ **goods left on hand** unsold goods left with the retailer or manufacturer ○ *They were left with half the stock on their hands.* **4.** □ **to hand** here or present □ **I have the invoice to hand** I have the invoice in front of me **5.** a worker ○ *to take on ten more hands*

hand in *phrasal verb* to deliver a letter by hand □ **he handed in his notice** *or* **resignation** he resigned

hand over *phrasal verb* to pass something to someone ○ *She handed over the documents to the lawyer.* □ **she handed over to her deputy** she passed her responsibilities to her deputy

handbill /'hændbɪl/ *noun* a sheet of printed paper handed out to members of the public as an advertisement

handbook /'hændbʊk/ *noun* a book which gives instructions on how to use something ○ *The handbook does not say how you open the photocopier.*

handle /'hænd(ə)l/ *verb* **1.** to deal with something or to organize something ○ *The accounts department handles all the cash.* ○ *We can handle orders for up to 15,000 units.* ○ *They handle all our overseas orders.* **2.** to sell or to trade in a type of product ○ *We do not handle foreign cars.* ○ *They will not handle goods produced by other firms.*

handling /'hændlɪŋ/ *noun* **1.** the moving of something by hand **2.** dealing with something

handling charge /'hændlɪŋ tʃɑrdʒ/ *noun* money to be paid for packing, invoicing, and dealing with goods which are being shipped

handmade /'hændmeɪd/ *adjective* made by hand, not by machine ○ *He writes all his letters on handmade paper.*

hand-operated /ˌhænd 'ɑpəreɪtɪd/ *adjective* worked by hand, not automatically ○ *a hand-operated machine*

handout /'hændaʊt/ *noun* **1.** a free gift, especially of money ○ *The company exists on handouts from the government.* **2.** money paid to help someone in difficulties

handover /'hændoʊvər/ *noun* the passing of responsibilities to someone else ○ *The handover from the old chairman to the new went very smoothly.* ○ *When the own-*

ership of a company changes, the handover period is always difficult. ○ *There was a smooth handover to the new management team.*

hands-on /ˌhændz 'ɑn/ *adjective* involving direct contact with the working of a system or organization ○ *We need a hands-on manager who will supervise operations closely.* ○ *More hands-on management means we will have to increase the technical input in our management training schemes.*

handwritten /ˌhænd'rɪt(ə)n/ *adjective* written by hand, not typed ○ *It is more professional to send in a typed rather than a handwritten letter of application.*

handy /'hændi/ *adjective* useful or convenient ○ *They are sold in handy-sized packs.* ○ *This small case is handy for use when traveling.*

hang /hæŋ/ *verb*

hang on *phrasal verb* to wait (while phoning) ○ *If you hang on a moment, the chairman will be off the other line soon.*

hang up *phrasal verb* to stop a telephone conversation by putting the telephone back on its hook ○ *When I asked him about the unpaid invoice, he hung up.*

happen /'hæpən/ *verb* to take place by chance ○ *The contract happened to arrive when the managing director was away on vacation.* ○ *He happened to be in the store when the customer placed the order.* □ **what has happened to?** what went wrong with? what is the matter with? where is? ○ *What has happened to that order for Japan?*

harass /'hærəs, hə'ræs/ *verb* to worry or to bother someone, especially by continually checking on them or making sexual approaches

harbor /'hɑrbər/ *noun* a port, place where ships come to load or unload (NOTE: The U.S. spelling is **harbor**.)

harbor dues /'hɑrbər duz/ *noun* payment which a ship makes to the harbor authorities for the right to use a harbor

harbor installations /ˌhɑrbər ˌɪnstə'leɪʃ(ə)nz/ *noun* the buildings or equipment in a harbor

hard /hɑrd/ *adjective* **1.** strong, not weak □ **to take a hard line in labor union negotiations** to refuse to compromise with the other side **2.** difficult ○ *It is hard to get* *good people to work on low salaries.* **3.** solid **4.** □ **after weeks of hard bargaining** after weeks of difficult discussions ■ *adverb* with a lot of effort ○ *The sales team sold the new product range hard into the supermarkets.* ○ *If all the work force works hard, the order should be completed on time.*

hard bargain /ˌhɑrd 'bɑrgɪn/ *noun* a bargain with difficult terms □ **to drive a hard bargain** to be a difficult negotiator □ **to strike a hard bargain** to agree a deal where the terms are favorable to you

hard cash /ˌhɑrd 'kæʃ/ *noun* money in bills and coins, as opposed to checks or credit cards

hard copy /ˌhɑrd 'kɑpi/ *noun* a printout of a text which is on a computer

hard currency /ˌhɑrd 'kʌrənsi/ *noun* the currency of a country which has a strong economy, and which can be changed into other currencies easily ○ *to pay for imports in hard currency* ○ *to sell raw materials to earn hard currency* Also called **scarce currency.** Opposite **soft currency**

hard disk /ˌhɑrd 'dɪsk/ *noun* a computer disk which has a sealed case and can store large quantities of information

"…hard disks help computers function more speedily and allow them to store more information" [*Australian Financial Review*]

hard drive /'hɑrd draɪv/ *noun* same as **hard disk**

harden /'hɑrd(ə)n/ *verb* to become more fixed or more inflexible ○ *The union's attitude to the management has hardened since the lockout.* □ **prices are hardening** prices are settling at a higher price

hardening /'hɑrd(ə)nɪŋ/ *adjective* **1.** (*of a market*) slowly moving upward □ **a hardening of prices** prices which are becoming settled at a higher level **2.** (*of prices*) becoming settled at a higher level

hard market /ˌhɑrd 'mɑrkət/ *noun* a market which is strong and not likely to fall

hardness /'hɑrdnəs/ *noun* □ **hardness of the market** the state of the market when it is strong and not likely to fall

hard sell /ˌhɑrd 'sel/ *noun* □ **to give a product the hard sell** to make great efforts to persuade people to buy a product □ **he tried to give me the hard sell** he put a lot of effort into trying to make me buy

hard selling /ˌhɑrd 'selɪŋ/ *noun* the act of selling by using great efforts ○ *A lot of hard selling went into that deal.*

hardware /'hɑrdwer/ *noun* **1.** machines used in data processing, including the computers and printers, but not the programs **2.** solid goods for use in the house, e.g., skillets or hammers ○ *a hardware store*

harm /hɑrm/ *noun* damage done ○ *The recession has done a lot of harm to export sales.* ■ *verb* to damage ○ *The bad publicity has harmed the company's reputation.*

hatchet man /'hætʃɪt mæn/ *noun* a recently appointed manager, whose job is to make staff redundant and reduce expenditure (*informal*)

hate site /'heɪt saɪt/ *noun* a website devoted to attacking a particular company or organization. A hate site often imitates the target organization's own site and is usually set up by a customer who has a complaint against the organization that he or she has been unable to express on the organization's own site. Also called **anti-site**

haul /hɔl/ *noun* a distance traveled with a load of cargo ○ *It is a long haul from Birmingham to Athens.*

haulage /'hɔlɪdʒ/ *noun* the cost of transporting goods by road ○ *Haulage is increasing by 5% per annum.*

haulage costs /'hɔlɪdʒ kɔsts/ *noun* the cost or rates of transporting goods by road

haulage firm /'hɔlɪdʒ fɜrm/ *noun U.K.* same as **trucking company**

hawk /hɔk/ *verb* to sell goods from door to door or in the street □ **to hawk something around** to take a product, an idea, or a project to various companies to see if one will accept it ○ *He hawked his idea for a plastic car body around to all the major car manufacturers.*

hawker /'hɔkər/ *noun* a person who sells goods from door to door or in the street

hazard /'hæzərd/ *noun* a danger

hazardous substance /ˌhæzərdəs 'sʌbstəns/ *noun* any substance that could be dangerous to people in the workplace, e.g., a poisonous raw material, fumes or byproduct from a production process. Employers have a duty to assess the risks from hazardous substances to their staff and customers, and to ensure that no one is exposed to danger.

head /hed/ *noun* **1.** the most important person **2.** a person ○ *Representatives cost on average $25,000 per head per annum.* **3.** the top part or first part ○ *Write the name of the company at the head of the list.* ■ *adjective* most important or main ○ *Ask the headwaiter for a table.* ■ *verb* **1.** to be the manager, to be the most important person ○ *We are looking for someone to head our sales department.* ○ *He is heading a buying mission to China.* **2.** to be first ○ *The two largest oil companies head the list of stock market results.*

head for *phrasal verb* to go toward □ **the company is heading for disaster** the company is going to collapse

head up *phrasal verb* to be in charge of ○ *He has been appointed to head up our European organization.*

"…reporting to the deputy managing director, the successful candidate will be responsible for heading up a team which provides a full personnel service" [*Times*]

head buyer /ˌhed ˈbaɪər/ *noun* the most important buyer in a store

headcount /ˈhedkaʊnt/ *noun* the total number of employees who work for an organization

headed paper /ˌhedɪd ˈpeɪpər/ *noun* notepaper with the name of the company and its address printed on it (NOTE: The U.S. term is **letterhead**.)

headhunt /ˈhedhʌnt/ *verb* to look for managers and offer them jobs in other companies □ **she was headhunted** she was approached by a headhunter and offered a new job

headhunter /ˈhedhʌntər/ *noun* a person or company whose job is to find suitable top managers to fill jobs in companies

heading /ˈhedɪŋ/ *noun* the words at the top of a piece of text ○ *Items are listed under several headings.* ○ *Look at the figure under the heading "Costs 2001–02".*

headlease /ˈhedlis/ *noun* a lease from the owner to a tenant

head office /ˌhed ˈɔfɪs/ *noun* an office building where the board of directors works and meets

head of the department /ˌhed əv ðə dɪˈpɑrtmənt/ *noun* a person in charge of a department

headquarters /hedˈkwɔrtərz/ *plural noun* the main office, where the board of directors meets and works ○ *The company's headquarters are in New York.* □ **to reduce headquarters staff** to have fewer people working in the main office. Abbreviation **HQ**

heads of agreement /ˌhedz əv ə ˈgrimənt/ *plural noun* a draft agreement with not all the details complete

health /helθ/ *noun* □ **to give a company a clean bill of health** to report that a company is trading profitably

"…the main U.S. banks have been forced to pull back from international lending as nervousness continues about their financial health" [*Financial Times*]

"…financial health, along with a dose of independence, has largely sheltered Japan's pharmaceutical companies from a global wave of consolidation. Those assets, however, are expected to soon lure foreign suitors too powerful to resist" [*Nikkei Weekly*]

health and safety /ˌhelθ ən ˈseɪfti/ *noun* the area of policy and legislation that deals with the physical well-being of people in the workplace. Employers have a legal duty to ensure that the working environment and working practices are safe and that the health of their employees is not harmed by the work that they do. In the U.S., health and safety in the workplace is coordinated by the Occupational Safety and Health Administration (OSHA). (NOTE: Health and safety within an organization is often co-ordinated by a particular person, but it is the responsibility of all employees.)

healthcare /ˈhelθker/ *noun* the provision of medical and related services aimed at maintaining good health

health insurance /ˈhelθ ɪnˌʃʊrəns/ *noun* insurance which pays the cost of treatment for illness

health maintenance organization /ˌhelθ ˈmeɪnt(ə)nəns ˌɔrgənaɪzeɪʃ(ə)n/ *noun* full form of **HMO**

healthy /ˈhelθi/ *adjective* □ **a healthy balance sheet** balance sheet which shows a good profit □ **the company made some very healthy profits**, **a very healthy profit** made a large profit

heavily /ˈhevɪli/ *adverb* □ **he is heavily in debt** he has many debts □ **they are heavily into property** they have large investments in property □ **the company has had to borrow heavily to repay its debts** the company has had to borrow large sums of money

"…the steel company had spent heavily on new equipment" [*Fortune*]

heavy /'hevi/ *adjective* **1.** large or in large quantities ○ *a program of heavy investment overseas* ○ *He suffered heavy losses on the Stock Exchange.* ○ *The government imposed a heavy tax on luxury goods.* □ **heavy costs** *or* **heavy expenditure** large sums of money that have to be spent **2.** which weighs a lot ○ *The post office refused to handle the package because it was too heavy.* **3.** used to describe a stock which has such a high price that small investors are reluctant to buy it (in which case the company may decide to split the stock so as to make it more attractive)

heavy equipment /ˌhevi ɪ'kwɪpmənt/ *noun* large machines, such as for making cars or for printing

heavy hitter /ˌhevi 'hɪtər/ *noun* an executive or company that performs extremely well (*slang*)

heavy industry /ˌhevi 'ɪndəstri/ *noun* an industry which deals in heavy raw materials such as coal or makes large products such as ships or engines

heavy machinery /ˌhevi mə'ʃinəri/ *noun* large machines

heavy truck /ˌhevi 'trʌk/ *noun* a very large truck which carries heavy loads

hectare /'hekter/ *noun* a measurement of area of land (= 2.47 acres)

hedge /hedʒ/ *noun* a protection against a possible loss, which involves taking an action which is the opposite of an action taken earlier □ **a hedge against inflation** investment which should increase in value more than the increase in the rate of inflation ○ *He bought gold as a hedge against exchange losses.* ■ *verb* to protect against the risk of a loss □ **to hedge your bets** to make investments in several areas so as to be protected against loss in one of them □ **to hedge against inflation** to buy investments which will rise in value faster than the increase in the rate of inflation

"…during the 1970s commercial property was regarded by investors as an alternative to equities, with many of the same inflation-hedge qualities" [*Investors Chronicle*]

"…the move saved it from having to pay its creditors an estimated \$270 million owed in connection with hedge contracts which began working against the company when the price of gold rose unexpectedly during September" [*Business in Africa*]

hedge fund /'hedʒ fʌnd/ *noun* a partnership open to a small number of rich investors, which invests in equities, currency futures and derivatives and may produce high returns but carries a very high risk

"…much of what was described as near hysteria was the hedge funds trying to liquidate bonds to repay bank debts after losing multi-million dollar bets on speculations that the yen would fall against the dollar" [*Times*]

"…hedge funds generally have in common an ability to sell short (that is, sell stocks you do not own), and to increase growth prospects – and risk – by borrowing to enhance the fund's assets" [*Money bserver*]

"…the stock is a hedge fund – limited by the Securities and Exchange Commission to only wealthy individuals and qualified institutions" [*Smart Money*]

COMMENT: Originally, hedge funds were funds planned to protect equity investments against possible falls on the stock market. Nowadays the term is applied to funds which take speculative positions in financial futures or equities, and are usually highly-leveraged: in other words, they do nothing to "hedge" their holdings.

hedging /'hedʒɪŋ/ *noun* the act of buying investments at a fixed price for delivery later, so as to protect against possible loss

height /haɪt/ *noun* **1.** a measurement of how tall or high something is ○ *What is the height of the desk from the floor?* ○ *He measured the height of the room from floor to ceiling.* **2.** highest point ○ *It is difficult to find hotel rooms at the height of the tourist season.*

heir /er/ *noun* a person who will receive property when someone dies ○ *His heirs split the estate between them.*

heiress /'eres/ *noun* a female heir

helicopter view /'helɪkɑptər vju/ *noun* a general or broad view of a problem as a whole, which does not go into details (*slang*)

help /help/ *noun* a thing which makes it easy to do something ○ *The company was set up with financial help from the government.* ○ *Her assistant is not much help –*

he can't type or drive. ■ *verb* to make it easy for something to be done ○ *the computer helps in the rapid processing of orders* or *helps us to process orders rapidly* ○ *He helped the salesman carry his case of samples.* ○ *The government helps exporting companies with easy credit.* (NOTE: You help someone *or* something **to do** something.)

hereafter /hɪrˈæftər/ *adverb* from this time on

hereby /hɪrˈbaɪ/ *adverb* in this way, by this letter ○ *We hereby revoke the agreement of January 1st 1982.*

hereditament /ˌherɪˈdɪtəmənt/ *noun* a property, including land and buildings

herewith /hɪrˈwɪð/ *adverb* together with this letter ○ *Please find the check enclosed herewith.*

hesitate /ˈhezɪteɪt/ *verb* not to be sure what to do next ○ *The company is hesitating about starting up a new computer factory.* ○ *She hesitated for some time before accepting the job.*

hidden /ˈhɪd(ə)n/ *adjective* not possible to see □ **hidden defect in the program** defect which was not noticed when the program was tested

hidden agenda /ˌhɪd(ə)n əˈdʒendə/ *noun* a secret plan which one party to discussions has, which the other party does not know about

hidden asset /ˌhɪd(ə)n ˈæset/ *noun* an asset which is valued much less in the company's accounts than its true market value

hidden economy /ˌhɪd(ə)n ɪˈkɑnəmi/ *noun* same as **black economy**

hidden reserves /ˌhɪd(ə)n rɪˈzɜrvz/ *plural noun* reserves which are not easy to identify in the company's balance sheet. Reserves which are illegally kept hidden are called "secret reserves".

hierarchical /haɪrˈrɑrkɪk(ə)l/ *adjective* referring to an organization which has several levels ○ *The company has a very traditional hierarchical structure.*

hierarchy /ˈhaɪrɑrki/ *noun* an organizational structure with several levels of responsibility or authority ○ *At the bottom of the hierarchy are the unskilled workers.*

high /haɪ/ *adjective* **1.** large, not low ○ *High overhead costs increase the unit price.* ○ *High prices put customers off.* ○

They are budgeting for a high level of expenditure. ○ *High interest rates are crippling small businesses.* □ **high sales** a large amount of revenue produced by sales □ **high taxation** taxation which imposes large taxes on incomes or profits □ **highest tax bracket** the group which pays the most tax □ **high volume (of sales)** a large number of items sold **2.** □ **the highest bidder** the person who offers the most money at an auction ○ *The property was sold to the highest bidder.* ■ *adverb* □ **prices are running high** prices are above their usual level ■ *noun* a point where prices or sales are very large ○ *Prices have dropped by 10% since the high of January 2nd.* □ **highs and lows on the Stock Exchange** a list of stock which have reached a new high or low price in the previous day's trading □ **sales volume has reached an all-time high** the sales volume has reached the highest point it has ever been at

high concept /haɪ ˈkɑnsept/ *noun* an important and persuasive idea expressed clearly and in few words

high finance /ˌhaɪ ˈfaɪnæns/ *noun* the lending, investing, and borrowing of very large sums of money organized by financiers

high flier /ˌhaɪ ˈflaɪr/ *noun* **1.** a person who is very successful or who is likely to rise to a very important position **2.** a stock whose market price is rising rapidly

high-grade /ˈhaɪ greɪd/ *adjective* of very good quality ○ *high-grade gasoline* □ **high-grade trade delegation** a delegation made up of very important people

high-income /ˌhaɪ ˈɪnkʌm/ *adjective* giving a large income ○ *high-income stocks* ○ *a high-income portfolio*

high-level /ˈhaɪ ˌlev(ə)l/ *adjective* very important □ **high-level decision** a decision taken by the most important person or group

high-level language /ˌhaɪ ˌlev(ə)l ˈlæŋgwɪdʒ/ *noun* programming language which uses normal words and figures

highly /ˈhaɪli/ *adverb* very □ **she is highly thought of by the managing director** the managing director thinks she is very competent

highly-leveraged company /ˌhaɪli ˌlev(ə)rɪdʒd ˈkʌmp(ə)ni/ *noun* company which has a high proportion of its funds from fixed-interest borrowings

highly-paid /ˌhaɪli 'peɪd/ *adjective* earning a large salary

highly-placed /ˌhaɪli 'pleɪst/ *adjective* occupying an important post ○ *The delegation met a highly-placed official in the Trade Ministry.*

highly-priced /ˌhaɪli 'praɪst/ *adjective* with a large price

high office /ˌhaɪ 'ɔfɪs/ *noun* an important position or job in the government or civil service

high official /ˌhaɪ ə'fɪʃ(ə)l/, **high-ranking official** /ˌhaɪ ræɪjkɪŋ ə'fɪʃ(ə)l/ *noun* an important person in a government department

high-powered /ˌhaɪ 'paʊrd/ *adjective* very capable and intelligent, and at the same time very energetic and forceful

high pressure /ˌhaɪ 'preʃər/ *noun* a strong insistence that somebody should do something □ **working under high pressure** working very hard, with a manager telling you what to do and to do it quickly, or with customers asking for supplies urgently

high-pressure salesman /ˌhaɪ ˌpreʃər 'seɪlzmən/, **high-pressure saleswoman** *noun* a salesman or saleswoman who forces a customer to buy something he or she does not really want

high-pressure sales technique /ˌhaɪ ˌpreʃər 'seɪlz tekˌnɪk/ *noun* an attempt to force a customer to buy something he or she does not really want

high-quality /ˌhaɪ 'kwɑləti/ *adjective* of very good quality ○ *high-quality goods* ○ *a high-quality product*

high season /ˌhaɪ 'siz(ə)n/ *noun* same as **peak season**

high-tech /haɪ 'tek/ *adjective* used to describe devices and methods that use advanced technology

hike /haɪk/ *noun* an increase ■ *verb* to increase

hire /'haɪə/ *noun* **1.** an arrangement whereby customers pay money to be able to use a car, boat or piece of equipment owned by someone else for a time (NOTE: The more usual term in the U.S. is **rent**) **2.** □ **"for hire"** sign on a taxi showing it is empty **3.** □ **to work for hire** to work free-

lance ■ *verb* **1.** to employ someone new to work for you □ **to hire staff** to employ someone new to work for you **2.** □ **to hire out cars** *or* **equipment** *or* **workers** to lend cars, equipment or workers to customers who pay for their use

hire and fire /ˌhaɪr ən 'faɪr/ *verb* to employ new staff and dismiss existing staff very frequently

hire car /'haɪr kɑr/ *noun U.K.* same as **rental car**

hire purchase /ˌhaɪr 'pɜrtʃɪs/ *noun U.K.* same as **installment plan** ○ *to buy a refrigerator on installment plan*

hiring /'haɪrɪŋ/ *noun* the act of employing new staff ○ *Hiring of new personnel has been stopped.*

histogram /'hɪstəgræm/ *noun* same as **bar chart**

historic /hɪ'stɔrɪk/, **historical** /hɪ'stɔrɪk(ə)l/ *adjective* dating back over a period of time

COMMENT: By tradition, a company's accounts are usually prepared on the historic(al) cost principle, i.e. that assets are costed at their purchase price. With inflation, such assets are undervalued, and current-cost accounting or replacement-cost accounting may be preferred.

historical figures /hɪˌstɔrɪk(ə)l 'fɪgərz/ *plural noun* figures which were current in the past

historic cost /hɪˌstɔrɪk 'kɔst/, **historical cost** /hɪˌstɔrɪk(ə)l 'kɔst/ *noun* the actual cost of purchasing something which was bought some time ago

hit /hɪt/ *noun* an action of accessing a website ○ *We are averaging over 3,500 hits a day.* ■ *verb* **1.** to reach something ○ *He hit his head against the table.* □ **we have hit our export targets** we have reached our targets **2.** to hurt or to damage someone or something ○ *The company was badly hit by the falling exchange rate.* ○ *Our sales of summer clothes have been hit by the bad weather.* ○ *The new legislation has hit the small companies hardest.* (NOTE: **hitting – hit**)

hive /haɪv/ *verb*
hive off *phrasal verb* to split off part of a large company to form a smaller subsidiary ○ *The new managing director hived off the retail sections of the company.*

HMO *noun* a healthcare organization whose members pay fees and receive medical care from participating doctors, hospitals, and other healthcare providers. Full form **health maintenance organization**

hoard /hɔrd/ *verb* **1.** to buy and store goods in case of need **2.** to keep cash instead of investing it

hoarder /'hɔrdər/ *noun* a person who buys and stores goods in case of need

hoarding /'hɔrdɪŋ/ *noun* **1.** □ **hoarding of supplies** the buying of large quantities of goods to keep in case of need **2.** *U.K.* same as **billboard 3.** a temporary fence put up around a construction site

hold /hoʊld/ *noun* **1.** the bottom part of a ship or aircraft, in which cargo is carried **2.** the action of keeping something ■ *verb* **1.** to own or to keep something ○ *She holds 10% of the company's stock.* □ **you should hold this stock – it looks likely to rise** you should keep this stock and not sell it **2.** to contain ○ *Each box holds 250 sheets of paper.* **3.** to make something happen ○ *The receiver will hold an auction of the company's assets.* **4.** □ **hold the line please** (*on the telephone*) please wait ○ *The chairman is on the other line – will you hold?* **5.** to have a certain job or status ○ *He holds the position of chairman.* (NOTE: **holding-held**)

"…as of last night, the bank's shareholders no longer hold any rights to the bank's shares" [*South China Morning Post*]

hold back *phrasal verb* to wait, not to do something at the present time □ **investors are holding back until after the Budget** investors are waiting until they hear the details of the Budget before they decide whether to buy or sell □ **he held back from signing the lease until he had checked the details** he delayed signing the lease until he had checked the details □ **payment will be held back until the contract has been signed** payment will not be made until the contract has been signed

hold down *phrasal verb* **1.** to keep at a low level ○ *We are cutting margins to hold our prices down.* **2.** □ **to hold down a job** to manage to do a difficult job

"…real wages have been held down; they have risen at an annual rate of only 1% in the last two years" [*Sunday Times*]

hold on *phrasal verb* to wait, not to change □ **the company's stockholders should hold on and wait for a better offer** they should keep their stock and not sell it until they are offered a higher price

hold out for *phrasal verb* to wait and ask for something □ **you should hold out for a 10% pay raise** you should not agree to a pay raise of less than 10%

hold over *phrasal verb* to postpone or put back to a later date ○ *Discussion of item 4 was held over until the next meeting.*

hold to *phrasal verb* not to allow something or someone to change □ **we will try to hold him to the contract** we will try to stop him going against the contract □ **the government hopes to hold wage increases to 5%** the government hopes that wage increases will not be more than 5%

hold up *phrasal verb* **1.** to stay at a high level ○ *Stock prices have held up well.* ○ *Sales held up during the tourist season.* **2.** to delay something ○ *The shipment has been held up at customs.* ○ *Payment will be held up until the contract has been signed.* ○ *The strike will hold up dispatch for some weeks.* ○ *The employees are holding up production as a form of protest against poor conditions.*

holdback /'hoʊlbæk/ *noun* a part of a loan to a property developer which is not paid until the development is almost finished

holder /'hoʊldər/ *noun* **1.** a person who owns or keeps something ○ *holders of government bonds* or *bondholders* ○ *holder of stock* or *of shares in a company* ○ *holder of an insurance policy* or *policy holder* **2.** a thing which keeps something, which protects something

holding /'hoʊldɪŋ/ *noun* a group of stocks owned ○ *She has sold all her holdings in the Far East.* ○ *The company has holdings in German manufacturing companies.*

holding company /'hoʊldɪŋ ˌkʌmp(ə)ni/ *noun* **1.** a company which owns more than 50% of the stock in another company. ◊ **subsidiary company 2.** a company which exists only or mainly to own stock in subsidiary companies. ◊ **subsidiary**

hold-up /'hoʊld ʌp/ *noun* a delay ○ *The bad weather caused hold-ups in the dispatch of goods.*

holiday /'hɒlɪdeɪ/ *noun* **1.** *U.K.* same as **vacation 2.** a day set aside by law or statute as exempt from regular labor or business activities ○ *a holiday to celebrate the life of Martin Luther King, Jr.*

holiday entitlement /'hɒlɪdeɪ ɪn̩ˌtaɪt(ə)lmənt/ *noun U.K.* same as **vacation entitlement**

holiday pay /'hɒlɪdeɪ peɪ/ *noun U.K.* same as **vacation pay**

hologram /'hɒləgræm/ *noun* a three-dimensional picture which is used on credit cards as a means of preventing forgery

home /hoʊm/ *noun* the place where a person lives

home address /ˌhoʊm ə'dres/ *noun* the address of a house or apartment where a person lives ○ *Please send the documents to my home address.*

home banking /ˌhoʊm 'bæŋkɪŋ/ *noun* a system of banking using a personal computer in your own home to carry out various financial transactions such as paying invoices or checking your bank account

home consumption /ˌhoʊm kən'sʌmpʃən/ *noun* use of something in the home

home country /ˌhoʊm 'kʌntri/ *noun* a country where a company is based

homegrown /'hoʊmgroʊn/ *adjective* which has been developed in a local area or in a country where the company is based ○ *a homegrown computer industry* ○ *India's homegrown car industry*

home loan /'hoʊm loʊn/ *noun* a loan by a bank or savings and loan to help someone buy a house

homemade /ˌhoʊm'meɪd/ *adjective* made in a home ○ *homemade jelly*

home market /ˌhoʊm 'mɑrkət/ *noun* the market in the country where the selling company is based ○ *Sales in the home market rose by 22%.*

homeowner /'hoʊmoʊnər/ *noun* a person who owns a private house or apartment

homeowner's insurance policy /ˌhoʊmoʊnəz ɪn'ʃʊrəns ˌpɑlɪsi/ *noun* insurance policy covering a house and its contents and the personal liability of the people living in it

homepage /'hoʊmpeɪdʒ/ *noun* the first page that is displayed when you visit a site on the Internet

home-produced product /ˌhoʊm prə,dust 'prɑdʌkt/ *noun* a product manufactured in the country where the company is based

home run /'hoʊm rʌn/ *noun* a very great achievement (*informal*)

home sales /ˌhoʊm 'seɪlz/ *noun* sales in the country where a company is based

home trade /ˌhoʊm 'treɪd/ *noun* trade in the country where a company is based

homeward /'hoʊmwərd/ *adjective* going toward the home country ○ *The ship is carrying homeward freight.* ○ *The liner left Buenos Aires on her homeward trip.*

homewards /'hoʊmwərdz/ *adverb* toward the home country ○ *cargo homewards*

homeworker /'hoʊmwɜrkər/ *noun* a person who works at home for a company

homeworking /'hoʊmwɜrkɪŋ/ *noun* a working method where employees work at home on computer terminals, and send the finished material back to the central office by modem. Also called **networking, teleworking**

homogenization /həˌmɑdʒənaɪ'zeɪʃ(ə)n/ *noun* the tendency for different products, markets and cultures to lose their characteristic differences and become the same (NOTE: Globalization is often blamed for homogenization.)

hon *abbreviation* honorary

honest /'ɑnɪst/ *adjective* respected, saying what is right □ **to play the honest broker** to act for the parties in a negotiation to try to make them agree to a solution

honor /'ɑnər/ *verb* to pay something because it is owed and is correct ○ *to honor a bill* (NOTE: The U.S. spelling is **honor.**) □ **to honor a signature** to pay something because the signature is correct

honorarium /ˌɑnə'reriəm/ *noun* money paid to a professional person such as an accountant or a lawyer when a specific fee has not been requested (NOTE: The plural is **honoraria.**)

honorary /'ɑnərəri/ *adjective* not paid a salary for the work done for an organization ○ *He is honorary president of the translators' association.*

honorary member /ˌɑnərəri ˈmembər/ *noun* a member who does not have to pay dues

hon sec honorary secretary

hope /houp/ *verb* to expect, to want something to happen ○ *We hope to be able to dispatch the order next week.* ○ *He is hoping to break into the U.S. market.* ○ *They had hoped the TV commercials would help sales.*

horizontal /ˌhɔrɪˈzɑnt(ə)l/ *adjective* at the same level or with the same status ○ *Her new job is a horizontal move into a different branch of the business.*

horizontal communication /ˌhɔrɪzɑnt(ə)l kəˌmjunɪˈkeɪʃ(ə)n/ *noun* communication between employees at the same level

horizontal integration /ˌhɔrɪzɑnt(ə)l ˌɪntɪˈɡreɪʃ(ə)n/ *noun* the process of joining similar companies or taking over a company in the same line of business as yourself

horse trading /ˈhɔrs ˌtreɪdɪŋ/ *noun* hard bargaining which ends with someone giving something in return for a concession from the other side

hostess /ˈhoʊstɪs/ *noun* a woman who looks after passengers or clients

hostile bid /ˌhɑstaɪl ˈbɪd/ *noun* same as **contested takeover**

hosting /ˈhoʊstɪŋ/ *noun* the business of putting websites onto the Internet so that people can visit them. ◊ **hosting option**

hosting option /ˌhoʊstɪŋ ˈɑpʃən/ *noun* any of the different kinds of hosting that a business may use when putting a website on the Internet and that are usually provided by specialist hosting companies. ◊ **collocation hosting**, **managed hosting**, **non-virtual hosting**, **virtual hosting**

host service /ˈhoʊst ˌsɜrvɪs/, **hosting service provider** /ˈhoʊstɪŋ ˌsɜrvɪs prəˌvaɪdər/ *noun* a company that provides connections to the Internet and storage space on its computers, which can store the files for a user's website

hot-desking /ˈhɑt ˌdeskɪŋ/ *noun* a flexible way of working that allows employees to use any free workspace rather than having a desk that they regard as their own

"…employees get "hot desks"--temporary desks that can be used by any employee on a given day. The employee removes all of his or her possessions by the end of the day so that the space can be used by someone else." [*InformationWeek*]

hotel /hoʊˈtel/ *noun* a building where you can rent a room for a night, or eat in a restaurant ○ *His hotel bills were paid by the insurance company.* ○ *She put her hotel expenses on her expense account.* ○ *Hotel staff had instructions not to let him into the hotel.*

hotel accommodationss /hoʊˌtel əˌkɑməˈdeɪʃ(ə)nz/ *noun* rooms available in hotels ○ *All hotel accommodations has been booked up for the exhibition.*

hotel chain /hoʊˈtel tʃeɪn/ *noun* a group of hotels owned by the same company

hotelier /hoʊˈtelieɪ/ *noun* a person who owns or manages a hotel

hoteling /hoʊˈtelɪŋ/ *noun* the practice of using a desk or workspace in an office belonging to someone who is not your employer. Hoteling is normally carried out by consultants or sales people, who spend more time with their customers than at their base.

hotel trade /hoʊˈtel treɪd/ *noun* the business of running hotels

hotline /ˈhɑtlaɪn/ *noun* a special telephone ordering service set up for a special period ○ *a Christmas hotline*

hot money /ˌhɑt ˈmʌni/ *noun* money which is moved from country to country to get the best returns

hour /aʊr/ *noun* **1.** a period of time lasting sixty minutes □ **to work a thirty-five hour week** to work seven hours a day each weekday □ **we work an eight-hour day** we work for eight hours a day, e.g. from 8.30 to 5.30 with one hour for lunch **2.** sixty minutes of work ○ *She earns $14 an hour.* ○ *We pay $16 an hour.* □ **to pay by the hour** to pay people a fixed amount of money for each hour worked **3.** □ **outside hours** *or* **out of hours** when the office is not open ○ *He worked on the accounts out of hours.*

hourly /ˈaʊrli/ *adjective, adverb* per hour

"…despite the Fed's long-standing fears that low unemployment will raise wage costs, average hourly earnings grew by just 3.6 per cent in the year to November" [*Investors Chronicle*]

hourly-paid /'aʊrli ˌpeɪd/ *adjective* paid at a fixed rate for each hour worked

hourly rate /ˌaʊrli 'reɪt/, **hourly wage** /ˌaʊrli 'weɪdʒ/ *noun* the amount of money paid for an hour worked

hourly wage /ˌaʊrli 'weɪdʒ/ *noun* the amount of money paid for an hour's work

hours of work /ˌaʊrz əv 'wɜrk/ *plural noun* the actual hours that an employee spends working, often many more than those stated in his or her contract of employment and sometimes not covered by overtime payments ○ *Our hours of work are 9.30 to 5.30, with an hour off for lunch.*

house /haʊs/ *noun* **1.** a company ○ *the largest London finance house* ○ *a brokerage house* ○ *a publishing house* **2.** *U.K.* the London Stock Exchange

house agent /'haʊz ˌeɪdʒənt/ *noun U.K.* a real estate agent who deals in buying or selling houses or apartments

housecleaning /'haʊsˌklinɪŋ/ *noun* a general reorganizing of a business ○ *She has mainly been performing housecleaning measures.*

household /'haʊshoʊld/ *noun* a unit formed of all the people living together in a single house or apartment, whether it is a single person living alone, a married couple, or a large family

householder /'haʊshoʊldər/ *noun* a person who owns a private house or apartment

household expenses /ˌhaʊshoʊld ɪk 'spensɪz/ *noun* money spent on running a private house

household insurance /ˌhaʊshoʊld ɪn'ʃʊrəns/ *noun* the act of insuring a house and its contents against damage

household insurance policy /ˌhaʊshoʊld ɪn'ʃʊrəns ˌpɑlɪsi/ *noun* insurance policy covering a house and its contents and the personal liability of the people living in it

household name /ˌhaʊshoʊld neɪm/ *noun* a brand name which is recognized by a large number of consumers

house journal /'haʊs ˌdʒɜrn(ə)l/, **house magazine** /'haʊs ˌmægəzin/ *noun* a magazine produced for the employees or stockholders in a company to give them news about the company

house phone /ˌhaʊs 'foʊn/ *noun* a telephone for calling from one room to another in an office or hotel

house property /'haʊs ˌprɑpərti/ *noun* private houses or apartments, not stores, offices, or factories

house starts /'haʊs 'stɑrts/, **housing starts** /'haʊzɪŋ 'stɑrts/ *plural noun* the number of new private houses or apartments of which the construction has begun during a year

house style /ˌhaʊs 'staɪl/ *noun* a company's own design which is used in all its products, including packaging and stationery

house-to-house /ˌhaʊs tə 'haʊs/ *adjective* going from one house to the next, asking people to buy something or to vote for someone ○ *house-to-house canvassing* ○ *He trained as a house-to-house salesman.* ○ *House-to-house selling is banned in this area.*

housewares /'haʊswerz/ *plural noun* items which are used in the home

housing market /'haʊzɪŋ ˌmɑrkət/ *noun* activity in the construction of new homes, used as a leading indicator in the U.S. of changes in economic trends

HP *abbreviation* hire purchase

HQ *abbreviation* headquarters

HR *abbreviation* human resources

HTML /ˌeɪtʃ ti em 'el/ *noun* the standard computer code used to build and develop webpages. Full form **HyperText Markup Language**

HTTP /ˌeɪtʃ ti ti 'pi/ *noun* the means used to transfer text, images, and sound over the World Wide Web. Full form **HyperText Transfer Protocol**

hub-and-spoke /ˌhʌb ən 'spoʊk/ *adjective* referring to any arrangement of component parts that is similar to a wheel, with a central hub and a series of spokes radiating outwards. The term can be applied to organizational structure, computer network design, work processes, methods of service delivery or transportation systems.

HUBZone /'hʌbzoʊn/ *noun* an area designated by the U.S. government as distressed, and in which the government is encouraging economic development and employment opportunities by offering special access to federal contracts

humanagement /hjuˈmænɪdʒmənt/ *noun* a style of management that emphasizes the empowerment of employees

human factors engineering /ˌhjumən ˈfæktəz endʒɪˌnɪrɪŋ/, **human factor engineering** /ˌhjumən ˈfæktər endʒɪˌnɪrɪŋ/ *noun* the work of designing activities, facilities and systems in the workplace on the basis of an analysis of human capabilities and needs so that the workplace can be fitted to the worker and employee performance can be improved (NOTE: Human factors engineering also tries to reduce risk by raising safety levels.)

human resources /ˌhjumən rɪˈsɔrsɪz/ *plural noun* the employees which an organization has available ○ *Our human resources must be looked after and developed if we are to raise productivity successfully.* Abbreviation **HR**. Also called **personnel**

human resources department /ˌhjumən rɪˈzɔrsɪz dɪˌpartmənt/ *noun* the section of the company which deals with its staff

human resources manager /ˌhjumən rɪˈzɔrsɪz ˌmænɪdʒər/ *noun* a person who is responsible for an organization's productive use of its employees ○ *She was appointed human resources manager because of her experience in manpower planning and recruitment.*

human resources officer /ˌhjumən rɪˈzɔrsɪz ˌɔfɪsər/ *noun* a person who deals with the staff in a company, especially interviewing candidates for new positions

hundredweight /ˈhʌndrədweɪt/ *noun* a weight of 112 pounds (about fifty kilos)

hungry /ˈhʌŋgri/ *adjective* wanting more sales, a bigger share of the market, etc. ○ *After the cutbacks in staff, the company is leaner and hungrier.*

hurry /ˈhʌri/ *noun* doing things fast ○ *There is no hurry for the figures, we do not need them until next week.* □ **in a hurry** very fast ○ *The sales manager wants the report in a hurry.* ■ *verb* to do something, to make something or to go very fast ○ *The production team tried to hurry the order through the factory.* ○ *The chairman does not want to be hurried into making a deci-sion.* ○ *The directors hurried into the meeting.*

hurry up *phrasal verb* to make something go faster ○ *Can you hurry up that order – the customer wants it immediately?*

hurry sickness /ˈhʌri ˌsɪknəs/ *noun* a state of anxiety caused by the feeling that you do not have enough time in the day to achieve everything that is required

hype /haɪp/ *noun* excessive claims made in advertising ○ *all the hype surrounding the launch of the new soap* ○ *Many consumers were actually put off by all the media hype surrounding the launch of the new magazine.* ■ *verb* to make excessive claims in advertising

hyper- /haɪpər/ *prefix* very large

hyperinflation /ˌhaɪpərɪnˈfleɪʃ(ə)n/ *noun* inflation which is at such a high percentage rate that it is almost impossible to reduce

hyperlink /ˈhaɪpərlɪŋk/ *noun* **1.** an image or a piece of text that a user clicks on in order to move directly from one webpage to another (NOTE: Hyperlinks can be added to webpages by using simple HTML commands; they can also be used in email messages, for example, to include the address of a company's website.) **2.** a series of commands attached to a button or word on one webpage that link it to another page, so that if a user clicks on the button or word, the hyperlink will move the user to another position or display another page

hypermarket /ˈhaɪpəmarkət/ *noun* a very large supermarket, usually outside a large town, with car-parking facilities

hypertext /ˈhaɪpərtekst/ *noun* a system of organizing information in which certain words in a document link to other documents and display the text when the word is selected

hypertext link /ˈhaɪpətekst lɪŋk/ *noun* same as **hyperlink**

HyperText Markup Language /ˌhaɪpərtekst ˈmarkʌp ˌlæŋgwɪdʒ/ *noun* full form of **HTML**

HyperText Transfer Protocol /ˌhaɪpərtekst ˈtrænsfɜr ˌproʊtəkal/ *noun* full form of **HTTP**

I

IBRD *abbreviation* International Bank for Reconstruction and Development (the World Bank)

ice /aɪs/ *noun* □ **to put something on ice** to file a plan or document as the best way of forgetting about it ○ *The whole expansion plan was put on ice.*

ICT *abbreviation* information and communications technologies

IDD *abbreviation* international direct dialing

idea hamster /aɪˈdɪə ˌhæmstər/ *noun* someone who appears to have an endless supply of new ideas (*slang*)

ideal /aɪˈdɪəl/ *adjective* perfect, very good for something ○ *This is the ideal site for a new hypermarket.*

Ideal Home Exhibition /aɪˌdɪəl ˈhoʊm ˌeksɪbɪʃən/ *noun* an annual exhibition in London showing new houses, new kitchens, etc.

idle /ˈaɪd(ə)l/ *adjective* **1.** not working ○ *2,000 employees were made idle by the recession.* **2.** □ **idle machinery, machines lying idle** machinery not being used □ **idle time** period of time when a machine is available for production but not doing anything

idle capital /ˌaɪd(ə)l ˈkæpɪt(ə)l/ *noun* capital which is not being used productively

i.e. /ˈaɪˈi, ˈðætˈɪz/ that is ○ *The largest companies, i.e. Smith's and Brown's, had a very good first quarter.* ○ *The import restrictions apply to expensive items, i.e. items costing more than $2,500.*

IHT *abbreviation* inheritance tax

illegal /ɪˈliːg(ə)l/ *adjective* not legal or against the law □ **illegal contract** contract which cannot be enforced in law (such as a contract to commit a crime)

illegality /ˌɪliˈɡælɪti/ *noun* the fact of being illegal

illegally /ɪˈliːɡəli/ *adverb* against the law ○ *He was accused of illegally laundering money.*

illicit /ɪˈlɪsɪt/ *adjective* not legal or not permitted ○ *the illicit sale of alcohol* ○ *trade in illicit alcohol*

illiquid /ɪˈlɪkwɪd/ *adjective* **1.** referring to an asset which is not easy to change into cash **2.** used to describe a person or business that lacks cash or assets such as securities that can readily be converted into cash

ILO *abbreviation* International Labour Organization

image /ˈɪmɪdʒ/ *noun* the general idea that the public has of a product, brand, or company ○ *They are spending a lot of advertising money to improve the company's image.* ○ *The company has adopted a downmarket image.* □ **to promote the corporate image** to publicize a company so that its reputation is improved

image-maker /ˈɪmɪdʒ ˌmeɪkər/ *noun* someone who is employed to create a favorable public image for an organization, product, or public figure

IMF *abbreviation* International Monetary Fund

imitate /ˈɪmɪteɪt/ *verb* to do what someone else does ○ *They imitate all our sales gimmicks.*

imitation /ˌɪmɪˈteɪʃ(ə)n/ *noun* something which is a copy of an original □ **beware of imitations** be careful not to buy low-quality goods which are made to look like other more expensive items ■ *adjective* which copies something ○ *He was caught selling imitation Rolex watches.*

immediate /ɪˈmiːdiət/ *adjective* happening at once ○ *We wrote an immediate letter of complaint.* ○ *Your order will receive immediate attention.*

immediate environment /ɪˌmidiət ɪn
'vaɪrənmənt/ *noun* elements or factors
outside a business organization which directly affect its work, such as the supply of
raw materials and demand for its products
○ *The unreliability of our suppliers is one
of the worst features of our immediate environment.*

immediately /ɪˈmidiətli/ *adverb* at
once ○ *He immediately placed an order
for 2,000 boxes.* ○ *As soon as he heard the
news he immediately faxed his office.* ○
*Can you phone immediately you get the in-
formation?*

immovable /ɪˈmuvəb(ə)l/ *adjective* impossible to move

immovable property /ɪˌmuvəb(ə)l
ˈprɑpərti/ *noun* houses and other buildings on land

immunity /ɪˈmjunɪti/ *noun* protection
against arrest □ **immunity from prosecution** not being liable to be prosecuted

impact /ˈɪmpækt/ *noun* a shock or
strong effect ○ *the impact of new technology on the cotton trade* ○ *The new design
has made little impact on the buying public.*

imperfect /ɪmˈpɜrfɪkt/ *adjective* having
defects ○ *They are holding a sale of imperfect items.* ○ *Check the batch for imperfect
products.*

imperfection /ˌɪmpəˈfekʃən/ *noun* a
defect in something ○ *to check a batch for
imperfections*

impersonal /ɪmˈpɜrs(ə)n(ə)l/ *adjective*
without any personal touch or as if done by
machines ○ *an impersonal style of management*

implement *noun* /ˈɪmplɪmənt/ a tool or
instrument used to do some work ○ *We
don't have the right implements for this
type of work.* ■ *verb* /ˈɪmplɪˌment/ to put
into action ○ *to implement an agreement* ○
to implement a decision

implementation /ˌɪmplɪmənˈteɪʃ(ə)n/
noun the process of putting something into
action ○ *the implementation of new rules*

import /ɪmˈpɔrt/ *verb* to bring goods
from abroad into a country for sale ○ *The
company imports television sets from Japan.* ○ *This car was imported from
France.*

importance /ɪmˈpɔrt(ə)ns/ *noun* considerable value or significance ○ *The bank
attaches great importance to the deal.*

important /ɪmˈpɔrtənt/ *adjective*
which matters a lot ○ *He left a pile of important papers in the taxi.* ○ *She has an
important meeting at 10.30.* ○ *I was promoted to a more important job.*

"…each of the major issues on the agenda at
this week's meeting is important to the
government's success in overall economic
management" [*Australian Financial
Review*]

importation /ˌɪmpɔˈteɪʃ(ə)n/ *noun* the
act of importing ○ *The importation of
arms is forbidden.* ○ *The importation of
livestock is subject to very strict controls.*

import ban /ˈɪmpɔrt bæn/ *noun* an order forbidding imports ○ *The government
has imposed an import ban on arms.*

import duty /ˈɪmpɔrt ˌduti/ *noun* a tax
on goods imported into a country

importer /ɪmˈpɔrtər/ *noun* a person or
company that imports goods ○ *a cigar importer* ○ *The company is a big importer of
foreign cars.*

import-export /ˌɪmpɔrt ˈekspɔrt/ *adjective, noun* referring to business which
deals with both bringing foreign goods
into a country and sending locally made
goods abroad ○ *Rotterdam is an important
center for the import-export trade.* ○ *She
works in import-export.*

importing /ɪmˈpɔrtɪŋ/ *adjective* bringing goods into a country ○ *oil-importing
countries* ○ *an importing company* ■
noun the act of bringing foreign goods
into a country for sale ○ *The importing of
arms into the country is illegal.*

import levy /ˈɪmpɔrt ˌlevi/ *noun* a tax
on imports, especially in the EU a tax on
imports of farm produce from outside the
EU

import license /ˈɪmpɔrt ˌlaɪs(ə)ns/,
import permit *noun* an official document
which allows goods to be imported

import quota /ˈɪmpɔrt ˌkwoʊtə/ *noun*
a fixed quantity of a particular type of
goods which the government allows to be
imported ○ *The government has imposed a
import quota on cars.*

import restrictions /ˈɪmpɔrt rɪ
ˌstrɪkʃ(ə)nz/ *plural noun* actions taken by
a government to reduce the level of imports by imposing quotas, duties, etc.

imports /ˈɪmpɔrts/ *plural noun* goods
brought into a country from abroad for
sale ○ *Imports from Poland have risen to*

$1m a year. (NOTE: Usually used in the plural, but the singular is used before a noun.)

import surcharge /ˈɪmpɔrt ˌsɜrtʃɑrdʒ/ *noun* the extra duty charged on imported goods, to try to stop them from being imported and to encourage local manufacture

import tariffs /ˌɪmpɔrt ˈtærɪfs/ *plural noun* taxes on imports

impose /ɪmˈpoʊz/ *verb* to give orders for something regarded as unpleasant or unwanted such as a tax or a ban ○ *to impose a tax on bicycles* ○ *They tried to impose a ban on smoking.* ○ *The government imposed a special duty on oil.*

imposition /ˌɪmpəˈzɪʃ(ə)n/ *noun* the act of imposing something

impossible /ɪmˈpɑsɪb(ə)l/ *adjective* which cannot be done ○ *Getting skilled staff is becoming impossible.* ○ *Government regulations make it impossible for us to export.*

impound /ɪmˈpaʊnd/ *verb* to take something away and keep it until a tax is paid ○ *customs impounded the whole cargo*

impounding /ɪmˈpaʊndɪŋ/ *noun* an act of taking something and keeping it until a tax is paid

imprest system /ˈɪmprest ˌsɪstəm/ *noun* a system of controlling petty cash, where cash is paid out against a written receipt and the receipt is used to get more cash to bring the float to the original level

improve /ɪmˈpruv/ *verb* to make something better, or to become better ○ *We are trying to improve our image with a series of TV commercials.* ○ *They hope to improve the company's market share.* ○ *We hope the cash flow position will improve or we will have difficulty in paying our bills.* □ **export trade has improved sharply during the first quarter** export trade has increased suddenly and greatly in the first period of the year

"…we also invest in companies whose growth and profitability could be improved by a management buyout" [*Times*]

improve on *phrasal verb* to do better than □ **she refused to improve on her previous offer** she refused to make a better offer

improved /ɪmˈpruvd/ *adjective* better ○ *an improved offer*

improvement /ɪmˈpruvmənt/ *noun* **1.** the process of getting better ○ *There is no improvement in the cash flow situation.* ○ *Sales are showing a sharp improvement over last year.* ○ *Employees have noticed an improvement in the working environment.* **2.** something which is better □ **an improvement on an offer** an act of making a better offer

"…the management says the rate of loss-making has come down and it expects further improvement in the next few years" [*Financial Times*]

impulse /ˈɪmpʌls/ *noun* a sudden decision □ **to do something on impulse** to do something because you have just thought of it, not because it was planned

impulse buyer /ˈɪmpʌls ˌbaɪər/ *noun* a person who buys something on impulse, not because he or she intended to buy it

impulse buying /ˈɪmpʌls ˌbaɪɪŋ/ *noun* the practice of buying items which you have just seen, not because you had planned to buy them

impulse purchase /ˈɪmpʌls ˌpɜrtʃɪs/ *noun* something bought as soon as it is seen

in. *abbreviation* inch

inactive /ɪnˈæktɪv/ *adjective* not active or not busy

inactive account /ɪnˌæktɪv əˈkaʊnt/ *noun* a bank account which is not used over a period of time

inactive market /ɪnˌæktɪv ˈmɑrkət/ *noun* a stock market with few buyers or sellers

Inc. *abbreviation* incorporated

incentive /ɪnˈsentɪv/ *noun* something which encourages a customer to buy, or employees to work better

incentive bonus /ɪnˈsentɪv ˌboʊnəs/, **incentive payment** /ɪnˈsentɪv ˌpeɪmənt/ *noun* an extra payment offered to employees to make them work better

incentive program /ɪnˈsentɪv ˌproʊɡræm/ *noun* a plan to encourage better work by paying higher commission or bonuses ○ *Incentive programs are boosting production.*

inch /ɪntʃ/ *noun* a measurement of length (= 2.54cm) ○ *a 31/2 inch disk* (NOTE: Usually written **in** or " after figures: *2in* or *2*". Note also that the inch is now no longer officially used in the U.K.)

incidental /ˌɪnsɪˈdent(ə)l/ *adjective* not important, but connected with something else

incidental expenses /ˌɪnsɪdent(ə)l ɪkˈspensɪz/ *plural noun* small amounts of money spent at various times in addition to larger amounts

include /ɪnˈkluːd/ *verb* to count something along with other things ○ *The charge includes sales tax.* ○ *The total is $140 not including insurance and freight.* ○ *The account covers services up to and including the month of June.*

inclusive /ɪnˈkluːsɪv/ *adjective* counting something in with other things ○ *inclusive of tax* ○ *not inclusive of sales tax* □ **inclusive of** including ○ *inclusive of tax* ○ *not inclusive of sales tax* □ **the conference runs from the 12th to the 16th inclusive** it starts on the morning of the 12th and ends on the evening of the 16th

inclusive charge /ɪnˌkluːsɪv ˈtʃɑːdʒ/, **inclusive sum** /ɪnˌkluːsɪv ˈsʌm/ *noun* a charge which includes all items or costs

income /ˈɪnkʌm/ *noun* **1.** money which a person receives as salary or dividends □ **lower income bracket, upper income bracket** the groups of people who earn low or high salaries considered for tax purposes **2.** money which an organization receives as gifts or from investments ○ *The hospital has a large income from gifts.*

income distribution /ˈɪnkʌm dɪstrɪˌbjuːʃ(ə)n/ *noun* the way in which the national income is distributed among the various classes and occupations in a country

income per head /ˈɪnkʌm pə/, **income per capita** *noun* same as **per capita income**

incomes policy /ˈɪnkʌmz ˌpɒlɪsi/ *noun* the government's ideas on how incomes should be controlled

income statement /ˈɪnkʌm ˌsteɪtmənt/ *noun* same as **profit and loss statement**

income stock /ˈɪnkʌm stɒk/ *plural noun* stock in an investment trust that receives income from the investments, but does not benefit from the rise in capital value of the investments

income tax /ˈɪnkʌm tæks/ *noun* **1.** the tax on a person's income, both earned and unearned **2.** the tax on the profits of a corporation

income tax form /ˈɪnkʌm tæks ˌfɔːm/ *noun* a form to be completed which declares all income to the tax office

income tax return /ˈɪnkʌm tæks rɪˌtɜːn/ *noun* a completed tax form, with details of income, exemptions, deductions, and credits. Also called **return, tax return**

income units /ˈɪnkʌm ˌjuːnɪts/ *plural noun* units in a mutual fund, from which the investor receives dividends in the form of income

incoming /ˈɪnkʌmɪŋ/ *adjective* **1.** □ **incoming call** a phone call coming into the office from someone outside □ **incoming mail** mail which comes into an office **2.** referring to someone who has recently been elected or appointed ○ *the incoming chairman* □ **the incoming board of directors** the new board which is about to start working

incompetent /ɪnˈkɒmpɪt(ə)nt/ *adjective* unable to work effectively ○ *The sales manager is incompetent.* ○ *The company has an incompetent sales director.*

inconvertible /ˌɪnkənˈvɜːtəb(ə)l/ *adjective* referring to currency which cannot be easily converted into other currencies

incorporate /ɪnˈkɔːpəreɪt/ *verb* **1.** to bring something in to form part of a main group ○ *Income from the 1998 acquisition is incorporated into the accounts.* **2.** to form a registered company ○ *an incorporated company* ○ *J. Doe Incorporated* ○ *a company incorporated in the U.S.*

incorporation /ɪnˌkɔːpəˈreɪʃ(ə)n/ *noun* an act of incorporating a company

incorrect /ˌɪnkəˈrekt/ *adjective* wrong ○ *The minutes of the meeting were incorrect and had to be changed.*

Incoterms /ˈɪŋkəʊtɜːmz/ *noun* a standard definition, by the International Chamber of Commerce, of terms such as "FOB" or "CIF" which are used in international trade

increase *noun* /ˈɪnkriːs/ **1.** an act of becoming larger ○ *There have been several increases in tax* or *tax increases in the last few years.* ○ *There is an automatic 5% increase in price* or *price increase on January 1st.* ○ *Profits showed a 10% increase* or *an increase of 10% on last year.* □ **increase in the cost of living** a rise in the annual cost of living **2.** a higher salary ○ *increase in pay* or *pay increase* ○ *The gov-*

ernment hopes to hold salary increases to 3%. □ **she had two increases last year** her salary went up twice **3.** □ **on the increase** growing larger, becoming more frequent ○ *Stealing in stores is on the increase.* ■ *verb* /ɪn'kriːs/ **1.** to grow bigger or higher ○ *Profits have increased faster than the increase in the rate of inflation.* ○ *Exports to Africa have increased by more than 25%.* ○ *The price of oil has increased twice in the past week.* □ **to increase in price** to cost more □ **to increase in size** *or* **value** to become larger or more valuable **2.** to make something bigger or higher □ **the company increased her salary to $50,000** the company gave her a raise in salary to $50,000

"…turnover has the potential to be increased to over 1 million dollars with energetic management and very little capital" [*Australian Financial Review*]

"…competition is steadily increasing and could affect profit margins as the company tries to retain its market share" [*Citizen (Ottawa)*]

increasing /ɪn'kriːsɪŋ/ *adjective* which is growing bigger ○ *increasing profits* ○ *The company has an increasing share of the market.*

increasingly /ɪn'kriːsɪŋli/ *adverb* more and more ○ *The company has to depend increasingly on the export market.*

increment /'ɪŋkrɪmənt/ *noun* a regular automatic increase in salary ○ *an annual increment* □ **salary which rises in annual increments of $1000** each year the salary is increased by $1000

incremental /ˌɪŋkrɪ'ment(ə)l/ *adjective* rising automatically in stages

incremental cost /ˌɪŋkrɪment(ə)l 'kɒst/ *noun* the cost of making extra units above the number already planned. This may then include further fixed costs.

incremental increase /ˌɪŋkrɪment(ə)l 'ɪnkriːs/ *noun* an increase in salary according to an agreed annual increment

incrementalism /ˌɪŋkrɪ'mentəlɪz(ə)m/ *noun* the philosophy or practice of making improvements by small and gradual steps. The is often used collectively term for the many initiatives of the 1980s and 1990s, e.g., total quality management, continuous improvement, and benchmarking, that took a small-step ap-

proach to improving quality and productivity and reducing costs.

incremental scale /ˌɪŋkrɪment(ə)l 'skeɪl/ *noun* a salary scale with regular annual salary increases

incur /ɪn'kɜːr/ *verb* to make yourself liable to something □ **to incur the risk of a penalty** to make it possible that you risk paying a penalty □ **the company has incurred heavy costs to implement the expansion program** the company has had to pay large sums of money

"…the company blames fiercely competitive market conditions in Europe for a £14m operating loss last year, incurred despite a record turnover" [*Financial Times*]

indebted /ɪn'detɪd/ *adjective* owing money to someone ○ *to be indebted to a property company*

indecisive /ˌɪndɪ'saɪsɪv/ *adjective* not able to make up one's mind or to decide on something important ○ *He is too indecisive to be a good manager.*

indemnification /ɪndemnɪfɪ'keɪʃən/ *noun* payment for damage

indemnify /ɪn'demnɪfaɪ/ *verb* to pay for damage ○ *to indemnify someone for a loss*

indemnity /ɪn'demnəti/ *noun* **1.** a guarantee of payment after a loss ○ *She had to pay an indemnity of $100.* **2.** compensation paid after a loss

indent *noun* /'ɪndent/ **1.** an order placed by an importer for goods from overseas ○ *They put in an indent for a new stock of soap.* **2.** a line of typing which starts several spaces from the left-hand margin ■ *verb* /ɪn'dent/ **1.** □ **to indent for something** to put in an order for something ○ *The department has indented for a new computer.* **2.** to start a line of typing several spaces from the left-hand margin ○ *Indent the first line three spaces.*

indenture /ɪn'dentʃər/ *verb* to contract with an apprentice who will work for some years to learn a trade ○ *He was indentured to a builder.*

indentures /ɪn'dentʃəz/ *plural noun* a contract by which an apprentice works for a master for some years to learn a trade

independent /ˌɪndɪ'pendənt/ *adjective* not under the control or authority of anyone else

independent company /ˌɪndɪpendənt 'kʌmp(ə)ni/ *noun* a company which is not controlled by another company

independents /ˌɪndɪˈpendənts/ *plural noun* stores or companies which are owned by private individuals or families

independent trader /ˌɪndɪpendənt ˈtreɪdər/, **independent store** /ˌɪndɪpendənt ˈstɔr/ *noun* a store which is owned by an individual proprietor, not by a chain

in-depth study /ˌɪn depθ ˈstʌdi/ *noun* a thorough painstaking study

index /ˈɪndeks/ *noun* **1.** a list of items classified into groups or put in alphabetical order **2.** a regular statistical report which shows rises and falls in prices, values, or levels **3.** a figure based on the current market price of stocks on a stock exchange ■ *verb* to link a payment to an index ○ *salaries indexed to the cost of living*

indexation /ˌɪndekˈseɪʃ(ə)n/ *noun* the linking of something to an index

indexation of wage increases /ˌɪndekseɪʃ(ə)n əv ˈweɪdʒ ˌɪnkrisɪz/ *noun* the linking of wage increases to the percentage rise in the cost of living

index card /ˈɪndeks kɑrd/ *noun* a card used to make a card catalog

indexed portfolio /ˌɪndekst pɔrt ˈfoʊlioʊ/ *noun* a portfolio of stocks in all the companies which form the basis of a stock exchange index

index fund /ˈɪndeks fʌnd/ *noun* an investment fund consisting of stocks in all the companies which are used to calculate a Stock Exchange index (NOTE: The plural is **indexes** or **indices**.)

indexing /ˈɪndeksɪŋ/ *noun* a method of showing changes in a value over time by starting with a simple base point such as 100, which then serves as a reference point for future years ○ *Indexing is used to show the rise in the cost of living over a ten-year period.*

index letter /ˈɪndeks ˌletər/ *noun* a letter of an item in an index

index-linked /ˌɪndeks ˈlɪŋkt/ *adjective* rising automatically by the percentage increase in the cost of living ○ *index-linked government bonds* ○ *Inflation did not affect her as she has an index-linked pension.*

index number /ˈɪndeks ˌnʌmbər/ *noun* **1.** a number of something in an index

2. a number showing the percentage rise of something over a period

indicate /ˈɪndɪkeɪt/ *verb* to show something ○ *The latest figures indicate a fall in the inflation rate.* ○ *Our sales for last year indicate a move from the home market to exports.*

indicator /ˈɪndɪkeɪtər/ *noun* something which indicates

indirect /ˌɪndaɪˈrekt/ *adjective* not direct

indirect costs /ˌɪndaɪrekt ˈkɑsts/, **indirect expenses** /ˌɪndaɪrekt ɪkˈspensɪz/ *plural noun* costs which are not directly related to the making of a product (such as cleaning, rent or administration)

indirect discrimination /ˌɪndaɪrekt ˌsekjuəl dɪsˌkrɪmɪˈneɪʃ(ə)n/ *noun* discrimination that takes place when, although people seem to be being treated equally, there is actually some special condition attached to getting a job, which rules out some of the people who are qualified to apply for it and which cannot be justified under anti-discrimination laws

indirect labor costs /ˌɪndaɪrekt ˈleɪbər ˌkɑsts/ *plural noun* the cost of paying employees not directly involved in making a product such as cleaners or cafeteria staff. Such costs cannot be allocated to a cost center.

indirect loss /ˌɪndaɪrekt ˈlɔs/ *noun* same as **consequential loss**

indirect tax /ˌɪndaɪrekt ˈtæks/ *noun* a tax such as sales tax paid to someone who then pays it to the government

indirect taxation /ˌɪndaɪrekt tæk ˈseɪʃ(ə)n/ *noun* taxes which are not paid direct to the government, e.g., sales tax ○ *The government raises more money by indirect taxation than by direct.*

individual /ˌɪndɪˈvɪdʒuəl/ *noun* one person ○ *a savings plan tailored to the requirements of the private individual* ■ *adjective* single or belonging to one person ○ *a pension plan designed to meet each person's individual requirements* ○ *We sell individual portions of ice cream.*

Individual Retirement Account /ˌɪndɪvɪdʒuəl rɪˈtaɪrmənt əˌkaʊnt/ *noun* a tax-deferred pension plan, that allows individuals to make contributions to a personal retirement fund. Abbreviation **IRA**

inducement /ɪnˈdusmənt/ *noun* something which helps to persuade someone to do something ○ *They offered her a company car as an inducement to stay.*

induction /ɪnˈdʌkʃən/ *noun* an introduction to a new organization or a new job

induction course /ɪnˈdʌkʃən kɔːrs/, **induction training** /ɪnˈdʌkʃən ˌtreɪnɪŋ/ *noun* a program intended to help a person entering an organization or starting a new job ○ *The company is organizing a two-day induction course for new employees.* ○ *The induction course spelled out the main objectives and procedures of the organization.*

industrial /ɪnˈdʌstriəl/ *adjective* referring to manufacturing work □ **to take industrial action** to go on strike or go-slow

industrial accident /ɪnˌdʌstriəl ˈæksɪd(ə)nt/ *noun* an accident which takes place at work

industrial arbitration tribunal /ɪnˌdʌstriəl ˌɑːrbɪˈtreɪʃ(ə)n traɪˌbjuːn(ə)l/ *noun* a court which decides in industrial disputes

industrial capacity /ɪnˌdʌstriəl kəˈpæsəti/ *noun* the amount of work which can be done in a factory or several factories

industrial center /ɪnˈdʌstriəl ˌsentər/ *noun* a large town with many industries

industrial consumption /ɪnˌdʌstriəl kənˈsʌmpʃən/ *noun* consumption of something by an industry

industrial court /ɪnˌdʌstriəl ˈkɔːrt/ *noun* a court which can decide in industrial disputes if both parties agree to ask it to judge between them

industrial design /ɪnˌdʌstriəl dɪˈzaɪn/ *noun* the design of products made by machines such as cars and refrigerators

industrial development /ɪnˌdʌstriəl dɪˈveləpmənt/ *noun* the planning and building of new industries in special areas

industrial dispute /ɪnˌdʌstriəl dɪˈspjuːt/ *noun* an argument between management and employees

industrial espionage /ɪnˌdʌstriəl ˈespiənɑːrʒ/ *noun* the practice of trying to find out the secrets of a competitor's work or products, usually by illegal means

industrial estate /ɪnˈdʌstriəl ɪˌsteɪt/ *noun U.K.* same as **industrial park**

industrial expansion /ɪnˌdʌstriəl ɪkˈspænʃən/ *noun* the growth of industries in a country or a region

industrial injury /ɪnˌdʌstriəl ˈɪndʒəri/ *noun* an injury to an employee that occurs in the workplace

industrialist /ɪnˈdʌstriəlɪst/ *noun* an owner or director of a factory

industrialization /ɪnˌdʌstriəlaɪˈzeɪʃ(ə)n/ *noun* the process of change by which an economy becomes based on industrial production rather than on agriculture

industrialize /ɪnˈdʌstriəˌlaɪz/ *verb* to set up industries in a country which had none before

industrialized society /ɪnˌdʌstriəlaɪzd səˈsaɪəti/ *noun* a country which has many industries

industrial park /ɪnˈdʌstriəl pɑːrk/ *noun* an area of land near a town where factories and warehouses are concentrated in accordance with local planning regulations (NOTE: The U.K. term is **industrial estate**)

industrial practices /ɪnˌdʌstriəl ˈpræktɪsɪz/ *plural noun* ways of managing or working in business, industry or trade (NOTE: also called **trade practices**)

industrial processes /ɪnˌdʌstriəl ˈprɑːsesɪz/ *plural noun* the various stages involved in manufacturing products in factories

industrial relations /ɪnˌdʌstriəl rɪˈleɪʃ(ə)nz/ *plural noun* relations between management and employees ○ *The company has a history of bad labor relations.*

"Britain's industrial relations climate is changing" [*Personnel Today*]

industrial revenue bond /ɪnˌdʌstriəl ˈrevənjuː ˌbɑːnd/ *noun* a bond issued by a state or local government to finance industrial or commercial projects for the public good

industrials /ɪnˈdʌstriəlz/ *plural noun* stock in manufacturing companies

industrial training /ɪnˌdʌstriəl ˈtreɪnɪŋ/ *noun* the training of new employees to work in an industry

industrial tribunal /ɪnˌdʌstriəl traɪˈbjuːn(ə)l/ *noun* a court which can decide in disputes about employment

"ACAS has a legal obligation to try and solve industrial grievances before they reach industrial tribunals" [*Personnel Today*]

industry /ˈɪndəstri/ *noun* **1.** all factories, companies, or processes involved in the manufacturing of products ○ *All sectors of industry have shown rises in output.* **2.** a group of companies making the same type of product or offering the same type of service ○ *the aircraft industry* ○ *the food-processing industry* ○ *the petroleum industry* ○ *the advertising industry*

industry rules /ˈɪndəstri rulz/ *plural noun* the unwritten rules that govern the ways in which organizations within a particular industry relate to and do business with one another

inefficiency /ˌɪnɪˈfɪʃ(ə)nsi/ *noun* the fact of not being able to work quickly and correctly ○ *The report criticized the inefficiency of the sales staff.*

inefficient /ˌɪnɪˈfɪʃ(ə)nt/ *adjective* not doing a job well or unable to work efficiently and correctly ○ *an inefficient sales director* ○ *Inefficient workers waste raw materials and fail to complete tasks on schedule.*

inelastic demand /ɪnɪˌlæstɪk dɪˈmænd/ *noun* demand which experiences a comparatively small percentage change in response to a percentage change in price ○ *Where a product is a household necessity, you almost always find an inelastic demand.*

inelastic supply /ɪnɪˌlæstɪk səˈplaɪ/ *noun* supply which experiences a comparatively small percentage change in response to a percentage change in price

ineligible /ɪnˈelɪdʒɪb(ə)l/ *adjective* not eligible

ineligible bill /ɪnˌelɪdʒəb(ə)l ˈbɪl/ *noun* a bill of exchange which cannot be discounted by a central bank

inertia selling /ɪˈnɜrʃə ˌselɪŋ/ *noun* a method of selling items by sending them when they have not been ordered and assuming that if the items are not returned, the person who has received them is willing to buy them

inexpensive /ˌɪnɪkˈspensɪv/ *adjective* cheap, not expensive

inexpensively /ɪnɪkˈspensɪvli/ *adverb* without spending much money

inferior /ɪnˈfɪriər/ *adjective* not as good as others ○ *products of inferior quality*

inflate /ɪnˈfleɪt/ *verb* **1.** □ **to inflate prices** to increase prices without any reason **2.** □ **to inflate the economy** to make the economy more active by increasing the money supply

inflated /ɪnˈfleɪtɪd/ *adjective* **1.** □ **inflated prices** prices which are increased without any reason ○ *Tourists don't want to pay inflated London prices.* **2.** □ **inflated currency** currency which is too high in relation to other currencies

inflation /ɪnˈfleɪʃ(ə)n/ *noun* a greater increase in the supply of money or credit than in the production of goods and services, resulting in higher prices and a fall in the purchasing power of money ○ *to take measures to reduce inflation* ○ *High interest rates tend to increase inflation.* □ **we have 3% inflation** *or* **inflation is running at 3%** prices are 3% higher than at the same time last year

inflationary /ɪnˈfleɪʃ(ə)n(ə)ri/ *adjective* tending to increase inflation ○ *inflationary trends in the economy* □ **the economy is in an inflationary spiral** the economy is in a situation where price increases encourage higher wage demands which in turn make prices rise

inflation-proof /ɪnˈfleɪʃ(ə)n pruf/ *adjective* referring to a pension, etc. which is index-linked, so that its value is preserved in times of inflation

inflow /ˈɪnfloʊ/ *noun* the act of coming in or being brought in □ **inflow of capital into the country** capital which is coming into a country in order to be invested

"…the dollar is strong because of capital inflows rather than weak because of the trade deficit" [*Duns Business Month*]

influence /ˈɪnfluəns/ *noun* an effect which is had on someone or something ○ *The price of oil has a marked influence on the price of manufactured goods.* ○ *We are suffering from the influence of a high exchange rate.* ■ *verb* to have an effect on someone or something ○ *The board was influenced in its decision by the memo from the managers.* ○ *The price of oil has influenced the price of manufactured goods.* ○ *High inflation is influencing our profitability.*

influx /ˈɪnflʌks/ *noun* an inflow, especially one where people or things come in in large quantities ○ *an influx of foreign currency into the country* ○ *an influx of cheap labor into the cities*

"…the retail sector will also benefit from the expected influx of tourists" [*Australian Financial Review*]

infomediary /ˈɪnfoʊˌmidiəri/ *noun* a business or website that collects information about customers for use by other companies (NOTE: The plural is **infomediaries**.)

"BioInformatics' position as an infomediary is facilitating the firm's expansion into markets adjacent to its current niche." [*Forbes*]

inform /ɪnˈfɔrm/ *verb* to tell someone officially ○ *I regret to inform you that your bid was not acceptable.* ○ *We are pleased to inform you that you have been selected for interview.* ○ *We have been informed by the Department that new regulations are coming into force.*

information /ˌɪnfərˈmeɪʃ(ə)n/ *noun* details which explain something ○ *to disclose a piece of information* ○ *to answer a request for information* ○ *Please send me information on* or *about vacations in the Southwest.* ○ *Have you any information on* or *about deposit accounts?* ○ *I enclose this leaflet for your information.* ○ *For further information, please write to Department 27.* □ **disclosure of confidential information** the act of telling someone information which should be secret

information and communications technologies /ˌɪnfərmeɪʃ(ə)n ən kə ˌmjunɪˈkeɪʃ(ə)nz tekˌnɑlədʒiz/ *plural noun* computer and telecommunications technologies considered together (NOTE: It is the coming together of information and communications technology that has made possible such things as the Internet, videoconferencing, groupware, intranets, and third-generation cell phones.)

information architecture /ˌɪnfərmeɪʃ(ə)n ˈɑrkɪtektʃər/ *noun* the methods used in designing the navigation, search and content layout for a website

information bureau /ˌɪnfərˈmeɪʃ(ə)n ˌbjʊroʊ/ *noun* an office which gives information to tourists or visitors

information management /ˌɪnfərmeɪʃ(ə)n ˈmænɪdʒmənt/ *noun* the task of controlling information and the flow of information within an organization, which involves acquiring, recording, organizing, storing, distributing, and retrieving it (NOTE: Good information management has been described as getting

the right information to the right person in the right format at the right time.)

information office /ˌɪnfərˈmeɪʃ(ə)n ˌɔfɪs/ *noun* an office which gives information to tourists or visitors

information officer /ˌɪnfərˈmeɪʃ(ə)n ˌɔfɪsər/ *noun* **1.** a person whose job is to give information about a company, an organization or a government department to the public **2.** a person whose job is to give information to other departments in the same organization

information overload /ˌɪnfərmeɪʃ(ə)n ˈoʊvərloʊd/ *noun* the act of burdening someone with too much information

information pack /ˌɪnfərˈmeɪʃ(ə)n pæk/ *noun* a folder containing information about a product, tourist attraction, etc. ○ *the conference agenda* or *the agenda of the conference is in the information pack given to delegates*

information retrieval /ˌɪnfərmeɪʃ(ə)n rɪˈtriv(ə)l/ *noun* the finding of stored data in a computer

information technology /ˌɪnfərmeɪʃ(ə)n tekˈnɑlədʒi/ *noun* working with data stored on computers (IT). Abbreviation **IT**

information technology outsourcing /ˌɪnfəmeɪʃ(ə)n tekˌnɑlədʒi ˈaʊtsɔrsɪŋ/ *noun* the practice of obtaining the services of information technology specialists from other companies rather than employing staff to provide IT services

infrastructure /ˈɪnfrəˌstrʌktʃər/ *noun* **1.** basic structure. Also called **social overhead capital 2.** basic services □ **a country's infrastructure** the road and rail systems of a country

infringe /ɪnˈfrɪndʒ/ *verb* to break a law or a right □ **to infringe a copyright** to copy a copyright text illegally □ **to infringe a patent** to make a product which works in the same way as a patented product and not pay a royalty to the patent holder

infringement /ɪnˈfrɪndʒmənt/ *noun* an act of breaking a law or a rule ○ *infringement of the company's rules*

infringement of copyright /ɪn ˌfrɪndʒmənt əv ˈkɑpɪraɪt/ *noun* the illegal copying of a work which is in copyright

infringement of patent /ɪn ˌfrɪndʒmənt əv ˈpeɪtənt/ *noun* an act of illegally using, making or selling an invention which is patented, without the permission of the patent holder

ingot /ˈɪŋɡət/ *noun* a bar of gold or silver

inherent vice /ɪnˌhɪrənt ˈvaɪs/ *noun* the tendency of some goods to spoil during transportation ○ *Inherent vice discouraged us from importing tropical fruit.*

inherit /ɪnˈherɪt/ *verb* to get something from a person who has died ○ *When her father died she inherited the store.* ○ *He inherited $10,000 from his grandfather.*

inheritance /ɪnˈherɪt(ə)ns/ *noun* property which is received from a dead person

inheritance tax /ɪnˈherɪt(ə)ns tæks/ *noun* tax paid on property received by inheritance or legal succession. Also called **death tax**

in-house /ˌɪn ˈhaʊs/ *adverb, adjective* done by someone employed by a company on their premises, not by an outside contractor ○ *the in-house staff* ○ *We do all our data processing in-house.*

in-house training /ˌɪn haʊs ˈtreɪnɪŋ/ *noun* training given to employees at their place of work

in in care of /ˌɪn ˈker ˌɒv/ *phrase* (*in an address*) words to show that the person is living at the address, but only as a visitor ○ *Herr Schmidt, in care of Mr W. Brown*

initial /ɪˈnɪʃ(ə)l/ *adjective* first or starting ○ *The initial response to the TV advertising has been very good.* ■ *verb* to write your initials on a document to show you have read it and approved ○ *to initial an amendment to a contract* ○ *Please initial the agreement at the place marked with an X.*

initial capital /ɪˌnɪʃ(ə)l ˈkæpɪt(ə)l/ *noun* capital which is used to start a business

initial public offering /ɪˌnɪʃ(ə)l ˌpʌblɪk ˈɒf(ə)rɪŋ/ *noun* the process of offering stock in a corporation for sale to the public for the first time. Abbreviation **IPO** (NOTE: The U.K. term is **offer for sale**.)

initials /ɪˈnɪʃ(ə)lz/ *plural noun* a first letters of the words in a name ○ *What do the initials IMF stand for?* ○ *The chairman wrote his initials by each alteration in the contract he was signing.*

initial sales /ɪˌnɪʃ(ə)l ˈseɪlz/ *plural noun* the first sales of a new product

initial yield /ɪˌnɪʃ(ə)l ˈjild/ *noun* the estimated yield of an investment fund at the time when it is launched

initiate /ɪˈnɪʃieɪt/ *verb* to start ○ *to initiate discussions*

initiative /ɪˈnɪʃətɪv/ *noun* the decision to start something □ **to take the initiative** to decide to do something

inject /ɪnˈdʒekt/ *verb* □ **to inject capital into a business** to put money into a business

injection /ɪnˈdʒekʃən/ *noun* □ **a capital injection of $100,000** *or* **an injection of $100,000 capital** putting $100,000 into an existing business

injunction /ɪnˈdʒʌŋkʃ(ə)n/ *noun* a court order telling someone not to do something ○ *He got an injunction preventing the company from selling his car.* ○ *The company applied for an injunction to stop their competition from marketing a similar product.*

injure /ˈɪndʒə/ *verb* to hurt someone ○ *Two workers were injured in the fire.*

injured party /ˌɪndʒərd ˈpɑrti/ *noun* a party in a court case which has been harmed by another party

injury /ˈɪndʒəri/ *noun* hurt caused to a person

injury benefit /ˈɪndʒəri ˌbenəfɪt/ *noun* money paid to an employee who has been hurt at work

inkjet printer /ˌɪŋkdʒet ˈprɪntər/ *noun* a printer which prints by sending a jet of ink onto the paper to form the characters (they give very good results, but cannot be used for multipart stationery)

inland /ˈɪnlənd/ *adjective* inside a country

inland carrier /ˌɪnlənd ˈkæriər/ *noun* company which transports goods from a port to a destination inside the country

inland freight charges /ˌɪnlənd ˈfreɪt ˌtʃɑrdʒɪz/ *plural noun* charges for carrying goods from one part of the country to another

inland port /ˌɪnlənd ˈpɔrt/ *noun* a port on a river or canal

inland postage /ˌɪnlənd ˈpoʊstɪdʒ/ *noun* postage for a letter to another part of the same country

innovate /'ɪnouveɪt/ *verb* to bring in new ideas or new methods

innovation /,ɪnə'veɪʃ(ə)n/ *noun* the development of new products or new ways of selling

innovative /'ɪnəveɪtɪv/ *adjective* referring to a person or thing which is new and makes changes

innovator /'ɪnəveɪtər/ *noun* **1.** a person or company that brings in new ideas and methods **2.** a person who buys a new product first

input /'ɪnpʊt/ *noun* what is contributed to an activity or project ○ *The amount of staff input in the company magazine is small.* □ **input of information, computer input** data fed into a computer ■ *verb* □ **to input information** to put data into a computer

input lead /'ɪnpʊt liːd/ *noun* a lead for connecting the electric current to a machine

inputs /'ɪnpʊts/ *plural noun* goods or services bought by a company and which may be liable to sales tax

inquire /ɪn'kwaɪə/ *verb* to ask questions about something ○ *He inquired if anything was wrong.* ○ *She inquired about the mortgage rate.* □ **"inquire within"** ask for more details inside the office or store

inquire into *phrasal verb* to investigate or try to find out about something ○ *We are inquiring into the background of the new supplier.*

inquiry /ɪn'kwaɪri/ *noun* a request for information about a product

inquiry office /ɪn'kwaɪri ,ɒfɪs/ *noun* an office which members of the public can go to to have their questions answered

inquorate /ɪn'kwɔːreɪt/ *adjective* without a quorum

COMMENT: If there is a quorum at a meeting, the meeting is said to be "quorate"; if there aren't enough people present to make a quorum, the meeting is "inquorate".

insert *noun* /'ɪnsɜːt/ a form or leaflet which is put inside something, usually a magazine or newspaper □ **an insert in a magazine mailing, a magazine insert** an advertising sheet put into a magazine when it is mailed ■ *verb* /ɪn'sɜːt/ to put something in ○ *to insert a clause into a contract* ○ *to insert a publicity piece into a magazine mailing*

in-service training /,ɪn ,sɜːvɪs 'treɪnɪŋ/ *noun* the training of staff while they are employed by an organization ○ *Management trainees will draw full salaries during the period of their in-service training.* Abbreviation **INSET**

inside /ɪn'saɪd/ *adjective, adverb* in, especially in a company's office or building ○ *We do all our design work inside.* ■ *preposition* in ○ *There was nothing inside the container.* ○ *We have a contact inside our competition's production department who gives us very useful information.*

inside director /,ɪnsaɪd daɪ'rektər/ *noun* a director who works full-time in a corporation, as opposed to an outside director

inside information /,ɪnsaɪd ,ɪnfə'meɪʃ(ə)n/ *noun* information which is passed from people working in a company to people outside, and which can be valuable to investors in the company

insider /ɪn'saɪdər/ *noun* a person who works in an organization and therefore knows its secrets

insider trading /ɪn,saɪdər 'dɪlɪŋ/, **insider buying** /ɪn,saɪdə 'treɪdɪŋ/, **insider dealing** *noun* the illegal buying or selling of stocks by staff of a company or other persons who have secret information about the company's plans

inside worker /'ɪnsaɪd ,wɜːkər/ *noun* an employee who works in an office or factory

insolvency /ɪn'sɒlvənsi/ *noun* the fact of not being able to pay debts. Opposite **solvency** □ **he was in a state of insolvency** he could not pay his debts

"…hundreds of thrifts found themselves on the brink of insolvency after a deregulation programme prompted them to enter dangerous financial waters" [*Times*]

insolvent /ɪn'sɒlvənt/ *adjective* not able to pay debts ○ *The company was declared insolvent.* (NOTE: see note at **insolvency**) □ **he was declared insolvent** he was officially stated to be insolvent

COMMENT: A company is insolvent when its liabilities are higher than its assets; if this happens it must cease operations.

inspect /ɪn'spekt/ *verb* to examine in detail ○ *to inspect a machine* or *an installation* ○ *The gas board is sending an engineer to inspect the central heating system.*

○ *Officials from the DTI have come to inspect the accounts.* □ **to inspect products for defects** to look at products in detail to see if they have any defects

inspection /ɪnˈspekʃ(ə)n/ *noun* the close examination of something ○ *to make an inspection* or *to carry out an inspection of a machine* or *an installation* ○ *the inspection of a product for defects* □ **to issue an inspection order** to order an official inspection

inspection stamp /ɪnˈspekʃən stæmp/ *noun* a stamp placed on something to show it has been inspected

inspector /ɪnˈspektər/ *noun* an official who inspects ○ *The inspectors will soon be round to make sure the building is safe.*

inspectorate /ɪnˈspekt(ə)rət/ *noun* all inspectors

inspector of factories /ɪnˌspektər əv ˈfækt(ə)riz/ *noun* a government official who inspects factories to see if they are safely run

inspector of weights and measures /ɪnˌspektər əv ˌweɪts ən ˈmeʒərz/ *noun* a government official who inspects weighing machines and goods sold in stores to see if the quantities and weights are correct

inst *abbreviation* instant □ **your letter of the 6th inst** your letter of the 6th of this month

instability /ˌɪnstəˈbɪləti/ *noun* the state of being unstable or moving up and down □ **a period of instability in the money markets** a period when currencies fluctuate rapidly

install /ɪnˈstɔl/ *verb* **1.** to put a machine into an office or into a factory ○ *We are planning to install the new machinery over the weekend.* ○ *They must install a new data processing system because the old one cannot cope with the mass of work involved.* **2.** to set up a piece of machinery or equipment, e.g., a new computer system, so that it can be used **3.** to configure a new computer program to the existing system requirements

installation /ˌɪnstəˈleɪʃ(ə)n/ *noun* **1.** the act of putting new machines into an office or a factory ○ *to supervise the installation of new equipment* **2.** machines, equipment and buildings ○ *Harbor installations were picketed by striking longshoremen.* ○ *The fire seriously damaged the oil installations.* **3.** the act of setting up a piece of equipment

installment /ɪnˈstɔlmənt/ *noun* a part of a payment which is paid regularly until the total amount is paid ○ *The first installment is payable on signature of the agreement.* (NOTE: The U.K. spelling is **instalment**.) □ **the final installment is now due** the last of a series of payments should be paid now □ **to pay $25 down and monthly installments of $20** to pay a first payment of $25 and the rest in payments of $20 each month □ **to miss an installment** not to pay an installment at the right time

installment plan /ɪnˈstɔlmənt plæn/, **installment sales** /ɪnˈstɔlmənt seɪlz/, **installment buying** /ɪnˌstɔlmənt ˈbaɪɪŋ/, **installment credit** *noun* a system of buying something by paying a sum regularly each month ○ *to buy a car on the installment plan* (NOTE: The U.K. term is **hire purchase**.)

instance /ˈɪnstəns/ *noun* a particular example or case ○ *In this instance we will overlook the delay.*

instant /ˈɪnstənt/ *adjective* **1.** immediately available ○ *Instant credit is available to checking account holders.* **2.** this month □ **our letter of the 6th instant** our letter of the 6th of this current month

instant access account /ˌɪnstənt ˈækses əˌkaʊnt/ *noun* a deposit account which pays interest and from which you can withdraw money immediately without penalty

instant messaging /ˌɪnstənt ˈmesɪdʒɪŋ/ *noun* a system that gives people on the Internet the ability to communicate in real time

institute /ˈɪnstɪtjut/ *noun* a society or organization which represents a particular profession or activity ○ *the Institute of Chartered Accountants* ○ *the Chartered Institute of Personnel and Development* ■ *verb* **1.** to start a new custom or procedure ○ *to institute a new staff payment scheme* **2.** to start ○ *to institute proceedings against someone*

institution /ˌɪnstɪˈtjuʃ(ə)n/ *noun* an organization or society set up for a particular purpose. ◊ **financial institution**

institutional /ˌɪnstɪˈtjuʃ(ə)n(ə)l/ *adjective* relating to an institution, especially a financial institution

institutional buying /ˌɪnstɪtjuʃ(ə)n(ə)l ˈbaɪɪŋ/ *noun* the buying of stocks by financial institutions

institutional buyout /ˌɪnstɪtjuʃ(ə)n(ə)l ˈbaɪaʊt/ *noun* a takeover of a company by a financial institution, which backs a group of managers who will run it. Abbreviation **IBO**

institutional investor /ˌɪnstɪtuʃ(ə)n(ə)l ɪnˈvestər/ *noun* **1.** a financial institution which invests money in securities **2.** an organization (such as a pension fund or insurance company) with large sums of money to invest

institutional selling /ˌɪnstɪˌtjuʃ(ə)n(ə)l ˈselɪŋ/ *noun* the selling of stocks by financial institutions

Institutional Shareholder Services, Inc. /ˌɪnstɪtjuʃ(ə)n(ə)l ˈʃerhoʊldər ˌsɜrvɪsɪz/ *noun* a company based in the U.S. that provides proxy voting services and corporate governance services worldwide. Abbreviation **ISS**

instruct /ɪnˈstrʌkt/ *verb* **1.** to give an order to someone □ **to instruct someone to do something** to tell someone officially to do something ○ *He instructed the credit controller to take action.* ○ *The foreman will instruct the men to stop working.* **2.** □ **to instruct a solicitor** to give information to a solicitor and to ask him to start legal proceedings on your behalf

instruction /ɪnˈstrʌkʃən/ *noun* an order which tells what should be done or how something is to be used ○ *She gave instructions to his stockbroker to sell the stock immediately.* □ **to await instructions** to wait for someone to tell you what to do □ **to issue instructions** to tell people what to do □ **in accordance with, according to instructions** as the instructions show

instructor /ɪnˈstrʌktə/ *noun* a person who shows how something is to be done ○ *Two new instructors are needed for the training courses.* ○ *Distance learning can be carried out without instructors.*

instrument /ˈɪnstrʊmənt/ *noun* **1.** a tool or piece of equipment ○ *The technician brought instruments to measure the output of electricity.* **2.** a legal document

insufficient funds /ˌɪnsəfɪʃ(ə)nt ˈfʌndz/ *noun* same as **non-sufficient funds**

insurable /ɪnˈʃʊrəb(ə)l/ *adjective* possible to insure

insurance /ɪnˈʃʊrəns/ *noun* an agreement that in return for regular payments called "premiums", a company will pay compensation for loss, damage, injury or death ○ *to take out insurance* ○ *Repairs will be paid for by the insurance.* □ **to take out insurance against fire** to pay a premium, so that, if a fire happens, compensation will be paid □ **the damage is covered by insurance** the insurance company will pay for the damage □ **to pay the insurance on a car** to pay premiums to insure a car

insurance adjuster /ˈlɔs əˌdʒʌstər/ *noun* a person who calculates how much insurance should be paid on a claim

insurance agent /ɪnˈʃʊrəns ˌeɪdʒənt/, **insurance broker** /ɪnˈʃʊrəns ˌbroʊkər/ *noun* a person who arranges insurance for clients

insurance certificate /ɪnˈʃʊrəns sərˌtɪfɪkət/ *noun* a document from an insurance company showing that an insurance policy has been issued

insurance claim /ɪnˈʃʊrəns kleɪm/ *noun* a request to an insurance company to pay compensation for damage or loss

insurance company /ɪnˈʃʊrəns ˌkʌmp(ə)ni/ *noun* a company whose business is insurance

insurance contract /ɪnˈʃʊrəns ˌkɑntrækt/ *noun* an agreement by an insurance company to insure

insurance cover /ɪnˈʃʊrəns ˌkʌvər/ *noun* protection guaranteed by an insurance policy ○ *Do you have cover against theft?*

insurance policy /ɪnˈʃʊrəns ˌpɑlɪsi/ *noun* a document which shows the conditions of an insurance contract

insurance premium /ɪnˈʃʊrəns ˌprimiəm/ *noun* an annual payment made by a person or a company to an insurance company

insurance rates /ɪnˈʃʊrəns reɪts/ *plural noun* the amount of premium which has to be paid per $1000 of insurance

insurance salesman /ɪnˈʃʊrəns ˌseɪlzmən/ *noun* a person who encourages clients to take out insurance policies

insure /ɪnˈʃʊə/ *verb* to have a contract with a company whereby, if regular small payments are made, the company will pay compensation for loss, damage, injury or death ○ *to insure a house against fire* ○ *to insure someone's life* ○ *to insure baggage against loss* ○ *to insure against loss of earnings* ○ *She was insured for $100,000.*

□ **the sum insured** the largest amount of money that an insurer will pay under an insurance policy

insurer /ɪnˈʃʊrər/ *noun* a company which insures (NOTE: For life insurance, U.K. English prefers to use **assurer**.)

intangible /ɪnˈtændʒɪb(ə)l/ *adjective* not possible to touch

intangible assets /ɪnˌtændʒɪb(ə)l ˈæsets/, **intangibles** /ɪnˈtændʒɪb(ə)lz/ *plural noun* assets which have a value, but which cannot be seen, e.g., goodwill, or a patent or a trademark

intangible fixed assets /ɪn ˌtændʒɪb(ə)l fɪkst ˈæsets/ *plural noun* assets which have a value, but which cannot be seen, e.g., goodwill, copyrights, patents or trademarks

integrate /ˈɪntɪɡreɪt/ *verb* to link things together to form one whole group

integration /ˌɪntɪˈɡreɪʃ(ə)n/ *noun* the act of bringing several businesses together under a central control

COMMENT: In a case of horizontal integration, a large supermarket might take over another smaller supermarket chain; on the other hand, if a supermarket takes over a food packaging company the integration would be vertical.

intellectual assets /ˌɪntəlektʃuəl ˈæsets/ *plural noun* the knowledge, experience, and skills possessed by its employees that an organization can use for its own benefit

intellectual property /ɪntɪˌlektjuəl ˈprɑpərti/ *noun* ideas, designs, and inventions, including copyrights, patents, and trademarks, that were created by and legally belong to an individual or an organization (NOTE: Intellectual property is protected by law in most countries, and the World Intellectual Property Organization is responsible for harmonizing the law in different countries and promoting the protection of intellectual property rights.)

intend /ɪnˈtend/ *verb* to plan or to expect to do something ○ *The company intends to open an office in New York next year.* ○ *We*

intend to offer jobs to 250 unemployed young people.

intensive farming /ɪnˌtensɪv ˈfɑrmɪŋ/ *noun* farming small areas of expensive land, using machines and fertilizers to obtain high crops

intent /ɪnˈtent/ *noun* something that someone plans to do

inter- /ɪntər/ *prefix* between □ **inter-company dealings** dealings between two companies in the same group □ **inter-company comparisons** comparing the results of one company with those of another in the same product area

interactive /ˌɪntərˈæktɪv/ *adjective* **1.** allowing the customer and seller to influence the presentation of information or the development of strategies **2.** referring to an online service, software program or television system that allows users to send information or instructions to it

"Last year Hongkong Telecom launched the first commercial interactive television (ITV) service in the world, offering video and music on demand, along with high-speed Internet access, to 70% of the city's homes." [*Economist*]

interactive media /ˌɪntəræktɪv ˈmidiə/ *plural noun* media that allow the customer to interact with the source of the message, receiving information and replying to questions, etc.

interactive voice response /ˌɪntəræktɪv ˈvɔɪs rɪˌspɑns/ *noun* a telephone or Internet system which is activated by the voice of the caller and responds to the caller's queries. Abbreviation **IVR**

inter-bank loan /ˌɪntər bæŋk ˈloʊn/ *noun* a loan from one bank to another

inter-city /ˌɪntər ˈsɪti/ *adjective* between cities ○ *Inter-city train services are often quicker than going by air.*

interest /ˈɪntrəst/ *noun* **1.** special attention ○ *The buyers showed a lot of interest in our new product range.* **2.** payment made by a borrower for the use of money, calculated as a percentage of the capital borrowed □ **high interest, low interest** interest at a high or low percentage **3.** money paid as income on investments or loans ○ *to receive interest at 5%* ○ *the loan pays 5% interest* ○ *deposit which yields or gives or produces or bears 5% interest* ○ *account which earns interest at 10%* or *which earns 10% interest* ○ *The bank pays*

10% interest on deposits. **4.** a part of the ownership of something, e.g., if you invest money in a company you acquire a financial share or interest in it □ **to acquire a substantial interest in the company** to buy a large number of shares in a company □ **to declare an interest** to state in public that you own stock in a company being discussed or that you are related to someone who can benefit from your contacts ■ *verb* to attract someone's attention ○ *She tried to interest several companies in her new invention.* ○ *The company is trying to interest a wide range of customers in its products.* □ **interested in** paying attention to ○ *The managing director is interested only in increasing profitability.*

interest-bearing deposits /ˌɪntrəst ˌberɪŋ dɪ'pɑzɪts/ *plural noun* deposits which produce interest

interest charges /'ɪntrəst ˌtʃɑrdʒɪz/ *plural noun* money paid as interest on a loan

interest coupon /'ɪntrəst ˌkupɑn/ *noun* a slip of paper attached to a government bond certificate which can be cashed to provide the annual interest

interested party /ˌɪntrestɪd 'pɑrti/ *noun* a person or company with a financial interest in a company

interest-free credit /ˌɪntrəst fri 'kredɪt/ *noun* a credit or loan where no interest is paid by the borrower ○ *The company gives its staff interest-free loans.*

interest rate /'ɪntrəst reɪt/ *noun* a figure which shows the percentage of the capital sum borrowed or deposited which is to be paid as interest. Also called **rate of interest**

interface /'ɪntərfeɪs/ *noun* **1.** the link between two different computer systems or pieces of hardware **2.** a point where two groups of people come into contact ■ *verb* to meet and act with ○ *The office PCs interface with the computer at head office.*

interfere /ˌɪntər'fɪr/ *verb* to get involved in or try to change something which is not your concern

interference /ˌɪntər'fɪrəns/ *noun* the act of interfering ○ *The sales department complained of continual interference from the accounts department.*

interfirm co-operation /ˌɪntərfɜrm koʊ ˌɑpəreɪʃ(ə)n/ *noun* co-operation between business organizations to enable them to achieve common goals more efficiently. Interfirm co-operation usually takes the form of a joint venture, strategic alliance or strategic partnering arrangement.

interim /'ɪntərɪm/ *adjective* made, measured or happening in the middle of a period, such as the financial year, and before the final result for the period is available ■ *noun* a statement of interim profits or dividends □ **in the interim** meanwhile, for the time being

"…the company plans to keep its annual dividend unchanged at 7.5 per share, which includes a 3.75 interim payout" [*Financial Times*]

interim dividend /ˌɪntərɪm 'dɪvɪdend/ *noun* a dividend paid at the end of a half-year

interim payment /ˌɪntərɪm 'peɪmənt/ *noun* a payment of part of a dividend

interim report /ˌɪntərɪm rɪ'pɔrt/, **interim statement** /ˌɪntərɪm 'steɪtmənt/ *noun* a report given at the end of a half-year

intermediary /ˌɪntə'midiəri/ *noun* a person who is the link between people or organizations who do not agree or who are negotiating ○ *He refused to act as an intermediary between the two directors.*

COMMENT: Banks, and savings and loans are types of financial intermediaries.

internal /ɪn'tɜrn(ə)l/ *adjective* **1.** inside a company □ **we decided to make an internal appointment** we decided to appoint an existing member of staff to the position, and not bring someone in from outside the company **2.** inside a country or a region

internal audit /ɪnˌtɜrn(ə)l 'ɔdɪt/ *noun* an audit carried out by a department inside the company

internal audit department /ɪnˌtɜrn(ə)l 'ɔdɪt dɪˌpɑrtmənt/ *noun* a department of a company which examines the internal accounting controls of that company

internal auditor /ɪnˌtɜrn(ə)l 'ɔdɪtər/ *noun* a member of staff who audits a company's accounts

internal differentiation analysis /ɪnˌtɜrn(ə)l ˌdɪfərenʃi'eɪʃ(ə)n əˌnæləsɪs/ *noun* analysis of the processes involved in the value chain in order to find out which of them make the product different as far as customers are concerned and so increase its value. By using internal differentiation analysis an organization can focus on improving the most important aspects of the value-creation process to maximize its competitive advantage.

internal flight /ɪn,tɜrn(ə)l 'flaɪt/ *noun* a flight to a town inside the same country

internal growth /ɪn,tɜrn(ə)l 'grouθ/ *noun* the development of a company by growing its existing business with its own finances, as opposed to acquiring other businesses. Also called **organic growth**. Opposite **external growth**

internalization /ɪn,tɜrnəlaɪ'zeɪʃ(ə)n/ *noun* a process by which individuals identify information which is relevant to them personally and so acquire values and norms which allow them to make decisions

internally /ɪn'tɜrn(ə)li/ *adverb* inside a company ○ *The job was advertised internally.* □ **the job was advertised internally** the job was advertised inside the company, but not in a public place such as a newspaper

internal rate of return /ɪn,tɜrn(ə)l reɪt əv rɪ'tɜrn/ *noun* a method used to evaluate a capital project that equates the present value of expected cash flows to the cost of the project

Internal Revenue Service /ɪn ,tɜrn(ə)l 'revənju ,sɜrvɪs/ *noun* in the United States, the branch of the federal government charged with collecting the majority of federal taxes. Abbreviation **IRS**

internal telephone /ɪn,tɜrn(ə)l 'telɪfoʊn/ *noun* a telephone which is linked to other telephones in an office

internal trade /ɪn,tɜrn(ə)l 'treɪd/ *noun* trade between various parts of a country. Opposite **external trade**

international /,ɪntər'næʃ(ə)nəl/ *adjective* working between countries

International Bank for Reconstruction and Development /,ɪntərnæʃ(ə)nəl bæŋk fər ,rɪkənstrʌkʃ(ə)n ən dɪ'veləpmənt/ *noun* the official name of the World Bank. Abbreviation **IBRD**

international call /,ɪntərnæʃ(ə)nəl 'kɔl/ *noun* a telephone call to another country

international (dialing) code /,ɪntərnæʃ(ə)nəl 'daɪlɪŋ koʊd/ *noun* the part of a telephone number used for dialing to another country

international direct dialing /,ɪntərnæʃ(ə)nəl daɪ,rekt 'daɪlɪŋ/ *noun* a system by which you can telephone direct to a number in another country without going through the operator. Abbreviation **IDD**

International Labour Organization /,ɪntərnæʃ(ə)nəl 'leɪbər ɔrgənaɪ ,zeɪʃ(ə)n/ *noun* a section of the United Nations which tries to improve working conditions and workers' pay in member countries. Abbreviation **ILO**

international law /,ɪntərnæʃ(ə)nəl 'lɔ/ *noun* laws referring to the way countries deal with each other

international lawyer /,ɪntərnæʃ(ə)nəl 'lɔjər/ *noun* a person who specializes in international law

international management /,ɪntərnæʃ(ə)nəl 'mænɪdʒmənt/ *noun* **1.** the management of an organization's production or market interests in other countries by either local or expatriate staff **2.** the management of a multinational business, made up of formerly independent organizations **3.** the particular type of skills, knowledge and understanding needed by managers who are in charge of operations that involve people from different countries and cultures

International Monetary Fund /,ɪntərnæʃ(ə)nəl 'mʌnɪt(ə)ri ,fʌnd/ *noun* a type of bank which is part of the United Nations and helps member states in financial difficulties, gives financial advice to members, and encourages world trade. Abbreviation **IMF**

international monetary system /,ɪntərnæʃ(ə)nəl 'mʌnɪt(ə)ri ,sɪstəm/ *noun* methods of controlling and exchanging currencies between countries

international (postal) reply coupon /,ɪntərnæʃ(ə)nəl ,poʊst(ə)l rɪ'plaɪ ,kupɑn/ *noun* a coupon which can be used in another country to pay the postage of a letter ○ *He enclosed an international reply coupon with his letter.*

international reserves /,ɪntərnæʃ(ə)nəl rɪ'zɜrvs/ *plural noun* same as **foreign currency reserves**

international trade /ˌɪntərnæʃ(ə)nəl ˈtreɪd/ *noun* trade between different countries

Internet /ˈɪntərnet/ *noun* an international network linking thousands of computers using telephone, cable, and satellite links ○ *Much of our business is done on the Internet.* ○ *Internet sales form an important part of our turnover.* ○ *He searched the Internet for information on cheap tickets to the U.S.*

Internet commerce /ˈɪntərnet ˌkɑmɜrs/ *noun* the part of e-commerce that consists of commercial business transactions conducted over the Internet

Internet marketing /ˈɪntərnet ˌmɑrkətɪŋ/ *noun* the marketing of products or services over the Internet

Internet merchant /ˈɪntərnet ˌmɜrtʃənt/ *noun* a businessman or businesswoman who sells a product or service over the Internet

Internet payment system /ˌɪntərnet ˈpeɪmənt ˌsɪstəm/ *noun* any mechanism that enables funds to be transferred from a customer to seller or from one business to another via the Internet

Internet security /ˌɪntərnet sɪˈkjʊrəti/ *noun* the means used to protect websites and other electronic files against attacks by hackers and viruses and to ensure that business can be safely conducted over the Internet

Internet selling /ˈɪntərnet ˌselɪŋ/ *noun* the act of selling of goods or services over the Internet

interoperability /ˌɪntərˌɑpərəˈbɪləti/ *noun* the ability of products made by different manufacturers to work together efficiently

interpersonal skills /ˌɪntərpɜrs(ə)n(ə)l ˈskɪlz/ *plural noun* skills used when communicating with other people, especially when negotiating

interpret /ɪnˈtɜrprət/ *verb* to translate what someone has said into another language ○ *My assistant knows Greek, so he will interpret for us.*

interpreter /ɪnˈtɜrprɪtər/ *noun* a person who translates what someone has said into another language ○ *My secretary will act as interpreter.*

Interstate Commerce Commission /ˌɪntəsteɪt ˈkɑmɜrs kəˌmɪʃ(ə)n/ *noun* a federal agency which regulates business activity involving two or more of the states in the U.S. Abbreviation **ICC**

interstitial /ˌɪntərˈstɪʃ(ə)l/ *noun* a page of advertising which is inserted into a website

intervene /ˌɪntərˈvin/ *verb* to try to make a change in a situation in which you have not been involved before □ **to intervene in a dispute** to try to settle a dispute

intervention /ˌɪntəˈvenʃən/ *noun* **1.** the act of becoming involved in a situation in order to change it ○ *the central bank's intervention in the banking crisis* ○ *the government's intervention in the labor dispute* **2.** an action taken by an outside agent to change the structure of a large company

interview /ˈɪntərvju/ *noun* **1.** a meeting in order to talk to a person who is applying for a job to find out whether they are suitable for it ○ *We called six people for interview.* ○ *I have an interview next week or I am going for an interview next week.* **2.** a meeting in order to ask a person questions as part of an opinion poll ■ *verb* to talk to a person applying for a job to see if they are suitable ○ *We interviewed ten candidates, but found no one suitable.*

interviewee /ˌɪntərvjuˈi/ *noun* the person who is being interviewed ○ *The interviewer did everything to put the interviewee at ease.* ○ *The interviewees were all nervous as they waited to be called into the interview room.*

interviewer /ˈɪntərvjuər/ *noun* the person who is conducting an interview

inter vivos /ˌɪntər ˈvivoʊs/ *phrase* a Latin phrase, "between living people"

intestacy /ɪnˈtestəsi/ *noun* the state of having died without having made a will

intestate /ɪnˈtestət/ *adjective* □ **to die intestate** to die without having made a will

COMMENT: When someone dies intestate, the property automatically goes to the parents or siblings of an unmarried person or, if married, to the surviving partner, unless there are children.

intranet /ˈɪntrənet/ *noun* a network of computers and telephone links that uses Internet technology but is accessible only to the employees of a particular organization

in transit /ˌɪn ˈtrænzɪt/ *adverb* □ **goods in transit** goods being transported

intrapreneurship /ˌɪntrəprəˈnɜrʃɪp/ *noun* entrepreneurship within an existing company, e.g., launching a new division or practice, which involves some risk

in tray /'ɪn treɪ/ *noun* a basket on a desk for letters or memos which have been received and are waiting to be dealt with

in-tray learning /'ɪn treɪ ˌlɜːnɪŋ/ *noun* a training exercise in which the trainee plays the role of a manager and has to deal with the contents of an in tray within a set period of time

introduce /ˌɪntrə'djuːs/ *verb* to make someone get to know somebody or something □ **to introduce a client** to bring in a new client and make them known to someone □ **to introduce a new product on the market** to produce a new product and launch it on the market

introduction /ˌɪntrə'dʌkʃ(ə)n/ *noun* **1.** a letter making someone get to know another person ○ *I'll give you an introduction to the CEO – he is an old friend of mine.* **2.** the act of bringing into use □ **the introduction of new technology** putting new machines (usually computers) into a business or industry

introductory offer /ˌɪntrədʌkt(ə)ri 'ɒfər/ *noun* a special price offered on a new product to attract customers

invalid /ɪn'vælɪd/ *adjective* not valid or not legal ○ *This permit is invalid.* ○ *The claim has been declared invalid.*

invalidate /ɪn'vælɪdeɪt/ *verb* to make something invalid ○ *Because the company has been taken over, the contract has been invalidated.*

invalidation /ɪnˌvælɪ'deɪʃən/ *noun* the act of making invalid

invalidity /ˌɪnvə'lɪdɪti/ *noun* the fact of being invalid ○ *the invalidity of the contract*

invent /ɪn'vent/ *verb* to make something which has never been made before ○ *She invented a new type of computer terminal.* ○ *Who invented shorthand?* ○ *The chief accountant has invented a new system of customer filing.*

invention /ɪn'venʃən/ *noun* **1.** something which has been invented ○ *He tried to sell his latest invention to a U.S. car manufacturer.* **2.** the creation of new products or processes which are then developed for commercial use through innovation

inventor /ɪn'ventər/ *noun* a person who invents something ○ *He is the inventor of the all-plastic car.*

inventory /'ɪnvənt(ə)ri/ *noun* **1.** *especially U.S.* all the stock or goods in a warehouse or store ○ *to carry a high inventory* ○ *to aim to reduce inventory* Also called **stock** □ **to take inventory** to count and record the quantity of each item in a warehouse or store **2.** a list of the contents of a building such as a house for sale or an office for rent ○ *to draw up an inventory of fixtures and fittings* □ **to agree the inventory** to agree that the inventory is correct ■ *verb* to make a list of stock or contents

inventory control /'ɪnvənt(ə)ri kən ˌtrəʊl/ *noun* the process of making sure that the correct level of inventory is maintained, to be able to meet demand while keeping the costs of holding inventory to a minimum

invest /ɪn'vest/ *verb* **1.** to put money into stocks, bonds, a savings and loan, etc., hoping that it will produce interest and increase in value ○ *He invested all his money in unit trusts.* ○ *She was advised to invest in real estate* or *in government bonds.* □ **to invest abroad** to put money into stocks or bonds in overseas countries **2.** to spend money on something which you believe will be useful ○ *to invest money in new machinery* ○ *to invest capital in a new factory*

"…we have substantial venture capital to invest in good projects" [*Times*]

investigate /ɪn'vestɪgeɪt/ *verb* to examine something which may be wrong ○ *The Serious Fraud Office has been asked to investigate his share dealings.*

investigation /ɪnˌvestɪ'geɪʃ(ə)n/ *noun* an examination to find out what is wrong ○ *They conducted an investigation into petty theft in the office.*

investigator /ɪn'vestɪgeɪtər/ *noun* a person who investigates ○ *government investigator*

investment /ɪn'vestmənt/ *noun* **1.** the placing of money so that it will produce interest and increase in value ○ *They called for more government investment in new industries.* ○ *She was advised to make investments in oil companies.* **2.** a stock, bond, or piece of property bought in the hope that it will produce more money than was used to buy it □ **long-term invest-**

ment, short-term investment stocks, etc., which are likely to increase in value over a long or short period □ **he is trying to protect his investments** he is trying to make sure that the money he has invested is not lost

investment adviser /ɪnˈvestmənt əd‚vaɪzər/ *noun* a person who advises people on what investments to make

investment grant /ɪnˈvestmənt grænt/ *noun* a government grant to a company to help it to invest in new machinery

investment income /ɪnˈvestmənt ‚ɪnkʌm/ *noun* income from investments, e.g., interest and dividends. Compare **earned income**

investment opportunities /ɪn ˈvestmənt ɑpə‚tunətiz/ *noun* possibilities for making investments or sales which will be profitable

investment trust /ɪnˈvestmənt trʌst/ *noun* a fund whose fixed number of shares can be bought on the Stock Exchange and whose business is to make money by buying and selling securities

investor /ɪnˈvestər/ *noun* a person who invests money

invisible /ɪnˈvɪzɪb(ə)l/ *adjective* not recorded or reflected in economic statistics

invisible assets /ɪn‚vɪzɪb(ə)l ˈæsets/ *plural noun* assets which have a value but which cannot be seen, e.g., goodwill or patents

invisible earnings /ɪn‚vɪzɪb(ə)l ˈɜːnɪŋz/ *plural noun* foreign currency earned by a country by providing services, receiving interests or dividends, but not by selling goods

invisible exports /ɪn‚vɪzəb(ə)l ˈeksports/ *plural noun* services such as banking, insurance, or tourism which do not involve selling a product and which are provided to foreign customers and paid for in foreign currency. Opposite **visible exports**

invisible imports /ɪn‚vɪzɪb(ə)l ˈɪmpɔrtz/ *noun* services such as banking, insurance, or tourism which do not involve selling a product and which are provided by foreign companies and paid for in local currency. Opposite **visible imports**

invisibles /ɪnˈvɪzɪb(ə)lz/ *plural noun* invisible imports and exports

invitation /‚ɪnvɪˈteɪʃ(ə)n/ *noun* an act of asking someone to do something ○ *to issue an invitation to someone to join the board* ○ *an invitation to subscribe a new issue.*

invite /ɪnˈvaɪt/ *verb* to ask someone to do something, or to ask for something ○ *to invite someone to an interview* ○ *to invite someone to join the board* ○ *to invite stockholders to subscribe to a new issue*

invoice /ˈɪnvɔɪs/ *noun* a note asking for payment for goods or services supplied ○ *your invoice dated November 10th* ○ *to make out an invoice for $250* ○ *to settle or to pay an invoice* ○ *They sent in their invoice six weeks late.* □ **the total is payable within thirty days of invoice** the total sum has to be paid within thirty days of the date on the invoice ■ *verb* to send an invoice to someone ○ *to invoice a customer* □ **we invoiced you on November 10th** we sent you the invoice on November 10th

invoice clerk /ˈɪnvɔɪs klɜrk/ *noun* an office employee who deals with invoices

invoice number /ˈɪnvɔɪs ‚nʌmbər/ *noun* the reference number printed on an invoice or order

invoice price /ˈɪnvɔɪs praɪs/ *noun* the price as given on an invoice, including any discount and tax

invoicing /ˈɪnvɔɪsɪŋ/ *noun* the work of sending invoices ○ *All our invoicing is done by computer.* □ **invoicing in triplicate** the preparation of three copies of invoices

invoicing department /ˈɪnvɔɪsɪŋ dɪ‚pɑrtmənt/ *noun* the department in a company which deals with preparing and sending invoices

inward /ˈɪnwərd/ *adjective* toward the home country

inward bill /‚ɪnwərd ˈbɪl/ *noun* a bill of lading for goods arriving in a country

inward investment /‚ɪnwərd ɪnˈvestmənt/ *noun* an investment from outside a country, as when a foreign company decides to set up a new factory there

inward mission /‚ɪnwərd ˈmɪʃ(ə)n/ *noun* a visit to your home country by a group of foreign businesspeople

IOU /‚aɪ oʊ ˈju/ *noun* "I owe you", a signed document promising that you will pay back money borrowed ○ *to pay a pile of IOUs* ○ *I have a pile of IOUs which need paying.*

IP address /ˌaɪ 'piː əˌdres/ *noun* a unique 32-bit number that defines the precise location of a computer connected to a network or the Internet

IPO *abbreviation* initial public offering

irrecoverable /ˌɪrɪˈkʌv(ə)rəb(ə)l/ *adjective* not possible to get back

irrecoverable debt /ɪrɪˌkʌv(ə)rəb(ə)l 'det/ *noun* a debt which will never be paid

irredeemable /ɪrɪˈdiːməb(ə)l/ *adjective* not possible to redeem

irredeemable bond /ɪrɪˌdiːməb(ə)l 'bɒnd/ *noun* a government bond which has no date of maturity and which therefore provides interest but can never be redeemed at full value

irregular /ɪˈreɡjʊlər/ *adjective* not correct or not done in the correct way ○ *The shipment arrived with irregular documentation.* ○ *This procedure is highly irregular.*

irregularities /ɪˌreɡjʊˈlærɪtiz/ *plural noun* things which are not done in the correct way and which are possibly illegal ○ *to investigate irregularities in the stock dealings*

"…the group, which asked for its shares to be suspended last week after the discovery of accounting irregularities, is expected to update investors about its financial predicament by the end of this week" [*Times*]

irregularity /ɪˌreɡjʊˈlærɪti/ *noun* the fact of not being regular ○ *the irregularity of the postal deliveries*

irrevocable /ɪˈrevəkəb(ə)l/ *adjective* unchangeable

irrevocable acceptance /ɪˌrevəkəb(ə)l əkˈseptəns/ *noun* an acceptance which cannot be withdrawn

irrevocable letter of credit /ɪˌrevəkəb(ə)l ˌletər əv 'kredɪt/ *noun* a letter of credit which cannot be canceled or changed, except if agreed between the two parties involved

IRS *abbreviation* Internal Revenue Service

ISDN /ˌaɪ es diː 'en/ *noun* a digital telephone network that supports advanced communications services and can be used for high-speed data transmission. Full form **Integrated Services Digital Network**

island site /ˈaɪlənd saɪt/, **island display** /ˈaɪlənd dɪsˌpleɪ/ *noun* an exhibition stand separated from others ○ *There are only two island sites at the exhibition and we have one of them.* ○ *An island site means that visitors can approach the stand from several directions.*

ISS *abbreviation* Institutional Shareholder Services, Inc

issue /ˈɪʃuː/ *noun* **1.** the number of a newspaper or magazine ○ *We have an ad in the January issue of the magazine.* **2.** an act of offering new shares for sale **3.** a problem being discussed ○ *To bring up the question of sales tax will only confuse the issue.* □ **to have issues around** to be concerned about something (*informal*) ■ *verb* to put out or to give out ○ *to issue a letter of credit* ○ *to issue stock in a new company* ○ *to issue a writ against someone* ○ *The government issued a report on air traffic.*

issued capital /ˌɪʃuːd 'kæpɪt(ə)l/ *noun* an amount of capital which is given out as shares to stockholders

issued price /ˌɪʃuːd 'praɪs/, **issue price** /ˈɪʃuː praɪs/ *noun* the price of shares in a new company when they are offered for sale for the first time

issuer /ˈɪʃuːər/ *noun* a financial institution that issues credit and debit cards and maintains the systems for billing and payment

issuing /ˈɪʃuːɪŋ/ *adjective* organizing an issue of shares

issuing bank /ˈɪʃuːɪŋ bæŋk/ *noun* a bank which organizes the selling of shares in a new company

IT *abbreviation* information technology

item /ˈaɪtəm/ *noun* **1.** something for sale □ **we are holding orders for out-of-stock items** we are holding orders for goods which are not in stock ○ *Please find enclosed an order for the following items from your catalog.* **2.** a piece of information ○ *items on a balance sheet* □ **the items on a profit and loss statement** the different entries on a profit and loss statement □ **item of expenditure** goods or services which have been paid for and appear in the accounts **3.** a point on a list □ **we will now take item four on the agenda** we will now discuss the fourth point on the agenda

itemize /ˈaɪtəmaɪz/ *verb* to make a detailed list of things ○ *Itemizing the sales figures will take about two days.*

itemized account /ˌaɪtəmaɪzd ə
'kaʊnt/ *noun* a detailed record of money
paid or owed

itemized deductions /ˌaɪtəmaɪzd dɪ
'dʌkʃ(ə)nz/ *noun* deductions from a person's taxable income which are listed on
his tax return

itemized invoice /ˌaɪtəmaɪzd 'ɪnvɔɪs/
noun an invoice which lists each item separately

itemized statement /ˌaɪtəmaɪzd
'steɪtmənt/ *noun* a bank statement where
each transaction is recorded in detail

itinerant worker /ɪˌtɪnərənt 'wɜrkər/
noun a worker who moves from place to
place, looking for work ○ *Most of the
workers hired during the summer are itinerant workers.* ○ *Much of the seasonal
work on farms is done by itinerant workers.*

itinerary /aɪ'tɪnərəri/ *noun* a list of
places to be visited on one trip ○ *a sales
representative's itinerary*

IVR *abbreviation* interactive voice response

J

jack /dʒæk/ *verb*

jack in *phrasal verb* to connect to something electronically, especially to connect to a network via a modem or similar device

jam /dʒæm/ *noun* a blockage ■ *verb* to stop working or to be blocked ○ *the paper feed has jammed* ○ *The switchboard was jammed with calls.* (NOTE: **jamming – jammed**)

janitor /'dʒænɪtər/ *noun* a person who looks after a building, making sure it is clean and that the rubbish is cleared away ○ *Go and ask the janitor to replace the light bulb.* (NOTE: The U.K. term is **caretaker**.)

Japanese management /,dʒæpəniz 'mænɪdʒmənt/ *noun* a combination of management styles that emphasizes human relations and teamworking and advanced manufacturing techniques such as just-in-time production and total quality management which is credited with bringing about the Japanese economic miracle that began in the 1960s (NOTE: Japanese management practices were studied in the rest of the world in the hope that other countries could imitate Japan's economic success, but the downturn in the Japanese economy that began in the 1990s has forced the Japanese themselves to reassess them.)

jargon /'dʒɑrgən/ *noun* a special sort of language used by a trade or profession or particular group of people

"The very term "open-source software" sounds like the kind of computer jargon most managers would prefer to leave to their IT experts." [*Harvard Business Review*]

Jiffy bag® /'dʒɪfi bæg/ *noun* a trade name for a padded bag, used for sending items by mail ○ *She sent the diskettes in a Jiffy bag.*

JIT *abbreviation* just-in-time

job /dʒɑb/ *noun* **1.** a piece of work □ **to do a job of work** to be given a job of work to do □ **to do odd jobs** to do various pieces of work ○ *He does odd jobs for us around the house.* □ **to be paid by the job** to be paid for each piece of work done **2.** an order being worked on ○ *We are working on six jobs at the moment.* ○ *The shipyard has a big job starting in August.* **3.** regular paid work ○ *She is looking for a job in the computer industry.* ○ *He lost his job when the factory closed.* ○ *Thousands of jobs will be lost if the factories close down.* □ **to give up your job** to resign or retire from your work □ **to look for a job** to try to find work □ **to retire from your job** to leave work and take a pension □ **to be out of a job** to have no work **4.** a difficulty ○ *They will have a job to borrow the money they need for the expansion program.* ○ *We had a job finding a qualified secretary.*

"…he insisted that the tax advantages he directed toward small businesses will help create jobs" [*Toronto Star*]

job analysis /'dʒɑb ə,næləsɪs/ *noun* a detailed examination and report on the duties involved in a job

job application /'dʒɑb æplɪ,keɪʃ(ə)n/ *noun* the process of asking for a job in writing

jobbing /'dʒɑbɪŋ/ *noun* the practice of doing small pieces of work

job center /'dʒɑb ,sentə/ *noun* a government office which lists jobs which are vacant ○ *There was a long line of unemployed people waiting at the job center.*

job classification /'dʒɑb klæsɪfɪ ,keɪʃ(ə)n/ *noun* the process of describing jobs listed in various groups

jobclub /'dʒɑbklʌb/ *noun* an organization which helps its members to find jobs ○ *Since joining the jobclub she has improved her interview techniques and gained self-confidence.*

job creation program /ˌdʒɑb kri
'eɪʃ(ə)n ˌprougræm/ *noun* a government-
backed program to make work for the unemployed

job cuts /'dʒɑb kʌts/ *plural noun* reductions in the number of jobs

job description /'dʒɑb dɪˌskrɪpʃən/
noun a description of what a job consists
of and what skills are needed for it ○ *The
letter enclosed an application form and a
job description.*

job evaluation /'dʒɑb ɪvæljuˌeɪʃ(ə)n/
noun the process of examining different
jobs within an organization to see what
skills and qualifications are needed to carry them out

jobless /'dʒɑbləs/ *plural noun* people
with no jobs, the unemployed (NOTE:
takes a plural verb)

"…the contradiction between the jobless
figures and latest economic review" [*Sunday
Times*]

job losses /'dʒɑb ˌlɔsɪz/ *noun* jobs
which no longer exist because workers
have been made redundant

job lot /ˌdʒɑb 'lat/ *noun* a group of miscellaneous items sold together ○ *They sold
the household furniture as a job lot.*

job opening /'dʒɑb ˌoup(ə)nɪŋ/ *noun* a
job which is empty and needs filling ○ *We
have job openings for office staff.*

job opportunities /'dʒɑb ɑpə
ˌtunətiz/ *plural noun* new jobs which are
available ○ *The increase in export orders
has created hundreds of job opportunities.*

job performance /'dʒɑb pəˌfɔrməns/
noun the degree to which a job is done
well or badly

job satisfaction /'dʒɑb sætɪsˌfækʃən/
noun an employee's feeling that he or she
is happy at work and pleased with the
work he or she does

job security /'dʒɑb sɪˌkjʊriti/ *noun* 1.
the likelihood that an employee will keep
his or her job for a long time or until retirement 2. an employee's feeling that he has
a right to keep his job, or that he will never
be made redundant

job-share /'dʒɑb ʃer/ *noun* a form of
employment in which two or more people
share a single job, each person working
part-time and being paid an amount pro-
portionate to the number of hours they
work

job sharing /'dʒɑb ˌʃerɪŋ/ *noun* a situation where one job is carried out by more
than one person, each working part-time

job specification /'dʒɑb
ˌspesɪfɪkeɪʃ(ə)n/ *noun* a very detailed description of what is involved in a job

job title /'dʒɑb ˌtaɪt(ə)l/ *noun* the name
given to the person who does a particular
job ○ *Her job title is "Chief Buyer".*

job vacancy /'dʒɑb ˌveɪkənsi/ *noun* a
job which is available for somebody to do

join /dʒɔɪn/ *verb* 1. to put things together
○ *The offices were joined together by making a door in the wall.* ○ *If the paper is too
short to take all the accounts, you can join
an extra piece on the bottom.* 2. □ **to join
a firm** to start work with a company □ **she
joined on January 1st** she started work on
January 1st 3. □ **to join an association** *or*
a group to become a member of an association or a group ○ *All the staff have joined
the company pension plan.* ○ *He was
asked to join the board.* ○ *Smith Inc. has
applied to join the trade association.*

joined-up /'dʒɔɪnd ʌp/ *adjective* involving two or more individuals or organizations who share information and co-or-
dinate their activities in order to achieve
their aims more effectively

joint /dʒɔɪnt/ *adjective* 1. carried out or
produced together with others ○ *a joint
undertaking* □ **joint discussions** discussions between management and workers
before something is done 2. one of two or
more people who work together or who
are linked ○ *They are joint beneficiaries of
the will.* ○ *She and her brother are joint
managing directors.* ○ *The two countries
are joint signatories of the treaty.*

joint account /'dʒɔɪnt əˌkaunt/ *noun* a
bank or savings and loan association account shared by two people ○ *Many married couples have joint accounts so that
they can pay for household expenses.*

joint commission of inquiry
/ˌdʒɔɪnt kəˌmɪʃ(ə)n əv ɪn'kwaɪri/ *noun*
a commission or committee with representatives of various organizations on it

jointly /'dʒɔɪntli/ *adverb* together with
one or more other people ○ *to own a property jointly* ○ *to manage a company jointly*
○ *They are jointly liable for damages.*

joint management /ˌdʒɔɪnt
'mænɪdʒmənt/ *noun* management done
by two or more people

joint ownership /ˌdʒɔɪnt ˈoʊnəʃɪp/ *noun* the owning of a property by several owners

joint-stock bank /ˌdʒɔɪnt ˈstɑk ˌbæŋk/ *noun* a bank which is a public company quoted on the Stock Exchange

joint-stock company /ˈdʒɔɪnt stɑk ˌkʌmp(ə)ni/ *noun* formerly, a public company in the U.K. whose stock was owned by very many people. Now called a Public Limited Company or Plc.

joint venture /ˌdʒɔɪnt ˈventʃə/ *noun* a situation where two or more companies join together for one specific large business project

journal /ˈdʒɜːn(ə)l/ *noun* **1.** a book with the account of sales and purchases made each day **2.** a magazine

journalist /ˈdʒɜːrn(ə)lɪst/ *noun* a person who writes for a newspaper

journey /ˈdʒɜːrni/ *noun* a long trip

judge /dʒʌdʒ/ *noun* a person who decides in a legal case ○ *The judge sent him to prison for embezzlement.* ■ *verb* to make an assessment about someone or something ○ *to judge an employee's managerial potential* ○ *He judged it was time to call an end to the discussions.*

judgment /ˈdʒʌdʒmənt/, **judgement** *noun* a legal decision or official decision of a court □ **to pronounce judgment, to give your judgment on something** to give an official or legal decision about something

judgment debtor /ˈdʒʌdʒmənt ˌdetər/ *noun* a debtor who has been ordered by a court to pay a debt

judicial /dʒuˈdɪʃ(ə)l/ *adjective* referring to the law

judicial processes /dʒu,dɪʃ(ə)l ˈprɑsesɪz/ *plural noun* the ways in which the law works

jump /dʒʌmp/ *noun* a sudden rise ○ *a jump in the cost-of-living index* ○ *There was a jump in unemployment figures in December.* ■ *verb* **1.** to go up suddenly ○ *Oil prices have jumped since the war started.* **2.** to go away suddenly □ **to jump the gun** to start to do something too early or before you should □ **to jump the line** to go in front of someone who has been waiting longer ○ *They jumped the line and got their export license before we did.*

junior /ˈdʒuniər/ *adjective* **1.** younger or lower in rank □ **John Smith, Junior** the younger John Smith (i.e. the son of John Smith, Senior) **2.** less important than something else ■ *noun* a barrister who is not a Queen's counsel

junior clerk /ˌdʒuniə ˈklɜːrk/ *noun* a clerk, usually young, who has lower status than a senior clerk

junior executive /ˌdʒuniə ɪg ˈzekjuːtɪv/, **junior manager** /ˈdʒuniə ˈmænɪdʒər/ *noun* a young manager in a company

junior management /ˌdʒuniə ˈmænɪdʒmənt/ *noun* the managers of small departments or deputies to departmental managers

junior partner /ˌdʒuniə ˈpɑrtnər/ *noun* a person who owns a small part of a partnership

junior staff /ˌdʒuniə ˈstæf/ *noun* **1.** younger members of staff **2.** people in less important positions in a company

junk bond /ˈdʒʌŋk bɑnd/ *noun* a corporate bond that offers high interest but at a high risk

"…the big U.S. textile company is running deep in the red, its junk bonds are trading as low as 33 cents on the dollar" [*Wall Street Journal*]

junk mail /ˈdʒʌŋk meɪl/ *noun* **1.** unsolicited advertising material sent through the mail and usually thrown away immediately by the people who receive it **2.** unsolicited advertising material sent by email

jurisdiction /ˌdʒʊrɪsˈdɪkʃən/ *noun* □ **within the jurisdiction of the court** in the legal power of a court

just-in-time /ˌdʒʌst ɪn ˈtaɪm/ *noun* a system in which goods are made or purchased just before they are needed, so as to avoid carrying high levels of inventory. Abbreviation **JIT**

K

K /keɪ/ *abbreviation* one thousand □ **"salary: $20K+"** salary more than $20,000 per annum

kaizen /kaɪ'zen/ *noun* the Japanese term for the continuous improvement of current working methods and processes. Kaizen makes use of a range of techniques, including small-group problem-solving, suggestion schemes, statistical analysis, brainstorming, and work studies to eliminate waste and encourage innovation and working to new standards. (NOTE: Kaizen is derived from the words "kai," meaning "change," and "zen," meaning "good" or "for the better.")

KAM *abbreviation* key account management

karat /'kærət/ *noun* **1.** a measure of the quality of gold (pure gold being 24 karat) ○ *a 22-karat gold ring* **2.** a measure of the weight of precious stones ○ *a 5-karat diamond*

COMMENT: Pure gold is 24 carats and is too soft to make jewellery. Most jewellery and other items made from gold are not pure, but between 19 and 22 carats. 22 carat gold has 22 parts of gold to two parts of alloy.

KBG *abbreviation* keiretsu business group

KD *abbreviation* knockdown

keen /kin/ *adjective* □ **keen prices** *U.K.* prices which are kept low so as to be competitive ○ *Our prices are the keenest on the market.*

keep /kip/ *verb* **1.** to go on doing something ○ *They kept working, even when the boss told them to stop.* ○ *The other secretaries complain that she keeps singing when she is typing.* **2.** to do what is necessary for something □ **to keep an appointment** to be there when you said you would be □ **to keep the books of a company, to keep a company's books** to note the ac-

counts of a company accurately **3.** to hold items for sale or for information □ **we always keep this item in stock** we always have this item in our warehouse or store **4.** to hold things at some level ○ *to keep spending to a minimum* ○ *We must keep our mailing list up to date.* ○ *The price of oil has kept the pound at a high level.* ○ *Lack of demand for the product has kept prices down.* (NOTE: **keeping – kept**)

keep back *phrasal verb* to hold on to something which you could give to someone ○ *to keep back information* or *to keep something back from someone* ○ *to keep $10 back from someone's salary*

keep on *phrasal verb* to continue to do something ○ *The factory kept on working in spite of the fire.* ○ *We keep on receiving orders for this item although it was discontinued two years ago.*

keep up *phrasal verb* to hold at a certain high level ○ *We must keep up the turnover in spite of the recession.* ○ *She kept up a rate of sixty words per minute for several hours.*

keiretsu, keiretsu business group a Japanese conglomerate company or business alliance whose members hold stock in the other member companies. Keiretsu business groups generally consist of firms that share close buyer-supplier relationships and are characterized by close internal control, policy co-ordination, and cohesiveness. Abbreviation **KBG**

"In the process they are freeing thousands of smaller businesses from the tyranny of keiretsu relationships where they were tied to certain suppliers and buyers in a semifeudal arrangement." [*Forbes*]

Keogh plan /'kioʊ ˌplæn/ *noun* a private pension plan allowing self-employed businesspeople and professionals to set up pension and retirement plans for themselves

key

226

key /kiː/ *adjective* important ○ *a key factor* ○ *key industries* ○ *key personnel* ○ *a key member of our management team* ○ *She has a key post in the organization.* ○ *We don't want to lose any key staff in the reorganization.* ■ *verb* □ **to key in data** to put information into a computer

key account /ˈkiː əˌkaʊnt/ *noun* an important account or client, e.g., of an advertising agency

key account management /ˈkiː əˌkaʊnt ˌmænɪdʒmənt/ *noun* the management of the small number of key accounts which represent the bulk of a company's business. Abbreviation **KAM**

keyboard /ˈkiːbɔːrd/ *noun* the part of a computer or other device with keys which are pressed to make letters or figures ■ *verb* to press the keys on a keyboard to type something ○ *She is keyboarding our address list.*

keyboarder /ˈkiːbɔːrdər/ *noun* a person who types information into a computer

keyboarding /ˈkiːbɔːrdɪŋ/ *noun* the act of typing on a keyboard ○ *Keyboarding costs have risen sharply.*

keyboarding speed /ˈkiːbɔːrdɪŋ ˌspiːd/ *noun* the number of words per minute which a keyboarder can enter

keyed /kiːd/ *adjective* which has a key

keyed advertisement /ˌkiːd ədˈvɜːrtɪsmənt/ *noun* an advertisement which asks people to write to a specially coded address which will indicate where they saw it, thus helping the advertisers to evaluate the effectiveness of advertising in that particular newspaper or magazine

key money /ˈkiː ˌmʌni/ *noun* a premium paid when taking over the keys of a apartment or office which you are renting

key-person insurance /ˈkiː pɜːrs(ə)n ɪnˌʃʊrəns/ *noun* an insurance policy taken out to cover the costs of replacing an employee who is particularly important to an organization if he or she dies or is ill for a long time

keyword /ˈkiːwɜːrd/ *noun* a word used by a search engine to help it locate a particular type of website (NOTE: Companies need to think very carefully about the keywords they place in their webpages in order to attract relevant search-engine traffic.)

keyword search /ˌkiːwɜːrd ˈsɜːrtʃ/ *noun* a search for documents containing one or more words that are specified by a search-engine user

kg *abbreviation* kilogram

kickback /ˈkɪkbæk/ *noun* an illegal commission paid to someone, especially a government official, who helps in a business deal

killing /ˈkɪlɪŋ/ *noun* a huge profit (*informal*) ○ *He made a killing on the stock market.*

kilo /ˈkiːloʊ/, **kilogram** /ˈkɪləgræm/ *noun* a measure of weight (= one thousand grams or 2.2 pounds) ○ *Packets weighing more than 2kg must go by parcel post.* (NOTE: Written **kg** after figures: *20kg*.)

kilobyte /ˈkɪloʊbaɪt/ *noun* a unit of storage in a computer (= 1,024 bytes)

kilometer /ˈkɪləˌmiːtə/ *noun* a measure of length (= one thousand meters or .6 mile) □ **the car does fifteen kilometers to the liter** the car uses a liter of gasoline to travel fifteen kilometers

king-size /ˈkɪŋ saɪz/ *adjective* **1.** referring to an extra large container of a product, usually comparatively economical to buy **2.** referring to a very large size of poster

kiosk /ˈkiːɑsk/ *noun* a small wooden shelter, for selling goods out of doors ○ *She had a newspaper kiosk near the station for 20 years.*

kite /kaɪt/ *noun* □ **to fly a kite** to put forward a proposal to try to interest people ■ *verb* **1.** to write checks on one account which may not be able to honor them and deposit them in another, withdrawing money from the second account before the checks are cleared **2.** to use stolen credit cards or check books

kite flier /ˈkaɪt ˌflaɪr/ *noun* a person who tries to impress people by putting forward a proposal

kite-flying /ˈkaɪt ˌflaɪɪŋ/ *noun* the practice of trying to impress people by putting forward grand plans

kitty /ˈkɪti/ *noun* money which has been collected by a group of people to be used later, such as for an office party ○ *We each put $5 into the kitty.*

km *abbreviation* kilometer

knock /nɑk/ *verb* □ **to knock the competition** to hit competing firms hard by vigorous selling

   knock down *phrasal verb* □ **to knock**

something down to a bidder to sell something to somebody at an auction ○ *The furniture was knocked down to him for $100.*

knock off *phrasal verb* **1.** to stop work ○ *We knocked off at 3p.m. on Friday.* **2.** to reduce a price by a particular amount ○ *She knocked $10 off the price for cash.*
■ *noun* a cheap copy of an established product, often an illegal copy of a famous named brand

knockdown /'nɑkdaʊn/ *noun* □ **knockdown goods** goods sold in parts, which must be assembled by the buyer

knockdown price /ˌnɑkdaʊn 'praɪs/ *noun* a very low price ○ *He sold me the car at a knockdown price.*

knocking copy /'nɑkɪŋ ˌkɑpi/ *noun* advertising material which criticizes competing products

knock-on effect /'nɑk ɑn ɪˌfekt/ *noun* the effect which an action will have on other situations ○ *The strike by customs officers has had a knock-on effect on car production by slowing down exports of cars.*

know /noʊ/ *verb* **1.** to learn or to have information about something ○ *I do not know how a computer works.* ○ *Does she know how long it takes to get to the airport?* ○ *The managing director's secretary does not know where he is.* ○ *He knows the African market very well.* ○ *I don't know how a computer works.* **2.** to have met someone ○ *Do you know Ms Jones, our new sales director?* (NOTE: **knowing – knew – known**)

know-how /'noʊ haʊ/ *noun* knowledge or skill in a particular field ○ *to acquire* computer know-how ○ *If we cannot recruit staff with the right know-how, we will have to initiate an ambitious training program.*

knowledge /'nɑlɪdʒ/ *noun* what is known □ **he had no knowledge of the contract** he did not know that the contract existed

knowledge-based /'nɑlɪdʒ beɪst/ *adjective* used to describe companies that rely on the ideas and knowledge of their employees to be successful

knowledge capital /'nɑlɪdʒ ˌkæpɪt(ə)l/ *noun* knowledge, especially specialist knowledge, that a company and its employees possess and that can be put to profitable use

knowledge management /'nɑlɪdʒ ˌmænɪdʒmənt/ *noun* **1.** the task of coordinating the specialist knowledge possessed by employees so that it can be exploited to create benefits and competitive advantage for the organization **2.** same as **information management**

knowledge portal /'nɑlɪdʒ ˌpɔrt(ə)l/ *noun* a website that provides links to information about a particular subject

knowledge worker /'nɑlɪdʒ ˌwɜrkər/ *noun* an employee whose value to an organization lies in the information, ideas and expertise that they possess

"…develop more offerings through which it can help customers streamline back-office operations and make their knowledge workers more efficient." [*InformationWeek*]

krona /'kroʊnə/ *noun* a unit of currency used in Sweden and Iceland

krone /'kroʊnə/ *noun* a unit of currency used in Denmark and Norway

L

l /el/ *abbreviation* litre

labeling /'leɪb(ə)lɪŋ/ *noun* the act of putting a label on something

labeling department /'leɪb(ə)lɪŋ dɪ ˌpɑrtmənt/ *noun* a section of a factory where labels are attached to the product

labeling program /'leɪb(ə)lɪŋ ˌproʊɡræm/ *noun* a word-processing program which allows you to print addresses from an address list onto labels

labor /'leɪbə/ *noun* **1.** heavy work (NOTE: The U.S. spelling is **labor.**) □ **to charge for materials and labor** to charge for both the materials used in a job and also the hours of work involved □ **labor is charged at $15 an hour** each hour of work costs $15 **2.** workers, the work force ○ *We will need to employ more labor if production is to be increased.* ○ *The costs of labor are rising in line with inflation.* (NOTE: The U.S. spelling is **labor.**) □ **labor shortage, shortage of labor** a situation where there are not enough workers to fill jobs **3.** (NOTE: The U.S. spelling is **labor.**) □ **labor disputes** arguments between management and workers □ **labor laws, labor legislation** laws relating to the employment of workers

"…the possibility that British goods will price themselves back into world markets is doubtful as long as sterling labour costs continue to rise faster than in competitor countries" [*Sunday Times*]

laboratory /'læb(ə)rət(ə)ri/ *noun* a place where scientific research is carried out ○ *The product was developed in the company's laboratories.* ○ *All products are tested in our own laboratories.* (NOTE: The plural is **laboratories.**)

laboratory technician /ˌlæb(ə)rət(ə)ri tek'nɪʃ(ə)n/ *noun* a person who deals with practical work in a laboratory

labor costs /'leɪbə kɔsts/ *noun* the cost of the employees employed to make a product, not including materials or overhead

laborer /'leɪbərər/ *noun* a person who does heavy work

labor force /'leɪbə fɔrs/ *noun* all the employees in a company or in an area ○ *The management has made an increased offer to the labor force.* ○ *We are opening a new factory in the Far East because of the cheap local labor force.*

"70 per cent of Australia's labour force is employed in service activity" [*Australian Financial Review*]

labor-intensive /ˌleɪbər ɪn'tensɪv/ *adjective* referring to an industry which needs large numbers of employees or where labor costs are high in relation to turnover ○ *As the business became more labor-intensive, so human resources management became more important.* ○ *With computerization, the business has become much less labor-intensive.*

labor-intensive industry /ˌleɪbər ɪn ˌtensɪv 'ɪndəstri/ *noun* an industry which needs large numbers of employees and where labor costs are high in relation to turnover

labor market /'leɪbər ˌmɑrkət/ *noun* the number of people who are available for work ○ *25,000 graduates have just come on to the labor market.*

labor relations /'leɪbə rɪˌleɪʃ(ə)nz/ *plural noun* relations between management and employees ○ *The company has a history of bad labor relations.*

labor-saving /'leɪbə ˌseɪvɪŋ/ *adjective* avoiding the need for work by someone ○ *Costs will be cut by the introduction of labor-saving devices.*

labor turnover /'leɪbə ˌtɜrnoʊvər/ *noun* the movement of employees with some leaving their jobs and others joining. Also called **turnover of labour**

labor union /'leɪbə ˌjʊnjən/ *noun* an organization which represents employees who are its members in discussions about wages and conditions of work with management (NOTE: The U.K. term is **trade union**.)

lack /læk/ *noun* the fact of not having enough □ **lack of data**, **lack of information** not having enough information ○ *The decision has been put back for lack of up-to-date information.* □ **lack of funds** not enough money ○ *The project was canceled because of lack of funds.* ■ *verb* not to have enough of something ○ *The company lacks capital.* ○ *The industry lacks skilled staff.* □ **the sales staff lack motivation** the sales staff are not motivated enough

ladder /'lædər/ *noun* a series of different levels through which an employee may progress

laden /'leɪd(ə)n/ *adjective* loaded □ **fully-laden ship** ship with a full cargo

lading /'leɪdɪŋ/ *noun* the work of putting goods on a ship

laggards /'lægərdz/ *plural noun* a category of buyers of a product who are the last to buy it or use it

lagging indicator /'lægɪŋ ˌɪndɪkeɪtər/ *noun* an indicator which shows a change in economic trends later than other indicators, e.g., the gross national product. Opposite **leading indicator**

laid up /ˌleɪd 'ʌp/ *adjective* **1.** not used because there is no work ○ *Half the shipping fleet is laid up by the recession.* **2.** (person who is) unable to work because of illness or injury ○ *Half the staff are laid up with flu.*

laissez-faire economy /ˌleseɪ 'fer ɪ ˌkɑnəmi/ *noun* an economy where the government does not interfere because it believes it is right to let the economy run itself

lakh /læk/ *noun* (*in India*) one hundred thousand (NOTE: Ten lakh equal one crore.)

lame duck /ˌleɪm 'dʌk/ *noun* **1.** a company which is in financial difficulties ○ *The government has refused to help lame duck companies.* **2.** an official who has not been re-elected and is finishing his term of office ○ *a lame-duck president*

LAN /læn/ *abbreviation* local area network

land /lænd/ *verb* to put goods or passengers onto land after a voyage by sea or by air ○ *The ship landed some goods at Mombasa.* ○ *The plane stopped for thirty minutes at the local airport to land passengers and mail.*

land agent /'lænd ˌeɪdʒənt/ *noun* a person who runs a farm or a large area of land for the owner

land bank /'lænd bæŋk/ *noun* undeveloped land which belongs to a property developer

landed costs /ˌlændɪd 'kɔsts/ *plural noun* the costs of goods which have been delivered to a port, unloaded, and passed through customs

landing card /'lændɪŋ kɑrd/ *noun* a card given to passengers who have passed through customs and can land from a ship or an aircraft

landing charges /'lændɪŋ ˌtʃɑrdʒɪz/ *plural noun* payments for putting goods on land and paying customs duties

landing order /'lændɪŋ ˌɔrdər/ *noun* a permit which allows goods to be unloaded into a bonded warehouse without paying customs duty

landlady /'lændleɪdi/ *noun* a woman who owns a property which she lets ○ *We pay our rent direct to the landlady every week.*

landlord /'lændlɔrd/ *noun* a person or company which owns a property which is rented

landowner /'lændoʊnər/ *noun* a person who owns large areas of land

land register /'lænd ˌredʒɪstər/ *noun* a list of pieces of land, showing who owns each and what buildings are on it

land registration /'lænd redʒɪ ˌstreɪʃ(ə)n/ *noun* a system of registering land and its owners

land tax /'lænd tæks/ *noun* a tax on the amount of land owned

lapse /læps/ *noun* □ **a lapse of time** a period of time which has passed ■ *verb* to stop being valid, or to stop being active ○ *The guarantee has lapsed.* □ **to let an offer lapse** to allow time to pass so that an offer is no longer valid

laptop /'læptɑp/ *noun* a small portable computer which you can hold on your knees to work ○ *I take my laptop with me so that I can write reports on the train.* ○ *Our reps all have laptops on which they can key their orders and email them back to the warehouse.*

large /lɑrdʒ/ *adjective* very big or important ○ *he is our largest customer* ○ *Our company is one of the largest suppliers of computers to the government.* ○ *Why has she got an office which is larger than mine?*

largely /ˈlɑrdʒli/ *adverb* mainly or mostly ○ *Our sales are largely in the home market.* ○ *They have largely pulled out of the American market.*

large-scale /ˈlɑrdʒ skeɪl/ *adjective* involving large numbers of people or large amounts of money ○ *large-scale investment in new technology* ○ *large-scale redundancies in the construction industry* ■ *noun* working with large or small amounts of investment, staff, etc.

laser cartridge /ˈleɪzər ˌkɑrtrɪdʒ/ *noun* a cartridge of toner for a laser printer

laser paper /ˈleɪzə ˌpeɪpər/ *noun* paper used in a laser printer

last /læst/ *adjective, adverb* **1.** coming at the end of a series ○ *Out of a line of twenty people, I was served last.* ○ *This is our last board meeting before we move to our new offices.* ○ *We finished the last items in the order just two days before the promised delivery date.* **2.** most recent or most recently ○ *Where is the last batch of invoices?* ○ *The last ten orders were only for small quantities.* □ **last week, last month, last year** the week, month or year before this one ○ *Last week's sales were the best we have ever had.* ○ *The sales managers have been asked to report on last month's drop in unit sales.* ○ *Last year's accounts have to be ready by the annual meeting.* ○ *Last year's accounts have to be ready in time for the annual meeting.* ■ *verb* to go on, to continue ○ *The boom started in the 1980s and lasted until the early 1990s.* ○ *The discussions over redundancies lasted all day.*

last in first out /ˌlæst ɪn ˌfɜrst ˈaʊt/ *noun* **1.** an employment policy using the principle that the people who have been most recently appointed are the first to be dismissed **2.** an accounting method where stock is valued at the price of the earliest purchases. Abbreviation **LIFO**. Compare **first in first out**

last quarter /ˌlæst ˈkwɔrtər/ *noun* a period of three months at the end of the financial year

last will and testament /ˌlæst ˌwɪl ən ˈtestəmənt/ *noun* a will, a document by which a person says what he or she wants to happen to their property when they die

late /leɪt/ *adjective* **1.** after the time stated or agreed ○ *We apologize for the late arrival of the plane from Amsterdam.* □ **there is a penalty for late delivery** if delivery is later than the agreed date, the supplier has to pay a fine **2.** at the end of a period of time □ **latest date for signature of the contract** the last acceptable date for signing the contract ■ *adverb* after the time stated or agreed ○ *The shipment was landed late.* ○ *The plane was two hours late.*

late majority /ˌleɪt məˈdʒɑrəti/ *noun* a category of buyers of a product who buy it later than the early majority but before the laggards

latent /ˈleɪt(ə)nt/ *adjective* present but not yet developed

latent demand /ˌleɪt(ə)nt dɪˈmænd/ *noun* a situation where there is demand for a product but potential customers are unable to pay for it ○ *We will have to wait for the economy to improve in countries where there is latent demand.* ○ *Situation analysis has shown that there is only latent demand.*

lateral /ˈlæt(ə)rəl/ *adjective* at the same level or with the same status ○ *Her transfer to Marketing was something of a lateral move.*

lateral diversification /ˌlæt(ə)rəl daɪ ˌvɜrsɪfɪˈkeɪʃ(ə)n/ *noun* the act of diversifying into a very different type of business

lateral integration /ˌlæt(ə)rəl ˌɪntə ˈgreɪʃ(ə)n/ *noun* the act of joining similar companies or taking over a company in the same line of business as yourself ○ *Lateral integration will allow a pooling of resources.* ○ *Lateral integration in the form of a merger will improve the efficiency of both businesses involved.*

lateral thinking /ˌlæt(ə)rəl ˈθɪŋkɪŋ/ *noun* an imaginative approach to problem-solving which involves changing established patterns of thinking to help make a breakthrough ○ *Lateral thinking resulted in finding a completely new use for an ex-*

isting product. ○ *Brainstorming sessions encourage lateral thinking and originality.*

latest /ˈleɪtɪst/ *adjective* most recent ○ *He always drives the latest model of car.* ○ *Here are the latest sales figures.*

launch /lɔntʃ/ *verb* **1.** to put a new product on the market, usually spending money on advertising it ○ *They launched their new car model at the motor show.* ○ *The company is spending thousands of pounds on launching a new brand of soap.* **2.** to put a company on the Stock Exchange for the first time ■ *noun* **1.** the act of putting a new product on the market ○ *The launch of the new model has been put back three months.* ○ *The management has decided on a September launch date.* ○ *The company is geared up for the launch of its first microcomputer.* **2.** the act of putting a company on the Stock Exchange for the first time

launching /ˈlɔntʃɪŋ/ *noun* the act of putting a new product on the market

launching costs /ˈlɔntʃɪŋ kɒsts/ *plural noun* the costs of publicity for a new product

launching date /ˈlɔntʃɪŋ deɪt/ *noun* the date when a new product is officially shown to the public for the first time

launching party /ˈlɔntʃɪŋ ˌpɑːti/ *noun* a party held to advertise the launching of a new product

launder /ˈlɔndər/ *verb* to pass illegal profits, money from selling drugs, money which has not been taxed, etc., into the banking system ○ *to launder money through an offshore bank*

"…it has since emerged that the bank was being used to launder drug money and some of its executives have been given lengthy jail sentences" [*Times*]

law /lɔː/ *noun* **1.** □ **inside** *or* **within the law** obeying the laws of a country □ **against** *or* **outside the law** not according to the laws of a country ○ *The company is possibly operating outside the law.* □ **to break the law** to do something which is not allowed by law ○ *He is breaking the law by trading without a license.* ○ *You will be breaking the law if you try to take that computer out of the country without an export license.* **2.** a rule governing some aspect of human activity made and enforced by the state □ **(the) law** all the laws

that are in force in a country considered as a body or system

law courts /ˈlɔː kɔːts/ *plural noun* a place where a judge listens to cases and decides who is right legally

lawful /ˈlɔːf(ə)l/ *adjective* acting within the law □ **lawful practice** action which is permitted by the law □ **lawful trade** trade which is allowed by law

lawfully /ˈlɔːfəli/ *adverb* acting within the law

law of diminishing returns /ˌlɔːr əv dɪˌmɪnɪʃɪŋ rɪˈtɜːnz/ *noun* a general rule that as more factors of production such as land, labor, and capital are added to the existing factors, so the amount they produce is proportionately smaller

law of supply and demand /ˌlɔːr əv səˌplaɪ ən dɪˈmænd/ *noun* a general rule that the amount of a product which is available is related to the needs of potential customers

lawsuit /ˈlɔːsuːt/ *noun* a case brought to a court □ **to bring a lawsuit against someone** to tell someone to appear in court to settle an argument □ **to defend a lawsuit** to appear in court to state your case

lawyer /ˈlɔːjər/ *noun* a person who has studied law and practices law as a profession

lay /leɪ/ *verb*

lay off *phrasal verb* **1.** to dismiss employees for a time until more work is available ○ *The factory laid off half its employees because of lack of orders.* □ **to lay off workers** to dismiss workers for a time (until more work is available) ○ *The factory laid off half its workers because of lack of orders.* **2. especially U.S.** to dismiss employees permanently □ **to lay off risks** to protect oneself against risk in one investment by making other investments

"…the company lost $52 million last year, and has laid off close to 2,000 employees" [*Toronto Star*]

lay out *phrasal verb* to spend money ○ *We had to lay out half our cash budget on equipping the new factory.*

lay up *phrasal verb* to stop using a ship because there is no work ○ *Half the shipping fleet is laid up by the recession.* ◊ **laid up**

"…while trading conditions for the tanker are being considered, it is possible that the ship could be laid up" [*Lloyd's List*]

lay-off /'leɪ ɔf/ *noun* an act of temporarily dismissing an employee for a period of more than four weeks ○ *The recession has caused hundreds of lay-offs in the car industry.*

layout /'leɪaʊt/ *noun* the arrangement of the inside space of a building or its contents ○ *They have altered the layout of the offices.*

lb *abbreviation* pound

LBO *abbreviation* leveraged buyout

L/C *abbreviation* letter of credit

LDC *abbreviation* least developed country

LDT *abbreviation* licensed deposit-taker

lead /lid/ *verb* **1.** to be the first, to be in front ○ *The company leads the market in cheap computers.* **2.** to be the main person in a group ○ *She will lead the trade mission to Nigeria.* ○ *The tour of American factories will be led by a Commerce Department official.* (NOTE: **leading – led**) ■ *noun* **1.** information which may lead to a sale ○ *It has been difficult starting selling in this territory with no leads to follow up.* ○ *I was given some useful leads by the sales rep who used to cover this territory.* **2.** a prospective purchaser who is the main decision-maker when buying a product or service ■ *adjective* most important, in/up front

lead (up) to *phrasal verb* to come before and be the cause of ○ *The discussions led to a big argument between the management and the union.* ○ *We received a series of approaches leading up to the takeover bid.*

leader /'lidər/ *noun* **1.** a person who manages or directs others ○ *the leader of the construction workers' union* or *the construction workers' leader* ○ *She is the leader of the trade mission to Nigeria.* **2.** a product which sells best **3.** an important stock, one which is often bought or sold on the Stock Exchange

leader pricing /'lidər ˌpraɪsɪŋ/ *noun* the practice of cutting prices on some goods in the hope that they attract customers to the store where more profitable sales can be made

leadership /'lidərʃɪp/ *noun* a quality that enables a person to manage or administer others ○ *Employees showing leadership potential will be chosen for management training.*

leading /'lidɪŋ/ *adjective* **1.** most important ○ *Leading industrialists feel the end of the recession is near.* ○ *Leading stocks rose on the Stock Exchange.* ○ *Leading stockholders in the company forced a change in management policy.* ○ *They are the leading company in the field.* **2.** which comes first

leading indicator /ˌlidɪŋ 'ɪndɪkeɪtər/ *noun* an indicator such as industrial production which shows a change in economic trends earlier than other indicators. Opposite **lagging indicator**

lead partner /'lid ˌpɑrtnər/ *noun* the organization that takes the leading role in a business alliance

lead time /'lid taɪm/ *noun* the time between deciding to place an order and receiving the product ○ *The lead time on this item is more than six weeks.*

leaflet /'liflət/ *noun* a sheet of paper giving information, used to advertise something ○ *to mail leaflets advertising a new hairdressing salon* ○ *They are handing out leaflets describing the financial services they offer.* ○ *We made a leaflet mailing to 20,000 addresses.*

leak /lik/ *verb* to pass on secret information ○ *Information on the contract was leaked to the press.* ○ *They discovered an employee was leaking information to a competitor.* ○ *The new manager was guilty of leaking confidential information about the organization to the press.*

leakage /'likɪdʒ/ *noun* an amount of goods lost in storage, e.g., by going bad or by being stolen or by leaking from the container

lean management /ˌlin 'mænɪdʒmənt/ *noun* a style of management, where few managers are employed, allowing decisions to be taken rapidly

lean production /lin prə'dʌkʃən/, **lean operation** /lin ɑpə'reɪʃ(ə)n/ *noun* a production method which reduces excessive expenditure on staff and concentrates on efficient low-cost manufacturing

leap-frogging /'lip ˌfrɑgɪŋ/ *adjective* □ **leap-frogging pay demands** pay demands where each section of employee asks for higher pay to do better than another section, which then asks for further increases in turn

Learning and Skills Council /ˌlɜrnɪŋ ən ˈskɪlz ˌkaʊnsəl/ *noun* a government organization responsible for the education and training of people over the age of 16

learning curve /ˈlɜrnɪŋ kɜrv/ *noun* a process of learning something that starts slowly and then becomes faster

learning disability /ˈlɜrnɪŋ ˌdɪsəbɪləti/ *noun* a condition which prevents someone from learning basic skills or assimilating information as easily as other people (NOTE: The plural is **learning disabilities**.)

learning organization /ˈlɜrnɪŋ ɔrgənaɪˌzeɪʃ(ə)n/ *noun* an organization whose employees are willing and eager to share information with each other, to learn from each other, and to work as a team to achieve their goals

learning relationship /ˈlɜrnɪŋ rɪˌleɪʃ(ə)nʃɪp/ *noun* a relationship between a supplier and a customer in which the supplier changes and adapts a product as it learns more about the customer's requirements

lease /lis/ *noun* **1.** a written contract for leasing or renting a building, a piece of land, or a piece of equipment for a period against payment of a fee ○ *to rent office space on a twenty-year lease* □ **the lease expires next year** *or* **the lease runs out next year** the lease comes to an end next year **2.** □ **to hold an oil lease in the North Sea** to have a lease on a section of the North Sea to explore for oil ■ *verb* **1.** to rent or rent offices, land or machinery for a period ○ *to lease offices to small firms* ○ *to lease equipment* **2.** to use an office, land or machinery for a time and pay a fee ○ *to lease an office from an insurance company* ○ *All our company cars are leased.*

  lease back *phrasal verb* to sell a property or machinery to a company and then take it back on a lease ○ *They sold the office building to raise cash, and then leased it back on a twenty-five year lease.*

lease-back /ˈlis bæk/ *noun* an arrangement where property is sold and then taken back on a lease ○ *They sold the office building and then took it back under a lease-back arrangement.*

leasehold /ˈlishoʊld/ *noun, adjective* possessing property on a lease, for a fixed time ○ *to buy a property leasehold* ○ *We are currently occupying a leasehold property.* ○ *The company has some valuable leaseholds.* ■ *noun* a property held on a lease from a freeholder ○ *The company has some valuable leaseholds.* ■ *adjective* on a lease from a freeholder ○ *to buy a property leasehold* ○ *We are currently occupying a leasehold property.*

leaseholder /ˈlishoʊldər/ *noun* a person who holds a property on a lease

leasing /ˈlisɪŋ/ *noun* the use of a lease or of equipment under a lease ○ *an equipment-leasing company* ○ *to run a copier under a leasing arrangement* ○ *The company has branched out into car leasing.* ◊ **lessee**

leave /liv/ *noun* permission to be away from work □ **six weeks' annual leave** six weeks' vacation each year □ **to go or be on leave** to be away from work ○ *She is away on sick leave* or *on maternity leave.* ■ *verb* **1.** to go away from ○ *He left his office early to go to the meeting.* ○ *The next plane leaves at 10.20.* **2.** to resign ○ *He left his job and bought a farm.* (NOTE: **leaving – left**)

  leave out *phrasal verb* not to include ○ *She left out the date on the letter.* ○ *The contract leaves out all details of marketing arrangements.*

leave of absence /ˌliv əv ˈæbsəns/ *noun* permission to be absent from work ○ *He asked for leave of absence to visit his mother in hospital.*

-led /led/ *suffix* which is led by something ○ *an export-led boom* ○ *the consumer-led rise in sales*

ledger /ˈledʒər/ *noun* a book in which accounts are written

left /left/ *adjective* on the side of the body which usually has the weaker hand, not right ○ *The numbers run down the left side of the page.* ○ *Put the debits in the left column.*

legacy /ˈlegəsi/ *noun* a piece of property given by someone to someone else in a will

legal /ˈlig(ə)l/ *adjective* **1.** according to the law or allowed by the law ○ *The company's action in sacking the accountant was completely legal.* **2.** referring to the law □ **to take legal action** to sue someone or to take someone to court □ **to take legal advice** to ask a lawyer to advise about a legal problem

legal adviser /ˌliːg(ə)l ədˈvaɪzər/ *noun* a person who advises clients about the law

legal claim /ˈliːg(ə)l kleɪm/ *noun* a statement that someone owns something legally ○ *He has no legal claim to the property.*

legal costs /ˈliːg(ə)l kɒsts/, **legal charges** /ˈliːg(ə)l ˌtʃɑːdʒɪz/, **legal expenses** /ˈliːg(ə)l ɪkˌspensɪz/ *plural noun* money spent on fees to lawyers ○ *The clerk could not afford the legal expenses involved in suing her boss.*

legal currency /ˌliːg(ə)l ˈkʌrənsi/ *noun* money which is legally used in a country

legal department /ˈliːg(ə)l dɪ ˌpɑːtmənt/ *noun* a section of a company dealing with legal matters

legal expert /ˈliːg(ə)l ˌekspɜːt/ *noun* a person who knows a lot about the law

legal holiday /ˌliːg(ə)l ˈhɒlɪdeɪ/ *noun* a day when banks and other businesses are closed

legality /lɪˈgæləti/ *noun* the fact of being allowed by law ○ *There is doubt about the legality of the company's action in dismissing him.*

legalization /ˌliːgəlaɪˈzeɪʃ(ə)n/ *noun* the act of making something legal ○ *the campaign for the legalization of cannabis*

legalize /ˈliːgəlaɪz/ *verb* to make something legal

legally /ˈliːgəli/ *adverb* according to the law □ **the contract is legally binding** according to the law, the contract has to be obeyed □ **the directors are legally responsible** the law says that the directors are responsible

legal proceedings /ˈliːg(ə)l prə ˌsiːdɪŋz/ *plural noun* legal action or a lawsuit

legal profession /ˈliːg(ə)l prəˌfeʃ(ə)n/ *noun* all qualified lawyers

legal tender /ˌliːg(ə)l ˈtendər/ *noun* coins or bills which can be legally used to pay a debt

legatee /ˌlegəˈtiː/ *noun* a person who receives property from someone who has died

legislation /ˌledʒɪˈsleɪʃ(ə)n/ *noun* laws

lemon /ˈlemən/ *noun* **1.** a product, especially a car, that is defective in some way **2.** an investment that is performing poorly

lend /lend/ *verb* to allow someone to use something for a period ○ *to lend something to someone* or *to lend someone something* ○ *to lend money against security* ○ *He lent the company money* or *He lent money to the company.* ○ *The bank lent her $50,000 to start her business.* (NOTE: **lending – lent**)

lender /ˈlendər/ *noun* a person who lends money

lender of the last resort /ˌlendər əv ðər ˌlɑːst rɪˈzɔːt/ *noun* a central bank which lends money to commercial banks

lending /ˈlendɪŋ/ *noun* an act of letting someone use money for a time

lending limit /ˈlendɪŋ ˌlɪmɪt/ *noun* a restriction on the amount of money a bank can lend

length /leŋθ/ *noun* **1.** a measurement of how long something is ○ *The boardroom table is twelve feet in length.* ○ *Inches and centimeters are measurements of length.* **2.** □ **to go to great lengths to get something** to do anything (even commit a crime) to get something ○ *They went to considerable lengths to keep the project secret.*

length of service /ˌleŋθ əv ˈsɜːvɪs/ *noun* the number of years someone has worked

less /les/ *adjective* smaller than, of a smaller size or of a smaller value ○ *We do not grant credit for sums of less than $100.* ○ *He sold it for less than he had paid for it.* ■ *preposition* minus, with a sum removed ○ *purchase price less 15% discount* ○ *interest less service charges* ■ *adverb* not as much

lessee /leˈsiː/ *noun* a person who has a lease or who pays money for a property he or she leases

lessor /leˈsɔː/ *noun* a person who grants a lease on a property

let /let/ *verb U.K.* same as **rent** □ **to let an office** to allow someone to use an office for a time in return for payment of rent □ **offices to let** offices which are available to be leased by companies ■ *noun* the period of the lease of a property ○ *They took the office on a short let.*

let go *phrasal verb* to make someone redundant or to fire someone (*euphemism*) (NOTE: **letting – let**)

let-out clause /ˈlet aʊt ˌklɔːz/ *noun* a clause which allows someone to avoid doing something in a contract ○ *He added a* *let-out clause to the effect that the payments would be revised if the exchange rate fell by more than 5%.*

letter /'letər/ *noun* **1.** a piece of writing sent from one person or company to another to ask for or to give information **2.** □ **to acknowledge receipt by letter** to write a letter to say that something has been received

> COMMENT: First names are commonly used between business people in the U.S. and U.K.; they are less often used in other European countries (France and Germany), for example, where business letters tend to be more formal.

letter box /'letər bɑks/ *noun* a place where incoming mail is put

letterhead /'letərhed/ *noun* **1.** the name and address of a company printed at the top of a piece of stationery **2.** a sheet of paper with the name and address of the company printed on it (NOTE: The U.K. term is **headed paper.**)

letter heading /'letər ˌhedɪŋ/ *noun* the name and address of a company printed at the top of a piece of notepaper

letter of acknowledgement /ˌletər əv ək'nɑlɪdʒmənt/ *noun* a letter which says that something has been received

letter of advice /ˌletər əv əd'vaɪs/ *noun* same as **advice note** ○ *The letter of advice stated that the goods would be at Miami on the morning of the 6th.* ○ *The letter of advice reminded the customer of the agreed payment terms.*

letter of application /ˌletər əv æplɪ'keɪʃ(ə)n/ *noun* a letter in which someone applies for a job

letter of appointment /ˌletər əv ə'pɔɪntmənt/ *noun* a letter in which someone is appointed to a job

letter of complaint /ˌletər əv kəm'pleɪnt/ *noun* a letter in which someone complains

letter of credit /ˌletə əv 'kredɪt/ *noun* a document issued by a bank on behalf of a customer authorizing payment to a supplier when the conditions specified in the document are met. Abbreviation **L/C**

letter of indemnity /ˌletər əv ɪn'demnəti/ *noun* a letter promising payment as compensation for a loss

letter of inquiry /ˌletər əv ɪn'kwaɪri/ *noun* a letter from a prospective buyer to a supplier inquiring about products and their prices ○ *The letter of inquiry requested us to send our catalogs and price lists.* ○ *We received a letter of inquiry concerning possible trade discounts.*

letter of intent /ˌletər əv ɪn'tent/ *noun* a letter which states what a company intends to do if something happens

letter of reference /ˌletər əv 'ref(ə)rəns/ *noun* a letter in which an employer recommends someone for a new job

letter post /'letər poʊst/ *noun* a service for sending letters or packages

letter rate /'letər reɪt/ *noun* postage (calculated by weight) for sending a letter or a parcel ○ *It is more expensive to send a packet letter rate but it will get there quicker.*

letter scale /'letər skeɪl/ *noun* special small scales for weighing letters

letters of administration /ˌletərz əv ədˌmɪnɪ'streɪʃ(ə)n/ *plural noun* a letter given by a court to allow someone to deal with the estate of a person who has died

letters patent /ˌletərz 'peɪtənt/ *plural noun* the official term for a patent

letting agency /'letɪŋ ˌeɪdʒənsi/ *noun* an agency which deals in property to rent

level /'lev(ə)l/ *noun* the position of something compared to others ○ *low levels of productivity* or *low productivity levels* ○ *to raise the level of employee benefits* ○ *to lower the level of borrowings* □ **high level of investment** large amounts of money invested □ **a decision taken at the highest level** a decision taken by the most important person or group ■ *verb* □ **to level off** or **to level out** to stop rising or falling ○ *Profits have leveled off over the last few years.* ○ *Prices are leveling out.*

level playing field /ˌlev(ə)l 'pleɪɪŋ ˌfild/ *noun* a situation in which the same rules apply for all competitors and none of them has any special advantage over the others

leverage /'livərɪdʒ/ *noun* **1.** an influence which you can use to achieve a goal ○ *He has no leverage over the chairman.* **2.** a ratio of capital borrowed by a company at a fixed rate of interest to the company's total capital (NOTE: The U.K. term is **gearing.**) **3.** (*act of borrowing money*) the act of borrowing money at fixed interest which is then used to produce more money than the interest paid

leveraged buyout /ˌlivərɪdʒd 'baɪaʊt/, **leveraged takeover** /ˌlivərɪdʒd 'teɪkoʊvər/ *noun* an act of buying all the stock in a company by borrowing money against the security of the stock to be bought. Abbreviation **LBO**

"…the offer came after management had offered to take the company private through a leveraged buyout for $825 million" [*Fortune*]

lever-arch file /ˌlivər ɑrtʃ 'faɪl/ *noun* a type of ring binder, where you lift up one side of the rings with a lever, place the document on the prongs of the other side and then close the rings together again

levy /'levi/ *noun* money which is demanded and collected by the government □ **levies on luxury items** taxes on luxury items ■ *verb* to demand payment of a tax or an extra payment and to collect it ○ *to levy a duty on the import of luxury items* ○ *The government has decided to levy a tax on imported cars.* □ **to levy members for a new club house** to ask members of the club to pay for the new building

"…royalties have been levied at a rate of 12.5% of full production" [*Lloyd's List*]

liabilities /ˌlaɪə'bɪlətiz/ *plural noun* the debts of a business, including dividends owed to stockholders ○ *The balance sheet shows the company's assets and liabilities.* □ **he was not able to meet his liabilities** he could not pay his debts □ **to discharge your liabilities in full** to pay everything which you owe

liability /ˌlaɪə'bɪləti/ *noun* **1.** a legal responsibility for damage, loss, or harm ○ *The two partners took out insurance to cover employers' liability.* □ **to accept liability for something** to agree that you are responsible for something □ **to refuse liability for something** to refuse to agree that you are responsible for something **2.** responsibility for a payment such as the repayment of a loan **3.** someone or something which represents a loss to a person or organization ○ *The sales director is an alcoholic and has become a liability to the company.*

liable /'laɪəb(ə)l/ *adjective* **1.** □ **liable for** legally responsible for ○ *The customer is liable for breakages.* ○ *The chairman was personally liable for the company's*

debts. ○ *The garage is liable for damage to customers' cars.* **2.** □ **liable to** which is officially due to be paid ○ *Employees' wages are liable to tax.*

libel /'laɪb(ə)l/ *noun* an untrue written statement which damages someone's character □ **action for libel**, **libel action** case in a law court where someone says that another person has written a libel ■ *verb* □ **to libel someone** to damage someone's character in writing

license¹ /'laɪs(ə)ns/ *noun* an official document which allows someone to do something (NOTE: The U.K. spelling is **licence.**) □ **goods manufactured under license** goods made with the permission of the owner of the copyright or patent

license² /'laɪs(ə)ns/ *verb* to give someone official permission to do something for a fee, e.g., when a company allows another company to manufacture its products abroad ○ *licensed to sell beers, wines and spirits* ○ *to license a company to manufacture spare parts* ○ *She is licensed to run an employment agency.*

license agreement /'laɪs(ə)ns ə ˌgrimənt/ *noun* a legal document which comes with a software product and defines how you can use the software and how many people are allowed to use it

licensed deposit-taker /ˌlaɪs(ə)nst dɪ'pɑzɪt ˌteɪkə/, **licensed institution** /ˌlaɪs(ə)nst ˌɪnstɪ'tjuʃ(ə)n/ *noun* a deposit-taking institution which is licensed to receive money on deposit from private individuals and to pay interest on it, e.g., a savings and loan, bank or friendly society. Abbreviation **LDT**

licensed premises /ˌlaɪs(ə)nst 'premɪsɪz/ *plural noun* shop, restaurant or public house which is licensed to sell alcohol

licensee /ˌlaɪs(ə)n'si/ *noun* a person who has a license, especially a license to sell alcohol or to manufacture something

licensing /'laɪs(ə)nsɪŋ/ *adjective* referring to licenses ○ *a licensing agreement* ○ *licensing laws*

licensing agreement /'laɪs(ə)nsɪŋ ə ˌgrimənt/ *noun* an agreement where a person or company is granted a license to manufacture something or to use something, but not an outright sale

licensing authorities /'laɪs(ə)nsɪŋ ɔr ˌθɑrətiz/ *noun* local authorities which have the right to grant licenses to sell alcohol

licensing hours /'laɪs(ə)nsɪŋ ˌaʊrz/ *plural noun* the hours of the day when alcohol can be sold

licensing laws /'laɪs(ə)nsɪŋ ˌlɔz/ *plural noun* the laws which control when and where alcohol can be sold

licensor /'laɪsensər/ *noun* a person who licenses someone

lien /'liən/ *noun* the legal right to hold someone's goods and keep them until a debt has been paid

lieu /lju/ *noun* □ **in lieu of** instead of □ **she was given two months' salary in lieu of notice** she was given two months' salary and asked to leave immediately

life /laɪf/ *noun* the period of time for which something or someone exists □ **for life** for as long as someone is alive ○ *His pension gives him a comfortable income for life.*

life annuity /'laɪf əˌnjuːti/ *noun* annual payments made to someone as long as they are alive

life assurance /'laɪf əˌʃʊrəns/ *noun* *U.K.* same as **life insurance**

life assured /ˌlaɪf ə'ʃʊrd/ *noun* the person whose life has been covered by a life insurance policy

lifeboat operation /ˌlaɪfbəʊt ˌapə'reɪʃ(ə)n/ *noun* actions taken to rescue of a company (especially of a bank) which is in difficulties

life cycle /'laɪf ˌsaɪk(ə)l/ *noun* a concept used for charting the different stages in the life of people, animals, or products

life expectancy /'laɪf ɪkˌspektənsi/ *noun* the number of years a person is likely to live

life insurance /'laɪf ɪnˌʃʊrəns/ *noun* insurance which pays a sum of money when someone dies, or at an agreed date if they are still alive

life interest /ˌlaɪf 'ɪntrəst/ *noun* a situation where someone benefits from a property as long as he or she is alive

LIFO /'laɪfəʊ/ *abbreviation* last in first out

light /laɪt/ *adjective* **1.** not heavy, not very busy or active **2.** not having enough of a certain type of stock in a portfolio ○ *His portfolio is light in banks.*

lighter /'laɪtər/ *noun* a boat used to take cargo from a cargo ship to shore

light industry /ˌlaɪt 'ɪndəstri/ *noun* an industry making small products such as clothes, books, or calculators

light pages /'laɪt ˌpeɪdʒɪz/ *noun* web pages that are less than 50KB in size, which enables them to be downloaded quickly

light pen /'laɪt pen/ *noun* a type of electronic pen that directs a beam of light which, when passed over a bar code, can read it and send information back to a computer

limit /'lɪmɪt/ *noun* the point at which something ends or the point where you can go no further □ **to set limits to imports, to impose import limits** to allow only a specific amount of imports ■ *verb* **1.** to stop something from going beyond a specific point, to restrict the number or amount of something □ **the banks have limited their credit** the banks have allowed their customers only a specific amount of credit □ **each agent is limited to twenty-five units** each agent is allowed only twenty-five units to sell **2.** to restrict the number or amount of something

limitation /ˌlɪmɪ'teɪʃ(ə)n/ *noun* the act of allowing only a specific quantity of something ○ *The contract imposes limitations on the number of cars which can be imported.* □ **limitation of liability** the fact of making someone liable for only a part of the damage or loss

limited /'lɪmɪtɪd/ *adjective* restricted

limited liability /ˌlɪmɪtɪd laɪə'bɪləti/ *noun* a situation where someone's liability for debt is limited by law

limited market /ˌlɪmɪtɪd 'markət/ *noun* a market which can take only a specific quantity of goods

limited partner /ˌlɪmɪtɪd 'partnər/ *noun* a partner who is responsible for the debts of the firm only up to the amount of money which he or she has provided to the business

limited partnership /ˌlɪmɪtɪd 'partnəʃɪp/ *noun* a registered business where the liability of the partners is limited to the amount of capital they have each provided to the business and where the partners may not take part in the running of the business

limiting /'lɪmɪtɪŋ/ *adjective* not allowing something to go beyond a point, restricting ○ *a limiting clause in a contract* ○ *The short tourist season is a limiting factor on the hotel trade.*

line /laɪn/ *noun* 1. a row of letters or figures on a page 2. a series of things, one after another 3. same as **product line** 4. a row of people waiting one after the other (NOTE: The U.K. term is **queue**.) 5. a short letter 6. □ **the line is busy** the person is already speaking on the phone 7. a type of goods produced or sold by someone

line chart /'laɪn tʃɑrt/ *noun* a chart or graph using lines to indicate values

line management /'laɪn ˌmænɪdʒmənt/ *noun U.K.* the organization of a company where each manager is responsible for doing what their superior tells them to do. Also called **line organization**

line manager /'laɪn ˌmænɪdʒər/ *noun* a manager responsible to a superior, but with authority to give orders to other employees

line of business /ˌlaɪn əv 'bɪznɪs/ *noun* a type of business or work

line of command /ˌlaɪn əv kə'mænd/ *noun* an organization of a business where each manager is responsible for doing what his superior tells him to do

line of credit /ˌlaɪn əv 'kredɪt/ *noun* 1. the amount of money made available to a customer by a bank as an overdraft □ **to open a line of credit** *or* **a credit line** to make credit available to someone 2. the borrowing limit on a credit card

line organization /'laɪn ɔrgənaɪˌzeɪʃ(ə)n/ *noun* same as **line management**

line printer /'laɪn ˌprɪntər/ *noun* a machine which prints information from a computer, printing one line at a time (the quality is not as good as laser printers or inkjet printers but line printers are the only type which print on multipart stationery)

line simplification /'laɪn sɪmplɪfɪˌkeɪʃ(ə)n/ *noun* the removal of some products from a product line to make the whole line more easily manageable

link /lɪŋk/ *verb* to join or to attach to something else ○ *to link pensions to inflation* ○ *to link bonus payments to productivity* ○ *His salary is linked to the cost of living.* ◊ **index-linked** ■ *noun* 1. same as

hyperlink 2. a connection or connecting device

linking /'lɪŋkɪŋ/ *noun* the process of connecting two or more websites or documents by inserting links that enable users to move from one to the other

liquid /'lɪkwɪd/ *adjective* easily converted to cash, or containing a large amount of cash

liquid assets /ˌlɪkwɪd 'æsets/ *plural noun* cash, or investments which can be quickly converted into cash

liquidate /'lɪkwɪdeɪt/ *verb* □ **to liquidate a company** to close a company and sell its assets, usually in order to pay debts □ **to liquidate a debt** to pay a debt in full □ **to liquidate stock** to sell stock to raise cash

liquidation /ˌlɪkwɪ'deɪʃ(ə)n/ *noun* 1. the sale of assets for cash, usually in order to pay debts □ **liquidation of a debt** payment of a debt 2. the winding up or closing of a company and selling of its assets □ **the company went into liquidation** the company was closed and its assets sold

liquidator /'lɪkwɪdeɪtər/ *noun* a person named to supervise the closing of a company which is in liquidation

liquidity /lɪ'kwɪdɪti/ *noun* 1. cash, or the fact of having cash or assets which can be changed into cash □ **liquidity crisis** not having enough cash or other liquid assets 2. assets which can be changed into cash

liquidity ratio /lɪ'kwɪdɪti ˌreɪʃioʊ/ *noun* an accounting ratio used to measure an organization's liquidity. It is calculated by taking the business's current assets, minus its stocks, divided by its current liabilities. Also called **acid test ratio**, **quick ratio**

liquor license /'lɪkər ˌlaɪs(ə)ns/ *noun* a government document allowing someone to sell alcohol

liquor store /'lɪkə stɔr/ *noun* a store which sells alcohol for drinking at home

lira /'lɪrə/ *noun* 1. a former unit of currency in Italy ○ *the book cost 2,700 lira or L2,700* (NOTE: **Lira** is usually written **L** before figures: **L2,700**.) 2. a unit of currency used in Turkey

list /lɪst/ *noun* 1. several items written one after the other ○ *They have an attractive list of products or product list.* ○ *I can't find that item on our stock list.* ○ *Please add this item to the list.* ○ *She* *crossed the item off her list.* **2.** a catalog ■ *verb* to write a series of items one after the other ○ *to list products by category* ○ *to list representatives by area* ○ *to list products in a catalog* ○ *The catalog lists ten models of fax machine.*

listed company /ˌlɪstɪd ˈkʌmp(ə)ni/ *noun* a company whose stock can be bought or sold on the Stock Exchange

listed securities /ˌlɪstɪd sɪˈkjʊrɪtiz/ *plural noun* stock which can be bought or sold on the Stock Exchange, shares which appear on the official Stock Exchange list

list host /ˈlɪst hoʊst/ *noun* a company that provides connections to the Internet and storage space on its computers which can store the files for a user's website (NOTE: also called a "host service *or* hosting service provider")

listing details /ˈlɪstɪŋ ˌditeɪlz/ *plural noun* **1.** details of a company which are published when the company applies for a stock exchange listing (the U.S. equivalent is the "registration statement") **2.** details of the institutions which are backing an issue

listing paper /ˈlɪstɪŋ ˌpeɪpər/ *noun* paper made as a long sheet, used in computer printers

listing particulars /ˈlɪstɪŋ pər ˌtɪkjʊləz/ *plural noun* same as **listing details**

list price /ˈlɪst praɪs/ *noun* the price for something as given in a catalog

liter /ˈlitə/ *noun* a measure of liquids (NOTE: The U.S. spelling is **liter**.) □ **the car does fifteen kilometers to the liter** *or* **fifteen kilometers per liter** the car uses one liter of gasoline to travel fifteen kilometers

literature /ˈlɪt(ə)rətʃər/ *noun* written information about something ○ *Please send me literature about your new product range.*

litigant /ˈlɪtɪɡənt/ *noun* a person who brings a lawsuit against someone

litigation /ˌlɪtɪˈɡeɪʃ(ə)n/ *noun* the bringing of a lawsuit against someone

Little Board /ˈlɪt(ə)l bɔrd/ *noun* same as **American Stock Exchange**

lively /ˈlaɪvli/ *adjective* □ **lively market** an active stock market, with many shares being bought or sold

livery /ˈlɪvəri/ *noun* a company's own special design and colors, used e.g., on uniforms, office decoration, and vehicles

living wage /ˌlɪvɪŋ ˈweɪdʒ/ *noun* not to earn enough to pay for essentials (food, heat, rent)

LLC *abbreviation* limited liability company

Lloyd's /lɔɪdz/ *noun* the central London insurance market

COMMENT: Lloyd's is an old-established insurance market. The underwriters who form Lloyd's are divided into syndicates, each made up of active underwriters who arrange the business and non-working underwriters (called "names") who stand surety for any insurance claims which may arise.

load /loʊd/ *noun* an amount of goods which are transported in a particular vehicle or aircraft □ **the load of a lorry** *or* **of a container** the goods carried by a truck or in a container □ **maximum load** the largest weight of goods which a truck or plane can carry ■ *verb* **1.** □ **to load a truck** *or* **a ship** to put goods into a truck or a ship for transporting ○ *to load cargo onto a ship* ○ *a truck loaded with boxes* ○ *a ship loaded with iron* □ **a fully loaded ship** a ship which is full of cargo **2.** (*of a ship*) to take on cargo ○ *The ship is loading a cargo of wood.* **3.** to put a program into a computer ○ *Load the word-processing program before you start keyboarding.* **4.** to add extra charges to a price

load-carrying capacity /ˈloʊd ˌkæriɪŋ kəˌpæsəti/ *noun* the amount of goods which a truck is capable of carrying

loaded price /ˌloʊdɪd ˈpraɪs/ *noun* a price which includes an unusually large extra payment for some service ○ *That company is notorious for loading its prices.*

load factor /ˈloʊd ˌfæktər/ *noun* a number of seats in a bus, plane or train which are occupied by passengers who have paid the full fare

loading /ˈloʊdɪŋ/ *noun* the process of assigning work to workers or machines ○ *The production manager has to ensure that careful loading makes the best use of human resources.*

loading bay /ˈloʊdɪŋ beɪ/ *noun* a section of road in a warehouse, where trucks can drive in to load or unload

loading dock /ˈloʊdɪŋ dɑk/ *noun* the part of a harbor where ships can load or unload

loading ramp /ˈloʊdɪŋ ræmp/ *noun* a raised platform which makes it easier to load goods onto a truck

load line /ˈloʊd laɪn/ *noun* a line painted on the side of a ship to show where the water should reach for maximum safety if the ship is fully loaded (NOTE: also called **Plimsoll line** on U.K. ships)

load time /ˈloʊd taɪm/ *noun* in computing, the time it takes for a page of data to open completely in a window

loan /loʊn/ *noun* money which has been lent ■ *verb* to lend something ○ *The truck has been loaned by the local haulage company.*

    "…over the last few weeks, companies raising new loans from international banks have been forced to pay more, and an unusually high number of attempts to syndicate loans among banks has failed" [*Financial Times*]

loan capital /ˈloʊn ˌkæpɪt(ə)l/ *noun* a part of a company's capital which is a loan to be repaid at a later date

loan shark /ˈloʊn ʃɑrk/ *noun* a person who lends money at a very high interest rate

loan stock /ˈloʊn stɑk/ *noun* stock issued to an organization in return for a loan. Loan stock earns interest.

lobby /ˈlɑbi/ *noun* a group that tries to persuade a government or law-makers to support a particular cause or interest □ **the energy-saving lobby** people who try to persuade government or law-makers to pass laws to save energy ■ *verb* to try to influence government, law-makers, etc ○ *The group lobbied the chairmen of all the committees.*

local /ˈloʊk(ə)l/ *adjective* located in or providing a service for a restricted area ■ *noun* a branch of a national labor union

local area network /ˌloʊk(ə)l ˌeriə ˈnetwɜrk/ *noun* a network of computers and associated devices such as printers linked by cable in an area and able to share resources. Abbreviation **LAN**

local authority /ˌloʊk(ə)l ɔrˈθɑrɪti/ *noun* an elected section of government which runs a small area of the country

local call /ˌloʊk(ə)l ˈkɔl/ *noun* a telephone call to a number on the same ex-

change as your own or to one on a neighboring exchange

local currency /ˌloʊk(ə)l ˈkʌrənsi/ *noun* the currency of a particular country where a transaction is being carried out ○ *Because of the weakness of the local currency, all payments are in dollars.*

local government /ˌloʊk(ə)l ˈgʌv(ə)nmənt/ *noun* elected authorities and administrative organizations which deal with the affairs of small areas of a country

localization /ˌloʊkəlaɪˈzeɪʃ(ə)n/ *noun* **1.** the process of restricting something to a particular area or adapting it for use in a particular area **2.** the translation of a website into a language or idiom that can be easily understood by the target user

local labor /ˌloʊk(ə)l ˈleɪbər/ *noun* workers who are recruited near a factory, and are not brought there from a distance

locally /ˈloʊk(ə)li/ *adverb* in the area near where an office or factory is based ○ *We recruit all our staff locally.*

local press /ˌloʊk(ə)l ˈpres/ *noun* newspapers which are sold in a small area of the country ○ *The product was only advertised in the local press as it was only being distributed in that area of the country.*

local time /ˈloʊk(ə)l ˌtaɪm/ *noun* the time in the country where something is happening ○ *If it is 12.00 noon in London, it will be 5 o'clock in the morning local time.*

locate /loʊˈkeɪt/ *verb* □ **to be located** to be in a certain place ○ *The warehouse is located near to the motorway.*

lock /lɑk/ *verb*

    lock up *phrasal verb* **1.** □ **to lock up a store, an office** to close and lock the door at the end of the day's work **2.** □ **to lock up capital** to have capital invested in such a way that it cannot be used for other investments

locking up /ˌlɑkɪŋ ˈʌp/ *noun* □ **the locking up of money in stock** the act of investing money in stock so that it cannot be used for other, possibly more profitable, investments

lockout /ˈlɑkaʊt/ *noun* an industrial dispute where the management will not let the workers into the factory until they have agreed to the management's conditions

lock-out /ˌlɑk ˈaʊt/ *noun* □ **to lock out workers** to shut the factory door so that workers cannot get in and so force them not to work until the conditions imposed by the management are met

lock-up premises /ˌlɑk ʌp ˈpremɪsɪz/ *plural noun* a store or other commercial building which has no living accommodations and which the proprietor locks at night when it is closed

lock-up shop /ˈlɑkʌp ˈʃɑp/ *noun* same as **lock-up premises**

lodge /lɑdʒ/ *verb* □ **to lodge a complaint against someone** to make an official complaint about someone □ **to lodge securities as collateral** to put securities into a bank to be used as collateral for a loan

log /lɔg/ *verb* to write down all that happens □ **to log phone calls** to note all details of phone calls made

> "I have just been trying to log onto a website for one hour – from 8.00 am to 9.00 am – to buy some shares. Their server just can't cope with the Monday morning rush to buy" [*Investors Chronicle*]

log off *phrasal verb* to stop work on a computer program and close down the program (NOTE: **logging – logged**)

log on *phrasal verb* to start a computer program by entering a password, and various other instructions

logistics /ləˈdʒɪstɪks/ *noun* the task or science of managing the movement, storage, and processing of materials and information in a supply chain (NOTE: Logistics includes the acquisition of raw materials and components, manufacturing or processing, and the distribution of finished products to the end user.)

logo /ˈloʊgoʊ/ *noun* a symbol, design, or group of letters used by a company as a mark on its products and in advertising

London gold fixing /ˌlʌndən ˈgoʊld ˌfɪksɪŋ/ *noun* a system whereby the world price for gold is set each day in London

long /lɑŋ/ *adjective* for a large period of time □ **in the long term** over a long period of time □ **to take the long view** to plan for a long period before current investment becomes profitable

long credit /ˌlɑŋ ˈkredɪt/ *noun* credit terms which allow the borrower a long time to pay

long-dated bill /ˌlɑŋ ˌdeɪtɪd ˈbɪl/ *noun U.K.* a bill which is payable in more than three months' time

long-dated stocks /ˌlɑŋ ˌdeɪtɪd ˈstɑks/ *plural noun* same as **longs**

long-distance /ˌlɑŋ ˈdɪstəns/ *adjective* □ **long-distance flight** flight to a destination which is a long way away

long-distance call /ˌlɑŋ ˌdɪstəns ˈkɔl/ *noun* a telephone call to a number which is not near

longhand /ˈlɑŋhænd/ *noun* handwriting where the words are written out in full and not typed or in shorthand ○ *Applications should be written in longhand and sent to the human resources manager.*

long-haul flight /ˌlɑŋ hɔl ˈflaɪt/ *noun* long-distance flight, especially one between continents

long-range /ˌlɑŋ ˈreɪndʒ/ *adjective* for a long period of time in the future □ **long-range economic forecast** a forecast which covers a period of several years

longs /lɑŋz/ *plural noun U.K.* government stocks which will mature in over fifteen years' time. Also called **long-dated stocks**

long-standing /ˌlɑŋ ˈstændɪŋ/ *adjective* which has been arranged for a long time ○ *a long-standing agreement* □ **long-standing customer, customer of long standing** a person who has been a customer for many years

long-term /ˌlɑŋ ˈtɜrm/ *adjective* **1.** relating to a long time into the future ○ *The management projections are made on a long-term basis.* ○ *Sound long-term planning will give the company more direction.* ○ *It is in the company's long-term interests to have a contented staff.* □ **on a long-term basis** continuing for a long period of time □ **long-term debts** debts which will be repaid many years later □ **long-term forecast** a forecast for a period of over three years □ **long-term loan** a loan to be repaid many years later □ **long-term objectives** aims which will take years to achieve **2.** used to describe an investment that is held for a long period of time, e.g., a bond that is held for at least 10 years

long-term unemployed /ˌlɑŋ tɜrm ˌʌnɪmˈplɔɪd/ *noun* people who have been out of work for more than a year

loophole /ˈluphoʊl/ *noun* □ **to find a loophole in the law** to find a means of legally avoiding the law □ **to find a tax loophole** to find a means of legally not paying tax

"...because capital gains are not taxed but money taken out in profits is taxed, owners of businesses will be using accountants and tax experts to find loopholes in the law" [*Toronto Star*]

loose /luːs/ *adjective* not packed together □ **to sell loose potatoes**, **to sell potatoes loose** to sell potatoes in quantities which are separately weighed, not in previously weighed bags

loose change /ˌluːs ˈtʃeɪndʒ/ *noun* money in coins

loose-leaf book /ˌluːs liːf ˈbʊk/ *noun* a book with loose pages which can be taken out and fixed back in again on rings

lorry /ˈlɒri/ *noun* U.K. same as **truck**

lorry-load /ˈlɒri ləʊd/ *noun* U.K. same as **truckload** ○ *They delivered six lorry-loads of coal.*

lose /luːz/ *verb* **1.** not to have something anymore □ **to lose an order** not to get an order which you were hoping to get ○ *During the strike, the company lost six orders to South American competitors.* □ **to lose control of a company** to find that you have less than 50% of the stock and so are no longer able to control the company □ **to lose customers** to have fewer customers ○ *Their service is so slow that they have been losing customers.* □ **she lost her job when the factory closed** she was made redundant **2.** to have less money ○ *He lost $25,000 in his father's computer company.* **3.** to drop to a lower price ○ *The dollar lost two cents against the yen.* ○ *Gold stocks lost 5% on the market yesterday.* □ **the dollar has lost value** the dollar is worth less

lose out *phrasal verb* to suffer as a result of something ○ *The company has lost out in the rush to make cheap computers.* ○ *We lost out to a Japanese company who put in a lower bid for the job.*

loss /lɒs/ *noun* **1.** the state or process of not having something anymore □ **loss of customers** not keeping customers because of bad service, high prices, etc. □ **loss of an order** not getting an order which was expected □ **the company suffered a loss of market penetration** the company found it had a smaller share of the market **2.** the state of having less money than be-

fore or of not making a profit □ **the company suffered a loss** the company did not make a profit □ **to report a loss** not to show a profit in the accounts at the end of the year ○ *The company reported a loss of $1m on the first year's trading.* □ **the car was written off as a dead loss** *or* **a total loss** the car was so badly damaged that the insurers said it had no value □ **at a loss** making a loss, not making any profit ○ *The company is trading at a loss.* ○ *We sold the store at a loss.* □ **to cut your losses** to stop doing something which is losing money **3.** the state of being worth less or having a lower value ○ *Stocks showed losses of up to 5% on the Stock Exchange.* **4.** the state of weighing less □ **loss in weight** goods which weigh less than when they were packed **5.** damage to property or destruction of property, which is then subject to an insurance claim □ **the cargo was written off as a total loss** the cargo was so badly damaged that the insurers said it had no value

loss adjuster /ˈlɒs əˌdʒʌstər/ *noun* U.K. same as **insurance adjuster**

loss-leader /ˈlɒs ˌliːdər/ *noun* an article which is sold at a loss to attract customers ○ *We use these cheap movies as a loss-leader.*

loss of earnings /ˌlɒs əv ˈɜːnɪŋz/ *plural noun* U.K. payment to someone who has stopped earning money or who is not able to earn money

loss of office /ˌlɒs əv ˈɒfɪs/ *noun* U.K. payment to a director who is asked to leave a company before his contract ends

lot /lɒt/ *noun* **1.** a large quantity ○ *a lot of people* or *lots of people are out of work* **2.** a group of items sold together at an auction ○ *to bid for lot 23* ○ *At the end of the auction half the lots were unsold.* **3.** a group of shares which are sold ○ *to sell a lot of shares* ○ *to sell shares in small lots* **4.** a piece of land, especially one to be used for redevelopment ○ *They bought a lot and built a house.*

lottery /ˈlɒtəri/ *noun* a game where numbered tickets are sold and prizes given for some of the numbers

low /ləʊ/ *adjective* not high or not much ○ *Low overhead costs keep the unit cost low.* ○ *We try to keep our wages bill low.* ○ *The company offered him a mortgage at a low rate of interest.* ○ *The pound is at a* *very low rate of exchange against the dollar.* □ **low volume of sales** small number of items sold ■ *noun* a point where prices or sales are very small ○ *the highs and lows on the stock market* ○ *Sales have reached a new low.* □ **highs and lows on the Stock Exchange** a list of stock which have reached a new high or low price in the previous day's trading □ **stocks have hit an all-time low** stocks have reached their lowest price ever

"...after opening at 79.1 the index touched a peak of 79.2 and then drifted to a low of 78.8" [*Financial Times*]

"...the pound which had been as low as $1.02 earlier this year, rose to $1.30" [*Fortune*]

low-cost /ˌloʊ ˈkɒst/ *adjective* not costing a lot

lower /ˈloʊr/ *adjective* smaller or less high ○ *a lower rate of interest* ○ *Sales were lower in December than in November.* ■ *verb* to make something smaller or less expensive ○ *to lower prices to secure a larger market share* ○ *Industrialists have asked the bank to lower interest rates.*

"Canadian and European negotiators agreed to a deal under which Canada could keep its quotas but lower its import duties" [*Globe and Mail (Toronto)*]

lowering /ˈloʊrɪŋ/ *noun* the act of making smaller or less expensive ○ *Lowering the prices has resulted in increased sales.* ○ *We hope to achieve low prices with no lowering of quality.*

low-grade /ˈloʊ ɡreɪd/ *adjective* **1.** not very important ○ *a low-grade official from the Department of Commerce* **2.** not of very good quality ○ *The car runs best on low-grade gasoline.*

low-income /ˌloʊ ˈɪŋkʌm/ *adjective* having a relatively small income, or used by people with on a relatively small income ○ *low-income housing*

low-level /ˌloʊ ˈlev(ə)l/ *adjective* not very important ○ *A low-level delegation visited the ministry.* ○ *A low-level meeting decided to put off making a decision.*

low-level computer language /ˌloʊ ˌlev(ə)l kəmˈpjuːtər ˌlæŋɡwɪdʒ/ *noun* programming language similar to machine code

low-pressure /ˌloʊ ˈpreʃər/ *adjective* □ **low-pressure sales** sales where the salesperson does not force someone to buy, but only encourages them to do so

low-quality /ˌloʊ ˈkwɑləti/ *adjective* not of good quality ○ *They tried to sell us some low-quality steel.*

low season /ˌloʊ ˈsiːz(ə)n/ *noun* a period when there are few travelers ○ *Air fares are cheaper in the low season.*

loyal /ˈlɔɪəl/ *adjective* **1.** always buying the same brand or using the same store ○ *The goal of the advertising is to keep the customers loyal.* **2.** referring to an employee who supports the company they work for (NOTE: You are loyal **to** someone or something.)

loyalty /ˈlɔɪəlti/ *noun* the state of being faithful to someone or something

Ltd. *abbreviation* limited company

lull /lʌl/ *noun* a quiet period ○ *After last week's hectic trading this week's lull was welcome.*

lump sum /ˌlʌmp ˈsʌm/ *noun* U.K. money paid in one single amount, not in several small sums ○ *When he retired he was given a lump-sum bonus.* ○ *She sold her house and invested the money as a lump sum.*

lunch hour /ˈlʌntʃ aʊə/, **lunchtime** /ˈlʌntʃtaɪm/ *noun* the time when people have lunch ○ *the office is closed during the lunch hour or at lunchtimes*

luxury /ˈlʌkʃəri/ *noun, adjective* referring to an expensive thing which is not necessary but which is good to have ○ *a black market in luxury articles* ○ *Luxury items are taxed very heavily.*

luxury goods /ˈlʌkʃəri ɡʊdz/, **luxury items** /ˈlʌkʃəri ˌaɪtəmz/ *plural noun* expensive items which are not basic necessities

M

m *abbreviation* **1.** metre **2.** million

Maastricht Treaty /'mæstrɪkt ˌtriti/ *noun* a treaty signed in 1992 which sets out the principles for a European Union and the convergence criteria for states wishing to join the EMU

machine /mə'ʃin/ *noun* a device which works with power from a motor

machine code /mə'ʃin koʊd/ *noun* instructions and information shown as a series of figures (0 and 1) which can be read by a computer

machine-made /mə'ʃin meɪd/ *adjective* manufactured by a machine, not by people

machine-readable code /mə ʃin ˌridəb(ə)l 'koʊd/ *noun* a set of signs or letters (such as a bar code or zip code) which can be read by computers

machinery /mə'ʃinəri/ *noun* **1.** machines **2.** an organization or a system ○ *the local government machinery* or *the machinery of local government is slow to act* ○ *the administrative machinery of a university* ○ *the machinery for awarding government contracts* ○ *The administrative machinery needs reviewing.*

machinery guard /mə'ʃinəri gɑrd/ *noun* a piece of metal to prevent workers from getting hurt by the moving parts of a machine

machine shop /mə'ʃin ʃɑp/ *noun* a place where working machines are placed

machine tool /mə'ʃin tul/ *noun* a tool worked by a motor, used to work on wood or metal

machinist /mə'ʃinɪst/ *noun* a person who operates a machine

macro- /mækroʊ/ *prefix* very large, covering a wide area

macroeconomics /ˌmækroʊikə'nɑmɪks/ *plural noun* a study of the economics of a whole area, a whole industry, a whole group of the population, or a whole country, in order to help in economic planning. Compare **microeconomics** (NOTE: takes a singular verb)

macroenvironment /'mækroʊ ɪn ˌvaɪrənmənt/ *noun* the general environmental factors that affect an organization, such as legislation or the country's economy ○ *We must develop a flexible planning system to allow for major changes in the macroenvironment.*

Macromedia Flash™ /ˌmækroʊmidiə 'flæʃ/ *noun* a trade name for a type of animation software used on the Web, which is characterized by small file sizes, easy scalability and the use of streaming technology

Madam /'mædəm/ *noun* a formal way of addressing a woman, especially one whom you do not know □ **Dear Madam** beginning of a letter to a woman whom you do not know

Madam Chairman /ˌmædəm 'tʃermən/, **Madam Chairwoman** /ˌmædəm 'tʃer,wʊmən/ *noun* a way of speaking to a female chairman of a committee or meeting

made /meɪd/ *adjective* produced or manufactured ○ *made in Japan* or *Japanese made* ◊ **make**

made-to-measure /ˌmeɪd tə 'meʒər/ *adjective* made to fit the requirements of the customer ○ *made-to-measure kitchen cabinets* ○ *a made-to-measure suit*

magazine /'mægəzin/ *noun* a special type of newspaper, usually published only weekly or monthly, often with a glossy cover and often devoted to a particular subject □ **magazine insert** an advertising sheet put into a magazine when it is mailed or sold □ **to insert a leaflet in a specialist magazine** to put an advertising leaflet into a magazine before it is mailed or sold

magazine mailing /ˈmægəzɪn ˌmeɪlɪŋ/ *noun* the sending of copies of a magazine by mail to subscribers

magnate /ˈmægneɪt/ *noun* an important businessman ○ *a shipping magnate*

magnetic strip /mægˌnetɪk ˈstrɪp/, **magnetic stripe** /mægˌnetɪk ˈstraɪp/ *noun* a black strip on credit cards and ATM cards, on which personal information about the account is recorded

mail /meɪl/ *noun* 1. a system of sending letters and parcels from one place to another ○ *The check was lost in the mail.* ○ *The invoice was put in the mail yesterday.* ○ *Mail to some of the islands in the Pacific can take six weeks.* □ **by mail** using the postal services, not sending something by hand or by messenger □ **to send a package by surface mail** to send a package by land or sea, not by air □ **by sea mail** sent by mail abroad, using a ship □ **by air mail** sent by mail abroad, using a plane □ **we sent the order by first-class mail** we sent the order by the most expensive mail service, designed to be faster 2. letters sent or received ○ *Has the mail arrived yet?* ○ *The first thing I do is open the mail.* ○ *The receipt was in this morning's mail.* 3. same as **email** ■ *verb* 1. to send something by post ○ *to mail a letter* ○ *We mailed our order last Wednesday.* ○ *They mailed their catalog to three thousand customers in Europe.* 2. same as **email**

mailbox /ˈmeɪlbɒks/ *noun* 1. one of several boxes where incoming mail is put in a large building 2. a number where email messages are received 3. a box where letters which are being sent are put to be collected 4. an area of a computer memory where emails are stored

mailer /ˈmeɪlər/ *noun* packaging made of folded cardboard, used to mail items which need protection ○ *a diskette mailer*

mailing list[1] /ˈmeɪlɪŋ/ *noun* the sending of something by mail ○ *the mailing of publicity material* □ **to buy a mailing list** to pay a society or other organization money to buy the list of members so that you can use it to mail publicity material

mailing list[2] /ˈmeɪlɪŋ lɪst/ *noun* a list of names and addresses of people who might be interested in a product, or a list of names and addresses of members of an organization ○ *to build up a mailing list* ○ *Your name is on our mailing list.*

mailing piece /ˈmeɪlɪŋ piːs/ *noun* a leaflet suitable for sending by direct mail

mailing tube /ˈmeɪlɪŋ tuːb/ *noun* a stiff cardboard or plastic tube, used for mailing large pieces of paper such as posters

mail merge /ˈmeɪl mɜrdʒ/ *noun* a word-processing program that allows a standard form letter to be printed out to a series of different names and addresses

mail order /ˌmeɪl ˈɔrdər/ *noun* a system of buying and selling from a catalog, placing orders, and sending goods by mail ○ *We bought our kitchen units by mail order.*

mail-order business /ˈmeɪl ˌɔrdər ˌbɪznɪs/ *noun* a company which sells its products by mail

mail-order catalog /ˈmeɪl ˌɔrdər ˌkætəlɒg/ *noun* a catalog from which a customer can order items to be sent by mail

mail-order selling /ˈmeɪl ˌɔrdər ˌselɪŋ/ *noun* a method of selling in which orders are taken and products are delivered by mail

mail room /ˈmeɪl ruːm/ *noun* a room in a building where the mail is sorted and sent to each department or collected from each department for sending

mail shot /ˈmeɪl ʃɒt/ *noun* leaflets sent by mail to possible customers. Also called **mailing shot**

main /meɪn/ *adjective* most important ○ *main office* ○ *main building* ○ *one of our main customers* ○ *The main building houses our admin and finance departments.*

mainframe /ˈmeɪnfreɪm/ *noun* a large computer ○ *The office PCs interface with the mainframe computer in the company headquarters.*

mainstream corporation tax /ˌmeɪnstrɪm ˌkɑːpəˈreɪʃ(ə)n tæks/ *noun* the total tax paid by a company on its profits less any advance corporation tax, which a company has already paid when distributing profits to its stockholders in the form of dividends. Abbreviation **MCT**

maintain /meɪnˈteɪn/ *verb* 1. to keep something going or working ○ *We try to maintain good relations with our customers.* ○ *Her trip aims to maintain contact with her important overseas markets.* 2. to keep something working at the same level ○ *to maintain an interest rate at 5%* ○ *The company has maintained the same volume* *of business in spite of the recession.* □ **to maintain a dividend** to pay the same dividend as the previous year

maintenance /'meɪntənəns/ *noun* **1.** the process of keeping things going or working ○ *Maintenance of contacts is important for a sales rep.* ○ *It is essential to ensure the maintenance of supplies to the factory.* **2.** the process of keeping a machine in good working order ○ *We offer a full maintenance service.*

"...responsibilities include the maintenance of large computerized databases" [*Times*]

"...the federal administration launched a full-scale investigation into the airline's maintenance procedures" [*Fortune*]

maintenance contract /'meɪntənəns ˌkɒntrækt/ *noun* a contract by which a company keeps a piece of equipment in good working order

majeure /mæˈʒɜr/ ♦ **force majeure**

major /'meɪdʒər/ *adjective* important ○ *There is a major risk of fire.* □ **major stockholder** a stockholder with a large number of shares

"...a client base which includes many major commercial organizations and nationalized industries" [*Times*]

majority /məˈdʒɒrəti/ *noun* **1.** more than half of a group □ **majority of the stockholders** more than 50% of the stockholders □ **the board accepted the proposal by a majority of three to two** three members of the board voted to accept the proposal and two voted against accepting it **2.** the number of votes by which a person wins an election ○ *He was elected store steward with a majority of three hundred.*

majority interest /məˈdʒɑrɪti ˈɪntrəst/ *noun* a situation where someone owns a majority or a minority of shares in a company ○ *He has a majority interest in a supermarket chain.*

majority shareholding /məˌdʒɒrəti ˈʃerhoʊldɪŋ/ *noun* a group of shares which are more than half the total

majority stockholder /məˌdʒɒrəti ˈstɑkhoʊldər/ *noun* a person who owns more than half the stock in a company

majority vote /məˈdʒɑrɪti voʊt/, **majority decision** /məˈdʒɑrɪti dɪˌsɪʒ(ə)n/ *noun* a decision which represents the wishes of the largest group as shown by a vote

make /meɪk/ *noun* a brand or type of product manufactured ○ *Japanese makes of cars* ○ *a standard make of equipment* ○ *What make is the new computer system* or *What's the make of the new computer system?* ■ *verb* **1.** to produce or to manufacture ○ *The employees spent ten weeks making the table.* ○ *The factory makes three hundred cars a day.* **2.** to earn money ○ *He makes $50,000 a year* or *$25 an hour.* **3.** to increase in value ○ *The stock made $2.92 in today's trading.* **4.** □ **to make a profit** to have more money after a deal □ **to make a loss** to have less money after a deal □ **to make a killing** to make a very large profit

make good *phrasal verb* **1.** to repair ○ *The company will make good the damage.* **2.** to be a success □ **a local boy made good** local person who has become successful

make out *phrasal verb* to write something ○ *to make out an invoice* ○ *The bill is made out to Smith Inc.* □ **to make out a check to someone** to write someone's name on a check

make over *phrasal verb* to transfer property legally ○ *to make over the house to your children*

make up *phrasal verb* **1.** to compensate for something □ **to make up a loss** *or* **difference** to pay extra so that the loss or difference is covered **2.** □ **to make up accounts** to complete the accounts

make up for *phrasal verb* to compensate for something ○ *to make up for a short payment* or *for a late payment* □ **to make up for a short order** to send items which were missing in the original order □ **to make up for a late payment** to pay more than is owed because the payment is late

maker /'meɪkər/ *noun* a person or company which makes something ○ *a major car maker* ○ *a furniture maker*

make-ready time /ˌmeɪk ˈredi ˌtaɪm/ *noun* a time to get a machine ready to start production

make-to-order /ˌmeɪk tu ˈɔrdər/ *noun* the making of goods or components to fulfill an existing order (NOTE: Make-to-order products are made to the customer's specification, and are often processed in small batches.)

making /'meɪkɪŋ/ *noun* the production of an item ○ *Ten tons of concrete were used in the making of the wall.*

maladministration /ˌmæləd.mɪnɪ'streɪʃ(ə)n/ *noun* incompetent administration

malfunction /mæl'fʌŋkʃən/ *noun* the fact of not working properly ○ *The data was lost due to a software malfunction.* ■ *verb* not to work properly ○ *Some of the keys on the keyboard have started to malfunction.*

mall /mɔl/ *noun* same as **shopping mall**

malware /'mælwer/ *noun* software such as viruses or trojans that are designed to do damage to a computer system

man /mæn/ *noun* a male worker, especially a manual worker without special skills or qualifications ○ *All the men went back to work yesterday.* ■ *verb* to provide the work force for something ○ *It takes six workers to man a shift.* ○ *We need volunteers to man the exhibition on Sunday.* ○ *The exhibition stand was manned by three salesgirls.* (NOTE: **manning – manned**. Note also **to man** does not mean only using men)

manage /'mænɪdʒ/ *verb* **1.** to direct or to be in charge of something ○ *to manage a branch office* ○ *A competent and motivated person is required to manage an important department in the company.* **2.** □ **to manage property** to look after rented property for the owner **3.** □ **to manage to** to be able to do something ○ *Did you manage to see the head buyer?* ○ *She managed to write six orders and take three phone calls all in two minutes.*

manageable /'mænɪdʒəb(ə)l/ *adjective* which can be dealt with ○ *The problems which the company faces are too large to be manageable by one person.*

managed fund /ˌmænɪdʒd 'fʌnd/ *noun* a mutual fund which is invested in specialist funds within the group and can be switched from one specialized investment area to another

managed hosting /ˌmænɪdʒd 'hoʊstɪŋ/ *noun* a hosting option in which the hosting company is mainly responsible for a client's servers, often supplying and managing not only the hardware but the software as well

management /'mænɪdʒmənt/ *noun* **1.** the process of directing or running a business ○ *a management graduate* or *a graduate in management* ○ *She studied management in college.* ○ *Good management* or *efficient management is essential in a large organization.* ○ *Bad management* or *inefficient management can ruin a business.* **2.** a group of managers or directors ○ *The management has decided to give everyone a pay increase.* (NOTE: Where **management** refers to a group of people it is sometimes followed by a plural verb.)

management accountant /'mænɪdʒmənt əˌkaʊntənt/ *noun* an accountant who prepares financial information for managers so that they can make decisions

management accounts /'mænɪdʒmənt əˌkaʊnts/ *plural noun* financial information prepared for a manager so that decisions can be made, including monthly or quarterly financial statements, often in great detail, with analysis of actual performance against the budget

management buyin /ˌmænɪdʒmənt 'baɪɪn/ *noun* the purchase of a subsidiary company by a group of outside directors. Abbreviation **MBI**

management buyout /ˌmænɪdʒmənt 'baɪaʊt/ *noun* the takeover of a company by a group of employees, usually senior managers and directors. Abbreviation **MBO**

management by exception /ˌmænɪdʒmənt baɪ ɪk'sepʃən/ *noun* a management system whereby deviations from plans are located and corrected

management by objectives /ˌmænɪdʒmənt baɪ əb'dʒektɪvz/ *noun* a way of managing a business by planning work for the managers to do and testing if it is completed correctly and on time

management by walking around /ˌmænɪdʒmənt baɪ ˌwɔrkɪŋ ə'raʊnd/ *noun* a way of managing where the manager moves round the office or shop floor, discusses problems with the staff and learns from them. Abbreviation **MBWA**

management committee /'mænɪdʒmənt kəˌmɪti/ *noun* a committee which manages something such as a club or a pension fund

management consultant /'mænɪdʒmənt kənˌsʌltənt/ *noun* a person who gives advice on how to manage a business

management course /'mænɪdʒmənt kɔrs/ *noun* a training course for managers

management function /'mænɪdʒmənt ˌfʌŋkʃən/ *noun* the duties of being a manager

management guru /ˌmænɪdʒmənt 'guru/ a management theorist (*informal*)

management information system /ˌmænɪdʒmənt ˌɪnfər'meɪʃ(ə)n ˌsɪstəm/ *noun* a computer-based information system that is specially designed to assist with management tasks and decision-making. Abbreviation **MIS**

management meeting /'mænɪdʒmənt ˌmitɪŋ/ *noun* a group of managers who meet

management standards /ˌmænɪdʒmənt 'stændərdz/ *plural noun* guidelines setting out the knowledge, understanding and personal competences that managers need to have if they are to be effective (NOTE: Management standards form the core criteria on which National Vocational Qualifications for managers in the United Kingdom are based and cover the management of activities, people, resources, information, energy, quality and projects.)

management style /'mænɪdʒmənt staɪl/, **style of management** the way in which managers work, in particular the way in which they treat their employees

management team /'mænɪdʒmənt tim/ *noun* all the managers who work in a particular company

management theorist /ˌmænɪdʒmənt 'θɪrɪst/ *noun* a person who develops original ideas and theories about the work of managers, usually on the basis of academic research or practical experience, and publishes them in books or journals

management trainee /ˌmænɪdʒmənt treɪ'ni/ *noun* a young member of staff who is being trained to be a manager

management training /ˌmænɪdʒmənt 'treɪnɪŋ/ *noun* the process of training staff to be managers, by making them study problems and work out solutions

manager /'mænɪdʒər/ *noun* **1.** the head of a department in a company ○ *She's a department manager in an engineering company.* ○ *Go and see the human resources manager if you have a problem.* ○ *The production manager has been with the company for only two weeks.* **2.** the person in charge of a branch or store ○ *Mr. Smith is the manager of our local Eastern Bank.* ○ *The manager of our London branch is in Boston for a series of meetings.*

manageress /ˌmænɪdʒə'res/ *noun* a woman who runs a store or a department

managerial /ˌmænɪ'dʒɪriəl/ *adjective* referring to managers ○ *All the managerial staff are sent for training every year.* □ **to be appointed to a managerial position** to be appointed a manager □ **decisions taken at managerial level** decisions taken by managers

managerial grid /ˌmænɪdʒɪriəl 'grɪd/ *noun* a type of management training in which trainees attempt to solve a number of problems in groups, and thereby discover their individual strengths and weaknesses

managerialism /ˌmænɪ'dʒɪriəlɪz(ə)m/ *noun* an outlook that emphasizes efficient management, and the use of systems, planning and management practices that improve efficiency (NOTE: Managerialism is often used as a term of criticism, implying either enthusiasm for efficiency at the expense of service or quality or a confrontational attitude toward labor unions.)

managership /'mænɪdʒərʃɪp/ *noun* the job of being a manager ○ *After six years, she was offered the managership of a branch in Scotland.*

managing change /ˌmænɪdʒɪŋ 'tʃeɪndʒ/ *noun* the process of managing the way changes in the working environment are implemented and how they affect the work force

managing director /ˌmænədʒɪŋ daɪ 'rektər/ *noun U.K.* the director who is in charge of a whole company. Abbreviation **MD**

mandate /'mændeɪt/ *noun* an order which allows something to take place

mandatory /'mændət(ə)ri/ *adjective* obligatory ○ *Wearing a suit is mandatory for all managerial staff.* □ **mandatory meeting** a meeting which all staff have to attend

manifest /'mænɪfest/ *noun* a list of goods in a shipment

manilla /mə'nɪlə/ *noun* thick brown paper ○ *a manilla envelope*

manipulate /mə'nɪpjʊleɪt/ *verb* □ **to manipulate the accounts** to make false accounts so that the company seems profitable □ **to manipulate the market** to work to influence stock prices in your favor

manning levels /'mænɪŋ ˌlev(ə)lz/ *plural noun* the number of people required in each department of a company to do the work efficiently

manpower /'mænpaʊr/ *noun* the number of employees in an organization, industry, or country (NOTE: **manpower** does not mean only men.)

manpower forecasting /'mænpaʊr ˌfɔrkæstɪŋ/ *noun* the process of calculating how many employees will be needed in the future, and how many will actually be available

manpower planning /'mænpaʊər ˌplænɪŋ/ *noun* the process of planning to obtain the right number of employees in each job

manpower requirements /'mænpaʊər rɪˌkwaɪəmənts/, **manpower needs** /'mænpaʊər nidz/ *plural noun* the number of employees needed

manpower shortage /'mænpaʊr ˌʃɔrtɪdʒ/ *noun* a lack of employees

manual /'mænjuəl/ *adjective* done by hand or done using the hands ■ *noun* a book of instructions, showing what procedures to follow

manual labor /ˌmænjuəl 'leɪbər/, **manual work** /'mænjuəl wɜrk/ *noun* heavy work done by hand

manual laborer /ˌmænjuəl 'leɪbərər/ *noun* a person who does heavy work with their hands

manually /'mænjuəli/ *adverb* done by hand, not by a machine ○ *Invoices have had to be typed manually because the computer has broken down.*

manual worker /ˌmænjuəl 'wɜrkər/ *noun* a person who works with his hands

manufacture /ˌmænjuˈfæktʃər/ *verb* to make a product for sale, using machines ○ *The company manufactures spare parts for cars.* ■ *noun* the making of a product for sale, using machines □ **products of foreign manufacture** products made in foreign countries

manufactured goods /ˌmænjufæktʃərd 'ɡʊdz/ *plural noun* items which are made by machine

manufacturer /ˌmænjuˈfæktʃərər/ *noun* a person or company that produces machine-made products ○ *a big Indian cotton manufacturer* ○ *Foreign manufacturers have set up factories here.*

manufacturer's recommended price /ˌmænjufæktʃərəz ˌrekəmendɪd 'praɪs/ *noun* a price at which the manufacturer suggests the product should be sold on the retail market, which is often reduced by the retailer ○ *"All china – 20% off the manufacturer's recommended price"* Abbreviation **MRP**

manufacturing /ˌmænjuˈfæktʃərɪŋ/ *noun* the production of machine-made products for sale ○ *We must try to reduce the manufacturing overhead.* ○ *Manufacturing processes are continually being updated.*

manufacturing capacity /ˌmænju 'fæktʃərɪŋ kəˌpæsəti/ *noun* the amount of a product which a factory is capable of making

manufacturing costs /ˌmænju 'fæktʃərɪŋ kɔsts/ *noun* the costs of making a product

manufacturing industries /ˌmænju 'fæktʃərɪŋ ˌɪndəstriz/ *plural noun* industries which take raw materials and make them into finished products

margin /'mɑrdʒɪn/ *noun* **1.** the difference between the money received when selling a product and the money paid for it □ **we are cutting our margins very fine** we are reducing our margins to the smallest possible in order to be competitive □ **our margins have been squeezed** profits have been reduced because our margins have to be smaller to stay competitive **2.** extra space or time allowed

marginal /'mɑrdʒɪn(ə)l/ *adjective* **1.** hardly worth the money paid **2.** not very profitable ○ *a marginal return on investment*

marginal cost /ˌmɑrdʒɪn(ə)l 'kɔst/ *noun* the cost of making a single extra unit above the number already planned

marginal costing /ˌmɑrdʒɪn(ə)l 'kɔstɪŋ/ *noun* the costing of a product on the basis of its variable costs only, excluding fixed costs

marginalization /ˌmɑrdʒɪnəlaɪ'zeɪʃ(ə)n/ *noun* loss of importance and status especially as a result of falling behind modern developments and being unable to participate in e.g., the Internet economy

marginal land /ˌmɑrdʒɪn(ə)l 'lænd/ *noun* land which is almost not worth farming

marginal pricing /ˌmɑrdʒɪn(ə)l 'praɪsɪŋ/ *noun* the practice of basing the selling price of a product on its variable costs of production plus a margin, but excluding fixed costs

marginal purchase /ˌmɑrdʒɪn(ə)l 'pɜrtʃɪs/ *noun* something which a buyer feels is only just worth buying

marginal rate of tax /ˌmɑrdʒɪn(ə)l reɪt əv 'tæks/, **marginal rate of taxation** /ˌmɑrdʒɪn(ə)l reɪt əv tæks'eɪʃ(ə)n/ *noun* the percentage of tax which a taxpayer pays at the top rate, which he or she therefore pays on every further dollar or pound he or she earns

marginal revenue /ˌmɑrdʒɪn(ə)l 'revɪnju/ *noun* the income from selling a single extra unit above the number already sold

marginal tax rate /ˌmɑrdʒɪn(ə)l 'tæks ˌreɪt/ *noun* same as **marginal rate of tax**

margin of error /ˌmɑrdʒɪn əv 'erər/ *noun* the number of mistakes which can be accepted in a document or in a calculation

margin of safety /ˌmɑrdʒɪn əv 'seɪfti/ *noun* the units produced or sales of such units which are above the break-even point

marine /mə'rin/ *adjective* referring to the sea

marine insurance /məˌrin ɪn'ʃʊrəns/ *noun* the insurance of ships and their cargoes

marine underwriter /məˌrin 'ʌndərraɪtər/ *noun* a person or company that insures ships and their cargoes

maritime /'mærɪtaɪm/ *adjective* referring to the sea

maritime law /ˌmærɪtaɪm 'lɔ/ *noun* laws referring to ships, ports, etc.

maritime lawyer /ˌmærɪtaɪm 'lɔjər/ *noun* a lawyer who specializes in legal matters concerning ships and cargoes

maritime trade /ˌmærɪtaɪm 'treɪd/ *noun* the transporting of commercial goods by sea

mark /mɑrk/ *noun* **1.** a sign put on an item to show something **2.** a former unit of currency in Germany ○ *The price was twenty-five marks.* ○ *The mark rose against the dollar.* (NOTE: Usually written **DM** after a figure: *25DM.*) ■ *verb* to put a sign on something ○ *to mark a product "for export only"* ○ *an article marked at $1.50* ○ *She used a black pen to mark the price on the book.*

mark down *phrasal verb* to make the price of something lower □ **to mark down a price** to lower the price of something ○ *This range has been marked down to $24.99.* ○ *We have marked all prices down by 30% for the sale.*

mark up *phrasal verb* to make the price of something higher □ **to mark prices up** to increase prices ○ *These prices have been marked up by 10%.*

mark-down /'mɑrk daʊn/ *noun* **1.** a reduction of the price of something to less than its usual price **2.** the percentage amount by which a price has been lowered ○ *There has been a 30% mark-down on all goods in the sale.*

marker pen /'mɑrkər pen/ *noun* a felt pen which makes a wide colored mark

market /'mɑrkət/ *noun* **1.** a place, often in the open air where farm produce and housewares are sold ○ *The fish market is held every Thursday.* ○ *The open-air market is held in the central square.* ○ *Here are this week's market prices for sheep.* **2.** □ **the Common Market** the European Union **3.** an area where a product might be sold or the group of people who might buy a product ○ *There is no market for this product.* ○ *Our share of the Far eastern market has gone down.* **4.** the possible sales of a specific product or demand for a specific product ○ *There's no market for word processors* ○ *The market for home computers has fallen sharply.* ○ *We have 20% of the U.K. car market.* **5.** □ **to pay black market prices** to pay high prices to get items which are not easily available **6.** a place where money or commodities are traded **7.** □ **to buy stocks on the open market** to buy stocks on the Stock Exchange, not privately □ **to come to the market** (*of a company*) to apply for a Stock Exchange listing, by offering existing shares for sale, or by offering a new issue **8.** a place where stocks are bought and sold ○ *The market in oil stocks was very* *active* or *There was a brisk market in oil stocks.* **9.** □ **to go up market, to go down market** to make products which appeal to a wealthy section of the market or to a wider, less wealthy section of the market **10.** □ **to be in the market for used cars** to look for used cars to buy □ **to come on to the market** to start to be sold ○ *This soap has just come on to the market.* □ **to put something on the market** to start to offer something for sale ○ *They put their house on the market.* ○ *I hear the company has been put on the market.* □ **the company has priced itself out of the market** the company has raised its prices so high that its products do not sell ■ *verb* to sell a product, or to present and promote a product in a way which will help to sell it ○ *This product is being marketed in all European countries.*

marketability /ˌmɑrkətəˈbɪlɪti/ *noun* the fact of being able to be sold easily ○ *the marketability of stocks in electronic companies*

marketable /ˈmɑrkɪtəb(ə)l/ *adjective* easily sold

market analysis /ˌmɑrkət əˈnæləsɪs/ *noun* the detailed examination and report of a market

market capitalization /ˌmɑrkɪt ˌkæpɪtəlaɪˈzeɪʃ(ə)n/ *noun* the total market value of a company, calculated by multiplying the price of its shares on the Stock Exchange by the number of shares outstanding ○ *company with a $1m capitalization*

market concentration /ˌmɑrkət ˌkɑns(ə)nˈtreɪʃ(ə)n/ *noun* same as **concentration**

market day /ˈmɑrkət deɪ/ *noun* the day when a market is regularly held ○ *Tuesday is market day, so the streets are closed to traffic.*

market dues /ˌmɑrkət ˈduz/ *plural noun* the rent to be paid for a stall in a market

market economist /ˌmɑrkət ɪˈkɑnəmɪst/ *noun* a person who specializes in the study of financial structures and the return on investments in the stock market

market economy /ˌmɑrkət ɪˈkɑnəmi/ *noun* same as **free market economy**

marketface /ˈmɑrkətfeɪs/ *noun* the point of contact between suppliers and their customers

market-facing /ˌmɑrkət ˈfeɪsɪŋ/ *adjective* referring to an enterprise that adapts itself to the needs of its markets and customers

market forces /ˌmɑrkət ˈfɔrsɪz/ *plural noun* the influences on the sales of a product which bring about a change in prices

market forecast /ˌmɑrkət ˈfɔrkæst/ *noun* a forecast of prices on the stock market

marketing /ˈmɑrkətɪŋ/ *noun* **1.** the business of presenting and promoting goods or services in such a way as to make customers want to buy them □ **marketing policy**, **marketing plans** ideas of how the company's products are going to be marketed ○ *to plan the marketing of a new product* **2.** the techniques used in selling a product, such as packaging and advertising

marketing agreement /ˈmɑrkətɪŋ əˌgrimənt/ *noun* a contract by which one company will market another company's products

marketing cost /ˈmɑrkətɪŋ kɔst/ *noun* the cost of selling a product, including advertising, packaging, etc.

marketing department /ˈmɑrkətɪŋ dɪˌpɑrtmənt/ *noun* the section of a company dealing with marketing and sales

marketing manager /ˈmɑrkətɪŋ ˌmænɪdʒər/ *noun* a person in charge of a marketing department ○ *The marketing manager has decided to start a new advertising campaign.*

marketing myopia /ˌmɑrkətɪŋ maɪ ˈoʊpiə/ *noun* a problem which occurs when a business is "nearsighted" and only views the world from its own perspective, and fails to see the point of view of the customer

marketing objectives /ˈmɑrkətɪŋ əb ˌdʒektɪvz/ *plural noun* aims set for an organization's marketing program, including sales, market share, and profitability

marketing plan /ˈmɑrkətɪŋ plæn/ *noun* a plan, usually annual, for a company's marketing activities, specifying expenditure and expected revenue and profits ○ *Has this year's marketing plan been drawn up yet?* ○ *The marketing plan is* *flexible enough to allow for an increase in advertising costs.*

market leader /ˌmɑrkət 'lidər/ *noun* **1.** a product which sells most in a market **2.** the company with the largest market share ○ *We are the market leader in home computers.*

market maker /'mɑrkɪt ˌmeɪkər/ *noun* a person or firm that buys and sells stocks on the stock market and offers to do so. Market makers list the securities they are willing to buy or sell and their bid and offer prices. If the prices are met, they immediately buy or sell and make their money by charging a commission on each transaction. Market makers play an important part in maintaining an orderly market.

market opening /'mɑrkət ˌoʊp(ə)nɪŋ/ *noun* the possibility of starting to do business in a new market

market opportunities /ˌmɑrkət ˌɑpər'tunətiz/ *noun* the possibility of finding new sales in a market

market opportunity /ˌmɑrkət ˌɑpər'tunəti/ *noun* the possibility of going into a market for the first time

market optimism /ˌmɑrkət 'ɑptɪˌmɪzəm/ *noun* a feeling that the stock market will rise

market penetration /ˌmɑrkət ˌpenɪ'treɪʃ(ə)n/ *noun* the percentage of a total market which the sales of a company cover

market pessimism /ˌmɑrkət 'pesɪmɪz(ə)m/ *noun* feeling that the stock market prices will fall

marketplace /'mɑrkətpleɪs/ *noun* **1.** the open space in the middle of a town where a market is held ○ *You can park in the marketplace when there is no market.* **2.** the situation and environment in which goods are sold ○ *Our salespeople find life difficult in the marketplace.* ○ *What's the reaction to the new car in the marketplace?* ○ *What's the marketplace reaction to the new car?*

market price /'mɑrkət praɪs/ *noun* the price at which a product can be sold

market profile /ˌmɑrkət 'proʊfaɪl/ *noun* the basic characteristics of a particular market

market rate /ˌmɑrkət 'reɪt/ *noun* the usual price in the market ○ *We pay the market rate for executive assistants* or *We pay executive assistants the market rate.*

market requirements /ˌmɑrkət rɪ'kwaɪrməntz/ *plural noun* things which are needed by the market

market research /ˌmɑrkət rɪ'sɜrtʃ/ *noun* the process of examining the possible sales of a product and the possible customers for it before it is put on the market

market sentiment /ˌmɑrkɪt 'sentɪmənt/ *noun* a general feeling among investors or financial analysts on a stock market

market share /ˌmɑrkət 'ʃer/ *noun* the percentage of a total market which the sales of a company's product cover ○ *We hope our new product range will increase our market share.*

market structure /ˌmɑrkət 'strʌktʃər/ *noun* the way in which a market is organized, including the concentration of suppliers or consumers, the ease of entry or barriers to entry, and the competitiveness of players in the market

market test /ˌmɑrkət 'test/ *noun* an examination to see if a sample of a product will sell in a market

market trends /ˌmɑrkət 'trendz/ *plural noun* gradual changes taking place in a market

market value /ˌmɑrkət 'vælju/ *noun* the value of an asset, a stock, a product, or a company if sold today

mark-up /'mɑrk ʌp/ *noun* **1.** an increase in price ○ *We put into effect a 10% mark-up of all prices in June.* ○ *Since I was last in the store they have put at least a 5% mark-up on the whole range of items.* **2.** the difference between the cost of a product or service and its selling price □ **we work to a 3.5 times mark-up** *or* **to a 350% mark-up** we take the unit cost and multiply by 3.5 to give the selling price

mart /mɑrt/ *noun* a place where things are sold

mass /mæs/ *noun* **1.** a large group of people **2.** a large number ○ *We have a mass of letters* or *masses of letters to write.* ○ *They received a mass of orders* or *masses of orders after the TV commercials.*

mass customization /ˌmæs ˌkʌstəmaɪ'zeɪʃ(ə)n/ *noun* a process that allows a standard, mass-produced item, e.g., a bicycle, to be altered to fit the specific requirements of individual customers

mass marketing /ˌmæs ˈmɑrkətɪŋ/ *noun* marketing which aims at reaching large numbers of people

mass media /ˌmæs ˈmidiə/ *noun* the means of communication by which large numbers of people are reached, e.g., radio, television, or newspapers

mass picketing /ˌmæs ˈpɪkɪtɪŋ/ *noun* the action of picketing by large numbers of pickets who try to frighten workers who want to work

mass-produce /ˌmæs prəˈdus/ *verb* to manufacture identical products in large quantities ○ *to mass-produce cars*

mass production /ˌmæs prəˈdʌkʃən/ *noun* the manufacture of large quantities of identical products

mass unemployment /ˌmæs ˌʌnɪm ˈplɔɪmənt/ *noun* unemployment affecting large numbers of people

master /ˈmæstər/ *adjective* main or original □ **master budget** a budget prepared by amalgamating budgets from various profit and cost centers such as sales, production, marketing, or administration in order to provide a main budget for the whole company □ **the master copy of a file** the main copy of a computer file, kept for security purposes ■ *noun* **1.** captain of a cargo ship ○ *Customs officers boarded the ship and arrested the master.* **2.** a skilled worker, qualified to train apprentices ○ *a master craftsman*

master franchise /ˈmæstər ˌfræntʃaɪz/ *noun* a franchise given to a single entrepreneur who then sells subsidiary franchises to others

mastermind /ˈmæstəmaɪnd/ *verb* to be in charge of a project

Master of Business Administration /ˌmæstər əv ˈbɪznɪs əd ˌmɪnɪstreɪʃ(ə)n/ *noun* full form of **M.B.A.**

masthead /ˈmæsthed/ *noun* the area at the top of a webpage, which usually contains the logo of the organization that owns the page, and often a search box and a set of links to important areas of the website

mate /meɪt/ *noun* an officer on a cargo ship below the rank of master

material /məˈtɪriəl/ *noun* a substance which can be used to make a finished product □ **materials control** a system to check that a company has enough materials in stock to do its work □ **material(s)**
cost cost of the materials used in making a product □ **materials handling** the moving of materials from one part of a factory to another in an efficient way

material requirement planning /mə ˌtɪriəl rɪˈkaɪrmənt ˌplænɪŋ/ *noun* a method of determining the materials that will be needed to meet manufacturing goals. Abbreviation **MRP**

maternity leave /məˈtɜrnɪti liv/ *noun* a period when a woman is away from work to have a baby but is often still paid

matrix management /ˈmeɪtrɪks ˌmænɪdʒmənt/ *noun* management that operates both through the hierarchical chain of command within the organization, and through relationships at the same level with other managers working in other locations or on different products or projects

matrix organization /ˈmeɪtrɪks ɔrgənaɪˌzeɪʃ(ə)n/ *noun* a flexible organization structure where authority depends on the expertise needed for a particular task and overall responsibility is shared between several people

matter /ˈmætər/ *noun* a question or problem to be discussed ○ *the most important matter on the agenda* ○ *We shall consider first the matter of last month's fall in prices.* ■ *verb* to be important ○ *Does it matter if one month's sales are down?*

mature /məˈtʃʊr/ *adjective* □ **mature economy** a fully developed economy ■ *verb* to become due □ **bills which mature in three weeks' time** bills which will be due for payment in three weeks

maturity /məˈtʃʊrəti/ *noun* **1.** the third stage in a product life cycle when a product is well established in the market though no longer enjoying increasing sales, after which sooner or later it will start to decline **2.** the time at which something becomes due for payment or repayment □ **amount payable on maturity** the amount received by the insured person when a policy matures

maturity date /məˈtʃʊrɪti deɪt/ *noun* a date when a government stock, an assurance policy or a debenture will become due for payment. Also called **date of maturity**

maturity yield /məˈtʃʊrɪti jild/ *noun* a calculation of the yield on a fixed-interest investment, assuming it is bought at a certain price and held to maturity

maximization /ˌmæksɪmaɪˈzeɪʃ(ə)n/ *noun* the process of making something as large as possible ○ *profit maximization* or *maximization of profit*

maximize /ˈmæksɪmaɪz/ *verb* to make something as large as possible ○ *Our goal is to maximize profits.* ○ *The cooperation of the work force will be needed if we are to maximize production.* ○ *She is paid on results, and so has to work flat out to maximize her earnings.*

maximum /ˈmæksɪməm/ *noun* the largest possible number, price or quantity ○ *It is the maximum the insurance company will pay.* (NOTE: The plural is **maximums** or **maxima**.) □ **up to a maximum of $10** no more than $30 □ **to increase exports to the maximum** to increase exports as much as possible ■ *adjective* largest possible ○ *40% is the maximum income tax rate* or *the maximum rate of tax.* ○ *The maximum load for the truck is one ton.* ○ *Maximum production levels were reached last week.* □ **to increase production to the maximum level** to increase it as much as possible

May Day /ˈmeɪ deɪ/ *noun* the change in practices on American Stock Exchanges which took place on 1st May 1975, with the removal of the system of fixed commissions. This allowed cheaper stock trading by brokers who did not offer any investment advice, and ultimately led to computerized financial dealing in general.

MB *abbreviation* megabyte

M.B.A. /ˌem bi ˈeɪ/ *noun* a degree awarded to graduates who have completed a further course in business studies. Full form **Master of Business Administration**

MBI *abbreviation* management buyin

MBO *abbreviation* management buyout

MBWA *abbreviation* management by walking around

MCT *abbreviation* mainstream corporation tax

MD *abbreviation* managing director ○ *She was appointed MD of a property company.*

mean /miːn/ *adjective* average ○ *The mean annual increase in sales is 3.20%.* □ **mean price** the average price of a stock in a day's trading ■ *noun* the average or number calculated by adding several quantities together and dividing by the number of quantities added ○ *Unit sales are over the mean for the first quarter* or *above the first-quarter mean.*

means /miːnz/ *noun* a way of doing something ○ *Do we have any means of copying all these documents quickly?* ○ *Bank transfer is the easiest means of payment.* (NOTE: The plural is **means.**) ■ *plural noun* money or resources ○ *The company has the means to launch the new product.* ○ *Such a level of investment is beyond the means of a small private company.*

means test /ˈmiːnz test/ *noun* an inquiry into how much money someone earns to see if they are eligible for state benefits ■ *verb* to find out how much money someone has in savings and assets ○ *All applicants will be means-tested.*

measure /ˈmeʒər/ *noun* **1.** a way of calculating size or quantity □ **as a measure of the company's performance** as a way of judging if the company's results are good or bad **2.** a type of action □ **to take measures to prevent something happening** to act to stop something happening □ **to take crisis**, **emergency measures** to act rapidly to stop a crisis developing ■ *verb* **1.** to find out the size or quantity of something or to be of a certain size or quantity ○ *to measure the size of a package* ○ *a package which measures 10cm by 25cm* or *a package measuring 10cm by 25cm* **2.** □ **to measure the government's performance** to judge how well the government is doing

measurement /ˈmeʒəmənt/ *noun* a way of judging something ○ *growth measurement* ○ *performance measurement* or *measurement of performance*

measurement of profitability /ˌmeʒəmənt əv ˌprɑfɪtəˈbɪlɪti/ *noun* a way of calculating how profitable something is

measurements /ˈmeʒəmənts/ *noun* size (in inches, centimeters, etc.) ○ *to write down the measurements of a package*

measuring tape /ˈmeʒərɪŋ teɪp/ *noun* a long tape with centimeters or inches marked on it, used to measure how long something is

mechanic /mɪˈkænɪk/ *noun* a person who works with engines or machines ○ *He got a job as a car mechanic before going to college.*

mechanical /mɪ'kænɪk(ə)l/ *adjective* worked by a machine ○ *a mechanical pump*

mechanism /'mekənɪz(ə)m/ *noun* the way in which something works ○ *the company's discount mechanism* ○ *a mechanism to slow down inflation* ○ *the company's salary review mechanism*

mechanization /ˌmekənaɪ'zeɪʃ(ə)n/ *noun* the act of using machines in place of workers ○ *farm mechanization* or *the mechanization of farms*

mechanize /'mekənaɪz/ *verb* to use machines in place of workers ○ *The country is aiming to mechanize its farming industry.*

media /'midiə/ *noun* the means of communicating a message about a product or service to the public (NOTE: **media** is followed by a singular or plural verb.) □ **the media, the mass media** means of communicating information to the public (such as television, radio, newspapers) ○ *the product attracted a lot of interest in the media* or *a lot of media interest*

media analysis /'midiə əˌnæləsɪs/ *noun* the examination of different types of media (such as the readers of newspapers, television viewers) to see which is best for promoting a certain type of product

media coverage /'midiə ˌkʌv(ə)rɪdʒ/ *noun* reports about something in the media ○ *We got good media coverage for the launch of the new model.*

median /'midiən/ *noun* the middle number in a list of numbers

mediate /'midieɪt/ *verb* to try to make the two sides in an argument come to an agreement ○ *The human resources director said she would try to mediate between the manager and his staff.* ○ *The government offered to mediate in the dispute.*

mediation /ˌmidɪ'eɪʃ(ə)n/ *noun* an attempt by a third party to make the two sides in an argument agree ○ *The employers refused an offer of government mediation.* ○ *The dispute was ended through the mediation of union officials.* ○ *Mediation by some third party is the only hope for ending the dispute.*

mediator /'midiəeɪtər/ *noun* a neutral person who attempts to make the two sides in an argument agree

medical certificate /'medɪk(ə)l sər'tɪfɪkət/ *noun* a certificate from a doctor to show that an employee has been ill

medical cover /'medɪk(ə)l ˌkʌvər/ *noun* same as **medical insurance**

medical insurance /'medɪk(ə)l ɪn'ʃʊrəns/ *noun* insurance which pays the cost of medical treatment, especially when someone is traveling abroad

medical profession /'medɪk(ə)l prə'feʃ(ə)n/ *noun* all doctors, nurses, and other professional people licensed to practice medicine

medium /'midiəm/ *adjective* middle or average ○ *The company is of medium size.* ■ *noun* a way of doing something, means of doing something

mediums /'midiəmz/ *plural noun* U.K. government stocks which mature in seven to fifteen years' time

medium-term /ˌmidiəm 'tɜrm/ *adjective* referring to a point between short term and long term □ **medium-term forecast** a forecast for two or three years □ **medium-term loan** a bank loan for three to five years

medium-term bond /ˌmidiəm tɜrm 'bɑnd/ *noun* a bond that is held for between two and ten years

meet /mit/ *verb* **1.** to come together with someone ○ *Union leaders came to meet the negotiating committee.* ○ *We met the agent at his hotel.* ○ *The two sides met in the lawyer's office.* **2.** to be satisfactory for something ○ *We must have a product which meets our requirements.* ○ *He was unable to meet his mortgage payments.* □ **to meet the demand for a new product** to fill the demand for a product □ **we will try to meet your price** we will try to offer a price which is acceptable to you □ **they failed to meet the deadline** they were not able to complete in time **3.** to pay for something ○ *The company will meet your expenses.* ○ *He was unable to meet his mortgage payments.* (NOTE: **meeting – met**)

meet with *phrasal verb* **1.** to come together with someone □ **I hope to meet with him in New York** I hope to meet him in New York **2.** □ **his request met with a refusal** his request was refused

meeting /'mitɪŋ/ *noun* an event at which a group of people come together in order to discuss matters of common interest to them □ **to hold a meeting** to organize a meeting of a group of people ○ *The meeting will be held in the committee room.* □ **to open a meeting** to start a meeting □ **to conduct a meeting** to be in the chair for a meeting □ **to close a meeting** to end a meeting □ **to address a meeting** to speak to a meeting □ **to put a resolution to a meeting** to ask a meeting to vote on a proposal

"...in proportion to your holding you have a stake in every aspect of the company, including a vote in the general meetings" [*Investors Chronicle*]

meeting place /'mitɪŋ pleɪs/ *noun* a room or area where people can meet

megabyte /'megəbaɪt/ *noun* storage unit in computers, equal to 1,048,576 bytes. Abbreviation **MB**

megacity /'megəsɪti/ *noun* a very large city, where there are powerful political institutions and media headquarters and which has key role in global information networks

member /'membər/ *noun* **1.** a person who belongs to a group, society, or organization ○ *Committee members voted on the proposal.* ○ *They were elected members of the board.* ○ *Every employer is a member of the employers' federation.* **2.** a stockholder in a company **3.** an organization which belongs to a larger organization ○ *the member companies of a trade association* ○ *The member states of the EU.* ○ *The members of the United Nations.*

"...it will be the first opportunity for party members and trade union members to express their views on the tax package" [*Australian Financial Review*]

membership /'membərʃɪp/ *noun* **1.** the fact of belonging to a group, society or organization ○ *membership qualifications* ○ *conditions of membership* ○ *membership card* ○ *to pay your membership or your membership fees* ○ *membership of the EU* **2.** all the members of a group ○ *The membership was asked to vote for the new president.* □ **the club has a membership of five hundred** the club has five hundred members

"...the bargaining committee will recommend that its membership ratify the agreement at a meeting called for June" [*Toronto Star*]

membership   secretary /'membərʃɪp ˌsekrətri/ *noun* a commit-

tee member who deals with the ordinary members of a society

members' voluntary winding up /ˌmembərz ˌvɑlənt(ə)ri ˌwaɪndɪŋ 'ʌp/ *noun* the winding up of a company by the stockholders themselves

memo /'memoʊ/ *noun* a short message sent from one person to another in the same organization ○ *She wrote a memo to the finance director.* ○ *The sales manager is going to send a memo to all the sales representatives.* ○ *According to your memo about debtors, the position is worse than last year.* ○ *I sent the managing director a memo about your complaint.*

memorandum /ˌmeməˈrændəm/ *noun* same as **memo**

memorandum and articles of association /ˌmeməˌrændəm ənd ˌɑrtɪk(ə)lz əv əˌsoʊsiˈeɪʃ(ə)n/, **memorandum   of   association** /ˌmemərændəm əv əˌsoʊsiˈeɪʃ(ə)n/ *noun U.K.* the legal documents which set up a limited company and give details of its name, aims, authorized share capital, conduct of meetings, appointment of directors and registered office

memory /'mem(ə)ri/ *noun* a facility for storing data in a computer

mental   handicap /ˌment(ə)l 'hændikæp/ *noun* same as **learning disability** (NOTE: This term is now generally considered unacceptable.)

mentee /men'ti/ *noun* a less experienced employee who is offered special guidance and support by a respected and trusted person with more experience (a mentor)

mention /'menʃ(ə)n/ *verb* to talk about something for a short time ○ *The chairman mentioned the work of the retiring managing director.* ○ *Can you mention to the secretary that the date of the next meeting has been changed?*

mentor /'mentɔr/ *noun* a person who is respected and trusted by a less experienced employee and offers special guidance and support to them

mentoring /'mentərɪŋ/ *noun* a form of training or employee development in which a trusted and respected person with a lot experience—the mentor—offers special guidance, encouragement and support to a less experienced employee

"I met Rick two years ago, after joining the Kansas City-based Helzberg Entrepreneurial Mentoring Program, which pairs company founders seeking help with more experienced entrepreneurs." [*BusinessWeek*]

menu /'menju/ *noun* a list of options or programs available to the user of a computer program

mercantile /'mɜrkəntaɪl/ *adjective* commercial □ **mercantile country** a country which earns income from trade □ **mercantile law** laws relating to business

mercantile agency /,mɜrkəntaɪl 'eɪdʒ(ə)nsi/ *noun* same as **credit bureau**

mercantile marine /,mɜrkəntaɪl mə 'rin/ *noun* all the commercial ships of a country

merchandise /'mɜrtʃəndaɪz/ *noun* goods which are for sale or which have been sold ○ *The merchandise is shipped through two ports.* ■ *verb* to sell goods by a wide variety of means, such as display, advertising, or sending samples ○ *to merchandise a product*

merchandiser /'mɜrtʃəndaɪzər/ *noun* a person or company that organizes the display and promotion of goods

merchandising /'mɜrtʃ(ə)n,daɪzɪŋ/ *noun* the process of organizing the display and promotion of goods in retail outlets ○ *the merchandising of a product* ○ *the merchandising department*

merchant /'mɜrtʃənt/ *noun* **1.** a businessperson who buys and sells, especially one who buys imported goods in bulk for retail sale ○ *a coal merchant* ○ *a wine merchant* **2.** a company, store or other business which accepts a credit card for purchases

merchant account /'mɜrtʃənt ə ,kaʊnt/ *noun* an account opened by an e-merchant at a financial institution to receive the proceeds of credit-card transactions

merchant bank /'mɜrtʃənt bæŋk/ *noun* a bank which arranges loans to companies, deals in international finance, buys and sells stocks and launches new companies on the Stock Exchange, but does not provide banking services to the general public

merchant banker /,mɜrtʃənt 'bæŋkər/ *noun* a person who has a high position in a merchant bank

merchantman /'mɜrtʃəntmən/ *noun* a commercial ship

merchant marine /,mɜrtʃənt mə'rin/ *noun* all the commercial ships of a country

merchant number /'mɜrtʃənt ,nʌmbər/ *noun* a number of the merchant, printed at the top of the report slip when depositing credit card payments

merchant ship /'mɜrtʃənt ʃɪp/ *noun* a commercial ship that carries a cargo

merge /mɜrdʒ/ *verb* to join together ○ *The two companies have merged.* ○ *The firm merged with its main competitor.*

merger /'mɜrdʒər/ *noun* the joining together of two or more companies ○ *As a result of the merger, the company is now the largest in the field.*

merit /'merɪt/ *noun* a quality which deserves reward

merit award /'merɪt ə,wɔrd/, **merit bonus** /'merɪt ,boʊnəs/ *noun* extra money given to an employee because they have worked well ○ *A merit bonus can encourage the better workers, but will discourage those who feel they cannot reach the required level.*

merit increase /'merɪt ,ɪnkris/ *noun* an increase in pay given to an employee because his or her work is good

meritocracy /,merɪ'tɑkrəsi/ *noun* a society or organization in which advancement is based on a person's natural ability rather than on his or her background

merit rating /'merɪt ,reɪtɪŋ/ *noun* the process of judging how well an employee works, so that payment can be according to merit

message /'mesɪdʒ/ *noun* **1.** a piece of news which is sent to someone ○ *He says he never received the message.* ○ *I'll leave a message with her assistant.* **2.** information given on a little screen on a computer, printer, fax machine, etc. ○ *We need more toner – the message is showing "TONER LOW".*

message board /'mesɪdʒ bɔrd/ *noun* a public bulletin board on which messages can be left (such as at a conference, or in a hotel lobby)

messenger /'mesɪndʒər/ *noun* a person who brings a message ○ *he sent the package by special messenger* or *by motorcycle messenger*

Messrs. /'mesərz/ *noun* plural form of Mr., used only in names of firms. ○ *Messrs. White, Inc.*

metadata /'metədeɪtə/ *noun* essential information contained in a document or web page, e.g., its publication date, author, keywords, title, and summary, which is used by search engines to find relevant websites in response to a search request from a user. ◊ **meta-tag** (NOTE: takes a singular or plural verb)

meta-tag /'metə tæg/ *noun* a keyword or description command used on a web page to enable it to be found by search engines

meter¹ /'mitər/ *noun* a device which measures the amount of something which has been used ○ *electricity meter* ○ *water meter* ■ *verb* to measure the amount of something which has been used

meter² /'mitər/ *noun* a measure of length (= 3.4 feet) (NOTE: Usually written **m** after figures: *the case is 2m wide by 3m long.*)

method /'meθəd/ *noun* a way of doing something ○ *They devised a new method of sending data.* ○ *What is the best method of payment?* ○ *Her organizing methods are out of date.* ○ *Their manufacturing methods or production methods are among the most modern in the country.*

metric /'metrɪk/ *adjective* using the meter as a basic measurement

metric system /'metrɪk ˌsɪstəm/ *noun* a system of measuring, using meters, liters and grams

metric ton /ˌmetrɪk 'tʌn/ *noun* 1000 kilograms

mezzanine financing /ˌmetsənin 'faɪnænsɪŋ/ *noun* financing provided to a company after it has received start-up financing

COMMENT: Mezzanine finance is slightly less risky than start-up finance, since the company has usually already started trading; it is, however, unsecured. This type of finance is aimed at consolidating a company's trading position before it is floated on a stock exchange.

mfg. *abbreviation* manufacturing

MFN *abbreviation* most favored nation

mg *abbreviation* milligram

mi *abbreviation* mile

micro- /maɪkroʊ/ *prefix* very small

microbrewery /'maɪɪroʊˌbruəri/ *noun* a small brewery, usually independently owned, that produces specialized beers in limited quantities

microbusiness /'maɪkroʊˌbɪznɪs/ *noun* a small business, typically with fewer than six employees, that does not have access to conventional sources of capital. Also called **microenterprise**

microeconomics /'maɪkroʊ ikəˌnɑmɪks/ *plural noun* the study of the economics of people or single companies. Compare **macroeconomics** (NOTE: takes a singular verb)

microenterprise /'maɪkroʊ ˌentərpraɪz/ *noun* same as **microbusiness**

microenvironment /'maɪkroʊɪnˌvaɪrənmənt/ *noun* the elements or factors outside a business organization which directly affect it, such as supply of raw materials, demand for its products, and competitive companies ○ *Unreliability of suppliers is one the greatest problems in our microenvironment.*

micromanage /'maɪkroʊˌmænɪdʒ/ *verb* to control a situation or employees by paying extreme attention to small details

mid- /mɪd/ *prefix* middle □ **from mid 2001** from the middle of 2001 ○ *The factory is closed until mid-July.*

middle /'mɪd(ə)l/ *adjective* in the center or between two points

middle-income /ˌmɪd(ə)l 'ɪŋkʌm/ *adjective* □ **people in the middle-income bracket** people with average incomes, not very high or very low

middleman /'mɪd(ə)lmæn/ *noun* a businessperson who buys from the manufacturer and sells to retailers or to the public ○ *We sell direct from the factory to the customer and cut out the middleman.* (NOTE: The plural is **middlemen**.)

middle management /ˌmɪd(ə)l 'mænɪdʒmənt/ *noun* department managers in a company, who carry out the policy set by the directors and organize the work of a group of employees

mid-month /ˌmɪd 'mʌnθ/ *adjective* happening in the middle of the month ○ *mid-month accounts*

mid-week /ˌmɪd 'wik/ *adjective* happening in the middle of a week ○ *the mid-week lull in sales*

mile /maɪl/ *noun* a measure of length (= 5,280 feet or 1.609 kilometers) □ **the car does twenty-five miles to the gallon, twenty-five miles per gallon** the car uses one gallon of gasoline to travel twenty-five miles

mileage /'maɪlɪdʒ/ *noun* **1.** a distance traveled in miles □ **the salesman's average annual mileage** the number of miles which a salesman drives in a year **2.** a distance which can be driven in a rented car, which may be charged to the person renting the car ○ *The car comes with unlimited free mileage.*

mileage allowance /'maɪlɪdʒ ə
ˌlaʊəns/ *noun* money allowed as expenses to someone who uses his or her own car for business travel

milk /mɪlk/ *verb* to make as much profit for as long as possible from a particular product or service ○ *We intend to milk the product hard for the next two years, before it becomes obsolete.*

mill /mɪl/ *noun* a building where some type of cloth is processed or made ○ *After lunch the visitors were shown round the mill.*

milligram /'mɪlɪɡræm/ *noun* one thousandth of a gram (NOTE: Usually written **mg** after figures.)

milliliter /'mɪlɪliːtə/ *noun* one thousandth of a liter (NOTE: The U.S. spelling is **milliliter**. Usually written **ml** after figures.)

millimeter /'mɪlɪmiːtə/ *noun* one thousandth of a meter (NOTE: The U.S. spelling is **millimeter**. Usually written **mm** after figures.)

million /'mɪljən/ *noun* the number 1,000,000 ○ *The company lost £10 million in the African market.* ○ *Our turnover has risen to $13.4 million.* ◊ **billion, trillion** (NOTE: Can be written **m** after figures: $5m (say "five million dollars.")))

millionaire /ˌmɪljə'neə/ *noun* a person who has more than one million pounds or dollars

min. *abbreviation* **1.** minute **2.** minimum

mindset /'maɪndset/ *noun* a way of thinking or general attitude to things

mine /maɪn/ *noun* a hole or tunnel in the ground for digging out coal, gold, iron, etc. ○ *The mines have been closed by a strike.* ○ *The main coal mines are in the west of the country.* ◊ **goldmine** ■ *verb* to dig and bring out coal, gold, etc. ○ *The*

company is mining coal in the south of the country.

mineral /'mɪn(ə)rəl/ *noun* a natural material (usually in the ground) which can be used

mineral resources /ˌmɪn(ə)rəl rɪ
'zɔːsɪz/ *noun* minerals (such as coal, iron ore, natural gas, etc.) which lie under the ground in a country and form part of the country's potential wealth

mineral rights /'mɪn(ə)rəl raɪts/ *noun* the right to extract minerals from the ground

mini- /mɪni/ *prefix* very small

minicontainer /'mɪnikən,teɪnər/ *noun* a small container

minimal /'mɪnɪm(ə)l/ *adjective* the smallest possible ○ *There was a minimal quantity of imperfections in the batch.* ○ *The head office exercises minimal control over the branch offices.*

minimart /'mɪnimɑːt/ *noun* a very small self-service store

minimize /'mɪnɪmaɪz/ *verb* to make something seem to be very small and not very important

minimum /'mɪnɪməm/ *noun* the smallest possible quantity, price or number ○ *to keep expenses to a minimum* ○ *to reduce the risk of a loss to a minimum* (NOTE: The plural is **minima** or **minimums.**) ■ *adjective* smallest possible □ **minimum dividend** the smallest dividend which is legal and accepted by the stockholders □ **minimum payment** the smallest payment necessary □ **minimum quantity** the smallest quantity which is acceptable □ **minimum stock level** lowest level of stock in a warehouse (when this level is reached more stock has to be ordered)

minimum wage /ˌmɪnɪməm 'weɪdʒ/ *noun* the lowest hourly wage which a company can legally pay its employees

mining concession /'maɪnɪŋ kən
ˌseʃ(ə)n/ *noun* the right to dig a mine on a piece of land

minister /'mɪnɪstər/ *noun* a member of a government who is in charge of a ministry ○ *a government minister* ○ *the Minister of Trade* or *the Trade Minister* ○ *the Minister of Foreign Affairs* or *the Foreign Minister* (NOTE: In the U.K. and U.S., they are called **secretary: the Foreign Secretary, Secretary of Commerce.**)

ministry /'mɪnɪstri/ *noun* a department in the government ○ *a ministry official* or *an official from the ministry* ○ *She works in the Ministry of Finance* or *the Finance Ministry.* ○ *He is in charge of the Ministry of Information* or *of the Information Ministry.* (NOTE: In the U.K. and the U.S., important ministries are called **departments: the Department of Trade and Industry, the Commerce Department**.)

minor /'maɪnər/ *adjective* less important ○ *Items of minor expenditure are not listed separately.* ○ *The minor stockholders voted against the proposal.* □ **a loss of minor importance** not a very serious loss ■ *noun* a person less than eighteen years old

minority /maɪ'nɑrɪti/ *noun* **1.** a number or quantity which is less than half of the total ○ *A minority of board members opposed the chairman.* □ **in the minority** being fewer than half ○ *Good salesmen are in the minority in our sales team.* **2.** a section of the population from a specific racial group, which does nor make up the majority of the population

minority shareholding /maɪ,nɑrɪti 'ʃerhoʊldɪŋ/ *noun* a group of shares which are less than half the total ○ *He acquired a minority shareholding in the company.*

minority stockholder /maɪ,nɑrɪti 'stɑkhoʊldər/ *noun* a person who owns a group of shares but less than half of the shares in a company

minus /'maɪnəs/ *preposition, adverb* less, without ○ *Net salary is gross salary minus tax and National Insurance deductions.* ○ *Gross profit is sales minus production costs.* ■ *adjective* □ **the accounts show a minus figure** the accounts show that more has been spent than has been received

minus factor /'maɪnəs ,fæktər/ *noun* an unfavorable factor ○ *To have lost sales in the best quarter of the year is a minus factor for the sales team.*

minute /'mɪnɪt/ *noun* **1.** one sixtieth part of an hour ○ *I can see you for ten minutes only.* ○ *If you do not mind waiting, Mr Smith will be free in about twenty minutes' time.* **2.** □ **the chairman signed the minutes of the last meeting** he signed them to show that they are a correct record of what was said and what decisions were taken □ **this will not appear in the minutes of the**

meeting this is unofficial and will not be noted as having been said ■ *verb* to write down something said at a meeting ○ *The chairman's remarks about the auditors were minuted.* □ **I do not want that to be minuted, I want that not to be minuted** do not put that remark into the minutes of the meeting

minutebook /'mɪnɪtbɑk/ *noun* a book in which the minutes of a meeting are kept

minutes /'mɪnɪts/ *plural noun* notes of what happened at a meeting, written by the secretary □ **to take the minutes** to write notes of what happened at a meeting

MIS *abbreviation* management information system

misappropriate /,mɪsə'proʊprieɪt/ *verb* to use illegally money which is not yours, but with which you have been trusted

misappropriation /,mɪsəproʊpri'eɪʃ(ə)n/ *noun* the illegal use of money by someone who is not the owner but who has been trusted to look after it

misc *abbreviation* miscellaneous

miscalculate /mɪs'kælkjʊleɪt/ *verb* to calculate wrongly, or to make a mistake in calculating something ○ *The salesman miscalculated the discount, so we hardly broke even on the deal.*

miscalculation /mɪs,kælkjʊ'leɪʃ(ə)n/ *noun* a mistake in calculating

miscellaneous /mɪsə'leɪniəs/ *adjective* various, mixed, or not all of the same sort ○ *miscellaneous items on the agenda* ○ *a box of miscellaneous pieces of equipment* ○ *Miscellaneous expenditure is not itemized in the accounts.*

miscount *noun* /'mɪskaʊnt/ a mistake in counting ■ *verb* /mɪs'kaʊnt/ to count wrongly, or to make a mistake in counting something ○ *The storekeeper miscounted, so we got twenty-five bars of chocolate instead of two dozen.*

misdirect /,mɪsdaɪ'rekt/ *verb* to give wrong directions

mismanage /mɪs'mænɪdʒ/ *verb* to manage something badly ○ *The company had been badly mismanaged under the previous CEO.*

mismanagement /mɪs'mænɪdʒmənt/ *noun* bad management ○ *The company failed because of the chairman's mismanagement.*

misrepresent /ˌmɪsreprɪˈzent/ *verb* to report facts or what someone says wrongly ○ *Our spokesman was totally misrepresented in the Sunday papers.*

misrepresentation /ˌmɪsreprɪzen ˈteɪʃ(ə)n/ *noun* the act of making a wrong statement in order to persuade someone to enter into a contract such as one for buying a product or service

miss /mɪs/ *verb* **1.** not to meet ○ *I arrived late, so missed most of the discussion.* □ **he missed the chairman by ten minutes** he left ten minutes before the chairman arrived **2.** to be late for ○ *He missed the last plane to Frankfurt.*

mission /ˈmɪʃ(ə)n/ *noun* a group of people going on a trip for a special purpose

mission statement /ˈmɪʃ(ə)n ˌsteɪtmənt/ *noun* a short statement of the reasons for the existence of an organization

mistake /mɪˈsteɪk/ *noun* an act or decision which is wrong, or something that has been done wrongly ○ *It was a mistake to let him name his own salary.* ○ *There was a mistake in the address.* □ **to make a mistake** to do something wrong ○ *The store made a mistake and sent the wrong items.* ○ *He made a mistake in addressing the letter.* □ **by mistake** in error, wrongly ○ *They sent the wrong items by mistake.* ○ *She put my letter into an envelope for the chairman by mistake.* ■ *verb* to think wrongly □ **I mistook him for his brother** I thought he was his brother

misunderstanding /ˌmɪsʌndər ˈstændɪŋ/ *noun* an act of not understanding something correctly ○ *There was a misunderstanding over my tickets.* ○ *There was a misunderstanding over the pay deal.*

misuse /mɪsˈjus/ *noun* a wrong use ○ *the misuse of funds* or *of assets*

mix /mɪks/ *noun* an arrangement of different things together ■ *verb* to put different things together ○ *I like to mix business with pleasure – why don't we discuss the deal over lunch?*

mixed /mɪkst/ *adjective* **1.** made up of different sorts or of different types of things together **2.** neither good nor bad

mixed economy /ˌmɪkst ɪˈkɑnəmi/ *noun* a system which contains both nationalized industries and private enterprise

mixed farm /ˌmɪkst ˈfɑrm/ *noun* a farm which has both animals and crops

ml *abbreviation* millilitre

mm *abbreviation* millimetre

mobile /ˈmoʊbaɪl/ *noun U.K.* same as **cell phone**

mobile phone /ˌmoʊbaɪl ˈfoʊn/ *noun U.K.* same as **cell phone**

mobility /moʊˈbɪlɪti/ *noun* the ability to move from one place to another

mobility of labor /moʊˌbɪlɪti əv ˈleɪbər/ *noun* movement of workers from one place to another to get work

mobilize /ˈmoʊbɪlaɪz/ *verb* to bring things or people together and prepare them for action, especially to fight □ **to mobilize capital** to collect capital to support something □ **to mobilize resources to defend a takeover bid** to get the support of stockholders, etc., to stop a company being taken over

mock-up /ˈmɑk ʌp/ *noun* the model of a new product for testing or to show to possible buyers ○ *The sales team were shown a mock-up of the new car.*

mode /moʊd/ *noun* a way of doing something □ **mode of payment** the way in which payment is made, e.g., cash or check

model /ˈmɑd(ə)l/ *noun* **1.** a small copy of something made to show what it will look like when finished ○ *They showed us a model of the new office building.* **2.** a style or type of product ○ *This is the latest model.* ○ *The model on display is last year's.* ○ *I drive a 2001 model Range Rover.* **3.** a person whose job is to wear new clothes to show them to possible buyers **4.** a description in the form of mathematical data ■ *adjective* which is a perfect example to be copied ○ *a model agreement* ■ *verb* to wear new clothes to show them to possible buyers ○ *She has decided on a career in modeling.* (NOTE: **modeling – modeled**)

modem /ˈmoʊdem/ *noun* a device which links a computer to a telephone line, allowing data to be sent from one computer to another

moderate /ˈmɑd(ə)rət/ *adjective* **1.** not too large ○ *The labor union made a moderate claim.* ○ *The government proposed a moderate increase in the tax rate.* **2.** not holding very extreme views ○ *a moderate labor union leader* ■ *verb* /ˈmɑdəreɪt/ to make less strong or less large ○ *The union was forced to moderate its claim.*

modern /'mɑdərn/ *adjective* referring to the recent past or the present time ○ *It is a fairly modern invention – it was patented only in the 1980s.*

modernization /,mɑdərnaɪ'zeɪʃ(ə)n/ *noun* the process of making something modern ○ *the modernization of the workshop*

modernize /'mɑdərnaɪz/ *verb* to make modern ○ *He modernized the whole product range.*

modest /'mɑdɪst/ *adjective* small ○ *Oil stocks showed modest gains over the week's trading.*

modification /,mɑdɪfɪ'keɪʃ(ə)n/ *noun* a change ○ *The board wanted to make or to carry out modifications to the plan.* ○ *The new model has had several important modifications.* ○ *The client pressed for modifications to the contract.*

modify /'mɑdɪfaɪ/ *verb* to change or to make something fit a different use ○ *The management modified its proposals.* ○ *This is the new modified agreement.* ○ *The car will have to be modified to pass the government tests.* ○ *The refrigerator was considerably modified before it went into production.* (NOTE: **modifies – modifying – modified**)

modular /'mɑdʒələr/ *adjective* made of various sections

moment of conception /,moumənt əv kən'sepʃən/ the moment at which an entrepreneur has the idea of founding a new organization to carry out a particular purpose

momentum /mou'mentəm/ *noun* a movement forward □ **to gain** *or* **lose momentum** to move faster or more slowly

monetary /'mʌnɪt(ə)ri/ *adjective* referring to money or currency

monetary policy /,mʌnɪt(ə)ri 'pɑlɪsi/ *noun* the government's policy relating to finance, e.g., bank interest rates, taxes, government expenditure, and borrowing

monetary standard /,mʌnɪt(ə)ri 'stændərd/ *noun* a fixed exchange rate for a currency

monetary targets /,mʌnɪt(ə)ri 'tɑrgɪtz/ *plural noun* figures which are given as targets by the government when setting out its budget for the forthcoming year, e.g., the money supply or the PSBR

monetary unit /'mʌnɪt(ə)ri ,junɪt/ *noun* a main item of currency of a country

money /'mʌni/ *noun* coins and bills used for buying and selling □ **to earn money** to have a wage or salary □ **to earn good money** to have a large wage or salary □ **to lose money** to make a loss, not to make a profit □ **the company has been losing money for months** the company has been working at a loss for months □ **to get your money back** to make enough profit to cover your original investment □ **to make money** to make a profit □ **to put money into the bank** to deposit money into a bank account □ **to put money into a business** to invest money in a business ○ *She put all her severance pay into a store.* □ **to put money down** to pay cash, especially as a deposit ○ *We put £25 down and paid the rest in installments.* □ **money up front** payment in advance ○ *They are asking for £10,000 up front before they will consider the deal.* ○ *He had to put money up front before he could clinch the deal.* □ **they are worth a lot of money** they are valuable

money at call /,mʌni ət 'kɔl/ *noun* same as **call money**

money-changer /'mʌni ,tʃeɪndʒər/ *noun* same as **changer**

moneylender /'mʌni,lendər/ *noun* a person who lends money at interest

money lying idle /,mʌni ,laɪɪŋ 'aɪd(ə)l/ *noun* money which is not being used to produce interest, which is not invested in business

money-making /'mʌni ,meɪkɪŋ/ *adjective* able to turn over a profit ○ *a money-making plan*

money market /'mʌni ,mɑrkɪt/ *noun* a place where large sums of money are lent or borrowed for a short period of time

money on call /,mʌni ɑn 'kɔl/ *noun* same as **call money**

money order /'mʌni ,ɔrdər/ *noun* a document which can be bought as a way of sending money through the mail

money rates /'mʌni reɪts/ *plural noun* rates of interest for borrowers or lenders

money-spinner /'mʌni ,spɪnər/ *noun* an item which sells very well or which is very profitable ○ *The home-delivery service has proved to be a real money-spinner.*

money supply /'mʌni sə,plaɪ/ *noun* the amount of money in a country's economy, consisting mainly of the money in

263 mortgage

circulation and that held in savings and checking accounts

monies /'mʌniz/ *plural noun* sums of money ○ *monies owing to the company* ○ *to collect monies due*

monitor /'mɒnɪtər/ *noun* a screen on a computer ○ *She brought up the information on the monitor.* ■ *verb* to check or to examine how something is working ○ *She is monitoring the progress of sales.* ○ *How do you monitor the performance of the sales reps?* ○ *How do you monitor the performance of a unit trust?*

monopolization /məˌnɒpəlaɪ'zeɪʃ(ə)n/ *noun* the process of making a monopoly

monopolize /mə'nɒpəlaɪz/ *verb* to create a monopoly or to get control of all the supply of a product

monopoly /mə'nɒpəli/ *noun* a situation where one person or company is the only supplier of a particular product or service ○ *to be in a monopoly situation* ○ *The company has the monopoly of imports of Brazilian wine.* ○ *The factory has the absolute monopoly of jobs in the town.*

monopsonist /mə'nɒpsənɪst/ *noun* a sole buyer of a particular product or service

monopsony /mə'nɒpsəni/ *noun* a situation where there is only one buyer for a particular product or service ○ *Monopsony gives the buyer leverage in demanding a low price.*

Monte Carlo method /ˌmɒnti 'kɑːloʊ ˌmeθəd/ *noun* a statistical analysis technique for calculating an unknown quantity which has an exact value by using an extended series of random trials (NOTE: The name refers to the fact that a roulette wheel in a casino, as in Monte Carlo, continually generates random numbers.)

month /mʌnθ/ *noun* one of twelve periods which make a year ○ *bills due at the end of the current month* ○ *The company pays him $1600 a month.* ○ *She earns $2,000 a month.* □ **paid by the month** paid once each month □ **to give a customer two months' credit** to allow a customer to pay not immediately, but after two months

month end /ˌmʌnθ 'end/ *noun* the end of a calendar month, when accounts have to be drawn up ○ *The accounts department are working on the month-end accounts.*

monthly /'mʌnθli/ *adjective* happening every month or which is received every month ○ *We get a monthly statement from the bank.* ○ *She makes monthly payments to the credit card company.* ○ *He is paying for his car by monthly installments.* ○ *My monthly salary check is late.* □ **monthly ticket** a ticket for travel which is good for one month ■ *adverb* every month ○ *She asked if she could pay monthly by direct debit.* ○ *The account is credited monthly.*

Moody's Investors Service /ˌmuːdiz ɪn'vestərz ˌsɜːvɪs/ *noun* an American rating organization, which gives a rating showing the reliability of a debtor organization (its ratings run from AAA to C). It also issues ratings on municipal bonds, running from MIG1 (the highest rating) to MIG4. ◊ **Standard & Poor's**

moonlight /'muːnlaɪt/ (*informal*) *noun* □ **to do a moonlight flit** to go away (at night) leaving many unpaid bills ■ *verb* to do a second job for cash, often in the evening, as well as a regular job

moonlighter /'muːnlaɪtər/ *noun* a person who moonlights

moonlighting /'muːnlaɪtɪŋ/ *noun* the practice of doing a second job ○ *He makes thousands a year from moonlighting.*

mooring(s) /'mʊərɪŋz/ *noun* a place where boats can be tied up in a harbor

morale /mə'ræl/ *noun* a feeling of confidence or satisfaction ○ *morale has been high since the new targets have been met* ○ *Employee morale is low due to the threat of unemployment.*

moral right /ˌmɒrəl 'raɪt/ *noun* a right of an editor or illustrator, etc., to have some say in the publication of a work to which he has contributed, even if he does not own the copyright

moratorium /ˌmɒrə'tɔːriəm/ *noun* a temporary stop to repayments of interest on loans or capital owed ○ *The banks called for a moratorium on payments.* (NOTE: The plural is **moratoria** or **moratoriums**.)

mortality tables /mɔːr'tæləti ˌteɪb(ə)lz/ *plural noun* chart, used by insurers, which shows how long a person of a certain age can be expected to live on average

mortgage /'mɔːrɡɪdʒ/ *noun* **1.** agreement where someone lends money to another person so that he or she can buy a property, the property being the security ○ *to take out a mortgage on a house* **2.** money lent on the security of a house or other property owned by the borrower, usually in order to enable the borrower to buy the property ○ *to buy a house with a £200,000 mortgage* □ **mortgage payments** money paid each month as interest on a mortgage, plus repayment of a small part of the capital borrowed □ **first mortgage** the main mortgage on a property □ **to pay off a mortgage** to pay back the principal and all the interest on a loan to buy a property ■ *verb* to use a property as security for a loan ○ *The house is mortgaged to the bank.* ○ *He mortgaged his house to set up in business.* □ **to foreclose on a mortgage** to sell a property because the owner cannot repay money which he or she has borrowed, using the property as security

"…mortgage payments account for just 20 per cent of the average first-time buyer's gross earnings against an average of 24 per cent during the past 15 years" [*Times*]

"…mortgage money is becoming tighter. Applications for mortgages are running at a high level and some building societies are introducing quotas" [*Times*]

"…for the first time since mortgage rates began falling a financial institution has raised charges on homeowner loans" [*Globe and Mail (Toronto)*]

mortgage bond /'mɔrgɪdʒ bɑnd/ *noun* a certificate showing that a mortgage exists and that property is security for it

mortgage debenture /'mɔrgɪdʒ dɪ,bentʃər/ *noun* a debenture where the lender can be repaid by selling the company's property

mortgagee /,mɔrgə'dʒi/ *noun* a person or company which lends money for someone to buy a property

mortgage famine /'mɔrgɪdʒ ,fæmɪn/ *noun* a situation where there is not enough money available to offer mortgages to house buyers

mortgager /'mɔrgɪdʒər/, **mortgagor** *noun* a person who borrows money to buy a property

mortgage REIT /'mɔrgɪdʒ reɪt/ *noun* a trust which provides mortgages to property developers. Full form **mortgage Real Estate Investment Trust**

most /moʊst/ *pronoun* very large amount or quantity ○ *Most of the staff are graduates.* ○ *Most of our customers live near the factory.* ○ *Most of the orders come in the early part of the year.* ■ *adjective* very large number of ○ *Most orders are dealt with the same day.* ○ *Most salesmen have had a course of on-the-job training.*

most-favoed-nation clause /moʊst ,feɪvərd 'neɪʃ(ə)n klɔz/ *noun* an agreement between two countries that each will offer the best possible terms in commercial contracts

most favored nation /,moʊst ,feɪvərd 'neɪʃ(ə)n/ *noun* a foreign country to which the home country allows the best trade terms. Abbreviation **MFN**

mostly /'moʊstli/ *adverb* mainly or generally ○ *The staff are mostly girls of twenty to thirty years of age.* ○ *He works mostly in the Los Angeles office.*

motion /'moʊʃ(ə)n/ *noun* a proposal which will be put to a meeting to be voted on ○ *to speak against* or *for a motion* ○ *Mr Brown will propose* or *move a motion congratulating the board on the results.* ○ *The meeting voted on the motion.* ○ *The motion was carried* or *was defeated by 220 votes to 196.* □ **to table a motion** to put forward a proposal for discussion by putting details of it on the table at a meeting

motion study /'moʊʃ(ə)n ,stʌdi/ *noun* a study of the movements of employees performing tasks in order to improve efficiency

motivate /'moʊtɪveɪt/ *verb* to encourage someone to do something, especially to work or to sell □ **highly motivated sales staff** sales staff who are very eager to sell

motivation /,moʊtɪ'veɪʃ(ə)n/ *noun* **1.** an encouragement to staff **2.** eagerness to work well or sell large quantities of a product □ **the sales staff lack motivation** the sales staff are not eager enough to sell

motive /'moʊtɪv/ *noun* something that forces someone to take a particular action

mount /moʊnt/ *verb*

mount up *phrasal verb* to increase rapidly ○ *Costs are mounting up.*

mountain /'maʊntɪn/ *noun* a pile, large heap ○ *I have mountains of typing to do.* ○ *There is a mountain of invoices on the sales manager's desk.*

mounting /'maʊntɪŋ/ *adjective* increasing ○ *He resigned in the face of mounting* *pressure from the stockholders.* ○ *The company is faced with mounting debts.*

mouse /maʊs/ *noun* a small movable device attached to a personal computer and used to move or select items on the screen (NOTE: The plural is **mouses** or **mice**.)

"…you can use a mouse to access pop-up menus and a keyboard for a word-processor" [*Byte*]

movable /'muvəb(ə)l/, **moveable** *adjective* possible to move ○ *All the movable property has been seized by the bailiffs.*

movables /'muvəb(ə)lz/, **moveables** *plural noun* movable property

move /muv/ *verb* **1.** to go from one place to another ○ *The company is moving from the suburbs to the center of town.* ○ *We have decided to move our factory to a site nearer the airport.* **2.** to be sold, or to sell ○ *Over Christmas the stock hardly moved at all but with the January sales it is finally starting to sell.* ○ *The sales staff will have to work hard if they want to move all that stock by the end of the month.* **3.** to propose formally that a motion be accepted by a meeting ○ *He moved that the accounts be agreed.* ○ *I move that the meeting should adjourn for ten minutes.*

movement /'muvmənt/ *noun* **1.** an act of changing position or going up or down ○ *movements in the money markets* ○ *cyclical movements of trade* **2.** a group of people working toward the same goal ○ *the labor movement* ○ *the free trade movement*

mover /'muvər/ *noun* **1.** a person who proposes a motion **2.** same as **moving company**

mover and shaker /,muvər ən 'ʃeɪkər/ *noun* an influential and dynamic person within an organization or group of people who makes things happen (*informal*)

moving average /,muvɪŋ 'æv(ə)rɪdʒ/ *noun* an average of stock prices on a stock market, where the calculation is made over a period which moves forward regularly

moving company /'muvɪŋ ,kʌmp(ə)ni/ *noun* a company that specializes in moving the contents of a house or an office to a new building. Also called **mover**

mpg *abbreviation* miles per gallon

Mr. Chairman /,mɪstər 'tʃermən/ *noun* a way of speaking to the male chairman of a committee meeting

MRP *abbreviation* **1.** manufacturer's recommended price **2.** material requirement planning

multi- /mʌlti/ *prefix* referring to many things or many of one thing

multibillion /,mʌlti'bɪljən/ *adjective* referring to several billion pounds or dollars ○ *They signed a multibillion pound deal.*

"…factory automation is a multi-billion-dollar business" [*Duns Business Month*]

multi-channel system /'mʌltɪ ,tʃæn(ə)l ,sɪstəm/ *noun* a distribution system used by a producer which makes use of more than one distribution channel

multicurrency /,mʌltɪ'kʌrənsi/ *adjective* in several currencies □ **multicurrency loan** a loan in several currencies

multilateral /,mʌlti'læt(ə)rəl/ *adjective* between several organizations or countries ○ *a multilateral agreement* □ **multilateral trade** trade between several countries

multimedia document /,mʌlti'midiə ,dɑkjəmənt/ *noun* an electronic document that contains interactive material from a range of different media such as text, video, sound, graphics, and animation

multimillion /,mʌlti'mɪljən/ *adjective* referring to several million pounds or dollars ○ *They signed a multimillion pound deal.*

multimillionaire /,mʌltimɪljə'ner/ *noun* a person who owns property or investments worth several million pounds or dollars

multinational /,mʌlti'næʃ(ə)nəl/ *noun, adjective* (a company) which has branches or subsidiary companies in several countries ○ *The company has been bought by one of the big multinationals.* Also called **transnational**

multipart stationery /,mʌltipɑrt 'steɪʃənri/ *noun* stationery, such as invoices, with several sheets usually in different colors, attached together and printed together ○ *Inkjet printers give very good results, but cannot print on multipart stationery.*

multiparty auction /ˌmʌltipɑːti ˈɔːkʃən/ *noun* a method of buying and selling on the Internet in which the people who wish to buy make electronic bids

multiple /ˈmʌltɪp(ə)l/ *adjective* many ■ *noun* **1.** □ **stock at a multiple of 5** a stock with a P or E ratio of 5 (i.e. 5 is the result when dividing the current market price of a share by the earnings per share) **2.** a company with stores in several different towns

multiple correlation /ˌmʌltɪp(ə)l kɒrəˈleɪʃ(ə)n/ *noun* a method for measuring the effect of several independent variables on one dependent variable

multiple entry visa /ˌmʌltɪp(ə)l ˈentri ˌviːzə/ *noun* a visa which allows a visitor to enter a country many times

multiple ownership /ˌmʌltɪp(ə)l ˈəʊnəʃɪp/ *noun* a situation where something is owned by several parties jointly

multiple store /ˈmʌltɪp(ə)l stɔː/ *noun* same as **chain store**

multiplication sign /ˌmʌltɪplɪ ˈkeɪʃ(ə)n saɪn/ *noun* a sign (x) used to show that a number is being multiplied by another

multiply /ˈmʌltɪplaɪ/ *verb* **1.** to calculate the sum of various numbers added together a particular number of times ○ *If you multiply twelve by three you get thirty-six.* ○ *Square measurements are calculated by multiplying length by width.* **2.** to grow or to increase ○ *Profits multiplied in the boom years.*

multiskilling /ˈmʌltiˌskɪlɪŋ/ *noun* a system of working where employees are trained to work in various types of job, and none are kept on the same type of work for very long, so as to allow flexibility in the deployment of the work force

multitasking /ˈmʌltiˌtæskɪŋ/ *noun* **1.** the action of performing several different tasks at the same time **2.** running several different software programs at the same time

"New research suggests that multi-tasking may be counterproductive. Mounting evidence shows that a crowded calendar calling for a lot of jumping back and forth between activities can diminish rather than enhance productivity." [*Harvard Business Review*]

municipal /mjuːˈnɪsɪp(ə)l/ *adjective* referring to a town or city ○ *We pay our municipal taxes by direct debit.* ○ *The municipal offices are in the center of the town.*

Murphy's law /ˌmɜːfiz ˈlɔː/ *noun* a law, based on wide experience, which says that in commercial life if something can go wrong it will go wrong, or that when you are thinking that things are going right, they will inevitably start to go wrong

mutual /ˈmjuːtʃuəl/ *adjective* belonging to two or more people ■ *noun* any commercial organization owned by its members, such as a savings and loan

mutual company /ˈmjuːtʃuəl ˌkʌmp(ə)ni/ *noun* same as **mutual insurance company**

mutual fund /ˈmjuːtʃuəl fʌnd/ *noun* an organization which takes money from small investors and invests it in stocks, bonds, and other securities for them (NOTE: The U.K. term is **unit trust**.)

mutual insurance company /ˈmjuːtʃuəl ˌkʌmp(ə)ni/ *noun* a company which belongs to insurance policy holders. Also called **mutual company**

MVA *abbreviation* market value adjuster

N

N *abbreviation* naira

nail /neɪl/ *noun* □ **to pay on the nail** to pay promptly, to pay rapidly

naira /'naɪrə/ *noun* a unit of currency used in Nigeria (NOTE: no plural; naira is usually written **N** before figures: **N2,000** say "two thousand naira")

named /neɪmd/ *adjective* □ **the person named in the policy** the person whose name is given on an insurance policy as the person insured

narrow market /ˌnærəʊ 'mɑːkət/ *noun* a market in a stock where very few shares are available for sale, and where the price can vary sharply

NASDAQ /'næzdæk/ *abbreviation* a system which provides quotations via computer for the U.S. electronic trading market, mainly in high tech stocks, and also for some large corporations listed on the NYSE, and publishes an index of stock price movements. Full form **National Association of Securities Dealers Automated Quotations system** (NOTE: The U.K. term is **SEAQ.**)

nation /'neɪʃ(ə)n/ *noun* a country and the people living in it

national /'næʃ(ə)nəl/ *adjective* referring to the whole of a particular country □ **national advertising** advertising in every part of a country, not just in the capital ○ *We took national advertising to promote our new 24-hour delivery service.* □ **national campaign** a sales or publicity campaign in every part of a country □ **national newspapers, the national press** newspapers which sell in all parts of a country

National Association of Realtors /ˌnæʃ(ə)nəl əˌsəʊsieɪʃ(ə)n əv 'rɪəltərz/ *noun* a professional organization that represents real estate brokers and agents

National Association of Securities Dealers Automated Quota-

tions system *noun* full form of **NASDAQ**

national bank /'næʃ(ə)nəl bæŋk/ *noun* a bank which is chartered by the federal government and is part of the Federal Reserve system as opposed to a "state bank"

National Council for Vocational Qualifications /ˌnæʃ(ə)nəl ˌkaʊns(ə)l fər vəʊˌkeɪʃ(ə)nəl ˌkwɑlɪfɪ'keɪʃ(ə)nz/ *noun* full form of **NCVQ**

National Debt /ˌnæʃ(ə)nəl 'det/ *noun* money borrowed by a government

national income /ˌnæʃ(ə)nəl 'ɪnkʌm/ *noun* the value of income from the sales of goods and services in a country

National Insurance contribution /ˌnæʃ(ə)nəl ɪn'ʃʊrəns kɑntrɪˌbjuʃ(ə)n/ *noun U.K.* a proportion of income paid each month by an employee and the employee's company to the National Insurance plan in the U.K., which helps to fund sickness and unemployment benefits and state pensions. Abbreviation **NIC**

nationality /ˌnæʃə'næliti/ *noun* the state of being a citizen of a particular country □ **he is of British nationality** he is a British citizen

nationalization /ˌnæʃ(ə)nəlaɪ'zeɪʃ(ə)n/ *noun* the taking over of private industry by the state

nationalize /'næʃ(ə)nəlaɪz/ *verb* to put a privately-owned industry under state ownership and control ○ *The government is planning to nationalize the banking system.*

nationalized industry /ˌnæʃ(ə)nəˌlaɪzd 'ɪndəstri/ *noun* an industry which was privately owned, but is now owned by the state

national press /ˌnæʃ(ə)nəl 'pres/ *noun* newspapers which sell in all parts of the country ○ *The new car has been advertised in the national press.*

nationwide /'neɪʃ(ə)nwaɪd/ *adjective* all over a country ○ *We offer a nationwide delivery service.* ○ *The new car is being launched with a nationwide sales campaign.*

natural /'nætʃ(ə)rəl/ *adjective* **1.** found in the earth ○ *The offices are heated by natural gas.* **2.** not made by people ○ *They use only natural fibers for their best cloths.*

natural capitalism /,nætʃ(ə)rəl 'kæpɪt(ə)lɪz(ə)m/ *noun* a capitalist philosophy that makes protection of the earth's resources a strategic priority

natural resources /,nætʃ(ə)rəl rɪ 'zɔːsɪz/ *plural noun* raw materials which are found in the earth, e.g., coal, gas, or iron

natural wastage /,nætʃ(ə)rəl 'weɪstɪdʒ/ *noun U.K.* same as **attrition**

nature /'neɪtʃə/ *noun* the kind or type ○ *What is the nature of the contents of the parcel?* ○ *The nature of his business is not known.*

NAV *abbreviation* net asset value

NB *abbreviation* from a Latin phrase meaning "note (this) well", i.e. pay attention to this. Full form **Nota bene**

NBV *abbreviation* net book value

NCVQ *noun* a government body set up to validate the system of national qualifications in vocational subjects. Full form **National Council for Vocational Qualifications**

necessary /'nesɪs(ə)ri/ *adjective* which has to be done, which is needed ○ *It is necessary to fill in the form correctly if you are not to have difficulty at customs.* ○ *Is it really necessary for the chairman to have six personal assistants?* ○ *You must have all the necessary documentation before you apply for a subsidy.*

necessity /nə'sesəti/ *noun* something which is vitally important, without which nothing can be done or no one can survive ○ *Being unemployed makes it difficult to afford even the basic necessities.* (NOTE: The plural is **necessities**.)

negative /'negətɪv/ *adjective* meaning "no" □ **the answer was in the negative** the answer was "no"

negative cash flow /,negətɪv 'kæʃ fləʊ/ *noun* a situation where more money

is going out of a company than is coming in

negative equity /,negətɪv 'ekwɪti/ *noun* a situation where a house bought with a mortgage becomes less valuable than the money borrowed to buy it because of falling house prices

negligence /'neglɪdʒəns/ *noun* **1.** a lack of proper care or failure to carry out a duty (with the result that a person or property is harmed) **2.** the act of not doing a job properly when one is capable of doing it

negligent /'neglɪdʒ(ə)nt/ *adjective* not taking appropriate care

negligible /'neglɪdʒɪb(ə)l/ *adjective* very small □ **not negligible** quite large

negotiable /nɪ'gəʊʃiəb(ə)l/ *adjective* transferable from one person to another or exchanged for cash □ **not negotiable** which cannot be exchanged for cash □ **"not negotiable"** words written on a check to show that it can be paid only to a specific person □ **negotiable check** a check made payable to bearer, i.e. to anyone who holds it

"…initial salary is negotiable around $45,000 per annum" [*Australian Financial Review*]

negotiable instrument /nɪ ,gəʊʃiəb(ə)l 'ɪnstrʊmənt/ *noun* a document which can be exchanged for cash, e.g., a bill of exchange or a check

negotiable paper /nɪ,gəʊʃiəb(ə)l 'peɪpər/ *noun* a document which can be transferred from one owner to another for cash

negotiate /nɪ'gəʊʃieɪt/ *verb* □ **to negotiate with someone** to discuss a problem or issue formally with someone, so as to reach an agreement ○ *The management refused to negotiate with the union.* □ **to negotiate terms and conditions** *or* **a contract** to discuss and agree upon the terms of a contract □ **he negotiated a $250,000 loan with the bank** he came to an agreement with the bank for a loan of $250,000

negotiating committee /nɪ 'gəʊʃieɪtɪŋ kə,mɪti/ *noun* a group of representatives of management and unions who negotiate a wage settlement

negotiation /nɪ,gəʊʃi'eɪʃ(ə)n/ *noun* the discussion of terms and conditions in order to reach an agreement □ **contract under negotiation** a contract which is being discussed □ **a matter for negotiation**

something which must be discussed before a decision is reached □ **to enter into** or **to start negotiations** to start discussing a problem □ **to resume negotiations** to start discussing a problem again, after talks have stopped for a time □ **to break off negotiations** to stop discussing a problem □ **to conduct negotiations** to negotiate □ **negotiations broke down after six hours** discussions stopped because no agreement was possible

negotiator /nɪˈɡoʊʃieɪtər/ noun a person who discusses a problem with the goal of achieving agreement between different people or groups of people □ **experienced union negotiator** a member of a union who has a lot of experience of discussing terms of employment with management

nepotism /ˈnepətɪz(ə)m/ noun the practice of giving preferential treatment to someone who is a relative or friend (especially giving a job to a member of the family who is less well qualified than other candidates) ○ The staff talked about nepotism when the training officer selected her nephew for management training. ○ So as not to be accused of nepotism, the sales manager refused to take his son into the department as a salesman.

nest egg /ˈnest eɡ/ noun money which someone has saved over a period of time, usually kept in an interest-bearing account and intended for use after retirement

net /net/ adjective **1.** referring to a price, weight, pay, etc., after all deductions have been made □ **net profit before tax** the profit of a company after expenses have been deducted but before tax has been paid **2.** □ **terms strictly net** payment has to be the full price, with no discount allowed ■ noun the Internet, international network linking millions of computers worldwide, using telephone, cable, and satellite links ○ He searched the Net for information on cheap tickets to the U.S. ■ verb to make a true profit ○ to net a profit of $10,000 (NOTE: **netting – netted**)

net asset value /net ˈæset ˌvælju/ noun the total value of a company after deducting the money owed by it (it is the value of stockholders' capital plus reserves and any money retained from profits). Abbreviation **NAV**. Also called **net worth**

net book value /net bʊk ˈvælju/ noun the historic cost of an asset less any accumulated depreciation or other provision for diminution in value, e.g., reduction to net realizable value, or asset value which has been revalued downward to reflect market conditions. Abbreviation **NBV**. Also called **written-down value**

net cash flow /ˌnet ˈkæʃ ˌfloʊ/ noun the difference between the money coming in and the money going out

net current assets /ˌnet ˌkʌrənt ˈæsets/ plural noun the current assets of a company, I.e. cash and stocks, less any liabilities. Also called **net working capital**

net earnings /ˌnet ˈɜrnɪŋz/ plural noun the total earnings of a business after tax and other deductions

Net imperative /ˌnet ɪmˈperətɪv/ noun the idea that an ability to use the Internet for business purposes is vital for organizations that wish to be successful in the future

net income /net ˈɪnkʌm/ noun a person's or organization's income which is left after taking away tax and other deductions

net loss /ˌnet ˈlɔs/ noun an actual loss, after deducting overhead

net margin /ˌnet ˈmɑrdʒɪn/ noun the percentage difference between received price and all costs, including overhead

net national product /ˌnet ˌnæʃ(ə)nəl ˈprɑdʌkt/ noun the gross national product less investment on capital goods and depreciation. Abbreviation **NNP**

net present value /ˌnet ˌprezənt ˈvælju/ noun the present value of the expected cash flows minus the cost of a project. Abbreviation **NPV**

net price /ˌnet ˈpraɪs/ noun the price of goods or services which cannot be reduced by a discount

net profit /ˌnet ˈprɑfɪt/ noun the amount by which income from sales is larger than all expenditure. Also called **profit after tax**

net receipts /ˌnet rɪˈsits/ plural noun receipts after deducting commission, tax, discounts, etc.

net salary /ˌnet ˈsæləri/ noun the salary which is left after deducting tax and National Insurance contributions

net sales /ˌnet 'seɪlz/ *plural noun* the total amount of sales less damaged or returned items and discounts to retailers

net turnover /net 'tɜrnˌoʊvər/ *noun* turnover before sales tax and after trade discounts have been deducted

net weight /ˌnet 'weɪt/ *noun* the weight of goods after deducting the packing material and container

network /'netwɜrk/ *noun* a system which links different points together ■ *verb* to link together in a network □ **to network a television program** to send out the same television program through several TV stations

network analysis /'netwɜrk əˌnæləsɪs/ *noun* an analysis of a project that charts the individual activities involved, each with the time needed for its completion, so that the timing of the whole can be planned and controlled

network culture /ˌnetwɜrk 'kʌltʃər/ *noun* a culture that is dependent on and greatly influenced by communication using global networks

networked system /ˌnetwɜrkt 'sɪstəm/ *noun* a computer system where several PCs are linked together so that they all draw on the same database or use the same server

networking /'netwɜrkɪŋ/ *noun* **1.** a working method where employees work at home on computer terminals, and send the finished material back to the central office by email **2.** the practice of keeping in contact with former colleagues, school friends, etc., so that all the members of the group can help each other in their careers

net working capital /net ˌwɜrkɪŋ 'kæpɪt(ə)l/ *noun* same as **net current assets**

network management /ˌnetwɜrk 'mænɪdʒmənt/ *noun* the management of co-ordinated computer systems and programs so as to enable a number of users to have access to and receive information through a local area or wide-area network

network organization /ˌnetwɜrk ˌɔrgənaɪ'zeɪʃ(ə)n/ *noun* an organization that operates as far as possible without a traditional organization structure. Instead, it creates teams to handle specific projects and, when those projects are completed, breaks up the teams and creates new ones. ◊ **virtual organization**

network revolution /ˌnetwɜrk ˌrevə'luʃ(ə)n/ *noun* the revolutionary change in business practices brought about by the growth of global networks

network society /'netwɜrk səˌsaɪəti/ *noun* a society that regularly uses global networks for the purposes of work, communication, and government

net worth /ˌnet 'wɜrθ/ *noun* the value of all the property of a person or company after taking away what the person or company owes ○ *The upmarket product is targeted at individuals of high net worth.*

net yield /ˌnet 'jild/ *noun* the profit from investments after deduction of tax

neurolinguistic programming /ˌnʊroʊlɪŋgwɪstɪk 'proʊgræmɪŋ/ *noun* a theory of behavior and communication based on how people avoid change and how to help them to change. Abbreviation **NLP**

new broom /ˌnu 'brum/ *noun* a manager or director brought into a company to change existing practices and possibly remove old-established staff

new entrant /ˌnu 'entrənt/ *noun* a company which is going into a market for the first time

"The virtuous cycle that the new entrants appear to be building will add pressure on established members to reform." [*BusinessWeek*]

new home sales /ˌnu 'hoʊm ˌseɪlz/ *noun* sales of new houses

new issue /nju 'ɪʃu/ *noun* securities that are being offered for sale to the public for the first time

news /nuz/ *noun* information about things which have happened ○ *She always reads the business news or financial news first in the paper.* ○ *Financial markets were shocked by the news of the devaluation.*

news agency /'nuz ˌeɪdʒənsi/ *noun* an office which distributes news to newspapers and television stations

newsagent /'njuzeɪdʒənt/ *noun U.K.* same as **news dealer**

news dealer /'nuz ˌdilərz/ *noun* a person who runs a store selling newspapers and magazines

newsletter /'nuzletər/ *noun* □ **company newsletter** a printed sheet or small newspaper giving news about a company

news release /'nuz rɪ‚lis/ *noun* a sheet giving information about a new event which is sent to newspapers and TV and radio stations so that they can use it ○ *The company sent out a news release about the new product launch.*

news stand /'nuz stænd/ *noun* a small wooden store on a sidewalk, for selling newspapers and magazines

new technology /‚nu tek'nɑlədʒi/ *noun* electronic devices which have recently been invented

New York Stock Exchange /‚nju jɔrk 'stɑk ɪks‚tʃeɪndʒ/ *noun* The older and larger of the two stock exchanges based in New York and the oldest in the United States. Abbreviation **NYSE** (NOTE: Also called the **Big Board**)

NIC *abbreviation* National Insurance contribution

niche /nɪtʃ/ *noun* a special place in a market, occupied by one company (a "niche company") ○ *They seem to have discovered a niche in the market.*

niche company /‚nɪtʃ 'kʌmp(ə)ni/ *noun* company specializing in a particular type of product or service, which occupies a market niche

niche market /‚nɪtʃ 'mɑrkət/ *noun* a small specialty market, where there is little competition

nickel /'nɪk(ə)l/ *noun* **1.** a valuable metal traded on commodity exchanges, such as the London Metal Exchange **2.** a five cent coin

Nielsen Index /'nilsən ‚ɪndeks/ *noun* an U.S. publication belonging to A.C. Nielsen, with a number of different retail and wholesale audit services referring to various types of outlet and different areas of the country

night depository /'naɪt dɪ‚pɑzɪt(ə)ri/ *noun* a safe in the outside wall of a bank, where money and documents can be deposited at night, using a special door

night duty /'naɪt ‚duti/ *noun* a period of work during the night

night rate /'naɪt reɪt/ *noun* a cheap rate for telephone calls at night

night shift /'naɪt ʃɪft/ *noun* a shift which works at night ○ *There are thirty men on the night shift.*

Nikkei Average /nɪ'keɪ ‚æv(ə)rɪdʒ/ an index of prices on the Tokyo Stock Exchange, based on about 200 leading stocks

nil /nɪl/ *noun* zero or nothing ○ *The advertising budget has been cut to nil.*

NLP *abbreviation* neurolinguistic programming

No., No *abbreviation* number

no-claims bonus /‚noʊ 'kleɪmz ‚boʊnəs/ *noun* **1.** a reduction of premiums on an insurance policy because no claims have been made **2.** a lower premium paid because no claims have been made against the insurance policy

nominal /'nɑmɪn(ə)l/ *adjective* (*of a payment*) very small ○ *They are paying a nominal rent.* ○ *The employment agency makes a nominal charge for its services.*

nominal ledger /‚nɑmɪn(ə)l 'ledʒər/ *noun* a book which records a company's transactions in the various accounts

nominal share capital /‚nɑmɪn(ə)l 'ʃer ‚kæpɪt(ə)l/ *noun* the total of the face value of all the shares which a company is authorized to issue according to its articles of incorporation

nominal value /‚nɑmɪn(ə)l 'vælju/ *noun* same as **face value**

nominate /'nɑmɪneɪt/ *verb* to suggest someone for a job □ **to nominate someone to a post** to appoint someone to a post without an election □ **to nominate someone as proxy** to name someone as your proxy

nomination /‚nɑmɪ'neɪʃ(ə)n/ *noun* the act of nominating someone for a position

nominee /‚nɑmɪ'ni/ *noun* a person who is nominated, especially someone who is appointed to deal with financial matters on your behalf

COMMENT: Stocks can be purchased and held in nominee accounts so that the identity of the owner of the stocks cannot be discovered easily.

nominee account /‚nɑmɪ'ni ə‚kaʊnt/ *noun* an account held on behalf of someone

COMMENT: Stocks can be purchased and held in nominee accounts so that the identity of the owner of the shares cannot be discovered easily.

non- /nɑn/ *prefix* not

non-acceptance /‚nɑn ək'septəns/ *noun* a situation in which the person who is to pay a bill of exchange does not accept it

non-contributory pension plan /nɑn kən,trɪbjʊt(ə)ri 'penʃən plæn/, **non-contributory pension scheme** /skiːm/ *noun U.K.* a pension plan in which a company, not the employee, pays all contributions ○ *The company pension plan is non-contributory.*

non-delivery /,nɑn dɪ'lɪv(ə)ri/ *noun* the failure to deliver goods that have been ordered

non-disclosure agreement /nɑn dɪs 'kloʊʒər ə,griːmənt/ *noun* a legally enforceable agreement that stops present or past employees from revealing commercially sensitive information belonging to their employer to anybody else

non-durables /,nɑn 'djʊrəb(ə)lz/, **non-durable goods** /,nɑn 'djʊrəb(ə)l ɡʊdz/ *plural noun* goods which are used up soon after they have been bought, e.g., food or newspapers

non-exec /,nɑn ɪɡ'zek/ *noun* same as **non-executive director**

non-executive director /nɑn ɪɡ ,zekjʊtɪv daɪ'rektər/ *noun* a director who attends board meetings and gives advice, but does not work full-time for the company. Also called **outside director**

non-feasance /,nɑn'fiːz(ə)ns/ *noun* a failure to do something which should be done by law

nonnegotiable instrument /,nɑnni ,ɡoʊʃəb(ə)l 'ɪnstrʊmənt/ *noun* a document which cannot be exchanged for cash, e.g., a crossed check

non-payment /,nɑn 'peɪmənt/ *noun* □ **non-payment of a debt** the act of not paying a debt that is due

nonprofit organization /,nɑn ,prɑfɪtmeɪkɪŋ ,ɔrɡənaɪ'zeɪʃən/ *noun* an organization which is not allowed by law to make a profit ○ *Nonprofitmaking organizations are exempted from tax.* Also called **not-for-profit organization** (NOTE: Nonprofit organizations include charities, professional associations, labor unions, and religious, arts, community, research, and campaigning bodies.)

non-recurring items /,nɑn rɪ,kɜrɪŋ 'aɪtəmz/ *plural noun* special items in a set of accounts which appear only once

non-refundable /,nɑn rɪ'fʌndəb(ə)l/ *adjective* not possible to refund ○ *You will be asked to make a non-refundable deposit.*

non-resident /,nɑn 'rezɪd(ə)nt/ *noun, adjective* a person who is not considered a resident of a country for tax purposes ○ *He has a non-resident bank account.*

non-returnable /,nɑn rɪ'tɜrnəb(ə)l/ *adjective* which cannot be returned

non-stop /,nɑn 'stɑp/ *adjective, adverb* without stopping ○ *They worked non-stop to finish the audit on time.*

non-sufficient funds /,nɑn sə,fɪʃənt 'fʌndz/ *noun* a lack of enough money in a bank account to pay a check drawn on that account. Abbreviation **NSF**. Also called **insufficient funds**, **not sufficient funds**

non-tariff barriers /,nɑn ,tærɪf 'bæriərz/ *noun* barriers to international trade other than tariffs. They include overcomplicated documentation; verification of goods for health and safety reasons and blocked deposits payable by importers to obtain foreign currency. Abbreviation **NTBs**

non-taxable /,nɑn 'tæksəb(ə)l/ *adjective* not subject to tax ○ *non-taxable income* ○ *Lottery prizes are non-taxable.*

non-union labor /,nɑn 'junjən ,leɪbər/ *noun* employees who do not belong to labor unions employed by a company

non-virtual hosting /,nɑn ,vɜrtjuəl 'hoʊstɪŋ/ *noun* the most basic type of hosting option, often provided free, in which clients do not have their own domain names, but attach their names to the web address of the hosting company (NOTE: This hosting option is only suitable for small companies and has the disadvantage that clients cannot change their hosting company without changing their web address.)

non-voting shares /,nɑn ,voʊtɪŋ 'ʃerz/ *plural noun* shares which do not allow the stockholder to vote at meetings

norm /nɔrm/ *noun* the usual quantity or the usual rate ○ *The output from this factory is well above the norm for the industry* or *well above the industry norm.*

normal /'nɔrm(ə)l/ *adjective* usual or which happens regularly ○ *Normal deliveries are made on Tuesdays and Fridays.* ○ *Now that supply difficulties have been resolved we hope to resume normal service as soon as possible.* □ **under normal**

conditions if things work in the usual way ○ *Under normal conditions a package takes ten days to get to Copenhagen.* ○ *Normal working will be resumed as soon as the men return to work on Monday.*

nosedive /'nouzdaɪv/ *verb* to fall very sharply ○ *The stock price nosedived after the chairman was arrested.*

no-strike agreement /nou 'straɪk ə ˌgrɪmənt/, **no-strike clause** /nou 'straɪk klɔz/ *noun* a clause in an agreement where the employees say that they will never strike

notary public /ˌnoutəri 'pʌblɪk/ *noun* a lawyer who has the authority to witness documents and spoken statements, making them official (NOTE: The plural is **notaries public**.)

note /nout/ *noun* 1. a short document or piece of writing, or a short piece of information ○ *to send someone a note* ○ *I left a note on her desk.* 2. same as **banknote** 3. paper showing that money has been borrowed ■ *verb* 1. to write down details of something and remember them ○ *your complaint has been noted* ○ *We note that the goods were delivered in bad condition.* ○ *Your order has been noted and will be dispatched as soon as we have stock.* 2. to notice an advertisement in a publication but not necessarily read or understand it

note of hand /ˌnout əv 'hænd/ *noun* a document stating that someone promises to pay an amount of money on an agreed date

not-for-profit organization /ˌnɑt fər 'prɑfɪt ˌɔrgənaɪzeɪʃ(ə)n/ *noun* same as **nonprofit organization**

notice /'noutɪs/ *noun* 1. a piece of written information ○ *The company secretary pinned up a notice about the pension plan.* 2. an official warning that a contract is going to end or that terms are going to be changed □ **until further notice** until different instructions are given ○ *You must pay £200 on the 30th of each month until further notice.* 3. official written information that an employee is leaving their job on a certain date □ **she gave in** *or* **handed in her notice** she resigned 4. the time allowed before something takes place ○ *We require three months' notice* □ **at short notice** with very little warning ○ *The bank manager will not see anyone at short no-*

tice. □ **you must give seven days' notice of withdrawal** you must ask to take money out of the account seven days before you want it 5. a legal document (such as telling a tenant to leave property which he is occupying) □ **to give someone notice, to serve notice on someone** to give someone a legal notice □ **to give a tenant notice to quit, to serve a tenant with notice to quit** to inform a tenant officially that he has to leave the premises by a certain date ○ *We have given our tenant notice to quitted.*

notification /ˌnoutɪfɪ'keɪʃ(ə)n/ *noun* the act of informing someone of something

notify /'noutɪfaɪ/ *verb* □ **to notify someone of something** to tell someone something formally ○ *They were notified of the arrival of the shipment.* ○ *The management were notified of the union's decision.*

notional /'nouʃ(ə)n(ə)l/ *adjective* probable but not known exactly or not quantifiable

not sufficient funds /ˌnɑt sə,fɪʃ(ə)nt 'fʌndz/ *noun* same as **non-sufficient funds**. abbreviation **NSF**

nought /nɔrt/ *noun* the figure 0 ○ *A million pounds can be written as "£1m" or as one and six noughts.* (NOTE: **Nought** is commoner in U.K. English; in U.S. English, **zero** is more usual.)

NPV *abbreviation* net present value

NTBs *abbreviation* non-tariff barriers

null /nʌl/ *adjective* 1. with no meaning 2. which cannot legally be enforced □ **the contract was declared null and void** the contract was said to be not valid □ **to render a decision null** to make a decision useless or to cancel it

nullification /ˌnʌlɪfɪ'keɪʃ(ə)n/ *noun* an act of making something invalid

nullify /'nʌlɪfaɪ/ *verb* to make something invalid or to cancel something (NOTE: **nullifying- nullified**)

number /'nʌmbər/ *noun* 1. a quantity of things or people ○ *The number of persons on the payroll has increased over the last year.* ○ *The number of days lost through strikes has fallen.* □ **a number of** some ○ *A number of the staff will be retiring this year.* 2. a printed or written figure that identifies a particular thing ○ *Please write your account number on the back of the* *check.* ○ *If you have a complaint to make, always quote the batch number.* ○ *She noted the check number in the ledger.* **3.** an amount in figures ■ *verb* to put a figure on a document ○ *to number an order* ○ *I refer to your invoice numbered 1234.*

numbered account /ˌnʌmbərd ə 'kaʊnt/ *noun* a bank account, usually in Switzerland, which is referred to only by a number, the name of the person holding it being kept secret

numeric /nu'merɪk/, **numerical** /nu 'merɪk(ə)l/ *adjective* referring to numbers

numerical order /njuˌmerɪk(ə)l 'ɔːrdər/ *noun* an arrangement by numbers ○ *Put these invoices in numerical order.*

numeric data /nuˌmerɪk 'deɪtə/ *noun* data in the form of figures

numeric keypad /nuˌmerɪk 'kipæd/ *noun* the part of a computer keyboard which is a programmable set of numbered keys

nursery /'nɜrs(ə)ri/ *noun* a special room or building where babies and small children can be looked after (not necessarily on the company's premises) ○ *The company offers nursery provision to its staff.* Compare **day care center**

NVQ *abbreviation* National Vocational Qualification

NYSE *abbreviation* New York Stock Exchange

O

O & M *abbreviation* organization and methods

OAP *abbreviation* old age pensioner

oath /oʊθ/ *noun* a legal promise stating that something is true □ **he was under oath** he had promised in court to say what was true

object /əbˈdʒekt/ *verb* to refuse to do something or to say that you do not accept something ○ *to object to a clause in a contract* (NOTE: You object **to** something.)

object and task technique /ˌɒbdʒekt ən ˈtæsk tekˌnik/ *noun* a method of budgeting in which the tasks required to achieve each objective are identified and the cost of each task is then estimated

objection /əbˈdʒekʃən/ *noun* □ **to raise an objection to something** to object to something ○ *The union delegates raised an objection to the wording of the agreement.*

objective /əbˈdʒektɪv/ *noun* something which you hope to achieve ○ *The company has achieved its objectives.* ○ *We set the sales forces specific objectives.* ○ *Our recruitment objectives are to have well-qualified and well-placed staff.* □ **long-term** *or* **short-term objective** a goal which you hope to achieve within a few years or a few months ■ *adjective* considered from a general point of view rather than from that of the person involved ○ *You must be objective in assessing the performance of the staff.* ○ *They have been asked to carry out an objective survey of the market.* Opposite **subjective**

obligate /ˈɒblɪɡeɪt/ *verb* □ **to be obligated to do something** to have a legal duty to do something

obligation /ˌɒblɪˈɡeɪʃ(ə)n/ *noun* **1.** a duty to do something ○ *There is no obligation to help out in another department* ○ *There is no obligation to buy.* □ **two weeks' free trial without obligation** the customer can try the item at home for two weeks without having to buy it at the end of the test □ **to be under an obligation to do something** to feel it is your duty to do something ○ *he is under no contractual obligation to buy* he has signed no contract which forces him to buy **2.** a debt □ **to meet your obligations** to pay your debts

obligatory /əˈblɪɡət(ə)ri/ *adjective* necessary according to the law or rules ○ *Each member of the sales staff has to pass an obligatory physical examination.*

oblige /əˈblaɪdʒ/ *verb* □ **to oblige someone to do something** to make someone feel he must do something ○ *He felt obliged to cancel the contract.*

o.b.o. *abbreviation* or best offer

observe /əbˈzɜrv/ *verb* **1.** to obey a rule or law ○ *Failure to observe the correct procedure will be punished.* ○ *Restaurants are obliged to observe the local fire regulations.* **2.** to watch or to notice what is happening ○ *Officials have been instructed to observe the conduct of the ballot for union president.*

obsolescence /ˌɒbsəˈles(ə)ns/ *noun* the process of a product going out of date because of progress in design or technology, and therefore becoming less useful or valuable

obsolescent /ˌɒbsəˈles(ə)nt/ *adjective* becoming out of date

obsolete /ˌɒbsəˈlit/ *adjective* no longer used ○ *Computer technology changes so fast that hardware soon becomes obsolete.*

COMMENT: A product or asset may become obsolete because it is worn out, or because new products have been developed to replace it.

obtain /əbˈteɪn/ *verb* to get ○ *to obtain supplies from abroad* ○ *to obtain an injunction against a company* ○ *We find* *these items very difficult to obtain.* ○ *He obtained control by buying the founder's shareholding.*

occasional /ə'keɪʒ(ə)n(ə)l/ *adjective* which happens from time to time

occupancy /'ɑkjʊpənsi/ *noun* the act of occupying a property (such as a house, an office, a room in a hotel) □ **with immediate occupancy** empty and available to be occupied immediately

"...while occupancy rates matched those of last year in July, August has been a much poorer month than it was the year before" [*Economist*]

occupancy rate /'ɑkjʊpənsi reɪt/ *noun* the average number of rooms occupied in a hotel over a period of time shown as a percentage of the total number of rooms ○ *During the winter months the occupancy rate was down to 50%.*

occupant /'ɑkjʊpənt/ *noun* a person or company which occupies a property

occupation /ˌɑkjʊ'peɪʃ(ə)n/ *noun* **1.** the act of living or staying in a place □ **occupation of a building** act of occupying a building **2.** a job or type of work ○ *What is her occupation?* ○ *His main occupation is house building.* ○ *It is not a well paid occupation.*

"...the share of white-collar occupations in total employment rose from 44 per cent to 49 per cent" [*Sydney Morning Herald*]

occupational /ˌɑkjʊ'peɪʃ(ə)nəl/ *adjective* referring to a job

occupational accident /ˌɑkjʊpeɪʃ(ə)nəl 'æksɪd(ə)nt/ *noun* an accident which takes place at work

occupational disease /ˌɑkjʊpeɪʃ(ə)nəl dɪ'ziz/ *noun* a disease which affects people in certain jobs

occupational hazard /ˌɑkjʊpeɪʃ(ə)nəl 'hæzərd/ *noun* a danger which applies to certain jobs ○ *Heart attacks are one of the occupational hazards of directors.*

occupational pension /ˌɑkjʊpeɪʃ(ə)nəl 'penʃən/ *noun* a pension which is paid by the company by which an employee has been employed

occupational pension plan /ˌɑkjʊpeɪʃ(ə)nəl 'penʃən ˌplæn/ *noun* a pension plan where the employee gets a pension from a fund set up by the company he or she has worked for, which is related to the salary he or she was earning. Also called **company pension scheme**

Occupational Safety and Health Administration full form of **OSHA**

occupier /'ɑkjʊpaɪr/ *noun* a person who lives in a property

occupy /'ɑkjʊpaɪ/ *verb* **1.** to live or work in a property (such as a house, an office, a hotel room) ○ *All the rooms in the hotel are occupied.* ○ *The company occupies three floors of an office building.* ○ *The office occupied by the personnel manager.* **2.** □ **to occupy a post** to be employed in a job

ocean terminal /ˌoʊʃ(ə)n 'tɜrmɪn(ə)l/ *noun* a building at a port where passengers arrive and depart

odd /ɑd/ *adjective* **1.** □ **a hundred odd** approximately one hundred **2.** one of a group □ **we have a few odd boxes left** we have a few boxes left out of the total shipment □ **to do odd jobs** to do various pieces of work

odd-job-man /ˌɑd 'dʒɑb ˌmæn/ *noun* a person who does various pieces of work

odd lot /ˌɑd 'lɑt/ *noun* **1.** a group of miscellaneous items for sale at an auction **2.** a group of less than 100 shares of stock bought or sold together. Also called **broken lot**, **uneven lot**

oddments /'ɑdmənts/ *plural noun* **1.** items left over **2.** left-over pieces of large items, sold separately

odd size /ˌɑd 'saɪz/ *noun* a size which is not usual

OECD *abbreviation* Organisation for Economic Co-operation and Development

"...calling for a greater correlation between labour market policies, social policies and education and training, the OECD warned that long-term unemployment would remain unacceptably high without a reassessment of labour market trends" [*Australian Financial Review*]

OEM *abbreviation* original equipment manufacturer

off /ɔf/ *adjective* not working or not in operation ○ *to take three days off* ○ *The agreement is off.* ○ *They called the strike off.* ○ *We give the staff four days off at Christmas.* ○ *It's my day off tomorrow.* ■ *adverb* **1.** lower than a previous price ○ *The stock closed 2% off.* **2.** □ **to be off** to be wrong in calculating something, or to be wrongly calculated ○ *the balance is*

$10 off □ **we are $20,000 off in our calculations** we have $20,000 too much or too little ■ *preposition* **1.** subtracted from ○ *to take $25 off the price* ○ *We give 10% off our usual prices.* **2.** not included □ **items off balance sheet** *or* **off balance sheet assets** financial items which do not appear in a company's balance sheet as assets, such as equipment acquired under an operating lease **3.** away from work ○ *to take time off work*

offer /'ɔfər/ *noun* **1.** a statement that you are willing to give or do something, especially to pay a specific amount of money to buy something ○ *to make an offer for a company* ○ *We made an offer of $10 a share.* ○ *We made a written offer for the house.* ○ *$1,000 is the best offer I can make.* ○ *We accepted an offer of $1,000 for the car.* □ **the house is under offer** *U.K.* someone has made an offer to buy the house and the offer has been accepted provisionally □ **we are open to offers** we are ready to discuss the price which we are asking □ **or best offer** *U.K.* or an offer of a price which is slightly less than the price asked ○ *The car is for sale at $2,000 or best offer.* **2.** a statement that you are willing to sell something **3.** a statement that you are willing to employ someone □ **she received six offers of jobs** *or* **six job offers** six companies told her she could have a job with them **4.** a statement that a company is prepared to buy another company's stock and take the company over ■ *verb* **1.** to say that you are willing to do something ○ *We offered to go with them to the meeting.* □ **to offer someone a job** to tell someone that they can have a job in your company ○ *She was offered a directorship with Smith Inc.* **2.** to say that you are willing to pay a specific amount of money for something ○ *to offer someone $100,000 for their house* ○ *She offered $10 a share.* **3.** to say that you are willing to sell something ○ *We offered the house for sale.* ○ *They are offering special prices on winter vacations in Europe.*

offer for sale /,ɔfər fər 'seɪl/ *noun* a situation in which a company advertises new shares for sale to the public as a way of launching itself on the Stock Exchange

offering /'ɔf(ə)rɪŋ/ *noun* an action of stating that you are prepared to sell something at some price

"…shares of newly public companies posted their worst performance of the year last month as a spate of initial public offerings disappointed followers" [*Wall Street Journal*]

"…if the partnership supports a sale, a public offering of shares would be set for as early as the fourth quarter" [*Wall Street Journal*]

offer period /'ɔfər ,pɪriəd/ *noun* a time during which a takeover bid for a company is open

offer price /'ɔfər praɪs/ *noun* the price at which investors buy new shares or units in a mutual fund. The opposite, i.e. the selling price, is called the "bid price", the difference between the two is the "spread".

office /'ɔfɪs/ *noun* **1.** a set of rooms where a company works or where business is done □ **for office use only** something which must only be used in an office **2.** a room where someone works and does business ○ *Come into my office.* ○ *The human resources manager's office is on the third floor.* **3.** a government department **4.** a post or position ○ *She holds* or *performs the office of treasurer*

office building /'ɔfɪs ,bɪldɪŋ/ *noun* a building which contains only offices

office design /,ɔfɪs dɪ'zaɪn/ *noun* the science or task of arranging the layout of an office so that work can be done as efficiently as possible

office equipment /'ɔfɪs ɪ,kwɪpmənt/ *noun* furniture and machines needed to make an office work

office furniture /,ɔfɪs 'fɜrnɪtʃər/ *noun* chairs, desks, filing cabinets used in an office ○ *an office furniture store* ○ *He deals in secondhand office furniture.*

office hours /,ɔfɪs 'aʊrz/ *plural noun* the time when an office is open ○ *Do not make private phone calls during office hours.*

office job /'ɔfɪs dʒɑb/ *noun* a job in an office

office junior /,ɔfɪs 'dʒuniər/ *noun* a young man or woman who does all types of work in an office

office messenger /,ɔfɪs 'mes(ə)ndʒər/ *noun* a person who carries messages from one person to another in a large office

Office of Fair Trading /,ɔfɪs əv fer 'treɪdɪŋ/ *noun* a department of the U.K. government that protects consumers against unfair or illegal business. Abbreviation **OFT**

Office of Management and Budget /ˌɒfɪs əv ˌmænɪdʒmənt ən 'bʌdʒɪt/ *noun* the department of the U.S. government that prepares the federal budget. Abbreviation **OMB**

Office of Thrift Supervision /ˌɒfɪs əv 'θrɪft supə,vɪʒ(ə)n/ *noun* a department of the U.S. government which regulates the Savings and Loan Associations. Abbreviation **OTS**

office park /'ɒfɪs pɑrk/ *noun* a group of office buildings concentrated in an area, often on landscaped grounds ○ *The dentist's office is in the office park near the mall.*

office politics /ˌɒfɪs 'pɑlɪtɪks/ *noun* the ways in which the people in a particular workplace relate to and behave toward each other, especially the ways in which people acquire power and status or use the power and status they have

"...established firms and renowned individuals who promise--for a fee--to help people become better executives, improve productivity and navigate office politics." [*Forbes*]

office premises /ˌɒfɪs 'premɪsɪz/ *plural noun* building which houses an office or store

officer /'ɒfɪsər/ *noun* a person who has an official position, especially an unpaid one in a club or other association ○ *The election of officers takes place next week.*

office space /'ɒfɪs speɪs/ *noun* a space available for offices or occupied by offices ○ *We are looking for extra office space.*

office staff /ˌɒfɪs 'stæf/ *noun* people who work in offices

office supplies /'ɒfɪs sə,plaɪz/ *noun* stationery and furniture used in an office

office worker /'ɒfɪs ˌwɜrkər/ *noun* a person who works in an office

official /ə'fɪʃ(ə)l/ *adjective* **1.** from a government department or organization ○ *She went to France on official business.* ○ *He left official documents in his car.* ○ *She received an official letter of explanation.* □ **speaking in an official capacity** speaking officially □ **to go through official channels** to deal with officials, especially when making a request **2.** done or approved by a director or by a person in authority ○ *This must be an official order – it is written on*

the company's headed paper. ○ *This is the union's official policy.* □ **the strike was made official** the local strike was approved by the main labor union office ■ *noun* a person working in a government department ○ *airport officials inspected the shipment* ○ *Government officials stopped the import license.* □ **minor official** a person in a low position in a government department ○ *Some minor official tried to stop my request for building permission.*

officialese /əˌfɪʃə'liz/ *noun* the language used in government documents which can be difficult to understand

official exchange rate /əˌfɪʃ(ə)l ɪks 'tʃeɪndʒ ˌreɪt/ *noun* an exchange rate which is imposed by the government ○ *The official exchange rate is ten to the dollar, but you can get fifty on the black market.*

officially /ə'fɪʃ(ə)li/ *adverb* according to what is said in public ○ *Officially he knows nothing about the problem, but unofficially he has given us a lot of advice about it.*

official mediator /əˌfɪʃ(ə)l 'midieɪtər/ *noun* a government official who tries to make the two sides in an industrial dispute agree

official receiver /əˌfɪʃ(ə)l rɪ'sivər/ *noun U.K.* a government official who is appointed to run a company which is in financial difficulties, to pay off its debts as far as possible and to close it down ○ *The company is in the hands of the official receiver.*

official strike /əˌfɪʃ(ə)l 'straɪk/ *noun* a strike which has been approved by the main office of a union

officio /ə'fɪʃioʊ/ ♦ **ex officio**

off-licence /'ɒf ˌlaɪs(ə)ns/ *noun U.K.* same as **liquor store**

offline /ˌɒf 'laɪn/ *adverb* not connected to a network or central computer

offload /ɒf'loʊd/ *verb* to pass something which you do not want to someone else □ **to offload excess stock** to try to sell excess inventory

off-peak /ˌɒf 'pik/ *adjective* not during the most busy time

off-peak period /ˌɒf 'pik ˌpɪriəd/ *noun* the time when business is less busy

off-peak tariff /ˌɔf pik 'tærɪf/ *noun* lower charges used when the service is not busy

off-season /'ɔf ˌsiz(ə)n/ *noun* the less busy season for travel, usually during the winter ○ *Air fares are cheaper in the off-season.*

off-season fare /ˌɔf ˌsiz(ə)n 'fer/ *noun* U.K. cheap fares which are charged in a season when there is less business

offset /ɔf'set/ *verb* to balance one thing against another so that they cancel each other out ○ *to offset losses against tax* ○ *Foreign exchange losses more than offset profits in the domestic market.* (NOTE: **off-setting – offset**)

offshore /'ɔfʃɔr/ *adjective, adverb* **1.** on an island or in the sea near to land ○ *an offshore oil field* ○ *an offshore oil platform* **2.** on an island which is a tax haven **3.** based outside a country, especially in a tax haven

offshore investment /ˌɔfʃɔr ɪn 'vestmənt/ *noun* an investment that is based outside the U.S., and usually in a country which has less strict taxation than in the U.S., such as the Bahamas

offshoring /'ɔfʃɔrɪŋ/ *noun* the practice of relocating manufacturing or services to a country that pays lower wages

offsite /ɔf'saɪt/ *adjective* not based or happening in an organization's principal place of business

off-the-job training /ˌɔf ðə dʒɑb 'treɪnɪŋ/ *noun* training given to employees away from their place of work, such as at a college or school

off-the-shelf /ˌɔf ðə 'ʃelf/ *adjective, adverb* ready-made according to a regular design

off-the-shelf company /ˌɔf ðə ˌʃelf 'kʌmp(ə)ni/ *noun* a company which has already been registered by an accountant or lawyer, and which is ready for sale to someone who wants to set up a new company quickly

000 *noun* **1.** U.K. same as **banker's bill 2.** same as **banknote**

oil /ɔɪl/ *noun* a natural liquid found in the ground, used to burn to give power

"…the biggest surprise of 1999 was the rebound in the price of oil. In the early months of the year commentators were talking about a fall to $5 a barrel but for the first time in two decades, the oil exporting countries got their act together, limited production and succeeded in pushing prices up" [*Financial Times*]

oil-exporting country /'ɔɪl ɪk ˌspɔrtɪŋ ˌkʌntri/ *noun* a country which produces oil and sells it to others

oil field /'ɔɪl fild/ *noun* an area of land or sea under which oil is found

oil-importing country /ˌɔɪ lɪm ˌpɔrtɪŋ 'kʌntri/ *noun* a country which imports oil

oil platform /ɔɪl 'plæt ˌfɔrm/ *noun* a large structure with equipment, used to for making holes to find oil in the ocean

oil-producing country /ɔɪl prə ˌdusɪŋ 'kʌntri/ *noun* a country which produces oil

oil well /'ɔɪl wel/ *noun* a hole in the ground from which oil is pumped

old boy network /'oʊld bɔɪ ˌnetwɜrk/ *noun* the practice of using long-standing key contacts to appoint people to jobs or to get a job or to do business. ◊ **networking**

old-established /ˌoʊld ɪs'tæblɪʃt/ *adjective* (company or brand) which has been in existence for a long time ○ *The old-established family business was bought by a group of entrepreneurs.*

OMB *abbreviation* Office of Management and Budget

ombudsman /'ɑmbʊdzmən/ *noun* **1.** a management employee who is given the freedom to move around the workplace to locate and remedy unfair practices (NOTE: The plural is **ombudsmen**.) **2.** an official who investigates complaints by the public against government departments or other large organizations

"…radical changes to the disciplinary system, including appointing an ombudsman to review cases where complainants are not satisfied with the outcome, are proposed in a consultative paper the Institute of Chartered Accountants issued last month" [*Accountancy*]

omission /oʊ'mɪʃ(ə)n/ *noun* a thing which has been omitted, or the act of omitting something

omit /oʊ'mɪt/ *verb* **1.** to leave something out, not to put something in ○ *Her assistant omitted the date when typing the contract.* **2.** not to do something ○ *He omitted to tell the managing director that he had lost the documents.* (NOTE: **omitting – omitted**)

omnibus agreement /ˈɒmnɪbəs ə ˌgrimənt/ *noun* an agreement which covers many different items

on /ɒn/ *preposition* **1.** being a member of a group ○ *to sit on a committee* ○ *She is on the boards of two companies.* ○ *We have 250 people on the payroll.* ○ *She is on our full-time staff.* **2.** in a certain way ○ *on a commercial basis* ○ *to buy something on approval* ○ *to get a mortgage on easy terms* ○ *He is still on probation.* ○ *She is employed on very generous terms.* □ **on the understanding that** on condition that, provided that ○ *We accept the terms of the contract, on the understanding that it has to be ratified by our main board.* **3.** at a time ○ *The store is closed on Wednesday afternoons.* ○ *We work 7 hours a day on weekdays.* ○ *The whole staff has the day off on May 24th.* **4.** doing something ○ *The director is on vacation.* ○ *She is in the States on business.* ○ *The switchboard operator is on duty from 6 to 9.*

on-demand /ˌɒn dɪˈmænd/ *adjective* used to describe stored Internet programming that allows users to access it whenever they want

one-man business /ˌwʌn mæn ˈbɪznɪs/, **one-man firm** /ˌwʌn mæn ˈfɜrm/, **one-man company** /ˌwʌn mæn ˈkʌmp(ə)ni/ *noun* a business run by one person alone with no staff or partners

one-off /ˌwʌn ˈɒf/ *adjective U.K.* done or made only once ○ *one-off item* ○ *one-off deal* ○ *one-off payment*

onerous /ˈɒunərəs/ *adjective* heavy, needing a lot of effort or money □ **the repayment terms are particularly onerous** the loan is particularly difficult to pay back

one-sided /ˌwʌn ˈsaɪdɪd/ *adjective* favoring one side and not the other in a negotiation

one-stop /ˈwʌn stɒp/ *adjective* offering a wide range of services to a customer, not necessarily services which are related to the product or services which the company normally sells

one-way fare /ˌwʌn weɪ ˈfer/ *noun* a fare for a trip from one place to another

one-way ticket /ˌwʌn weɪ ˈtɪkɪt/ *noun* a ticket for a trip from one place to another

one-way trade /ˌwʌn weɪ ˈtreɪd/ *noun* a situation in which one country sells to another, but does not buy anything in return

online /ɒnˈlaɪn/; /ˈɒnlaɪn/ *adjective, adverb* linked via a computer directly to another computer, a computer network or, especially, the Internet; on the Internet ○ *The sales office is online to the warehouse.* ○ *We get our data online from the stock control department.*

online community /ˌɒnlaɪn kəˈmjunɪti/ *noun* a network of people who communicate with one another and with an organization through interactive tools such as e-mail, discussion boards and chat systems

o.n.o. *abbreviation* or near offer

on-site /ˌɒn ˈsaɪt/ *adjective* based or happening in an organization's principal place of business

on-the-job training /ˌɒn ðə dʒɒb ˈtreɪnɪŋ/ *noun* training given to employees at their place of work

on the side /ˌɒn ðə ˈsaɪd/ *adverb* separate from your normal work, and hidden from your employer ○ *He works in an accountant's office, but he runs a construction company on the side.* ○ *Her salary is too small to live on, so the family lives on what she can make on the side.*

on time /ˌɒn ˈtaɪm/ *adverb* the right time ○ *the plane was on time* ○ *you will have to hurry if you want to get to the meeting on time* or *if you want to be on time for the meeting*

OPEC /ˈoupek/ *abbreviation* Organization of Petroleum Exporting Countries

op-ed /ˌɒp ˈed/ *noun* in a newspaper, a page that has signed articles expressing personal opinions, usually found opposite the editorial page

open /ˈoupən/ *adjective* **1.** at work, not closed ○ *The store is open on Sunday mornings.* ○ *Our offices are open from 9 to 6.* ○ *They are open for business every day of the week.* **2.** ready to accept something □ **the job is open to all applicants** anyone can apply for the job □ **we will keep the job open for a month** we will not give the job to anyone else for a month □ **open to offers** ready to accept a reasonable offer □ **the company is open to offers for the empty factory** the company is ready to discuss an offer which is lower than the suggested price ■ *verb* **1.** to start a new business ○ *She has opened a store on Main Street.* ○ *We have opened a branch in London.* **2.** to start work, to be at work ○ *The* *office opens at 9 a.m.* ○ *We open for business on Sundays.* **3.** to begin something □ **to open negotiations** to begin negotiating ○ *She opened the discussions with a description of the product.* ○ *The chairman opened the meeting at 10.30.* **4.** to set something up or make something available ○ *to open a bank account* ○ *to open a line of credit* ○ *to open a loan* **5.** □ **stocks opened lower** stock prices were lower at the beginning of the day's trading

  open up *phrasal verb* □ **to open up new markets** to work to start business in markets where such business has not been done before

open account /ˌoʊpən əˈkaʊnt/ *noun* an account where the supplier offers the purchaser credit without security

open check /ˌoʊpən ˈtʃek/ *noun* same as **uncrossed check**

open communication /ˌoʊpən kəˌmjuːnɪˈkeɪʃ(ə)n/ *noun* a policy intended to ensure that employees are able to find out everything they want to know about their organization

open credit /ˌoʊpən ˈkredɪt/ *noun* credit given to good customers without security

open-door policy /ˌoʊpən ˈdɔr ˌpɑlɪsi/ *noun* a policy in which a country accepts imports from all other countries on equal terms

open-end /ˌoʊpən ˈend/ *adjective* with no fixed limit or with some items not specified

open-ended /ˌoʊpən ˈendɪd/ *adjective* with no fixed limit or with some items not specified ○ *They signed an open-ended agreement.* ○ *The candidate was offered an open-ended contract with a good career plan.* Also called **open-end**

open-ended credit /ˌoʊpən ˌendɪd ˈkredɪt/ *noun* same as **revolving credit**

open general license /ˌoʊpən ˌdʒen(ə)rəl ˈlaɪs(ə)ns/ *noun* an import license for all goods which are subject to special import restrictions

opening /ˈoʊp(ə)nɪŋ/ *noun* **1.** the act of starting a new business ○ *the opening of a new branch* ○ *the opening of a new market* or *of a new distribution network* **2.** an available job ○ *She's applied for the opening in the sales department.* **3.** an opportunity to do something ■ *adjective* being at the beginning, or the first of several

opening balance /ˈoʊp(ə)nɪŋ ˌbæləns/ *noun* a balance at the beginning of an accounting period

opening bid /ˌoʊp(ə)nɪŋ ˈbɪd/ *noun* the first bid at an auction

opening entry /ˈoʊp(ə)nɪŋ ˌentri/ *noun* the first entry in an account

opening hours /ˈoʊp(ə)nɪŋ aʊrz/ *plural noun* the hours when a store or business is open

opening price /ˌoʊp(ə)nɪŋ ˈpraɪs/ *noun* a price at the start of a day's trading

opening session /ˌoʊp(ə)nɪŋ ˈseʃ(ə)n/ *noun* the first part or last part of a conference

opening stock /ˌoʊp(ə)nɪŋ ˈstɑk/ *noun U.K.* same as **beginning inventory**

opening time /ˈoʊp(ə)nɪŋ taɪm/ *noun* the time when a store or office starts work

open market /ˌoʊpən ˈmɑrkət/ *noun* a market where anyone can buy or sell

open-plan office /ˌoʊpən plæn ˈɔfɪs/ *noun* a large room divided into smaller working spaces with no fixed divisions between them

open pricing /ˌoʊpən ˈpraɪsɪŋ/ *noun* the attempt by companies to achieve some cooperation and conformity in pricing ○ *Representatives from the major companies in the industry are meeting to establish an open-pricing policy.*

open standard /ˌoʊpən ˈstændərd/ *noun* a standard that allows computers and similar pieces of equipment made by different manufacturers to operate with each other

open system /ˈoʊpən ˌsɪstəm/ *noun* **1.** a flexible type of organization, which allows employees freedom to work in their own way ○ *An open system can allow employees to choose their own working hours.* **2.** a computer operating system that users are freely allowed to develop applications for

open systems thinking /ˌoʊpən ˌsɪstəmz ˈθɪŋkɪŋ/ *noun* an approach to learning and problem-solving in which people the behavior of a system, then explore possible ways for improving it

open ticket /ˌoʊpən ˈtɪkɪt/ *noun* a ticket which can be used on any date

operate /ˈɑpəreɪt/ *verb* **1.** to be in force ○ *The new terms of service will operate from January 1st.* ○ *The rules operate on* *domestic postal services only.* **2.** to make something work or function □ **to operate a machine** to make a machine work ○ *He is learning to operate the new telephone switchboard.* **3.** to do business, or to run a business or a machine

operating /ˈɑpəreɪtɪŋ/ *noun* the general running of a business or of a machine

operating budget /ˈɑpəreɪtɪŋ ˌbʌdʒət/ *noun* a forecast of income and expenditure over a period of time

operating costs /ˈɑpəreɪtɪŋ ˌkɔsts/ *plural noun* the costs of the day-to-day activities of a company. Also called **operating expenses, running costs**

operating earnings /ˌɑpəreɪtɪŋ ˈɜrnɪŋz/ *plural noun* same as **operating income**

operating expenses /ˌɑpəreɪtɪŋ ɪk ˈspenss/ *plural noun* same as **operating costs**

operating income /ˈɑpəreɪtɪŋ ˌɪnkʌm/, **operating profit** /ˈɑpəreɪtɪŋ ˌprɑfɪt/ *noun* the profit made by a company in its usual business. Also called **operating earnings**

operating manual /ˈɑpəreɪtɪŋ ˌmænjuəl/ *noun* a book which shows how to work a machine

operating statement /ˈɑpəreɪtɪŋ ˌsteɪtmənt/ *noun* a financial statement which shows a company's expenditure and income and consequently its final profit or loss ○ *The operating statement shows unexpected electricity costs.* ○ *Let's look at the operating statement to find last month's expenditure.*

operating system /ˈɑpəreɪtɪŋ ˌsɪstəm/ *noun* the main program which operates a computer

operation /ˌɑpəˈreɪʃ(ə)n/ *noun* **1.** an activity or a piece of work, or the task of running something ○ *the company's operations in West Africa* ○ *He heads up the operations in Northern Europe.* **2.** □ **in operation** working or being used ○ *The system will be in operation by June.* ○ *The new system came into operation on January 1st.*

operational /ˌɑpəˈreɪʃ(ə)nəl/ *adjective* **1.** referring to the day-to-day activities of a business or to the way in which something is run **2.** working or in operation □ **the system became operational on June 1st** the system began working on June 1st

operational audit /ˌɑpəreɪʃ(ə)nəl ˈɔdɪt/ *noun* a systematic review of the systems and procedures used in an organization in order to assess whether they are being carried out efficiently and effectively. Also known as **management audit, operations audit**

operational budget /ˌɑpəreɪʃ(ə)nəl ˈbʌdʒət/ *noun* a forecast of expenditure on running a business

operational costs /ˌɑpəreɪʃ(ə)nəl ˈkɔsts/ *plural noun* the costs of running a business

operational planning /ˌɑpəreɪʃ(ə)nəl ˈplænɪŋ/ *noun* the planning of how a business is to be run

operational research /ˌɑpəreɪʃ(ə)nəl rɪˈsɜrtʃ/ *noun* a study of a company's way of working to see if it can be made more efficient and profitable

operations review /ˌɑpəreɪʃ(ə)nz rɪ ˈvju/ *noun* an act of examining the way in which a company or department works to see how it can be made more efficient and profitable

operative /ˈɑp(ə)rətɪv/ *adjective* operating or working ○ *The new system has been operative since June 1st* □ **to become operative** to start working ■ *noun* a person who operates a machine which makes a product ○ *A skilled operative can produce 250 units per hour.*

operator /ˈɑpəreɪtər/ *noun* **1.** a person who works a machine ○ *a keyboard operator* ○ *a computer operator* **2.** a person who works a telephone switchboard ○ *switchboard operator* ○ *to call the operator* or *to dial the operator* ○ *to place a call through* or *via the operator* **3.** a person who runs a business **4.** (*on the Stock Exchange*) a person who buys and sells stocks hoping to make a quick profit

"…a number of block bookings by American tour operators have been cancelled" [*Economist*]

opinion /əˈpɪnjən/ *noun* a piece of expert advice ○ *the lawyers gave their opinion* ○ *to ask an adviser for his opinion on a case*

opinion leader /əˈpɪnjən ˌfɔrmər/ *noun* someone well known whose opinions influence others in society ○ *A popstar is the ideal opinion-leader if we are aiming at the teenage market.*

opinion poll /ə'pɪnjən poʊl/ *noun* the activity of asking a sample group of people what their opinion is, so as to guess the opinion of the whole population ○ *Opinion polls showed that the public preferred butter to margarine.* ○ *Before starting the new service, the company carried out nationwide opinion polls.*

OPM *abbreviation* other people's money

opportunity /ˌɑpər'tunəti/ *noun* a chance to do something successfully

opportunity and threat analysis /ɑpərˌtunəti ən 'θret əˌnæləsɪs/ *noun* a company's analysis of both the advantages and disadvantages in its situation, done in order to ensure sound strategic planning

opportunity cost /ˌɑpər'tjunɪti kɔst/ *noun* the cost of a business initiative in terms of profits that could have been gained through an alternate plan ○ *It's a good investment plan and we will not be deterred by the opportunity cost.*

oppose /ə'poʊz/ *verb* to try to stop something happening; to vote against something ○ *A minority of board members opposed the motion.* ○ *We are all opposed to the takeover.*

opposite number /ˌɑpəzɪt 'nʌmbər/ *noun* a person who has a similar job in another company □ **John is my opposite number in Smith's** John has the same job in Smith's as I have here

optimal /'ɑptɪm(ə)l/ *adjective* best

optimum /'ɑptɪməm/ *adjective* best ○ *The market offers optimum conditions for sales.*

opt-in /'ɑpt ɪn/ *noun* a method by which users can register with a website if they want to receive particular information or services from it. In opt-in, users must provide their e-mail addresses, so that the website owner can send them e-mails.

option /'ɑpʃən/ *noun* the opportunity to buy or sell something, such as a security, within a fixed period of time at a fixed price □ **to have first option on something** to have the right to be the first to have the possibility of deciding something □ **to grant someone a six-month option on a product** to allow someone six months to decide if they want to manufacture the product □ **to take up an option** *or* **to exercise an option** to accept the option which has been offered and to put it into action ○ *They exercised their option* or

they took up their option to acquire sole marketing rights to the product. □ **I want to leave my options open** I want to be able to decide what to do when the time is right

optional /'ɑpʃən(ə)l/ *adjective* able to be done or not done, taken or not taken, as a person chooses ○ *The insurance cover is optional.* ○ *Attendance at staff meetings is optional, although the management encourages employees to attend.*

optional extra /ˌɑpʃən(ə)l 'ekstrə/ *noun* an item that is not essential but can be added if wanted

option contract /'ɑpʃən ˌkɑntrækt/ *noun* a right to buy or sell a specific number of shares at a fixed price

option dealing /'ɑpʃən ˌdilɪŋ/ *noun* the activity of buying and selling stock options

option to purchase /ˌɑpʃən tə 'pɜrtʃɪs/ *noun* an option which gives someone the possibility to buy something within a period of time

orange goods /'ɑrɪndʒ gʊdz/ *plural noun* goods which are not bought as often as fast-moving items but are replaced from time to time, e.g., clothing. Compare **red goods, yellow goods**

order /'ɔrdər/ *noun* **1.** the way in which records such as filing cards or invoices are arranged ○ *in alphabetical or numerical order* **2.** working arrangement □ **machine in full working order** a machine which is ready and able to work properly □ **the telephone is out of order** the telephone is not working □ **is all the documentation in order?** are all the documents valid and correct? **3.** an official request for goods to be supplied ○ *to give someone an order* or *to place an order with someone for twenty filing cabinets* ○ *The management ordered the work force to leave the factory.* □ **to fill an order, to fulfill an order** to supply items which have been ordered ○ *We are so understaffed we cannot fulfill anymore orders before Christmas.* □ **items available to order only** items which will be manufactured only if someone orders them □ **on order** ordered but not delivered ○ *This item is out of stock, but is on order.* **4.** an item which has been ordered ○ *The order is to be delivered to our warehouse.* ○ *That filing cabinet contains staff records ordered by name.* **5.** an instruction **6.** a document which allows money to be paid to someone ○ *She sent us an order on the Bank of America.* **7.** □ **pay to Mr Smith or order** pay money to Mr. Smith or as he orders. □ **pay to the order of Mr Smith** pay money directly to Mr. Smith or to his account. ■ *verb* **1.** to ask for goods to be supplied ○ *They ordered a new BMW for the managing director.* **2.** to give an official request for something to be done or for something to be supplied ○ *to order twenty filing cabinets to be delivered to the warehouse* **3.** to put in a certain way ○ *The address list is ordered by country.* ○ *That filing cabinet contains invoices ordered by date.*

order book /'ɔrdər bʊk/ *noun* a book which records orders received

order confirmation /'ɔrdər kɑnf ˌmeɪʃ(ə)n/ *noun* an email message informing a purchaser that an order has been received

order form /'ɔrdər fɔrm/ *noun* a pad of blank forms for orders to be written on

order fulfillment /'ɔrdər fʊl,fɪlmənt/ *noun* the process of supplying items which have been ordered

order number /'ɔrdər ,nʌmbər/ *noun* the reference number printed on an order

order picking /'ɔrdər ,pɪkɪŋ/ *noun* the process of collecting various items in a warehouse in order to make up an order to be sent to a customer

order processing /'ɔrdər ,prɑsesɪŋ/ *noun* the work of dealing with orders

ordinary member /,ɔrd(ə)n(ə)ri 'membər/ *noun* a person who pays dues to belong to a group

ordinary resolution /,ɔrd(ə)n(ə)ri ,rezə'luʃ(ə)n/ *noun* a resolution put before an annual meeting, usually referring to some general procedural matter, and which requires a simple majority of votes to be accepted

ordinary shares /'ɔrd(ə)n(ə)ri ʃerz/ *plural noun U.K.* same as **common stock**

organic growth /ɔ,gænɪk 'groʊθ/ *noun* same as **internal growth**

Organisation for Economic Co-operation and Development /,ɔrgənaɪzeɪʃ(ə)n fər ikə,nɑmɪk koʊ ,ɑpəreɪʃ(ə)n ən dɪ'veləpmənt/ *noun* an organization representing the industrialized countries, aimed at encouraging international trade, wealth and employment in member countries. Abbreviation **OECD**

organization /,ɔrgənaɪ'zeɪʃ(ə)n/ *noun* **1.** a way of arranging something so that it works efficiently ○ *the organization of the head office into departments* ○ *The chairman handles the organization of the annual meeting.* ○ *The organization of the group is too centralized to be efficient.* **2.** a group or institution which is arranged for efficient work

organizational /,ɔrgənaɪ'zeɪʃ(ə)n(ə)l/ *adjective* referring to the way in which something is organized ○ *The paper gives a diagram of the company's organizational structure.*

organizational analysis /,ɔrgənaɪzeɪʃ(ə)n(ə)l ə'næləsɪs/ *noun* a type of analysis carried out by an organization that is intended to identify areas where it is inefficient and ways in which it can be restructured so as to become more efficient

organizational chart /,ɔrgənaɪ 'zeɪʃ(ə)n(ə)l tʃɑrt/ *noun* a chart showing the hierarchical relationships between employees in a company

organizational development /,ɔrgənaɪzeɪʃ(ə)n(ə)l dɪ'veləpmənt/ *noun* **1.** a form of management training designed to affect the whole organization as well as the individual employees **2.** planning that is directed toward bringing about far-reaching changes in an organization that will enable it to adapt to changing market conditions and set itself new objectives

organization and methods /,ɔrgənaɪzeɪʃ(ə)n ən 'meθədz/ *noun* a process of examining how an office works, and suggesting how it can be made more efficient. Abbreviation **O & M**

organization chart /,ɔrgənaɪ 'zeɪʃ(ə)n tʃɑrt/ *noun* same as **organizational chart**

organization hierarchy /,ɔrgənaɪzeɪʃ(ə)n 'haɪrɑrki/ *noun* the traditional way that authority is structured within an organization, that is, in a series of layers arranged vertically, each layer consisting of people of equal rank who are superior to the people in the layers below and subordinate to the people in the layers above. During the later 20th and early 21st centuries the numbers of layers within the hierarchies of large organizations have often been greatly reduced as a result of downsizing, leading to so-called flat organizations where there is greater employee empowerment.

Organization of Petroleum Exporting Countries /ˌɔːgənaɪzeɪʃ(ə)n əv pəˌtrəʊliəm ekˌspɔːtɪŋ ˈkʌntriz/ *noun* a group of major countries who are producers and exporters of oil. Abbreviation **OPEC**

organization pyramid /ˌɔːgənaɪ ˈzeɪʃ(ə)n ˌpɪrəmɪd/ *noun* a structure of an organization with many employees at lower levels and fewer at the top

organization theory /ˌɔːgənaɪ ˈzeɪʃ(ə)n ˌθɪəri/ *noun* the study of organizations, especially of organizations as units or structures, rather than of the behavior of people within organizations

organize /ˈɔːgənaɪz/ *verb* **1.** to set up a system for doing something ○ *The company is organized into six profit centers.* ○ *The group is organized by sales areas.* **2.** to arrange something so that it works

organized labor /ˌɔːgənaɪzd ˈleɪbər/ *noun* employees who are members of labor unions

"…governments are coming under increasing pressure from politicians, organized labour and business to stimulate economic growth" [*Duns Business Month*]

organizer *noun* a person who arranges things efficiently ○ *Address any queries about the venue to the conference organizer.*

organizing committee /ˌɔːgənaɪzɪŋ kəˈmɪti/ *noun* a group of people who arrange something ○ *He is a member of the organizing committee for the conference.*

oriented /ˈɔːrientɪd/, **orientated** /ˈɔːrienteɪtəd/ *adjective* working in a certain direction ○ *a market-orientated approach* □ **export-oriented company** company which produces goods mainly for export

origin /ˈɔrɪdʒɪn/ *noun* the place where something or someone originally comes from ○ *spare parts of European origin*

original /əˈrɪdʒən(ə)l/ *adjective* which was used or made first ○ *They sent a copy of the original invoice.* ○ *He kept the original receipt for reference.* ■ *noun* the first copy made ○ *Send the original and file two copies.*

original equipment manufacturer /əˌrɪdʒən(ə)l ɪˌkwɪpmənt ˌmænjə

ˈfæktʃərər/ *noun* a company that makes or assembles pieces of equipment that are designed to work with a basic and common product such as a computer

originally /əˈrɪdʒən(ə)li/ *adverb* first or at the beginning

O's ◊ four O's

OS *abbreviation* outsize

O/S *abbreviation* out of stock

OSHA *noun* the federal agency in the U.S. that is responsible for health and safety in the workplace. Full form **Occupational Safety and Health Administration**

other people's money (OPM) /ˌʌðər ˌpiːp(ə)lz ˈmʌni/ money which a business "borrows" from its creditors (such as by not paying invoices on schedule) and so avoids using its own funds

OTS *abbreviation* Office of Thrift Supervision

ounce /aʊns/ *noun* a measure of weight (= 28 grams) (NOTE: Usually written **oz** after figures: *25oz.* Note also that the ounce is now no longer officially used in the U.K.)

out /aʊt/ *adverb* **1.** on strike ○ *The workers have been out on strike for four weeks.* ○ *As soon as the management made the offer, the staff came out.* ○ *The shop stewards called the work force out.* **2.** away from work because of illness (NOTE: The U.K. term for this sense is **off**.)

outbid /aʊtˈbɪd/ *verb* to offer a better price than someone else ○ *We offered £100,000 for the warehouse, but another company outbid us.* (NOTE: **outbidding – outbid**)

outfit /ˈaʊtfɪt/ *noun* a small, sometimes badly run company ○ *They called in a public relations outfit.* ○ *He works for some finance outfit.*

outflow /ˈaʊtfləʊ/ *noun* □ **outflow of capital from a country** capital which is sent out of a country for investment abroad

outgoing /ˌaʊtˈgəʊɪŋ/ *adjective* **1.** □ **outgoing mail** mail which is being sent out **2.** □ **the outgoing chairman, the outgoing president** chairman or president who is about to retire

outgoings /ˈaʊtgəʊɪŋz/ *plural noun* money which is paid out

outlay /ˈaʊtleɪ/ *noun* money spent, expenditure □ **for a modest outlay** for a small sum ○ *For a modest outlay he was able to take control of the business.*

outlet /'aʊtlət/ *noun* a place where something can be sold

outline /'aʊtlaɪn/ *noun* a general description, without giving many details ○ *They drew up the outline of a plan* or *an outline plan.* ■ *verb* to make a general description ○ *The chairman outlined the company's plans for the coming year.*

outlook /'aʊtlʊk/ *noun* a view of what is going to happen in the future ○ *The economic outlook is not good.* ○ *The stock market outlook is worrying.*

"American demand has transformed the profit outlook for many European manufacturers" [*Duns Business Month*]

out of court /ˌaʊt əv 'kɔrt/ *adverb, adjective* □ **a settlement was reached out of court** a dispute was settled between two parties privately without continuing a court case

out-of-date /ˌaʊt əv 'deɪt/ *adjective, adverb* old-fashioned or no longer modern ○ *Their computer system is years out of date.* ○ *They're still using out-of-date equipment.*

out-of-house /ˌaʊt əv 'haʊs/ *adjective, adverb* working outside a company's buildings ○ *the out-of-house staff* ○ *We do all our data processing out-of-house.*

out of pocket /ˌaʊt əv 'pɑkɪt/ *adjective, adverb* having paid out money personally ○ *The deal has left me out of pocket.*

out-of-pocket expenses /ˌaʊt əv ˌpɑkɪt ɪk'spɛnsɪz/ *plural noun* an amount of money paid back to an employee who has spent his or her personal money on company business

out of stock /ˌaʊt əv 'stɑk/ *adjective, adverb* with no inventory left ○ *Those books are temporarily out of stock.* ○ *Several out-of-stock items have been on order for weeks.* Abbreviation **O/S**

out of the loop /ˌaʊt əv ðə 'lup/ *adverb* deliberately or accidentally excluded from decision-making processes and the flow of information around an organization (*informal*) (NOTE: A person who is out of the loop is likely to feel isolated and will be unable to contribute fully to the organization.)

out of work /ˌaʊt əv 'wɜrk/ *adjective, adverb* with no job ○ *The recession has put millions out of work.* ○ *The company was set up by three out-of-work engineers.*

outperform /ˌaʊtpər'fɔrm/ *verb* to do better than other companies

"...on the fairly safe assumption that there is little to be gained in attempting to find the share or trust that outperforms everything else, there is every reason to buy an index-tracking fund" [*Money Observer*]

output /'aʊtpʊt/ *noun* **1.** the amount which a company, person, or machine produces ○ *Output has increased by 10%.* ○ *25% of our output is exported.* **2.** information which is produced by a computer. Opposite **input** ■ *verb* to produce (by computer) ○ *The printer will output color graphics.* ○ *That is the information outputted from the computer.* ○ *The printer will output color graphs.* (NOTE: **outputting – outputted**)

output bonus /'aʊtpʊt ˌboʊnəs/, **output-based bonus** /ˌaʊtpʊt beɪst 'boʊnəs/ *noun* an extra payment for increased production

output per hour /ˌaʊtpʊt pər 'aʊr/ *noun* the amount of something produced in one hour

output tax /'aʊtpʊt tæks/ *noun* sales tax charged by a company on goods or services sold, and which the company pays to the government

outright /aʊt'raɪt/ *adverb, adjective* completely □ **to purchase something outright, to make an outright purchase** to buy something completely, including all rights in it

outsell /aʊt'sɛl/ *verb* to sell more than someone ○ *The company is easily outselling its competitors.* (NOTE: **outselling – outsold**)

outside /'aʊtsaɪd/ *adjective, adverb* **1.** not in a company's office or building □ **to send work to be done outside** to send work to be done in other offices **2.** □ **outside office hours** not during office hours, when the office is not open

outside dealer /ˌaʊtsaɪd 'dilər/ *noun* a person who is not a member of the Stock Exchange but is allowed to trade

outside director /ˌaʊtsaɪd daɪ'rɛktər/ *noun* a director who is not employed by the company, a non-executive director

outside line /ˌaʊtsaɪd 'laɪn/ *noun* a line from an internal office telephone system to the main telephone exchange ○ *You dial 9 to get an outside line.*

outside stockholder /ˌaʊtsaɪd 'stɒkhoʊldər/ same as **minority stockholder**

outside worker /'aʊtsaɪd ˌwɜːrkər/ *noun* an employee who does not work in a company's offices

outsize /'aʊtsaɪz/ *noun* a size which is larger than usual. Abbreviation **OS** □ **outsize order** a very large order

outsource /'aʊtsɔːrs/ *verb* to use a source outside a company or business to do the work that is needed

"The services unit won outsourcing contracts from the Environmental Protection Agency and NASA, which the company says played a significant part in the increase." [*InformationWeek*]

outsourcer /'aʊtsɔːrsər/ *noun* a company that obtains services from other companies rather than employing full-time staff members to provide them

outsourcing /'aʊtsɔːrsɪŋ/ *noun* **1.** the practice of obtaining services from specialist bureaus or other companies, rather than employing full-time staff members to provide them **2.** the transfer of work previously done by employees of an organization to another organization, usually one that specializes in that type of work (NOTE: Things that have usually been outsourced in the past include legal services, transportation, catering, and security, but nowadays IT services, training, and public relations are often added to the list.)

outstanding /aʊt'stændɪŋ/ *adjective* not yet paid or completed □ **outstanding debts** debts which are waiting to be paid □ **outstanding orders** orders received but not yet filled □ **what is the amount outstanding?** how much money is still owed? □ **matters outstanding from the previous meeting** questions which were not settled at the previous meeting

COMMENT: Note the difference between "outstanding" and "overdue". If a debtor has 30 days credit, then his debts are outstanding until the end of the 30 days, and they only become overdue on the 31st day.

outstrip /aʊt'strɪp/ *verb* to become larger than something else ○ *Wage increases are outstripping inflation.* (NOTE: **outstripped – outstripping**)

out tray /'aʊt treɪ/ *noun* a basket on a desk for letters or memos which have been dealt with and are ready to be dispatched

outturn /'aʊttɜːrn/ *noun* an amount produced by a country or company

outvote /aʊt'voʊt/ *verb* to defeat someone in a vote □ **the chairman was outvoted** the majority voted against the chairman

outward /'aʊtwərd/ *adjective* going away from the home country ○ *the ship is outward bound* ○ *On the outward voyage the ship will call in at the West Indies.*

outward cargo /ˌaʊtwərd 'kɑːrgoʊ/ *noun* goods which are being exported

outward mission /ˌaʊtwərd 'mɪʃ(ə)n/ *noun* a visit by a group of businesspeople to a foreign country

outwork /'aʊtwɜːrk/ *noun* work which a company pays someone to do at home

outworker /'aʊtwɜːrkər/ *noun* a person who works at home for a company

over /oʊvər/ *preposition* **1.** more than ○ *the carpet costs over $1000* ○ *The increase in turnover was over 25%.* **2.** compared with ○ *Increase in output over last year.* ○ *Increase in debtors over the last quarter's figure.* **3.** during ○ *Over the last half of the year profits doubled.* ■ *adverb* □ **held over to the next meeting** postponed, put back to the next meeting

over- /oʊvər/ *prefix* more than □ **store which caters to the over-60s** a store which has goods which appeal to people who are more than sixty years old

overall /ˌoʊvər'ɔːl/ *adjective* covering or including everything □ **the company reported an overall fall in profits** the company reported a general fall in profits □ **overall plan** a plan which covers everything

overbook /ˌoʊvər'bʊk/ *verb* to book more people than there are seats or rooms available ○ *The hotel or The flight was overbooked.*

overbooking /ˌoʊvər'bʊkɪŋ/ *noun* the act of taking more bookings than there are seats or rooms available

overborrowed /ˌoʊvər'bɑːroʊd/ *adjective* referring to a company which has very high borrowings compared to its assets, and has difficulty in meeting its interest payments

overbought /ˌoʊvər'bɔːt/ *adjective* having bought too much □ **the market is**

overbought prices on the stock market are too high, because there have been too many people wanting to buy

"...they said the market was overbought when the index was between 860 and 870 points" [*Australian Financial Review*]

overcapacity /ˌoʊvərkə'pæsɪti/ *noun* an unused capacity for producing something

"...with the present overcapacity situation in the airline industry the discounting of tickets is widespread" [*Business Traveller*]

overcapitalized /ˌoʊvər'kæpɪtəlaɪzd/ *adjective* referring to a company with more capital than it needs

overcharge *noun* /'oʊvərtʃɑrdʒ/ a charge which is higher than it should be ○ *to pay back an overcharge* ■ *verb* /ˌoʊvər'tʃɑrdʒ/ to ask someone for too much money ○ *They overcharged us for our meals.* ○ *We asked for a refund because we'd been overcharged.*

overdraft /'oʊvərdræft/ *noun* **1.** an amount of money which a company or person can withdraw from a bank account, with the bank's permission, despite the fact that the account is empty ○ *The bank has allowed me an overdraft of £5,000.* Abbreviation **O/D** (NOTE: The U.S. term is **overdraft protection**.) □ **we have exceeded our overdraft facilities** we have taken out more than the overdraft allowed by the bank **2.** a negative amount of money in an account, i.e. a situation where a check is more than the money in the account on which it is drawn

overdraft facilities /'oʊvərdræft fəˌsɪlɪtiz/ *plural noun* an arrangement with a bank to have an overdraft

overdraw /ˌoʊvər'drɔ/ *verb* to take out more money from a bank account than there is in it □ **your account is overdrawn, you are overdrawn** you have paid out more money from your account than you have in it

overdue /ˌoʊvər'du/ *adjective* having not been paid on time □ **interest payments are three weeks overdue** interest payments which should have been made three weeks ago

overestimate /ˌoʊvər'estɪmeɪt/ *verb* to think something is larger or worse than it really is ○ *She overestimated the amount of time needed to fit out the factory.* ○ *They*

overestimated the costs of moving the offices to Manhattan.

overextend /ˌoʊvərɪk'stend/ *verb* □ **the company overextended itself** the company borrowed more money than its assets would allow

overhang /'oʊvərhæŋ/ *verb* to put downward pressure on stock or commodity prices ○ *Major uncertainties about the economy are overhanging the market.*

overhead /'oʊvərhed/ *noun* the indirect costs of the day-to-day running of a business, i.e. not money spent on producing goods, but money spent on such things as renting or maintaining buildings and machinery ○ *The sales revenue covers the manufacturing costs but not the overhead.* (NOTE: The U.K. term is **overheads**.)

overhead budget /ˌoʊvərhed 'bʌdʒət/ *noun* a plan of probable overhead costs

overhead costs /ˌoʊvərhed 'kɔsts/, **overhead expenses** /ˌoʊvərhed ɪk'spensɪz/ *plural noun* same as **overhead**

overheads /'oʊvərhedz/ *plural noun* U.K. same as **overhead**

overlook /ˌoʊvər'lʊk/ *verb* not to pay attention to ○ *In this instance we will overlook the delay.*

overmanning /ˌoʊvər'mænɪŋ/ *noun* U.K. same as **overstaffing**

overpaid /ˌoʊvər'peɪd/ *adjective* paid too much ○ *Our staff are overpaid and underworked.*

overpay /ˌoʊvər'peɪ/ *verb* **1.** to pay too much to someone or for something ○ *We overpaid the invoice by $245.* **2.** to pay an extra amount to reduce the total capital borrowed on a mortgage

overpayment /ˌoʊvər'peɪmənt/ *noun* an act of paying too much

overproduce /ˌoʊvərprə'dus/ *verb* to produce too much of a product

overproduction /ˌoʊvərprə'dʌkʃən/ *noun* the manufacturing of too much of a product

overrated /ˌoʊvər'reɪtɪd/ *adjective* valued more highly than it should be ○ *The effect of the dollar on European business cannot be overrated.* ○ *Their "first-class service" is very overrated.*

overrider /'oʊvərraɪdər/, **overriding commission** /ˌoʊvərraɪdɪŋ kə'mɪʃ(ə)n/

noun a special extra commission which is above all other commissions

overrun /ˌoʊvər'rʌn/ *verb* to go beyond a limit ○ *The construction company overran the time limit set to complete the factory.* ○ *The workers overran the time limit set by the production manager.* (NOTE: **overrunning – overran – overrun**)

overs /'oʊvərz/ *plural noun* extra items above the agreed total ○ *The price includes 10% overs to compensate for damage.*

overseas *adjective* /'oʊvərsiz/, *adverb* /ˌoʊvər'siz/ across the sea, or to or in foreign countries ○ *Management trainees knew that they would be sent overseas to learn about the export markets.* ○ *Some workers are going overseas to find new jobs.* ■ *noun* /ˌoʊvər'siz/ foreign countries ○ *The profits from overseas are far higher than those of the home division.*

overseas call /ˌoʊvərsiz 'kɔl/ *noun* a call to another country

overseas division /ˌoʊvərsiz dɪ'vɪʒ(ə)n/ *noun* the section of a company dealing with trade with other countries

overseas markets /ˌoʊvərsiz 'mɑrkəts/ *plural noun* markets in foreign countries

overseas trade /ˌoʊvərsiz 'treɪd/ *noun* same as **foreign trade**

overseer /'oʊvərsɪr/ *noun* a person who supervises other workers

oversell /ˌoʊvər'sel/ *verb* to sell more than you can produce □ **he is oversold** he has agreed to sell more product than he can produce □ **the market is oversold** stockmarket prices are too low, because there have been too many sellers

overspend /ˌoʊvər'spend/ *verb* to spend too much □ **to overspend your budget** to spend more money than is allowed in your budget

overspending /ˌoʊvər'spendɪŋ/ *noun* the act of spending more than is allowed ○ *The board decided to limit the overspending by the production departments.*

overstaffed /ˌoʊvər'stæft/ *adjective* employing more people than are needed to do the work of the company

overstaffing /ˌoʊvər'stæfɪŋ/ *noun* the state of having more employees than are needed to do a company's work

overstock /ˌoʊvər'stɑk/ *verb* to have a bigger stock, or inventory, of something than is needed □ **to be overstocked with spare parts** to have too many spare parts in stock

overstocks /'oʊvərstɑks/ *plural noun* more stock than is needed to supply orders ○ *We will have to sell off the overstocks to make room in the warehouse.*

oversubscribe /ˌoʊvərsəb'skraɪb/ *verb* □ **the share offer was oversubscribed six times** people agreed to buy six times as many new shares as were available

over-the-counter /ˌoʊvər ðə 'kaʊntər/ *adjective* involving stock that is not listed on a Stock Exchange. Abbreviation **OTC**

over-the-counter sales /ˌoʊvər ðə 'kaʊntər ˌseɪlz/ *plural noun* the legal selling of stock that is not listed on a Stock Exchange, usually carried out by telephone

overtime /'oʊvərtaɪm/ *noun* hours worked in addition to your usual working hours ○ *to work six hours' overtime* ○ *The overtime rate is one and a half times normal pay.* ■ *adverb* □ **to work overtime** to work longer hours than stated in the contract of employment

overtime ban /'oʊvərtaɪm bæn/ *noun* an order by a labor union which forbids overtime work by its members

overtime pay /'oʊvərtaɪm peɪ/ *noun* pay for extra time worked

overtrading /ˌoʊvər'treɪdɪŋ/ *noun* a situation where a company increases sales and production too much and too quickly, so that it runs short of cash

overvalue /ˌoʊvər'vælju/ *verb* to give a higher value to something or someone than is right □ **this stock is overvalued at $12.53** the stock is worth less than the $12.53 for which it is selling □ **the pound is overvalued against the dollar** the exchange rate gives too many dollars to the pound, considering the strength of the two countries' economies

"...the fact that sterling has been overvalued for the past three years shows that currencies can remain above their fair value for very long periods" [*Investors Chronicle*]

overweight /ˌoʊvər'weɪt/ *adjective* □ **the package is sixty grams overweight** the package weighs sixty grams too much

overworked /ˌoʊvərˈwɜrkt/ *adjective* having too much work to do ○ *Our staff complain of being underpaid and overworked.*

owe /oʊ/ *verb* to have to pay money ○ *He owes the bank $250,000.* □ **they still owe the company for the stock they purchased last year** they have still not paid for the stock

owing /ˈoʊɪŋ/ *adjective* **1.** owed ○ *money owing to the directors* ○ *How much is still owing to the company by its debtors?* **2.** □ **owing to** because of ○ *The plane was late owing to fog.* ○ *I am sorry that owing to pressure of work, we cannot supply your order on time.*

own /oʊn/ *verb* to have or to possess ○ *She owns 50% of the stock.* □ **a wholly-owned subsidiary** a subsidiary which belongs completely to the parent company

own brand /ˌoʊn ˈbrænd/ *noun* the name of a store which is used on products which are specially packed for that store

own-brand goods /ˌoʊn brænd ˈɡʊdz/ *plural noun* products specially packed for a store with the store's name on them

owner /ˈoʊnər/ *noun* the person who controls a private company

owner-occupier /ˌoʊnər ˈɑkjʊpaɪr/ *noun* a person who owns the property in which he or she lives

ownership /ˈoʊnəʃɪp/ *noun* the fact of owning something □ **the ownership of the company has passed to the banks** the banks have become owners of the company

own label /ˌoʊn ˈleɪb(ə)l/ *noun* goods specially produced for a store with the store's name on them

own-label goods /ˌoʊn ˌleɪb(ə)l ˈɡʊdz/ *plural noun* goods specially produced for a store with the store's name on them

oz *abbreviation* ounce(s)

P

P2P /ˌpi tə ˈpi/ *adjective* used to describe a file-sharing connection between computer users, without a central server being involved. Full form **peer-to-peer**

PA *abbreviation* personal assistant

p.a. *abbreviation* per annum

pacemaker /ˈpeɪsmeɪkər/ *noun* an organization which helps another to change by giving advice or offering support

Pacific Rim /pəˌsɪfɪk ˈrɪm/ *noun* the countries on the edge of the Pacific Ocean: especially Hong Kong, Japan, Korea, Malaysia, Singapore, Thailand and Taiwan

pack /pæk/ *noun* **1.** items put together in a container or shrink-wrapped for selling □ **items sold in packs of 200** items sold in boxes containing 200 items **2.** a folder containing documents about something ■ *verb* to put things into a container for selling or sending ○ *to pack goods into cartons* ○ *Your order has been packed and is ready for shipping.* ○ *The biscuits are packed in plastic wrappers.*

package /ˈpækɪdʒ/ *noun* **1.** goods packed and wrapped for sending by mail ○ *The USPS does not accept bulky packages.* ○ *The goods are to be sent in airtight packages.* **2.** a box or bag in which goods are sold ○ *Instructions for use are printed on the package.* **3.** a group of different items joined together in one deal **4.** a different items of software sold together ○ *a payroll package* ○ *The computer is sold with accounting and word-processing packages.* ○ *The company's area of specialization is accounts packages for small businesses.* ■ *verb* **1.** □ **to package goods** to wrap and pack goods in an attractive way **2.** □ **to package vacations** to sell a vacation package including travel, hotels, and food

package deal /ˌpækɪdʒ ˈdil/ *noun* an agreement which covers several different things at the same time ○ *They agreed on a package deal which involves the construction of the factory, training of staff, and purchase of the product.*

package tour /ˈpækɪdʒ tʊr/, **packagetrip** /ˈpækɪdʒ trɪp/ *noun* a vacation whose price includes transportation and accommodations, and sometimes also meals ○ *The travel company is arranging a package tour to the international trade fair.*

packaging /ˈpækɪdʒɪŋ/ *noun* **1.** the act of putting things into packages **2.** material used to protect goods which are being packed ○ *bubble wrap and other packaging material* ○ *The fruit is sold in airtight packaging.* **3.** material used to wrap goods for display

packer /ˈpækər/ *noun* a person who packs goods

packet /ˈpækət/ *noun* a small box of goods for selling ○ *We need two packets of filing cards.* □ **item sold in packets of 20** items are sold in boxes containing 20 items each

packing /ˈpækɪŋ/ *noun* **1.** the act of putting goods into boxes and wrapping them for shipping ○ *What is the cost of the packing?* ○ *Packing is included in the price.* **2.** material used to protect goods ○ *packed in airtight packing* ○ *The fruit is packed in airtight packing.*

packing charges /ˈpækɪŋ ˌtʃɑrdʒɪz/ *plural noun* money charged for putting goods into boxes

packing list /ˈpækɪŋ lɪst/ *noun* a list of goods which have been packed, sent with the goods to show they have been checked

Pac-man /ˈpæk mæn/ *noun* a method of defence against a takeover bid, where the target company threatens to take over the company which is trying to take it over

page pushing /ˈpeɪdʒ ˌpʊʃɪŋ/ *noun* same as **co-browsing**

paid /peɪd/ *adjective* **1.** for which money has been given ○ *The invoice is marked "paid".* **2.** □ **paid holidays** holidays where the worker's wages are still paid even though he or she is not working **3.** referring to an amount which has been settled ○ *The order was sent carriage paid.* □ **paid bills** bills which have been settled

paid assistant /ˌpeɪd əˈsɪst(ə)nt/ *noun* an assistant who receives a salary

paid-up /ˌpeɪd ˈʌp/ *adjective* paid in full

paid-up capital /ˌpeɪd ʌp ˈkæpɪt(ə)l/, **paid-up share capital** /ˌpeɪd ʌp ˈʃer ˌkæpɪt(ə)l/ *noun* an amount of money paid for the issued capital shares (it does not include called-up capital which has not yet been paid for)

paid-up shares /ˌpeɪd ʌp ˈʃerz/ *noun* shares which have been completely paid for by the stockholders

pallet /ˈpælət/ *noun* a flat wooden base on which goods can be stacked for easy handling by a fork-lift truck, and on which they remain for the whole of their transportation

palletize /ˈpælətaɪz/ *verb* to put goods on pallets ○ *palletized cartons*

palmtop /ˈpɑlmtɒp/ *noun* a very small computer which can be held in your hand and which usually has a character recognition screen instead of a keyboard

pamphlet /ˈpæmflət/ *noun* a small booklet of advertising material or of information

P&L *abbreviation* profit and loss

panel /ˈpæn(ə)l/ *noun* **1.** a flat vertical surface **2.** a group of people who give advice on a problem ○ *a panel of experts*

Panel on Takeovers and Mergers /ˌpæn(ə)l ɒn ˌteɪkouvərz ən ˈmɜrdʒərz/ *noun* a non-statutory body which examines takeovers and applies the Takeover Code

panic buying /ˈpænɪk ˌbaɪɪŋ/ *noun* a rush to buy something at any price because stocks may run out

paper /ˈpeɪpər/ *noun* **1.** □ **on paper** in theory ○ *On paper the system is ideal, but we have to see it working before we will sign the contract.* **2.** a document which can represent money, e.g., a bill of exchange or a promissory note **3.** a newspaper **4.** shares in the form of share certificates

paper feed /ˈpeɪpər fid/ *noun* a device which puts paper into a printer or photocopier

paper gain /ˌpeɪpər ˈɡeɪn/ *noun* same as **paper profit**

"...the profits were tax-free and the interest on the loans they incurred qualified for income tax relief; the paper gains were rarely changed into spending money" [*Investors Chronicle*]

paperless office /ˌpeɪpələs ˈɒfɪs/ *noun* an office where all work is done on computers, which should mean that less paper is used (in fact, such offices usually use far more paper than old-fashioned offices)

paper loss /ˌpeɪpər ˈlɒs/ *noun* a loss made when an asset has fallen in value but has not been sold

paper mill /ˈpeɪpər mɪl/ *noun* a factory where wood is made into paper

paper millionaire /ˌpeɪpər ˌmɪljəˈner/ *noun* a person who owns stock which, if sold, would be worth one million pounds or dollars

paper money /ˌpeɪpər ˈmʌni/ *noun* payments in paper form, e.g., checks

paper profit /ˌpeɪpər ˈprɑfɪt/ *noun* a profit on an asset which has increased in price but has not been sold ○ *He is showing a paper profit of $25,000 on his investment.* Also called **paper gain**, **unrealised profit**

paperwork /ˈpeɪpərwɜrk/ *noun* an office work, especially writing memos and filling in forms ○ *Exporting to Russia involves a large amount of paperwork.*

par /pɑr/ *adjective* equal, at the same price □ **shares at par** shares whose market price is the same as their face value

paragraph /ˈpærəɡræf/ *noun* a group of several lines of writing which makes a separate section ○ *the first paragraph of your letter* or *paragraph one of your letter* ○ *Please refer to the paragraph in the contract on "shipping instructions".*

parallel economy /ˌpærəlel ɪˈkɑnəmi/ *noun* same as **black economy**

parameter /pəˈræmɪtər/ *noun* a fixed limit ○ *The budget parameters are fixed by the finance director.* ○ *Spending by each department has to fall within agreed parameters.*

parastatal /ˌpærəˈsteɪt(ə)l/ *noun* in Africa, a large state-controlled organization

"...the minister did reveal that the accumulated losses of major parastatals totalled $0.4 billion in mid-year" [*Business in Africa*]

parcel delivery service /ˌpɑːs(ə)l dɪ ˈlɪv(ə)ri ˌsɜːvɪs/ *noun* a private company which delivers packages within a specific area

parcel post /ˈpɑːs(ə)l pəʊst/ *noun* a mail service for sending packages ○ *Send the order by parcel post.*

parcels office /ˈpɑːs(ə)lz ˌɒfɪs/ *noun* an office where packages can be handed in for sending by mail

parent company /ˈpeərənt ˌkʌmp(ə)ni/ *noun* a company which owns more than 50% of the stock in another company

Pareto's Law /pəˈriːtəʊz lɔː/, **Pareto Effect** /pəˈriːtəʊ ɪˌfekt/ *noun* the theory that incomes are distributed in the same way in all countries, whatever tax regime is in force, and that a small percentage of a total is responsible for a large proportion of value or resources. Also called **eighty/twenty law**

COMMENT: Also called the 80/20 law, because 80/20 is the normal ratio between majority and minority figures: so 20% of accounts produce 80% of turnover; 80% of GDP enriches 20% of the population, etc.

pari passu /ˌpæri ˈpæsuː/ *adverb* a Latin phrase meaning "equally" ○ *The new shares will rank pari passu with the existing ones.*

Paris Club /ˈpærɪs ˈklʌb/ *noun* the Group of Ten, the major world economic powers working within the framework of the IMF (there are in fact eleven: Belgium, Canada, France, Germany, Italy, Japan, Netherlands, Sweden, Switzerland, United Kingdom and the United States. It is called the "Paris Club" because its first meeting was in Paris)

parity /ˈpærəti/ *noun* the state of being equal □ **the female staff want parity with the men** they want to have the same rates of pay and conditions as the men □ **the pound fell to parity with the dollar** the pound fell to a point where one pound equaled one dollar

"...the draft report on changes in the international monetary system casts doubt about any return to fixed exchange-rate parities" [*Wall Street Journal*]

parity bit /ˈpærəti bɪt/ *noun* an odd or even digit that is used to check computer data for errors

Parkinson's law /ˈpɑːkɪnsənz ˌlɔː/ *noun* a law, based on wide experience, that in business the amount of work increases to fill the time available for it. The principle is named after the book written in 1958 by C. Northcote Parkinson.

part /pɑːt/ *noun* **1.** a piece or section; some ○ *Part of the shipment was damaged.* ○ *Part of the work force is on overtime.* ○ *Part of the expenses will be refunded.* **2.** □ **in part** not completely ○ *to contribute in part to the costs* or *to pay the costs in part*

part delivery /pɑːt dɪˈlɪv(ə)ri/ *noun* a delivery that contains only some of the items in an order

part exchange /ˌpɑːt ɪksˈtʃeɪndʒ/ *noun U.K.* same as **trade-in**

partial /ˈpɑːʃ(ə)l/ *adjective* not complete □ **partial loss** a situation where only part of the insured property has been damaged or lost □ **he got partial compensation for the damage to his house** he was compensated for part of the damage □ **partial payment** payment of part of a whole payment

participation /pɑːˌtɪsɪˈpeɪʃ(ə)n/ *noun* the act of taking part ○ *The workers are demanding more participation in the company's affairs.* ○ *Participation helps to make an employee feel part of the organization.*

participative /pɑːˈtɪsɪpətɪv/ *adjective* where both sides take part ○ *We do not treat management-worker relations as a participative process.*

particular /pəˈtɪkjʊlər/ *adjective* special, different from others ○ *The color printer only works with a particular type of paper.* ■ *noun* **1.** □ **to give full particulars of something** to list all the known details about something **2.** □ **in particular** specially, as a special point ○ *Fragile goods, in particular glasses, need special packing.*

particular average /pəˌtɪkjʊlə ˈæv(ə)rɪdʒ/ *noun* a situation in which part of a shipment is lost or damaged and the insurance costs are borne by the owner of the lost goods and not shared among all the owners of the shipment

particular lien /pəˌtɪkjʊlə ˈliːən/ *noun* a right of a person to keep possession of another person's property until debts relating to that property have been paid

particulars /pəˈtɪkjʊləz/ *noun* details ○ *sheet which gives particulars of the items for sale* ○ *The inspector asked for particulars of the missing car.*

partly /ˈpɑːtli/ *adverb* not completely □ **partly-secured creditors** creditors whose debts are not fully covered by the value of the security

partly-paid capital /ˌpɑːt(ə)li peɪd ˈkæpɪt(ə)l/ *noun* capital which represents partly-paid shares

partly-paid up shares /ˌpɑːt(ə)li peɪd ʌp ˈʃeəz/, **partly-paid shares** /ˌpɑːt(ə)li peɪd ˈʃeəz/ *plural noun* shares in which the stockholders have not paid the full face value

partner /ˈpɑːtnər/ *noun* a person who works in a business and has an equal share in it with other partners ○ *I became a partner in a law firm.*

partnership /ˈpɑːtnərʃɪp/ *noun* an unregistered business where two or more people (but not more than twenty) share the risks and profits according to a partnership agreement ○ *to go into partnership with someone* ○ *to join with someone to form a partnership* □ **to offer someone a partnership, to take someone into partnership with you** to have a working business and bring someone in to share it with you □ **to dissolve a partnership** to bring a partnership to an end

part order /ˌpɑːt ˈɔːdər/ *noun* same as **part delivery**

part-owner /ˌpɑːt ˈoʊnər/ *noun* a person who owns something jointly with one or more other people ○ *I am part-owner of the restaurant.*

part-ownership /ˌpɑːt ˈoʊnərʃɪp/ *noun* a situation where two or more persons own the same property

part payment /ˌpɑːt ˈpeɪmənt/ *noun* the paying of part of a whole payment ○ *I gave him $250 as part payment for the car.*

part shipment /ˌpɑːt ˈʃɪpmənt/ *noun* same as **part delivery**

part-time /ˌpɑːt ˈtaɪm/ *adjective, adverb* not working for the whole working week ○ *a part-time employee* ○ *It is a part-time job that* ○ *We are looking for part-time staff to work our computers.* ○ *She only works part-time as she has small children to look after.*

part-timer /ˌpɑːt ˈtaɪmər/ *noun* a person who works part-time

part-time work /ˌpɑːt taɪm ˈwɜːk/, **part-time employment** /ˌpɑːt taɪm ɪm ˈplɔɪmənt/ *noun* work for part of a working week (officially, between 8 and 16 hours per week) ○ *He is trying to find part-time work when the children are in school.*

party /ˈpɑːti/ *noun* a person or organization involved in a legal dispute or legal agreement ○ *How many parties are there to the contract?* ○ *The company is not a party to the agreement.*

par value /ˌpɑː ˈvæljuː/ *noun* same as **face value**

pass /pæs/ *noun* **1.** a permit to allow someone to go into a building ○ *You need a pass to enter the ministry offices.* ○ *All members of staff must show a pass.* **2.** a permit to allow someone to travel ■ *verb* **1.** □ **to pass a dividend** to pay no dividend in a certain year **2.** to approve something ○ *The finance director has to pass an invoice before it is sent out.* ○ *The loan has been passed by the board.* □ **to pass a resolution** to vote to agree to a resolution ○ *The meeting passed a proposal that salaries should be frozen.* **3.** to be successful in an examination or test ○ *He passed his typing test.* ○ *She has passed all her exams and now is a qualified accountant.*

pass off *phrasal verb* □ **to pass something off as something else** to pretend that something is another thing in order to cheat a customer ○ *She tried to pass off the wine as French, when in fact it came from Romania.*

passbook /ˈpæsbʊk/ *noun* same as **bank book**

"…instead of customers having transactions recorded in their passbooks, they will present plastic cards and have the transactions printed out on a receipt" [*Australian Financial Review*]

passenger ferry /ˈpæsɪndʒər ˌferi/ *noun* a ferry which only carries passengers

passenger manifest /ˌpæsɪndʒər ˈmænɪfest/ *noun* a list of passengers on a ship or plane

passenger terminal /ˈpæsɪndʒər ˌtɜːmɪn(ə)l/ *noun* an air terminal for people going on planes, not for cargo

passenger train /ˈpæsɪndʒər treɪn/ *noun* a train which carries passengers but not freight

passport /'pæspɔrt/ *noun* an official document proving that you are a citizen of a country, which you have to show when you travel from one country to another ○ *We had to show our passports at the customs post.* ○ *His passport is out of date.* ○ *The passport officer stamped my passport.*

password /'pæswɜrd/ *noun* a word or character which identifies a user and allows them access to a computer system

patent /'peɪtənt, 'pætənt/ *noun* an official document showing that a person has the exclusive right to make and sell an invention ○ *to take out a patent for a new type of light bulb* ○ *to apply for a patent for a new invention* □ **to forfeit a patent** to lose a patent because payments have not been made □ **to infringe a patent** to make and sell a product which works in the same way as a patented product and not pay a royalty for it □ **to file a patent application** to apply for a patent ■ *verb* □ **to patent an invention** to register an invention with the patent office to prevent other people from copying it

patent agent /'peɪtənt ,eɪdʒənt/ *noun* a person who advises on patents and applies for patents on behalf of clients

patented /'peɪtəntɪd, 'pætəntɪd/ *adjective* which is protected by a patent

patent medicine /,peɪtənt 'med(ə)sɪn/ *noun* a medicine which is registered as a patent

patent office /'peɪtənt ,ɒfɪs/ *noun* a government office which grants patents and supervises them

patent pending /,peɪtənt 'pendɪŋ/ *noun* a situation where an invention is put on the market before a patent is granted

patent rights /'peɪtənt raɪts/ *plural noun* the rights which an inventor holds because of a patent

paternity leave /pə'tɜrnɪti liv/ *noun* a short period of leave given to a father to be away from work when his partner has a baby

pathfinder prospectus /'pæθfaɪndər prə,spektəs/ *noun* a preliminary prospectus about a company which is going to be launched on the Stock Exchange, sent to potential major investors before the issue date, giving details of the company's background, but not giving the price at which stock will be sold

patron /'peɪtrən/ *noun* a regular customer, e.g., of a hotel, restaurant, etc. ○ *The parking lot is for the use of hotel patrons only.*

patronage /'pætrənɪdʒ/ *noun* the use of a store by regular shoppers □ **to lose someone's patronage** to do something which makes a regular customer go to another store

patronize /'pætrənaɪz/ *verb* to be a regular customer ○ *I stopped patronizing that restaurant when their prices went up.*

pattern /'pæt(ə)n/ *noun* the general way in which something usually happens ○ *The pattern of sales* or *The sales pattern is very different this year.*

pattern book /'pæt(ə)n bʊk/ *noun* a book showing examples of design

pattern of trade /,pæt(ə)n əv 'treɪd/ *noun* a general way in which trade is carried on ○ *The company's trading pattern shows high export sales in the first quarter and high home sales in the third quarter.*

pawn /pɔn/ *noun* □ **to put something in pawn** to leave a valuable object with someone in exchange for a loan which has to be repaid if you want to take back the object □ **to take something out of pawn** to repay the loan and so get back the object which has been pawned ■ *verb* □ **to pawn a watch** to leave a watch with a pawnbroker who gives a loan against it

pawnbroker /'pɔnbroʊkər/ *noun* a person who lends money against the security of valuable objects

pawnshop /'pɔnstɔr/ *noun* a pawnbroker's store

pawn ticket /'pɔn ,tɪkɪt/ *noun* a receipt given by the pawnbroker for an object left in pawn

pay /peɪ/ *noun* a salary or wages, money given to someone for regular work □ **vacation with pay** a vacation which an employee can take by contract and for which he or she is paid ■ *verb* **1.** to give money to buy an item or a service ○ *to pay $1,000 for a car* ○ *How much did you pay to have the office cleaned?* (NOTE: **paying – paid**) □ **to pay in advance** to pay before you receive the item bought or before the service has been completed ○ *We had to pay in advance to have the new telephone system installed.* □ **to pay in installments** to pay for an item by giving small amounts regularly ○ *We are buying the van by paying install-*

ments of $500 a month. □ **to pay cash** to pay the complete sum in cash □ **to pay by check** to pay by giving a check, not by using cash or credit card □ **to pay by credit card** to pay using a credit card, not a check or cash **2.** to produce or distribute money (NOTE: **paying – paid**) □ **to pay a dividend** to give stockholders a part of the profits of a company ○ *This stock pays a dividend of $150.* □ **to pay interest** to give money as interest on money borrowed or invested ○ *Some building societies pay interest of 5%.* **3.** to give an employee money for work done ○ *The work force has not been paid for three weeks.* ○ *We pay good wages for skilled workers.* ○ *How much do they pay you per hour?* (NOTE: **paying – paid**) □ **to be paid by the hour** to get money for each hour worked □ **to be paid at piecework rates** to get money for each piece of work finished **4.** to give money which is owed or which has to be paid ○ *He was late paying the bill.* ○ *We phoned to ask when they were going to pay the invoice.* ○ *You will have to pay duty on these imports.* ○ *She pays tax at the highest rate.* (NOTE: **paying – paid**) □ **to pay on demand** to pay money when it is asked for, not after a period of credit □ **please pay the sum of $10** please give $10 in cash or by check **5.** □ **to pay a check into an account** to deposit money in the form of a check (NOTE: **paying – paid**)

pay back *phrasal verb* to give money back to someone ○ *Banks are warning students not to take out loans which they cannot pay back.* ○ *I lent him $50 and he promised to pay me back in a month.* ○ *She has never paid me back the money she borrowed.*

pay down *phrasal verb* □ **to pay money down** to make a deposit ○ *They paid $50 down and the rest in monthly installments.*

pay off *phrasal verb* **1.** to finish paying money which is owed for something ○ *He won the lottery and paid off his mortgage.* ○ *She is trying to pay off the loan by monthly installments.* **2.** to terminate somebody's employment and pay all wages that are due ○ *When the company was taken over the factory was closed and all the employees were paid off.*

pay out *phrasal verb* to give money ○ *The company pays out thousands of pounds in legal fees.* ○ *We have paid out*

half our profits in dividends.

pay up *phrasal verb* to give money which is owed ○ *The company only paid up when we sent them a letter from our solicitor.* ○ *She finally paid up six months late.*

payable /ˈpeɪəb(ə)l/ *adjective* due to be paid □ **payable in advance** which has to be paid before the goods are delivered □ **payable on delivery** which has to be paid when the goods are delivered □ **payable at sixty days** which has to be paid by sixty days after the date on the invoice □ **check made payable to bearer** a check which will be paid to the person who has it, not to any particular name written on it □ **electricity charges are payable by the tenant** the tenant (and not the landlord) must pay for the electricity

pay as you earn /ˌpeɪ əz jʊ ˈɜːn/ *noun* a tax system, where income tax is deducted from the salary before it is paid to the worker. Abbreviation **PAYE** (NOTE: The U.S. term is **pay-as-you-go**.)

pay-as-you-go /ˌpeɪ əz ju ˈɡoʊ/ *noun* a payment system where the purchaser pays in small installments as he or she uses the service

payback /ˈpeɪbæk/ *noun* the act of paying back money which has been borrowed

payback clause /ˈpeɪbæk klɔːz/ *noun* a clause in a contract which states the terms for repaying a loan

payback period /ˈpeɪbæk ˌpɪriəd/ *noun* **1.** a period of time over which a loan is to be repaid or an investment is to pay for itself **2.** the length of time it will take to earn back the money invested in a project

paycheck /ˈpeɪtʃek/ *noun* a monthly check by which an employee is paid (NOTE: The U.K. spelling is **pay cheque**.)

pay comparability /ˈpeɪ kɑmp(ə)rəˌbɪlɪti/ *noun* a similar pay system in two different companies

pay day /ˈpeɪ deɪ/ *noun* a day on which wages are paid to employees, usually Friday for employees paid once a week and during the last week of the month for employees who are paid once a month

pay desk /ˈpeɪ desk/ *noun* a place in a store where you pay for goods bought

pay differentials /ˈpeɪ dɪfəˌrenʃəlz/ *plural noun* the difference in salary between employees in similar types of jobs.

Also called **salary differentials, wage differentials**

paydown /'peɪdaʊn/ *noun* a repayment of part of a sum which has been borrowed

PAYE *abbreviation* pay as you earn

payee /peɪ'iː/ *noun* a person who receives money from someone, or the person whose name is on a check

pay envelope /'peɪ ˌenvəloʊp/ *noun* an envelope containing the pay slip and the cash pay

payer /'peɪər/ *noun* a person who gives money to someone

pay hike /'peɪ haɪk/ *noun* an increase in salary

paying /'peɪɪŋ/ *adjective* **1.** making a profit ○ *It is a paying business.* □ **it is not a paying proposition** it is not a business which is going to make a profit **2.** producing money, source of money ■ *noun* the act of giving money

paying-in book /ˌpeɪɪŋ 'ɪn bʊk/ *noun* *U.K.* a book of deposit slips

paying-in slip /ˌpeɪɪŋ 'ɪn slɪp/ *noun* *U.K.* same as **deposit slip**

pay levels /'peɪ ˌlev(ə)lz/ *plural noun* rates of pay for different types of work. Also called **wage levels**

payload /'peɪloʊd/ *noun* the cargo or passengers carried by a ship, train, or plane for which payment is made

payment /'peɪmənt/ *noun* **1.** the act of giving money in exchange for goods or a service ○ *We always ask for payment in cash* or *cash payment and not payment by check.* ○ *The payment of interest* or *the interest payment should be made on the 22nd of each month.* □ **payment on account** paying part of the money owed □ **payment on invoice** paying money as soon as an invoice is received □ **payment in kind** paying by giving goods or food, but not money □ **payment by results** money given which increases with the amount of work done or goods produced **2.** money paid □ **repayable in easy payments** repayable with small sums regularly

payment gateway /'peɪmənt ˌgeɪtweɪ/ *noun* software that processes online credit-card payments. It gets authorization for the payment from the credit-card company and transfers money into the retailer's bank account.

payment in full /ˌpeɪmənt ɪn 'fʊl/ *noun* payment of all the money owed

pay negotiations /'peɪ nɪgoʊʃɪ ˌeɪʃ(ə)nz/, **pay talks** /'peɪ tɔːks/ *plural noun* discussions between management and employees about pay increases

payoff /'peɪɒf/ *noun* **1.** money paid to finish paying something which is owed, such as money paid to an employee when his or her employment is terminated **2.** a profit or reward ○ *One of the payoffs of a university degree is increased earning power.*

"…the finance director of the group is to receive a payoff of about £300,000 after deciding to leave the company and pursue other business opportunities" [*Times*]

payout /'peɪaʊt/ *noun* **1.** money paid to help a company or person in difficulties, a subsidy ○ *The company only exists on payouts from the government.* **2.** money paid to help someone in difficulties

"…after a period of recession followed by a rapid boost in incomes, many tax payers embarked upon some tax planning to minimize their payouts" [*Australian Financial Review*]

pay package /'peɪ ˌpækɪdʒ/ *noun* the salary and other benefits offered with a job ○ *The job carries an attractive pay package.*

pay parity /'peɪ ˌpærɪti/ *noun* earning the same pay for the same job (NOTE: also called **wage parity**)

pay-per-click /ˌpeɪ pe 'klɪk/ *noun* same as **pay-per-view**

pay-per-play /ˌpeɪ pe 'pleɪ/ *noun* a website where the user has to pay to play an interactive game over the Internet

pay-per-view /ˌpeɪ pər 'vjuː/ *noun* a website where the user has to pay to see digital information, e.g., an e-book or e-magazine. Also called **pay-per-click**

pay phone /'peɪ foʊn/ *noun* a public telephone which works if you put coins into it

pay raise /'peɪ raɪz/ *noun* an increase in pay

pay restraint /'peɪ rɪˌstreɪnt/ *noun* the process of keeping increases in wages under control

pay review /'peɪ rɪˌvjuː/ *noun* an occasion when an employee's salary is considered and usually increased ○ *I'm soon due for a pay review and hope to get a rise.*

payroll /'peɪroʊl/ *noun* **1.** the list of people employed and paid by a company ○ *The company has 250 on the payroll.* **2.** the money paid by a company in salaries ○ *The office has a weekly payroll of $10,000.*

payroll clerk /'peɪroʊl klɑrk/ *noun* a person employed to administer the payment of employees. Also called **wages clerk**

payroll deduction /ˌpeɪroʊl dɪ'dʌkʃ(ə)n/ *noun* money taken from an employee's gross pay for taxes, social security and pension contributions

payroll ledger /'peɪroʊl ˌledʒər/ *noun* a list of staff and their salaries

payroll tax /'peɪroʊl tæks/ *noun* a tax on the people employed by a company

pay round /'peɪ raʊnd/ *noun* an annual series of wage bargaining negotiations in various industries

pay scale /'peɪ skeɪl/ *noun* a hierarchy of wage levels, typically varying according to job title, salary or length of service. Also called **salary scale**, **wage scale**

pay slip /'peɪ slɪp/, **pay statement** /'peɪ ˌsteɪtmənt/ *noun* a piece of paper showing the full amount of an employee's pay, and the money deducted as tax, pension and National Insurance contributions

pay threshold /'peɪ ˌθreʃhoʊld/ *noun* a point at which pay increases because of a threshold agreement

pc *abbreviation* per cent

PC *abbreviation* personal computer

PCB *abbreviation* petty cash book

PDA *abbreviation* personal digital assistant

PDF /ˌpi di 'ef/ *noun* a format for electronic documents that enables all their original features, including page layout, text, photographs and colors, to be viewed on different computers or systems. Full form **portable document format**

P/E *abbreviation* price/earnings

peak /pik/ *noun* the highest point ○ *The stock reached its peak in January.* ○ *The stock index has fallen 10% since the peak in January.* ○ *Withdrawals from bank accounts reached a peak in the week before Christmas.* ○ *He has reached the peak of his career.* ■ *verb* to reach the highest point ○ *Productivity peaked in January.* ○ *Shares have peaked and are beginning to slip back.* ○ *He peaked early and never*

achieved his ambition of becoming managing director. ○ *Demand peaks in August, after which sales usually decline.*

peak output /ˌpik 'aʊtpʊt/ *noun* the highest output

peak period /'pik ˌpɪriəd/ *noun* the time of the day when something is at its highest point, e.g., when most commuters are traveling or when most electricity is being used

peak season /pik 'siz(ə)n/ *noun* the period when there are the most travelers and tourists

peak year /ˌpik 'jɪr/ *noun* the year when the largest quantity of products was produced or when sales were highest

pecuniary /pɪ'kjuniəri/ *adjective* referring to money □ **he gained no pecuniary advantage** he made no profit

peddle /'ped(ə)l/ *verb* to sell goods from door to door or in the street

pedestrian precinct /pə,destriən 'prisɪŋkt/ *noun* the part of a town which is closed to traffic so that people can walk about and shop

peer-to-peer /ˌpɪr tə 'pɪr/ *adjective* full form of **P2P**

peg /peg/ *verb* to maintain or fix something at a specific level □ **to peg prices** to fix prices to stop them rising □ **to peg wage increases to the cost-of-living index** to limit increases in wages to the increases in the cost-of-living index

P/E multiple /ˌpi'i ˌmʌltɪp(ə)l/ *noun* same as **price/earnings ratio**

penalize /'pinəlaɪz/ *verb* to punish or fine someone ○ *to penalize a supplier for late deliveries* ○ *They were penalized for bad time-keeping.*

penalty /'pen(ə)lti/ *noun* a punishment, often a fine, which is imposed if something is not done or is done incorrectly or illegally

penalty clause /'pen(ə)lti klɔz/ *noun* a clause which lists the penalties which will be imposed if the terms of the contract are not fulfilled ○ *The contract contains a penalty clause which fines the company 1% for every week the completion date is late.*

pence /pens/ *plural noun* ♦ **penny**

pending /'pendɪŋ/ *adjective* waiting ■ *preposition* □ **pending advice from our**

lawyers while waiting for advice from our lawyers

pending tray /'pendɪŋ treɪ/ *noun* a basket on a desk for papers which cannot be dealt with immediately

penetrate /'penɪtreɪt/ *verb* □ **to penetrate a market** to get into a market and capture a share of it

penetration /ˌpenɪ'treɪʃ(ə)n/ *noun* **1.** the percentage of a target market that accepts a product **2.** the percentage of a target audience reached by an advertisement

penny /'peni/ *noun* **1.** *U.K.* a small coin, of which one hundred make a pound (NOTE: Written **p** after a figure: *26p*. The plural is **pence**.) **2.** a small coin, one cent (*informal*) (NOTE: The plural in U.S. English is **pennies**. In U.K. English, say "pee" for the coin, and "pee" or "pence" for the amount: **a five "pee" coin; it costs ten "pee"** *or* **ten "pence"**. In U.S. English, say **"pennies"** for coins and **"cents"** for the amount.)

penny stock /'peni 'stɑr/ *noun* a very cheap stock, often costing less than $1 (NOTE: The U.K. term is **penny share**.)

COMMENT: These stocks can be considered as a good speculation, since buying even large numbers of them does not involve a large amount of money, and the stock price of some companies can rise dramatically; the price can of course fall, but in the case of penny stocks, the loss is not likely to be as much as with stocks with a higher market value.

pension /'penʃən/ *noun* money paid regularly to someone who no longer works ■ *verb* □ **to pension someone off** to ask someone to retire and take a pension

pensionable /'penʃənəb(ə)l/ *adjective* able to receive a pension

pensionable age /ˌpenʃənəb(ə)l 'eɪdʒ/ *noun* an age after which someone can stop working and take a pension

pension contributions /'penʃən kəntrɪˌbjuʃ(ə)nz/ *plural noun* money paid by a company or employee into a pension fund

pension entitlement /'penʃən ɪnˌtaɪt(ə)lmənt/ *noun* the amount of pension which someone has the right to receive when he or she retires

pensioner /'penʃənər/ *noun* a person who receives a pension

pension fund /'penʃən fʌnd/ *noun* a large sum of money made up of contributions from employees and their employer which provides pensions for retired employees

pension plan /'penʃən plæn/ *noun* an arrangement by which an employer and, usually, an employee pay into a fund which is invested for the employee's retirement

people skills /'pip(ə)l skɪlz/ *plural noun* the techniques used in forming relationships and dealing with other people ○ *Good people skills are essential for anyone working in customer service.*

peppercorn rent /ˌpepəkɔrn 'rent/ *noun* a very small or nominal rent ○ *to lease a property for* or *at a peppercorn rent* ○ *The charity pays only a peppercorn rent.*

per /pər, pər/ *preposition* **1.** □ **as per invoice** as stated in the invoice □ **as per sample** as shown in the sample □ **as per previous order** according to the details given in our previous order **2.** for each □ **we pay $10 per hour** we pay $10 for each hour worked □ **the car was traveling at twenty-five miles per hour** at a speed which covered 25 miles in one hour □ **the earnings per share** the dividend received for each share □ **the average sales per representative** the average sales achieved by one representative **3.** out of ○ *The rate of imperfect items is about twenty-five per thousand.* ○ *The birth rate has fallen to twelve per hundred.*

"…a 100,000 square-foot warehouse generates $600 in sales per square foot of space" [*Duns Business Month*]

PER *abbreviation* price/earnings ratio

per annum /pər 'ænəm/ *adverb* in a year ○ *What is their turnover per annum?* ○ *What is his total income per annum?* ○ *She earns over $100,000 per annum.*

P/E ratio /ˌpi 'i ˌreɪʃioʊ/ *noun* same as **price/earnings ratio**

per capita /pər 'kæpɪtə/ *adjective, adverb* for each person

per-capita expenditure /pər ˌkæpɪtə ɪk'spendɪtʃər/ *noun* the total money spent divided by the number of people involved

per capita income /pər ˌkæpɪtə 'ɪnkʌm/ *noun* the average income of one person. Also called **income per capita**, **income per head**

percent /pərˈsent/ *adjective, adverb* out of each hundred, or for each hundred □ **10 percent** ten in every hundred ○ *What is the increase percent?* ○ *Fifty percent of nothing is still nothing.*

"...this would represent an 18 per cent growth rate – a slight slackening of the 25 per cent turnover rise in the first half" [*Financial Times*]

"...buildings are depreciated at two per cent per annum on the estimated cost of construction" [*Hongkong Standard*]

percentage /pərˈsentɪdʒ/ *noun* an amount shown as part of one hundred

"...state-owned banks cut their prime rates a percentage point to 11%" [*Wall Street Journal*]

"...a good percentage of the excess stock was taken up during the last quarter" [*Australian Financial Review*]

"...the Federal Reserve Board, signalling its concern about the weakening American economy, cut the discount rate by one-half percentage point to 6.5%" [*Wall Street Journal*]

percentage discount /pərˌsentɪdʒ dɪsˈkaʊnt/ *noun* a discount calculated at an amount per hundred

percentage increase /pərˌsentɪdʒ ˈɪnkriːs/ *noun* an increase calculated on the basis of a rate for one hundred

percentage point /pərˈsentɪdʒ pɔɪnt/ *noun* 1 per cent

percentile /pərˈsentaɪl/ *noun* one of a series of ninety-nine figures below which a percentage of the total falls

per contra /ˌpɜr ˈkɒntrə/ *adverb* words showing that a contra entry has been made

perfect *adjective* /ˈpɜrfɪkt/ completely correct with no mistakes ○ *We check each batch to make sure it is perfect.* ○ *She did a perfect keyboarding test.* ■ *verb* /pəˈfekt/ to develop or improve something until it is as good as it can be ○ *They perfected the process for making high-grade steel.*

perfect competition /ˌpɜrfɪkt ˌkɒmpəˈtɪʃ(ə)n/ *noun* (*in economic theory*) the ideal market, where all products are equal in price and all customers are provided with all information about the products. Also called **atomistic competition**

perform /pərˈfɔrm/ *verb* to do well or badly □ **how did the stock perform?** did

the stock go up or down? □ **the company, the stock performed badly** the company's stock price fell

performance /pərˈfɔrməns/ *noun* 1. the way in which someone or something acts ○ *Last year saw a dip in the company's performance.* □ **the poor performance of the stock on the stock market** the fall in the stock price on the stock market □ **performance of staff against objectives** how staff have worked, measured against the objectives set 2. the way in which a stock increases in value

"...inflation-adjusted GNP edged up at a 1.3% annual rate, its worst performance since the economic expansion began" [*Fortune*]

performance evaluation /pərˈfɔrməns ɪˌvæljuˌeɪʃ(ə)n/ *noun* an examination of how well an employee is doing his or her job

performance fund /pərˈfɔrməns fʌnd/ *noun* an investment fund designed to produce a high return, reflected in the higher risk involved

performance management /pərˌfɔrməns ˈmænɪdʒmənt/ *noun* management that specializes in finding ways to enable people to carry out their work to the best of their ability, and to reach and if possible exceed performance targets and standards. Successful performance management usually relies on the establishment of a culture of collective and individual responsibility for the continuing improvement of business processes, and on encouraging individuals to develop their own skills.

performance measurement /pərˈfɔrməns ˌmeʒərmənt/ *noun* a way of calculating how something or someone (a stock or a person) has performed

performance rating /pərˈfɔrməns ˌreɪtɪŋ/ *noun* a judgment of how well a stock or a company has performed

performance-related pay /pəˈfɔrməns peɪ/, **performance pay** /pəˈfɔrməns rɪˌleɪtɪd peɪ/ *noun* pay which is linked to the employee's performance of their duties. Abbreviation **PRP**

performance review /pərˈfɔrməns rɪˌvjuː/ *noun* a yearly interview between a manager and each employee to discuss how the employee has worked during the year

per head /pər 'hed/ *adverb* for each person ○ *Allow $15 per head for expenses.* ○ *Representatives cost on average $50,000 per head per annum.*

per hour /ˌpər 'aʊr/ *adverb* for each hour ○ *The rate is $5 per hour.*

period /'pɪriəd/ *noun* a length of time ○ *for a period of time* or *for a period of months* or *for a six-year period* ○ *sales over a period of three months* ○ *sales over the holiday period* ○ *to deposit money for a fixed period*

periodic /ˌpɪri'ɑdɪk/, **periodical** /ˌpɪri'ɑdɪk(ə)l/ *adjective* happening from time to time ○ *a periodic review of the company's performance*

periodical /ˌpɪri'ɑdɪk(ə)l/ *noun* a magazine which comes out regularly, usually once a month or once a week

period of notice /ˌpɪriəd əv 'nəʊtɪs/ *noun* a time stated in the contract of employment which the worker or company has to allow between resigning or being fired and the worker actually leaving his job ○ *we require three months' notice* ○ *he gave six months' notice* ○ *We gave him three months' wages in lieu of notice.*

period of validity /ˌpɪriəd əv və'lɪdɪti/ *noun* the length of time for which a document is valid

peripherals /pə'rɪf(ə)rəlz/ *plural noun* items of hardware (such as terminals, printers, monitors, etc.) which are attached to a main computer system

perishables /'perɪʃəb(ə)lz/ *plural noun* goods which can go bad easily

perjure /'pɜrdʒər/ *verb* □ **to perjure yourself** to tell lies when you have made an oath to say what is true

perjury /'pɜrdʒəri/ *noun* an act of telling lies when you have made an oath in court to say what is true ○ *He was sent to prison for perjury.* ○ *She appeared in court on a perjury charge.*

perk /pɜrk/ *noun* an extra item given by a company to employees in addition to their salaries, e.g., company cars or private health insurance (*informal*) ○ *She earns a good salary and in addition has all sorts of perks.*

permanency /'pɜrmənənsi/ *noun* the fact of being permanent ○ *There is a lack of permanency about the company.*

permanent /'pɜrmənənt/ *adjective* which will last for a long time or for ever ○ *the permanent staff and part-timers* ○ *She has found a permanent job.* ○ *She is in permanent employment.*

permanently /'pɜrmənəntli/ *adverb* always or for ever ○ *The company is permanently in debt.*

permission /pər'mɪʃ(ə)n/ *noun* the activity of allowing something to happen □ **to give someone permission to do something** to allow someone to do something

permission marketing /pər'mɪʃ(ə)n ˌmɑrkətɪŋ/ *noun* any form of online direct marketing that requires the seller to get permission from each recipient, usually through an opt-in, before sending him or her any promotional material

permit *noun* /'pɜrmɪt/ an official document which allows someone to do something ■ *verb* /pə'mɪt/ to allow someone to do something ○ *This document permits you to export twenty-five computer systems.* ○ *The ticket permits three people to go into the exhibition.* ○ *Will we be permitted to use her name in the advertising copy?* ○ *Smoking is not permitted in the design studio.* (NOTE: **permitting – permitted**)

perpetual inventory system /pɜr ˌpetjʊəl 'ɪnventəri ˌsɪstəm/ *noun* a stock control system by which the stock is continually counted as it moves into and out of the warehouse, so avoiding having to close the warehouse for annual stock checks. Abbreviation **PIS**

per pro /pər 'prəʊ/ *abbreviation* per procurationem ○ *The secretary signed per pro the manager.*

per procurationem /pər ˌprɑkjʊræsɪ 'əʊnəm/ *preposition* "a Latin phrase meaning "on behalf of" or "acting as the representative of"'"

perquisite /'pɜrkwɪzɪt/ *noun* same as **perk**

per se /ˌpɜr 'seɪ/ *adverb* by itself or in itself

person /'pɜrs(ə)n/ *noun* □ **in person** by doing something or going somewhere yourself, not through another person or means □ **this important package is to be delivered to the chairman in person** the package has to be given to the chairman himself (and not to his secretary, assistant, etc.) □ **she came to see me in person** she came to see me

personal /'pɜrs(ə)n(ə)l/ *adjective* **1.** referring to one person □ **the car is for his personal use** the car is for him to use himself **2.** private ○ *The envelope was marked "Personal".* ○ *I want to see the director on a personal matter.*

personal assets /ˌpɜrs(ə)n(ə)l 'æsets/ *plural noun* movable assets which belong to a person

personal assistant /ˌpɜrs(ə)n(ə)l ə'sɪstənt/ *noun* a person who performs various secretarial and administrative tasks for someone in authority such as a director

personal call /'pɜrs(ə)n(ə)l kɔl/ *noun* **1.** a telephone call where you ask the operator to connect you with a particular person **2.** a telephone call not related to business ○ *Staff are not allowed to make personal calls during office hours.*

personal computer /ˌpɜrs(ə)n(ə)l kəm'pjutə/ *noun* a small computer which can be used by one person in the home or office. Abbreviation **PC**

personal day /'duveɪ deɪ/ *noun* a day on which an employer allows an employee to call in and say that they do not feel like coming to work and will be absent (NOTE: Organizations that allow personal days do not usually make them part of written policy, limit them to two or three per year and sometimes only offer them to key employees. The U.K. term is **duvet day**.)

personal development /ˌpɜrs(ə)n(ə)l dɪ'veləpmənt/ *noun* the process of gaining additional knowledge, skills and experience in order to improve the way you do your present job and your prospects of future employment and promotion, and, more generally, to develop your own talents and fulfil your own potential (NOTE: also called **self-development**)

personal digital assistant /ˌpɜrs(ə)n(ə)l ˌdɪdʒɪt(ə)l ə'sɪstənt/ *noun* a small handheld computer with facilities for taking notes, storing information such as addresses, and keeping a calendar. Abbreviation **PDA**

personal effects /ˌpɜrs(ə)n(ə)l ɪ'fekts/ *plural noun* things which belong to someone

Personal Identification Number /ˌpɜrs(ə)n(ə)l aɪˌdentɪfɪ'keɪʃ(ə)n ˌnʌmbər/ *noun* a unique number allocated to the holder of an ATM card or credit card, by which he or she can enter an automatic banking system, as e.g., to withdraw cash from an ATM or to pay in a store. Abbreviation **PIN**

personal income /ˌpɜrs(ə)n(ə)l 'ɪnkʌm/ *noun* the income received by an individual person before tax is paid

personalization /ˌpɜrs(ə)nəlaɪ'zeɪʃ(ə)n/ *noun* the process by which a website presents customers with information that is selected and adapted to meet their specific needs

personalized /'pɜrs(ə)nəlaɪzd/ *adjective* with the name or initials of a person printed on it ○ *She has a personalized briefcase.*

personal letter /ˌpɜrs(ə)n(ə)l 'letər/ *noun* a letter which deals with personal matters (NOTE: also called **private letter**)

personally /'pɜrs(ə)n(ə)li/ *adverb* in person ○ *He personally opened the envelope.* ○ *She wrote to me personally.*

personal organizer /ˌpɜrs(ə)n(ə)l 'ɔrgənaɪzər/ *noun* a very small pocket computer in which you can enter details of names, addresses, telephone numbers, appointments, meetings, etc.

personal pension plan /ˌpɜrs(ə)n(ə)l 'penʃən plæn/ *noun* a pension plan which applies to one employee only, usually a self-employed person, not to a group. Abbreviation **PPP**

personal property /ˌpɜrs(ə)n(ə)l 'prɑpərti/ *noun* things which belong to a person ○ *The fire caused considerable damage to personal property.*

personnel /ˌpɜrsə'nel/ *noun* all the people who work for an organization or at a particular location ○ *The personnel of the warehouse* or *the warehouse personnel have changed their shift system.* ○ *The company is famous for the way it looks after its personnel.* (NOTE: now replaced in some cases by **human resources**)

personnel department /ˌpɜrsə'nel dɪˌpɑrtmənt/ *noun* same as **human resources department**

personnel management /ˌpɜrsənel 'mænɪdʒmənt/ *noun* organizing and training of staff so that they work well and profitably

personnel manager /ˌpɜrsəˈnel ˌmænɪdʒər/ *noun* same as **human resources manager**

personnel officer /ˌpɜrsəˈnel ˌɒfɪsər/ *noun* same as **human resources officer**

person-to-person call /ˌpɜrs(ə)n tə ˈpɜrs(ə)n kɔl/ *noun* a telephone call where you ask the operator to connect you with a named person

persuade /pəˈsweɪd/ *verb* to talk to someone and get them to do what you want ○ *We could not persuade the French company to sign the contract.*

PERT /pɜrt/ *abbreviation* programme evaluation and review technique

peseta /pəˈseɪtə/ *noun* a unit of currency used before the euro in Spain (NOTE: Usually written **ptas** after a figure: *2,000ptas.*)

peso /ˈpeɪsoʊ/ *noun* a unit of currency used in Mexico and many other countries such as Argentina, Bolivia, Chile, Colombia, Cuba, the Dominican Republic, the Philippines and Uruguay

peter /ˈpitər/ *verb*

  peter out *phrasal verb* to come to an end gradually

  "…economists believe the economy is picking up this quarter and will do better in the second half of the year, but most expect growth to peter out next year" [*Sunday Times*]

Peter principle /ˈpitər ˌprɪnsɪp(ə)l/ *noun* a law, based on wide experience, that people are promoted until they occupy positions for which they are incompetent

petition /pəˈtɪʃ(ə)n/ *noun* an official request ■ *verb* to make an official request ○ *He petitioned the government for a special pension.*

petrocurrency /ˈpetroʊˌkʌrənsi/ *noun* a foreign currency which is earned by exporting oil

petrodollar /ˈpetroʊˌdɑlər/ *noun* a dollar earned by a country from exporting oil, then invested outside that country

petrol /ˈpetrəl/ *noun U.K.* same as **gasoline**

petroleum /pəˈtroʊliəm/ *noun* raw natural oil, found in the ground

petroleum-exporting countries /pəˌtroʊliəm ˌeksˌpɔrtɪŋ ˈkʌntriz/ *noun* countries which produce petroleum and sell it to others

petroleum industry /pəˈtroʊliəm ˌɪndəstri/ *noun* an industry which uses petroleum to make other products such as gasoline or soap

petroleum products /pəˌtroʊliəm ˈprɑdʌkts/ *plural noun* products such as gasoline, soap and paint which are made from crude petroleum

petroleum revenues /pəˈtroʊliəm ˌrevənjuz/ *plural noun* income from selling oil

petty cash /ˌpeti ˈkæʃ/ *noun* a small amount of money kept in an office to pay small debts. Abbreviation **P/C**

petty cash book /ˌpeti ˈkæʃ ˌbʊk/ *noun* a book in which petty cash payments are noted. Abbreviation **PCB**

petty cash box /ˌpeti ˈkæʃ ˌbɑks/ *noun* a locked metal box in an office where the petty cash is kept

petty cash voucher /ˌpeti ˈkæʃ ˌvaʊtʃər/ *noun* a piece of paper on which cash expenditure is noted so that an employee can be reimbursed for what he or she has spent on company business

petty expenses /ˌpeti ɪkˈspensɪz/ *plural noun* small sums of money spent

PGP /ˌpi dʒi ˈpi/ *noun* a method of encrypting information so that only the intended recipient can read the message; often used to send credit card details via electronic mail. Full form **pretty good privacy**

phase /feɪz/ *noun* a period or part of something which takes place ○ *the first phase of the expansion program*

  phase in *phrasal verb* to bring something in gradually ○ *The new invoicing system will be phased in over the next two months.*

  "…the budget grants a tax exemption for $500,000 in capital gains, phased in over the next six years" [*Toronto Star*]

  phase out *phrasal verb* to remove something gradually ○ *Smith Inc. will be phased out as a supplier of spare parts.*

phishing /ˈfɪʃɪŋ/ *noun* the act of tricking someone into providing bank or credit-card information by sending a fraudulent email claiming to be from a bank, Internet provider, etc. asking for account and password information

phoenix company /ˈfinɪks ˌkʌmp(ə)ni/ *noun* a company formed by the directors of a company which has gone into receivership, which trades in the same way as the first company, and in most respects (except its name) seems to be exactly the same as the first company

"…the prosecution follows recent calls for a reform of insolvency legislation to prevent directors from leaving behind a trail of debt while continuing to trade in phoenix companies – businesses which fold only to rise again, often under a slightly different name in the hands of the same directors and management" [*Financial Times*]

phoenixism /'finɪksɪzm/ *noun* a situation where phoenix companies can easily be set up

phone /fəʊn/ *verb* □ **to phone someone** to call someone by telephone ○ *Don't phone me, I'll phone you.* ○ *His secretary phoned to say he would be late.* ○ *He phoned the order through to the warehouse.* □ **to phone for something** to make a phone call to ask for something ○ *he phoned for a taxi* □ **to phone about something** to make a phone call to speak about something ○ *He phoned about the January invoice.*

phone back *phrasal verb* to reply by phone ○ *The chairman is in a meeting, can you phone back in about half an hour?* ○ *Mr Smith called while you were out and asked if you would phone him back.*

phone book /'fəʊn bʊk/ *noun* a book which lists names of people or companies with their addresses and telephone numbers

phone call /'fəʊn kɔːl/ *noun* an act of speaking to someone on the phone

phone pad /'fəʊn pæd/ *noun* a pad of paper kept by a telephone for noting messages

photocopier /'fəʊtəʊkɒpiər/ *noun* a machine which makes a copy of a document by photographing and printing it

photocopy /'fəʊtəʊkɒpi/ *noun* a copy of a document made by photographing and printing it ○ *Make six photocopies of the contract.* ■ *verb* to make a copy of a document by photographing and printing it ○ *she photocopied the contract*

photocopying /'fəʊtəʊˌkɒpiɪŋ/ *noun* making photocopies ○ *Photocopying costs are rising each year.* □ **there is a mass of photocopying to be done** there are many documents waiting to be photocopied

photo opportunity /'fəʊtəʊ ˌɒpətunəti/ *noun* an arranged situation where a famous person can be filmed or photographed by journalists

physical inventory /ˌfɪzɪk(ə)l 'ɪnvənt(ə)ri/ *noun* the actual items of inventory held in a warehouse

physical inventory check /ˌfɪzɪk(ə)l 'ɪnvənt(ə)ri ˌtʃek/ *noun* an act of counting actual items of inventory (and then checking this figure against inventory records)

physical retail shopping /ˌfɪzɪk(ə)l 'riːteɪl ˌʃɒpɪŋ/ *noun* shopping that involves visiting actual stores rather than buying online

physical stock /ˌfɪzɪk(ə)l 'stɒk/ *noun* *U.K.* same as **physical inventory**

physical stock check /ˌfɪzɪk(ə)l 'stɒk ˌtʃek/ *noun U.K.* same as **physical inventory check**

pick /pɪk/ *verb* to choose ○ *The board picked the finance director to succeed the retiring CEO.* ○ *The Association has picked Paris for its next meeting.*

pick out *phrasal verb* to choose (something or someone) out of a lot ○ *He was picked out for promotion by the chairman.*

pick up *phrasal verb* **1.** to get better or to improve ○ *Business or Trade is picking up.* **2.** to fetch something or someone in a vehicle ○ *The company sent a driver to pick him up at the airport.* ○ *We sent a courier to pick up the packet and deliver it to the designer.*

picket /'pɪkɪt/ *noun* a striking employee who stands at the entrance to a place of work to try to persuade other employees not to go to work □ **to cross a picket line** to go into a place to work, even though pickets are trying to prevent employees from going in ■ *verb* □ **to picket a factory** to stand at the entrance of a place of work to try to prevent other employees from going to work

picketing /'pɪkətɪŋ/ *noun* the act of standing at the entrance of a place of work to try to prevent other employees going to work □ **lawful picketing** picketing which is allowed by law □ **peaceful picketing** picketing which does not involve aggression

picket line /'pɪkɪt laɪn/ *noun* a line of pickets at the entrance of a place of work

○ *to man a picket line* or *to be on the picket line*

picking /'pɪkɪŋ/ *noun* the selecting of a product according to its packaging or place on the shelf, rather than by making a conscious decision to buy

picking list /'pɪkɪŋ lɪst/ *noun* a list of items in an order, listed according to where they can be found in the warehouse

pickup /'pɪkʌp/ *noun* a type of small van for transporting goods

pickup and delivery service /,pɪkʌp ən dɪ'lɪv(ə)ri ,sɜːvɪs/ *noun* **1.** a service which takes goods from the warehouse and delivers them to the customer **2.** a service which takes something away for cleaning or servicing and returns it to the owner when finished

picture messaging /'pɪktʃər ,mesɪdʒɪŋ/ *noun* the transmission of images and photographs from one cell phone to another

piece /piːs/ *noun* a small part of something ○ *to sell something by the piece* ○ *The price is 25p the piece.*

piece rate /'piːs reɪt/ *noun* a rate of pay calculated as an amount for each product produced or for each piece of work done and not as an amount for each hour worked ○ *to earn piece rates*

piecework /'piːswɜːk/ *noun* work for which employees are paid in accordance with the number of products produced or pieces of work done and not at an hourly rate

pieceworker /'piːswɜːkər/ *noun* a person who is employed at a piece rate

pie chart /'paɪ tʃɑːt/ *noun* a diagram where information is shown as a circle cut up into sections of different sizes

pigeonhole /'pɪdʒənhəʊl/ *noun* one of a series of small spaces for filing documents or for putting letters for delivery to separate offices ○ *I looked in my pigeonhole but there were no letters for me.* ■ *verb* to file a plan or document as the best way of forgetting about it ○ *The whole expansion plan was pigeonholed.*

pile /paɪl/ *noun* a lot of things put one on top of the other ○ *The Managing Director's desk is covered with piles of paper.* ○ *She put the letter on the pile of letters waiting to be signed.* ■ *verb* to put things on top of one another ○ *He piled the papers on his desk.*

pile up *phrasal verb* to put or get into a pile ○ *The invoices were piled up on the table.* ○ *Complaints are piling up about the after-sales service.*

pilferage /'pɪlfərɪdʒ/, **pilfering** /'pɪlfərɪŋ/ *noun* the stealing of small amounts of money or small items from an office or store

pilot /'paɪlət/ *adjective* used as a test, which if successful will then be expanded into a full operation ○ *The company set up a pilot project to see if the proposed manufacturing system was efficient.* ○ *The pilot factory has been built to test the new production processes.* ○ *She is directing a pilot program for training unemployed young people.* ■ *verb* to test a project on a small number of people, to see if it will work in practice ■ *noun* a test project, undertaken to see whether something is likely to be successful or profitable

pilot's case /'paɪləts keɪs/ *noun* a strong square leather case for carrying documents, used by salesmen to carry samples, order forms, etc.

PIN /pɪn/ *abbreviation* Personal Identification Number

pink advertising /,pɪŋk 'ædvətaɪzɪŋ/ *noun* advertising aimed specifically at the gay and lesbian market

pink market /'pɪŋk ,mɑːkət/ *noun* the market that consists of gay and lesbian people

pin money /'pɪn ,mʌni/ *noun* a small amount of money earned, used for personal expenditure ○ *She does some typing at home to earn some pin money.*

PIN number /'pɪn ,nʌmbər/ same as **Personal Identification Number** (*informal*)

pint /paɪnt/ *noun* a measure of liquids (= 0.568 of a litre)

pioneer /,paɪə'nɪə/ *noun* the first to do a type of work ■ *verb* to be the first to do something ○ *The company pioneered developments in the field of electronics.*

pioneer project /,paɪənɪr 'prɒdʒekt/ *noun* a project or development which is new and has never been tried before

pipeline /'paɪplaɪn/ *noun* a distribution channel from the manufacturer through wholesalers and retailers to the customer ○ *How many different businesses are involved in the product's pipeline?*

piracy /'paɪrəsi/ *noun* the copying of patented inventions or copyright works

pirate /'paɪrət/ *noun* a person who copies a patented invention or a copyright work and sells it ■ *verb* to copy a copyright work ○ *a pirated book* ○ *The designs for the new dress collection were pirated in the Far East.* ■ *adjective* copied without permission ○ *a pirate copy of a book*

pit /pɪt/ *noun* **1.** a coal mine **2.** the area of a stock exchange or of a commodities exchange where dealers trade

pitch /pɪtʃ/ *noun* a presentation by an advertising agency to a potential customer

pix /pɪks/ *plural noun* pictures used in advertising or design (*informal*)

place /pleɪs/ *noun* **1.** where something is or where something happens □ **to take place** to happen ○ *The meeting will take place in our offices.* **2.** a position (in a competition) ○ *Three companies are fighting for first place in the home computer market.* **3.** a job ○ *He was offered a place with an insurance company.* ○ *She turned down three places before accepting the one we offered.* **4.** a position in a text ○ *She marked her place in the text with a red pen.* ○ *I have lost my place and cannot remember where I have reached in my filing.* ■ *verb* **1.** to put □ **to place money in an account** to deposit money in an account □ **to place a contract** to decide that a certain company shall have the contract to do work □ **to place something on file** to file something **2.** □ **to place an order** to order something ○ *He placed an order for 250 cartons of paper.* ○ *She placed an order for 100 shares of IBM.* **3.** □ **to place staff** to find jobs for staff □ **how are you placed for work?** have you enough work to do?

placement /'pleɪsmənt/ *noun* the act of finding work for someone ○ *The bureau specializes in the placement of former executives.*

place of work /ˌpleɪs əv 'wɜːk/ *noun* an office, factory, etc., where people work

placing /'pleɪsɪŋ/ *noun* the act of finding a single buyer or a group of institutional buyers for a large number of shares in a new company or a company that is going public □ **the placing of a block of shares** finding a purchaser for a block of shares which was overhanging the market

plain /pleɪn/ *adjective* **1.** easy to understand ○ *We made it plain to the union that* 5% *was the management's final offer.* **2.** simple ○ *The design of the package is in plain blue and white squares.* ○ *We want the cheaper models to have a plain design.*

plain cover /ˌpleɪn 'kʌvər/ *noun* □ **to send something under plain cover** to send something in an ordinary envelope with no company name printed on it

plain paper /ˌpleɪn 'peɪpər/ *noun* ordinary white paper

plain paper copier /ˌpleɪn ˌpeɪpər 'kɒpiər/ *noun* a copier which uses ordinary white paper, not special copier paper

plain paper fax /ˌpleɪn ˌpeɪpər 'fæks/ *noun* a fax machine which uses ordinary white paper and not special fax paper

plain text e-mail /ˌpleɪn tekst 'i ˌmeɪl/ *noun* e-mail in a basic simple format that is cheap to produce and can be read even by older e-mail systems, which may be unable to receive HTML messages

plaintiff /'pleɪntɪf/ *noun* a person who starts an action against someone in the civil courts (NOTE: Since April 1999, this term has been replaced by **claimant**.)

plan /plæn/ *noun* **1.** an idea of how something should be done, which has been decided on and organized in advance □ **the government's economic plans** the government's proposals for running the country's economy **2.** an organized way of doing something ○ *an investment plan* ○ *a pension plan* ○ *a savings plan* **3.** a drawing which shows how something is arranged or how something will be built ○ *The designers showed us the first plans for the new offices.* **4.** a way of saving or investing money ■ *verb* **1.** to organize carefully how something should be done in the future □ **to plan for an increase in bank interest charges** to change a way of doing things because you think there will be an increase in bank interest charges □ **to plan investments** to propose how investments should be made **2.** to decide on and organize something in advance (NOTE: **planning – planned**)

planned economy /ˌplænd ɪ'kɒnəmi/ *noun* a system where the government plans all business activity, regulates supply, sets production targets and itemizes work to be done. Also called **command economy, central planning**

planned obsolescence /ˌplænd ˌɒbsə'les(ə)ns/ *adjective* built-in obsolescence ○ *Planned obsolescence was condemned by the consumer organization as a cynical marketing ploy.*

planner /'plænər/ *noun* a person who plans □ **the government's economic planners** people who plan the future economy of the country for the government

planning /'plænɪŋ/ *noun* the process of organizing how something should be done in the future ○ *Setting up a new incentive program with insufficient planning could be a disaster.* ○ *The long-term planning or short-term planning of the project has been completed.*

planning and zoning department /ˌplænɪŋ ən 'zoʊnɪŋ dɪˌpɑrtmənt/ *noun* the part of local government that deals with issues relating to the use and development of land

plant /plænt/ *noun* **1.** industrial machinery and equipment **2.** a large factory ○ *to set up a new plant* ○ *They are planning to build a car plant near the river.* ○ *They closed down six plants in the north of the country.* ○ *He was appointed plant manager.*

plastic[1] /'plæstɪk/ *noun* a plastic card, especially a credit or debit card, for use as a means of payment

plastic[2] /ˌplæstɪk 'mʌni/ *noun* credit cards and charge cards □ **do you take plastic?** can I pay by credit card?

plateau /plæ'toʊ/ *noun* a level point, e.g., when sales or costs stop increasing

platform /'plætfɔrm/ *noun* **1.** a basic product that can be added to in order to develop more complex products **2.** a system that can be used to deliver services, e.g., a communications network is a platform for delivering information

Plc, PLC, plc *abbreviation* public limited company

plead /plid/ *verb* **1.** to speak on behalf of a client in court **2.** to answer a charge in a criminal court □ **to plead guilty** to say at the beginning of a trial that you did commit the crime of which you are accused □ **to plead not guilty** to say at the beginning of a trial that you did not commit the crime of which you are accused

pledge /pledʒ/ *noun* an object given to a pawnbroker as security for money borrowed □ **to redeem a pledge** to pay back a loan and interest and so get back the security ■ *verb* □ **to pledge share certificates**

to deposit share certificates with a lender as security for money borrowed (the title to the certificates is not transferred and the certificates are returned when the debt is repaid)

plenary meeting /'plinəri 'mitɪŋ/, **plenary session** /'plinəri ˌseʃ(ə)n/ *noun* a meeting at a conference when all the delegates meet together

Plimsoll Line /'plɪmsəl laɪn/ *noun* a line painted on the side of a ship to show where the water should reach for maximum safety if the ship is fully loaded. Also called **load line**

plow /plaʊ/ *verb*
plow back *phrasal verb* □ **to plow back profits into the company** to invest the profits in the business (and not pay them out as dividends to the stockholders) by using them to buy new equipment or to create new products (NOTE: The U.K. spelling is **plough back**.)

plug /plʌg/ *noun* □ **to give a plug to a new product** to publicize a new product ■ *verb* **1.** □ **to plug in** to attach a machine to the electricity supply ○ *The fax machine was not plugged in.* **2.** to publicize or advertise ○ *They ran six commercials plugging vacations in Spain.* (NOTE: **plugging–plugged**) **3.** to block or to stop ○ *The company is trying to plug the drain on cash reserves.* (NOTE: **plugging – plugged**)

plug and play /ˌplʌg ən 'pleɪ/ *adjective* used to describe a new member of staff who does not need training (*slang*)

plummet /'plʌmɪt/, **plunge** /plʌndʒ/ *verb* to fall sharply ○ *Stock prices plummeted or plunged on the news of the devaluation.*

"…in the first six months of this year secondhand values of tankers have plummeted by 40%" [*Lloyd's List*]

"…crude oil output plunged during the past month" [*Wall Street Journal*]

plus /plʌs/ *preposition* added to ○ *Her salary plus commission comes to more than $45,000.* ○ *Production costs plus overhead are higher than revenue.* ■ *adverb* more than □ **houses valued at $100,000 plus** houses valued at over $100,000 ■ *adjective* favorable, good and profitable ○ *A plus factor for the company is that the market is much larger than they had originally thought.* □ **the plus side of**

the account the credit side of the account □ **on the plus side** this is a favorable point ○ *On the plus side, we must take into account the new product line.* ■ *noun* a good or favorable point ○ *To have achieved $1m in new sales in less than six months is certainly a plus for the sales team.* ○ *His marketing experience is a definite plus.*

p.m. /ˌpiː 'em/ *adverb* in the afternoon or in the evening, after 12 o'clock midday ○ *The train leaves at 6.50 p.m.* ○ *If you phone New York after 6 p.m. the calls are at a cheaper rate.* (NOTE: The U.S. spelling is **P.M.**)

PO *abbreviation* post office

pocket /'pɑkɪt/ *noun* □ **to be $25 in pocket** to have made a profit of $25 □ **to be $25 out of pocket** to have lost $25

pocket envelope /ˌpɑkɪt 'envəloʊp/ *noun* a type of envelope with the flap at the end, on the shorter side (an envelope with a flap along the longer side, is called a "wallet envelope")

point /pɔɪnt/ *noun* **1.** a place or position **2.** same as **decimal point 3.** a unit for calculations □ **the dollar gained two points** the dollar increased in value against another currency by two hundredths of a cent □ **the exchange fell ten points** the stock market index fell by ten units ■ *verb* □ **to point out** to show ○ *The report points out the mistakes made by the company over the last year.* ○ *He pointed out that the results were better than in previous years.*

point of sale /ˌpɔɪnt əv 'seɪl/ *noun* a place where a product is sold, e.g., a store. Abbreviation **POS**

point-of-sale material /ˌpɔɪnt əv 'seɪl məˌtɪriəl/ *noun* a display material to advertise a product where it is being sold, e.g., posters or dump bins. Abbreviation **POS material**

point of sale terminal /ˌpɔɪnt əv 'seɪl ˌtɜrmɪn(ə)l/ *noun* an electronic cash terminal at a pay desk which records transactions and stock movements automatically when an item is bought. Abbreviation **POS terminal**

poison pill /ˌpɔɪz(ə)n 'pɪl/ *noun* an action taken by a company to make itself less attractive to a potential takeover bid

police record /pəˌlis 'rekɔrd/ *noun* a note of previous crimes for which someone has been convicted ○ *He did not say that he had a police record.*

policy /'pɑləsi/ *noun* **1.** a course of action or set of principles determining the general way of doing something ○ *a company's trading policy* ○ *The country's economic policy seems to lack any direction.* ○ *We have a policy of only hiring qualified staff.* ○ *Our policy is to submit all contracts to the legal department.* □ **company policy** the company's agreed plan of action or the company's way of doing things ○ *What is the company policy on credit?* ○ *It is against company policy to give more than thirty days' credit.* **2.** a course of action or set of principles **3.** a contract for insurance □ **to take out a policy** to sign the contract for insurance and start paying the premiums ○ *She took out a life insurance policy* or *a house insurance policy.* □ **the insurance company made out a policy, drew up a policy** the company wrote the details of the contract on the policy

policyholder /'pɑlɪsi ˌhoʊldər/ *noun* a person who is insured by an insurance company

policy statement /'pɑlɪsi ˌsteɪtmənt/ *noun* the government declared in public what its plans were

polite /pə'laɪt/ *adjective* behaving in a pleasant way ○ *We insist on our sales staff being polite to customers.* ○ *We had a polite letter from the CEO.*

political /pə'lɪtɪk(ə)l/ *adjective* referring to a certain idea of how a country should be run

political levy /pəˌlɪtɪk(ə)l 'levi/ *noun* a part of the subscription of a member of a labor union which the union pays to support a political party

political party /pə'lɪtɪk(ə)l ˌpɑrti/ *noun* a group of people who believe a country should be run in a certain way

poll /poʊl/ *noun* same as **opinion poll** ■ *verb* □ **to poll a sample of the population** to ask a sample group of people what they feel about something □ **to poll the members of the club on an issue** to ask the members for their opinion on an issue

pollster /'poʊlstər/ *noun* an expert in understanding what polls mean

pool /puːl/ *noun* **1.** an unused supply ○ *a pool of unemployed labor* or *of expertise* **2.** a group of mortgages and other collateral used to back a loan ■ *verb* □ **to pool resources** to put all resources together so as to be more powerful or profitable

poor /pɔr/ *adjective* **1.** without much money ○ *The company tries to help the poorest members of staff with loans.* ○ *It is one of the poorest countries in the world.* **2.** not very good ○ *poor quality* ○ *poor service* ○ *poor performance by office staff* ○ *poor organization of working methods*

poorly /'pɔli/ *adverb* badly ○ *The offices are poorly laid out.* ○ *The plan was poorly presented.* □ **poorly-paid staff** staff with low wages

popular /'pɑpjələr/ *adjective* liked by many people ○ *This is our most popular model.* ○ *The South Coast is the most popular area for vacations.*

popular price /ˌpɑpjələr 'praɪs/ *noun* a price which is low and therefore liked

population /ˌpɑpjʊ'leɪʃ(ə)n/ *noun* **1.** all the people living in a particular country or area ○ *Paris has a population of over three million.* ○ *Population statistics show a rise in the 18–25 age group.* ○ *Population trends have to be taken into account when drawing up economic plans.* ○ *The working population of the country is getting older.* **2.** the group of items or people in a survey or study

population forecast /ˌpɑpjə'leɪʃ(ə)n ˌfɔrkæst/ *noun* a calculation of how many people will be living in a country or in a town at some point in the future

pop-under ad /'pɑp ʌndər ˌæd/ *noun* a web advertisement that appears in a separate browser window from the rest of a website

pop-up menu /ˌpɑp ʌp 'menju/ *noun* **1.** a menu of options that can be displayed at any time, usually covering part of other text on the screen in the process **2.** a small window that pops up covering part of a browser page, usually carrying an advertisement

pork bellies /'pɔrk ˌbeliz/ *plural noun* meat from the underside of pig carcasses used to make bacon, traded as futures on some American exchanges

portable /'pɔrtəb(ə)l/ *adjective* possible to carry ○ *a portable computer* ■ *noun* □ **a portable** a computer or typewriter which can be carried ○ *He keys all his orders on his portable and then emails them to the office.*

portable document format /ˌpɔrtəb(ə)l 'dɑkjəmənt ˌfɔrmæt/ *noun* full form of **PDF**

portable pension /ˌpɔrtəb(ə)l 'penʃən/, **portable pension plan** /ˌpɔrtəb(ə)l 'penʃən plæn/ *noun* a pension entitlement which can be moved from one company to another without loss (as an employee changes jobs)

portal /'pɔrt(ə)l/ *noun* a website that provides access and links to other sites and pages on the web (NOTE: Search engines and directories are the most common portal sites.)

port authority /'pɔrt ɔˌθɑrəti/ *noun* an organization which runs a port

port charges /'pɔrt ˌtʃɑrdʒɪz/ *noun* payment which a ship makes to the port authority for the right to use the port

portfolio /pɔrt'foʊlioʊ/ *noun* □ **a portfolio of stocks** all the stocks owned by a single investor

portfolio management /pɔrt'foʊlioʊ ˌmænɪdʒmənt/ *noun* the systematic buying and selling stocks in order to make the highest-possible profits for a single investor

portfolio working /pɔrt'foʊlioʊ ˌwɜrkɪŋ/ *noun* a way of organizing your working life in which, instead of working full-time for one employer and pursuing a single career, you work for several different employers, do several different jobs and follow several different career paths all at the same time

port installations /ˌpɔrt ɪnstə'leɪʃ(ə)nz/ *plural noun* the buildings and equipment of a port

port of embarkation /ˌpɔrt əv ˌɪmbɑr'keɪʃ(ə)n/ *noun* a port at which you get on to a ship

port of registry /ˌpɔrt əv 'redʒɪstri/ *noun* a port where a ship is registered

POS /pɑz/, **p.o.s.** *abbreviation* point of sale

position /pə'zɪʃ(ə)n/ *noun* **1.** a situation or state of affairs □ **what is the cash position?** what is the state of the company's checking account? **2.** a point of view **3.** a job or paid work in a company ○ *to apply for a position as manager* ○ *We have several positions vacant.* ○ *All the vacant positions have been filled.* ○ *She retired from her position in the accounts department.* □ **he is in a key position** he has an important job

positioning /pə'zɪʃ(ə)nɪŋ/ *noun* **1.** the creation of an image for a product in the minds of consumers **2.** the promotion of a product in a particular area of a market

position of trust /pə‚zɪʃ(ə)n əv ‚trʌst/ *noun* a job in which a person is trusted to act correctly and honestly

positive /ˈpɑzətɪv/ *adjective* meaning "yes" ○ *The board gave a positive reply.*

positive cash flow /‚pɑzətɪv ˈkæʃ ‚floʊ/ *noun* a situation where more money is coming into a company than is going out

possess /pəˈzes/ *verb* to own something ○ *The company possesses property in the center of the town.* ○ *He lost all he possessed in the collapse of his company.* Compare **repossess**

possession /pəˈzeʃ(ə)n/ *noun* the fact of owning or having something □ **the documents are in his possession** he is holding the documents

possessions /pəˈzeʃ(ə)nz/ *plural noun* property, things owned ○ *They lost all their possessions in the fire.* Compare **repossession**

possibility /‚pɑsɪˈbɪlɪti/ *noun* the state of being likely to happen ○ *There is a possibility that the plane will be early.* ○ *There is no possibility of the chairman retiring before next Christmas.*

possible /ˈpɑsɪb(ə)l/ *adjective* which might happen ○ *The 25th and 26th are possible dates for our next meeting.* ○ *It is possible that production will be held up by industrial action.* □ **there are two possible candidates for the job** two candidates are good enough to be appointed

post /poʊst/ *noun* **1.** *U.K.* same as **mail 2.** *U.K.* letters sent or received ○ *Has the post arrived yet?* ○ *The first thing I do is open the post.* ○ *The receipt was in this morning's post.* ○ *The letter didn't arrive by the first post this morning.* (NOTE: U.K. English uses both **mail** and **post** but American English only uses **mail**) **3.** job, paid work in a company ○ *to apply for a post as cashier* ○ *we have three posts vacant* ○ *All our posts have been filled.* ○ *We advertised three posts in the "Times".* ■ *verb* **1.** *U.K.* same as **mail 2.** to send a letter or package by post **3.** to record or enter something □ **to post an entry** to transfer an entry to an account □ **to post up a ledger** to keep a ledger up to date **4.** □ **to post up a notice** to put a notice on a wall or on a bulletin board **5.** □ **to post an increase** to let people know that an increase has taken place

"Toronto stocks closed at an all-time high, posting their fifth day of advances in heavy trading" [*Financial Times*]

post- /poʊst/ *prefix* after

postage /ˈpoʊstɪdʒ/ *noun* payment for sending a letter or package by mail ○ *What is the postage for this airmail packet to China?*

postage stamp /ˈpoʊstɪdʒ stæmp/ *noun* a small piece of gummed paper which you buy from a post office and stick on a letter or parcel to pay for the postage ○ *You'll need two $1 postage stamps for the parcel.*

postal /ˈpoʊst(ə)l/ *adjective* referring to the mail

postal charges /ˈpoʊst(ə)l ‚tʃɑrdʒɪz/ *plural noun* money to be paid for sending letters or packages by mail ○ *Postal charges are going up by 10% in September.*

postal order /ˈpoʊst(ə)l ‚ɔrdər/ *noun* a document bought at a post office, used as a method of paying small amounts of money by mail

post-balance sheet event /‚poʊst ‚bæləns ʃit ɪˈvent/ *noun* something which happens after the date when the balance sheet is drawn up, and before the time when the balance sheet is officially approved by the directors, which affects a company's financial position

postcode /ˈpoʊstkoʊd/ *noun U.K.* same as **ZIP code**

postdate /‚poʊstˈdeɪt/ *verb* to put a later date on a document ○ *He sent us a postdated check.* ○ *Her check was postdated to June.*

poster /ˈpoʊstər/ *noun* a large eye-catching notice or advertisement which is stuck up outdoors or placed prominently inside a store

poste restante /‚poʊst ‚restænt/ *noun U.K.* same as **general delivery**

Post-it ® Notes /ˈpoʊst ɪt ‚noʊtz/ *noun* a trademark for small pieces of paper, partially sticky on one side, sold in pads (you write on a note and then stick it onto a document, a telephone, a computer monitor, etc.) ○ *She left me a Post-it Note with the telephone number on my computer keyboard.*

postmark /ˈpoʊstmɑrk/ *noun* a mark stamped by the post office on a letter, covering the postage stamp, to show that the post office has accepted it ○ *a letter with a Cleveland postmark* ■ *verb* to stamp a letter with a postmark ○ *The letter was postmarked New York.*

post office /'poʊst ˌɒfɪs/ *noun* **1.** a building where the postal services are based ○ *main post office* **2.** a store where you can buy stamps, send packages, etc. **3.** a national organization which deals with sending letters and packages ○ *Post Office officials* or *officials of the Post Office* ○ *The Post Office van was collecting mail from the box.*

> "…travellers cheques cost 1% of their face value and can be purchased from any bank, main post offices, travel agents and several building societies" [*Sunday Times*]

post office box number /ˌpoʊst ˌɒfɪs 'bɑks ˌnʌmbər/ *noun* a reference number given for delivering mail to a post office, so as not to give the actual address of the person who will receive it

postpaid /poʊst'peɪd/ *adjective* with the postage already paid ○ *The price is $5.95 postpaid.*

postpone /poʊst'poʊn/ *verb* to arrange for something to take place later than planned ○ *He postponed the meeting to tomorrow.* ○ *They asked if they could postpone payment until the cash situation was better.*

postponement /poʊst'poʊnmənt/ *noun* the act of arranging for something to take place later than planned ○ *I had to change my appointments because of the postponement of the board meeting.*

post room /'poʊst rum/ *noun* U.K. same as **mail room**

post scriptum /ˌpoʊst 'skrɪptəm/, **postscript (P.S.)** /'poʊskrɪpt/ *Latin phrase meaning* "after what has been written": an additional note at the end of a letter

potential /pə'tenʃəl/ *adjective* possible □ **potential customers** people who could be customers □ **potential market** a market which could be exploited □ **the product has potential sales of 100,000 units** the product will possibly sell 100,000 units □ **she is a potential managing director** she is the sort of person who could become managing director ■ *noun* the possibility of becoming something □ **a stock with a growth potential** *or* **with a potential for**

growth a stock which is likely to increase in value □ **a product with considerable sales potential** a product which is likely to have very large sales □ **to analyze the market potential** to examine the market to see how large it possibly is

pound /paʊnd/ *noun* **1.** a measure of weight (= 0.45 kilos) ○ *to sell oranges by the pound* ○ *a pound of oranges* ○ *Oranges cost 50p a pound.* (NOTE: Usually written **lb** after a figure: **25lb**. Note also that the pound is now no longer officially used in the U.K.) **2.** a unit of currency used in the U.K. and many other countries including Cyprus, Egypt, Lebanon, Malta, Sudan, Syria and, before the euro, Ireland

poundage /'paʊndɪdʒ/ *noun* **1.** a rate charged per pound in weight **2.** tax charged per pound in value

pound sterling /paʊnd 'stɜrlɪŋ/ *noun* the official term for the U.K. currency

poverty /'pɑvərti/ *noun* the condition of being poor ○ *He lost all his money and died in poverty.*

poverty trap /'pɑvərti træp/ *noun* a situation where a poor person lives on government benefits and cannot afford to earn more money because he or she would then lose the benefits and be worse off

power /'paʊr/ *noun* **1.** strength or ability □ **the power of a consumer group** ability of a group to influence the government or manufacturers **2.** a force or legal right □ **the full power of the law** the full force of the law when applied ○ *We will apply the full power of the law to get possession of our property again.* ○ *There was a power struggle in the boardroom, and the finance director had to resign.*

power brand /'paʊr brænd/ *noun* a very powerful brand which covers several best-selling products and is known worldwide

power center /ˌpaʊr 'sentər/ *noun* the most powerful part of an organization, the one that has the greatest influence on policy

power of attorney /ˌpaʊr əv ə'tɜrni/ *noun* a legal document which gives someone the right to act on someone's behalf in legal matters

power structure /'paʊr ˌstrʌktʃər/ *noun* the way in which authority and influence are divided up among the different groups or individuals who make up an organization

p.p. *abbreviation* per procurationem ■ *verb* □ **to p.p. a letter** to sign a letter on behalf of someone ○ *Her assistant p.p.'d the letter while the manager was at lunch.*

PR *abbreviation* public relations ○ *A PR firm is handling all our publicity.* ○ *She works in PR.* ○ *The PR people gave away 100,000 balloons.*

practice /'præktɪs/ *noun* **1.** a way of doing things, a custom or habit ○ *Her practice was to arrive at work at 7.30 and start counting the cash.* □ **to depart from normal practice** to act in a different way from the normal way of doing things **2.** □ **in practice** when actually done ○ *The marketing plan seems very interesting, but what will it cost in practice?*

"…the EC demanded international arbitration over the pricing practices of the provincial boards" [*Globe and Mail (Toronto)*]

pre- /priː/ *prefix* before ○ *a pre-stocktaking sale* ○ *There will be a pre-annual meeting board meeting* or *There will be a board meeting pre the annual meeting.* ○ *The pre-Christmas period is always very busy.*

precautionary measure /prɪ'kɔːʃ(ə)n(ə)ri ˌmeʒər/ *noun* an action taken to prevent something unwanted taking place

precautions /prɪ'kɔːʃ(ə)nz/ *plural noun* measures taken to avoid something unpleasant ○ *We intend to take precautions to prevent thefts in the office.* ○ *The company did not take proper fire precautions.*

precinct /'priːsɪŋkt/ *noun* **1.** a separate area **2.** an administrative district in a town

predator /'predətə/ *noun* an individual (or company) who spends most of the time looking for companies to purchase cheaply

predecessor /'priːdɪsesər/ *noun* a person who had a job or position before someone else ○ *He took over from his predecessor last May.* ○ *She is using the same office as her predecessor.*

predict /prɪ'dɪkt/ *verb* to say that something will happen in the future

preempt /priː'empt/ *verb* to stop something happening or stop someone doing something by taking action quickly before anyone else can ○ *They staged a management buyout to preempt a takeover bid.*

preemptive /priː'emptɪv/ *adjective* done before anyone else takes action in order to stop something happening □ **preemptive strike against a takeover bid** rapid action taken to prevent a takeover bid

preemptive right /prɪˌemptɪv 'raɪt/ *noun* **1.** a right of a government or of a local authority to buy a property before anyone else **2.** the right of a stockholder to be first to buy a new stock issue

prefer /prɪ'fɜr/ *verb* to like something better than another thing ○ *We prefer the small corner store to the large supermarket.* ○ *Most customers prefer to choose clothes themselves, rather than take the advice of the sales assistant.*

preference /'pref(ə)rəns/ *noun* **1.** a thing which someone prefers ○ *the customers' preference for small corner stores* **2.** a thing which has an advantage over something else

preference shares /'pref(ə)rəns ʃerz/ *plural noun* U.K. same as **preferred stock**

COMMENT: Preference shares, because they have less risk than ordinary shares, normally carry no voting rights.

preferential /ˌprefə'renʃəl/ *adjective* showing that something is preferred more than another

preferential creditor /ˌprefərenʃ(ə)l 'kredɪtə/ *noun* a creditor who must be paid first if a company is in liquidation. Also called **preferred creditor**

preferential duty /ˌprefərenʃ(ə)l 'duːti/ *noun* a special low rate of tax

preferential terms /ˌprefərenʃ(ə)l 'tɜrmz/ *noun* terms or a way of dealing which is better than usual ○ *Subsidiary companies get preferential treatment when it comes to subcontracting work.*

preferred creditor /prɪˌfɜrd 'kredɪtər/ *noun* same as **preferential creditor**

preferred provider organization /prɪˌfɜrd prəˌvaɪdər ˌɔrgənaɪ'zeɪʃ(ə)n/ *noun* a group of hospitals and doctors that agree to provide healthcare under a particular health insurance plan

preferred stock /prɪˌfɜrd 'ʃerz/ *plural noun* stock with no voting rights. Holders receive their dividend before all other stockholders and are repaid first at face value if the company goes into liquidation. (NOTE: The U.K. term is **preference shares**.)

pre-financing /ˌpri ˈfaɪnænsɪŋ/ *noun* financing in advance

prejudice /ˈpredʒʊdɪs/ *noun* **1.** bias or unjust feelings against someone **2.** harm done to someone □ **without prejudice** without harming any interests (a phrase spoken or written in letters when trying to negotiate a settlement, meaning that the negotiations cannot be referred to in court or relied upon by the other party if the discussions fail) □ **to act to the prejudice of a claim** to do something which may harm a claim ■ *verb* to harm ○ *to prejudice someone's claim*

preliminary /prɪˈlɪmɪn(ə)ri/ *adjective* early, happening before anything else □ **preliminary discussion, a preliminary meeting** discussion or meeting which takes place before the main discussion or meeting starts

"…preliminary indications of the level of business investment and activity during the March quarter will be available this week" [*Australian Financial Review*]

preliminary prospectus /prɪˌlɪmɪn(ə)ri prəˈspektəs/ *noun* same as **pathfinder prospectus**

premises /ˈpremɪsɪz/ *plural noun* building and the land it stands on □ **on the premises** in the building ○ *There is a doctor on the premises at all times.*

premium /ˈpriːmiəm/ *noun* **1.** a regular payment made to an insurance company for the protection provided by an insurance policy **2.** an amount to be paid to a landlord or a tenant for the right to take over a lease ○ *apartment to rent with a premium of $10,000* ○ *annual rent: $8,500, premium: $25,000* **3.** an extra sum of money in addition to a usual charge, wage, price or other amount □ **shares at a premium** shares whose price is higher than their face value ○ *New shares whose market price is higher than their issue price.* **4.** a gift, discount or other incentive to encourage someone to buy ■ *adjective* **1.** of very high quality **2.** very high

premium offer /ˈpriːmiəm ˌɒfə/ *noun* a free gift offered to attract more customers

premium pricing /ˈpriːmiəm ˌpraɪsɪŋ/ *noun* the act of giving products or services high prices either to give the impression

that the product is worth more than it really is, or as a means of offering customers an extra service

premium quality /ˈpriːmiəm ˌkwɒlɪti/ *noun* top quality

prepack /priːˈpæk/, **prepackage** /priːˈpækɪdʒ/ *verb* to pack something before putting it on sale ○ *The fruit are prepacked in plastic trays.* ○ *The watches are prepacked in attractive display boxes.*

prepackaged choice /ˌpriːpækɪdʒd ˈtʃɔɪs/ *noun* a set of multimedia computer material that cannot be customized by the user

prepaid /priːˈpeɪd/ *adjective* paid in advance

prepaid reply card /ˌpriːpeɪd rɪˈplaɪ ˌkɑːd/ *noun* a stamped addressed card which is sent to someone so that they can reply without paying the postage

prepay /priːˈpeɪ/ *verb* to pay something in advance (NOTE: **prepaying – prepaid**)

prepayment /priːˈpeɪmənt/ *noun* a payment in advance, or the act of paying in advance □ **to ask for prepayment of a fee** to ask for the fee to be paid before the work is done

present /ˈprez(ə)nt/ *noun* something which is given ○ *these calculators make good presents* ○ *The office gave her a present when she got married.* ■ *adjective* **1.** happening now ○ *The stock is too expensive at their present price.* ○ *What is the present address of the company?* **2.** being there when something happens ○ *Only six directors were present at the board meeting.* ■ *verb* /prɪˈzent/ **1.** to give someone something ○ *He was presented with a watch on completing twenty-five years' service with the company.* **2.** to bring or send and show a document □ **to present a bill for acceptance** to present a bill for payment by the person who has accepted it □ **to present a bill for payment** to send a bill to be paid **3.** *vti* to give a talk about or demonstration of something ○ *I've been asked to present at the sales conference.* ○ *The HR director will present the new staff structure to the Board.*

presentation /ˌprez(ə)nˈteɪʃ(ə)n/ *noun* **1.** the showing of a document □ **check payable on presentation** a check which will be paid when it is presented □ **free admission on presentation of this card** you do not pay to go in if you show this card **2.** a demonstration or exhibition of a proposed plan ○ *The distribution company gave a presentation of the services they could offer.* ○ *We have asked two PR firms to make presentations of proposed publicity campaigns.*

presenteeism /ˌprez(ə)nˈtiːz(ə)m/ *noun* the practice of spending more hours at work or in the workplace than is healthy, necessary or productive, e.g., when an employee comes to work when sick for fear of losing their job or letting the company down

present value /ˌprez(ə)nt ˈvæljuː/ *noun* **1.** the value something has now ○ *In 1984 the pound was worth five times its present value.* **2.** the value now of a specified sum of money to be received in the future, if invested at current interest rates. Abbreviation **PV 3.** a price which a stock must reach in the future to be the equivalent of today's price, taking inflation into account

COMMENT: The present value of a future sum of money is found by discounting that future sum, and can be used to decide how much money to invest now at current interest rates in order to receive the sum you want to have in a given number of years' time.

preside /prɪˈzaɪd/ *verb* to be chairman ○ *The CEO will preside over the meeting.* ○ *The meeting was held in the committee room, Mr Smith presiding.*

president /ˈprezɪd(ə)nt/ *noun* the head of a company, society or club ○ *She was elected president of the sports club.* ○ *After many years on the board, A.B. Smith has been appointed president of the company.*

COMMENT: In the U.K., president is sometimes a title given to a non-executive former chairman of a company; in the U.S., the president is the main executive of a company.

press /pres/ *noun* newspapers and magazines ○ *We plan to give the product a lot of press publicity.* ○ *There was no mention of the new product in the press.* ◇ **press the flesh** /ˌpres ðə ˈfleʃ/ to shake hands with people at a business function (*informal*)

press clipping /ˈpres ˌklɪpɪŋ/ *noun* a copy of a news item kept by a company because it contains important business information or is a record of news published

about the company ○ *We have kept a file of press clippings about the new car.*

press clipping agency /ˈpres ˌklɪpɪŋ ˌeɪdʒənsi/ *noun* a company which cuts out references to clients from newspapers and magazines and sends them on to them

press conference /ˈpres ˌkɒnf(ə)rəns/ *noun* a meeting where newspaper and TV reporters are invited to hear news of something such as a new product or a takeover bid

press coverage /ˈpres ˌkʌv(ə)rɪdʒ/ *noun* reports about something in newspapers, and magazines and other media ○ *The company had good press coverage for the launch of its new model.*

press cutting /ˈpres ˌkʌtɪŋ/ *noun U.K.* same as **press clipping**

pressing /ˈpresɪŋ/ *adjective* urgent □ **pressing engagements** meetings which have to be attended □ **pressing bills** bills which have to be paid

press office /ˈpres ˌɒfɪs/ *noun* an office in a company which deals with relations with the press, sends out press releases, organizes press conferences, etc.

press officer /ˈpres ˌɒfɪsər/ *noun* a person who works in a press office

press release /ˈpres rɪˌliːs/ *noun* a sheet giving news about something which is sent to newspapers and TV and radio stations so that they can use the information ○ *The company sent out a press release about the launch of the new car.*

pressure /ˈpreʃər/ *noun* something which forces you to do something □ **he was under considerable financial pressure** he was forced to act because he owed money □ **to put pressure on someone to do something** to try to force someone to do something ○ *The group tried to put pressure on the government to act.* ○ *The banks put pressure on the company to reduce its borrowings.*

pressure group /ˈpreʃər gruːp/ *noun* a group of people who try to influence the government or some other organization

prestige /preˈstiːʒ/ *noun* importance because of factors such as high quality or high value □ **prestige product** an expensive luxury product □ **prestige offices** expensive offices in a good area of the town

prestige advertising /preˈstiːʒ ˌædvərtaɪzɪŋ/ *noun* advertising in high-quality magazines to increase a company's reputation

presume /prɪˈzjuːm/ *verb* to suppose something is correct ○ *I presume the account has been paid.* ○ *The company is presumed to be still solvent.* ○ *We presume the shipment has been stolen.*

presumption /prɪˈzʌmpʃən/ *noun* something which is assumed to be correct

pretax /ˈpriːtæks/, **pre-tax** *adjective* before tax has been deducted or paid

"…the company's goals are a growth in sales of up to 40 per cent, a rise in pre-tax earnings of nearly 35 per cent and a rise in after-tax earnings of more than 25 per cent" [*Citizen (Ottawa)*]

"EC regulations which came into effect in July insist that customers can buy cars anywhere in the EC at the local pre-tax price" [*Financial Times*]

pretax profit /ˌpriːtæks ˈprɒfɪt/ *noun* the amount of profit a company makes before taxes are deducted ○ *The dividend paid is equivalent to one quarter of the pretax profit.* Also called **profit before tax**, **profit on ordinary activities before tax**

pretend /prɪˈtend/ *verb* to act like someone else in order to trick, to act as if something is true when it really is not ○ *He got in by pretending to be a telephone engineer.* ○ *The chairman pretended he knew the final profit.* ○ *She pretended she had flu and asked to have the day off.*

prevent /prɪˈvent/ *verb* to stop something happening ○ *We must try to prevent the takeover bid.* ○ *The police prevented anyone from leaving the building.* ○ *We have changed the locks on the doors to prevent the former CEO from getting into the building.*

preventive /prɪˈventɪv/ *adjective* which tries to stop something happening □ **to take preventive measures against theft** to try to stop things from being stolen

previous /ˈpriːviəs/ *adjective* happening earlier or which existed before ○ *List all previous positions with the salaries earned.* □ **he could not accept the invitation because he had a previous engagement** because he had earlier accepted another invitation to go somewhere

previously /ˈpriːviəsli/ *adverb* happening earlier ○ *Previously our distribution was handled by Smith Inc.* ○ *His résumé*

stated that he had previously been a salesman with Jones & Co.

price /praɪs/ *noun* money which has to be paid to buy something □ **to sell goods off at half price** to sell goods at half the price at which they were being sold before □ **cars in the $18–19,000 price range** cars of different makes, selling for between $18,000 and $19,000 □ **price ex warehouse** the price for a product which is to be collected from the manufacturer's or agent's warehouse and so does not include delivery □ **to increase in price** to become more expensive ○ *Gasoline has increased in price* or *the price of gasoline has increased.* □ **to increase prices**, **to raise prices** to make items more expensive □ **we will try to meet your price** we will try to offer a price which is acceptable to you □ **to cut prices** to reduce prices suddenly □ **to lower prices, to reduce prices** to make items cheaper ■ *verb* to give a price to a product ○ *We have two used cars for sale, both priced at $5,000.* □ **the company has priced itself out of the market** the company has raised its prices so high that its products do not sell

price ceiling /ˈpraɪs ˌsiːlɪŋ/ *noun* the highest price which can be reached

price controls /ˈpraɪs kənˌtrəʊlz/ *plural noun* legal measures to prevent prices rising too fast

price cutting /ˈpraɪs ˌkʌtɪŋ/ *noun* a sudden lowering of prices

price-cutting war /ˈpraɪs ˌkʌtɪŋ wɔː/ *noun* same as **price war**

price deflation /ˈpraɪs diːˌfleɪʃ(ə)n/ *noun* a gradual fall in prices because of increased competition. Compare **disinflation**

price differential /ˈpraɪs ˌdɪfəˌrenʃəl/ *noun* the difference in price between products in a range

price/earnings ratio /ˌpraɪs ˈɜːnɪŋz ˌreɪʃiəʊ/ *noun* a ratio between the current market price of a share of stock and the earnings per share (the current dividend it produces), calculated by dividing the market price by the earnings per share ○ *This stock sells at a P/E ratio of 7* Also called **P/E ratio.** Abbreviation **PER**

COMMENT: The P/E ratio is an indication of the way investors think a company will perform in the future, as a high market price suggests that investors expect earnings to grow and this gives a high P/E figure; a low P/E figure implies that investors feel that earnings are not likely to rise.

price elasticity /'praɪs ɪlæ,stɪsəti/ *noun* a situation where a change in price has the effect of causing a big change in demand

price fixing /'praɪs ,fɪksɪŋ/ *noun* an illegal agreement between companies to charge the same price for competing products

price-insensitive /,praɪs ɪn'sensətɪv/ *adjective* used to describe a good or service for which sales remain constant no matter what its price because it is essential to buyers

price label /'praɪs ,leɪb(ə)l/ *noun* a label which shows a price

price list /'praɪs lɪst/ *noun* a sheet giving prices of goods for sale

price maintenance /'praɪs ,meɪntənəns/ *noun* an agreement between producers or distributors on a minimum price for a product

price range /'praɪs reɪndʒ/ *noun* a series of prices for similar products from different suppliers

price-sensitive /,praɪs 'sensətɪv/ *adjective* referring to a product for which demand will change significantly if its price is increased or decreased

price tag /'praɪs tæg/ *noun* a label attached to an item being sold that shows its price

price war /'praɪs wɔr/ *noun* a competition between companies to get a larger market share by cutting prices. Also called **price-cutting war**

pricing /'praɪsɪŋ/ *noun* the act of giving a price to a product

pricing policy /'praɪsɪŋ ,pɑlisi/ *noun* a company's policy in giving prices to its products ○ *Our pricing policy aims at producing a 35% gross margin.*

primarily /'praɪm(ə)rɪli/ *adverb* mainly ○ *The company trades primarily in the South American market.*

primary /'praɪməri/ *adjective* **1.** basic **2.** first, most important

primary commodities /,praɪməri kə'mɑdətiz/ *plural noun* **1.** farm produce grown in large quantities, e.g., corn, rice or cotton **2.** raw materials or food

primary industry /,praɪməri 'ɪndəstri/ *noun* an industry dealing with basic raw materials such as coal, wood, or farm produce

primary products /,praɪməri 'prɑdʌkts/ *plural noun* products which are basic raw materials, e.g., wood, milk, or fish

prime /praɪm/ *adjective* **1.** most important **2.** basic ■ *noun* same as **prime rate**

prime bills /,praɪm 'bɪlz/ *plural noun* bills of exchange which do not involve any risk

prime cost /,praɪm 'kɔst/ *noun* the cost involved in producing a product, excluding overhead

prime rate /'praɪm reɪt/ *noun* the best rate of interest at which a bank lends to its customers. Also called **prime**

prime sites /,praɪm 'saɪts/ *plural noun* the most valuable commercial sites, i.e. in main shopping streets, as opposed to secondary sites

prime time /'praɪm taɪm/ *noun* the most expensive advertising time for TV commercials ○ *We are putting out a series of prime-time commercials.*

priming /'praɪmɪŋ/ *noun* ♦ **pump priming**

principal /'prɪnsɪp(ə)l/ *noun* **1.** a person or company that is represented by an agent ○ *The agent has come to Chicago to see his principals.* **2.** a person acting for him or herself, such as a market maker buying securities on his or her own account **3.** money invested or borrowed on which interest is paid ○ *to repay principal and interest* ○ *We try to repay part of principal each month.* (NOTE: Do not confuse with **principle.**) ■ *adjective* most important ○ *The principal stockholders asked for a meeting.* ○ *The country's principal products are paper and wood.* ○ *The company's principal asset is its design staff.*

principle /'prɪnsɪp(ə)l/ *noun* a basic point or general rule □ **in principle** in agreement with a general rule □ **agreement in principle** agreement with the basic conditions of a proposal

print /prɪnt/ *noun* words made (on paper) with a machine □ **to read the small print, the fine print on a contract** to read the conditions of a contract which are often printed very small so that people will not be able to read them easily ■ *verb* **1.** to make letters on paper with a machine ○ *The health warning is printed on the front of the packet.* ○ *We use a standard printed agreement for installment sales.* **2.** to write by hand using letters that are separated by space ○ *Please print your name and address on the top of the form.*

print out *phrasal verb* to print information from a computer through a printer

printed matter /ˈprɪntɪd ˌmætər/ *noun* printed items, e.g., books, newspapers, and publicity sheets

printer /ˈprɪntər/ *noun* a machine which prints

printer ribbon /ˈprɪntər ˌrɪbən/ *noun* an inked ribbon in a cartridge which is put into a line printer

prior /ˈpraɪr/ *adjective* earlier □ **prior agreement** an agreement which was reached earlier □ **without prior knowledge** without knowing before □ **prior charge** (capital) ranking before other capital in terms of distributions of profits and repayment when a company goes into liquidation

priority /praɪˈɔrəti/ *noun* □ **to have priority** to have the right to be first □ **to have priority over** *or* **to take priority over something** to be more important than something ○ *Reducing overhead takes priority over increasing turnover.* □ **to give something top priority** to make something the most important item

privacy /ˈprɪvəsi/ *noun* a situation of not being disturbed by other people, especially the knowledge that communications are private and cannot be accessed by others

private /ˈpraɪvət/ *adjective* **1.** belonging to a single person or to individual people, not to a company or the state □ **a letter marked "private and confidential"** a letter which must not be opened by anyone other than the person it is addressed to **2.** □ **in private** away from other people ○ *He asked to see the managing director in private.* ○ *In public he said the company would break even soon, but in private he was less optimistic.* ○ *In public the union said it would never go back to the negotiating table, but in private they were already having discussions with the company representatives.*

private client /ˌpraɪvət ˈklaɪənt/ *noun* a client dealt with by a salesman as a person, not as a company

private enterprise /ˌpraɪvət ˈentərpraɪz/ *noun* businesses that are owned privately, not nationalized ○ *The project is completely funded by private enterprise.*

private income /ˌpraɪvət ˈɪnkʌm/ *noun* income from dividends, interest, or rent which is not part of a salary

private letter /ˌpraɪvət ˈletər/ *noun* a letter which deals with personal matters. Same as **personal letter**

private limited company /ˌpraɪvət ˌlɪmɪtɪd ˈkʌmp(ə)ni/ *noun U.K.* **1.** a company with a small number of stockholders, whose stock is not traded on the Stock Exchange **2.** a subsidiary company whose stock is not listed on the Stock Exchange, while that of its parent company is ▶ abbreviation **Pty Ltd**

privately /ˈpraɪvətli/ *adverb* away from other people ○ *The deal was negotiated privately.*

private means /ˌpraɪvət ˈminz/ *plural noun* income from dividends, interest, or rent which is not part of someone's salary

private ownership /ˌpraɪvət ˈoʊnərʃɪp/ *noun* a situation in which a company is owned by private stockholders

private property /ˌpraɪvət ˈprɑpərti/ *noun* property which belongs to a private person, not to the public

private sector /ˈpraɪvət ˌsektər/ *noun* all privately-owned businesses, organizations, farms, etc., that are operated for profit and are not controlled by the government ○ *The expansion is completely funded by the private sector.* ○ *Salaries in the private sector have increased faster than in the public sector.*

privatization /ˌpraɪvətaɪˈzeɪʃ(ə)n/ *noun* the process of selling a nationalized industry to private owners

privatize /ˈpraɪvətaɪz/ *verb* to sell a nationalized industry to private owners

pro /proʊ/ *preposition* for

PRO *abbreviation* public relations officer

proactive /proʊˈæktɪv/ *adjective* taking the initiative in doing something (as opposed to reacting to events)

probable /ˈprɑbəb(ə)l/ *adjective* likely to happen ○ *They are trying to prevent the probable collapse of the company.* ○ *It is probable that the company will collapse if* *a rescue package is not organized before the end of the month.*

probably /ˈprɑbəbli/ *adverb* likely ○ *The CEO is probably going to retire next year.* ○ *This store is probably the best in town for service.*

probate /ˈproʊbeɪt/ *noun* legal acceptance that a document, especially a will, is valid □ **the executor was granted probate** *or* **obtained a grant of probate** the executor was told officially that the will was valid

Probate Registry /ˈproʊbeɪt ˌredʒɪstri/ *noun* a court which examines wills to see if they are valid

probation /prəˈbeɪʃ(ə)n/ *noun* a period when a new employee is being tested before getting a permanent job ○ *He is on three months' probation.* ○ *We will take her on probation.* ○ *The accountant was appointed on three months' probation at the end of which he was not found to be satisfactory.*

probationary /prəˈbeɪʃ(ə)n(ə)ri/ *adjective* while someone is being tested ○ *We will take her for a probationary period of three months.* ○ *After the probationary period the company decided to offer him a full-time contract.*

problem /ˈprɑbləm/ *noun* something to which it is difficult to find an answer ○ *The company suffers from staff problems.* □ **to solve a problem** to find an answer to a problem ○ *Problem solving is a test of a good manager.* ○ *Problem solving is the test of a good manager.*

problem area /ˈprɑbləm ˌeriə/ *noun* an area of a company's work which is difficult to run ○ *Overseas sales is one of our biggest problem areas.*

problem-solving /ˈprɑbləm ˌsɑlvɪŋ/ *noun* the task of dealing with problems that occur within an organization and the methods that managers use to solve them (NOTE: The most widely used method of problem-solving proceeds through the following stages: recognizing that a problem exists and defining it; generating a range of solutions; evaluating the possible solutions and choosing the best one; implementing the solution and evaluating its effectiveness in solving the problem.)

procedure /prəˈsidʒər/ *noun* a way in which something is done ○ *The inquiry found that the company had not followed*

the approved procedures. □ **this procedure is very irregular** this is not the proper way to do something □ **accounting procedures** set ways of doing the accounts of a company

"…this was a serious breach of disciplinary procedure and the dismissal was unfair" [*Personnel Management*]

proceed /prəˈsid/ *verb* to go on, to continue ○ *The negotiations are proceeding slowly.* □ **to proceed against someone** to start a legal action against someone □ **to proceed with something** to go on doing something ○ *Shall we proceed with the committee meeting?*

proceedings /prəˈsidɪŋz/ *plural noun* □ **to institute proceedings against someone** to start a legal action against someone

proceeds /ˈproʊsidz/ *plural noun* money received from selling something □ **the proceeds of a sale** money received from a sale after deducting expenses ○ *He sold his store and invested the proceeds in a computer repair business.*

process /ˈprɑses/ *noun* **1.** □ **decision-making processes** ways in which decisions are reached **2.** □ **the due processes of the law** the formal work of a legal action ■ *verb* **1.** □ **to process figures** to sort out information to make it easily understood ○ *The sales figures are being processed by our accounts department.* ○ *The data is being processed by our computer.* **2.** to deal with something in the usual routine way ○ *It usually takes at least two weeks to process an insurance claim.* ○ *Orders are processed in our warehouse.*

processing /ˈprɑsesɪŋ/ *noun* **1.** the act of sorting information ○ *the processing of information* or *of statistics by a computer* **2.** □ **the processing of a claim for insurance** putting a claim for insurance through the usual office routine in the insurance company

procurement /prəˈkjʊrmənt/ *noun* the act of buying equipment or raw materials for a company ○ *Procurement of raw materials is becoming very complicated with the entry of so many new suppliers into the market.*

produce *noun* /ˈprɑdjus/ products from farms and gardens, especially fruit and vegetables ○ *home produce* ○ *agricultural produce* ○ *farm produce* ■ *verb* /prəˈdus/ **1.** to bring something out and show it ○ *He* produced documents to prove his claim. ○ *The negotiators produced a new set of figures.* ○ *The customs officer asked him to produce the relevant documents.* **2.** to make or manufacture something ○ *The factory produces cars* or *engines.* □ **to mass produce** to make large quantities of a product **3.** to give an interest ○ *investments which produce about 10% per annum*

producer /prə'dusər/ *noun* a person, company, or country that manufactures ○ *a country which is a producer of high-quality watches* ○ *The company is a major car producer.* Also called **supplier**

producer prices /prə,dusər 'praisiz/ *noun* prices of goods when they leave the manufacturer

producing /prə'dusɪŋ/ *adjective* which produces

producing capacity /prə'dusɪŋ kə ,pæsəti/ *noun* the capacity to produce

product /'pradʌkt/ *noun* **1.** something which is made or manufactured **2.** a manufactured item for sale

product advertising /'pradʌkt ,ædvərtaizɪŋ/ *noun* the advertising of a particular named product, not the company which makes it

product analysis /,pradʌkt ə 'næləsɪs/ *noun* an examination of each separate product in a company's range to find out why it sells, who buys it, etc.

product churning /'pradʌkt ,tʃɜrnɪŋ/ *noun* the practice of putting many new products onto the market in the hope that one of them will become successful (NOTE: Product churning is especially prevalent in Japan.)

product design /'pradʌkt dɪ,zain/ *noun* the design of consumer products

product development /,pradʌkt dɪ 'veləpmənt/ *noun* the process of improving an existing product line to meet the needs of the market

product diversification /,pradʌkt dai,vɜrsɪfɪ'keɪʃ(ə)n/ *noun* adding new types of products to the range already made

product endorsement /'pradʌkt ɪn ,dɔrsmənt/ *noun* advertising which makes use of famous or qualified people to endorse a product ○ *Which celebrities have agreed to contribute to our endorsement advertising?* ○ *Product endorsement*

will, we hope, help our fund-raising campaign.

product engineer /,pradʌkt ,endʒɪ 'nɪr/ *noun* an engineer in charge of the equipment for making a product

production /prə'dʌkʃən/ *noun* **1.** the act of showing something □ **on production of** when something is shown ○ *The case will be released by customs on production of the relevant documents.* ○ *Goods can be exchanged only on production of the sales slip.* **2.** the work of making or manufacturing goods for sale ○ *We are hoping to speed up production by installing new machinery.* ○ *Higher production is rewarded with higher pay.*

production cost /prə'dʌkʃən kɔst/ *noun* the cost of making a product

production department /prə 'dʌkʃən dɪ,partmənt/ *noun* the section of a company which deals with the making of the company's products

production line /prə'dʌkʃən lain/ *noun* a system of making a product, where each item such as a car moves slowly through the factory with new sections added to it as it goes along ○ *He works on the production line.* ○ *She is a production-line employee.*

production manager /prə'dʌkʃən ,mænɪdʒər/ *noun* the person in charge of the production department

production rate /prə'dʌkʃ(ə)n reit/ *noun* same as **rate of production**

production standards /prə'dʌkʃən ,stændərdz/ *plural noun* the quality levels relating to production

production target /prə'dʌkʃən ,targət/ *noun* the amount of units a factory is expected to produce

production unit /prə'dʌkʃən ,junɪt/ *noun* a separate small group of employees producing a product

productive /prə'dʌktɪv/ *adjective* producing something, especially something useful □ **productive discussions** useful discussions which lead to an agreement or decision

productive capital /prə,dʌktɪv 'kæpɪt(ə)l/ *noun* capital which is invested to give interest

productively /prə'dʌktɪvli/ *adverb* in a productive way

productivity /ˌprɒdʌk'tɪvəti/ *noun* the rate of output per employee or per machine in a factory ○ *Bonus payments are linked to productivity.* ○ *The company is aiming to increase productivity.* ○ *Productivity has fallen* or *risen since the company was taken over.*

productivity agreement /ˌprɒdʌk'tɪvəti əˌgriːmənt/ *noun* an agreement to pay a productivity bonus

productivity bonus /ˌprɒdʌk'tɪvəti ˌbəʊnəs/ *noun* an extra payment made to employees because of increased production per employee

productivity drive /ˌprɒdʌk'tɪvəti draɪv/ *noun* an extra effort to increase productivity

product line /'prɒdʌkt laɪn/ *noun* a series of different products which form a group, all made by the same company ○ *We do not stock that line.* ○ *Computers are not one of our best-selling lines.* ○ *They produce an interesting line in garden tools.*

product management /ˌprɒdʌkt 'mænɪdʒmənt/ *noun* the process of directing the making and selling of a product as an independent item

product mix /'prɒdʌkt mɪks/ *noun* a range of different products which a company has for sale

profession /prə'feʃ(ə)n/ *noun* **1.** an occupation for which official qualifications are needed and which is often made a lifelong career ○ *The managing director is an accountant by profession.* ○ *HR management is now more widely recognized as a profession.* **2.** a group of specialized workers ○ *the accounting profession* ○ *the legal profession*

"…one of the key advantages of an accountancy qualification is its worldwide marketability. Other professions are not so lucky: lawyers, for example, are much more limited in where they can work" [*Accountancy*]

professional /prə'feʃ(ə)n(ə)l/ *adjective* **1.** referring to one of the professions ○ *The accountant sent in his bill for professional services.* ○ *We had to ask our lawyer for professional advice on the contract.* ○ *The professional institute awards diplomas.* □ **professional man**, **professional woman** a man or woman who works in one of the professions such as a

lawyer, doctor or accountant **2.** expert or skilled ○ *Her work is very professional.* ○ *They did a very professional job in designing the new office.* **3.** doing work for money ○ *a professional tennis player* □ **he is a professional troubleshooter** he makes his living by helping companies to sort out their problems ■ *noun* a skilled person or a person who does skilled work for money

professional qualification /prə ˌfeʃ(ə)n(ə)l ˌkwɒlɪfɪ'keɪʃ(ə)n/ *noun* a document which shows that someone has successfully finished a course of study which allows him or her to work in one of the professions

proficiency /prə'fɪʃ(ə)nsi/ *noun* a skill in doing something at more than a basic level ○ *Her proficiency in languages should help in the export department.* ○ *To get the job he had to pass a proficiency test.*

proficient /prə'fɪʃ(ə)nt/ *adjective* capable of doing something well ○ *She is quite proficient in Spanish.* ○ *She is quite proficient in accountancy.*

profile /'prəʊfaɪl/ *noun* a brief description of the characteristics of something or someone ○ *They asked for a profile of the possible partners in the joint venture.* ○ *Her résumé provided a profile of her education and career to date.*

profit /'prɒfɪt/ *noun* money gained from a sale which is more than the money spent on making the item sold or on providing the service offered □ **to take your profit** to sell stock at a higher price than was paid for it, and so realize the profit, rather than to keep it as an investment □ **to show a profit** to make a profit and state it in the company accounts ○ *We are showing a small profit for the first quarter.* □ **to make a profit** to have more money as a result of a deal □ **to move into profit** to start to make a profit ○ *The company is breaking even now, and expects to move into profit within the next two months.* □ **to sell at a profit** to sell at a price which gives you a profit □ **healthy profit** a good or large profit

profitability /ˌprɒfɪtə'bɪləti/ *noun* **1.** the ability to make a profit ○ *We doubt the profitability of the project.* **2.** the amount of profit made as a percentage of costs

profitable /'prɑfɪtəb(ə)l/ *adjective* making a profit ○ *She runs a very profitable employment agency.*

profitably /'prɑfɪtəbli/ *adverb* making a profit ○ *The goal of every company must be to trade profitably.*

profit after tax /ˌprɑfɪt æftər 'tæks/ *noun* same as **net profit**

profit and loss account /ˌprɑfɪt ən 'lɔs əˌkaʊnt/ same as **profit and loss statement**

profit and loss statement /ˌprɑfɪt ən 'lɔs əˌkaʊnt/ *noun* the accounts for a company showing expenditure and income over a period of time, usually one calendar year, balanced to show a final profit or loss. Also called **income statement, profit and loss account, P&L statement** (NOTE: The U.K. term is **consolidated profit and loss account**.)

profit before tax /ˌprɑfɪt bɪ'fɔr 'tæks/ *noun* same as **pretax profit**

profit center /'prɑfɪt ˌsentər/ *noun* a person, unit, or department within an organization which is considered separately for the purposes of calculating a profit ○ *We count the kitchen equipment division as a single profit center.*

profiteer /ˌprɑfɪ'tɪr/ *noun* a person who makes too much profit, especially when goods are rationed or in short supply

profiteering /ˌprɑfɪ'tɪrɪŋ/ *noun* the practice of making too much profit

profit-making /'prɑfɪt ˌmeɪkɪŋ/ *adjective* making a profit, or operated with the primary objective of making a profit ○ *The whole project was expected to be profit-making by 2001 but it still hasn't broken even.* ○ *We hope to make it into a profit-making concern.*

profit margin /'prɑfɪt ˌmɑrdʒɪn/ *noun* the percentage difference between sales income and the cost of sales

profit motive /'prɑfɪt 'moʊtɪv/ *noun* an idea that profit is the most important goal of a business

profit on ordinary activities before tax /ˌprɑfɪt ɑn ˌɔrd(ə)n(ə)ri æk'tɪvətiz bɪˌfɔr 'tæks/ *noun* same as **pretax profit**

profit-oriented company /ˌprɑfɪt ˌɔrientɪd 'kʌmp(ə)ni/ *noun* company which does everything to make a profit

profit-sharing /'prɑfɪt ˌʃerɪŋ/ *noun* an arrangement whereby employees get a share of the profits of the company they work for ○ *The company runs a profit-sharing scheme.*

profit squeeze /'prɑfɪt skwiz/ *noun* a strict control of the amount of profits which companies can pay out as dividend

profits tax /'prɑfɪts tæks/ *noun* a tax to be paid on profits

profit-taking /'prɑfɪt ˌteɪkɪŋ/ *noun* the act of selling investments to realize the profit, rather than keeping them ○ *Stock prices fell under continued profit-taking.*

"…some profit-taking was seen yesterday as investors continued to lack fresh incentives to renew buying activity" [*Financial Times*]

pro forma /proʊ 'fɔrmə/ *adverb* "for the sake of form" ■ *verb* to issue a pro forma invoice ○ *Can you pro forma this order?* ■ *adjective* used to describe an early version of a document that is issued before all the relevant data is available and is usually followed by a final version

pro forma invoice /ˌproʊ ˌfɔrmə 'ɪnvɔɪs/, **pro forma** /proʊ 'fɔrmə/ *noun* an invoice sent to a buyer before the goods are sent, so that payment can be made or so that goods can be sent to a consignee who is not the buyer ○ *They sent us a pro forma invoice.* ○ *We only supply that account on pro forma.*

program[1] /'proʊgræm/ *noun* **1.** a set of instructions telling a computer to perform some task **2.** a set of instructions that tell a computer to carry out specific tasks ■ *verb* to write a program for a computer □ **to program a computer** to install a program in a computer ○ *The computer is programmed to print labels.*

program[2] /'proʊgræm/ *noun U.K.* same as **program**

program evaluation and review technique /ˌproʊgræm ɪˌvælju,eɪʃ(ə)n ən rɪ'vju tekˌnik/ *noun* a way of planning and controlling a large project, concentrating on scheduling and completion on time. Abbreviation **PERT**

programmable /'proʊgræməb(ə)l/ *adjective* possible to program

programming engineer /'proʊgræmɪŋ ˌendʒɪnɪr/ *noun* an engineer in charge of programming a computer system

programming language /'proʊgræmɪŋ ˌlæŋgwɪdʒ/ *noun* a system of signs, letters and words used to instruct a computer

progress noun /'prougres/ the movement of work toward completion ○ *to report on the progress of the work* or *of the negotiations* □ **to make a progress report** to report how work is going □ **in progress** which is being done but is not finished ○ *negotiations in progress* ○ *work in progress* ■ verb /prou'gres/ to move forward, to go ahead ○ *The contract is progressing through various departments.*

progress chaser /'prougres ˌtʃeɪsər/ noun a person whose job is to check that work is being carried out on schedule, that orders are being fulfilled on time, etc.

progressive /prə'gresɪv/ adjective moving forward in stages

progressive taxation /prəˌgresɪv tæk'seɪʃ(ə)n/ noun a taxation system where tax levels increase as the income is higher. Also called **graduated taxation**. Compare **regressive taxation**

progress payment /'prougres ˌpeɪmənt/ noun a payment made as a particular stage of a contract is completed ○ *The fifth progress payment is due in March.*

progress report /'prougres rɪˌpɔrt/ noun a document which describes what progress has been made

prohibitive /prou'hɪbɪtɪv/ adjective with a price so high that you cannot afford to pay it ○ *The cost of redesigning the product is prohibitive.*

project /'prɑdʒekt/ noun **1.** a plan ○ *She has drawn up a project for developing new markets in Europe.* **2.** a particular job of work which follows a plan ○ *We are just completing an engineering project in North Africa.* ○ *The company will start work on the project next month.*

project analysis /'prɑdʒekt əˌnæləsɪs/ noun the examination of all the costs or problems of a project before work on it is started

projected /prə'dʒektɪd/ adjective planned or expected □ **projected sales** a forecast of sales ○ *Projected sales next year should be over $1m.*

project engineer /ˌprɑdʒekt ˌendʒɪ'nɪr/ noun an engineer in charge of a project

projection /prə'dʒekʃən/ noun a forecast of something which will happen in the future ○ *Projection of profits for the next three years.* ○ *The sales manager was asked to draw up sales projections for the next three years.*

project management /ˌprɑdʒekt 'mænɪdʒmənt/ noun the coordination of the financial, material, and human resources needed to complete a project and the organization of the work that the project involves

project manager /ˌprɑdʒekt 'mænɪdʒər/ noun the manager in charge of a project

promise /'prɑmɪs/ noun an act of saying that you will do something □ **to keep a promise** to do what you said you would do ○ *He says he will pay next week, but he never keeps his promises.* □ **to go back on a promise** not to do what you said you would do ○ *The management went back on its promise to increase salaries across the board.* □ **a promise to pay** a promissory note ■ verb to say that you will do something ○ *They promised to pay the last installment next week.* ○ *The personnel manager promised he would look into the grievances of the office staff.*

promissory note /'prɑmɪsəri ˌnout/ noun a document stating that someone promises to pay an amount of money on a specific date

promote /prə'mout/ verb **1.** to give someone a more important job or to move someone to a higher grade ○ *He was promoted from salesman to sales manager.* **2.** to advertise a product □ **to promote a new product** to increase the sales of a new product by a sales campaign, by TV commercials or free gifts, or by giving discounts **3.** □ **to promote a new company** to organize the setting up of a new company

promotion /prə'mouʃ(ə)n/ noun **1.** the fact of being moved up to a more important job ○ *I ruined my chances of promotion when I argued with the managing director.* ○ *The job offers good promotion chances* or *promotion prospects.* □ **to earn promotion** to work hard and efficiently and so be promoted **2.** all means of conveying the message about a product or service to potential customers, e.g., publicity, a sales campaign, TV commercials or free gifts ○ *Our promotion budget has been doubled.* ○ *The promotion team has put forward plans for the launch.* ○ *We are* offering free vacations in Mexico as part of our special in-store promotion. ○ We a running a special promotion offering two for the price of one. □ **promotion of a product** selling a new product by publicity, by a sales campaign, TV commercials, free gifts, or by giving special discounts ○ The promotion budget has been increased to $500,000. ○ He is leading the promotion team in charge of the launch. ○ We a running a special promotion offering two for the price of one. **3.** □ **promotion of a company** the setting up of a new company

promotional /prə'mouʃən(ə)l/ adjective used in an advertising campaign ○ The admen are using balloons as promotional material.

promotional budget /prə ˌmouʃən(ə)l 'bʌdʒət/ noun a forecast of the cost of promoting a new product

promotion ladder /prə'mouʃ(ə)n ˌlædər/ noun a series of steps by which employees can be promoted ○ By being appointed sales manager, she moved several steps up the promotion ladder.

prompt /prɑmpt/ adjective rapid or done immediately ○ We got very prompt service at the complaints desk. ○ Thank you for your prompt reply to my letter. □ **prompt payment** payment made rapidly □ **prompt supplier** a supplier who delivers orders rapidly

promptly /'prɑmptli/ adverb rapidly ○ He replied to my letter very promptly.

proof /pruf/ noun evidence which shows that something is true

-proof /pruf/ suffix preventing something getting in or getting out or harming something ○ a dustproof cover ○ an inflation-proof pension ○ a soundproof studio

prop /prɑp/ noun same as **proprietor**

propaganda /ˌprɑpə'gændə/ noun an attempt to spread an idea through clever use of the media and other forms of communication ○ The charity has been criticized for spreading political propaganda.

property /'prɑpəti/ noun **1.** land and buildings ○ Property taxes are higher in the inner city. ○ They are assessing damage to property or property damage after the storm. ○ The commercial property market is booming. **2.** a building ○ We have several properties for sale in the center of the town. **3.** things which a person or organization owns

property company /'prɑpəti ˌkʌmp(ə)ni/ noun a company which buys buildings to lease them

property developer /'prɑpəti dɪ ˌveləpər/ noun a person who buys old buildings or empty land and plans and builds new houses or factories for sale or rent

proportion /prə'pɔrʃ(ə)n/ noun a part of a total ○ A proportion of the pre-tax profit is set aside for contingencies. ○ Only a small proportion of our sales comes from retail stores. □ **in proportion to** compared to something else, by an amount related to something else ○ Profits went up in proportion to the fall in overhead costs. ○ Sales in Europe are small in proportion to those in the U.S.

proportional /prə'pɔrʃ(ə)n(ə)l/ adjective directly related ○ The increase in profit is proportional to the reduction in overhead.

proportionately /prə'pɔrʃ(ə)nətli/ adverb in a way that is directly related

proposal /prə'pouz(ə)l/ noun **1.** a suggestion, thing which has been suggested ○ to make a proposal or to put forward a proposal to the board □ **the committee turned down the proposal** the committee refused to accept what was suggested **2.** an official document with details of a property or person to be insured which is sent to the insurance company when asking for an insurance

propose /prə'pouz/ verb **1.** to suggest that something should be done □ **to propose a motion** to ask a meeting to vote for a motion and explain the reasons for this □ **to propose someone as president** to ask a group to vote for someone to become president **2.** □ **to propose to** to say that you intend to do something ○ I propose to repay the loan at $20 a month.

proposer /prə'pouzər/ noun a person who proposes a motion at a meeting

proposition /ˌprɑpə'zɪʃ(ə)n/ noun a commercial deal which is suggested □ **it will never be a commercial proposition** it is not likely to make a profit

proprietary /prə'praɪət(ə)ri/ noun, adjective a product, e.g., a medicine which is made and owned by a company

proprietary drug /prə ˌpraɪət(ə)ri 'drʌg/ noun a drug which is made by a particular company and marketed under a brand name

proprietor /prə'praɪətər/ *noun* the owner of a business, especially in the hospitality industry ○ *She is the proprietor of a hotel* or *a hotel proprietor.* ○ *The restaurant has a new proprietor.*

pro rata /,proʊ 'rɑːtə/ *adjective, adverb* at a rate which varies according to the size or importance of something ○ *When part of the shipment was destroyed we received a pro rata payment.* ○ *The full-time pay is $800 a week and the part-timers are paid pro rata.* □ **dividends are paid pro rata** dividends are paid according to the number of shares held

prosecute /'prɑsɪkjuːt/ *verb* to bring someone to court to answer a criminal charge ○ *He was prosecuted for embezzlement.*

prosecuting attorney /,prɑsəkjuːtɪŋ ə'tɜːni/ *noun* a lawyer acting for the prosecution

prosecution /,prɑsɪ'kjuːʃ(ə)n/ *noun* **1.** the act of bringing someone to court to answer a charge ○ *his prosecution for embezzlement* **2.** a party who brings a criminal charge against someone ○ *The costs of the case will be borne by the prosecution.*

prosecution counsel /,prɑsɪ 'kjuːʃ(ə)n ,kaʊnsəl/ *noun U.K.* same as **prosecuting attorney**

prospect /'prɑspekt/ *noun* **1.** a chance or possibility that something will happen in the future □ **her job prospects are good** she is very likely to find a job □ **prospects for the market, market prospects are worse than those of last year** sales in the market are likely to be lower than they were last year **2.** the possibility that something will happen ○ *There is no prospect of negotiations coming to an end soon.* **3.** a person who may become a customer ○ *The sales force were looking out for prospects.*

prospective /prə'spektɪv/ *adjective* possibly happening in the future □ **a prospective buyer** someone who may buy in the future ○ *There is no shortage of prospective buyers for the computer.*

prospective dividend /prə,spektɪv 'dɪvɪdend/ *noun* a dividend which a company expects to pay at the end of the current year

prospects /'prɑspekts/ *plural noun* the possibilities for the future

prospectus /prə'spektəs/ *noun* **1.** *U.K.* same as **brochure 2.** a document which gives information about a company whose stock is being sold to the public for the first time (NOTE: plural is **prospectuses**)

prosperity /prɑ'sperɪti/ *noun* the state of being rich □ **in times of prosperity** when people are rich

prosperous /'prɑsp(ə)rəs/ *adjective* rich ○ *a prosperous shopkeeper* ○ *a prosperous town*

protection /prə'tekʃən/ *noun* the imposing of tariffs to protect domestic producers from competition from imports

protectionism /prə'tekʃənɪz(ə)m/ *noun* the practice of protecting producers in the home country against foreign competitors by banning or taxing imports or by imposing import quotas

protective cover /prə,tektɪv 'kʌvər/ *noun* a cover which protects a machine

protective tariff /prə,tektɪv 'tærɪf/ *noun* a tariff which tries to ban imports to stop them competing with local products

pro tem /,proʊ 'tem/ *adverb* temporarily, for a time

protest *noun* /'proʊtest/ **1.** a statement or action to show that you do not approve of something ○ *to make a protest against high prices* □ **in protest at** showing that you do not approve of something ○ *The staff occupied the offices in protest at the low pay offer.* □ **to do something under protest** to do something, but say that you do not approve of it **2.** an official document which proves that a bill of exchange has not been paid ■ *verb* /prə'test/ **1.** □ **to protest against something** to say that you do not approve of something ○ *The importers are protesting against the ban on luxury goods.* **2.** □ **to protest a bill** to draw up a document to prove that a bill of exchange has not been paid

protest strike /'proʊtest straɪk/ *noun* a strike in protest, intended to call attention to a particular grievance

prototype /'proʊtətaɪp/ *noun* the first model of a new product before it goes into production ○ *a prototype car* ○ *a prototype plane* ○ *The company is showing the prototype of the new model at the exhibition.*

provide /prə'vaɪd/ *verb* **1.** to give or supply something **2.** □ **to provide for** to allow for something which may happen in the future ○ *The contract provides for an annual increase in charges.* ○ *$10,000 of expenses have been provided for in the budget.* **3.** to put money aside in accounts to cover expenditure or loss in the future ○ *$25,000 is provided against bad debts.* □ **to provide someone with something** to supply something to someone ○ *Each rep is provided with a company car.* ○ *Staff uniforms are provided by the hotel.*

provided that /prə'vaɪdɪd 'ðæt/, **providing** /prə'vaɪdɪŋ/ *conjunction* on condition that ○ *the goods will be delivered next week provided* or *providing the drivers are not on strike*

provident /'prɑvɪd(ə)nt/ *adjective* providing benefits in case of illness, old age or other cases of need ○ *a provident fund* ○ *a provident society*

province /'prɑvɪns/ *noun* a large division of a country ○ *the provinces of Canada*

provinces /'prɑvɪnsɪz/ *noun* parts of any country away from the main capital town ○ *There are fewer retail outlets in the provinces than in the capital.*

provincial /prə'vɪnʃ(ə)l/ *adjective* referring to a province or to the provinces ○ *a provincial government* ○ *a provincial branch of a national bank*

provincial government /prə,vɪnʃ(ə)l 'gʌv(ə)nmənt/ *noun* an organization dealing with the affairs of a province or of a state

provision /prə'vɪʒ(ə)n/ *noun* **1.** □ **to make provision for** to see that something is allowed for in the future □ **there is no provision for** *or* **no provision has been made for car parking in the plans for the office building** the plans do not include space for cars to park **2.** a legal condition □ **we have made provision to this effect** we have put into the contract terms which will make this work **3.** an amount of money put aside in accounts for anticipated expenditure where the timing or amount of expenditure is uncertain, often for doubtful debts ○ *The bank has made a $2m provision for bad debts* or *a $5bn provision against Third World loans.*

"...landlords can create short lets of dwellings which will be free from the normal security of tenure provisions" [*Times*]

provisional /prə'vɪʒ(ə)n(ə)l/ *adjective* temporary, not final or permanent ○ *She was given a provisional posting to see* ○ *The sales department has been asked to make a provisional forecast of sales.* ○ *The provisional budget has been drawn up for each department.* ○ *They faxed their provisional acceptance of the contract.*

provisionally /prə'vɪʒ(ə)nəli/ *adverb* not finally ○ *The contract has been accepted provisionally.*

proviso /prə'vaɪzoʊ/ *noun* a condition ○ *We are signing the contract with the proviso that the terms can be discussed again after six months.* (NOTE: The plural is **provisos** or **provisoes**.)

proxy /'prɑksi/ *noun* **1.** a document which gives someone the power to act on behalf of someone else ○ *to sign by proxy* **2.** a person who acts on behalf of someone else ○ *She asked the chairman to act as proxy for her.*

proxy form /'prɑksi fɔrm/, **proxy card** /'prɑksi kɑrd/ *noun* a form that stockholders receive with their invitations to attend an annual meeting, and that they fill in if they want to appoint a proxy to vote for them on a resolution

proxy vote /'prɑksi voʊt/ *noun* a vote made by proxy ○ *The proxy votes were all in favor of the board's recommendation.*

P's ♦ **four P's**

P.S. /'pi'es/ *short for* additional note at the end of a letter ○ *Did you read the P.S. at the end of the letter?* Full form **post scriptum**

PSBR *abbreviation* Public Sector Borrowing Requirement

pt *abbreviation* pint

ptas *abbreviation* pesetas

Pte *abbreviation* (in Singapore) private limited company

Pty. *abbreviation* proprietary company

public /'pʌblɪk/ *adjective* **1.** referring to all the people in general **2.** referring to the government or the state ■ *noun* □ **the public, the general public** the people □ **in public** in front of everyone ○ *In public he said that the company would soon be in profit, but in private he was less optimistic.*

publication /,pʌblɪ'keɪʃ(ə)n/ *noun* **1.** the act of making something public by publishing it ○ *the publication of the latest trade figures* **2.** a printed document which is to be sold or given to the public ○ *We asked the library for a list of government* *publications.* □ **the company has six business publications** the company publishes six magazines or newspapers referring to business

public company /ˌpʌblɪk 'kʌmp(ə)ni/ *noun* same as **public limited company**

public expenditure /ˌpʌblɪk ɪk'spendɪtʃər/ *noun* money spent by the local or central government

public finance /ˌpʌblɪk 'faɪnæns/ *noun* the raising of money by governments by taxes or borrowing, and the spending of it

public funds /ˌpʌblɪk 'fʌndz/ *plural noun* government money available for expenditure

public holiday /ˌpʌblɪk 'hɒlɪdeɪ/ *noun* a day when all employees are entitled to take a holiday

public image /ˌpʌblɪk 'ɪmɪdʒ/ *noun* an idea which the people have of a company or a person ○ *The mayor is trying to improve her public image.*

publicity /pʌ'blɪsəti/ *noun* the process of attracting the attention of the public to products or services by mentioning them in the media

publicity agency /pʌ'blɪsəti ˌeɪdʒənsi/ *noun* an office which organizes publicity for companies who do not have publicity departments

publicity budget /pʌ'blɪsəti ˌbʌdʒət/ *noun* money allowed for expenditure on publicity

publicity campaign /pʌ'blɪsəti kæmˌpeɪn/ *noun* a planned period when publicity takes place ○ *They are working on a campaign to launch a new brand of soap.*

publicity copy /pʌ'blɪsəti ˌkɒpi/ *noun* the text of a proposed advertisement before it is printed ○ *She writes publicity copy for a travel firm.*

publicity department /pʌ'blɪsəti dɪˌpɑːtmənt/ *noun* the section of a company which organizes the company's publicity

publicity director /pʌ'blɪsəti daɪˌrektər/ *noun* the person in charge of a publicity department

publicity expenditure /pʌ'blɪsəti ɪkˌspendɪtʃər/ *noun* money spent on publicity

publicity handout /pʌ'blɪsəti ˌhændaʊt/ *noun* an information sheet which is given to members of the public

publicity material /pʌ'blɪsəti məˌtɪriəl/ *noun* leaflets, adverts, etc., used in publicity (NOTE: no plural in this meaning)

publicity slogan /pʌ'blɪsəti ˌsləʊgən/ *noun* a group of words which can be easily remembered and which is used in publicity for a product ○ *We are using the slogan "Smiths can make it" on all our publicity.*

publicize /'pʌblɪsaɪz/ *verb* to attract people's attention to a product for sale, a service, or an entertainment ○ *The campaign is intended to publicize the services of the tourist board.* ○ *We are trying to publicize our products by advertisements on buses.*

public limited company /ˌpʌblɪk ˌlɪmɪtɪd 'kʌmp(ə)ni/ *noun U.K.* a company whose stock can be bought on the Stock Exchange. Abbreviation **Plc, PLC, plc.** Also called **public company**

publicly held company /ˌpʌblɪkli held 'kʌmp(ə)ni/ *noun* a company controlled by a few stockholders or its directors, but which is quoted on the Stock Exchange and which allows the public to hold a few shares

public monopoly /ˌpʌblɪk mə'nɒpəli/ *noun* a situation where an organization owned and run by the state (e.g., the Post Office) is the only supplier of a product or service

public opinion /ˌpʌblɪk ə'pɪnjən/ *noun* what people think about something

public ownership /ˌpʌblɪk 'əʊnəʃɪp/ *noun* a situation in which the government owns a business, i.e. where an industry is nationalized

public relations /ˌpʌblɪk rɪ'leɪʃ(ə)nz/ *plural noun* the practice of building up and keeping good relations between an organization and the public, or an organization and its employees, so that people know and think well of what the organization is doing ○ *She works in public relations.* ○ *A public relations firm handles all our publicity.* ○ *The company's internal public relations were improved by setting up the house journal.* Abbreviation **PR** (NOTE: takes a singular verb)

public relations department /ˌpʌblɪk rɪ'leɪʃ(ə)nz dɪˌpɑːtmənt/ *noun* the section of a company which deals with relations with the public. Abbreviation **PR department**

public relations exercise /ˌpʌblɪk rɪ 'leɪʃ(ə)nz ˌeksəsaɪz/ *noun* a campaign to improve public relations

public relations officer /ˌpʌblɪk rɪ 'leɪʃ(ə)nz ˌɔfɪsər/ *noun* a person in an organization who is responsible for public relations activities. Abbreviation **PRO**

public sector /'pʌblɪk ˌsektər/ *noun* nationalized industries and services ○ *a report on wage increases in the public sector* or *on public-sector wage increases* Also called **government sector**

Public Sector Borrowing Requirement /ˌpʌblɪk ˌsektər 'bɑroʊɪŋ rɪ ˌkwaɪrmənt/ *noun* the amount of money which a government has to borrow to pay for its own spending. Abbreviation **PBSR**

public transportation /ˌpʌblɪk ˌtrænspər'teɪʃ(ə)n/ *noun* transportation which is used by any member of the public, e.g., buses and trains

public transportation system /ˌpʌblɪk ˌtrænspər'teɪʃ(ə)n ˌsɪstəm/ *noun* a system of trains, buses, etc., used by the general public

public works /ˌpʌblɪk 'wɜrks/ *noun* large construction schemes which benefit the public in general (such as motorways, hospitals, etc.)

publish /'pʌblɪʃ/ *verb* to have a document such as a catalog, book, magazine or newspaper written and printed and then sell or give it to the public ○ *The society publishes its list of members annually.* ○ *The government has not published the figures on which its proposals are based.* ○ *The company publishes six magazines for the business market.*

publisher /'pʌblɪʃər/ *noun* a person or company which publishes books, magazines, etc.

pull /pʊl/ *verb*
  pull off *phrasal verb* to succeed in negotiating a deal (*informal*)
  pull out *phrasal verb* to stop being part of a deal or agreement ○ *Our Australian partners pulled out of the contract.*

pump /pʌmp/ *verb* to put something in by force ○ *Venture capitalists have been pumping money into the company to keep it afloat.*

"…in each of the years 1986 to 1989, Japan pumped a net sum of the order of $100bn into foreign securities, notably into U.S. government bonds" [*Financial Times Review*]

pump priming /'pʌmp ˌpraɪmɪŋ/ *noun* government investment in new projects which it hopes will benefit the economy

punch /pʌntʃ/ *verb*
  punch in *phrasal verb* (*of a worker*) to record the time of arriving for work by putting a card into a special timing machine ○ *If workers do not punch in on arrival at the factory, they may be sent a written warning.*
  punch out *phrasal verb* to record the time of leaving work by putting a card into a time clock

punt /pʌnt/ *noun* **1.** a former unit of currency in the Republic of Ireland **2.** a gamble, bet (*informal*) ○ *That stock is worth a punt.* ○ *He took a punt on the exchange rate falling.* ■ *verb* to gamble or to bet (on something)

punter /'pʌntər/ *noun* **1.** a person who gambles or who hopes to make money in the stock market ○ *The stock price shot up as punters rushed to buy.* **2.** a customer (*informal*) ○ *The product looks attractive but will the punters like it?*

"…if punters don't come in for their regular packet of cigarettes, then they are unlikely to make any impulse buys" [*The Grocer*]

pup /pʌp/ *noun* a worthless item (*informal*) ○ *I've been sold a pup* ○ *That street trader sold me a pup.*

purchase /'pɜrtʃɪs/ *noun* a product or service which has been bought □ **to make a purchase** to buy something ■ *verb* to buy something □ **to purchase something for cash** to pay cash for something

purchase ledger /'pɜrtʃɪs ˌledʒər/ *noun* a book in which purchases are recorded

purchase order /'pɜrtʃɪs ˌɔrdər/ *noun* an official order made out by a purchasing department for goods which a company wants to buy ○ *We cannot supply you without a purchase order number.*

purchase price /'pɜrtʃɪs praɪs/ *noun* a price paid for something

purchaser /'pɜrtʃɪsər/ *noun* a person or company that purchases ○ *The company has found a purchaser for its warehouse.* □ **the company is looking for a purchaser**

the company is trying to find someone who will buy it

purchase requisition /ˌpɜːtʃɪs ˌrekwɪˈzɪʃ(ə)n/ *noun* an instruction from a department within an organization to its purchasing department to buy goods or services, stating the kind and quantity required, and forming the basis of a purchase order

purchase tax /ˈpɜːtʃɪs tæks/ *noun* a tax paid on things which are bought

purchasing /ˈpɜːtʃɪsɪŋ/ *noun, adjective* buying

purchasing department /ˈpɜːtʃɪsɪŋ dɪˌpɑːtmənt/ *noun* the section of a company which deals with the buying of stock, raw materials, equipment, etc.

purchasing manager /ˈpɜːtʃɪsɪŋ ˌmænɪdʒər/ *noun* the head of a purchasing department

purchasing officer /ˈpɜːtʃɪsɪŋ ˌɒfɪsər/ *noun* a person in a company or organization who is responsible for buying stock, raw materials, equipment, etc.

purchasing power /ˈpɜːtʃɪsɪŋ ˌpaʊər/ *noun* the quantity of goods which can be bought by a particular group of people or with a particular sum of money ○ *the purchasing power of the school market* ○ *The purchasing power of the pound has fallen over the last five years.*

purpose /ˈpɜːpəs/ *noun* a goal or plan □ **we need the invoice for tax purposes, for the purpose of declaration to the tax authorities** in order for it to be declared to the tax authorities

push the envelope /ˌpʊʃ ðɪ ˈenvələʊp/ *verb* to go beyond normal limits, especially to attempt to do something that is highly innovative and rather risky

"This work is yet another example of how Lucent continues to push the envelope and lead the evolution towards high-speed mobile data." [*Forbes*]

put /pʊt/ *noun* same as **put option** ■ *verb* to place or to fix □ **the accounts put the stock value at $10,000** the accounts state that the value of the stock is $10,000 □ **to put a proposal to the vote** to ask a meeting to vote for or against a proposal □ **to put a proposal to the board** to ask the board to consider a suggestion

put down *phrasal verb* **1.** to make a deposit ○ *to put down money on a house* **2.** to write an item in a ledger or an account

book ○ *to put down a figure for expenses*

put in *phrasal verb* □ **to put an ad in a paper** to have an ad printed in a newspaper □ **to put in a bid for something** to offer to buy something, usually in writing □ **to put in an estimate for something** to give someone a written calculation of the probable costs of carrying out a job □ **to put in a claim for damage** to ask an insurance company to pay for damage □ **the union put in a 6% wage claim** the union asked for a 6% increase in wages

put into *phrasal verb* □ **to put money into a business** to invest money in a business

put off *phrasal verb* to arrange for something to take place later than planned ○ *The meeting was put off for two weeks.* ○ *She asked if we could put the visit off until tomorrow.*

put on *phrasal verb* **1.** □ **to put an item on the agenda** to list an item for discussion at a meeting □ **to put an embargo on trade** to forbid trade **2.** □ **property shares put on gains of 10%-15%** shares in property companies increased in value by 10%-15%

put out *phrasal verb* to send something out for other people to work on ○ *We are planning to put out most of the work to freelancers.* □ **to put work out to contract** to decide that work should be done by a company on a contract, rather than employ members of staff to do it

put up *phrasal verb* **1.** □ **who put up the money for the store?** who provided the investment money for the store to start? □ **to put something up for sale** to advertise that something is for sale ○ *When he retired he decided to put his condo up for sale.* **2.** to increase something, to make something higher ○ *The store has put up all its prices by 5%.*

put option /ˈpʊt ˌɒpʃən/ *noun* an option to sell a specified number of shares at a specified price within a specified period of time. Also called **put**. Opposite **call option**

PV *abbreviation* present value

pyramid /ˈpɪrəmɪd/ *noun* a hierarchical staff structure in an organization, with few employees at the top and many more at the bottom

pyramiding /'pɪrəmɪdɪŋ/ *noun* **1.** the process of building up a major group by acquiring controlling interests in many different companies, each larger than the original company **2.** the illegal practice of using new investors' deposits to pay the interest on the deposits made by existing investors

pyramid selling /'pɪrəmɪd ˌselɪŋ/ *noun* an illegal way of selling goods or investments to the public, where each selling agent pays for the franchise to sell the product or service, and sells that right on to other agents together with stock, so that in the end the person who makes the most money is the original franchiser, and sub-agents or investors may lose all their investments

Q

QC *abbreviation* quality circle

qty. *abbreviation* quantity

quadruple /'kwɑdrʊp(ə)l/ *verb* to multiply four times ○ *The company's profits have quadrupled over the last five years.*

quadruplicate /kwa'drʊplɪkət/ *noun* □ **in quadruplicate** with the original and three copies ○ *The invoices are printed in quadruplicate.* ○ *The application form should be completed in quadruplicate.*

qualification /,kwɑlɪfɪ'keɪʃ(ə)n/ *noun* a document or some other formal proof of the fact that someone has successfully completed a specialized course of study or has acquired a skill ○ *You must have the right qualifications for the job.* ○ *Job-hunting is difficult if you have no qualifications.*

"...personnel management is not an activity that can ever have just one set of qualifications as a requirement for entry into it" [*Personnel Management*]

qualification of accounts /,kwɑlɪfɪkeɪʃ(ə)n əv ə'kaʊnts/ *noun* same as **auditors' qualification**

qualified /'kwɑlɪfaɪd/ *adjective* **1.** same as **certified** □ **highly qualified** with very good results in examinations or a lot of experience or skills ○ *All our staff are highly qualified.* ○ *They employ twenty-six highly qualified engineers.* **2.** with some reservations or conditions ○ *qualified acceptance of a contract* ○ *The plan received qualified approval from the board.*

"...applicants will be professionally qualified and ideally have a degree in Commerce and postgraduate management qualifications" [*Australian Financial Review*]

qualified accounts /,kwɑlɪfaɪd ə'kaʊnts/ *plural noun* accounts which have been noted by the auditors because they contain something with which the auditors do not agree

qualified auditors' report /,kwɑlɪfaɪd 'ɔdɪtəz rɪ,pɔrt/ *noun* a report from a company's auditors which points out areas in the accounts with which the auditors do not agree or about which they are not prepared to express an opinion or where the auditors believe the accounts as a whole have not been prepared correctly or where they are unable to decide whether the accounts are correct or not

qualify /'kwɑlɪfaɪ/ *verb* **1.** □ **to qualify for** to be entitled to something ○ *The company does not qualify for a government grant.* ○ *She qualifies for unemployment benefit.* **2.** □ **to qualify as** to follow a specialized course of study and pass examinations so that you can do a certain job ○ *She has qualified as an accountant.* ○ *He will qualify as a solicitor next year.* **3.** □ **the auditors have qualified the accounts** the auditors have found something in the accounts of the company which has made them unable to agree that they show a "true and fair" view of the company's financial position

"...federal examiners will also determine which of the privately insured savings and loans qualify for federal insurance" [*Wall Street Journal*]

qualifying period /'kwɑlɪfaɪɪŋ ,pɪriəd/ *noun* a time which has to pass before something or someone qualifies for something, e.g., a grant or subsidy ○ *There is a six-month qualifying period before you can get a grant from the local authority.*

qualifying shares /,kwɑlɪfaɪɪŋ 'ʃerz/ *plural noun* the number of shares you need to hold to get a bonus issue or to be a director of the company, etc.

quality /'kwɑləti/ *noun* what something is like or how good or bad something is ○ *The poor quality of the service led to many complaints.* ○ *There is a market for good-*

quality secondhand computers. □ **we sell only quality farm produce** we sell only farm produce of the best quality

quality circle /'kwɑlɪti ˌsɜrk(ə)l/ *noun* a group of employees in a company who meet to discuss quality controls and working practices. Abbreviation **QC**

quality control /'kwɑləti kənˌtroʊl/ *noun* the process of making sure that the quality of a product is good

quality controller /'kwɑləti kənˌtroʊlər/ *noun* a person who checks the quality of a product

quality label /'kwɑləti ˌleɪb(ə)l/ *noun* a label which states the quality of something

quality of working life /ˌkwɑləti əv 'wɜrkɪŋ laɪf/ *noun* the general satisfaction with your life at work, including the environment, career structure and pay. Abbreviation **QWL**

quango /'kwæŋɡoʊ/ *noun* an official body, set up by a government to investigate or deal with a special problem (NOTE: The plural is **quangos**.)

quantifiable /'kwɑntɪfaɪəb(ə)l/ *adjective* possible to quantify ○ *The effect of the change in the discount structure is not quantifiable.*

quantify /'kwɑntɪfaɪ/ *verb* □ **to quantify the effect of something** to show the effect of something in figures ○ *It is impossible to quantify the effect of the new legislation on our turnover.*

quantity /'kwɑntəti/ *noun* **1.** the amount or number of items ○ *a small quantity of illegal drugs* ○ *She bought a large quantity of spare parts.* **2.** an amount, especially a large amount

quantity discount /ˌkwɑntəti 'dɪskaʊnt/ *noun* a discount given to people who buy large quantities

quantity purchase /'kwɑntəti ˌpɜrtʃɪs/ *noun* a large quantity of goods bought at one time ○ *The company offers a discount for quantity purchase.*

quantity survey /'kwɑntəti ˌsɜrveɪ/ *noun* the process of calculating the amount of materials and cost of labor needed for a construction project

quantity surveyor /ˌkwɑntəti sə'veɪər/ *noun* a person who calculates the amount of materials and cost of labor needed for a construction project

quart /kwɔrt/ *noun* an old measure of liquids or of loose goods, such as seeds (= 1.136 litres)

quarter /'kwɔrtər/ *noun* **1.** one of four equal parts (25%) ○ *She paid only a quarter of the list price.* □ **a quarter of an hour** 15 minutes **2.** a period of three months ○ *The installments are payable at the end of each quarter.* **3.** a 25 cent coin (*informal*)

"…corporate profits for the first quarter showed a 4 per cent drop from last year's final three months" [*Financial Times*]

"…economists believe the economy is picking up this quarter and will do better still in the second half of the year" [*Sunday Times*]

quarter day /'kwɔrtər deɪ/ *noun* a day at the end of a quarter, when rents, fees etc. should be paid

quarterly /'kwɔrtərli/ *adjective, adverb* happening once every three months ○ *There is a quarterly charge for electricity.* ○ *The bank sends us a quarterly statement.* ○ *We agreed to pay the rent quarterly* or *on a quarterly basis.* ■ *noun* the results of a corporation, produced each quarter

quartile /'kwɔrtaɪl/ *noun* one of a series of three figures below which 25%, 50% or 75% of the total falls

quasi- /kweɪzaɪ/ *prefix* almost or which seems like ○ *a quasi-official body*

quasi-public corporation /ˌkweɪzaɪ ˌpʌblɪk ˌkɔrpə'reɪʃ(ə)n/ *noun* a U.S. institution which is privately owned, but which serves a public function, such as the Federal National Mortgage Association

quay /ki/ *noun* the place in a port where ships can tie up □ **price ex quay**, **price ex dock** price of goods after they have been unloaded, not including transportation from the harbor

query /'kwɪri/ *noun* a question ○ *The chief accountant had to answer a mass of queries from the auditors.* ■ *verb* to ask a question about something, to suggest that something may be wrong ○ *The stockholders queried the payments to the chairman's son.*

question /'kwestʃ(ə)n/ *noun* **1.** words which need an answer ○ *The managing director refused to answer questions about redundancies.* ○ *The market research team prepared a series of questions to test the public's reactions to color and price.* ○ *The training manager prepared a series of* questions to test the trainees' reactions in different sales situations. **2.** a problem ○ the main question is that of cost ○ The board discussed the question of redundancy payments. ○ The main question is that of the cost of the training program. ■ **verb 1.** to ask questions ○ The police questioned the accounts staff for four hours. ○ She questioned the chairman on the company's investment policy. **2.** to show doubt about something or suggest that something may be wrong ○ We all question how accurate the data is.

questionnaire /ˌkwestʃə'ner/ noun a printed list of questions aiming at collecting data in an unbiased way, especially used in market research ○ We'll send out a questionnaire to test the opinions of users of the system. ○ We were asked to answer or to fill in a questionnaire about vacations abroad. ○ Questionnaires were handed to the staff asking them about their attitudes to work conditions.

queue /kju/ noun **1.** U.K. same as **line 4 2.** a series of documents such as orders or application forms which are dealt with in order □ **his order went to the end of the queue** his order was dealt with last □ **mortgage queue** a list of people waiting for mortgages ■ verb U.K. to form a line one after the other for something ○ We queued for hours to get tickets.

queuing theory /'kjuin ˌθɪri/ noun a theoretical framework, based on studies of people waiting in lines, that can help to establish the best way of providing a service. Average waiting and service times are calculated using mathematical formulae, and on the basis of these it is possible to decide what would be the most cost-effective number of service facilities and the most efficient way of organizing a process. (NOTE: Queuing theory was first applied to the provision of telephone switching equipment but is now used in many areas, including machine maintenance, production lines, and air transportation.)

quick ratio /ˌkwɪk 'reɪʃiʊ/ noun same as **liquidity ratio**

quid /kwɪd/ noun U.K. one pound Sterling (slang)

quid pro quo /ˌkwɪd proʊ 'kwoʊ/ noun money paid or an action carried out in return for something ○ She agreed to re-

pay the loan early, and as a quid pro quo the bank released the collateral.

quit /kwɪt/ verb to resign or leave a job ○ He quit after an argument with the managing director. ○ Several of the managers are quitting to set up their own company. (NOTE: **quitting – quit**)

quite /kwaɪt/ adverb **1.** more or less ○ she can type quite fast ○ He is quite a good salesman. ○ Sales were quite satisfactory in the first quarter. **2.** very or completely ○ He is quite capable of running the department alone. ○ The company is quite possibly going to be sold. **3.** □ **quite a few, quite a lot** many ○ Quite a few of our sales staff are women. ○ Quite a lot of orders come in the pre-Christmas period.

quorate /'kwɔreɪt/ adjective (meeting) with enough people to form a quorum

COMMENT: If there is a quorum at a meeting, the meeting is said to be "quorate"; if there aren't enough people present to make a quorum, the meeting is "inquorate".

quorum /'kwɔrəm/ noun a minimum number of people who have to be present at a meeting to make it valid □ **to have a quorum** to have enough people present for a meeting to go ahead ○ Do we have a quorum?

quota /'kwoʊtə/ noun a limited amount of something which is allowed to be produced, imported, etc.

quota system /'kwoʊtə ˌsɪstəm/ noun **1.** a system where imports or supplies are regulated by fixed maximum amounts **2.** an arrangement for distribution which allows each distributor only a specific number of items

quotation /kwoʊ'teɪʃ(ə)n/ noun an estimate of how much something will cost ○ They sent in their quotation for the job. ○ In reply please quote this number. ○ We accepted the lowest quotation.

quotation on the Stock Exchange /kwoʊˌteɪʃ(ə)n ɑn ði 'stɑk ɪkˌstʃeɪndʒ/ noun the highest bid or lowest asking price at any given time for a stock on the Stock Exchange

quote /kwoʊt/ verb **1.** to repeat words or a reference number used by someone else ○ He quoted figures from the annual report. ○ In reply please quote this number. ○ When making a complaint please quote *the batch number printed on the box.* ○ *She replied, quoting the number of the account.* **2.** to estimate what a cost or price is likely to be ○ *to quote a price for supplying stationery* ○ *Their prices are always quoted in dollars.* ○ *He quoted me a price of $1,026.* ○ *Can you quote for supplying 20,000 envelopes?* ■ *noun* an estimate of how much something will cost (*informal*) ○ *to give someone a quote for supplying computers* ○ *We have asked for quotes for refitting the store.* ○ *Her quote was the lowest of three.* ○ *We accepted the lowest quote.*

quoted company /ˌkwoʊtɪd ˈkʌmp(ə)ni/ *noun* a company whose stock can be bought or sold on the Stock Exchange

quoted investments /ˌkwoʊtɪd ɪn ˈvestmənts/ *noun* investments which are listed on a Stock Exchange

quoted shares /ˌkwoʊtɪd ˈʃerz/, **quoted stocks** *plural noun* stock which can be bought or sold on the Stock Exchange

qwerty keyboard /ˈkwɜrti ˌkibɔrd/ *noun* an English language keyboard, where the first letters of the top row are Q-W-E-R-T-Y ○ *The computer has a normal qwerty keyboard.*

QWL *abbreviation* quality of working life

R

racial discrimination /ˌreɪʃ(ə)l dɪsˌkrɪmɪˈneɪʃ(ə)n/ *noun* the practice of treating a person differently (usually worse) because of their race ○ *The organization was accused of racial discrimination in selecting managers.*

rack /ræk/ *noun* a frame to hold items for display ○ *a magazine rack* ○ *Put the birthday-card display rack near the checkout.* ○ *We need a bigger display rack for these magazines.*

racket /ˈrækɪt/ *noun* an illegal deal which makes a lot of money ○ *She runs a cut-price ticket racket.*

racketeer /ˌrækɪˈtɪr/ *noun* a person who runs a racket

racketeering /ˌrækɪˈtɪrɪŋ/ *noun* the crime of carrying on an illegal business to make money

"...he was charged with 98 counts of racketeering and securities fraud and went on to serve two years in jail. He was banned for life from the securities industry" [*Times*]

rack jobber /ˈræk ˌdʒɑbər/ *noun* a wholesaler who sells goods by putting them on racks in retail stores

rack rent /ˈræk rent/ *noun* **1.** a very high rent **2.** full yearly rent of a property rented on a normal lease

radio frequency identification /ˈreɪdioʊ ˌfrikwənsi aɪˌdentɪfɪkeɪʃ(ə)n/ *noun* a method of using radio waves to transfer data between a scanner and a tag on a product that is located at some distance away. Abbreviation **RFID**

raid /reɪd/ *noun* a sudden attack

raider /ˈreɪdər/ *noun* a person or company that buys a stake in another company before making a hostile takeover bid. Also called **corporate raider**

"...bear raiding involves trying to depress a target company's share price by heavy selling of its shares, spreading adverse rumours or a combination of the two. As an added refinement, the raiders may sell short. The aim is to push down the price so that the raiders can buy back the shares they sold at a lower price" [*Guardian*]

rail /reɪl/ *noun* a railroad system ○ *Six million commuters travel to work by rail each day.* ○ *We ship all our goods by rail.* ○ *Rail travelers are complaining about rising fares.* ○ *Rail travel is cheaper than air travel.* □ **free on rail (FOR)** a price including all the seller's costs until the goods are delivered to the railroad for shipment

railhead /ˈreɪlhed/ *noun* the end of a railroad line ○ *The goods will be sent to the railhead by truck.*

railroad /ˈreɪlroʊd/ *noun* a system using trains to carry passengers and goods ○ *The country's railroad network is being modernized.*

railway /ˈreɪlweɪ/ *noun* U.K. same as **railroad**

raise /reɪz/ *noun* an increase in salary ○ *He asked the boss for a raise.* ○ *She is pleased – she has had her raise.* ○ *She got her raise last month.* (NOTE: The U.K. term is **rise**.) ■ *verb* **1.** to ask a meeting to discuss a question ○ *to raise a question* or *a point at a meeting* ○ *In answer to the questions raised by Mr Smith.* ○ *The chairman tried to prevent the question of redundancies being raised.* **2.** to increase or to make higher ○ *The government has raised the tax levels.* ○ *Air fares will be raised on June 1st.* ○ *The company raised its dividend by 10%.* ○ *When the company raised its prices, it lost half of its share of the market.* ○ *The organization will raise wages if inflation gets worse.* ○ *This increase in production will raise the standard of living in the area.* **3.** to obtain money ○ *The company is trying to raise the capital to fund its expansion program.* ○ *The government raises more money by indirect taxation than by direct.* ○ *Where* *will he raise the money from to start up his business?*

"...the company said yesterday that its recent share issue has been oversubscribed, raising A$225.5m" [*Financial Times*]

"...investment trusts can raise capital, but this has to be done as a company does, by a rights issue of equity" [*Investors Chronicle*]

"...over the past few weeks, companies raising new loans from international banks have been forced to pay more" [*Financial Times*]

rake /reɪk/ *verb*

    rake in *phrasal verb* to gather something together □ **to rake in cash**, **to rake it in** to make a lot of money

rake-off /'reɪk ɔf/ *noun* a person's share of profits from a deal, especially if obtained illegally ○ *The group gets a rake-off on all the company's sales.* ○ *He got a $100,000 rake-off for introducing the new business.* (NOTE: The plural is **rake-offs**.)

rally /'ræli/ *noun* a rise in price when the trend has been downward ○ *Stocks staged a rally on the Stock Exchange.* ○ *After a brief rally shares fell back to a new low.* ■ *verb* to rise in price, when the trend has been downward ○ *Stocks rallied on the news of the latest government figures.*

"...when Japan rallied, it had no difficulty in surpassing its previous all-time high, and this really stretched the price-earnings ratios into the stratosphere" [*Money Observer*]

"...bad news for the U.S. economy ultimately may have been the cause of a late rally in stock prices yesterday" [*Wall Street Journal*]

RAM /ræm/ *abbreviation* random access memory

ramp /ræmp/ *noun* an act of buying shares in order to force up the price (as when a company buys its own shares illegally during a takeover bid)

R&D *abbreviation* research and development

random /'rændəm/ *adjective* done without making any special selection □ **at random** without special selection ○ *The director picked out two sales reports at random.*

random access memory /,rændəm 'ækses ,mem(ə)ri/ *noun* memory that allows access to any location in any order without having to access the rest of memory. Abbreviation **RAM**

random check /,rændəm 'tʃek/ *noun* a check on items taken from a group without any special selection

random error /,rændəm 'erər/ *noun* a computer error for which there is no special reason

random sample /,rændəm 'sæmpəl/ *noun* a sample taken without any selection

random sampling /,rændəm 'sæmplɪŋ/ *noun* the action of choosing samples for testing without any special selection

range /reɪndʒ/ *noun* **1.** a series of items ○ *Their range of products* or *product range is too narrow.* ○ *We offer a wide range of sizes* or *range of styles.* ○ *There are a whole range of alternatives for the new salary plan.* **2.** a spread of sizes or amounts within fixed limits ○ *We make shoes in a wide range of prices.* ○ *The company's salary scale ranges from $5,000 for a trainee to $50,000 for the managing director.* **3.** a set of activities or products of the same general type or variety ○ *This falls within the company's range of activities.* ■ *verb* to be within a group of sizes or amounts falling within fixed limits ○ *The company sells products ranging from cheap downmarket pens to imported luxury items.* ○ *The company's salary scale ranges from $10,000 for a trainee to $150,000 for the managing director.* ○ *Our activities range from mining in the U.S. to computer services in Scotland.*

rank /ræŋk/ *noun* a position in a company or an organization, especially one which shows how important someone is relative to others ○ *All managers are of equal rank.* ○ *Promotion means moving up from a lower rank.* □ **in rank order** in order according to position of importance ■ *verb* **1.** to classify in order of importance ○ *Candidates are ranked in order of their test results.* **2.** to be in a position ○ *The non-voting shares rank equally with the voting shares.* □ **all managers rank equally** all managers have the same status in the company

rank and file /,ræŋk ən 'faɪl/ *noun* the ordinary members of a labor union or other association ○ *The rank and file of the labor union membership.* ○ *The decision was not liked by the rank and file.* □ **rank-and-file members** ordinary members

ranking /'ræŋkɪŋ/ *adjective* in a certain position ○ *a high-ranking official* □ **she is the top-ranking, the senior-ranking official in the delegation** she is the member of the delegation who occupies the highest official post

rare /rer/ *adjective* not common ○ *Experienced salesmen are rare these days.* ○ *It is rare to find a small business with good cash flow.*

rarely /'rerli/ *adverb* not often ○ *The company's stock is rarely sold on the Stock Exchange.* ○ *The chairman is rarely in his office on Friday afternoons.*

rata /'rɑtə/ ♦ **pro rata**

ratable value /ˌreɪtəb(ə)l 'vælju/ *noun* ♦ **rateable value**

rate /reɪt/ *noun* **1.** the money charged for time worked or work completed **2.** an amount of money paid, e.g., as interest or dividend, shown as a percentage **3.** the value of one currency against another ○ *What is today's rate* or *the current rate for the dollar?* □ **to calculate costs on a fixed exchange rate** to calculate costs on an exchange rate which does not change **4.** an amount, number or speed compared with something else ○ *the rate of increase in lay-offs* ○ *The rate of absenteeism* or *The absenteeism rate always increases in fine weather.* ■ *verb* □ **to rate someone highly** to value someone, to think someone is very good

rateable value /ˌreɪtəb(ə)l 'vælju/ *noun U.K.* a value of a property as a basis for calculating local taxes (NOTE: The U.S. spelling of "rateable" is "ratable")

rate card /reɪt kɑrd/ *noun* a list of charges for advertising issued by a newspaper or magazine

rate of exchange /ˌreɪt əv ɪks 'tʃeɪndʒ/ *noun* same as **exchange rate** ○ *The current rate of exchange is $1.60 to the pound.*

rate of inflation /ˌreɪt əv ɪn'fleɪʃ(ə)n/ *noun* the percentage increase in prices over a twelve-month period

rate of interest /ˌreɪt əv 'ɪntrəst/ *noun* same as **interest rate**

rate of production /ˌreɪt əv prə 'dʌkʃən/ *noun* the speed at which items are made. Also called **production rate**

rate of return /ˌreɪt əv rɪ't3rn/ *noun* the amount of interest or dividend which comes from an investment, shown as a percentage of the money invested

rate of sales /ˌreɪt əv 'seɪlz/ *noun* the speed at which units are sold

rate of unemployment /ˌreɪt əv ˌʌnɪm'plɔɪmənt/ *noun* same as **unemployment rate**

ratification /ˌrætɪfɪ'keɪʃ(ə)n/ *noun* official approval ○ *The agreement has to go to the board for ratification.*

ratify /'rætɪfaɪ/ *verb* to approve officially ○ *The agreement has to be ratified by the board.* (NOTE: **ratifies – ratifying – ratified**)

rating /'reɪtɪŋ/ *noun* the act of giving something a value, or the value given

rating officer /'reɪtɪŋ ˌɔfɪsər/ *noun U.K.* same as **assessor**

ratings /'reɪtɪŋz/ *plural noun* the estimated number of people who watch TV programs ○ *The show is high in the ratings, which means it will attract good publicity.*

ratio /'reɪʃioʊ/ *noun* a proportion or quantity of something compared to something else ○ *the ratio of successes to failures* ○ *Our product outsells theirs by a ratio of two to one.* ○ *With less manual work available, the ratio of employees to managers is decreasing.*

ration /'ræʃ(ə)n/ *verb* to allow someone only a certain amount (of food or money) ○ *to ration investment capital* or *to ration funds for investment* □ **to ration mortgages** to make only a certain amount of money available for house mortgages, and so restrict the number of mortgages which can be given ○ *Mortgages are rationed for first-time buyers.*

rationale /ˌræʃə'nɑrl/ *noun* a set of reasons for doing something ○ *I do not understand the rationale behind the decision to sell the warehouse.*

rationalization /ˌræʃ(ə)nəlaɪ'zeɪʃ(ə)n/ *noun* a process designed to make an organization efficient and profitable again when its performance or results have been poor, which usually involves changes in organization structure, employee dismissals, plant closures and cutbacks in supplies and resources

rationalize /'ræʃ(ə)nəlaɪz/ *verb* to make something more efficient ○ *The rail company is trying to rationalize its freight* *services.* ○ *The organization is trying to rationalize its salary scales.*

rationing /ˈræʃ(ə)nɪŋ/ *noun* the act of allowing only a certain amount of something to be sold ○ *There may be a period of food rationing this winter.* ○ *Building societies are warning of mortgage rationing.*

rat race /ˈræt reɪs/ *noun* competition for success in business or in a career ○ *He decided to get out of the rat race and buy a small farm.*

raw data /ˌrɔ ˈdeɪtə/ *noun* data as it is put into a computer, without being analyzed

raw materials /ˌrɔ məˈtɪriəlz/ *plural noun* basic materials which have to be treated or processed in some way before they can be used, e.g., wood, iron ore, or crude petroleum

Rd *abbreviation* road

R/D *abbreviation* refer to drawer

re /ri/ *preposition* about, concerning or referring to ○ *re your inquiry of May 29th* ○ *re: Smith's memo of yesterday* ○ *re: the agenda for the annual meeting*

re- /ri/ *prefix* again

react /riˈækt/ *verb* □ **to react to** to do or to say something in reply to what someone has done or said ○ *Stocks reacted sharply to the fall in the exchange rate.* ○ *How will the chairman react when we tell him the news?*

readjust /ˌriəˈdʒʌst/ *verb* to adjust something again or in a new way, or to change in response to new conditions ○ *to readjust prices to take account of the rise in the costs of raw materials* ○ *to readjust salary scales* ○ *Stock prices readjusted quickly to the news of the devaluation.*

readjustment /ˌriəˈdʒʌstmənt/ *noun* an act of readjusting ○ *a readjustment in pricing* ○ *After the devaluation there was a period of readjustment in the exchange rates.*

read only memory (ROM) /ˌrid ˌoʊnli ˈmeməri/ *noun* a computer memory device that has had data written into it when it is manufactured, and so can only be read but not written to

readvertise /riˈædvərtaɪz/ *verb* to advertise again ○ *All the candidates failed the test so we will just have to readvertise.*

□ **to readvertise a post** to put in a second advertisement for a vacant position

readvertisement /ˌriədˈvɜrtɪsmənt/ *noun* a second advertisement for a vacant position ○ *The readvertisement attracted only two new applicants.*

ready /ˈredi/ *adjective* **1.** fit to be used or to be sold ○ *The order will be ready for delivery next week.* ○ *The driver had to wait because the shipment was not ready.* **2.** quick □ **these items find a ready sale in the Middle East** these items sell rapidly or easily in the Middle East

ready cash /ˌredi ˈkæʃ/ *noun* money which is immediately available for payment

ready-made /ˌredi ˈmeɪd/, **ready-to-wear** /ˌredi tə ˈwer/ *adjective* referring to clothes which are mass-produced and not made for each customer personally ○ *The ready-to-wear trade has suffered from foreign competition.*

ready money /ˌredi ˈmʌni/ *noun* cash or money which is immediately available

real /riəl/ *adjective* **1.** genuine and not an imitation ○ *His briefcase is made of real leather* or *he has a real leather briefcase.* ○ *That car is a real bargain at $300.* **2.** (*of prices or amounts*) shown in terms of money adjusted for inflation □ **in real terms** actually or really ○ *Salaries have gone up by 3% but with inflation running at 5% that is a fall in real terms.*

real earnings /ˌriəl ˈɜrnɪŋz/, **real wages** /ˌriəl ˈweɪdʒɪz/ *plural noun* income which is available for spending after tax and other contributions have been deducted, corrected for inflation. Also called **real income**, **real wages**

real estate /ˈriəl ɪˌsteɪt/ *noun* property in the form of land or buildings

"…on top of the cost of real estate, the investment in inventory and equipment to open a typical warehouse comes to around $5 million" [*Duns Business Month*]

real estate agency /ˈriəl ɪˌsteɪt ˌeɪdʒənsi/ *noun* an office which arranges for the sale of properties

real estate agent /ˈriəl ɪˌsteɪt ˌeɪdʒənt/, **real estate broker** *noun* a person who sells property for customers

real estate developer /ˈriəl ɪˌsteɪt dɪˌveləpər/ *noun* a person or company that erects buildings on vacant land or improves buildings to increase their value

real estate investment trust /ˌrɪəl ɪ ˌsteɪt ɪnˈvestmənt trʌst/ *noun* a public trust company which invests only in property. Abbreviation **REIT**

realign /ˌriəˈlaɪn/ *verb* to change the relationship between things ○ *to realign currencies*

realignment /ˌriəˈlaɪnmənt/ *noun* the process of changing a system, so that different parts are in a different relationship to each other □ **a currency realignment** a change in the international exchange rates

real income /ˌrɪəl ˈɪnkʌm/ *noun* same as **real earnings**

realisable assets /ˌrɪəlaɪzəb(ə)l ˈæsets/ *noun* assets which can be sold for money

realization /ˌrɪəlaɪˈzeɪʃ(ə)n/ *noun* **1.** a gradual understanding ○ *The chairman's realization that he was going to be outvoted.* **2.** the act of making real □ **the realization of a project** putting a project into action ○ *The plan moved a stage nearer realization when the contracts were signed.*

realization of assets /ˌrɪəlaɪzeɪʃ(ə)n əv ˈæsets/ *noun* the act of selling of assets for money

realize /ˈrɪəlaɪz/ *verb* **1.** to understand clearly ○ *He soon realized the meeting was going to vote against his proposal.* ○ *The small storekeepers realized that the hypermarket would take away some of their trade.* ○ *When she went into the manager's office she did not realize she was going to be promoted.* **2.** to make something become real □ **to realize a project or a plan** to put a project or a plan into action **3.** to sell for money ○ *The company was running out of cash, so the board decided to realize some property or assets.* ○ *The sale realized $100,000.*

realized profit /ˌrɪəlaɪzd ˈprɒfɪt/ *noun* an actual profit made when something is sold, as opposed to paper profit

really /ˈrɪəli/ *adverb* in fact ○ *The company is really making an acceptable profit.* ○ *The office building really belongs to the chairman's father.* ○ *The shop is really a general store, though it does carry some books.*

real time /ˈrɪəl taɪm/ *noun* the time when a computer is working on the processing of data while the event to which the data refers is actually taking place ○ *The website allows you to check stock prices in real time or gives real time information on share prices.*

real time company /ˌrɪəl taɪm ˈkʌmp(ə)ni/ *noun* a company that can respond immediately to customer demands by communicating over the Internet

real time credit card processing /ˌrɪəl taɪm ˈkredɪt kɑːd ˌprəsesɪŋ/ *noun* online checking of a credit card that either approves or rejects it for use during a transaction

real time manager /ˌrɪəl taɪm ˈmænɪdʒər/ *noun* a manager who uses the Internet or similar technologies to provide the immediate service that customers expect

real-time system /ˈrɪəl taɪm ˌsɪstəm/ *noun* a computer system where data is inputted directly into the computer which automatically processes it to produce information which can be used immediately

real time transaction /ˌrɪəl taɪm trænˈzækʃən/ *noun* an Internet payment transaction that is either approved or rejected immediately when the customer completes the online order form

Realtor™ /ˈrɪəltər/ *trademark* a trademark, used by a real estate agent or broker who is a member of the National Association of Realtors

realty /ˈrɪəlti/ *noun* property or real estate

real wages /rɪəl ˈweɪdʒɪz/ *plural noun* same as **real earnings**

reapplication /ˌriæplɪˈkeɪʃ(ə)n/ *noun* a second or subsequent application for a job

reapply /ˌriəˈplaɪ/ *verb* to apply again ○ *When he saw that the job had still not been filled, he reapplied for it.* (NOTE: **reapplies – reapplying – reapplied**)

reappoint /ˌriəˈpɔɪnt/ *verb* to appoint someone again ○ *She was reappointed chairman for a further three-year period.*

reappointment /ˌriəˈpɔɪntmənt/ *noun* the act of being reappointed ○ *On her reappointment as chairman, she thanked the board for their support.* ○ *The board decided to offer him reappointment for a further two years at the end of his fixed-term contract.*

reason /ˈriːz(ə)n/ *noun* an explanation as to why something has happened ○ *the airline gave no reason for the plane's late ar-*

rival ○ *The chairman was asked for his reasons for canceling the meeting.* ○ *The company gave no reason for the sudden closure of the factory.*

reasonable /'riz(ə)nəb(ə)l/ *adjective* **1.** sensible, or not annoyed ○ *The manager of the store was very reasonable when I tried to explain that I had left my credit cards at home.* □ **no reasonable offer refused** we will accept any offer which is not extremely low **2.** moderate or not expensive ○ *The union has decided to put in a reasonable wage claim.*

reassess /,riə'ses/ *verb* to assess again ○ *The manager was asked to reassess the department staff, after the assessments were badly done by the supervisors.*

reassessment /,riə'sesmənt/ *noun* a new assessment

reassign /,riə'saɪn/ *verb* to assign something again or to assign someone to a new position

reassignment /,riə'saɪnmənt/ *noun* a new assignment

reassure /,riə'ʃʊr/ *verb* to make someone calm or less worried ○ *The markets were reassured by the government statement on import controls.* ○ *The manager tried to reassure her that she would not lose her job.*

rebate /'ribeɪt/ *noun* **1.** a reduction in the amount of money to be paid ○ *We are offering a 10% rebate on selected goods.* **2.** money returned to someone because they have paid too much ○ *She got a tax rebate at the end of the year.*

rebound /rɪ'baʊnd/ *verb* to go back up again quickly ○ *The market rebounded with the news of the government's decision.*

recall /rɪ'kɔl/ *verb* (*of a manufacturer*) to ask for products to be returned because of possible faults ○ *They recalled 10,000 washing machines because of a faulty electrical connection.* ■ *noun* the ability to remember an advertisement

recapitalization /riˌkæpɪt(ə)laɪ'zeɪʃ(ə)n/ *noun* a change in the capital structure of a company as when new shares are issued, especially when undertaken to avoid the company going into liquidation

recapitalize /riˈkæpɪt(ə)laɪz/ *verb* to change the capital structure of a company

(as by issuing new shares), especially to avoid the company going into liquidation

recd. *abbreviation* received

receipt /rɪ'sit/ *noun* **1.** a piece of paper showing that money has been paid or that something has been received ○ *He kept the customs receipt to show that he had paid duty on the goods.* ○ *She lost her taxi receipt.* ○ *Keep the receipt for items purchased in case you need to change them later.* **2.** the act of receiving something ○ *Goods will be supplied within thirty days of receipt of order.* ○ *Invoices are payable within thirty days of receipt.* ○ *On receipt of the notification, the company lodged an appeal.* □ **to acknowledge receipt of a letter** to write to say that you have received a letter ○ *We acknowledge receipt of your letter of the 15th.* ◊ **receipts** ■ *verb* to stamp or to sign a document to show that it has been received, or to stamp an invoice to show that it has been paid ○ *Receipted invoices are filed in the ring binder.*

receipt book /rɪ'sit bʊk/ *noun* a book of blank receipts to be filled in when purchases are made

receipts /rɪ'sits/ *plural noun* money taken in sales ○ *to itemize receipts and expenditure* ○ *Receipts are down against the same period of last year.*

receipts and payments basis /rɪˌsits ən 'peɪmənts ˌbeɪsɪs/ *noun U.K.* same as **cash basis**

receivable /rɪ'sivəb(ə)l/ *adjective* able to be received

receivables /rɪ'sivəb(ə)lz/ *plural noun* money which is owed to a company

receive /rɪ'siv/ *verb* to get something which is given or delivered to you ○ *We received the payment ten days ago.* ○ *The employees have not received any salary for six months.* ○ *The goods were received in good condition.* □ **"received with thanks"** words put on an invoice to show that a sum has been paid

receiver /rɪ'sivər/ *noun* **1.** a person who receives something ○ *He signed as receiver of the shipment.* **2.** same as **official receiver** ■ a person appointed by a court to help a company which is insolvent to avoid liquidation (NOTE: The U.K. term is **administrator**)

receivership /rɪ'sivəʃɪp/ *noun* □ **the company went into receivership** the company was put into the hands of a receiver

"...it suggests a classic case for receivership. There appear to be good businesses to be sold to the right owner within a group that is terminally sick" [*Times*]

receiving /rɪ'siviŋ/ *noun* an act of getting something which has been delivered

receiving clerk /ri'siviŋ klɜrk/ *noun* an official who works in a receiving office

receiving department /ri'siviŋ dɪ ˌpɑrtmənt/ *noun* a section of a company which deals with incoming goods or payments

receiving office /rɪ'siviŋ ˌɔfɪs/ *noun* an office where goods or payments are received

receiving order /ri'siviŋ ˌɔrdər/ *noun* an order from a court appointing an official receiver to a company

reception /rɪ'sepʃən/ *noun* a place in a hotel or office where visitors register or say who they have come to see

reception clerk /rɪ'sepʃ(ə)n klɜrk/ *noun* a person who works at a reception desk

reception desk /rɪ'sepʃ(ə)n desk/ *noun* a desk where customers or visitors check in

receptionist /rɪ'sepʃənɪst/ *noun* a person in a hotel or office who meets guests or clients, answers the phone, etc.

recession /rɪ'seʃ(ə)n/ *noun* a period where there is a decline in trade or in the economy ○ *The recession has reduced profits in many companies.* ○ *Several firms have closed factories because of the recession.*

COMMENT: There are various ways of deciding if a recession is taking place: the usual one is when the GNP falls for three consecutive quarters.

recipient /rɪ'sɪpiənt/ *noun* a person who receives something ○ *She was the recipient of an allowance from the company.* ○ *He was the recipient of the award for salesperson of the year.* ○ *A registered letter must be signed for by the recipient.*

reciprocal /rɪ'sɪprək(ə)l/ *adjective* done by one person, company, or country to another one, which does the same thing in return ○ *We signed a reciprocal agreement* or *a reciprocal contract with a Russian company.*

reciprocal holdings /rɪˌsɪprək(ə)l 'hoʊldɪŋz/ *plural noun* a situation in which two companies own stock in each other to prevent takeover bids

reciprocal trade /rɪˌsɪprək(ə)l 'treɪd/ *noun* trade between two countries

reciprocate /rɪ'sɪprəkeɪt/ *verb* to do the same thing for someone as that person has done for you ○ *They offered us an exclusive agency for their cars and we reciprocated with an offer of the agency for our buses.*

reckon /'rekən/ *verb* **1.** to calculate something ○ *to reckon the costs at $25,000* ○ *We reckon the loss to be over $1m.* ○ *They reckon the insurance costs to be too high.* **2.** □ **to reckon on** to depend on, to expect something to happen ○ *They reckon on being awarded the contract.* ○ *He can reckon on the support of the managing director.*

reclaim /rɪ'kleɪm/ *verb* to claim something which you owned before ○ *After he stopped paying the installments, the finance company tried to reclaim his car.*

recognize /'rekəgnaɪz/ *verb* □ **to recognize a union** to agree that a union can act on behalf of employees in a company ○ *Although more than half the staff had joined the union, the management refused to recognize it.*

recognized agent /ˌrekəgnaɪzd 'eɪdʒənt/ *noun* an agent who is approved by the company for which they act

recommend /ˌrekə'mend/ *verb* **1.** to suggest that something should be done ○ *The investment adviser recommended buying supermarket stocks.* ○ *We do not recommend bank stocks as a safe investment.* ○ *The management consultant recommended a different form of pay structure.* **2.** to say that someone or something is good ○ *He recommended a store in the mall for shoes.* ○ *I certainly would not recommend Miss Smith for the job.* ○ *The board meeting recommended a dividend of 10 cents a share.* ○ *Can you recommend a good hotel in Chicago?*

"...the supermarkets have been fair with pricing – not trying to beat us down as many people might think. They are all selling at the recommended price which means the same as our smaller retail customers" [*The Grocer*]

recommendation /ˌrekəmen'deɪʃ(ə)n/ *noun* an act of saying that someone or something is good ○ *We appointed him on the recommendation of his former employer.*

recommended retail price /ˌrekəmendɪd 'riːteɪl ˌpraɪs/ *noun* the price at which a manufacturer suggests a product should be sold on the retail market, though this may be reduced by the retailer. Abbreviation **RRP**. Also called **administered price**

reconcile /'rekənsaɪl/ *verb* **1.** to make two financial accounts or statements agree ○ *She is trying to reconcile one account with another* or *to reconcile the two accounts.* **2.** to make two things agree ○ *Their manager tried to reconcile the different points of view.*

reconciliation /ˌrekənsɪli'eɪʃ(ə)n/, **reconcilement** /'rekənsaɪlmənt/ *noun* the act of making two accounts or statements agree

reconciliation statement /ˌrekənsɪli 'eɪʃ(ə)n ˌsteɪtmənt/ *noun* a statement which explains how two accounts can be made to agree

reconsider /ˌriːkən'sɪdər/ *verb* to think again about a decision which has already been made ○ *The union asked management to reconsider their decision on closing the factory.* ○ *The interim agreement will provide a breathing space while both sides reconsider their positions.*

reconstruction /ˌriːkən'strʌkʃən/ *noun* **1.** the process of building again ○ *The economic reconstruction of an area after a disaster.* **2.** new way of organizing □ **the reconstruction of a company** restructuring the finances of a company by transferring the assets to a new company

record *noun* /'rekɔːd/ **1.** a report of something which has happened ○ *The chairman signed the minutes as a true record of the last meeting.* ○ *She has a very poor time-keeping record.* □ **for the record** *or* **to keep the record straight** in order that everyone knows what the real facts of the matter are ○ *For the record, I should like to say that these sales figures have not yet been checked by the sales department.* □ **on record** reported in a published document, e.g. in a newspaper ○ *The chairman is on record as saying that profits are set to rise.* □ **off the record** un-

officially, in private ○ *He made some remarks off the record about the disastrous home sales figures.* **2.** a description of what has happened in the past ○ *the salesperson's record of service* or *service record* ○ *the company's record in industrial relations* **3.** a success which is better than anything before ○ *Last year was a record year for the company.* ○ *Our top sales rep has set a new record for sales per call.* □ **record sales, record losses, record profits** sales, losses or profits which are higher than ever before □ **we broke our record for June** we sold more than we have ever sold before in June ○ *Sales last year equaled the record set in 1997.* ■ *verb* /rɪ'kɔːd/ to note or report something ○ *The company has recorded another year of increased sales.*

record-breaking /'rekɔːd ˌbreɪkɪŋ/ *adjective* better or worse than anything which has happened before ○ *We are proud of our record-breaking profits in 2000.*

record date /'rekɔːd deɪt/ *noun* the date when a computer data entry or record is made

recorded delivery /ˌsɜːtɪfaɪd 'meɪl/ *noun U.K.* same as **certified mail**

recording /rɪ'kɔːdɪŋ/ *noun* the act of making a note of something ○ *the recording of an order* or *of a complaint*

records /'rekɔːdz/ *plural noun* documents which give information ○ *The names of customers are kept in the company's records.* ○ *We find from our records that our invoice number 1234 has not been paid.*

recoup /rɪ'kuːp/ *verb* □ **to recoup your losses** to get back money which you thought you had lost

recourse /rɪ'kɔːs/ *noun* a right of a lender to compel a borrower to repay money borrowed □ **to decide to have recourse to the courts to obtain money due** to decide in the end to sue someone to obtain money owed □ **without recourse** words used to show that the endorser of a bill (as an agent acting for a principal) is not responsible for paying it

recover /rɪ'kʌvər/ *verb* **1.** to get back something which has been lost ○ *to recover damages from the driver of the car* ○ *to start a court action to recover property* ○ *He never recovered his money.* ○ *The ini-*

tial investment was never recovered. **2.** to get better, to rise ○ *The market has not recovered from the rise in oil prices.* ○ *The stock market fell in the morning, but recovered during the afternoon.*

recoverable /rɪˈkʌv(ə)rəb(ə)l/ *adjective* possible to get back

recovery /rɪˈkʌv(ə)ri/ *noun* **1.** the act of getting back something which has been lost ○ *to start an action for recovery of property* ○ *We are aiming for the complete recovery of the money invested.* **2.** a movement upward of stock or of the economy ○ *signs of recovery after a slump* ○ *The economy staged a recovery.*

recovery stock /rɪˈkʌv(ə)ri stɒk/ *noun* a stock which is likely to go up in value because the company's performance is improving

recruit /rɪˈkruːt/ *verb* □ **to recruit new staff** to search for and appoint new staff to join a company ○ *We are recruiting staff for our new store.* ■ *noun* a new member of staff ○ *The induction program for recruits begins on Wednesday.*

recruitment /rɪˈkruːtmənt/, **recruiting** /rɪˈkruːtɪŋ/ *noun* □ **the recruitment of new staff** the process of looking for new staff to join a company

rectification /ˌrektɪfɪˈkeɪʃ(ə)n/ *noun* correction

rectify /ˈrektɪfaɪ/ *verb* to correct something, to make something right ○ *to rectify an entry* (NOTE: **rectifies – rectifying – rectified**)

recurrent /rɪˈkʌrənt/ *adjective* happening again and again ○ *a recurrent item of expenditure* ○ *There is a recurrent problem in supplying this part.*

recycle /riˈsaɪk(ə)l/ *verb* **1.** to take waste material and process it so that it can be used again **2.** to use money in a different way (as by investing profits from industry in developing environmental resources)

red /red/ *noun* the color of debit or overdrawn balances in some bank statements □ **in the red** showing a debit or loss ○ *My bank account is in the red.* ○ *The company went into the red in 1998.* ○ *The company is out of the red for the first time since 1990.*

redeem /rɪˈdiːm/ *verb* **1.** to pay off a loan or a debt ○ *to redeem a mortgage* ○ *to re-*

deem a debt **2.** □ **to redeem a bond** to sell a bond for cash

redeemable /rɪˈdiːməb(ə)l/ *adjective* referring to a bond which can be sold for cash

redemption /rɪˈdempʃən/ *noun* **1.** the repayment of a loan □ **redemption before due date** paying back a loan before the date when repayment is due **2.** the repayment of a debt ○ *redemption of a mortgage*

redemption date /rɪˈdempʃən deɪt/ *noun* a date on which a loan or debt is due to be repaid

redemption value /rɪˈdempʃən ˌvæljuː/ *noun* a value of a security when redeemed

redemption yield /rɪˈdempʃən jiːld/ *noun* a yield on a security including interest and its redemption value

redeploy /ˌriːdɪˈplɔɪ/ *verb* to move employees from one place to another or from one type of job to another ○ *We closed the design department and redeployed the work force in the publicity and sales departments.*

redeployment /ˌriːdɪˈplɔɪmənt/ *noun* the act of moving employees from one place of work to another or from one type of job to another

redevelop /ˌriːdɪˈveləp/ *verb* to knock down the buildings on a site, and build new ones

redevelopment /ˌriːdɪˈveləpmənt/ *noun* the action of knocking down of existing buildings to replace them with new ones ○ *The redevelopment plan was rejected by the planning committee.*

red goods /ˈred gʊdz/ *plural noun* fast-selling convenience goods, especially food items. Compare **orange goods**, **yellow goods**

red ink /ˌred ˈɪŋk/ *noun* a financial loss or deficit

redistribute /ˌriːdɪˈstrɪbjuːt/ *verb* to move items, work or money to different areas or people ○ *The government aims to redistribute wealth by taxing the rich and giving grants to the poor.* ○ *The orders have been redistributed among the company's factories.*

redistribution of wealth /ˌriːdɪstrɪbjuːʃən əv ˈwelθ/ *noun* the process of sharing wealth among the whole population

redraft /riːˈdræft/ *verb* to draft again ○ *The whole contract had to be redrafted to take in the objections from the chairman.*

red tape /ˌred ˈteɪp/ *noun* official paperwork which takes a long time to complete ○ *The start of the new project has been held up by extra checks and government red tape.*

reduce /rɪˈdʊs/ *verb* **1.** to make something smaller or lower ○ *We must reduce expenditure if we want to stay in business.* ○ *They have reduced prices in all departments.* ○ *We were expecting the government to reduce taxes not to increase them.* ○ *We have dismissed some employees to reduce overstaffing.* ○ *The company reduced output because of a fall in demand.* ○ *The government's policy is to reduce inflation to 5%.* □ **to reduce staff** to dismiss employees in order to have a smaller number of staff **2.** to lower the price of something ○ *Carpets have been reduced from $100 to $50.*

reduced /rɪˈdʊst/ *adjective* lower ○ *Reduced prices have increased unit sales.* ○ *Prices have fallen due to a reduced demand for the goods.*

reduced rate /rɪˌdʊst ˈreɪt/ *noun* an especially low price or charge

reduction /rɪˈdʌkʃən/ *noun* an act of making something smaller or less ○ *Reduction in demand has led to the cancellation of several new projects.* ○ *The company was forced to make reductions in its advertising budget.* ○ *Price reductions have had no effect on our sales.* ○ *Working only part-time will mean a significant reduction in take-home pay.*

redundancy /rɪˈdʌndənsi/ *noun U.K.* **1.** the dismissal of a person whose job no longer needs to be done **2.** a person who has lost a job because they are not needed anymore ○ *The takeover caused 250 redundancies.*

redundancy package /rɪˈdʌndənsi ˌpækɪdʒ/ *noun U.K.* various benefits and payments given to a worker who is being made redundant

redundancy payment /rɪˈdʌndənsi ˌpeɪmənt/ *noun U.K.* a payment made to an employee to compensate for losing his or her job

redundant /rɪˈdʌndənt/ *adjective* **1.** more than is needed, useless ○ *a redundant clause in a contract* ○ *The new legislation has made clause 6 redundant.* ○ *Retraining can help employees whose old skills have become redundant.* **2.** □ **to make someone redundant** *U.K.* to dismiss an employee who is not needed anymore

redundant staff /rɪˌdʌndənt ˈstæf/ *noun U.K.* staff who have lost their jobs because they are not needed anymore

re-elect /ˌriː ɪˈlekt/ *verb* to elect again ○ *he was re-elected chairman*

reelection /ˌriːɪˈlekʃən/ *noun* the process of being elected again □ **she is eligible to stand for reelection** it is possible for her to be re-elected if she wants

re-employ /ˌriː ɪmˈplɔɪ/ *verb* to employ someone again ○ *He came back to the factory hoping to be re-employed.*

reemployment /ˌriːɪmˈplɔɪmənt/ *noun* the act of employing someone again

reengage /ˌriːɪnˈɡeɪdʒ/ *verb* to re-employ someone, but not necessarily in the same job □ **to reengage staff** to employ staff again

reengineering /ˌriːendʒɪˈnɪrɪŋ/ *noun* a management theory that encourages the reorganization of a business by taking account of the market value each department adds to the products the business produces

re-entry /ˌriː ˈentri/ *noun* an act of coming back in again

re-entry visa /ˌriː ˈentri ˌviːzə/ *noun* a visa which allows someone to leave a country and go back in again

reexamination /ˌriːɪɡzæmɪˈneɪʃən/ *noun* an act of examining something which has already been examined before

re-examine /ˌriːɪɡˈzæmɪn/ *verb* to examine something again

re-export /ˌriːɪekˈspɔrt/ *noun* the exporting of goods which have been imported ○ *The port is a center for the re-export trade.* ○ *We import wool for re-export.* ○ *The value of re-exports has increased.* ■ *verb* to export something which has been imported

reexportation /riːˌekspɔrˈteɪʃ(ə)n/ *noun* the exporting of goods which have been imported

ref *abbreviation* reference

refer /rɪˈfɜr/ *verb* **1.** to mention, to deal with or to write about something ○ *referring to your letter of June 4th* ○ *We refer to your estimate of May 26th.* ○ *He referred* to an article which he had seen in the *"Times"*. **2.** to pass a problem on to someone else to solve ○ *The board has decided to refer the question to a committee.* ○ *We have referred your complaint to our supplier.* **3.** □ **"refer to drawer"** words written on a check which a bank refuses to pay and returns it to the person who wrote it. Abbreviation **R** *or* **D** □ **the bank referred the check to drawer** the bank returned the check to person who wrote it because there was not enough money in the account to pay it

referee /ˌrefəˈriː/ *noun* a person such as a former employer or teacher who can give a report on someone's character, ability or job performance ○ *She gave the name of her boss as a referee.* ○ *When applying please give the names of three referees.* ○ *He chose his former headmaster as referee.*

reference /ˈref(ə)rəns/ *noun* **1.** the process of mentioning or dealing with something ○ *with reference to your letter of May 25th* **2.** a series of numbers or letters which make it possible to find a document which has been filed ○ *our reference: PC/MS 1234* ○ *Thank you for your letter (reference 1234).* ○ *Please quote this reference in all correspondence.* **3.** a written report on someone's character or ability ○ *to write someone a reference* or *to give someone a reference* ○ *to ask applicants to supply references* □ **to ask a company for trade references** *or* **for bank references** to ask for reports from traders or a bank on the company's financial status and reputation **4.** a person such as a former employer or teacher who can give a report on someone's character, ability or job performance ○ *He gave the name of his former manager as a reference.* ○ *Please use me as a reference if you wish.*

reference site /ˈref(ə)rəns saɪt/ *noun* a customer site where a new technology is being used successfully

refinance /riːˈfaɪnæns/ *verb* **1.** to replace one source of financing with another **2.** to extend a loan by exchanging it for a new one (normally done when the terms of the new loan are better)

refinancing /riːˈfaɪnænsɪŋ/ *noun* □ **refinancing of a loan** the act of taking out a new loan to pay back a previous loan

"…the refinancing consisted of a two-for-five rights issue, which took place in September this year, to offer 55.8m shares at 2p and raise about œ925,000 net of expenses" [*Accountancy*]

refit /riːˈfɪt/ *verb* to fit out (a store, factory or office) again ○ *the store is being refitted* (NOTE: **refitting – refitted**)

refitting /riːˈfɪtɪŋ/ *noun* the process of fitting out (a store, factory or office) again ○ *The refitting of the store is more expensive than we thought.* ○ *Refitting the conference room has disturbed the office routine.*

reflate /riːˈfleɪt/ *verb* □ **to reflate the economy** to stimulate the economy by increasing the money supply or by reducing taxes, often leading to increased inflation ○ *The government's attempts to reflate the economy were not successful.*

reflation /riːˈfleɪʃ(ə)n/ *noun* an act of stimulating the economy by increasing the money supply or by reducing taxes

reflationary measures /riːˌfleɪʃ(ə)n(ə)ri ˈmeʃərz/ *plural noun* actions which are likely to stimulate the economy

refresher course /rɪˈfreʃər kɔːrs/ *noun* a course of study designed to bring existing skills or knowledge up to date ○ *Refresher courses were given to anyone who had not used this machinery for some time.* ○ *She went on a refresher course in bookkeeping.*

refund *noun* /ˈriːfʌnd/ money paid back ○ *The shoes don't fit – I'm going to ask for a refund.* ○ *She got a refund after complaining to the manager.* ■ *verb* /rɪˈfʌnd/ **1.** to pay back money ○ *to refund the cost of postage* ○ *All money will be refunded if the goods are not satisfactory.* **2.** to borrow money to repay a previous debt

refundable /rɪˈfʌndəb(ə)l/ *adjective* possible to pay back ○ *We ask for a refundable deposit of $20.* ○ *The entrance fee is refundable if you purchase $5 worth of goods.*

refusal /rɪˈfjuːz(ə)l/ *noun* an act of saying no □ **his request met with a refusal** his request was refused □ **to give someone (the right of) first refusal of something** to allow someone to be the first to decide if they want something or not

refuse /rɪˈfjuːz/ *verb* to say that you will not do something or will not accept something ○ *they refused to pay* ○ *the customer refused the goods* or *refused to accept the goods* ○ *The bank refused to lend the company any more money.* ○ *He asked for a rise but it was refused.* ○ *The loan was refused by the bank.* (NOTE: You refuse **to do something** or refuse **something**.)

regard /rɪˈɡɑrd/ *noun* □ **with regard to** concerning or dealing with ○ *with regard to your request for unpaid leave*

regarding /rɪˈɡɑrdɪŋ/ *preposition* concerning or dealing with ○ *Instructions regarding the shipment of goods to Africa.*

regardless /rɪˈɡɑrdləs/ *adjective* □ **regardless of** in spite of □ **the chairman furnished his office regardless of expense** without thinking of how much it would cost

regeneration /rɪˌdʒenəˈreɪʃ(ə)n/ *noun* the redevelopment of areas that are in economic decline, in order to increase employment and stimulate new business activity

"They are creating jobs and spurring economic regeneration--despite obstacles such as heavy taxes and red tape that have long discouraged the Continent's entrepreneurs." [*BusinessWeek*]

region /ˈridʒən/ *noun* **1.** a large area of a country ○ *Her territory consists of all the eastern region of the country.* **2.** □ **in the region of** about or approximately ○ *She was earning a salary in the region of $35,000.* ○ *The house was sold for a price in the region of $300,000.*

regional /ˈridʒ(ə)nəl/ *adjective* referring to a region

regional planning /ˌridʒ(ə)nəl ˈplænɪŋ/ *noun* the work of planning the industrial development of a region

register /ˈredʒɪstər/ *noun* **1.** an official list ○ *to enter something in a register* ○ *to keep a register up to date* ○ *people on the register of electors* **2.** a large book for recording details (as in a hotel, where guests sign in, or in a registry where deaths are recorded) ■ *verb* **1.** to write something in an official list ○ *to register a fall in the numbers of unemployed teenagers* ○ *To register a company you must pay a fee to Companies House.* ○ *When a property is sold, the sale is registered at the Land Registry.* **2.** to arrive at a hotel or at a conference, sign your name and write your address on a list ○ *They registered at the hotel under* the name of Macdonald. **3.** to send a letter by registered mail ○ *I registered the letter, because it contained some money.*

registered /ˈredʒɪstərd/ *adjective* having been noted on an official list ○ *a registered stock transaction*

registered letter /ˌredʒɪstərd ˈletər/, **registered parcel** /ˌredʒɪstərd ˈpɑrs(ə)l/ *noun* a letter or parcel which is noted by the post office before it is sent, so that the sender can claim compensation if it is lost

registered mail *noun* a system where a letter or parcel is noted by the post office before it is sent, so that compensation can be claimed if it is lost ○ *to send documents by registered mail* or *registered post*

registered office /ˌredʒɪstərd ˈɒfɪs/ *noun* the office address of a company which is officially registered with the Companies' Registrar

registered trademark /ˌredʒɪstərd ˈtreɪdmɑrk/ *noun* a name, design, or symbol which has been registered by the manufacturer and which cannot be used by other manufacturers. It is an intangible asset. ○ *You can't call your beds "Softn'kumfi" – it is a registered trademark.*

register of debentures /ˌredʒɪstər əv dɪˈbentjʊəz/ *noun* a list of debenture holders of a company

register of stockholders /ˌredʒɪstər əv ˈstɒkhoʊldərz/ *noun* a list of stockholders in a company along with their addresses

registrar /ˌredʒɪˈstrɑr/ *noun* a person who keeps official records

registration /ˌredʒɪˈstreɪʃ(ə)n/ *noun* the act of having something noted on an official list ○ *the registration of a trademark* or *of a stock transaction*

registration fee /ˌredʒɪˈstreɪʃ(ə)n fi/ *noun* **1.** money paid to have something registered **2.** money paid to attend a conference

registration number /ˌredʒɪˈstreɪʃ(ə)n ˌnʌmbər/ *noun* an official number, e.g., the number of a car

registry /ˈredʒɪstri/ *noun* a place where official records are kept

registry office /ˈredʒɪstri ˌɒfɪs/ *noun* an office where records of births, marriages and deaths are kept

regressive taxation /rɪˌgresɪv tæk
'seɪʃ(ə)n/ *noun* a system of taxation in
which tax gets progressively less as income rises. Compare **progressive taxation**

regular /'regjələr/ *adjective* **1.** occurring at the same time each day, each week,
each month or each year ○ *His regular
train is the 12.45.* ○ *The regular flight to
Athens leaves at 06.00.* **2.** ordinary or
standard ○ *The regular price is $1.25, but
we are offering them at 99 cents.*

regular customer /ˌregjələr
'kʌstəmər/ *noun* a customer who always
buys from the same store

regular income /ˌregjələr 'ɪnkʌm/
noun an income which comes in every
week or month ○ *She works freelance so
she does not have a regular income.*

regularly /'regjʊləli/ *adverb* happening
often each day, week, month or year ○ *The
first train in the morning is regularly late.*

regular size /'regjələr saɪz/ *noun* the
standard size (smaller than economy size
or family size)

regular staff /ˌregjələr 'stæf/ *noun* the
full-time staff

regulate /'regjəleɪt/ *verb* **1.** to adjust
something so that it works well or is correct **2.** to change or maintain something by
law □ **prices are regulated by supply and
demand** prices are increased or lowered
according to supply and demand □ **government-regulated price** a price which is
imposed by the government

regulation /ˌregjə'leɪʃ(ə)n/ *noun* **1.** a
law or rule ○ *the new government regulations on housing standards* ○ *Fire regulations or Safety regulations were not observed at the restaurant.* ○ *Regulations
concerning imports and exports are set out
in this leaflet.* **2.** the use of laws or rules
stipulated by a government or regulatory
body, such as the Securities and Exchange
Commission, to provide orderly procedures and to protect consumers and investors ○ *government regulation of trading
practices*

Regulation Q /ˌregjʊleɪʃ(ə)n 'kju/
noun a federal regulation which limits the
amount of interest banks can pay on deposits

Regulation S-X /ˌregjʊleɪʃ(ə)n es
'eks/ *noun* the rule of the U.S. Securities

and Exchange Commission which regulates annual reports from companies

regulator /'regjəleɪtər/ *noun* a person
whose job it is to see that regulations are
followed

regulatory /'regjʊlət(ə)ri/ *adjective*
applying regulations

regulatory body /ˌregjʊlət(ə)ri 'bɒdi/
noun an independent organization, usually
established by a government, that makes
rules and sets standards for an industry and
oversees the activities of companies within
it

"Management of PharmaPlus is facing
opposition from the regulatory body of
pharmacists, which has authority over a
pharmacy's operations and the stakeholders
in the current industry structure." [*Harvard
Business Review*]

regulatory powers /'regjʊlət(ə)ri
ˌpaʊrz/ *noun* powers to enforce government regulations

reimburse /ˌriːm'bɜrs/ *verb* □ **to reimburse someone their expenses** to pay
someone back for money which they have
spent ○ *You will be reimbursed for your
expenses* or *Your expenses will be reimbursed.*

reimbursement /ˌriːm'bɜrsmənt/
noun the act of paying back money ○ *reimbursement of expenses*

reimport *noun* /riː'ɪmpɔrt/ the importing
of goods which have been exported from
the same country ■ *verb* /ˌriːm'pɔrt/ to
import goods which have already been exported

reimportation /ˌriːmpɔ'teɪʃ(ə)n/ *noun*
the importing of goods which have already
been exported

reinstate /ˌriːn'steɪt/ *verb* to allow
someone to return to a job from which they
were dismissed ○ *The union demanded
that the sacked workers should be reinstat-
ed.*

reinstatement /ˌriːn'steɪtmənt/ *noun*
1. the act of putting someone back into a
job from which they were dismissed **2.** the
act of giving a borrower back his or her
former credit status after he or she has paid
off outstanding debts

reinsurance /ˌriːn'ʃʊrəns/ *noun* insurance where a second insurer (the reinsurer)
agrees to cover part of the risk insured by
the first insurer

reinsure /ˌriːn'ʃʊr/ *verb* to spread the insurance risk, by having another insurance company cover part of it and receive part of the original premium

reinsurer /ˌriːn'ʃʊrər/ *noun* an insurance company which agrees to insure part of the risk for another insurer

reinvest /ˌriːn'vest/ *verb* to invest money again ○ *She sold her shares and reinvested the money in government stocks.*

reinvestment /ˌriːn'vestmənt/ *noun* **1.** the act of investing money again in the same securities **2.** the act of investing a company's earnings in its own business by using them to create new products for sale

"...many large U.S. corporations offer shareholders the option of reinvesting their cash dividend payments in additional company stock at a discount to the market price. But to some big securities firms these discount reinvestment programs are an opportunity to turn a quick profit" [*Wall Street Journal*]

reissue /riː'ɪʃuː/ *noun* an issue of something again; thing which has been issued again ○ *This is a reissue of the government guidelines first issued in 1995.* ■ *verb* to issue something again ○ *The company reissued its catalog with a new price list.*

REIT *abbreviation* real estate investment trust. ◊ **mortgage REIT**

reject¹ *noun* /'riːdʒekt/, *adjective* (something) which has been thrown out because it is not of the usual standard ○ *sale of rejects* or *of reject items* ○ *to sell off reject stock* ■ *verb* /rɪ'dʒekt/ to refuse to accept something, or to say that something is not satisfactory ○ *The board rejected the draft budget.* □ **the company rejected the takeover bid** the directors recommended that the stockholders should not accept the bid

reject² /'riːdʒekt stɔr/ *noun U.K.* same as **seconds store**

rejection /rɪ'dʒekʃən/ *noun* a refusal to accept something, such as a refusal to give a customer credit ○ *The rejection of the company's offer meant that the negotiations had to start again.* ○ *After the union's rejection of the offer, management came back with new redundancy terms.*

related /rɪ'leɪtɪd/ *adjective* connected or linked ○ *related items on the agenda*

related company /rɪˌleɪtɪd 'kʌmp(ə)ni/ *noun* a company in which another company makes a long-term capital investment in order to gain control or influence

relating to /rɪ'leɪtɪŋ tu/ *adverb* referring to or connected with ○ *documents relating to the agreement*

relational database /rɪˌleɪʃ(ə)n(ə)l 'deɪtəbeɪs/ *noun* a computer database in which different types of data are linked for analysis

relations /rɪ'leɪʃ(ə)nz/ *plural noun* relationships with other people, companies or countries ○ *we maintain good relations with our customers* ○ *we are taking advantage of improving international relations in that area to expand our exports* ○ *Relations between the management and the work force have been strained recently.* ○ *Relations between management and work force have never been good in this factory.* □ **to break off relations with someone** to stop dealing with someone

relative /'relətɪv/ *adjective* compared to something else

relative error /ˌrelətɪv 'erər/ *noun* the difference between an estimate and its correct value

relatively /'relətɪvli/ *adverb* more or less ○ *We have appointed a relatively new PR firm to handle our publicity.*

relaunch /'riːlɔːnʃ/ *noun* the act of putting a product back on the market again, after adapting it to changing market conditions ○ *The relaunch is scheduled for August.*

release /rɪ'liːs/ *noun* **1.** the act of setting someone free or of making something or someone no longer subject to an obligation or restriction ○ *release from a contract* ○ *the release of goods from customs* ○ *She was offered early release so that she could take up her new job.* **2.** the act of making something public, or a public announcement **3.** the act of putting something on the market, or something put on the market **4.** □ **new release** a new CD or a piece of software put on the market ■ *verb* **1.** to free something or someone ○ *to release goods from customs* ○ *to release someone from a debt* ○ *Customs released the goods against payment of a fine.* **2.** to end an employee's contract early **3.** to make something public ○ *The company released information about the new mine in Australia.* ○ *The government has refused to release figures for the number of unemployed* *women.* **4.** to put something on the market ○ *They released several new CDs this month.* □ **to release dues** to send off orders which had been piling up while a product was out of stock

relevant /'reləv(ə)nt/ *adjective* having to do with what is being discussed or the current situation ○ *Which is the relevant government department?* ○ *Can you give me the relevant papers?* ○ *The new assistant does not have any relevant experience.*

reliability /rɪˌlaɪə'bɪləti/ *noun* the fact of being reliable ○ *The product has passed its reliability tests.*

reliable /rɪ'laɪəb(ə)l/ *adjective* which can be trusted ○ *We are looking for a reliable bookkeeper to deal with the payroll.* ○ *The sales manager is completely reliable.* ○ *We have reliable information about our competitor's sales.* ○ *The company makes a very reliable product.*

relief /rɪ'liːf/ *noun* help

relief shift /rɪ'liːf ʃɪft/ *noun* a shift which comes to take the place of another shift, usually the shift between the day shift and the night shift

relocate /ˌriːloʊ'keɪt/ *verb* to establish an organization in a new place, or to be established in a new place ○ *The board decided to relocate the company in Scotland.* ○ *When the company moved its headquarters, 1500 people had to be relocated.* ○ *If the company moves down south, all the managerial staff will have to relocate.*

relocation /ˌriːloʊ'keɪʃ(ə)n/ *noun* the act of moving to a different place ○ *We will pay all the staff relocation costs.*

rely /ri'laɪ/ *verb*

rely on *phrasal verb* to depend on or to trust ○ *The chairman relies on the finance department for information on sales.* ○ *We rely on part-time staff for most of our mail-order business.* ○ *Do not rely on the agents for accurate market reports.*

remainder /rɪ'meɪndər/ *noun* things left behind ○ *The remainder of the stock will be sold off at half price.* ■ *verb* □ **to remainder books** to sell new books off cheaply ○ *The store was full of piles of remaindered books.*

remainder merchant /rɪ'meɪndər ˌmɜːtʃənt/ *noun* a book dealer who buys unsold new books from publishers at a very low price

remainders /rɪ'meɪndərz/ *plural noun* new books sold cheaply

remind /rɪ'maɪnd/ *verb* to make someone remember ○ *I must remind my secretary to book the flight for New York.* ○ *He reminded the chairman that the meeting had to finish at 6:30.*

reminder /rɪ'maɪndər/ *noun* a letter to remind a customer that he or she has not paid an invoice ○ *to send someone a reminder*

remission of taxes /rɪˌmɪʃ(ə)n əv 'tæksɪz/ *noun U.K.* same as **tax refund**

remit /rɪ'mɪt/ *verb* to send money ○ *to remit by check* (NOTE: **remitting – remitted**)

remittance /rɪ'mɪt(ə)ns/ *noun* money which is sent to pay back a debt or to pay an invoice ○ *Please send remittances to the treasurer.* ○ *The family lives on a weekly remittance from their father in the U.S.*

remnant /'remnənt/ *noun* an odd piece of a large item such as, a carpet or fabric sold separately ○ *a sale of remnants* or *a remnant sale*

remortgage /riː'mɔːɡɪdʒ/ *verb* to mortgage a property which is already mortgaged ○ *The bank offered him better terms than the building society, so he decided to remortgage the house.*

removal /rɪ'muːv(ə)l/ *noun* **1.** the act of moving to a new house or office ○ *Staff are allowed removal expenses on joining the company.* **2.** the act of sacking someone (usually a director) from a job ○ *The removal of the managing director is going to be very difficult.*

removal company /rɪ'muːv(ə)l ˌkʌmp(ə)ni/, **removals company** /rɪ'muːv(ə)lz ˌkʌmp(ə)ni/ *noun U.K.* same as **moving company**

remove /rɪ'muːv/ *verb* to take something away ○ *We can remove his name from the mailing list.* ○ *The government has removed the ban on imports from Japan.* ○ *The minister has removed the embargo on the sale of computer equipment.* □ **two directors were removed from the board at the annual meeting** two directors were dismissed from the board

remunerate /rɪ'mjuːnəreɪt/ *verb* to pay someone for doing something ○ *The company refused to remunerate them for their services.*

remuneration /rɪ,mjunə'reɪʃ(ə)n/ *noun* payment for services ○ *The job is interesting but the remuneration is low.* ○ *She receives a small remuneration of $400 a month.* ○ *No one will work hard for such poor remuneration.*

COMMENT: Remuneration can take several forms: e.g. a regular salary or wage check or cash payment for hours worked or for work completed.

remuneration package /rɪ,mjunə 'reɪʃ(ə)n ,pækɪdʒ/ *noun* the salary, pension contributions, bonuses and other forms of payment or benefit that make up an employee's total remuneration

remunerative /rɪ'mjunərətɪv/ *adjective* referring to a job which pays well ○ *She is in a highly remunerative job.*

render /'rendər/ *verb* □ **to render an account** to send in an account ○ *Please find enclosed payment per account rendered.*

renew /rɪ'nju/ *verb* to continue something for a further period of time ○ *We have asked the bank to renew the bill of exchange.* ○ *The tenant wants to renew his lease.* ○ *Her contract was renewed for a further three years.* □ **to renew a subscription** to pay a subscription for another year □ **to renew an insurance policy** to pay the premium for another year's insurance

renewal /rɪ'nuəl/ *noun* the act of renewing ○ *renewal of a lease* or *of a subscription* or *of a bill* ○ *renewal of a contract* ○ *Her contract is up for renewal* ○ *When is the renewal date of the bill?* □ **to be up for renewal** to be due to be renewed ○ *His contract is up for renewal in January.* ○ *The lease is up for renewal next month.*

renewal notice /rɪ'nuəl ,noutɪs/ *noun* a note sent by an insurance company asking the insured person to renew the insurance

renewal premium /rɪ'nuəl ,primiəm/ *noun* a premium to be paid to renew insurance

rent /rent/ *noun* money paid to use an office, house or factory for a period of time □ **high rent, low rent** expensive or cheap rent ○ *to pay three months' rent in advance* ○ *Rents are high in the centre of the town.* ○ *We cannot afford to pay High Street rents.* □ **the apartment is let at an economic rent** at a rent which covers all costs to the landlord □ **nominal rent** a

very small rent ■ *verb* **1.** to pay money to hire an office, house, factory or piece of equipment for a period of time ○ *to rent an office* or *a car* ○ *He rents an office in the center of town.* ○ *They were driving a rented car when they were stopped by the police.* **2.** to allow the use of a house, an office or a farm to someone for the payment of rent (NOTE: The U.K. term is **let**.)

rental /'rent(ə)l/ *noun* money paid to use an office, house, factory, car, piece of equipment, etc., for a period of time ○ *The car rental bill comes to over $1000 a quarter.*

"…top quality office furniture: short or long-term rental 50% cheaper than any other rental company" [*Australian Financial Review*]

"…until the vast acres of empty office space start to fill up with rent-paying tenants, rentals will continue to fall and so will values. Despite the very sluggish economic recovery under way, it is still difficult to see where the new tenants will come from" [*Australian Financial Review*]

rental car /'rent(ə)l kɑr/ *noun* a car that has been leased

rental income /'rent(ə)l ,ɪnkʌm/ *noun* income from letting offices or houses, etc.

rent control /'rent kən,troul/ *noun* government regulation of rents

rent income /'rent ,ɪnkʌm/ *noun* income from letting offices, houses, etc.

renunciation /rɪ,nʌnsi'eɪʃ(ə)n/ *noun* an act of giving up ownership of shares

reopen /ri'oupən/ *verb* to open again ○ *The office will reopen soon after its refit.* ○ *The management agreed to reopen discussions with the union.*

reopening /ri'oup(ə)nɪŋ/ *noun* the act of opening again ○ *the reopening of the store after refitting*

reorder /ri'ɔrdər/ *noun* a further order for something which has been ordered before ○ *The product has only been on the market ten days and we are already getting reorders.* ■ *verb* to place a new order for something ○ *We must reorder these items because stock is getting low.*

reorder level /ri'ɔrdər ,lev(ə)l/ *noun* a minimum amount of an item which a company holds in stock, such that, when stock falls to this amount, the item must be reordered

reorder quantity /ri'ɔrdər ,kwɑntəti/ *noun* a quantity of a product which is reordered, especially the economic order quantity (EOQ)

reorganization /rɪˌɔːɡənaɪ'zeɪʃ(ə)n/ noun **1.** the act of organizing something in a new way ○ *His job was downgraded in the office reorganization* or *in the reorganization of the office.* **2.** the process of organizing a company in a different way, as in the U.S. when a bankrupt company applies to be treated under Chapter 11 to be protected from its creditors while it is being reorganized □ **the reorganization of a company, a company reorganization** restructuring the finances of a company

reorganize /riˈɔːɡənaɪz/ verb to organize something in a new way ○ *We have reorganized all our reps' territories.*

rep /rep/ (informal) noun same as **representative** ○ *to hold a reps' meeting* ○ *Our reps make on average six calls a day.* ■ verb same as **represent** ○ *He reps for two firms on commission.* (NOTE: **repping – repped**)

repack /riˈpæk/ verb to pack again

repacking /riˈpækɪŋ/ noun the act of packing again

repair /rɪˈpeə/ noun mending or making good something which was broken ○ *to carry out repairs to the machinery* ○ *His car is in the garage for repair.* ■ verb to mend, to make good something which is broken ○ *the photocopier is being repaired*

repairer /rɪˈpeərə/, **repair man** /rɪ ˈpeəmən/ noun a person who carries out repairs ○ *The repair man has come to mend the photocopier.*

repairing lease /rɪˈpeərɪŋ liːs/ noun a lease where the tenant is responsible for repairs to the building which he or she is renting

repair shop /rɪˈpeə ʃɒp/ noun a small factory where machines are repaired

repay /rɪˈpeɪ/ verb to pay something back, or to pay back money to someone ○ *to repay money owed* ○ *The company had to cut back on expenditure in order to repay its debts.* □ **he repaid me in full** he paid me back all the money he owed me

repayable /rɪˈpeɪəb(ə)l/ adjective possible to pay back ○ *loan which is repayable over ten years*

repayment /rɪˈpeɪmənt/ noun the act of paying money back or money which is paid back ○ *The loan is due for repayment*

next year. □ **he fell behind with his mortgage payments** U.K. he was late in paying back the installments on his mortgage

repayment mortgage /rɪˈpeɪmənt ˌmɔːɡɪdʒ/ noun a mortgage where the borrower pays back both interest and capital over the period of the mortgage. This is opposed to an endowment mortgage, where only the interest is repaid, and insurance is taken out to repay the capital at the end of the term of the mortgage.

repeat /rɪˈpiːt/ verb **1.** to do or say something again ○ *He repeated his address slowly so that the saleswoman could write it down.* ○ *When asked what the company planned to do, the chairman repeated "Nothing".* ○ *We'll have to repeat the survey next year.* **2.** □ **to repeat an order** to order something again

repeat order /rɪˌpiːt 'ɔːdə/ noun a new order for something which has been ordered before ○ *The product has been on the market only ten days and we are already flooded with repeat orders.*

repetitive strain injury /rɪˌpetɪtɪv 'streɪn ˌɪndʒəri/, **repetitive stress injury** /rɪˌpetɪtɪv 'stres ˌɪndʒəri/ noun a pain in the arm felt by someone who performs the same movement many times over a certain period, such as when keyboarding. Abbreviation **RSI**

replace /rɪˈpleɪs/ verb to put someone or something in the place of someone or something else ○ *the photocopier needs replacing* ○ *The cost of replacing damaged stock is very high.* ○ *The company will replace any defective item free of charge.* ○ *We are replacing all our salaried staff with freelancers.*

replacement /rɪˈpleɪsmənt/ noun **1.** an item which replaces something ○ *We are out of stock and are waiting for replacements.* **2.** a person who replaces someone ○ *My assistant leaves us next week, so we are advertising for a replacement.*

replacement cost /rɪˈpleɪsmənt kɒst/ noun the cost of an item to replace an existing asset. Also called **cost of replacement**

replacement value /rɪˈpleɪsmənt ˌvæljuː/ noun the value of something for insurance purposes if it were to be replaced ○ *The computer is insured at its replacement value.*

reply coupon /rɪˈplaɪ ˌkupɑn/ *noun* a form attached to a coupon ad which has to be filled in and returned to the advertiser

reply paid card /rɪˌplaɪ ˈpeɪd ˌkɑrd/ *noun* a card or letter to be sent back to the sender with a reply, the sender having already paid for the return postage

repo /ˈripoʊ/ *noun* same as **repurchase agreement** (*informal*) (NOTE: The plural is **repos**)

report /rɪˈpɔrt/ *noun* **1.** a statement describing what has happened or describing a state of affairs ○ *to make a report* or *to present a report* or *to send in a report on market opportunities in the Far East* ○ *The accountants are drafting a report on salary scales.* ○ *The sales manager reads all the reports from the sales team.* ○ *The chairman has received a report from the insurance company.* □ **the treasurer's report** a document from the honorary treasurer of a society to explain the financial state of the society to its members **2.** an official document from a government committee ○ *The government has issued a report on the credit problems of exporters.* ○ *They reported for work at the usual time.* ■ *verb* **1.** to make a statement describing something ○ *The sales force reported an increased demand for the product.* ○ *He reported the damage to the insurance company.* ○ *We asked the bank to report on his financial status.* **2.** □ **to report to someone** to be responsible to or to be under someone ○ *She reports directly to the vice president.* ○ *The sales force reports to the sales director.* **3.** to go to a place or to attend ○ *She has been asked to report for an interview.* ○ *Please report to our main office for training.* **4.** to publish the results of a company for a period and declare the dividend

repossess /ˌripəˈzes/ *verb* to take back an item which someone is buying under an installment plan, or a property which someone is buying under a mortgage, because the purchaser cannot continue the payments

repossession /ˌripəˈzeʃ(ə)n/ *noun* an act of repossessing ○ *Repossessions are increasing as people find it difficult to meet mortgage payments.*

represent /ˌreprɪˈzent/ *verb* **1.** to work for a company, showing goods or services to possible buyers ○ *He represents an American car firm in Europe.* ○ *Our French distributor represents several other competing firms.* **2.** to act on behalf of someone ○ *He sent his solicitor and accountant to represent him at the meeting.* ○ *Three managers represent the work force in discussions with the directors.*

re-present /ˌri prɪˈzent/ *verb* to present something again ○ *She re-presented the check two weeks later to try to get payment from the bank.*

representation /ˌreprɪzenˈteɪʃ(ə)n/ *noun* **1.** the right to sell goods for a company, or a person or organization that sells goods on behalf of a company ○ *We offered them exclusive representation in the U.S.* ○ *They have no representation in Europe.* **2.** the fact of having someone to act on your behalf ○ *The minority stockholders want representation on the board.* ○ *The ordinary store floor workers want representation on the committee.* **3.** a complaint made on behalf of someone ○ *The managers made representations to the board on behalf of the hourly-paid members of staff.*

representative /ˌreprɪˈzentətɪv/ *adjective* which is an example of what all others are like ○ *We displayed a representative selection of our product range.* ○ *The sample chosen was not representative of the whole batch.* ■ *noun* **1.** a company which works for another company, selling their goods ○ *We have appointed Smith & Co our exclusive representatives in Europe.* **2.** a person who acts on someone's behalf ○ *He sent his solicitor and accountant to act as his representatives at the meeting.* ○ *The board refused to meet the representatives of the work force.* **3.** same as **salesperson**

reprice /riˈpraɪs/ *verb* to change the price on an item, usually to increase it

repudiate /rɪˈpjudieɪt/ *verb* to refuse to accept something □ **to repudiate an agreement** to refuse to continue with an agreement

repudiation /rɪˌpjudiˈeɪʃ(ə)n/ *noun* a refusal to accept something such as a debt

repurchase /riˈpɜrtʃɪs/ *verb* to buy something again, especially something which you have recently bought and then sold

repurchase agreement /riˈpɜrtʃɪs əˌgrimənt/ *noun* an agreement, where a bank agrees to buy something and sell it back later (in effect, giving a cash loan to the seller; this is used especially to raise short-term financing)

reputable /'repjʊtəb(ə)l/ *adjective* with a good reputation ○ *we only use reputable carriers* ○ *a reputable firm of accountants*

reputation /ˌrepjʊ'teɪʃ(ə)n/ *noun* an opinion of someone or something held by other people ○ *company with a reputation for quality* ○ *He has a reputation for being difficult to negotiate with.*

request /rɪ'kwest/ *noun* an act of asking for something ○ *They put in a request for a government subsidy.* ○ *His request for a loan was turned down by the bank.* □ **on request** if asked for ○ *We will send samples on request* or *"samples available on request".* ■ *verb* to ask for ○ *to request assistance from the government* ○ *I am sending a catalog as requested.*

request for quotation, request for proposal *noun* a request to a company or individual to submit a competitive bid

require /rɪ'kwaɪə/ *verb* **1.** to ask for or to demand something ○ *to require a full explanation of expenditure* ○ *The law requires you to submit all income to the tax authorities.* **2.** to need something ○ *The document requires careful study.* ○ *Writing the program requires a specialist knowledge of computers.*

requirement /rɪ'kwaɪəmənt/ *noun* **1.** something which someone wants or needs ○ *We hope the items will meet the customer's requirements.* ○ *If you will supply us with a list of your requirements, we shall see if we can meet them.* **2.** something which is necessary to enable something to be done ○ *Are computing skills a requirement for this job?*

requisition /ˌrekwɪ'zɪʃ(ə)n/ *noun* an official order for something ○ *What is the reference number of your latest requisition?* ■ *verb* to put in an official order for something or to ask for supplies to be sent ○ *We have requisitioned three trucks to move the stock.*

resale /'riːseɪl/ *noun* the selling of goods which have been bought ○ *to purchase something for resale* ○ *The contract forbids resale of the goods to Canada.*

resale price maintenance /ˌriːseɪl 'praɪs ˌmeɪntənəns/ *noun* a system in which the price for an item is fixed by the manufacturer, and the retailer is not allowed to sell it at a lower price. Abbreviation **RPM**

reschedule /riː'skedʒəl/ *verb* **1.** to arrange a new timetable for something ○ *She missed her plane, and all the meetings had to be rescheduled.* **2.** to arrange new credit terms for the repayment of a loan ○ *Third World countries which are unable to keep up the interest payments on their loans from western banks have asked for their loans to be rescheduled.*

rescind /rɪ'sɪnd/ *verb* to annul or to cancel something ○ *to rescind a contract* or *an agreement*

rescue operation /'reskju ɑpə ˌreɪʃ(ə)n/ *noun* an arrangement by a group of people to save a company from collapse ○ *The banks planned a rescue operation for the company.*

research /rɪ'sɜrtʃ/ *noun* the process of trying to find out facts or information □ **research and development costs** the costs involved in R & D ■ *verb* to study or try to find out information about something ○ *They are researching the market for their new product.*

COMMENT: Research costs can be divided into (a) applied research, which is the cost of research leading to a specific aim, and (b) basic, or pure, research, which is research carried out without a specific aim in mind: these costs are written off in the year in which they are incurred. Development costs are the costs of making the commercial products based on the research.

research and development /rɪˌsɜrtʃ ən dɪ'veləpmənt/ *noun* a scientific investigation which leads to making new products or improving existing products ○ *The company spends millions on research and development.* Abbreviation **R&D**

research department /rɪ'sɜrtʃ dɪ ˌpɑrtmənt/ *noun* the section of a company which carries out research

researcher /rɪ'sɜrtʃər/ *noun* a person who carries out research ○ *Government statistics are a useful source of information for the desk researcher.*

research institute /rɪ'sɜrtʃ ˌɪnstɪtjut/ *noun* a place which exists only to carry out research

research unit /rɪ'sɜrtʃ ˌjunɪt/ *noun* a separate small group of research workers

research worker /rɪˈsɜːtʃ ˌwɜːkər/ *noun* a person who works in a research department

resell /riˈsel/ *verb* to sell something which has just been bought ○ *The car was sold in June and the buyer resold it to an dealer two months later.* (NOTE: **reselling – resold**)

reseller /riˈselər/ *noun* somebody in the marketing chain who buys to sell to somebody else, e.g., wholesalers, distributors, and retailers

reservation /ˌrezəˈveɪʃ(ə)n/ *noun* an advance booking of a seat, table, or room ○ *I want to make a reservation on the train to Plymouth tomorrow evening.*

reserve /rɪˈzɜːv/ *noun* **1.** money from profits not paid as dividend but kept back by a company in case it is needed for a special purpose □ **reserve for bad debts** money kept by a company to cover debts which may not be paid **2.** □ **in reserve** kept to be used at a later date ○ *to keep something in reserve* ○ *We are keeping our new product in reserve until the launch date.* ■ *verb* □ **to reserve a room, a table, a seat** to make arrangements in advance for a room, table, or seat ○ *I want to reserve a table for four people.* ○ *Can your secretary reserve a seat for me on the train to Glasgow?*

COMMENT: The accumulated profits retained by a company usually form its most important reserve.

reserve currency /rɪˈzɜːv ˌkʌrənsi/ *noun* a strong currency used in international finance, held by other countries to support their own weaker currencies

reserved market /rɪˌzɜːvd ˈmɑːkət/ *noun* a market in which producers agree not to sell more than a specific amount in order to control competition. Also called **restricted market**

reserve fund /rɪˈzɜːv fʌnd/ *noun* profits in a business which have not been paid out as dividend but have been plowed back into the business

reserve price /rɪˈzɜːv praɪs/ *noun* the lowest price which a seller will accept, e.g., at an auction or when selling securities through a broker ○ *The painting was withdrawn when it failed to reach its reserve price.*

reserve requirement /rɪˈzɜːv rɪˌkwaɪrmənt/ *noun* the amount of reserves which an American bank has to hold on deposit with a Federal Reserve Bank

reserves /rɪˈzɜːvz/ *plural noun* supplies kept in case of need ○ *Our reserves of fuel fell during the winter.* ○ *The country's reserves of gas* or *gas reserves are very large.*

residence /ˈrezɪd(ə)ns/ *noun* **1.** a house or apartment where someone lives ○ *He has a country residence where he spends his weekends.* **2.** the fact of living or operating officially in a country

residence permit /ˈrezɪd(ə)ns ˌpɜːmɪt/ *noun* an official document allowing a foreigner to live in a country ○ *He has applied for a residence permit.* ○ *She was granted a residence permit for one year* or *a one-year residence permit.*

resident /ˈrezɪd(ə)nt/ *noun, adjective* a person or company considered to be living or operating in a country for official or tax purposes ○ *The company is resident in France.*

residual /rɪˈzɪdjuəl/ *adjective* remaining after everything else has gone

residue /ˈrezɪduː/ *noun* money left over ○ *After paying various bequests the residue of his estate was split between his children.*

resign /rɪˈzaɪn/ *verb* to give up a job ○ *He resigned from his post as treasurer.* ○ *He has resigned with effect from July 1st.* ○ *She resigned as finance director.*

resignation /ˌrezɪgˈneɪʃ(ə)n/ *noun* the act of giving up a job ○ *He wrote his letter of resignation to the chairman.* □ **to hand in** *or* **to give in** *or* **to send in your resignation** to resign from your job

resist /rɪˈzɪst/ *verb* to fight against something, not to give in to something ○ *The chairman resisted all attempts to make him resign.* ○ *The company is resisting the takeover bid.*

resistance /rɪˈzɪstəns/ *noun* opposition felt or shown by people to something ○ *There was a lot of resistance from the team to the new plan.* ○ *The chairman's proposal met with strong resistance from the banks.* ○ *There was a lot of resistance from the stockholders to the new plan.*

resolution /ˌrezəˈluːʃ(ə)n/ *noun* a decision to be reached at a meeting □ **to put a resolution to a meeting** to ask a meeting to vote on a proposal ○ *The meeting carried* or *adopted a resolution to go on* *strike.* ○ *The meeting rejected the resolution* or *The resolution was defeated by ten votes to twenty.* ○ *A resolution was passed to raise salaries by six percent.*

resolve /rɪ'zɑlv/ *verb* to decide to do something ○ *The meeting resolved that a dividend should not be paid.*

resource productivity /rɪˌzɔrs ˌprɑdʌk'tɪvɪti/ *noun* an approach to production that is concerned to increase the productivity of resources in order to reduce waste and preserve the environment

resources /rɪ'sɔrsɪz/ *plural noun* **1.** a supply of something □ **we are looking for a site with good water resources** a site with plenty of water available **2.** the money available for doing something □ **the cost of the new project is easily within our resources** we have more than enough money to pay for the new project

respect /rɪ'spekt/ *noun* □ **with respect to** concerning ■ *verb* to pay attention to ○ *to respect a clause in an agreement* ○ *The company has not respected the terms of the contract.*

respectively /rɪ'spektɪvli/ *adverb* referring to each one separately ○ *Mr. Smith and Mr. Jones are respectively CEO and Sales Director of Smith Inc.*

response /rɪ'spɑns/ *noun* a reply or reaction ○ *There was no response to our mailing shot.* ○ *We got very little response to our complaints.*

response rate /rɪ'spɑns reɪt/ *noun* the proportion of people who respond to a questionnaire or survey

responsibility /rɪˌspɑnsɪ'bɪlɪti/ *noun* the fact of being responsible ○ *There is no responsibility on the company's part for loss of customers' property.* ○ *The management accepts no responsibility for loss of goods in storage.* ○ *The manager has overall responsibility for the welfare of the staff in her department.*

responsible /rɪ'spɑnsɪb(ə)l/ *adjective* **1.** □ **responsible to someone** being under someone's authority ○ *She is directly responsible to the managing director.* □ **responsible for** directing or being in charge of doing a certain job ○ *He is responsible for all sales.* ○ *He is responsible for the staff in his department.* **2.** (person) who is sensible or who can be trusted □ **a responsible job** job where important decisions have to be taken or where the employee

has many responsibilities ○ *He is looking for a responsible job in marketing.*

rest /rest/ *noun* what is left ○ *The chairman went home, but the rest of the directors stayed in the boardroom.* ○ *We sold most of the stock before Christmas and hope to clear the rest in a sale.* ○ *The rest of the money is invested in gilts.*

restitution /ˌrestɪ'tjuʃ(ə)n/ *noun* **1.** the act of giving back property ○ *The court ordered the restitution of assets to the company.* **2.** compensation or payment for damage or loss

restock /ri'stɑk/ *verb* to order more stock or inventory ○ *to restock after the Christmas sales*

restocking /ri'stɑkɪŋ/ *noun* the ordering of more stock or inventory

restraint /rɪ'streɪnt/ *noun* control

restraint of trade /rɪˌstreɪnt əv 'treɪd/ *noun* **1.** a situation where employees are not allowed to use their knowledge in another company on changing jobs **2.** an attempt by companies to fix prices, create monopolies, or reduce competition, which could affect free trade

restrict /rɪ'strɪkt/ *verb* to limit something or to impose controls on something ○ *to restrict credit* ○ *to restrict the flow of trade* or *to restrict imports* ○ *We are restricted to twenty staff by the size of our offices.* □ **to sell into a restricted market** to sell goods into a market where the supplier has agreed to limit sales to avoid competition

restricted market /rɪˌstrɪktɪd 'mɑrkət/ *noun* same as **reserved market**

restriction /rɪ'strɪkʃ(ə)n/ *noun* a limit or control ○ *import restrictions* or *restrictions on imports* □ **to impose restrictions on imports** *or* **credit** to start limiting imports or credit □ **to lift credit restrictions** *or* **import restrictions** to allow credit to be given freely or imports to enter the country freely

restrictive /rɪ'strɪktɪv/ *adjective* not allowing something to go beyond a point, limiting

restrictive trade practices /rɪˌstrɪktɪv 'treɪd ˌpræktɪsɪz/, **restrictive practices** /rɪˌstrɪktɪv 'præktɪsɪz/ *plural noun* an arrangement between companies to fix prices or to share the market in order to restrict trade

restructure /riˈstrʌktʃər/ *verb* to reorganize the financial basis of a company

restructuring /riˈstrʌktʃərɪŋ/ *noun* the process of reorganizing the financial basis of a company

result /rɪˈzʌlt/ *noun* **1.** a profit or loss account for a company at the end of a trading period ○ *The company's results for last year were an improvement on those of the previous year.* **2.** something which happens because of something else ○ *What was the result of the price investigation?* ○ *The company doubled its sales force with the result that the sales rose by 26%.* □ **the expansion program has produced results** has produced increased sales ■ *verb* **1.** □ **to result from** to happen because of ○ *We have to fill several vacancies resulting from the recent internal promotions* **2.** □ **to result in** to produce as a result ○ *The doubling of the sales force resulted in increased sales.* ○ *The extra orders resulted in overtime work for all the factory staff.*

"…the company has received the backing of a number of oil companies who are willing to pay for the results of the survey" [*Lloyd's List*]

"…some profit-taking was noted, but underlying sentiment remained firm in a steady stream of strong corporate results" [*Financial Times*]

result-driven /rɪˈzʌlt ˌdrɪv(ə)n/ *adjective* used to describe a strategy or organization that focuses mainly on results and achievements rather than on improving procedures (NOTE: A result-driven organization concentrates on achieving its aims, and delivering products at the required time, cost, and quality, and considers performance to be more important than procedures.)

resume /rɪˈzjuːm/ *verb* to start again ○ *The discussions resumed after a two hour break.*

résumé /ˈrezuˌmeɪ/, **resume** /rɪˈzuːm/ *noun* a summary of a person's work experience and qualifications sent to a prospective employer by someone applying for a job ○ *Candidates should send a letter of application with a résumé to the HR manager.* ○ *The résumé listed all the candidate's previous jobs and her reasons for leaving them.* (NOTE: The U.K. term is **curriculum vitae.**)

resumption /rɪˈzʌmpʃən/ *noun* an act of starting again □ **we expect an early re**sumption of negotiations we expect negotiations will start again soon

retail /ˈriːteɪl/ *noun* the sale of small quantities of goods to the general public □ **the goods in stock have a retail value of $1m** the value of the goods if sold to the public is $1m, before discounts and other factors are taken into account ■ *adverb* □ **he buys wholesale and sells retail** he buys goods in bulk at a wholesale discount and sells in small quantities to the public ■ *verb* **1.** □ **to retail goods** to sell goods direct to the public **2.** to sell for a price □ **these items retail at** or **for $2.50** the retail price of these items is $2.50

retail dealer /ˈriːteɪl ˌdiːlər/ *noun* a person who sells to the general public

retailer /ˈriːteɪlər/ *noun* a person who runs a retail business, selling goods direct to the public

retailing /ˈriːteɪlɪŋ/ *noun* the selling of full-price goods to the public ○ *From car retailing the company branched out into car leasing.*

retail outlet /ˈriːteɪl ˌaʊtlet/ *noun* a store which sells to the general public

retail price /ˈriːteɪl ˌpraɪs/ *noun* the price at which the retailer sells to the final customer

retail price index /ˌriːteɪl ˈpraɪs ˌɪndeks/, **retail prices index** /ˌriːteɪl ˈpraɪsɪz ˌɪndeks/ *noun U.K.* same as **Consumer Price Index**

COMMENT: In the U.K., the RPI is calculated on a group of essential goods and services; it includes both sales tax and mortgage interest; the U.S. equivalent is the Consumer Price Index.

retail store /ˈriːteɪl stɔːr/ *noun* a store which sells goods to the general public

retail trade /ˈriːteɪl treɪd/ *noun* all people or businesses selling goods retail

retain /rɪˈteɪn/ *verb* **1.** to keep something or someone ○ *measures to retain experienced staff* ○ *Out of the profits, the company has retained $50,000 as provision against bad debts.* **2.** □ **to retain a lawyer to act for a company** to agree with a lawyer that he or she will act for you (and pay him or her a fee in advance)

retained earnings /rɪˌteɪnd ˈɜːnɪŋz/ *plural noun* an amount of profit after tax which a company does not pay out as dividend to the stockholders, but which is kept to be used for the further development of the business. Also called **retentions**

retained income /rɪˌteɪnd ˈɪnkʌm/, **retained profit** /rɪˌteɪnd ˈprɒfɪt/ *noun* same as **retained earnings**

retainer /rɪˈteɪnər/ *noun* money paid in advance to someone so that they will work for you, and not for someone else ○ *We pay them a retainer of $1,000.*

retention /rɪˈtenʃ(ə)n/ *noun* the process of keeping the loyalty of existing employees and persuading them not to work for another company

retentions /rɪˈtenʃənz/ *plural noun* same as **retained earnings**

retire /rɪˈtaɪr/ *verb* **1.** to stop work and take a pension ○ *She retired with a $15,000 pension.* ○ *The founder of the company retired at the age of 85.* ○ *The store is owned by a retired policeman.* **2.** to make an employee stop work and take a pension ○ *They decided to retire all staff over 50.* **3.** to come to the end of an elected term of office ○ *The treasurer retires from the council after six years.* ○ *Two retiring directors offer themselves for reelection.*

retiree /rɪˌtaɪˈriː/ *noun* a person who has retired or is about to retire

retirement /rɪˈtaɪrmənt/ *noun* **1.** the act of retiring from work ○ *I am looking forward to my retirement.* ○ *Older staff are planning what they will do in retirement.* □ **to take early retirement** to retire from work before the usual age **2.** the period when a person is retired

retirement age /rɪˈtaɪrmənt eɪdʒ/ *noun* the age at which people retire. In the U.S. this is usually 65.

retrain /riːˈtreɪn/ *verb* to train someone for a new job, or to do the same job in a more efficient way ○ *She went back to college to be retrained.*

retraining /riːˈtreɪnɪŋ/ *noun* the act of training again ○ *The store is closed for staff retraining.* ○ *He had to attend a retraining session.* ○ *Retraining is necessary to keep up with new production methods.*

retrench /rɪˈtrentʃ/ *verb* to reduce expenditure or to shelve expansion plans because money is not available

retrenchment /rɪˈtrentʃmənt/ *noun* a reduction of expenditure or of new plans ○ *The company is in for a period of retrenchment.*

retrieval /rɪˈtriːv(ə)l/ *noun* the act of getting something back

retrieval system /rɪˈtriːv(ə)l ˌsɪstəm/ *noun* a system which allows information to be retrieved

retrieve /rɪˈtriːv/ *verb* **1.** to get back (something) which has been lost ○ *The company is fighting to retrieve its market share.* **2.** to get back (information) which is stored in a computer ○ *All of the information was accidentally wiped off the computer so we cannot retrieve our sales figures for the last month.*

retroactive /ˌretroʊˈæktɪv/ *adjective* which takes effect from a time in the past ○ *They got a pay raise retroactive to last January.*

"The salary increases, retroactive from April of the current year, reflect the marginal rise in private sector salaries" [*Nikkei Weekly*]

retroactively /ˌretroʊˈæktɪvli/ *adverb* going back to a time in the past

return /rɪˈtɜrn/ *noun* **1.** the act of going back or coming back **2.** the act of sending something back □ **these goods are all on sale or return** if the retailer does not sell them, he sends them back to the supplier, and pays only for the items sold **3.** a profit or income from money invested ○ *We are buying technology stocks because they bring in a quick return.* **4.** an official statement or form that has to be sent in to the authorities **5.** same as **income tax return** ■ *verb* **1.** to send back ○ *to return unsold stock to the wholesaler* ○ *to return a letter to sender* **2.** to report ○ *to return income of $15,000 to the tax authorities*

"…with interest rates running well above inflation, investors want something that offers a return for their money" [*Business Week*]

returnable /rɪˈtɜrnəb(ə)l/ *adjective* which can be returned ○ *These bottles are not returnable.*

return address /rɪˈtɜrn əˌdres/ *noun* the address to which you send back something

returner /rɪˈtɜrnər/ *noun* a person who goes back to work after being away for a time

return journey /rɪˌtɜrn ˈdʒɜrni/ *noun* *U.K.* same as **round trip**

return on assets /rɪˌtɜrn ɒn ˈæsets/, **return on capital employed** /rɪˌtɜrn ɒn ˈekwɪti/, **return on equity** *noun* a profit shown as a percentage of the capital or money invested in a business. Abbreviation **ROA, ROCE, ROE**

return on capital employed /rɪˈtɜrn ən ˈkæpɪt(ə)l ɪmˈplɔɪd/, **return on assets** /rɪˌtɜrn ən ˈæsets/, **return on equity** /rɪˌtɜrn ən ˈekwɪti/ noun a profit shown as a percentage of the capital or money invested in a business. Abbreviation **ROCE, ROA, ROE**

return on investment /rɪˌtɜrn ən ɪn ˈvestmənt/ noun a ratio of the profit made in a financial year as a percentage of an investment. Abbreviation **ROI**

returns /rɪˈtɜrnz/ plural noun **1.** profits or income from investment ○ The company is looking for quick returns on its investment. **2.** unsold goods, especially books, newspapers, or magazines, sent back to the supplier

return ticket /rɪˌtɜrn ˈtɪkɪt/ noun U.K. same as **round-trip ticket** ○ I want two returns to Edinburgh.

revaluation /riˌvæljuˈeɪʃən/ noun **1.** an act of revaluing ○ The balance sheet takes into account the revaluation of the company's properties. **2.** the increasing of the value of a currency ○ The revaluation of the dollar against the euro.

revalue /riˈvælju/ verb to value something again, usually setting a higher value on it than before ○ The company's properties have been revalued. ○ The dollar has been revalued against all world currencies.

revenue /ˈrevənju/ noun **1.** money received ○ revenue from advertising or advertising revenue ○ Oil revenues have risen with the rise in the dollar. **2.** money received by a government in tax

revenue accounts /ˈrevənju əˌkaʊnts/ plural noun accounts of a business which record money received as sales, commission, etc.

revenue model /ˌrevənju ˈmɑd(ə)l/ noun a description of any of the methods by which an organization obtains income

revenue officer /ˈrevənju ˌɒfɪsər/ noun a person working in the government tax offices

revenue stream /ˈrevənju strim/ noun the income obtained by an organization from a particular source or activity

reversal /rɪˈvɜrs(ə)l/ noun a change from being profitable to unprofitable ○ The company suffered a reversal in the Far East.

reverse /rɪˈvɜrs/ adjective opposite or in the opposite direction ■ verb to change a decision to the opposite ○ The committee reversed its decision on import quotas.

reverse charge call /rɪˌvɜrs tʃɑrdʒ ˈkɔl/ noun a telephone call where the person receiving the call agrees to pay for it

reverse takeover /rɪˌvɜrs ˈteɪkoʊvər/ noun a takeover in which the company that has been taken over ends up owning the company which has taken it over. The acquiring company's stockholders give up their stock in exchange for stock in the target company.

reversion /rɪˈvɜrʃ(ə)n/ noun a return of property to an original owner □ **he has the reversion of the estate** he will receive the estate when the present lease ends

reversionary /rɪˈvɜrʃ(ə)n(ə)ri/ adjective referring to property which passes to another owner on the death of the present one

reversionary annuity /rɪˌvɜrʃ(ə)n(ə)ri əˈnuəti/ noun an annuity paid to someone on the death of another person

review /rɪˈvju/ noun **1.** a general examination ○ to conduct a review of distributors □ **she had a salary review last April** her salary was examined (and increased) in April ○ The company has decided to review freelance payments in light of the rising cost of living. **2.** a magazine, monthly or weekly journal ○ We read it in last month's international business review. ■ verb to examine something generally □ **to review salaries** to look at all salaries in a company to decide on increases ○ His salary will be reviewed at the end of the year. □ **to review discounts** to look at discounts offered to decide whether to change them

revise /rɪˈvaɪz/ verb to change something which has been calculated or planned ○ Sales forecasts are revised annually. ○ The chairman is revising his speech to the annual meeting.

revival of trade /rɪˌvaɪv(ə)l əv ˈtreɪd/ noun an increase in trade after a recession

revive /rɪˈvaɪv/ verb to make more lively; to increase (after a recession) ○ The government is introducing measures to revive trade. ○ Industry is reviving after the recession.

revoke /rɪ'vəʊk/ *verb* to cancel something ○ *to revoke a decision* or *a clause in an agreement* ○ *The quota on luxury items has been revoked.*

revolving credit /rɪ,vɒlvɪŋ 'kredɪt/ *noun* a system where someone can borrow money at any time up to an agreed amount, and continue to borrow while still paying off the original loan. Also called **open-ended credit**

reward /rɪ'wɔːd/ *verb* to give a person something in return for effort or achievement ○ *The work is hard and not very rewarding financially.*

"...an additional incentive is that the Japanese are prepared to give rewards where they are due" [*Management Today*]

reward package /rɪ'wɔːd ,pækɪdʒ/ *noun* the total of all money and benefits given to an employee (including salary, bonuses, company car, pension plans, medical insurance, etc.)

rich /rɪtʃ/ *adjective* **1.** having a lot of money ○ *a rich stockbroker* ○ *a rich oil company* **2.** having a lot of natural resources ○ *The country is rich in minerals.* ○ *The oil-rich territory has attracted several international companies.*

-rich /rɪtʃ/ *suffix* meaning "which contains or has a large amount of something"

rid /rɪd/ □ **to get rid of something** to throw something away because it is useless ○ *The company is trying to get rid of all its old stock.* ○ *Our department has been told to get rid of twenty staff.* ○ *The department has been told to get rid of twenty staff.*

rider /'raɪdər/ *noun* an additional clause ○ *to add a rider to a contract*

rig /rɪɡ/ *verb* to arrange illegally or dishonestly for a result to be changed ○ *They tried to rig the election of officers.* □ **to rig the market** to make stock prices go up or down so as to make a profit

right /raɪt/ *noun* a legal entitlement to something ○ *There is no automatic right of renewal to this contract.* ○ *She has a right to the property.* ○ *He has no right to the patent.* ○ *The staff have a right to know how the company is doing.*

rightful /'raɪtf(ə)l/ *adjective* legally correct

rightful claimant /,raɪtf(ə)l 'kleɪmənt/ *noun* a person who has a legal claim to something (NOTE: This term has now replaced **plaintiff**. The other side in a case is the **defendant**.)

rightful owner /,raɪtf(ə)l 'əʊnər/ *noun* a legal owner

right-hand man /,raɪt hænd 'mæn/ *noun* a man who is the main assistant to someone

right of way /,raɪt əv 'weɪ/ *noun* a legal title to go across someone's property

rights issue /'raɪts ,ɪʃuː/ *noun* an arrangement which gives stockholders the right to buy more stock at a lower price (NOTE: The U.S. term is **rights offering**.)

right-sizing /'raɪt ,saɪzɪŋ/ *noun* the process of reducing a company's work force to its most economical size, usually by dismissing some of its employees

"...intense competition and rapid change are destroying predictability. Virtual organizations and many current managerial practices, such as reengineering, continuous improvement, matrix management, and "rightsizing," ignore this human need." [*Harvard Business Review*]

right to strike /,raɪt tə 'straɪk/ *noun* a legal right of employees to stop working if they have a good reason for it

ring /rɪŋ/ *noun* **1.** a group of people who try to fix prices so as not to compete with each other and still make a large profit **2.** a trading floor on a commodity exchange

ring back *phrasal verb U.K.* same as **call back**

rise /raɪz/ *noun* **1.** an increase ○ *A rise in the price of raw materials.* ○ *Oil price rises brought about a recession in world trade.* ○ *There has been a rise in sales of 10%* or *Sales show a rise of 10%.* ○ *Salaries are increasing to keep up with the rises in the cost of living.* ○ *The recent rise in interest rates has made mortgages dearer.* ○ *There needs to be an increase in salaries to keep up with the rise in the cost of living.* **2.** an increase in pay ○ *She asked her boss for a rise.* ○ *He had a 6% rise in January.* (NOTE: The U.S. term is **raise**.) ■ *verb* to move upward or to become higher ○ *Prices* or *Salaries are rising faster than inflation.* ○ *Interest rates have risen to 15%.* ○ *Salaries are rising faster than inflation.* (NOTE: **rising – rose – risen**)

risk /rɪsk/ *noun* **1.** possible harm or a chance of danger □ **to run a risk** to be likely to suffer harm □ **to take a risk** to do something which may make you lose money or suffer harm **2.** □ **at owner's risk** a situation where goods shipped or stored are insured by the owner, not by the transportation company or the storage company ○ *Goods left here are at owner's risk.* ○ *The shipment was sent at owner's risk.* **3.** loss or damage against which you are insured **4.** □ **he is a good** *or* **bad risk** it is not likely or it is very likely that the insurance company will have to pay out against claims where he is concerned

risk arbitrage /ˌrɪsk ˈɑrbɪtrɑrʒ/ *noun* the business of buying stock in companies which are likely to be taken over and so rise in price

risk assessment /ˈrɪsk əˌsesmənt/ *noun* the process of working out how risky any particular course of action may be. Risk assessments are important in areas such as health and safety and environmental management, in which safety can sometimes be improved, but can also be used to estimate economic and social risk and play a part in strategic planning.

risk-averse /ˌrɪsk əˈvɜrs/ *adjective* not wanting to take risks

risk capital /ˈrɪsk ˌkæpɪt(ə)l/ *noun* same as **venture capital**

risk factor /ˈrɪsk ˌfæktər/ *noun* the amount of risk involved in carrying out a project or other business activity

risk-free /ˌrɪsk ˈfri/, **riskless** /ˈrɪskləs/ *adjective* with no risk involved ○ *a risk-free investment*

risky /ˈrɪski/ *adjective* dangerous or which may cause harm ○ *We lost all our money in some risky ventures in South America.*

rival /ˈraɪv(ə)l/ *noun* a person or company that competes in the same market ○ *a rival company* ○ *to undercut a rival*

road haulage /ˈroʊd ˌhɔlɪdʒ/ *noun* the moving of goods by road

road haulage depot /roʊd ˈhɔlɪdʒ ˌdepoʊ/ *noun* a center for goods which are being moved by road, and the trucks which carry them

road hauler /ˈroʊd ˌhɔlər/ *noun* a company which transports goods by road

robot /ˈroʊbɑt/ *noun* a machine which can be programmed to work like a person ○ *The car is made by robots.*

ROCE *abbreviation* return on capital employed

rock /rɑk/ *noun* □ **the company is on the rocks** the company is in great financial difficulties

rock bottom /ˌrɑk ˈbɑtəm/ *noun* □ **sales have reached rock bottom** sales have reached the lowest point possible

rocket /ˈrɑkət/ *verb* to rise fast ○ *Investors are rushing to cash in on rocketing stock prices.* ○ *Prices have rocketed on the commodity markets.*

ROI *abbreviation* return on investment

roll /roʊl/ *noun* something which has been turned over and over to wrap round itself ○ *The desk calculator uses a roll of paper.* ○ *We need to order some more rolls of fax paper.* ■ *verb* **1.** to make something go forward by turning it over or pushing it on wheels ○ *They rolled the computer into position.*

    roll over *phrasal verb* □ **to roll over a credit** to make credit available over a continuing period

rolling account /ˈroʊlɪŋ əˌkaʊnt/ *noun* a system where there are no fixed account days, but stock exchange transactions are paid at a fixed period after each transaction has taken place, as opposed to the U.K. system, where an account day is fixed each month

rolling budget /ˌroʊlɪŋ ˈbʌdʒɪt/ *noun* a budget which moves forward on a regular basis, such as a budget covering a twelve-month period which moves forward each month or quarter

rolling launch /ˌroʊlɪŋ ˈlɔntʃ/ *noun* a gradual launch of a new product onto the market by launching it in different areas over a period

rolling plan /ˌroʊlɪŋ ˈplæn/ *noun* a plan which runs for a period of time and is updated regularly for the same period

rolling settlement /ˌroʊlɪŋ ˈset(ə)lmənt/ *noun* same as **rolling account**

rolling stock /ˈroʊlɪŋ stɑk/ *noun* wagons, etc., used on the railroad

roll on/roll off (RORO) /ˌroʊl ɑn ˌroʊl ˈɔf/ *adjective* (ferry) where trucks and cars can drive straight into or off the boat

rollout /ˈroʊlaʊt/ *noun* same as **rolling launch**

ROM /rɑm/ *abbreviation* read only memory

room /rum/ *noun* **1.** a part of a building, divided off from other parts by walls ○ *The chairman's room is at the end of the corridor.* **2.** a bedroom in a hotel ○ *I want a room with bath for two nights.* **3.** a space ○ *The filing cabinets take up a lot of room.* ○ *There is no more room in the computer file.*

room divider /'rum dɪˌvaɪdər/ *noun* a movable low wall, which can be used to make a "room" in an open-plan office

room reservations /'rum ˌrezəveɪʃ(ə)nz/ *noun* a department in a hotel which deals with bookings for rooms ○ *Can you put me through to reservations?*

room service /'rum ˌsɜrvɪs/ *noun* arrangement in a hotel where food or drink can be served in a guest's bedroom

rootless capitalism /ˌrutləs 'kæpɪt(ə)lɪz(ə)m/ *noun* capitalism that is not restricted to one particular country or economy

rota /'routə/, **roster** /'rastər/ *noun* a list showing when different members of staff will do certain duties ○ *We are drawing up a new roster for Saturday afternoon work.*

rotation /rou'teɪʃ(ə)n/ *noun* the act of taking turns □ **to fill the post of chairman by rotation** to let each member of the group act as chairman for a period then give the post to another member □ **two directors retire by rotation** two directors retire because they have been directors longer than any others, but can offer themselves for reelection

rough /rʌf/ *adjective* **1.** approximate, not very accurate **2.** not finished

rough out *phrasal verb* to make a draft or a general design of something, which may be changed later ○ *The finance director roughed out a plan of investment.*

rough calculation /ˌrʌf ˌkælkjʊ'leɪʃ(ə)n/ *noun* a way of working out a mathematical problem approximately, or the approximate result arrived at ○ *I made some rough calculations on the back of an envelope.*

rough copy /ˌrʌf 'kɑpi/ *noun* a draft of a document which, it is expected, will have changes made to it

rough draft /ˌrʌf 'dræft/ *noun* a plan of a document which may have changes made to it before it is complete

roughly /'rʌfli/ *adverb* more or less ○ *The turnover is roughly twice last year's.*

○ *The development cost of the project will be roughly $25,000.*

round *noun* a series (of meetings) ○ *a round of pay negotiations* ■ *phrasal verb* to make a fractional figure a full figure, by increasing or decreasing it ○ *Some figures have been rounded to the nearest cent.*

round down *phrasal verb* to decrease a fractional figure to the nearest full figure

round up *phrasal verb* to increase a fractional figure to the nearest full figure ○ *to round up the figures to the nearest pound*

"…each cheque can be made out for the local equivalent of œ100 rounded up to a convenient figure" [*Sunday Times*]

round lot /ˌraʊnd 'lɑt/ *noun* a group of 100 shares of stock bought or sold together. Also called **even lot, full lot**

roundtable /raʊnd'teɪb(ə)l/ *noun* a discussion or negotiation between several parties or groups who all take part on equal terms

round trip /'raʊnd trɪp/ *noun* a trip from one place to another and back again ○ *She bought a round-trip ticket.* ○ *The round-trip fare is twice the one-way fare.*

round-trip ticket /rɪˌtɜrn 'tɪkɪt/ *noun* a ticket for a journey to a place and back again ○ *I want two returns to Edinburgh.*

route /rut/ *noun* a way which is regularly taken ○ *Companies were warned that normal shipping routes were dangerous because of the war.*

router /'raʊtər/ *noun* a device that switches telephone calls to another network that may offer cheaper rates

routine /ru'tin/ *noun* a normal or regular way of doing something ○ *Refitting the conference room has disturbed the office routine.* ■ *adjective* normal or which happens regularly ○ *routine work* ○ *a routine call* ○ *They carried out a routine check of the fire equipment.*

royalty /'rɔɪəlti/ *noun* money paid to an inventor, writer, or the owner of land for the right to use their property, usually a specific percentage of sales, or a specific amount per sale ○ *The country will benefit from rising oil royalties.* ○ *He is still receiving substantial royalties from his invention.*

RPI *abbreviation* retail price index

RPM *abbreviation* resale price maintenance

RRP *abbreviation* recommended retail price

RSI *abbreviation* repetitive strain injury

R.S.V.P. letters on an invitation asking the person invited to reply. Full form **répondez s'il vous plaît**

ruble /'rub(ə)l/ *noun* a unit of currency used in Russia and Belarus (NOTE: The U.S. spelling is **ruble**.)

rule /rul/ *noun* **1.** a statement that directs how people should behave ○ *It is a company rule that smoking is not allowed in the offices.* ○ *The rules of the organization are explained during the induction sessions.* □ **as a rule** usually ○ *As a rule, we do not give discounts over 20%.* **2.** □ **to work to rule** to work strictly according to the rules agreed by the company and union, and therefore to work very slowly ■ *verb* **1.** to give an official decision ○ *The commission of inquiry ruled that the company was in breach of contract.* ○ *The judge ruled that the documents had to be deposited with the court.* **2.** to be in force or to be current ○ *Prices which are ruling at the moment.* ○ *The current ruling agreement is being redrafted.*

rulebook /'rulbʊk/ *noun* a set of rules by which the members of a self-regulatory organization must operate

rule of thumb /ˌrul əv 'θʌm/ *noun* an easily remembered way of doing a simple calculation

ruling /'rulɪŋ/ *adjective* in operation at the moment, current ○ *We will invoice at ruling prices.* ■ *noun* a decision ○ *The inquiry gave a ruling on the case.* ○ *According to the ruling of the court, the contract was illegal.*

run /rʌn/ *noun* **1.** a period of time during which a machine is working □ **a check run** a series of checks processed through a computer **2.** a rush to buy something ○ *The Post Office reported a run on the new stamps.* □ **a run on the bank** a rush by customers to take deposits out of a bank which they think may close down □ **a run on the pound** a rush to sell pounds and buy other currencies **3.** a regular route (of a plane or bus) ○ *He flies the Chicago-New York run.* ■ *verb* **1.** to be in force ○ *The lease runs for twenty years.* ○ *The lease has only six months to run.* **2.** to amount to ○ *The costs ran into thousands of pounds.* **3.** to manage or to organize something ○

She runs a mail-order business from home. ○ *They run a staff sports club.* ○ *He is running a multimillion-pound company.* (NOTE: **running – ran – run**) **4.** to work on a machine ○ *Do not run the photocopier for more than four hours at a time.* ○ *The computer was running invoices all night.* **5.** (*of buses, trains, etc.*) to be working ○ *this train runs on weekdays* ○ *There is an evening plane running between Manchester and Paris.* (NOTE: **running – ran – has run**) ■ **1.** to be in a particular state or to be taking place in a particular way ○ *The meeting was running late.* **2.** to continue or to last ○ *The lease runs for twenty years.* ○ *The lease has only six months to run.* (NOTE: **running – ran – has run**)

run down *phrasal verb* **1.** to reduce a quantity gradually ○ *We decided to run down stocks* or *to let stocks run down at the end of the financial year.* **2.** to slow down the business activities of a company before it is going to be closed ○ *The company is being run down.*

run into *phrasal verb* **1.** □ **to run into debt** to start to have debts **2.** to amount to ○ *Costs have run into thousands of pounds.* □ **he has an income running into five figures** he earns more than $10,000

run out of *phrasal verb* to have nothing left of something, to use up all the stock of something ○ *We have run out of headed notepaper.* ○ *The printer has run out of paper.*

run up *phrasal verb* to make debts or costs go up quickly ○ *He quickly ran up a bill for $250.*

runaway inflation /ˌrʌnəweɪ ɪn'fleɪʃ(ə)n/ *noun* very rapid inflation, which is almost impossible to reduce

running /'rʌnɪŋ/ *noun* □ **the company has made a profit for six years running** the company has made a profit for six years one after the other

running costs /'rʌnɪŋ kɒsts/ *plural noun* money spent on the day-to-day cost of keeping a business going

running total /ˌrʌnɪŋ 'təʊt(ə)l/ *noun* the total carried from one column of figures to the next

rupee /ru'pi/ *noun* a unit of currency used in India, Mauritius, Nepal, Pakistan and Sri Lanka (NOTE: Written **Rs** before the figure: *Rs. 250.*)

rush /rʌʃ/ *noun* doing something rapidly ■ *verb* to make something go fast ○ *to rush an order through the factory*

rush hour /'rʌʃ aʊr/ *noun* the time when traffic is worst, when everyone is trying to travel to work or from work back home ○ *The taxi was delayed in the rush hour traffic.*

rush job /'rʌʃ dʒɑb/ *noun* a job which has to be done fast

rush order /ˌrʌʃ 'ɔrdər/ *noun* an order which has to be supplied fast

S

sack /sæk/ *verb U.K.* same as **fire**

sackful /'sækful/ *noun* a large amount, the contents of a sack ○ *We got sackfuls of replies to our TV ad.*

s.a.e. *abbreviation* stamped addressed envelope ○ *Send your application form to the personnel officer, with an s.a.e. for reply.*

safe /seɪf/ *noun* a heavy metal box which cannot be opened easily, in which valuable documents and money can be kept ○ *Put the documents in the safe.* ○ *We keep the petty cash in the safe.* ■ *adjective* out of danger □ **keep the documents in a safe place** in a place where they cannot be stolen or destroyed

safe deposit /'seɪf dɪ,pɑzɪt/ *noun* a bank safe where you can leave jewelry or documents

safe deposit box /,seɪf dɪ'pɑzɪt ,bɑks/ *noun* a small box which you can rent to keep jewelry or documents in a bank's safe

safeguard /'seɪfgɑrd/ *verb* to protect something or someone ○ *The duty of the directors is to safeguard the interests of the stockholders.* ■ *noun* something that provides protection

safe investment /,seɪf ɪn'vestmənt/ *noun* something, e.g., a stock, which is not likely to fall in value

safe keeping /,seɪf 'kipɪŋ/ *noun* the fact of being looked after carefully ○ *We put the documents into the bank for safe keeping.*

safely /'seɪfli/ *adverb* without being harmed ○ *The cargo was unloaded safely from the sinking ship.*

safety /'seɪfti/ *noun* **1.** the fact of being free from danger or risk □ **to take safety precautions** *or* **safety measures** to act to make sure something is safe **2.** □ **for safety** to make something safe, to be safe ○ *to*

take a copy of the disk for safety ○ *Put the documents in the cupboard for safety.*

safety margin /'seɪfti ,mɑrdʒɪn/ *noun* a time or space allowed to make sure that something can be done safely

safety measures /'seɪfti ,meʒərz/ *plural noun* actions to make sure that something is safe

safety precautions /'seɪfti prɪ,kɔrʃ(ə)nz/ *plural noun* actions to try to make sure that something is safe

safety regulations /'seɪfti regjʊ,leɪʃ(ə)nz/ *plural noun* rules to make a place of work safe for the employees

salability /,seɪlə'bɪləti/, **saleability** *noun* a quality in an item which makes it easy to sell

salable /'seɪləb(ə)l/, **saleable** *adjective* which can easily be sold ○ *The company is not readily salable in its present state.*

salaried /'sælərid/ *adjective* earning a salary ○ *The company has 250 salaried staff.*

salary /'sæləri/ *noun* **1.** a regular payment for work done, made to an employee usually as a check at the end of each month ○ *The company froze all salaries for a six-month period.* ○ *If I get promoted, my salary will go up.* ○ *The salary may be low, but the fringe benefits attached to the job are good.* ○ *She got a salary increase in June.* **2.** an amount paid to an employee, shown as a monthly, quarterly or yearly total (NOTE: The plural is **salaries**.)

salary ceiling /'sæləri ,silɪŋ/ *noun* **1.** the maximum amount which can be earned for a particular job or by a particular class of employee, as set by a government or by an agreement between a trade union and an employer **2.** the highest level on a pay scale that a particular employee can achieve under his or her contract

salary check /'sæləri tʃek/ *noun* a check by which a salaried employee is paid

salary cut /'sæləri kʌt/ *noun* a sudden reduction in salary

salary deductions /'sæləri dɪ,dʌkʃənz/ *plural noun* money which a company removes from salaries to pay to the government as tax, National Insurance contributions, etc.

salary package /'sæləri ,pækɪdʒ/ *noun* same as **pay package**

salary review /'sæləri rɪ,vjuː/ *noun* same as **pay review** ○ *She had a salary review last April* or *Her salary was reviewed last April.*

salary scale /'sæləri skeɪl/ *noun* same as **pay scale** ○ *He was appointed at the top end of the salary scale.*

salary structure /'sæləri ,strʌktʃər/ *noun* the organization of salaries in a company with different rates of pay for different types of job

sale /seɪl/ *noun* **1.** an act of giving an item or doing a service in exchange for money, or for the promise that money will be paid □ **for sale** ready to be sold □ **to offer something for sale** *or* **to put something up for sale** to announce that something is ready to be sold ○ *They put the factory up for sale.* ○ *His store is for sale.* ○ *These items are not for sale to the general public.* □ **sale or return** a system where the retailer sends goods back if they are not sold, and pays the supplier only for goods sold ○ *We have taken 4,000 items on sale or return.* □ **on sale** ready to be sold in a store ○ *These items are on sale in most druggists.* **2.** an act of selling goods at specially low prices ○ *The store is having a sale to clear old stock.* ○ *The sale price is 50% of the usual price.*

sale and lease-back /,seɪl ən 'liːs bæk/ *noun* a situation where a company sells a property to raise cash and then leases it back from the purchaser

saleroom /'seɪlruːm/ *noun* a room where an auction takes place

sales /seɪlz/ *plural noun* **1.** money received for selling something ○ *Sales have risen over the first quarter.* **2.** items sold, or the number of items sold **3.** □ **the sales** period when major stores sell many items at specially low prices ○ *I bought this in*

the sales or at the sales or in the January sales.

sales analysis /'seɪlz ə,næləsɪs/ *noun* an examination of the reports of sales to see why items have or have not sold well

sales appeal /'seɪlz ə,piːl/ *noun* a quality in a product which makes customers want to buy it

sales book /'seɪlz bʊk/ *noun* a record of sales

sales budget /'seɪlz ,bʌdʒət/ *noun* a plan of probable sales

sales campaign /'seɪlz kæm,peɪn/ *noun* a series of planned activities to achieve higher sales

sales channel /'seɪlz ,tʃæn(ə)l/ *noun* any means by which products can be brought into the marketplace and offered for sale, either directly to the customer or indirectly through retailers or dealers

sales chart /'seɪlz tʃɑːt/ *noun* a diagram showing how sales vary from month to month

sales clerk /'seɪlz klɜːk/ *noun* a person who sells goods to customers in a store

sales conference /'seɪlz ,kɑnf(ə)rəns/ *noun* a meeting of sales managers, representatives, publicity staff, etc., to discuss results and future sales plans

sales curve /'seɪlz kɜːv/ *noun* a graph showing how sales increase or decrease

sales day book /,seɪlz 'deɪ ,bʊk/ *noun* a book in which non-cash sales are recorded with details of customer, invoice, amount and date; these details are later posted to each customer's account in the sales ledger. Abbreviation **SDB**

sales department /'seɪlz dɪ,pɑːtmənt/ *noun* the section of a company which deals with selling the company's products or services

sales drive /'seɪlz draɪv/ *noun* a vigorous effort to increase sales

sales executive /'seɪlz ɪg,zekjʊtɪv/ *noun* a person in a company or department in charge of sales

sales figures /'seɪlz ,fɪgərz/ *plural noun* total sales

sales force /'seɪlz fɔːs/ *noun* a group of sales staff

sales forecast /'seɪlz ,fɔːkæst/ *noun* an estimate of future sales

sales invoice /'seɪlz ˌɪnvɔɪs/ *noun* an invoice relating to a sale

sales journal /'seɪlz ˌdʒɜrn(ə)l/ *noun* the book in which non-cash sales are recorded with details of customer, invoice, amount and date. These details are later posted to each customer's account in the sales ledger.

sales ledger /'seɪlz ˌledʒər/ *noun* a book in which sales to each customer are entered

sales ledger clerk /'seɪlz ˌledʒər ˌklɜrk/ *noun* an office employee who deals with the sales ledger

sales literature /'seɪlz ˌlɪt(ə)rətʃər/ *noun* printed information which helps sales, e.g., leaflets or prospectuses

salesman /'seɪlzmən/ *noun* a man who sells an organization's products or services to customers, especially to retail shops ○ *He is the head salesman in the carpet department.* ○ *His only experience is as a used-car salesman.* ○ *Salesmen are paid a basic salary plus commission.*

sales manager /'seɪlz ˌmænɪdʒər/ *noun* a person in charge of a sales department

salesmanship /'seɪlzmənʃɪp/ *noun* the art of selling or of persuading customers to buy

sales mix /'seɪlz mɪks/ *noun* the sales and profitability of a wide range of products sold by a single company

sales outlet /'seɪlz ˌaʊt(ə)let/ *noun* a store which sells to the general public

"...that aims to offer a one-stop sales outlet for companies that need to sell a diverse mix of used equipment and surplus inventory." [*InformationWeek*]

salesperson /'seɪlzˌpɜrs(ə)n/ *noun* **1.** a person who sells goods or services to members of the public **2.** a person who sells products or services to retail stores on behalf of a company (NOTE: The plural is **salespeople**.)

sales pitch /'seɪlz pɪtʃ/ *noun* a talk by a salesperson to persuade someone to buy

sales report /'seɪlz rɪˌpɔrt/ *noun* a report made showing the number of items or amount of money received for selling stock ○ *In the sales reports all the European countries are bracketed together.*

sales representative /'seɪlz reprɪˌzentətɪv/, **sales rep** /'seɪlz rep/ *noun*

same as **salesperson** ○ *We have six sales representatives in Europe.* ○ *They have vacancies for sales representatives to call on accounts in the Midwest.*

sales return /'seɪlz rɪˌtɜrn/ *noun* a report of sales made each day or week or quarter

sales revenue /'seɪlz ˌrevənju/ *noun* the income from sales of goods or services

sales sheet /'seɪlz ʃit/ *noun* paper which gives details of a product and explains why it is good

sales slip /'seɪlz slɪp/ *noun* a paper showing that an article was bought at a specific store ○ *Goods can be exchanged only on production of a sales slip.*

sales target /'seɪlz ˌtɑrgət/ *noun* the amount of sales a sales representative is expected to achieve

sales tax /'seɪlz tæks/ *noun* a tax which is paid on each item sold and is collected when the purchase is made. Also called **turnover tax**

sales team /'seɪlz tim/ *noun* all representatives, sales staff, and sales managers working in a company

sales volume /'seɪlz ˌvɑljum/ *noun* the number of units sold (NOTE: The U.K. term is **turnover**.)

saleswoman /'seɪlzwʊmən/ *noun* **1.** a woman who sells an organization's products or services to customers **2.** a woman in a store who sells goods to customers (NOTE: The plural is **saleswomen**.)

salvage /'sælvɪdʒ/ *noun* **1.** the work of saving a ship or a cargo from being destroyed **2.** goods saved from a wrecked ship, from a fire or from some other accident ○ *a sale of flood salvage items* (NOTE: no plural) ■ *verb* **1.** to save goods or a ship from being destroyed ○ *We are selling off a warehouse full of salvaged goods.* **2.** to save something from loss ○ *The company is trying to salvage its reputation after the managing director was sent to prison for fraud.* ○ *The receiver managed to salvage something from the collapse of the company.*

salvage money /'sælvɪdʒ ˌmʌni/ *noun* payment made by the owner of a ship or a cargo to the person who has saved it

salvage value /'sælvɪdʒ ˌvælju/ *noun* the value of an asset if sold for scrap

salvage vessel /'sælvɪdʒ ˌves(ə)l/ *noun* a ship which specializes in saving other ships and their cargoes

same /seɪm/ *adjective* being or looking exactly alike

"...previously, only orders received by 11 a.m. via the Internet could be delivered the same day, and then only for a limited range of items. With fast packaging and inspection, same-day delivery is now possible anywhere in Tokyo" [*Nikkei Weekly*]

same-store sales /ˌseɪm stɔr 'seɪlz/ *noun* sales for the same stores over an earlier period

"...it led the nation's department stores over the crucial Christmas season with an 11.7% increase in same-store sales" [*Fortune*]

"...its consistent double-digit same-store sales growth also proves that it is not just adding revenue by adding new locations" [*Fortune*]

sample /'sæmpəl/ *noun* **1.** a small part of an item which is used to show what the whole item is like ○ *Can you provide us with a sample of the cloth* or *a cloth sample?* **2.** a small group which is studied in order to show what a larger group is like ○ *We interviewed a sample of potential customers.* ■ *verb* **1.** to test or to try something by taking a small amount of it ○ *to sample a product before buying it* **2.** to ask a representative group of people questions to find out what the reactions of a much larger group would be ○ *They sampled 2,000 people at random to test the new drink.*

sample book /'sæmpəl bʊk/ *noun* a book showing samples of different types of cloth, paper, etc.

sampling /'sæmplɪŋ/ *noun* **1.** the testing of a product by taking a small amount ○ *a sampling of European Union produce* **2.** the testing of the reactions of a small group of people to find out the reactions of a larger group of consumers

sampling error /'sæmplɪŋ ˌerər/ *noun* the difference between the results achieved in a survey using a small sample and what the results would be if you used the entire population

sanction /'sæŋkʃən/ *noun* permission ○ *You will need the sanction of the local authorities before you can knock down the office building.* ■ *verb* to approve ○ *The*

board sanctioned the expenditure of $1.2m on the development project.

"...members of the new Association of Coffee Producing Countries voted to cut their exports by 20 per cent to try to raise prices. The Association voted also on ways to enforce the agreement and to implement sanctions if it is breached" [*Times*]

S&L *abbreviation* savings and loan

sandwich board /'sændwɪtʃ bɔrd/ *noun* a pair of boards with advertisements on them that is suspended from shoulder straps in front of and behind the person wearing them

sandwich course /'sændwɪtʃ kɔrs/ *noun* a course of study where students at a college or institute spend a period of time working in a factory, office or other organization as part of gaining their qualification

sandwich lease /'sændwɪtʃ lis/ *noun* a lease held by someone who sublets the property he is leasing

satisfaction /ˌsætɪs'fækʃən/ *noun* a good feeling of happiness and contentment ○ *He finds great satisfaction in the job even though the pay is bad.*

satisfy /'sætɪsfaɪ/ *verb* **1.** to give satisfaction or to please (NOTE: **satisfies – satisfying – satisfied**) □ **to satisfy a client** to make a client pleased with what they have purchased □ **a satisfied customer** a customer who has gotten what they wanted **2.** to fill the requirements for a job (NOTE: **satisfies – satisfying – satisfied**) □ **to satisfy a demand** to fill a demand ○ *We cannot produce enough to satisfy the demand for the product.*

saturate /'sætʃəreɪt/ *verb* to fill something completely ○ *They are planning to saturate the market with cheap cell phones.* ○ *The market for home computers is saturated.*

saturation /ˌsætʃə'reɪʃ(ə)n/ *noun* the process of filling completely □ **saturation of the market**, **market saturation** a situation where the market has taken as much of the product as it can buy □ **the market has reached saturation point** the market is at a point where it cannot buy anymore of the product

saturation advertising /ˌsætʃə 'reɪʃ(ə)n ˌædvərtaɪzɪŋ/ *noun* a highly intensive advertising campaign ○ *Saturation advertising is needed when there are large* numbers of competitive products on the market.

save /seɪv/ verb **1.** to keep, not to spend (money) ○ He is trying to save money by walking to work. ○ She is saving to buy a house. **2.** not to waste, to use less ○ To save time, let us continue the discussion in the taxi to the airport. ○ The government is encouraging companies to save energy. **3.** to store data on a computer disk ○ Don't forget to save your files when you have finished keyboarding them.

save on phrasal verb not to waste, to use less ○ By introducing shift work we find we can save on fuel.

save up phrasal verb to put money aside for a special purpose ○ They are saving up for a vacation in Europe.

save-as-you-earn /ˌseɪv əz ju ˈɜːn/ noun U.K. a scheme where employees can save money regularly by having it deducted automatically from their wages and invested in National Savings. Abbreviation **SAYE**

saver /ˈseɪvər/ noun a person who saves money

saving /ˈseɪvɪŋ/ noun the action of using less ○ We are aiming for a 10% saving in fuel. ○ The new heating system has produced remarkable savings in fuel. ■ suffix which uses less

savings /ˈseɪvɪŋz/ plural noun money saved (i.e. money which is not spent) ○ She put all her savings into a deposit account.

savings account /ˈseɪvɪŋz əˌkaʊnt/ noun an account where you put money in regularly and which pays interest, often at a higher rate than a deposit account

savings and loan /ˈseɪvɪŋz ən ˈloʊn/, **savings and loan association** /ˈseɪvɪŋz ən ˈloʊn əˌsoʊsieɪʃ(ə)n/ noun a financial association which accepts and pays interest on deposits from investors and lends money to people who are buying property. The loans are in the form of mortgages on the security of the property being bought. S&Ls are regulated by the Office of Thrift Supervision and are protected by the Savings Association Insurance Fund. Abbreviation **S&L**. Also called **thrift** (NOTE: The U.K. term is **building society**.)

COMMENT: Because of deregulation of interest rates in 1980, many S&Ls found that they were forced to raise in-

terest on deposits to current market rates in order to secure funds, while at the same time they still were charging low fixed-interest rates on the mortgages granted to borrowers. This created considerable problems and many S&Ls had to be rescued by the Federal government.

savings bank /ˈseɪvɪŋz bæŋk/ noun a bank where you can deposit money and receive interest on it

SAYE abbreviation save-as-you-earn

SBA abbreviation Small Business Administration

SBU abbreviation strategic business unit

scale /skeɪl/ noun **1.** a system which is graded into various levels □ **scale of charges** or **scale of prices** a list showing various prices □ **scale of salaries** a list of salaries showing different levels of pay in different jobs in the same company **2.** □ **to start in business on a small scale** to start in business with a small staff, few products or little capital

scale down phrasal verb to lower something in proportion

scale up phrasal verb to increase something in proportion

scales /skeɪlz/ noun a machine for weighing

scalp /skælp/ verb to buy or sell to make a quick profit

scam /skæm/ noun a fraud, an illegal or dishonest scheme (informal) ○ Many financial scams only come to light by accident.

scandal /ˈskænd(ə)l/ noun a wrong action that produces a general feeling of public anger ○ The government was brought down by the scandal over the slush funds.

"...frauds have always been perpetrated, but the growth of the capital markets in the last 30 years has led to an explosion in trading scandals" [Times]

scanner /ˈskænər/ noun a device for examining written or recorded data, e.g., for reading a product bar code for inventory and pricing purposes

scarce /skers/ adjective not easily found or not common ○ scarce raw materials ○ Reliable trained staff are scarce.

scarceness /ˈskersnəs/, **scarcity** /ˈskersɪti/ noun the state of being scarce ○ There is a scarcity of trained staff.

scarcity value /'skersəti ˌvælju/ *noun* the value something has because it is rare and there is a large demand for it

scenario /sɪ'neriəʊ/ *noun* the way in which a situation may develop, or a description or forecast of possible future developments

scenario planning /sɪ'neriəʊ ˌplænɪŋ/ *noun* a planning technique in which the planners write down several different descriptions of what they think might happen in the future and how future events, good or bad, might affect their organization (NOTE: Scenario planning can help managers to prepare for changes in the business environment, to develop strategies for dealing with unexpected events, and to choose between alternate strategic options.)

schedule /'skedʒəl/ *noun* **1.** a timetable, a plan of how time should be spent, drawn up in advance ○ *The managing director has a busy schedule of appointments.* ○ *Her assistant tried to fit us into her schedule.* □ **on schedule** at the time or stage set down in the schedule ○ *The launch took place on schedule.* □ **to be ahead of schedule** to be early ○ *The building was completed ahead of schedule.* □ **to be on schedule** to be on time ○ *The project is on schedule.* ○ *We are on schedule to complete the project at the end of May.* □ **to be behind schedule** to be late ○ *I am sorry to say that we are three months behind schedule.* **2.** a list, especially a list forming an additional document attached to a contract ○ *the schedule of territories to which a contract applies* ○ *Please find enclosed our schedule of charges.* ○ *See the attached schedule* or *as per the attached schedule.* **3.** a list of interest rates **4.** a form relating to a particular kind of income liable for U.K. income tax **5.** details of the items covered by insurance, sent with the policy ■ *verb* **1.** to list officially ○ *We offer a 10% reduction on scheduled prices* or *scheduled charges to selected customers.* **2.** to plan the time when something will happen ○ *The building is scheduled for completion in May.*

scheduled /'skedʒəld/ *adjective* listed in a separate schedule

scheduled flight /ˌskedʒəld 'flaɪt/ *noun* a regular flight which is in the airline timetable ○ *He left for Helsinki on a scheduled flight.*

scheduling /'skedʒulɪŋ/ *noun* the process of drawing up a plan or a timetable

scheme /skim/ *noun* U.K. a plan, arrangement or way of working ○ *Under the bonus scheme all employees get 10% of their annual pay as a Christmas bonus.* ○ *She has joined the company pension scheme.* ○ *We operate a profit-sharing scheme for managers.* ○ *The new payment scheme is based on reward for individual effort.*

science /'saɪəns/ *noun* study or knowledge based on observing and testing

science park /'saɪəns pɑrk/ *noun* an area near a town or university set aside for technological industries

scientific management /ˌsaɪəntɪfɪk 'mænɪdʒmənt/ *noun* a theory of management which believes in the rational use of resources in order to maximize output, thus motivating workers to earn more money

scientific research /ˌsaɪəntɪfɪk rɪ'sɜrtʃ/ *noun* study to try to find out information ○ *He is engaged in research into the packaging of the new product line.* ○ *The company is carrying out research into finding a medicine to cure colds.*

scope /skoʊp/ *noun* an opportunity or possibility ○ *There is considerable scope for expansion into the export market.* □ **there is scope for improvement in our sales performance** the sales performance could be improved

scorched-earth policy /ˌskɔrtʃt 'ɜrθ ˌpɑlɪsi/ *noun* a way of combating a takeover bid, where the target company sells valuable assets or purchases unattractive assets. ◊ **poison pill**

SCORE /skɔr/ *noun* a program run by the Small Business Administration in which volunteer retired executives provide counseling and seminars for small businesses. Full form **Service Corps of Retired Executives**

S corporation /'es ˌkɔrpəreɪʃ(ə)n/ *noun* In the U.S., a corporation with only a few stockholders that is not taxed as a corporation, but is able to pass its income, losses, and other tax items on to its shareholders. Also called **Subchapter S corporation**

scrap /skræp/ *noun* **1.** material left over after an industrial process, and which still has some value, as opposed to waste, which has no value ○ *to sell a ship for scrap* **2.** pieces of metal to be melted down to make new metal ingots ■ *verb* **1.** to give up, to stop working on ○ *We scrapped all our plans for expansion.* **2.** to throw (something) away as useless ○ *They had to scrap 10,000 spare parts.* (NOTE: **scrapping – scrapped**)

scrap dealer /'skræp ˌdiːlər/ *noun* a person who deals in scrap

scrap value /'skræp ˌvæljuː/ *noun* the value of an asset if sold for scrap ○ *Its scrap value is $2,500.*

screen /skriːn/ *noun* **1.** a glass surface on which computer information or TV pictures can be shown ○ *She brought up the information on the screen.* ○ *I'll just call up details of your account on the screen.* **2.** a flat panel which acts as a form of protection ■ *verb* to examine something carefully to evaluate or assess it □ **to screen candidates** to examine candidates to see if they are completely suitable

screen-based activity /ˌskriːn ˌbeɪst ækˈtɪvɪti/ *noun* a task that has to be done using a computer

screening /'skriːnɪŋ/ *noun* □ **the screening of candidates** the examining of candidates to see if they are suitable

screensaver /'skriːnˌseɪvər/ *noun* a program that shows moving images on the screen when a computer is not being used, because a static image can damage the monitor by burning itself into the phosphor coating on the inside of the screen

scrip /skrɪp/ *noun* a security, e.g., a share, bond, or the certificate issued to show that someone has been allotted a share or bond

"…under the rule, brokers who fail to deliver stock within four days of a transaction are to be fined 1% of the transaction value for each day of missing scrip" [*Far Eastern Economic Review*]

scrip issue /'skrɪp ˌɪʃuː/ *noun* an issue of shares whereby a company transfers money from reserves to share capital and issues free extra shares to the stockholders. The value of the company remains the same, and the total market value of stockholders' shares remains the same, the market price being adjusted to account for the

new shares. Also called **free issue, capitalization issue**

S-curve /'es kɜːrv/ *noun* a curve shaped like the letter "S" that describes the adoption and life-cycle of a product, especially a high-tech product

SDB *abbreviation* sales day book

seal /siːl/ *noun* **1.** a special symbol, often one stamped on a piece of wax, which is used to show that a document is officially approved by the organization that uses the symbol □ **contract under seal** a contract which has been legally approved with the seal of the company **2.** a piece of paper, metal, or wax attached to close something, so that it can be opened only if the paper, metal, or wax is removed or broken ■ *verb* **1.** to close something tightly ○ *The computer disks were sent in a sealed container.* **2.** to attach a seal, to stamp something with a seal ○ *Customs sealed the shipment.*

sealed bid /ˌsiːld 'bɪd/ *noun* a bid sent in a sealed envelope that will be opened with others at a specific time (NOTE: The U.K. term is **sealed tender.**)

SEAQ *noun* a computerized information system giving details of current stock prices and stock market transactions on the London Stock Exchange. Dealers list their offer and bid prices on SEAQ, and transactions are carried out on the basis of the information shown on the screen and are also recorded on the SEAQ database in case of future disputes. Full form **Stock Exchange Automated Quotations system**

search /sɜːrtʃ/ *noun* **1.** an examination of records by the lawyer acting for someone who wants to buy a property, to make sure that the vendor has the right to sell it **2.** the facility that enables visitors to a website to look for the information they want

search engine /'sɜːrtʃ ˌendʒɪn/ *noun* a computer program that searches through a number of documents, especially on the Internet, for particular keywords and provides the user with a list of the documents in which those keywords appear

search engine registration /'sɜːrtʃ ˌendʒɪn redʒɪˌstreɪʃ(ə)n/ *noun* the process of registering a website with a search engine, so that the site can be selected when a user requests a search

season /'siːz(ə)n/ *noun* **1.** one of four parts into which a year is divided, i.e.

spring, summer, fall, and winter **2.** a period of time when some activity usually takes place ○ *the selling season*

seasonal /'siz(ə)n(ə)l/ *adjective* which lasts for a season or which only happens during a particular season ○ *seasonal variations in sales patterns* ○ *The demand for this item is very seasonal.*

seasonal adjustment /ˌsiz(ə)n(ə)l ə 'dʒʌstmənt/ *noun* a change made to figures to take account of seasonal variations

seasonal demand /ˌsiz(ə)n(ə)l dɪ 'mænd/ *noun* a demand which exists only during the high season

seasonal employment /'siz(ə)n(ə)l ɪm,plɔɪmənt/, **seasonal work** /'siz(ə)n(ə)l wɜːk/ *noun* a job which is available at certain times of the year only (such as in a ski resort)

seasonally adjusted /ˌsiz(ə)nəli ə 'dʒʌstɪd/ *adjective* referring to statistics which are adjusted to take account of seasonal variations

seasonal product /'siz(ə)n(ə)l ˌprɑdʌkt/ *noun* a product such as skis or New Year cards which is only bought for use at a specific time of year

seasonal unemployment /ˌsiz(ə)nəl ˌʌnɪm'plɔɪmənt/ *noun* unemployment which rises and falls according to the season

season ticket /'siz(ə)n ˌtɪkɪt/ *noun* a rail or bus ticket which can be used for any number of trips over a period (normally 1, 3, 6 or 12 months)

sec *abbreviation* secretary

SEC *abbreviation* Securities and Exchange Commission

second /'sekənd/ *noun, adjective* the thing which comes after the first ■ *verb* /sɪ 'kʌnd/ **1.** /'sekənd/; /sɪ'kʌnd/ □ **to second a motion** to be the first person to support a proposal put forward by someone else ○ *Mrs. Smith seconded the motion* or *The motion was seconded by Mrs. Smith.* **2.** to lend a member of staff to another company, organization or department for a fixed period of time ○ *He was seconded to the Department of Trade for two years.*

secondary /'sekənd(ə)ri/ *adjective* second in importance

secondary action /ˌsekənd(ə)ri 'ækʃən/, **secondary strike** /ˌsekənd(ə)ri 'straɪk/, **secondary pick-**

eting /ˌsekənd(ə)ri 'pɪkɪtɪŋ/ *noun* the picketing by striking workers of a factory which is not the one with which they are in direct dispute, often to prevent it from supplying the striking factory or receiving supplies from it. Also called **secondary picketing, secondary strike**

secondary bank /ˌsekənd(ə)ri 'bæŋks/ *noun* a finance company which provides money for installment-plan deals

secondary industry /'sekənd(ə)ri ˌɪndəstri/ *noun* an industry which uses basic raw materials to produce manufactured goods

secondary picketing /ˌsekənd(ə)ri 'pɪkɪtɪŋ/ *noun* same as **secondary action**

secondary products /'sekənd(ə)ri ˌprɑdʌkts/ *plural noun* products which have been processed from raw materials (as opposed to primary products)

secondary strike /ˌsekənd(ə)ri 'straɪk/ *noun* same as **secondary action**

second-class /ˌsekənd 'klɑrs/ *adjective, adverb* referring to a less expensive or less comfortable way of traveling ○ *The group will travel second-class to Holland.* ○ *The price of a second-class ticket is half that of a first class.*

second-class mail /ˌsekənd klæs 'meɪl/ *noun* a less expensive, slower mail service ○ *The letter took three days to arrive because he sent it second-class.*

second decile /ˌsekənd 'desaɪəl/ *noun* a number below which fifty percent of numbers fall ○ *This group falls within the second decile.*

seconder /'sekəndər/ *noun* a person who seconds a proposal ○ *There was no seconder for the motion so it was not put to the vote.*

second half /ˌsekənd 'hæf/ *noun* a period of six months from 1st July to 31st December ○ *The figures for the second half are up on those for the first part of the year.*

second half-year /ˌsekənd ˌhæf 'jɪr/ *noun* the six-month period from July to the end of December

secondhand /ˌsekənd'hænd/ *adjective, adverb* which has been owned by someone before ○ *a secondhand car* ○ *the market in secondhand computers* or *the secondhand computer market* ○ *to buy something secondhand*

secondhand dealer /ˌsekəndhænd 'dilər/ *noun* a dealer who buys and sells secondhand items

secondment /sɪ'kɑndmənt/ *noun* the fact or period of being seconded to another job for a period ○ *She is on three years' secondment to an Australian college.*

second mortgage /ˌsekənd 'mɔrgɪdʒ/ *noun* a further mortgage on a property which is already mortgaged

second quarter /ˌsekənd 'kwɔrtər/ *noun* a period of three months from April to the end of June

second-rate /ˌsekənd 'reɪt/ *adjective* not of good quality ○ *never buy anything second-rate*

seconds /'sekəndz/ *plural noun* items which have been turned down by the quality controller as not being top quality ○ *The store has a sale of seconds.*

seconds store /'sekənz stɔr/ *noun* a store which specializes in the sale of goods which have not passed all of their producers quality-control tests, but which are still suitable for sale at a reduced price

secret /'sikrət/ *adjective* being deliberately kept hidden from people, or which is not known about by many people ○ *The CEO kept the contract secret from the rest of the board.* ○ *The management signed a secret deal with a foreign supplier.* ■ *noun* something which is kept hidden or which is not known about by many people ○ *to keep a secret* □ **to keep a secret** not to tell secret information which you have been told

secretarial /ˌsekrɪ'teriəl/ *adjective* referring to the work of a secretary ○ *She is taking a secretarial course.* ○ *He is looking for secretarial work.* ○ *We need extra secretarial help to deal with the mailings.* ○ *Their secretarial duties are not onerous, just boring.* ○ *Secretarial work is seen as a step toward management positions.*

secretarial college /ˌsekrɪ'teriəl ˌkɑlɪdʒ/ *noun* a college which teaches skills which a secretary needs, such as shorthand, typing and word-processing

secretariat /ˌsekrɪ'teriət/ *noun* an important office and the officials who work in it ○ *the United Nations secretariat*

"…a debate has been going on over the establishment of a general secretariat for the G7. Proponents argue that this would give the G7 a sense of direction and continuity" [*Times*]

secretary /'sekrət(ə)ri/ *noun* **1.** a person who helps to organize work, types letters, files documents, arranges meetings, etc., for someone ○ *My secretary deals with incoming orders.* ○ *Her secretary phoned to say she would be late.* **2.** an official of a company or society whose job is to keep records and write letters **3.** a member of the government in charge of a department ○ *the Trade Secretary* ○ *the Foreign Secretary* ○ *the Education Secretary*

secretary and personal assistant /ˌsekrət(ə)ri ən ˌpɜrs(ə)n(ə)l ə'sɪst(ə)nt/ *noun* a secretary to a top-level member of an organization, such as director, or senior manager

Secretary of State /ˌsekrət(ə)ri əv 'steɪt/ *noun* **1.** *U.K.* a member of the government in charge of a department ○ *the Secretary of State for Trade and Industry* **2.** the U.S. government official and cabinet member who is in charge of foreign affairs (NOTE: The U.K. term is **Foreign Secretary.**)

Secretary of the Treasury /ˌsekrət(ə)ri əv ðə 'treʒəri/ *noun* a senior member of the government in charge of financial affairs

secret ballot /ˌsikrət 'bælət/ *noun* an election where the voters vote in secret

section /'sekʃən/ *noun* a part of something ○ *You should read the last section of the report – it is very interesting.*

sector /'sektər/ *noun* a part of the economy or the business organization of a country ○ *All sectors of the economy suffered from the fall in the exchange rate.* ○ *Technology is a booming sector of the economy.*

secure /sɪ'kjuə/ *adjective* safe, which cannot change □ **secure job** a job from which you are not likely to be made redundant □ **secure investment** an investment where you are not likely to lose money ■ *verb* **1.** □ **to secure a loan** to pledge an asset as a security for a loan **2.** to get something safely into your control ○ *He is visiting several banks in an attempts to secure funds for his project.* ○ *He secured the backing of an Australian group.*

secured /sɪ'kjurd/ *adjective* used to describe a type of borrowing such as a mortgage where the lender has a legal right to take over an asset or assets of the borrower, if the borrower does not repay the loan

secured creditor /sɪˌkjʊrd ˈkredɪtər/ *noun* a person who is owed money by someone, and can legally claim the same amount of the borrower's property if the borrower fails to pay back the money owed

secured debt /sɪˌkjʊrd ˈdet/ *noun* a debt which is guaranteed by assets which have been pledged

secured loan /sɪˈkjʊrd loʊn/ *noun* a loan which is guaranteed by the borrower giving assets as security

secure server /sɪˌkjʊr ˈsɜrvər/ *noun* a combination of hardware and software that makes e-commerce credit card transactions safe by stopping unauthorized people from gaining access to credit card details online

secure sockets layer /sɪˌkjʊr ˈsɑkɪts ˌleɪər/ *noun* full form of **SSL**

secure website /sɪˌkjʊr ˈwebsaɪt/ *noun* a website on the Internet that encrypts the messages between the visitor and the site to ensure that no hacker or eavesdropper can intercept the information

securities /sɪˈkjʊrɪtiz/ *plural noun* **1.** investments in stocks and bonds **2.** certificates to show that someone owns stocks and bonds

Securities and Exchange Commission /sɪˈkjʊrɪtiz ən ɪksˈtʃeɪndʒ kəˈmɪʃ(ə)n/ *noun* the official body which regulates the securities markets in the U.S. Abbreviation **SEC**

securities market /sɪˈkjʊrɪtiz ˌmɑrkət/ *noun* a Stock Exchange, a place where stocks and bonds can be bought or sold

securities trader /sɪˈkjʊrɪtiz ˌtreɪdər/ *noun* a person whose business is buying and selling stocks and bonds

securitise /sɪˈkjʊrətaɪz/, **securitize** *verb* to make a loan into a security which can be traded (e.g., by issuing an IOU for a loan)

security /sɪˈkjʊrəti/ *noun* **1.** the fact of being protected against attack □ **office security** the act of protecting an office against theft **2.** the fact of being kept secret □ **security in this office is nil** nothing can be kept secret in this office **3.** a guarantee that someone will repay money borrowed ○ *to give something as security for a debt*

○ *to use a house as security for a loan* ○ *The bank lent him $20,000 without security.* □ **to stand security for someone** to guarantee that if the person does not repay a loan, you will repay it for him

security guard /sɪˈkjʊrɪti gɑrd/ *noun* a person who protects an office or factory against burglars

security of employment /sɪˌkjʊrɪti əv ɪmˈplɔɪmənt/ *noun* a feeling by an employee that he or she will be able to stay in the same job until retirement

security of tenure /sɪˌkjʊrɪti əv ˈtenjər/ *noun* a right to keep a job or rented accommodations provided conditions are met

security printer /sɪˈkjʊrɪti ˌprɪntər/ *noun* a printer who prints material that has to be kept secure, such as paper money, share prospectuses or secret government documents

seed capital /ˈsid ˈkæpɪtəl/, **seed money** /ˈsid ˌmʌni/, **seedcorn** /ˈsidkɔrn/ *noun* capital invested when a new project is starting up, before it is brought to the stock market

seedcorn /ˈsidkɔrn/, **seed money** /ˈsid ˌmʌni/ *noun* venture capital invested when a new project is starting up (and therefore more risky than secondary financing or mezzanine financing) ○ *They had their ranch house to operate out of, a used printer and seed money from friends.*

see-safe /ˈsi seɪf/ *adverb* under an agreement where a supplier will give credit for unsold goods at the end of a period if the retailer cannot sell them ○ *We bought the stock see-safe.*

segment /ˈsegmənt/ *noun* a part of the sales of a large business defined by specific criteria

segmentation /ˌsegmənˈteɪʃ(ə)n/ *noun* the division of the market or consumers into categories according to their buying habits

seize /siz/ *verb* to take hold of something, to take possession of something ○ *Customs seized the shipment of books.* ○ *The court ordered the company's funds to be seized.*

seizure /ˈsiʒər/ *noun* an act of taking possession of something ○ *the court ordered the seizure of the shipment* or *of the company's funds*

select /sɪ'lekt/ *adjective* of top quality or specially chosen ○ *The firm offers a select range of merchandise.* ○ *Our customers are a select group.* ■ *verb* to choose ○ *The board will meet to select three candidates for a second interview.* □ **selected items are reduced by 25%** some items have been reduced by 25%

selection /sɪ'lekʃən/ *noun* **1.** a choice **2.** a thing which has been chosen ○ *Here is a selection of our product line.*

selection board /sɪ'lekʃən bɔːd/ *noun* a committee which chooses a candidate for a job

selection procedure /sɪ'lekʃən prə ,sidʒər/ *noun* the general method of choosing a candidate for a job

selective /sɪ'lektɪv/ *adjective* choosing carefully

selective strikes /sɪ,lektɪv 'straɪks/ *noun* strikes in certain areas or at certain factories, but not everywhere

self /self/ *pronoun* your own person □ **"pay self"** (*on cheques*) pay the person who has signed the check

self- /self/ *prefix* referring to yourself

self-assessment /self ə'sesmənt/ *noun* the process of calculating how much tax you should pay and reporting it to the Inland Revenue on time ○ *Self-assessment forms should be returned to the tax office by 31st January.*

self-contained office /,self kən ,teɪnd 'ɒfɪs/ *noun* an office which has all facilities inside it, and its own entrance, so that it is separate from other offices in the same building

self-dealing /,self 'diːlɪŋ/ *noun* the benefiting or attempting to benefit from a financial transaction carried out on the behalf of someone else

self-employed /,self ɪm'plɔɪd/ *adjective* working for yourself or not on the payroll of a company ○ *a self-employed engineer* ○ *He worked for a bank for ten years but is now self-employed.* ■ *plural noun* □ **the self-employed** people who work for themselves

self-financed /,self faɪ'nænst/ *adjective* □ **the project is completely self-financed** the project pays its development costs out of its own revenue, with no subsidies

self-financing /,self faɪ'nænsɪŋ/ *noun* the financing of development costs, the purchase of capital assets, etc. by a company from its own resources ■ *adjective* □ **the company is completely self-financing** the company finances its development costs, capital assets, etc. from its own resources

self-made man /,self meɪd 'mæn/ *noun* a man who is rich and successful because of his own work, not because he inherited money or position

self-made woman /,self meɪd 'wʊmən/ *noun* a woman who is rich and successful because of her own work, not because she inherited money or position

self-managed (work) team /,self mænɪdʒd 'tim/, **self-managing (work) team** *noun* same as **autonomous work group**

self-regulating organization /,self ,regjuleɪtɪŋ ,ɔːgənaɪ'zeɪʃ(ə)n/ *noun* same as **self-regulatory organization**

self-regulation /,self ,regjə'leɪʃ(ə)n/ *noun* the regulation of an industry by itself, through a committee which issues a rulebook and makes sure that members of the industry follow the rules

self-regulatory /self ,regjʊ'leɪt(ə)ri/ *adjective* referring to an organization which regulates itself

self-regulatory organization /,self ,regjʊlət(ə)ri ,ɔːgənaɪ'zeɪʃ(ə)n/ *noun* an organization, such as the Securities and Futures Authority, which regulates the way in which its own members carry on their business. Abbreviation **SRO**

self-seal envelope /,self ,sil 'envələʊp/ *noun* an envelope which sticks closed when you press the flap down

self-service store /,self 'sɜːvɪs ,stɔː/ *noun* a store where customers take goods from the shelves and pay for them at the checkout

self-starter /,self 'stɑːtər/ *noun* a person who can be relied on to take the initiative in a new situation without asking for instructions

self-sufficiency /,self sə'fɪʃ(ə)nsi/ *noun* the state of being self-sufficient

self-sufficient /,self sə'fɪʃ(ə)nt/ *adjective* producing enough food or raw materials for its own needs ○ *The country is self-sufficient in oil.*

self-supporting /ˌself səˈpɔːtɪŋ/ *adjective* which finances itself from its own resources, with no subsidies

sell /sel/ *noun* an act of selling □ **to give a product the hard sell** to make great efforts to persuade customers to buy it ■ *verb* **1.** to exchange something for money ○ *to sell something on credit* ○ *The store sells washing machines and refrigerators.* ○ *They tried to sell their house for $100,000.* ○ *Their products are easy to sell.* **2.** to be bought ○ *These items sell well in the pre-Christmas period.* ○ *Those packs sell for $25 a dozen.* ◊ **hard sell** (NOTE: **selling – sold**)

sell forward *phrasal verb* to sell foreign currency, commodities, etc. for delivery at a later date

sell off *phrasal verb* to sell goods quickly to get rid of them

sell out *phrasal verb* **1.** □ **to sell out of an item** to sell all the stock of an item ○ *to sell out of a product line* ○ *We have sold out of plastic bags.* ○ *This item has sold out.* **2.** to sell your business ○ *They sold out and retired to the seaside.*

sell up *phrasal verb* to sell a business and all the stock ○ *He sold up and bought a farm.*

sell and build /ˌsel ən ˈbɪld/ *noun* a type of manufacturing in which the producer first receives an order and payment from the customer and then makes a product, rather than making products for stock

sell-by date /ˈsel baɪ ˌdeɪt/ *noun* a date on a food packet which is the last date on which the food is guaranteed to be good

seller /ˈselər/ *noun* **1.** a person who sells ○ *There were few sellers in the market, so prices remained high.* **2.** something which sells ○ *This book is a steady seller.*

seller's market /ˌselərz ˈmɑːkət/ *noun* a market where the seller can ask high prices because there is a large demand for the product. Opposite **buyer's market**

-selling /ˈselɪŋ/ *suffix* □ **best-selling car** a car which sells better than other models

selling costs /ˈselɪŋ kʌsts/, **selling overhead** /ˌselɪŋ ˈoʊvərhed/ *plural noun* the amount of money to be paid for the advertising, reps' commissions, and other expenses involved in selling something

selling price /ˈselɪŋ praɪs/ *noun* the price at which someone is willing to sell something

sellout /ˈselaʊt/ *noun* □ **this item has been a sellout** all the stock of the item has been sold

sell-side /ˈsel saɪd/ *noun* a broker or brokerage firm that sells securities to its customers. ◊ **buy-side**

semi- /ˈsemi/ *prefix* half or part

semi-finished product /ˌsemi ˈfɪnɪʃt ˌprɑdʌkt/ *noun* a product which is partly finished

seminar /ˈsemɪnɑːr/ *noun* a meeting for the purposes of learning and discussion with a relatively small number of participants ○ *He attended a seminar on direct selling.* ○ *She is running a seminar for senior managers.*

semi-skilled /ˌsemi ˈskɪld/ *adjective* having had or involving some training □ **semi-skilled jobs** jobs which require some training or experience

send /send/ *verb* to make someone or something go from one place to another ○ *She sent a letter to our lawyers.* ○ *The order was sent to the warehouse.* ○ *The company is sending him to Australia to be general manager of the Sydney office.* ○ *Send the letter airmail if you want it to arrive next week.* ○ *The shipment was sent by rail.* (NOTE: **sending – sent**)

send away for *phrasal verb* to write asking for something to be sent to you ○ *We sent away for the new catalog.*

send for *phrasal verb* **1.** to ask someone to come; to ask for something to be brought ○ *He sent for the chief accountant.* ○ *She sent for the papers on the contract.* **2.** to write to ask for something to be sent to you ○ *We sent for the new catalog.* (NOTE: **U.K.** English uses **send away for, send off for** in this meaning.)

send in *phrasal verb* to send (a letter) ○ *he sent in his resignation* ○ *she sent in an application*

send off *phrasal verb* to put (a letter) in the mail

send off for *phrasal verb* to write asking for something to be sent to you ○ *We sent off for the new catalog.*

send on *phrasal verb* to mail a letter which you have received, and address it to someone else ○ *He sent the letter on to* *his agent in Australia.*

sender /'sendər/ *noun* a person who sends □ **"return to sender"** words on an envelope or package to show that it is to be sent back to the person who sent it

senior /'siniər/ *adjective* **1.** referring to an employee who is more important **2.** referring to an employee who is older or who has been employed longer than another **3.** referring to a sum which is repayable before others

senior debt /ˌsiniər 'det/ *noun* a debt which must be repaid in preference to other debts (such as a first mortgage over a second mortgage)

seniority /ˌsini'ɑrɪti/ *noun* **1.** the fact of being more important ○ *in order of seniority* **2.** the fact of being older or having been an employee of the company longer

senior management /ˌsiniər 'mænɪdʒmənt/ *noun* the main directors of a company

senior manager /ˌsiniə 'mænɪdʒər/, **senior executive** /ˌsiniər ɪg'zekjʊtɪv/ *noun* a manager or director who has a higher rank than others

senior partner /ˌsiniər 'pɑrtnər/ *noun* the most important partner in law firm or firm of accountants

senior staff /ˌsiniər 'stæf/ *noun* **1.** older members of staff **2.** people in more important positions in a company

senior vice president /ˌsiniər vaɪs 'prezɪd(ə)nt/ *noun* one of a few main executive directors of a company

SEP *abbreviation* Simplified Employee Pension Plan

separate *adjective* /'sep(ə)rət/ not connected with something □ **to send something under separate cover** to send something in a different envelope ■ *verb* /'sepəreɪt/ to divide ○ *The personnel are separated into part-timers and full-time staff.*

separately /'sep(ə)rətli/ *adverb* not together ○ *each job was invoiced separately*

sequester /sɪ'kwestə/, **sequestrate** /'sikwɪstreɪt, sɪ'kwestreɪt/ *verb* to take and keep a bank account or property because a court has ordered it ○ *The union's funds have been sequestrated.*

sequestration /ˌsikwe'streɪʃ(ə)n/ *noun* the act of taking and keeping property on the order of a court, especially of seizing property from someone who is in contempt of court

sequestrator /'sikwɪstreɪtər, sɪ'kwestreɪtər/ *noun* a person who takes and keeps property on the order of a court

serial entrepreneur /ˌsiriəl ˌɑntrəprə'nɜr/ *noun* an entrepreneur who starts up many new businesses, one after the other

serial number /'siriəl ˌnʌmbər/ *noun* a number in a series ○ *This batch of shoes has the serial number 25–02.*

series /'siriz/ *noun* a group of items following one after the other ○ *A series of successful takeovers made the company one of the largest in the trade.* (NOTE: The plural is **series.**)

serious /'siriəs/ *adjective* **1.** bad ○ *the storm caused serious damage* ○ *The damage to the computer was not very serious.* **2.** thoughtful ○ *The management is making serious attempts to improve working conditions.*

seriously /'siriəsli/ *adverb* **1.** badly ○ *The cargo was seriously damaged by water.* **2.** in a thoughtful way ○ *We are taking the threat from our competitors very seriously.*

servant /'sɜrvənt/ *noun* a person who is paid to work in someone's house

serve /sɜrv/ *verb* **1.** to deal with a customer □ **to serve a customer** to take a customer's order and provide what he wants □ **to serve in a store** *or* **in a restaurant** to deal with customers' orders **2.** □ **to serve someone with a writ** *or* **to serve a writ on someone** to give someone a writ officially, so that they have to receive it

server /'sɜrvər/ *noun* a computer or program which provides a function to a network

server farm /'sɜrvər fɑrm/ *noun* a place that contains a large number of server computers and usually runs these servers for the benefit of many different organizations

service /'sɜrvɪs/ *noun* **1.** a piece of work done to help someone as a duty or a favor ○ *After a lifetime's service to the company he was rewarded with a generous golden handshake.* **2.** a form of business (e.g., insurance, banking, or transportation) that provides help in some form when it is needed, as opposed to making or selling goods **3.** the fact of working for an employer, or the period of time during which an employee has worked for an employer ○ *retiring after twenty years service to the company* ○ *The amount of your pension depends partly on the number of your years of service.* **4.** the work of dealing with customers ○ *The service in that restaurant is extremely slow* **5.** payment for help given to the customer ○ *to add on 10% for service* □ **the bill includes service** the bill includes a charge added for the work involved ○ *The service in that restaurant is extremely slow.* **6.** the act of keeping a machine in good working order ○ *the routine service of equipment* ○ *The machine has been sent in for service.* **7.** the business of providing help in some form when it is needed **8.** □ **to put a machine into service** to start using a machine **9.** the regular working of a public organization ○ *the postal service is efficient* ○ *The bus service is very irregular.* ○ *We have a good train service to the city.* □ **the civil service** the organization and personnel which administer a country ○ *you have to pass an examination to get a job in the civil service* or *to get a civil service job* ○ *civil service pensions are index-linked* ○ *He has a job in the civil service.* ■ *verb* **1.** to keep a machine in good working order ○ *The car needs to be serviced every six months.* ○ *The computer has gone back to the manufacturer for servicing.* **2.** □ **to service a debt** to pay interest on a debt ○ *The company is having problems in servicing its debts.*

service agreement /'sɜrvɪs ə,grɪmənt/ *noun* a contract between a company and a director showing all conditions of work ○ *The service agreement says very little about hours of work.*

service bureau /'sɜrvɪs ,bjʊroʊ/ *noun* an office which specializes in helping other offices

service center /'sɜrvɪs ,sentər/ *noun* an office or workshop which specializes in keeping machines in good working order

service charge /'sɜrvɪs tʃɑrdʒ/ *noun* **1.** a charge added to the check in a restaurant to pay for service **2.** an amount paid by tenants in an apartment block or office building for general maintenance, insurance and cleaning **3.** a charge which a bank or business makes for carrying out work for a customer (NOTE: The U.K. term is **bank charge**.)

service contract /'sɜrvɪs ,kɑntrækt/ *noun* a contract between a company and a director showing all conditions of work ○ *She worked unofficially with no service contract.*

Service Corps of Retired Executives /,sɜrvɪs kɔr əv rɪ,taɪrd ɪg'zekjʊtɪvz/ *noun* full form of **SCORE**

service department /'sɜrvɪs dɪ,pɑrtmənt/ *noun* the section of a company which keeps customers' machines in good working order

service engineer /'sɜrvɪs endʒɪ,nɪr/ *noun* an engineer who specializes in keeping machines in good working order

service handbook /'sɜrvɪs ,hændbʊk/ *noun* a book which shows how to service a machine

service industry /'sɜrvɪs ,ɪndəstri/ *noun* an industry which does not produce raw materials or manufacture products but offers a service such as banking, retailing or accountancy

service level agreement /'sɜrvɪs ,lev(ə)l ə,grɪmənt/ *noun* an agreement between a supplier and a customer which stipulates the level of services to be rendered. Abbreviation **SLA**

service manual /'sɜrvɪs ,mænjʊəl/ *noun* a book showing how to service a machine

services /'sɜrvɪsɪz/ *plural noun* benefits which are sold to customers or clients, e.g., transportation or education ○ *We give advice to companies on the marketing of services.* ○ *We must improve the exports of both goods and services.*

service sector /'sɜrvɪs ,sektər/ *noun* the part of an economy that consists of service industries

service station /'sɜrvɪs ,steɪʃ(ə)n/ *noun* a garage where you can buy gasoline and have small repairs done to a car

session /'seʃ(ə)n/ *noun* a period of time spent on a specific activity, especially as part of a larger event ○ *The morning session* or *the afternoon session will be held in the conference room.*

"…statistics from the stock exchange show that customer interest in the equity market has averaged just under £700m in recent trading sessions" [*Financial Times*]

set /set/ *noun* a group of items which go together, which are used together, or which are sold together ○ *a set of tools* ■

adjective fixed, or which cannot be changed ○ *There is a set fee for all our consultants.* ■ *verb* to fix or to arrange something ○ *We have to set a price for the new computer.* ○ *The price of the calculator has been set low, so as to achieve maximum unit sales.* (NOTE: **setting – set**) □ **the auction set a record for high prices** the prices at the auction were the highest ever reached □ **to set the bar** to motivate staff by setting targets that are above their current level of achievement

set against *phrasal verb* to balance one group of figures against another group to try to make them cancel each other out ○ *to set the costs against the sales revenue* ○ *Can you set the expenses against tax?*

set aside *phrasal verb* to decide not to apply a decision ○ *The arbitrator's award was set aside on appeal.*

set back *phrasal verb* to make something late ○ *The project was set back six weeks by bad weather.*

set out *phrasal verb* to put clearly in writing ○ *to set out the details in a report*

set up *phrasal verb* to begin something, or to organize something new ○ *to set up a new department* □ **to set up a company** to start a company legally □ **to set up in business** to start a new business ○ *She set up in business as an insurance broker.* ○ *He set himself up as a freelance representative.*

setback /'setbæk/ *noun* something that stops progress ○ *The company has suffered a series of setbacks over the past two years.*

"…a sharp setback in foreign trade accounted for most of the winter slowdown" [*Fortune*]

setting up costs /ˌsetɪŋ 'ʌp kɔsts/, **setup costs** /'setʌp kɔsts/ *plural noun* the costs of getting a machine or a factory ready to make a new product after finishing work on the previous one

settle /'set(ə)l/ *verb* **1.** □ **to settle an account** to pay what is owed **2.** to solve a problem or dispute □ **to settle a claim** to agree to pay what is asked for ○ *The insurance company refused to settle his claim for storm damage.* □ **the two parties settled out of court** the two parties reached an agreement privately without continuing the court case

settle on *phrasal verb* to leave property to someone when you die ○ *He settled his property on his children.*

settlement /'set(ə)lmənt/ *noun* **1.** the payment of an account □ **we offer an extra 5% discount for rapid settlement** we take a further 5% off the price if the customer pays quickly □ **settlement in cash** *or* **cash settlement** payment of an invoice in cash, not by check **2.** an agreement after an argument or negotiations ○ *a wage settlement* □ **to effect a settlement between two parties** to bring two parties together to make them agree

settlement date /'set(ə)lmənt deɪt/ *noun* **1.** a date when a payment has to be made **2.** the day on which stock that has been bought must be paid for, usually three business days from the day of trade (NOTE: The U.K. term is **settlement day**)

setup /'setʌp/ *noun* **1.** arrangement or organization □ **the setup in the office** the way the office is organized **2.** a commercial firm ○ *He works for a PR setup.*

"…for sale: top quality office furniture, which includes executive desks, filing cabinets, typewriters and complete office setup" [*Australian Financial Review*]

several /'sev(ə)rəl/ *adjective* more than a few, some ○ *Several managers are retiring this year.* ○ *Several of our products sell well in Japan.*

severally /'sev(ə)rəli/ *adverb* separately, not jointly □ **they are jointly and severally liable** they are liable both as a group and as individuals for the total amount

severance pay /'sev(ə)rəns peɪ/ *noun* money paid as compensation to an employee whose job is no longer needed

sexual discrimination /ˌsekʃuəl dɪskrɪmɪ'neɪʃ(ə)n/, **sex discrimination** /ˌseks dɪskrɪmɪ'neɪʃ(ə)n/ *noun* the practice of treating men and women in different ways (usually favoring men) ○ *The company was accused of sex discrimination in its appointment of managers.* ○ *Sex discrimination has made it difficult for women to reach managerial posts in the organization.*

sexual harassment /ˌsekʃuəl 'hærəsmənt/ *noun* the practice of making unpleasant sexual gestures, comments or approaches to someone ○ *She complained of sexual harassment by the manager.*

shadow economy /ˌʃædoʊ ɪ'kɑnəmi/ *noun* same as **black economy**

shady /'ʃeɪdi/ *adjective* not honest ○ *The newspapers reported that he had been involved in several shady deals.*

shake /ʃeɪk/ *verb* **1.** to move something quickly from side to side □ **to shake hands** to hold someone's hand when meeting to show you are pleased to meet them or to show that an agreement has been reached ○ *The two negotiating teams shook hands and sat down at the conference table.* □ **to shake hands on a deal** to shake hands to show that a deal has been agreed **2.** to surprise or to shock ○ *The markets were shaken by the company's results.* (NOTE: **shaking – shook – has shaken**)

shakeout /,ʃeɪk 'aʊt/ *noun* **1.** a complete change, where weak or inefficient people or companies are removed ○ *Only three companies were left after the shakeout in the computer market.* **2.** a reorganization in a company, in which some people are left, but others go ○ *a shakeout in the top management*

shakeup /'ʃeɪkʌp/ *noun* a total reorganization ○ *The managing director ordered a shakeup of the sales departments.*

shaky /'ʃeɪki/ *adjective* not very sure or not very reliable ○ *He only has the shakiest idea of what he should be doing.*

shape up or ship out /ʃeɪp ˌʌp ɔr ʃɪp 'aʊt/ *interjection* an order to improve your performance at work because if you do not you will be fired

share /ʃer/ *noun* **1.** a part of something that has been divided up among several people or groups □ **to have a share in** to take part in or to contribute to ○ *to have a share in management decisions* **2.** one of many equal parts into which a company's capital is divided ○ *He bought a block of stock in Microsoft.* ○ *Stocks fell on Wall Street.* □ **to allot shares** to give a certain number of shares to people who have subscribed to them ■ *verb* **1.** to own or use something together with someone else ○ *It is very awkward having to share a telephone.* ○ *I don't want to share an office with her because she smokes.* **2.** to divide something up among several people or groups ○ *to share computer time* ○ *to share the profits among the senior executives* ○ *Three companies share the market.* □ **to share information** *or* **data** to give someone information which you have

share above par /,ʃer əˌbʌv 'pɑr/ *noun* a share with a market price which is higher than its par value

share allocation /ʃer ˌælə'keɪʃ(ə)n/ *noun* the act of spreading a small number of shares among a large number of people who have subscribed to them

share allotment /'ʃer əˌlɑtmənt/ *noun* the act of giving some shares in a new company to people who have subscribed to them ○ *Payment must be made in full on allotment.*

share at par /,ʃer ət 'pɑr/ *noun* a share whose value on the stock market is the same as its face value

share buyback /'ʃer ˌbaɪbæk/ *noun* same as **stock buyback**

share capital /'ʃer ˌkæpɪt(ə)l/ *noun* the value of the assets of a company held as shares

share certificate /'ʃer səˌtɪfɪkət/ *noun* a document proving that you own shares

shareholder /'ʃerhoʊldər/ *noun U.K.* same as **stockholder**
"…as of last night the bank's shareholders no longer hold any rights to the bank's shares" [*South China Morning Post*]
"…the company said that its recent issue of 10.5% convertible preference shares at A\$8.50 has been oversubscribed, boosting shareholders' funds to A\$700 million plus" [*Financial Times*]

shareholding /'ʃerhoʊldɪŋ/ *noun* a group of shares in a company owned by one owner

share issue /'ʃer ˌɪʃu/ *noun* an act of selling new shares in a company to the public

share option /'ʃer ˌɑpʃən/ *noun U.K.* same as **stock option**

share option scheme /'ʃer ˌɑpʃən ˌskim/ *noun U.K.* same as **stock option plan**

share ownership scheme /,ʃer 'oʊnəʃɪp skim/, **share incentive scheme** *noun U.K.* same as **stock ownership plan**

share warrant /'ʃer ˌwɑrənt/ *noun* a document which says that someone has the right to a number of shares in a company

sharing /'ʃerɪŋ/ *noun* the act of dividing up ◇ **time-sharing 1.** owning a property in part, with the right to use it for a period each year **2.** sharing a computer system with different users using different terminals

sharp /ʃɑrp/ *adjective* sudden ○ *There was a sharp rally on the stock market.* ○ *Last week's sharp drop in prices has been reversed.*

sharp practice /ˌʃɑrp ˈpræktɪs/ *noun* a way of doing business which is not honest, but is not illegal

shed /ʃed/ *verb* to lose (NOTE: **shedding – shed**) □ **to shed staff** to lose staff by dismissing them

sheet /ʃit/ *noun* □ **sheet of paper** a piece of paper

sheet feed /ˈʃit fid/ *noun* a device which puts one sheet of paper at a time into a printer

shelf barker /ˈʃelf ˌbɑrkə/ *noun* a card placed on or hung from a shelf to promote an item for sale. Also called **shelf talker**, **shelf wobbler**

shelf filler /ˈʃelf ˌfɪlər/ *noun* a person whose job is to make sure that the shelves in a store are kept full of items for sale

shelf life /ˈʃelf laɪf/ *noun* the length of time during which a product can stay in the store and still be good to use

shelf space /ˈʃelf speɪs/ *noun* the amount of space on shelves in a store

shelf talker /ˈʃelf ˌwɑblər/, **shelf wobbler** *noun* same as **shelf barker**

shell company /ˈʃel ˌkʌmp(ə)ni/ *noun* a company that has ceased to trade but is still registered, especially one sold to enable the buyer to begin trading without having to establish a new company (NOTE: The U.S. term is **shell corporation**.)

"…shell companies, which can be used to hide investors' cash, figure largely throughout the twentieth century" [*Times*]

shelter /ˈʃeltər/ *noun* a protected place ■ *verb* to give someone or something protection

shelve /ʃelv/ *verb* to postpone or to put back to another date ○ *The project was shelved.* ○ *Discussion of the problem has been shelved.*

shelving /ˈʃelvɪŋ/ *noun* postponing ○ *The shelving of the project has resulted in six redundancies.*

shift /ʃɪft/ *noun* **1.** a group of employees who work for a period, and then are replaced by another group □ **they work double shifts** two groups of workers are working shifts together **2.** a period of time worked by a group of employees **3.** a movement or change ○ *a shift in the company's marketing strategy* ○ *The company is taking advantage of a shift in the market toward higher-priced goods.* ■ *verb* to move, to sell ○ *We shifted 20,000 items in one week.*

shift work /ˈʃɪft wɜrk/ *noun* a system of work with shifts

shilling /ˈʃɪlɪŋ/ *noun* a unit of currency used in Kenya, Somalia, Tanzania and Uganda

ship /ʃɪp/ *verb* to send goods, but not always on a ship ○ *to ship goods to Kansas* ○ *We ship all our goods by rail.* ○ *The consignment of cars was shipped abroad last week.*

shipbroker /ˈʃɪpˌbroʊkər/ *noun* a person who arranges shipping or transportation of goods for customers on behalf of ship owners

ship chandler /ˌʃɪp ˈtʃændlər/ *noun* a person who supplies goods such as food to ships

ship laden in bulk /ˌʃɪp ˌleɪd(ə)n ɪn ˈbʌlk/ *noun* a ship which has a loose cargo (such as corn) which is not packed in containers

shipment /ˈʃɪpmənt/ *noun* **1.** goods which have been sent or are going to be sent ○ *Two shipments were lost in the fire.* ○ *A shipment of computers was damaged.* **2.** an act of sending goods ○ *We make two shipments a week to France.*

shipper /ˈʃɪpər/ *noun* a person who sends goods or who organizes the sending of goods for other customers

shipping /ˈʃɪpɪŋ/ *noun* the sending of goods ○ *shipping charges* ○ *shipping costs* (NOTE: **shipping** does not always mean using a ship.)

shipping agent /ˈʃɪpɪŋ ˌeɪdʒənt/ *noun* a company which specializes in the sending of goods

shipping clerk /ˈʃɪpɪŋ klɜrk/ *noun* a clerk who deals with shipping documents

shipping company /ˈʃɪpɪŋ ˌkʌmp(ə)ni/ *noun* a company whose business is in transporting goods or passengers in ships

shipping confirmation /ˈʃɪpɪŋ kənfəˌmeɪʃ(ə)n/ *noun* an email message informing the purchaser that an order has been shipped

shipping instructions /'ʃɪpɪŋ ɪn ˌstrʌkʃənz/ *plural noun* the details of how goods are to be shipped and delivered

shipping line /'ʃɪpɪŋ laɪn/ *noun* a large shipping or aircraft company which carries passengers or cargo ○ *Profits of major airlines have been affected by the rise in fuel prices.*

shipping note /'ʃɪpɪŋ noʊt/ *noun* a note which gives details of goods being shipped

shoot /ʃut/ *verb*
  shoot up *phrasal verb* to go up fast ○ *Prices have shot up during the strike.* (NOTE: **shooting – shot**)

shop /ʃɒp/ *noun* **1.** *U.K.* a retail outlet where goods of a certain type are sold ○ *a computer shop* (NOTE: The usual U.S. term is **store**.) **2.** a workshop, the place in a factory where goods are made ■ *verb* to go to stores to make purchases (NOTE: **shopping – shopped**) □ **to shop (for)** to look for things in shops
  shop around *phrasal verb* to go to various stores or suppliers and compare prices before making a purchase or before placing an order ○ *You should shop around before getting your car serviced.* ○ *He's shopping around for a new computer.* ○ *It pays to shop around when you are planning to get a mortgage.*

shop assistant /'ʃɒp ə,sɪstənt/ *noun U.K.* same as **sales clerk**

shopbot /'ʃɒpbɑt/ *noun* an Internet search device that searches for particular products or services and allows the user to compare prices and specifications

shop floor /ˌʃɒp 'flɔr/ *noun U.K.* same as **store floor**

shop front /'ʃɒp frʌnt/ *noun U.K.* same as **store front**

shopkeeper /'ʃɒpkipər/ *noun U.K.* same as **storekeeper**

shoplifter /'ʃɒplɪftər/ *noun* a person who steals goods from stores

shoplifting /'ʃɒplɪftɪŋ/ *noun* the practice of stealing goods from stores

shopper /'ʃɒpər/ *noun* a person who buys goods in a store ○ *The store stays open until midnight to cater to late-night shoppers.*

shoppers' charter /ˌʃɒpərz 'tʃɑrtər/ *noun U.K.* a law which protects the rights of shoppers against storekeepers who are not honest or against manufacturers of defective goods

shopping /'ʃɒpɪŋ/ *noun* **1.** goods bought in a store ○ *a basket of shopping* **2.** the act of going to stores to buy things ○ *to do your shopping in the local supermarket* □ **shopping around** looking at prices in various stores before buying what you want

shopping arcade /'ʃɒpɪŋ ɑr,keɪd/ *noun* a covered passageway with small stores on either side

shopping cart /'ʃɒpɪŋ kɑrt/ *noun* **1.** a software package that records the items that an online buyer selects for purchase together with associated data, e.g., the price of the item and the number of items required **2.** a metal basket on wheels, used by shoppers to put their purchases in as they go around a supermarket

shopping centre /'ʃɒpɪŋ ,sentər/ *noun U.K.* same as **shopping mall**

shopping experience /'ʃɒpɪŋ ɪk ,spɪriəns/ *noun* the virtual environment in which a customer visits an e-merchant's website, selects items, places them in an electronic shopping cart, and notifies the merchant of the order (NOTE: The shopping experience does not include a payment transaction, which is initiated by a message to a point-of-sale program when the customer signals that he or she has finished shopping and wishes to pay.)

shopping mall /'ʃɒpɪŋ mɔl/ *noun* an enclosed covered area for shopping, with stores, restaurants, banks, and other facilities. Also called **mall**

shopping precinct /'ʃɒpɪŋ ,prisɪŋkt/ *noun* a part of a town where the streets are closed to traffic so that people can walk about and shop

shop-soiled /'ʃɒp sɔɪld/ *adjective* dirty because of having been on display in a store ○ *These items are shop-soiled and cannot be sold at full price.*

shop steward /ʃɒp 'stjuərd/ *noun* an elected labor union official who represents employees in day-to-day negotiations with the management

shopwalker /'ʃɒpwɔkər/ *noun* an employee of a department store who advises the customers and supervises the store assistants in a department

shop window /ˌʃɒp ˈwɪndoʊ/ *noun* U.K. same as **store window**

shop window website /ˌʃɒp ˈwɪndoʊ ˌwebsaɪt/ *noun U.K.* a website that provides information about an organization and its products, but does not allow visitors to interact with it

short /ʃɔːt/ *adjective, adverb* **1.** for a small period of time □ **in the short term** in the near future or very soon **2.** less than what is expected or desired ○ *The shipment was three items short.* ○ *My change was $2 short.* □ **when we cashed out we were $10 short** we had $10 less than we should have had □ **to give short weight** to sell something which is lighter than it should be □ **short of** lacking ○ *We are short of staff* or *short of money.* ○ *The company is short of new ideas.* ■ *verb* to sell short ○ *He shorted the stock at $35 and continued to short it as the price moved up.*

shortage /ˈʃɔːtɪdʒ/ *noun* a lack or low availability of something ○ *a shortage of skilled staff* ○ *We employ part-timers to make up for staff shortages.* ○ *The import controls have resulted in the shortage of spare parts.* □ **there is no shortage of investment advice** there are plenty of people who want to give advice on investments

short-change /ˌʃɔːt ˈtʃeɪndʒ/ *verb* to give a customer less change than is right, either by mistake or in the hope that it will not be noticed

short credit /ˌʃɔːt ˈkredɪt/ *noun* terms which allow the customer only a little time to pay

short-dated bill /ˌʃɔːt ˌdeɪtɪd ˈbɪl/ *noun* a bill which is payable within a few days

short-dated securities /ˌʃɔːt ˌdeɪtɪd sɪˈkjʊərɪtiz/ *plural noun* same as **shorts**

shorten /ˈʃɔːt(ə)n/ *verb* to make shorter ○ *to shorten credit terms* □ **to shorten a credit period** to make a credit period shorter, so as to improve the company's cash position

shortfall /ˈʃɔːtfɔːl/ *noun* an amount which is missing which would make the total expected sum ○ *We had to borrow* money to cover the shortfall between expenditure and revenue.

shorthand /ˈʃɔːthænd/ *noun* a rapid way of writing using a system of signs □ **to take shorthand** to write using shorthand ○ *He took down the minutes in shorthand.*

shorthanded /ʃɔːtˈhændɪd/ *adjective* without enough staff ○ *We're rather shorthanded at the moment.*

shorthand notebook /ˌʃɔːthænd ˈnoʊtbʊk/ *noun* a small notebook for taking shorthand dictation

shorthand secretary /ˌʃɔːthænd ˈsekrɪt(ə)ri/ *noun* a secretary who takes dictation in shorthand

shorthand typist /ˌʃɔːthænd ˈtaɪpɪst/ *noun U.K.* same as **stenographer**

short-haul flight /ˌʃɔːt hɔːl ˈflaɪt/ *noun* a flight over a short distance (up to 1,000 km)

short lease /ˌʃɔːt ˈliːs/ *noun* a lease which runs for up to two or three years ○ *We have a short lease on our current premises.*

shortlist /ˈʃɔːtlɪst/ *noun* a list of candidates who can be asked to come for a test or interview (drawn up after all applications have been examined and the most obviously unsuitable candidates have been rejected) ○ *to draw up a shortlist* ○ *She is on the shortlist for the job.* ■ *verb* to make a shortlist ○ *Four candidates have been shortlisted.* ○ *Shortlisted candidates will be asked for an interview.*

short-range forecast /ˌʃɔːt reɪndʒ ˈfɔːkæst/ *noun* a forecast which covers a period of a few months

shorts /ʃɔːts/ *plural noun* government stocks which mature in less than five years' time

short sale /ˌʃɔːt ˈseliŋ/, **short selling** *noun* the act of arranging to sell something in the future which you think you can buy for less than the agreed selling price

short-staffed /ˌʃɔːt ˈstæft/ *adjective* with not enough staff ○ *We're rather short-staffed at the moment.*

short-stay /ˌʃɔːt ˈsteɪ/ *noun* customers who spend only a few nights at a hotel

short-term /ˌʃɔːt ˈtɜːm/ *adjective* for a period of weeks or months ○ *to place money on short-term deposit* ○ *She is employed on a short-term contract.* □ **on a short-term basis** for a short period

short-term debt /ˌʃɔrt tɜrm 'det/ *noun* a debt which has to be repaid within a few weeks

short-term forecast /ˌʃɔrt tɜrm 'fɔrkæst/ *noun* a forecast which covers a period of a few months

short-term gain /ˌʃɔrt tɜrm 'geɪn/ *noun* an increase in price made over a short period

short-termism /ˌʃɔrt 'tɜrmɪz(ə)m/ *noun* a type of thinking or planning that concentrates on achieving results in the near future rather than on long-term objectives

short-term loan /ˌʃɔrt tɜrm 'loʊn/ *noun* a loan which has to be repaid within a few weeks or some years

short time /ˌʃɔrt 'taɪm/ *noun* reduced working hours resulting in less than half a normal week's pay ○ *Several machinists will be on short time as long as the shortage of orders lasts.* ○ *The company has had to introduce short-time working because of lack of orders.*

short ton /ˌʃɔrt 'tʌn/ *noun* same as **ton**

show /ʃoʊ/ *noun* an exhibition or display of goods or services for sale ○ *a motor show* ○ *a computer show* ■ *verb* to make something be seen ○ *to show a gain or a fall* ○ *to show a profit or a loss* (NOTE: **showing – showed – has shown**)

showcard /'ʃoʊkɑrd/ *noun* a piece of cardboard with advertising material, put near an item for sale

showcase /'ʃoʊkeɪs/ *noun* 1. a cupboard with a glass front or top to display items 2. the presentation of someone or something in a favorable setting ■ *verb* to present someone or something in a way that is designed to attract attention and admiration

show house /'ʃoʊ haʊs/ *noun* a house or apartment built and furnished so that possible buyers can see what similar houses could be like

show of hands /ˌʃoʊ əv 'hændz/ *noun* a vote where people show how they vote by raising their hands ○ *The motion was carried on a show of hands.*

showroom /'ʃoʊrum/ *noun* a room where goods are displayed for sale ○ *a car showroom*

shred /ʃred/ *verb* to tear (paper) into thin strips, which can then be thrown away or used as packing material ○ *They sent a pile of old invoices to be shredded.* ○ *She told the police that the manager had told her to shred all the documents in the file.*

shredder /'ʃredər/ *noun* a machine for shredding paper

shrink /ʃrɪŋk/ *verb* to get smaller ○ *The market has shrunk by 20%.* ○ *The company is having difficulty selling into a shrinking market.* (NOTE: **shrinking – shrank – has shrunk**)

shrinkage /'ʃrɪŋkɪdʒ/ *noun* 1. the amount by which something gets smaller ○ *to allow for shrinkage* 2. losses of inventory through theft, especially by the store's own staff (*informal*)

shrink-wrapped /'ʃrɪŋk ræpt/ *adjective* covered in tight plastic protective cover

shrink-wrapping /'ʃrɪŋk ˌræpɪŋ/ *noun* the act of covering (a book, fruit, record, etc.) in a tight plastic cover

shroff /ʃrɒf/ *noun* 1. (*in the Far East*) an accountant 2. (*in the Far East*) an accounts clerk

shut /ʃʌt/ *adjective* not open for business ○ *The office is shut on Saturdays.* ■ *verb* to close ○ *to shut a store* or *a warehouse* (NOTE: **shutting – shut**)

shut down *phrasal verb* to make a factory or office stop working for a time ○ *The offices will shut down for Christmas.* ○ *Six factories have shut down this month.*

shutdown /'ʃʌtdaʊn/ *noun* the shutting of a factory or office

shutout /'ʃʌtaʊt/ *noun* the locking of the door of a factory or office to stop the staff getting in

sick building syndrome /ˌsɪk 'bɪldɪŋ ˌsɪndroʊm/ *noun* a condition where many people working in a building feel ill or have headaches, caused by blocked air-conditioning ducts in which stale air is recycled round the building, often carrying allergenic substances or bacteria

sick leave /'sɪk liv/ *noun* time when a worker is away from work because of illness

sick pay /'sɪk peɪ/ *noun* pay paid to an employee who is sick, even if he cannot work

sideline /'saɪdlaɪn/ *noun* a business which is extra to your normal work ○ *He* *runs a profitable sideline selling postcards to tourists.*

sight bill /'saɪt bɪl/ *noun* a bill of exchange which is payable at sight

sight draft /'saɪt dræft/ *noun* a bill of exchange which is payable when it is presented

sign /saɪn/ *noun* a board or notice which advertises something ○ *They have asked for planning permission to put up a large red store sign.* ○ *Advertising signs cover most of the buildings in the center of the town.* ■ *verb* to write your name in a special way on a document to show that you have written it or approved it ○ *The letter is signed by the managing director.* ○ *Our company checks are not valid if they have not been signed by the finance director.* ○ *The new recruit was asked to sign the contract of employment.* □ **the warehouse manager signed for the goods** the manager signed a receipt to show that the goods had been received

sign off *phrasal verb* □ **to sign off the accounts** (*of directors*) to sign the final form of a company's accounts to show that they are approved, before sending them to Companies House

sign on *phrasal verb* to start work, by signing your name in the human resources office □ **to sign on for the dole** to register as unemployed

signatory /'sɪɡnət(ə)ri/ *noun* a person who signs a contract, etc. ○ *You have to get the permission of all the signatories to the agreement if you want to change the terms.*

signature /'sɪɡnətʃər/ *noun* a person's name written by themselves on a check, document or letter ○ *She found a pile of checks on his desk waiting for signature.* ○ *All our company's checks need two signatures.* ○ *The contract of employment had the personnel director's signature at the bottom.*

sign in /'saɪn ɪn/ *noun* he signed the stock report to show that the goods had arrived or had been dispatched

silent partner /ˌsaɪlənt 'pɑrtnər/ *noun* a partner who has a share of the business but does not work in it

simple interest /ˌsɪmpəl 'ɪntrəst/ *noun* interest calculated on the capital invested only, and not added to it

Simplified Employee Pension Plan /ˌsɪmplɪfaɪd ɪmˌplɔɪi 'penʃ(ə)n ˌplæn/ a tax-deferred retirement plan that allows employers to contribute to their own and their employees' Individual Retirement Accounts (IRAs). Abbreviation **SEP**

simultaneous management /ˌsɪm(ə)lteɪniəs 'mænɪdʒmənt/ *noun* a style of management in which managers try to integrate different tasks and deal with them at the same time rather than keeping them separate and dealing with them one after the other

single /'sɪŋɡ(ə)l/ *adjective* 1. one alone 2. □ **in single figures** less than ten ○ *Sales are down to single figures.* ○ *Inflation is now in single figures.*

single-entry bookkeeping /ˌsɪŋɡ(ə)l ˌentri 'bʊkkipɪŋ/ *noun* a method of bookkeeping where payments or sales are noted with only one entry per transaction, usually in the cash book

single European market /ˌsɪŋɡ(ə)l ˌjʊrəpiən 'mɑrkət/, **single market** /ˌsɪŋɡ(ə)l 'mɑrkət/ *noun* the EU considered as one single market, with no tariff barriers between its member states

single fare /'sɪŋɡ(ə)l fer/ *noun U.K.* a fare or ticket for one trip from one place to another

single-figure inflation /ˌsɪŋɡ(ə)l ˌfɪɡər ɪn'fleɪʃ(ə)n/ *noun* inflation rising at less than 10% per annum

single premium policy /ˌsɪŋɡ(ə)l ˌprimiəm 'pɑlɪsi/ *noun* an insurance policy where only one premium is paid rather than regular annual premiums

single ticket /ˌsɪŋɡ(ə)l 'tɪkɪt/ *noun U.K.* same as **one-way ticket**

single union agreement /ˌsɪŋɡ(ə)l 'junjən əˌɡrimənt/ *noun* agreement between management and one union, that the union will represent all the workers in the company (whatever type of job they have)

sink /sɪŋk/ *verb* 1. to go down suddenly ○ *Prices sank at the news of the closure of the factory.* 2. to invest money into something ○ *He sank all his savings into a car-hire business.* (NOTE: **sinking – sank – sunk**)

sinking fund /'sɪŋkɪŋ fʌnd/ *noun* a fund built up out of amounts of money put aside regularly to meet a future need, such as the repayment of a loan

sir /sɜr/ *noun* □ **Dear Sir** way of addressing a letter to a man whom you do not know or to a limited company □ **Dear Sirs** way of addressing a letter to a firm

sister company /'sɪstə ˌkʌmp(ə)ni/ *noun* another company which is part of the same group

sister ship /'sɪstə ʃɪp/ *noun* a ship which is of the same design and belongs to the same company as another ship

sit-down protest /'sɪt daʊn ˌprəʊtest/, **sit-down strike** /'sɪt daʊn ˌstraɪk/ *noun* a strike where the employees stay in their place of work and refuse to work or to leave ○ *They staged a sit-down strike but were forced to leave the premises by the police.*

site /saɪt/ *noun* **1.** the place where something is located ○ *We have chosen a site for the new factory.* ○ *The supermarket is to be built on a site near the station.* **2.** a website which is created by a company, organization or individual, and which anyone can visit ○ *How many hits did we have on our site last week?* ■ *verb* to place or position □ **to be sited** to be placed ○ *The factory will be sited near the motorway.*

site engineer /'saɪt endʒɪˌnɪr/ *noun* an engineer in charge of a building being constructed

sit-in /'sɪt ɪn/ *noun* a strike where the employees stay in their place of work and refuse to work or leave (NOTE: The plural is **sit-ins**.)

sitting tenant /ˌsɪtɪŋ 'tenənt/ *noun* a tenant who is occupying a building when the freehold or lease is sold ○ *The block of apartments is for sale with four apartments vacant and two with sitting tenants.*

situated /'sɪtʃueɪtɪd/ *adjective* placed ○ *The factory is situated on the edge of the town.* ○ *The office is situated near the railroad station.*

situation /ˌsɪtʃu'eɪʃ(ə)n/ *noun* **1.** a state of affairs ○ *the financial situation of a company* ○ *the general situation of the economy* **2.** a job **3.** a place where something is ○ *The factory is in a very pleasant situation by the sea.*

situations vacant /ˌsɪtʃueɪʃ(ə)nz 'veɪkənt/ *noun* a list in a newspaper of jobs which are available

sixth decile /ˌsɪksθ 'desaɪəl/ *noun* a number below which sixty percent of numbers fall ○ *This group falls within the sixth decile of consumers.*

size /saɪz/ *noun* measurements of something, of how big something is or of how many there are of something ○ *What is the size of the container?* ○ *The size of the staff has doubled in the last two years.* ○ *This packet is the maximum size allowed by the post office.*

size of firm /ˌsaɪz əv 'fɜrm/ *noun* a method of classifying companies according to their size used in government statistics. Companies are usually classified either as microbusinesses, small businesses, medium-sized businesses, or large-sized businesses.

skeleton staff /'skelɪt(ə)n stæf/ *noun* a small number of staff who are left to carry on essential work while most of the work force is away

skid /skɪd/ *noun* a flat wooden base on which goods can be stacked for easy handling by a fork-lift truck (NOTE: The U.K. term is **pallet**.)

skill /skɪl/ *noun* an ability to do something because you have been trained ○ *We are badly in need of technical skills now that we have computerized the production line.* ○ *She has acquired some very useful office management skills.* ○ *He was not appointed because he didn't have the skills required for the job.*

"Britain's skills crisis has now reached such proportions that it is affecting the nation's economic growth" [*Personnel Today*]

"…we aim to add the sensitivity of a new European to the broad skills of the new professional manager" [*Management Today*]

skilled /skɪld/ *adjective* having learned certain skills

skilled workers /skɪld 'wɜrkərz/, **skilled labor** /skɪld 'leɪbə/ *noun* workers who have special skills or who have had long training

SKU /ˌes keɪ 'ju/ *noun* a unique code made up of numbers or letters and numbers which is assigned to a product by a retailer for identification and inventory control. Full form **stockkeeping unit**

SLA *abbreviation* service level agreement

slack /slæk/ *adjective* not busy ○ *Business is slack at the end of the week.* ○ *January is always a slack period.* ○ *The foreman decided to tighten up on slack workers.*

slacken /'slæk(ə)n/ *verb*
slacken off *phrasal verb* to become less
busy ○ *Trade has slackened off.*

slack season /'slæk ˌsiz(ə)n/ *noun* a
period when a company is not very busy

slander /'slændər/ *noun* an untrue spoken statement which damages someone's
character □ **action for slander, slander
action** case in a law court where someone
says that another person had slandered him
or her ■ *verb* □ **to slander someone** to
damage someone's character by saying
untrue things about him or her. Compare
libel

slash /slæʃ/ *verb* to reduce something
sharply ○ *We have been forced to slash
credit terms.* ○ *Prices have been slashed
in all departments.* ○ *The banks have
slashed interest rates.*

sleeping partner /ˌslipɪŋ 'partnər/
noun U.K. same as **silent partner**

slide /slaɪd/ *verb* to move down steadily
○ *Prices slid after the company reported a
loss.* (NOTE: **sliding – slid**)

sliding /'slaɪdɪŋ/ *adjective* rising in
steps

sliding scale /ˌslaɪdɪŋ 'skeɪl/ *noun* a
list of charges which rises gradually according to value, quantity, time, etc.

slight /slaɪt/ *adjective* not very large, not
very important ○ *There was a slight improvement in the balance of trade.* ○ *We
saw a slight increase in sales in February.*

slightly /'slaɪtli/ *adverb* not very much
○ *Sales fell slightly in the second quarter.*
○ *The Swiss bank is offering slightly better
terms.*

slip /slɪp/ *noun* **1.** a small piece of paper
2. a mistake ○ *He made a couple of slips
in calculating the discount.* ■ *verb* to go
down and back ○ *Profits slipped to $1.5m.*
○ *Stocks slipped back at the close.* (NOTE:
slipping – slipped)

"…with long-term fundamentals reasonably
sound, the question for brokers is when does
cheap become cheap enough? The Bangkok
and Taipei exchanges offer lower p/e ratios
than Jakarta, but if Jakarta p/e ratios slip to
the 16–18 range, foreign investors would
pay more attention to it" [*Far Eastern
Economic Review*]

slip up *phrasal verb* to make a mistake
○ *We slipped up badly in not signing the
agreement with the Chinese company.*

slip-up /'slɪp ʌp/ *noun* a mistake ○
*There has been a slip-up in the customs
documentation.* (NOTE: The plural is **slip-
ups.**)

slot /slɒt/ *noun* the period of time available for a TV or radio commercial ○ *They
took six 30-second slots at peak viewing
time.*

slow /sloʊ/ *adjective* not going fast ○
*The sales got off to a slow start, but picked
up later.* ○ *Business is always slow after
Christmas.* ○ *They were slow to reply* or
*slow in replying to the customer's com-
plaints.* ○ *The board is slow to come to a
decision.* ○ *There was a slow improvement
in sales in the first half of the year.* ■ *verb*
to go less fast

"…cash paid for stock: overstocked lines,
factory seconds, slow sellers" [*Australian
Financial Review*]

"…a general price freeze succeeded in
slowing the growth in consumer prices"
[*Financial Times*]

"…the fall in short-term rates suggests a
slowing economy" [*Financial Times*]

slow down *phrasal verb* to stop rising,
moving or falling, or to make something
go more slowly ○ *Inflation is slowing
down.* ○ *The fall in the exchange rate is
slowing down.* ○ *The management decided to slow down production.*

slowdown /'sloʊdaʊn/ *noun* a reduction in business activity ○ *a slowdown in
the company's expansion*

slow payer /ˌsloʊ 'peɪər/ *noun* a person
or company that does not pay debts on
time ○ *The company is well known as a
slow payer.*

sluggish /'slʌgɪʃ/ *adjective* not moving
very fast ○ *The economy is still sluggish,
and is taking a long time to get out of recession.*

"…the association said sluggish earnings by
supermarkets are due to consumers' concern
about income and job prospects" [*Nikkei
Weekly*]

slump /slʌmp/ *noun* **1.** a rapid fall ○ *the
slump in the value of the dollar* ○ *We experienced a slump in sales* or *a slump in profits.* **2.** a period of economic collapse with
high unemployment and loss of trade ○ *We
are experiencing slump conditions.* **3.** the
world economic crisis of 1929–33 ■ *verb*
to fall fast ○ *Profits have slumped.* ○ *The
dollar slumped on the foreign exchange
markets.*

slush fund /'slʌʃ fʌnd/ *noun* money kept to one side to give to people to persuade them to do what you want ○ *The government was brought down by the scandal over the slush funds.* ○ *The party was accused of keeping a slush fund to pay foreign businessmen.*

small ads /'smɔl ædz/ *plural noun U.K.* short private advertisements in a newspaper, e.g., selling small items or asking for jobs

small business /ˌsmɔl 'bɪznɪs/ *noun* a little company with low turnover and few employees

Small Business Administration /ˌsmɔl 'bɪznɪs ədˌmɪnɪstreɪʃ(ə)n/ *noun* a federal agency that advises small businesses and helps them obtain loans to finance their businesses. Abbreviation **SBA**

small businessman /ˌsmɔl 'bɪznɪsmæn/ *noun* a man who owns a small business

small change /ˌsmɔl 'tʃeɪndʒ/ *noun* coins

small-claims court /ˌsmɔl 'kleɪmz ˌkɔrt/ *noun U.K.* a court which deals with disputes over small amounts of money

small investor /ˌsmɔl ɪn'vestər/ *noun* a person with a small sum of money to invest

small print /'smɔl prɪnt/ *noun* items printed at the end of an official document such as a contract in smaller letters than the rest of the text. People sometimes do not pay attention to the small print, but it can contain important information, and unscrupulous operators may deliberately try to hide things such as additional charges, unfavorable terms, or loopholes in it.

"An emergency fiscal program is on the table providing for tax cuts next year. But there's some small print that provides for new taxes two years down the road." [*BusinessWeek*]

small-scale /'smɔl skeɪl/ *adjective* working in a small way, with few staff and not much money

small-scale enterprise /ˌsmɔl skeɪl 'entəpraɪz/ *noun* a small business

small storekeeper /ˌsmɔl 'stɔrkipər/ *noun* an owner of a small store

smart card /'smɑrt kɑrd/ *noun* a credit card with a microchip, used for withdrawing money from ATMs, or for purchases at EFTPOS terminals

smart market /ˌsmɑrt 'mɑrkət/ *noun* a market where all business is conducted electronically using network communications

smartsizing /'smɑrtsaɪzɪŋ/ *noun* the process of reducing the size of a company by making incompetent and inefficient employees redundant

smash /smæʃ/ *verb* to break (a record), to do better than (a record) ○ *The factory is aiming to smash all production records this year.* ○ *Sales have smashed all records for the first half of the year.*

SMEs *abbreviation* small and medium-sized enterprises

smokestack industries /'smoʊkstæk ˌɪndəstriz/ *plural noun* heavy industries, such as steel-making

smuggle /'smʌg(ə)l/ *verb* to take goods illegally into a country or without declaring them to customs ○ *They had to smuggle the spare parts into the country.*

smuggler /'smʌglər/ *noun* a person who smuggles

smuggling /'smʌglɪŋ/ *noun* the practice of taking goods illegally into a country or without declaring them to customs ○ *They made their money in arms smuggling.*

snap /snæp/ *adjective* rapid or sudden ○ *they carried out a snap inspection of the expense accounts* ○ *The board came to a snap decision.*

snap up *phrasal verb* to buy something quickly ○ *to snap up a bargain* ○ *She snapped up 15% of the company's stock.* (NOTE: **snapping – snapped**)

soar /sɔr/ *verb* to go up rapidly ○ *Stock prices soared on the news of the takeover bid* or *the news of the takeover bid sent stock prices soaring.* ○ *Food prices soared during the cold weather.*

social /'soʊʃ(ə)l/ *adjective* referring to society in general

social audit /ˌsoʊʃ(ə)l 'ɔdɪt/ *noun* a systematic assessment of an organization's effects on society or on all those who can be seen as its stakeholders. A social audit covers such issues as internal codes of conduct, business ethics, human resource development, environmental impact, and the organization's sense of social responsibility. ○ *The social audit focused on the effects of pollution in the area.* ○ *The social audit showed that the factory could pro-*

vide jobs for five percent of the unemployed in the small town nearby.

social capital /ˌsouʃ(ə)l ˈkæpɪt(ə)l/ *noun* the social and interpersonal skills of employees, considered as an intangible asset of an organization

social costs /ˈsouʃ(ə)l kɔsts/ *plural noun* the ways in which something will affect people

social investing /ˌsouʃ(ə)l ˌɪnˈvestɪŋ/ *noun* U.K. same as **socially responsible investment**

socially responsible investment /ˌsouʃ(ə)li rɪˌspansɪb(ə)l ɪnˈvestmənt/ *noun* the practice of investing in companies that follow ethical practices, e.g.,paying fair wages and protecting the environment

social overhead capital /ˌsouʃ(ə)l ˈouvərhed ˌkæpɪt(ə)l/ *noun* same as **infrastructure**

social purpose ventures /ˌsouʃ(ə)l ˌpərpəs ˈventʃərz/ *plural noun* businesses and organizations that are concerned with human society and the welfare of others

social responsibility /ˌsouʃ(ə)l rɪˌspansəˈbɪləti/ *noun* a business's obligation to be concerned with the welfare of its customers, employees, and the community

social security /ˌsouʃ(ə)l sɪˈkjurəti/ *noun* a government program where employers, employees, and the self-employed make regular contributions to a fund which provides unemployment pay, sickness pay, or retirement pensions ○ *He expects to receive $1,000 a month in social security payments.* ○ *She became disabled and subsequently lived on social security for years.*

Social Security Administration /ˌsouʃ(ə)l sɪˈkjurɪti ədˌmɪnɪstreɪʃ(ə)n/ *noun* The agency of the U.S. government that administers the social security program, which includes paying retirement, survivor, and disability benefits

social system /ˈsouʃ(ə)l ˌsɪstəm/ *noun* the way society is organized

society /səˈsaɪəti/ *noun* **1.** the way in which the people in a country are organized **2.** a club for a group of people with the same interests ○ *We have joined a computer society.*

socio-economic /ˌsouʃiou ˌikə ˈnamɪk/ *adjective* referring to social and economic conditions, social classes and income groups ○ *We have commissioned a thorough socio-economic analysis of our potential market.*

socio-economic groups /ˌsouʃiou ikəˌnamɪk ˈgrups/ *plural noun* groups in society divided according to income and position

soft currency /ˌsaft ˈkʌrənsi/ *noun* the currency of a country with a weak economy, which is cheap to buy and difficult to exchange for other currencies. Opposite **hard currency**

soft landing /sɔft ˈlændɪŋ/ *noun* a change in economic strategy to counteract inflation, which does not cause unemployment or a fall in the standard of living, and has only minor effects on the bulk of the population

soft loan /ˌsɔft ˈloun/ *noun* a loan from a company to an employee or from one government to another at a very low rate of interest or with no interest payable at all

soft market /ˌsɔft ˈmarkət/ *noun* a market where there is not enough demand, and where prices fall

soft sell /ˌsɔft ˈsel/ *noun* the process of persuading people to buy, by encouraging and not forcing them to do so

software /ˈsɔftwer/ *noun* computer programs

sole /soul/ *adjective* only

sole agency /ˌsoul ˈeɪdʒənsi/ *noun* an agreement to be the only person to represent a company or to sell a product in a particular area ○ *He has the sole agency for Ford cars.*

sole agent /ˌsoul ˈeɪdʒənt/ *noun* a person who has the sole agency for a company in an area ○ *She is the sole agent for Ford cars in the locality.*

sole distributor /ˌsoul dɪˈstrɪbjətər/ *noun* a retailer who is the only one in an area who is allowed to sell a product

solemn /ˈsaləm/ *adjective* □ **solemn and binding agreement** an agreement which is not legally binding, but which all parties are supposed to obey

sole owner /ˌsoul ˈounər/ *noun* a person who owns a business on their own, with no partners, and has not formed a company

sole proprietor /ˌsoul prəˈpraɪətər/, **sole trader** /ˌsoul ˈtreɪdər/ *noun* a person who runs a business, usually by him- or herself, but has not registered it as a corporation

solicit /sə'lɪsɪt/ *verb* □ **to solicit orders** to ask for orders, to try to get people to order goods

solus (advertisement) /'souləs əd ˌvɜrtɪsmənt/ *noun* an advertisement which does not appear near other advertisements for similar products

solution /sə'luʃ(ə)n/ *noun* the answer to a problem ○ *to look for a solution to the company's financial problems* ○ *to look for a solution to the company's manpower crisis* ○ *The programmer came up with a solution to the systems problem.* ○ *We think we have found a solution to the problem of getting skilled staff.*

solution brand /sə'luʃ(ə)n brænd/ *noun* a combination of a product and related services, e.g., a computer system plus installation and maintenance, that meets a customer's needs more effectively than the product on its own

solve /salv/ *verb* to find an answer to a problem ○ *The loan will solve some of our short-term problems.* ○ *The new rates of pay should solve some of our short-term recruitment problems.*

solvency /'salv(ə)nsi/ *noun* the state of being able to pay all debts on due date. Opposite **insolvency**

solvent /'salv(ə)nt/ *adjective* having enough money to pay debts ○ *When she bought the company it was barely solvent.*

sort /sɔrt/ *verb* to put (a lot of things) in order ○ *She is sorting index cards into alphabetical order.*

sort out *phrasal verb* **1.** to put into order ○ *Did you sort out the accounts problem with the auditors?* **2.** to settle a problem

sort code /'sɔrt koʊd/ *noun* a combination of numbers that identifies a bank branch on official documentation, such as bank statements and checks (NOTE: The U.S. term is **routing number.**)

sort field /'sɔrt fild/ *noun* a special area of computer storage used to identify data so that it can be easily classified and arranged in order

sound /saʊnd/ *adjective* reasonable, which can be trusted ○ *The company's financial situation is very sound.* ○ *He gave us some very sound advice.*

soundness /'saʊndnəs/ *noun* the state of being reasonable

source /sɔrs/ *noun* the place where something comes from ○ *What is the source of her income?* ○ *You must declare income from all sources to the IRS.* □ **income which is taxed at source** income where the tax is removed and paid to the government by the employer before the income is paid to the employee ■ *verb* to get supplies from somewhere ○ *We source these spare parts in Germany.*

source and application of funds statement /ˌsɔrs ən ˌæplɪkeɪʃ(ə)n əv 'fʌndz ˌsteɪtmənt/, **sources and uses of funds statement** /ˌsɔrsɪz ən ˌjuzɪz əv 'fʌndz ˌsteɪtmənt/ *noun* a statement in a company's annual accounts, showing where new funds came from during the year, and how they were used

source credibility /'sɔrs kredəˌbɪləti/ *noun* the image people have of someone which will determine that person's credibility

sourcing /'sɔrsɪŋ/ *noun* the process of finding suppliers of goods or services ○ *The sourcing of spare parts can be diversified to suppliers outside Europe.* ◊ **outsourcing**

space /speɪs/ *noun* an empty place or empty area □ **to take advertising space in a newspaper** to place a large advertisement in a newspaper

space out *phrasal verb* to place things with spaces between them ○ *The company name is written in spaced-out letters.* ○ *Payments can be spaced out over a period of ten years.*

spam /spæm/ *noun* articles that have been posted to more than one newsgroup, and so are likely to contain unsolicited commercial messages

span of control /ˌspæn əv kən'troʊl/ *noun* the number and type of employees that a manager is responsible for supervising ○ *The job has a large amount of responsibility with a wide span of control.* ○ *Too wide a span of control can lead to inefficient supervision.*

spare /sper/ *adjective* extra, not being used ○ *He has invested his spare capital in a computer store.* □ **to use up spare capacity** to make use of time or space which has not been fully used

spare part /ˌsper 'pɑrt/ *noun* a small piece of machinery used to replace part of a machine which is broken ○ *The photocopier will not work – it needs a spare part.*

spare time /ˌsper 'taɪm/ *noun* the time when you are not at work ○ *He built himself a car in his spare time.*

speakerphone /'spikərfoʊn/ *noun* a telephone that has a loudspeaker and microphone so that several people can listen to a conversation and speak

spec /spek/ *noun* same as **specification** □ **to buy something on spec** to buy something without being sure of its value

special /'speʃ(ə)l/ *adjective* better than usual ○ *He offered us special terms.* ○ *The car is being offered at a special price.*

special delivery /ˌspeʃ(ə)l dɪ'lɪv(ə)ri/ *noun* a type of postal service for rapid delivery of letters and packets

special deposits /ˌspeʃ(ə)l dɪ'pɑzɪts/ *plural noun* large sums of money which commercial banks have to deposit with the Bank of England

special drawing rights /ˌspeʃ(ə)l 'drɔɪŋ ˌraɪts/ *plural noun* units of account used by the International Monetary Fund, allocated to each member country for use in loans and other international operations. Their value is calculated daily on the weighted values of a group of currencies shown in dollars. Abbreviation **SDRs**

specialist /'speʃəlɪst/ *noun* a person or company that deals with one particular type of product or one subject ○ *You should go to a specialist in computers or to a computer specialist for advice.* ○ *We need a manager who can grasp the overall picture rather than a narrow specialist.*

specialization /ˌspeʃələɪ'zeɪʃ(ə)n/ *noun* the act of dealing with one specific type of product ○ *The company's area of specialization is accounts packages for small businesses.*

specialize /'speʃəlaɪz/ *verb* to deal with one particular type of skill, product, or service ○ *The company specializes in electronic components.* ○ *They have a specialized product line.* ○ *He sells very specialized equipment for the electronics industry.* ○ *After working in all the departments, he finally decided to specialize in distribution.*

special offer /ˌspeʃ(ə)l 'ɔfər/ *noun* a situation where goods are put on sale at a specially low price ○ *We have a range of men's shirts on special offer.*

special resolution /ˌspeʃ(ə)l ˌrezə'luʃ(ə)n/ *noun* a resolution concerning an important matter, such as a change to the company's bylaws

specialty /ˌspeʃi'æləti/ *noun* the specific business interest or specific type of product that a company has ○ *Their specialty is computer programs.*

specialty store /'speʃ(ə)lti stɔr/ *noun* a store selling a limited range of items of good quality

specie /'spiʃi/ *noun* money in the form of coins

specification /ˌspesɪfɪ'keɪʃ(ə)n/ *noun* detailed information about what or who is needed or about a product to be supplied ○ *to detail the specifications of a computer system* □ **to work to standard specifications** to work to specifications which are acceptable anywhere in an industry □ **the work is not up to specification** *or* **does not meet our specifications** the product is not made in the way which was detailed

specify /'spesɪfaɪ/ *verb* to state clearly what is needed ○ *to specify full details of the goods ordered* ○ *Do not include sales tax on the invoice unless specified.* ○ *Candidates are asked to specify which of the three positions they are applying for.* (NOTE: **specifies – specifying – specified**)

specimen /'spesɪmɪn/ *noun* something which is given as a sample □ **to give specimen signatures on a bank mandate** to write the signatures of all the people who can sign checks for an account so that the bank can recognize them

speculate /'spekjʊleɪt/ *verb* to take a risk in business which you hope will bring you profits □ **to speculate on the Stock Exchange** to buy stock which you hope will rise in value

speculation /ˌspekjʊ'leɪʃ(ə)n/ *noun* a risky deal which may produce a short-term profit ○ *He bought the company as a speculation.* ○ *She lost all her money in Stock Exchange speculations.*

speculative bubble /ˌspekjʊlətɪv 'bʌb(ə)l/ *noun* same as **bubble**

speculative builder /ˌspekjʊlətɪv 'bɪldər/ *noun* a builder who builds houses in the hope that someone will want to buy them

speculative stock /'spekjʊlətɪv stɑk/ *noun* a stock that may go sharply up or down in value

speculator /'spekjʊleɪtə/ *noun* a person who buys goods, stock or foreign currency in the hope that it will rise in value ○ *a property speculator* ○ *a currency speculator* ○ *a speculator on the Stock Exchange* or *a Stock Exchange speculator*

speed /spid/ *verb*
  speed up *phrasal verb* to make something go faster ○ *We are aiming to speed up our delivery times.*

spend /spend/ *verb* **1.** to pay money ○ *They spent all their savings on buying the store.* ○ *The company spends thousands of dollars on research.* **2.** to use time ○ *The company spends hundreds of person-hours on meetings.* ○ *The chairman spent yesterday afternoon with the auditors.* (NOTE: **spending – spent**) ■ *noun* an amount of money spent ○ *What's the annual spend on marketing?*

spending /'spendɪŋ/ *noun* the act of paying money for goods and services ○ *Both cash spending and credit card spending increase at Christmas.*

spending money /'spendɪŋ ˌmʌni/ *noun* money for ordinary personal expenses

spending power /'spendɪŋ ˌpaʊr/ *noun* **1.** the fact of having money to spend on goods ○ *the spending power of the student market* **2.** the amount of goods which can be bought for a sum of money ○ *The spending power of the dollar has fallen over the last ten years.*

sphere /sfɪr/ *noun* an area ○ *a sphere of activity* ○ *a sphere of influence*

spin /spɪn/ *verb*
  spin off *phrasal verb* □ **to spin off a subsidiary company** to split off part of a large company to form a smaller subsidiary, giving stock in the subsidiary to the existing stockholders

spin doctor /'spɪn ˌdɑktər/ *noun* a person who explains news in a way that makes it flattering to the person or organization employing him or her (*informal*) ○ *Government spin doctors have been having some difficulty in dealing with the news items about the rise in unemployment.*

spinoff /'spɪnɔf/ *noun* **1.** a useful product developed as a secondary product from a main item ○ *One of the spinoffs of the research program has been the development of the electric car.* **2.** a corporate reorganization in which a subsidiary becomes an independent company

spiral /'spaɪrəl/ *noun* something which twists round and round getting higher all the time ■ *verb* to twist round and round, getting higher all the time ○ *a period of spiraling prices* □ **spiraling inflation** inflation where price rises make employees ask for higher wages which then increase prices again

splash page /'splæʃ peɪdʒ/ *noun* a page, usually containing advertisements, that is displayed to visitors to a website before they reach the homepage

split /splɪt/ *noun* **1.** an act of dividing up **2.** a lack of agreement ○ *a split in the family stockholders* ■ *verb* **1.** □ **the stock split two for one** two shares of a stock at half the price are issued for each share held **2.** □ **to split the difference** to come to an agreement over a price by dividing the difference between the amount the seller is asking and amount the buyer wants to pay and agreeing on a price between the two ■ *adjective* divided into parts

split commission /ˌsplɪt kəˈmɪʃ(ə)n/ *noun* a commission which is divided between brokers or agents

split-level investment trust /ˌsplɪt ˌlev(ə)l ɪnˈvestmənt ˌtrʌst/ *noun* U.K. an investment trust with two categories of shares: income shares which receive income from the investments, but do not benefit from the rise in their capital value, and capital shares, which increase in value as the value of the investments rises, but do not receive any income. Also called **split trust, split-capital trust**

split payment /ˌsplɪt ˈpeɪmənt/ *noun* a payment which is divided into small units

spoil /spɔɪl/ *verb* to ruin, to make something bad ○ *Half the shipment was spoiled by water.* ○ *The company's results were spoiled by a disastrous last quarter.*

sponsor /'spɑnsər/ *noun* **1.** a person who recommends another person for a job **2.** a company which pays part of the cost of making a TV program by taking advertising time on the program **3.** a person or company which pays money to help research or to pay for a business venture **4.** a company which pays to help a sport, in return for advertising rights ■ *verb* **1.** to act as a sponsor for something ○ *a government-sponsored trade exhibition* ○ *The company has sponsored the soccer match.* ○ *Six of the management trainees have been sponsored by their companies.* **2.** to play an active part in something, such as a pension plan for employees ○ *If you're single and not covered by an employer-sponsored retirement plan.*

sponsorship /'spɒnsərʃɪp/ *noun* the act of sponsoring ○ *the sponsorship of a season of concerts* ○ *The training course could not be run without the sponsorship of several major companies.*

spot /spɒt/ *noun* **1.** a place for an advertisement on a TV or radio show **2.** the buying of something for immediate delivery

spot cash /ˌspɒt 'kæʃ/ *noun* cash paid for something bought immediately

spot market /'spɒt ˌmɑːkət/ *noun* a market that deals in commodities or foreign exchange for immediate rather than future delivery

spot price /'spɒt praɪs/, **spot rate** /ˌspɒt 'reɪt/ *noun* a current price or rate for something which is delivered immediately. Also called **cash price**

"…the average spot price of Nigerian light crude oil for the month of July was 27.21 dollars per barrel" [*Business Times (Lagos)*]

spread /spred/ *noun* **1.** same as **range** **2.** the difference between buying and selling prices, i.e. between the bid and offer prices ■ *verb* to space something out over a period of time ○ *to spread payments over several months* □ **to spread a risk** to make the risk of insurance less great by asking other companies to help cover it

"…dealers said markets were thin, with gaps between trades and wide spreads between bid and ask prices on the currencies" [*Wall Street Journal*]

"…to ensure an average return you should hold a spread of different shares covering a wide cross-section of the market" [*Investors Chronicle*]

spreadsheet /'spredˌʃiːt/ *noun* a computer printout or program that shows a series of columns or rows of figures

spyware /'spaɪweər/ *noun* software that is installed on a computer without a user's knowledge. It tracks Internet use and key

strokes and can be used in marketing activities.

square /skweər/ *noun* a way of measuring area, by multiplying the length by the width ○ *The office is ten meters by twelve – its area is one hundred and twenty square meters.* ■ *adjective* **1.** with four right angles and four equal straight sides **2.** settled, not owing anything (*informal*) □ **now we're all square** we do not owe each other anything ■ *verb* □ **to square a bill** to pay a bill □ **to square away** to put (papers) in order

square cut file /ˌskweər kʌt 'faɪl/ *noun* a simple folded card file, with one side taller than the other, used for filing documents (the file is inserted into a suspension file)

squared paper /ˌskweəd 'peɪpər/ *noun* paper printed with a series of small squares, like graph paper

square measure /ˌskweər 'meʒər/ *noun* an area in square feet or meters, calculated by multiplying width and length

squeeze /skwiːz/ *noun* government control carried out by reducing the availability of something ■ *verb* to crush or to press; to make smaller ○ *to squeeze margins or profits or credit*

"…the real estate boom of the past three years has been based on the availability of easy credit. Today, money is tighter, so property should bear the brunt of the credit squeeze" [*Money Observer*]

SRO *abbreviation* self-regulatory organization

SSL /ˌes es 'el/ *abbreviation* a method of providing a safe channel over the Internet to allow a user's credit card or personal details to be safely transmitted ○ *I only purchase goods from a web site that has SSL security installed.* ○ *The little key logo on my web browser appears when I am connected to a secure site with SSL.* Full form **secure sockets layer**

SSP *abbreviation* statutory sick pay

St *abbreviation* street

stability /stə'bɪləti/ *noun* the state of being steady or not moving up or down ○ *price stability* ○ *a period of economic stability* ○ *the stability of the currency markets*

stabilization /ˌsteɪbɪlaɪ'zeɪʃ(ə)n/ *noun* the process of making something stable, e.g., preventing sudden changes in prices □ **stabilization of the economy** keeping the economy stable by preventing inflation from rising, cutting high interest rates and excess money supply

stabilize /'steɪbəlaɪz/ *verb* to become steady, or to make something steady □ **prices have stabilized** prices have stopped moving up or down □ **to have a stabilizing effect on the economy** to make the economy more stable

stable /'steɪb(ə)l/ *adjective* steady or not moving up or down ○ *stable prices* ○ *a stable exchange rate* ○ *a stable currency* ○ *a stable economy*

staff /stæf/ *noun* people who work for a company or organization ○ *The office staff have complained about the lack of heating.* (NOTE: **staff** refers to a group of people and so is often followed by a plural verb.) □ **to be on the staff** *or* **a member of staff** *or* **a staff member** to be employed permanently by a company ■ *verb* to employ workers ○ *to have difficulty in staffing the factory* ○ *The department is staffed by skilled part-timers.*

staff agency /'stæf ˌeɪdʒənsi/ *noun* an agency which looks for office staff for companies

staff appointment /'stæf əˌpɔɪntmənt/ *noun* a job on the staff

staff appraisal /stæf əˈpreɪz(ə)l/, **staff assessment** /stæf əˈsesmənt/ *noun* a report on how well a member of staff is working

staff association /'stæf əsoʊsiˌeɪʃ(ə)n/ *noun* a society formed by members of staff of a company to represent them to the management and to organize entertainments

staff club /'stæf klʌb/ *noun* a club for the staff of a company, which organizes staff parties, sports and meetings

staffed /stæft/ *adjective* with someone working on it

staffer /'stæfər/ *noun* a member of the permanent staff

staff incentives /ˌstæf ɪnˈsentɪvz/ *plural noun* higher pay and better conditions offered to employees to make them work better

staffing /'stæfɪŋ/ *noun* the provision of staff for a company or the number of people needed to do a work process

staffing levels /'stæfɪŋ ˌlev(ə)lz/ *plural noun* the numbers of employees required in a department of a company for it to work efficiently

staffing policy /'stæfɪŋ ˌpɑlɪsi/ *noun* the company's views on staff – how many are needed for each department, if they should be full-time or part-time, what the salaries should be, etc.

staff meeting /'stæf ˌmitɪŋ/ *noun* a meeting of a group of staff or their representatives

staff training /ˌstæf ˈtreɪnɪŋ/ *noun* the process of teaching staff better and more profitable ways of working

stag /stæg/ *noun* **1.** a person who buys initial public offerings at the offering price and sells them immediately to make a profit **2.** a dealer in stocks who is not a member of a Stock Exchange ■ *verb* □ **to stag an issue** to buy an initial public offering at the offering price not as an investment, but to sell immediately not as at a profit. Also called **flip**

stage /steɪdʒ/ *noun* a period, one of several points in a process of development ○ *the different stages of the production process* □ **the contract is still in the drafting stage** the contract is still being drafted □ **in stages** in different steps ○ *The company has agreed to repay the loan in stages.*

staged payments /ˌsteɪdʒd ˈpeɪmənts/ *plural noun* payments made in stages

stage-gate model /'steɪdʒ geɪt ˌmɑd(ə)l/ *noun* a business model for developing a new product from conception to its launch, where the development is divided into several stages at the end of which is a "gate" where the management has to make a decision as to how to proceed to the next stage

stagflation /stægˈfleɪʃ(ə)n/ *noun* inflation and stagnation happening at the same time in an economy

stagger /'stægər/ *verb* to arrange vacations or working hours so that they do not all begin and end at the same time ○ *Staggered vacations help the tourist industry.* ○ *We have to stagger the lunch hour so that there is always someone on the switchboard.* ○ *We asked our supplier to stagger deliveries so that the warehouse can cope.*

stagnant /'stægnənt/ *adjective* not active, not increasing ○ *Turnover was stagnant for the first half of the year.* ○ *A stagnant economy is not a good sign.*

stagnate /stæg'neɪt/ *verb* not to increase, not to make progress ○ *The economy is stagnating.* ○ *After six hours the talks were stagnating.*

stagnation /stæg'neɪʃ(ə)n/ *noun* the state of not making any progress, especially in economic matters ○ *The country entered a period of stagnation.*

stake /steɪk/ *noun* an amount of money invested □ **to have a stake in a business** to have money invested in a business □ **to acquire a stake in a business** to buy stock in a business ○ *He acquired a 25% stake in the company.* ■ *verb* □ **to stake money on something** to risk money on something

stakeholder /'steɪkhoʊldər/ *noun* **1.** a person such as a stockholder, employee, or supplier who has a stake in a business **2.** a person or body that is directly or indirectly involved with a company or organization and has an interest in ensuring that it is successful (NOTE: A stakeholder may be an employee, customer, supplier, partner, or even the local community within which an organization operates.)

stakeholder pension /'steɪkhoʊldər ˌpenʃən/ *noun* a pension, provided through a private company, in which the income a person has after retirement depends on the amount of contributions made during their working life (NOTE: Stakeholder pensions are designed for people without access to an occupational pension scheme.)

stakeholder theory /'steɪkhoʊldər ˌθɪəri/ *noun* the theory that it is possible for an organization to promote the interests of its stockholders without harming the interests of its other stakeholders such as its employees, suppliers, and the wider community

stakeholder value analysis /ˌsteɪkhoʊldər ˌvælju ə'næləsɪs/ *noun* a form of analysis that identifies the various people and organizations who have a stake in a company and finds out their views on various issues so that these views may be taken into account when making strategic and operational decisions

stall /stɔl/ *noun* a small movable wooden booth, used for selling goods in a market

stallholder /'stɔlhoʊldər/ *noun* a person who has a stall in a market and pays rent for the site it occupies

stamp /stæmp/ *noun* a device for making marks on documents; a mark made in this way ○ *The invoice has the stamp "Received with thanks" on it.* ○ *The customs officer looked at the stamps in her passport.* □ **rubber stamp** stamp made of hard rubber cut to form words ■ *verb* **1.** to mark a document with a stamp ○ *to stamp an invoice "Paid"* ○ *The documents were stamped by the customs officials.* **2.** to put a postage stamp on an envelope or parcel

stamp duty /'stæmp ˌdjuti/ *noun* a tax on legal documents such as those used, e.g., for the sale or purchase of stock or the conveyance of a property to a new owner

stamped addressed envelope /ˌstæmpd əˌdresd 'envəloʊp/ *noun* an envelope with your own address written on it and a stamp stuck on it to pay for return postage ○ *Please send a stamped addressed envelope for further details and our latest catalog.* Abbreviation **s.a.e.**

stamp pad /'stæmp pæd/ *noun* a soft pad of cloth with ink on which a stamp is pressed, before marking the paper

stand /stænd/ *noun* an arrangement of shelves or tables at an exhibition for showing a company's products ■ *verb* to be or to stay □ **the company's balance stands at $24,000** the balance is $24,000

stand down *phrasal verb* to withdraw your name from an election ○ *At the last minute the two other candidates stood down, so she was elected chairman.*

stand in for *phrasal verb* to take someone's place ○ *Mrs. Smith is standing in for the chairman, who is ill.* (NOTE: **standing – stood**)

standard /'stændərd/ *noun* the usual quality or usual conditions which other things are judged against □ **up to standard** of acceptable quality ○ *This batch is not up to standard or does not meet our standards.* ■ *adjective* normal or usual ○ *a standard model car* ○ *We have a standard charge of $25 for a thirty-minute session.*

standard agreement /ˌstændərd ə'grimənt/, **standard contract** /ˌstændərd 'kɑntrækt/ *noun* a normal printed contract form

Standard & Poor's /ˌstændərd ən 'pʊrz/ *noun* an American corporation which rates bonds according to the creditworthiness of the organizations issuing them. Abbreviation **S&P**

standard costing /ˌstændərd 'kɒstɪŋ/ *noun* the process of planning costs for the period ahead and, at the end of the period, comparing these figures with actual costs in order to make necessary adjustments in planning

standard deduction /ˌstændərd dɪ 'dʌkʃ(ə)n/ *noun* an amount that can be deducted from income on a federal income tax form, if deductions are not itemized

standardization /ˌstændərdaɪ 'zeɪʃ(ə)n/ *noun* the process of making sure that everything fits a standard or is produced in the same way ○ *standardization of measurements throughout the EU* ○ *Standardization of design is necessary if we want to have a uniform company style.* □ **standardization of products** the process of reducing a large number of different products to a series which have the same measurements, design, packaging, etc.

standardize /'stændərdaɪz/ *verb* to make sure that everything fits a standard or is produced in the same way

standard letter /ˌstændərd 'letər/ *noun* a letter which is sent without change to various correspondents

standard of living /ˌstændərd əv 'lɪvɪŋ/ *noun* the quality of personal home life (such as amount of food or clothes bought, size of family car, etc.)

standard rate /'stændərd reɪt/ *noun* a basic rate of income tax which is paid by most taxpayers

Standard Rate & Data Service /ˌstændərd reɪt ən 'deɪtə ˌsɜrvɪs/ *noun* an American publication listing advertising rates, circulation, and other details of major American magazines, newspapers, and other advertising media. Abbreviation **SRDS** (NOTE: The comparable U.K. publication is **U.K. Rate and Data.**)

Standard Time /'stændərd taɪm/ *noun* normal time as in the winter months

standby arrangements /'stændbaɪ ə ˌreɪndʒmənts/ *plural noun* plans for what should be done if an emergency happens, especially money held in reserve in the International Monetary Fund for use by a country in financial difficulties

standby credit /'stændbaɪ ˌkredɪt/ *noun* credit which is available if a company needs it, especially credit guaranteed by a euronote

standby fare /'stændbaɪ fer/ *noun* a cheap fare for a standby ticket

standby ticket /'stændbaɪ ˌtɪkɪt/ *noun* a cheap air ticket which allows the passenger to wait until the last moment to see if there is an empty seat on the plane

standing /'stændɪŋ/ *noun* a good reputation ○ *The financial standing of a company.* □ **company of good standing** very reputable company

standing order /ˌstændɪŋ 'ɔrdər/ *noun* an order written by a customer asking a bank to pay money regularly to an account ○ *I pay my subscription by standing order.*

standstill /'stændstɪl/ *noun* a situation where work has stopped ○ *Production is at a standstill.* ○ *The strike brought the factory to a standstill.*

staple /'steɪp(ə)l/ *verb* □ **to staple papers together** to attach papers with staples ○ *He could not take away separate pages, because the documents were stapled together.*

staple commodity /ˌsteɪp(ə)l kə 'mɒdəti/ *noun* a basic food or raw material

staple industry /ˌsteɪp(ə)l 'ɪndəstri/ *noun* the main industry in a country

staple product /ˌsteɪp(ə)l 'prɒdʌkt/ *noun* the main product

start /stɑrt/ *noun* the beginning ■ *verb* to begin to do something □ **to start a business from cold** *or* **from scratch** to begin a new business, with no previous turnover to base it on

starting /'stɑrtɪŋ/ *noun* the act of beginning

starting date /'stɑrtɪŋ deɪt/ *noun* a date on which something starts

starting point /'stɑrtɪŋ pɔɪnt/ *noun* the place where something starts

starting salary /'stɑrtɪŋ ˌsæləri/ *noun* a salary for an employee when he or she starts work with a company

start-up /'stɑrt ʌp/ *noun* **1.** the beginning of a new company or new product ○ *We went into the red for the first time because of the costs for the start-up of our new subsidiary.* **2.** a new, usually small business that is just beginning its operations, especially a new business supported by venture capital and in a sector where new technologies are used

"It's unusual for a venture capitalist to be focused tightly on a set of companies with a common technology base, and even more unusual for the investment fund manager to be picking start-ups that will be built on a business he's currently running." [*InformationWeek*]

start-up financing /'stɑrt ʌp ˌfaɪnænsɪŋ/ *noun* the first stage in financing a new project, which is followed by several rounds of investment capital as the project gets under way (NOTE: The plural is **start-ups**.)

start-up model /'stɑrt ʌp ˌmɑd(ə)l/ *noun* a business model in which the objective is rapid short-term success. In this model the typical goal is to acquire venture capital, grow, then quickly list the company on the stock exchange or sell it off, so as to produce profit for the founders but not necessarily for the business.

state /steɪt/ *noun* **1.** an independent country **2.** a semi-independent section of a federal country such as the U.S. **3.** the government of a country ■ *verb* to say clearly ○ *The document states that all revenue has to be declared to the tax office.*

"...the unions had argued that public sector pay rates had slipped behind rates applying in state and local government areas" [*Australian Financial Review*]

state bank /steɪt 'bæŋk/ *noun* in the U.S., a commercial bank licensed by the authorities of a state, and not necessarily a member of the Federal Reserve system, as opposed to a national bank

state-controlled /'steɪt kənˌtroʊld/ *adjective* run by the state ○ *state-controlled television*

state enterprise /ˌsteɪt 'entərpraɪz/ *noun* a company run by the state

statement /'steɪtmənt/ *noun* **1.** something said or written which describes or explains something clearly □ **to make a false statement** to give wrong details □ **statement of expenses** a detailed list of money spent **2.** □ **statement (of account)** a list of invoices and credits and debits sent by a supplier to a customer at the end of each month □ **monthly** *or* **quarterly statement** a statement which is sent every month or every quarter by the bank

Statement of Financial Accounting Standards /ˌsteɪtmənt əv faɪˌnænʃ(ə)l əˈkaʊntɪŋ ˌstændərdz/ *noun* in the U.S., a statement detailing the standards to be adopted for the preparation of financial statements. Abbreviation **SFAS**

state of emergency /ˌsteɪt əv ɪ ˈmɜrdʒənsi/ *noun* the government decided that the situation was so dangerous that the police or army had to run the country

state of indebtedness /ˌsteɪt əv ɪn ˈdetɪdnəs/ *noun* the fact of being in debt, owing money

state-of-the-art /ˌsteɪt əv ði 'ɑrt/ *adjective* as technically advanced as possible

state-owned /ˌsteɪt 'oʊnd/ *adjective* owned by the state or by a state

"...state-owned banks cut their prime rates a percentage point to 11%" [*Wall Street Journal*]

state-owned industry /ˌsteɪt oʊnd ˈɪndəstri/ *noun* an industry which is nationalized

state ownership /steɪt 'oʊnəʃɪp/ *noun* a situation in which an industry is nationalized

static market /ˌstætɪk 'mɑrkət/ *noun* a market which does not increase or decrease significantly over a period of time

stationery /'steɪʃ(ə)n(ə)ri/ *noun* **1.** office supplies for writing, such as paper, carbons, pens, etc. ○ *We use the same stationery supplier for all our office stationery.* **2.** in particular, letter paper, envelopes, etc., with the company's name and address printed on them ○ *The letter was typed on his office stationery.*

statistical /stəˈtɪstɪk(ə)l/ *adjective* based on statistics ○ *statistical information* ○ *They took two weeks to provide the statistical analysis of the opinion-poll data.*

statistical discrepancy /stə ˌtɪstɪk(ə)l dɪˈskrepənsi/ *noun* the amount by which sets of figures differ

statistician /ˌstætɪˈstɪʃ(ə)n/ *noun* a person who analyzes statistics

statistics /stəˈtɪstɪks/ *plural noun* **1.** facts or information in the form of figures ○ *to examine the sales statistics for the previous six months* ○ *Government trade statistics show an increase in imports.* ○ *The statistics on unemployment did not take school-leavers into account.* (NOTE: takes a plural verb) **2.** the study of facts in the form of figures (NOTE: takes a singular verb)

status /'steɪtəs/ *noun* **1.** the importance of someone or something relative to others, especially someone's position in society □ **the chairman's car is a status symbol** the size of the car shows how important the chairman is □ **loss of status** the act of becoming less important in a group **2.** □ **legal status** legal position

status inquiry /'steɪtəs ɪnˌkwaɪri/ *noun* an act of checking on a customer's credit rating

status quo /ˌsteɪtəs 'kwoʊ/ *noun* the state of things as they are now ○ *The contract does not alter the status quo.*

statute /'stætʃut/ *noun* an established written law, especially an Act of Parliament. Also called **statute law**

statute book /'stætʃut bʊk/ *noun* all laws passed by Parliament which are still in force

statute law /'stætʃut lɔr/ *noun* same as **statute**

statute of limitations /ˌstætʃut əv ˌlɪmɪ'teɪʃ(ə)nz/ *noun* a law which allows only a fixed period of time, usually six years, for someone to start legal proceedings to claim property or compensation for damage

statutory /'stætʃʊt(ə)ri/ *adjective* fixed by law ○ *There is a statutory period of probation of thirteen weeks.* ○ *Are all the employees aware of their statutory rights?*

statutory holiday /ˌstætʃʊt(ə)ri 'hɑlɪdeɪ/ *noun* a holiday which is fixed by law ○ *The office is closed for the statutory Christmas holiday.*

statutory regulations /ˌstætʃʊt(ə)ri ˌregjʊ'leɪʃ(ə)nz/ *plural noun* regulations covering financial dealings which are based on Acts of Parliament, such as the Financial Services Act, as opposed to the rules of self-regulatory organizations which are non-statutory

statutory sick pay /ˌstætʃʊt(ə)ri 'sɪk ˌpeɪ/ *noun* payment made each week by an employer to an employee who is away from work because of sickness. Abbreviation **SSP**

stay /steɪ/ *noun* a length of time spent in one place ○ *The tourists were in town only for a short stay.* ■ *verb* to stop at a place ○ *The chairman is staying at the Hilton.* ○ *Profits have stayed below 10% for two*

years. ○ *Inflation has stayed high in spite of the government's efforts to bring it down.*

stay of execution /ˌsteɪ əv ˌeksɪ'kjuʃ(ə)n/ *noun* the temporary stopping of a legal order ○ *The court granted the company a two-week stay of execution.*

steadily /'stedɪli/ *adverb* in a regular or continuous way ○ *Output increased steadily over the last two quarters.* ○ *The company has steadily increased its market share.*

steadiness /'stedɪnəs/ *noun* the fact of being firm, not fluctuating ○ *The steadiness of the markets is due to the government's intervention.*

steady /'stedi/ *adjective* continuing in a regular way ○ *The company can point to a steady increase in profits.* ○ *The market stayed steady in spite of the collapse of the bank.* ○ *There is a steady demand for computers.* ○ *He has a steady job in the supermarket.* ■ *verb* to become firm, to stop fluctuating ○ *The markets steadied after last week's fluctuations.* ○ *Prices steadied on the commodity markets.* ○ *The government's figures had a steadying influence on the exchange rate.*

steal /stil/ *verb* to take something which does not belong to you ○ *The competition stole our best clients.* ○ *One of our biggest problems is stealing in the wine department.* (NOTE: **stealing – stole – has stolen**)

steep /stip/ *adjective* referring to an increase which is very great and usually sudden or a price which is very high ○ *a steep increase in interest charges* ○ *a steep decline in overseas sales*

steeply /'stipli/ *adverb* sharply, suddenly ○ *Prices rose steeply after the budget.*

"…if oil prices should fall steeply it may lead to an equally steep fall in naira value if supply cannot meet demand. Then there might be political consequences if devaluation leads to inflation" [*Business in Africa*]

stenographer /stə'nɑgrəfər/ *noun* a typist who can take dictation in shorthand and then type it

step /step/ *noun* **1.** a type of action ○ *The first step taken by the new CEO was to analyze all the expenses.* □ **to take steps to prevent something happening** to act to stop something happening **2.** a movement forward ○ *Becoming assistant to the CEO is a step up the promotion ladder.* □ **in step with** moving at the same rate as ○ *The pound rose in step with the dollar.* □ **out of step with** not moving at the same rate as ○ *The pound was out of step with other European currencies.* ○ *Wages are out of step with the cost of living.*

step down *phrasal verb* to retire from a position ○ *The chairman will be 70 this month and he is stepping down from his post to give way to his nephew.* (NOTE: **stepping – stepped**)

"…the chairman of the investment bank is to step down after less than 12 months in the job" [*Times*]

step up *phrasal verb* to increase ○ *The union is stepping up its industrial action.* ○ *The company has stepped up production of the latest models.* (NOTE: **stepping – stepped**)

sterling /'stɜrlɪŋ/ *noun* a standard currency used in the United Kingdom ○ *to quote prices in sterling* or *to quote sterling prices*

"…it is doubtful that British goods will price themselves back into world markets as long as sterling labour costs continue to rise faster than in competitor countries" [*Sunday Times*]

sterling area /'stɜrlɪŋ ˌeriə/ *noun* formerly, an area of the world where the pound sterling was the main trading currency

sterling balances /ˌstɜrlɪŋ 'bælənsɪz/ *plural noun* a country's trade balances expressed in pounds sterling

sterling crisis /'stɜrlɪŋ ˌkraɪsɪs/ *noun* a fall in the exchange rate of the pound sterling

sterling millionaire /ˌstɜrlɪŋ ˌmɪljə'ner/ *noun* a person who has more than one million pounds sterling (NOTE: To be specific, you can say **dollar millionaire, peso millionaire, etc.**)

stevedore /'stivədɔr/ *noun* a person who works in a port, loading or unloading ships

steward /'stjuərd/ *noun* a man who serves drinks or food on a ship or plane ○ *She called the steward and asked for a glass of water.*

stewardess /ˌstjuə'des/ *noun* a woman who serves drinks or food on a ship or plane

stick /stɪk/ *verb* to stay still, not to move ○ *Sales have stuck at $2m for the last two years.* (NOTE: **sticking – stuck**)

sticker /'stɪkər/ *verb* to put a price sticker on an article for sale ○ *We had to sticker all the inventory.*

stickiness /'stɪkinəs/ *noun* a website's ability to retain the interest of visitors and to keep them coming back

sticky site /'stɪki saɪt/ *noun* a website that holds the interest of visitors for a substantial amount of time and is therefore effective as a marketing vehicle

stimulate /'stɪmjuleɪt/ *verb* to make something or someone become more active ○ *What can the government do to stimulate the economy?* ○ *The goal of the subsidies is to stimulate trade with the Middle East.*

stimulus /'stɪmjuləs/ *noun* a thing which encourages activity (NOTE: The plural is **stimuli.**)

stipulate /'stɪpjuleɪt/ *verb* to state something specifically as a binding condition in a contract ○ *to stipulate that the contract should run for five years* ○ *They found it difficult to pay the stipulated charges.* ○ *The company failed to pay on the date stipulated in the contract.* ○ *The contract stipulates that the seller pays the buyer's legal costs.*

stipulation /ˌstɪpju'leɪʃ(ə)n/ *noun* a condition in a contract ○ *The contract has a stipulation that the new manager has to serve a three-month probationary period.*

stock /stɑk/ *noun* **1.** the available supply of raw materials ○ *large stocks of oil or coal* ○ *the country's stocks of butter or sugar* **2.** *especially U.K.* the quantity of goods for sale in a warehouse or retail outlet. Also called **inventory** □ **to buy a store with stock at valuation** when buying a store, to pay a price for the stock which is the same as its value as estimated by the valuer □ **to purchase stock at valuation** to pay the price that stock has been valued at □ **in stock** available in the warehouse or store □ **to take stock** to count the items in a warehouse **3.** shares in a company **4.** investments in a company, represented by shares or fixed interest securities ■ *adjective* usually kept in stock ○ *Butter is a stock item for any good grocer.* ■ *verb* to hold goods for sale in a warehouse or store

○ *The average supermarket stocks more than 4500 lines.*

stock up *phrasal verb* to buy supplies of something which you will need in the future ○ *They stocked up with computer paper.*

stockbroker /ˈstɑkbroʊkər/ *noun* a person who buys or sells stock for clients

stockbroker's commission /stɑk ˌbroʊkəz kəˈmɪʃ(ə)n/ *noun* the payment to a broker for a deal carried out on behalf of a client

stockbroking /ˈstɑkbroʊkɪŋ/ *noun* the business of dealing in stock for clients ○ *a stockbroking firm*

stock buyback /ˈstɑk ˌbaɪbæk/ *noun* an arrangement where a company buys some of its own stock on the stock market (NOTE: The U.K. term is **share buyback**.)

stock certificate /ˈstɑk sərˌtɪfɪkət/ *noun* a document proving that someone owns stock in a company

stock control /ˈstɑk kənˌtroʊl/ *noun* U.K. same as **inventory control**

stock dividend /ˈstɑk ˌdɪvɪdend/ *noun* a dividend paid to a stockholder in the form of additional stock rather than cash

Stock Exchange /ˈstɑk ɪksˌtʃeɪndʒ/ *noun* a place where stocks and bonds are bought and sold ○ *He works on the Stock Exchange.* ○ *Shares in the company are traded on the Stock Exchange.*

"…the news was favourably received on the Sydney Stock Exchange, where the shares gained 40 cents to A\$9.80" [*Financial Times*]

Stock Exchange listing /ˈstɑk ɪks ˌtʃeɪndʒ ˌlɪstɪŋ/ *noun* the fact of being on the official list of stocks which can be bought or sold on the Stock Exchange ○ *The company is planning to obtain a Stock Exchange listing.*

Stock Exchange operation /ˌstɑk ɪksˌtʃeɪndʒ ˌɑpəˈreɪʃ(ə)n/ *noun* the activity of buying or selling of stocks on the Stock Exchange

stock figures /ˈstɑk ˌfɪgərz/ *plural noun* details of how many goods are in the warehouse or store

stockholder /ˈstɑkhoʊldər/ *noun* a person who holds stock in a company

stockholders' equity /ˌstɑkhoʊldərz ˈekwɪti/ *noun* the value of a company which is the property of its stockholders (the company's assets less its liabilities)

stockholding /ˈstɑkhoʊldɪŋ/ *noun* the stock in a company held by someone

stocking filler /ˈstɑkɪŋ ˌfɪlər/ *noun* a small item which can be used to put into a Christmas stocking

stock-in-hand /ˌstɑk ɪn ˈhænd/ *noun* stock held in a store or warehouse

stock-in-trade /ˌstɑk ɪn ˈtreɪd/ *noun* goods held by a business for sale

stockist /ˈstɑkɪst/ *noun* a person or store that stocks an item

stockkeeping /ˈstɑkˌkipɪŋ/ *noun* the process of making sure that the correct level of stock is maintained (to be able to meet demand while keeping the costs of holding stock to a minimum)

stockkeeping unit /ˈstɑkkipɪŋ ˌjunɪt/ *noun* full form of **SKU**

stock ledger /ˈstɑk ˌledʒər/ *noun* a book which records quantities and values of stock

stock level /ˈstɑk ˌlev(ə)l/ *noun* the quantity of goods kept in stock ○ *We try to keep stock levels low during the summer.*

stocklist /ˈstɑklɪst/ *noun* a list of items carried in stock

stock market /ˈstɑk ˌmɑrkɪt/ *noun* a place where stocks are bought and sold, i.e. a stock exchange ○ *stock market price* or *price on the stock market*

stock market manipulation /ˈstɑk ˌmɑrkət məˌnɪpjʊleɪʃ(ə)n/ *noun* the practice of trying to influence the price of stocks by buying or selling in order to give the impression that the stocks are widely traded

stock market manipulator /ˌstɑk ˌmɑrkət məˈnɪpjʊleɪtər/ *noun* a person who tries to influence the price of stocks in his or her own favor

stock market valuation /ˌstɑk ˌmɑrkət ˌvæljuˈeɪʃ(ə)n/ *noun* a value of a company based on the current market price of its stock

stock movements /ˈstɑk ˌmuvmənts/ *noun* passing of goods into or out of a warehouse ○ *All stock movements are logged by the computer.*

stock option /ˈstɑk ˌɑpʃən/ *noun* a right to buy stock at a fixed price given by a company as a form of compensation to its employees

stock option plan /'ʃer ˌɑpʃən ˌskim/ *noun* a plan that gives company employees the right to buy shares in the company which employs them, often at a special price

stockout /'stɑkoʊt/ *noun* a situation where an item is out of stock

stock ownership plan /ˌʃer 'oʊnəʃɪp skim/, **stock incentive plan** *noun* a plan whereby employees in a company can buy shares in it and so share in the profits ○ *Stock ownership plans help employees to identify more closely with the company they work for.*

stockpile /'stɑkpaɪl/ *noun* the supplies kept by a country or a company in case of need ○ *a stockpile of raw materials* ■ *verb* to buy items and keep them in case of need ○ *to stockpile canned food*

stockroom /'stɑkrum/ *noun* a room where stores are kept

stock size /'stɑk saɪz/ *noun* a standard size ○ *We only carry stock sizes of shoes.*

stock split /stɑk splɪt/ *noun* the issuing of additional free shares to stockholders in such a way that value of the company remains the same, and the total market value of stockholders' shares remains the same, the market price being adjusted to account for the new shares ○ *After the stock split we own 2000 shares at $20 a share instead of 1000 shares at $40 a share.*

stocktaking /'stɑkteɪkɪŋ/, **stocktake** /'stɑkteɪk/ *noun* the counting of goods in stock at the end of an accounting period ○ *The warehouse is closed for the annual stocktaking.*

stocktaking sale /'stɑkteɪkɪŋ ˌseɪl/ *noun* a sale of goods cheaply to clear a warehouse before stocktaking

stock transfer form /ˌstɑk 'trænsfər ˌfɔrm/ *noun* a form to be signed by the person transferring stock

stock turn /'stɑk tɜrn/, **stock turnaround** /ˌstɑk 'tɜrnəˌraʊnd/, **stock turnover** /ˌstɑk 'tɜrnoʊvər/ *noun* the total value of stock sold in a year divided by the average value of goods in stock

stock valuation /ˌstɑk ˌvælju'eɪʃ(ə)n/ *noun* an estimation of the value of stock at the end of an accounting period

stop /stɑp/ *noun* 1. the end of an action ○ *Work came to a stop when the company could not pay the workers' wages.* ○ *The new finance director put a stop to the reps'*

inflated expense claims. 2. a situation in which someone is not supplying or not paying something □ **account on stop** an account which is not supplied because it has not paid its latest invoices ○ *We put their account on stop and sued them for the money they owed.* □ **to put a stop on a check** to tell the bank not to pay a check which you have written ■ *verb* 1. to make something not move or happen anymore ○ *The shipment was stopped by customs.* ○ *The government has stopped the import of luxury items.* 2. not to do anything anymore ○ *The work force stopped work when the company could not pay their wages.* *The office staff stop work at 5:30.* ○ *We have stopped supplying Smith & Co.* 3. □ **to stop an account** not to supply an account anymore on credit because bills have not been paid □ **to stop payment on a check** to ask a bank not to pay a check you have written □ **to stop payments** not to make any further payments

stop over *phrasal verb* to stay for a short time in a place on a long trip ○ *We stopped over in Hong Kong on the way to Australia.*

stop-loss order /ˌstɑp 'lɔs ˌɔrdər/ *noun* an instruction to a stockbroker to sell a stock if the price falls to an specified level (NOTE: The U.S. term is **stop order**.)

stopover /'stɑpoʊvər/ *noun* an act of staying for a short time in a place on a long trip ○ *The ticket allows you two layovers between London and Tokyo.*

stoppage /'stɑpɪdʒ/ *noun* 1. the act of stopping ○ *stoppage of payments* ○ *Bad weather was responsible for the stoppage of deliveries.* ○ *Deliveries will be late because of stoppages on the production line.* 2. a sum of money taken regularly from an employee's wages for insurance, tax, etc.

storage /'stɔrɪdʒ/ *noun* 1. the act of keeping something in store or in a warehouse ○ *We rent our house and put the furniture into storage.* □ **to put a plan into cold storage** to postpone work on a plan, usually for a very long time 2. the cost of keeping goods in store ○ *Storage rose to 10% of value, so we scrapped the stock.* 3. the facility for storing data in a computer ○ *a disc with a storage capacity of 100Mb*

storage capacity /'stɔrɪdʒ kəˌpæsəti/ *noun* the space available for storage

storage company /ˈstɔrɪdʒ ˌkʌmp(ə)ni/ *noun* a company which keeps items for customers

storage facilities /ˈstɔrɪdʒ fəˌsɪlətiz/ *plural noun* equipment and buildings suitable for storage

storage unit /ˈstɔrɪdʒ ˌjunɪt/ *noun* a device attached to a computer for storing information on disc or tape

store /stɔr/ *noun* 1. a place where goods are kept 2. a quantity of items or materials kept because they will be needed ○ *I always keep a store of envelopes ready in my desk.* 3. a shop ■ *verb* 1. to keep in a warehouse ○ *to store goods for six months* 2. to keep for future use ○ *We store our pay records on computer.*

store card /ˈstɔr kɑrd/ *noun* a credit card issued by a large department store, which can only be used for purchases in that store

store floor /ˌʃɑp ˈflɔr/ *noun* 1. the space in a store given to the display of goods for sale 2. □ **on the shop floor** in the factory or among the ordinary workers ○ *The feeling on the shop floor is that the manager does not know his job.*

store front /ˈʃɑp frʌnt/ *noun* a part of a store which faces the street, including the entrance and windows

storekeeper[1] /ˈʃɑpkipər/ *noun* a person who owns or runs a store

storekeeper[2] /ˈstɔrkipər/, **storeman** /ˈstɔrmən/ *noun* a person in charge of a storeroom

storeroom /ˈstɔrum/ *noun* a room or small warehouse where stock can be kept

store window /ˌʃɑp ˈwɪndoʊ/ *noun* a large window in a store front, where customers can see goods displayed

straight line depreciation /ˌstreɪt laɪn dɪˌpriʃiˈeɪʃ(ə)n/ *noun* depreciation calculated by dividing the cost of an asset, less its remaining value, by the number of years it is likely to be used

COMMENT: Various methods of depreciating assets are used; under the "straight line method", the asset is depreciated at a constant percentage of its cost each year, while with the "reducing balance method" the asset is depreciated at the same percentage rate each year, but calculated on the value after the previous year's depreciation has been deducted.

strategic /strəˈtidʒɪk/ *adjective* based on a plan of action

strategic alliance /strəˌtidʒɪk əˈlaɪəns/ *noun* an agreement between two or more organizations to cooperate with each other and share their knowledge and expertise in a particular business activity, so that each benefits from the others' strengths and gains a competitive edge (NOTE: Strategic alliances can reduce the risk and costs involved in relationships with suppliers and the development of new products and technologies and have been seen as a response to globalization and the increasing uncertainty in the business environment.)

strategic business unit /strəˌtidʒɪk ˈbɪznɪs ˌjunɪt/ *noun* a part or division of a large company which forms its own business strategy. Abbreviation **SBU**

strategic management /strəˌtidʒɪk ˈmænɪdʒmənt/ *noun* management that focuses on developing corporate strategy, ensuring that the organization operates and makes decision in accordance with that strategy, and on achieving and maintaining a strong competitive advantage

strategic partnering /strəˌtidʒɪk ˈpɑrtnərɪŋ/ *noun* collaboration between organizations in order to enable them to take advantage of market opportunities together, or to respond to customers more effectively than they could if each operated separately. Strategic partnering allows the partners to pool information, skills, and resources and to share risks.

strategic planning /strəˌtidʒɪk ˈplænɪŋ/ *noun* the process of planning the future work of a company

strategy /ˈstrætədʒi/ *noun* a course of action, including the specification of resources required, to achieve a specific objective ○ *a marketing strategy* ○ *a financial strategy* ○ *a sales strategy* ○ *a pricing strategy* ○ *What is the strategy of the HR department to deal with long-term manpower requirements?* ○ *Part of the company's strategy to meet its marketing objectives is a major recruitment and retraining program.* (NOTE: The plural is **strategies**.)

streaming /ˈstrimɪŋ/ *noun* technology that allows material to be downloaded from the Web and viewed at the same time. For example, a user can download enough of a multimedia file to start viewing or listening to it, while the rest of the file is downloaded in the background.

streamline /'strimlaɪn/ *verb* to make something more efficient or more simple ○ *to streamline the accounting system* ○ *to streamline distribution services*

streamlined /'strimlaɪnd/ *adjective* efficient or rapid ○ *We need a more streamlined payroll system.* ○ *The company introduced a streamlined system of distribution.*

streamlining /'strimlaɪnɪŋ/ *noun* the process of making something efficient

street directory /'strit daɪ,rekt(ə)ri/ *noun* a list of people living in a street; a map of a town which lists all the streets in alphabetical order in an index

street plan /'strit plæn/ *noun* a map of a town showing streets and buildings

street vendor /'strit ,vendər/ *noun* a person who sells food or small items in the street

strength /streŋθ/ *noun* the fact of being strong, or being at a high level ○ *The company took advantage of the strength of the demand for cell phones.* ○ *The strength of the pound increases the possibility of high interest rates.* Opposite **weakness**

stress /stres/ *noun* nervous tension or worry, caused by overwork, difficulty with managers, etc. ○ *People in positions of responsibility suffer from stress-related illnesses.* ○ *The new work schedules caused too much stress on the shop floor.*

"…manual and clerical workers are more likely to suffer from stress-related diseases. Causes of stress include the introduction of new technology, job dissatisfaction, fear of job loss, poor working relations with the boss and colleagues, and bad working conditions" [*Personnel Management*]

stressful /'stresf(ə)l/ *adjective* which causes stress ○ *Psychologists claim that repetitive work can be just as stressful as more demanding but varied work.*

stress management /'stres ,mænɪdʒmənt/ *noun* a way of coping with stress-related problems at work

stretch /stretʃ/ *verb* to pull out or to make longer ○ *The investment program has stretched the company's resources.* □ **he is not fully stretched** his job does not make him work as hard as he could

strict /strɪkt/ *adjective* exact ○ *The partners are listed in strict order of seniority.*

strike /straɪk/ *noun* **1.** the stopping of work by the workers (because of lack of agreement with management or because of orders from a union) **2.** □ **to take strike action** to go on strike **3.** □ **to come out on strike, to go on strike** to stop work ○ *The office workers are on strike for higher pay.* □ **to call the work force out on strike** to tell the workers to stop work ○ *The union called its members out on strike.* ■ *verb* **1.** to stop working because there is no agreement with management ○ *to strike for higher wages* or *for shorter working hours* ○ *to strike in protest against bad working conditions* (NOTE: **striking – struck**) □ **to strike in sympathy with the postal workers** to strike to show that you agree with the postal workers who are on strike **2.** □ **to strike a bargain with someone** to come to an agreement □ **a deal was struck at $25 a unit** we agreed the price of $25 a unit

strike ballot /'straɪk ,bælət/, **strike vote** /'straɪk vout/ *noun* a vote by employees to decide if a strike should be held

strikebound /'straɪkbaund/ *adjective* not able to work or to move because of a strike ○ *Six ships are strikebound in the docks.*

strikebreaker /'straɪkbreɪkər/ *noun* an employee who goes on working while everyone else is on strike

strike call /'straɪk kɔl/ *noun* a demand by a union for a strike

strike fund /'straɪk fʌnd/ *noun* money collected by a labor union from its members, used to pay strike pay

strike pay /'straɪk peɪ/ *noun* wages paid to striking employees by their labor union

strike price /'straɪkɪŋ praɪs/, **striking price** *noun* **1.** *U.K.* a price at which a new issue of stock is offered for sale **2.** *U.K.* the lowest selling price when selling a new issue of stock by tender (applicants who tendered at a higher price will get stock; those who tendered at a lower price will not) **3.** a specified price at which a holder of an option can buy or sell a security upon exercising the contract. Also called **exercise price**

striker /'straɪkər/ *noun* an employee who is on strike ○ *Strikers marched to the company headquarters.*

strong /strɒŋ/ *adjective* with a lot of force or strength ○ *This Christmas saw a strong demand for cell phones.* ○ *The company needs a strong chairman.*

"...everybody blames the strong dollar for U.S. trade problems" [*Duns Business Month*]

"...in a world of floating exchange rates the dollar is strong because of capital inflows rather than weak because of the nation's trade deficit" [*Duns Business Month*]

strongbox /'strɒŋbɒks/ *noun* a heavy metal box which cannot be opened easily, in which valuable documents and money can be kept

strong currency /ˌstrɒŋ 'kʌrənsi/ *noun* a currency which has a high value against other currencies

strong pound /ˌstrɒŋ 'paʊnd/ *noun* a pound which is high against other currencies

strongroom /'strɒŋrum/ *noun* a special room in a bank where valuable documents, money and gold can be kept

structural /'strʌktʃ(ə)rəl/ *adjective* referring to a structure ○ *to make structural changes in a company*

structural unemployment /ˌstrʌktʃ(ə)rəl ˌʌnɪm'plɔɪmənt/ *noun* unemployment caused by the changing structure of an industry or the economy

structure /'strʌktʃər/ *noun* the way in which something is organized ○ *the price structure in the small car market* ○ *the career structure within a corporation* ○ *The paper gives a diagram of the company's organizational structure.* ○ *The company is reorganizing its discount structure.* ■ *verb* to arrange in a specific way ○ *to structure a meeting*

structured systems analysis and design method /ˌstrʌktʃərd ˌsɪstəmz əˌnæləsɪs ən dɪˌzaɪn 'meθəd/ *noun* a method of analyzing and designing computer systems, which proceeds in a series of logical steps, beginning with a feasibility study and moving through requirements analysis, requirements specification, and logical system specification to physical design. Each stage must be completed before the next stage can begin. Abbreviation **SSADM**

stub /stʌb/ *noun* a slip of paper left after writing a check, an invoice or a receipt, as a record of the deal which has taken place

studio /'stjudioʊ/ *noun* a place where designers, movie producers, artists, etc., work

study /'stʌdi/ *noun* an act of examining something carefully ○ *The company has asked the consultants to prepare a study of new production techniques.* ○ *He has read the government study on sales opportunities.* □ **to carry out a feasibility study on a project** to examine the costs and possible profits to see if the project should be started ■ *verb* to examine something carefully ○ *We are studying the possibility of setting up an office in New York.* ○ *The government studied the committee's proposals for two months.* ○ *You will need to study the market carefully before deciding on the design of the product.*

stuff /stʌf/ *verb* to put papers into envelopes ○ *We pay casual workers by the hour for stuffing envelopes* or *for envelope stuffing.*

style /staɪl/ *noun* a way of doing or making something ○ *a new style of product* ○ *old-style management techniques*

sub /sʌb/ *noun* **1.** wages paid in advance **2.** same as **subscription**

sub- /sʌb/ *prefix* under or less important

sub-agency /'sʌb ˌeɪdʒənsi/ *noun* a small agency which is part of a large agency

sub-agent /'sʌb ˌeɪdʒənt/ *noun* a person who is in charge of a sub-agency

Subchapter S corporation /ˌsʌbtʃæptər 'es ˌkɔrpəreɪʃ(ə)n/ *noun* same as **S corporation**

subcommittee /'sʌbkəˌmɪti/ *noun* a small committee which is part of or set up by a main committee ○ *The next item on the agenda is the report of the finance subcommittee.*

subcontract *noun* /'sʌbˌkɒntrækt/ a contract between the main contractor for a whole project and another firm which will do part of the work ○ *They have been awarded the subcontract for all the electrical work in the new building.* ○ *We will put the electrical work out to subcontract.* ■ *verb* /ˌsʌbkən'trækt/ (*of a main contractor*) to agree with a company that they will do part of the work for a project

○ *The electrical work has been subcontracted to Smith Inc.*

subcontractor /ˈsʌbkənˌtræktər/ *noun* a company which has a contract to do work for a main contractor

subdivision /ˈsʌbdɪvɪʒ(ə)n/ *noun* a piece of empty land to be used for building new houses

subjective /səbˈdʒektɪv/ *adjective* considered from the point of view of the person involved, and not from any general point of view ○ *Her assessments of the performance of her staff are quite subjective.* Opposite **objective**

subject line /ˈsʌbdʒɪkt laɪn/ *noun* the space at the top of an email template in which the sender types the title or subject of the email. It is the only part of the email, apart from the sender's name, that can be read immediately by the receiver.

subject to /ˈsʌbdʒɪkt tu/ *adjective* **1.** depending on □ **the contract is subject to government approval** the contract will be valid only if it is approved by the government □ **offer subject to availability** the offer is valid only if the goods are available **2.** □ **these articles are subject to import tax** import tax has to be paid on these articles

sub judice /ˌsʌb ˈdʒudɪsi/ *adverb* being considered by a court (and so not to be mentioned in the media) ○ *The papers cannot report the case because it is still sub judice.*

sublease *noun* /ˈsʌblis/ a lease from a tenant to another tenant ○ *They signed a sublease for the property.* ■ *verb* /sʌbˈlis/ to lease a leased property from another tenant ○ *They subleased a small office in the center of town.*

sublessee /ˌsʌbleˈsi/ *noun* a person or company that takes a property on a sublease

sublessor /ˌsʌbleˈsɔr/ *noun* a tenant who leases a leased property to another tenant

sublet /sʌbˈlet/ *verb* to rent a leased property to another tenant ○ *We have sublet part of our office to a financial consultancy.* (NOTE: **subletting – sublet**)

subliminal advertising /sʌb ˌlɪmɪn(ə)l ˈædvərtaɪzɪŋ/ *noun* advertising that attempts to leave impressions on the subconscious mind of the person who

sees it or hears it without that person realizing that this is being done

submit /səbˈmɪt/ *verb* to put something forward to be examined ○ *The planners submitted the proposal to the committee.* ○ *He submitted a claim to the insurers.* ○ *The reps are asked to submit their expenses claims once a month.* ○ *The union has submitted a claim for a ten percent wage increase.* (NOTE: **submitting – submitted**)

subordinate /səˈbɔrdɪnət/ less important □ **subordinate to** governed by, which depends on ■ *noun* a person in a lower position in an organization ○ *Her subordinates find her difficult to work with.* ○ *Part of the manager's job is to supervise the training of their subordinates.*

subpoena /səˈpinə/ *noun* a court order telling someone to appear as a witness (NOTE: an old term, now called a **witness summons**) ■ *verb* to order someone to appear in court ○ *The finance director was subpoenaed by the prosecution.*

sub-post office /ˌsʌb ˈpoʊst ˌɔfɪs/ *noun* a small post office, usually part of a general store

subscribe /səbˈskraɪb/ *verb* **1.** □ **to subscribe to a magazine or website** to pay for a series of issues of a magazine or for information available on a website **2.** □ **to subscribe to a new issue** to to agree to buy stock in a new company

subscriber /səbˈskraɪbər/ *noun* **1.** □ **subscriber to a magazine, magazine subscriber** a person who has paid in advance for a series of issues of a magazine or to have access to information on a website ○ *The extra issue is sent free to subscribers.* **2.** □ **subscriber to a new issue** a person who has agreed to buy stock in a new company **3.** a user who chooses to receive information, content, or services regularly from a website

subscription /səbˈskrɪpʃən/ *noun* **1.** money paid in advance for a series of issues of a magazine or for access to information on a website ○ *Did you remember to pay the subscription to the computer magazine?* □ **to take out a subscription to a magazine** to start paying for a series of issues of a magazine □ **to cancel a subscription to a magazine** to stop paying for a series of issues of a magazine **2.** □ **sub-**

scription to a new issue agreement to buy stock in a new company

subscription-based publishing /səbˌskrɪpʃən beɪst ˈpʌblɪʃɪŋ/ *noun* a form of publishing in which content from a website, magazine, book, or other publication is delivered regularly by email or other means to a group of subscribers

subscription list /səbˈskrɪpʃən lɪst/ *noun* a list of subscribers to a new stock issue

subscription process /səbˈskrɪpʃən ˌprɑses/ *noun* the process by which users register and pay to receive information, content, or services, from a website

subscription rate /səbˈskrɪpʃən reɪt/ *noun* the amount of money to be paid for a series of issues of a magazine

subsidiary /səbˈsɪdiəri/ *adjective* less important ○ *They agreed to most of the conditions in the contract but queried one or two subsidiary items.* ■ *noun* same as **subsidiary company** ○ *Most of the group profit was contributed by the subsidiaries in the Far East.*

subsidiary company /səbˌsɪdiəri ˈkʌmp(ə)ni/ *noun* a company which is more than 50% owned by a holding company, and where the holding company controls the board of directors

subsidize /ˈsʌbsɪdaɪz/ *verb* to help by giving money ○ *The government has refused to subsidize the car industry.*

subsidized accommodations /ˌsʌbsɪdaɪzd əˌkɑməˈdeɪʃ(ə)nz/ *noun* cheap accommodations which are partly paid for by an employer or a local authority

subsidy /ˈsʌbsɪdi/ *noun* **1.** money given to help something which is not profitable ○ *The industry exists on government subsidies.* ○ *The government has increased its subsidy to the car industry.* **2.** money given by a government to make something cheaper ○ *the subsidy on rail transportation* (NOTE: The plural is **subsidies**.)

subsistence /səbˈsɪstəns/ *noun* a minimum amount of food, money, housing, etc., which a person needs □ **to live at subsistence level** to have only just enough money to live on

subsistence allowance /səbˈsɪstəns əˌlauəns/ *noun* money paid by a company to cover the cost of hotels, meals, etc., for an employee who is traveling on business

substantial /səbˈstænʃəl/ *adjective* large or important □ **she was awarded substantial damages** she received a large sum of money as damages

substitute /ˈsʌbstɪtut/ *noun* a person or thing that takes the place of someone or something else ■ *adjective* taking the place of another person or thing ■ *verb* to take the place of someone or something else

subtenancy /sʌbˈtenənsi/ *noun* an agreement to sublet a property

subtenant /sʌbˈtenənt/ *noun* a person or company to which a property has been sublet

subtotal /ˈsʌbˌtout(ə)l/ *noun* the total of one section of a complete set of figures ○ *She added all the subtotals to make a grand total.*

subtract /səbˈtrækt/ *verb* to take away something from a total ○ *The credit note should be subtracted from the figure for total sales.* ○ *If the profits from the Far Eastern operations are subtracted, you will see that the group has not been profitable in the European market.*

subtraction /səbˈtrækʃən/ *noun* an act of taking one number away from another

subvention /səbˈvenʃ(ə)n/ *noun* same as **subsidy**

succeed /səkˈsid/ *verb* **1.** to do well, to be profitable ○ *The company has succeeded best in the overseas markets.* ○ *Her business has succeeded more than she had expected.* **2.** to do what was planned ○ *She succeeded in passing her computing test.* ○ *They succeeded in putting their competition out of business.* **3.** to take over from someone in a post ○ *Mr. Smith was succeeded as chairman by Mr.s. Jones.*

success /səkˈses/ *noun* **1.** an act of doing something well ○ *The launch of the new model was a great success.* ○ *The company has had great success in the Japanese market.* **2.** an act of doing what was intended ○ *We had no success in trying to sell the lease.* ○ *She has been looking for a job for six months, but with no success.*

successful /səkˈsesf(ə)l/ *adjective* having got the desired result ○ *a successful businessman* ○ *a successful selling trip to Germany* ○ *The successful candidates will be advised by letter.*

successfully /səkˈsesf(ə)li/ *adverb* well or getting the desired result ○ *She* *successfully negotiated a new contract with the unions.* ○ *The new model was successfully launched last month.*

successor /sək'sesər/ *noun* a person who takes over from someone ○ *Mr. Smith's successor as chairman will be Mr.s Jones.*

sue /su/ *verb* to take someone to court, to start legal proceedings against someone to get money as compensation ○ *They are planning to sue the construction company for damages.* ○ *He is suing the company for $50,000 compensation.*

suffer /'sʌfə/ *verb* to be in a bad situation, to do badly ○ *Exports have suffered during the last six months.* □ **to suffer from something** to do badly because of something ○ *The company's products suffer from bad design.* ○ *The group suffers from bad management.*

"…the bank suffered losses to the extent that its capital has been wiped out" [*South China Morning Post*]

"…the holding company has seen its earnings suffer from big writedowns in conjunction with its agricultural loan portfolio" [*Duns Business Month*]

sufficient /sə'fɪʃ(ə)nt/ *adjective* enough ○ *The company has sufficient funds to pay for its expansion program.*

suggest /sə'dʒest/ *verb* to put forward a proposal ○ *The chairman suggested (that) the next meeting should be held in October.* ○ *We suggested Mr Smith for the post of treasurer.*

suggestion /sə'dʒestʃən/ *noun* an idea which is put forward

suggestion box /sə'dʒestʃən bɑks/, **suggestions box** /sə'dʒestʃənz bɑks/ *noun* a place in a company where employees can put forward their ideas for making the company more efficient and profitable

suggestion scheme /sə'dʒestʃən skim/ *noun* a program in which employees are asked to suggest ways in which the work they do or the way their organization operates can be improved and receive a gift or cash reward for useful suggestions

suitable /'sutəb(ə)l/ *adjective* convenient or which fits ○ *Wednesday is the most suitable day for board meetings.* ○ *We had to readvertise the job because there were no suitable candidates.*

sum¹ /sʌm/ *noun* **1.** a quantity of money ○ *A sum of money was stolen from the human resources office.* ○ *He lost large sums on the Stock Exchange.* ○ *She received the sum of $5000 in compensation.* □ **the sum insured** the largest amount which an insurer will pay under the terms of an insurance **2.** the total of a series of figures added together ○ *The sum of the various subtotals is $18,752.*

sum² /sʌm/ *noun* a unit of currency used in Uzbekistan

summary /'sʌməri/ *noun* a short account of what has happened or of what has been written ○ *The CEO gave a summary of her discussions with the German trade delegation.* ○ *The sales department has given a summary of sales in Europe for the first six months.*

summons /'sʌmənz/ *noun* an official order from a court requiring someone to appear in court to be tried for a criminal offense or to defend a civil action ○ *He threw away the summons and went on holiday to New York.*

sums chargeable to the reserve /ˌsʌmz ˌtʃɑrdʒəb(ə)l tə ðə rɪ'zɜrv/ *plural noun* sums which can be debited to a company's reserves

Sunday closing /ˌsʌndeɪ 'kloʊzɪŋ/ *noun* the practice of not opening a store on Sundays

Sunday trading laws /ˌsʌndeɪ 'treɪdɪŋ ˌlɔz/ *plural noun* regulations which govern business activities on Sundays (NOTE: The U.S. term is **Blue Laws**.)

sundries /'sʌndriz/ *plural noun* various small additional items, often of little value, that are not included under any of the main headings in accounts

sundry /'sʌndri/ *adjective* various

sundry items /ˌsʌndri 'aɪtəmz/ *noun* small items which are not listed in detail

sunrise industries /'sʌnraɪz ˌɪndəstriz/ *plural noun* companies in the fields of electronics and other high-tech areas

sunset industries /'sʌnset ˌɪndəstriz/ *plural noun* old-style industries which are being replaced by new technology

superannuation /ˌsupərænju'eɪʃ(ə)n/ *noun* a pension paid to someone who is too old or ill to work any more

superannuation plan /ˌsupərænju'eɪʃ(ə)n plæn/ *noun* a pension plan

superindustrial society
/ˌsupərɪndʌstriəl səˈsaɪəti/ *noun* a society in which both the personal and working lives of people are dominated by technology

superintend /ˌsupərɪnˈtend/ *verb* to be in charge of work, to watch carefully, to see that work is well done ○ *He superintends the company's overseas sales.*

superintendent /ˌsupərɪnˈtendənt/ *noun* the title of an official in charge

superior /suˈpɪriər/ *adjective* better, of better quality ○ *Our product is superior to all competing products.* ○ *Their sales are higher because of their superior distribution service.* ■ *noun* a more important person ○ *Each manager is responsible to their superior for accurate reporting of sales.*

supermarket /ˈsupərmɑrkət/ *noun* a large store, usually selling food and housewares, where customers serve themselves and pay at a checkout ○ *Sales in supermarkets* or *Supermarket sales account for half the company's turnover.*

supermarket trolley /ˈsupərmɑrkət ˌtrɑli/ *noun U.K.* same as **shopping cart**

superstore /ˈsupərstɔr/ *noun* a very large self-service store (more than 25,000 square feet) which sells a wide range of goods ○ *We bought the laptop at a computer superstore.*

supertanker /ˈsupətæŋkər/ *noun* a very large oil tanker

supervise /ˈsupərvaɪz/ *verb* to monitor work carefully to see that it is being done well ○ *The move to the new offices was supervised by the administrative manager.* ○ *She supervises six people in the accounts department.*

supervision /ˌsupəˈvɪʒ(ə)n/ *noun* the fact of being supervised ○ *New staff work under supervision for the first three months.* ○ *She is very experienced and can be left to work without any supervision.* ○ *The cash was counted under the supervision of the finance manager.*

supervisor /ˈsupəvaɪzər/ *noun* a person who supervises ○ *The supervisor was asked to write a report on the workers' performance.*

supervisory /ˈsupərvaɪzəri/ *adjective* as a supervisor ○ *Supervisory staff checked the trainees' work.* ○ *He works in*

a supervisory capacity. ○ *The supervisory staff have asked for a pay raise.*

supplement *noun* something which is added ○ *The company gives him a supplement to his pension.* ■ *verb* to add ○ *We will supplement the warehouse staff with six part-timers during the Christmas rush.*

supplementary /ˌsʌplɪˈment(ə)ri/ *adjective* in addition to

supplementary unemployment benefits /ˌsʌplɪment(ə)ri ˌʌnɪmˈplɔɪmənt ˌbenəfɪts/ *noun* payments made by a company to workers who have been laid off, in addition to regular unemployment insurance payments

supplier /səˈplaɪr/ *noun* a person or company that supplies or sells goods or services ○ *We use the same office equipment supplier for all our stationery purchases.* ○ *They are major suppliers of spare parts to the auto industry.* Also called **producer**

supply /səˈplaɪ/ *noun* **1.** the act of providing something which is needed **2.** □ **in short supply** not available in large enough quantities to meet the demand ○ *Spare parts are in short supply because of the strike.* **3.** stock of something which is needed ○ *Garages were running short of supplies of gasoline.* ○ *Supplies of coal to the factory have been hit by the rail strike.* ○ *Supplies of stationery have been reduced.* ■ *verb* to provide something which is needed ○ *to supply a factory with spare parts* ○ *The finance department supplied the committee with the figures.* ○ *Details of staff addresses and phone numbers can be supplied by the HR department.*

supply and demand /səˌplaɪ ən dɪ ˈmænd/ *noun* the amount of a product which is available and the amount which is wanted by customers

supply chain /səˈplaɪ tʃeɪn/ *noun* the manufacturers, wholesalers, distributors, and retailers who produce goods and services from raw materials and deliver them to consumers, considered as a group or network

"Only companies that build supply chains that are agile, adaptable, and aligned get ahead of their rivals." [*Harvard Business Review*]

supply chain management /səˈplaɪ tʃeɪn ˌmænɪdʒmənt/ *noun* the work of coordinating all the activities connected with supplying of finished goods (NOTE: Supply chain management covers the processes of materials management, logistics, physical distribution management, purchasing, and information management.)

supply price /sə'plaɪ praɪs/ *noun* the price at which something is provided

supply-side economics /sə'plaɪ saɪd ikə,nɒmɪks/ *plural noun* an economic theory that governments should encourage producers and suppliers of goods by cutting taxes, rather than encourage demand by making more money available in the economy (NOTE: takes a singular verb)

support /sə'pɔːt/ *noun* **1.** actions or money intended to help someone or something ○ *The government has provided support to the car industry.* ○ *We have no financial support from the banks.* **2.** agreement or encouragement ○ *The chairman has the support of the committee.* ■ *verb* **1.** to give money to help someone or something ○ *The government is supporting the car industry to the tune of $2m per annum.* ○ *We hope the banks will support us during the expansion period.* **2.** to encourage someone, or to agree with someone ○ *She hopes the other members of the committee will support her.* ○ *The market will not support another price increase.*

surcharge /'sɜːtʃɑːdʒ/ *noun* an extra charge

surety /'ʃʊərəti/ *noun* **1.** a person who guarantees that someone will do something ○ *to stand surety for someone* **2.** deeds, share certificates, etc., deposited as security for a loan

surface transportationation /,sɜːfɪs ,trænspɔː'teɪʃ(ə)n/ *noun* transportation on land or sea

surplus /'sɜːpləs/ *noun* **1.** more of something than is needed □ **these items are surplus to our requirements** we do not need these items **2.** an amount of money remaining after all liabilities have been met □ **to absorb a surplus** to take a surplus into a larger amount ■ *adjective* more than is needed ○ *Profit figures are lower than planned because of surplus labor.* ○ *Some of the machines may have to be sold off as there is surplus production capacity.* ○ *We are proposing to put our surplus staff on short time.*

surrender /sə'rendər/ *noun* the act of giving up of an insurance policy before the contracted date for maturity ■ *verb* □ **to surrender a policy** to give up an insurance policy before the date on which it matures

surrender value /sə'rendər ,væljuː/ *noun* the money which an insurer will pay if an insurance policy is given up

surtax /'sɜːtæks/ *noun* an extra tax on high income

survey *noun* /'sɜːveɪ/ **1.** a general report on a problem ○ *The government has published a survey of population trends.* ○ *We have asked the sales department to produce a survey of competing products.* **2.** a careful examination of something, such as a building, to see if it is in good enough condition ○ *We have asked for a survey of the house before buying it.* ○ *The insurance company is carrying out a survey of the damage.* **3.** the process of examining and measuring something exactly ■ *verb* /sə'veɪ/ **1.** to make a survey of a building ○ *A buildings surveyor was called in to survey the damage caused by the fire.* **2.** to measure land in order to produce a plan or map ○ *They're surveying the area where the new motorway will be built.*

surveyor /sə'veɪə/ *noun* a person who examines buildings to see if they are in good condition; person who surveys land ○ *the surveyor's report was favorable*

suspend /sə'spend/ *verb* **1.** to stop doing something for a time ○ *We have suspended payments while we are waiting for news from our agent.* ○ *Sailings have been suspended until the weather gets better.* ○ *Work on the construction project has been suspended.* ○ *The management decided to suspend negotiations.* **2.** to stop someone working for a time ○ *He was suspended on full pay while the police investigations were going on.*

suspense account /sə'spens ə,kaʊnt/ *noun* an account into which payments are put temporarily when the accountant cannot be sure where they should be entered

suspension /sə'spenʃən/ *noun* **1.** an act of stopping something for a time ○ *There has been a temporary suspension of payments.* ○ *We are trying to avoid a suspension of deliveries during the strike.* **2.**

the act of stopping someone working for a time

suspension file /sə'spenʃ(ə)n faɪl/ *noun* a stiff card file, with metal edges, which can be hooked inside the drawer of a filing cabinet so that it hangs loose

suspension file cart /sə,spenʃ(ə)n faɪl 'kɑrt/ *noun* a cart which carries rows of suspension files, and can easily be moved from place to place in an office

sustainability /sə,steɪnə'bɪlɪti/ *noun* the ability of communities to promote economic growth while protecting quality of life for the future

sustainable advantage /sə ,steɪnəb(ə)l əd'væntɪdʒ/ *noun* a competitive advantage that can be preserved over a long period of time, as opposed to one that results from a short-term tactical promotion

sustainable development /sə 'steɪnəb(ə)l dɪ'veləpmənt/ *noun* development that will be able to continue for a long time into the future because it is based on renewable resources and respects the environment rather consuming resources recklessly to meet the needs of the present

sustainable investment /səs ,teɪnəb(ə)l ɪŋ'vestmənt/ *noun* investment in companies whose operations cause little or no harm to the environment

swap /swɒp/ *noun* an exchange of one thing for another ■ *verb* to exchange one thing for another ○ *He swapped his old car for a new motorcycle.* □ **they swapped jobs** each of them took the other's job

swatch /swɒtʃ/ *noun* a small sample of a fabric ○ *The interior designer showed us swatches of the curtain fabric.*

sweated labor /,swetɪd 'leɪbər/ *noun* **1.** people who work hard for very little money ○ *Of course the firm makes a profit – it employs sweated labor.* ○ *Most of the immigrant farmworkers are sweated labor.* **2.** hard work which is very badly paid

sweatshop /'swetʃɒp/ *noun* a factory using sweated labor

sweetener /'swit(ə)nər/ *noun* an incentive offered to help persuade somebody to take a particular course of action, a bribe (*informal*)

sweetheart agreement /'swithɑrt ə ,grimənt/ *noun* (*in Australia and New Zealand*) an agreement reached between

employees and their employer without the need for arbitration

swipe /swaɪp/ *verb* to pass a credit card or charge card through a reader ○ *He swiped the card but it didn't register.*

Swiss franc /,swɪs 'fræŋk/ *noun* a unit of currency used in Switzerland and Liechtenstein (normally considered a very stable currency)

switch /swɪtʃ/ *verb* to change from one thing to another ○ *to switch funds from one investment to another* ○ *The job was switched from our Tennessee factory to the Philippines.*

switch over to *phrasal verb* to change to something quite different ○ *We have switched over to a French supplier.* ○ *The factory has switched over to gas for heating.*

switchboard /'swɪtʃbɔrd/ *noun* central point in a telephone system, where all lines meet

switchboard operator /'swɪtʃbɔrd ,ɑpəreɪtər/ *noun* a person who works the central telephone system

switch selling /'swɪtʃ ,selɪŋ/ *verb* the practice of offering an apparently good bargain as bait in order to gain the attention of prospective customers then approaching them with a different offer which is more profitable to the seller

swop /swɒp/ *verb* same as **swap**

SWOT analysis /'swɒt ə,næləsɪs/ *noun* a method of assessing a person, company, or product by considering their Strengths, Weaknesses, and external factors which may provide Opportunities or Threats to their development. Full form **Strengths, Weaknesses, Opportunities, Threats**

symbol /'sɪmbəl/ *noun* a sign, picture, or object which represents something ○ *They use a bear as their advertising symbol.*

sympathy strike /'sɪmpəθi straɪk/ *noun* a strike to show that workers agree with another group of workers who are already on strike

syndicate *noun* /'sɪndɪkət/ a group of people or companies working together to make money ○ *a German finance syndicate* ■ *verb* /'sɪndɪkeɪt/ **1.** to produce an article, a cartoon, etc., which is then published in several newspapers or magazines

2. to arrange for a large loan to be underwritten by several international banks

syndicated /'sɪndɪkeɪtɪd/ *adjective* (article which is) published in several newspapers or magazines ○ *He writes a syndicated column on personal finance.*

synergy /'sɪnərdʒi/ *noun* the process of producing greater effects by joining forces than by acting separately ○ *There is considerable synergy between the two companies.*

synthetic /sɪn'θetɪk/ *adjective* artificial, made by man

synthetic fibers /sɪnˌθetɪk 'faɪbərz/ *noun* materials made as products of a chemical process

synthetic materials /sɪnˌθetɪk mə'tɪriəlz/ *plural noun* substances made as products of a chemical process

system /'sɪstəm/ *noun* an arrangement or organization of things which work together ○ *Our accounting system has worked well in spite of the large increase in orders.* ○ *What system is being used for filing data on personnel?* □ **to operate a quota system** to regulate supplies by fixing quantities which are allowed ○ *We arrange our distribution using a quota system – each agent is allowed only a specific number of units.*

systematic /ˌsɪstə'mætɪk/ *adjective* in order, using method ○ *He ordered a systematic report on the distribution service.*

systems analysis /'sɪstəmz əˌnæləsɪs/ *noun* the process of using a computer to suggest how a company can work more efficiently by analyzing the way in which it works at present

systems analyst /'sɪstəmz ˌænəlɪst/ *noun* a person who specializes in systems analysis

systems approach /ˌsɪstəmz ə'proutʃ/ *noun* an approach to decision-making and problem-solving within organizations that is based on the idea that when the various components of a system work together they produce an effect greater than the sum of the effects made by each individual part

systems audit /ˌsɪstəmz 'ɔrdɪt/ *noun* an audit that uses the systems method to assess the internal control system of an organization, e.g., to assess the quality of the accounting system and the level of testing required from the financial statements

systems design /ˌsɪstəmz dɪ'zaɪn/ *noun* the process of designing a computer system or program to carry out a particular function or achieve a particular objective

systems engineering /ˌsɪstəmz ˌendʒɪ'nɪrɪŋ/ *noun* the process of planning, designing, creating, testing and operating complex systems

systems method /ˌsɪstəmz 'meθəd/ *noun* a method of exploring the nature of complex business situations, which involves creating a mathematical or computer model in which all the activities to be studied are represented

T

TA *abbreviation* transactional analysis

tab /tæb/ *noun* same as **tabulator** (*informal*)

table /'teɪb(ə)l/ *noun* **1.** a diagram or chart **2.** a list of figures or facts set out in columns ■ *verb* **1.** to put items of information on the table before a meeting ○ *The report of the finance committee was tabled.* □ **to table a motion** to put forward a proposal for discussion at a meeting **2.** □ **to table a proposal** to remove a proposal from discussion ○ *The motion to hold a new election was tabled.*

table of contents /ˌteɪb(ə)l əv 'kɒntents/ *noun* a list of contents in a book

tabular /'tæbjələr/ *adjective* □ **in tabular form** arranged in a table

tabulate /'tæbjʊleɪt/ *verb* to set something out in a table

tabulation /ˌtæbjə'leɪʃ(ə)n/ *noun* the arrangement of figures in a table

tabulator /'tæbjəleɪtər/ *noun* a feature on a computer which sets words or figures automatically in columns

tachograph /'tækəgræf/ *noun* a device attached to the engine of a truck, which records details of the distance traveled and the time of trips

tacit /'tæsɪt/ *adjective* agreed but not stated ○ *The committee gave the proposals their tacit approval.* ○ *I think we have their tacit agreement to the proposal.*

tactic /'tæktɪk/ *noun* a way of doing things so as to be at an advantage ○ *Securing a key position at an exhibition is an old tactic which always produces good results* ○ *Concentrating our sales force in that area could be a good tactic.* ○ *The directors planned their tactics before going into the meeting.*

tael /taɪl/ *noun* a measurement of the weight of gold, used in the Far East (= 1.20oz/38g)

tailor /'teɪlər/ *verb* to design something for a specific purpose ○ *We mail out press releases tailored to the reader interests of each particular newspaper or periodical.*

take /teɪk/ *noun* **1.** the money received in a store ○ *Our weekly take is over $5,000.* **2.** a profit from any sale ■ *verb* **1.** to receive or to get □ **she takes home $450 a week** her salary, after deductions for tax, etc. is $450 a week **2.** to perform an action □ **to take action** to do something ○ *You must take immediate action if you want to stop thefts.* □ **to take a call** to answer the telephone □ **to take the chair** to be chairman of a meeting ○ *In the absence of the chairman his deputy took the chair.* □ **to take dictation** to write down what someone is saying ○ *The secretary was taking dictation from the managing director.* □ **to take stock** to count the items in a warehouse □ **to take stock of a situation** to examine the state of things before deciding what to do **3.** to need a time or a quantity ○ *It took the factory six weeks* or *The factory took six weeks to clear the backlog of orders.* ○ *It will take her all morning to do my letters.* ○ *It took six men and a crane to get the computer into the building.* (NOTE: **taking – took – has taken**)

take away *phrasal verb* **1.** to remove one figure from a total ○ *If you take away the home sales, the total turnover is down.* **2.** to remove ○ *We had to take the work away from the supplier because the quality was so bad.* ○ *The police took away piles of documents from the office.* □ **sales of food to take away** *U.K.* cooked food sold by a store to be eaten at some other place

take back *phrasal verb* **1.** to return with something ○ *When the watch went* *wrong, he took it back to the shop.* ○ *If you do not like the color, you can take it back to change it.* **2.** □ **to take back employees** to re-employ former employees

take in *phrasal verb* □ **the store takes in $5,000 a week** the store receives $5,000 a week in sales

take into *phrasal verb* to take inside ○ *to take items into stock* or *into the warehouse*

take off *phrasal verb* **1.** to remove or to deduct something ○ *He took $25 off the price.* **2.** to start to rise fast ○ *Sales took off after the TV commercials.* **3.** □ **she took the day off** she decided not to work for the day

take on *phrasal verb* **1.** to agree to employ someone ○ *to take on more staff* **2.** to agree to do something ○ *She took on the job of preparing the sales tax returns.* ○ *He has taken on a lot of extra work.*

take out *phrasal verb* **1.** to remove something ○ *She's taken all the money out of her account.* **2.** □ **to take out a patent for an invention** to apply for and receive a patent □ **to take out insurance against theft** to pay a premium to an insurance company, so that if a theft takes place the company will pay compensation

"…capital gains are not taxed, but money taken out in profits and dividends is taxed" [*Toronto Star*]

take over *phrasal verb* **1.** to start to do something in place of someone else ○ *Miss Black took over from Mr Jones on May 1st.* **2.** □ **to take over a company** to buy a business by offering to buy most of its stock ○ *The company was taken over by a large multinational.*

take up *phrasal verb* □ **to take up a rights issue** to agree to buy rights in stock that has been offered ○ *Half the rights issue was not taken up by the stockholders.*

takeaway /ˈteɪkəweɪ/ *noun U.K.* same as **takeout**

take-home pay /ˈteɪk hoʊm ˌpeɪ/ *noun* same as **disposable personal income** ○ *After all the deductions, her take-home pay is only $600 a week.*

takeout /ˈteɪkaʊt/ *noun* **1.** a store which sells food to be eaten at some other place ○ *There's a Chinese takeout on the corner of the street.* **2.** the food sold by a takeout

take-out /ˈteɪk aʊt/ *noun* the act of removing capital which you had originally invested in a new company by selling your stock

takeover /ˈteɪkoʊvər/ *noun* **1.** an act of buying a controlling interest in a business by buying more than 50% of its stock. Compare **acquisition 2.** the act of starting to do something in place of someone else **3.** the period when one person is taking over work from another

takeover bid /ˈteɪkoʊvər bɪd/ *noun* an offer to buy all or a majority of the stock in a company so as to control it ○ *They made a takeover bid for the company.* ○ *She had to withdraw her takeover bid when she failed to find any backers.* ○ *Stock prices rose sharply on the disclosure of the takeover bid.* □ **to make a takeover bid for a company** to offer to buy the majority of the stock in a company □ **to withdraw a takeover bid** to say that you no longer offer to buy the stock in a company

takeover target /ˈteɪkoʊvər ˌtɑrgɪt/ *noun* a company which is the object of a takeover bid

takeover timetable /ˈteɪkoʊvər ˌtaɪmteɪb(ə)l/ *noun* a timetable of the various events during a takeover bid

taker /ˈteɪkər/ *noun* a person who wants to buy something ○ *There were very few takers for the special offer.*

take up rate /ˈteɪk ʌp ˌreɪt/ *noun* the percentage of acceptances for a rights issue

take your pick /ˌteɪk jə ˈpɪk/ *phrase* choose what you want

takings /ˈteɪkɪŋz/ *plural noun* the money received in a store or a business ○ *The week's takings were stolen from the cash desk.*

talk offline /ˌtɔːk ɔfˈlaɪn/ *noun* to express an opinion that is different from or contrary to the official policy of the organization that is employing you

tall organization /ˌtɔːl ˌɔrgənaɪˈzeɪʃ(ə)n/ *noun* an organization that has a hierarchy with many different levels of management. Opposite **flat organization**

tally /ˈtæli/ *noun* a note of things counted or recorded ○ *to keep a tally of stock movements* or *of expenses* ■ *verb* to agree, to be the same ○ *The invoices do not tally.* ○ *The accounts department tried to make the figures tally.*

tally clerk /'tæli klɜrk/ *noun* a person whose job is to note quantities of cargo

tally sheet /'tæli ʃit/ *noun* a sheet on which quantities are noted

tangible assets /,tændʒɪb(ə)l 'æsets/, **tangible fixed assets** /,tændʒɪb(ə)l 'prɑpəti/, **tangible property** *plural noun* assets that are physical, such as buildings, cash and stock. Leases and securities, although not physical in themselves, are classed as tangible assets because the underlying assets are physical.

tanker /'tæŋkə/ *noun* a special ship or vehicle for carrying liquids (especially oil)

tare /ter/ *noun* **1.** the weight of a container and packing or the weight of a vehicle ○ *to allow for tare* **2.** an allowance made for the weight of a container and packing which is deducted from the total weight, or an allowance made for the weight of a vehicle in calculating transportation costs

target /'tɑrgət/ *noun* something to aim for ○ *performance targets* □ **to set targets** to fix amounts or quantities which employees have to produce or reach □ **to meet a target** to produce the quantity of goods or sales which are expected □ **to miss a target** not to produce the amount of goods or sales which are expected ○ *They missed the target figure of $2m turnover.* ■ *verb* to aim to sell to somebody ○ *I'll follow up your idea of targeting our address list with a special mailing.* □ **to target a market** to plan to sell goods in a specific market ○ *an advertising campaign which targets teenagers*

target market /'tɑrgət ,mɑrkət/ *noun* the market in which a company is planning to sell its goods

tariff /'tærɪf/ *noun* **1.** a tax to be paid on imported goods. Also called **customs tariff**. Compare **import levy**, **import tariffs 2.** a rate of charging for something such as electricity, hotel rooms, or train tickets

tariff barrier /'tærɪf ,bæriər/ *noun* the customs duty intended to make imports more difficult ○ *to impose tariff barriers on* or *to lift tariff barriers from a product*

task /tæsk/ *noun* work which has to be done ○ *The job involves some tasks which are unpleasant and others which are more rewarding.* ○ *The candidates are given a series of tasks to complete within a time limit.* □ **to list task processes** to make a list of various parts of a job which have to be done ■ *verb* to give someone a task to do

task analysis /'tæsk ə,næləsɪs/ *noun* the analysis of the various activities involved in carrying out a particular task, used especially to examine the activities of people who are interacting with computerized or other systems (NOTE: The purpose of task analysis is to find the most efficient way of integrating the human element into automated systems.)

task culture /'tæsk ,kʌltʃər/ *noun* a type of corporate culture that focuses on the carrying out of individual projects by small teams

task force /'tæsk fɔrs/ *noun* a special group of workers or managers who are chosen to carry out a special job or to deal with a special problem ○ *He is heading the government task force on inner city poverty.*

tax /tæks/ *noun* **1.** money taken by the government or by an official body to pay for government services □ **mainstream corporation tax (MCT)** total tax paid by a company on its profits (less any ACT which the company will already have paid) **2.** an amount of money charged by government as part of a person's income or on goods bought □ **basic tax** income tax paid at the normal rate □ **to levy** *or* **impose a tax** to make a tax payable ○ *The government has imposed a 15% tax on gasoline.* □ **to lift a tax** to remove a tax ○ *The tax on fuel charges has been lifted.* ○ *The tax on company profits has been lifted.* □ **tax deducted at source** tax which is removed from a salary or interest before the money is paid out ■ *verb* to make someone pay a tax, to impose a tax on something ○ *Businesses are taxed at 40%.* ○ *Income is taxed at 35%.* ○ *Luxury items are heavily taxed.*

tax abatement /'tæks ə,beɪtmənt/ *noun* a reduction of tax

taxable /'tæksəb(ə)l/ *adjective* able to be taxed

taxable income /,tæksəb(ə)l 'ɪnkʌm/ *noun* income on which a person has to pay tax

taxable items /'tæksəb(ə)l ,aɪtəmz/ *plural noun* items on which a tax has to be paid

tax adjustments /'tæks ə,dʒʌstmənts/ *plural noun* changes made to tax

tax adviser /'tæks əd,vaızər/, **tax consultant** /'tæks kən,sʌltənt/ *noun* a person who gives advice on tax problems

taxation /tæk'seıʃ(ə)n/ *noun* the act of taxing

tax avoidance /'tæks ə,vɔıd(ə)ns/ *noun* the practice of legally trying to pay as little tax as possible

tax bracket/'tæks ,brækıt/ *noun* a section of people paying a particular level of income tax

tax collector /'tæks kə,lektər/ *noun* a person who collects taxes which are owed

tax concession /'tæks kən,seʃ(ə)n/ *noun* an act of allowing less tax to be paid

tax credit /'tæks ,kredıt/ *noun* **1.** a sum of money which can be offset against tax **2.** the part of a dividend on which the company has already paid tax, so that the stockholder is not taxed on it **3.** an amount that can be subtracted directly to reduce an individual's income tax liability

tax-deductible /,tæks dı'dʌktıb(ə)l/ *adjective* possible to deduct from an income before tax is calculated □ **these expenses are not tax-deductible** tax has to be paid on these expenses

tax deduction /'tæks dı,dʌkʃ(ə)n/ *noun* a subtraction for some expense items that reduces income tax liability

tax deductions /'tæks dı,dʌkʃənz/ *plural noun* **1.** money removed from a salary to pay tax **2.** business expenses which can be claimed against tax

tax-deferred /tæks dı'fɜrd/ *adjective* not taxable until a later time, often after retirement

tax evasion /'tæks ı,veıʒ(ə)n/ *noun* the practice of illegally trying to not pay tax

tax-exempt /,tæks ıg'zempt/ *adjective* **1.** referring to a person or organization not required to pay tax **2.** not subject to tax

tax exemption /'tæks ıg,zempʃən/ *noun* **1.** the fact of being free from payment of tax **2.** the part of income which a person is allowed to earn and not pay tax on

tax exile /'tæks ,eksaıl/ *noun* a person who lives in a country where taxes are low in order to avoid paying tax at home

tax form /'tæks fɔrm/ *noun* a blank form to be filled in annually with details of income, exemptions, deductions, and credits, and submitted to the Internal Revenue Service and tax departments in most states

tax-free /,tæks 'fri/ *adjective* with no tax having to be paid ○ *tax-free goods*

tax harmonization /,tæks ,hɑrmənaı'zeıʃ(ə)n/ *noun* the enactment of taxation laws in different jurisdictions, such as neighboring countries, provinces, or states of the United States, that are consistent with one another

tax haven /'tæks ,heıv(ə)n/ *noun* a country or area where taxes are low, encouraging companies to set up their main offices there

tax holiday /'tæks ,hɑlıdeı/ *noun* a period when a new business is exempted from paying tax

tax incentive /'tæks ın,sentıv/ *noun* a tax reduction afforded to people for particular purposes, e.g., sending their children to college

tax inspector /'tæks ın,spektər/ *noun* a government employee who investigates taxpayers' declarations

tax loophole /'tæks ,luphoʊl/ *noun* a legal means of not paying tax

tax loss /'tæks lɔs/ *noun* a loss made by a company during an accounting period, for which relief from tax is given

taxpayer /'tækspeıər/ *noun* a person or company that has to pay tax ○ *basic taxpayer* or *taxpayer at the basic rate* ○ *Corporate taxpayers are being targeted by the government.*

tax point /'tæks pɔınt/ *noun* the date on which goods or services are supplied, which is the date when sales tax becomes is due

tax refund /'tæks ,rifʌnd/ *noun* a refund of taxes that have been overpaid

tax relief /'tæks rı,lif/ *noun U.K.* same as **tax deduction**

tax return /'tæks rı,tɜrn/ *noun* same as **income tax return**

tax schedules /'tæks ,skedʒəlz/ *plural noun* tables that show the rates at which different income levels are taxed. See Comment at **schedule**

tax shelter /'tæks ,ʃeltə/ *noun* a financial arrangement such as a pension plan where investments can be made without tax

tax threshold /'tæks ˌθreʃhoʊld/ *noun* a point at which another percentage of tax is payable ○ *The government has raised the minimum tax threshold from $4,000 to $4,500.*

tax year /'tæks ˌjɪr/ *noun* a twelve month period on which taxes are calculated. In the U.S. this is either January 1 to December 31, or in the case of a company, it may be a fiscal year.

T-bill /'ti bɪl/ same as **Treasury bill** (*informal*)

T-bond /'ti bɑnd/ same as **Treasury bond**

TCO *abbreviation* total cost of ownership

team /tim/ *noun* a group of people who work together and cooperate to share work and responsibility

team-building /'tim ˌbɪldɪŋ/ *noun* a set of training sessions designed to instill cooperation and solidarity in a group of employees who work together as a team

teamster /'timstər/ *noun* a truck driver

teamwork /'timwɜrk/ *noun* a group effort applied to work

tear sheet /'ter ʃit/ *noun* a page taken from a published magazine or newspaper, sent to an advertiser as proof that their advertisement has been run

teaser /'tizər/, **teaser ad** /'tizər æd/ *noun* an advertisement that gives a little information about a product in order to attract customers by making them curious to know more

technical /'teknɪk(ə)l/ *adjective* **1.** referring to a particular machine or process ○ *The document gives all the technical details on the new computer.* **2.** referring to influences inside a market, e.g., volumes traded and forecasts based on market analysis, as opposed to external factors such as oil-price rises, wars, etc.

technical correction /ˌteknɪk(ə)l kə 'rekʃ(ə)n/ *noun* a situation in which a stock price or a currency moves up or down because it was previously too low or too high

technician /tek'nɪʃ(ə)n/ *noun* a person who is specialized in industrial work ○ *Computer technicians worked to install the new system.*

technique /tek'nik/ *noun* a skilled way of doing a job ○ *The company has developed a new technique for processing steel.*

○ *We have a special technique for answering complaints from customers.* □ **marketing techniques** skill in marketing a product

technocracy /tek'nɑkrəsi/ *noun* an organization controlled by technical experts. ◊ **bureaucracy**

"The heyday of technocracy taught us that progress was the Manhattan Project and Apollo to the moon: bureaucratically managed programs aimed at specific goals, with each step plotted in advance."

technological /ˌteknə'lɑdʒɪk(ə)l/ *adjective* referring to technology □ **the technological revolution** the changing of industry by introducing new technology

technology /tek'nɑlədʒi/ *noun* the application of scientific knowledge to industrial processes □ **the introduction of new technology** putting new electronic equipment into a business or industry

technology adoption life cycle /tek ˌnɑlədʒi ə,dɑpʃən 'laɪf ˌsaɪk(ə)l/ *noun* a model that describes the stages in which various types of individuals and organizations start to use new technologies. The individual and organizations are usually classified as innovators, early adopters, early majority, late majority, or technology laggards.

technology laggard /tek'nɑlədʒi ˌlægərd/ *noun* an individual or organization that is very slow or reluctant to adopt new technology

technology transfer /tek'nɑlədʒi ˌtrænsfɜr/ *noun* the process of transferring the scientific findings of research facilities to the commercial sector in order to produce useful products, reward researchers, and contribute to economic growth

tel *abbreviation* telephone

telecommunications /ˌtelɪkə,mjunɪ 'keɪʃ(ə)nz/ *plural noun* systems of passing messages over long distances (by cable, radio, etc.)

telecoms /'telɪkɑmz/ *noun* same as **telecommunications** (*informal*)

teleconference /'teli,kɑnf(ə)rəns/ *noun* a discussion between several people in different places, using the telephone, microphones and loudspeakers

telegram /'telɪgræm/ *noun* a message sent by telegraph ○ *to send a telegram to an agent in South Africa*

telegraph /'telɪgræf/ *noun* a system of sending messages along wires ○ *to send a message by telegraph* ■ *verb* to send a message by telegraph ○ *to telegraph an order*

telegraphic /ˌtelɪ'græfɪk/ *adjective* referring to a telegraph system

telegraphic transfer /ˌtelɪgræfɪk 'trænsfər/ *noun* a transfer of money from one account to another by telegraph

telemarketing /'telɪˌmɑːkətɪŋ/ *noun* the selling of a product or service by telephone

telephone /'telɪfoʊn/ *noun* a machine used for speaking to someone over a long distance ○ *We had a new telephone system installed last week.* □ **to be on the telephone** to be speaking to someone using the telephone ○ *The managing director is on the telephone to Hong Kong.* ○ *She has been on the telephone all day.* □ **by telephone** using the telephone ○ *to place an order by telephone* ○ *to reserve a room by telephone* □ **to make a telephone call** to speak to someone on the telephone □ **to answer the telephone, to take a telephone call** to speak in reply to a call on the telephone ■ *verb* □ **to telephone a place, a person** to call a place or someone by telephone ○ *His secretary telephoned to say he would be late.* □ **he telephoned the order through to the warehouse** he telephoned the warehouse to place an order □ **to telephone about something** to make a telephone call to speak about something ○ *He telephoned about the January invoice.* □ **to telephone for something** to make a telephone call to ask for something ○ *he telephoned for a taxi*

telephone book /'telɪfoʊn bʊk/ *noun* a book which lists all people and businesses in alphabetical order with their telephone numbers ○ *He looked up the number of the company in the telephone book.*

telephone booth /'telɪfoʊn buːð/ *noun* a public box with a telephone

telephone call /'telɪfoʊn kɔːl/ *noun* an act of speaking to someone on the telephone

telephone directory /'telɪfoʊn daɪˌrekt(ə)ri/ *noun* a book which lists all people and businesses in alphabetical order with their phone numbers ○ *To find his address you will have to look up his number in the telephone directory.*

telephone exchange /'telɪfoʊn ɪksˌtʃeɪndʒ/ *noun* a center where the telephones of a whole district are linked

telephone kiosk /'telɪfoʊn ˌkiɑsk/ *noun* a shelter with a public telephone in it ○ *There are two telephone kiosks outside the post office.*

telephone line /'telɪfoʊn laɪn/ *noun* a wire along which telephone messages travel

telephone number /'telɪfoʊn ˌnʌmbər/ *noun* a set of figures for a particular telephone subscriber ○ *Can you give me your telephone number?*

telephone operator /ˌtelɪfoʊn ˌɑpə'reɪtər/ *noun* a person who operates a telephone switchboard

telephone order /'telɪfoʊn ˌɔrdər/ *noun* an order received by telephone ○ *Since we mailed the catalog we have received a large number of telephone orders.*

telephone research /'telɪfoʊn rɪˌsɜrtʃ/ *noun* same as **telephone survey**

telephone selling /'telɪfoʊn ˌselɪŋ/ *noun* the practice of making sales by phoning prospective customers and trying to persuade them to buy

telephone subscriber /ˌtelɪfoʊn səb'skraɪbər/ *noun* a person who has a telephone

telephone survey /'telɪfoʊn ˌsɜrveɪ/ *noun* an act of interviewing respondents by telephone for a survey ○ *How many people in the sample hung up before replying to the telephone survey?*

telephone switchboard /ˌtelɪfoʊn 'swɪtʃbɔrd/ *noun* central point in a telephone system where all internal and external lines meet

telesales /'teliˌseɪlz/ *plural noun* sales made by telephone

teleshopping /'telɪˌʃɑpɪŋ/ *noun* shopping from home by means of a television screen and a home computer

television network /ˌtelɪvɪʒ(ə)n 'netwɜrk/ *noun* a system of linked television stations covering the whole country

teleworking /'teliwɜrkɪŋ/ *noun* a working method where an employee works at home on computer, and sends the finished material back to the central office by modem. Also called **homeworking**, **networking**

teller /'telər/ *noun* a person who takes cash from or pays cash to customers at a bank

tem /tem/ ◊ **pro tem**

temp /temp/ *noun* a temporary office worker ○ *We have had two temps working in the office this week to clear the backlog of letters.* ■ *verb* to work as a temporary office worker

temp agency /'temp ,eɪdʒənsi/ *noun* an office which deals with finding temporary secretaries for offices

temping /'tempɪŋ/ *noun* the practice of working as a temporary office worker ○ *He can earn more money from temping than from a full-time job.*

temporarily /,temp(ə)'rerəli/ *adverb* lasting only for a short time

temporary /'temp(ə)rəri/ *adjective* which only lasts a short time ○ *to take temporary measures* ○ *He was granted a temporary export license.* ○ *She has a temporary post with a construction company.* ○ *He has a temporary job as a filing clerk* or *he has a job as a temporary filing clerk.*

temporary employment /,temp(ə)rəri ɪm'plɔɪmənt/, **temporary work** /'temp(ə)rəri wɜrk/ *noun* full-time work which does not last for more than a few days or months

temporary staff /'temp(ə)rəri stæf/, **temporary employees** /,temp(ə)rəri ɪm 'plɔɪiz/, **temporary workers** /'temp(ə)rəri ,wɜrkərz/ *plural noun* members of staff who are appointed for a short time ○ *We need to recruit temporary staff for the busy summer season.*

tenancy /'tenənsi/ *noun* **1.** an agreement by which a tenant can occupy a property **2.** a period during which a tenant has an agreement to occupy a property

tenant /'tenənt/ *noun* a person or company which rents a house, apartment or office to live or work in ○ *The tenant is liable for repairs.*

tend /tend/ *verb* to be likely to do something ○ *He tends to appoint young girls to his staff.*

tendency /'tendənsi/ *noun* the condition of being likely to do something ○ *The market showed an upward tendency.* ○ *There has been a downward tendency in*

the market for several days. □ **the market showed a tendency to stagnate** the market seemed to stagnate rather than advance

tender /'tendər/ *noun* an offer to do something for a specific price ○ *a successful tender* ○ *an unsuccessful tender* ◊ **bid** □ **to sell shares by tender** *U.K.* to ask people to offer in writing a price for shares ■ *verb* **1.** to sell a stock, usually at a price above the current price, in response to a tender offer. ◊ **bid 2.** □ **to tender your resignation** to resign, to give in your resignation **3.** to offer money ○ *please tender the correct fare*

tenderer /'tendərər/ *noun U.K.* same as **bidder**

tendering /'tendərɪŋ/ *noun* same as **bidding**

tender offer /'tendər ,ɔfər/ *noun* a takeover bid in which stockholders are invited to sell their stock, usually at a price higher than the current price

tentative /'tentətɪv/ *adjective* not certain ○ *They reached a tentative agreement over the proposal.* ○ *We suggested Wednesday May 10th as a tentative date for the next meeting.*

tentatively /'tentətɪvli/ *adverb* without being sure ○ *We tentatively suggested Wednesday as the date for our next negotiating meeting.*

tenure /'tenjər/ *noun* **1.** the right to hold property or a position **2.** the time when a position is held ○ *during his tenure of the office of chairman*

term /tɜrm/ *noun* **1.** a period of time when something is legally valid ○ *during his term of office as chairman* ○ *the term of a lease* ○ *We have renewed her contract for a term of six months.* ○ *The term of the loan is fifteen years.* **2.** a period of time **3.** a part of a legal or university year

term assurance /'tɜrm ə,ʃʊrəns/ *noun U.K.* same as **term insurance**

term deposit /'tɜrm dɪ,pɑzɪt/ *noun* money invested for a fixed period at a higher rate of interest

terminable /'tɜrmɪnəb(ə)l/ *adjective* which can be terminated

terminal /'tɜrmɪn(ə)l/ *noun* the building where you end a trip ■ *adjective* at the end

terminal bonus /,tɜrmɪn(ə)l 'bɔɪnəs/ *noun* a bonus received when insurance comes to an end

terminate /'tɜrmɪneɪt/ *verb* **1.** to end something or to bring something to an end ○ *His employment was terminated.* **2.** to dismiss someone ○ *His employment was terminated.*

termination /ˌtɜrmɪ'neɪʃ(ə)n/ *noun* **1.** the process of bringing to an end **2.** the end of a contract of employment; leaving a job (resigning, retiring, or being fired or made redundant) ○ *Both employer and employee agreed that termination was the only way to solve the problem.*

termination clause /ˌtɜrmɪ'neɪʃ(ə)n klɔz/ *noun* a clause which explains how and when a contract can be terminated

term insurance /'tɜrm ɪnˌʃʊrəns/ *noun* a life insurance which covers a person's life for a period of time. At the end of the period, if the person is still alive he receives nothing from the insurance.

term loan /'tɜrm loʊn/ *noun* a loan for a fixed period of time

terms /tɜrmz/ *plural noun* the conditions or duties which have to be carried out as part of a contract, or the arrangements which have to be agreed upon before a contract is valid ○ *to negotiate for better terms* ○ *She refused to agree to some of the terms of the contract.* ○ *By or Under the terms of the contract, the company is responsible for all damage to the property.* □ **"terms: cash with order"** the terms of sale showing that payment has to be made in cash when the order is placed

terms of employment /ˌtɜrmz əv ɪm 'plɔɪmənt/ *noun* the conditions set out in a contract of employment

terms of payment /ˌtɜrmz əv 'peɪmənt/ *plural noun* the conditions for paying something

terms of reference /ˌtɜrmz əv 'ref(ə)rəns/ *plural noun* areas which a committee or an inspector can deal with ○ *Under the terms of reference of the committee, it cannot investigate complaints from the public.* ○ *The committee's terms of reference do not cover exports.*

terms of sale /ˌtɜrmz əv 'seɪl/ *plural noun* the conditions attached to a sale

territorial waters /ˌterɪtɔriəl 'wɔrtərz/ *noun* sea waters near the coast of a country, which are part of the country and governed by the laws of that country □ **outside territorial waters** in international waters, over which no single country has jurisdiction

territory /'terɪt(ə)ri/ *noun* an area visited by a salesperson ○ *We are adding two new reps and reducing all the reps' territories.* ○ *Her territory covers all of the Northeast.*

tertiary industry /ˌtɜrʃəri 'ɪndəstri/ *noun* an industry which does not produce raw materials or manufacture products but offers a service such as banking, retailing, or accountancy

tertiary sector /'tɜrʃəri ˌsektər/ *noun* the section of the economy containing the service industries

test /test/ *noun* an examination to see if something works well or is possible ■ *verb* to examine something to see if it is working well ○ *We are still testing the new computer system.* □ **to test the market for a product** to show samples of a product in a market to see if it will sell well ○ *We are testing the market for the toothpaste in New Jersey.*

test case /'test keɪs/ *noun* a legal action where the decision will fix a principle which other cases can follow

test certificate /'test səˌtɪfɪkət/ *noun* a certificate to show that something has passed a test

test-drive /'test draɪv/ *verb* □ **to test-drive a car** to drive a car before buying it to see if it works well

testimonial /ˌtestɪ'moʊniəl/ *noun* a written report about someone's character or ability ○ *She has asked me to write her a testimonial.*

testing /'testɪŋ/ *noun* the act of examining something to see if it works well ○ *During the testing of the system several defects were corrected.*

test-market /'test ˌmɑrkət/ *verb* □ **to test-market a product** to show samples of a product in a market to see if it will sell well ○ *We are test-marketing the toothpaste in New Jersey.*

test run /'test rʌn/ *noun* a trial made on a machine

text /tekst/ *noun* a written part of something ○ *He wrote notes at the side of the text of the agreement.* ■ *verb* to send a text message on a cell phone or pager

text message /'tekst ˌmesɪdʒ/ *noun* a message sent in text form, especially from one cellular phone or pager to another

text processing /'tekst ˌprɑsesɪŋ/ *noun* working with words, using a computer to produce, check and change documents, reports, letters, etc.

thanks /θæŋks/ *plural noun* word showing that someone is grateful ○ *"Many thanks for your letter of June 25th."*

thanks to /'θæŋks tʊ/ *adverb* because of ○ *The company was able to continue trading thanks to a loan from the bank.* □ **it was no thanks to the bank that we avoided making a loss** we avoided making a loss in spite of what the bank did

the first half /ˌði fɜrst 'hæf/ *noun* the periods from January 1st to June 30th and from June 30th to December 31st

theft /θeft/ *noun* the act of stealing ○ *to take out insurance against theft* ○ *We have brought in security guards to protect the store against theft.* ○ *They are trying to cut their losses by theft.*

theory /'θiəri/ *noun* a statement of the general principle of how something should work □ **in theory the plan should work** the plan may work, but it has not been tried in practice

think tank /'θɪŋk tæŋk/ *noun* a group of experts who advise or put forward plans

third /θɜrd/ *noun* one part of something which is divided into three □ **to sell everything at one third off** to sell everything at a discount of 33% □ **the company has two thirds of the total market** the company has 66% of the total market

third party /ˌθɜrd 'pɑrti/ *noun* a person other than the two main parties involved in a contract, e.g., in an insurance contract, anyone who is not the insurance company nor the person who is insured □ **the case is in the hands of a third party** the case is being dealt with by someone who is not one of the main interested parties

third party insurance /ˌθɜrd ˌpɑrti ɪn'ʃʊrəns/ *noun* insurance to cover damage to any person who is not one of the people named in the insurance contract (that is, not the insured person nor the insurance company)

third quarter /ˌθɜrd 'kwɔrtər/ *noun* a period of three months from July to September

Third World /ˌθɜrd 'wɜrld/ *noun* ♦ **developing world** (*dated*) ○ *We sell tractors into the Third World* or *to Third World countries.*

three-part /θri'pɑrt/ *adjective* paper (for computers or typewriters) with a top sheet for the original and a two sheets for copies ○ *three-part invoices* ○ *three-part stationery*

360 degree appraisal /ˌθri hʌndrəd ən ˌsɪksti dɪgri ə'preɪz(ə)l/ *noun* an assessment of the performance of a person working for an organization, to which colleagues ranking above, below and of equal rank contribute

threshold /'θreʃhoʊld/ *noun* the point at which something changes

threshold agreement /'θreʃhoʊld ə ˌgrimənt/ *noun* a contract which says that if the cost of living goes up by more than an agreed amount, pay will go up to match it

thrift /θrɪft/ *noun* **1.** a careful attitude toward money, shown by saving it spending wisely **2.** a private local bank, savings and loan association or credit union, which accepts and pays interest on deposits from small investors

"…the thrift, which had grown from $4.7 million in assets in 1980 to 1.5 billion this year, has ended in liquidation" [*Barrons*]

"…some thrifts came to grief on speculative property deals, some in the high-risk junk bond market, others simply by lending too much to too many people" [*Times*]

thrifty /'θrɪfti/ *adjective* careful not to spend too much money

thrive /θraɪv/ *verb* to grow well, to be profitable ○ *The country has a thriving economy based on oil.* ○ *There is a thriving black market in car radios.* ○ *The company is thriving in spite of the recession.*

throughput /'θrupʊt/ *noun* an amount of work done or of goods produced in a certain time ○ *We hope to increase our throughput by putting in two new machines.* ○ *The invoice department has a throughput of 6,000 invoices a day.*

throw out *phrasal verb* **1.** to reject or to refuse to accept ○ *The proposal was thrown out by the planning committee.* ○ *The board threw out the draft contract submitted by the union.* ○ *The union negotiators threw out the management offer.* **2.** to get rid of something which is not wanted ○ *The annual meeting threw out the old board of directors.* ○ *He was thrown out of the company for disobedience.* (NOTE: **throwing – threw – thrown**)

tick /'tɪkə/ *noun* **1.** credit (*informal*) ○ *All the furniture in the house is bought on tick.* **2.** a mark on paper to show that something is correct or that something is approved ○ *Put a tick in the box marked "R".* (NOTE: The U.S. term is **check** in this meaning.) ■ *verb* to mark with a sign to show that something is correct ○ *Tick the box marked "R" if you require a receipt.* (NOTE: The U.S. term is **check** in this meaning.)

ticker /'tɪkər/ *noun* a machine (operated by telegraph) which prints details of stock prices and transactions rapidly (formerly printed on paper tape called "ticker tape", but is now shown online on computer terminals)

ticket /'tɪkət/ *noun* **1.** a piece of paper or card which allows you to do something **2.** a piece of paper or card which allows you to travel ○ *train ticket* or *bus ticket* or *plane ticket* **3.** paper which shows something

ticket agency /'tɪkɪt ,eɪdʒənsi/ *noun* a store which sells tickets to theaters

ticket counter /'tɪkət ,kaʊntər/ *noun* a place where tickets are sold

ticket office /'tɪkət ,ɔfɪs/ *noun* an office where tickets can be bought

tie /taɪ/ *verb*
tie in *phrasal verb* to link an insurance policy to a mortgage
tie up *phrasal verb* **1.** to attach or to fasten something tightly ○ *The parcel is tied up with string.* ○ *The ship was tied up to the dock.* □ **he is rather tied up at the moment** he is very busy **2.** to invest money in one way, so that it cannot be used for other investments ○ *He has $100,000 tied up in long-term bonds.* ○ *The company has $250,000 tied up in stock which no one wants to buy.*
"…a lot of speculator money is said to be tied up in sterling because of the interest-rate differential between U.S. and British rates" [*Australian Financial Review*]

tie-in /'taɪ ɪn/ *noun* an advertisement linked to advertising in another media, e.g., a magazine ad linked to a TV commercial (NOTE: The plural is **tie-ins**.)

tie-in promotion /,taɪ ɪn prə 'moʊʃ(ə)n/ *noun* a special display linking the product to a major advertising campaign, or to a TV program

tie-on label /,taɪ ɑn 'leɪb(ə)l/ *noun* a label with a piece of string attached so that it can be tied to an item

tie-up /'taɪ ʌp/ *noun* a link or connection ○ *The company has a tie-up with a German distributor.* (NOTE: The plural is **tie-ups**.)

tight /taɪt/ *adjective* which is controlled, which does not allow any movement ○ *The manager has a very tight schedule today – she cannot fit in any more appointments.* ○ *Expenses are kept under tight control.*
"…mortgage money is becoming tighter" [*Times*]
"…a tight monetary policy by the central bank has pushed up interest rates and drawn discretionary funds into bank deposits" [*Far Eastern Economic Review*]
"…the U.K. economy is at the uncomfortable stage in the cycle where the two years of tight money are having the desired effect on demand" [*Sunday Times*]

-tight /taɪt/ *suffix* which prevents something getting in ○ *The computer is packed in a watertight case.* ○ *Send the movies in an airtight container.*

tighten /'taɪt(ə)n/ *verb* to make something tight, to control something ○ *The accounts department is tightening its control over departmental budgets.*
"…the decision by the government to tighten monetary policy will push the annual inflation rate above the previous high" [*Financial Times*]
tighten up on *phrasal verb* to control something more strictly ○ *The government is tightening up on tax evasion.* ○ *We must tighten up on the reps' expenses.*

tight money /,taɪt 'mʌni/ *noun* money which has to be borrowed at a high interest rate, and so restricts expenditure by companies

tight money policy /taɪt 'mʌni ,pɑlɪsi/ *noun* a government policy to restrict money supply

till /tɪl/ *noun* a drawer for keeping cash in a store

time /taɪm/ *noun* **1.** a period during which something takes place, e.g., one hour, two days, or fifty minutes **2.** a hour of the day (such as 9.00, 12.15, ten o'clock at night, etc.) ○ *the time of arrival* or *the* *arrival time is indicated on the screen* ○ *Departure times are delayed by up to fifteen minutes because of the volume of traffic.* **3.** a system of hours on the clock **4.** the number of hours worked **5.** a period before something happens □ **to keep within the time limits** *or* **within the time schedule** to complete work by the time stated

time and a half /ˌtaɪm ənd ə 'hæf/ *noun* the normal rate of pay plus 50% extra

time and method study /ˌtaɪm ən 'meθəd ˌstʌdi/ *noun* a process of examining the way in which something is done to see if a cheaper or quicker way can be found

time and motion expert /ˌtaɪm ən 'mouʃ(ə)n ˌekspɜrt/ *noun* a person who analyzes time and motion studies and suggests changes in the way work is done

time and motion study /ˌtaɪm ən 'mouʃ(ə)n ˌstʌdi/ *noun* a study in an office or factory of the time taken to do specific jobs and the movements employees have to make to do them

time-card /'taɪm kɑrd/ *noun* a special card which a worker puts into the time clock when punching in or out of work

time clock /'taɪm klɑk/ *noun* a machine which records when an employee arrives at or leaves work

time deposit /'taɪm dɪˌpɑzɪt/ *noun* a deposit of money for a fixed period, during which it cannot be withdrawn

time-keeping /'taɪm ˌkipɪŋ/ *noun* the fact of being on time for work ○ *He was warned for bad time-keeping.*

time limit /'taɪm ˌlɪmɪt/ *noun* the maximum time which can be taken to do something ○ *to set a time limit for acceptance of the offer* ○ *The work was finished within the time limit allowed.* ○ *The time limit on applications to the industrial tribunal is three months.*

time limitation /'taɪm lɪmɪˌteɪʃ(ə)n/ *noun* the restriction of the amount of time available

time management /'taɪm ˌmænɪdʒmənt/ *noun* analysis and control of the amount of time spent on different work activities, in order to maximize personal efficiency. The most important aspect of time management involves listing different work tasks in order of priority so that you can concentrate on those that are most important. (NOTE: Time management involves analyzing how you spend your time, deciding how important each of your different work tasks is and reorganizing your activities so that you spend most time on the tasks that are most important.)

"""When people feel that others are just a keystroke away, they fail to employ any time-management skills," says Sabath. "People should gather their thoughts and pull their questions together before they start typing. It saves everyone time."" [*Forbes*]

time of peak demand /ˌtaɪm əv pik dɪ'mænd/ *noun* the time when something is being used most

time rate /'taɪm reɪt/ *noun* a rate for work which is calculated as money per hour or per week, and not money for work completed

time-saving /'taɪm ˌseɪvɪŋ/ *adjective* which saves time ○ *a time-saving device* ■ *noun* the practice of trying to save time ○ *The management is keen on time-saving.*

timescale /'taɪmskeɪl/ *noun* the time which will be taken to complete work ○ *Our timescale is that all work should be completed by the end of August.* ○ *He is working to a strict timescale.*

time share /'taɪm ʃer/ *noun* a system where several people each own part of a property, each being able to use it for a certain period each year

time-sharing /'taɪm ˌʃerɪŋ/ *noun* **1.** same as **time share 2.** an arrangement for sharing a computer system, with different users using different terminals

time sheet /'taɪm ʃit/ *noun* a record of when an employee arrives at and leaves work, or one which shows how much time a person spends on different jobs each day

time sovereignty /'taɪm ˌsɑvrɪnti/ the ability to control the way you spend your time so that you can arrange your working life to suit your own situation, e.g., by working flexible hours

timetable /'taɪmteɪb(ə)l/ *noun* **1.** a list showing times of arrivals and departures of buses, trains, planes, etc. ○ *According to the timetable, there should be a train to Baltimore at 10.22.* ○ *The bus company has brought out its winter timetable.* **2.** a list of appointments or events ○ *The manager has a very full timetable, so I doubt if he will be able to see you today.* ◊ **takeo-**

ver timetable ■ *verb* to make a list of times

time work /'taɪm wɜrk/ *noun* work which is paid for at a rate per hour or per day, not per piece of work completed

time zone /'taɪm zoʊn/ *noun* one of 24 bands in the world in which the same standard time is used ○ *When you fly across the U.S. you cross several time zones.*

"…time-zone differences are an attraction for Asian speculators. In Hongkong, it is 5 p.m. when the London exchange opens and 9.30 or 10 p.m. when New York starts trading" [*Far Eastern Economic Review*]

timing /'taɪmɪŋ/ *noun* a way in which something happens at a particular time ○ *The timing of the conference is very convenient, as it comes just before my summer vacation.* ○ *His arrival ten minutes after the meeting finished was very bad timing.*

tip /tɪp/ *noun* **1.** money given to someone who has helped you ○ *The staff are not allowed to accept tips.* **2.** a piece of advice on buying or doing something which could be profitable ○ *The newspaper gave several stock market tips.* ○ *She gave me a tip about a stock which was likely to rise because of a takeover bid.* ■ *verb* to give money to someone who has helped you ○ *He tipped the receptionist $5.* (NOTE: **tipping – tipped**)

tip sheet /'tɪp ʃɪt/ *noun* a newspaper which gives information about stocks which should be bought or sold

TIR *abbreviation* Transports Internationaux Routiers

title /'taɪt(ə)l/ *noun* **1.** a right to own a property ○ *She has no title to the property.* ○ *He has a good title to the property.* **2.** name given to a person in a certain job ○ *He has the title "Chief Executive".*

title deeds /'taɪt(ə)l ˌdidz/ *plural noun* a document showing who is the owner of a property

token /'toʊkən/ *noun* something which acts as a sign or symbol

token charge /ˌtoʊkən 'tʃɑrdʒ/ *noun* a small charge which does not cover the real costs ○ *A token charge is made for heating.*

token payment /'toʊkən ˌpeɪmənt/ *noun* a small payment to show that a payment is being made

token rent /ˌtoʊkən 'rent/ *noun* a very low rent payment to show that some rent is being asked

token strike /ˌtoʊkən 'straɪk/ *noun* a short strike to show that workers have a grievance

toll /toʊl/ *noun* a payment for using a service, usually a bridge or a road ○ *We had to cross a toll bridge to get to the island.* ○ *You have to pay a toll to cross the bridge.*

toll call /'toʊl kɔl/ *noun* a long-distance telephone call

toll free /ˌtoʊl 'fri/ *adverb*, *adjective* without having to pay a charge for a long-distance telephone call ○ *to call someone toll free* ○ *a toll-free number*

COMMENT: Toll-free numbers usually start with the digits 800.

ton /tʌn/ *noun* a measure of weight

toner cartridge /'toʊnər ˌkɑrtrɪdʒ/ *noun* a sealed plastic box containing toner

tonnage /'tʌnɪdʒ/ *noun* a space for cargo in a ship, measured in tons

"…in the dry cargo sector a total of 956 cargo vessels of 11.6m tonnes are laid up – 3% of world dry cargo tonnage" [*Lloyd's List*]

tonne /tʌn/ *noun* a metric ton, 1,000 kilos

"Canada agreed to the new duty-free quota of 600,000 tonnes a year" [*Globe and Mail (Toronto)*]

tool /tul/ *noun* an instrument used for doing manual work, e.g., a hammer or screwdriver

tool up *phrasal verb* to put machinery into a factory

top /tɑp/ *noun* **1.** the upper surface or upper part ○ *Do not put coffee cups on top of the computer.* **2.** the highest point or most important place ○ *She rose to the top of her profession.* ■ *verb* to go higher than ○ *Sales topped $1m in the first quarter.* (NOTE: **topping – topped**) ■ *adjective* highest or most important □ **to give something top priority** to make something the most important item, so that it is done very fast

"…the base lending rate, or prime rate, is the rate at which banks lend to their top corporate borrowers" [*Wall Street Journal*]

"…gross wool receipts for the selling season appear likely to top $2 billion" [*Australian Financial Review*]

top out *noun* a period of peak demand for a product ∎ *phrasal verb* to finish the roof of a new building

top up *phrasal verb* **1.** to fill up something which is not full ○ *to top up stocks before the Christmas rush* **2.** to add to something to make it more complete ○ *He topped up his pension contributions to make sure he received the maximum allowable pension when he retired.*

top copy /ˌtɒp ˈkɒpi/ *noun* the first or top sheet of a document which is typed with carbon copies

top-down approach /ˌtɒp ˈdaʊn ə ˌproʊtʃ/ *noun* a style of leadership, considered a feature of large bureaucracies, in which plans are made and decisions taken by senior management and are then passed down to the other members of the organization. Opposite **bottom-up approach**

top-down information /ˌtɒp ˈdaʊn ɪnfərˌmeɪʃ(ə)n/ *noun* a system of passing information down from management to the work force

topflight /ˌtɒp ˈflaɪt/ *adjective* in the most important position ○ *Topflight managers can earn very high salaries.* Also called **top-ranking**

top-grade /ˈtɒp greɪd/ *adjective* of the best quality ○ *top-grade gasoline*

top-hat pension /ˌtɒp hæt ˈpenʃən/ *noun* a special extra pension for senior managers

top management /ˌtɒp ˈmænɪdʒmənt/ *noun* the main directors of a company

top official /ˌtɒp əˈfɪʃ(ə)l/ *noun* a very important person in a government department

topping-out ceremony /ˌtɒpɪŋ ˈaʊt ˌserɪməni/ *noun* a ceremony when the roof of a new building is finished

top quality /ˌtɒp ˈkwɒlɪti/ *noun* very best quality ○ *We specialize in top quality imported goods.*

top-ranking /ˌtɒp ˈræŋkɪŋ/ *adjective* same as **topflight**

top-selling /ˌtɒp ˈselɪŋ/ *adjective* which sells better than all other products ○ *top-selling brands of toothpaste*

tort /tɔːt/ *noun* harm done to a person or property which can be the basis of a civil lawsuit

total /ˈtoʊt(ə)l/ *adjective* complete, or with everything added together ○ *The total amount owed is now $1000.* ○ *The company has total assets of over $1bn.* ○ *The total cost was much more than expected.* ○ *Total expenditure on publicity is twice that of last year.* ○ *Our total income from exports rose last year.* □ **the cargo was written off as a total loss** the cargo was so badly damaged that the insurers said it had no value ∎ *noun* an amount which is complete, with everything added up ○ *The total of the charges comes to more than $1,000.* ∎ *verb* to add up to ○ *costs totaling more than $25,000* (NOTE: **totaling – totaled**. The U.S. spelling is **totaling – totaled**.)

total cost of ownership /ˌtoʊt(ə)l kɒst əv ˈoʊnəʃɪp/ *noun* a systematic method of calculating the total cost of buying and using a product or service. It takes into account not only the purchase price of an item but also related costs such as ordering, delivery, subsequent use and maintenance, supplier costs, and after-delivery costs.

total invoice value /ˌtoʊt(ə)l ˈɪnvɔɪs ˌvælju/ *noun* the total amount on an invoice, including transportation, sales tax, etc.

total loss control /ˌtoʊt(ə)l lɒs kən ˈtroʊl/ *noun* an approach to risk management that involves the implementation of safety procedures to minimize the effects of a total or partial loss of an organization's physical assets or its employees on its performance

totally /ˈtoʊt(ə)li/ *adverb* completely ○ *The factory was totally destroyed in the fire.* ○ *The cargo was totally ruined by water.*

total quality management /ˌtoʊt(ə)l ˌkwɒləti ˈmænɪdʒmənt/ *noun* a management style which demands commitment to maintain and improve quality throughout the work force (with control of systems, quality, inspection of working practices, etc.). Abbreviation **TQM**

total systems approach /ˌtoʊt(ə)l ˈsɪstəmz əˌproʊtʃ/ *noun* a way of organizing a large company, in which the systems in each section are all seen as part of the total corporate system

tourism /'tʊrɪz(ə)m/ *noun* the business of providing travel, hotel rooms, food, entertainment, etc., for tourists

tourist /'tʊrɪst/ *noun* a person who goes on vacation to visit places away from home

tourist bureau /'tʊrɪst ,bjʊroʊ/ *noun* an office which gives information to tourists about the place where it is situated

tourist class /'tʊrɪst klæs/ *noun* a lower quality or less expensive way of traveling ○ *He always travels first class, because he says tourist class is too uncomfortable.*

tourist information /,tʊrɪst ,ɪnfə'meɪʃ(ə)n/ *noun* information for tourists

tourist season /'tʊrɪst ,siz(ə)n/ *noun* a period when there are many people on vacation

tourist visa /'tʊrɪst ,vizə/ *noun* a visa which allows a person to visit a country for a short time on vacation

tour operator /'tʊər ,ɑpəreɪtər/ *noun* a person or company which organizes tours

tout /taʊt/ *noun* a person who sells tickets (to games or shows) for more than the price printed on them ■ *verb* **1.** □ **to tout for custom** to try to attract customers **2.** to make extravagant publicity for a product

TQM *abbreviation* total quality management

trace /treɪs/ *noun* a very small amount ○ *There was a trace of powder on his coat.* ○ *She showed no trace of anger.* ■ *verb* **1.** to find where someone or something is ○ *we couldn't trace the order* **2.** to copy a drawing, etc., by placing a sheet of transparent paper over it and drawing on it ○ *she traced the map*

tracing paper /'treɪsɪŋ ,peɪpər/ *noun* transparent paper for copying drawings, etc. ○ *This is a copy I made on tracing paper.*

track /træk/ *noun* □ **to keep track of** to keep an account, to keep yourself informed about ○ *I like to keep track of new developments in computer technology.* □ **to lose track of someone or something** not to know where someone or something is ○ *We lost track of our rep in Turkey.* ■ *verb* to follow someone or something; to follow how something develops, such as one of the stock market indices ○ *This fund tracks the Footsie Index.*

"…tracking the stock market is a good way of providing for the long term, if you're prepared to ride the ups and downs" [*Investors Chronicle*]

tracker fund /'trækə fʌnd/ *noun* a fund which tracks one of the stock market indices, such as the FTSE

track record /'træk ,rekɔrd/ *noun* the success or failure of a company or salesperson in the past ○ *He has a good track record as a secondhand car salesman.* ○ *The company has no track record in the computer market.* ○ *We are looking for someone with a track record in the computer market.*

tractor-trailer /,træktər 'treɪlər/ *noun* a large truck for carrying heavy loads and made up of two parts, the first pulling the second

trade /treɪd/ *noun* **1.** the business of buying and selling □ **to do a good trade in a range of products** to sell a large number of a range of products **2.** □ **to impose trade barriers on** to restrict the import of some goods by charging high duty **3.** a particular type of business, or people or companies dealing in the same type of product ○ *He's in the used car trade.* ○ *She's very well known in the clothing trade.* ■ *verb* to buy and sell, to carry on a business ○ *We trade with all the countries of the EU.* ○ *She trades on the Stock Exchange.* ○ *The company has stopped trading.* ○ *The company trades under the name "Eeziphitt".*

trade in *phrasal verb* **1.** to buy and sell specific items ○ *The company trades in imported goods.* ○ *They trade in French wine.* **2.** to give in an old item as part of the payment for a new one ○ *The chairman traded in his old Mercedes for a new model.*

trade agreement /'treɪd ə,grimənt/ *noun* an international agreement between countries over general terms of trade

trade association /'treɪd əsoʊsi,eɪʃ(ə)n/ *noun* a group which links together companies in the same trade

trade balance /treɪd 'bæləns/ *noun* same as **balance of trade**

trade barrier /'treɪd ,bæriər/ *noun* a limitation imposed by a government on the free exchange of goods between countries. Also called **import restriction** (NOTE:

NTBs, safety standards, and tariffs are typical trade barriers.)

trade bill /'treɪd bɪl/ *noun* a bill of exchange between two companies who are trading partners. It is issued by one company and endorsed by the other.

trade bureau /'treɪd ˌbjʊroʊ/ *noun* an office which specializes in commercial inquiries

trade counter /'treɪd ˌkaʊntər/ *noun* a store in a factory or warehouse where goods are sold to retailers

trade creditors /'treɪd ˌkredɪtəz/ *plural noun* companies which are owed money by a company. The amount owed to trade creditors is shown in the annual accounts.

trade cycle /'treɪd ˌsaɪk(ə)l/ *noun* a period during which trade expands, then slows down, then expands again

trade debtor /'treɪd ˌdetər/ *noun* a debtor who owes money to a company in the normal course of that company's trading

trade deficit /'treɪd ˌdefɪsɪt/ *noun* the difference in value between a country's low exports and higher imports. Also called **balance of payments deficit**, **trade gap**

trade description /ˌtreɪd dɪ'skrɪpʃən/ *noun* a description of a product to attract customers

Trade Descriptions Act /ˌtreɪd dɪ'skrɪpʃənz ækt/ *noun* an act which limits the way in which products can be described so as to protect customers from wrong descriptions made by manufacturers

trade directory /'treɪd daɪˌrekt(ə)ri/ *noun* a book which lists all the businesses and businesspeople in a town

trade discount /treɪd 'dɪskaʊnt/ *noun* a reduction in price given to a customer in the same trade

trade fair /'treɪd fer/ *noun* a large exhibition and meeting for advertising and selling a specific type of product ○ *There are two trade fairs running in Atlanta at the same time – the carpet manufacturers' and the cell phone companies'.*

trade figures /'treɪd ˌfɪgərz/ *noun* government statistics showing the value of a country's trade with other countries

trade gap /'treɪd gæp/ *noun* same as **trade deficit**

trade-in /'treɪd ɪn/ *noun* an old item, e.g., a car or washing machine, given as part of the payment for a new one ○ *She bought a new car and gave her old one as a trade-in.*

trade-in allowance /'treɪd ɪn ə ˌlaʊəns/ *noun* an amount allowed by the seller for an old item being traded in for a new one

trade journal /'treɪd ˌdʒɜrn(ə)l/ *noun* a magazine or newspaper produced for people and companies in a certain trade

trade magazine /'treɪd ˌmægəzin/ *noun* a magazine aimed at working people in a specific industry

trademark /'treɪdmɑrk/, **trade name** /'treɪd neɪm/ *noun* same as **registered trademark**

trade mission /'treɪd ˌmɪʃ(ə)n/ *noun* a visit by a group of businesspeople to discuss trade ○ *He led a trade mission to China.*

tradeoff /'treɪd ɔf/ *noun* an act of exchanging one thing for another as part of a business deal (NOTE: The plural is **tradeoffs**.)

trade paper /ˌtreɪd 'peɪpər/ *noun* a newspaper aimed at people working in a specific industry

trade practices /'treɪd ˌpræktɪsɪz/ *plural noun* same as **industrial practices**

trade press /'treɪd pres/ *noun* all magazines produced for people working in a certain trade

trade price /'treɪd praɪs/ *noun* a special wholesale price paid by a retailer to the manufacturer or wholesaler

trader /'treɪdər/ *noun* **1.** a person who does business **2.** a person who buys or sells stocks, bonds, and options

trade secret /ˌtreɪd 'sikrət/ *noun* information (especially about manufacturing) which a company has and will not give to other companies

tradesman /'treɪdzmən/ *noun* **1.** a storekeeper **2.** a skilled craftsman (NOTE: [all senses] The plural is **tradesmen**.)

tradespeople /'treɪdzˌpip(ə)l/ *plural noun* storekeepers

trade surplus /'treɪd ˌsɜrpləs/ *noun* the difference in value between a country's high exports and lower imports

"Brazil's trade surplus is vulnerable both to a slowdown in the American economy and a pick-up in its own" [*Economist*]

trade terms /'treɪd tɜrmz/ *plural noun* a special discount for people in the same trade

trade union /ˌtreɪd 'junjən/, **trades union** /ˌtreɪdz 'junjən/ *noun U.K.* same as **labor union**

trade-weighted index /treɪd ˌweɪtɪd 'ɪndeks/ *noun* an index of the value of a currency calculated against a basket of currencies

trading /'treɪdɪŋ/ *noun* **1.** the business of buying and selling **2.** an area of a brokerage firm where dealing in securities is carried out by phone, using monitors to display current prices and stock exchange transactions

trading account /'treɪdɪŋ əˌkaʊnt/ *noun* an account of a company's gross profit

trading area /'treɪdɪŋ ˌeriə/ *noun* a group of countries which trade with each other

trading bloc /'treɪdɪŋ blɑk/ *noun* a group of countries which trade with each other on special terms

trading company /'treɪdɪŋ ˌkʌmp(ə)ni/ *noun* a company which specializes in buying and selling goods

trading estate /'treɪdɪŋ ɪˌsteɪt/ *noun* an area of land near a town specially for building factories and warehouses

trading floor /'treɪdɪŋ flɔr/ *noun* same as **dealing floor**

trading loss /ˌtreɪdɪŋ 'lɔs/ *noun* a situation where a company's receipts are less than its expenditure

trading partner /'treɪdɪŋ ˌpɑrtnər/ *noun* a company or country which trades with another

trading profit /'treɪdɪŋ ˌprɑfɪt/ *noun* a result where the company' receipts are higher than its expenditure

trading session /'treɪdɪŋ ˌseʃ(ə)n/ *noun* one period (usually a day) during which trading takes place on a stock exchange

trading stamp /'treɪdɪŋ stæmp/ *noun* a special stamp given away by a store, which the customer can collect and exchange later for free goods

traffic /'træfɪk/ *noun* **1.** the movement of cars, trucks, trains or planes; movement of people or goods in vehicles ○ *there is an increase in commuter traffic* or *goods traffic on the motorway* ○ *Passenger traffic on the commuter lines has decreased during the summer.* **2.** an illegal trade ○ *drugs traffic* or *traffic in drugs* ■ *verb* to deal illegally ○ *they are trafficking in drugs* (NOTE: **trafficking – trafficked**)

trailor-tractor /ɑrˌtɪkjʊleɪtɪd 'lɑri/ *noun* a large truck formed of two parts, the second pulled by the first

train /treɪn/ *verb* **1.** to teach someone to do something ○ *She trained as an accountant.* ○ *The company has appointed a trained lawyer as its managing director.* **2.** to learn how to do something

trainee /treɪ'ni/ *noun* a person who is learning how to do something ○ *We take five graduates as trainees each year.* ○ *Office staff with leadership potential are selected for courses as trainee managers.* ○ *We employ an additional trainee accountant at peak periods.*

traineeship /treɪ'niʃɪp/ *noun* a post as a trainee

training /'treɪnɪŋ/ *noun* the process of being taught how to do something ○ *There is a ten-week training period for new staff.* ○ *The store is closed for staff training.* ○ *After six months' training he thought of himself as a professional salesman.*

training board /'treɪnɪŋ bɔrd/ *noun* a government organization set up by each industry to provide and coordinate training for that industry

training levy /'treɪnɪŋ ˌlevi/ *noun* a tax to be paid by companies to fund the government's training schemes

training officer /'treɪnɪŋ ˌɔfɪsər/ *noun* a person who deals with the training of staff in a company

training unit /'treɪnɪŋ ˌjunɪt/ *noun* a special group of teachers who organize training for companies

tranche /trænʃ/ *noun* one of a series of installments, used when referring to loans to companies, government securities which are issued over a period of time, or money withdrawn by a country from the IMF ○ *The second tranche of interest on the loan is now due for payment.*

transact /træn'zækt/ *verb* □ **to transact business** to carry out a piece of business

transaction /træn'zækʃən/ *noun* an instance of doing business, e.g., a purchase in a store or a withdrawal of money from savings □ **a transaction on the Stock Exchange** a purchase or sale of stock on the Stock Exchange ○ *The paper publishes a daily list of Stock Exchange transactions.* □ **fraudulent transaction** a transaction which aims to cheat someone

transactional analysis /træn ˌzækʃ(ə)nəl ə'næləsɪs/ *noun* a psychological theory, sometimes used in education and training, that describes patterns of feeling, thought, and behavior that influence how individuals interact with, communicate with, and relate to each other ○ *Transactional analysis sessions have helped many of our managers deal more effectively with subordinates.*

transfer /'trænsfɜr/ *noun* an act of moving an employee to another job in the same organization ○ *She applied for a transfer to our branch in British Columbia.* ∎ *verb* **1.** to move someone or something to a different place, or to move someone to another job in the same organization ○ *The accountant was transferred to our Canadian branch.* ○ *He transferred his shares to a family trust.* ○ *She transferred her money to a deposit account.* **2.** to move an employee to another job in the same organization **3.** to change from one type of travel to another ○ *When you get to Newark airport, you have to transfer onto an internal flight.* (NOTE: **transferring – transferred**)

transferable /træns'fɜrəb(ə)l/ *adjective* possible to pass to someone else □ **the season ticket is not transferable** the ticket cannot be given or lent to someone else to use

transfer of property /ˌtrænsfɜr əv 'prɑpəti/, **transfer of shares** /ˌtrænsfɜr əv 'ʃerz/ *noun* the act of moving the ownership of property or shares of stock from one person to another

Transfer of Undertakings (Protection of Employment) full form of **TUPE**

transfer passenger /'trænsfɜr ˌpæsɪndʒər/ *noun* a traveler who is changing from one aircraft or train or bus to another, or to another form of transportation

transfer pricing /'trænsfɜr ˌpraɪsɪŋ/ *noun* prices used in a large organization for selling goods or services between departments in the same organization; also used in multinational corporations to transfer transactions from one country to another to avoid paying tax

transferred charge call /træns,fɜrd 'tʃɑrdʒ ˌkɔl/ *noun* a phone call where the person receiving the call agrees to pay for it

transformative potential /træns ˌfɔrmətɪv pə'tenʃ(ə)l/ *noun* the ability of something such as information technology to change the economy, society and business

tranship /træn'ʃɪp/ *verb* another spelling of **transship**

transit /'trænsɪt/ *noun* the movement of passengers or goods on the way to a destination ○ *Some of the goods were damaged in transit.* □ **goods in transit** goods being transported from warehouse to customer

transit visa /'trænsɪt ˌvizə/ *noun* a document which allows someone to spend a short time in one country while traveling to another country

translate /træns'leɪt/ *verb* **1.** to put something which is said or written in one language into another language ○ *He asked his secretary to translate the letter from the German agent.* ○ *We have had the contract translated from French into Japanese.* **2.** to change something into another form

translation /træns'leɪʃ(ə)n/ *noun* something which has been translated ○ *She passed the translation of the letter to the accounts department.*

translation bureau /ˌtrænsˈleɪʃ(ə)n ˌbjʊroʊ/ *noun* an office which translates documents for companies

translator /træns'leɪtə/ *noun* a person who translates

transmission /trænz'mɪʃ(ə)n/ *noun* sending ○ *transmission of a message*

transmit /trænz'mɪt/ *verb* to send (a message) (NOTE: **transmitting – transmitted**)

transnational /trænz'næʃ(ə)nəl/ *noun* same as **multinational**

transnational corporation /ˌtrænz ˌnæʃ(ə)nəl ˌkɔrpəˈreɪʃ(ə)n/ *noun* a large company which operates in various countries

transport /'trænspɔːt/ *noun U.K.* same as **transportation** ■ *verb* /træns'pɔːt/ to move goods or people from one place to another in a vehicle ○ *The company transports millions of tons of goods by rail each year.* ○ *The visitors will be transported to the factory by air or by helicopter or by taxi.*

transportable /træns'pɔːtəb(ə)l/ *adjective* which can be moved

transportation /ˌtrænspər'teɪʃ(ə)n/ *noun* **1.** the moving of goods or people from one place to another ○ *air transportation* or *transportation by air* ○ *rail transportation* or *transportation by rail* ○ *road transportation* or *transportation by road* ○ *the public transportation services into Boston* ○ *What means of transportation will you use to get to the factory?* **2.** vehicles used to move goods or people from one place to another ○ *The company will provide transportation to the airport.*

transporter /træns'pɔːtər/ *noun* a company which transports goods

Transports Internationaux Routiers /ˌtrɒnspɔːz ˌæntenæsjə'nʊ ˌrutieɪ/ *noun* a system of international documents which allows dutiable goods to cross several European countries by road without paying duty until they reach their final destination. Abbreviation **TIR**

transship /træns'ʃɪp/, **tranship** *verb* to move cargo from one ship to another. Another spelling of **tranship**

travel /'træv(ə)l/ *noun* the moving of people from one place to another or from one country to another ○ *Overseas travel is a very important part of the job.* ■ *verb* **1.** to move from one place to another or from one country to another ○ *He travels to the States on business twice a year.* ○ *In her new job, she has to travel abroad at least ten times a year.* **2.** to go from one place to another, showing a company's goods to buyers and taking orders from them ○ *She travels throughout the Midwest for an insurance company.* (NOTE: **traveling – traveled**)

travel agency /'træv(ə)l ˌeɪdʒənsi/ *noun* an office which arranges travel for customers

travel agent /'træv(ə)l ˌeɪdʒənt/ *noun* a person in charge of a travel agency

travel allowance /'træv(ə)l əˌlaʊəns/ *noun* money which an employee is allowed to spend on traveling

traveler /'træv(ə)lər/ *noun* a person who travels (NOTE: The U.K. spelling is **traveller.**)

traveler's checks /'træv(ə)ləz tʃeks/ *plural noun* checks bought by a traveler which can be cashed in a foreign country

travel expenses /'træv(ə)l ɪk ˌspensɪz/ *plural noun* money spent on traveling and hotels for business purposes

traveling expenses /'træv(ə)lɪŋ ek ˌspensɪz/ *plural noun* money spent on traveling and hotels for business purposes

travel magazine /'træv(ə)l ˌmægəzin/ *noun* a magazine with articles on vacations and travel

travel organization /'træv(ə)l ˌɔːgənaɪzeɪʃ(ə)n/ *noun* a body representing companies in the travel business

travel trade /'træv(ə)l treɪd/ *noun* all businesses which organize travel for people

treasurer /'treʒərər/ *noun* **1.** a person who looks after the money or finances of a club or society, etc. **2.** the main financial officer of a company **3.** (*in Australia*) the finance minister in a government

Treasury /'treʒəri/ *noun* **1.** a government department which deals with the country's finance (NOTE: The term is used in both the U.K. and the U.S.; in most other countries this department is called the **Ministry of Finance.**) **2.** a Treasury bond, bill, or note issued by the U.S. Treasury

Treasury bill /'treʒəri bɪl/ *noun* a short-term financial instrument which does not give any interest and is sold by the government at a discount through the central bank. In the U.K., their term varies from three to six months, in the U.S., they are for 91 or 182 days, or for 52 weeks. Also called **T-bill**

Treasury bond /'treʒəri bɒnd/ *noun* a long-term bond issued by the British or U.S. government. Also called **T-bond**

Treasury note /'treʒəri nəʊt/ *noun* a medium-term bond issued by the U.S. government

Treasury Secretary /'treʒəri ˌsekrət(ə)ri/ *noun* same as **Secretary of the Treasury**

treasury tag /ˈtreʒəri tæg/ *noun* a short piece of string with two metal pieces at the ends, which are put through holes in sheets of paper or cards to hold them together

treaty /ˈtriːti/ *noun* **1.** an agreement between countries ○ *The two countries signed a commercial treaty.* **2.** an agreement between individual persons

treble /ˈtreb(ə)l/ *verb* to increase three times, or to make something three times larger ○ *The company's borrowings have trebled.* ○ *The acquisition of the chain of stores has trebled the group's turnover.* ■ *adverb* three times ○ *Our borrowings are treble what they were last year.*

trend /trend/ *noun* a general way in which things are developing ○ *a downward trend in investment* ○ *There is a trend away from old-established food stores.* ○ *The report points to inflationary trends in the economy.* ○ *We notice a general trend toward selling to the student market.* ○ *We have noticed an upward trend in sales.*

trial /ˈtraɪəl/ *noun* **1.** a court case to judge a person accused of a crime ○ *He is on trial* or *is standing trial for embezzlement.* **2.** a test to see if something is good □ **on trial** in the process of being tested ○ *The product is on trial in our laboratories.* ■ *verb* *U.K.* to test a product to see how good it is (NOTE: **trialling – trialled**)

trial balance /ˈtraɪəl ˌbæləns/ *noun* the draft calculation of debits and credits to see if they balance

trial period /ˌtraɪəl ˈpɪriəd/ *noun* the time when a customer can test a product before buying it

trial sample /ˈtraɪəl ˌsæmpəl/ *noun* a small piece of a product used for testing

tribunal /traɪˈbjuːn(ə)l/ *noun* an official court which examines special problems and makes judgments

trigger /ˈtrɪɡər/ *noun* a thing which starts a process ■ *verb* to start a process

"…the recovery is led by significant declines in short-term interest rates, which are forecast to be roughly 250 basis points below their previous peak. This should trigger a rebound in the housing markets and consumer spending on durables" [*Toronto Globe & Mail*]

trigger point /ˈtrɪɡər pɔɪnt/ *noun* a point in acquiring stock in a company where the purchaser has to declare an interest or to take certain action

trillion /ˈtrɪljən/ *noun* one million millions (NOTE: In the U.K., trillion now has the same meaning as in the U.S.; formerly in U.K. English it meant one million million millions, and it is still sometimes used with this meaning; see also the note at **billion**.)

"…if land is assessed at roughly half its current market value, the new tax could yield up to ¥10 trillion annually" [*Far Eastern Economic Review*]

"…behind the decline was a 6.1% fall in exports to ¥47.55 trillion, the second year of falls. Automobiles and steel were among categories showing particularly conspicuous drops" [*Nikkei Weekly*]

"…the London Stock Exchange said that the value of domestic U.K. equities traded during the year was £1.4066 trillion, more than the capitalization of the entire London market and an increase of 36 per cent compared with previous year's total of £1.037 trillion" [*Times*]

trip /trɪp/ *noun* a journey

triple /ˈtrɪp(ə)l/ *verb* to become three times larger, or to multiply something three times ○ *The company's debts tripled in twelve months.* ○ *The acquisition of the chain of stores has tripled the group's turnover.* ■ *adjective* three times as much ○ *The cost of airfreighting the goods is triple their manufacturing cost.*

triplicate /ˈtrɪplɪkət/ *noun* □ **in triplicate** with an original and two copies ○ *The invoices are printed in triplicate.* ○ *The application form should be completed in triplicate.* □ **invoicing in triplicate** the preparing of three copies of invoices

trojan /ˈtroʊdʒən/ *noun* a computer program containing a hidden function that causes damage to other programs while appearing to perform a valid function

trouble /ˈtrʌb(ə)l/ *noun* a problem or difficult situation ○ *we are having some computer trouble* or *some trouble with the computer* ○ *we are having some union trouble* or *some trouble with the union* ○ *There was some trouble in the warehouse after the manager was fired.*

troubleshooter /ˈtrʌb(ə)lʃuːtər/ *noun* a person whose job is to solve problems in a company ○ *They brought in a troubleshooter to try to sort out the management problems.*

trough /trɔf/ *noun* a low point in the economic cycle

troy ounce /ˌtrɔɪ ˈaʊns/ *noun* a measurement of weight (= 31.10 grams) (NOTE: In writing, often shortened to **troy oz.** after figures: **25.2 troy oz.**)

troy weight /ˌtrɔɪ ˈweɪt/ *noun* a system of measurement of weight used for gold and other metals, such as silver and platinum

truck /trʌk/ *noun* 1. a large motor vehicle for carrying goods 2. *U.K.* an open railroad car for carrying goods

trucker /ˈtrʌkər/ *noun* a person who drives a truck

trucking /ˈtrʌkɪŋ/ *noun* the carrying of goods in trucks ○ *a trucking firm*

trucking company /ˈtrʌkɪŋ ˌkʌmp(ə)ni/ *noun* a company that transports goods by road

truckload /ˈtrʌkloʊd/ *noun* a quantity of goods that fills a truck

true /tru/ *adjective* correct or accurate

true and fair view /ˌtru ən fer ˈvju/ *noun* a correct statement of a company's financial position as shown in its accounts and confirmed by the auditors

Trueblood Report /ˈtrublʌb rɪˌpɔrt/ *noun* a report, "Objectives of Financial Statements," published by the American Institute of Certified Public Accountants in 1971, that recommended a conceptual framework for financial accounting and led to the Statements of Financial Accounting Concepts issued by the Financial Accounting Standards Board in the United States

true copy /ˌtru ˈkɑpi/ *noun* an exact copy ○ *I certify that this is a true copy.* ○ *It is certified as a true copy.*

trunk call /ˈtrʌŋk kɔl/ *noun* a call to a number in a different zone or area

trust /trʌst/ *noun* 1. the fact of being confident that something is correct or will work □ **we took his statement on trust** we accepted his statement without examining it to see if it was correct 2. a legal arrangement to pass goods, money or valuables to someone who will look after them well ○ *She left his property in trust for her grandchildren.* 3. the management of money or property for someone ○ *They set up a family trust for their grandchildren.* 4. a small group of companies which control the supply of a product ■ *verb* □ **to trust someone with something** to give something to someone to look after ○ *Can he be trusted with all that cash?*

trustbusting /ˈtrʌstbʌstɪŋ/ *noun* the breaking up of trusts to encourage competition

trust company /ˈtrʌst ˌkʌmp(ə)ni/ *noun* an organization which supervises the financial affairs of private trusts, executes wills, and acts as a bank to a limited number of customers

trust deed /ˈtrʌst did/ *noun* a document which sets out the details of a private trust

trustee /trʌˈsti/ *noun* a person who has charge of money in trust ○ *the trustees of the pension fund*

trust fund /ˈtrʌst fʌnd/ *noun* assets such as money, securities or property held in trust for someone

trustworthy /ˈtrʌstwɜrði/ *adjective* (person) who can be trusted ○ *our cashiers are completely trustworthy*

Truth in Lending Act /ˌtruθ ɪn ˈlendɪŋ ækt/ *noun* a U.S. Act of 1969, which requires lenders to state the full terms of their interest rates to borrowers

TUC *abbreviation* Trades Union Congress

tune /tun/ *noun* □ **the bank is backing him to the tune of $10,000** the bank is helping him with a loan of $10,000

TUPE *noun* the legislation that protects employees' rights and contract terms when one company is bought by another. Full form **Transfer of Undertakings (Protection of Employment)**

turbulence /ˈtɜrbjʊləns/ *noun* rapid and unexpected changes within an organization or in external conditions, which affect the organization's performance

"Heinz's location insulates the company from much of the turbulence affecting the IT labor market in other parts of the country." [*InformationWeek*]

turkey /ˈtɜrki/ *noun* a bad investment, an investment which has turned out to be worthless (*informal*)

turn /tɜrn/ *noun* 1. a movement in a circle, or a change of direction 2. a profit or commission ○ *She makes a turn on everything he sells.* ■ *verb* to change direction, to go round in a circle

turn around *phrasal verb* to make a company change from making a loss to becoming profitable □ **they turned the company round in less than a year** they made the company profitable in less than a year

turn down *phrasal verb* to refuse something ○ *The bank turned down their request for a loan.* ○ *The application for a license was turned down.* ○ *He turned down the job he was offered.* ○ *The board turned down the proposal.*

turn out *phrasal verb* to produce ○ *The factory turns out fifty units per day.*

turn over *phrasal verb* **1.** to have a specific amount of sales ○ *We turn over $2,000 a week.* **2.** to pass something to someone ○ *She turned over the documents to the lawyer.* (NOTE: In this meaning, the usual U.K. term is **hand over**.)

turnaround /ˈtɜrnəˌraʊnd/ *noun* **1.** the value of goods sold during a year divided by the average value of goods held in stock (NOTE: The U.K. term is **turnround**.) **2.** the action of emptying a ship, plane, etc., and getting it ready for another commercial trip (NOTE: The U.K. term is **turnround**.) **3.** the act of making a company profitable again (NOTE: The U.K. term is **turnround**.) **4.** processing orders and sending out the goods

turnaround time /ˈtɜrnəraʊnd ˌtaɪm/ *noun* the time taken from receiving an order and supplying the goods

turnkey contract /ˈtɜrnki ˌkɑntrækt/ *noun* an agreement by which a contractor undertakes to design, construct, and manage something and only hand it over to the client when it is in a state where it is ready for immediate use

turnkey operation /ˈtɜrnki ɑpəˌreɪʃ(ə)n/ *noun* a deal where a company takes all responsibility for constructing, fitting and staffing a building (such as a school, hospital or factory) so that it is completely ready for the purchaser to take over

turnover /ˈtɜrnoʊvər/ *noun* **1.** the amount of sales of goods or services by a company ○ *The company's turnover has increased by 235%.* ○ *We based our calculations on the forecast turnover.* **2.** the number of times something is used or sold in a period, usually one year, expressed as a percentage of a total

turnover of labor /ˈtɜrnoʊvər əv ˈleɪbər/ *noun* same as **labor turnover**

turnover tax /ˈtɜrnoʊvər tæks/ *noun* same as **sales tax**

TV spot /ˌti ˈvi ˌspɑt/ *noun* a short period on TV which is used for commercials ○ *We are running a series of TV spots over the next three weeks.*

TV station /ˌti ˌvi ˈsteɪʃ(ə)n/ *noun* a building where TV or radio programs are produced

24–7 /ˌtwenti fɔr ˈsev(ə)n/, **24/7** *adverb* 24 hours a day, 7 days a week

24/7 /ˌtwenti fɔr ˈsev(ə)n/ *adverb* twenty-four hours a day, every day of the week (NOTE: Businesses often advertise themselves as being "open 24/7.")

24-hour banking /ˌtwentifɔr aʊr ˈbæŋkɪn/ *noun* a banking service provided during the whole day (e.g., by cash dispensers in the street and online services)

COMMENT: 24-hour trading is now possible because of instant communication to Stock Exchanges in different time zones; the Tokyo Stock Exchange closes about two hours before the London Stock Exchange opens; the New York Stock Exchange opens at the same time as the London one closes

24-hour service /ˌtwenti fɔr aʊr ˈsɜrvɪs/ *noun* help which is available for the whole day

two-bin system /ˌtu bɪn ˈsɪstəm/ *noun* a warehousing system, where the first bin contains the current working stock, and the second bin has the backup stock

two-part /ˌtu ˈpɑrt/ *adjective* paper (for computers or typewriters) with a top sheet for the original and a second sheet for a copy ○ *two-part invoices* ○ *two-part stationery*

two-way trade /ˌtu weɪ ˈtreɪd/ *noun* trade between two countries or partners

tycoon /taɪˈkun/ *noun* an important businessman

typewriter /ˈtaɪpraɪtər/ *noun* a machine which prints letters or figures on a piece of paper when keys are pressed ○ *portable typewriter* ○ *electronic typewriter*

typewritten /ˈtaɪprɪt(ə)n/ *adjective* written on a computer keyboard, not handwritten ○ *He sent in a typewritten job application.*

typing /'taɪpɪŋ/ *noun* the act of keying words on a keyboard □ **copy typing** typing documents from handwritten originals, not from dictation

typing error /'taɪpɪŋ ˌerər/ *noun* a mistake made when typing ○ *The secretary must have made a typing error.*

typist /'taɪpɪst/ *noun* a person whose job is to write letters using a computer keyboard ○ *The HR department needs more typists to deal with all the correspondence.* □ **copy typist** person who types documents from handwritten originals not from dictation

U

ultimate /'ʌltɪmət/ *adjective* last or final

ultimate consumer /ˌʌltɪmət kən'sumər/ *noun* the person who actually uses the product

ultimately /'ʌltɪmətli/ *adverb* in the end ○ *Ultimately, the management had to agree to the demands of the union.*

ultimatum /ˌʌltɪ'meɪtəm/ *noun* a statement to someone that unless they do something within a period of time, action will be taken against them ○ *The union officials argued among themselves over the best way to deal with the ultimatum from the management.* (NOTE: The plural is **ultimatums** or **ultimata**.)

umbrella organization /ʌm'brelə ˌɔrɡənaɪzeɪʃ(ə)n/ *noun* a large organization which includes several smaller ones

UN *abbreviation* United Nations

unacceptable /ˌʌnək'septəb(ə)l/ *adjective* which cannot be accepted ○ *The terms of the contract are quite unacceptable.*

unaccounted for /ˌʌnə'kaʊntɪd fɔr/ *adjective* lost without any explanation ○ *Several thousand units are unaccounted for in the stocktaking.*

unanimous /ju'nænɪməs/ *adjective* where everyone agrees or votes in the same way ○ *There was a unanimous vote against the proposal.* ○ *They reached unanimous agreement.*

unanimously /ju'nænɪməsli/ *adverb* with everyone agreeing ○ *The proposals were adopted unanimously.*

unaudited /ʌn'ɔdɪtɪd/ *adjective* having not been audited ○ *unaudited accounts*

unauthorized /ʌn'ɔθəraɪzd/ *adjective* not permitted ○ *unauthorized access to the company's records* ○ *unauthorized expenditure* ○ *No unauthorized persons are allowed into the laboratory.*

unavailability /ˌʌnəveɪlə'bɪləti/ *noun* the fact of not being available ○ *The unavailability of any reliable sales data makes forecasting difficult.*

unavailable /ˌʌnə'veɪləb(ə)l/ *adjective* not available ○ *The following items on your order are temporarily unavailable.*

unavoidable /ˌʌnə'vɔɪdəb(ə)l/ *adjective* which cannot be avoided ○ *Flights are subject to unavoidable delays.*

unbalanced /ʌn'bælənst/ *adjective* referring to a budget which does not balance or which is in deficit

unbanked /ʌn'bæŋkt/ *adjective* **1.** referring to a person who does not have a bank account **2.** referring to a check which has not been deposited in a bank account

unbundling /ʌn'bʌnd(ə)lɪŋ/ *noun* **1.** the process of separating companies from a conglomerate (the companies were independent in the past, and have been acquired by the conglomerate over a period of time) **2.** the practice of charging separately for each different service provided

uncalled /ʌn'kɔld/ *adjective* referring to capital which a company is authorized to raise and has been issued but for which payment has not yet been requested

uncashed /ʌn'kæʃt/ *adjective* having not been cashed ○ *uncashed checks*

unclaimed baggage /ˌʌnkleɪmd 'bæɡɪdʒ/ *noun* cases which have been left with someone and have not been claimed by their owners ○ *unclaimed property or unclaimed baggage will be sold by auction after six months*

uncollected /ˌʌnkə'lektɪd/ *adjective* which has not been collected ○ *uncollected subscriptions* ○ *uncollected taxes*

unconditional /ˌʌnkən'dɪʃ(ə)nəl/ *adjective* with no conditions or provisions attached ○ *unconditional acceptance of the offer by the board*

unconditionally /ˌʌnkən'dɪʃ(ə)n(ə)li/ *adverb* without imposing any conditions ○ *The offer was accepted unconditionally by the labor union.*

unconstitutional /ˌʌnkɑnstɪ 'tjuːʃ(ə)n(ə)l/ *adjective* not allowed by the rules of an organization or by the laws of a country ○ *The chairman ruled that the meeting was unconstitutional.*

uncontrollable /ˌʌnkən'trəʊləb(ə)l/ *adjective* not possible to control ○ *uncontrollable inflation*

uncrossed check /ˌʌnkrɒst 'tʃek/ *noun U.K.* a check which does not have two lines across it, and can be cashed anywhere

undated /ʌn'deɪtɪd/ *adjective* with no date indicated or written ○ *She tried to cash an undated check.*

undated bond /ʌnˌdeɪtɪd 'bɒnd/ *noun* a bond with no maturity date

under /'ʌndər/ *preposition* **1.** lower than or less than ○ *The interest rate is under 10%.* ○ *Under half of the stockholders accepted the offer.* **2.** controlled by, according to ○ *Under the terms of the agreement, the goods should be delivered in October.* ○ *He is acting under rule 23 of the union constitution.*

under- /ʌndər/ *prefix* less important than or lower than

underbid /ˌʌndər'bɪd/ *verb* to bid less than someone (NOTE: **underbidding – underbid**)

underbidder /'ʌndərbɪdər/ *noun* a person who bids less than the person who buys at an auction

undercapitalized /ˌʌndə 'kæpɪtəlaɪzd/ *adjective* without enough capital ○ *The company is severely undercapitalized.*

undercharge /ˌʌndər'tʃɑrdʒ/ *verb* to ask someone for too little money ○ *She undercharged us by $25.*

underclass /'ʌndəˌklɑrs/ *noun* a group of people who are underprivileged in a way that appears to exclude them from mainstream society

undercut /ˌʌndər'kʌt/ *verb* to offer something at a lower price than someone else ○ *They increased their market share by undercutting their competitors.* (NOTE: **undercutting – undercut**)

underdeveloped /ˌʌndərdɪ'veləpt/ *adjective* which has not been developed ○ *Japan is an underdeveloped market for our products.*

underdeveloped countries /ˌʌndərdɪvˌeləpt 'kʌntriz/ *plural noun* countries which are not fully industrialized

underemployed /ˌʌndərɪm'plɔɪd/ *adjective* with not enough work ○ *The staff is underemployed because of the cutback in production.*

underemployed capital /ˌʌndərɪmplɔɪd 'kæpɪt(ə)l/ *noun* capital which is not producing enough interest

underemployment /ˌʌndərɪm 'plɔɪmənt/ *noun* **1.** a situation where workers in a company do not have enough work to do **2.** a situation where there is not enough work for all the workers in a country

underequipped /ˌʌndərɪ'kwɪpt/ *adjective* with not enough equipment

underestimate *noun* /ˌʌndər'estɪmət/ an estimate which is less than the actual figure ○ *The figure of $50,000 in turnover was a considerable underestimate.* ■ *verb* /ˌʌndər'estɪmeɪt/ to think that something is smaller or not as bad as it really is ○ *They underestimated the effects of the strike on their sales.* ○ *He underestimated the amount of time needed to finish the work.*

underlease /'ʌndərlis/ *noun* a lease from a tenant to another tenant

underlying inflation rate /ˌʌndərlaɪɪŋ ɪn'fleɪʃ(ə)n reɪt/ *noun* the basic inflation rate calculated on a series of prices of consumer items, gasoline, gas and electricity, and interest rates

undermanned /ˌʌndər'mænd/ *adjective U.K.* same as **understaffed**

undermanning /ˌʌndər'mænɪŋ/ *noun U.K.* same as **understaffing**

undermentioned /ˌʌndər'menʃ(ə)nd/ *adjective* mentioned lower down in a document ○ *See the undermentioned list of countries to which these terms apply.*

underpaid /ˌʌndər'peɪd/ *adjective* not paid enough ○ *Our staff say that they are underpaid and overworked.*

underperform /ˌʌndərpər'fɔrm/ *verb* □ **to underperform the market** to perform worse than the rest of the market ○

The hotel group has underperformed the sector this year.

underperformance /ˌʌndərpər
'fɔrməns/ *noun* the fact of performing worse than others ○ *The underperformance of the stock has worried investors.*

"Australia has been declining again. Because it has had such a long period of underperfomance, it is now not as vulnerable as other markets" [*Money Observer*]

underrate /ˌʌndər'reɪt/ *verb* to value someone or something less highly than they should be ○ *Do not underrate the strength of the competition in the European market.* ○ *The power of the yen is underrated.*

undersell /ˌʌndər'sel/ *verb* to sell more cheaply than someone ○ *to undersell a competitor* □ **the company is never undersold** no other company sells goods as cheaply as this one

undersigned /ˌʌndər'saɪnd/ *noun* a person who has signed a letter □ **we, the undersigned** we, the people who have signed below

underspend /ˌʌndər'spend/ *verb* to spend less than you should have spent or were allowed to spend □ **he has underspent his budget** he has spent less than was allowed in the budget

understaffed /ˌʌndər'stæft/ *adjective* with not enough staff to do the company's work

understaffing /ˌʌndər'stæfɪŋ/ *noun* a situation of having too few staff than are needed to do the company's work

understand /ˌʌndər'stænd/ *verb* to know or to see what something means (NOTE: **understanding – understood**)

understanding /ˌʌndər'stændɪŋ/ *noun* a private agreement ○ *to come to an understanding about the divisions of the market*

understate /ˌʌndər'steɪt/ *verb* to make something seem less than it really is ○ *The company accounts understate the real profit.*

understudy /'ʌndərstʌdi/ *noun* a person who is learning how to do a job which is currently being done by someone else, so as to be able to take over the job if the present incumbent retires or is ill ○ *They have planned to put understudies into each of the key management posts.* ○ *The production manager made sure his under-*

study could run the factory if called upon to do so. (NOTE: The plural is **understudies**.) ■ *verb* to learn how to do a job by working alongside the present incumbent, so as to be able to take over if he retires or is ill ○ *He is understudying the production manager.* (NOTE: **understudies – understudying – understudied**)

undersubscribed /ˌʌndərsʌb'skraɪbd/ *adjective* referring to a new issue in which not all shares are sold, and part of the issue remains with the underwriters

undertake /ˌʌndər'teɪk/ *verb* **1.** to agree to do something ○ *We asked the research unit to undertake an investigation of the market.* ○ *They have undertaken not to sell into our territory.* (NOTE: **undertaking – undertook – undertaken**) **2.** to carry out ○ *They are undertaking a study on employee reactions to pay restraint.* ○ *We asked the research unit to undertake an investigation of the market.*

undertaking /'ʌndəteɪkɪŋ/ *noun* **1.** a business ○ *He is the CEO of a large commercial undertaking.* **2.** a promise, especially a legally binding one ○ *They have given us a written undertaking not to sell their products in competition with ours.*

under-the-counter sales /ˌʌndər ðə ˌkaʊntə 'seɪlz/ *plural noun* black-market sales

underutilized /ˌʌndə'juːtɪlaɪzd/ *adjective* not used enough

undervaluation /ˌʌndərvæljuˈeɪʃ(ə)n/ *noun* the state of being valued, or the act of valuing something, at less than the true worth

undervalued /ˌʌndər'væljud/ *adjective* not valued highly enough ○ *The dollar is undervalued on the foreign exchanges.* ○ *The properties are undervalued on the company's balance sheet.*

underweight /ˌʌndər'weɪt/ *adjective* not heavy enough □ **the pack is twenty ounces underweight** the pack weighs twenty ounces less than it should

underworked /ˌʌndər'wɜrkt/ *adjective* not given enough work to do ○ *The directors think our staff are overpaid and underworked.*

underwrite /ˌʌndər'raɪt/ *verb* **1.** to accept responsibility for something □ **to underwrite a share issue** to guarantee that a new issue will be sold by agreeing to buy all shares which are not subscribed ○ *The issue was underwritten by three underwriting companies.* **2.** to insure, to cover a risk ○ *to underwrite an insurance policy* **3.** to agree to pay for costs ○ *The government has underwritten the development costs of the project.* (NOTE: **underwriting – underwrote – has underwritten**)

"…under the new program, mortgage brokers are allowed to underwrite mortgages and get a much higher fee" [*Forbes Magazine*]

underwriter /'ʌndəraɪtə/ *noun* a person or company that underwrites a new issue or an insurance policy

underwriting syndicate /'ʌndəraɪtɪŋ ˌsɪndɪkət/ *noun* a group of underwriters who insure a large risk

undischarged bankrupt /ˌʌndɪstʃɑːdʒd 'bæŋkrʌpt/ *noun* a person who has been declared bankrupt and has not been released from that state

undistributable reserves /ˌʌndɪstrɪbjutəb(ə)l rɪ'zɜːvz/ *plural noun* same as **capital reserves**

undistributed profit /ˌʌndɪstrɪbjutɪd 'prɑːfɪt/ *noun* a profit which has not been distributed as dividends to stockholders

unearned income /ˌʌnɜːnd 'ɪnkʌm/ *noun* same as **investment income**

uneconomic /ˌʌnikə'nɑːmɪk/ *adjective* which does not make a commercial profit □ **it is an uneconomic proposition** it will not be commercially profitable

uneconomic rent /ˌʌnikənɑːmɪk 'rent/ *noun* a rent which is not enough to cover costs

unemployed /ˌʌnɪm'plɔɪd/ *adjective* not having any paid work ■ *noun* □ **the unemployed** the people without any jobs

unemployment /ˌʌnɪm'plɔɪmənt/ *noun* the state of not having any work

"…tax advantages directed toward small businesses will help create jobs and reduce the unemployment rate" [*Toronto Star*]

unemployment benefit /ˌʌnɪm'plɔɪmənt ˌbenəfɪt/ *noun* a payment from the government made to someone who is unemployed (NOTE: The U.S. term is **unemployment compensation**.)

unemployment pay /ˌʌnɪm'plɔɪmənt peɪ/ *noun* money given by the government to someone who is unemployed

unemployment rate /ˌʌnɪm'plɔɪmənt reɪt/ *noun* the number of peo-

ple out of work, shown as a percentage of the total number of people available for work. Also called **rate of unemployment**

uneven lot /ˌʌnivən 'lɑːt/ *noun* same as **odd lot**

uneven playing field /ˌʌniv(ə)n 'pleɪɪŋ fild/ *noun* a situation where the competing groups do not compete on the same terms and conditions. Opposite **level playing field**

unfair competition /ˌʌnfer ˌkɑːmpə'tɪʃ(ə)n/ *noun* the practice of trying to do better than another company by using techniques such as importing foreign goods at very low prices or by wrongly criticizing a competitor's products

unfair dismissal /ˌʌnfer dɪs'mɪs(ə)l/ *noun* the act of removing someone from a job for reasons which are not fair

unfulfilled /ˌʌnfʊl'fɪld/ *adjective* (*of an order*) which has not yet been supplied

unfulfilled orders /ˌʌnfʊlfɪld 'ɔːdərz/ *plural noun* orders received in the past and not yet supplied

ungeared /ʌn'ɡɪrd/ *adjective* with no borrowings

ungluing /ʌn'ɡluɪŋ/ *noun* the process of breaking up an established supply chain or group of collaborating organizations by taking control of the shared element or interest that previously kept the partners together

unilateral /ˌjuni'læt(ə)rəl/ *adjective* on one side only or done by one party only ○ *They took a unilateral decision to cancel the contract.*

unilaterally /ˌjuni'læt(ə)rəli/ *adverb* by one party only ○ *The decision was taken to cancel the contract unilaterally.*

uninsured /ˌʌnɪn'ʃʊrd/ *adjective* not insured ○ *his art collection is uninsured* ○ *She was charged with driving while uninsured.*

union /'junjən/ *noun* same as **labor union**

"…the blue-collar unions are the people who stand to lose most in terms of employment growth" [*Sydney Morning Herald*]

union agreement /'junjən əˌɡrimənt/ *noun* an agreement between management and a labor union over wages and conditions of work

union dues /ˌjunjən 'djuz/, **union subscriptions** /'junjən səbˌskrɪpʃənz/

plural noun payment made by workers to belong to a union

unionism /'junjənɪz(ə)m/ *noun* the fact of being a member of a labor union

unionist /'juniənɪst/ *noun* a member of a labor union

unionized /'junjənaɪzd/ *adjective* referring to a company where the members of staff belong to a labor union

"...after three days of tough negotiations, the company reached agreement with its 1,200 unionized workers" [*Toronto Star*]

union officials /ˌjunjən ə'fɪʃ(ə)lz/ *plural noun* paid organizers of a union

union recognition /ˌjunjən ˌrekəg 'nɪʃ(ə)n/ *noun* the act of agreeing that a labor union can act on behalf of staff in a company

unique /ju'nik/ *adjective* unlike anything else

unique selling point /juˌnik 'selɪŋ ˌpɔɪnt/, **unique selling proposition** /ju ˌnik 'selɪŋ ˌprɑpəzɪʃ(ə)n/ *noun* a special quality of a product which makes it different from other goods and is used as a key theme in advertising ○ *A five-year guarantee is a USP for this product.* ○ *What's this product's unique selling proposition?* Abbreviation **USP**

unissued capital /ˌʌnɪʃud 'kæpɪt(ə)l/ *noun* capital which a company is authorized to issue but has not issued as shares

unit /'junɪt/ *noun* **1.** a single product for sale **2.** a separate piece of equipment or furniture **3.** a group of people set up for a special purpose **4.** a single share in a mutual fund □ **accumulation units** units in a mutual fund, where the dividend is left to accumulate as new units

unit cost /'junɪt kɔst/ *noun* the cost of one item, i.e. the total product costs divided by the number of units produced

unite /ju'naɪt/ *verb* to join together ○ *The directors united with the managers to reject the takeover bid.* ○ *The three unions in the factory united to present their wage claims to the management.*

United Nations /juˌnaɪtɪd 'neɪʃ(ə)nz/ *noun* an organization which links almost all the countries of the world to promote good relations between them

unit-linked insurance /ˌjunɪt lɪŋkd ɪn'ʃʊrəns/ *noun U.K.* an insurance policy which is linked to the security of units in a unit trust or fund

unit of account /ˌjunɪt əv ə'kaʊnt/ *noun* a standard unit used in financial transactions among members of a group, e.g., SDRs in the IMF

unit price /'junɪt praɪs/ *noun* the price of one item

unit trust /'junɪt trʌst/ *noun U.K.* same as **mutual fund**

Universal Product Code /juni ˌvɜrs(ə)l 'prɑdʌkt ˌkoʊd/ *noun* the code which identifies an article for sale, usually printed as a bar code on the package or item itself. Abbreviation **UPC**

unladen /ʌn'leɪd(ə)n/ *adjective* without a cargo ○ *The ship was unladen when she arrived in port.*

unlawful /ʌn'lɔrf(ə)l/ *adjective* against the law, not legal

unlimited /ʌn'lɪmɪtɪd/ *adjective* with no limits ○ *The bank offered him unlimited credit.*

unlimited liability /ʌnˌlɪmɪtɪd ˌlaɪə 'bɪləti/ *noun* a situation where a sole proprietor or each partner is responsible for all a firm's debts with no limit on the amount each may have to pay

unlined paper /ˌʌnlaɪnd 'peɪpər/ *noun* paper with no lines printed on it

unlisted /ʌn'lɪstɪd/ *adjective* (telephone number) which is not printed in the telephone book

unlisted securities /ʌnˌlɪstɪd sɪ 'kjʊrɪtiz/ *plural noun* stocks that are not listed on the Stock Exchange

unload /ʌn'loʊd/ *verb* **1.** to take goods off a ship, truck etc. ○ *The ship is unloading at Hamburg.* ○ *We need a forklift to unload the truck.* ○ *We unloaded the spare parts at New Orleans.* ○ *There are no unloading facilities for container ships.* **2.** to sell stocks which do not seem attractive ○ *We tried to unload our shareholding as soon as the company published its accounts.*

unobtainable /ˌʌnəb'teɪnəb(ə)l/ *adjective* which cannot be obtained ○ *This spare part is currently unobtainable.*

unofficial /ˌʌnə'fɪʃ(ə)l/ *adjective* done without authority

unofficial strike /ˌʌnəfɪʃ(ə)l 'straɪk/ *noun* a strike by local employees which has not been approved by the main labor union

unpaid /ʌn'peɪd/ *adjective* not paid

unpaid invoices /ʌnˌpeɪd 'ɪnvɔɪsɪz/ *plural noun* invoices which have not been paid

unpaid vacation /ˌʌnpeɪd 'hɑlɪdeɪ/, **unpaid leave** /ʌnˌpeɪd 'liv/ *noun* leave during which the employee does not receive any pay

unprofitable /ʌn'prɑfɪtəb(ə)l/ *adjective* not profitable

unquoted shares /ˌʌnkwoʊtɪd 'ʃerz/ *plural noun* stocks that have no Stock Exchange quotation

unrealized profit /ʌnˌrɪəlaɪzd 'prɑfɪt/ *noun* same as **paper profit**

unredeemed pledge /ˌʌnrɪdimd 'pledʒ/ *noun* a pledge which the borrower has not claimed back because he or she has not paid back the loan

unregistered /ʌn'redʒɪstərd/ *adjective* referring to a company which has not been registered

unreliable /ˌʌnrɪ'laɪəb(ə)l/ *adjective* which cannot be relied on ○ *The postal service is very unreliable.*

unsealed envelope /ˌʌnsild 'envəloʊp/ *noun* an envelope where the flap has been pushed into the back of the envelope, not stuck down

unsecured creditor /ˌʌnsɪkjʊrd 'kredɪtər/ *noun* a creditor who is owed money, but has no security from the debtor for the debt

unsecured debt /ˌʌnsɪkjʊrd 'det/ *noun* a debt which is not guaranteed by a charge on assets or by any collateral

unsecured loan /ˌʌnsɪkjʊrd 'loʊn/ *noun* a loan made with no security

unseen /ʌn'sin/ *adverb* not seen

unsettled /ʌn'set(ə)ld/ *adjective* which changes often or which is upset

unskilled /ʌn'skɪld/ *adjective* not having specific skills or training ○ *Using unskilled labor will reduce labor costs.* ○ *Nowadays there is relatively little work for an unskilled work force* or *for unskilled workers.*

unsold /ʌn'soʊld/ *adjective* not sold ○ *Unsold items will be scrapped.*

unsolicited /ˌʌnsə'lɪsɪtɪd/ *adjective* which has not been asked for ○ *an unsolicited gift*

unsolicited testimonial /ˌʌnsəlɪsɪtɪd ˌtestɪ'moʊniəl/ *noun* a letter praising

someone or a product, without the writer having been asked to write it

unstable /ʌn'steɪb(ə)l/ *adjective* not stable, changing frequently ○ *unstable exchange rates*

unsubsidized /ʌn'sʌbsɪdaɪzd/ *adjective* with no subsidy

unsuccessful /ˌʌnsək'sesf(ə)l/ *adjective* not successful ○ *an unsuccessful businessman* ○ *The project was expensive and unsuccessful.* ○ *He made six unsuccessful job applications before he finally got a job.*

unsuccessfully /ˌʌnsək'sesf(ə)li/ *adverb* with no success ○ *The company unsuccessfully tried to break into the South American market.* ○ *He unsuccessfully applied for the job of marketing manager.*

untrue /ʌn'tru/ *adjective* not true

unused /ʌn'juzd/ *adjective* which has not been used ○ *We are trying to sell off six unused computers.*

unwaged /ʌn'weɪdʒd/ *noun* □ **the unwaged** people with no jobs

unwritten agreement /ʌnˌrɪt(ə)n ə'grimənt/ *noun* agreement which has been reached in speaking (such as in a telephone conversation) but has not been written down

up /ʌp/ *adverb, preposition* in or to a higher position ○ *The inflation rate is going up steadily.* ○ *Stocks were up slightly at the end of the day.* ○ *She worked her way up to become sales director.*

UPC *abbreviation* Universal Product Code

update /'ʌpdeɪt/ *noun* information added to something to make it up to date ○ *Here is the latest update on sales.* ■ *verb* /ʌp'deɪt/ to revise something so that it is always up to date ○ *The figures are updated annually.*

up front /ˌʌp 'frʌnt/ *adverb* in advance

upgrade /ʌp'greɪd/ *verb* to increase the importance of someone or of a job ○ *Her job has been upgraded to senior manager level.*

upkeep /'ʌpkip/ *noun* the cost of keeping a building or machine in good order

uplift /'ʌplɪft/ *noun* an increase ○ *The contract provides for an annual uplift of charges.*

up market /ˌʌp 'mɑrkət/ *noun* a stock market which is rising or is at its highest level ○ *How your emerging growth fund* *performs in a down market is just as important as in an up market.*

upmarket /ˌʌp'mɑrkət/ *adverb, adjective* more expensive or appealing to a wealthy section of the population □ **the company has decided to move upmarket** the company has decided to start to produce more luxury items

upset price /'ʌpset praɪs/ *noun* the lowest price which the seller will accept at an auction

upstream /ʌp'strim/ *adjective* referring to the operations of a company at the beginning of a process (as drilling for oil as an operation of a petroleum company). Compare **downstream**

upstream progress /ˌʌpstrim prou'gres/ *noun* progress made despite opposition or difficult conditions. Opposite **downstream progress**

up to /'ʌp tu/ *preposition* as far as, as high as ○ *We will buy at prices up to $25.*

up-to-date /ˌʌp tə 'deɪt/ *adjective, adverb* current, recent, or modern ○ *an up-to-date computer system* □ **to bring something up to date** to add the latest information or equipment to something □ **to keep something up to date** to keep adding information to something so that it always has the latest information in it ○ *We spend a lot of time keeping our mailing list up to date.*

upturn /'ʌptɜrn/ *noun* a movement toward higher sales or profits ○ *an upturn in the economy* ○ *an upturn in the market*

urgent /'ɜrdʒənt/ *adjective* which has to be done quickly ○ *This is an urgent delivery – it has to be in New York tomorrow afternoon.*

urgently /'ɜrdʒəntli/ *adverb* immediately

U.S., USA *abbreviation* United States (of America)

usage /'jusɪdʒ/ *noun* the way in which something is used

usance /'juzəns/ *noun* the time between the date when a bill of exchange is presented and the date when it is paid

use *noun* /jus/ a way in which something can be used □ **to make use of something** to use something □ **in use** being worked ○

The computer is in use twenty-four hours a day. □ **items for personal use** items which a person will use for himself, not on behalf of the company □ **he has the use of a company car** he has a company car which he uses privately ■ *verb* /juz/ to take something, e.g., a machine, a company or a process, and work with it ○ *We use airmail for all our overseas correspondence.* ○ *The photocopier is being used all the time.* ○ *They use freelancers for most of their work.*

use-by date /'juz baɪ ˌdeɪt/ *noun* a date printed on a packet of food showing the last date on which the contents should be used. Compare **best-before date**, **sell-by date**

useful /'jusf(ə)l/ *adjective* which can help

user /'juzər/ *noun* a person who uses something

user-friendly /ˌjuzər 'frendli/ *adjective* which a user finds easy to work ○ *These programs are really user-friendly.*

user's guide /'juzərz gaɪd/, **user's handbook** /'juzərz ˌhændbʊk/, **user's manual** /'juzərz ˌmænjuəl/ *noun* a book showing someone how to use something

USP *abbreviation* **1.** unique selling point **2.** unique selling proposition

usual /'juʒuəl/ *adjective* normal or ordinary ○ *Our usual terms* or *usual conditions are thirty days' credit.* ○ *The usual practice is to have the contract signed by the CEO.* ○ *The usual hours of work are from 9.30 to 5.30.*

usury /'juʒəri/ *noun* the lending of money at high interest

utilisation /ˌjutɪlaɪ'zeɪʃ(ə)n/, **utilization** *noun* the act of making use of something

"…control permits the manufacturer to react to changing conditions on the plant floor and to keep people and machines at a high level of utilization" [*Duns Business Month*]

utility /ju'tɪləti/ *noun* a public service company, such as one that supplies water, gas or electricity or runs public transportation ○ *Stocks in utility companies* or *utilities offer good dividends.*

utilize /'jutɪlaɪz/ *verb* to use something

V

vacancy /'veɪkənsi/ *noun* **1.** a job which is to be filled ○ *There are two vacancies in the human resources department.* ○ *We advertised the vacancy both internally and in the local press.* ○ *We have been unable to fill the vacancy for a skilled machinist.* ○ *They have a vacancy for a secretary.* **2.** an empty place, empty room

vacancy rate /'veɪkənsi reɪt/ *noun* **1.** the average number of rooms empty in a hotel over a period of time, shown as a percentage of the total number of rooms **2.** the average number of office buildings, stores, etc., which are not rented at a particular time **3.** the number of jobs which are available shown as a proportion of the total work force

vacant /'veɪkənt/ *adjective* empty, not occupied

"…the current vacancy rate in Tokyo stands at 7%. The supply of vacant office space, if new buildings are built at the current rate, is expected to take up to five years to absorb" [*Nikkei Weekly*]

vacant possession /ˌveɪkənt pə'zeʃ(ə)n/ *adjective* being able to occupy a property immediately after buying it because it is empty ○ *The property is to be sold with vacant possession.*

vacate /və'keɪt/ *verb* □ **to vacate the premises** to leave premises, so that they become empty

vacation /və'keɪʃ(ə)n/ *noun* **1.** a period when the law courts are closed **2.** a period when an employee does not work, but rests, goes away and does things for pleasure ○ *The CEO is on vacation in Montana.* ○ *He was given two weeks' vacation after his wife's death.* ○ *The job comes with a month's annual vacation.* (NOTE: The U.K. term is **holiday**.) □ **the job carries five weeks' vacation** one of the conditions of the job is that you have five weeks' vacation time

vacation entitlement /'hɑlɪdeɪ ɪnˌtaɪt(ə)lmənt/ *noun* the number of days of paid holiday which an employee has the right to take ○ *She has not used up all her vacation entitlement.*

vacation pay /'hɑlɪdeɪ peɪ/ *noun* a salary which is still paid during the holiday

valid /'vælɪd/ *adjective* **1.** which is acceptable because it is true ○ *That is not a valid argument* or *excuse.* ○ *The intelligence test is not valid since it does not accurately measure basic mental skills.* ○ *The contract is not valid if it has not been signed by both parties.* **2.** which can be used lawfully ○ *ticket which is valid for three months* ○ *The contract is not valid if it has not been witnessed.* ○ *He was carrying a valid passport.*

validate /'vælɪdeɪt/ *verb* **1.** to check to see if something is correct ○ *The document was validated by the bank.* **2.** to make something valid

validation /ˌvælɪ'deɪʃ(ə)n/ *noun* the act of making something valid

validity /və'lɪdəti/ *noun* effectiveness or usefulness ○ *The validity of these tests is questionable since applicants have also managed to pass them who have been unsatisfactory in subsequent employment.*

valorem /və'lɔrəm/ *noun* ♦ **ad valorem duty**

VALS /vælz/ *noun* a system of dividing people into segments according to their way of living. Full form **Values and Lifestyles**

valuable /'væljʊəb(ə)l/ *adjective* which is worth a lot of money

valuable property /ˌvæljʊəb(ə)l 'prɑpəti/ *noun* personal items which are worth a lot of money

valuation /ˌvælju'eɪʃ(ə)n/ *noun* an estimate of how much something is worth ○ *to ask for a valuation of a property before making an offer for it* □ **to buy a store with stock at valuation** when buying a store, to pay a price for the stock which is equal to the value as estimated by the valuer □ **to purchase stock at valuation** to pay the price for stock which it is valued at

value /'vælju/ *noun* the amount of money which something is worth ○ *the fall in the value of the dollar* ○ *She imported goods to the value of $2500.* ○ *The valuer put the value of the stock at $25,000.* □ **good value (for money)** a bargain, something which is worth the price paid for it ○ *That restaurant gives value for money.* ○ *Buy that computer now – it is very good value.* ○ *Vacations in Mexico are a good value because of the exchange rate.* □ **to rise** *or* **fall in value** to be worth more or less ■ *verb* to estimate how much money something is worth ○ *He valued the stock at $25,000.* ○ *We are having the jewelry valued for insurance.*

value added /ˌvælju 'ædɪd/ *noun* **1.** the difference between the cost of the materials purchased to produce a product and the final selling price of the finished product **2.** the amount added to the value of a product or service, being the difference between its cost and the amount received when it is sold. Also called **net output 3.** the features that make one product or service different from or better than another and so create value for the customer (NOTE: Value added in this sense is based on the customer's view of what makes a product or service more desirable than others and worth a higher price.)

value-added reseller /ˌvælju ˌædɪd 'riselər/ *noun* a merchant who buys products at retail prices and packages them with additional items for resale to customers

value-added services /ˌvælju ˌædɪd 'sɜːvɪsɪz/ *plural noun* services which add value to a service or product being sold

Value Added Tax /ˌvælju ædɪd 'tæks/ *noun* full form of **VAT**

value-adding intermediary /ˌvælju ˌædɪŋ ˌɪntər'midiəri/ *noun* a distributor who increases the value of a product before selling it to a customer, e.g., by installing software in a computer

value chain /'vælju tʃeɪn/ *noun* **1.** the sequence of activities a company carries out as it designs, produces, markets, delivers, and supports its product or service, each of which is thought of as adding value **2.** the pattern that people traditionally have in mind when considering their career prospects, which involves them identifying at each stage in their careers what the next, most obvious, upward move should be

"Competition is no longer limited to the realm of the enterprise. Entire value chains are now starting to act as formidable entities, competing against each other for similar markets." [*Harvard Business Review*]

value map /'vælju mæp/ *noun* an indication of the amount of value that the market considers a product or service to have, which helps to differentiate it from its competitors

value network /ˌvælju 'netwɜːrk/ *noun* the links between an organization and the various collaborators who external contributors to its value chain

valuer /'væljuər/ *noun* a person who estimates how much money something is worth

variability /ˌveriə'bɪləti/ *noun* the condition of being variable

variable /'veriəb(ə)l/ *adjective* changeable ■ *noun* something which varies

variable annuity /ˌveriəb(ə)l ə'njuəti/ *noun* a type of insurance contract in which the insurance company invests the premiums and makes future payments to someone, usually at retirement. The size of the payments depends on the how well the investments do. ◊ **annuity, fixed annuity**

variable costs /ˌveriəb(ə)l 'kɔsts/ *plural noun* production costs which increase with the quantity of the product made, e.g., wages or raw materials

variable pricing /ˌveriəb(ə)l 'praɪsɪŋ/ *noun* the practice of giving a product or service different prices in different places or at different times

variable rate /ˌveriəb(ə)l 'reɪt/ *noun* a rate of interest on a loan which is not fixed, but can change with the current bank interest rates. Also called **floating rate**

variance /'veriəns/ *noun* the difference between what was expected and the actual results □ **at variance with** not in agreement with ○ *The actual sales are at variance with the sales reported by the reps.*

variation /ˌveriˈeɪʃ(ə)n/ *noun* the amount by which something changes □ **seasonal variations** variations which take place at different times of the year ○ *seasonal variations in buying patterns* ○ *There are marked seasonal variations in unemployment in the hotel industry.*

variety /vəˈraɪəti/ *noun* different types of things ○ *The store stocks a variety of goods.* ○ *We had a variety of visitors at the office today.*

variety store /vəˈraɪəti stɔr/ *noun* a store selling a wide range of usually cheap items

vary /ˈveri/ *verb* to change or to differ ○ *The gross margin varies from quarter to quarter.* ○ *We try to prevent the flow of production from varying in the factory.*

VAT /ˌviː eɪ ˈtiː, væt/ *noun U.K.* same as **sales tax**

VC *abbreviation* venture capitalist

VCT *abbreviation* venture capital trust

VDT *abbreviation* visual display terminal

VDU *abbreviation* visual display unit

vending /ˈvendɪŋ/ *noun* selling

vending machine /ˈvendɪŋ məˌʃin/ *noun* same as **automatic vending machine**

vendor /ˈvendər/ *noun* **1.** a person who sells something, especially a property ○ *the solicitor acting on behalf of the vendor* **2.** a person who sells goods

venture /ˈventʃər/ *noun* a commercial deal which involves a risk ○ *They lost money on several import ventures.* ○ *She's started a new venture – a computer store.* ■ *verb* to risk money

venture capital /ˌventʃə ˈkæpɪt(ə)l/ *noun* capital for investment which may easily be lost in risky projects, but can also provide high returns. Also called **risk capital**

venture capital fund /ˌventʃə ˈkæpɪt(ə)l fʌnd/ *noun* a fund which invests in finance houses providing venture capital

"…the Securities and Exchange Board of India allowed new companies to enter the primary market provided venture capital funds took up 10 per cent of the equity. At present, new companies are allowed to make initial public offerings provided their projects have been appraised by banks or financial institutions which take up 10 per cent of the equity" [*The Hindu*]

venture capitalist /ˌventʃə ˈkæpɪt(ə)lɪst/ *noun* a finance house or private individual specializing in providing venture capital. Abbreviation **VC**

"…along with the stock market boom of the 1980s, the venture capitalists piled more and more funds into the buyout business, backing bigger and bigger deals with ever more extravagant financing structures" [*Guardian*]

venture capital trust /ˌventʃə ˈkæpɪt(ə)l trʌst/ *noun* a trust which invests in smaller firms which need capital to grow. Abbreviation **VCT**

venture management /ˌventʃə ˈmænɪdʒmənt/ *noun* a type of management in which various sections within an organization, typically research and development, corporate planning, marketing, finance and purchasing, work together to encourage an entrepreneurial spirit among employees, to increase innovation, and to develop new products more quickly

venture philanthropy /ˌventʃər fɪˈlænθrəpi/ *noun* the practice of donating to charities using the same principles as investing in profit-making companies, in which the donor's contributions are contingent upon the charity showing results

venue /ˈvenju/ *noun* a place where a meeting is to be held ○ *The venue for the exhibition has been changed from the library to the conference center.* ○ *The lecture theater is not a good venue for informal presentations.* ○ *We're having trouble finding a suitable venue for our annual show this year.*

verbal /ˈvɜrb(ə)l/ *adjective* using spoken words, not writing

verbal agreement /ˌvɜrb(ə)l əˈgrimənt/ *noun* an agreement which is spoken (such as over the telephone)

verbal contract /ˌvɜrb(ə)l ˈkɑntrækt/ *noun* same as **verbal agreement**

verbally /ˈvɜrbəli/ *adverb* using spoken words, not writing ○ *They agreed to the terms verbally, and then started to draft the contract.* ○ *He was warned verbally that his work was not up to standard.*

verbal permission /ˌvɜrb(ə)l pəˈmɪʃ(ə)n/ *noun* an act of telling someone that they are allowed to do something

verification /ˌverɪfɪˈkeɪʃ(ə)n/ *noun* the process of checking if something is correct ○ *The shipment was allowed into the country after verification of the documents by customs.*

verify /ˈverɪfaɪ/ *verb* to check to see if something is correct

version /ˈvɜːʒ(ə)n/ *verb* to adapt a website for different categories of customer by maintaining different versions of it

vertical /ˈvɜːtɪk(ə)l/ *adjective* upright, straight up or down

vertical communication /ˌvɜːtɪk(ə)l kəˌmjuːnɪˈkeɪʃ(ə)n/ *noun* communication between senior managers via the middle management to the work force

vertical integration /ˌvɜːtɪk(ə)l ˌɪntɪˈɡreɪʃ(ə)n/ *noun* the extent to which supply-chain activities are controlled within an organization. Same as **backward integration**

vertical linkage analysis /ˌvɜːtɪk(ə)l ˌlɪŋkɪdʒ əˈnæləsɪs/ *noun* a type of analysis that considers the value chain as extending beyond the organization itself and including both suppliers and users. In this way it maximizes the number of points in the chain where value can be created for customers.

vessel /ˈves(ə)l/ *noun* a ship

vested interest /ˌvestɪd ˈɪntrəst/ *noun* a special interest in keeping an existing state of affairs □ **she has a vested interest in keeping the business working** she wants to keep the business working because she will make more money if it does

vet /vet/ *verb* to examine something carefully ○ *All candidates have to be vetted by the managing director.* ○ *The contract has been sent to the legal department for vetting.* (NOTE: **vetting – vetted**)

via /ˈvaɪə/ *preposition* using (a means or a route) ○ *The shipment is going via the Suez Canal.* ○ *We are sending the check via our office in New York.* ○ *They sent the message via email.*

viability /ˌvaɪəˈbɪlɪti/ *noun* the fact of being viable or being able to make a profit

viable /ˈvaɪəb(ə)l/ *adjective* which can work in practice

vice- /vaɪs/ *prefix* deputy or second in command ○ *He is the vice-chairman of an industrial group.* ○ *She was appointed to the vice-chairmanship of the committee.*

vice president /ˌvaɪs ˈprezɪd(ə)nt/ *noun* one of the executive directors of a company

victimization /ˌvɪktɪmaɪˈzeɪʃ(ə)n/ *noun* the unfair or unreasonable treatment of one employee by their employer or by other employees ○ *Victimization can come from senior employees' fear of losing their jobs to juniors, or from racial and sexual prejudice.*

videoconference /ˈvɪdɪoʊˌkɒnf(ə)rəns/ *noun* a system linking video, audio and computer signals from different locations so that distant people can talk and see each other, as if in the same conference room

videoconferencing /ˈvɪdɪoʊˌkɒnf(ə)rənsɪŋ/ *noun* the use of live video links that enable people in different locations to see and hear one another and so to discuss matters and hold meetings without being physically present together in one place

view /vjuː/ *noun* a way of thinking about something ○ *We asked the sales manager for his views on the reorganization of the reps' territories.* ○ *The chairman takes the view that credit should never be longer than thirty days.* □ **to take the long view** to plan for a long period before your current investment will become profitable □ **in view of** because of ○ *In view of the falling exchange rate, we have redrafted our sales forecasts.*

VIP *abbreviation* very important person □ **we laid on VIP treatment for our visitors, we gave our visitors a VIP reception** we arranged for our visitors to be looked after and entertained well

VIP lounge /ˌviː aɪ ˈpiː ˌlaʊndʒ/ special room at an airport for important travelers

viral effect /ˈvaɪrəl ɪˌfekt/ *noun* the number of recipients of a message who forward the message on to others

viral marketing /ˈvaɪrəl ˌmɑːkətɪŋ/ *noun* marketing by word of mouth or by spreading advertising messages on the Internet

"…investment in new technology enabled marketing programs, such as viral marketing and E-care systems, to remain relevant to the changing needs of online buyers" [*InformationWeek*]

virement /'vaɪrmənt/ *noun* a transfer of money from one account to another or from one section of a budget to another

virtual hosting /ˌvɜːtʃuəl 'hoʊstɪŋ/ *noun* a hosting option, suitable for small and medium-sized businesses, in which the customer shares space on the hosting company's server that with other organizations (NOTE: In virtual hosting, the hosting company carries out basic maintenance on hardware, but the customer is responsible for managing the content and software.)

virtualization /ˌvɜːtʃuəlaɪ'zeɪʃ(ə)n/ *noun* the creation of a product, service or organization that exists only in electronic systems and has no physical existence

"As an important part of implementing our adaptive enterprise strategy, we do a lot of consolidation of the server environment and a lot of virtualisation of the storage environment." [*Forbes*]

virtual office /ˌvɜːtʃuəl 'ɒfɪs/ *noun* a workplace that has no physical location but is created when a number of employees use information and communications technologies to do their work and collaborate with one another (NOTE: A virtual office is characterized by the use of teleworkers, telecenters, mobile workers, hot-desking and hoteling.)

virtual organization /ˌvɜːtʃuəl ˌɔːɡənaɪ'zeɪʃ(ə)n/ *noun* an organization that often has only a temporary existence and consists of a network of companies, suppliers, or employees who work together using information and communications technology to supply a particular service or product

virtual team /ˌvɜːtʃuəl 'tiːm/ *noun* a group of employees working in different locations who use communications technologies such as groupware, email, an intranet, or videoconferencing to collaborate with each other and work as a team

virus /'vaɪrəs/ *noun* a computer program that is part of another and inserts copies of itself, often damaging the integrity of stored data. It travels with the program that contains it.

visa /'viːzə/ *noun* a special document, special stamp in a passport which allows someone to enter a country ○ *You will need a visa before you go to the U.S.* ○ *He filled in his visa application form.*

VISA™ /'viːzə/ *trademark* a trademark for an international credit card system

visible /'vɪzɪb(ə)l/ *adjective* referring to real products which are imported or exported

visible exports /ˌvɪzɪb(ə)l 'ekspɔːts/ *plural noun* real products which are exported, as opposed to services

visible imports /ˌvɪzɪb(ə)l 'ɪmpɔːts/ *plural noun* real products which are imported, as opposed to services

visit /'vɪzɪt/ *noun* a short stay in a place ○ *We are expecting a visit from our German agents.* ○ *He is on a business visit to Kansas City.* ○ *We had a visit from the safety inspector.* ■ *verb* to go to a place, to see someone for a short time ○ *He spent a week in Scotland, visiting clients in Edinburgh and Glasgow.* ○ *The trade delegation visited the Ministry of Commerce.*

visitor /'vɪzɪtə/ *noun* **1.** a person who visits ○ *The chairman showed the Japanese visitors round the factory.* **2.** a person who visits a website

"During the week to December 19, the number of visitors to consumer e-commerce sites jumped 37% compared with the same week last year" [*Times*]

visitors' bureau /'vɪzɪtəz ˌbjʊroʊ/ *noun* an office which deals with visitors' questions and promotes an area's tourist industry

visual display terminal /ˌvɪzjuəl dɪ 'spleɪ ˌtɜːminəl/, **visual display unit** /ˌvɪʒuəl dɪ'spleɪ ˌjuːnɪt/ *noun* a screen attached to a computer which shows the information stored in the computer. Abbreviation **VDT, VDU**

vivos /'vaɪvoʊs/ ▸ **inter vivos**

vocation /voʊ'keɪʃ(ə)n/ *noun* an occupation that you feel strongly you should do and have the right skills for ○ *He found his vocation as a special needs teacher.* ○ *He followed his vocation and became an accountant.*

vocational /voʊ'keɪʃ(ə)n(ə)l/ *adjective* referring to a choice of career or occupation which a person wishes to follow

vocational guidance /voʊˌkeɪʃ(ə)nəl 'ɡaɪd(ə)ns/ *noun* the process of helping young people to choose a suitable job

vocational training /voʊˌkeɪʃ(ə)nəl 'treɪnɪŋ/ *noun* training for a particular job

voicemail /'vɔɪsmeɪl/ *noun* an electronic communications system which stores digitized recordings of telephone messages for later playback

voice over Internet protocol /ˌvɔɪs ouvər 'ɪntərnet ˌprouːtəkəl/ *noun* full form of **VoIP**

void /vɔɪd/ *adjective* not legally valid ■ *verb* □ **to void a contract** to make a contract invalid

VoIP /vɔɪp/ *noun* a technology that enables phone calls to be made over the Internet. Full form **voice over Internet protocol**

volatile /'vɑlətaɪl/ *adjective* referring to a market or price which is not stable, but which rises and falls sharply ○ *The stock has been very volatile since it was launched.*

"…blue chip stocks are the least volatile while smaller stocks are the most volatile" [*The Times*]

"…the investment markets appear to have become ever more volatile, with interest rates moving at times to extreme levels, and the stock market veering wildly from boom to slump and back again" [*Financial Times Review*]

"…the FTSE 100 Index ended another volatile session a net 96.3 easier at 6027" [*Financial Times*]

volatility /ˌvɑlə'tɪləti/ *noun* the fact of being volatile ○ *Investors are recommended to keep their money in savings and loan accounts because the increasing volatility of the stock market.*

"…while the technology sector has certainly captured the imagination of private investors, the enthusiasm it has aroused among them is likely to cause extreme share price volatility in the short term" [*Financial Times*]

volume /'vɑljum/ *noun* **1.** a quantity of items **2.** the quantity of shares traded on a stock market ○ *average daily volume: 130,000 shares*

volume business /'vɑljum ˌbɪznəs/ *noun* dealing in large quantities of items

volume discount /'vɑljum ˌdɪskaunt/ *noun* the discount given to a customer who buys a large quantity of goods

volume of business /ˌvɑljum əv 'bɪznɪs/ *noun* the number of items sold, or the number of shares sold on the Stock Exchange during a day's trading ○ *The company has maintained the same volume of business in spite of the recession.*

volume of output /ˌvɑljum əv 'autput/ *noun* the number of items produced

volume of sales /ˌvɑljum əv 'seɪlz/ *noun* the number of items sold □ **low or high volume of sales** a small or large number of items sold

volume of trade /ˌvɑljum əv 'treɪd/ *noun* same as **volume of business**

voluntarily /ˌvɑlən'terəli/ *adverb* without being forced or paid

voluntary /'vɑlənˌteri/ *adjective* **1.** done freely without anyone forcing you to act **2.** done without being paid

voluntary chain /'vɑlənt(ə)ri tʃeɪn/, **voluntary group** /'vɑlənt(ə)ri grup/ *noun* a group of distributors who join together to buy from suppliers so as to enjoy quantity discounts ○ *After joining the voluntary chain the store saved up to 20% in buying.*

voluntary liquidation /ˌvɑlənt(ə)ri ˌlɪkwɪ'deɪʃ(ə)n/ *noun* a situation where a company itself decides it must close and sell its assets

voluntary organization /'vɑlənt(ə)ri ˌɔrgənaɪzeɪʃ(ə)n/ *noun* an organization which does not receive funding from the government, but relies on contributions from the public

volunteerism /ˌvɑlən'tɪrɪz(ə)m/ *noun* the practice of using volunteer workers, especially in community service or educational organizations and programs

vostro account /'vɑstrou əˌkaunt/ *noun* an account held by a correspondent bank for a foreign bank

vote /vout/ *noun* the act of marking a paper or holding up your hand, to show your opinion or to show who you want to be elected □ **to take a vote on a proposal, to put a proposal to the vote** to ask people present at a meeting to say if they do or do not agree with the proposal ■ *verb* to show an opinion by marking a paper or by holding up your hand at a meeting ○ *The meeting voted to close the factory.* ○ *52% of the members voted for Mr Smith as chairman.* ○ *Most of the staff voted for a strike.* □ **to vote for or against a proposal** to say that you agree or do not agree with a proposal □ **two directors were voted off the board at the annual meeting** the annual meeting voted to dismiss two directors □ **she was**

voted on to the committee she was elected a member of the committee

vote of thanks /ˌvəʊt əv ˈθæŋks/ *plural noun* official vote at a meeting to show that the meeting is grateful for what someone has done ○ *The meeting passed a vote of thanks to the organizing committee for their work in setting up the international conference.*

voter /ˈvəʊtər/ *noun* a person who votes

voting /ˈvəʊtɪŋ/ *noun* the act of making a vote

voting rights /ˈvəʊtɪŋ raɪts/ *plural noun* the rights of stockholders to vote at company meetings

voting shares /ˈvəʊtɪŋ ʃerz/ *plural noun* shares which give the holder the right to vote at company meetings

voucher /ˈvaʊtʃər/ *noun* **1.** a piece of paper which is given instead of money **2.** a written document from an auditor to show that the accounts are correct or that money has really been paid

W

wage /weɪdʒ/ *noun* the money paid to an employee in return for work done, especially when it is paid weekly and in cash ○ *She is earning a good wage* or *good wages for a young person.* (NOTE: The plural **wages** is more usual when referring to the money earned, but **wage** is used before other nouns.)

"European economies are being held back by rigid labor markets and wage structures" [*Duns Business Month*]

"…real wages have been held down dramatically: they have risen at an annual rate of only 1% in the last two years" [*Sunday Times*]

COMMENT: The term "wages" refers to hourly pay for workers. For employees who are paid a set amount per week or month, the term used is "salary."

wage adjustments /'weɪdʒ əˌdʒʌstmənts/ *plural noun* changes made to wages

wage claim /'weɪdʒ kleɪm/ *noun* an act of asking for an increase in wages

wage differentials /'weɪdʒ dɪfəˌrenʃəlz/ *plural noun* same as **pay differentials**

wage-earner /'weɪdʒ ˌɜrnər/ *noun* a person who earns a wage

wage-earning /'weɪdʒ ˌɜrnɪŋ/ *adjective* □ **the wage-earning population** people who have jobs and earn money

wage freeze /'weɪdʒ friz/ *noun* a period when wages are not allowed to increase. Also called **freeze on wages**, **wages freeze**

wage levels /'weɪdʒ ˌlev(ə)lz/ *plural noun* same as **pay levels**

wage negotiations /'weɪdʒ nɪɡoʊʃiˌeɪʃ(ə)nz/ *plural noun* same as **pay negotiations**

wage parity /'weɪdʒ ˌpærəti/ *noun* same as **pay parity**

wage policy /'weɪdʒ ˌpɑlɪsi/ *noun* a government policy on what wages, especially the minimum wage should be

wage-price spiral /ˌweɪdʒ 'praɪs ˌspaɪərəl/ *noun* a situation where price rises encourage higher wage demands which in turn make prices rise

wage review /'weɪdʒ rɪˌvju/ *noun* the examination of salaries or wages in a company to see if the employees should earn more

wages and prices freeze /ˌweɪdʒɪz ən 'praɪsɪz ˌfriz/ *noun* a period when wages and prices are not allowed to be increased

wage scale /'weɪdʒ skeɪl/ *noun* same as **pay scale**

wagon /'wægən/ *noun U.K.* an open railroad car that carries freight

waive /weɪv/ *verb* to give up a right ○ *He waived his claim to the estate.* □ **to waive a payment** to say that payment is not necessary

waiver /'weɪvər/ *noun* an act of giving up a right or removing the conditions of a rule ○ *If you want to work without a permit, you will have to apply for a waiver.*

waiver clause /'weɪvər klɔz/ *noun* a clause in a contract giving the conditions under which the rights in the contract can be given up

walk /wɔk/ *verb*
walk off *phrasal verb* to stop working and leave an office, factory or task as a protest ○ *The builders walked off the job because they said the site was too dangerous.*
walk out *phrasal verb* to stop working and leave an office or factory as a protest ○ *The whole work force walked out at the news of her dismissal.*

walk-in /'wɔk ɪn/ *noun* a person who approaches an organization for a job, without knowing if any jobs are available (NOTE: The plural is **walk-ins**.)

walk-out /'wɔrk aʊt/ *noun* a strike or stopping work ○ *Production has been held up by the walk-out of the workers.* ○ *Production has been held up by a workers' walk-out.* (NOTE: The plural is **walk-outs**.)

wallet envelope /ˌwɑlɪt 'envəloʊp/ *noun* a type of envelope with the flap along the longer side (an envelope with a flap at the end, on the shorter side, is called a "pocket envelope")

wallet file /'wɑlɪt faɪl/ *noun* a cardboard file, with a wide pocket on one side and a flap which folds down

wall safe /'wɔl seɪf/ *noun* a safe installed in a wall

Wall Street /'wɔl strit/ *noun* **1.** a street in New York where the New York Stock Exchange is situated **2.** the U.S. financial center ○ *Wall Street analysts predict a rise in interest rates.* ○ *She writes the Wall Street column in the newspaper.*

want ads /'wɑnt ædz/ *plural noun* advertisements listed in a newspaper under special headings such as "property for sale" or "jobs wanted"

WAP /wæp/ *noun* a technical language and set of processing rules that enables users of cell phones to access websites (NOTE: WAP stands for Wireless Application Protocol and is the equivalent of HTML for cell phones.)

warehouse /'werhaʊs/ *noun* a large building where goods are stored □ **price ex warehouse** the price for a product which is to be collected from the manufacturer's or agent's warehouse and so does not include delivery ■ *verb* to store goods in a warehouse ○ *Our offices are in St. Louis but our stock is warehoused in Kansas.*

warehouse capacity /'werhaʊs kə ˌpæsəti/ *noun* the space available in a warehouse

warehouseman /'werhaʊsmən/ *noun* a person who works in a warehouse (NOTE: The plural is **warehousemen**.)

warehousing /'werhaʊzɪŋ/ *noun* the act of storing goods in a warehouse ○ *Warehousing costs are rising rapidly.*

war for talent /ˌwɔr fər 'tælənt/ *noun* competition between different organizations to recruit and retain talented staff

warn /wɔrn/ *verb* to say that there is a possible danger ○ *He warned the stockholders that the dividend might be cut.* ○ *The government warned of possible import duties.* ○ *He was warned that any further instances of absenteeism would be punished by stopping his pay.* (NOTE: You warn someone **of** something or **that** something may happen.)

warning /'wɔrnɪŋ/ *noun* a notice of possible danger ○ *Warning notices were put up around the construction site.* □ **to issue a profits warning** to state that profits will not be as good as last year, or much as predicted

warrant /'wɑrənt/ *noun* an official document which allows someone to do something ■ *verb* **1.** to guarantee ○ *All the spare parts are warranted.* **2.** to show that something is reasonable ○ *The company's volume of trade with the U.S. does not warrant six trips a year to New York by the sales director.*

"…the rights issue will grant shareholders free warrants to subscribe for further new shares" [*Financial Times*]

warrantee /ˌwɑrən'ti/ *noun* a person who is given a warranty

warrantor /ˌwɑrən'tɔr/ *noun* a person who gives a warranty

warranty /'wɑrənti/ *noun* **1.** a legal document which promises that a machine will work properly or that an item is of good quality ○ *The car is sold with a twelve-month warranty.* ○ *The warranty covers spare parts but not labor costs.* **2.** a promise in a contract **3.** a statement made by an insured person which declares that the facts stated by him are true

wastage /'weɪstɪdʒ/ *noun* an amount lost by being wasted ○ *Allow 10% extra material for wastage.*

waste /weɪst/ *noun* material left over from a production process which is of no value and is thrown away ■ *adjective* not used ○ *Waste materials are collected from the factory each week.* ○ *Cardboard is made from recycled waste paper.* ■ *verb* to use more than is needed ○ *to waste money* or *paper* or *electricity* or *time* ○ *The CEO does not like people wasting her time with minor details.* ○ *We turned off all the heating so as not to waste energy.*

COMMENT: Industrial waste has no value, as opposed to scrap which may be sold to a scrap dealer.

wastebasket /ˈweɪstbæskɪt/ *noun* a container into which paper or pieces of trash can be thrown. Also called **waste paper basket**

wasteful /ˈweɪstf(ə)l/ *adjective* which wastes a lot of something ○ *This photocopier is very wasteful of paper.*

waste management /weɪst ˈmænɪdʒmənt/, **waste control** *noun* control of the waste produced by an organization to avoid the excessive use of resources and damage to the environment through processes such as recycling and to promote the efficient use of materials

waste paper basket /ˌweɪst ˈpeɪpər ˌbæskɪt/ *noun* same as **wastebasket**

wasting asset /ˌweɪstɪŋ ˈæsɪt/ *noun* an asset which becomes gradually less valuable as time goes by, e.g., a short lease on a property

waybill /ˈweɪbɪl/ *noun* a list of goods being transported, made out by the carrier

weak market /ˌwik ˈmɑrkət/ *noun* a stock market in which prices tend to fall because there are no buyers

weakness /ˈwiknəs/ *noun* the fact of being weak or at a low level

"…indications of weakness in the U.S. economy were contained in figures from the Fed on industrial production" [*Financial Times*]

wealth /welθ/ *noun* a large quantity of money owned by a person

wealth tax /ˈwelθ tæks/ *noun U.K.* a tax on money, property or investments owned by a person

wealthy /ˈwelθi/ *adjective* very rich ○ *The company is owned by a wealthy American businessman.*

wear and tear /ˌwer ən ˈter/ *noun* the deterioration of a tangible fixed asset as a result of normal use. This is recognized for accounting purposes by depreciation.

web /web/ *noun* same as **World Wide Web**

web-based /ˈweb ˌbeɪst/ *adjective* available or accessible on the World Wide Web ○ *a web-based training program*

web bug /ˈweb bʌg/ *noun* a small computer file, placed in a website user's browser so that the user's actions can be

tracked the next time he or she visits the site

web commerce /ˈweb ˌkɑmɜrs/ *noun* same as **e-commerce**

web form /ˈweb fɔrm/ *noun* an electronic document similar to a printed form, which can be used to collect information from a visitor to a website. When the form has been filled in the form, it is usually returned to the owner of the website by e-mail.

webinar /ˈwebɪnɑr/ *noun* a seminar that is given on the World Wide Web

web log /ˈweb lɑg/ *noun* **1.** a record of activity taking place on a website, which can provide important marketing information, e.g., on how many users are visiting the site and what they are interested in, as well as highlighting any technical problems. Also called **server log 2.** a personal journal published on the Internet, which often encourages other users to make comments. Also called **blog**

web marketing /ˈweb ˌmɑrkətɪŋ/ *noun* marketing that uses websites to advertise products and services and to reach potential customers

web marketplace /ˈweb ˌmɑrkətpleɪs/ *noun* a network of connections that enables business buyers and sellers to contact one another and do business on the web (NOTE: There are three types of web marketplace: online catalogs, auctions, and exchanges.)

webmaster /ˈwebmæstər/ *noun* the person who looks after a website, changing and updating the information it contains and noting how many people visit it (NOTE: Several different people within an organization may share the job of webmaster.)

webpage /ˈwebpeɪdʒ/ *noun* a single file of text and graphics, forming part of a website

website /ˈwebsaɪt/ *noun* a position on the web, which is created by a company, organization or individual, and which anyone can visit ○ *How many hits did we have on our website last week?*

website classification /ˌwebsaɪt ˌklæsɪfɪˈkeɪʃ(ə)n/ *noun* the organization of the materials on a website into different categories, so that they can be easily identified and found by users

week /wik/ *noun* a period of seven days (from Sunday to Saturday) ○ *He earns $900 a week* or *per week*. ○ *She works thirty-five hours per week* or *she works a thirty-five-hour week*. □ **to be paid by the week** to be paid a certain amount of money each week

weekday /'wikdeɪ/ *noun* a normal working day (not Saturday or Sunday)

weekly /'wikli/ *adjective* done every week ○ *The weekly rate for the job is $750.*

weekly magazine /ˌwikli ˌmægə'zin/ *noun* a magazine which is published each week

weigh /weɪ/ *verb* **1.** to measure how heavy something is ○ *He weighed the packet at the post office.* **2.** to have a certain weight ○ *the packet weighs twenty-five grams*

weighbridge /'weɪbrɪdʒ/ *noun* a platform for weighing a truck and its load

weighing machine /'weɪɪŋ məˌʃin/ *noun* a machine which measures how heavy a thing or a person is

weight /weɪt/ *noun* a measurement of how heavy something is □ **to sell fruit by weight** the price is per pound or per kilo of the fruit □ **to give short weight** to give less than you should ■ *verb* to give an extra value to a factor

weighted average /ˌweɪtəd 'æv(ə)rɪdʒ/ *noun* an average which is calculated taking several factors into account, giving some more value than others

weighted index /ˌweɪtɪd 'ɪndeks/ *noun* an index where some important items are given more value than less important ones

weighting /'weɪtɪŋ/ *noun U.K.* an additional salary or wages paid to compensate for living in an expensive part of the country

weightlessness /'weɪtləsnəs/ *noun* a quality considered to be characteristic of an economy that is based on intangible assets such as knowledge rather than physical assets

weight limit /'weɪt ˌlɪmɪt/ *noun* the maximum weight ○ *The packet is over the weight limit for a letter, so it will have to go by parcel post.*

welfare /'welfer/ *noun* **1.** the practice of looking after people ○ *The chairman is in-* terested in the welfare of the workers' families. **2.** money paid by the government to people who need it ○ *With no job and no savings, he was forced to live on welfare.*

"California become the latest state to enact a program forcing welfare recipients to work for their benefits" [*Fortune*]

welfare state /ˌwelfer 'steɪt/ *noun* a country which looks after the health, education, etc., of the people

well-known /ˌwel 'nəʊn/ *adjective* known by many people

well-paid /ˌwel 'peɪd/ *adjective* earning a high salary ○ *She has a well-paid job in an accountancy firm.*

wet goods /'wet gʊdz/ *plural noun* goods that are sold in liquid form ○ *Special plastic containers have to be used for wet goods.* ○ *Inflammable wet goods are the most dangerous type of product to transport.*

WFM *abbreviation* workflow management

wharf /wɔrf/ *noun* a place in a dock where a ship can tie up to load or unload (NOTE: The plural is **wharfs** or **wharves**.)

wharfage /'wɔrfɪdʒ/ *noun* a charge for tying up at a wharf

wharfinger /'wɔrfɪndʒər/ *noun* a person who works on a wharf

wheeler-dealer /ˌwilər 'dilər/ *noun* a person who lives on money from a series of profitable business deals

whereof /wer'ɑv/ *adverb* □ **in witness whereof I sign my hand** I sign as a witness that this is correct (*formal*)

whistleblower /'wɪs(ə)l‚bloʊr/ *noun* a person who reveals dishonest practices (*informal*)

white-collar /ˌwaɪt 'kɑlər/ *adjective* referring to office workers

"...the share of white-collar occupations in total employment rose from 44 per cent to 49 per cent" [*Sydney Morning Herald*]

white-collar crime /ˌwaɪt ˌkɑlər 'kraɪm/ *noun* crimes committed by business people or office workers (such as embezzlement, computer fraud or insider dealing)

white-collar job /ˌwaɪt 'kɑlər ˌdʒɑb/ *noun* a job in an office

white-collar union /waɪt ˌkɑlər 'junjːən/ *noun* a labor union formed of white-collar workers

white-collar worker /waɪt ˌkɑlər ˈwɜrkər/ *noun* a worker in an office, not in a factory

white goods /ˈwaɪt ɡʊdz/ *plural noun* **1.** machines which are used in the kitchen, e.g., refrigerators, washing machines **2.** household linen, e.g., sheets and towels

white knight /waɪt ˈnaɪt/ *noun* a person or company which rescues a firm in financial difficulties, especially one which saves a firm from being taken over by an unacceptable purchaser

white sale /ˌwaɪt ˈseɪl/ *noun* a sale of sheets, towels, etc.

white squire /ˌwaɪt ˈskwaɪr/ *noun* a stockholder who purchases a large number of shares, but not a controlling interest, in a company in order to prevent it from being taken over

whizz-kid /ˈwɪz kɪd/ *noun* a brilliant young person who quickly becomes successful in business ○ *She was a whizz-kid who reached head of department in five years.*

whole-life insurance /ˌhoʊl ˈlaɪf ɪnˌʃʊrəns/, **whole-life policy** /ˌhoʊl ˈlaɪf ˌpɑlɪsi/ *noun* an insurance policy where the insured person pays a fixed premium each year and the insurance company pays a sum when he or she dies. Also called **whole-of-life assurance**

wholesale /ˈhoʊlseɪl/ *adjective, adverb* referring to the business of buying goods from manufacturers and selling them in large quantities to traders (retailers) who then sell in smaller quantities to the general public ○ *I persuaded him to give us a wholesale discount.* □ **he buys wholesale and sells retail** he buys goods in bulk at a wholesale discount and then sells in small quantities to the public

wholesale dealer /ˈhoʊlseɪl ˌdilər/ *noun* a person who buys in bulk from manufacturers and sells to retailers

wholesale price /ˈhoʊlseɪl praɪs/ *noun* the price charged to customers who buy goods in large quantities in order to resell them in smaller quantities to others

wholesale price index /ˌhoʊlseɪl ˈpraɪs ˌɪndeks/ *noun* an index showing the rises and falls of prices of manufactured goods as they leave the factory

wholesaler /ˈhoʊlseɪlər/ *noun* a person who buys goods in bulk from manufacturers and sells them to retailers

wholly-owned subsidiary /ˌhoʊli oʊnd səbˈsɪdjəri/ *noun* a subsidiary which belongs completely to the parent company

Wi-Fi /ˈwaɪ faɪ/ *trademark* a certification trademark used to certify that wireless local area network products work with one another

wildcat strike /ˈwaɪldkæt straɪk/ *noun* a strike organized suddenly by workers without the approval of the main union office

will /wɪl/ *noun* a legal document where someone says what should happen to his or her property when he or she dies ○ *He wrote his will in 1984.* ○ *According to her will, all her property is left to her children.*

COMMENT: A will should best be drawn up by a lawyer; it can also be written on a form which can be bought from a stationery shop. To be valid, a will must be dated and witnessed by a third party (i.e. by someone who is not mentioned in the will).

win /wɪn/ *verb* to be successful □ **to win a contract** to be successful in bidding on a contract ○ *The company announced that it had won a contract worth $25m to supply buses and trucks.*

wind /waɪnd/ *verb*
   wind up *phrasal verb* **1.** to end a meeting, or to close down a business or organization and sell its assets ○ *She wound up the meeting with a vote of thanks to the committee.* **2.** □ **to wind up a company** to put a company into liquidation ○ *The court ordered the company to be wound up.*

windfall /ˈwɪndfɔl/ *noun* a sudden winning of money or a sudden profit which is not expected

windfall profit /ˌwɪndfɔl ˈprɑfɪt/ *noun* a sudden profit which is not expected

windfall profits tax /ˈwɪndfɔl ˌprɑfɪts tæks/, **windfall tax** /ˈwɪndfɔl tæks/ *noun* a tax on companies that have made large profits because of circumstances outside their usual trading activities. A windfall tax was imposed on the privatized utility companies in 1997.

winding up /ˌwaɪndɪŋ ˈʌp/ *noun* liquidation, the act of closing a company and selling its assets □ **a compulsory winding up order** an order from a court saying that a company must be wound up

window /ˈwɪndoʊ/ *noun* a short period when something is available or possible

window display /ˈwɪndoʊ dɪˌspleɪ/ *noun* the display of goods in a store window

window dressing /ˈwɪndoʊ ˌdresɪŋ/ *noun* 1. the practice of putting goods on display in a store window, so that they attract customers 2. the practice of putting on a display to make a business seem better or more profitable or more efficient than it really is

window envelope /ˌwɪndoʊ ˈenvəloʊp/ *noun* an envelope with a hole covered with film so that the address on the letter inside can be seen

window of opportunity /ˌwɪndoʊ əv ˌɑpərˈtuːnɪti/ *noun* a short period which allows an action to take place

window shopping /ˈwɪndoʊ ˌʃɑpɪŋ/ *noun* the practice of looking at goods in store windows, without buying anything

win-win situation /ˌwɪn wɪn ˌsɪtjuˈeɪʃ(ə)n/ *noun* a situation in which, whatever happens or whatever choice is made, the people involved will benefit

WIP *abbreviation* work in progress

wireless /ˈwaɪrləs/ *adjective* referring to communications systems and devices that use cell phone technology

withdraw /wɪðˈdrɔr/ *verb* 1. to take money out of an account ○ *to withdraw money from the bank or from your account* ○ *You can withdraw up to $50 from any ATM by using your card.* 2. to take back an offer ○ *When he found out more about the candidate, the HR manager withdrew the offer of a job.* ○ *When the employees went on strike, the company withdrew its revised pay offer.* (NOTE: **withdrawing – withdrew**) □ **one of the company's backers has withdrawn** he or she stopped supporting the company financially ○ *We expect they will withdraw their takeover bid.* ○ *The chairman asked him to withdraw the remarks he has made about the finance director.*

withdrawal /wɪðˈdrɔrəl/ *noun* the act of removing money from an account ○ *to give seven days' notice of withdrawal* ○ *Withdrawals from bank accounts reached a peak in the week before Christmas.* □ **withdrawal without penalty at seven days' notice** money can be taken out of a deposit account, without losing any inter-

est, provided that seven days' notice has been given

withholding tax /wɪðˈhoʊldɪŋ ˌtæks/ *noun* 1. a tax which removes money from interest or dividends before they are paid to the investor, usually applied to non-resident investors 2. an amount deducted from a person's income which is an advance payment of tax owed 3. income tax deducted from the paycheck of an employee before they are paid

with profits /ˌwɪθ ˈprɑfɪts/ *adverb* used to describe an insurance policy which guarantees the policyholder a share in the profits of the fund in which the premiums are invested

witness /ˈwɪtnəs/ *noun* a person who sees something happen □ **to act as a witness to a document, a signature** to sign a document to show that you have watched the main signatory sign it ○ *The CEO signed as a witness.* ○ *The contract has to be signed in front of two witnesses.* ■ *verb* to sign (a document) to show that you guarantee that the other signatures on it are genuine ○ *the two directors were asked to witness the agreement* or *the signature*

witness summons /ˈwɪtnəs ˌsʌmənz/ *noun* a court order requiring someone to appear as a witness (NOTE: This term has now replaced **subpoena**.)

women's magazine /ˈwɪmɪnz ˌmæɡəzɪn/ *noun* a magazine aimed at the women's market

wording /ˈwɜrdɪŋ/ *noun* a series of words ○ *Did you read the wording on the contract?*

work /wɜrk/ *noun* 1. things done using the hands or brain 2. a job, something done to earn money ○ *It is not the work itself that the employees are complaining about* ○ *He goes to work by bus.* ○ *She never gets home from work before 8 p.m.* ○ *His work involves a lot of traveling.* ○ *He is still looking for work.* ○ *She has been out of work for six months.* ■ *verb* 1. to do things with your hands or brain, for money ○ *The factory is working hard to complete the order.* ○ *She works better now that she has been promoted.* □ **to work a machine** to make a machine function □ **to work to rule** to work strictly according to rules agreed between the company and the labor union e.g. by not doing overtime, as a protest **2.** to have a paid job ○ *She works in an office.* ○ *He works at Smith's.*

"...the quality of the work environment demanded by employers and employees alike" [*Lloyd's List*]

work out *phrasal verb* **1.** to calculate ○ *He worked out the costs on the back of an envelope.* ○ *He worked out the discount at 15%.* ○ *She worked out the discount on her calculator.* **2.** □ **he is working out his notice** he is working during the time between resigning and actually leaving the company

workaholic /ˌwɜrkəˈhɑlɪk/ *noun* a person who works all the time, and is unhappy when not working

worker /ˈwɜrkər/ *noun* **1.** a person who is employed □ **worker representation on the board** the fact of having a representative of the workers as a director of the company **2.** a person who works hard ○ *She's a real worker.* ○ *She's a hard worker.*

worker control /ˌwɜrkər kənˈtroʊl/ *noun* the control of an organization by its own employees, or the involvement of employees in management

worker director /ˌwɜrkər daɪˈrektər/ *noun* a director of a company who is a representative of the work force

worker participation /ˌwɜrkər pɑrtɪsɪˈpeɪʃ(ə)n/ *noun* the practice of employees sharing in the company's planning and decision-making

work ethic /ˈwɜrk ˌeθɪk/ *noun* a belief that work is morally good or that people have a moral or religious duty to work hard and try to better themselves (NOTE: The work ethic originated among Protestants, being central to the views of Martin Luther and John Calvin, and played an important role in the achievements of the Industrial Revolution.)

work experience /ˈwɜrk ɪkˌspɪriəns/ *noun* the practice of a student working for a company to gain experience of how businesses work

work flow /ˈwɜrk floʊ/ *noun* **1.** the sequence of jobs which results in a final product or service ○ *A flow chart on the wall showed the work flow for the coming month.* **2.** the rate of progress of work done by a business, department or individual

"The people who fill these jobs ... will be faced with accelerated work flows, faster project hand-offs, and more projects being done simultaneously." [*BusinessWeek*]

workflow management /ˌwɜrkfloʊ ˈmænɪdʒmənt/ *noun* the process of controlling the flow of material that has to be processed to the department, individual or machine that has to process it. Abbreviation **WFM**

work force /ˈwɜrk fɔrs/ *noun* the total number of employees in an organization, industry or country

working /ˈwɜrkɪŋ/ *adjective* **1.** referring to a person who works or who performs tasks ○ *The new rules apply to the whole working population of the country.* ○ *How large is the working population of the country?* **2.** referring to work

working capital /ˈwɜrkɪŋ ˌkæpɪt(ə)l/ *noun* capital in the form of cash, stocks, and debtors but not creditors, used by a company in its day-to-day operations. Also called **circulating capital, floating capital, net current assets**

working conditions /ˈwɜrkɪŋ kən ˌdɪʃ(ə)nz/ *plural noun* the general state of the place where people work, e.g., whether it is hot, noisy, dark or dangerous

working lunch /ˌwɜrkɪŋ ˈlʌntʃ/ *noun* a midday meal during which people continue to work or to do business. Also called **power lunch**

working partner /ˈwɜrkɪŋ ˌpɑrtnər/ *noun* a partner who works in a partnership

working party /ˈwɜrkɪŋ ˌpɑrti/ *noun* a group of experts who study a problem ○ *The government has set up a working party to study the problems of industrial waste.* ○ *Professor Smith is the chairman of the working party on computers in society.*

working week /ˌwɜrkɪŋ ˈwik/ *noun* the usual number of hours worked per week ○ *Even though he is a freelance, he works a normal working week.*

work in progressprocess /ˌwɜrk ɪn ˈprɑses/ *noun* the value of goods being manufactured which are not complete at the end of an accounting period ○ *Our current assets are made up of stock, goodwill, and work in progress.* Abbreviation **WIP** (NOTE: The U.K. term is **work in progress**.)

work-life balance /ˌwɜrk ˈlaɪf ˌbæləns/ *noun* the balance between the amount of time and effort someone devotes to work and the amount they devote to other aspects of life (NOTE: Work-life balance is the subject of widespread debate on how to allow employees more control over their working arrangements so that they have more time for their outside activities and responsibilities, but in a way that will still benefit the organizations they work for.)

workload /'wɜrkloʊd/ *noun* the amount of work which a person has to do ○ *He has difficulty in coping with his heavy workload.*

workman /'wɜrkmən/ *noun* a man who works with his hands (NOTE: The plural is **workmen**.)

workmanship /'wɜrkmənʃɪp/ *noun* the skill of a good workman □ **bad** *or* **shoddy workmanship** bad work done by a workman

work permit /'wɜrk ˌpɜrmɪt/ *noun* an official document which allows someone who is not a citizen to work in a country

workplace /'wɜrkpleɪs/ *noun* a place where you work

"...every house and workplace in Britain is to be directly involved in an energy efficiency campaign" [*Times*]

works /wɜrks/ *noun* a factory ○ *There is a small engineering works in the same street as our office.* ○ *The steel works is expanding.* (NOTE: takes a singular or plural verb)

works committee /'wɜrks kəˌmɪti/, **works council** /'wɜrks ˌkaʊnsəl/ *noun* a committee of employees and management which discusses the organization of work in a factory

work-sharing /'wɜrk ˌʃerɪŋ/ *noun* **1.** a system that allows two or more part-timers to share one job, each doing part of the work for part of the pay **2.** a system where employees agree to share work when there is less work available, so as to avoid redundancies

workshop /'wɜrkʃɑp/ *noun* a small factory

works manager /'wɜrks ˌmænɪdʒər/ *noun* a person in charge of a works

workspace /'wɜrkspeɪs/ *noun* the memory or space available on a computer for temporary work

workstation /'wɜrkˌsteɪʃ(ə)n/ *noun* a desk, usually with a computer terminal, printer, telephone and other office items at which an employee in an office works

work study /'wɜrk ˌstʌdi/ *noun* the analysis of activities carried out by employees in the course of their work for an organization in order to improve efficiency or as part of quality management

work-to-rule /ˌwɜrk tə 'rul/ *noun* an act of working strictly according to the rules agreed between the union and management e.g., by not doing any overtime, as a protest

workweek /'wɜrkwik/ *noun* the usual number of hours worked per week ○ *She works a normal 35-hour workweek.*

world /wɜrld/ *noun* the people in a specific business or people with a special interest ○ *the world of big business* ○ *the world of lawyers* or *the legal world*

World Bank /wɜrld 'bæŋk/ *noun* a central bank, controlled by the United Nations, whose funds come from the member states of the UN and which lends money to member states

world rights /ˌwɜrld 'raɪts/ *plural noun* the right to sell the product anywhere in the world

World Trade Organization /wɜrld 'treɪd ɔrgənaɪˌzeɪʃ(ə)n/ *noun* an international organization set up with the goal of reducing restrictions in trade between countries. Abbreviation **WTO**

worldwide /'wɜrldwaɪd/; /wɜrld'waɪd/ *adjective, adverb* everywhere in the world ○ *The company has a worldwide network of distributors.* ○ *Worldwide sales* or *Sales worldwide have topped two million units.* ○ *This make of computer is available worldwide.*

World Wide Web /ˌwɜrld waɪd 'web/ *noun* an information system on the Internet that allows documents to be linked to one another by hypertext links and accommodates websites and makes them accessible. Also called **web**

worth /wɜrθ/ *adjective* having a value or a price ○ *Don't get it repaired – it's worth only $25.* ○ *The car is worth $6,000 used.* □ **he is worth $10m** he owns property, investments, etc., which would sell for $10m □ **what are ten pounds worth in dollars?** what is the equivalent of £10 in dollars? ■ *noun* a value □ **give me ten dollars' worth of gasoline** give me as much gasoline as $10 will buy

worthless /'wɜːθləs/ *adjective* having no value ○ *The check is worthless if it is not signed.*

wrap /ˌræp 'ʌp/, **wrap up** *verb* to cover something all over in paper ○ *He wrapped (up) the package in green paper.* □ **to gift-wrap a present** to wrap a present in attractive paper

wreck /rek/ *noun* the fact of collapsing, or a company which has collapsed ○ *He managed to save some of his investment from the wreck of the company.* ○ *Investors lost thousands of pounds in the wreck of the investment trust.* ■ *verb* to damage something badly or to ruin it ○ *They are trying to salvage the wrecked tanker.* ○ *The negotiations were wrecked by the unions.*

writ /ˌrɪt əv 'sʌmənz/, **writ of summons** *noun U.K.* a legal document which begins an action in the High Court ○ *The court issued a writ to prevent the labor union from going on strike.* ○ *The company obtained a writ to prevent the labor union from going on strike.*

write /raɪt/ *verb*

write down *phrasal verb* to note an asset at a lower value than previously ○ *written down value* ○ *The car is written down in the company's books.*

write off *phrasal verb* to cancel a debt, or to remove an asset from the accounts as having no value ○ *We had to write off $20,000 in bad debts.* □ **two cars were written off after the accident** the insurance company considered that both cars were a total loss □ **the cargo was written off as a total loss** the cargo was so badly damaged that the insurers said it had no value

"$30 million from usual company borrowings will either be amortized or written off in one sum" [*Australia Financial Review*]

write out *phrasal verb* to write something in full ○ *She wrote out the minutes of the meeting from her notes.* □ **to write out a check** to write the words and figures on a check and then sign it

writedown /'raɪtdaʊn/ *noun* a reduction in the recorded value of an asset to comply with the concept of prudence. The valuation of stock at the lower of cost or net realizable value may require the values of some stock to be written down.

"...the holding company has seen its earnings suffer from big writedowns in conjunction with its $1 billion loan portfolio" [*Duns Business Month*]

write-off /'raɪt ɔːf/ *noun* **1.** the total loss or cancellation of a bad debt, or the removal of an asset's value from a company's accounts ○ *to allow for write-offs in the yearly accounts* **2.** something which is so badly damaged that it cannot be repaired (*informal*) ○ *The car was a write-off.*

writing /'raɪtɪŋ/ *noun* something which has been written ○ *to put the agreement in writing* ○ *He had difficulty in reading the candidate's writing.*

written-down value /ˌrɪt(ə)n daʊn 'væljuː/ *noun* a value of an asset in a company's accounts after it has been written down or recorded at a lower value than previously

written permission /ˌrɪt(ə)n pə'mɪʃ(ə)n/ *noun* a document which allows someone to do something

wrongful /'rɒŋf(ə)l/ *adjective* unlawful

wrongful dismissal /ˌrɒŋf(ə)l dɪs'mɪs(ə)l/ *noun* the act of removing someone from a job for reasons which are wrong

WTO *abbreviation* World Trade Organization

XYZ

XBRL *noun* a computer language used for financial reporting that allows companies to exchange or publish financial information through the Internet. Full form **Extensible Business Reporting Language**

xd *abbreviation* ex dividend

Xerox™ /'zɪrɑks/ *noun* a trademark for a type of photocopier

yard /jɑrd/ *noun* **1.** a measure of length (= 0.91 meters) (NOTE: Can be written **yd.** or **yds** after numbers: **10 yd.**) **2.** a factory which builds ships ○ *This yard builds mainly fishing boats.*

yd. *abbreviation* yard

year /jɪr/ *noun* a period of twelve months

yearbook /'jɪrbʊk/ *noun* a reference book which is published each year with updated or new information

year end /ˌjɪr 'end/ *noun* the end of the financial year, when a company's accounts are prepared ○ *The accounts department has started work on the year-end accounts.*

yearly /'jɪrli/ *adjective* happening once a year ○ *We make a yearly payment of $1000.* ○ *His yearly insurance premium has risen to $550.* ○ *For the past few years she has had a yearly pay raise of 10%.*

year planner /'jɪr ˌplænər/ *noun* a large wall planner covering all the days of a whole year

year to date /ˌjɪr tə 'deɪt/ *noun* the period between the beginning of a calendar or financial year and the present time. A variety of financial information, such as a company's profits, losses, or sales, may be displayed in this way. Abbreviation **YTD**

yellow goods /'jeloʊ gʊdz/ *plural noun* high-priced goods which are kept in use for a relatively long time and so are not replaced very frequently. Compare **orange goods, red goods**

Yellow Pages /ˌjeloʊ 'peɪdʒɪz/ *trademark* a section of a telephone directory printed on yellow paper which lists businesses under various headings such as computer stores or airlines

yen /jen/ *noun* a unit of currency used in Japan (NOTE: It is usually written as ¥ before a figure: **¥2,700** (say two thousand seven hundred yen).)

yes-man /'jes mæn/ *noun* a man who always agrees with what his boss says

yield /jild/ *noun* the money produced as a return on an investment, shown as a percentage of the money invested ■ *verb* to produce an amount or percentage as interest or dividend ○ *government stocks which yield a small interest* ○ *stocks which yield 10%*

"...if you wish to cut your risks you should go for shares with yields higher than average" [*Investors Chronicle*]

COMMENT: To work out the yield on an investment, take the gross dividend per annum, multiply it by 100 and divide by the price you paid for it (in cents): an investment paying a dividend of 20 cents per share and costing $3.00, is yielding 6.66%.

yours faithfully /ˌjɔrz 'feɪθf(ə)li/ *adverb* used as an ending to a formal business letter not addressed to a named person (NOTE: not used in U.S. English)

Yours sincerely /ˌjɔrz sɪn'sɪrli/ *adverb* words used as an ending to a business letter addressed to a named person

Yours truly /ˌjɔrz 'truli/ *adverb* ending to a formal business letter where you do not know the person you are writing to

zero /'zɪroʊ/ *noun* **1.** nought, the number 0 ○ *The code for international calls is zero zero (00).* **2.** *U.K.* same as **zero dividend preference share**

zero dividend preference share /ˌzɪroʊ ˌdɪvɪdend 'pref(ə)rəns ˌʃerz/

noun U.K. a bond which pays no dividend, but has a fixed term and a fixed redemption price, which is a little higher than the redemption price on similar gilts though the redemption price is not in fact guaranteed. Abbreviation **ZDPS**. Also called **zero**

zero inflation /ˌzɪroʊ ɪnˈfleɪʃ(ə)n/ *noun* inflation at 0%

zero-rated /ˌzɪroʊ ˈreɪtɪd/ *adjective* referring to an item which has a sales tax rate of 0%

zero-rating /ˈzɪroʊ ˌreɪtɪŋ/ *noun* the rating of a product or service at 0% sales tax

ZIP code /ˈzɪp koʊd/ *noun* a series of numbers and letters which forms part of an address, indicating the street and the town in a way which can be read by a scanner (NOTE: The U.K. term is **postcode**.)

zipper clause /ˈzɪpər klɔz/ *noun* a clause in a contract of employment which prevents any discussion of employment conditions during the term of the contract

zone /zoʊn/ *noun* an area of a town or country for administrative purposes ■ *verb* to divide a town into different areas for planning and development purposes □ **land zoned for light industrial use** land within an area that has been zoned so that small factories for light industry can be built on it

zoning regulations /ˈzoʊnɪŋ ˌreɡjʊleɪʃ(ə)nz/ *noun* local laws which regulate the types of building and land use in a town

Z-score /ˈzi skɔr/ *noun* same as **Altman Z-score**

SUPPLEMENTS

International Dialing Codes
Local Times Around the World
International Currencies
Weights and Measures
SWOT Analysis
Sample Business Letters
How to say the Alphabet and Numbers
Using the Telephone

International Dialing Codes

Afghanistan	93	Djibouti	253
Albania	355	Dominica	767
Algeria	213	Dominican Republic	809
Andorra	376	Ecuador	593
Angola	244	Egypt	20
Anguilla	264	El Salvador	503
Antigua and Barbuda	268	Equatorial Guinea	240
Argentina	54	Estonia	372
Armenia	374	Ethiopia	251
Australia	61	Falkland Islands	500
Austria	43	Fiji	679
Bahamas	242	Finland	358
Bahrain	973	France	33
Bangladesh	880	French Guiana	594
Barbados	246	Gabon	241
Belarus	375	Gambia	220
Belgium	32	Georgia	679
Belize	501	Germany	49
Benin	229	Ghana	233
Bermuda	441	Gibraltar	350
Bhutan	975	Great Britain	44
Bolivia	591	Greece	30
Bosnia	387	Grenada	473
Botswana	267	Guatemala	502
Brazil	55	Guinea	224
Brunei	673	Guinea-Bissau	245
Bulgaria	359	Guyana	592
Burkina Faso	226	Haiti	509
Burma (*see* Myanmar)		Honduras	504
Burundi	257	Hong Kong	852
Cambodia	855	Hungary	36
Cameroon	237	Iceland	354
Canada	1	India	91
Cape Verde Islands	238	Indonesia	62
Cayman Islands	345	Iran	98
Central African Republic	236	Iraq	964
Chad	235	Irish Republic	353
Chile	56	Israel	972
China	86	Italy	39
Colombia	57	Ivory Coast	225
Comoros	269	Jamaica	876
Congo (Republic of the)	242	Japan	81
Congo	243	Jordan	962
(Democratic Republic of the)		Kazakhstan	7
Costa Rica	506	Kenya	254
Croatia	385	Kuwait	965
Cuba	53	Kyrgyzstan	996
Cyprus	357	Laos	856
Czech Republic	420	Latvia	371
Denmark	45	Lebanon	961

International Dialing Codes *continued*

Lesotho	266	Romania	40
Liberia	231	Russia	7
Libya	218	Rwanda	250
Liechtenstein	423	St. Lucia	758
Lithuania	370	St. Vincent	784
Luxembourg	352	Samoa	378
Macao	853	Saudi Arabia	966
Macedonia	389	Senegal	221
(Former Yugoslav Republic of)		Serbia and Montenegro	381
Madagascar	261	Seychelles	248
Madeira	351	Sierra Leone	232
Malawi	265	Singapore	65
Malaysia	60	Slovakia	42
Maldives	960	Slovenia	386
Mali	223	Somalia	252
Malta	356	South Africa	27
Mauritania	222	South Korea	82
Mauritius	230	Spain	34
Mexico	52	Sri Lanka	94
Moldova	373	Sudan	249
Monaco	377	Suriname	597
Mongolia	976	Swaziland	268
Montserrat	664	Sweden	46
Morocco	212	Switzerland	41
Mozambique	258	Syria	963
Myanmar	95	Taiwan	886
Namibia	264	Tanzania	255
Nauru	674	Thailand	66
Nepal	977	Togo	228
Netherlands	31	Tonga	676
New Zealand	64	Trinidad & Tobago	868
Nicaragua	505	Tunisia	216
Niger	227	Turkey	90
Nigeria	234	Turkmenistan	993
North Korea	850	Tuvalu	688
Norway	47	Uganda	256
Oman	968	Ukraine	380
Pakistan	92	United Arab Emirates	971
Panama	507	United Kingdom	44
Papua New Guinea	675	U.S.A.	1
Paraguay	595	Uruguay	598
Peru	51	Uzbekistan	998
Philippines	63	Vanuatu	678
Poland	48	Venezuela	58
Portugal	351	Vietnam	84
Puerto Rico	787	Yemen	967
Qatar	974	Zambia	260
Réunion	262	Zimbabwe	263

Local Times Around the World

Universal Time (UT)	1200	Universal Time (UT)	1200
Abu Dhabi	1600	Luanda	1300
Adelaide	2130	Luxembourg	1300
Algiers	1300	Madagascar	1500
Amsterdam	1300	Madrid	1300
Ankara	1400	Malé	1700
Astana	1800	Malta	1300
Athens	1400	Manila	2000
Baghdad	1500	Mexico	0600
Bangkok	1900	Minsk	1400
Beijing	2000	Montevideo	0900
Beirut	1400	Montreal	0700
Berlin	1300	Moscow	1500
Bern(e)	1300	Mumbai	1730
Bogota	0700	Nairobi	1500
Brasilia	0900	Nassau	0700
Brazzaville	1300	New York	0700
Brussels	1300	Oslo	1300
Bucharest	1400	Ottawa	0700
Budapest	1300	Panama	0700
Buenos Aires	0900	Paris	1300
Cairo	1400	Perth	2000
Calcutta (Kolkata)	1730	Phnom Penh	1900
Canberra	2200	Prague	1300
Cape Town	1400	Pretoria	1400
Caracas	0800	Pyongyang	2100
Chicago	0600	Quebec	0700
Colombo	1730	Rangoon	1830
Copenhagen	1300	Reykjavik	1200
Costa Rica	0600	Rio de Janeiro	0900
Damascus	1400	Riyadh	1500
Delhi	1730	Rome	1300
Dhaka	1800	San Francisco	0400
Dublin	1200	Santiago	0800
Gibraltar	1300	Seoul	2100
Hanoi	1900	Seychelles	1600
Harare	1400	Singapore	2000
Helsinki	1400	Stockholm	1300
Hong Kong	2000	Sydney	2200
Honolulu	0200	Taipei	2000
Istanbul	1400	Tallinn	1400
Jakarta	1900	Tbilisi	1600
Jerusalem	1400	Tehran	1530
Kabul	1630	Tirana	1300
Karachi	1700	Tokyo	2100
Khartoum	1400	Toronto	0700
Kiev	1400	Tripoli	1300
Kinshasa	1400	Tunis	1300
Kuala Lumpur	2000	Ulan Bator	2000
Kuwait	1500	Vienna	1300
Lagos	1300	Warsaw	1300
La Paz	0800	Washington, D.C.	0700
Lima	0700	Wellington	0000 (+1 day)
Lisbon	1200	Yaoundé	1300
London	1200		

International Currencies

In the following list, units of currency marked (*) usually have no plural: e.g. 1 kyat (one kyat), 200 kyat (two hundred kyat), etc.

Country	Currency	Divided into	Abbreviation
Afghanistan	Afghani*	puli	Af or Afs
Albania	Lek*	qindars	Lk
Algeria	Algerian dinar	centimes	DA
Andorra	Euro	cents	€
Angola	Kwanza*	lwei	Kzrl
Antigua	East Caribbean dollar	cents	Ecar$ or EC$
Argentina	Argentinian peso	australes	
Australia	Australian dollar	cents	A$
Austria	Euro	cents	€
Bahamas	Bahamian dollar	cents	B$
Bahrain	Bahraini dinar	fils	BD
Bangladesh	Taka*	poisha	Tk
Barbados	Barbados dollar	cents	Bd$ or BD$
Belarus	Rouble	kopeks	
Belgium	Euro	cents	€
Belize	Belize dollar	cents	BZ$
Benin	CFA franc	centimes	CFA Fr
Bermuda	Bermuda dollar	cents	Bda$
Bhutan	Ngultrum*	chetrum	N
Bolivia	Boliviano or Bolivian peso	centavos	$b
Bosnia	Marka	para	
Botswana	Pula	thebe	P
Brazil	Real	centavos	R$
Brunei	Brunei dollar	sen	B$
Bulgaria	Lev*	stotinki	Lv
Burkina Faso	CFA franc	centimes	CFA Fr
Burma (see Myanmar)			
Burundi	Burundi franc	centimes	Bur Fr or FrBr
Cambodia	Riel*	sen	RI
Cameroon	CFA franc	centimes	CFA Fr
Canada	Canadian dollar	cents	Can$ or C$
Cape Verde Islands	Escudo Caboverdiano	centavos	CV esc
Cayman Islands	Cayman Island dollar	cents	CayI$
Central African Republic	CFA franc	centimes	CFA Fr
Chad	CFA franc	centimes	CFA Fr
Chile	Chilean peso	centavos	Ch$
China	Yuan* or renminbi*	fen	Y
Colombia	Colombian peso	centavos	Col$
Comoros	CFA franc	centimes	CFA Fr
Congo (Republic of)	CFA franc	centimes	CFA Fr

International Currencies *continued*

Country	Currency	Divided into	Abbreviation
Congo (Democratic Republic of)	Congolese franc	centimes	
Costa Rica	Colón*	centimos	₡
Croatia	Kuna	lipas	
Cuba	Cuban peso	centavos	Cub$
Cyprus	Cyprus pound	cents	£C *or* C£
Czech Republic	Koruna	haleru	Kč
Dahomey *(see Benin)*			
Denmark	Krone	öre	DKr *or* DKK
Djibouti	Djibouti franc	centimes	Dj Fr
Dominica	East Caribbean dollar	cents	EC$
Dominican Republic	Dominican peso	centavos	DR$
Ecuador	Sucre*	centavos	Su
Egypt	Egyptian pound	piastres	£E *or* E£
Eire *(see Irish Republic)*			
El Salvador	Colón*	centavos	ES¢
Equatorial Guinea	CFA franc	centimes	CFA Fr
Estonia	Kroon	sents	
Ethiopia	Birr* *or* Ethiopian dollar	cents	EB
Fiji	Fiji dollar	cents	$F *or* F$
Finland	Euro	cents	€
France	Euro	cents	€
French Guiana	Euro	cents	€
Gabon	CFA franc	centimes	CFA Fr
Gambia, The	Dalasi*	butut	Di
Germany	Euro	cents	€
Ghana	Cedi*	pesewas	¢
Georgia	Lari	tetri	
Great Britain *(see United Kingdom)*			
Greece	Euro	cents	€
Grenada	East Caribbean dollar	cents	Ecar$ *or* EC$
Guatemala	Quetzal	centavos	Q
Guinea	Guinea franc	centimes	
Guinea-Bissau	CFA franc	centimes	CFA Fr
Guyana	Guyana dollar	cents	G$ *or* Guy$
Haiti	Gourde*	centimes	Gde
Holland *(see Netherlands)*			
Honduras	Lempira*	centavos	La
Hong Kong	Hong Kong dollar	cents	HK$
Hungary	Forint	filler	Ft
Iceland	Króna	aurar	Ikr
India	Rupee	paisa	R *or* Re *or* R$
Indonesia	Rupiah*	sen	IDR

International Currencies *continued*

Country	Currency	Divided into	Abbreviation
Iran	Rial*	dinars	RI
Iraq	Iraqi dinar	fils	ID
Irish Republic	Euro	cents	€
Israel	Shekel	agora	IS
Italy	Euro	cents	€
Ivory Coast	CFA franc	centimes	CFA Fr
Jamaica	Jamaican dollar	cents	J$
Japan	Yen*	sen	Y *or* ¥
Jordan	Jordanian Dinar	fils	JD
Kazakhstan	Tenge		
Kenya	Kenya shilling	cents	KSh *or* Sh
Korea (North)	North Korean won*	chon	NK W
Korea (South)	South Korean won*	jeon	SK W
Kuwait	Kuwaiti dinar	fils	KD
Kyrgystan	Som	tyin	
Laos	Kip*	at	K *or* Kp
Latvia	Lat	santims	
Lebanon	Lebanese pound	piastres	£Leb *or* L£
Lesotho	Loti*	lisente	L
Liberia	Liberian dollar	cents	L$
Libya	Libyan dinar	dirhams	LD
Liechtenstein	Swiss franc	centimes	SFr *or* FS
Lithuania	Lita		
Luxembourg	Euro	cents	€
Macedonia	Dinar	paras	
Macau	Pataca*	avos	P *or* $
Madeira	Euro	cents	€
Malagasy Republic	Malagasy franc	centimes	FMG *or* Mal Fr
Malawi	Kwacha*	tambala	K *or* MK
Malaysia	Ringgit *or* Malaysian Dollar	sen	M$
Maldives	Rufiyaa	laaris	MvRe
Mali	CFA franc	cents	CFA Fr
Malta	Maltese pound *or* lira	cents	£M *or* M£
Mauritania	Ouguiya*	khoums	U
Mauritius	Mauritius rupee	cents	Mau Rs *or* R
Mexico	Peso	centavos	Mex$
Moldova	Leu		
Monaco	Euro	cents	€
Mongolian Republic	Tugrik*	möngös	Tug
Montserrat	East Caribbean dollar	cents	Ecar$ *or* EC$
Morocco	Dirham	centimes	DH
Mozambique	Metical*	centavos	M
Myanmar	Kyat*	pyas	Kt
Namibia	Namibian dollar	cents	

Country	Currency	Divided into	Abbreviation
Nauru	Australian dollar	cents	A$
Nepal	Nepalese rupee	paise	NR *or* Nre
Netherlands	Euro	cents	€
New Hebrides *(see Vanuatu)*			
New Zealand	New Zealand dollar	cents	NZ$
Nicaragua	Córdoba	centavos	C$ *or* C
Niger	CFA franc	centimes	CFA Fr
Nigeria	Naira*	kobo	N *or* ₦
Norway	Krone	ore	NKr
Oman	Rial Omani	baizas	RO
Pakistan	Pakistan rupee	paise	R *or* Pak Re
Panama	Balboa	centesimos	Ba
Papua New Guinea	Kina*	toea	Ka *or* K
Paraguay	Guarani*	centimos	G
Peru	Sol	cents	S
Philippines	Philippine peso	centavos	P *or* PP
Poland	Zloty	groszy	Zl
Portugal	Euro	cents	€
Puerto Rico	U.S. dollar	cents	$ *or* US$
Qatar	Qatar Riyal	dirhams	QR
Reunion	CFA franc	centimes	CFA Fr
Romania	Leu*	bani	L *or* l
Russia	Rouble	kopeks	Rub
Rwanda	Rwanda franc	centimes	Rw Fr
St. Lucia	East Caribbean dollar	cents	Ecar$ *or* EC$
St. Vincent	East Caribbean dollar	cents	Ecar$ *or* EC$
Samoa	Tala	sene	
Saudi Arabia	Saudi riyal *or* rial	halala	SA R
Senegal	CFA franc	centimes	CFA Fr
Seychelles	Seychelles rupee	cents	Sre *or* R
Sierra Leone	Leone	cents	Le
Singapore	Singapore dollar	cents	S$ *or* Sing$
Slovakia	Koruna	haliers	Sk
Slovenia	Tolar	stotin	SIT
Solomon Islands	Solomon Island dollar	cents	SI$
Somalia	Somali shilling	cents	Som Sh *or* So Sh
South Africa	Rand*	cents	R
Spain	Euro	cents	€
Sri Lanka	Sri Lankan rupee	cents	SC Re
Sudan	Sudanese dinar	pounds	SD
Suriname	Suriname guilder	cents	S Gld
Swaziland	Lilangeni*	cents	Li *or* E
Sweden	Krona	örer	SKr

International Currencies *continued*

Country	Currency	Divided into	Abbreviation
Syria	Syrian pound	piastres	S£
Taiwan	New Taiwan dollar	cents	T$ *or* NT$
Tanzania	Tanzanian shilling	cents	TSh
Thailand	Baht*	satang	Bt
Togo	CFA franc	centimes	CFA Fr
Tonga	Pa'anga	seniti	
Trinidad & Tobago	Trinidad & Tobago dollar	cents	TT$
Tunisia	Tunisian dinar	millimes	TD
Turkey	Turkish lira	kurus	TL
Turkmenistan	Manat	tenesi	
Tuvalu	Australian dollar	cents	$A
Uganda	Uganda Shilling	cents	Ush
Ukraine	Hryvna	kopiykas	
United Arab Emirates	UAE dirham	fils	UAE Dh *or* UD
United Kingdom	Pound sterling	pence	£ *or* £Stg
U.S.A.	Dollar	cents	$ *or* US$
Uruguay	Uruguayan peso	centesimos	N$
Uzbekistan	Sum	tiyin	
Vanuatu	Vatu	centimes	
Venezuela	Bolívar	centimos	BS
Vietnam	Dong*	xu	D
Virgin Islands	U.S. dollar	cents	US$
Yemen	Riyal	fils	YR
Yugoslavia	Dinar	paras	DN
Zambia	Kwacha*	ngwee	K
Zimbabwe	Zimbabwe dollar	cents	Z$

Weights and Measures

Imperial Measures

Length

1 inch		= 2.54 cm
1 foot	= 12 inches	= 0.3048 m
1 yard	= 3 feet	= 0.9144 m
1 rod	= 5.5 yards	= 4.0292 m
1 chain	= 22 yards	= 20.117 m
1 furlong	= 10 chains	= 201.17 m
1 mile (statute)	= 1,760 yards	= 1.6093 km

Weight or **Mass**

1 ounce (oz)	= 437.6 grains	= 28.35 g
1 pound (lb)	= 16 ounces	= 0.4536 kg
1 stone (*U.K.*)	= 14 pounds	= 6.3503 kg
1 hundredweight	= 112 pounds	= 50.802 kg
1 (short) ton	= 2,000 pounds	= 0.907 tonnes

Area

1 square inch		= 6.4516 cm^2
1 square foot	= 144 sq. ins	= 0.0929 m^2
1 square yard	= 9 sq. ft	= 0.8361 m^2
1 acre	= 4,840 sq. yds	= 4046.9 m^2
1 square mile	= 640 acres	= 259 hectares

Capacity or **Volume**

1 cubic inch		= 16.387 cm^3
1 cubic foot	= 1,728 cu. ins	= 0.0283 m^3
1 cubic yard	= 27 cu. ft	= 0.7646 m^3
1 fluid ounce (fl. oz, *U.S.*)		= 29.573 cm^3
1 pint (*U.S.*)	= 16 fl.oz	= 0.473 liters
1 quart (*U.S.*)	= 2 pints	= 0.946 liters
1 gallon (*U.S.*)	= 8 pints	= 3.785 liters

Metric Measures

Length

1 millimeter (mm)		= 0.0394 in
1 centimeter (cm)	= 10 mm	= 0.3937 in
1 meter (m)	= 100 cm	= 1.0936 yds
1 kilometer (km)	= 1,000 m	= 0.6214 mile

Weight or **Mass**

1 milligram (mg)		= 0.0154 grain
1 gram (g)	= 1,000 mg	= 0.0353 oz
1 kilogram (kg)	= 1,000 g	= 2.2046 lb
1 tonne (t)	= 1,000 kg	= 0.9842 t

Area

1 square centimeter (cm^2)	= 100 mm^2	= 0.155 sq. in.
1 square meter (m^2)	= 10,000 cm^2	= 1.196 sq. yds
1 are (a)	= 100 m^2	= 119.6 sq. yds
1 hectare (ha)	= 100 a	= 2.4711 acres
1 kilometer (km)	= 100 ha	= 0.3861 sq. mile

Capacity or **Volume**

1 cubic centimeter (cm^3)		= 0.061 cu. in
1 cubic decimeter (dm^3)	= 1,000 cm^3	= 61 cu. in.
1 liter (l)	= 1 dm^3	= 0.22 gallon
1 cubic meter (m^3)	= 1,000 dm^3	= 1.308 cu. yds

SWOT Analysis

Organization

Strengths

The services, products, or skills which the organization is good at doing or making

Weaknesses

The services, products, or skills which the organization can't do or doesn't do well

Market

Opportunities

Segments of the market which are attractive, and where changes in the market might work in favor of the organization

Threats

Segments of the market or changes taking place in the market which make it difficult for the organization to work there

Sample Business Letters

Carter & Perry, Inc.
123 N Capitol Street
NY 10516

April 15th, 2005

Dear Sirs,

We would be grateful if you could send us a copy of your current catalog and price list.

Yours faithfully,

....
Pamela Williams
Purchasing Manager

****

Ms P. Williams
Purchasing Manager
Black & White
42 Peachtree Road NE
NY 10321

Our ref: 1234

April 25th, 2005

Dear Ms Williams,

Thank you for your letter of April 15th. Please find enclosed this year's catalog and our current price list. Please let me know if there is any further information you need.

Yours sincerely,

....
Thomas Crane
Carter & Perry, Inc.

Encl.

Carter & Perry, Inc.
123 N Capitol Street
NY 10516

May 20th, 2005

Dear Sirs,

Order Number: PW/5678/5/01

From your current catalog, please supply the following items:
    20 x 8765/WB
    10 x 6543/QA
    2 x 3210/ZP
Please deliver with an invoice in triplicate to the following address:
    Black & White
    42 Peachtree Road NE
    NY 10321

Yours faithfully

....
Pamela Williams
Purchasing Manager

****

Ms P. Williams
Purchasing Manager
Black & White
42 Peachtree Road NE
NY 10321

Our ref: 1456

May 27th, 2005

Dear Ms Williams,

Order Number: PW/5678/5/01

Thank you for your order. We are able to supply all the items listed immediately, with the exception of 6543/QA which is currently out of stock. We expect new stock to be delivered within the next two weeks, and that part of your order will be supplied as soon as stock is in our warehouse.

Yours sincerely,

....
Thomas Crane
Carter & Perry, Inc.

Sample Business Letters *continued*

Carter & Perry, Inc.
123 N Capitol Street
NY 10516

June 20th, 2005

Dear Sirs,

Invoice SB/1097

Our Order Number: PW/5678/5/01

We have received the items ordered, but one box of 8765/WB was badly damaged when delivered and some of the contents are unusable. We would be grateful if you could replace it as soon as possible.

Yours faithfully

....

Pamela Williams
Purchasing Manager

****

Black & White
42 Peachtree Road NE
NY 10321

Attn: Ms P. Williams
         Purchasing Manager

September 1st, 2005

Dear Ms Williams,

Invoice SB/1097

We note that this invoice has not been paid and would be grateful if you could settle it within seven days.

Yours sincerely,

....

Accounts Dept
Carter & Perry, Inc.

How to say ...

The Alphabet

A	/eɪ/	N	/en/
B	/bi/	O	/oʊ/
C	/si/	P	/pi/
D	/di/	Q	/kju/
E	/i/	R	/ɑr/
F	/ef/	S	/es/
G	/dʒi/	T	/ti/
H	/eɪtʃ/	U	/ju/
I	/aɪ/	V	/vi/
J	/dʒeɪ/	W	/'dʌbəlju/
K	/keɪ/	X	/eks/
L	/el/	Y	/waɪ/
M	/em/	Z	/zi/

Numbers

1, 2, 3, 4 (I,II, III, IV)	one, two, three, four
1st, 2nd, 3rd, 4th	first, second, third, fourth
5, 6, 7, 8 (V VI, VII, VIII)	five, six, seven, eight
5th, 6th, 7th, 8th	fifth, sixth, seventh, eighth
9, 10, 11, 12 (IX, X, XI, XII)	nine, ten, eleven, twelve
9th, 10th 11th, 12th	ninth, tenth, eleventh, twelfth
13, 14, 15, 16 (XIII, XIV, XV, XVI)	thirteen, fourteen, fifteen, sixteen
13th, 14th,15th, 16th	thirteenth, fourteenth, fifteenth, sixteenth
17, 18, 19, 20 (XVII, XVIII, XIX, XX)	seventeen, eighteen, nineteen, twenty
17th, 18th,19th, 20th	seventeenth, eighteenth, nineteenth, twentieth
21, 22, 23 (XX1, XXII, XXIII)	twenty-one, twenty-two, twenty-three
21st, 22nd, 23rd	twenty-first, twenty-second, twenty-third
30, 31, 32 (XXX, XXX1, XXXII)	thirty, thirty-one, thirty-two
40, 50, 60, 70, 80, 90 (XL, L, LX, LXX, LXXX, XC)	forty, fifty, sixty, seventy, eighty, ninety
40th, 50th, 60th, 70th, 80th, 90th	fortieth, fiftieth, sixtieth, seventieth, eightieth, ninetieth
100 (C)	one hundred, a hundred
101 (CI)	one hundred and one, a hundred and one
200, 300, 400, 500 (CC, CCC, CCCC, D)	two hundred, three hundred, four hundred, five hundred
1,000 (M)	one thousand, a thousand
10,000	ten thousand
1,000,000	one million, a million
1,000,000,000	one billion, a billion
1,000,000,000,000	one trillion, a trillion

How to say ...

Decimals

0.5	zero point five, point five
0.25	zero point two five, point two five
2.5	two point five

Money

$1	one dollar, a dollar
10¢	a dime, ten cents
25¢	a quarter, twenty-five cents
$1.25	one dollar twenty-five, a dollar twenty-five, one twenty-five

Telephone numbers

617 502 1505	six-one-seven, five-oh-two, one-five-oh-five

Years

1905	nineteen oh five, nineteen hundred and five
1998	nineteen ninety-eight
the 1900s, the 1900's	the nineteen hundreds
2000	two thousand, the year two thousand
2005	two thousand and five

Dates

1.2.98 or 1/2/98	February first, nineteen ninety eight, or *(U.K.)* the second of January, nineteen ninety eight (NOTE: European and British dates are written with the day before the month, American dates are written with the month before the day.)

Some words with numbers

911, *(U.K.)* 999, *(Aus)* 000	nine one one, *(U.K.)* nine nine nine, *(Aus)* triple oh (NOTE: the number to phone in an emergency)
24/7	twenty-four seven (NOTE: means "all the time")
A1	/ˌei 'wʌn/ (NOTE: means "excellent")

Numbers are sometimes used as abbreviations in e-mails, text messages, or adverts.

2day	today	CUL8R	see you later	L8R	later
4U	for you	F2F	face to face	M8	mate
B4	before	GR8	great	P2P	person to person

Using the Telephone

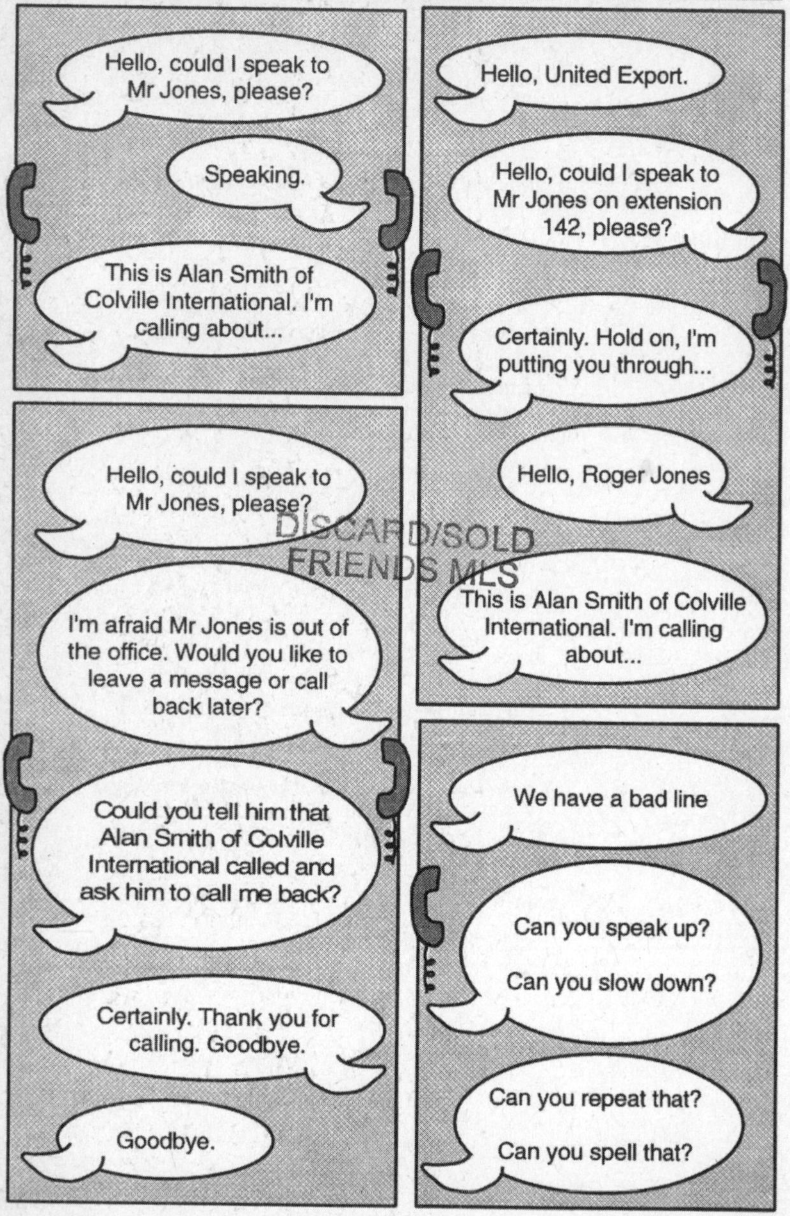